STRATEGIC
MANAGEMENT

FIFTH EDITION
STRATEGIC MANAGEMENT

FRED R. DAVID
FRANCIS MARION UNIVERSITY

PRENTICE HALL
Englewood Cliffs, New Jersey 07632

Library of Congress Cataloging-in-Publication Data

David, Fred R.
   Strategic management / Fred R. David.—5th ed.
     p. cm.
    Includes bibliographical references and indexes.
    ISBN 0-02-327861-7
    1. Strategic planning—Case studies.   2. Strategic planning.
    I. Title.
HD30.28.D385   1995   94-28863
658.4'012—dc20   CIP

Acquisitions Editor: Natalie Anderson
Production Editor: Katherine Evancie
Managing Editor: Fran Russello
Interior/Cover Designer: Michaelis/Carpellis Design Associates, Inc.
Design Director: Linda Fiordilino
Buyer: Paul Smolenski
Assistant Editor: Lisamarie Brassini
Editorial Assistant: Nancy Proyect
Cover art: Adam Niklewicz

© 1995, 1993, 1991, 1989, 1987 by Prentice Hall, Inc.
A Simon & Schuster Company
Englewood Cliffs, New Jersey 07632

Printed in the United States of America

10 9 8 7 6 5 4 3 2

ISBN 0-02-327861-7

Prentice Hall International (UK) Limited, *London*
Prentice Hall of Australia Pty. Limited, *Sydney*
Prentice Hall Canada Inc., *Toronto*
Prentice Hall Hispanoamericana, S.A., *Mexico*
Prentice Hall of India Private Limited, *New Delhi*
Prentice Hall of Japan, Inc., *Tokyo*
Simon & Schuster Asia Pte. Ltd., *Singapore*
Editora Prentice Hall do Brasil, Ltda., *Rio de Janeiro*

*Joy, Forest, Byron, and Meredith—my wife and children—
for their encouragement and love*

PREFACE

The mission of Prentice Hall and me in preparing the fifth edition of *Strategic Management* was "to create the premier business policy textbook on the market, a book that is interesting and valuable to students and from which professors will enjoy teaching." To achieve this mission, Prentice Hall spared no expense, published this edition in color, and financed development of the most elaborate ancillary package available. This mission has led to inclusion of exceptionally current business policy cases and the newest strategic management research and practice. Prentice Hall and I believe you will find this textbook to be better than any other for communicating both the excitement and value of strategic management.

A SPECIAL NOTE TO PROFESSORS

This textbook meets all AACSB guidelines for the business policy and strategic management course. Previous editions of this text have been used at more than 400 colleges and universities. Although the structure of this edition parallels the last, great improvements have been made in readability and coverage. Every page has undergone rethinking and rewriting to streamline, update, and improve the caliber of presentation. The entire research base for this text has been revised and updated since the previous edition. A net result of this activity is that every chapter is shorter in length, yet the chapters include all new examples and many new concepts. The most current concepts and practices in strategic management are presented in a style that is clear, focused, and relevant. The changes in this edition add up to the biggest revision ever made on this popular text.

The first four editions achieved a reputation for excellence and differentiation in three primary areas:

1. The cases are exceptionally up-to-date and offer a good mix of large and small firms across a variety of industries.
2. The chapter material is presented in a skills-oriented, practical manner, supported by Experiential Exercises.
3. The writing style is conversational, logical, concise, interesting, and lively.

This fifth edition builds upon these traditional strengths. New with this edition is an exercise at the end of each chapter that directs students to contact or visit local businesses to investigate important strategic-management topics. *All* of the cases in this edition include year-end 1992 or 1993 information. A new Experiential Exercise at the end of each chapter directs students into the business community to explore strategic-management issues.

This is the only business policy text on a two-year revision cycle, reflecting the author's and publisher's commitment to keeping up-to-date. This cycle allows a continuous stream of fresh, current cases. Markets, economics, and global factors affecting strategic decisions are changing more rapidly than ever and the body of knowledge that comprises strategic management increases continually. The two-year revision cycle allows the chapter material to stay current.

Improved Model. The comprehensive strategic-management model that appears in all chapters of this text has been improved and simplified to incorporate the latest thought and practice.

New Collection of Cases. This edition has a total of thirty-five cases. Thirteen of the cases are new and 22 of the cases are updated from the previous edition. Some of the new cases focus on large firms in trouble, such as IBM—1994 and Borden—1994, and some focus on small businesses, such as Dave's Pit Stop Cafe and Norwood Furniture. The cases in this text are organized clearly by type of industry and size of firm. A breakdown of the cases is as follows:

- Sixteen service-oriented cases, such as Audubon Zoo—1994 and Citicorp—1994.
- Nineteen manufacturing-oriented cases, such as Boeing—1994 and Winnebago Industries—1994.
- Twenty international cases, such as Playboy Enterprises—1994 and Weyerhaeuser Corporation—1994.
- Four nonprofit cases, such as Classic Car Club of America—1994 and Walnut Creek Baptist Church—1993.
- Ten small business strategy cases, such as Circus Circus Enterprises—1994 and Splatterball—1993.

All cases have been class tested to ensure that they are interesting, challenging, and effective for illustrating strategic-management concepts. Most were written exclusively for this text and are designed to reflect current strategic-management problems and practices. This collection of cases complements virtually any approach in teaching business policy or strategic management. An industry note precedes each group of cases in this edition. The notes provide a list of top competitors as well as important opportunities and threats facing firms in each industry.

Chapter Themes. The following three themes permeate all the chapters in this text:
1. Communication is a key to successful strategic management.
2. Global considerations affect virtually all strategic decisions.
3. Preserving the natural environment is an important strategic issue.

Chapter Changes
- Chapter 1—More emphasis is devoted to intuitive thinking and empowering managers and employees through participation in strategic-management activities. A new Experiential Exercise focuses on "The Ethics of Spying on Competitors."
- Chapter 2—The examples of strategies in action are all new. There is also new coverage of strategic management in small businesses, nonprofit organizations, and governmental agencies.
- Chapter 3—New material on corporate vision statements contrast this document with the mission statement. Ten new mission statements are presented and evaluated. Two new exercises challenge students in mission statement theory and practice.
- Chapter 4—More coverage is devoted to international issues. All tables and examples are updated. The Library Search Experiential Exercise has been changed.
- Chapter 5—The chapter has been streamlined and shortened in length. A new exercise has students developing a Competitive Profile Matrix for colleges and universities in your state. More emphasis is given to product quality, customer service, and organizational culture.

- Chapter 6—Expanded coverage is given to behavioral and cultural aspects of strategy analysis and choice. The QSPM has been improved in theory and structure. Two new exercises challenge students.
- Chapter 7—Important topics include organizational structure, linking performance and pay to strategies, developing a supportive corporate culture, empowering employees through participation, creating Employee Stock Ownership Plans (ESOPs), and operating in a green (environmental) manner.
- Chapter 8—Expanded coverage is given to finance/accounting and marketing issues central to strategy implementation. New organizational charts are provided. Two new exercises focus on managing strategic-management activities.
- Chapter 9—New coverage is provided for conducting an environmental audit. Emphasis is given to contingency planning and using computers to evaluate strategies.
- Chapter 10—Totally revamped, this chapter gives up-to-date coverage of NAFTA, Europe, Russia, and Japan. Increased emphasis on culture is also provided.

Global Perspectives. This edition provides a new Global Perspective boxed insert in each chapter to illustrate how global factors affect virtually all strategic decisions. The concluding chapter on international strategic management issues has been expanded and updated. Guidelines for being a successful global competitor are provided.

Natural Environment Perspectives. This edition also provides a new Natural Environment boxed insert in each chapter to highlight the benefits of conducting manufacturing and marketing operations in an environmentally sound manner. The strategic efforts of both companies and countries to preserve the natural environment are described.

Appendix on "Using the Software." An appendix in this edition gives students all the information needed to use the *Strategy Formulator* and *Case Analyst* software materials that are available free upon adoption of this text. This new software instructional material appears in Part Six of the text.

Updated New Cohesion Case on Hershey Foods Corporation. Thoroughly revised to include new global, ethical, and natural environment issues, the Cohesion Case focuses on Hershey Foods Company in 1994. Based in Hershey, Pennsylvania, this well-known multinational company manufactures and markets candy and pasta products. Appearing at the end of Chapter 1, the Cohesion Case allows student to apply strategic-management concepts and techniques to a real organization as chapter material is covered. Experiential exercises at the end of each chapter apply textual material to the Cohesion Case. This integrative (cohesive) approach readies students for case analysis. The Hershey Foods Company encourages professors and students to call (1-800-468-1714) for additional information.

Fifty-three Experiential Exercises. This edition features a total of fifty-three end-of-chapter Experiential Exercises, including eighteen exercises that apply text material to the Cohesion Case and ten that apply textual material to a college or university. In addition, four exercises focus on the *Strategy Formulator* and *Case Analyst* software and ten involve outside library or research activities. The Experiential Exercises are relevant, interesting, challenging, contemporary, and enjoyable.

AACSB Guidelines. AACSB guidelines advocate that business policy texts become more practitioner-oriented. The exercises and writing style of this text focus on applications and skills development. This continues to be a trademark of this text.

The AACSB also encourages greater emphasis on business ethics. Business ethics is introduced in the first chapter and permeates the entire text.

Respect for the natural environment is emerging as an important concern for consumers, companies, society, and the AACSB. Environmental issues are thus discussed throughout the text and cases.

The new international emphasis described above is aimed at meeting AACSB guidelines for internationalizing business courses and curriculum.

Paperback Editions Available. For instructors who desire a text containing only concepts or only cases, separate paperback editions of the chapters and case sections of this text are available. *Concepts of Strategic Management* (fifth edition) contains all ten chapters of this text, as well as the Cohesion Case, Experiential Exercises and the appendix. *Cases in Strategic Management* (fifth edition) includes all thirty-five cases, the Cohesion Case, the case analysis material, and the new appendix.

SPECIAL ANCILLARY MATERIALS

This text is accompanied by the most elaborate auxiliary package available with any business policy text. As described below, seven separate supplements are available free from Prentice Hall with adoption of this text.

Comprehensive Case Solutions Manual. Prepared solely by the author, the *Case Solutions Manual* provides comprehensive teacher's notes for each case. The teacher's notes feature detailed analyses, classroom discussion questions with answers, an external and internal assessment, specific recommendations, strategy-implementation material, and an epilogue for each case. Diskettes for the *Case Analyst* and *Strategy Formulator* software are provided on the back cover of the *Case Solutions Manual.*

Elaborate Instructor's Manual. Also prepared by the author, the *Instructor's Manual* provides lecture notes and teaching tips for all sections of each chapter, as well as additional examples and references for each chapter. This manual includes answers to all end-of-chapter Experiential Exercises and Review Questions, as well as fifteen additional Experiential Exercises not in the text. An elaborate set of 185 transparency masters is included in this manual. Also included is a glossary with definitions of all end-of-chapter key terms and concepts. Sample course syllabi and a test bank of 1,364 questions with answers also are provided.

Seventeen Color Case Video Segments. To accompany the Cohesion Case, a 21-minute color video prepared by Hershey Foods Corporation is available to adopters free of charge. Shown near the beginning of the course, the Hershey Foods video can arouse students' interest in studying the Cohesion Case and completing Experiential Exercises that apply chapter material to this case.

In addition, a collection of sixteen other color case video segments is available free of charge. The segments average 15 minutes each and were professionally prepared by firms used in cases in this text. Videos are provided to accompany the following cases: The Limited, Promus Corporation, Winnebago Industries, Playboy Enterprises, Weyerhaeuser Corporation, WTD Industries, Banc One, Audubon Zoo, W.L. Gore, Borden, Nike, Pilgrim's Pride, Whirlpool, Rykä, Georgia Pacific, and McDonnell Douglas.

Updated Case Analyst *Software.* Free for all adopters of this text, *Case Analyst* is a diskette that contains income statement and balance sheet data from all cases in the text. Information on the disk is organized in Lotus 1-2-3 format. The text gives clear instructions so that IBM-compatible spreadsheet packages can be used to access the data files. Special instructions are given for the EXCEL and ENABLE spreadsheet products.

Packaged on the back cover of the *Case Solutions Manual,* the *Case Analyst* diskette is not copyright protected. Rather, professors are encouraged to make copies of the disk for students who have access to a personal computer and who want to generate pro forma financial statements for the cases being analyzed. Exceptionally fast and user-friendly, *Case Analyst* shows students the impact their recommendations will have on the firms' financial condition. Familiarity with spreadsheets is needed to use *Case Analyst* initially.

New Strategy Formulator *Software.* The *Strategy Formulator* software is packaged inside the back cover of the *Case Solutions Manual.* Clear instructions for using *Strategy Formulator* are given in the text. No prior experience with computers, spreadsheets, databases, or programming is needed to use *Strategy Formulator.* Prentice Hall has purchased the strategic planning software most widely used among corporations and is making that available free for students who use this text. *Strategy Formulator* thus is a totally new software package that gives students hands-on experience using actual strategic planning software. The new *Strategy Formulator* software follows the approach presented in the chapters for formulating strategies in any type organization.

Transparency Masters. A total of 185 transparency masters are available with this text. Half of the transparencies are from exhibits and figures in the text, while the other half are from sources outside the text.

Printed and Computerized Test Bank. The test bank for this text includes 737 True/False questions, 425 multiple choice questions, and 202 essay questions for the text chapters. Sample comprehensive tests for Chapters 1–5 and Chapters 6–10 are also given, and answers to all objective questions are provided. The test questions given in the *Instructor's Manual* are also available on computerized test software to facilitate preparing and grading tests.

A SPECIAL NOTE TO STUDENTS

Welcome to business policy. This is a challenging and exciting course that will allow you to function as the owner or chief executive officer of different organizations. Your major task in this course will be to make strategic decisions and to justify those decisions through oral and written communication. Strategic decisions determine the future direction and competitive position of an enterprise for a long time. Decisions to expand geographically or to diversify are examples of strategic decisions.

Strategic decision making occurs in all types and sizes of organizations, from General Motors to a small hardware store. Many people's lives and jobs are affected by strategic decisions, so the stakes are very high. An organization's very survival is often at stake. The overall importance of strategic decisions makes this course especially exciting and challenging. You will be called upon in business policy to demonstrate how your strategic decisions could be successfully implemented.

In this course you can look forward to making strategic decisions both as an individual and as a member of a team. No matter how hard employees work, an organization is in real trouble if strategic decisions are not made effectively. Doing the right things (effectiveness) is more important than doing things right (efficiency). For example, IBM was prosperous in the 1980s, but ineffective strategies led to annual billion dollar losses in the 1990s.

You will have the opportunity in this course to make actual strategic decisions, perhaps for the first time in your academic career. Do not hesitate to take a stand and defend specific strategies that you determine to be the best. The rationale for your strategic decisions will be more important than the actual decision, because no one knows for sure what the best strategy is for a particular organization at a given point in time. This fact accents the subjective, contingency nature of the strategic-management process. Use the concepts and tools presented in this text, coupled with your own intuition, to recommend strategies that you can defend as being most appropriate for the organizations that you study. You will also need to integrate knowledge acquired in previous business courses. For this reason, business policy is often called a capstone course; you may want to keep this book for your personal library.

This text is practitioner-oriented and applications-oriented. It presents strategic-management concepts that will enable you to formulate, implement, and evaluate strategies in all kinds of profit and nonprofit organizations. The end-of-chapter Experiential Exercises allow you to apply what you've read in each chapter to the Hershey Foods Cohesion Case and to your own university.

Be sure to use *Case Analyst* and *Strategy Formulator* because this software will save you time in performing analyses and will make your work look professional. Read and follow the guidelines provided in the appendices for using the software and for making oral presentations. Work hard in policy this term and have fun. Good luck!

ACKNOWLEDGMENTS

Many persons have contributed time, energy, ideas, and suggestions for improving this text over four editions. The strength of this text is largely attributed to the collective wisdom, work, and experiences of business policy professors, strategic-management researchers, students, and practitioners. Names of particular individuals whose published research is referenced in the fourth edition of this text are listed alphabetically in the Name Index. To all individuals involved in making this text so popular and successful, I am indebted and thankful.

Many special persons and reviewers contributed valuable material and suggestions for this edition. I would like to thank my colleagues and friends at Auburn University, Mississippi State University, East Carolina University, and Francis Marion University. These are universities where I have served on the management faculty. Professors at these schools who shaped development of this text are Bill Holley, Achilles Armenakis, and Bob Neibuhr at Auburn University; Johnny Giglioni, Dennis Ray, and Dan Cochran at Mississippi State University; Louis Eckstein, Tilton Wilcox, and Buc Keush at East Carolina University; and Tom Stanton, Jery Kinard, Don Kelley, Jim Fenton, Bob Pugh, Lucretia Zienert, and Bob Barrett at Francis Marion University.

Individuals who develop cases for the North American Case Research Association Meeting, the Midwest Society for Case Research Meeting, the Eastern Casewriters Association Meeting, the European Case Research Association Meeting, and Harvard Case Services are vitally important for continued progress in the field of strategic management. From a research perspective, there is no question that writing business policy cases represents a valuable scholarly activity among faculty. Extensive research is required to structure business policy cases in a way that exposes strategic issues, decisions, and behavior. Pedagogically, business policy cases are essential for students in learning how to apply concepts, evaluate situations, formulate strategies, and resolve implementation problems. Without a continuous stream of up-to-date business policy cases, the strategic-management course and discipline would lose much of its energy and excitement.

The following individuals wrote cases that were selected for inclusion in this text. These persons helped develop the most current compilation of cases ever assembled in a business policy text: Claire Anderson, Old Dominion University; Robert Anderson, College of Charleston; Jill Austin, Middle Tennessee State University;

Stephen Barndt, Pacific Lutheran University; Henry Beam, Western Michigan University; Lynn Brumfield, Middle Tennessee State University; Carol Cumber, South Dakota State University; Jim Fenton, Francis Marion University; Caroline Fisher, Loyola University; Phil Fisher, University of South Dakota; Barbara Gottfried, Bentley College; Michelle Greene, Francis Marion University; Walter Greene, Pan American University; James Harbin, East Texas State University; Marilyn Helms, University of Tennessee at Chattanooga; Diane Hoadley, University of South Dakota, Neil Jacobs, Northern Arizona University; Mike Keeffe, Southwest Texas State University; Ted Legatski, Sam Houston State University; Dean Lewis, Sam Houston State University; Charles Manz, Arizona State University; Paula Maynes, University of Tennessee at Chattanooga; Steve McCutcheon, University of Tennessee at Chattanooga; Bill Middlebrook, Southwest Texas State University; Kent Nassen, Iowa State University; Sharon Oswald, Auburn University; Valerie J. Porciello, Bentley College; Paul Reed, Sam Houston State University; John Ross, Southwest Texas State University; Frank Shipper, Arizona State University; Charles Shrader, Iowa State University; Matthew Sonfield, Hofstra University; Randall White, Auburn University at Montgomery.

Prentice Hall employees and salespersons have worked diligently behind the scenes to make this text a leader in the business policy market. Natalie Anderson, Lisamarie Brassini, Nancy Proyect, Jo-Anne DeLuca, Tom Nixon, Bill Oldsey, Katherine Evancie, and Paul Smolenski, for example, have supported this text immensely. I appreciate the continued hard work of all Prentice Hall employees and salespersons.

I also want to thank you, the reader, for investing time and effort reading and studying this text. As we approach the twenty-first century together, this book will help you formulate, implement, and evaluate strategies for organizations with which you become associated. I hope you come to share my enthusiasm for the rich subject area of strategic management and for the systematic learning approach taken in this text.

I need to thank Mary Greene, Nichole Greene, and Angela White—my special editorial assistants at Francis Marion University—for doing an excellent job.

Finally, I want to welcome and invite your suggestions, ideas, thoughts, and comments and questions regarding any part of this text or the ancillary materials. Please call me at 803-661-1419 or write me at the School of Business, Francis Marion University, Florence, South Carolina 29501. I appreciate and need your input to continually improve this text in future editions. Drawing my attention to specific errors or deficiencies in coverage or exposition will especially be appreciated. Thank you for using this text.

F. R. D.

BRIEF CONTENTS

CONTENTS

PART 2
Strategy Formulation   85

PART 6
Case Analysis

PART 7
Cases

MANUFACTURING ORGANIZATIONS

[a]Denotes an international organization

[b]Denotes a case updated from fourth edition of the text

[c]Denotes a new case appearing for first time in text

PART · 1

Overview of Strategic Management

Chapter 1

THE NATURE OF STRATEGIC MANAGEMENT

OBJECTIVES

After studying this chapter, you should be able to:

- Describe the strategic-management process.
- Explain the need for integrating analysis and intuition in strategic management.
- Define and give examples of key terms in strategic management.
- Discuss the nature of strategy formulation, implementation, and evaluation activities.
- Describe the benefits of good strategic management.
- Explain why "good ethics is good business" in strategic management.

*T*his chapter provides an overview of strategic management. It introduces a practical, integrative model of the strategic-management process and defines basic activities and terms in strategic management. It presents the benefits of strategic management and discusses the importance of business ethics.

This chapter initiates several themes that permeate all chapters of this text. First, *communication is a key to successful strategic management*. The strategic-management process is more important than resultant documents, because through involvement in the process, managers and employees become committed to supporting the organization. Dialogue and participation are essential ingredients. The chief executive officer of Rockwell International explains, "We believe that fundamental to effective strategic management is fully informed employees at all organizational levels. We expect every business segment to inform every employee about the business objectives, the direction of the business, the progress towards achieving objectives, and our customers, competitors and product plans."

A second theme is that *global considerations impact virtually all strategic decisions!* The boundaries of countries can no longer define the limits of our imaginations. To see and appreciate the world from the perspective of others has become a matter of survival for businesses. The underpinnings of strategic management hinge upon managers' gaining an understanding of competitors, markets, prices, suppliers, distributors, governments, creditors, shareholders, and customers worldwide. The price and quality of a firm's products and services must be competitive on a worldwide basis, not just a local basis. A Global Perspective is provided in all chapters of this text to emphasize the importance of global factors in strategic management.

A third theme in this text is that *the natural environment has become an important strategic issue*. With the demise of communism and the end of the Cold War, perhaps no greater threat exists to business and society than the continuous exploitation and decimation of our natural environment. Mark Starik at George Washington University says, "The 1990s decade is critical in halting and reversing worldwide ecological destruction and deterioration; this is a strategic issue that needs immediate and substantive attention by all businesses and managers." A Natural Environment Perspective is provided in all chapters to illustrate how firms are addressing environmental concerns.

WHAT IS STRATEGIC MANAGEMENT?

Once there were two company presidents who competed in the same industry. These two presidents decided to go on a camping trip to discuss a possible merger. They hiked deep into the woods. Suddenly, they came upon a grizzly bear that rose up on its hind legs and snarled. Instantly, the first president took off his knapsack and got out a pair of jogging shoes. The second president said, "Hey, you can't outrun that bear." The first president responded, "Maybe I can't outrun that bear, but I can surely outrun you!" This story captures the notion of strategic management.

Defining Strategic Management. Strategic management can be defined as the art and science of formulating, implementing, and evaluating cross-functional decisions that enable an organization to achieve its objectives. As this definition implies, strategic management focuses on integrating management, marketing, finance/accounting, production/operations, research and development, and computer information systems to achieve organizational success. The term "strategic management" is used at many colleges and universities as the title for the capstone course in business administration, "business policy," which integrates material from all business courses.

Stages of Strategic Management. The *strategic-management process* consists of three stages: strategy formulation, strategy implementation, and strategy evaluation. *Strategy formulation* includes developing a business mission, identifying an organization's external opportunities and threats, determining internal strengths and weaknesses, establishing long-term objectives, generating alternative strategies, and choosing particular strategies to pursue. Strategy-formulation issues include deciding what new businesses to enter, what businesses to abandon, how to allocate resources, whether to expand operations or diversify, whether to enter international markets, whether to merge or form a joint venture, and how to avoid a hostile takeover.

Since no organization has unlimited resources, strategists must decide which alternative strategies will benefit the firm most. Strategy-formulation decisions commit an organization to specific products, markets, resources, and technologies over an extended period of time. Strategies determine long-term competitive advantages. For better or worse, strategic decisions have enduring effects on an organization and major multifunctional consequences. Top managers have the best perspective to fully understand the ramifications of formulation decisions; they have the authority to commit the resources necessary for implementation.

Strategy-implementation requires a firm to establish annual objectives, devise policies, motivate employees, and allocate resources so that formulated strategies can be executed; strategy implementation includes developing a strategy-supportive culture, creating an effective organizational structure, redirecting marketing efforts, preparing budgets, developing and utilizing information systems, and linking employee compensation to organizational performance.

Strategy-implementation is often called the action stage of strategic management. *Implementing* means mobilizing employees and managers to put formulated strategies into action. Often considered to be the most difficult stage in strategic management, strategy implementation requires personal discipline, commitment, and sacrifice. Successful strategy implementation hinges upon managers' ability to motivate employees, which is more an art than a science. Strategies formulated but not implemented serve no useful purpose.

Interpersonal skills are especially critical for successful strategy implementation. Strategy-implementation activities affect all employees and managers in an organization. Every division and department must decide on answers to questions such as "What must we do to implement our part of the organization's strategy?" and "How best can we get the job done?" The challenge of implementation is to stimulate managers and employees throughout an organization to work with pride and enthusiasm toward achieving stated objectives.

Strategy evaluation is the final stage in strategic management. Managers desperately need to know when particular strategies are not working well; strategy evaluation is the primary means for obtaining this information. All strategies are subject to future modification because external and internal factors are constantly changing. Three fundamental strategy-evaluation activities are (1) reviewing external and internal factors that are the bases for current strategies, (2) measuring performance, and (3) taking corrective actions. Strategy evaluation is needed because success today is no guarantee of success tomorrow! Success always creates new and different problems; complacent organizations experience demise.

Strategy formulation, implementation, and evaluation activities occur at three hierarchical levels in a large organization: corporate, divisional or strategic business unit, and functional. By fostering communication and interaction among managers and employees across hierarchical levels, strategic management helps a firm function as a competitive team. Most small businesses and some large businesses do not have divisions or strategic business units; they have only the corporate and functional levels. Nevertheless, managers and employees at these two levels should be actively involved in strategic-management activities.

Peter Drucker says the prime task of strategic management is thinking through the overall mission of a business:

> ...that is, of asking the question "What is our Business?" This leads to the setting of objectives, the development of strategies, and the making of today's decisions for tomorrow's results. This clearly must be done by a part of the organization that can see the entire business; that can balance objectives and the needs of today against the needs of tomorrow; and that can allocate resources of men and money to key results.[1]

Integrating Intuition and Analysis. The strategic-management process can be described as an objective, logical, systematic approach for making major decisions in an organization. It attempts to organize qualitative and quantitative information in a way that allows effective decisions to be made under conditions of uncertainty. Yet, strategic management is not a pure science that lends itself to a nice, neat, one-two-three approach.

Based on past experiences, judgment, and feelings, *intuition* is essential to making good strategic decisions. Intuition is particularly useful for making decisions in situations of great uncertainty or little precedent. It is also helpful when highly interrelated variables exist, when there is immense pressure to be right, or when it is necessary to choose from several plausible alternatives.[2] These situations describe the very nature and heart of strategic management.

Some managers and owners of businesses profess to have extraordinary abilities for using intuition alone in devising brilliant strategies. For example, Will Durant, who organized General Motors Corporation, was described by Alfred Sloan as "a man who would proceed on a course of action guided solely, as far as I could tell, by some intuitive flash of brilliance. He never felt obliged to make an engineering hunt for the facts. Yet at times he was astoundingly correct in his judgment."[3] Albert Einstein acknowledged the importance of intuition when he said, "I believe in intuition and inspiration. At times I feel certain that I am right while not knowing the reason. Imagination is more important than knowledge, because knowledge is limited, whereas imagination embraces the entire world."[4]

Although some organizations today may survive and prosper because they have intuitive geniuses managing them, most are not so fortunate. Most organizations can benefit from strategic management, which is based upon integrating intuition and analysis in decision making. Choosing an intuitive or analytic approach to decision making is not an either-or proposition. Managers at all levels in an organization should inject their intuition and judgment into strategic-management analyses. Analytical thinking and intuitive thinking complement each other.

Operating from the "I've already made up my mind, don't bother me with the facts" mode is not management by intuition; it is management by ignorance.[5] Drucker says, "I believe in intuition only if you discipline it. 'Hunch' artists, who make a diagnosis but don't check it out with the facts, are the ones in medicine who kill people, and in management kill businesses."[6] In a sense, the strategic-management process is an attempt to duplicate what goes on in the mind of a brilliant intuitive person who knows the business. Successful strategic management hinges upon effective integration of intuition and analysis, as Henderson notes:

> The accelerating rate of change today is producing a business world in which customary managerial habits in organizations are increasingly inadequate. Experience alone was an adequate guide when changes could be made in small increments. But intuitive and experience-based management philosophies are grossly inadequate when decisions are strategic and have major, irreversible consequences.[7]

Adapting to Change. The strategic-management process is based on the belief that organizations should continually monitor internal and external events and trends so that timely changes can be made as needed. The rate and magnitude of changes that affect organizations are increasing dramatically. Consider, for example, palmtop computers, color fax machines, voice mail, monoclonal antibodies, completion of the English Channel tunnel, the aging population, collapse of the Soviet Union, potential collapse of the Yeltsin-led government in Russia, the Hong Kong annexation, and unification of Western Europe. To survive, all organizations must be capable of astutely identifying and adapting to change. The strategic-management process is aimed at allowing organizations to effectively adapt to change over the long run.

> In today's business environment, more than any preceding era, the only constant is change. Successful organizations effectively manage change, continuously adapting their bureaucracies, strategies, systems, products, and cultures to survive the shocks and prosper from the forces that decimate the competition.[8]

Information technology and globalization are external changes that are transforming business and society today. On a political map, the boundaries between countries are as clear as ever, but on a competitive map showing the real flows of financial and industrial activity, the boundaries have largely disappeared.[9] Speedy flow of information has eaten away at national boundaries so that people worldwide readily see for themselves how other people live. People are traveling abroad more; ten million Japanese travel abroad annually. People are emigrating more; East Germans to West Germany and Mexicans to the United States are examples. As the Global Perspective

A GLOBAL PERSPECTIVE
THE WORLD'S LARGEST COMPANIES

Wall Street Journal's annual ranking of the world's largest companies revealed in 1993 that 30 of the world's 100 largest companies are Japanese, compared to 23 in 1992. Japan dominates especially among financial institutions. As shown below, the five largest banks in the world are Japanese, as are four of the five largest insurance companies, and three of the five largest securities firms.

BANKS	INSURANCE COMPANIES	SECURITIES FIRMS
Dai-Ichi Kangyo Bank	Nippon Life	Nomura Securities
Sumitomo Bank	Prudential Insurance (US)	Merrill Lynch (US)
Sakura Bank	Zerkyoren	Daiwa Securities
Fuji Bank	Dai-Ichi Mutual Life	Nikko Securities
Sanwa Bank	Sumitomo Life	Salomon (US)

Japan's new prime minister, Morihiro Hosokawa, elected in August 1993, is pleased at these results. He would like to see Japan controlling world financial markets and currencies by the year 2000.

Source: Adapted from *Wall Street Journal*, September 27, 1993, pp. R26–R27.

indicates, we are becoming a borderless world with global citizens, global competitors, global customers, global suppliers, and global distributors!

The need to adapt to change leads organizations to key strategic-management questions, such as: What kind of business should we become? Are we in the right fields? Should we reshape our business? What new competitors are entering our industry? What strategies should we pursue? How are our customers changing? Are new technologies being developed that could put us out of business?

KEY TERMS IN STRATEGIC MANAGEMENT

Before we go any further in discussing strategic management, we should define eight key terms: strategists, mission statements, external opportunities and threats, internal strengths and weaknesses, long-term objectives, strategies, annual objectives, and policies.

Strategists. Strategists are individuals who are most responsible for the success or failure of an organization. Strategists have various job titles, such as chief executive officer, president, owner, chairman of the board, executive director, chancellor, dean, or entrepreneur. Jonas, Fry, and Srivastva recently reported that strategists' three principal responsibilities in organizations are creating a context for change, building commitment and ownership, and balancing stability and innovation.[10]

Strategists in the 1990s are expected to change in ways outlined in Table 1–1. For example, strategists in the year 2000 will provide more visionary leadership, will better link compensation to performance, will communicate more frequently with employees, and will emphasize business ethics more. Coverage of these topics is expanded in this edition of this text.

Strategists differ as much as organizations themselves, and these differences must be considered in the formulation, implementation, and evaluation of strategies. Strategists differ in their attitudes, values, ethics, willingness to take risks, concern for social responsibility, concern for profitability, concern for short-run versus long-run aims, and management style. Some strategists will not consider some types of strategies due to their personal philosophy. For example, David Wickins, who replaced Colin Chapman as chairman of the board of Lotus, the car manufacturer, says, "Lotus has never been run with the objective of being a profitable company. Colin Chapman was quite simply interested in making cars go fast. I have a different viewpoint."[11]

Some strategists agree with Ralph Nader, who proclaims that organizations have tremendous social obligations. Others agree with Milton Friedman, an economist, who maintains that organizations have no obligation to do any more for society than is legally required. Most strategists agree that the first social responsibility of any business must be to make enough profit to cover the costs of the future, because if this is not achieved, no other social responsibility can be met. Strategists should examine social problems in terms of potential costs and benefits to the firm, and address social issues that could benefit the firm most.

Mission Statements. Mission statements are "enduring statements of purpose that distinguish one business from other similar firms. A mission statement identifies the scope of a firm's operations in product and market terms."[12] It addresses the basic question that faces all strategists: "What is our Business?" A clear mission statement describes the values and priorities of an organization. Developing a business mission compels strategists to think about the nature and scope of present operations and to

TABLE 1-1 What Traits CEOs Have—and Will Need: Percent Describing Traits or Talents Dominant Now in the CEO and Important for the CEO of 2000

PERSONAL BEHAVIOR	NOW	YEAR 2000	KNOWLEDGE AND SKILLS	NOW	YEAR 2000
Conveys strong sense of vision	75%	98%	Strategy formulation	68%	78%
Links compensation to performance	66%	91%	Human resource management	41%	53%
Communicates frequently with employees	59%	89%	International economics and politics	10%	19%
Emphasizes ethics	74%	85%	Science and technology	11%	15%
Plans for management succession	56%	85%	Computer literacy	3%	7%
Communicates frequently with customers	41%	78%	Marketing and sales	50%	48%
Reassigns or terminates unsatisfactory employees	34%	71%	Negotiation	34%	24%
Rewards loyalty	48%	44%	Accounting and finance	33%	24%
Makes all major decisions	39%	21%	Handling media and public speaking	16%	13%
Behaves conservatively	32%	13%	Production	21%	9%

Source: Lester Korn, "How the Next CEO Will Be Different," *Fortune* (22 May 1989): 157. Note: This information is based on a Columbia University survey of 1,500 senior executives, 870 of them CEOs, in 20 countries.

assess the potential attractiveness of future markets and activities. A mission statement broadly charts the future direction of an organization.

Research suggests that 60 percent of all organizations have developed a formal mission statement and that high-performing firms have more well developed mission statements than low-performing firms.[13] The current mission statement of Adolph Coors Company is the following:

We are a highly successful, innovative company of stand alone and self-sustaining businesses. We are leaders in technology, quality products and services that provide recognizably superior customer satisfaction. We are growth and profit oriented, developing new businesses from internally generated technology and synergistic acquisitions. Our business is known for quality relationships which are honest, ethical, and caring. Our employees grow personally as the company grows. Our work life is exciting, challenging and rewarding in a friendly atmosphere of teamwork and mutual respect. We are socially responsible and strive for the betterment of society.[14]

External Opportunities and Threats. Other key terms in our study of strategic management are *external opportunities* and *external threats.* These terms refer to economic, social, cultural, demographic, environmental, political, legal, governmental, technological, and competitive trends and events that could significantly benefit or harm an organization in the future. Opportunities and threats are largely beyond the control of a single organization, thus the term "external." The computer revolution, biotechnology, population shifts, changing work values and attitudes, space exploration, recyclable packages, and increased competition from foreign companies are examples of opportunities or threats for companies. These types of changes are creating a different type of consumer and consequently a need for different types of products, services, and strategies. Other opportunities and threats may include the passage of a new law, the introduction of a new product by a competitor, a national catastrophe, or the declining value of the dollar. A competitor's strength could be a threat. Unrest in Eastern Europe, rising interest rates, or the war against drugs could represent an opportunity or a threat.

A basic tenet of strategic management is that firms need to formulate strategies to take advantage of external opportunities and to avoid or reduce the impact of external threats. For this reason, identifying, monitoring, and evaluating external opportunities and threats is essential for success. This process of conducting research and gathering and assimilating external information is sometimes called environmental scanning or industry analysis.

Internal Strengths and Weaknesses. *Internal strengths* and *internal weaknesses* are controllable activities within an organization that are performed especially well or poorly. Management, marketing, finance/accounting, production/operations, research and development, and computer information systems activities of a business are areas where internal strengths or weaknesses arise. The process of identifying and evaluating organizational strengths and weaknesses in the functional areas of a business is an essential strategic-management activity. Organizations strive to pursue strategies that capitalize on internal strengths and improve on internal weaknesses.

Strengths and weaknesses are determined relative to competitors. "Relative" deficiency or superiority is important information. Also, strengths and weaknesses can be determined by elements of "being rather than performance." For example, a strength may involve ownership of natural resources or a historic reputation for quality. Strengths and weaknesses may be determined relative to a firm's own objectives. For example, high levels of inventory turnover may not be a strength to a firm that seeks never to stock-out.

Internal factors can be determined in a number of ways that include computing ratios, measuring performance, and comparing to past periods and industry averages. Various types of surveys can also be developed and administered to examine internal factors such as employee morale, production efficiency, advertising effectiveness, and customer loyalty. Robert H. Short, chief executive officer of Portland General Corporation, describes his firm's strategy in terms of strengths and weaknesses:

> First and foremost we are an energy company for the people of Oregon. Indeed, energy is our fundamental strength, and we intend to pursue growth aggressively in this business. To build on our strengths, however, we must mitigate or eliminate our weaknesses. I am proud of the way Portland General is drawing on its strengths to build for another century of success.[15]

Long-term Objectives. *Objectives* can be defined as specific results that an organization seeks to achieve in pursuing its basic mission. *Long-term* means more than one year. Objectives are essential for organizational success because they provide direction, aid in evaluation, create synergy, reveal priorities, allow coordination, and provide a basis for effective planning, organizing, motivating, and controlling activities. Objectives should be challenging, measurable, consistent, reasonable, and clear. In a multidivisional firm, objectives should be established for the overall company and for each division. Minnesota Power's long-term objectives are to achieve a 13 percent return on equity (ROE) in their core electric utility, 14 percent ROE on water resource operations, and

15 percent on support businesses. Minnesota Power also strives to stay in the top 25 percent of electric utilities in the United States in terms of common stock's market-to-book ratio, and to maintain an annual growth in earnings per share of 5 percent.

Strategies. *Strategies* are the means by which long-term objectives will be achieved. Business strategies may include geographic expansion, diversification, acquisition, product development, market penetration, retrenchment, divestiture, liquidation, and joint venture. Strategies currently being pursued by Polaroid Corporation and Sears, Roebuck & Company are described in Table 1–2.

Annual Objectives. *Annual objectives* are short-term milestones that organizations must achieve to reach long-term objectives. Like long-term objectives, annual objectives should be measurable, quantitative, challenging, realistic, consistent, and prioritized. They should be established at the corporate, divisional, and functional levels in a large organization. Annual objectives should be stated in terms of management, marketing, finance/accounting, production/operations, research and development, and information systems accomplishments. A set of annual objectives is needed for each long-term objective. Annual objectives are especially important in strategy implementation, whereas long-term objectives are particularly important in strategy formulation. Annual objectives represent the basis for allocating resources.

Campbell Soup Corporation has an annual objective to achieve 20 percent growth in earnings, a 20 percent return on equity, and a 20 percent return on invested cash. The company calls this ERC, for earnings, returns, and cash.

The Tribune Company (the nation's fifth-largest publisher of newspapers and owner of the Chicago Cubs baseball team) is another firm that has clear annual objectives. Stanton Cook, president and chief executive officer of Tribune, emphasizes annual objectives. Tribune strives to have an 18-percent annual return on equity (net income divided by average stockholders' investment) and a 30-percent debt to total capital ratio.

Policies. The final key term to be highlighted here is *policies*—the means by which annual objectives will be achieved. Policies include guidelines, rules, and procedures

---

TABLE 1-2 Two Organizations' Strategies

Polaroid Corporation is one of only a few American companies today pursuing a conglomerate diversification strategy which carries the firm into a new industry. Polaroid is getting out of the photography business and moving into the electronic imaging business. Instant photography accounts for 85 percent of Polaroid's sales in 1993; company plans by the year 2000 are to obtain 85 percent of sales from medical imaging and graphic arts.

Sears, Roebuck & Company's strategy from the mid–1990s include focusing on women customers, increasing apparel offerings, closing catalog operations and stores, cutting more than 50,000 employees, closing more than 100 unprofitable stores, refurbishing more than 500 profitable stores, moving furniture out of all Sears stores and into a new chain of shops called Homelife, divesting of Coldwell Banker, and selling a 20 percent stake in Allstate.

established to support efforts to achieve stated objectives. Policies are guides to decision making and address repetitive or recurring situations.

Policies are most often stated in terms of management, marketing, finance/accounting, production/operations, research and development, and computer information systems activities. Policies can be established at the corporate level and apply to an entire organization, at the divisional level and apply to a single division, or at the functional level and apply to particular operational activities or departments. Policies, like annual objectives, are especially important in strategy implementation because they outline an organization's expectations of its employees and managers. Policies allow consistency and coordination within and between organizational departments.

Most firms have policies against drinking at work. The Centers for Disease Control recently reported that states with the highest alcohol consumption per employee were Wisconsin, New Hampshire, Minnesota, Montana, the Dakotas, Texas, and Hawaii.

Substantial research suggests that a healthier work force can more effectively and efficiently implement strategies. The National Center for Health Promotion estimates that more than 80 percent of all American corporations have "No Smoking" policies. "No Smoking" policies are usually derived from annual objectives that seek to reduce corporate medical costs associated with absenteeism and to provide a healthy workplace. Pullman Company in Garden Grove, California, charges smokers ten dollars more each month for health insurance than it charges nonsmokers.

THE STRATEGIC-MANAGEMENT MODEL

The strategic-management process can best be studied and applied using a model. Every model represents some kind of process. The framework illustrated in Figure 1–1 is a widely accepted, comprehensive model of the strategic-management process.[16] This model does not guarantee success, but it does represent a clear and practical approach for formulating, implementing, and evaluating strategies. Relationships among major components of the strategic-management process are shown in the model, which appears in all subsequent chapters with appropriate areas shaded to show the particular focus of each chapter.

Identifying an organization's existing mission, objectives, and strategies is the logical starting point for strategic management because a firm's present situation and condition may preclude certain strategies and may even dictate a particular course of action. Every organization has a mission, objectives, and strategy, even if these elements are not consciously designed, written, or communicated. The answer to where an organization is going can be determined largely by where the organization has been!

The strategic-management process is dynamic and continuous. A change in any one of the major components in the model can necessitate a change in any or all of the other components. For instance, a shift in the economy could represent a major opportunity and require a change in long-term objectives and strategies; or a failure to accomplish annual objectives could require a change in policy; or a major competitor could announce a change in strategy that requires a change in the firm's mission. Therefore, strategy formulation, implementation, and evaluation activities should be performed on a continual basis, not just at the end of the year or semi-annually. The strategic-management process never really ends.

The strategic-management process is not as cleanly divided and neatly performed in practice as the strategic-management model suggests. Strategists do not go through the process in lockstep fashion. Generally, there is give-and-take among hierarchical levels of an organization. Many organizations conduct formal meetings semiannually to

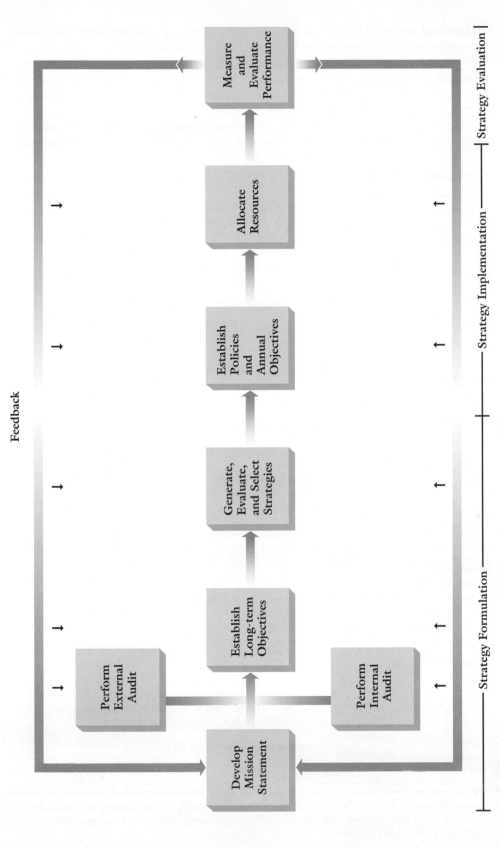

Feedback

Perform
External
Audit

Develop
Mission
Statement

Perform
Internal
Audit

Establish
Long-term
Objectives

Generate,
Evaluate,
and Select
Strategies

Establish
Policies
and
Annual
Objectives

Allocate
Resources

Measure
and
Evaluate
Performance

Strategy Formulation ——— Strategy Implementation ——— Strategy Evaluation

FIGURE 1-1 A Comprehensive Strategic-Management Model

discuss and update the firm's mission, opportunities/threats, strengths/weaknesses, strategies, objectives, policies, and performance. These meetings are commonly held off-premises and called "retreats." The rationale for periodically conducting strategic-management meetings away from the work site is to encourage more creativity and candor among participants. Good communication and feedback are needed throughout the strategic-management process.

As shown in Figure 1–2, a number of different forces affect the formality of strategic management in organizations. Size of organization is a key factor; smaller firms

FIGURE 1-2 Forces Influencing Design of Strategic-Management Systems

Source: Reprinted with permission of the Free Press, a Division of Macmillan, Inc., from *Strategic Planning: What Every Manager Must Know* by George A. Steiner (New York: Free Press, 1979), p. 54. Copyright 1979 by the Free Press.

are less formal in performing strategic-management tasks. Other variables that affect formality are management styles, complexity of environment, complexity of production processes, nature of problems, and purpose of planning system.

BENEFITS OF STRATEGIC MANAGEMENT

Strategic management allows an organization to be more proactive than reactive in shaping its own future; it allows an organization to initiate and influence (rather than just respond to) activities, and thus to exert control over its own destiny. Small business owners, chief executive officers, presidents, and managers of many for-profit and nonprofit organizations have recognized and realized the benefits of strategic management.

Historically, the principal benefit of strategic management has been to help organizations make better strategies through the use of a more systematic, logical, and rational approach to strategic choice. This certainly continues to be a major benefit of strategic management, but research studies now indicate that the process, rather than the decision or document, is the more important contribution of strategic management.[17]

The manner in which strategic management is carried out thus is exceptionally important. A major aim of the process is to achieve understanding and commitment from all managers and employees. Understanding may be the most important benefit of strategic management, followed by commitment. When managers and employees understand what the organization is doing and why, they often feel a part of the firm and become committed to assisting it. This is especially true if employees also understand linkages between their own compensation and organizational performance. Managers and employees become surprisingly creative and innovative when they understand and support the firm's mission, objectives, and strategies. A great benefit of strategic management, then, is the opportunity that the process provides to empower individuals! *Empowerment* is the act of strengthening an individual's sense of effectiveness.[18]

More and more organizations are decentralizing the strategic-management process, recognizing that planning must involve lower-level managers and employees. The notion of centralized staff planning is being replaced in organizations by decentralized line manager planning. The process is a learning, helping, educating, and supporting activity, not merely a paper-shuffling activity among top executives. Strategic-management dialogue is more important than a nicely bound strategic-management document.[19] The worst thing strategists can do is develop strategic plans themselves and then present them to operating managers to execute. Through involvement in the process, line managers become "owners" of the strategy. Ownership of strategies by the people who have to execute them is a key to success!

Although making good strategic decisions is the major responsibility of an organization's owner or chief executive officer, managers and employees both must also be involved in strategy formulation, implementation, and evaluation activities. Participation is a key to gaining commitment for needed changes.

An increasing number of corporations and institutions are using strategic management to make effective decisions. Over 75 percent of all companies now use strategic-management techniques, compared to less than 25 percent in 1979.[20] But strategic-management is not a guarantee for success; it can be dysfunctional if conducted haphazardly. The benefits of strategic management to Rockwell International Corporation, Columbia Gas System Service Corporation, and Ogden Corporation are evidenced in Table 1-3. Waterman recently discovered the following benefit of strategic management for IBM Corporation:

TABLE 1-3   Top Managers Discuss Strategic Management in Their Firms

ROCKWELL INTERNATIONAL CORPORATION

We expect every business segment head to be responsible for the strategic direction of the business and the business team to be very knowledgeable about their business in the worldwide marketplace, to know where they are taking the business long term; and how they are going to position the business vis-a-vis worldwide competition, as well as the market place as a whole. We also expect every business to make full use of the corporation's resources in developing functionally-integrated implementation strategies that will beat the best of the competition. We will distinguish ourselves as a strategically managed worldwide company through the care and thoroughness with which our strategic management is linked to operational decision making. (Donald Beall, chief executive officer of Rockwell International, *Internal Report*, 1990.)

COLUMBIA GAS SYSTEM SERVICE CORPORATION

Headquartered in Wilmington, Delaware, Columbia Gas System's Strategic Plan forms the basis of all other planning activities—marketing plans, capital programs, financial plans, and so forth. Strategic management goes far beyond operational planning that has been traditional throughout Columbia. We are not just looking at projections of how much gas we'll need and where it will come from. The first part of our Strategic Plan is the Mission Statement, which sets the direction for the company. All operating units have their own mission statements, defining their business and their corporate reason for existing. These in turn are followed by long-term objectives which are broad statements of what the company intends to do, followed by annual objectives which for the most part are quantified. (James D. Little, executive vice president of Columbia Gas System, *Columbia Today*, Winter 1985–86, p. 2.)

OGDEN CORPORATION

The best long-run results come from good strategic decisions, which ensure doing the right things (effectiveness), and the combination of design, technology, and automation, which ensure doing things right (efficiency). To predict...without the ability to adapt is simply to foresee one's own end! The strategic objectives Ogden has achieved have enabled the adaptation necessary to cope with the changing economic environment for the balance of this century. We are describing a classic example of evolution; in this case, corporate evolution. To survive, both organisms and corporations must adapt to new circumstances. (Ralph Ablon, chairman of the board, Ogden Corporation)

I was blown away by the experience of talking with Chief Executive John Akers of IBM and learning how effective and elaborate IBM's strategic-management system was. At IBM, people explained it wasn't just a plan, it was a way of communicating with each other. Strategic management is important because it helps generate information and helps you communicate.[21]

William Dearden of Hershey Foods Corporation attributes his company's success to strategic management:

There is the strategic-management process. Planning for the long-term future has been entrenched as a way of life at Hershey, and we certainly plan to strengthen and rely on the process going forward.[22]

Financial Benefits. Research studies indicate that organizations using strategic-management concepts are more profitable and successful than those that do not. For example, a longitudinal study of 101 retail, service, and manufacturing firms over a 3-year period concluded that businesses using strategic-management concepts showed significant improvement in sales, profitability, and productivity compared to firms without systematic planning activities; another study reported that up to 80 percent of the improvement possible in a firm's profitability is achieved through changes in a company's strategic direction; Cook and Ferris reported that the practices of high-performing firms reflect a more strategic orientation and longer-term focus. [23] High-performing firms tend to do systematic planning to prepare for future fluctuations in their external and internal environments. Firms with planning systems more closely resembling strategic-management theory generally exhibit superior long-term financial performance relative to their industry.

High-performing firms seem to make more informed decisions with good anticipation of both short- and long-term consequences. On the other hand, firms that perform poorly often engage in activities that are shortsighted and do not reflect good forecasting of future conditions. Michael Allen found that strategic management demonstrated impressive power by dramatically improving the performance of a number of major companies that had implemented it, including General Electric, American Express, Allied Corporation, Dun & Bradstreet, and Pitney Bowes.[24] Strategists of low-performing organizations are often preoccupied with solving internal problems and meeting paperwork deadlines. They typically underestimate their competitors' strengths and overestimate their own firm's strengths. They often attribute weak performance to uncontrollable factors such as a poor economy, technological change, or foreign competition.

Dun & Bradstreet reports that nearly 100,000 businesses in the United States failed in 1993. Hawaii, Connecticut, and California had the highest increases in number of failures. Business failures include bankruptcies, foreclosures, liquidations, and court-mandated receiverships. Although many factors besides a lack of effective strategic management obviously can lead to business failure, these statistics suggest that strategic-management concepts could yield substantial financial benefits for many organizations.

Nonfinancial Benefits. Besides helping firms avoid financial demise, strategic management offers other tangible benefits, such as an enhanced awareness of external threats, an improved understanding of competitors' strategies, increased employee productivity, reduced resistance to change, and a clearer understanding of performance-reward relationships. Strategic management enhances the problem-prevention capabilities of organizations because it promotes interaction among managers at all divisional and functional levels. Interaction can enable firms to "turn on" their managers and employees by nurturing them, sharing organizational objectives with them, empowering them to help improve the product or service, and recognizing their contributions. According to Tom Peters, the difference between a turned-on and a turned-off worker is not 5 percent or 10 percent, but 100 percent to 200 percent.[25]

In addition to empowering managers and employees, strategic management often brings order and discipline to an otherwise floundering firm. It can be the beginning of an efficient and effective managerial system. Strategic management may renew confidence in the current business strategy or point to the need for corrective actions. The strategic-management process provides a basis for identifying and rationalizing the need for change to all managers and employees of a firm; it helps them view change as an opportunity rather than a threat.

Greenley stresses that strategic management offers the following benefits:

1. It allows for identification, prioritization, and exploitation of opportunities.
2. It provides an objective view of management problems.
3. It represents a framework for improved coordination and control of activities.
4. It minimizes the effects of adverse conditions and changes.
5. It allows major decisions to better support established objectives.
6. It allows more effective allocation of time and resources to identified opportunities.
7. It allows fewer resources and less time to be devoted to correcting erroneous or ad hoc decisions.
8. It creates a framework for internal communication among personnel.
9. It helps to integrate the behavior of individuals into a total effort.
10. It provides a basis for the clarification of individual responsibilities.
11. It gives encouragement to forward thinking.
12. It provides a cooperative, integrated, and enthusiastic approach to tackling problems and opportunities.
13. It encourages a favorable attitude towards change.
14. It gives a degree of discipline and formality to the management of a business.[26]

BUSINESS ETHICS AND STRATEGIC MANAGEMENT

Business ethics can be defined as principles of conduct within organizations that guide decision making and behavior. Good business ethics is a prerequisite for good strategic management; good ethics is just good business!

A rising tide of consciousness about the importance of business ethics is sweeping America and the world. Strategists are the individuals primarily responsible for assuring that high ethical principles are espoused and practiced in an organization. All strategy formulation, implementation, and evaluation decisions have ethical ramifications.

Newspapers and business magazines daily report legal and moral breaches of ethical conduct by both public and private organizations. As the Natural Environment Perspective indicates, harming the natural environment is unethical, illegal, and costly. Dow Chemical, however, is a role model company in this regard.

A new wave of ethics issues related to product safety, employee health, sexual harassment, AIDS in the workplace, smoking, acid rain, affirmative action, waste disposal, foreign business practices, cover-ups, takeover tactics, conflicts of interest, employee privacy, inappropriate gifts, security of company records, and layoffs has accented the need for strategists to develop a clear code of business ethics. United Technologies Corporation recently revealed a 21-page Code of Ethics and named a new vice president of business ethics. Baxter Travenol Laboratories, IBM, Caterpillar Tractor, Chemical Bank, Exxon, Dow Corning, and Celanese are firms that have a formal code of business ethics. Note how clearly BellSouth's code of business ethics in Table 1–4 outlines the standards of behavior expected of all managers and employees.

A business code of ethics can provide a basis on which policies can be devised to guide daily behavior and decisions at the work site. Merely having a code of ethics, however, is not sufficient to assure ethical business behavior. A code of ethics can be viewed as a public relations gimmick, or a set of platitudes, or window dressing. To ensure that the code is read, understood, believed, and remembered, organizations need to conduct periodic ethics workshops to sensitize people to workplace circumstances in which ethics issues may arise.[27] Chemical Bank, the nation's sixth-largest bank, has an extensive ethics education program whereby all new employees attend sessions and sign Chemical's code of ethics. In a survey conducted by the national accounting firm Touche-Ross, 63 percent of corporate executives believed that high ethical standards strengthened, rather than weakened, a firm's competitive position.

An ethics "culture" needs to permeate organizations! To help create an ethics culture, Citicorp has developed a business ethics board game that is played by 40,000 employees in 45 countries. Called "The Work Ethic," this game asks players business ethics questions, such as how to deal with a customer who offers you football tickets in exchange for a new, backdated IRA. Diana Robertson at the Wharton School believes the game is effective because it is interactive. Many organizations, such as Prime Computer and Kmart, have developed a code-of-conduct manual outlining ethical expectations and giving examples of situations that commonly arise in their businesses. Harris Corporation's managers and employees are warned that failing to report an ethical violation by others could bring discharge.

One reason strategists' salaries are high compared to those of other individuals in an organization is that strategists must take the moral risks of the firm. Strategists are responsible for developing, communicating, and enforcing the code of business ethics for their organization. Although primary responsibility for ensuring ethical behavior rests with a firm's strategists, an integral part of the responsibility of all managers is to provide ethics leadership by constant example and demonstration. Managers hold positions that enable them to influence and educate many people. This makes managers responsible for the development and implementation of ethical decision making. Gellerman and Drucker respectively offer some good advice for managers:

> All managers risk giving too much because of what their companies demand from them. But the same superiors who keep pressing you to do more, or to do it better, or faster, or less expensively, will turn on you should you cross that fuzzy line between right and wrong. They will blame you for exceeding instructions or for ignoring their warnings. The smartest managers already know that the best answer to the question, "How far is too far?" is don't try to find out.[28]

A man (or woman) might know too little, perform poorly, lack judgment and ability, and yet not do too much damage as a manager. But if that person lacks in character and integrity—no matter how knowledgeable, how brilliant, how successful—he

TABLE 1-4　　BellSouth's Code of Conduct

COUNT ON US!

We are committed to the highest ethical standards because we want people to know they can count on us. This commitment flows naturally from our responsibilities to our customers, our owners, our vendors and suppliers, our families, the communities where we live and work, and to each other. Trust is at the heart of these connections, and trust can only be built on honesty and dependability—on ethical conduct.

Our Customers Can Count on Us

We believe our first responsibility is to the people who count on us for their telecommunications needs—in the office, on the road, at home, wherever they might be. All else hinges on this. We will deal with customers straightforwardly and honestly. They will know they can depend not only on our products and services, but on our word and our character. We will promise only what we can deliver. When we err, we will make things right.

Our Owners Can Count on Us

We will provide the highest quality at a reasonable price. As we do so, we will earn a fair return on our owners' investment. Our aim is to increase the value of their investment over the years.

Our Vendors and Suppliers Can Count on Us

Vendors and suppliers must know we will be fair. BellSouth's interests will dictate our decisions about what products and services to buy; our decisions will be based on factors such as quality, price, service, and reliability.

Our Families Can Count on Us

We want our families to be proud of our character as individuals in the jobs we do and proud that we work for a company known for its integrity. We seek a healthy balance between our work and our family life.

Our Communities Can Count on Us

Beyond the quality, day-to-day service they expect from us in telecommunications, the cities and towns where we operate can also count on us for help in civic, charitable and other community activities.

We Can Count on Each Other

We take pride in the quality of our collective efforts at BellSouth; we take pride in the integrity of our company. A company's reputation is built on what its people do every day. BellSouth's reputation was built on the honesty of hundreds of thousands of people over the years, and we recognize that we can diminish that reputation in one single instant. We also know, however, that we can reinforce it every day. And since you and I inherited a company with a reputation for honesty and integrity, we are obligated to pass that heritage on to the women and men who follow us.

We will be even-handed with everyone around us—in scheduling work, in assigning jobs, in awarding incentives and promotions and in the way we treat one another generally.

Each of us expects to be heard and we in turn pledge to listen. We want honesty and openness—about mistakes as well as successes.

We will speak out when we see ethical lapses. We expect that no one will ask us to do anything wrong. Likewise, we will not ask anyone else to do anything wrong.

Satisfying the letter of the law is not enough. Ours is a higher standard. BellSouth's obligations are for the long term—not just for this quarter or this year. These obligations demand this pledge of us on professional, industry and personal ethics: We will build on BellSouth's heritage of integrity so that people will have an abiding trust in the company and our employees; they will know they can count on us. That is our pledge.

Source: BellSouth Corporation, *Internal Report*, 1993.

destroys. He destroys people, the most valuable resource of the enterprise. He destroys spirit. And he destroys performance. This is particularly true of the people at the head of an enterprise. For the spirit of an organization is created from the top. If an organization is great in spirit, it is because the spirit of its top people is great. If it decays, it does so because the top rots, as the proverb has it, "Trees die from the top." No one should ever become a strategist unless he or she is willing to have his or her character serve as the model for subordinates.[29]

According to John Akers of IBM, ethics and competitiveness are inseparable. [30] No society anywhere in the world can compete very long or successfully with people stealing from one another or not trusting one another, with every bit of information requiring notarized confirmation, with every disagreement ending up in litigation, or with government having to regulate businesses to keep them honest. Akers says being unethical is a recipe for headaches, inefficiency, and waste. History has proven that the greater the trust and confidence of people in the ethics of an institution or society, the greater its economic strength. Business relationships are built mostly on mutual trust and reputation. Short-term decisions based on greed and questionable ethics will preclude the necessary self-respect to gain the trust of others. More and more firms believe that ethics training and an ethics culture create strategic advantage.

In a recent *Academy of Management Executive* article, Susan Harrington emphasizes that ethics training programs should include messages from the CEO emphasizing ethical business practices, development and discussion of codes of ethics, and procedures for discussing and reporting unethical behavior.[31] Harrington suggests that firms can align ethical and strategic decision making by incorporating ethical considerations into long-term planning, integrating ethical decision making into the performance appraisal process, encouraging "whistle-blowing" or the reporting of unethical practices, and monitoring departmental and corporate performance regarding ethical issues.

In a final analysis, ethical standards come out of history and heritage. Our fathers and mothers and brothers and sisters of the past left to us an ethical foundation to build upon. Even the legendary football coach Vince Lombardi knew that some things were worth more than winning, as he required his players to have three kinds of loyalty: to God, to their families, and to the Green Bay Packers, "in that order."

COMPARING BUSINESS AND MILITARY STRATEGY

A strong military heritage underlies the study of strategic management. Terms such as *objectives, mission, strengths,* and *weaknesses* were first formulated to address problems on the battlefield. In many respects, business strategy is like military strategy, and military strategists have learned much over the centuries that can benefit business strategists today. Both business and military organizations try to use their own strengths to exploit competitors' weaknesses. If an organization's overall strategy is wrong (ineffective), then all the efficiency in the world may not be enough to allow success. Business or military success is generally not the happy result of accidental strategies. Rather, success is the product of continuous attention to changing external and internal conditions and the formulation and implementation of insightful adaptations to those conditions. The element of surprise provides great competitive advantages in both military and business strategy; information systems that provide data on opponents or competitors' strategies and resources are also vitally important.

Of course, a fundamental difference between military and business strategy is that business strategy is formulated, implemented, and evaluated with an assumption of *competition,* whereas military strategy is based on an assumption of *conflict.* Nonetheless, military conflict and business competition are so similar that many strategic-management techniques apply equally to both. Business strategists have access to valuable insights that military thinkers have refined over time. Superior strategy formulation and implementation can overcome an opponent's superiority in numbers and resources.

Both business and military organizations must adapt to change and constantly improve to be successful. Too often, firms do not change their strategies when their environment and competitive conditions dictate the need to change. Gluck offers a classic military example of this:

> When Napoleon won it was because his opponents were committed to the strategy, tactics, and organization of earlier wars. When he lost—against Wellington, the Russians, and the Spaniards—it was because he, in turn, used tried-and-true strategies against enemies who thought afresh, who were developing the strategies not of the last war, but of the next.[32]

CONCLUSION

All firms have a strategy, if it is informal, unstructured, and sporadic. All organizations are heading somewhere, but unfortunately some organizations do not know where. The old saying "If you do not know where you are going, then any road will lead you there!" accents the need for organizations to use strategic-management concepts and techniques. The strategic-management process is becoming more and more widely used by small firms, large companies, nonprofit institutions, governmental organizations, and multinational conglomerates alike. The process of "empowering" managers and employees has almost limitless benefits.

Organizations should take a proactive rather than a reactive approach in their industry, and should strive to influence, anticipate, and initiate rather than just respond to events. The strategic-management process embodies this approach to decision making. It represents a logical, systematic, and objective approach for determining an enterprise's future direction. The stakes are generally too high for strategists to use intuition alone in choosing among alternative courses of action. Successful strategists take the time to think about their business, where they are with the business, and what they want to be as an organization, and then implement programs and policies to get from where they are to where they want to be in a reasonable period of time.

It is a known and accepted fact that people and organizations that plan ahead are much more likely to become what they want to become than those who do not plan at all. A "good" strategist plans and controls his plans, while a "bad" strategist never plans and then tries to control people! This textbook is devoted to providing you with the tools necessary to be a "good" strategist.

KEY TERMS AND CONCEPTS

Annual Objectives
Business Ethics
Code of Business Ethics
Corporate Evolution
Empowerment
Environmental Scanning
External Audit
External Opportunities
External Threats

Forward Integration
Horizontal Diversification
Internal Audit
Internal Strengths
Internal Weaknesses
Intuition
Long-term Objectives
Mission Statement
Policies

Strategic Management
Strategic-Management Process
Strategies
Strategists

Strategy Evaluation
Strategy Formulation
Strategy Implementation

1. Explain why business policy is often called a "capstone course."

2. Select one of the suggested readings at the end of this chapter. Go to your college library and find that article. Read the article. Prepare a one-page written summary that includes your personal thoughts on the subject.

3. What aspect of strategy formulation do you think requires the most time? Why?

4. Why is strategy implementation often considered the most difficult stage in the strategic-management process?

5. Why is it so important to integrate intuition and analysis in strategic management?

6. Explain the importance of a formal mission statement.

7. Discuss relationships among objectives, strategies, and policies.

8. Why do you think some chief executive officers fail to use a strategic-management approach to decision making? Can you identify and describe a good alternative approach?

9. Discuss the importance of feedback in the strategic-management model.

10. How can strategists best assure that strategies formulated will be effectively implemented?

11. Give an example of a recent political development that changed the overall strategy of an organization.

12. Who are the major competitors of your college or university? What are their strengths and weaknesses? What are their strategies? How successful are these institutions compared to your college?

13. If you owned a small business, would you develop a code of business conduct? If yes, what variables would you include? If no, how would you assure that ethical business standards were being followed by your employees?

14. Would strategic-management concepts and techniques benefit foreign businesses as much as domestic firms? Justify your answer.

15. What do you believe are some potential pitfalls or risks in using a strategic-management approach to decision making?

16. In your opinion, what is the single major benefit of using a strategic-management approach to decision making? Justify your answer.

17. Compare business strategy and military strategy.

18. What do you feel is the relationship between personal ethics and business ethics? Are they, or should they be, the same?

1. Peter Drucker, *Management: Tasks, Responsibilities, and Practices* (New York: Harper & Row, 1974): 611.

2. Weston Agor, "How Top Executives Use Their Intuition to Make Important Decisions," *Business Horizons* 29, no. 1 (January–February 1986): 6. Also, see Andrew Campbell, "Brief Case: Strategy and Intuition—A Conversation with Henry Mintzberg," *Long Range Planning* 24, no. 2. (April 1991):108–110.

3. Alfred Sloan, Jr., *Adventures of the White Collar Man* (New York: Doubleday, 1941), 104.

4. Quoted in Eugene Raudsepp, "Can You Trust Your Hunches?" *Management Review* 49, no. 4 (April 1960): 7.

5. Stephen Harper, "Intuition: What Separates Executives from Managers," *Business Horizons* 31, no. 5 (September–October 1988): 16.

6. Ron Nelson, "How to Be a Manager," *Success* (July–August 1985): 69.

7. Bruce Henderson, *Henderson on Corporate Strategy* (Boston: Abt Books, 1979), 6.

8. Robert Waterman, Jr., *The Renewal Factor: How the*

Best Get and Keep the Competitive Edge (New York: Bantam, 1987). See also Business Week (14 September 1987): 100. Also, see Academy of Management Executive III, no. 2 (May 1989): 115.

9. Kenichi Ohmae, "Managing in a Borderless World," Harvard Business Review 67, no. 3 (May–June 1989): 153.

10. Harry Jonas III, Ronald Fry, and Suresh Srivastva, "The Office of the CEO: Understanding the Executive Experience," Academy of Management Executive 4, no. 3 (August 1990): 36.

11. Rosemary Brady, "World Class," Forbes (18 June 1984): 133. See also Harry S. Jonas III, Ronald E. Fry, and Suresh Srivastva, "The Person of the CEO: Understanding the Executive Experience," Academy of Management Executive III, no. 3 (August 1989): 205.

12. John Pearce II and Fred David, "The Bottom Line on Corporate Mission Statements," Academy of Management Executive 1, no. 2 (May 1987): 109.

13. Ibid., 112. See also John A. Pearce and Fred R. David, "Corporate Mission Statements: The Bottom Line," Academy of Management Executive 1, no. 2 (May 1987): 109; and Fred R. David, "How Companies Define Their Mission," Long Range Planning 22, no.1 (February 1989): 90.

14. Adolph Coors Company, Annual Report (1988), 1.

15. Portland General Corporation, Annual Report (1986), 2, 3.

16. Fred R. David, "How Companies Define Their Mission," Long Range Planning 22, no. 1 (February 1989): 91.

17. Ann Langley, "The Roles of Formal Strategic Planning," Long Range Planning 21, no. 3 (June 1988): 40.

18. Jay Conger, "Leadership: The Art of Empowering Others," Academy of Management Executive III, no. 1 (February 1989): 18. See also D. Keith Denton and Barry L. Wisdom, "Shared Vision," Business Horizons 32, no. 4 (July–August 1989): 67.

19. Bernard Reimann, "Getting Value from Strategic Planning," Planning Review 16, no. 3 (May–June 1988): 42.

20. Michael Allen, "Strategic Management Hits Its Stride," Planning Review 13, no. 5 (September–October 1985): 6.

21. Robert Waterman, Jr., "How the Best Get Better," Business Week (14 September 1987): 99.

22. Hershey Foods Corporation, Annual Report, 1983, 3.

23. Richard Robinson, Jr., "The Importance of Outsiders in Small Firm Strategic Planning," Academy of Management Journal 25, no. 1 (March 1982): 80. Also, S. Schoeffler, Robert Buzzell, and Donald Heany, "Impact of Strategic Planning on Profit Performance," Harvard Business Review (March 1974): 137; Lawrence Rhyne, "The Relationship of Strategic Planning to Financial Performance," Strategic Management Journal 7 (1986): 432; and Deborah Cook and Gerald Ferris, "Strategic Human Resource Management and Firm Effectiveness in Industries Experiencing Decline," Human Resource Management 25, no. 3 (Fall 1986): 454.

24. Allen, 6.

25. Tom Peters, "Passion for Excellence," Public Broadcasting System videotape, 1987.

26. Gordon Greenley, "Does Strategic Planning Improve Company Performance?" Long Range Planning 19, no. 2 (April 1986): 106.

27. Saul Gellerman, "Managing Ethics from the Top Down," Sloan Management Review (Winter 1989): 77.

28. Saul Gellerman, "Why 'Good' Managers Make Bad Ethical Choices," Harvard Business Review 64, no. 4 (July–August 1986): 88.

29. Drucker, 462, 463.

30. John Akers, "Ethics and Competitiveness—Putting First Things First," Sloan Management Review (Winter 1989): 69–71.

31. Susan Harrington, "What Corporate America is Teaching About Ethics," Academy of Management Executive 5, no. 1 (February 1991): 24.

32. Frederick Gluck, "Taking the Mystique out of Planning," Across the Board (July–August 1985): 59.

CURRENT READINGS

Badaracco, Joseph L., Jr. "Business Ethics: Four Spheres of Executive Responsibility." California Management Review 34, no. 3 (Spring 1992): 64–79.

Basadur, Min. "Managing Creativity: A Japanese Model." The Executive VI, no. 2 (May 1992): 29–42.

Burrows, Brian. "Essay Review—The Greening of Business and Its Relationship to Business Ethics." Long Range Planning 26, no.1 (February 1993): 130–139.

Coplin, William D., and Michael K. O'Leary. "Brave New World?" Planning Review 22, no. 3 (May–June 1993): 34–41.

Dhebar, Anirudh. "Managing the Quality of Quantitative Analysis." Sloan Management Review 34, no. 2 (Winter 1993): 69–76.

Friedman, Frank B. "The Changing Role of the Environmental Manager." *Business Horizons* 35, no. 2 (March–April 1992): 25–28.

Garvin, David A. "Building a Learning Organization." *Harvard Business Review* 71, no. 4 (July–August 1993): 78–92.

Glassman, Myron, and Bruce McAfee. "Integrating the Personnel and Marketing Functions: The Challenge of the 1990s." *Business Horizons* 35, no. 3 (May –June 1992): 52–59.

Gustafson, James M. "The Booming Business of Busi-ness Ethics." *Business and Society Review* 81 (Spring 1992): 84–86.

Hart, Stuart L. "An Integrative Framework for Strategy-Making Processes." *The Academy of Management Review* 17, no. 2 (April 1992): 327–351.

Havens, Tim, M.D. "Strategy and the Art of Reinventing Value." *Harvard Business Review* 71, no. 5 (September–October 1993): 39–53.

Hemphill, Thomas A. "Can New Environmental Laws Overcome Old Flaws?" *Business and Society Review* 83 (Fall 1992): 46–49.

Ireland, R. Duane, Michael A. Hitt, and J. Clifton Williams. "Self-Confidence and Decisiveness: Prerequisites for Effective Management in the 1990s." *Business Horizons* 35, no. 1 (January–February 1992): 36–43.

McWilliams, Abagail, and Dennis L. Smart. "Efficiency v. Structure–Conduct–Performance: Implications for Strategy Research and Practice." *Journal of Management* 19, no. 1 (March 1993): 63–68.

Meyer, Christopher. "2020 Vision." *Planning Review* 20, no. 5 (September–October 1992): 39–41.

Moore, James F. "Predators and Prey: A New Ecology of Competition." *Harvard Business Review* (May–June 1993): 75–86.

Murphy, Emmett C., with Michael Snell. "The Genius of Sitting Bull: 13 Heroic Strategies for Today's Business Leaders." *Academy of Management Executive* VII, no. 2 (May 1993): 98–99.

Peattie, Ken. "Strategic Planning: Its Role in Organizational Politics." *Long Range Planning* 26, no. 3 (June 1993): 10–17.

Petry, Edward S., Jr., and Fred Tietz. "Can Ethics Officers Improve Office Ethics?" *Business and Society Review* 82 (Summer 1992): 21–25.

Savage, J. A., and J. M. Majot. "Industry Preaches Green but Is Far from Clean." *Business and Society Review* 83 (Fall 1992): 39–42.

Stacey, Ralph. "Strategy as Order Emerging from Chaos." *Long Range Planning* 26, no. 1 (February 1993): 10–17.

Stark, Andrew. "What's the Matter with Business Ethics?" *Harvard Business Review* (May–June 1993): 38–48.

Strati, Antonio. "Aesthetic Understanding of Organizational Life." *Academy of Management Review* 17, no. 3 (July 1992): 568–581.

Tenaglia, Mason, and Alistair Davidson. "A Directory of Strategic Management Software Tools." *Planning Review* 22, no. 4 (July–August 1993): 38–48.

Thakur, Manab, and Luis Ma. R. Calingo. "Strategic Thinking Is Hip, but Does It Make a Difference?" *Business Horizons* 35, no. 5 (September–October 1992): 47–54.

Trevino, Linda Klebe, and Bart Victor. "Reporting Unethical Behavior: A Social Context Perspective." *Academy of Management Journal* 35, no. 1 (March 1992): 38–64.

Vogel, David. "The Globalization of Business Ethics: Why America Remains Distinctive." *California Management Review* 35, no. 1 (Fall 1992): 30–49.

Watson, Charles. "The Meaning of Service in Business." *Business Horizons* 35, no. 1 (January–February 1992): 55–61.

Watson, Gregory H. "How Process Benchmarking Supports Corporate Strategy." *Planning Review* 22, no. 1 (January–February 1993): 12–15.

Wolfe, Art. "We've Had Enough Business Ethics." *Business Horizons* 36, no. 3 (May–June 1993): 1–3.

Woodman, Richard W., John E. Sawyer, and Ricky W. Griffin. "Toward a Theory of Organizational Creativity." *Academy of Management Review* 18, no. 2 (April 1993): 293–321.

THE COHESION CASE AND EXPERIENTIAL EXERCISES

Two special features of this text are introduced here: (1) the Cohesion Case and (2) the Experiential Exercises. As strategic-management concepts and techniques are introduced in this text, they are applied to the Cohesion Case through Experiential Exercises. The Cohesion Case centers on Hershey Foods Corporation in 1993. As the term "cohesion" implies, the Hershey Foods case and related exercises integrate material presented throughout the text. At least one exercise at the end of each chapter applies textual material to the Hershey Foods case. The Cohesion Case and

Experiential Exercises thus work together to give students practice applying strategic-management concepts and tools as they are presented in the text. In this way, students become prepared to perform case analyses as the policy course progresses.

Based in Hershey, Pennsylvania, and a leading manufacturer of candy and pasta, Hershey Foods was selected as the Cohesion Case for several important reasons. First, Hershey is a multinational corporation, so global issues can be discussed in class. Second, Hershey is a multidivisional organization, thus allowing strategic-management concepts to be applied at the corporate, divisional, and functional levels. Third, Hershey is undergoing extensive strategic changes and recently was rumored to be a takeover target by a larger competitor, Nestlé. Fourth, you have probably eaten Hershey candy and pasta; this familiarity will help you "learn this business." Fifth, Hershey is an exemplary organization in terms of business ethics and social responsibility; a significant part of Hershey Foods' profits go toward operating the Milton Hershey School for Orphaned Children. Finally, Hershey is very cooperative with students and professors; Hershey has a toll-free number (1-800-468-1714) that students or professors can call to obtain additional information about the company.

Some Experiential Exercises in the text do not relate specifically to the Cohesion Case. At least one exercise at the end of each chapter applies textual material to your university. As a business administration student nearing graduation, you are quite knowledgeable about your university. Apply strategic-management concepts learned in this course to assist your institution. More and more colleges and universities are instituting strategic management.

Part Six of this text provides information on preparing a case analysis and giving an oral presentation. After reading the text and applying concepts and tools to the Cohesion Case through Experiential Exercises, you should be well prepared to analyze business policy cases. The objectives of the case method are

1. To give you experience applying strategic-management concepts and techniques to different organizations.
2. To give you experience applying and integrating the knowledge you have gained in prior courses and work experience.
3. To give you decision-making experience in actual organizations.
4. To improve your understanding of relationships among the functional areas of business and the strategic-management process.
5. To improve your self-confidence; since there is no one right answer to a case, you will gain experience justifying and defending your own ideas, analyses, and recommendations.
6. To improve your oral and written communication skills.
7. To sharpen your analytical and intuitive skills.

The Appendix in Part Six provides information on the strategic-management software that comes with this text. Two computer packages are available, *Case Analyst* and *Strategy Formulator*. Both packages include IBM-formatted diskettes.

The *Case Analyst* program contains income statements and balance sheets from all cases in the text. This data is provided in spreadsheet form so projected financial statements can be developed. To use *Case Analyst* well, you need some experience and knowledge of financial spreadsheets.

The *Strategy-Formulator* software provides organizations with a structured approach for doing strategic planning, and thereby aids students in preparing case analyses. *Strategy Formulator* is very easy to use and requires no computer skills.

HERSHEY FOODS CORPORATION—1994

Do you know which of the following candies are made by Hershey Foods: Mr. Goodbar, Reese's, Kit Kat, Big Block, Whatchamacallit, Allsorts, Rolo, Krackel, BarNone, Mounds, Almond Joy, 5th Avenue, Snickers, and Baby Ruth? The answer is all of them except Snickers, made by M&M Mars, and Baby Ruth, by Nestlé. Mars and Nestlé are Hershey's two major competitors. Snickers is the best-selling candy bar in the world.

In Hershey, Pennsylvania, you can walk down Chocolate Avenue, stroll sidewalks lit with lights in the shape of Hershey Kisses, visit the Hershey Zoo, and see the Chocolate Kiss Tower in Hershey Park. Hershey is the home of Hershey Foods Corporation, which produces more than 33 million Hershey Kisses every day. Since the turn of this century, Hershey Foods has grown from a one-product, one-plant operation to a $2 billion company with many U.S. and international plants providing an array of quality chocolate and confectionery products and services. According to Hershey, chocolate is low in cholesterol, caffeine, and sodium, as shown in Exhibit 1.

Hershey entered 1994 as the largest candy maker in the United States, with a 21.5 percent share of a $10 billion retail market. M&M Mars is second, with a 20 percent market share. Hershey also is the largest pasta manufacturer in the United States, having recently surpassed Borden. Hershey manufactures and sells pasta under a variety of names, including American Beauty, San Giorgio, Skinner, Perfection, Light 'n Fluffy, P&R, and Delmonico.

All but 11 percent of Hershey's sales and 2 percent of profits are generated in domestic markets. How long can Hershey survive as an almost exclusively domestic producer of candy and pasta, while its competitors gain economies of scale and experience in world markets?

HISTORY

Milton Hershey's love for candy making began with a childhood apprenticeship under candy maker Joe Royer of Lancaster, Pennsylvania. Hershey was eager to own a candy-making business. After numerous attempts and even bankruptcy, he finally gained success in the caramel business. Upon seeing the first chocolate-making equipment at the Chicago Exhibition in 1893, Hershey envisioned endless opportunities for the chocolate industry. He founded the Hershey Chocolate Company in 1893.

By 1901, the chocolate industry in America was growing rapidly. Hershey's sales reached $662,000 that year, creating the need for a new factory. Milton Hershey moved his company to Derry Church, Pennsylvania, which was renamed Hershey in 1906. The new Hershey factory provided a means of mass-producing a single chocolate product. In 1909, the Milton Hershey School for Orphans was founded. Mr. and Mrs. Hershey could not have children, so for years the Hershey Chocolate

Company operated mainly to provide funds for the orphanage. Hershey's sales reached $5 million in 1911.

In 1918, the entire Hershey business was donated to the Milton Hershey School for Orphans. In 1927, the Hershey Chocolate Company was incorporated under the laws of the state of Delaware and listed on the New York Stock Exchange. That same year, 20 percent of Hershey's stock was sold to the public. Between 1930 and 1960, Hershey went through tremendous growth; the name "Hershey" became a household word. Milton Hershey died in 1945.

EXHIBIT 1   Chocolate Myths: Some Questions and Answers as Provided by Hershey

IS CHOCOLATE HIGH IN SATURATED FAT, THE FAT THAT RAISES BLOOD CHOLESTEROL LEVELS?

Milk chocolate is actually low in cholesterol. A 1.55-ounce *Hershey's* milk chocolate bar contains only 10 milligrams of cholesterol, all of which comes from the milk used in the milk chocolate. (An 8-ounce glass of whole milk has approximately 36 milligrams of cholesterol.)

Cocoa is cholesterol-free and, because it is low in fat (14 percent by weight), it is the only chocolate baking ingredient included in fat-restricted diets by the American Heart Association.

WHAT IS VANILLIN AND WHY DOES HERSHEY USE IT IN ITS MILK CHOCOLATE?

Vanillin is a vanilla-like flavoring used in some of our products. It is more readily available, less expensive and more consistent in quality than vanilla. It has been used by virtually all chocolate manufacturers for many years.

IS CHOCOLATE HIGH IN CAFFEINE?

Related to the hyperactivity issue is the belief that chocolate contains large amounts of caffeine. The reality is, however, that a 1.55-ounce *Hershey's* milk chocolate bar contains only 10 milligrams of caffeine. How does this compare to other foods? A 5-ounce cup of regular automatic drip coffee contains 137 milligrams, a 12-ounce can of a regular cola beverage contains approximately 30–46 milligrams, and a 5-ounce cup of instant decaffeinated coffee contains approximately 3 milligrams of caffeine.

DOES CHOCOLATE CONTAIN HIGH LEVELS OF CHOLESTEROL?

It was once believed that all dietary saturated fats increased blood cholesterol levels. Not anymore. Recent studies have shown that stearic acid, one of the primary saturated fats found in chocolate, behaves differently from other saturated fats. In fact, stearic acid has no effect on, or may actually lower, blood cholesterol levels.

DOES CHOCOLATE PROMOTE TOOTH DECAY?

Tooth decay is a food-related disease. Sugars, as a group, play a role in tooth decay as do most foods. Tooth decay occurs for a variety of reasons, such as genetic makeup, lack of good oral hygiene, food lingering in the mouth, consistency of the food and the frequency of consumption. A fact not commonly known, however, is that chocolate promotes less tooth decay than do crackers, raisins, or granola bars. Chocolate actually appears to modify the cavity-causing potential of its sugar. It contains a component that blocks the production of plaque, the first stage of tooth decay. In addition, the cocoa butter in chocolate melts quickly and helps to clear the mouth, thereby reducing the potential to cause cavities.

IS CHOCOLATE HIGH IN SODIUM?

A 1.55-ounce *Hershey's* milk chocolate bar contains only 40 milligrams of sodium; a *Special Dark* chocolate bar contains 5 milligrams; a *Mr. Goodbar* chocolate bar contains 20 milligrams. In fact, by Food and Drug Administration standards, many of *Hershey's* products qualify as "low sodium." Much higher amounts of sodium are found in other common foods. For example, an ounce of cheddar cheese has 198 milligrams, and a slice of whole wheat bread has 132 milligrams.

Source: Hershey Foods Corporation

In 1963, Hershey acquired the H. B. Reese Candy Company, maker of Reese's Peanut Butter Cups, Reese's Pieces, and Reese's Peanut Butter Chips. Later acquisitions included San Giorgio Macaroni and Delmonico Foods, both pasta manufacturers, in 1966, and the Cory Corporation, a provider of coffee services to U.S. and Canadian businesses, in 1967. In 1968, Hershey Chocolate Corporation changed its name to Hershey Foods Corporation. Between 1976 and 1984, William Dearden served as Hershey's chief executive officer. An orphan who grew up in the Milton Hershey School for Orphans, Dearden diversified the company to reduce its dependence on fluctuating cocoa and sugar prices.

In 1977, Hershey acquired Y&S Candy Corporation, a manufacturer of licorice-type products, such as Y&S Twizzlers, Nibs, and Bassett's Allsorts. In 1978, Hershey purchased Procino-Rossi, a pasta company, and in 1979 it acquired Skinner Macaroni Company and Friendly Ice Cream Corporation. Richard Zimmerman replaced William Dearden as chief executive officer of Hershey in 1984. That year, Zimmerman divested the company of Hershey's Cory Foods division and acquired A. B. Marabou of Sweden. He purchased Franklin Restaurants in 1985. In 1986, Hershey acquired the Dietrich Corporation, maker of Luden's Throat Drops, Luden's Mellomints, Queen Anne chocolate-covered cherries, and 5th Avenue candy bars. On April 28, 1986, Dearden retired from Hershey's board of directors after a lifetime association and 29-year career with the corporation.

Hershey acquired the Canadian confectionery and snack nut operations of Nabisco Brands Ltd. in June 1987. These businesses include bar and bagged candy items such as Oh Henry!, Eat-More, Cherry Blossom, Glosettes, Lowney, Life Savers, Breath Savers, Planter nuts, Beaver nuts, Chipits chocolate chips, Moirs boxed chocolates, Care*Free gum, and Bubble Yum gum. Hershey's debt as a percentage of total capitalization increased to 29 percent by year-end 1987, but the company achieved record sales, earnings, and dividends that year.

In 1988, Hershey acquired Peter Paul/Cadbury's U.S. candy operations, which included plant facilities in Hazleton and York, Pennsylvania, and Naugatuck, Connecticut. This agreement allowed Hershey to manufacture and market the following new products in the United States: Mounds, Almond Joy, York Peppermint Pattie, Cadbury Dairy Milk, Cadbury Fruit & Nut, Cadbury Caramello, and Cadbury Creme Eggs. Hershey received rights to market the Peter Paul products worldwide. This acquisition cost Hershey $285 million, plus assumption of $30 million of Cadbury's debt. The York facility was closed on January 20, 1989, and its operations moved to Hershey's Reading, Pennsylvania, plant.

Hershey Foods revised its mission statement in 1989 to read as below:

Hershey Foods Corporation's mission is to become a major diversified food company and a leading company in every aspect of our business as:

The number one confectionery company in North America, moving toward worldwide confectionery market share leadership.

A respected and valued supplier of high-quality, branded consumer food products in North America and selected international markets.

During 1989, Hershey's Sherbrooke Canadian plant was closed, and other Canadian manufacturing facilities were combined into Hershey's existing facility at Smith Falls, Ontario. Also during 1989, Hershey introduced five new baking items, and the Symphony chocolate bar moved into national distribution. Hershey test-marketed the first microwave pasta, called Perfection. A newly formed venture group introduced a line of chocolate bar flavored puddings to selected East Coast markets in late 1989.

In 1990, Hershey acquired Ronzoni Foods Corporation from Kraft General Foods Corporation for $80 million. The purchase included the dry pasta, pasta sauces, and cheese businesses of Ronzoni Foods. The acquired businesses had sales of approximately $85 million and strengthened Hershey's position as the number two branded pasta supplier in the United States.

In 1991, Hershey acquired Gubor Schokoladen, a German manufacturer and marketer of high-quality assorted pralines and seasonal chocolates. Gubor has two manufacturing plants in Germany and provided Hershey with increased European presence. Also in 1991, Hershey established an employee stock ownership plan (ESOP), which was funded by a 7.75 percent loan of $47.9 million from the company. In October 1991, Hershey purchased Nacional de Dulces (NDD) and renamed this company Hershey Mexico. Hershey Mexico has its main offices and manufacturing plant in Guadalajara, Mexico. It produces, imports, and markets chocolate products for the Mexican market under the Hershey brand name.

In April 1992, Hershey divested of Petybon S. A., its pasta and biscuit manufacturer in Brazil. Also in 1992, Hershey divested its stake in Freia Marabou, a Norwegian confectioner, for $220 million in cash. Company plans for 1993 include spending $200 million of this cash to repurchase its own common stock. Hershey's revenues and net income increased 11 percent in 1992, while long-term debt fell to $174 million, the lowest level in a decade.

Hershey Foods Corporation today is comprised of five divisions: Hershey Chocolate U.S.A., Hershey Canada, Inc., Hershey International, Ltd., Hershey Refrigerated Products, and Hershey Pasta Group. For the corporation as a whole, strategic objectives are to achieve a return on net assets of 12 percent without acquisitions and 10 percent with a major acquisition. Growth in earnings per share is targeted to be double-digit, and an "A" debt rating is to be maintained. Hershey's current organizational chart is provided in Exhibit 2.

Hershey Foods' mission statement today is given as follows:

Hershey Foods Corporation's mission is to be a focused food company and a leader in every aspect of our business as:

The number one confectionery company and number one branded pasta company in North America, and moving toward worldwide confectionery market share leadership.

A respected and valued supplier of other high quality, branded consumer food products in North America and selected international markets.

HERSHEY CHOCOLATE U.S.A.

Hershey has chocolate and confectionery manufacturing operations in Hershey, Pennsylvania; Oakdale, California; Stuarts Draft, Virginia; Reading, Pennsylvania; Hazleton, Pennsylvania; Lancaster, Pennsylvania; and Naugatuck, Connecticut. Hershey Chocolate U.S.A. produces an extensive line of products, including bar candies, bagged candies, syrup, baking ingredients, chocolate drink mixes, granola bars, dessert toppings, and dessert puddings. These products are produced in numerous packaged forms, marketed under more than 40 brand names, and sold in over one million retail outlets in the United States.

Hershey Chocolate U.S.A. achieved record sales and earnings in 1992, as indicated in Exhibit 3. Several new products were introduced during the year, including

EXHIBIT 2   Hershey's Organizational Chart

Source: Adapted from information in Hershey's 1992 *Annual Report*.

Amazin' Fruit gummy bears fruit candy. Hershey worked closely with McDonald's Corporation and the Nickelodeon cable television network to initially provide Amazin' Fruit. Y&S Twizzlers and Nibs candies are Hershey's other major non-chocolate candies. Hershey also is the leader in licorice-type candies. Another new product introduction by the Hershey Chocolate division is the Cookies 'n' Mint chocolate bar. Established candy brands that contributed significantly to growth included Hershey's Miniatures chocolate bars, Reese's Peanut Butter Cups, York

EXHIBIT 3 Hershey's Sales and Income by Product Area (in millions of dollars; 1993 and 1994 figures are estimated)

	1992	PERCENTAGE CHANGE	1993	PERCENTAGE CHANGE	1994	PERCENTAGE CHANGE
NET REVENUES						
Hershey Chocolate USA	$2,420.8	11	$2,650.0	9	$2,850.0	8
Pasta Operations	366.0	8	395.0	8	440.0	11
Canadian Operations	233.0	1	250.0	7	280.0	12
International Operations	200.0	33	285.0	43	375.0	32
Total Revenues	$3,219.8	11	$3,580.0	11	$3,945.0	10
OPERATING PROFITS						
Hershey Chocolate USA	$412.2	6	$449.0	9	$481.0	7
Operating Profit Margin	17.0%		16.9%		16.9%	
Pasta Operations	$ 36.8	12	$ 39.5	7	$ 44.6	13
Operating Profit Margin	10.1%		10.0%		10.1%	
Canadian Operations	$ 14.8	0	$ 15.5	5	$ 17.2	11
Operating Profit Margin	6.4%		6.2%		6.1%	
International Operations	$9.0	0	$ 14.1	57	$ 20.2	43
Operating Profit Margin	4.5%		4.9%		5.4%	
Total Operating Margin	$472.8	6	$518.1	10	$563.0	9
Operating Profit Margin	14.7%		14.5%		14.3%	

Source: *Hershey Internal Report.*

Peppermint Patties, Kit Kat bars, Y&S Twizzlers candy, Mr. Goodbar, Mounds, Almond Joy, Symphony, and Whatchamacallit candy bar. All of Hershey Chocolate U.S.A.'s confectionery and grocery products are listed below:

CONFECTIONERY PRODUCTS

Amazin' Fruit Gummy Bears Candy
BarNone Candy Bar
Cadbury's Dairy Milk Chocolate Bar
Cadbury's Krisp Chocolate Bar
Cadbury's Roast Almond Chocolate Bar
5th Avenue Candy Bar
Hershey's Cookies 'n' Mint Chocolate Bar
Hershey's Golden Collection Almond
Hershey's Kisses Chocolates
Hershey's Milk Chocolate Bar
Hugs
Krackel Chocolate Bar
Mr. Goodbar Chocolate Bar
Nibs Candy
Reese's Peanut Butter Cups

Almond Joy Candy Bar
Cadbury's Creme Eggs Candy
Cadbury's Fruit & Nut Chocolate Bar
Cadbury's Mini Eggs Candy
Caramello Candy Bar
Helps Cough Suppressant Tablets
Hershey's Golden Collection Solitaires
Hershey's Kisses with Almonds Chocolates
Hershey's Milk Chocolate Bar with Almonds
Hershey's Miniatures Chocolate Bars
Kit Kat Wafer Bar
Luden's Throat Drops
Mounds Candy Bar
Reese's Crunchy Peanut Butter Cup
Reese's Peanut Butter Chips

Reese's Pieces Candy
Skor Toffee Bar
Super Twizzlers Candy
Symphony Chocolate Bar with Almonds
  and Toffee Chips
Whatchamacallit Candy Bar

Rolo Caramels in Milk Chocolate
Special Dark Chocolate Bar
Symphony Chocolate Bar
Twizzlers Candy
Y&S Candy
York Peppermint Pattie

GROCERY PRODUCTS

Hershey's Baking Chocolate
Hershey's Chocolate Drink
Hershey's Chocolate Milk Mix
Hershey's Cocoa
Hershey's Mint Chips
Hershey's Premium Chocolate Chunks
Hershey's Syrup
Hershey's Vanilla Chunks
Reese's Peanut Butter

Hershey's Chocolate Chips
Hershey's Chocolate Milk
Hershey's Chocolate Shoppe Toppings
Hershey's Fudge Toppings
Hershey's Premium Baking Bars
Hershey's Sweetened Coconut Flakes
Hershey's Vanilla Chips
Mini Chips Semi-Sweet Chocolate

Hershey faces seasonal demand for its products. Confectionery sales are generally lowest during the second quarter of the year and highest during the third and fourth quarters, due largely to the holiday seasons. For example, in 1992, Hershey generated only 19 percent of annual sales during the second quarter. In contrast, 30 percent of annual sales were generated during the fourth quarter. For the third quarter of 1993, Hershey's confection volume was up 14 percent, due partly to strong demand for Hugs and Cookies 'n' Mint. Analysts estimate sales of $100 million of Hugs and $400 million of Kisses.

Conventional wisdom in the candy industry is that a person rarely selects the same candy bar twice in a row; consequently, product variety is crucial to success. In addition, marketing issues relative to health, nutrition, and weight consciousness are important. Hershey's marketing strategy for its products is based on consistently superior product quality, mass distribution, and best possible consumer value in terms of price and weight. The firm utilizes a variety of advertising and promotional programs to implement its strategy. The media Hershey uses most for advertising are network television, followed by syndicated television, spot (local) television, magazines, and network and spot radio. Hershey's advertising expenses increased 21 percent in 1992 to $536 million. A comparison of candy advertising expenditures for Hershey versus Mars is given in Exhibit 4.

For the year ended August 31, 1993, Hershey's confectionery market share rose 1.4 percent, to 33.8 percent. The quality of share improvement is reinforced by M&M Mars' 12-month market share drop of 2.8 percent, to 26.5 percent. The market share gap between the two companies is an unprecedented 7.3 share points (the gap rarely reaches 6 percent). At the end of the second quarter 1993, the share gap was 6.5 points.

Hershey Chocolate U.S.A. recently completed construction of a 160,000-square-foot chocolate-processing facility in Hershey, Pennsylvania. The facility operates with a team concept among employees and managers to foster a sense of ownership. Adjoining this new facility is another new 180,000-square-foot chocolate plant. Building these new facilities has been in response to the U.S. confectionery market's growing 4 percent annually in sales volume. The nonchocolate segment, which accounts for about one-third of the overall sweets market, is growing at 6.5 percent

EXHIBIT 4   First-Quarter 1993 Advertising Expenditures for Candy by Hershey Foods Corporation and Mars Inc. (in millions of dollars)

	1992	1993	PERCENTAGE CHANGE
HERSHEY FOODS CORP.			
Hershey's Bar None candy bar	—	4.8	—
Reese's peanut butter cups	3.5	4.2	20.0%
Hershey's Chocolate Kisses	2.6	3.9	50.0%
York Peppermint Patties	—	3.7	—
Kit Kat candy bar	4.0	3.6	(10.0%)
Amazin' Fruit candies	0.1	3.4	—
Hershey's candy bars	3.4	3.2	(5.9%)
Hershey Symphony bar	3.4	3.1	(8.8%)
Cadbury Creme Eggs	2.1	2.6	23.8%
Fifth Avenue candy bar	1.3	2.5	92.3%
Mr. Goodbar candy	1.3	1.5	15.4%
Peter Paul Mounds and Almond Joy	2.5	1.2	(52.0%)
Reese's Pieces candy	1.3	0.9	(30.8%)
Cadbury Caramello candy	1.6	0.9	(43.8%)
Hershey's candies	—	0.6	—
Twizzlers	—	0.3	—
Others	1.8	0.3	(83.3%)
Total	28.9	40.5	40.1%
MARS INC.			
M&M candies	8.8	5.6	(36.4%)
Snickers candy bar	7.9	4.0	(49.4%)
Dove candy bar	0.2	3.9	1,850%
Snickers Peanut Butter candy bar	—	2.6	—
Twix candy bar	1.5	2.1	40.0%
Milky Way Dark candy	—	1.7	—
Milky Way candy	0.6	1.5	83.3%
Skittles candy	1.0	1.1	10.0%
Milky Way II candy	—	0.4	—
3 Musketeers candy bar	0.5	0.2	(60.0%)
Starburst candies	—	0.1	—
Bounty coconut candy bar	—	0.1	—
Others	7.6	0.1	(98.7%)
Total	28.1	23.4	(16.7%)

Source: Company Data.

annually, while the chocolate segment is growing at 2.5 percent. Hershey has only 4 percent of the nonchocolate confectionery market, while the leader is RJR Nabisco, with 18 percent. RJR's Life Savers and Gummy Life Savers compete with Hershey's Amazin' Fruit Gummy Bears.

Hershey Canada has manufacturing facilities in Smith Falls, Ontario, Montreal, Quebec, and Dartmouth, Nova Scotia. Hershey Canada has attained market share leadership in practically every phase of the Canadian confectionery market, despite a 9 percent decline in the Canadian dollar exchange rate in 1992. Some Hershey Canada candy products that sell especially well are the Oh Henry! and Lowney brand names, hard candy sold under the brand names Life Savers and Breath Savers, nuts under the Planters name, gum under the Care*Free and Bubble Yum brands, and the Skor toffee bar.

Canadian tax on confectionery sales was reduced from 13.5 percent to 7 percent in 1991. This tax reduction action continues to benefit Hershey Canada sales. The Canadian division of Hershey markets the following products:

CONFECTIONERY PRODUCTS

Almondillos Chocolates
Bridge Mixture Candy
Eat-More Candy
Goodies Candy
Hershey Chocolate-Covered Almonds
Hershey Milk Chocolate Bar
Life Savers Candy
Moirs Chocolates
Oh Henry! Chocolate Bar
Planters Nuts
Skor Toffee Candy Bar
Special Dark Chocolate Bar

Breath Savers Mints
Cherry Blossom Candy
Glosette Candy
Hershey Almond Bar
Hershey Kisses Milk Chocolates
Hershey Raisins and Almonds Bar
Lowney Candy
Nibs Candy
Ovation Chocolate Covered Sticks
Reese's Peanut Butter Cups Candy
Special Crisp Candy Bar
Twizzlers candy
Y&S Candy

GROCERY PRODUCTS

Brown Cow Chocolate Syrup
Chipits Chocolate Chips
Hershey's Chocolate Chips
Hershey's Instant Chocolate Syrup
Strawberry Cow Strawberry Syrup

Chipits Baking Chocolate
Chipits Cocoa
Hershey's Cocoa
Hershey's Syrup
Top Scotch Butterscotch Syrup

Hershey's Canadian operation generates $250 million in annual sales, about 7 percent of the company total. The Canadian confectionery market is estimated at approximately $1 billion wholesale, with chocolate bars accounting for about 56 percent. Hershey is number three in chocolate bars and number one in boxed chocolates, a fast-growing segment that accounts for 16 percent of the market. Hershey's first-quarter 1993 Canadian sales rose 7 percent, but this increase was negated by a drop in the value of the Canadian dollar. Third-quarter 1993 Canadian sales increased another 7 percent, the result of a 17 percent volume increase and a 10 percent price decline due again to a weakening Canadian dollar. This quarter also was the first time in history when a Hershey candy product became the best seller in Canada. The product was Oh Henry!

Hershey's export sales have been increasing in recent years, benefiting immensely from a weak U.S. dollar in most foreign countries. Much of the results were due to higher sales of Hershey Kisses chocolates, Hershey's milk chocolate bar with almonds and Almond Joy bars in Mexico and higher sales of Hershey Kisses in the Philippines, South Korea, and Singapore. A new market for Hershey products was established in New Zealand in 1992. Exhibit 5 provides export information for confectionery products.

Hershey's recent sales and earnings in Mexico and Germany, however, have been lower than expected. Hershey International's licensing revenues have been growing recently, especially the Snow Brand Milk Products venture in Japan and the Maeil Dairy

EXHIBIT 5 International Trade in Confectionery Products, 1989–91 (in thousands of dollars)

	EXPORTS		
COUNTRY	1989	1990	1991
Canada	43,363	102,003	118,655
Mexico	40,346	42,039	54,917
Japan	34,446	33,151	26,130
South Korea	12,342	14,477	10,046
Philippines	6,056	6,212	9,415
Hong Kong	6,006	6,135	7,113
Taiwan	8,289	7,555	6,260
Australia	2,245	3,829	4,438
Saudi Arabia	2,181	2,029	3,751
Venezuela	417	1,159	2,359
All others	21,886	23,025	27,791
Total	177,577	241,614	270,875

	IMPORTS		
	1989	1990	1991
Canada	29,334	52,022	80,608
Germany	36,507	40,356	59,986
United Kingdom	17,893	22,080	30,797
Italy	12,081	12,239	18,220
Netherlands	30,885	34,640	15,933
Brazil	17,322	17,951	15,198
Mexico	10,586	10,704	13,425
Switzerland	8,239	14,056	13,195
Spain	10,075	10,630	10,811
France	6,083	5,891	8,291
All others	66,924	68,986	74,001
Total	245,929	289,555	340,465

Source: U.S. Department of Commerce, Bureau of the Census.

Industry venture in South Korea. In 1992, Hershey divested itself of its Petybon pasta operations in Brazil and acquired 100 percent ownership of the Hershey Japan operations.

Hershey's international division contributes about $200 million to annual sales, or 6 percent of the total. The division focuses heavily on the German and Mexican markets, both of which have been weak. Together, sales in Mexico and Germany were off 5 percent (down 3 percent in price, down 2 percent in volume) in the first quarter of 1993. However, exports to both countries increased, and the overall international operating income rose 15 percent on better cost controls. Total exports now amount to about $60 million and are increasing rapidly. Hershey recently consolidated its Japanese operation, which added $15–20 million in sales. Elsewhere, Hershey has licensing agreements in Korea and New Zealand. Analysts foresee annual sales growth of 10 to 15 percent in foreign markets, with profits growing at a double-digit clip. However, at current growth rates, the international business will remain a small part of Hershey's business. Analysts believe Hershey should expand geographically, perhaps through a major acquisition.

For the first quarter of 1993, Hershey's international sales declined another 5 percent, and volume fell 2 percent. Lack of presence anywhere in the world except Mexico, Germany, and Japan severely hurts Hershey.

HERSHEY REFRIGERATED PRODUCTS

The Refrigerated Products division of Hershey recently introduced Hershey's Free chocolate bar flavor puddings. This product is cholesterol-free, contains no artificial sweeteners, and has only 100 calories per serving. Introduction of this new product, though, hurt Hershey's regular puddings, which experienced a decline in volume for the first time ever.

HERSHEY PASTA GROUP

What is pasta? Pasta is paste or dough made from semolina milled from durum wheat, a class of hard wheat grown in the United States, primarily in North Dakota. It is formed into shapes such as spaghetti and macaroni, then dried, boxed, and readied for sale. Hershey's pasta sales have been growing 5 percent annually compared to an industry growth rate of 2.5 percent. Hershey's Ronzoni, San Giorgio, and American Beauty brands overtook Borden's Creamette brand in 1993, with 27.7 percent share to Borden's 27.6 percent. Two other major competitors in the U.S. pasta market, Quaker Oats and CPC, continue to lose market share to Hershey and Borden.

Hershey first expanded its business from cocoa-based confectionery products into pasta with the acquisition in 1966 of San Giorgio Macaroni, Inc., of Lebanon, Pennsylvania. Later that year Hershey acquired a Louisville, Kentucky, firm known as Delmonico Foods, Inc. Subsequently, Hershey acquired additional pasta product companies in a variety of regions, including Procino-Rossi Corp., Auburn, New York, in 1978; Skinner Macaroni Company, Omaha, Nebraska (1979); American Beauty Brand (purchased from Pillsbury Company) (1984); G&R Pasta Company, Inc., Philadelphia, Pennsylvania (1986); Ronzoni Foods Corporation (from Kraft General Foods) (1990); and American Italian Pasta Company, Excelsior Springs, Missouri (1990). With these regional acquisitions Hershey's Pasta Group is able to manufacture and distribute pasta throughout the United States under the following brand names: San Giorgio, Skinner, Delmonico, P&R, Light 'n Fluffy, American Beauty, Perfection, Pastamania, and Ronzoni.

Products of the Hershey Pasta Group are divided into four general categories: long goods, short cuts, egg products and specialties. A brief listing of the major items in each category follows:

Long Goods

Capellini	Fettucine
Linguine	Margherite
Perciatelli/Long Macaroni	Spaghetti
Spaghettini	Vermicelli
Angel Hair	

Short Cuts

Alphabets	Ditalini/Salad Macaroni
Dumplings	Ancini Pepe
Elbows	Fusilli
Orzo	Ridged Mostaccioli
Fideo Cortado	Radiatore
Occhi Dilupo	Rigatoni
Rings/Spaghetti Rings	Rotelle Curly-Macaroni/Twirls
Mafalda	Rotini/Twists
Shells	Ziti
Macarrones	Tubetti
Mezzani rigati	Mezzani

Egg Products

Egg Fettucini	Kluski
Egg Pastina	Noodles Fine, Medium, Extra-wide
Pot Pie Bows	Pot Pie Squares
Spinach Noodles	

Specialties

Long Fusilli	Jumbo Shells
Lasagne	Manicotti
Healthy Ribbons	Cannelloni

The popularity of pasta has increased over the last ten years. Per capita consumption of pasta has grown from 12.8 pounds in 1980 to almost 20 pounds today. Hershey recently expanded pasta production capacity in its Winchester, Virginia, plant. This is a state-of-the-art facility that provides Hershey with much-needed capacity. Foreign manufacturers of pasta, especially companies in Italy and Turkey, are now marketing pasta in the United States at accelerating rates.

HERSHEY'S OPERATIONS

Social Responsibility. Hershey Foods Corporation is committed to the values of its founder, Milton S. Hershey—the highest standard of quality, honesty, fairness, integrity, and respect. The firm makes annual contributions of cash, products, and services to a variety of national and local charitable organizations. The corporation operates the Milton Hershey School for socially disadvantaged children and is the sole sponsor of the Hershey National Track and Field Youth Program. Hershey also makes contributions to the Children's Miracle Network, a national program benefiting children's hospitals across the United States.

Research and Development. Hershey engages in research and development activities to develop new products, improve the quality of existing products, and improve and modernize production processes. The company's recent research and development expenditures are listed below (in millions of dollars):

Year	Research and Development
1984	$9.9
1985	11.2
1986	12.5
1987	12.9
1988	15.7
1989	16.1
1990	19.2
1991	22.8
1992	24.2

Hershey recently completed a test market of its reduced calorie and fat candy bar. Test results suggest that consumers desire the real thing—calories, fat and all—when they indulge in a candy bar. This finding is consistent with a general trend in the U.S. away from fitness, exercise, and nutrition toward a more sedentary life-style.

Finance. Hershey's 1992 financial statements are given in Exhibits 6 through 9. Note that both revenues and net income increased 11 percent in 1992, while long-term debt declined 38 percent. Hershey's total number of full-time employees declined to 13,700 in 1992. For 1993, revenues of Hershey Chocolate, Pasta, Canadian, and International operations are expected to increase 9, 8, 7, and 43 percent, respectively.

Advertising and Promotion. M&M Mars in the early 1990s seemed lethargic in terms of advertising, promotion, and new product introductions. Hershey has tried to capitalize on this by spending more on advertising and promotion, which increased 21 percent in 1992 alone. Hershey's recent expenditures on advertising and promotion are given below (in millions of dollars):

Year	Advertising	Promotion
1987	$ 97	$171
1988	99	230
1989	121	256
1990	146	315
1991	117	325
1992	137	398

GLOBAL ISSUES

The chocolate/cocoa products industry is SIC 2066 while candy/confectionery is SIC 2064. Demand for chocolate increased nearly 4 percent in both 1991 and 1992, following a sharp decline in 1990 when price increases reduced consumption. The confectionery industry introduced nearly 400 new candy products in 1991 and 1992.

U.S. exports of candy increased 32 percent in 1992 to $359 million, while imports increased 24 percent to $420 million. Canada and Mexico represent about 64 percent

EXHIBIT 6   Hershey Food Corporation, Consolidated Statements of Income
(in thousands of dollars except per share amounts)

FOR THE YEARS ENDED DECEMBER 31,	1992	1991	1990
Net Sales	$3,219,805	$2,899,165	$2,715,609
Costs and Expenses:			
Cost of sales	1,833,388	1,694,404	1,588,360
Selling, marketing and administrative	958,189	814,459	776,668
Total costs and expenses	2,791,577	2,508,863	2,365,028
Gain on Business Restructuring, Net	—	—	35,540
Income before Interest and Income Taxes	428,228	390,302	386,121
Interest expense, net	27,240	26,845	24,603
Income before Income Taxes	400,988	363,457	361,518
Provision for income taxes	158,390	143,929	145,636
Net Income	$ 242,598	$ 219,528	$ 215,882
Net Income per Share	$ 2.69	$ 2.43	$ 2.39
Cash Dividends Paid per Share:			
Common Stock—Regular	$ 1.030	$ .940	$ .840
Common Stock—Special	—	—	.150
Class B Common Stock—Regular	.935	.850	.755
Class B Common Stock—Special	—	—	.135

Source: *Annual Report*, 1992.

of total export value, while Canada and Germany represent 41 percent of the import value. Mexico's candy tariffs currently are 20 percent compared to the U.S. tariff of 7 percent. Note that none of the high-candy-consumption countries of Western Europe are major markets for U.S.-made candy.

The main distribution channels for chocolate are grocery, drug, and department stores as well as vending machine operators. Almost all of these distributors are local, regional, or national; only a few are multinational. While chocolate producers have not yet developed globally uniform marketing programs, the situation is changing. European unification extended grocery and department store channels of distribution. For example, Safeway, a U.S. grocery chain, now operates stores in

EXHIBIT 7 Hershey Foods Corporation, Consolidated Balance Sheets
(in thousands of dollars)

DECEMBER 31,	1992	1991
ASSETS		
Current Assets:		
Cash and cash equivalents	$ 24,114	$ 71,124
Accounts receivable—trade	173,646	159,805
Inventories	457,179	436,917
Prepaid expenses and other	105,966	76,633
Investment interest	179,076	—
Total current assets	939,981	744,479
Property, Plant, and Equipment, Net	1,295,989	1,145,666
Intangibles Resulting from Business Acquisitions	399,768	421,694
Other Assets	37,171	29,983
LIABILITIES AND STOCKHOLDERS' EQUITY	$2,672,909	$2,341,822
Current Liabilities:		
Accounts payable	$ 127,175	$ 137,890
Accrued liabilities	240,816	226,267
Accrued income taxes	5,682	22,000
Short-term debt	259,045	57,620
Current portion of long-term debt	104,224	26,955
Total current liabilities	736,942	470,732
Long-term Debt	174,273	282,933
Other Long-term Liabilities	92,950	80,907
Deferred Income Taxes	203,465	171,999
Total liabilities	$1,207,630	$1,006,571
Stockholders' Equity		
Preferred Stock, outstanding shares: none in 1992 and 1991	—	—
Common Stock, outstanding shares:		
74,929,057 in 1992 and 74,921,282 in 1991	74,929	74,921
Class B Common Stock, outstanding shares:		
15,257,279 in 1992 and 15,265,054 in 1991	15,257	15,265
Additional paid-in capital	52,129	52,509
Cumulative foreign currency translation adjustments	2,484	26,424
Unearned ESOP compensation	(44,708)	(47,902)
Retained earnings	1,365,188	1,214,034
Total stockholders' equity	1,465,279	1,335,251
Source: Annual Report, 1992	$2,672,909	$2,341,822

EXHIBIT 8   Hershey Foods Corporation, Consolidated Statements of Cash Flows

FOR THE YEARS ENDED DECEMBER 31,	1992	1991
Cash Flows Provided from (Used by) Operating Activities		
Net income	$ 242,598	$ 219,528
Adjustments to reconcile net income to net cash provided from operations:		
Depreciation and amortization	97,087	85,413
Deferred income taxes	21,404	20,654
Gain on business restructuring, net	—	—
Changes in assets and liabilities, net of effects from business acquisitions:		
Accounts receivable—trade	(13,841)	(6,404)
Inventories	(20,262)	(43,949)
Accounts payable	(10,715)	4,070
Other assets and liabilities	(20,707)	94,270
Other, net	649	(26,242)
Net Cash Provided from Operating Activities	296,213	347,340
Cash Flows Provided from (Used by) Investing Activities		
Capital additions	(249,795)	(226,071)
Business acquisitions	—	(44,108)
Sale of equity interest	—	—
Purchase of investment interest	(179,076)	—
Other, net	6,581	(1,510)
Net Cash (Used by) Investing Activities	(422,290)	(271,689)
Cash Flows Provided from (Used by) Financing Activities		
Net increase in short-term debt	201,425	56,489
Long-term borrowings	1,259	23,620
Repayment of long-term debt	(32,173)	(27,861)
Repayment of assumed debt	—	—
Loan to ESOP	—	(47,902)
Proceeds from sale of Common Stock to ESOP	—	47,902
Cash dividends paid	(91,444)	(83,401)
Net Cash Provided from (Used by) Financing Activities	79,067	(31,153)
Increase (Decrease) in Cash and Cash Equivalents	(47,010)	44,498
Cash and Cash Equivalents as of January 1	71,124	26,626
Cash and Cash Equivalents as of December 31	$ 24,114	$ 71,124
Interest Paid	$ 29,515	$ 24,468
Income Taxes Paid	$ 151,490	$ 119,038

Source: Annual Report, 1992

EXHIBIT 9 Hershey Foods Corporation, Net Sales, Income and Income Taxes, and Assets by Geographic Segments (in thousands of dollars)

DECEMBER 31,	1992	1991	1990
Net sales:			
Domestic	$2,871,438	$2,566,448	$2,508,542
International	348,367	332,717	207,067
Total	$3,219,805	$2,899,165	$2,715,609
Income before interest and income taxes:			
Domestic	$ 419,317	$ 381,549	$ 344,303
International	8,911	8,753	6,278
Gain on Business Restructuring, Net	---	---	35,540
Total	$ 428,228	$ 390,302	$ 386,121
Identifiable assets as of December 31:			
Domestic	$2,353,230	$2,003,425	$1,820,434
International	319,679	338,397	258,394
Total	$2,672,909	$2,341,822	$2,078,828

Source: Annual Report, 1992

Canada, Britain, Germany, and Saudi Arabia. As global channels of distribution become more available for chocolate manufacturers, global marketing uniformity will become more prevalent in the industry. Global cultural convergence is accelerating the need for more global marketing uniformity in the confectionery industry. Despite the global success of the movie E.T., about an extraterrestrial being who happens to be fond of Hershey's Reese's Pieces, Hershey did not promote this product globally.

The confectionery industry is characterized by high manufacturing economies of scale. Hershey's U.S. factory, for example, occupies more than two million square feet, is highly automated, and contains a great deal of heavy equipment, vats, and containers. It is the largest chocolate plant in the world. High manufacturing costs in any industry encourage global market expansion, globally standardized products, and globally centralized production.

The confectionery industry is also characterized by high transportation costs for moving milk and sugar, the primary raw materials. This fact motivates companies such as Hershey to locate near their supply sources. Since milk can be obtained in large volumes in many countries, chocolate producers have many options in locating plants. This is true also because producing chocolate is not labor-intensive, and it does not require highly skilled labor.

Product development costs in the confectionery industry are relatively low, since the process largely involves mixing different combinations of the same ingredients. Whenever product development costs are low in an industry, firms are spurred to globalize existing brands rather than develop new ones.

Industry analysts expect the candy industry to continue to grow. Consumption of chocolate, according to industry analysts, is closely related to national income, although the Far East is an exception to this rule. Candy consumption varies in the major markets of the developed nations. Americans consume about 22 pounds of candy annually per person, and Europeans consume about 27 pounds of candy per person.

Chocolate accounts for about 54 percent of all candy consumed. Northern Europeans consume almost twice as much chocolate per capita as Americans. Among European countries, Switzerland, Norway, and the United Kingdom consume the most chocolate, while Finland, Yugoslavia, and Italy consume the least. The Japanese consume very little chocolate—about 1.4 kilos per capita. Throughout Asia and southern Europe, there is a preference for types of sweets other than chocolate, partly because of a high incidence of lactose intolerance (difficulty in digesting dairy products).

Many consumers worldwide are becoming more and more weight-conscious and health-oriented. Numerous organizations and individuals discourage candy consumption and promote the need for exercise and nutrition. The teenage customer base that historically has consumed so much chocolate is shrinking in the United States and most other countries. This clientele is being replaced by older, wealthier consumers, who prefer more sophisticated chocolates. In countries where birth rates and numbers of youth are still growing, disposable income tends to be low, posing a barrier to entry. The confectionery industry overall is thus undergoing transition.

Cocoa beans are the most important raw material used in the production of Hershey's products. This commodity is imported from West Africa, South America, and Far Eastern equatorial regions. West Africa accounts for approximately 60 percent of the world's crop. Cocoa beans exhibit wide fluctuations in price, flavor, and quality, due to (a) weather and other conditions affecting crop size; (b) consuming countries' demand requirements; (c) producing countries' sales policies; (d) speculative influences; and (e) international economics and currency movements. Cocoa bean prices are determined by a provisional International Cocoa Agreement formed by certain producing and consuming countries. The average price of cocoa beans for 1993 had fallen to 9 cents per pound, down from 53 cents per pound in 1991. To minimize the effects of cocoa bean price fluctuations, Hershey purchases large inventories of cocoa beans and cocoa products. Hershey also purchases and sells cocoa future contracts. Hershey maintains West African and Brazilian crop-forecasting operations and continually monitors economic and political factors affecting market conditions.

Hershey's second most important raw material is sugar. Sugar is subject to price supports under domestic farm legislation. Due to import quotas and duties, sugar prices paid by U.S. users are substantially higher than prices on the world market. The average wholesale list price for refined sugar has remained stable at 30 cents per pound over recent years.

Other raw materials that Hershey Corporation purchases in substantial quantities include semolina milled from durum wheat, milk, peanuts, almonds, and coconut. The prices of milk and peanuts are affected by federal marketing orders and subsidy programs of the U.S. Department of Agriculture. Raising and lowering price supports on milk and peanuts greatly affect the cost of Hershey's raw materials. Market prices of peanuts and almonds are generally determined in the latter months of each year, following harvest time.

Tariffs imposed by different countries can greatly impede or promote globalization within an industry, especially in the country where the product is manufactured. For example, U.S. tariffs on chocolate are very low, ranging from 35 cents per pound for mass- produced chocolate to about $2.50 per pound for some premium brands. Even a ten-cent difference in price among competing brands, however, makes a big difference to consumers.

Nationalistic tariffs as they impact candy are falling but still are high enough to be a concern. Japan, Korea, and Taiwan, for example, have reduced their tariffs on imported chocolate from 20 percent to 10 percent. Europe is retaining its 12 percent tariff on chocolate imports from outside Europe. The United States has a 5 percent tariff on solid chocolate products and a 7 percent tariff on all other chocolate confectionery products. Technology standards across countries are similar to tariffs in that they vary and can impact global strategy plans. Japan, for example, prohibits the sale of chocolates that contain the additives BHT and TBHQ, which are approved by the U.S. Food and Drug Administration.

COMPETITORS

The $10 billion U.S. confectionery industry is composed of six major competitors, who control nearly 70 percent of the market: Hershey, Mars, Jacobs Suchard of Switzerland, Nestlé of Switzerland, RJR Nabisco, and Leaf Inc. The remaining 30 percent is divided among many local and regional candy manufacturers.

Based in Switzerland, Nestlé clearly has an edge internationally, being the world leader in many food categories including candy, with 98 percent of its revenues coming from international sales. Hershey's other competitors also do much of their business in foreign markets. For example, Jacobs Suchard obtains 95 percent from international sales, Cadbury-Schweppes, 50 percent, and Mars, 50 percent, while Hershey is the least with 10 percent. Hershey's two major candy competitors are Mars and Nestlé.

Nestlé's chocolate business generally totals $4.5 billion wholesale, Jacobs Suchard, $1.8 billion, Mars, $4.5 billion, Cadbury, $2 billion, and Hershey, $4.5 billion. In total, all firms in the chocolate business sell $20 billion wholesale annually, and revenues are growing at 10 percent worldwide each year.

Mars. Hershey overtook Mars in 1988 as the leading candy manufacturer in the United States, but Mars has a stronger presence in Europe, Asia, Mexico, and Japan. Mars gained 12 percent of the market in Mexico after only one year of entering that market. Analysts estimate Mars' worldwide sales and profits to be just over $7 billion and $1 billion respectively. Mars was recently successful in introducing its Bounty chocolate, originally a European candy, into the United States without prior test marketing. Mars, unlike Hershey, uses uniform marketing globally. For example, the company's M&M candies slogan, "It melts in your mouth, not in your hands," is used worldwide. In contrast, Hershey's successful BarNone candy is named Temptation in Canada.

Based in Hackettstown, New Jersey, Mars is controlled by the Mars family through two brothers, John and Forrest, Jr. A marketing executive at Mars recently said, "Being no. 2 doesn't sit well with the brothers, and that's the biggest motivator." Mars was the first candy company to persuade merchants to put candy displays near cash registers in 1979. Mars is one of the world's largest private, closely held companies. It is a secretive company, unwilling to divulge financial information and corporate strategies. Recently, Mars has not been performing well, and there are reports of high turnover in its executive and sales ranks.

Unlike Hershey, Mars has historically relied upon extensive marketing and advertising expenditures to gain market share, rather than on product innovation. Mars has been repackaging, restyling, and reformulating its leading brands, including Snickers, M&Ms, Milky Way, and 3 Musketeers, but that strategy is now being supplemented with extensive product development. New Mars products include Bounty, Balisto, and PB Max. It also successfully developed and marketed frozen Snickers ice cream bars. The product was so successful that it dislodged Eskimo Pie and Original Klondike from the number one ice cream snack slot without any assistance from promotional advertising. Mars has world-class production facilities in Hackettstown, New Jersey; from that plant it ships products worldwide. In addition, it has manufacturing plants in Mexico and in several European locations.

Mars entered Russia in 1992 and today virtually owns the chocolate market there. Kentave, one of the three Mars distributors in Moscow, sells $5 million of Mars candy monthly. Kentave estimates Mars's total monthly sales in Russia to be about $20 million.

Nestlé. Nestlé, according to many analysts, is the number one food company in the world, with sizable exposure in Europe, the Far East, and South America. Nestlé sells products in over 360 countries on all five continents, many in the Third World. It is the world's largest instant coffee manufacturer, with Nescafé the dominant product. Nestlé also produces and markets chocolate and malt drinks and is the world's largest producer of milk powder and condensed milk. Its coffee creamer product, Carnation Coffeemate, holds a sizable portion of that market.

Nestlé's chocolate and confectionery products carry some popular brand names, including Callier, Crunch, and Yes. With the acquisition of Rowntree, additional notable brands were added to the product line, including Kit Kat, Smarties, After Eight, and Quality Street. The Perugina division produces Baci. Through the RJR Nabisco acquisition, Nestlé acquired Curtiss Brand, a U.S. confectionery producer with such products as Baby Ruth and Butterfinger. Nestlé manufactures chocolate in 23 countries, notably Switzerland and Latin America. Each factory is highly automated, employing an average of 250 people.

Another major product concentration for Nestlé is frozen foods and other refrigerated products. Findus in Europe and Stouffer in the United States, with well-known brands such as Lean Cuisine, represent the bulk of the group's frozen food sales. Nestlé also manufactures a fast-developing range of fresh pasta and sauces in Europe and the United States under the name Contadina. Through the Carnation division, it also manufactures and sells pet foods, including Friskies, Gourmet, and Fancy Feast.

Other Nestlé businesses include the Stouffer hotel chain in the United States and Mexico. Nestlé also has some presence in pharmaceuticals and cosmetics, including a majority interest in Alcon, a manufacturer of eye-care products in the United States, and a 28 percent interest in L'Oreal, the world's largest cosmetics manufacturer.

Nestlé's financial performance, due to its international emphasis, can be dramatically affected by currency value fluctuations. Because of downward fluctuations in foreign currencies against the Swiss franc, Nestlé recorded a conservative 8 percent reduction in profits in 1990. The decline in profits was also influenced by the recession in the United States and worldwide, the Persian Gulf War, and the deterioration of the Brazilian economy. Since 25 percent of Nestlé's revenues and profits come from coffee, any adverse economic occurrences in South America, particularly Brazil, affect the company. Nestlé plans to continue to play to its strength, international markets outside the United States, to combat Hershey.

Hershey's global market share in the chocolate confectionery industry is only 10 percent, lowest among its competitors. A major strategic issue facing Hershey today is where, when, and how to best expand geographically. Perhaps Hershey should expand into Russia, since Mars is doing so well there already. China is another large untapped market.

More and more firms are becoming environmentally proactive in their manufacturing and service delivery processes. Environmentally responsible firms market themselves and their products as being "green-sensitive." Concern for the natural environment is an issue Hershey should address before competitors seize the initiative. Developing environmentally safe products and packages, reducing industrial waste, recycling, and establishing an environmental audit process are strategies that could benefit Hershey.

Some analysts contend that Hershey's organizational chart reflects an outdated structure. Some corporate positions could be consolidated; Hershey divisions perhaps should be based on product rather than on geographic area. Alternatives to the organization's present structure may be needed to effectively expand manufacturing and marketing operations globally.

Hershey's recent divestiture of Freia Marabou, a Norwegian confectioner, for $220 million adds more working capital for a major acquisition. Analysis is needed to identify and value specific acquisition candidates. In developing an overall strategic plan, what specific recommendations would you present to CEO Richard Zimmerman? What relative emphasis should Hershey place on chocolate versus pasta in 1994 through 1996? Should Hershey diversify more into nonchocolate candies since that segment is growing most rapidly? Should a new manufacturing plant be built in Asia or Europe? Design global marketing strategy that could enable Hershey to boost exports of both chocolate and pasta. Should Hershey increase its long-term debt or issue stock to raise the capital needed to implement your recommended strategies? Develop pro forma financial statements to fully assess and evaluate the impact of your proposed strategies.

EXPERIENTIAL EXERCISES

Experiential Exercise 1A

STRATEGY ANALYSIS FOR HERSHEY FOODS

PURPOSE

The purpose of this exercise is to give you experience identifying an organization's opportunities, threats, strengths, and weaknesses. This information is vital to generating and selecting among alternative strategies.

INSTRUCTIONS

Step 1 Identify what you consider to be Hershey's major opportunities, threats, strengths, and weaknesses. On a separate sheet of paper, list these key factors under separate headings. Be sure to state each factor in specific terms.

Step 2 Through class discussion, compare your external and internal factors to those developed by other students. From the discussion, add to your list of factors. Keep this information for use in later exercises.

Experiential Exercise 1B

DEVELOPING A CODE OF BUSINESS ETHICS FOR HERSHEY FOODS

PURPOSE

This exercise can give you practice developing a code of business ethics. Research was recently conducted to examine codes of business ethics from large manufacturing and service firms in the United States. The twenty-eight variables listed below were found to be included in a sample of more than eighty codes of business ethics. The variables are presented in order of how frequently they occurred. Thus, the first variable, "Conduct business in compliance with all laws," was the variable most often included in the sample documents; "Firearms at work are prohibited" was least often included.

1. Conduct business in compliance with all laws.
2. Payments for unlawful purposes are prohibited.
3. Avoid outside activities that impair duties.
4. Comply with all antitrust and trade regulations.
5. Comply with accounting rules and controls.
6. Bribes are prohibited.
7. Maintain confidentiality of records.
8. Participate in community and political activities.
9. Provide products and services of the highest quality.
10. Exhibit standards of personal integrity and conduct.
11. Do not propagate false or misleading information.
12. Perform assigned duties to the best of your ability.

13. Conserve resources and protect the environment.
14. Comply with safety, health, and security regulations.
15. Racial, ethnic, religious, and sexual harassment at work is prohibited.
16. Report unethical and illegal activities to your manager.
17. Convey true claims in product advertisements.
18. Make decisions without regard for personal gain.
19. Do not use company property for personal benefit.
20. Demonstrate courtesy, respect, honesty, and fairness.
21. Illegal drugs and alcohol at work are prohibited.
22. Manage personal finances well.
23. Employees are personally accountable for company funds.
24. Exhibit good attendance and punctuality.
25. Follow directives of supervisors.
26. Do not use abusive language.
27. Dress in businesslike attire.
28. Firearms at work are prohibited.[1]

INSTRUCTIONS

Step 1 On a separate sheet of paper, write a code of business ethics for Hershey. Include as many variables listed above as you believe appropriate to Hershey's business. Limit your document to one hundred words or less.

Step 2 Read your code of ethics to the class. Comment on why you did or did not include certain variables.

Step 3 Explain why having a code of ethics is not sufficient for assuring ethical behavior in an organization. What else does it take?

NOTES

1. Donald Robin, Michael Giallourakis, Fred R. David, and Thomas E. Moritz, "A Different Look at Codes of Ethics," *Business Horizons* 32, no. 1 (January February 1989): 66–73.

Experiential Exercise 1C

THE ETHICS OF SPYING ON COMPETITORS

PURPOSE

This exercise gives you an opportunity to discuss ethical and legal issues in class as related to methods being used by many companies to spy on competing firms. Gathering and using information about competitors is an area of strategic management that Japanese firms do much better than American firms.

INSTRUCTIONS

On a separate sheet of paper, number from 1 to 18. For the eighteen spy activities listed below, indicate whether or not you believe the activity is Ethical or Unethical and Legal or Illegal. Place an E for ethical or U for unethical and an L for legal or an I for illegal. Compare your answers to your classmates' answers and discuss any differences.

1. Buying competitors' garbage.
2. Dissecting competitors' products.
3. Taking plant tours anonymously.
4. Counting tractor-trailer trucks leaving competitors' loading bays.
5. Studying aerial photographs.
6. Analyzing labor contracts.
7. Analyzing help wanted ads.
8. Quizzing customers and buyers about the sales of competitors' products.
9. Infiltrating customers' and competitors' business operations.
10. Quizzing suppliers about competitors' level of manufacturing.
11. Using customers to buy out phony bids.
12. Encouraging key customers to reveal competitive information.
13. Quizzing competitors' former employees.
14. Interviewing consultants who may have worked with competitors.
15. Hiring key managers away from competitors.
16. Conducting phony job interviews to get competitors' employees to reveal information.
17. Sending engineers to trade meetings to quiz competitors' technical employees.
18. Quizzing potential employees who in the past may have worked with competitors.

Experiential Exercise 1D

STRATEGIC PLANNING FOR MY UNIVERSITY

PURPOSE

External and internal factors are the underlying bases of strategies formulated and implemented by organizations. Your college or university faces numerous external opportunities/threats and has many internal strengths/weaknesses. The purpose of this exercise is to illustrate the process of identifying critical external and internal factors.

External influences include trends in the following areas: economic, social, cultural, demographic, environmental, technological, political, legal, governmental, and competitive. External factors could include declining numbers of high school graduates; population shifts; community relations; increased competitiveness among colleges and universities; rising number of adults returning to college; decreased support from local, state, and federal agencies; and increasing number of foreign students attending American colleges.

Internal factors of a college or university include faculty, students, staff, alumni, athletic programs, physical plant, grounds and maintenance, student housing, administration, fundraising, academic programs, food services, parking, placement, clubs, fraternities, sororities, and public relations.

INSTRUCTIONS

Step 1 On a separate sheet of paper, make four headings: External Opportunities, External Threats, Internal Strengths, and Internal Weaknesses.

Step 2 As related to your college or university, list ten factors under each of the four headings.

Step 3 Discuss the factors as a class. Write the factors on the board.

Step 4 What new things did you learn about your university from the class discussion? How could this type of discussion benefit an organization?

STRATEGIC PLANNING AT A LOCAL COMPANY

PURPOSE

This activity is aimed at giving you practical knowledge about how organizations in your city are doing strategic planning. This exercise will also give you experience interacting on a professional basis with local business leaders.

INSTRUCTIONS

Step 1 Use the telephone to contact several local business owners or top managers. Find an organization that does strategic planning. Conduct a phone interview with the president, chief executive officer, or owner of that business.

Step 2 Seek answers to the following questions during the interview:

a. How does your firm actually conduct strategic planning? Who is involved in the process?
b. Does your firm have a formal mission statement? How was the statement developed? When was the statement last changed?
c. What are the benefits of engaging in strategic planning?
d. What are the major costs or problems in doing strategic planning in your business?
e. Do you anticipate making any changes in the strategic planning process at your company? If yes, please explain.

Step 3 Report your findings to the class.

Chapter 2

STRATEGIES IN ACTION

O B J E C T I V E S   After studying this chapter, you should be able to:

■ Identify sixteen types of business strategies.

■ Identify numerous examples of organizations pursuing different types of strategies.

■ Discuss guidelines when generic strategies are most appropriate to pursue.

■ Discuss Porter's generic strategies.

■ Describe strategic management in nonprofit, governmental, and small organizations.

*T*his chapter brings strategic management to life with many contemporary examples. Sixteen types of strategies are defined and exemplified, including Michael Porter's generic strategies: cost leadership, differentiation, and focus. Guidelines are presented for determining when different types of strategies are most appropriate to pursue. An overview of strategic management in nonprofit organizations, governmental agencies, and small firms is provided.

TYPES OF STRATEGIES

The model illustrated in Figure 2–1 provides a conceptual basis for applying strategic management. Defined and exemplified in Table 2–1, alternative strategies that an enterprise could pursue can be categorized into thirteen actions: forward integration, backward integration, horizontal integration, market penetration, market development, product development, concentric diversification, conglomerate diversification, horizontal diversification, joint venture, retrenchment, divestiture, liquidation, and a combination strategy. Each alternative strategy has countless variations. For example, market penetration can include adding salespersons, increasing advertising expenditures, couponing, and using similar actions to increase market share in a given geographic area.

INTEGRATION STRATEGIES

Forward integration, backward integration, and horizontal integration are sometimes collectively referred to as vertical integration strategies. Vertical integration strategies allow a firm to gain control over distributors, suppliers, and/or competitors.

Forward Integration. *Forward integration* involves gaining ownership or increased control over distributors or retailers. A company that is betting a large part of its future on forward integration is Coca-Cola. Coke continues to purchase domestic and foreign bottlers, most recently the second-largest bottling firm in the United States, Johnson Coca-Cola Bottling in Chattanooga, for $450 million. Johnson accounts for about 11 percent of all Coca-Cola soft drink products bottled and canned in the United States. Coke has been able to improve its acquired bottlers' efficiency in production and distribution.

An effective means of implementing forward integration is franchising. Approximately 2,000 companies in about fifty different industries in the United States use franchising to distribute their products or services. Businesses can expand rapidly by franchising because costs and opportunities are spread among many individuals. Total sales by franchises in the United States increased to over $800 billion in 1993.

Backward Integration. Both manufacturers and retailers purchase needed materials from suppliers. *Backward integration* is a strategy of seeking ownership or increased control of a firm's suppliers. This strategy can be especially appropriate when a firm's current suppliers are unreliable, too costly, or cannot meet the firm's needs.

More and more, consumers are buying products according to environmental considerations which include recyclability of the package. Some firms are thus using back-

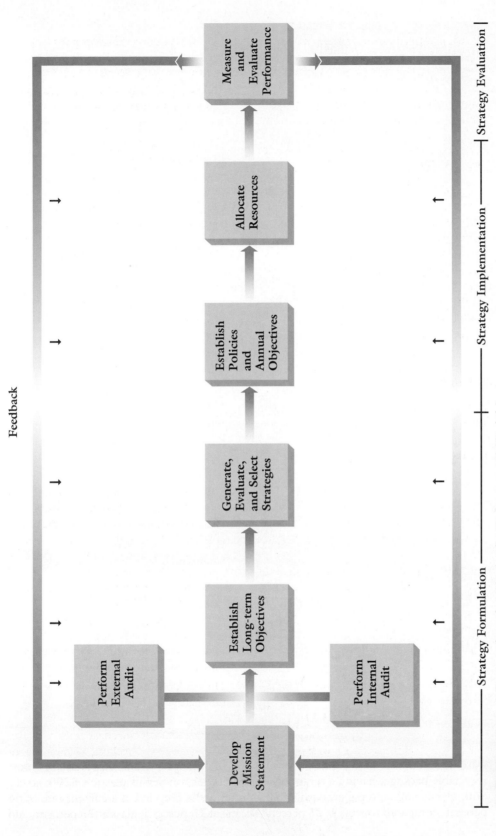

FIGURE 2-1 A Comprehensive Strategic–Management Model

TABLE 2-1   Alternative Strategies Defined and Exemplified

STRATEGY	DEFINITION	EXAMPLE
Forward Integration	Gaining ownership or increased control over distributors or retailers	Tandy Corporation opens new Radio Shack stores.
Backward Integration	Seeking ownership or increased control of a firm's suppliers	Kmart requires suppliers to sell its goods on consignment.
Horizontal Integration	Seeking ownership or increased control over competitors	Merck, the world's largest drug company, acquires Medco Containment Services, the nation's largest marketer of discount prescription drugs.
Market Penetration	Seeking increased market share for present products or services in present markets through greater marketing efforts	Walt Disney pays Nancy Kerrigan $1 million for appearances.
Market Development	Introducing present products or services into new geographic area	Corning Inc. becomes one of Russia's first major suppliers of optical fiber.
Product Development	Seeking increased sales by improving present products or services or developing new ones	Rayovac develops an alkaline battery recharger.
Concentric Diversification	Adding new, but related, products or services	Sonoco Products Company, a maker of industrial packages, acquires Engraph Inc., a maker of consumer packages.
Conglomerate Diversification	Adding new, unrelated products or services	Seagram acquires 13.1 percent of Time Warner.
Horizontal Diversification	Adding new, unrelated products or services for present customers	Stratus Computer, a maker of fault-tolerant computers, acquires Shared Financial Systems, a software maker.
Joint Venture	Two or more sponsoring firms forming a separate organization for cooperative purposes	Home Shopping Network and Sumitomo offer television shopping in Japan.
Retrenchment	Regrouping through cost and asset reduction to reverse declining sales and profits	U.S. Surgical declares bankruptcy.
Divestiture	Selling a division or part of an organization	Ryder System, the truck-leasing company divests its aviation business.
Liquidation	Selling all of a company's assets, in parts, for their tangible worth	The Bank of Credit and Commerce International (BCCI) liquidates.

ward integration to gain control over suppliers of packages. Aluminum is still the most recyclable package, having a scrap value of $650 per ton versus plastic's $200, steel's $60, glass's $50, and paperboard's $30. Aluminum is recycled at a current rate of 64 percent, compared to steel at 25 percent, plastic at 15 percent, glass at 25 percent, and paperboard at 25 percent. Coca-Cola Company and PepsiCo are currently experimenting with bottles made completely from other recycled bottles.

Some industries in the United States (such as the automotive and aluminum industries) are reducing their historical pursuit of backward integration. Instead of owning their suppliers, companies negotiate with several outside suppliers. Ford and Chrysler buy over half of their components parts from outside suppliers such as TRW, Eaton, General Electric, and Johnson Controls. De-integration makes sense in industries that have global sources of supply. *Outsourcing,* whereby companies use outside suppliers, shop around, play one seller against another, and go with the best deal, is becoming widely practiced.

Global competition is also spurring firms to reduce their number of suppliers and to demand higher levels of service and quality from those they keep. For example, Motorola recently reduced its number of suppliers from 10,000 to 3,000, Xerox cut its suppliers from 5,000 to 500, Digital Equipment cut from 9,000 to 3,000, General Motors from 10,000 to 5,500, and Texas Instruments from 22,000 to 14,000. Although traditionally relying on many suppliers to ensure uninterrupted supplies and low prices, American firms are now following the lead of Japanese firms, who have far fewer suppliers and closer, long-term relationships with those few. "Keeping track of so many suppliers is onerous," says Mark Shimelonis of Xerox.

Horizontal Integration. *Horizontal integration* refers to a strategy of seeking ownership of or increased control over a firm's competitors. One of the most significant trends in strategic management today is the increased use of horizontal integration as a growth strategy. Mergers, acquisitions, and takeovers among competitors allow for increased economies of scale and enhanced transfer of resources and competencies. This was a major reason why Renault acquired Volvo recently to become Europe's third-largest auto maker behind Volkswagen and General Motors. At the time of the acquisition, Renault, a French firm, had 10.6 percent of the market, and Volvo, a Swedish firm, had 1.4 percent. It is among the top three. Kenneth Davidson makes the following observation about horizontal integration:

> The trend towards horizontal integration seems to reflect strategists' misgivings about their ability to operate many unrelated businesses. Mergers between direct competitors are more likely to create efficiencies than mergers between unrelated businesses, both because there is a greater potential for eliminating duplicate facilities and because the management of the acquiring firm is more likely to understand the business of the target.[1]

Mattel, Inc., maker of Barbie, Hot Wheels, and Disney toys, recently acquired rival toy maker Fisher-Price, to surpass Hasbro as the largest toy company in the world. More than half of Mattel's sales are outside the United States.

INTENSIVE STRATEGIES

Market penetration, market development, and product development are sometimes referred to as "intensive strategies" because they require intensive efforts to improve a firm's competitive position with existing products.

Market Penetration. A *market penetration* strategy seeks to increase market share for present products or services in present markets through greater marketing efforts. This strategy is widely used alone and in combination with other strategies. Market penetration includes increasing the number of salespersons, increasing advertising expenditures, offering extensive sales promotion items, or increasing publicity efforts. Procter & Gamble is an example of this, spending heavily on advertising to increase market share of Venezia, its upscale perfume. Its advertising campaign includes full-page ads with scent strips in glossy magazines.

Market Development. *Market development* involves introducing present products or services into new geographic areas. The climate for international market development is becoming more and more favorable as illustrated in the Global Perspective. In many industries, it is going to be hard to maintain a competitive edge by staying close to home. This certainly is true in the soft-drink industry. Pepsi is spending $500 million in Poland alone this year to combat Coke, which has gained a 35 percent market share throughout eastern Europe.

Expansion into world markets is no guarantee of success. A company that is striving to slow down, rather than speed up, global expansion is L. L. Bean, the famous mail-order company based in Freeport, Maine. L.L. Bean guarantees "100 percent satisfaction or your money back." L. L. Bean's problem is that $82 million worth of goods, or about 14 percent of Bean's $588 million in sales, is returned yearly. Bean's strategy to slow down market development is intended to allow greater care in quality control and customer service.

Product Development. *Product development* is a strategy that seeks increased sales by improving or modifying present products or services. Product development usually entails large research and development expenditures. Firms in the beer industry, for example, continually allocate large sums of money to product development. Anheuser-Busch recently developed and tested O'Douls, a no-alcohol beer, and Busch Light, a draft-light beer. Stroh Brewery successfully developed an alcohol-free fruit and sparkling water mix called Sundance. Coors recently developed and introduced George Killian's Irish Red beer, Herman Joseph's beer, and two lower-priced beers, Keystone and Keystone Light.

Large expenditures in product development are a major reason why automotive and computer firms, such as General Motors, Ford, IBM, and Apple, do not own their distributors or dealers. Tandy is the only computer company that owns its distributors, which are Radio Shack stores. One of the most expensive new-product flops of the 1980s was Premier, RJR Nabisco's "smokeless" cigarette. After spending 10 years developing this product, and test marketing it for 5 months, RJR abandoned plans to introduce Premier.

DIVERSIFICATION STRATEGIES

There are three general types of diversification strategies: concentric, horizontal, and conglomerate. Overall, diversification strategies are becoming less and less popular as organizations are finding it more and more difficult to manage diverse business activities. In the 1960s and 1970s, the trend was to diversify so as not to be dependent on any single industry, but the 1980s saw a general reversal of that thinking. Diversification is now on the retreat. Michael Porter of the Harvard Business School says, "Management found they couldn't manage the beast." Hence, businesses are selling, or closing, less profitable divisions in order to focus on core businesses.

Peters and Waterman's advice to firms is to "stick to the knitting" and not to stray too far from the firm's basic areas of competence. However, diversification is still an appropriate and successful strategy sometimes. For example, Philip Morris derives 60 percent of its profits from sales of Marlboro cigarettes. Hamish Maxwell, Philip Morris's CEO, says, "We want to become a consumer-products company." Diversification makes sense for Philip Morris because cigarette consumption is declining, product liability suits are a risk, and some investors reject tobacco stocks on principle. In a diversification move, Philip Morris spent $12.9 billion in a hostile takeover of Kraft General Foods, the world's second-largest food producer behind Nestlé.

Concentric Diversification. Adding new, but related, products or services is widely called *concentric diversification*. An example of this strategy is the recent entry of Bell Atlantic Corporation, a telephone company, into the video programming business. The cable industry had lobbied heavily against allowing telephone companies to sell programming.

Another example of a concentrically diversifying firm is Iowa-Illinois Gas & Electric, which is developing the first major U.S. wind energy project outside California. The firm's wind farm will cost $225 million and involves putting large wind turbines on agricultural land to generate 250 megawatts of power. Pacific Gas, the nation's largest utility, gets up to 8 percent of its power from the wind. The new Iowa wind project will produce electricity for about five cents a kilowatt-hour, making wind power cheaper than coal power, considering air pollution and other environmental costs. A growing number of states now require utilities to include "hidden environmental costs" in strategic planning.

Horizontal Diversification. Adding new, unrelated products or services for present customers is called *horizontal diversification*. This strategy is not as risky as conglomerate diversification, because a firm should already be familiar with its present customers. For example, Motorola recently entered the cordless phone market by introducing a flip-top, 7.5-ounce cordless phone to be sold initially only through Sears Roebuck. AT&T dominates the $700 million U.S.

cordless market with a 48 percent market share, followed by Panasonic with a 10 percent share and Sony with 8 percent. Motorola is producing the new phones in its Grayslake, Illinois, factory.

Another example of horizontal diversification is Sony Corporation's purchase of Columbia Pictures Entertainment Company. Totaling $3.4 billion, this acquisition represented Japan's largest entry ever into the U.S. entertainment industry. A final example of horizontal diversification is Anheuser-Busch's acquisition of Harcourt Brace Jovanovich's Sea World, near Orlando, and six other theme parks.

Conglomerate Diversification. Adding new, unrelated products or services is called *conglomerate diversification*. Some firms pursue conglomerate diversification based in part on an expectation of profits from breaking up acquired firms and selling divisions piecemeal. Richard West, dean of New York University's School of Business, says, "The stock market is rewarding deconglomerations, saying company assets are worth more separately than together. There is a kind of antisynergy, the whole being worth less than the parts."

Of the seven regional companies created by the breakup of AT&T, U.S. West has pursued the most risky diversification strategy. U.S. West, a telecommunications firm, now owns operations in industries such as cable TV, equipment financing, advertising services, real estate development, cellular telephones, and publishing. Based in Denver, U.S. West recently purchased Financial Security Assurance for $345 million, further diversifying into financial services.

General Electric is an example of a firm that is highly diversified. GE makes locomotives, light bulbs, power plants, and refrigerators; GE manages more credit cards than American Express; GE owns more commercial aircraft than American Airlines.

DEFENSIVE STRATEGIES

In addition to integrative, intensive, and diversification strategies, organizations could also pursue joint venture, retrenchment, divestiture, or liquidation.

Joint Venture. *Joint venture* is a popular strategy that occurs when two or more companies form a temporary partnership or consortium for the purpose of capitalizing on some opportunity. This strategy can be considered defensive only because the firm is not undertaking the project alone. Often, the two or more sponsoring firms form a separate organization and have shared equity ownership in the new entity. Other types of *cooperative arrangements* include research and development partnerships, cross-distribution agreements, cross-licensing agreements, cross-manufacturing agreements, and joint-bidding consortia.

Joint ventures and cooperative arrangements are being used increasingly because they allow companies to improve communications and networking, to globalize operations, and to minimize risk. Kathryn Rudie Harrigan, professor of strategic management at Columbia University, summarizes the trend toward increased joint venturing:

> In today's global business environment of scarce resources, rapid rates of technological change, and rising capital requirements, the important question is no longer, "Shall we form a joint venture?" Now the question is, "Which joint ventures and cooperative arrangements are most appropriate for our needs and expectations?" followed by, "How do we manage these ventures most effectively?"[2]

Cooperative agreements even between competitors are becoming popular. For example, Canon supplies photocopies to Kodak, France's Thomson and Japan's FVC manufacture videocassette recorders, Siemens and Fujitsu work together, and General Motors and Toyota assemble automobiles. For collaboration between competitors to succeed, both firms must contribute something distinctive, such as technology, distribution, basic research, or manufacturing capacity. But a major risk is that unintended transfers of important skills or technology may occur at organizational levels below where the deal was signed.[3] Information not covered in the formal agreement often gets traded in day-to-day interactions and dealings of engineers, marketers, and product developers. American firms often give away too much information to foreign firms when operating under cooperative agreements! Tighter formal agreements are needed, and Western companies must become better learners since leadership in many industries has shifted to the Far East and Europe.

Retrenchment. *Retrenchment* occurs when an organization regroups through cost and asset reduction to reverse declining sales and profits. Sometimes called a turnaround or reorganizational strategy, retrenchment is designed to fortify an organization's basic distinctive competence. During retrenchment, strategists work with limited resources and face pressure from shareholders, employees, and the media. Retrenchment can entail selling off land and buildings to raise needed cash, pruning product lines, closing marginal businesses, closing obsolete factories, automating processes, reducing the number of employees, and instituting expense control systems.

In some cases, *bankruptcy* can be an effective type of retrenchment strategy. Bankruptcy can allow a firm to avoid major debt obligations and to void union contracts. While reorganizing under Chapter 11 bankruptcy in 1989, Revco received a $925 million takeover offer from the Bass Group. There are five major types of bankruptcy: Chapter 7, Chapter 9, Chapter 11, Chapter 12, and Chapter 13.

Chapter 7 bankruptcy is a liquidation procedure used only when a corporation sees no hope of being able to operate successfully or to obtain the necessary creditor agreement. All the organization's assets are sold in parts for their tangible worth.

Chapter 9 bankruptcy applies to municipalities. The most recent municipality successfully declaring bankruptcy is Bridgeport, the largest city in Connecticut. Some states do not allow municipalities to declare bankruptcy.

Chapter 11 bankruptcy allows organizations to reorganize and "come back" after filing a petition for protection. Declaring Chapter 11 bankruptcy allowed the Manville Corporation and Continental Products to gain protection from liability suits filed over their manufacture of asbestos products. Million-dollar judgments against these companies would have required liquidation, so bankruptcy was a good strategy for these two firms. Similarly, Wang Laboratories recently emerged from Chapter 11 with one of the strongest balance sheets in the computer industry. Carlisle Retailers, Ohio's oldest family-run department store, recently filed for protection from creditors under Chapter 11.

Chapter 12 bankruptcy was created by the Family Farmer Bankruptcy Act of 1986. This law became effective in 1987 and provides special relief to family farmers with debt equal to or less than $1.5 million.

Chapter 13 bankruptcy is a reorganization plan similar to Chapter 11 but available only to small businesses owned by individuals with unsecured debts of less than $100,000 and secured debts of less than $350,000. The Chapter 13 debtor is allowed to operate the business while a plan is being developed to provide for the successful operation of the business in the future.

Divestiture.   Selling a division or part of an organization is called *divestiture.* Divestiture is often used to raise capital for further strategic acquisitions or investments. Divestiture can be part of an overall retrenchment strategy to rid an organization of businesses that are unprofitable, that require too much capital, or that do not fit well with the firm's other activities.

Liquidation.   Selling all of a company's assets, in parts, for their tangible worth is called *liquidation.* Liquidation is a recognition of defeat and consequently can be an emotionally difficult strategy. However, it may be better to cease operating than to continue losing large sums of money. Container-shipping pioneer Malcolm P. McLean recently liquidated McLean Industries, the 115-year-old shipping company. Reorganization under Chapter 11 bankruptcy had failed. Based in Charlotte, North Carolina, the company was 85-percent owned by Mr. McLean.

Combination.   Many, if not most, organizations pursue a combination of two or more strategies simultaneously, but a combination strategy can be exceptionally risky if carried too far. No organization can afford to pursue all the strategies that might benefit the firm. Difficult decisions must be made. Priorities must be established. Organizations, like individuals, have limited resources. Both organizations and individuals must choose among alternative strategies and avoid excessive indebtedness.

Organizations cannot do too many things well because resources and talents get spread thin and competitors gain advantage. In large diversified companies, a combination strategy is commonly employed when different divisions pursue different strategies. Also, organizations struggling to survive may employ a combination of several defensive strategies, such as divestiture, liquidation, and retrenchment, simultaneously.

GUIDELINES FOR PURSUING STRATEGIES

Table 2–2 reveals situations, conditions, and guidelines for when various alternative strategies are most appropriate to pursue. For example, note that a market development strategy is generally most appropriate when new channels of distribution are available that are reliable, inexpensive, and of good quality; when an organization is very successful at what it does; when new untapped or unsaturated markets exist; when an organization has the needed capital and human resources to manage expanded operations; and when an organization has excess production capacity; when an organization's basic industry is rapidly becoming global in scope.

MERGERS AND LEVERAGED BUYOUTS

Acquisition and merger are two commonly used ways to pursue strategies. An *acquisition* occurs when a large organization purchases (acquires) a smaller firm, or vice versa. A *merger* occurs when two organizations of about equal size unite to form one enterprise. When an acquisition or merger is not desired by both parties, it can be called a *takeover* or *hostile takeover.* Regarding "merger mania" restructuring in the United States, *Business Week* offers the following conclusion:

> It is clear now that restructurings are driven by a lot more than tax considerations, low stock prices, raiders' desire for a quick buck, and aggressive merger merchants on Wall Street.... Restructuring continues because U.S. industry needs it. Deregulation in industries from financial services to energy, from communications to transportation, has exposed manager-

TABLE 2-2   Guidelines for Situations When Particular Strategies Are Most Effective

Forward Integration

- When an organization's present distributors are especially expensive, or unreliable, or incapable of meeting the firm's distribution needs
- When the availability of quality distributors is so limited as to offer a competitive advantage to those firms that integrate forward
- When an organization competes in an industry that is growing and is expected to continue to grow markedly; this is a factor because forward integration reduces an organization's ability to diversify if its basic industry falters
- When an organization has both the capital and human resources needed to manage the new business of distributing its own products
- When the advantages of stable production are particularly high; this is a consideration because an organization can increase the predictability of the demand for its output through forward integration
- When present distributors or retailers have high profit margins; this situation suggests that a company could profitably distribute its own products and price them more competitively by integrating forward

Backward Integration

- When an organization's present suppliers are especially expensive, or unreliable, or incapable of meeting the firm's needs for parts, components, assemblies, or raw materials
- When the number of suppliers is few and the number of competitors is many
- When an organization competes in an industry that is growing rapidly; this is a factor because integrative-type strategies (forward, backward, and horizontal) reduce an organization's ability to diversify in a declining industry
- When an organization has both the capital and human resources needed to manage the new business of supplying its own raw materials
- When the advantages of stable prices are particularly important; this is a factor because an organization can stabilize the cost of its raw materials and the associated price of its product through backward integration
- When present supplies have high profit margins, which suggests that the business of supplying products or services in the given industry is a worthwhile venture
- When an organization needs to acquire a needed resource quickly

Horizontal Integration

- When an organization can gain monopolistic characteristics in a particular area or region without being challenged by the federal government for "tending substantially" to reduce competition
- When an organization competes in a growing industry
- When increased economies of scale provide major competitive advantages
- When an organization has both the capital and human talent needed to successfully manage an expanded organization
- When competitors are faltering due to a lack of managerial expertise or a need for particular resources that your organization possesses; note that horizontal integration would not be appropriate if competitors are doing poorly because overall industry sales are declining

Market Penetration

- When current markets are not saturated with your particular product or service
- When the usage rate of present customers could be significantly increased
- When the market shares of major competitors have been declining while total industry sales have been increasing

TABLE 2-2   *Continued*

- When the correlation between dollar sales and dollar marketing expenditures has historically been high
- When increased economies of scale provide major competitive advantages

Market Development

- When new channels of distribution are available that are reliable, inexpensive, and of good quality
- When an organization is very successful at what it does
- When new untapped or unsaturated markets exist
- When an organization has the needed capital and human resources to manage expanded operations
- When an organization has excess production capacity
- When an organization's basic industry is rapidly becoming global in scope

Product Development

- When an organization has successful products that are in the maturity stage of the product life cycle; the idea here is to attract satisfied customers to try new (improved) products as a result of their positive experience with the organization's present products or services
- When an organization competes in an industry that is characterized by rapid technological developments
- When major competitors offer better quality products at comparable prices
- When an organization competes in a high-growth industry
- When an organization has especially strong research and development capabilities

Concentric Diversification

- When an organization competes in a no-growth or a slow-growth industry
- When adding new, but related, products would significantly enhance the sales of current products
- When new, but related, products could be offered at highly competitive prices
- When new, but related, products have seasonal sales levels that counterbalance an organization's existing peaks and valleys
- When an organization's products are currently in the decline stage of the product life cycle
- When an organization has a strong management team

Conglomerate Diversification

- When an organization's basic industry is experiencing declining annual sales and profits
- When an organization has the capital and managerial talent needed to compete successfully in a new industry
- When the organization has the opportunity to purchase an unrelated business that is an attractive investment opportunity
- When there exists financial synergy between the acquired and acquiring firm; note that a key difference between concentric and conglomerate diversification is that the former should be based on some commonality in markets, products, or technology, whereas the latter should be based more on profit considerations
- When existing markets for an organization's present products are saturated
- When antitrust action could be charged against an organization that has historically concentrated on a single industry

TABLE 2-2   *Continued*

Horizontal Diversification

- When revenues derived from an organization's current products or services would significantly increase by adding the new, unrelated products
- When an organization competes in a highly competitive and/or a no-growth industry, as indicated by low industry profit margins and returns
- When an organization's present channels of distribution can be used to market the new products to current customers
- When the new products have countercyclical sales patterns compared to an organization's present products

Joint Venture

- When a privately owned organization is forming a joint venture with a publicly owned organization; there are some advantages of being privately held, such as close ownership; there are some advantages of being publicly held, such as access to stock issuances as a source of capital. Sometimes, the unique advantages of being privately and publicly held can be synergistically combined in a joint venture
- When a domestic organization is forming a joint venture with a foreign company; joint venture can provide a domestic company with the opportunity for obtaining local management in a foreign country, thereby reducing risks such as expropriation and harassment by host country officials
- When the distinctive competencies of two or more firms complement each other especially well
- When some project is potentially very profitable, but requires overwhelming resources and risks; the Alaskan pipeline is an example
- When two or more smaller firms have trouble competing with a large firm
- When there exists a need to introduce a new technology quickly

Retrenchment

- When an organization has a clearly distinctive competence, but has failed to meet its objectives and goals consistently over time
- When an organization is one of the weaker competitors in a given industry
- When an organization is plagued by inefficiency, low profitability, poor employee morale, and pressure from stockholders to improve performance
- When an organization has failed to capitalize on external opportunities, minimize external threats, take advantage of internal strengths, and overcome internal weaknesses over time; that is, when the organization's strategic managers have failed (and possibly been replaced by more competent individuals)
- When an organization has grown so large so quickly that major internal reorganization is needed

Divestiture

- When an organization has pursued a retrenchment strategy and it failed to accomplish needed improvements
- When a division needs more resources to be competitive than the company can provide
- When a division is responsible for an organization's overall poor performance
- When a division is a misfit with the rest of an organization; this can result from radically different markets, customers, managers, employees, values, or needs
- When a large amount of cash is needed quickly and cannot be reasonably obtained from other sources
- When government antitrust action threatens an organization

TABLE 2-2   *Continued*

Liquidation

- When an organization has pursued both a retrenchment strategy and a divestiture strategy, and neither has been successful

- When an organization's only alternative is bankruptcy; liquidation represents an orderly and planned means of obtaining the greatest possible cash for an organization's assets. A company can legally declare bankruptcy first and then liquidate various divisions to raise needed capital

- When the stockholders of a firm can minimize their losses by selling the organization's assets

Source: Adapted from F. R. David, "How Do We Choose Among Alternative Growth Strategies?" *Managerial Planning* 33, no. 4 (January–February 1985): 14–17, 22.

ial complacency and inefficient practices caused by years of shelter from market forces.... Plenty of companies have simply recognized that if they want to compete globally, they must slim down, toughen up, and focus on a narrower range of businesses.[4]

Among mergers, acquisitions, and takeovers in recent years, same-industry combinations have predominated. For example, Columbia Hospital and Galen Health Care merged recently to create one of the largest health-care providers in the United States, Columbia Healthcare Corporation. The company now operates 99 hospitals in 19 states and two foreign countries. In the aerospace industry, Martin Marietta and Grumman merged in 1994 to create one of the largest defense firms in the United States. A general market consolidation is occurring in many industries, especially pharmaceuticals, food, airlines, accounting, publishing, computers, retailing, financial services, and biotechnology. Table 2–3 shows some mergers and acquisitions completed in 1993 and 1994. There are many reasons for mergers and acquisitions, including the following:

- To provide improved capacity utilization
- To make better use of existing sales force
- To reduce managerial staff
- To gain economies of scale
- To smooth out seasonal trends in sales
- To gain access to new suppliers, distributors, and creditors
- To gain new technology
- To reduce tax obligations

Spurred by high stock prices, merger activity in 1993 more than doubled the pace in 1992. Instead of being financed by junk-bond debt, the latest merger boom is being funded largely by stock.

Leveraged Buyouts (LBOs).   A *leveraged buyout* (LBO) occurs when a corporation's shareholders are bought out (hence "buyout") by the company's management and other private investors using borrowed funds (hence "leveraged").[5] Besides trying to avoid a hostile takeover, other reasons for initiating an LBO are senior management decisions that particular divisions do not fit into an overall corporate strategy or must be sold to raise cash, or receipt of an attractive offering price. An LBO takes a corporation private. There were nearly 2,000 LBOs consummated in the United States during the 1980s.

TABLE 2-3   Some Examples of Merger and Acquisitions
Completed in 1993 and 1994

ACQUIRING FIRM	ACQUIRED FIRM
Viacom	Paramount Communications
Cadbury Schweppes	A&W Brands
Bell Atlantic	Tele-Communications
Paramount Communications	Chris-Craft Industries
Akzo	Nobel Industries
New York Times	Affiliated Publications
UniHealth America	Blue Shield of California
AH Belo	Dallas Morning News
Banc One	Liberty National Bancorp
Renault	Volvo
QVC	Home Shopping Network
AT&T	McCaw Cellular Communications
Bass PLC	Prague Breweries
Merck	Medco
Southwest Airlines	Morris Air

Borg-Warner, Owen-Illinois, and Jim Walter are companies that recently experienced leveraged buyouts. Under this arrangement, the debt is paid back later through funds from operations and the sale of assets. Many banks, insurance companies, and other financial institutions are getting into the buyout business, sometimes called "merchant banking."

Merchant bankers usually sell companies acquired in leveraged buyouts in pieces and at high profits. In the most profitable leveraged buyout ever recorded, Kohlberg, Kravis, Roberts (KKR) and Company acquired RJR Nabisco for $25 billion and then began selling divisions separately at premiums. RJR's divestitures included selling its fresh-fruit business for $875 million to Polly Peck, a London-based food company, and its Del Monte canned food business for about $1.48 billion to another leveraged buyout group led by Citicorp Venture Capital.

In most situations, the capital structure of a newly acquired LBO company will have 85 percent or more debt on the initial balance sheet. This debt can be divided into two categories: senior debt, which is supplied by commercial lenders, and subordinated debt, which is raised in the public market. In most cases, subordinated debt providers become equity partners by negotiating options or warrants, known as *equity kickers*. When a management group "buys" a business in an LBO, the group usually ends up with about 15 percent of the equity of that business.[6] Even if a management group does not seek substantial equity in the new business, a strong management group is usually essential to have in place before financial institutions or other investors are willing to participate in the buyout.

Many firms that were taken private during the 1980s in leveraged buyouts are today selling shares back to the public. Called a *reverse* LBO, this activity is being used to improve the companies' debt-laden balance sheets. The largest recent reverse LBOs occurred at Duracell where $365 million of capital was raised through equity.

Probably the three most widely read books on competitive analysis in the 1980s were Michael Porter's *Competitive Strategy* (Free Press, 1980), *Competitive Advantage* (Free Press, 1985), and *Competitive Advantage of Nations* (Free Press, 1989). According to Porter, strategies allow organizations to gain competitive advantage from three different bases: cost leadership, differentiation, and focus. Porter calls these bases "generic strategies."[7] *Cost leadership* emphasizes producing standardized products at very low per-unit cost for consumers who are price-sensitive. *Differentiation* is a strategy aimed at producing products and services considered unique industrywide and directed at consumers who are relatively price-insensitive. *Focus* means producing products and services that fulfill the needs of small groups of consumers.

Porter's strategies imply different organizational arrangements, control procedures, and incentive systems. Larger firms with greater access to resources typically compete on a cost leadership and/or differentiation basis, whereas smaller firms often compete on a focus basis.

Porter stresses the need for strategists to perform cost-benefit analyses to evaluate "sharing opportunities" among a firm's existing and potential business units. Sharing activities and resources enhances competitive advantage by lowering costs or raising differentiation. In addition to prompting sharing, Porter stresses the need for firms to "transfer" skills and expertise among autonomous business units effectively in order to gain competitive advantage. Depending upon factors such as type of industry, size of firm, and nature of competition, various strategies could yield advantages in cost leadership, differentiation, and focus.

Cost Leadership Strategies. A primary reason for pursuing forward, backward, and horizontal integration strategies is to gain cost leadership benefits. But cost leadership generally must be pursued in conjunction with differentiation. A number of cost elements affect the relative attractiveness of generic strategies, including economies or diseconomies of scale achieved, learning and experience curve effects, the percentage of capacity utilization achieved, and linkages with suppliers and distributors.[8] Other cost elements to consider in choosing among alternative strategies include the potential for sharing costs and knowledge within the organization, R&D costs associated with new product development or modification of existing products, and labor costs, tax rates, energy costs, and shipping costs.

Striving to be the low-cost producer in an industry can be especially effective when the market is comprised of many price-sensitive buyers, when there are few ways to achieve product differentiation, when buyers do not care much about differences from brand to brand, or when there are a large number of buyers with significant bargaining power. The basic idea is to underprice competitors and thereby gain market share and sales, driving some competitors out of the market entirely.

A successful cost leadership strategy usually permeates the entire firm, as evidenced by high efficiency, low overhead, limited perks, intolerance of waste, intensive screening of budget requests, wide spans of control, rewards linked to cost containment, and broad employee participation in cost control efforts. Some risks of pursuing cost leadership are that competitors may imitate the strategy, thus driving overall industry profits down, technological breakthroughs in the industry may make the strategy ineffective, or buyer interest may swing to other differentiating features besides price. Several example firms that are well known for their low-cost leadership strategies are Wal-Mart, BIC, McDonald's, Black and Decker, Lincoln Electric, and Briggs and Stratton.

Differentiation Strategies. Different strategies offer different degrees of differentiation. Differentiation does not guarantee competitive advantage, especially if standard products sufficiently meet customer needs or if rapid imitation by competitors is possible. Durable products protected by barriers to quick copying by competitors are best. Successful differentiation can mean greater product flexibility, greater compatibility, lower costs, improved service, less maintenance, greater convenience, or more features. Product development is an example of a strategy that offers the advantages of differentiation.

A differentiation strategy should be pursued only after careful study of buyers' needs and preferences, to determine the feasibility of incorporating one or more differentiating features into a unique product that features the desired attributes. A successful differentiation strategy allows a firm to charge a higher price for its product and to gain customer loyalty since consumers may become strongly attached to the differentiation features. Special features to differentiate one's product can include superior service, spare parts availability, engineering design, product performance, useful life, gas mileage, or ease of use.

A risk of pursuing a differentiation strategy is that the unique product may not be valued highly enough by customers to justify the higher price. When this happens, a cost leadership strategy will easily defeat a differentiation strategy. Another risk of pursuing a differentiation strategy is that competitors may develop ways to quickly copy the differentiating features. Firms thus must find durable sources of uniqueness that cannot be quickly or cheaply imitated by rival firms.

Common organizational requirements for a successful differentiation strategy include strong coordination among the R&D and marketing functions and substantial amenities to attract scientists and creative people. Firms pursuing a differentiation strategy include Dr. Pepper, Jenn-Air, The Limited, BMW, Grady-White, Ralph Lauren, Maytag, and Cross. As indicated in this chapter's Natural Environment Perspective, an increasing number of firms are developing differentiation strategies that capitalize on consumer concern for preserving the natural environment.

Focus Strategies. A successful focus strategy depends upon an industry segment that is of sufficient size, has good growth potential, and is not crucial to the success of other major competitors. Strategies such as market penetration and market development offer substantial focusing advantages. In an article refining Porter's work, Peter Wright emphasizes that midsize and large firms can effectively pursue focus-based strategies only in conjunction with differentiation or cost leadership-based strategies.[9] Fulmer and Goodwin concur by emphasizing that all firms in essence follow a differentiated strategy. Since only one firm can differentiate itself with the lowest cost, the remaining firms in the industry must find other ways to differentiate their products.[10]

Focus strategies are most effective when consumers have distinctive preferences or requirements and when rival firms are not attempting to specialize in the same target segment. Firms pursuing a focus strategy include Midas, Red Lobster, Federal Express, US Sprint, MCI, Coors Brewers, and Schwinn.

Risks of pursuing a focus strategy include the possibility that numerous competitors recognize the successful focus strategy and copy the strategy, or that consumer preferences drift toward the product attributes desired by the market as a whole. An organization using a focus strategy may concentrate on a particular group of customers, geographic markets, or product line segments in order to serve a well-defined but narrow market better than competitors who serve a broader market.

The Value Chain. According to Porter, the business of a firm can best be described as a value chain in which total revenues minus total costs of all activities undertaken to develop and market a product or service yields value. All firms in a given industry have a similar value chain, which includes activities such as obtaining raw materials, designing products, building manufacturing facilities, developing cooperative agreements, and providing customer service. A firm will be profitable as long as total revenues exceed the total costs incurred in creating and delivering the product or service. Firms should strive to understand not only their own value chain operations, but also their competitors', suppliers', and distributors' value chains.

The Competitive Advantage of Nations. Some countries around the world, such as Brazil, offer abundant natural resources, while others, such as Mexico, offer cheap labor. Others, such as Japan, offer a high commitment to education, while still others, such as the United States, offer innovativeness and entrepreneurship. Countries differ in what they have to offer businesses, and more and more firms are relocating various parts of their value chain operations to take advantage of what different countries have to offer.

Porter reveals in his most recent book that some countries seem to have a disproportionate share of successful firms in particular industries. Examples are the United States in entertainment, Italy in ceramic tile, Sweden in trucks, Japan in banking, Switzerland in candy, and Germany in cars. Porter attributes these differences to four decisive elements: (1) availability of strengths in certain narrow, technical fields; (2) high demand in the home country; (3) related and supporting industries in the home country; and (4) strong domestic rivals.[11] Local rivalry, for example, often stimulates growth in local distributors and suppliers. Organizations should strive to pursue strategies that effectively enable the firm to capitalize on the relative strengths of various nations. According to Porter, comparative differences among nations result in the following generalizations for strategic management: devaluation is bad for competitiveness; relaxing antitrust is bad; relaxing product safety and environmental regulations is bad; deregulation is good; promoting interfirm cooperation is bad; orderly marketing agreements are bad; and increasing defense contracts is bad.

STRATEGIC MANAGEMENT IN NONPROFIT AND GOVERNMENTAL ORGANIZATIONS

The strategic-management process is being used effectively by countless nonprofit and governmental organizations, such as the Girl Scouts and Boy Scouts, the Red Cross, chambers of commerce, educational institutions, medical institutions, public utilities, libraries, government agencies, and churches. The nonprofit sector, surprisingly, is by far America's largest employer, with 80 million Americans giving on average nearly 5 hours each week to one or more nonprofit organizations.[12] Many nonprofit and governmental organizations outperform private firms and corporations on innovativeness, motivation, productivity, and strategic management.[13] For example, the Salvation Army in Florida is able to rehabilitate 80 percent of persons convicted of their first offense. The Daisy Scouts, a Girl Scout program for 5-year-olds, has grown rapidly to more than 100,000 strong after being initiated only a few years ago.

Compared to for-profit firms, nonprofit and governmental organizations often function as a monopoly, produce a product or service that offers little or no measurability of performance, and are totally dependent on outside financing. Especially for these organizations, strategic management provides an excellent vehicle for developing and justifying requests for needed financial support.

Educational Institutions. Educational institutions are using strategic-management techniques and concepts more frequently. Richard Cyert, president of Carnegie-Mellon University, says, "I believe we do a far better job of strategic management than any company I know."[14] Population shifts nationally from the Northeast and Midwest to the Southeast and West are but one factor causing trauma for educational institutions that have not planned for changing enrollments. Ivy League schools in the Northeast are recruiting more heavily in the Southeast and West. This trend represents a significant change in the competitive climate for attracting the best high school graduates each year.

Schools of Business in more and more colleges and universities are developing and offering custom courses for individual companies. At Northwestern University's Kellogg School, for example, custom courses for companies such as Ernst & Young and Johnson & Johnson now comprise 40 percent of all executive education offerings. Custom courses account for 59 percent of executive education offerings at the University of Pennsylvania's Wharton School. "In the past, schools felt they were teaching the truth, and everyone would come kneel at their feet," says Nancy Hartigan at Kellogg. "Now companies are much more selective. Schools have to become more responsive to what organizations want." To become accredited by the American Association of Collegiate Schools of Business (AACSB), an elaborate strategic plan must be prepared by the applying school.

Medical Organizations. The $200-billion American hospital industry is experiencing declining margins, excess capacity, bureaucratic overburdening, poorly planned and executed diversification strategies, soaring health care costs, reduced federal support, and high administrator turnover. The seriousness of this problem is accented by a 20 percent annual decline in inpatient use nationwide. Declining occupancy rates, deregulation, and accelerating growth of health maintenance organizations (HMOs), preferred provider organizations (PPOs), urgent care centers, outpatient surgery centers, diagnostic centers, specialized clinics, and group practices are other major threats facing hospitals today. Many private and state-supported medical institutions are in financial trouble as a result of traditionally taking a reactive rather than a proactive approach in dealing with their industry.

Hospitals—originally intended to be warehouses for people dying of tuberculosis, smallpox, cancer, pneumonia, and infectious diseases—are creating new strategies today as advances in the diagnosis and treatment of chronic diseases are undercutting that earlier mission. Hospitals are beginning to bring services to the patient as much as bringing the patient to the hospital; in 20 years, health care will be concentrated in the home and in the residential community, not on the hospital campus.[15] Chronic care will require day treatment facilities, electronic monitoring at home, user-friendly ambulatory services, decentralized service networks, and laboratory testing. A successful hospital strategy for the future will require renewed and deepened collaboration with physicians, who are central to hospitals' well-being, and a reallocation of resources from acute to chronic care in home and community settings.

Current strategies being pursued by many hospitals include creating home health services, establishing nursing homes, and forming rehabilitation centers. Backward integration strategies that some hospitals are pursuing include acquiring ambulance services, waste disposal services, and diagnostic services. The Stuart Circle Hospital in Richmond, Virginia, is using newspaper, radio, and outdoor advertising as part of a market penetration strategy. Archbold Memorial Hospital in Thomasville, Georgia, is pursuing a product development strategy by creating an outpatient mental health service, a nurse midwife service, and a substance abuse center. The Children's Memorial Hospital in Chicago has developed a new program called "Pediatric Excellence" that provides nursing care at home for medically fragile children. This strategy could be considered concentric diversification, as could the strategies of building fitness centers and diet centers. Desert Hospital in Palm Springs, California, has moved its non-invasive cardiac catheterization services out of the hospital and into a joint venture arrangement with physicians.

The ten most successful hospital strategies today are providing freestanding outpatient surgery centers, freestanding outpatient diagnostic centers, physical rehabilitation centers, home health services, cardiac rehabilitation centers, preferred provider services, industrial medicine services, women's medicine services, skilled nursing units, and psychiatric services.[16]

Due largely to increasing costs, more and more hospitals are contracting with outside companies to perform services such as providing 24-hour emergency room and life-support systems. Psicor in San Diego, for example, leases equipment and provides technicians for open-heart surgery in eighty hospitals across the country. At least 1,000 hospitals nationwide have contracted with firms such as Coastal Emergency Services in Durham, North Carolina, to provide emergency room services.

Government Agencies and Departments. Federal, state, county, and municipal agencies and departments, such as police departments, chambers of commerce, forestry associations, and health departments, are responsible for formulating, implementing, and evaluating strategies that use taxpayers' dollars in the most cost-effective way to provide services and programs. Strategic-management concepts are increasingly being used to enable governmental organizations to be more effective and efficient.

But strategists in governmental organizations operate with less strategic autonomy than their counterparts in private firms. Public enterprises generally cannot diversify into unrelated businesses or merge with another firm. Governmental strategists usually enjoy little freedom in altering the organization's mission or redirecting objectives. Legislators and politicians often have direct or indirect control over major decisions and resources. Strategic issues get discussed and debated in the media and legislatures. Issues become politicized, resulting in fewer strategic choice alternatives. There is more predictability in the management of public sector enterprises.

On the surface, it may seem that strategic management is not applicable to government organizations, but the opposite is true. Government agencies and departments are finding that their employees get excited about the opportunity to participate in the strategic-management process and thereby have an effect on the organization's mission, objectives, strategies, and policies. In addition, government agencies are using a strategic-management approach to develop and substantiate formal requests for additional funding.

STRATEGIC MANAGEMENT IN SMALL FIRMS

Strategic management is vital for large firms' success, but what about small firms? The strategic-management process is just as vital for small companies. From their inception, all organizations have a strategy, even if the strategy just evolves from day-to-day operations. Even if conducted informally or by a single owner/entrepreneur, the strategic-management process can significantly enhance small firms' growth and prosperity. Recent data clearly show that an ever-increasing number of men and women in the United States are starting their own businesses. This means more individuals are becoming strategists. Widespread corporate layoffs have contributed to an explosion in small businesses and new ideas. For example, although less than one percent of the 900,000 auto mechanics in the U.S. are women, Janet Brown of Newport News, Virginia, recently opened and is successfully operating the Women's Auto Clinic, which features women mechanics.

Numerous magazine and journal articles have focused on applying strategic-management concepts to small businesses.[17] A major conclusion of these articles is that a lack of strategic-management knowledge is a serious obstacle for many small business owners. Other problems often encountered in applying strategic-management concepts to small businesses are a lack of sufficient capital to exploit external opportunities and a "day-to-day" cognitive frame of reference. Recent research also indicates that strategic management in small firms is more informal than in large firms, but small firms that engage in strategic management outperform those that do not.

CONCLUSION

The main appeal of any managerial approach is the expectation that it will enhance organizational performance. This is especially true of strategic management. Through involvement in strategic-management activities, managers and employees achieve a better understanding of an organization's priorities and operations.

Strategic management allows organizations to be efficient, but more importantly, it allows them to be effective. Although strategic management does not guarantee organizational success, the process allows proactive rather than reactive decision making. Strategic management may represent a radical change in philosophy for some organizations, so strategists must be trained to anticipate and constructively respond to questions and issues as they arise. The sixteen strategies discussed in this chapter can represent a new beginning for many firms, especially if managers and employees in the organization understand and support the plan for action.

KEY TERMS AND CONCEPTS

Acquisition	Horizontal Integration
Backward Integration	Integrative Strategies
Bankruptcy	Intensive Strategies
Combination Strategy	Joint Venture
Concentric Diversification	Leveraged Buyout
Conglomerate Diversification	Liquidation
Cooperative Arrangements	Market Development
Cost Leadership	Market Penetration
Differentiation	Merchant Banking
Diversification Strategies	Merger
Divestiture	Outsourcing
Equity Kickers	Product Development
Focus	Retrenchment
Forward Integration	Reverse LBO
Franchising	Takeover
Generic Strategies	Value Chain
Horizontal Diversification	Vertical Integration

ISSUES FOR REVIEW AND DISCUSSION

1. How does strategy formulation differ for a small versus a large organization? For a for-profit versus a nonprofit organization?

2. Give recent examples of market penetration, market development, and product development.

3. Give recent examples of forward integration, backward integration, and horizontal integration.

4. Give recent examples of concentric diversification, horizontal diversification, and conglomerate diversification.

5. Give recent examples of joint venture, retrenchment, divestiture, and liquidation.

6. Select one of the suggested readings at the end of this chapter and find that article in your college library. Read the article and prepare a 5-minute oral report on the topic.

7. Do you think hostile takeovers are unethical? Why or why not?

8. What are the major advantages and disadvantages of diversification?

9. What are the major advantages and disadvantages of an integrative strategy?

10. How does strategic management differ in profit and nonprofit organizations?

11. Why is it not advisable to pursue too many strategies at once?

12. Explain Porter's value chain concept.

13. Describe the mechanics of a leveraged buyout.

14. What are the implications of Porter's "competitive advantage of nations" research?

1. Kenneth Davidson, "Do Megamergers Make Sense?" *Journal of Business Strategy* 7, no. 3 (Winter 1987): 45.

2. Kathryn Rudie Harrigan, "Joint Ventures: Linking for a Leap Forward," *Planning Review* 14, no. 4 (July–August 1986):10.

3. Gary Hamel, Yves Doz, and C. K. Prahalad, "Collaborate with Your Competitors—and Win," *Harvard Business Review* 67, no. 1 (January–February 1989): 133.

4. "Why Nothing Seems to Make a Dent in Dealmaking," *Business Week* (20 July 1987): 75.

5. Dan Dalton, "The Ubiquitous Leveraged Buyout (LBO): Management Buyout or Management Sellout?" *Business Horizons* 32, no. 4 (July–August 1989): 36.

6. Marc Schwartz and Edward Weinstein, "So You Want to Do a Leveraged Buyout," *Journal of Business Strategy* 9, no. 1 (January/February 1989): 10.

7. Michael Porter, *Competitive Strategy: Techniques for Analyzing Industries and Companies* (New York: Free Press, 1980); also, Michael Porter, *Competitive Advantage: Creating and Sustaining Superior Performance* (New York: Free Press, 1985).

8. Porter, *Competitive Strategy*, 70–83.

9. Peter Wright, "A Refinement of Porter's Strategies," *Strategic Management Journal* 8, no. 1 (January–February 1987): 94.

10. William Fulmer and Jack Goodwin, "Differentiation: Begin with the Consumer," *Business Horizons* 66, no. 5 (September–October 1988): 56.

11. Bernard Reimann, "Selected Highlights of the 1988 Strategic Management Society Conference," *Planning Review* (January–February 1989): 26–27. See also Michael Porter, *Competitive Advantage of Nations* (New York: Free Press, 1989).

12. Peter Drucker, "What Business Can Learn from Nonprofits," *Harvard Business Review* 67, no. 4 (July–August 1989): 88.

13. Ibid., 90.

14. "How Academia Is Taking a Lesson from Business," *Business Week* (27 August 1984): 58.

15. Jeff Goldsmith, "A Radical Prescription for Hospitals," *Harvard Business Review* 67, no. 3 (May–June 1989): 104–111.

16. *Hospital,* May 5, 1991, p.16.

17. Some of these articles are P. H. Thurston, "Should Smaller Companies Make Formal Plans?" *Harvard Business Review* 61, no. 5 (September–October 1983): 162–188; R. Robinson, J. Pearce, G. Vozikis, and T. Mescon, "The Relationship Between Stage of Development and Small Firm Planning and Performance," *Journal of Small Business Management* 22, no. 2 (April 1984): 45–52; L. Nagel, "Strategy Formulation for the Smaller Firm: A Practical Approach," *Long Range Planning* 14, no. 4 (August 1981): 115–120; P.G. Holland and W. Boulton, "Balancing the 'Family' and the 'Business' in Family Business," *Business Horizons* 27, no. 2 (March–April 1984): 16–21; F. R. David, "Computer Assisted Strategic Planning for Small Businesses," *Journal of Systems Management* 36, no. 7 (July 1985): 24–33.

Barr, Stephen. "Bankruptcy: No Longer a Dirty Word?" *Management Review* (April 1992): 22–27.

Belohlav, James A. "Quality, Strategy, and Competitiveness." *California Management Review* 35, no. 3 (Spring 1993): 55–67.

Bowman, E. H., and H. Singh. "Corporate Restructuring: Reconfiguring the Firm." *Strategic Management Journal* 14, Special Issue (Summer 1993): 5–14.

Braun, David, and Thomas Bertsch. "Breakthroughs in Corporate Nurturing Strategies." *Business Horizons* 36, no. 4 (July–August 1993): 28–33.

Cannella, A. A., and D. C. Hambrick. "Effects of Executive Departures on the Performance of Acquired Firms." *Strategic Management Journal* 14, Special Issue (Summer 1993): 137–152.

Cascio, Wayne F. "Downsizing: What Do We Know? What Have We Learned?" *The Executive* VII, no. 1 (February 1993): 95–104.

D'Aveni, Richard A., and Anne Y. Ilinitch. "Complex Patterns of Vertical Integration in the Forest Products Industry: Systematic and Bankruptcy Risks." *Academy of Management Journal* 35, no.3 (August 1992): 596–625.

Dollinger, Marc J., and Peggy A. Golden. "Interorganizational and Collective Strategies in Small Firms: Environmental Effects and Performance." *Journal of Management* 18, no. 4 (December 1992): 695–716.

Ettlie, John E., and Ernesto M. Reza. "Organizational Integration and Process Innovation." *Academy of Management Journal* 35, no. 4 (October 1992): 795–827.

Foster, M. John. "Scenario Planning for Small Businesses." *Long Range Planning* 26, no. 1 (February 1993): 123–129.

Fox, Isaac, and Alfred Marcus. "The Causes and Consequences of Leveraged Management Buyouts." *Academy of Management Review* 17, no. 1 (January 1992): 62–87.

Goold, Michael, and Kathleen Luchs. "Why Diversify? Four Decades of Management Thinking." *Academy of Management Executive* 7, no. 3 (August 1993): 7–25.

Grundy, Tony. "Putting Value on a Strategy." *Long Range Planning* 26, no. 3 (June 1993): 87–94.

Gutknecht, John E., and J. Bernard Keys. "Mergers, Acquisitions and Takeovers: Maintaining Morale of Survivors and Protecting Employees." *Academy of Management Executive* 7, no. 3 (August 1993): 26–36.

Hamilton, R. T., and Y. K. Chow. "Why Managers Divest—Evidence New Zealand's Largest Companies." *Strategic Management Journal* 14, no. 6 (September 1993): 479–484.

Hench, Thomas J., James C. Chrisman, and David M. Schweiger. "The Case of the Enigmatic Entrepreneur." *The Executive* VI, no. 2 (May 1992): 83–100.

Jones, Gareth R., and John E. Butler. "Managing Internal Corporate Entrepreneurship: An Agency Theory." *Journal of Management* 18, no. 4 (December 1992): 733–716.

Kim, W. C., P. Hwang, and W. P. Burgers. "Strategic Redirection in Large Management Buyouts: The Evidence from Post-Buyout Restructuring Activity." *Strategic Management Journal* 14, no. 4 (May 1993): 251–274.

Lubatkin, M., H. Merchant, and N. Srinivasan. "Construct Validity of Some Unweighted Product-Count Diversification Measures." *Strategic Management Journal* 14, no. 6 (September 1993): 433–449.

McCarthy, Mark, Martha Pointer, David Ricks, and Robert Rolfe. "Managers' Views on Potential Investment Opportunities." *Business Horizons* 36, no. 4 (July–August 1993): 54.

Miles, G., C. C. Snow, and M. P. Sharfman. "Industry Variety and Performance." *Strategic Management Journal* 14, no. 3 (March 1993): 163–178.

Moulton, W. N., and H. Thomas. "Bankruptcy as a Deliberate Strategy: Theoretical Considerations and Empirical Evidence." *Strategic Management Journal* 14, no. 2 (February 1993): 125–136.

Nutt, Paul C., and Robert W. Backoff. "Transforming Public Organizations with Strategic Management and Strategic Leadership." *Journal of Management* 19, no. 2 (Summer 1993): 299–348.

Osborne, Richard L. "Entrepreneurial Renewal." *Business Horizons* 35, no. 6 (November–December 1992): 58–63.

Rubenson, George C., and Anil K. Gupta. "Replacing the Founder: Exploding the Myth of the Entrepreneur's Disease." *Business Horizons* 35, no. 6 (November–December 1992): 53–57.

Schilit, W. Keith. "The Globalization of Venture Capital." *Business Horizons* 35, no. 1 (January–February 1992): 17–23.

Seth, A., and J. Easterwood. "Strategic Redirection in Large Management Buyouts: The Evidence from Post-Buyout Restructuring Activity." *Strategic Management Journal* 14, no. 4 (May 1993): 251–274.

Slevin, D. P. "Entrepreneurship and the Concept of Fit: A Model and Empirical Tests." *Strategic Management Journal* 14, no. 2 (February 1993): 137–154.

Stuckey, John, and David White. "When and When Not to Vertically Integrate." *Sloan Management Review* 34, no. 3 (Spring 1993): 71–84.

Thomas, James B., Shawn M. Clark, and Dennis A. Gioia. "Strategic Sensemaking and Organizational Performance: Linkages Among Scanning, Interpretation, Action, and Outcomes." *Academy of Management Journal* 36, no. 2 (April 1993): 239–270.

Waalewijn, Philip, and Peter Segaar. "Strategic Management: The Key to Profitability in Small Companies." *Long Range Planning* 26, no. 2, (April 1993): 24–30.

Welch, James A., and P. Ranganath Nayak. "Strategic Sourcing: A Progressive Approach to the Make-or-Buy Decision." *The Executive* VI, no. 1 (February 1992): 23–31.

Winsemius, Pieter, and Ulrich Guntram. "Responding to the Environmental Challenge." *Business Horizons* 35, no. 2 (March–April 1992): 12–20.

EXPERIENTIAL EXERCISES

WHAT HAPPENED AT HERSHEY FOODS IN 1993/1994?

PURPOSE

In performing business policy case analysis, you will need to find epilogue information about the respective companies to determine what strategies were actually employed since the time of the case. Comparing "what actually happened" with "what you would have recommended and expected to happen" is an important part of business policy case analysis. Do not recommend what the firm actually did, unless in-depth analysis of the situation at the time reveals those strategies to have been best among all feasible alternatives. This exercise gives you experience conducting library research to determine what strategies Hershey, Mars, and Nestlé pursued in 1993 and 1994.

INSTRUCTIONS

Step 1 Go to your college library and look up Hershey Foods Corporation, Mars, and Nestlé Corporation in indexes such as the *Funk & Scott Index, Business Periodicals Index*, and *Wall Street Journal/Barron's Index*. Find some recent articles about firms in the confectionery industry. Scan Moody's, Dun & Bradstreet, and Standard & Poors publications for information.

Step 2 Summarize your findings in a three-page report titled "Hershey Foods' Strategies in the 1990s." Include information about Mars and Nestlé. Also include your personal reaction to Hershey's strategies in terms of their attractiveness.

EXAMINING STRATEGY ARTICLES

PURPOSE

Strategy articles can be found weekly in journals, magazines, and newspapers. By reading and studying strategy articles, you can gain a better understanding of the strategic-management process. Several of the best journals in which to find corporate strategy articles are *Planning Review, Long Range Planning, Journal of Business Strategy*, and *Strategic Management Journal*. These journals are devoted to reporting the results of empirical research in strategic management. They apply strategic-management concepts to specific organizations and industries. They introduce new strategic-management techniques and provide short case studies on selected firms.

Other good journals in which to find strategic-management articles are *Harvard Business Review, Sloan Management Review, Business Horizons, California Manage-*

ment Review, Academy of Management Review, Academy of Management Journal, Academy of Management Executive, Journal of Management, and *Journal of Small Business Management.*

In addition to journals, many magazines regularly publish articles that focus on business strategies. Several of the best magazines in which to find applied strategy articles are *Dun's Business Month, Fortune, Forbes, Business Week, Inc. Magazine,* and *Industry Week.* Newspapers such as *USA Today, The Wall Street Journal, The New York Times,* and *Barrons* cover strategy events when they occur—for example, a joint venture announcement, a bankruptcy declaration, a new advertising campaign start, acquisition of a company, divestiture of a division, a chief executive officer's hiring or firing, or a hostile takeover attempt.

In combination, journal, magazine, and newspaper articles can make the business policy course especially exciting. They allow current strategies of profit and nonprofit organizations to be identified and studied.

INSTRUCTIONS

Step 1 Go to your college library and find a recent journal article that focuses on a strategic-management topic. Select your article from one of the journals listed above. Copy the article and bring it to class.

Step 2 Give a 3-minute oral report summarizing the most important information in your article. Include comments giving your personal reaction to the article. Pass your article around in class.

Experiential Exercise 2C

CLASSIFYING 1994 STRATEGIES

PURPOSE

This exercise can improve your understanding of various strategies by giving you experience classifying strategies. This skill will help you use the strategy-formulation tools presented later. Consider the following strategies being implemented in 1994 by various firms:

1. Coors Brewing and Whittle Communications starting a new all-female professional baseball team called the Colorado Silver Bullets.
2. R. H. Macy & Company remaining under Chapter 11 bankruptcy until 1995.
3. AT&T developing new phones to funnel information from TV, PC's, VCR's, and fax machines.
4. Toys "Я" Us buying back up to $1 billion of its stock and opening 155 new stores in new geographic areas.
5. Four months after losing Absolut Vodka, Grand Met selling Stolichnaya.
6. Rite Aid selling four noncore businesses and closing 200 drugstores.
7. Food Lion closing 88 supermarkets.
8. Chase Manhattan Corporation and Keystone, Inc. creating a new business called Insurance Partners.
9. The New York Times acquiring The Boston Globe.
10. Apple Computer beginning to offer products from L. L. Bean and Tiffany's on CD-ROM discs.

11. The activist shareholder rights organization, United Shareholders Association, closing its doors.

12. Pharmaceutical Resources rebuilding the firm's product line to over 100 drugs.

13. SmithKline Beecham giving a $10 cash rebate on its anti-ulcer drug, Tagamet, to spur sales.

14. Wal-Mart acquiring 91 PACE membership warehouses from rival Kmart.

15. Pacific Telesis Group spinning off its cellular operation into a separate company.

16. Baxter International cutting 4,500 jobs.

17. Mellon Bank swapping $1.7 billion in stock for mutual-funds giant Dreyfus.

18. MCA building a $2 billion theme park in Osaka, Japan.

19. Walt Disney perhaps closing its $4 billion theme park near Paris due to low attendance.

20. Carnival Cruise Lines entering the riverboat gaming business.

21. Walt Disney entering the cruise business with Carnival.

22. Bell Atlantic spending $25 million to build the first leg of the Information Superhighway.

23. Union Camp Corporation spending $100 million to turn office paper into recycled pulp.

24. Apple Computer launching a Visa and Mastercard with Citibank.

25. M&M Mars expanding aggressively into Russia.

INSTRUCTIONS

Step 1 On a separate sheet of paper, number from 1 to 25. These numbers correspond to the strategies described above.

Step 2 What type of strategy best describes the 25 actions cited above? Indicate your answers on the separate sheet of paper.

Step 3 Exchange papers with a classmate and grade each other's paper as your instructor gives the right answers.

STRATEGIC MANAGEMENT AT THE DYNAMIC COMPUTER COMPANY

PURPOSE

This exercise can give you experience choosing among alternative growth strategies for a specific company. Remember that organizations cannot pursue all the strategies that potentially may benefit the firm. Difficult decisions have to be made to eliminate some options. Use the guidelines given in Table 2–2 to complete this exercise.

BACKGROUND

Dynamic Computer, Inc. (DCI) is a highly regarded personal computer manufacturer based in central California. DCI designs, develops, produces, markets, and services personal computer systems for individuals' needs in business, education, science, engineering, and the home. The company's main product is the Dynamic II personal computer system, complete with optional accessories and software. The company has recently announced a new system, the Dynamic III, that is aimed at large business firms. It is much more expensive than the Dynamic II. Dynamic's computer systems are distributed in the United States and Canada by 1,000 independent retail stores and internationally through 21 independent distributors, who resell to 850 foreign retail outlets. Approximately 700 of the retail outlets in the United States and Canada are authorized service centers for Dynamic products, but none of the outlets sell Dynamic products exclusively. Many of these outlets are not marketing Dynamic's products effectively.

The American computer industry grew at an inflation-adjusted, compound annual rate of about 20 percent from 1958 through the late 1980s. In the 1990s, real annual growth in the computer industry is expected to average about 18 percent a year. The outlook for personal computers continues to be positive. However, this market is highly competitive and is characterized by rapid technological advances in both hardware and software. Margins on software are nearly double operating margins on hardware. New firms are entering the industry at an increasing rate, and this has resulted in a decline in Dynamic's sales, earnings, and market share in recent years. Many computer companies expect software sales and services to represent 50 percent of their total revenues by 1995. Dynamic is concerned about its future direction and competitiveness. Selected financial information for Dynamic is given in Table 2D–1.

INSTRUCTIONS

The owners of DCI have indicated a willingness to explore a number of alternative growth strategies for the future. They have hired you as a consultant to assist them in making strategic decisions regarding the future allocation of resources. The feeling is that to sustain growth, the company must make some critical decisions. Dynamic is financially capable of investing in several projects. The owners wish to use their resources wisely to produce the highest possible return on investment in the future. They are considering five alternative strategies:

1. Market penetration—establish a nationwide sales force to market Dynamic products to large firms that do not buy through independent retailers.
2. Product development—develop an "easier to use" computer for small business firms.
3. Forward integration—offer major new incentives to distributors who sell and service Dynamic products.
4. Backward integration—purchase a major outside supplier of software.
5. Conglomerate diversification—acquire Toys Unlimited, a large and successful toy manufacturer.

TABLE 2D-1

	1993	1994	1995
Sales	$ 13,000,000	$ 12,000,000	$ 10,000,000
Net Income	3,000,000	1,000,000	500,000
Total Assets	180,000,000	200,000,000	250,000,000
Market Share	15%	12%	10%

Based on the strategy guidelines given in Chapter 2, your task is to offer specific recommendations to the strategists of DCI. Follow these steps:

Step 1 Across the top of a separate sheet of paper, set up five columns, with the following headings:

Individual Percentage Allocations	*Group Percentage Allocations*	*Expert Percentage Allocations*	*The Absolute Difference Between Colunms 1 and 3*	*The Absolute Difference Between Columns 2 and 3*

Down the left side of your paper, number from 1 to 5. These numbers correspond to the five strategies listed above.

Step 2 Take 10 minutes to determine how you would allocate DCI's resources among the five alternative strategies. Record your answers by placing individual percentage values for strategies 1 through 5 under column 1. Your only constraint is that the total resources allocated must equal 100%. Distribute resources in the manner you think will offer the greatest future return on investment and profitability.

Step 3 Join with two other students in class. Develop a set of group percentage allocations and record these values for strategies 1 through 5 under column 2. Do not change your individual percentage allocations once discussion begins in your group.

Step 4 As your professor reveals the right answer and supporting rationale, record these values for strategies 1 through 5 under column 3.

Step 5 For each row, subtract column 3 values from column 1 values and record the absolute difference (ignore negatives) in column 4. Then, sum the column 4 values.

Step 6 For each row, subtract column 3 values from column 2 values and record the absolute difference (ignore negatives) in column 5. Then, sum the column 5 values.

Step 7 If the sum of column 4 values exceeds the sum of column 5 values, then your group allocation of DCI's resources was better than your individual allocation. However, if the sum of column 4 values is less than the sum of column 5 values, you were a better strategist than your group on this exercise.

Strategic-management research indicates that group strategic decisions are almost always better than individual strategic decisions. Did you do better than your group?

HOW RISKY ARE VARIOUS ALTERNATIVE STRATEGIES?

PURPOSE

This exercise focuses on how risky various alternative strategies are for organizations to pursue. Different degrees of risk are based largely on varying degrees of *externality*, defined as movement away from present business into new markets and products.

In general, the greater the degree of externality, the greater the probability of loss resulting from unexpected events. High-risk strategies are generally less attractive than low-risk strategies.

INSTRUCTIONS

Step 1 On a separate sheet of paper, number vertically from 1 to 10. Think of 1 as "most risky," 2 as "next most risky," and so forth to 10, "least risky."

Step 2 Write the following strategies beside the appropriate number to indicate how risky you believe the strategy is to pursue: horizontal integration, horizontal diversification, liquidation, forward integration, backward integration, product development, market development, market penetration, joint venture, and conglomerate diversification.

Step 3 Grade your paper as your professor gives you the right answers and supporting rationale. Each correct answer is worth ten points. This exercise is based on a commonly accepted and published classification of strategies given in the footnote.[1]

NOTES

1. James Belohlav and Karen Giddens-Emig, "Selecting a Master Strategy," *Journal of Business Strategy* 7, no. 3 (Winter 1987): 77.

Experiential Exercise 2F

DEVELOPING ALTERNATIVE STRATEGIES FOR MY UNIVERSITY

PURPOSE

It is important for representatives from all areas of a college or university to identify and discuss alternative strategies that could benefit faculty, students, alumni, staff, and other constituencies. As you complete this exercise, notice the learning and understanding that occurs as people express differences of opinions. Recall that *the process of planning is more important than the document.*

INSTRUCTIONS

Step 1 Recall or locate the external opportunity/threat and internal strength/weakness factors that you identified as part of Experiential Exercise 1D. If you did not do that exercise, discuss now as a class important external and internal factors facing your college or university.

Step 2 Identify and put on the chalkboard alternative strategies that you feel could benefit your college or university. Your proposed actions should allow the institution to capitalize on particular strengths, improve upon certain weaknesses, avoid external threats, and/or take advantage of particular external opportunities. List at least twenty possible strategies on the board. Number the strategies as they are written on the board.

Step 3 On a separate sheet of paper, number from 1 to the total number of strategies listed on the board. Everyone in class should individually rate the strategies identified, using a 1 to 3 scale, where 1 = I do not support implementation, 2 = I am neutral about implementation, 3 = I strongly support implementation. In rating the strategies, recognize that your institution cannot do everything desired or potentially beneficial.

Step 4 Go to the board and record your ratings in a row beside the respective strategies. Everyone in class should do this, going to the board perhaps by rows in the class.

Step 5 Sum the ratings for each strategy so that a prioritized list of recommended strategies is obtained. This prioritized list reflects the collective wisdom of your class. Strategies with the highest score are deemed best.

Step 6 Discuss how this process could enable organizations to achieve understanding and commitment from individuals.

Step 7 Share your class results with a university administrator and ask for comments regarding the process and top strategies recommended.

PART · 2

Strategy Formulation

Chapter 3

THE BUSINESS MISSION

NOTABLE QUOTES

··

A business is not defined by its name, statutes, or articles of incorporation. It is defined by the business mission. Only a clear definition of the mission and purpose of the organization makes possible clear and realistic business objectives. —Peter Drucker

A corporate vision can focus, direct, motivate, unify, and even excite a business into superior performance. The job of a strategist is to identify and project a clear vision. —John Keane

Where there is no vision, the people perish. —Proverbs 29:18

Customers are first, employees second, shareholders third, and the community fourth. That's the credo at H. B. Fuller, the century-old adhesives maker in St. Paul. —Patricia Sellers

What is especially difficult is getting different departments working together in the best interest of customers. Yet managers at all levels are the critical link to aligning the entire organization toward the customer. —Richard Whiteley

For strategists, there's a trade-off between the breadth and detail of information needed. It's a bit like an eagle hunting for a rabbit. The eagle has to be high enough to scan a wide area in order to enlarge his changes of seeing prey, but he has to be low enough to see the detail—the movement and features that will allow him to recognize his target. Continually making this trade-off is the job of a strategist—it simply can't be delegated. —Frederick Gluck

The best laid schemes of mice and men often go awry. —Robert Burns (paraphrased)

A strategist's job is to see the company not as it is … but as it can become. —John W. Teets, Chairman of Greyhound, Inc.

That business mission is so rarely given adequate thought is perhaps the most important single cause of business frustration. —Peter Drucker

OBJECTIVES

After studying this chapter, you should be able to:

■ Describe the nature and role of mission statements in strategic management.

■ Discuss why the process of developing a mission statement is as important as the resulting document.

■ Identify the components of mission statement documents.

■ Discuss how a clear mission statement can benefit other strategic-management activities.

■ Evaluate mission statements of different organizations.

■ Write good mission statements.

*T*his chapter focuses on the concepts and tools needed to evaluate and write business mission statements. A practical framework for developing mission statements is provided. Actual mission statements from large and small organizations and for-profit and nonprofit enterprises are presented and critically examined. The process of creating a mission statement is discussed.

WHAT IS OUR BUSINESS?

Current thought on mission statements is based largely on guidelines set forth in the mid-1970s by Peter Drucker, often called "the father of modern management" for his pioneering studies at General Motors Corporation and for his twenty-two books and hundreds of articles. *Harvard Business Review* calls Drucker, age 79, "the preeminent management thinker of our time."

Drucker says asking the question, "What is our business?" is synonymous with asking the question, "What is our mission?" An enduring statement of purpose that distinguishes one organization from other similar enterprises, the *mission statement* is a declaration of an organization's "reason for being." It answers the pivotal question, "What is our business?" A clear mission statement is essential for effectively establishing objectives and formulating strategies.

Sometimes called a *creed statement,* a statement of purpose, a statement of philosophy, a statement of beliefs, a statement of business principles, a vision statement, or a statement "defining our business," a mission statement reveals the long-term vision of an organization in terms of what it wants to be and whom it wants to serve. All organizations have a reason for being, even if strategists have not consciously transformed this into writing. As illustrated in Figure 3–1, a carefully prepared statement of mission is widely recognized by both practitioners and academicians as the first step in strategic management.

> A business mission is the foundation for priorities, strategies, plans, and work assignments. It is the starting point for the design of managerial jobs and, above all, for the design of managerial structures. Nothing may seem simpler or more obvious than to know what a company's business is. A steel mill makes steel, a railroad runs trains to carry freight and passengers, an insurance company underwrites fire risks, and a bank lends money. Actually, "What is our business?" is almost always a difficult question and the right answer is usually anything but obvious. The answer to this question is the first responsibility of strategists. Only strategists can make sure that this question receives the attention it deserves and that the answer makes sense and enables the business to plot its course and set its objectives.[1]

We can perhaps best understand a business mission by focusing on a business when it is first started. In the beginning, a new business is simply a collection of ideas. Starting a new business rests on a set of beliefs that the new organization can offer some product or service, to some customers, in some geographic area, using some type of technology, at a profitable price. A new business owner typically believes that the management philosophy of the new enterprise will result in a favorable public image and that this concept of the business can be communicated to, and will be adopted by, important constituencies. When the set of beliefs about a business at its inception are put into writing, the resulting document mirrors the same basic ideas that compose a mission statement. As a business grows, owners or managers find it necessary to revise the founding set of beliefs, but those original ideas usually are reflected in the revised statement of mission.

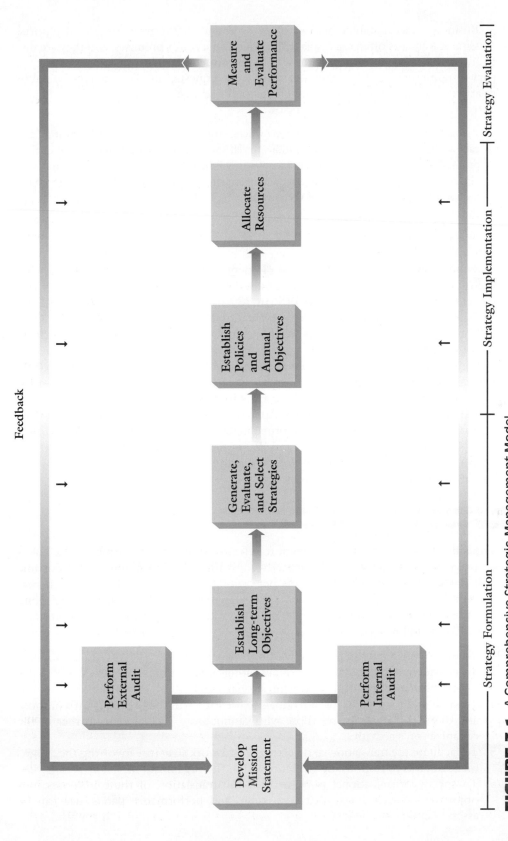

FIGURE 3-1 A Comprehensive Strategic-Management Model

Feedback

Perform External Audit

Develop Mission Statement

Establish Long-term Objectives

Generate, Evaluate, and Select Strategies

Establish Policies and Annual Objectives

Allocate Resources

Measure and Evaluate Performance

Perform Internal Audit

Strategy Formulation — Strategy Implementation — Strategy Evaluation

Business mission statements can often be found in the front of annual reports. Mission statements often are displayed throughout a firm's premises, and they are distributed with company information sent to constituencies. The mission statement is a part of numerous internal reports, such as loan requests, supplier agreements, labor relations contracts, business plans, and customer service agreements. Barnett Bank's current mission statement is given below:

> Barnett's mission is to create value for its owners, customers and employees by creating and capitalizing on market leadership positions to sell and service a broad range of high quality, profitable financial services. Our sales emphasis will be full service to consumers and businesses in our communities and advisory and processing services to others. We will operate at the lowest possible cost consistent with maintaining high service quality and market leadership.[2]

A good mission statement describes an organization's purpose, customers, products or services, markets, philosophy, and basic technology. According to Vern McGinnis, a mission statement should (1) define what the organization is and what the organization aspires to be, (2) be limited enough to exclude some ventures and broad enough to allow for creative growth, (3) distinguish a given organization from all others, (4) serve as a framework for evaluating both current and prospective activities, and (5) be stated in terms sufficiently clear to be widely understood throughout the organization.[3]

Some strategists spend almost every moment of every day on administrative and tactical concerns, and strategists who rush quickly to establish objectives and implement strategies often overlook developing a mission statement. This problem is widespread even among large organizations. Approximately 40 percent of large corporations in America have not yet developed a formal mission statement, including Walt Disney Company, Grumman Corporation, and Wal★Mart Stores. However, 60 percent do have a formal mission document.[4] An increasing number of organizations every day are developing formal mission statements.

THE IMPORTANCE OF A CLEAR MISSION

The importance of a mission statement to effective strategic management is well documented in the literature. A recent study comparing mission statements of Fortune 500 firms performing well and firms performing poorly concluded that high performers have more comprehensive mission statements than low performers.[5] King and Cleland recommend that organizations carefully develop a written mission statement for the following reasons:

1. To ensure unanimity of purpose within the organization.
2. To provide a basis, or standard, for allocating organizational resources.
3. To establish a general tone or organizational climate.
4. To serve as a focal point for individuals to identify with the organization's purpose and direction; and to deter those who cannot from participating further in the organization's activities.
5. To facilitate the translation of objectives into a work structure involving the assignment of tasks to responsible elements within the organization.
6. To specify organizational purposes and the translation of these purposes into objectives in such a way that cost, time, and performance parameters can be assessed and controlled.[6]

Reuben Mark, CEO of Colgate, maintains that a clear mission increasingly must make sense internationally. Colgate's mission can be summarized in five words: "We can be the best." Mark's thoughts on a mission statement are as follows:

> When it comes to rallying everyone to the corporate banner, it's essential to push one vision globally rather than trying to drive home different messages in different cultures. The trick is to keep the vision simple but elevated: "We make the world's fastest computers" or "Telephone service for everyone." You're never going to get anyone to charge the machine guns only for financial objectives. It's got to be something that makes them feel better, feel a part of something.[7]

Vision Versus Mission. Some organizations develop both a mission statement and a vision statement. Whereas the mission statement answers the question "What is our business?" the vision statement answers the question "What do we want to become?" Two example companies that have both a mission and vision statement are Amoco Corporation and Harley-Davidson Corporation, as given in Table 3–1.

The Process of Developing a Mission Statement. As indicated in the strategic-management model, a clear mission statement is needed before alternative strategies can be formulated and implemented. It is important to involve as many managers as possible in the process of developing a mission statement, because through involvement, people become committed to an organization. Mark's comment above about machine guns accents the need for a good mission statement.

A widely used approach to developing a mission statement is to first select several articles about mission statements and ask all managers to read these as background information. Then ask managers to personally prepare a mission statement for the organization. A facilitator, or committee of top managers, then should merge these statements into a single document and distribute this draft mission statement to all managers. A request for modifications, additions, and deletions is needed next, along with a meeting to revise the document. To the extent that all managers have input into and support the final mission statement document, organizations can more easily obtain managers' support for other strategy formulation, implementation, and evaluation activities. Thus, the process of developing a mission statement represents a great opportunity for strategists to obtain needed support from all managers in the firm.

During the process of developing a mission statement, some organizations use discussion groups of managers to develop and modify the mission statement. Some organizations hire an outside consultant or facilitator to manage the process and help draft the language. Sometimes an outside person with expertise in developing mission statements and "unbiased" views can manage the process more effectively than an internal group or committee of managers. Decisions on how best to communicate the mission to all managers, employees, and external constituencies of an organization are needed when the document is in final form. Some organizations even develop a videotape to explain the mission statement and how it was developed.[8]

A recent article by Campbell and Yeung emphasizes that the process of developing a mission statement should create an "emotional bond" and "sense of mission" between the organization and its employees.[9] Commitment to a company's strategy and intellectual agreement on the strategies to be pursued do not necessarily translate into an emotional bond; hence strategies that have been formulated may not be implemented. These researchers stress that an emotional bond comes when an individual personally identifies with the underlying values and behavior of a firm, thus turning intellectual agreement and commitment to strategy into a sense of mission.

TABLE 3-1   Two Companies' Mission and Vision Statements

AMOCO CORPORATION

Mission Statement

Amoco is a worldwide integrated petroleum and chemical company. We find and develop petroleum resources and provide quality products and services for our customers. We conduct our business responsibly to achieve a superior financial return balanced with our long-term growth, benefiting shareholders and fulfilling our commitment to the community and the environment.

Vision Statement

Amoco will be a global business enterprise, recognized throughout the world as preeminent by employees, customers, competitors, investors and the public. We will be the standard by which other businesses measure their performance. Our hallmarks will be the innovation, initiative and teamwork of our people and our ability to anticipate and effectively respond to change and to create opportunity.

HARLEY-DAVIDSON

Mission Statement

Stay true to the things that make a Harley-Davidson a Harley-Davidson. Keep the heritage alive. From the people in the front office to the craftsmen on our factory floor, that is what we do. And it's why each new generation of Harley-Davidson motorcycles, well refined, contains the best of the ones before it. We have a passion for our product few companies understand. But when you see the result, it all becomes clear. We're not just building motorcycles. We're carrying on a legend. Ask anyone who's ever owned a Harley-Davidson. It gets in your blood. Becomes a part of your life. And once it does, it never leaves. It's something you can't compare with anything else. We know because we've been there. That's why, for 90 years, we've remained firm in our commitment to building the kind of motorcycles that deserve the intense loyalty that Harley-Davidson enjoys. The styling is still pure. The engines still rumble. It's also why you'll see us at major rallies and rides throughout the year, listening and talking to our customers. Staying close to riders and to the sport is how we've kept alive the things that make a Harley-Davidson a Harley-Davidson. Our approach has always been different. But again, so has owning a Harley-Davidson. We wouldn't have it any other way.

Vision Statement

Harley-Davidson Inc. is an action oriented, international company—a leader in its commitment to continuously improve the quality of profitable relationships with stakeholders (customers, employees, suppliers, shareholders, governments, and society). Harley-Davidson believes the key to success is to balance stakeholders' interests through the empowerment of all employees to focus on value-added activities.

Our Vision is our corporate conscience and helps us to eliminate short-term thinking, such as "cashing in" on demand for our motorcycles by giving quantity precedence over quality or cutting corners in recreational or commercial vehicles to save a few dollars per unit. It also encourages every employee in our organization to be acutely aware of his or her role in satisfying our stakeholders.

Equally important to our Vision, we live by a Code of Business Conduct that is driven by a value system which promotes honesty, integrity, and personal growth in all our dealings with stakeholders. Our values are the rules by which we operate: Tell the truth; be fair; keep your promises; respect the individual; and encourage intellectual curiosity.

In addition, we never lose sight of the issues we feel must be addressed in order to be successful in the 1990s: Quality, participation, productivity, and cash flow. As a shareholder, you should expect no less from us.

Campbell and Yeung also differentiate between the terms vision and mission, saying vision is "a possible and desirable future state of an organization" that includes specific goals, whereas mission is more associated with behavior and with the present.

THE NATURE OF A BUSINESS MISSION

A Declaration of Attitude. A mission statement is a declaration of attitude and outlook more than a statement of specific details. It is usually broad in scope for at least two major reasons. First, a good mission statement allows for the generation and consideration of a range of feasible alternative objectives and strategies without unduly stifling management creativity. Excess specificity would limit the potential of creative growth for the organization. On the other hand, an overly general statement that does not exclude any strategy alternatives could be dysfunctional. Apple Computer's mission statement, for example, should not open the possibility for diversification into pesticides, or Ford Motor Company's into food processing.

Second, a mission statement needs to be broad to effectively reconcile differences among an organization's diverse stakeholders, the individuals and groups of persons who have a special stake or claim on the company. Stakeholders include employees, managers, stockholders, boards of directors, customers, suppliers, distributors, creditors, governments (local, state, federal, and foreign), unions, competitors, environmental groups, and the general public. Stakeholders affect and are affected by an organization's strategies, yet the claims and concerns of diverse constituencies vary and often conflict. For example, the general public is especially interested in social responsibility, whereas stockholders are more interested in profitability. Claims on any business may literally number in the thousands, and often include clean air, jobs, taxes, investment opportunities, career opportunities, equal employment opportunities, employee benefits, salaries, wages, clean water, and community services. All stakeholders' claims on an organization cannot be pursued with equal emphasis. A good mission statement indicates the relative attention that an organization will devote to meeting the claims of various stakeholders. As indicated in this chapter's Natural Environment Perspective, more and more firms are becoming environmentally proactive in response to the concerns of stakeholders.

Reaching the fine balance between specificity and generality is difficult to achieve, but is well worth the effort. George Steiner offers the following insight on the need for a mission statement to be broad in scope:

> Most business statements of mission are expressed at high levels of abstraction. Vagueness nevertheless has its virtues. Mission statements are not designed to express concrete ends, but rather to provide motivation, general direction, an image, a tone, and a philosophy to guide the enterprise. An excess of detail could prove counterproductive since concrete specification could be the base for rallying opposition. Precision might stifle creativity in the formulation of an acceptable mission or purpose. Once an aim is cast in concrete it creates a rigidity in an organization and resists change. Vagueness leaves room for other managers to fill in the details, perhaps even to modify general patterns. Vagueness permits more flexibility in adapting to changing environments and internal operations. It facilitates flexibility in implementation.[10]

An effective mission statement arouses positive feelings and emotions about an organization; it is inspiring in the sense that it motivates readers to action. An effective mission statement generates the impression that a firm is successful, has direction, and is worthy of time, support, and investment. Japanese firms believe strongly in the emotional aspect of a mission statement, as revealed in this chapter's Global Perspective.

It reflects judgments about future growth directions and strategies based upon forward-looking external and internal analyses. A business mission should provide useful criteria for selecting among alternative strategies. A clear mission statement provides a basis for generating and screening strategic options. The statement of mission should be dynamic in orientation, allowing judgments about the most promising growth directions and those considered less promising.

A Resolution of Divergent Views. What are the reasons some strategists are reluctant to develop a statement of their business mission? First, the question "What is our business?" can create controversy. Raising the question often reveals differences among strategists in the organization. Individuals who have worked together for a long time and who think they know each other may suddenly realize that they are in fundamental disagreement. For example, in a college or university, divergent views regarding the relative importance of teaching, research, and service are often expressed during the mission statement development process. Negotiation, compromise, and eventual agreement on important issues is needed before focusing on more specific strategy-formulation activities.

"What is our mission?" is a genuine decision; and a genuine decision must be based on divergent views to have a chance to be a right and effective decision. Developing a business mission is always a choice between alternatives, each of which rests on different assumptions regarding the reality of the business and its environment. It is always a high-risk decision. A change in mission always leads to changes in objectives, strategies, organization, and behavior. The mission decision is far too important to be made by acclamation. Developing a business mission is a big step toward management effectiveness. Hidden or half-understood disagreements on the definition of a business mission underlie many of the personality problems, communication problems, and irritations that tend to divide a top-management group. Establishing a mission should never be made on plausibility alone, never should be made fast, and never should be made painlessly.[11]

Considerable disagreement among an organization's strategists over basic purpose and mission can cause trouble if not resolved. For example, unresolved disagreement over the business mission was one of the reasons for W. T. Grant's bankruptcy and eventual liquidation. As one executive reported,

> There was a lot of dissension within the company whether we should go the Kmart route or go after the Montgomery Ward and J. C. Penney position. Ed Staley and Lou Lustenberger (two top executives) were at loggerheads over the issue, with the upshot being we took a position between the two and that consequently stood for nothing.[12]

Too often, strategists develop a statement of business mission only when their organization is in trouble. Of course it is needed then. Developing and communicating a clear mission during troubled times may indeed have spectacular results and may even reverse decline. However, to wait until an organization is in trouble to develop a mission statement is a gamble that characterizes irresponsible management! According to Drucker, the most important time to ask seriously "What is our business?" is when a company has been successful:

> Success always obsoletes the very behavior that achieved it, always creates new realities, and always creates new and different problems. Only the fairy story ends "They lived happily ever after." It is never popular to argue with success or to rock the boat. The ancient Greeks knew that the penalty of success can be severe. The management that does not ask "What is our mission?" when the company is successful is, in effect, smug, lazy, and arrogant. It will not be long before success will turn into failure. Sooner or later, even the most successful answer to the question "What is our business?" becomes obsolete.[13]

A Customer Orientation. A good mission statement reflects the anticipations of customers. Rather than developing a product and then trying to find a market, the operating philosophy of organizations should be to identify customers' needs and then provide a product or service to fulfill those needs. Good mission statements identify the utility of a firm's products to its customers. This is why AT&T's mission statement focuses on communication rather than telephones, Exxon's mission statement focuses on energy rather than oil and gas, Union Pacific's mission statement focuses on transportation rather than railroads, and Universal Studios' mission statement focuses on entertainment instead of movies. The following utility statements are relevant in developing a mission statement:

Do not offer me things.

Do not offer me clothes. Offer me attractive looks.

Do not offer me shoes. Offer me comfort for my feet and the pleasure of walking.

Do not offer me a house. Offer me security, comfort, and a place that is clean and happy.

Do not offer me books. Offer me hours of pleasure and the benefit of knowledge.

Do not offer me records. Offer me leisure and the sound of music.

Do not offer me tools. Offer me the benefit and the pleasure of making beautiful things.

Do not offer me furniture. Offer me comfort and the quietness of a cozy place.

Do not offer me things. Offer me ideas, emotions, ambience, feelings, and benefits.

Please, do not offer me things.

A major reason for developing a business mission is to attract customers who give meaning to an organization. A classic description of the purpose of a business reveals the relative importance of customers in a statement of mission:

It is the customer who determines what a business is. It is the customer alone whose willingness to pay for a good or service converts economic resources into wealth and things into goods. What a business thinks it produces is not of first importance, especially not to the future of the business and to its success. What the customer thinks he/she is buying, what he/she considers value, is decisive—it determines what a business is, what it produces, and whether it will prosper. And what the customer buys and considers value is never a product. It is always utility, meaning what a product or service does for him. The customer is the foundation of a business and keeps it in existence.[14]

A Declaration of Social Policy. The words *social policy* embrace managerial philosophy and thinking at the highest levels of an organization. For this reason, social policy affects the development of a business mission statement. Social issues mandate that strategists consider not only what the organization owes its various stakeholders but also what responsibilities the firm has to consumers, environmentalists, minorities, communities, and other groups. After decades of debate on the topic of social responsibility, many firms still struggle to determine appropriate social policies.

The issue of social responsibility arises when a company establishes its business mission. The impact of society on business and vice versa, is becoming more pronounced each year. Social policies directly affect a firm's customers, products and services, markets, technology, profitability, self-concept, and public image. An organization's social policy should be integrated into all strategic-management activities, including the development of a mission statement. Carroll and Hoy assert that corporate social policy should be designed and articulated during strategy formulation, set and administered during strategy implementation, and reaffirmed or changed during strategy evaluation.[15] The emerging view of social responsibility holds that social issues should be attended to both directly and indirectly in determining strategies.

Firms should strive to engage in social activities that have economic benefits. For example, Merck & Company recently developed the drug ivermectin for treating river blindness, a disease caused by a fly-borne parasitic worm endemic in poor tropical areas of Africa, the Middle East, and Latin America. In an unprecedented gesture that reflected its corporate commitment to social responsibility, Merck then made ivermectin available at no cost to medical personnel throughout the world. Merck's action highlights the dilemma of "orphan drugs," which offer pharmaceutical companies no economic incentive for development and distribution.

Despite differences in approaches, most American companies try to assure outsiders that they conduct business in a socially responsible way. The mission statement is an effective instrument for conveying this message. The Norton Company, for example, concludes its mission statement by saying:

> In order to fulfill this mission, Norton will continue to demonstrate a sense of responsibility to the public interest and to earn the respect and loyalty of its customers, employees, shareholders, and suppliers, and the communities in which it does business.[16]

COMPONENTS OF A MISSION STATEMENT

Mission statements can and do vary in length, content, format, and specificity. Most practitioners and academicians of strategic management consider an effective statement to exhibit nine characteristics or components. Since a mission statement is often the most visible and public part of the strategic-management process, it is important that it includes all of these essential components. Components and corresponding questions that a mission statement should answer are given here.

1. *Customers:* Who are the firm's customers?
2. *Products or services:* What are the firm's major products or services?
3. *Markets:* Where does the firm compete?
4. *Technology:* Is technology a primary concern of the firm?
5. *Concern for survival, growth, and profitability:* Is the firm committed to economic objectives?
6. *Philosophy:* What are the basic beliefs, values, aspirations, and philosophical priorities of the firm?
7. *Self-concept:* What is the firm's distinctive competence or major competitive advantage?
8. *Concern for public image:* Is the firm responsive to social, community, and environmental concerns?
9. *Concern for employees:* Are employees considered to be a valuable asset of the firm?

Excerpts from the mission statements of different organizations are provided in Table 3–2 to exemplify the nine essential components.

WRITING AND EVALUATING MISSION STATEMENTS

Perhaps the best way to develop a skill for writing and evaluating mission statements is to study actual company missions. Therefore, eleven mission statements are presented in Table 3–3. These statements are then evaluated in Table 3–4 based on the nine criteria presented in the previous section.

TABLE 3-2   Examples of the Nine Essential Components of a Mission Statement

1. *Customers*

We believe our first responsibility is to the doctors, nurses, and patients, to mothers and all others who use our products and services. (Johnson & Johnson)

2. *Products or Services*

AMAX's principal products are molybdenum, coal, iron ore, copper, lead, zinc, petroleum and natural gas, potash, phosphates, nickel, tungsten, silver, gold, and magnesium. (AMAX)

Standard Oil Company (Indiana) is in business to find and produce crude oil, natural gas, and natural gas liquids; to manufacture high quality products useful to society from these raw materials; and to distribute and market those products and to provide dependable related services to the consuming public at reasonable prices. (Standard Oil Company)

3. *Markets*

We are dedicated to the total success of Corning Glass Works as a worldwide competitor. (Corning Glass Works)

Our emphasis is on North American markets, although global opportunities will be explored. (Blockway)

4. *Technology*

Control Data is in the business of applying micro-electronics and computer technology in two general areas: computer-related hardware; and computing-enhancing services, which include computation, information, education and finance (Control Data)

The common technology in these areas is discrete particle coatings. (Nashua)

5. *Concern for Survival, Growth, and Profitability*

In this respect, the company will conduct its operations prudently, and will provide the profits and growth which will assure Hoover's ultimate success. (Hoover Universal)

To serve the worldwide need for knowledge at a fair profit by gathering, evaluating, producing and distributing valuable information in a way that benefits our customers, employees, authors, investors, and our society. (McGraw-Hill)

6. *Philosophy*

We believe human development to be the worthiest of the goals of civilization and independence to be the superior condition for nurturing growth in the capabilities of people. (Sun Company)

It's all part of the Mary Kay philosophy—a philosophy based on the golden rule. A spirit of sharing and caring where people give cheerfully of their time, knowledge, and experience. (Mary Kay Cosmetics)

7. *Self-concept*

Crown Zellerbach is committed to leapfrogging competition within 1,000 days by unleashing the constructive and creative abilities and energies of each of its employees. (Crown Zellerbach)

8. *Concern for public image*

To share the world's obligation for the protection of the environment. (Dow Chemical)

To contribute to the economic strength of society and function as a good corporate citizen on a local, state, and national basis in all countries in which we do business. (Pfizer)

9. *Concern for employees*

To recruit, develop, motivate, reward, and retain personnel of exceptional ability, character and dedication by providing good working conditions, superior leadership, compensation on the basis of performance, an attractive benefit program, opportunity for growth, and a high degree of employment security. (The Wachovia Corporation)

To compensate its employees with remuneration and fringe benefits competitive with other employment opportunities in its geographical area and commensurate with their contributions toward efficient corporate operations. (Public Service Electric and Gas Company)

There is no one best mission statement for a particular organization, so good judgment is required in evaluating mission statements. In Table 3–4, a "yes" indicates that the given mission statement answers satisfactorily the question posed in Table 3–3 for the respective evaluative criteria. For example, the "yes" under "customers" for the Chase Manhattan mission statement means this statement answers "Who are our customers?" Notice that Chase Manhattan's customers are "individuals, industries, communities, and countries." A "no" would mean a particular mission statement does not answer or answers unsatisfactorily the key question associated with one of the nine evaluative criteria. For example, note that the Apple Computer, AT&T, BellSouth, and Corning mission statements do not identify the organization's customers. To determine whether a particular statement satisfactorily includes a given component, ask yourself the following question: "If I were responsible for writing a mission statement for this organization, would I have communicated this component better?" If your answer is yes, then record a "no" in the evaluation matrix.

Table 3–4 indicates that the Bancorp Hawaii mission statement is the "best" and the Corning mission statement is the "worst" of the examples. Overall, the example mission statements are weakest in the areas of "technology," "philosophy," and "concern for survival, growth, and profitability." The statements are strongest in the areas of "products or services," "markets," and "self-concept."

Let's focus specifically for a moment on the Apple Computer mission statement. Note that the statement does include coverage of the "customer" component, which could be individuals, businesses, educational institutions, and governmental agencies. Apple's statement does include the "product/service" component in saying, "We provide exceptional personal computing products and innovative customer services." The Apple statement includes coverage of the "market" component in saying, "We help people around the world" and includes the technology component in saying, "We find innovative ways to use computing technology." No mention of "concern for survival, growth, and profitability" is given in the statement. Nor is coverage of the "philosophy," "concern for public image," or "concern for employees" components. The Apple mission statement includes coverage of "self-concept" by mentioning "education," which is a segment of the industry that Apple does especially well. Overall, the Apple statement includes only four of the nine essential mission statement components.

In multidivisional organizations, strategists should ensure that divisional units perform strategic-management tasks, including the development of a statement of mission. Each division should involve its own managers and employees in developing a mission statement consistent with and supportive of the corporative mission. Anchor Hocking is an example of a multinational organization that has developed an overall corporate mission statement and a statement for each of its eight divisions. Notice that the Nicholls State and Sam Houston State mission statements that are given in Table 3–3 are for those in situations at the College of Business rather than in the university at large.

An organization that fails to develop a comprehensive and inspiring mission statement loses the opportunity to present itself favorably to existing and potential stakeholders. All organizations need customers, employees, and managers, and most firms need creditors, suppliers, and distributors. The business mission statement is an effective vehicle for communicating with important internal and external stakeholders. The principal value of a mission statement as a tool of strategic management is derived from its specification of the ultimate aims of a firm:

TABLE 3-3   Mission Statements of Eleven Organizations

American Home Products

American Home Products Corporation makes a significant contribution to health care worldwide as a leader in researching, developing, manufacturing and marketing products that meet important health needs.

Our prescription drugs, nutritionals, over-the-counter medications, and medical devices, supplies and instrumentation benefit millions of people. We also produce and market well-known quality food brands in the United States and Canada.

We are focused on improving health care by finding and commercializing innovative, cost-effective therapies and technologies. Key to our efforts are efficient manufacturing, global distribution and marketing, and strict financial controls.

In 1992, American Home Products Corporation achieved record sales and earnings, and the company increased its dividend for the 41st consecutive year.

Pfizer, Inc.

Pfizer, Inc. is a research-based, global health care company. Our principal mission is to apply scientific knowledge to help people around the world enjoy longer, healthier and more productive lives. The company has four business segments: health care, consumer health care, food science and animal health. We manufacture in 39 countries, and our products are available worldwide.

Chase Manhattan Corporation

We provide financial services that enhance the well-being and success of individuals, industries, communities and countries around the world.

Through our shared commitment to those we serve, we will be the best financial services company in the world.

Customers will choose us first because we deliver the highest quality service and performance.

People will be proud and eager to work here.

Investors will buy our stock as a superior long-term investment.

To be the best for our customers, we are team players who show respect for our colleagues and commit to the highest standards of quality and professionalism.

Customer focus

Respect for each other

Teamwork

Quality

Professionalism

Food Lion, Inc.

The Food Lion team will work hard to use our *talents* and *resourcefulness* to satisfy every customer by providing Extra Low Prices on a wide variety of quality products in a *clean, convenient,* and *friendly* environment.

Apple Computer

It is Apple's mission to help transform the way customers work, learn and communicate by providing exceptional personal computing products and innovative customer services.

We will pioneer new directions and approaches, finding innovative ways to use computing technology to extend the bounds of human potential.

Apple will make a difference: our products, services and insights will help people around the world shape the ways business and education will be done in the 21st century.

TABLE 3-3   *Continued*

AT&T

We are dedicated to being the world's best at bringing people together—giving them easy access to each other and to the information and services they want—anytime, anywhere.

Bancorp Hawaii, Inc.

The mission of Bancorp Hawaii is to be the finest, most effective financial services organization in the state of Hawaii and the Pacific markets we serve.

As a family of companies built around an outstanding regional bank, we will sell and deliver a broad range of services that meet the needs of our customers at prices which are competitive and consistent with our profit goals.

Our basic business strategy is to identify, understand and then satisfy the financial needs and wants of consumers, businesses, and governments. We will be alert to changes which impact our businesses and exercise initiative to capitalize on new opportunities.

The geographic scope of our business will be expanded only to areas where our unique background, experience and capabilities will give us a competitive advantage and a reasonable opportunity for an adequate financial return. We will introduce only those new financial services which we can perform well.

Two primary goals are to achieve significant reductions in noninterest expense through enhanced productivity and automation and to increase noninterest income by marketing fee-based services.

We want to conduct our business under conditions largely determined by ourselves and will, therefore, always maintain a strong financial position. Our goal is to consistently rank among the top 10 percent of our peer group in terms of financial performance. This will ensure that we will fulfill our responsibility to increase the value of our shareholders' investment.

We will maintain a stimulating work environment—one that encourages, recognizes, and rewards high achievers, at all levels of the organization.

We will always conduct ourselves with integrity and endeavor to be a good neighbor and a responsible corporate citizen.

BellSouth Corporation

BellSouth Corporation provides information services in local exchange and exchange access markets in its nine-state franchised territory. It also provides communications services and products such as advertising and publishing, mobile cellular telephone service, paging, and telecommunications and computer systems through its entities, in both the nine-state region and other major U.S. and international markets.

Corning, Inc.

Our purpose is to deliver superior, long-range economic benefits to our customers, our employees, our shareholders, and to the communities in which we operate. We accomplish this by living our corporate values.

Nicholls State University (College of Business)

The principal mission of the College of Business is to prepare students to participate in society and the work force as educated individuals able to compete in a dynamic global economy. In order to enrich the learning process, the College also contributes to scholarship through applied research and instructional development. In addition to providing support to the employer community through the development of marketable skills in potential employees, the College also enhances the competitive capabilities of regional businesses by providing continuing education courses and consulting services through the Small Business Development Center (SBDC) and the individual efforts of faculty. The faculty advances the welfare of the University, the community, and academic and professional organizations through professional interactions.

TABLE 3-3   *Continued*

Sam Houston State University (College of Business Administration)

The mission of the College of Business Administration is to support Sam Houston State University's mission by providing students with the educational experience in the field of business necessary to become productive citizens, to develop successful business-related careers and to provide interested students with the background necessary to pursue advanced studies in the field of business and related fields. The educational experience at the undergraduate and master's levels is designed to provide students with the intellectual flexibility to be successful in a dynamic business environment.

The highest priority of the College of Business Administration is teaching, primarily at the undergraduate level. In addition, the College encourages faculty professional development, scholarly productivity, and service to benefit all stakeholders: students, alumni, donors, regional businesses, and the State of Texas.

It provides managers with a unity of direction that transcends individual, parochial, and transitory needs. It promotes a sense of shared expectations among all levels and generations of employees. It consolidates values over time and across individuals and interest groups. It projects a sense of worth and intent that can be identified and assimilated by company outsiders. Finally, it affirms the company's commitment to responsible action, which is symbiotic with its need to preserve and protect the essential claims of insiders for sustained survival, growth, and profitability of the firm.[17]

CONCLUSION

Every organization has a unique purpose and reason for being. This uniqueness should be reflected in a statement of mission. The nature of a business mission can represent either a competitive advantage or disadvantage for the firm. An organization achieves a heightened sense of purpose when strategists, managers, and employees develop and communicate a clear business mission. Drucker says developing a clear business mission is the "first responsibility of strategists." A good mission statement reveals an organization's customers, products or services, markets, technology, concern for survival, philosophy, self-concept, concern for public image, and concern for employees. These nine basic components serve as a practical framework for evaluating and writing mission statements. Being the first step in strategic-management, the mission statement provides direction for all planning activities.

A well-designed mission statement is essential for formulating, implementing, and evaluating strategy. Developing and communicating a clear business mission is one of the most commonly overlooked tasks in strategic management. Without a clear statement of mission, a firm's short-term actions can be counterproductive to long-term interests. A mission statement should always be subject to revision, but, if carefully prepared, it will require major changes only infrequently. Organizations usually reexamine their mission statement annually. Effective mission statements stand the test of time.

A mission statement is an essential tool for strategists, a fact illustrated in a short story told by Porsche CEO Peter Schultz:

Three people were at work on a construction site. All were doing the same job, but when each was asked what his job was, the answers varied. "Breaking rocks," the first replied,

TABLE 3-4   An Evaluation Matrix of Mission Statements

EVALUATIVE CRITERIA

COMPANY	CUSTOMERS	PRODUCTS/ SERVICES	MARKETS	TECHNOLOGY	CONCERN FOR SURVIVAL, GROWTH, AND PROFITABILITY
American Home Products	Yes	Yes	Yes	Yes	Yes
Pfizer, Inc.	Yes	Yes	Yes	No	No
Chase Manhattan Corporation	Yes	Yes	Yes	No	Yes
Food Lion, Inc.	Yes	No	No	No	No
Apple Computer	No	Yes	Yes	Yes	No
AT&T	No	No	Yes	No	No
Bancorp Hawaii, Inc.	Yes	Yes	Yes	No	Yes
BellSouth Corporation	No	Yes	Yes	No	No
Corning, Inc.	No	No	No	No	No
Nicholls State University	Yes	Yes	No	No	No
Sam Houston State University	Yes	Yes	Yes	No	No

COMPANY	PHILOSOPHY	CONCERN FOR SELF-CONCEPT	CONCERN FOR PUBLIC IMAGE	EMPLOYEES
American Home Products	No	Yes	No	No
Pfizer, Inc.	No	No	No	No
Chase Manhattan Corporation	Yes	Yes	Yes	Yes
Food Lion, Inc.	No	Yes	No	No
Apple Computer	No	Yes	No	No
AT&T	No	Yes	No	No
Bancorp Hawaii, Inc.	Yes	Yes	Yes	Yes
BellSouth Corporation	No	No	No	No
Corning, Inc.	Yes	No	Yes	Yes
Nicholls State University	No	Yes	Yes	Yes
Sam Houston State University	No	Yes	Yes	Yes

"Earning a living," responded the second. "Helping to build a cathedral," said the third. Few of us can build cathedrals. But to the extent we can see the cathedral in whatever cause we are following, the job seems more worthwhile. Good strategists and a clear mission help us find those cathedrals in what otherwise could be dismal issues and empty causes.[18]

KEY TERMS AND CONCEPTS

Concern for Employees
Concern for Public image
Concern for Survival, Growth, and Profitability
Creed Statement
Customers
Markets
Mission Statement
Mission Statement Components

Philosophy
Products or Services
Self-Concept
Social Policy
Stakeholders
Technology
Vision

ISSUES FOR REVIEW AND DISCUSSION

1. Do local service stations need to have written mission statements? Why or why not?

2. Why do you think organizations that have a comprehensive mission tend to be high performers? Does having a comprehensive mission cause high performance?

3. Explain why a mission statement should not include strategies and objectives.

4. What is your college or university's self-concept? How would you state that in a mission statement?

5. Explain the principal value of a mission statement.

6. Why is it important for a mission statement to be reconciliatory?

7. In your opinion, what are the three most important components to include in writing a mission statement? Why?

8. How would the mission statements of a for-profit and a nonprofit organization differ?

9. Write a business mission statement for an organization of your choice.

10. Go to your nearest library and look in the annual reports of corporations. Find a mission statement, make a photocopy of the document, bring the copy to class, and evaluate the document.

11. Who are the major stakeholders of the bank that you do business with locally? What are the major claims of those stakeholders?

12. Select one of the current readings at the end of this chapter. Look up that article in your college library and give a 5-minute oral report to the class summarizing the article.

1. Peter Drucker, *Management: Tasks, Responsibilities, and Practices* (New York: Harper & Row, 1974), 61.

2. Barnett Bank, Internal document, (1993).

3. Vern McGinnis, "The Mission Statement: A Key Step in Strategic Planning," *Business* 31, no. 6 (November–December 1981): 41.

4. Fred David, "How Companies Define Their Mission," *Long Range Planning* 22, no. 1 (February 1989): 90–92. Also, see John Pearce II and Fred David, "Corporate Mission Statements: The Bottom Line," *Academy of Management Executive* 1, no. 2 (May 1987): 110.

5. John Pearce II and Fred David, "Corporate Mission Statements: The Bottom Line," *Academy of Management Executive* 1, no. 2 (May 1987): 110.

6. W. R. King and D. I. Cleland, *Strategic Planning and Policy* (New York: Van Nostrand Reinhold, 1979), 124.

7. Brian Dumaine, "What the Leaders of Tomorrow See," *Fortune* (July 3, 1989): 50.

8. Patrick Murphy, "Creating Ethical Corporate Structures," *Sloan Management Review* (Winter 1989): 81.

9. Andrew Campbell and Sally Yeung, "Creating a Sense of Mission," *Long Range Planning* 24, no. 4 (August 1991): 17.

10. George Steiner, *Strategic Planning: What Every Manager Must Know* (New York: The Free Press, 1979): 160.

11. Drucker, 78, 79.

12. "How W. T. Grant Lost $175 Million Last Year," *Business Week* (February 25, 1975): 75.

13. Drucker, 88.

14. Drucker, 61.

15. Archie Carroll and Frank Hoy, "Integrating Corporate Social Policy into Strategic Management," *Journal of Business Strategy* 4, no. 3 (Winter 1984): 57.

16. The Norton Company, *Annual Report* (1981).

17. John Pearce II, "The Company Mission as a Strategic Tool," *Sloan Management Review* 23, no. 3 (Spring 1982): 74.

18. Robert Waterman, Jr., *The Renewal Factor: How the Best Get and Keep the Competitive Edge* (New York: Bantam, 1987). Also, *Business Week* (September 14, 1987): 120.

Ackoff, Russell. "Mission Statements." Planning Review 15, no. 4 (July–August 1987): 30–32.

Bertodo, R. "The Role of Suppliers in Implementing a Strategic Vision." Long Range Planning 24, no. 3 (June 1991): 40–48.

Byars, Lloyd. "Organizational Philosophy and Mission Statements." Planning Review 15, no. 4 (July–August 1987): 32–36.

Campbell, Andrew. "The Power of Mission: Aligning Strategy and Culture." Planning Review 20, no. 5 (Septem-ber–October 1992): 10–12.

Campbell, Andrew, and Sally Yeung. "Creating a Sense of Mission." Long Range Planning 24, no. 4 (August 1991): 10–20.

Campbell, Andrew, and Sally Yeung, "Brief Case: Mission, Vision and Strategic Intent." Long Range Planning 24, no. 4 (August 1991): 145–147.

David, Fred R. "How Companies Define Their Mission." Long Range Planning 22, no. 1 (February 1989): 90–97.

Dowling, G.R. "Developing Your Company Image into a Corporate Asset." Long Range Planning 26, no. 2 (April 1993): 101–109.

Ireland, R. Duane, and Michael A. Hitt. "Mission Statements: Importance, Challenge, and Recommen-dations for Development." Business Horizons 35, no. 3 (May–June 1992): 34–42.

Kamfer, Louis. "Enscaling the Mission Statement as a Procedure for Organizational Diagnosis." South African Journal of Business Management 22, no. 1 (1991): 1–8.

Klemm, Mary, Stuart Sanderson, and George Luffman. "Mission Statements: Selling Corporate Values to Employ-ees." Long Range Planning 24, no. 3 (June 1991): 73–78.

Kolesar, Peter J. "Vision, Values, and Milestones: TQM at Alcoa." California Management Review 35, no. 3 (Spring 1993): 133–165.

Lavin, Douglas. "Robert Eaton Thinks 'Vision' Is Overrated and He's Not Alone." Wall Street Journal, October 4, 1993: A1 and A8.

Meyer, Christopher. "2020 Vision." Planning Review 20, no. 5 (September–October 1992): 39–41.

Osborne, Richard L. "Core Value Statements: The Corporate Compass." Business Horizons 34, no. 5 (September/October 1991): 28–34.

Rogers, James E., Jr. "Adopting and Implementing a Corporate Environmental Charter." Business Horizons 35, no. 2 (March–April 1992): 29–33.

Schoemaker, Paul, J. H. "How to Link Strategic Vision to Core Capabilities." Sloan Management Review 34, no. 1 (Fall 1992): 67–82.

EXPERIENTIAL EXERCISES

EVALUATING MISSION STATEMENTS

PURPOSE

A business mission statement is an integral part of strategic management. It provides direction for formulating, implementing, and evaluating strategic activities. This exercise will give you practice evaluating mission statements, a skill that is prerequisite to writing a good mission statement.

INSTRUCTIONS

Step 1   Your instructor will select some or all of the following mission statements to evaluate. On a separate sheet of paper, construct an evaluation matrix like the one presented in Table 3–3. Evaluate the mission statements based on the nine criteria presented in the chapter.

Step 2   Record a "yes" in all cells of the evaluation matrix where the respective mission statement satisfactorily meets the desired criteria. Record a "no" in all cells where the respective mission statement does not meet the stated criteria.

Mission Statements

Carolina Power & Light Company. It is the mission of the Carolina Power & Light Company to provide the best service to present and future customers at the lowest rates consistent with fair compensation to employees. A fair return to those who have invested in the Company, safety for employees and the public, reasonable protection of the environment, and the development of technology to provide future service. Through the development and contribution of all employees, to the maximum of their potential, the Company will assure total quality performance that results in the highest achievable levels of customer satisfaction and recognition for excellence.

John B. Stetson University. The mission of Stetson University is to provide students with an excellent education in an intellectually challenging and collaborative learning community. We pursue excellence through superior teaching, close student-faculty interaction, creative activity, and programs solidly grounded in liberal learning. We seek academically talented students with leadership potential and records of personal growth and community service. We prepare them for rewarding careers, selective graduate and professional programs, and a lifetime of learning. Stetson pursues truth in an open, caring, diverse environment, and encourages all members of its community to be morally sensitive and effective citizens committed to active forms of social responsibility. (*Stetson College Catalog,* 1993–1994, p. 5)

CSX Corporation. CSX is a transportation company committed to being a leader in railroad, inland water and containerized distribution markets.

To attract the human and financial resources necessary to achieve this leadership position, CSX will support our three major constituencies:

For our customers, we will work as a partner to provide excellent service and meet all agreed-upon commitments.

For our employees, we will create a work environment that motivates and allows them to grow and develop and perform their jobs to the maximum of their capacity.

For our shareholders, we will meet our goals to provide them with sustainable superior returns.

University of North Carolina at Chapel Hill. The University of North Carolina at Chapel Hill has been built by the people of the state and has existed for two centuries as the nation's first state university. Through its excellent undergraduate programs, it has provided higher education to ten generations of students, many of whom have become leaders of the State and the nation. Since the nineteenth century, it has offered distinguished graduate and professional programs.

The university is a research university. Fundamental to this designation is a faculty actively involved in research, scholarship, and creative work, whose teaching is transformed by discovery and whose service is informed by current knowledge.

The mission of the University is to serve all the people of the state, and indeed the nation, as a center for scholarship and creative endeavor. The university exists to expand the body of knowledge; to teach students at all levels in an environment of research, free inquiry, and personal responsibility; to improve the condition of human life through service and publication; and to enrich our culture.

To fulfill this mission, the university must:

acquire, discover, preserve, synthesize, and transmit knowledge;

provide high quality undergraduate instruction to students within a community engaged in original inquiry and creative expression, while committed to intellectual freedom, to personal integrity and justice, and to those values that foster enlightened leadership for the state and the nation;

provide graduate and professional programs of national distinction at the doctoral and other advanced levels to future generations of research scholars, educators, professionals, and informed citizens;

extend knowledge-based services and other resources of the university to the citizens of North Carolina and their institutions to enhance the quality of life for all people in the State; and

address, as appropriate, regional, national, and international needs.

This mission imposes special responsibilities upon the faculty, students, staff, administration, trustees, and other governance structures and constituencies of the university in their service and decision-making on behalf of the university. (*UNC College Catalog*, 1993–1994, p. 2)

Federal Express. Federal Express is committed to our people-service-profit philosophy. We will produce outstanding financial returns by providing totally reliable, competitively superior global air-ground transportation of high priority goods and documents that require rapid, time-certain delivery. Equally important, positive control of each package will be maintained utilizing real time electronic tracking and tracing systems. A complete record of each shipment and delivery will be presented with our request for payment. We will be helpful, courteous and professional to each other and the public. We will strive to have a satisfied customer at the end of each transaction.

Experiential Exercise 3B

WRITING A MISSION STATEMENT FOR HERSHEY FOODS

PURPOSE

Although there is no one best mission statement for a given organization, analysts feel the Hershey mission statement provided in the Cohesion Case can be improved. Writing a mission statement that includes desired components … and at the same time is inspiring and reconciliatory requires careful thought. Mission statements should not be too lengthy; statements under 200 words are desirable.

INSTRUCTIONS

Step 1   Take 15 minutes to write a mission statement for Hershey Foods that does not exceed 200 words. Scan the case for needed details as you prepare your mission statement.

Step 2   Join with three other classmates to form a group of four people. Read each other's mission statements silently. As a group, select the best of your group's mission statements.

Step 3   Read that best mission statement to the class.

Experiential Exercise 3C

WRITING A MISSION STATEMENT FOR MY UNIVERSITY

PURPOSE

Most universities have a mission statement, as indicated by the examples provided in this chapter. The purpose of this exercise is to give you practice writing a mission statement for a nonprofit organization such as your own university.

INSTRUCTIONS

Step 1   Take 15 minutes to write a mission statement for your university. Your statement should not exceed 200 words.

Step 2   Read your mission statement to the class.

Step 3   Determine whether your institution has a mission statement. Look in the front of the college handbook. If your institution has a written statement, contact an appropriate administrator of the institution to inquire about how and when the statement was prepared. Share this information with the class.

CONDUCTING MISSION STATEMENT RESEARCH

PURPOSE

This exercise gives you the opportunity to study the nature and role of mission statements in strategic management.

INSTRUCTIONS

Step 1 Call various organizations in your city or county to identify firms that have developed a formal mission statement. Contact nonprofit organizations and government agencies in addition to small and large businesses. Ask to speak with the director, owner, or chief executive officer of one organization. Explain that you are studying mission statements in class and are conducting research as part of a class activity.

Step 2 Ask several executives the following four questions and record their answers.

1. When did your organization first develop a formal mission statement? Who was primarily responsible for its development?
2. How long has your current mission statement existed? When was it last modified? Why was it modified at that point in time?
3. By what process is your firm's mission statement altered?
4. How is your mission statement used in the firm? How does it affect the firm's strategic-planning process?

Step 3 Provide an overview of your findings to the class.

ARE MISSION STATEMENTS ESOTERIC?[1]

PURPOSE

Some large American corporations have recently and publicly denounced the importance of having a clear mission. Louis Gerstner, CEO of IBM, recently said, "The last thing IBM needs now is a vision." Robert Eaton, CEO of Chrysler, recently said, "Internally we don't use the word vision (mission). I believe in quantifiable short-term results—things we can all relate to—as opposed to some esoteric thing no one can quantify." William Gates, CEO of Microsoft Corporation, recently said, "Being a visionary (concerned with mission) is trivial." Douglas Lavin of *Wall Street Journal* recently said, "Vision (mission) may not exactly be dead in corporate America, but a surprising number of CEOs are casting aside their crystal balls to concentrate on the nuts-and-bolts of running their businesses in these leaner times; CEOs whose notion of vision (mission) is a sharp eye on the bottom line include John Sculley at Apple Computer, Ronald Compton at Aetna Life & Casualty, and John Smith, Jr., at General Motors."

INSTRUCTIONS

Step 1   Decide whether you agree or disagree with the CEO comments cited above. Do you agree with these persons that mission statements are esoteric or crystal ballish? Discuss this issue with several local business executives.

Step 2   Write a two page essay explaining your personal views regarding the importance of mission statements.

Step 3   Summarize your views in a one minute presentation to the class.

1. This exercise is adapted from "Robert Eaton Thinks 'Vision' Is Overrated and He's Not Alone," *Wall Street Journal* (Oct. 4, 1993) pp. A1, A8.

Experiential Exercise 3F

USING THE *STRATEGY FORMULATOR* SOFTWARE

PURPOSE

The purpose of this exercise is to get you familar using the new *Strategy Formulator* strategic planning software that accompanies this text. Developing a mission statement is one of the first activities in the software program. At the end of Chapters 4, 5, and 6, there also will appear software exercises, so go ahead and begin to get familiar with this software. *Strategy Formulator* is useful in preparing case analyses and also is widely used by businesses actually doing strategic planning.

INSTRUCTIONS

Use the software to prepare a mission statement for your university. Do this in conjuction with Experiential Exercise 3C if possible. Bring a printout of your work to class.

Chapter 4

THE EXTERNAL ASSESSMENT

OBJECTIVES

After studying this chapter, you should be able to:

■ Describe how to conduct an external strategic-management audit.

■ Discuss ten major external forces that affect organizations: economic, social, cultural, demographic, environmental, political, governmental, legal, technological, and competitive.

■ Identify key sources of external information.

■ Discuss important forecasting tools used in strategic management.

■ Discuss the importance of monitoring external trends and events.

■ Explain how to develop an EFE Matrix.

■ Explain how to develop a Competitive Profile Matrix.

■ Discuss the importance of gathering competitive intelligence.

■ Describe the trend toward cooperation among competitors.

113

*T*his chapter examines the tools and concepts needed to conduct an external strategic-management audit (sometimes called environmental scanning or industry analysis). An *external audit* focuses on identifying and evaluating trends and events beyond the control of a single firm, such as increased foreign competition, population shifts to the Sunbelt, an aging society, information technology, and the computer revolution. An external audit reveals key opportunities and threats confronting an organization so that managers can formulate strategies to take advantage of the opportunities and avoid or reduce the impact of threats. This chapter presents a practical framework for gathering, assimilating, and analyzing external information.

THE NATURE OF AN EXTERNAL AUDIT

The purpose of an external audit is to develop a finite list of opportunities that could benefit a firm, and threats that should be avoided. As the term "finite" suggests, the external audit is not aimed at developing an exhaustive list of every possible factor that could influence the business. Rather, it is aimed at identifying key variables that offer actionable responses. Firms should be able to respond either offensively or defensively to the factors by formulating strategies that take advantage of external opportunities or that minimize the impact of potential threats. Figure 4–1 illustrates how the external audit fits into the strategic-management process.

Key External Forces. External forces can be divided into five broad categories: (1) economic forces; (2) social, cultural, demographic, and environmental forces; (3) political, governmental, and legal forces; (4) technological forces; and (5) competitive forces. Relationships among these forces and an organization are depicted in Figure 4–2. External trends and events significantly affect all products, services, markets, and organizations in the world.

Changes in external forces translate into changes in consumer demand for both industrial and consumer products and services. External forces affect the types of products developed, the nature of positioning and market segmentation strategies, the types of services offered, and the choice of businesses to acquire or sell. External forces directly affect both suppliers and distributors. Identifying and evaluating external opportunities and threats enables organizations to develop a clear mission, to design strategies to achieve long-term objectives, and to develop policies to achieve annual objectives.

Some organizations survive solely because they recognize and take advantage of external opportunities. For example, Larson Company in Tucson, Arizona, has capitalized upon the growing concern for our natural environment by creating "naturalistic environments" for zoos, aquariums, shopping centers, amusement parks, and resort hotels. Larson's sales have grown dramatically to over $20 million annually. Larson contends that large, flashy nature exhibits are a big tourist draw. The new Mirage hotel and casino in Las Vegas, for example, attributes its success to the extensive use of artificial environments, ranging from a giant aquarium behind the registration desk to a 60-foot-high volcano outside the hotel.

The increasing complexity of business today is evidenced by more countries' developing the capacity and will to compete aggressively in world markets. Foreign businesses and countries are willing to learn, adapt, innovate, and invent to compete successfully in the marketplace. There are more competitive new technologies in Europe and the Far East today than ever before. American businesses can no longer

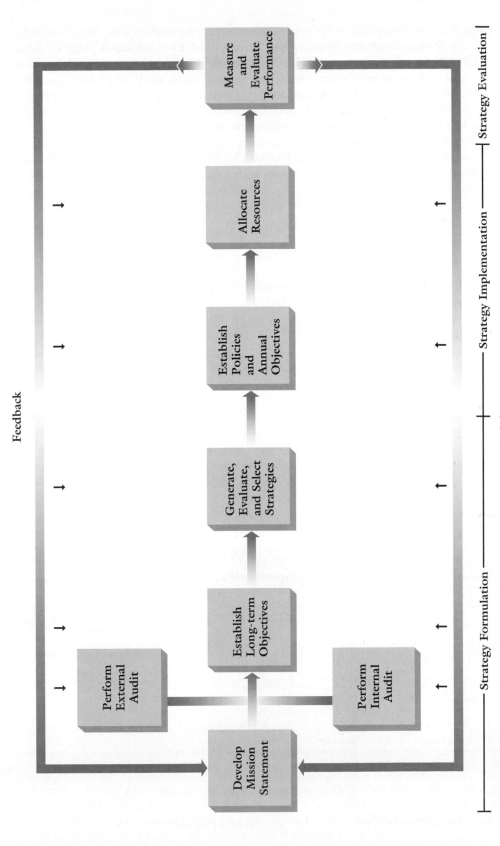

Feedback

Perform
External
Audit

Develop
Mission
Statement

Perform
Internal
Audit

Establish
Long-term
Objectives

Generate,
Evaluate,
and Select
Strategies

Establish
Policies
and
Annual
Objectives

Allocate
Resources

Measure
and
Evaluate
Performance

├── Strategy Formulation ──┤├── Strategy Implementation ──┤├── Strategy Evaluation ──┤

FIGURE 4-1 A Comprehensive Strategic-Management Model

beat foreign competitors with ease. For example, the world's four largest manufacturers of industrial and farm equipment are Mitsubishi of Japan, INI of Spain, Mannesmann of Germany, and BTR of Britain; the world's two largest jewelry and silverware companies are Citizen Watch and Seiko of Japan; the world's two largest rubber and plastic products companies are Bridgestone of Japan and Michelin of France. In publishing and printing, no U.S. company ranks among the six largest; in textiles, no U.S. company ranks among the eight largest.

Most organizations practice some form of external analysis as part of their planning process. Nearly 75 percent of chief executive officers of the Fortune 500 companies report that their firms perform external analysis and achieve numerous benefits from doing so.[1] Another 16 percent report that they do not have organized external analysis but probably should. Only 11 percent report that their firms do not conduct external audits and have no plans to begin.

The Process of Performing an External Audit. The process of performing an external audit must include involvement of as many managers and employees as possible. As emphasized in earlier chapters, involvement in the strategic-management process can lead to understanding and commitment from organizational members. Individuals appreciate having the opportunity to contribute ideas and to gain a better understanding of their firm's industry, competitors, and markets.

To perform an external audit, a company must first gather competitive intelligence and information about social, cultural, demographic, environmental, economic, political, legal, governmental, and technological trends. Individuals can be asked to monitor various sources of information such as key magazines, trade journals, and newspapers. These persons can submit periodic scanning reports to a committee of managers charged with performing the external audit. This approach provides a continuous stream of timely strategic information and involves many individuals in the external-audit process. On-line data bases provide another source for gathering strategic information, as does use of corporate, university, and public libraries. Suppliers, distributors, salespersons, customers, and competitors represent other sources of vital information.

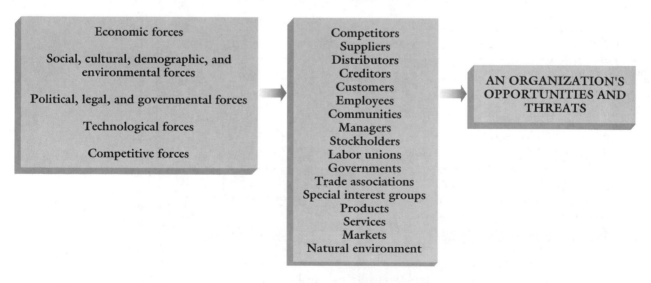

FIGURE 4-2 Relationships Between Key External Forces and an Organization

Once information is gathered, it should be assimilated and evaluated. A meeting or series of meetings of up to twenty managers is needed to collectively identify the most important opportunities and threats facing the firm. Critical success factors should be listed on flip charts or a blackboard. A prioritized list of these factors could be obtained by requesting all managers to rank the factors identified, from 1 for the most important opportunity/threat to 20 for the least important opportunity/threat. Critical success factors can vary over time and by industry. Relationships with suppliers or distributors are often a critical success factor. Other variables commonly used include market share, breath of competing products, world economies, foreign affiliates, proprietary and key account advantages, price competitiveness, technological advancements, population shifts, interest rates, and pollution abatement.

Freund emphasizes that critical success factors should be (1) important to achieving long-term and annual objectives, (2) measurable, (3) relatively few in number, (4) applicable to all competing firms, and (5) hierarchical in the sense that some will pertain to the overall company and others will be more narrowly focused on functional or divisional areas.[2] A final list of the most important critical success factors should be communicated and distributed widely in the organization. Both opportunities and threats can be critical success factors.

Information Technology. *Information technology* (IT) has become a powerful tool for conducting an external audit. The quantity and quality of industry and competitive information available to organizations has increased dramatically in recent years. Advanced computer technology, telecommunications, data access and storage devices, fax machines, on-line data bases, graphics, and software represent efficient and effective vehicles for identifying and evaluating opportunities and threats.

Information technology (IT) itself is changing the very nature of opportunities and threats by altering the life cycles of products, increasing the speed of distribution, creating new products and services, erasing limitations of traditional geographic markets, and changing the historical trade-off between production standardization and flexibility. IT is altering economies of scale, changing entry barriers, and redefining the relationship between industries and various suppliers, creditors, customers, and competitors. As an example, consider the airline industry's business travel market:

> Given the current rate of development in telecommunications and office technology, video conferences may become a major substitute for some business air travel soon. This would significantly affect the airline industry's business travel market. Strategists today must address a crucial question: What impact will IT have on our industry over the next five to ten years in terms of products and services, markets, and production economies?[3]

The era of the mainframe computer is giving way to a proliferation of affordable microcomputers that are almost as powerful. This trend is creating a new basis for competition in virtually all industries and has generated new buyers, suppliers, products, and services. The microcomputer revolution especially represents an opportunity for innovative young companies. Entrenched industrial leaders face more competition than ever from small firms using advanced microcomputer technology.

To effectively capitalize on information technology, a number of organizations are establishing two new positions in the firm, chief information officer (CIO) and chief technology officer (CTO).[4] This trend reflects the growing importance of information technology in strategic management. A CIO and CTO work together to assure that information needed to formulate, implement, and evaluate strategies is available where and when it is needed. These persons are responsible for developing, maintaining, and updating a company's information data base. The CIO is more a manager, managing the overall external-audit process; the CTO is more a technician, focusing on technical issues such as data acquisition, data processing, decision support systems, and software and hardware acquisition.

ECONOMIC FORCES

Low inflation and high unemployment in the 1990s have caused sweeping changes in the buying patterns of consumers. As consumers perceive that more money is buying them less, many adopt the "buy now, save later" motto. Both consumer debt and governmental debt levels have soared at the expense of future security. As a percent of disposable income, consumer savings has fallen to below 4 percent. Interest rates have dropped to the lowest levels in decades. Banks are hesitant to lend money and businesses are reluctant to obtain additional debt; consumers are reluctant to make purchases. Many states are increasing taxes. Four states already have a state income tax higher than 10 percent: Massachusetts, North Dakota, Vermont, and California. Nine states have no state income tax: Alaska, Florida, Nevada, New Hampshire, South Dakota, Tennessee, Texas, Washington, and Wyoming.

Increasing numbers of two-income households are an economic trend in America. As affluence increases, individuals place a premium on time. Improved customer service, immediate availability, trouble-free operation of products, and dependable maintenance and repair services are becoming more important. Americans today are more willing than ever to pay for good service if it limits inconvenience.

Economic factors have a direct impact on the potential attractiveness of various strategies. For example, if interest rates rise, then funds needed for capital expansion become more costly or unavailable. Also, as interest rates rise, discretionary income declines, and the demand for discretionary goods falls. As stock prices increase, the desirability of equity as a source of capital for market development increases. Also, as the market rises, consumer and business wealth expands. A summary of economic variables that often represent opportunities and threats for organizations is provided in Table 4–1.

Trends in the dollar's value have significant and unequal effects on companies in different industries and in different locations. For example, the pharmaceutical, tourism, entertainment, motor vehicle, aerospace, and forest products industries benefit greatly with the dollar's fall against the yen, franc, and mark. Agricultural and petroleum industries are hurt by the dollar's rise against the currencies of Mexico, Brazil, Venezuela, and Australia. Generally, a strong or high dollar makes American goods more expensive on overseas markets. This worsens America's trade deficit. When the value of the dollar falls, tourism-oriented firms benefit, since Americans do not travel abroad as much when the value of the dollar is low; rather, foreigners visit and vacation more in the United States. The value of the dollar hit a post–World War II low of 103 yen in mid-1993.

A low value of the dollar means lower imports and higher exports; it helps U.S. companies' competitiveness in world markets. This was the case in 1992, when U.S. exports reached a record $448 billion, up 6.2 percent from 1991. The United States is the number one exporting country in the world, followed by Germany and then Japan.

America's eight largest exporting firms are Boeing, General Motors, General Electric, IBM, Ford Motor, Chrysler, McDonnell Douglas, and Philip Morris. The top ten countries that receive U.S. exports, in rank order, are Canada, Japan, Mexico, Britain, Germany, South Korea, France, The Netherlands, Taiwan, and Belgium/Luxembourg.

TABLE 4-1   Key Economic Variables to Be Monitored

Shift to a service economy in the U.S.	Demand shifts for different categories of goods and services
Availability of credit	
Level of disposable income	Income differences by region and consumer groups
Propensity of people to spend	
Interest rates	Price fluctuations
Inflation rates	Exportation of labor and capital from the U.S.
Economies of scale	
Money market rates	Monetary policies
Federal government budget deficits	Fiscal policies
Gross national product trend	Tax rates
Consumption patterns	European Economic Community (ECC) policies
Unemployment trends	
Worker productivity levels	Organization of Petroleum Exporting Countries (OPEC) policies
Value of the dollar in world markets	
Stock market trends	Coalitions of Lesser Developed Countries (LDC) policies
Foreign countries' economic conditions	
Import/export factors	

Every business day, an average of 2,389 American workers learn they will lose their jobs. More than 500,000 annual employee layoffs by U.S. firms in the early 1990s resulted in terms such as "downsizing," "rightsizing," and "decruiting" becoming common. The U.S. and world economy faces a sustained period of slow, low-inflationary expansion, global overcapacity, high unemployment, price wars, and increased competitiveness. Thousands of laid-off workers are being forced to become entrepreneurs to make a living. The United States is becoming more entrepreneurial every day.

SOCIAL, CULTURAL, DEMOGRAPHIC, AND ENVIRONMENTAL FORCES

Social, cultural, demographic, and environmental changes have a major impact upon virtually all products, services, markets, and customers. Small and large and for-profit and nonprofit organizations in all industries are being staggered and challenged by the opportunities and threats arising from changes in social, cultural, demographic, and environmental variables. In every way, the United States is much different in 1994 than it was in 1984, and the year 2004 promises even greater changes.

Social, cultural, demographic, and environmental trends are shaping the way Americans live, work, produce, and consume. New trends are creating a different type of consumer and consequently a need for different products, different services, and different strategies. There are now more American households with people living alone or with unrelated people than there are households consisting of married couples with children. Census data suggest that Americans are not returning to traditional life-styles. Church membership fell substantially during the 1980s for nearly all religious denominations, except Southern Baptists and Mormons.[5]

Significant trends for the 1990s include consumers becoming more educated, the population aging, narcissism replacing the Protestant work ethic, minorities becoming more influential, people looking for local rather than federal solutions to problems, fixation on youth decreasing, more emphasis being placed on preserving the natural environment, and more women entering the work force. The United States Census Bureau projects that the number of Hispanics will increase from 9 percent of the population in 1994 to 15 percent by 2021, when they will become a larger minority group than blacks in America. The percentage of blacks in America will increase from 12 percent to 14 percent between 1994 and 2021. Eight states currently have more than 500,000 Hispanics as registered voters: California, New Mexico, Arizona, Texas, Florida, New York, Illinois, and New Jersey.[6]

During the 1990s, the number of individuals aged 50 and over will increase 18.5 percent, to 76 million. In contrast, the number of Americans under age 50 will grow by just 3.5 percent. The trend toward an older America is good news for restaurants, hotels, airlines, cruise lines, tours, resorts, theme parks, luxury products and services, recreational vehicles, home builders, furniture producers, computer manufacturers, travel services, pharmaceutical firms, auto makers, and funeral homes. Older Americans are especially interested in health care, financial services, travel, crime prevention, and leisure.

The aging American population affects the strategic orientation of nearly all organizations. Apartment complexes for the elderly, with one meal a day, transportation, and utilities included in the rent, have increased to over 200,000 units nationwide. Called lifecare facilities, the number of complexes is expected to increase to 815,000 by 1995. Some well-known companies building these facilities include Avon, Marriott, and Hyatt. By the year 2005, individuals aged 65 and older in the United States will rise to 13 percent of the total population; Japan's elderly population ratio will rise to 17 percent, and West Germany's to 19 percent.

Americans are on the move in a population shift to the South and West (Sunbelt) and away from the Northeast and Midwest (Frostbelt). The Internal Revenue Service provides the Census Bureau with massive computer files of demographic data. By comparing individual address changes from year to year, the Census Bureau now publishes extensive information about population shifts across the country. For example, Arizona will be the fastest growing state during the 1990s as its population increases 23 percent. Nevada, New Mexico, and Florida are close behind with projected growth rates above 20 percent. Wyoming will remain the nation's least populated state and California the most populated state. Texas will replace New York as the most populous state. States incurring the greatest loss of people for the 1990s are North Dakota, Wyoming, Pennsylvania, Iowa, and West Virginia.[7] This type of information can be essential for successful strategy formulation, including where to locate new plants and distribution centers and where to focus marketing efforts.

Americans are becoming less and less interested in fitness and exercise. Fitness participants declined in the United States by 4.8 percent in 1991 and again by 2.7 percent in 1992. Makers of fitness products, such as Nike, Reebok International, and CML Group, which makes NordicTrack, are experiencing declines in sales growth. American Sports Data in Hartsdale, New York, reports that "the one American in five who exercises regularly is now outnumbered by three couch potatoes."

Mark Starik at George Washington University argues that with the thawing of the Cold War, no greater threat to business and society exists than the voracious, continuous decimation and degradation of our natural environment. The U.S. Clean Air Act went into effect in 1994. The U.S. Clean Water Act went into effect in 1984. As indicated in the Natural Environment Perspective, American firms planning to begin and expand operations in Mexico face immense pollution and health problems. A summary

TABLE 4-2   Key Social, Cultural, Demographic, and Environmental Variables

Childbearing rates	Government regulation
Number of special interest groups	Attitudes toward retirement
Number of marriages	Attitudes toward leisure time
Number of divorces	Attitudes toward product quality
Number of births	Attitudes toward customer service
Number of deaths	Pollution control
Immigration and emigration rates	Attitudes toward foreign peoples
Social security programs	Energy conservation
Life expectancy rates	Social programs
Per capita income	Number of churches
Location of retailing, manufacturing, and service businesses	Number of church members
	Social responsibility
Attitudes toward business	Attitudes toward authority
Life-styles	Attitudes toward careers
Traffic congestion	Population changes by race, age, sex, and level of affluence
Inner-city environments	
Average disposable income	Population changes by city, county, state, region, and country
Value placed on leisure time	
Trust in government	Regional changes in tastes and preferences
Attitudes toward government	Number of women and minority workers
Attitudes toward work	Number of high school and college graduates by geographic area
Buying habits	
Ethical concerns	Recycling
Attitudes toward saving	Waste management
Sex roles	Air pollution
Attitudes toward investing	Water pollution
Racial equality	Ozone depletion
Use of birth control	Endangered species
Average level of education	

of important social, cultural, demographic, and environmental variables that represent opportunities or threats for virtually all organizations is given in Table 4–2.

POLITICAL, GOVERNMENTAL, AND LEGAL FORCES

Federal, state, local, and foreign governments are major regulators, deregulators, subsidizers, employers, and customers of organizations. Political, governmental, and legal factors can therefore represent key opportunities or threats for both small and large organizations. For industries and firms that depend heavily on government contracts or subsidies, political forecasts can be the most important part of an external audit. Changes in patent laws, antitrust legislation, tax rates, and lobbying activities can affect firms significantly.

The U.S. government recently lifted trade sanctions against imports of Japanese laptop computers as a concession to Japan for agreeing to a new bilateral semiconductor accord. This action was followed by a surge of new Japanese competitors entering the U.S. laptop computer market, including Fujitsu, Kyocera, and Hitachi. IBM, Compaq Computer, and Tandy are lowering prices and adding features to their laptops in response to the lifting of sanctions. Although the U.S. market for personal computers has been growing only 3 percent annually, the market for laptops is growing about 32 percent annually.

Irvine Companies, Baldwin Company, and Santa Margarita Company in California were recently forced to abandon strategies to further develop the southern California coastline because the federal government added the California coastal gnatcatcher to the endangered species list. This tiny California songbird faces possible extinction because its habitat, the low scrub and sagebrush that dots the southern California coast, was being destroyed by the firms cited.

Firms such as Chambers Development, Waste Management, and Browning-Ferris, which build and operate large private dumps, are poised for the Environmental Protection Agency (EPA) to close about 6,000 municipal, public solid-waste landfills operating below standards in the United States. New EPA landfill rules set standards for location, design, operation, and closure of public landfills, as well as groundwater-monitoring procedures.

The increasing global interdependence among economies, markets, governments, and organizations makes it imperative that firms consider the possible impact of political variables on the formulation and implementation of competitive strategies. A number of nationally known firms forecast political, governmental, and legal variables, including Frost & Sullivan, Probe International, and Arthur D. Little (ADL). ADL forecasts the political climate in foreign countries by examining five criteria: (1) social development, (2) technological advancement, (3) abundance of natural resources, (4) level of domestic tranquility, and (5) type of political system. ADL has found that political unrest follows whenever a country's development in any one of

A NATURAL ENVIRONMENT PERSPECTIVE
MEXICO'S NATURAL ENVIRONMENT

Mexico is one of the most polluted countries in the world and this situation was a stumbling block in the North American Free Trade Agreement (NAFTA) that recently became law. The natural environment presents both opportunities and threats for American firms doing business in Mexico.

Numerous Mexican cities have no sewage system; they dump millions of gallons of raw sewage daily into rivers and dumping sites. Ciudad Juarez, for example, is a large city near the U.S. border that has no sewage system, and that dumps 22 million gallons of raw sewage a day. Air pollution is another huge problem in Mexico. The ozone levels in Mexico City recently hit 342, a poisonous level far exceeding the less than 100 satisfactory level. All Mexico City schools closed, children stayed indoors, hundreds of people wore face masks, scores of businesses closed, and all hospital incinerators shut down. Smokestack industries in Mexico City, a metropolis of nearly 20 million inhabitants, emit tons of sulfur and heavy metals daily into the air.

President Salinas of Mexico is committed to reversing Mexico's natural environment record, but many analysts say his programs of environmental reform are too little too late. Hundreds of species of Mexican fauna and flora have become extinct in the last two decades; 80 percent of Mexico's huge Lacandona jungle has been destroyed. The incidence of lung cancer, heart disease, typhoid fever, polio, hepatitis, cholera, and numerous other diseases is more than 10 times higher in Mexico than in the United States. The 2,000-mile U.S.-Mexico border is a polluted industrial corridor of assembly factories known as *maquilas*.

Will NAFTA worsen or enhance the monumental natural environment problems that plague Mexico? Reduced tariffs will mean more U.S. companies will locate facilities in Mexico. U.S. firms will export more products to Mexico, such as pollution control equipment, and Mexico will export more products to the United States, such as lettuce and tomatoes. Will implementation of NAFTA mutually benefit both countries?

Source: Adapted from Stephen Mumme, "Clearing the Air: Environmental Reform in Mexico." *Environment* 33, no. 10 (December 1991): 7–30.

these areas gets too far ahead of the others. Ford, Du Pont, Singer, and PepsiCo are among the many companies that use forecasts developed by outside firms to identify key political and governmental opportunities and threats.

Political forecasting can be especially critical and complex for multinational firms that depend on foreign countries for natural resources, facilities, distribution of products, special assistance, or customers. *Planning Review* annually publishes an extensive political risk forecast for eighty-five countries worldwide; an excerpt from a recent political forecast is given in Table 4–3.

Strategists today must possess skills to deal more legalistically and politically than previous strategists, whose attention was directed more to economic and technical affairs of the firm.[8] Strategists today are spending more time anticipating and influencing public policy actions. They spend more time meeting with government officials, attending important hearings and government-sponsored conferences, giving public speeches, and meeting with trade groups, industry associations, and government agency directors. Before entering or expanding international operations, strategists need a good understanding of the political and decision-making processes in countries where their firm may conduct business. For example, the republics that comprise the new Commonwealth of Independent States differ greatly in wealth, resources, language, and life-style.

Increasing global competition toward the year 2000 accents the need for accurate political, governmental, and legal forecasts. Many strategists will have to become familiar with political systems in Europe and Asia and with trading currency futures. East Asian countries have already become world leaders in labor-intensive industries. Frederick Gluck, director of McKinsey & Company, concludes that a world market is emerging from what previously was a multitude of distinct national markets, and that the climate for international business in the 1990s is much more favorable than in the 1980s. Mass communication and high technology are creating similar patterns of consumption in diverse cultures worldwide! This means that many companies may find it difficult to survive by relying solely on domestic markets.

It is no exaggeration that in an industry that is, or is rapidly becoming, global, the riskiest possible posture is to remain a domestic competitor. The domestic competitor will watch as more aggressive companies use this growth to capture economies of scale and learning. The domestic competitor will then be faced with an attack on domestic markets using different

TABLE 4-3 Risk Forecast for 85 Countries to 1998

COUNTRY	REGIME	INFLATION	TURMOIL	TRANSFER	INVESTMENT	EXPORT	GROWTH
U.S.	Clinton	4.5%	Low	A	A	A	3.0%
China	Pragmatists	9.5%	Low	A–	B+	B+	7.0%
Libya	Qaddafi	20.0%	Moderate	B+	B–	B–	4.5%
France	Socialist	3.2%	Low	A	A+	A	2.8%
Sudan	Moderate Military	150.0%	Very High	D+	D+	C	5.0%
Russia	Yeltsin	100.0%	Very High	C	D+	C–	1.5%
Israel	Labor Coalition	15.0%	High	C+	B+	B	5.0%
Brazil	Franco	200.0%	High	C+	C	C	2.2%

Source: William Coplin and Michael O'Leary, "1993–1998 World Political Risk Forecast," *Planning Review* (May/June1993): 34–41. (Note: Only 8 of 85 countries are included here.)

TABLE 4-4   Important Political, Governmental, and Legal Variables

Government regulations or deregulations	Sino-American relationships
Changes in tax laws	Russian-American relationships
Special tariffs	European-American relationships
Political action committees	African-American relationships
Voter participation rates	Import-export regulations
Number, severity, and location of government protests	Government fiscal and monetary policy changes
Number of patents	Political conditions in foreign countries
Changes in patent laws	Special local, state, and federal laws
Environmental protection laws	Lobbying activities
Level of defense expenditures	Size of government budgets
Legislation on equal employment	World oil, currency, and labor markets
Level of government subsidies	Location and severity of terrorist activities
Antitrust legislation	Local, state, and national elections

(and possibly superior) technology, product design, manufacturing, marketing approaches, and economies of scale. A few examples suggest how extensive the phenomenon of world markets has already become. Hewlett-Packard's manufacturing chain reaches halfway around the globe, from well-paid, skilled engineers in California to low-wage assembly workers in Malaysia. General Electric has survived as a manufacturer of inexpensive audio products by centralizing its world production in Singapore.[9]

Local, state, and federal laws, regulatory agencies, and special interest groups can have a major impact on the strategies of small, large, for-profit, and nonprofit organizations. Many companies have altered or abandoned strategies in the past because of political or governmental actions. For example, many nuclear power projects have been halted and many steel plants shut down because of pressure from the Environmental Protection Agency (EPA). Other federal regulatory agencies include the Food and Drug Administration (FDA), the National Highway Traffic and Safety Administration (NHTSA), the Occupational Safety and Health Administration (OSHA), the Consumer Product Safety Commission (CPSC), the Federal Trade Commission (FTC), the Securities Exchange Commission (SEC), the Equal Employment Opportunity Commission (EEOC), the Federal Communications Commission (FCC), the Federal Maritime Commission (FMC), the Interstate Commerce Commission (ICC), the Federal Energy Regulatory Commission (FERC), the National Labor Relations Board (NLRB), and the Civil Aeronautics Board (CAB). A summary of political, governmental, and legal variables that can represent key opportunities or threats to organizations is provided in Table 4–4.

TECHNOLOGICAL FORCES

Revolutionary technological changes and discoveries such as superconductivity, computer engineering, "thinking" computers, robotics, unmanned factories, miracle drugs, space communications, space manufacturing, lasers, cloning, satellite networks, fiber optics, biometrics, and electronic funds transfer are having a dramatic impact on organizations. Superconductivity advancements alone, which increase the power of electrical products by lowering resistance to current, are expected to revolutionize business operations in the 1990s, especially in the transportation, utility, health-care, electrical, and computer industries.

New microprocesser-based equipment and process technologies, such as computer-aided design and manufacturing (CAD/CAM), direct numerical control (DNC), computer-centralized numerical control (CNC), flexible production centers (FPC), equipment and process technology (EPT), and computer-integrated manufacturing (CIM), are burgeoning.

Technological forces represent major opportunities and threats that must be considered in formulating strategies. Technological advancements can dramatically affect organizations' products, services, markets, suppliers, distributors, competitors, customers, manufacturing processes, marketing practices, and competitive position. Technological advancements can create new markets, result in a proliferation of new and improved products, change the relative competitive cost positions in an industry, and render existing products and services obsolete. Technological changes can reduce or eliminate cost barriers between businesses, create shorter production runs, create shortages in technical skills, and result in changing values and expectations of employees, managers, and customers. Technological advancements can create new competitive advantages that are more powerful than existing advantages. No company or industry today is insulated against emerging technological developments. In high-tech industries, identification and evaluation of key technological opportunities and threats can be the most important part of the external strategic-management audit.

Organizations that have traditionally limited technology expenditures to what they can fund after meeting marketing and financial requirements urgently need a reversal in thinking. The pace of technological change is increasing and literally wiping out more and more businesses every day. An emerging consensus holds that technology management is one of the key responsibilities of strategists. Firms should pursue strategies that take advantage of technological opportunities to achieve sustainable, competitive advantages in the marketplace.

> Technology-based issues will underlie nearly every important decision that strategists make. Crucial to those decisions will be the ability to approach technology planning analytically and strategically. . . . technology can be planned and managed using formal techniques similar to those used in business and capital investment planning. An effective technology strategy is built on a penetrating analysis of technology opportunities and threats, and an assessment of the relative importance of these factors to overall corporate strategy.[10]

In practice, critical decisions about technology are too often delegated to lower organizational levels or are made without an understanding of their strategic implications. Many strategists spend countless hours determining market share, positioning products in terms of features and price, forecasting sales and market size, and monitoring distributors; yet too often technology does not receive the same respect:

> The impact of this oversight is devastating. Firms not managing technology to ensure their futures may eventually find their futures managed by technology. Technology's impact reaches far beyond the "high-tech" companies. Although some industries may appear to be relatively technology-insensitive in terms of products and market requirements, they are not immune from the impact of technology; companies in smokestack as well as service industries must carefully monitor emerging technological opportunities and threats.[11]

Not all sectors of the economy are equally affected by technological developments. The communications, electronics, aeronautics, and pharmaceutical industries are much more volatile than the textile, forestry, and metals industries. For strategists in industries affected by rapid technological change, identifying and evaluating technological opportunities and threats can represent the most important part of an external audit. Key questions about technology that should be asked during the external audit are presented in Table 4–5.

Some technological advancements expected before the year 2000 in the computer and medical industry are computers that recognize handwriting, voice-controlled computers, gesture-controlled computers, color fax, picture phones, and defeat of heart disease, AIDS, rheumatoid arthritis, multiple sclerosis, leukemia, and lung cancer.[12] New technological advancements from Japan include tape recorders the size of a matchbox, television sets with flat screens that can be hung on the wall, translation telephones, microminiaturized personal computers, robots that wash windows, and sports cars that rival Lamborghinis but cost half as much.[13]

Electronic data interchange (EDI) is one information technology that is changing the way America does business. EDI allows companies to lower inventory levels, improve customer service, and reduce payroll expenses by sending specially formatted documents such as invoices and purchase orders from one company's computer to another's. EDI is enabling organizations to perform external audits more effectively and to gain competitive advantages in world markets. *Business Week* gives the following example of EDI in use:

> In businesses such as the $55 billion textile industry, which has suffered as retailers doubled their purchases of cheap Asian apparel over the past five years, adopting EDI has become a way to get an edge over foreign rivals. Led by textile magnate Roger Milliken, 220 top retail

TABLE 4-5   Key Questions to Ask in Assessing the Technological Environment

- What are the technologies within the corporation?
- Which technologies are utilized in the firm's business? products? components and parts?
- How critical is each technology to each of these products and businesses?
- Which technologies are contained in purchased parts and material?
- Which of these external technologies might become critical and why? Will they remain available outside the firm?
- What was the evolution of these technologies over time? In which companies were these technological changes initiated?
- What is the likely evolution of these technologies in the future?
- What have been the firm's investments in critical technologies over time?
- What were the investments and investment patterns of its leading technological competitors? Historical? Planned?
- What has been the investment in the product and in the process side of these technologies? For the firm and for its competitors? Design? Production? Implementation and service?
- What is the subjective ranking of different firms in each of these technologies?
- What are the firm's businesses and products?
- What are the parts and components of these products?
- What is the cost and value-added structure of these parts, components, products, and businesses?
- What has been the historical financial and strategic performance of the business, and what are the implications of these trends? In terms of cash generation and earnings characteristics? Investment requirements? Growth? Market position and market share?
- What are the applications of the firm's technologies?
- In which does the firm currently participate and why? In which does the firm not participate and why?
- How attractive is each of these applications as an investment opportunity in terms of its market growth, its potential for profit improvement, and/or its potential for increasing technological leadership?

  —Underlying growth charateristics?

  —Evolution of customer needs and requirements?

  —Current and emeging market segments; segment growth rates?

  —Competitive positioning and likely strategies of key competitors?

- How critical are the firm's technologies to each of these applications?
- What other technologies are critical to the external applications?
- How do the technologies differ in each of these applications?
- What are the competing technologies in each application? What are the determinations of substitution dynamics?
- What is and will be the degree of technological change in each of these technologies?
- What are the applications that the firm should consider entering?
- What should be the priorities of technological resource investment?
- What technological resources are required for the firm to achieve its current business objectives?
- What should be the level and rate of corporate technology investments?
- Which technological investments should be curtailed or eliminated?
- What additional technologies will be required in order to achieve the current corporate business objectives?
- What are the implications of the technology and business portfolios for corporate strategy?

Source: Boris Petrov, "The Advent of the Technology Portfolio." Reprinted by permission from the *Journal of Business Strategy,* Fall 1982. Published by Warren, Gorham & Lamont, Inc. Boston, Mass. Copyright © 1982. All rights reserved.

and clothing executives convened earlier this year to back industry-standard formats for purchase orders, shipping documents, and other forms. Their purpose is to beat Asian rivals by making it easier for retailers to deal with U.S. suppliers. "This is the beginning of a revolution in our industry," says Milliken.[14]

COMPETITIVE FORCES

The top five competitors in four different industries are identified in Table 4–6. An important part of an external audit is to identify rival firms and to determine their strengths, weaknesses, capabilities, opportunities, threats, objectives, and strategies.

Collecting and evaluating information on competitors is essential for successful strategy formulation. Identifying major competitors is not always easy because many firms have divisions that compete in different industries. Most multidivisional firms

TABLE 4-6   The Five Top U.S. Competitors in Four Different Industries in 1993

	1993 SALES IN $ MILLIONS	PERCENTAGE CHANGE FROM 1992	1993 PROFITS IN $ MILLIONS	PERCENTAGE CHANGE FROM 1992
AEROSPACE				
Boeing	25,438	–16	1,244	–20
United Technologies	21,081	–4	487	—
McDonnell Douglas	14,474	–17	359	–49
Lockheed	13,071	+29	422	+21
Grumman	3,249	–7	66	–45
FOREST PRODUCTS				
International Paper	13,685	+1	289	+104
Georgia Pacific	12,330	+4	–34	+73
Weyerhaeuser	9,544	+3	+579	+56
Kimberly Clark	6,972	–2	+510	+278
Champion International	5,068	+3	–65	—
COMPUTERS				
IBM	62,716	–3	–8,101	–63
Hewlett-Packard	20,317	+24	+1,177	+114
Xerox	14,601	–1	–126	+88
Digital Computer	13,636	–4	–93	—
Unisys	7,742	–8	+565	+57
PUBLISHING				
Time Warner	6,581	+4	–164	—
Dun & Bradstreet	4,710	–1	+428	–23
Times Mirror	3,714	+3	+165	+365
Gannett	3,641	+5	398	+15
Reader's Digest	2,822	0	272	+7

generally do not provide sales and profit information on a divisional basis for competitive reasons. Also, privately held firms do not publish any financial or marketing information.

Despite the problems mentioned above, financial information on leading competitors in particular industries can be found in publications such as *Moody's Manuals, Standard Corporation Descriptions, Value Line Investment Surveys, Ward's Business Directory, Dun's Business Rankings, Standard and Poor's Industry Surveys, Industry Week, Forbes, Fortune, Business Week,* and *Inc.* In addition, the *Million Dollar Directory* lists key personnel, products, divisions, and SIC codes for over 160,000 U.S. public and private companies whose revenues exceed $500,000. *Standard and Poor's Register of Corporate Directors and Executives* and the *Directory of Corporate Affiliations* are other excellent sources of competitive information. Questions about competitors such as those presented in Table 4–7 are important to address in performing an external audit.

Competition in virtually all industries can be described as intense, and sometimes cutthroat. For example, when RJR Nabisco was seriously wounded with management changes and a record $25 billion leveraged buyout, its major competitor, Philip Morris, did everything it could to take advantage of the situation. Philip Morris used pricing tactics and expanded its sales force in a direct effort to muscle RJR out of the market. "I can assure you that we plan to take advantage of any opportunities the changed situation at RJR may bring," said Philip Morris's William Murray. One analyst commented, "These are war games."

In a recent article, seven characteristics were given that describe the most competitive companies in America: (1) Market share matters; The 90th share point isn't as important as the 91st, and nothing is more dangerous than falling to 89; (2)

TABLE 4-7   Key Questions About Competitors

1. What are the major competitors' strengths?
2. What are the major competitors' weaknesses?
3. What are the major competitors' objectives and strategies?
4. How will the major competitors most likely respond to current economic, social, cultural, demographic, geographic, political, governmental, technological, and competitive trends affecting our industry?
5. How vulnerable are the major competitors to our alternative company strategies?
6. How vulnerable are our alternative strategies to successful counterattack by our major competitors?
7. How are our products or services positioned relative to major competitors?
8. To what extent are new firms entering and old firms leaving this industry?
9. What key factors have resulted in our present competitive position in this industry?
10. How have the sales and profit rankings of major competitors in the industry changed over recent years? Why have these rankings changed that way?
11. What is the nature of supplier and distributor relationships in this industry?
12. To what extent could substitute products or services be a threat to competitors in this industry?

Understand and remember precisely what business you are in; (3) Whether it's broke or not, fix it—make it better, not just products, but the whole company if necessary; (4) Innovate or evaporate; particularly in technology-driven businesses, nothing quite recedes like success; (5) Acquisition is essential to growth; the most successful purchases are in niches that add a technology or a related market; (6) People make a difference; tired of hearing it? Too bad; (7) There is no substitute for quality and no greater threat than failing to be cost competitive on a global basis; these are complementary concepts, not mutually exclusive ones.[15]

Competitive Intelligence Programs. Good competitive intelligence in business, as in the military, is one of the keys to success. The more information and knowledge a firm can obtain about its competitors, the more likely it can formulate and implement effective strategies. Major competitors' weaknesses can represent external opportunities; major competitors' strengths may represent key threats.

Firms need an effective competitive intelligence (CI) program. The three basic missions of a CI program are (1) to provide a general understanding of an industry and its competitors, (2) to identify areas in which competitors are vulnerable and to asseses the impact strategic actions would have on competitors, and (3) to identify potential moves that a competitor might make that would endanger a firm's position in the market.[16] Competitive information is equally applicable for strategy formulation, implementation, and evaluation decisions. An effective CI program allows all areas of a firm to access consistent and verifiable information in making decisions. All members of an organization, from the chief executive officer to custodians, are valuable intelligence agents and should feel a part of the CI process. Special characteristics of a successful CI program include flexibility, usefulness, timeliness, and cross-functional cooperation.

The increasing emphasis on competitive analysis in the United States is evidenced by more and more corporations putting this function on their organizational charts under job titles such as Director of Competitive Analysis, Competitive Strategy Manager, Director of Information Services, or Associate Director of Competitive Assessment. The responsibilities of a Director of Competitive Analysis include planning, collecting data, analyzing data, facilitating the process of gathering and analyzing information, disseminating intelligence on a timely basis, researching special issues, and recognizing what information is important and who needs to know. Competitive intelligence is not corporate espionage because 95 percent of the information a company needs to make strategic decisions is available and accessible to the public. Dialog, for example, is a large data base that offers an exclusive menu of competitive intelligence information. Other excellent sources of competitive information include trade journals, want ads, newspaper articles, and government filings, as well as customers, suppliers, distributors, and competitors themselves.

Computer-based filing systems are often used to assimilate newspaper clippings, annual reports, and similar information about competitors. The *Thomas Register* and *Directory of American Firms Operating in Foreign Countries* are helpful for identifying suppliers, distributors, and potential competitors. Telephone interviews can also be an efficient and effective means of gathering competitive intelligence. For example, to learn details about expansion of a competitor's facility, strategists could call the local tax assessor. The Occupational Safety and Health Administration could be called to obtain information about production capacity and utilization in a given industry. It is important to study an organization's competitors carefully when preparing a business policy case analysis.

Marriott is one American company that does an excellent job gathering and using competitive intelligence. Before building Fairfield Inns, a team of Marriott employees spent 6 months traveling the country staying in rival hotels/motels and gathering information about service, quality, walls, beds, food, and service. This team identified rival firms' strengths and weaknesses in nearly every aspect of hotel/motel operations, from soap to soundproof rooms. Intelligence officers agree that unethical tactics should never be used to obtain information. However, poorly performing firms sometimes resort to this practice. Table 4–8 reveals some new ways to battle unethical information-gathering tactics.

Some CI activities are illegal and/or unethical, but determining which is often a matter of opinion for a jury to decide. Mindy Kotler, president of Search Associates, says, "If you talk to a Japanese executive, he says, 'Of course information gathering is part of the job.' If you ask a typical Harvard MBA, he says, 'It's the company librarian's job.' " Gathering competitive intelligence should be a part of everyone's job in an organization. Marriott and Motorola—another American company that does a particularly good job of gathering competitive intelligence—agree that all the information you could wish for can be collected without resorting to unethical tactics. They keep their intelligence staffs small, usually under five people, and spend less than $200,000 per year on gathering competitive intelligence.[17]

Cooperation Among Competitors. Strategies that stress cooperation among competitors are being used more and more. Three of Europe's largest computer firms recently changed from foe to friend as they agreed to work together on a strategy to link Europe's diverse computer systems. The three companies, Germany's Siemens-Nixdorf Information Systems AG, France's Cie des Machines Bull, and Italy's Ing. C. Olivetti & Co., excluded the United Kingdom firm ICL Ltd., which is 80-percent owned by Fujitsu.

Corning has successfully formed fifteen joint ventures with foreign rival firms, including agreements with BICC in Britain, Ciba-Geigy in Switzerland, Cie Financiere des Fibres Optiques in France, Siemens in West Germany, Finimi in Belgium, Asahi Glass in Japan, Beijing Electronic Glass Engineering Technology in China, NGK Insulators in Japan, Samsung Group in South Korea, and Australian Consolidated Industries in Australia. The perceived need for cooperation between competitors has turned even bitter enemies into friends. For example, Warner-Lambert Inc. of the United States recently agreed to pool all of its nonprescription drug operations with the United Kingdom drug makers Wellcome PLC and Galaxo Holdings PLC.

Grossack and Heenan assert that the idea of joining forces with a competitor is not easily accepted by Americans, who often view cooperation and partnerships with skepticism and suspicion.[18] Indeed, joint ventures and cooperative arrangements among competitors demand a certain amount of trust to combat paranoia about whether one firm will injure the other. However, multinational firms are becoming more globally cooperative, and increasing numbers of domestic firms are joining forces with competitive foreign firms to reap mutual benefits.

Intel and Texas Instruments recently agreed to a cooperative mutual-gain strategy whereby the two firms will swap semiconductor designs and manufacturing technologies for developing computer chips and act as alternate suppliers for each other. This technology exchange will allow both companies to gain market share in the burgeoning market for application-specific integrated circuits (ASICs), the fastest growing segment of the semiconductor industry. Kathryn Harrigan at Columbia University says: "Within a decade most companies will be members of teams that compete against each other."

TABLE 4-8   New Ways to Battle Corporate Spooks

Though the vast majority of companies don't resort to James Bond tactics when gathering information on competitors, a few just can't resist. Hitachi tried to pay $525,000 to IBM employees for some of the Big Blue's trade secrets in the early 1980s but was caught in a sophisticated sting operation. Before that, a competitor flew a plane over a Du Pont plant and snapped pictures to help figure out the factory's capacity. More recently, Procter & Gamble has charged that a number of companies used spies to get hold of its secret recipe for soft cookies.

How can you avoid being victimized? Educating employees about the seriousness of leaking sensitive information is a good place to start. Warn your workers about companies that hire head-hunting firms to grill unwitting job candidates on business plans and R & D secrets. Assume that any consulting firm or organization that calls and says it is doing an industry study is digging up nuggets for the competition. Ben Zour, a senior analyst for business research at Eastman Kodak, says, "You have to make employees sensitive to the fact that if they leak, they will lose their jobs." Or worse—if the breach is serious enough, an employee could face criminal prosecution.

Every company tries to keep competitors from hiring away its best employees. But be careful too about pulling that trick yourself. In a recent case in Scotland, an American electronics firm hired an accomplished marketing manager from a competing multinational. A month later he returned to his old company—with some of the firm's European business plans.

Next to leaks, electronic eavesdropping poses the biggest threat to your trove of secrets. Unless you've done a thorough electronic sweep recently, assume anything you communicate by telex, electronic mail, fax, or phone is up for grabs. An estimated seventy foreign governments have the ability to read what multinationals transmit into their countries. Jan Herring, a consultant with Futures Group of Glastonbury, Connecticut, warns that often an American executive will attend an important meeting in, say, Japan and have the conference room swept for electronic bugs, then will return to his hotel and tell his U.S. colleagues the results of the meeting—over a phone line tapped by a competitor. Says Herring, "You find companies that lose by $600 on a $6 million bid, and you wonder why."

Electronic eavesdropping devices are getting ever more sophisticated. At Spy Shops International in Miami, a particularly popular device is a laser gun that can hear conversations up to a half mile away by measuring sound vibrations in an office window. Another gadget can read your computer screen some two blocks away by picking up radio waves emitted by the machine. Naturally, the store also sells countermeasures: an apparent cigarette pack that vibrates in your pocket when someone who's wired walks in, for example, or a computer that foils wire taps by scrambling messages.

If you discover a bug, don't despair. Companies that resort to illegal or unethical spying are very likely in desperate straits. If you can pinpoint what they're trying to learn by spying on your company, chances are you have spotted a weakness and can strike back.

Source: Brian Dumaine, "Corporate Spies Snoop to Conquer," used by permission of *Fortune* (November 7, 1988): 72.

American companies often enter alliances primarily to avoid investments, being more interested in reducing the costs and risks of entering new businesses or markets than in acquiring new skills. In contrast, "learning from the partner" is a major reason why Asian and European firms enter into cooperative agreements. American firms too should place "learning" high on the list of reasons to cooperate with competitors. American companies often form alliances with Asian firms to gain an understanding of their manufacturing excellence, but Asian competence in this area is not easily transferable. Manufacturing excellence is a complex system that includes employee training and involvement, integration with suppliers, statistical process controls, value engineering, and design. In contrast, American know-how in technology and related areas can more easily be imitated. American firms thus need to be careful not to give away more "intelligence" than they receive in cooperative agreements with rival Asian firms.

SOURCES OF EXTERNAL INFORMATION

A wealth of strategic information is available to organizations from both published and unpublished sources. Unpublished sources include customer surveys, market research, speeches at professional and shareholders' meetings, television programs, interviews, and conversations with stakeholders. Published sources of strategic information include periodicals, journals, reports, government documents, abstracts, books, directories, newspapers, and manuals. Computerization has made it easier today for firms to gather, assimilate, and evaluate information. Recall that information technology is a key dimension in performing an external audit.

Indexes. A number of excellent indexes reveal the location of strategic information by subject, topic, source, author, company, and industry. Indexes can save managers considerable time and effort in identifying and evaluating opportunities and threats. A description of major indexes available for locating information is provided in Table 4–9.

On-line Data Bases. In addition to indexes, on-line data bases are being used increasingly to locate strategic information. On-line data bases allow individuals who have no computer programming skills to search hundreds of publications efficiently for information by subject, industry, name of organization, Standard Industrial Classification (SIC) code, type of product, geographic area, or type of publication. There are approximately 2,000 organizations offering data bases. The *Directory of Online Databases* is an excellent reference book on data bases. It is published quarterly and describes over 4,000 on-line data bases.

An excellent on-line data base for accessing economic information is *Economics Abstracts International.* For social, cultural, demographic, and environmental information, *Sociological Abstracts* is a good on-line data base. A widely used data base for political, governmental, and legal information is the *Public Affairs Information Service* (PAIS) *International.* The *National Technical Information Service* (NTIS) is an excellent on-line data base for technology-related information. An excellent index for locating information on competitors is *PIS Indexes,* which incorporates the *F & S Index of Corporations & Industries.*

Several other data bases are widely used, including *ABI/Inform,* the largest reference business data base. *ABI/Inform* has 650 business and management publications on-line and makes information accessible from many areas, including finance, economics, manufacturing, technology, human resources, and data processing. Most of the data accessible by *ABI/Inform* is updated weekly.

Compact Disclosure is another on-line data base that includes financial and statistical information on about 12,000 publicly owned companies and is updated weekly. In addition, *CD/International* provides operating data and ratios on 2,000 American and 1,400 foreign firms, as well as evaluative comments to accompany the data. A printed version of these data is called *Worldscope.* *Compustat* is another excellent on-line data base that provides financial and performance data on 6,250 companies in over 200 industries.

PTS U.S. Time Series and *PTS International Time Series* are data bases that monitor over 150,000 time series. Time series measure variables such as productivity rates,

TABLE 4-9   Major Indexes That Reference Economic, Social, Political, Technological, and Competitive Information

Name of Index	Type of Information	Description
Applied Science & Technology Index	Technological	A subject index that covers over 200 selected journals in the fields of aeronautics and space science, automation, chemistry, construction, earth sciences, electricity and electronics, engineering, industrial and mechanical arts, materials, mathematics, metallurgy, physics, telecommunication, transportation, and related subjects. *ASTI* is published monthly.
Business Periodicals Index	Economic Social Political Technological Competitive	This is probably the best known index for its overall subject coverage of selected periodicals in the following fields of business: accounting, advertising and public relations, automation, banking, communications, economics, finance and investments, insurance, labor, management, marketing, taxation, and also specific businesses, industries, and trades. This index also includes a review of books appearing in the journals it indexes, listed together under the heading "Book Reviews." *BPI* is published monthly.
Funk & Scott Index of Corporations & Industries	Competitive	This is the best index for current information on companies and industries. It covers a wide selection of business, industrial, and financial periodicals and also a few brokerage house reports. The yellow pages in the weeklies and the green pages in cumulated issues list articles (or data in articles) on all SIC (Standard Industrial Classification) industries; the white pages list articles on companies. Since many of the entries refer to very brief citations, it is important to note that major articles are designated by a black dot, which precedes the abbreviated title of the journal. *F & S* is published weekly.
F & S Index International	Competitive Political	A companion of the index above, covering articles on foreign companies and industries that have appeared in some 1,000 foreign and domestic periodicals and other documents. It is arranged in three parts: (1) by SIC number or product; (2) by region and country; (3) by company. *F & SI* is published monthly.

consumption patterns, prices, foreign trade, population statistics, income levels, and agricultural factors over a period of time. The *PTS U.S. Time Series* is updated three times a year and the *PTS International Time Series* is updated monthly; graphic displays of information from these sources are available.

Another commonly used data base is the *Harvard Business Review/Online*, also called the *HBR/Online*. It covers a wide range of subjects that include accounting, organizational behavior, marketing, industry analysis, international trade, business ethics, computers, time management, and strategic management. The subscriber can

TABLE 4-9 *Continued*

Public Affairs Information Service Bulletin	Social[a] Political	This is a selective listing in the areas of economic and social conditions, public administration, and international relations, published in English throughout the world. The important differences in this index are (1) it only selectively indexes journals, to cover those articles pertinent to its subject coverage; (2) it covers not only periodical articles but also selected books, pamphlets, government publications, and reports of public and private agencies. There is a companion index called *Public Affairs Information Service: Foreign Language Index*. The *PAIS* is published weekly.
Readers' Guide to Periodical Literature	Economic Social Political Technological Competitive	A very popular author and subject index to periodicals published in the United States. The *RGPL* is published bimonthly.
Social Sciences Index	Social Economic Political	A subject and author index to articles in over 260 journals that cover the fields of anthropology, area studies, economics, environmental science, geography, law and criminology, medical sciences, political science, psychology, public administration, sociology, and related subjects. At the back of each issue is an author listing of book reviews that appear in the indexed journals. The *SSI* is published quarterly.
New York Times Index	Economic Social Political Technological Competitive	This is an excellent and very detailed index of articles published by the *New York Times* newspaper. The index is arranged alphabetically and includes many helpful cross-references. The *NYTI* is published bimonthly.
Wall Street Journal/ Barrons Index	Economic Social Political Technological Competitive	A valuable index of *Wall Street Journal* and *Barrons* articles. Each issue is in two parts, corporate news and general news. The index includes a list of book reviews. The *WSJI* is published monthly.

[a]"Social" includes cultural, demographic, and environmental information; "Political" includes governmental and legal information.

Source: Adapted from Lorna M. Daniells, *Business Information Sources* (Los Angeles: University of California Press, 1976), 14–17.

print a full text of every article, citation, or abstract published in the *Harvard Business Review* from 1976 to the present. Three other excellent data bases tailored for home users are *Compuserve, The Source,* and *Dow Jones On Line.* All three of these services have grown over 100 percent annually since 1980.

Library Publications. Important published sources of strategic information are provided in Tables 4–10 through 4–14. Some of the most widely used sources are described in Table 4–15.

TABLE 4-10   Sources of Economic Information

Economic Outlook

American Register of Exporters and Importers

Worldcasts

Federal Reserve Bank of St. Louis, *Rate of Change in Economic Data for Ten Industrial Countries*

Handbook of Basic Economic Statistics

National Bureau of Economic Research publications

Marketing Economic Guide

U.S. Council of Economic Advisors, *Economic Indicators*

Chase Econometric Associates' publications

U.S. Bureau of Labor Statistics, *Monthly Labor Review*

U.S. Bureau of Labor Statistics, *Handbook of Labor Statistics*

U.S. Bureau of the Census, *Statistical Abstract of the United States*

Survey of Business

Business Conditions Digest

Survey of Manufacturers

U.S. Department of Commerce, *Survey of Current Business*

U.S. Department of Commerce, *Business Statistics*

U.S. Department of Commerce, *Long-Term Economic Growth*

U.S. Department of Commerce, *Foreign Economic Trends and Their Implications for the United States*

U.S. Industrial Outlook

Securities and Exchange Commission, *Survey of Buying Power*

United Nations, *Yearbook of International Trade Statistics*

U.S. Board of Governors of the Federal Reserve System, *Federal Reserve Bulletin*

Kiplinger Washington Letter

Guide to Foreign Trade Statistics

Census of Retail Trade

Census of Wholesale Trade

Index of Economic Articles

TABLE 4-11   Sources of Social, Cultural, Demographic, and Environmental Information

American Statistics Index

Demographic Yearbook

Social Indicators and Social Reporting

Brookings Institute Report

Ford Foundation Report

World Bank Atlas

Annals of the American Academy of Political and Social Sciences

Conference Board, *Business Outlook*

Yearbook of International Organizations

Chamber of Commerce publications

Great Britain Central Statistical Office, *Social Trends*

County Business Patterns

Census of Populations

Census of Housing

Census of Agriculture

Census of Manufacturers

Guide to Consumer Markets

County and City Data Book

United Nations Educational, Scientific, andCultural Organization, *Statistical Yearbook*

Dun & Bradstreet, *Principal International Business*

Telephone directories

City directories

Public opinion polls

TABLE 4-12   Sources of Political, Governmental, and Legal Information

Monthly *Catalog of United States Government Publications*	Chamber of Commerce publications
Federal Register	*Kiplinger Washington Letter*
Directory of American Firms Operating in Foreign Countries	Lobbyists
	U.S. Congress, *Official Congressional Directory*
Code of Federal Regulations	*Census of Governments*
Congressional Information Service publications	*American Statistics Index*
Bureau of National Affairs publications	*Congressional Information Service Annual*

TABLE 4-13   Sources of Technological Information

Scientific and Technical Information Source	*World Guide to Trade Associations*
Trade journals and industrial reports	University reports
Department of Defense Annual Reports	Congressional reports
Research and Development Directory	Patent records
Proceedings to professional meetings	
Annual Report of the National Science Foundation	

FORECASTING TOOLS AND TECHNIQUES

Forecasts are educated assumptions about future trends and events. Forecasting is a complex activity due to factors such as technological innovation, cultural changes, new products, improved services, stronger competitors, shifts in government priorities, changing social values, unstable economic conditions, and unforeseen events. Managers often must rely upon published forecasts to identify key external opportunities and threats effectively.

Many of the publications cited in Tables 4–10 through 4–14 forecast external variables. Several examples include *Industry Week's* "Trends and Forecasts," *Business Week's* "Investment Outlook," Standard & Poor's *Earnings Forecaster,* and the *U.S. Industrial Outlook.* The reputation and continued success of these publications depend to some extent upon accurate forecasts, so published sources of information can offer the best projections available for some variables.

When published forecasts of key external or internal variables are not available, organizations must develop their own projections. Most organizations forecast (project) their own revenues and profits annually. Organizations sometimes

TABLE 4-14   Sources of Information on Competitors

Annual reports of companies	Trade association publications
Directory of Corporate Affiliations	*County Business Patterns*
Securities and Exchange Commission, 10K Reports	*County and City Data Book*
U.S. Industrial Outlook	*Fortune*
Value Line Investment Survey	*Dun's Business Month*
Moody's Industrial Manual	*Industry Week*, "Trends and Forecasts"
Moody's Investors Service	*Industry Week*, "Financial Analysis of Industry"
Moody's Handbook of Common Stocks	*Business Week*, "Survey of Capital Requirements of Nonfinancial Corporations"
Moody's Bank and Finance Manual	
Moody's Municipal & Government Manual	*Business Week*, "Annual Survey of International Corporate Performance"
Moody's Public Utilities Manual	
Moody's Transportation Manual	*Business Week*, "Survey of Corporate Performance"
Dun & Bradstreet, *Million Dollar Directory*	*Business Week*, "Investment Outlook"
Dun & Bradstreet, *Reference Book*	*Business Week*, "Annual Survey of Bank Performance"
Dun & Bradstreet, *Key Business Ratios*	*Barron's*
Standard & Poor's Corp., *Industry Surveys*	*Forbes*, "Annual Report on American Industry"
Standard & Poor's Corp., *Standard Corporation Records*	*Nation's Business*, "Lesson of Leadership"
Standard & Poor's Corp., *Analyst's Handbook*	*Census of Manufacturers*
Standard & Poor's Corp., *Earnings Forecast*	*Encyclopedia of Associations*
Standard & Poor's Corp., *Bond Guide*	*Facts on File*
Standard & Poor's Corp., *Security Owners Stock Guide*	U.S. Department of Commerce, *Overseas Business Reports*
Standard & Poor's Corp., *The Outlook*	
Standard & Poor's *Register of Corporations, Directors and Executives*	Conference Board, *Business Outlook*
	Starch Marketing
Barometer of Small Business	*U.S. Industrial Directory*
Dow Jones & Co., *Dow Jones Investor's Handbook*	*Fortune 500 Directory*
U.S. Internal Revenue Service, *Statistics of Income: Corporation Income Tax Returns*	*Wall Street Transcript*
	F & S Index of Corporate Change
Robert Morris Associates, *Annual Statement Studies*	*Investment Dealers' Digest*
Troy, Leo, *Almanac of Business and Industrial Financial Ratios*	*Conference Board Record*
	Local newspapers
U.S. Department of Commerce, *International Economic Indicators and Competitive Trends*	

forecast market share or customer loyalty in local areas. Since forecasting is so important in strategic management and since the ability to forecast (in contrast to the ability to use a forecast) is essential, selected forecasting tools are examined further here.

Forecasting tools can be broadly categorized into two groups: quantitative techniques and qualitative techniques. Quantitative forecasts are most appropriate when historical data are available and when the relationships among key variables are expected to remain the same in the future. The three basic types of quantitative forecasting techniques are econometric models, regression, and trend extrapolation. *Econometric models* are based on simultaneous systems of regression equations that forecast variables such as interest rates and money supply. With the advent of sophisticated computers, econometric models have become the most widely used approach for forecasting economic variables.

All quantitative forecasts, regardless of statistical sophistication and complexity, are based on historical relationships among key variables. *Linear regression,* for example, is based on the assumption that the future will be just like the past—which, of course, it never is. As historical relationships become less stable, quantitative forecasts becomes less accurate.

The six basic qualitative approaches to forecasting are (1) sales-force estimate, (2) juries of executive opinion, (3) anticipatory surveys or market research, (4) scenario forecasts, (5) delphi forecasts, and (6) brainstorming. Qualitative or judgmental forecasts are particularly useful when historical data are not available or when constituent variables are expected to change significantly in the future.

Due to advancements in computer technology, quantitative forecasting techniques are usually cheaper and faster than qualitative methods. Quantitative techniques such as multiple regression can generate "measures of error" that allow a manager to estimate the degree of confidence associated with a given forecast. Forecasting tools must be used carefully or the results can be more misleading than helpful, but qualitative techniques require more intuitive judgment than do quantitative ones. Managers sometimes erroneously "forecast" what they would like to occur. The cost, popularity, and complexity of different forecasting techniques are compared in the following table.

The Costs, Popularity, and Complexity of Quantitative Versus Qualitative Forecasting Techniques

	COST	POPULARITY	COMPLEXITY
QUANTITATIVE TECHNIQUES			
Economic Models	High	High	High
Regression	High	High	Medium
Trend Exploration	Medium	High	Medium
QUALITATIVE TECHNIQUES			
Sales-force Estimate	Low	High	Low
Nominal Grouping Technique	Low	High	Low
Juries of Executive Opinion	Low	High	Low
Anticipatory Surveys and Market Research	Medium	Medium	Medium
Scenario	Low	Medium	Low
Delphi	Low	Medium	Medium
Brainstorming	Low	Medium	Medium

Source: Adapted in part from J. A. Pearce II and R. B. Robinson, Jr., "Environmental Forecasting: Key to Strategic Management," *Business* (July–September 1983): 6.

TABLE 4-15   Key Sources of External Information

SOURCE	BRIEF DESCRIPTION
Statistical Abstract of the U.S. (published annually)	Provides social, demographic, environmental, political, and economic information about the United States.
United States Industrial Outlook (published annually)	Provides industry forecasts, profiles, data, trends, and projections. Industries are classified by type of business and by SIC Code.
Survey of Business (published quarterly)	Provides information concerning the economic outlook of specific industries. Many graphs are given.
Business Conditions Digest (published monthly)	Provides charts and graphs of past, present, and forecasted unemployment rates, productivity and income data, consumption patterns, and prices of products and services.
Survey of Manufacturers (published annually)	Provides manufacturing data for many industries, including the value of inventories, plant and equipment expenditures, book value of assets, rental payments, etc.
Predicasts (published quarterly)	A guide to corporate organization developments, including liquidations, name changes, new companies, joint ventures, bankruptcies, and divestitures.
Survey of Buying Power (published annually)	Provides information on households, population shifts, disposable income, and retail sales by geographic area.
Federal Reserve Bulletin (published monthly)	Includes congressional reports, staff studies, announcements, legal developments in the monetary and banking systems.
Forbes (published weekly)	A magazine that focuses on current business issues and topics.
Business Week (published weekly)	A magazine that contains current business news, including corporate strategy articles.
Fortune (published biweekly)	A popular magazine that reports news and events in the business world.

No forecast is perfect, and some forecasts are even wildly inaccurate. This fact accents the need for strategists to devote sufficient time and effort to study the underlying bases for published forecasts and to develop internal forecasts of their own. Key external opportunities and threats can be effectively identified only through good forecasts. Accurate forecasts can provide major competitive advantages for organizations. Forecasts are vital to the strategic-management process and to the success of organizations.

Making Assumptions. Planning would be impossible without assumptions! McConkey defines assumptions as "best present estimates of the impact of major external factors, over which the manager has little if any control, but which may exert a significant impact on performance or the ability to achieve desired results.[19] Strategists are faced with countless variables

TABLE 4-15   *Continued*

Federal Register (published daily)	Gives all public regulations and legal notices issued by federal agencies.
Trade journals	Provide news, forecasts, changes, and developments in particular industries. Examples are *Hardware Ace* and *The Underwriter*.
Securities and Exchange Commission's *10K Reports* (published annually)	Gives detailed descriptive and financial information on a specific company.
Annual reports (published annually)	Published by corporations for shareholders and interested parties. Reveal company plans, organization, and financial condition.
Moody's Industrial Manual (published annually)	Provides information on firms' capital structures, histories, financial conditions, and bond ratings.
The Dun & Bradstreet Corporation	Publishes many reference indexes, including *Market Profile Analysis, Dun's Business Rankings, The Billion Dollar Directory, Who Owns Whom,* and *Principal International Businesses.*
United States Census of Manufacturers (published annually)	Presents manufacturing data by state and area within states. Includes data on employment, payroll, number of workers, hours, wages, capital expenditures, and the like.
Value Line (published weekly)	Provides investment information on companies and industries. Evaluates companies and industries on financial criteria.
Guide to Consumer Markets (published annually)	Provides detailed consumer information on the distribution and prices of goods and services, labor force changes, and other key areas.
Chambers of Commerce	Provide valuable local business information such as traffic patterns, locations of particular businesses, household income levels, etc.
Facts on File (published weekly)	Weekly summaries of world business news are provided.

and imponderables that can be neither controlled nor predicted with 100-percent accuracy.

By identifying future occurrences that could have a major effect on the firm and making reasonable assumptions about those factors, strategists can carry the strategic-management process forward. Assumptions are needed only for future trends and events that are most likely to have a significant effect on the company's business. Based on the best information at the time, assumptions serve as checkpoints on the validity of strategies. If future occurrences deviate significantly from assumptions, strategists know that corrective actions may be needed. Without reasonable assumptions, the strategy-formulation process could not proceed effectively. Firms that have the best information generally make the most "accurate" assumptions, and this can lead to major competitive advantages.

Illustrated in Figure 4–3, Porter's five-forces model of competitive analysis is a widely used approach for developing strategies in many industries. The intensity of competition among firms varies widely across industries. According to Porter, the nature of competitiveness in a given industry can be viewed as a composite of five forces:

1. Rivalry among competitive firms.
2. Potential entry of new competitors.
3. Potential development of substitute products.
4. Bargaining power of suppliers.
5. Bargaining power of consumers.

Rivalry Among Competing Firms. Rivalry among competing firms is usually the most powerful of the five competitive forces. The strategies pursued by one firm can be successful only to the extent that they provide competitive advantage over the strategies being pursued by rival firms. Changes in strategy by one firm may be met with retaliatory countermoves, such as lowering price, enhancing quality, adding features, providing services, extending warranties, and increasing advertising.

The intensity of rivalry among competing firms tends to increase as the number of competitors increases, as competitors become more equal in size and capability, as demand for the industry's products declines, and as price cutting becomes common. Rivalry also increases when consumers can switch brands easily, when barriers to leaving the market are high, when fixed costs are high, when the product is perishable, when rival firms are diverse in strategies, origins, and culture, and when mergers and acquisitions are common in the industry. As rivalry among competing firms intensifies, industry profits decline, in some cases to the point where an industry becomes inherently unattractive.

FIGURE 4-3 The Five-forces Model of Competition

Potential Entry of New Competitors. Whenever new firms can easily enter a particular industry, the intensity of competitiveness among firms increases. Barriers to entry, however, can include the need to gain economies of scale quickly, the need to gain technology and specialized know-how, the lack of experience, strong customer loyalty, strong brand preferences, large capital requirements, lack of adequate distribution channels, government regulatory policies, tariffs, lack of access to raw materials, possession of patents, undesirable locations, counterattack by entrenched firms, and potential saturation of the market.

Despite numerous barriers to entry, new firms sometimes enter industries with higher-quality products, lower prices, and substantial marketing resources. Compaq's entering the personal computer market and Wal-Mart's entering the discount market are examples. The strategist's job is, therefore, to identify potential new firms entering the market, to monitor the new rival firms' strategies, to counterattack as needed, and to capitalize on existing strengths and opportunities.

Development of Substitute Products. In many industries, firms are in close competition with producers of substitute products in other industries. Examples are plastic container producers competing with glass, paperboard, and aluminum can producers, or acetaminophen manufacturers competing with other manufacturers of pain and headache remedies. The presence of substitute products puts a ceiling on the price that can be charged before the consumers will switch to the substitute product.

Competitive pressures arising from substitute products increase as the relative price of substitute products declines and as consumers' switching costs decrease. The competitive strength of substitute products is best measured by the inroads into market share those products obtain, as well as those firms' plans for increased capacity and market penetration.

Bargaining Power of Suppliers. The bargaining power of suppliers affects the intensity of competition in an industry, especially when there is a large number of suppliers, when there are only a few good substitute raw materials, or when the cost of switching raw materials is especially costly. It is often in the best interest of both suppliers and producers to assist each other with reasonable prices, improved quality, development of new services, just-in-time deliveries, and reduced inventory costs, thus enhancing long-term profitability for all concerned.

Firms may pursue a backward integration strategy to gain control or ownership of suppliers. This strategy is especially effective when suppliers are unreliable, too costly, or not capable of meeting the firm's needs on a consistent basis. Firms can generally negotiate more favorable terms with suppliers when backward integration is a commonly used strategy among rival firms in an industry.

Bargaining Power of Consumers. When customers are concentrated, large, or buy in volume, their bargaining power represents a major force affecting intensity of competition in an industry. Rival firms may offer extended warranties or special services to gain customer loyalty whenever the bargaining power of consumers is substantial. Bargaining power of consumers is also higher when the products being purchased are standard or undifferentiated. When this is the case, consumers can often negotiate selling price, warranty coverage, and accessory packages to a greater extent.

INDUSTRY ANALYSIS: THE EXTERNAL FACTOR EVALUATION (EFE) MATRIX

An *External Factor Evaluation (EFE) Matrix* allows strategists to summarize and evaluate economic, social, cultural, demographic, environmental, political, governmental, legal, technological, and competitive information.[20] There are five steps in developing an EFE Matrix:

1. List critical success factors as identified in the external-audit process. Include a total of from ten to twenty factors, including both opportunities and threats affecting the firm and its industry. List the opportunities first and then the threats. Be as specific as possible, using percentages, ratios, and comparative numbers whenever possible.

2. Assign to each factor a weight that ranges from 0.0 (not important) to 1.0 (very important). The weight indicates the relative importance of that factor to being successful in the firm's industry. Opportunities often receive higher weights than threats, but threats too can receive high weights if they are especially severe or threatening. Appropriate weights can be determined by comparing successful with unsuccessful competitors or by discussing the factor and reaching a group consensus. The summation of all weights assigned to the factors must equal 1.0.

3. Assign a 1-to-4 rating to each critical success factor to indicate how effectively the firm's current strategies respond to the factor, where 4 = the response is superior, 3 = the response is above average, 2 = the response is average, and 1 = the response is poor. Ratings are based on effectiveness of the firm's strategies. Ratings are thus company-based, whereas the weights in Step 2 are industry-based!

4. Multiply each factor's weight by its rating to determine a weighted score.

5. Sum the weighted scores for each variable to determine the total weighted score for the organization.

Regardless of the number of key opportunities and threats included in an EFE Matrix, the highest possible total weighted score for an organization is 4.0 and the lowest possible total weighted score is 1.0. The average total weighted score is 2.5. A total weighted score of 4.0 indicates that an organization is responding in an outstanding way to existing opportunities and threats in its industry. In other words, the firm's strategies effectively take advantage of existing opportunities and minimize the potential adverse effect of external threats. A total score of 1.0 indicates the firm's strategies are not capitalizing on opportunities or avoiding external threats.

An example of an EFE Matrix is provided in Table 4–16. Note that "consumers are more willing to pay for biodegradable packages" is the most important factor affecting this industry, as indicated by the weight of 0.14. The firm in this example is pursuing strategies that effectively capitalize on this opportunity, as indicated by the rating of 4. The total weighted score of 2.64 indicates that this firm is just above average in its effort to pursue strategies that capitalize on external opportunities and avoid threats. It is important to note here that a thorough understanding of the factors being used in the EFE Matrix is more important than the actual weights and ratings assigned.

TABLE 4-16   A Sample External Factor Evaluation Matrix

CRITICAL SUCCESS FACTORS	WEIGHT	RATING	WEIGHTED SCORE
OPPORTUNITIES			
1. The U.S./Canadian Free Trade Agreement is spurring growth	.08	3	.24
2. Equity markets are healthy	.06	2	.12
3. Disposable income is increasing 3 percent annually	.11	1	.11
4. Consumers are more willing to pay for biodegradable packages	.14	4	.56
5. New software can shorten product life cycle	.09	4	.36
THREATS			
1. Japanese markets are closed to many U.S. products	.10	2	.20
2. The European Community has imposed new tariffs	.12	4	.48
3. The Russian Republic is unstable politically	.07	3	.21
4. Federal and state support for business is declining	.13	2	.26
5. Unemployment rates are increasing	.10	1	.10
TOTAL	1.00		2.64

Note: (1) The ratings indicate how effectively the firm's strategies respond to each factor, where 4 = the response is superior, 3 = the response is above average, 2 = the response is average, and 1 = the response is poor. (2) The total weighted score of 2.64 is above the average of 2.50.

THE COMPETITIVE PROFILE MATRIX (CPM)

The *Competitive Profile Matrix* identifies a firm's major competitors and their particular stengths and weaknesses in relation to a sample firm's strategic position. The weights and total weighted scores in both a CPM and EFE have the same meaning. However, the factors in a CPM include both internal and external issues; the ratings refer to strengths and weaknesses. There are some important differences between the EFE and CPM. First of all, the critical success factors in a CPM are broader; they do not include specific or factual data and may even focus on internal issues. The critical success factors in a CPM also are not grouped into opportunities and threats as they are in an EFE. In a CPM, the ratings and total weighted scores for rival firms can be compared to the sample firm. This comparative analysis provides important internal strategic information.

TABLE 4-17   A Competitive Profile Matrix

CRITICAL SUCCESS FACTORS	WEIGHT	SAMPLE COMPANY		COMPETITOR 1		COMPETITOR 2	
		RATING	WEIGHTED SCORE	RATING	WEIGHTED SCORE	RATING	WEIGHTED SCORE
Market Share	0.20	3	0.6	2	0.4	2	0.4
Price Competitiveness	0.20	1	0.2	4	0.8	1	0.2
Financial Position	0.40	2	0.8	1	0.4	4	1.6
Product Quality	0.10	4	0.4	3	0.3	3	0.3
Customer Loyalty	0.10	3	0.3	3	0.3	3	0.3
Total	1.00		2.3		2.2		2.8

Note: (1) The ratings values are as follows: 1 = major weakness, 2 = minor weakness, 3 = minor strength, 4 = major strength. (2) As indicated by the total weighted score of 2.8, Competitor 2 is strongest. (3) Only five critical success factors are included for simplicity; this is too few in actuality.

A sample Competitive Profile Matrix is provided in Table 4–17. In this example, "financial position" is the most important critical success factor, as indicated by a weight of 0.40. The sample company's "product quality" is superior, as evidenced by a rating of 4; competitor 1's "financial position" is poor, as indicated by a rating of 1; competitor 2 is the strongest firm overall as indicated by a total weighted score of 2.8.

A word on interpretation: Just because one firm receives a 3.2 rating and another receives a 2.8 rating in a Competitive Profile Matrix, it does not follow that the first firm is 20 percent better than the second. Numbers reveal the relative strength of firms, but their implied precision is an illusion. Numbers are not magic. The aim is not to arrive at a single magic number, but rather to assimilate and evaluate information in a meaningful way that aids in decision making.

Due to increasing turbulence in markets and industries around the world, the external audit has become an explicit and vital part of the strategic-management process. This chapter provides a framework for collecting and evaluating economic, social, cultural, demographic, environmental, political, governmental, legal, technological, and competitive information. Firms that do not mobilize and empower their managers and employees to identify, monitor, forecast, and evaluate key external forces may fail to anticipate emerging opportunities and threats and, consequently, may pursue ineffective strategies, miss opportunities, and invite organizational demise.

A major responsibility of strategists is to ensure development of an effective external-audit system. This includes using information technology to devise a competitive intelligence system that works. The external-audit approach described in this chapter can be effectively used by any size or type of organization. Typically the external-audit process is more informal in small firms, but the need to understand key trends and events is no less important for these firms. The EFE Matrix and five-forces model can help strategists evaluate the market and industry, but these tools must be accompanied by good intuitive judgment. Multinational firms especially need a systematic and effective external-audit system because external forces vary so greatly among foreign countries.

KEY TERMS AND CONCEPTS

Business Periodicals Index
Chief Information Officer (CIO)
Chief Technology Officer (CTO)
Competitive Advantage
Competitive Analysis
Competitive-Information System
Competitive Intelligence (CI)
Competitive Profile Matrix (CPM)
Computer-Aided Design and Manufacturing (CAD/CAM)
Cooperative Mutual Gain Strategies
Critical Success Factors
Director of Competitive Analysis
Directory of Online Databases
Econometric Models
Electronic Data Interchange (EDI)
Environmental Scanning

External Audit
External Factor Evaluation (EFE) Matrix
F & S Index of Corporations & Industries
Five-forces Model
Industry Analysis
Information Technology (IT)
Linear Regression
Multinational Corporations (MNCs)
On-line Data Bases
Spying on Competitors
Standard and Poor's *Industry Surveys*
Statistical Abstract of the United States
Total Weighted Score
Trend Extrapolation
U.S. Industrial Outlook
Value Line Investment Survey
Wall Street Journal/Barron's Index

ISSUES FOR REVIEW AND DISCUSSION

1. Explain how to conduct an external strategic-management audit.

2. Identify a recent economic, social, political, or technological trend that significantly affects financial institutions.

3. Discuss the following statement: Major opportunities and threats usually result from an interaction among key environmental trends rather than from a single external event or factor.

4. Identify two industries experiencing rapid technological changes and three industries that are experiencing little technological change. How does the need for technological forecasting differ in these industries? Why?

5. Use Porter's five-forces model to evaluate competitiveness within the U.S. banking industry.

6. What major forecasting techniques would you use to identify (1) economic opportunities and threats and (2) demographic opportunities and threats? Why are these techniques most appropriate?

7. How does the external audit affect other components of the strategic-management process?

8. As the owner of a small business, explain how you would organize a strategic-information scanning system. How would you organize such a system in a large organization?

9. Construct an EFE Matrix for an organization of your choice.

10. Make an appointment with a librarian at your university to learn how to use on-line data bases. Report your findings in class.

11. Give some advantages and disadvantages of cooperative versus competitive strategies.

12. As a local bank strategist, explain when you would use qualitative versus quantitative forecasts.

13. What is your forecast for interest rates and the stock market in the next several months? As the stock market moves up, do interest rates always move down? Why? What are the strategic implications of these trends?

14. Explain how information technology affects strategies of the organization where you most recently worked.

15. Let's say your boss develops an EFE Matrix that includes sixty-two factors. How would you suggest reducing the number of factors to twenty?

16. Select one of the current readings at the end of this chapter. Prepare a one-page written summary that includes your personal opinion of the article.

17. Discuss the ethics of gathering competitive intelligence.

18. Discuss the ethics of cooperating with rival firms.

1. John Diffenbach, "Corporate Environmental Analysis in Large U.S. Corporations," *Long Range Planning* 16, no. 3 (June 1983): 109.

2. York Freund, "Critical Success Factors," *Planning Review* 16, no. 4 (July–August 1988): 20.

3. Gregory Parsons, "Information Technology: A New Competitive Weapon," *Sloan Management Review* 25, no. 1 (Fall 1983): 5.

4. Michael Ashmore, "A New Approach for Managing Information Technology," *Journal of Business Strategy* 10, no. 1 (January/February 1989): 57–59.

5. Thomas Stewart, "Turning Around the Lord's Business," *Fortune* (September 25, 1989): 124.

6. Joe Schwartz and Thomas Exter, "All Our Children," *American Demographics* (May 1989): 36.

7. Judith Walop, "2010," *American Demographics* (February 1989): 20.

8. Sue Greenfield, Robert Winder, and Gregory Williams, "The CEO and the External Environment," *Business Horizons* 31, no. 6 (November–December 1988): 20–25.

9. Frederick Gluck, "Global Competition in the 1990s," *Journal of Business Strategy* (Spring 1983): 22, 24.

10. John Harris, Robert Shaw, Jr., and William Sommers, "The Strategic Management of Technology," *Planning Review* 11, no. 1 (January–February 1983): 28, 35.

11. Susan Levine and Michal Yalowitz, "Managing Technology: The Key to Successful Business Growth," *Management Review* 72, no. 9 (September 1983): 44.

12. Gene Bylinsky, "Technology in the Year 2000," *Fortune* (July 18, 1988): 92–98.

13. Gene Bylinsky, "Where Japan Will Strike Next," *Fortune* (September 25, 1989): 42.

14. Susan Gelford, "An Electronic Pipeline That's Changing the Way America Does Business," *Business Week* 3, no. 4 (August 1987): 80.

15. Bill Saporito, "Companies That Compete Best," *Fortune* (May 22, 1989): 36.

16. John Prescott and Daniel Smith, "The Largest Survey of 'Leading-Edge' Competitor Intelligence Managers," *Planning Review* 17, no. 3 (May–June 1989): 6–13.

17. Brian Duamaine, "Corporate Spies Snoop to Conquer," *Fortune* (November 7, 1989): 68–76.

18. Irvin Grossack and David Heenan, "Cooperation, Competition, and Antitrust: Two Views," *Business Horizons* 29, no. 5 (September–October 1986): 27.

19. Dale McConkey, "Planning in a Changing Environment," *Business Horizons* 31, no. 5 (September–October 1988): 67.

20. Robert Mockler, "A Catalog of Commercially Available Software for Strategic Planning," *Planning Review* 19, no. 3 (May–June 1991): 33.

CURRENT READINGS

Bartmess, Andrews, and Keith Cerny. "Building Competitive Advantage: A Capability-Centered Approach." *California Management Review* 35, no. 2 (Winter 1993): 78–103.

Burgers, W. P., C. W. L. Hill, and W. C. Kim. "A Theory of Global Strategic Alliances: The Case of the Global Auto Industry." *Strategic Management Journal* 14, no. 6 (September 1993): 419–432.

Coplin, William D., and Michael K. O'Leary. "1992–97 World Political Risk Forecast." *Planning Review* 20, no. 2 (March–April 1992): 24–31.

Jennings, Daniel F., and James R. Lumpkin. "Insights Between Environmental Scanning Activities and Porter's Generic Strategies: An Empirical Analysis." *Journal of Management* 18, no. 4 (December 1992): 791–804.

Jordan D. Lewis. "The New Power of Strategic Alliances." *Planning Review* 20, no. 5 (September–October 1992): 45–46.

Lado, Augustine A., Nancy G. Boyd, and Peter Wright. "A Competency-Based Model of Sustainable Competitive Advantage: Toward a Conceptual Integration." *Journal of Management* 18, no. 1 (March 1992): 77–92.

Lasserre, Philippe. "Gathering and Interpreting Strategic Intelligence in Asia Pacific." *Long Range Planning* 26, no. 3 (June 1993): 56–66.

Lei, David. "Offensive and Defensive Uses of Alliances." *Long Range Planning* 26, no. 4 (August 1993): 32–41.

Lev, Baruch. "Information Disclosure Strategy." *California Management Review* 34, no. 4 (Summer 1992): 9–32.

Mockler, Robert J. "Strategic Intelligence Systems: Competitive Intelligence Systems to Support Strategic Management Decision Making." *SAM Advanced Management Journal* 57, no. 1 (Winter 1992): 4–9.

Moore, James F. "Predators and Prey: A New Ecology of Competition." *Harvard Business Review* (May–June 1993): 75–86.

O'Sullivan, Leonard, and Michael J. Geringer. "Harnessing the Power of Your Value Chain." *Long Range Planning* 26, no. 2 (April 1993): 59–68.

Parkhe, Arvind. "Strategic Alliance Structuring: A Game Theoretic and Transaction Cost Examination of Interfirm Cooperation." *Academy of Management Journal* 36, no. 4 (August 1993): 794–829.

Peteraf, M.A. "The Cornerstones of Competitive Advantage: A Resource-based View." *Strategic Management Journal* 14, no. 3 (March 1993): 179–192.

Thomas, Lee M. "The Business Community and the Environment: An Important Partnership." *Business Horizons* 35, no. 2 (March–April 1992): 21–24.

Wheelwright, Steven C., and Kim B. Clark. "Competing Through Development Capability in a Manufacturing-Based Organization." *Business Horizons* 35, no. 4 (July–August 1992): 29–43.

Williams, Jeffrey R. "How Sustainable Is Your Competitive Advantage?" *California Management Review* 34, no. 3 (Spring 1992): 29–51.

Zahra, Shaker A., and Sherry S. Chaples. "Blind Spots in Competitive Analysis." *Academy of Management Executive* VII, no. 2 (May 1993): 7–28.

EXPERIENTIAL EXERCISES

DEVELOPING AN EFE MATRIX FOR HERSHEY FOODS

PURPOSE

This exercise will give you practice developing an EFE Matrix. An EFE Matrix summarizes the results of an external audit. This is an important tool widely used by strategists.

INSTRUCTIONS

Step 1 Join with two other students in class and jointly prepare an EFE Matrix for Hershey Foods. Refer back to the Cohesion Case and to Experiential Exercise 1A if needed to identify external opportunities and threats.

Step 2 All three-person teams participating in this exercise should record their team's EFE total weighted score on the board. Put your initials after your score to identify it as your team's.

Step 3 Compare the total weighted scores. Which team's score came closest to the instructor's answer? Discuss reasons for variation in the scores reported on the board.

THE LIBRARY SEARCH

PURPOSE

This exercise will help you become familiar with important sources of external information available in your college library. A key part of preparing an external audit is to examine published sources of information for relevant economic, social, cultural, demographic, environmental, political, governmental, technological, and competitive trends and events. External opportunities and threats must be identified and evaluated before strategies can be formulated effectively.

INSTRUCTIONS

Step 1 Select a company or business located in your county. Go to your college library and conduct an external audit for this company. Find opportunities and threats in recent issues of the local newspaper. Also check magazines and *Value Line Investment Survey* and *U.S. Industrial Outlook*. Conduct a computer search if possible.

Step 2 On a separate sheet of paper, list ten opportunities and ten threats that face this company. Be specific in stating each factor by including percentages and numbers wherever possible.

Step 3 Include a bibliography page to reveal where you found the information.

Step 4 Share your information with a manager of that company. Ask for his or her comments and additions.

Step 5 Write a three-page summary of your findings and submit it to your professor.

DEVELOPING AN EFE MATRIX FOR MY UNIVERSITY

PURPOSE

More and more colleges and universities are embarking upon the strategic-management process. Institutions are consciously and systematically identifying and evaluating external opportunities and threats facing higher education in your state, the nation, and the world.

INSTRUCTIONS

Step 1 Join with two other individuals in class and jointly prepare an EFE Matrix for your institution.

Step 2 Go to the board and record your total weighted score in a column that includes the scores for all three-person teams participating. Put your initials after your score to identify it as your team's.

Step 3 Which team viewed your college's strategies most positively; which team viewed your college's strategies most negatively? Discuss the nature of the differences.

USING THE *STRATEGY FORMULATOR* SOFTWARE

PURPOSE

The purpose of this exercise is to give you experience using the *Strategy Formulator* software that is available with this text. This software can make it easier for you to develop, revise, update, and print various strategy-formulation analyses.

INSTRUCTIONS

Step 1 Use the *Strategy Formulator* software to develop a list of opportunities and threats facing your university (Experiential Exercise 4C).

Step 2 Bring a printout of your work to class. Discuss any problems or questions you encountered in using this software.

DEVELOPING A COMPETITIVE PROFILE MATRIX FOR HERSHEY FOODS

PURPOSE

Monitoring competitors' performance and strategies is a key aspect of an internal audit. This exercise is designed to give you practice evaluating the competitive position of organizations in a given industry, and assimilating that information in the form of a Competitive Profile Matrix.

INSTRUCTIONS

Step 1 Turn back to the Cohesion Case and review the section on competitors.

Step 2 On a separate sheet of paper, prepare a Competitive Profile Matrix that includes Hershey Foods, Nestlé, and Mars.

Step 3 Turn your Competitive Profile Matrix in for a classwork grade.

DEVELOPING A COMPETITIVE PROFILE MATRIX FOR MY UNIVERSITY

PURPOSE

Your college or university competes with all other educational institutions in the world, especially those in your own state. Competition for state funds, students, faculty, staff, endowments, gifts, and federal funds are areas of competitiveness. The purpose of this exercise is to give you practice thinking competitively about the business of education in your state.

INSTRUCTIONS

Step 1 Identify two colleges or universities in your state that compete directly with your institution for students. Interview several persons who are aware of particular strengths and weaknesses of those universities. Record information about the two competing universities.

Step 2 Prepare a Competitive Profile Matrix that includes your institution and the two competing institutions. Include the following factors in your analysis.

1. Tuition costs
2. Quality of faculty
3. Academic reputation
4. Average class size
5. Campus landscaping
6. Athletic programs
7. Quality of students
8. Graduate programs
9. Location of campus
10. Campus culture

Step 3 Submit your Competitive Profile Matrix to your professor for evaluation.

Chapter 5

THE INTERNAL ASSESSMENT

OBJECTIVES   After studying this chapter, you should be able to:

■ Describe how to perform an internal strategic-management audit.

■ Discuss key interrelationships among the functional areas of business.

■ Identify the basic functions or activities that comprise management, marketing, finance/accounting, production/operations, research and development, and computer information systems.

■ Explain how to determine and prioritize a firm's internal strengths and weaknesses.

■ Explain the importance of financial ratio analysis.

■ Discuss the nature and role of computer information systems in strategic management.

■ Develop an Internal Factor Evaluation (IFE) Matrix.

*T*his chapter focuses on identifying and evaluating a firm's strengths and weaknesses in the functional areas of business, including management, marketing, finance/accounting, production/operations, research and development, and computer information systems. Relationships among these areas of business are examined. Strategic implications of important functional area concepts are examined. The process of performing an internal audit is described.

THE NATURE OF AN INTERNAL AUDIT

All organizations have strengths and weaknesses in the functional areas of business. No enterprise is equally strong or weak in all areas. Maytag, for example, is known for excellent production and product design, whereas Procter & Gamble is known for superb marketing. Internal strengths/weaknesses, coupled with external opportunities/threats and a clear statement of mission, provide the basis for establishing objectives and strategies. Objectives and strategies are established with the intention of capitalizing upon internal strengths and overcoming weaknesses! The internal-audit part of the strategic-management process is highlighted in Figure 5–1.

Key Internal Forces. It is not possible in a business policy text to review in depth all the material presented in courses such as marketing, finance, accounting, management, computer information systems, and production/operations; there are many subareas within these functions, such as customer service, warranties, advertising, packaging, and pricing under marketing.

For different types of organizations, such as hospitals, universities, and government agencies, the functional business areas, of course, differ. In a hospital, for example, functional areas may include cardiology, hematology, nursing, maintenance, physician support, and receivables. Functional areas of a university can include athletic programs, placement services, housing, fund-raising, academic research, counseling, and intramural programs. Within large organizations, each division has certain strengths and weaknesses. For example, AT&T is strong in communications and weak in computers.

A firm's strengths that cannot be easily matched or imitated by competitors are called *distinctive competencies*. Building competitive advantages involves taking advantage of distinctive competencies. For example, 3M exploits its distinctive competence in research and development by producing a wide range of innovative products. Strategies are designed in part to improve on a firm's weaknesses, turning them into strengths, and maybe even into distinctive competencies.

Some researchers emphasize the importance of the internal audit part of the strategic-management process by comparing it to the external audit. Robert Grant concludes that the internal audit is more important, saying:

> In a world where customer preferences are volatile, the identity of customers is changing, and the technologies for serving customer requirements are continually evolving, an externally focused orientation does not provide a secure foundation for formulating long-term strategy. When the external environment is in a state of flux, the firm's own resources and capabilities may be a much more stable basis on which to define its identity. Hence, a definition of a business in terms of what it is capable of doing may offer a more durable basis for strategy than a definition based upon the needs which the business seeks to satisfy.[1]

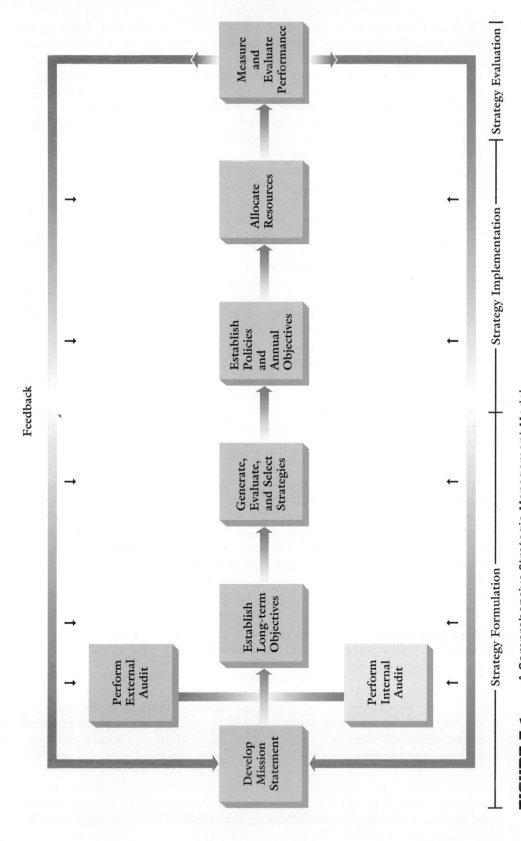

FIGURE 5-1 A Comprehensive Strategic-Management Model

The Process of Performing an Internal Audit. The process of performing an internal audit closely parallels the process of performing an external audit. Representative managers and employees from throughout the firm need to be involved in determining a firm's strengths and weaknesses. The internal audit requires gathering and assimilating information about the firm's management, marketing, finance/accounting, production/operations, research and development, and computer information systems operations. Key factors should be prioritized as described in Chapter 4 so that the firm's most important strengths and weaknesses can be collectively determined.

Compared to the external audit, the process of performing an internal audit provides more opportunity for participants to understand how their jobs, departments, and divisions fit into the whole organization. This is a great benefit because managers and employees perform better when they understand how their work affects other areas and activities of the firm. For example, when marketing and manufacturing managers jointly discuss issues related to internal strengths and weaknesses, they gain a better appreciation of issues, problems, concerns, and needs in all the functional areas. In organizations that do not use strategic management, marketing, finance, and manufacturing managers often do not interact with each other in significant ways. Performing an internal audit thus is an excellent vehicle or forum for improving the process of communication in the organization. "Communication" may be the most important word in management.

Performing an internal audit requires gathering, assimilating, and evaluating information about the firm's operations. Critical success factors, consisting of both strengths and weaknesses, can be identified and prioritized in the manner discussed in Chapter 4. According to William King, a task force of managers from different units of the organization, supported by staff, should be charged with determining the ten to twenty most important strengths and weaknesses that should influence the future of the organization:

> The development of conclusions on the ten to twenty most important organizational strengths and weaknesses can be, as any experienced manager knows, a difficult task, when it involves managers representing various organizational interests and points of view. Developing a twenty page list of strengths and weaknesses could be accomplished relatively easily, but a list of the ten to fifteen most important ones involves significant analysis and negotiation. This is true because of the judgments that are required and the impact which such a list will inevitably have as it is used in the formulation, implementation, and evaluation of strategies.[2]

RELATIONSHIPS AMONG THE FUNCTIONAL AREAS OF BUSINESS

Strategic management is a highly interactive process that requires effective coordination among management, marketing, finance/accounting, production/operations, R & D, and computer information systems managers. Although the strategic-management process is overseen by strategists, success requires that managers and employees from all functional areas work together to provide ideas and information. Financial managers, for example, may need to restrict the number of feasible options available to operations managers, or R & D managers may develop such good products that marketing managers need to set higher objectives. A key to organizational success is effective coordination and understanding among managers from all functional business areas! Through involvement in performing an internal strategic-management audit, managers from different departments and divisions of the firm come to understand the nature and effect of decisions in other functional business areas in their firm. Knowledge of these relationships is critical for effectively establishing objectives and strategies.

A failure to recognize and understand relationships among the functional areas of business can be detrimental to strategic management, and the number of those relationships that must be managed increases dramatically with a firm's size, diversity, geographic dispersion, and the number of products or services offered. Governmental and nonprofit enterprises have traditionally not placed sufficient emphasis on relationships among the business functions. For example, some state governments, utilities, universities, and hospitals have only recently begun to establish marketing objectives and policies that are consistent with their financial capabilities and limitations. Some firms place too great an emphasis on one function at the expense of others. Ansoff explains:

> During the first fifty years, successful firms focused their energies on optimizing the performance of one of the principal functions: production/operations, R & D, or marketing. Today, due to the growing complexity and dynamism of the environment, success increasingly depends on a judicious combination of several functional influences. This transition from a single function focus to a multifunction focus is essential for successful strategic management.[3]

Financial ratio analysis exemplifies the complexity of relationships among the functional areas of business. A declining return on investment or profit margin ratio could be the result of ineffective marketing, poor management policies, research and development errors, or a weak computer information system. The effectiveness of strategy formulation, implementation, and evaluation activities hinges upon a clear understanding of how major business functions affect one another. For strategies to succeed, a coordinated effort among all the functional areas of business is needed. In the case of planning, George says:

> We may conceptually separate planning for the purpose of theoretical discussion and analysis, but in practice, neither is it a distinct entity nor is it capable of being separated. The planning function is mixed with all other business functions and, like ink once mixed with water, it cannot be set apart. It is spread throughout and is a part of the whole of managing an organization.[4]

Integrating Strategy and Culture.   Relationships among a firm's functional business activities can perhaps be exemplified best by focusing on organizational culture, an internal phenomenon that permeates all departments and divisions of an organization. *Organizational culture* can be defined as "a pattern of behavior developed by an organization as it learns to cope with its problem of external adaptation and internal integration, that has worked well enough to be considered valid and to be taught to new members as the correct way to perceive, think, and feel."[5] This definition emphasizes the importance of matching external with internal factors in making strategic decisions.

Organizational culture captures the subtle, elusive, and largely unconscious forces that shape a workplace. Remarkably resistant to change, culture can represent a major strength or weakness for the firm. It can be an underlying reason for strengths or weaknesses in any of the major business functions.

Defined in Table 5–1, cultural products include values, beliefs, rites, rituals, ceremonies, myths, stories, legends, sagas, language, metaphors, symbols, heroes, and heroines. These products or dimensions are levers that strategists can use to influence and direct strategy formulation, implementation, and evaluation activities. An organization's culture compares to an individual's personality in the sense that no organization has the same culture and no individual has the same personality. Both culture and personality are fairly enduring and can be warm, aggressive, friendly, open, innovative, conservative, liberal, harsh, or likable.

Dimensions of organizational culture permeate all the functional areas of business. It is something of an art to uncover the basic values and beliefs that are buried deeply in an organization's rich collection of stories, language, heroes, and rituals, but cultural products can represent important strengths and weaknesses. Culture is an aspect of organizations that can no longer be taken for granted in perform-

TABLE 5-1 Cultural Products and Associated Definitions

Rites	Relatively elaborate, dramatic, planned sets of activities that consolidate various forms of cultural expressions into one event, carried out through social interactions, usually for the benefit of an audience.
Ceremonial	A system of several rites connected with a single occasion or event.
Ritual	A standardized, detailed set of techniques and behaviors that manage anxieties, but seldom produce intended, technical consequences of practical importance.
Myth	A dramatic narrative of imagined events, usually used to explain origins or transformations of something. Also, an unquestioned belief about the practical benefits of certain techniques and behaviors that is not supported by facts.
Saga	An historical narrative describing the unique accomplishments of a group and its leaders, usually in heroic terms.
Legend	A handed-down narrative of some wonderful event that is based on history but has been embellished with fictional details.
Story	A narrative based on true events, sometimes a combination of truth and fiction.
Folktale	A completely fictional narrative.
Symbol	Any object, act, event, quality, or relation that serves as a vehicle for conveying meaning, usually by representing another thing.
Language	A particular form or manner in which members of a group use sounds and written signs to convey meanings to each other.
Metaphors	Shorthand words used to capture a vision or to reinforce old or new values.
Values	Life-directing attitudes that serve as behavioral guidelines.
Belief	An understanding of a particular phenomenon.
Heroes/ Heroines	Individuals whom the organization has legitimized to model behavior for others.

Source: Adapted from H. M. Trice and J. M. Beyer, "Studying Organizational Cultures Through Rites and Ceremonials," *Academy of Management Review* 9, no. 4 (October 1984): 655.

ing an internal strategic-management audit, because culture and strategy must work together.

The strategic-management process takes place largely within a particular organization's culture. Lorsch found that executives in successful companies are emotionally committed to the firm's culture, but he concluded that culture can inhibit strategic management in two basic ways. First, managers frequently miss the significance of changing external conditions because they are blinded by strongly held beliefs. Second, when a particular culture has been effective in the past, the natural response is to stick with it in the future, even during times of major strategic change.[6] An organization's culture must support the collective commitment of its people to a common purpose. It must foster competence and enthusiasm among managers and employees.

Organizational culture significantly affects business decisions and thus must be evaluated during an internal strategic-management audit. If strategies can capitalize on cultural strengths, such as a strong work ethic or highly ethical beliefs, then management can often implement changes swiftly and easily. However, if the firm's culture is not supportive, strategic changes may be ineffective or even counterproductive. A firm's culture can become antagonistic to new strategies, with the result being confusion and disorientation. An organization's culture should infuse individuals with enthusiasm for implementing strategies. Allarie and Firsirotu emphasize the need to understand culture:

> Culture provides an explanation for the insuperable difficulties a firm encounters when it attempts to shift its strategic direction. Not only has the "right" culture become the essence and foundation of corporate excellence, it is also claimed that success or failure of reforms hinges on management's sagacity and ability to change the firm's driving culture in time and in tune with required changes in strategies.[7]

The potential value of organizational culture has not been fully realized in the study of strategic management. Ignoring the effect that culture can have on relationships among the functional areas of business can result in barriers to communication, lack of coordination, and an inability to adapt to changing conditions. Some tension between culture and a firm's strategy is inevitable, but the tension should be monitored so that it does not reach a point at which relationships are severed and the culture becomes antagonistic. The resulting disarray among members of the organization would disrupt strategy formulation, implementation, and evaluation. On the other hand, a supportive organizational culture can make managing much easier. One firm struggling to manage its culture is NationsBank, created from the merger of NCNB and C&S/Sovran. NCNB was a highly centralized company with a hard-charging, maverick style of management, whereas C&S/Sovran was highly decentralized and conservative in management style.

Internal strengths and weaknesses associated with a firm's culture are sometimes overlooked due to the interfunctional nature of this phenomenon. It is important, therefore, for strategists to understand their firm as a sociocultural system. Success is often determined by linkages between a firm's culture and strategies. The challenge of strategic management today is to bring about the changes in organizational culture and individual mind-sets necessary to support the formulation, implementation, and evaluation of strategies. As indicated in the Global Perspective, this challenge becomes greater as a firm initiates or expands multinational operations.

Operating as if the Natural Environment Matters. Both employees and consumers are becoming especially resentful of firms that take more than they give from the natural environment; likewise, people today are especially appreciative of firms that conduct operations in a way that mends rather than harms the environment.

The U.S. Justice Department recently issued new guidelines for companies to uncover environmental wrongdoing among their managers and employees without exposing themselves to potential criminal liability. The new guidelines give nine hypothetical examples to illustrate the new legal requirements. The examples include Company A, which regularly conducts a comprehensive environmental audit, goes straight to the government as soon as something wrong is turned up, disciplines the responsible people in the company, and gives their names as well as all relevant documentation to the government. The Justice Department will prosecute but be lenient in this case. The extreme example is Company K, which tries to cover up an environmental violation and does not cooperate with the government or provide names. Its audit is narrow, and its compliance program is "no more than a collection of paper." No leniency is likely for this firm. United Technologies Corporation, for example, recently was a Company K and incurred a $5.3 million fine for abuses in handling and discharging hazardous wastes.

A GLOBAL PERSPECTIVE
How Cultures of Countries Vary

There are two basic types of cultures in the world—high-context and low-context. High-context cultures are oral cultures where what a person says in writing is *less important* than who a person is and what the social context is surrounding a business agreement. In low-context cultures, what a person says in writing is *more important* than who a person is and what the social context is surrounding a business agreement. The following diagram gives an arrangement of high-context and low-context cultures worldwide:

Chinese	High-Context Culture
Korean	
Japanese	
Vietnamese	
Arab	
Greek	
Spanish	
Italian	
English	
North American	
Scandinavian	
Swiss	
German	Low-Context Culture

There are numerous implications of the high-context/low-context culture analysis that should be considered in doing business globally. For example:

1. In high-context countries, casual conversations have a level of business significance far beyond the content being discussed. High-context foreign nationals want to know a lot about people personally and about their companies before making business commitments.
2. Businesspeople in high-context cultures expect a presentation to be in short, separate segments to allow time for questions and digestion of what has been presented. Frequent deviations from the major business topic are expected. High-context persons are not time- or efficiency-oriented and thus like to relax some during business meetings.
3. In high-context cultures, age, seniority, and experience are very important, so sending a "young expert" to conduct a meeting or close a sale would often be interpreted negatively.
4. A passive, impersonal style of communication is best with low-context cultures. Avoid exaggeration, hyperbole, superlatives, and egocentrism.

Adapted from Ronald Dulek, John Fielden, and John Hill, "International Communication: An Executive Primer." *Business Horizons* **(January–February 1991): 19–25. Also, Edward Hall, "How Cultures Collide."** *Psychology Today* **(July 1976): 67–74.**

The functions of management consist of five basic activities: planning, organizing, motivating, staffing, and controlling. An overview of these activities is provided in Table 5–2.

Planning. The only thing certain about the future of any organization is change, and *planning* is the essential bridge between the present and the future that increases the likelihood of achieving desired results. Planning is the cornerstone of effective strategy formulation. But even though it is considered the foundation of management, it is commonly the task that managers neglect most. Planning is essential for successful strategy implementation and strategy evaluation, largely because organizing, motivating, staffing, and controlling activities are dependent upon good planning.

The process of planning must include involvement of managers and employees throughout an organization. As noted in Figure 5–2, the time horizon for planning

TABLE 5-2   The Basic Functions of Management

FUNCTION	DESCRIPTION	MOST IMPORTANT AT WHAT STAGE OF THE STRATEGIC-MANAGEMENT PROCESS?
Planning	Planning consists of all those managerial activities related to preparing for the future. Specific tasks include forecasting, establishing objectives, devising strategies, developing policies, and setting goals.	Strategy Formulation
Organizing	Organizing includes all those managerial activities that result in a structure of task and authority relationships. Specific areas include organizational design, job specialization, job descriptions, job specifications, span of the control, unity of command, coordination, job design, and job analysis.	Strategy Implementation
Motivating	Motivating involves efforts directed toward shaping human behavior. Specific topics include leadership, communication, work groups, behavior modification, delegation of authority, job enrichment, job satisfaction, needs fulfillment, organizational change, employee morale, and managerial morale.	Strategy Implementation
Staffing	Staffing activities are centered on personnel or human resource management. Included are wage and salary administration, employee benefits, interviewing, hiring, firing, training, management development, employee safety, affirmative action, equal employment opportunity, union relations, career development, personnel research, discipline policies, grievance procedures, and public relations.	Strategy Implementation
Controlling	Controlling refers to all those managerial activities directed toward assuring that actual results are consistent with planned results. Key areas of concern include quality control, financial control, sales control, inventory control, expense control, analysis of variances, rewards, and sanctions.	Strategy Evaluation

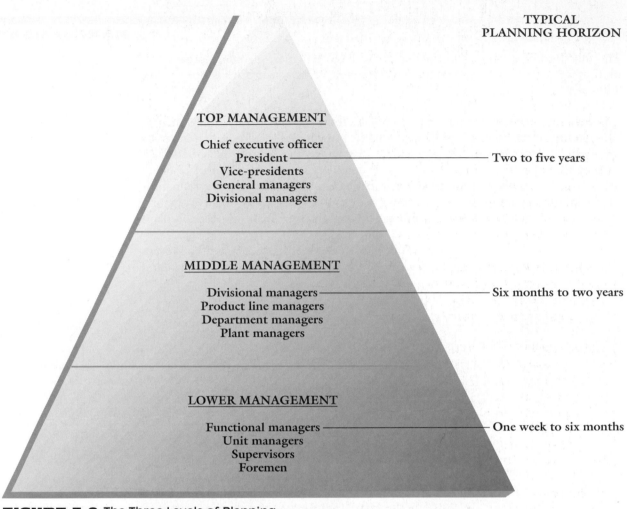

TOP MANAGEMENT

Chief executive officer
President ——————————————————— Two to five years
Vice-presidents
General managers
Divisional managers

MIDDLE MANAGEMENT

Divisional managers ——————————— Six months to two years
Product line managers
Department managers
Plant managers

LOWER MANAGEMENT

Functional managers ——————————— One week to six months
Unit managers
Supervisors
Foremen

FIGURE 5-2 The Three Levels of Planning

decreases from two to five years for top to less than six months for lower-level managers. The important point is that all managers do planning and should involve subordinates in the process to facilitate employee understanding and commitment.

Planning can have a positive impact on organizational and individual performance. Planning allows an organization to identify and take advantage of external opportunities and minimize the impact of external threats. Planning is more than extrapolating from the past and present into the future. It also includes developing a mission, forecasting future events and trends, establishing objectives, and choosing strategies to pursue.

An organization can develop synergy through planning. *Synergy* exists when everyone pulls together as a team that knows what it wants to achieve; synergy is the 2 + 2 = 5 effect. By establishing and communicating clear objectives, employees and managers can work together toward desired results. Synergy can result in powerful competitive advantages. The strategic-management process itself is aimed at creating synergy in an organization.

Planning allows a firm to adapt to changing markets and thus shape its own destiny. Strategic management can be viewed as a formal planning process that allows an organization to pursue proactive rather than reactive strategies. Successful organizations strive to control their own futures rather than merely react to external forces and events as they occur. Historically, organisms and organizations that have not adapted to changing conditions have become extinct. Swift adaptation is needed today more than ever before because changes in markets, economies, and competitors worldwide are accelerating.

Organizing. The purpose of *organizing* is to achieve coordinated effort by defining task and authority relationships. Organizing means determining who does what and who reports to whom. There are countless examples in history of well-organized enterprises successfully competing against, and in some cases defeating, much stronger but less well-organized firms. A well-organized firm generally has motivated managers and employees who are committed to seeing the organization succeed. Resources are allocated more effectively and used more efficiently in a well-organized firm than in a disorganized firm.

The organizing function of management can be viewed as consisting of three sequential activities: breaking tasks down into jobs (work specialization), combining jobs to form departments (departmentalization), and delegating authority. Breaking tasks down into jobs requires development of job descriptions and job specifications. These tools clarify for both managers and employees what particular jobs entail. In *Wealth of Nations* published in 1776, Adam Smith cited the advantages of work specialization in the manufacture of pins:

> One man draws the wire, another straightens it, a third cuts it, a fourth points it, a fifth grinds it at the top for receiving the head. Ten men working in this manner can produce 48,000 pins in a single day, but if they had all wrought separately and independently, each might at best produce twenty pins in a day.[8]

Combining jobs to form departments results in an organizational structure, span of control, and a chain of command. Changes in strategy often require changes in structure because new positions may be created, deleted, or merged. Organizational structure dictates how resources are allocated and how objectives are established in a firm. Allocating resources and establishing objectives geographically, for example, is much different from doing so by product or customer.

The most common forms of departmentalization are functional, divisional, strategic business unit, and matrix. These types of structure are discussed further in Chapter 7. Sears recently reorganized its 825 stores into six broad divisions: electronics and appliances, home fashions, home improvement products, men's and children's products, women's apparel, and automotive and recreational products.

Delegating authority is an important organizing activity, as evidenced in the old saying that "you can tell how good a manager is by observing how his or her department functions when he or she isn't there." Employees today are more educated and more capable of participating in organizational decision making than ever before. In most cases, they expect to be delegated authority and responsibility, and to be held accountable for results. Delegation of authority is embedded in the strategic-management process.

Motivating. *Motivating* can be defined as the process of influencing people to accomplish specific objectives.[9] Motivation explains why some people work hard and others do not. Objectives, strategies, and policies have little chance of succeeding if employees and managers are not motivated to implement strategies once they are formulated. The motivating function of management includes at least four major components: leadership, group dynamics, communication, and organizational change.

When managers and employees of a firm strive to achieve high levels of productivity, this indicates that the firm's strategists are good leaders. Good leaders establish rapport with subordinates, empathize with their needs and concerns, set a good example, and are trustworthy and fair. Leadership includes developing a vision of the firm's future and inspiring people to work hard to achieve that vision. Kirkpatrick and Locke recently reported that certain traits also characterize effective leaders: knowledge of the business, cognitive ability, self-confidence, honesty, integrity, and drive.[10]

Research suggests that democratic behavior on the part of leaders results in more positive attitudes toward change and higher productivity than does autocratic behavior. Drucker says:

> Leadership is not a magnetic personality. That can just as well be demagoguery. It is not "making friends and influencing people." That is flattery. Leadership is the lifting of a person's vision to higher sights, the raising of a person's performance to a higher standard, the building of a person's personality beyond its normal limitations.[11]

Group dynamics play a major role in employee morale and satisfaction. Informal groups or coalitions form in every organization. The norms of coalitions can range from being very positive to very negative toward management. It is important, therefore, that strategists identify the composition and nature of informal groups in an organization to facilitate strategy formulation, implementation, and evaluation. Leaders of informal groups are especially important in formulating and implementing strategy changes.

Communication, perhaps the most important word in management, is a major component in motivation. An organization's system of communication determines whether strategies can be implemented successfully. Good two-way communication is vital for gaining support for departmental and divisional objectives and policies. Top-down communication encourages bottom-up communication. The strategic-management process becomes a whole lot easier when subordinates are encouraged to discuss their concerns, reveal their problems, provide recommendations, and give suggestions. A primary reason for instituting strategic management is to build and support effective communication networks throughout the firm.

> The manager of tomorrow must be able to get his people to commit themselves to the business, whether they are machine operators or junior vice presidents. Ah, you say, participative management. Have a cigar. But just because most managers tug a forelock at the P word doesn't mean they know how to make it work. In the 1990s, throwing together a few quality circles won't suffice. The key issue will be empowerment, a term whose strength suggests the need to get beyond merely sharing a little information and a bit of decision-making.[12]

Staffing. The management function of *staffing*, also called *personnel management* or *human resource management*, includes activities such as recruiting, interviewing, testing, selecting, orienting, training, developing, caring for, evaluating, rewarding, disciplining, promoting, transferring, demoting, and dismissing employees. Staffing activities play a major role in strategy-implementation efforts, and for this reason human resource managers are becoming more actively involved in the strategic-management process. Strengths and weaknesses in the staffing area are important to identify.

The complexity and importance of human resource activities have increased to such a degree that all but the smallest organizations now need a full-time human resource manager. Numerous court cases that directly affect staffing activities are decided each day. Organizations and individuals can be penalized severely for not following federal, state, and local laws and guidelines related to staffing.[13] Line managers simply cannot stay abreast of all the legal developments and requirements regarding staffing. The human resources department coordinates staffing decisions in the firm so that an organization as a whole meets legal requirements. This department also provides needed consistency in administering company rules, wages, and policies.

Human resources management is particularly challenging for international companies. For example, the inability of spouses and children to adapt to new surroundings has become a major staffing problem in overseas transfers. The problems include premature returns, job performance slumps, resignation, discharge, low morale, marital discord, and general discontent. Firms such as Ford Motor and Exxon have begun screening and interviewing spouses and children before assigning persons to overseas positions. 3M Corporation introduces children to peers in the target country and offers spouses educational benefits.

Strategists are becoming increasingly aware of how important human resources are to effective strategic management. Human resource managers are becoming more involved and more proactive in formulating and implementing strategies. They provide leadership for organizations that are restructuring, such as Union Carbide, which reduced its workforce by 14.5 percent, or 5,500 employees, between 1992 and 1994.

Waterman describes staffing activities among successful companies:

> Successful (renewing) companies are busy taking out layers of management, cutting staff, and pushing decisions down. Nucor Corporation runs a successful, near billion-dollar steel enterprise from a headquarters office and complement of seven people in a Charlotte, N.C., shopping mall. At Dana Corporation, President Woody Morcott and others take extraordinary pride in the fact that today there are only five layers between the chief executive's office and the person on the factory floor. In the mid-1970s there were 14. . . . Leaner organizations set the stage for success (renewal). They make each one of us more important. They empower the individual.[14]

Controlling. The *controlling* function of management includes all those activities undertaken to assure that actual operations conform to planned operations. All managers in an organization have controlling responsibilities, such as conducting performance evaluations and taking necessary action to minimize inefficiencies. The controlling function of management is particularly important for effective strategy evaluation. Controlling consists of four basic steps:

1. Establishing performance standards
2. Measuring individual and organizational performance
3. Comparing actual performance to planned performance standards
4. Taking corrective actions

Measuring individual performance is often conducted ineffectively or not at all in organizations. Some reasons for this shortcoming are that evaluation can create confrontations that most managers prefer to avoid, can take more time than most managers are willing to give, and can require skills that many managers lack. No single approach to measuring individual performance is without limitations. For this reason, an organization should examine various methods, such as the graphic rating scale, the behaviorally anchored rating scale, and the critical incident method, and then develop or select a performance appraisal approach that best suits the firm's needs.

Increasingly, firms are striving to link organizational performance with managers' and employees' pay. This topic is discussed further in Chapter 7.

MARKETING

Marketing can be described as the process of defining, anticipating, creating, and fulfilling customers' needs and wants for products and services. Joel Evans and Barry Bergman suggest that there are nine basic *functions of marketing*: (1) customer analysis, (2) buying supplies, (3) selling products/services, (4) product and service planning, (5) pricing, (6) distribution, (7) marketing research, (8) opportunity analysis, and (9) social responsibility.[15] Understanding these functions helps strategists identify and evaluate marketing strengths and weaknesses.

Customer Analysis. *Customer analysis*—the examination and evaluation of consumer needs, desires, and wants—involves administering customer surveys, analyzing consumer information, evaluating market positioning strategies, developing customer profiles, and determining optimal market segmentation strategies. The information generated by customer analysis can be essential in developing an effective mission statement. Customer profiles can reveal the demographic characteristics of an organization's customers. Buyers, sellers, distributors, salespeople, managers, wholesalers, retailers, suppliers, and creditors can all participate in gathering information to identify customers' needs and wants successfully. Successful organizations continually monitor present and potential customers' buying patterns.

Buying Supplies. The second function of marketing is buying supplies needed to produce and sell a product or service. Buying consists of evaluating alternative suppliers or vendors, selecting the best suppliers, arranging acceptable terms with suppliers, and procuring the supplies. The buying process can be complicated by such factors as price controls, recession, foreign trade restrictions, strikes, walkouts, and machine breakdowns. Even the weather can significantly disrupt procurement of needed supplies. Quite often, the question arises whether to "make or buy" needed supplies and services. Recall that backward integration, gaining control over suppliers, is a particularly attractive strategy when suppliers are unreliable, costly, or incapable of meeting company needs.

Selling Products/Services. Successful strategy implementation generally rests upon the ability of an organization to sell some product or service. *Selling* includes many marketing activities such as advertising, sales promotion, publicity, personal selling, sales-force management, customer relations, and dealer relations. These activities are especially critical when a firm pursues a market penetration strategy. The effectiveness of various selling tools for consumer and industrial products varies. Personal selling is most important for industrial goods companies, and advertising is most important for consumer goods companies. Determining organizational strengths and weaknesses in the selling function of marketing is an important part of performing an internal strategic-management audit.

Product and Service Planning. *Product and service planning* includes activities such as test marketing; product and brand positioning; devising warranties; packaging; determining product options, product features, product style, and product quality; deleting old products; and providing for customer service. Product and service planning is particularly important when a company is pursuing product development or diversification.

One of the most effective product and service planning techniques is *test marketing*. Test markets allow an organization to test alternative marketing plans and to forecast future sales of new products. In conducting a test market project, an organization must decide how many cities to include, which cities to include, how long to run the test, what information to collect during the test, and what action to take after the test has been completed. Test marketing is more frequently used by consumer goods companies than by industrial goods companies. Test marketing can allow an organization to avoid substantial losses by revealing weak products and ineffective marketing approaches before large-scale production begins.

Pricing. Five major stakeholders affect *pricing* decisions: consumers, governments, suppliers, distributors, and competitors. Sometimes an organization will pursue a forward integration strategy primarily to gain better control over prices charged to consumers. Governments can impose constraints on price-fixing, price discrimination, minimum prices, unit pricing, price advertising, and price controls. For example, the Robinson-Patman Act prohibits manufacturers and wholesalers from discriminating in price among channel member purchasers (suppliers and distributors) if competition is injured.

Competing organizations must be careful not to coordinate discounts, credit terms, or condition of sale; not to discuss prices, markups, and costs at trade association meetings; and not to arrange to issue new price lists on the same date, to rotate low bids on contracts, or to uniformly restrict production to maintain high prices. Strategists should view price from both a short-run and a long-run perspective, because competitors can copy price changes with relative ease. Often a dominant firm will aggressively match all price cuts by competitors.

Distribution. *Distribution* includes warehousing, distribution channels, distribution coverage, retail site locations, sales territories, inventory levels and location, transportation carriers, wholesaling, and retailing. Most producers today do not sell their goods directly to consumers. Various marketing entities act as intermediaries; they bear a variety of names such as wholesalers, retailers, brokers, facilitators, agents, middlemen, vendors, or simply distributors.

Distribution becomes especially important when a firm is striving to implement a market development or forward integration strategy. Some of the most complex and challenging decisions facing a firm concern product distribution. Intermediaries flourish in our economy because many producers lack the financial resources and expertise to carry out direct marketing. Manufacturers who could afford to sell directly to the public often can gain greater returns by expanding and improving their manufacturing operations. Even General Motors would find it very difficult to buy out its more than 18,000 independent dealers.

Successful organizations identify and evaluate alternative ways to reach their ultimate market. Possible approaches vary from direct selling to using just one or many wholesalers and retailers. Strengths and weaknesses of each channel alternative should be determined according to economic, control, and adaptive criteria. Organizations should consider the costs and benefits of various wholesaling and retailing options. They must consider the need to motivate and control channel members and the need to adapt to changes in the future. Once a marketing channel is chosen, an organization usually must adhere to it for an extended period of time.

Marketing Research. *Marketing research* is the systematic gathering, recording, and analyzing of data about problems relating to the marketing of goods and services. Marketing research can uncover critical strengths and weaknesses, and marketing researchers employ numerous scales, instruments, procedures, concepts, and techniques to gather information. Marketing research activities support all of the major business functions of an organization. Organizations that possess excellent marketing research skills have a definite strength in pursuing generic strategies.

> The President of PepsiCo says, "Looking at the competition is the company's best form of market research. The majority of our strategic successes are ideas that we borrow from the marketplace, usually from a small regional or local competitor. In each case, we spot a promising new idea, improve on it, and then out-execute our competitor."[16]

Opportunity Analysis. The eighth function of marketing is *opportunity analysis*, which involves assessing the costs, benefits, and risks associated with marketing decisions. Three steps are required to perform a cost/benefit analysis: (1) compute the total costs associated with a decision, (2) estimate the total benefits from the decision, and (3) compare the total costs with the total benefits. As expected benefits exceed total costs, an opportunity becomes more attractive. Sometimes the variables included in a cost/benefit analysis cannot be quantified or even measured, but usually reasonable estimates can be made to allow the analysis to be performed. One key factor to be considered is risk. Cost/benefit analyses should also be performed when a company is evaluating alternative ways to be socially responsible.

Social Responsibility. The final function of marketing according to Evans and Berman is to determine how best to meet the firm's social responsibility obligations. *Social responsibility* can include offering products and services that are safe and reasonably priced. Demands by special interest groups on business organizations greatly increased during the 1980s. Arguments still rage today, though, about how socially responsible firms should be. A clear social policy can represent a major strength for organizations, whereas a poor social policy can be a weakness.

Some strategists view social responsibility as a focus that detracts from, or is counter to, their profit-minded pursuits. Although there may be some clearly distinct economic versus social concerns, there is a rather broad area in which economic and social concerns are consistent with one another. Many corporate activities are profitable, and at the same time are socially responsible. When a firm engages in social activities, it must do so in a way that receives economic advantages.

FINANCE/ACCOUNTING

Financial condition is often considered the single best measure of a firm's competitive position and overall attractiveness to investors. Determining an organization's financial strengths and weaknesses is essential to formulating strategies effectively. A firm's liquidity, leverage, working capital, profitability, asset utilization, cash flow, and equity can eliminate some strategies as being feasible alternatives. Financial factors often alter existing strategies and change implementation plans.

Finance/Accounting Functions. According to James Van Horne, the *functions of finance/accounting* comprise three decisions: the investment decision, the financing decision, and the dividend decision.[17] Financial ratio analysis is the most widely used method for determining an organization's strengths and weaknesses in the investment, financing, and dividend areas. Since the functional areas of business are so closely related, financial ratios can signal strengths or weaknesses in management, marketing, production, research and development, and computer information systems activities.

The *investment decision*, also called *capital budgeting*, is the allocation and reallocation of capital and resources to projects, products, assets, and divisions of an organization. Once strategies are formulated, capital budgeting decisions are required to implement strategies successfully. The *financing decision* concerns determining the best capital structure for the firm and includes examining various methods by which the firm can raise capital (for example, by issuing stock, increasing debt, selling assets, or using a combination of these approaches). The financing decision must consider both short-term and long-term needs for working capital. Two key financial ratios that indicate whether a firm's financing decisions have been effective are the debt-to-equity ratio and the debt-to-total-assets ratio.

Dividend decisions concern issues such as the percentage of earnings paid to stockholders, the stability of dividends paid over time, and the repurchase or issuance of stock. Dividend decisions determine the amount of funds that are retained in a firm compared to the amount paid out to stockholders. Three financial ratios that are helpful in evaluating a firm's dividend decisions are the earnings-per-share ratio, the dividends-per-share ratio, and the price-earnings ratio. The benefits of paying dividends to investors must be balanced against the benefits of retaining funds internally, and there is no set formula on how to balance this trade-off. For the reasons listed here, dividends are sometimes paid out even when funds could be better reinvested in the business or when the firm has to obtain outside sources of capital:

1. Paying cash dividends is customary. Failure to do so could be thought of as a stigma. A dividend change is considered a signal about the future.
2. Dividends represent a sales point for investment bankers. Some institutional investors can buy only dividend-paying stocks.
3. Shareholders often demand dividends, even in companies with great opportunities for reinvesting all available funds.
4. A myth exists that paying dividends will result in a higher stock price.

Basic Types of Financial Ratios. Financial ratios are computed from an organization's income statement and balance sheet. Computing financial ratios is like taking a picture, because the results reflect a situation at just one point in time. Comparing ratios over time and to industry averages is more likely to result in meaningful statistics that can be used to identify and evaluate strengths and weaknesses. Trend analysis, illustrated in Figure 5–3, is a useful technique that incorporates both the time and industry average dimensions of financial ratios. Note that the dotted line reveals projected ratios. Four major sources of industry-average financial ratios are

1. Dun & Bradstreet's *Industry Norms and Key Business Ratios*—Fourteen different ratios are calculated in an industry-average format for 800 different types of businesses. The ratios are presented by Standard Industrial Classification (SIC) number and are grouped by annual sales into three size categories.
2. Robert Morris Associates, *Annual Statement Studies*—Sixteen different ratios are calculated in an industry-average format. Industries are referenced by SIC numbers

published by the Bureau of the Census. The ratios are presented in four size categories by annual sales and "for all firms" in the industry.

3. Troy, Leo's *Almanac of Business & Industrial Financial Ratios*—Twenty-two financial ratios and percentages are provided in an industry-average format for all major industries. The ratios and percentages are given for twelve different company-size categories and for all firms in a given industry.

4. Federal Trade Commission Reports—The FTC publishes quarterly financial data including ratios on manufacturing companies. FTC reports include analyses by industry group and asset size.

Table 5–3 provides a summary of key financial ratios showing how each ratio is calculated and what each ratio measures. However, all the ratios are not significant for all industries and companies. For example, accounts receivable turnover and average collection period are not very meaningful to a company that does primarily a cash receipts business. Key financial ratios can be classified into the following five types:

1. *Liquidity ratios* measure a firm's ability to meet maturing short-term obligations.
Current ratio
Quick or acid-test ratio
2. *Leverage ratios* measure the extent to which a firm has been financed by debt.
Debt-to-total-assets ratio
Debt-to-equity ratio
Long-term debt-to-equity ratio
Times-interest-earned (or coverage) ratio

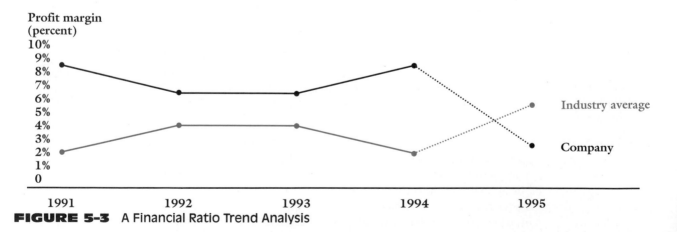

FIGURE 5-3 A Financial Ratio Trend Analysis

TABLE 5-3   A Summary of Key Financial Ratios

RATIO	HOW CALCULATED	WHAT IT MEASURES
LIQUIDITY RATIOS		
Current ratio	Current assets / Current liabilities	The extent to which a firm can meet its short-term obligations
Quick ratio	Current assets minus inventory / Current liabilities	The extent to which a firm can meet its short-term obligations without relying upon the sale of its inventories
LEVERAGE RATIOS		
Debt-to-total-assets ratio	Total debt / Total assets	The percentage of total funds that are provided by creditors
Debt-to-equity ratio	Total debt / Total stockholders' equity	The percentage of total funds provided by creditors versus by owners
Long-term debt-to-equity ratio	Long-term debt / Total stockholders' equity	The balance between debt and equity in a firm's long-term capital structure
Times-interest-earned ratio	Profits before interest and taxes / Total interest charges	The extent to which earnings can decline without the firm becoming unable to meet its annual interest costs
ACTIVITY RATIOS		
Inventory turnover	Sales / Inventory of finished goods	Whether a firm holds excessive stocks of inventories and whether a firm is selling its inventories slowly compared to the industry average
Fixed-assets turnover	Sales / Fixed assets	Sales productivity and plant and equipment utilization
Total-assets turnover	Sales / Total assets	Whether a firm is generating a sufficient volume of business for the size of its asset investment
Accounts-receivable turnover	Annual credit sales / Accounts receivable	(in percentage terms) The average length of time it takes a firm to collect credit sales
Average collection period	Accounts receivable / Total sales/365 days	(in days) The average length of time it takes a firm to collect on credit sales

3. *Activity ratios* measure how effectively a firm is using its resources.
  Inventory-turnover ratio
  Total-assets turnover
  Fixed-assets turnover
  Average collection period

TABLE 5-3 *Continued*

PROFITABILITY RATIOS

Gross profit margin	$$\frac{\text{Sales minus cost of goods sold}}{\text{Sales}}$$	The total margin available to cover operating expenses and yield a profit
Operating profit margin	$$\frac{\text{Earnings before interest and taxes (EBIT)}}{\text{Sales}}$$	Profitability without concern for taxes and interest
Net profit margin	$$\frac{\text{Net income}}{\text{Sales}}$$	After-tax profits per dollar of sales
Return on total assets (ROA)	$$\frac{\text{Net income}}{\text{Total assets}}$$	After-tax profits per dollar of assets; this ratio is also called return on investment (ROI)
Return on stockholders' equity (ROE)	$$\frac{\text{Net income}}{\text{Total stockholders' equity}}$$	After-tax profits per dollar of stockholders' investment in the firm
Earning per share (EPS)	$$\frac{\text{Net income}}{\text{Number of shares of common stock outstanding}}$$	Earnings available to the owners of common stock

GROWTH RATIOS

Sales	Annual percentage growth in total sales	Firm's growth rate in sales
Income	Annual percentage growth in profits	Firm's growth rate in profits
Earnings per share	Annual percentage growth in EPS	Firm's growth rate in EPS
Dividends per share	Annual percentage growth in dividends per share	Firm's growth rate in dividends per share
Price-earning ratio	$$\frac{\text{Market price per share}}{\text{Earnings per share}}$$	Faster-growing and less risky firms tend to have higher price-earnings ratios

4. *Profitability ratios* measure management's overall effectiveness as shown by the returns generated on sales and investment.
      Gross profit margin
      Operating profit margin
      Net profit margin
      Return on total assets (ROA)
      Return on stockholders' equity (ROE)
      Earnings per share
5. *Growth ratios* measure the firm's ability to maintain its economic position in the growth of the economy and industry.
      Sales
      Net income
      Earnings per share
      Dividends per share
      Price-earnings ratio

Financial ratio analysis is not without some limitations. First of all, financial ratios are based on accounting data, and firms differ in their treatment of such items as depreciation, inventory valuation, research and development expenditures, pension plan costs, mergers, and taxes. Also, seasonal factors can influence comparative ratios. Therefore, conformity to industry composite ratios does not establish with certainty that a firm is performing normally or that it is well managed. Likewise, departures from industry averages do not always indicate that a firm is doing especially well or badly. For example, a high inventory-turnover ratio could indicate efficient inventory management and a strong working capital position, but it could also indicate a serious inventory shortage and a weak working capital position.

It is important to recognize that a firm's financial condition depends not only on the functions of finance, but also on many other factors that include (1) management, marketing, production/operations, research and development, and computer information systems decisions; (2) actions by competitors, suppliers, distributors, creditors, customers, and shareholders; and (3) economic, social, demographic, political, governmental, and technological trends. Even natural environment liabilities can affect financial ratios, as indicated in the Natural Environment Perspective. So, financial ratio analysis, like all other analytical tools, should be used wisely.

PRODUCTION/OPERATIONS

The *production/operations function* of a business consists of all those activities that transform inputs into goods and services. Production/operations management deals with inputs, transformations, and outputs that vary across industries and markets. A manufacturing operation transforms or converts inputs such as raw materials, labor, capital, machines, and facilities into finished goods and services. As indicated in Table 5–4, Roger Schroeder suggests that production/operations management comprises five functions or decision areas: process, capacity, inventory, workforce, and quality.

TABLE 5-4	The Basic Functions of Production Management
FUNCTION	**DESCRIPTION**
1. Process	Process decisions concern the design of the physical production system. Specific decisions include choice of technology, facility layout, process flow analysis, facility location, line balancing, process control, and transportation analysis.
2. Capacity	Capacity decisions concern determination of optimal output levels for the organization—not too much and not too little. Specific decisions include forecasting, facilities planning, aggregate planning, scheduling, capacity planning, and queuing analysis.
3. Inventory	Inventory decisions involve managing the level of raw materials, work in process, and finished goods. Specific decisions include what to order, when to order, how much to order, and materials handling.
4. Workforce	Workforce decisions are concerned with managing the skilled, unskilled, clerical, and managerial employees. Specific decisions include job design, work measurement, job enrichment, work standards, and motivation techniques.
5. Quality	Quality decisions are aimed at assuring that high-quality goods and services are produced. Specific decisions include quality control, sampling, testing, quality assurance, and cost control.

Source: Adapted from R. Schroeder, *Operations Management* (New York: McGraw-Hill Book Co., 1981): 12.

Production/operations activities often represent the largest part of an organization's human and capital assets. In most industries, the major costs of producing a product or service are incurred within operations, so production/operations can have great value as a competitive weapon in a company's overall strategy. Strengths and weaknesses in the five functions of production can mean the success or failure of an enterprise.

Many production/operations managers are finding that cross-training of employees can help their firms respond to changing markets faster. Cross-training of workers can increase efficiency, quality, productivity, and job satisfaction. For example, at General Motors' Detroit Gear & Axle plant, costs related to product defects were reduced 400 percent in two years as a result of cross-training workers. A shortage of qualified labor in America is another reason cross-training is becoming a common management practice.

TABLE 5-5   Impact of Strategy Elements on Production Management

POSSIBLE ELEMENTS OF STRATEGY	CONCOMITANT CONDITIONS THAT MAY AFFECT THE OPERATIONS FUNCTION AND ADVANTAGES AND DISADVANTAGES
1. Compete as low-cost provider of goods or services	Discourages competition. Broadens market. Requires longer production runs and fewer product changes. Requires special-purpose equipment and facilities.
2. Compete as high-quality provider	Often possible to obtain more profit per unit, and perhaps more total profit from a smaller volume of sales. Requires more quality-assurance effort and higher operating cost. Requires more precise equipment, which is more expensive. Requires highly skilled workers, necessitating higher wages and greater training efforts.
3. Stress customer service	Requires broader development of service people and service parts and equipment. Requires rapid response to customer needs or changes in customer tastes, rapid and accurate information system, careful coordination. Requires a higher inventory investment.
4. Provide rapid and frequent introduction of new products	Requires versatile equipment and people. Has higher research and development costs. Has high retraining costs and high tooling and changeover in manufacturing. Provides lower volumes for each product and fewer opportunities for improvements due to the learning curve.
5. Strive for absolute growth	Requires accepting some projects or products with lower marginal value, which reduces ROI. Diverts talents to areas of weakness instead of concentrating on strengths.
6. Seek vertical integration	Enables company to control more of the process. May not have economies of scale at some stages of process. May require high capital investment as well as technology and skills beyond those currently available within the organization.

There is much reason for concern that many organizations have not taken sufficient account of the capabilities and limitations of the production/operations function in formulating strategies. Scholars contend that this neglect has had unfavorable consequences on corporate performance in America. In Table 5–5, James Dilworth outlines several types of strategic decisions that a company might make and considers production/operations implications of those decisions. Production capabilities and policies can also greatly affect strategies:

Given today's decision-making environment with shortages, inflation, technological booms, and government intervention, a company's production/operations capabilities and policies may not be able to fulfill the demands dictated by strategies. In fact, they may dictate corporate strategies. It is hard to imagine that an organization can formulate strategies today without first considering the constraints and limitations imposed by its existing production/operations structure.[18]

TABLE 5-5   *Continued*

7. Maintain reserve capacity for flexibility	Provides ability to meet peak demands and quickly implement some contingency plans if forecasts are too low. Requires capital investment in idle capacity. Provides capability to grow during the lead time normally required for expansion.
8. Consolidate processing (Centralize)	Can result in economies of scale. Can locate near one major customer or supplier. Vulnerability: one strike, fire, or flood can halt the entire operation.
9. Disperse processing of service (Decentralize)	Can be near several market territories. Requires more complex coordination network: perhaps expensive data transmission and duplication of some personnel and equipment at each location. If each location produces one product in the line, then other products still must be transported to be available at all locations. If each location specializes in a type of component for all products, the company is vulnerable to strike, fire, flood, etc. If each location provides total product line, then economies of scale may not be realized.
10. Stress the use of mechanization, automation, robots	Requires high capital investment. Reduces flexibility. May affect labor relations. Makes maintenance more crucial.
11. Stress stability of employment	Serves the security needs of employees and may develop employee loyalty. Helps to attract and retain highly skilled employees. May require revisions of make-or-buy decisions, use of idle time, inventory, and subcontractors as demand fluctuates.

The fifth major area of internal operations that should be examined for specific strengths and weaknesses is research and development (R & D). Many firms today conduct no R & D, and yet many other companies depend on successful R & D activities for survival. Firms pursuing a product development strategy especially need to have a strong R & D orientation. Table 5–6 gives R & D information for ten American industries in 1992. Note that health-care firms on average spend the most money on R & D as a percentage of revenues, while food companies spend the least.

Organizations invest in R & D because they believe that such investment will lead to superior product or services and give them competitive advantages. Research and development expenditures are directed at developing new products before competitors do, improving product quality, or improving manufacturing processes to reduce costs.[19]

A recent article emphasizes that effective management of the R & D function today requires a strategic and operational partnership between R & D and the other vital business functions. A spirit of partnership and mutual trust between general and R & D managers is evident in the best managed firms today. Managers in these firms jointly explore, assess, and decide the what, when, why, and how much of R & D. Priorities, costs, benefits, risks, and rewards associated with R & D activities are discussed openly and shared. The overall mission of R & D has thus become broad-based, including supporting existing businesses, helping launch new businesses, developing new products, improving product quality, improving manufacturing efficiency, and deepening or broadening the company's technological capabilities.[20]

The best managed firms today seek to organize R & D activities in a way that breaks the isolation of R & D from the rest of the company and promotes a spirit of partnership between R & D managers and other managers in the firm. R & D decisions and plans must be integrated and coordinated across departments and divisions by sharing experiences and information. The strategic-management process facilitates this new cross-functional approach to managing the R & D function.

TABLE 5-6   R & D Expenditure Information for U.S. Firms

INDUSTRY	TOTAL R & D EXPENDITURES 1992 VERSUS 1991 (PERCENT CHANGE)	TOTAL R & D EXPENDITURES AS A PERCENT OF SALES
Chemicals	+06	4.3
Health care	+18	9.7
Electrical	+07	6.0
Manufacturing	+08	3.0
Food	+08	0.7
Leisure Time	+08	5.7
Office Equipment	+06	8.4
Automotive	+07	4.0
Aerospace	+16	4.4
Telecommunications	-03	3.1
All Industries in 1992	+07	3.7

Source: Adapted from *Business Week*, June 28, 1993, p. 105.

When companies are acquired, R & D departments are often pared down or eliminated due to "redundancy." For example, when General Electric acquired RCA, it sold RCA's research laboratories to SRI International. The proliferation of mergers, acquisitions, and takeovers in the United States is one reason for forecasters' fears that total R & D spending in the United States is poised for a downturn. Other worrisome trends are burgeoning trade deficits, waning competitiveness, and the rapidly rising cost of R & D. Declines in R & D would hurt virtually all the types of strategies described in Chapter 2, especially product development.

Internal and External R & D. Cost distributions among R & D activities vary by company and industry, but total R & D costs generally do not exceed manufacturing and marketing start-up costs. Four approaches to determining R & D budget allocations are commonly used: (1) financing as many project proposals as possible, (2) using a percentage-of-sales method, (3) budgeting about the same amount that competitors spend for R & D, or (4) deciding how many successful new products are needed and working backward to estimate the required R & D investment.

R & D in organizations can take two basic forms: (1) internal R & D, in which an organization operates its own R & D department, and/or (2) contract R & D, in which a firm hires independent researchers or independent agencies to develop specific products. Many companies use both approaches to develop new products. For example, Grumman Corporation spends roughly half of its $200 million R & D budget internally and half externally. A widely used approach for obtaining outside R & D assistance is to pursue a joint venture with another firm. R & D strengths (capabilities) and weaknesses (limitations) play a major role in strategy formulation and strategy implementation.

Most firms have no choice but to continually develop new and improved products because of changing consumer needs and tastes, new technologies, shortened product life cycles, and increased domestic and foreign competition. A shortage of ideas for new products, increased global competition, increased market segmentation, strong special interest groups, and increased government regulation are several factors making the successful development of new products more and more difficult, costly, and risky. In the pharmaceutical industry, for example, only one out of every 10,000 drugs created in the laboratory ends up on pharmacists' shelves. Scarpello, Boulton, and Hofer emphasize that different strategies require different R & D capabilities:

> The focus of R & D efforts can vary greatly depending on a firm's competitive strategy. Some corporations attempt to be market leaders and innovators of new products, while others are satisfied to be market followers and developers of currently available products. The basic skills required to support these strategies will vary, depending on whether R & D becomes the driving force behind competitive strategy. In cases where new product introduction is the driving force for strategy, R & D activities must be extensive. The R & D unit must then be able to advance scientific and technological knowledge, exploit that knowledge, and manage the risks associated with ideas, products, services, and production requirements.[21]

COMPUTER INFORMATION SYSTEMS

Information ties all business functions together and provides the basis for all managerial decisions. It is the cornerstone of all organizations. Information represents a major source of competitive advantage or disadvantage. Assessing a firm's internal strengths and weaknesses in information systems is a critical dimension of performing an internal audit. The company motto of Mitsui, a large Japanese trading company, is "Information is the lifeblood of the company." A satellite network connects Mitsui's 200 worldwide offices.

A computer information system's purpose is to improve the performance of an enterprise by improving the quality of managerial decisions. An effective information system thus collects, codes, stores, synthesizes, and presents information in such a manner that it answers important operating and strategic questions. The heart of an information system is a data base containing the kinds of records and data important to managers.

A computer information system receives raw material from both the external and internal evaluation of an organization. It gathers data about marketing, finance, production, and personnel matters internally, and social, cultural, demographic, environmental, economic, political, government, legal, technological, and competitive factors externally. Data are integrated in ways needed to support managerial decision making.

There is a logical flow of material in a computer information system, whereby data are input to the system and transformed into output. Outputs include computer printouts, written reports, tables, charts, graphs, checks, purchase orders, invoices, inventory records, payroll accounts, and a variety of other documents. Payoffs from alternative strategies can be calculated and estimated. *Data* become *information* only when they are evaluated, filtered, condensed, analyzed, and organized for a specific purpose, problem, individual, or time.

An effective computer information system utilizes computer hardware, software, models for analysis, and a data base. Some people equate information systems with the advent of the computer, but historians have traced record keeping and noncomputer data processing to Babylonian merchants living in 3500 B.C. Benefits of an effective information system include an improved understanding of business functions, improved communications, more informed decision making, analysis of problems, and improved control.

Because organizations are becoming more complex, decentralized, and globally dispersed, the function of information systems is growing in importance. Spurring this advance is the falling cost and increasing power of computers. There are costs and benefits associated with obtaining and evaluating information, just as with equipment and land. Like equipment, information can become obsolete and may need to be purged from the system. An effective information system is like a library, collecting, categorizing, and filing data for use by managers throughout the organization. Information systems are a major strategic resource, monitoring environment changes, identifying competitive threats, and assisting in the implementation, evaluation, and control of strategy.

We are truly in an information age. Firms whose information-system skills are weak are at a competitive disadvantage. On the other hand, strengths in information systems allow firms to establish distinctive competencies in other areas. Low-cost manufacturing and good customer service, for example, can depend on a good information system.

Watson and Rainer recently found that executive information systems provide managerial support in six key areas: electronic mail, access to external news, access to external data bases, word processing, spreadsheet, and automated filing.[22] A good executive information system provides graphic, tabular, and textual information. Graphic capabilities are needed so current conditions and trends can be examined quickly; tables provide greater detail and enable variance analyses; textual information adds insight and interpretation to data.

Electronic data interchange (EDI) can represent a strength or weakness of a firm's computer information system. EDI provides an electronic exchange of agreements and documents between trading partners. By 1995, analysts expect that more than 400,000 companies all over the world will be using EDI directly or indirectly.[23]

Strategic Planning Software. The computer revolution today is being compared in magnitude to the industrial revolution. Computers are now common at the desks of almost every professional and administrative employee of industry, government, and academia. The proliferation of computers has aided strategic management because software products can be designed to enhance participation and to provide integration, uniformity, analysis, and economy. Strategic planning software can allow firms to tap the knowledge base of everyone in the firm. There are a number of commercially available strategic planning software products designed to train and assist managers in strategic planning, including *Business Advantage, Business Simulator, SUCCESS, ANSPLAN-A, Strategy!, CheckMATE, EXCEL, STRATPAC, SIMPLAN, REVEAL, COSMOS,* and *BASICS P-C.*[24]

Some strategic decision support systems, however, are too sophisticated, expensive, or restrictive to be used easily by managers in a firm. This is unfortunate because the strategic management process must be a "people process" to be successful. People make the difference! Strategic planning software thus should be simple and unsophisticated. Simplicity allows wide participation among managers in a firm and participation is essential for effective strategy implementation.

One strategic planning software product that offers managers and executives a simple yet effective approach for developing organizational strategies is *CheckMATE*. This IBM-compatible, personal computer software performs planning analyses and generates strategies a firm could pursue. *CheckMATE* incorporates the most modern strategic planning techniques. No previous experience with computers or knowledge of strategic planning is required of the user. *CheckMATE* thus promotes communication, understanding, creativity, and forward thinking among users.

CheckMATE is not a spreadsheet or data-base program; it is a structured brainstorming tool that enhances participation in strategic planning. A major strength of the new *CheckMATE* strategic planning software is its simplicity and participative approach. The user is asked appropriate questions, responses are recorded, information is assimilated, and results are printed. Individuals can work through the software independently, and then meet to develop joint recommendations for the firm.

The *CheckMATE* software utilizes the most modern strategic planning analytical matrices to generate alternative strategies firms could pursue. Specific analytical procedures included in the *CheckMATE* program are Strategic Planning and Action Evaluation (SPACE) analysis, Threats-Opportunities-Weaknesses-Strengths (TOWS) analysis, Internal-External (IE) analysis, and Grand Strategy Matrix analysis. These widely used strategic planning analyses are described in Chapter 6.

INTERNAL-AUDIT CHECKLISTS

The checklists of questions provided in this section can be helpful in determining specific strengths and weaknesses in the functional area of business. An answer of "no" to any question could indicate a potential weakness, although the strategic significance and implications of negative answers will of course vary by organization, industry, and severity of the weakness. Positive or "yes" answers to the checklist questions suggest potential areas of strength. The questions provided in Table 5–7 are not all-inclusive, but they can facilitate internal-audit efforts.

TABLE 5-7   Internal Audit Checklist of Questions

MANAGEMENT

1. Does the firm use strategic-management concepts?
2. Are company objectives and goals measurable and well-communicated?
3. Do managers at all hierarchical levels plan effectively?
4. Do managers delegate authority well?
5. Is the organization's structure appropriate?
6. Are job descriptions and job specifications clear?
7. Is employee morale high?
8. Is employee turnover and absenteeism low?
9. Are organizational reward and control mechanisms effective?

MARKETING

1. Are markets segmented effectively?
2. Is the organization positioned well among competitors?
3. Has the firm's market share been increasing?
4. Are present channels of distribution reliable and cost-effective?
5. Does the firm have an effective sales organization?
6. Does the firm conduct market research?
7. Is product quality and customer service good?
8. Are the firm's products and services priced appropriately?
9. Does the firm have an effective promotion, advertising, and publicity strategy?
10. Is marketing planning and budgeting effective?
11. Do the firm's marketing managers have adequate experience and training?

TABLE 5-7 *Continued*

FINANCE

1. Where is the firm financially strong and weak as indicated by financial ratio analyses?
2. Can the firm raise needed short-term capital?
3. Can the firm raise needed long-term capital through debt and/or equity?
4. Does the firm have sufficient working capital?
5. Are capital budgeting procedures effective?
6. Are dividend payout policies reasonable?
7. Does the firm have good relations with its investors and stockholders?
8. Are the firm's financial managers experienced and well-trained?

PRODUCTION

1. Are suppliers of raw materials, parts, and subassemblies reliable and reasonable?
2. Are facilities, equipment, machinery, and offices in good condition?
3. Are inventory-control policies and procedures effective?
4. Are quality-control policies and procedures effective?
5. Are facilities, resources, and markets strategically located?
6. Does the firm have technological competencies?

RESEARCH AND DEVELOPMENT

1. Does the firm have R & D facilities? Are they adequate?
2. If outside R & D firms are used, are they cost-effective?
3. Are the organization's R & D personnel well-qualified?
4. Are R & D resources allocated effectively?
5. Are management information and computer systems adequate?
6. Is communication between R & D and other organizational units effective?
7. Are present products technologically competitive?

COMPUTER INFORMATION SYSTEMS

1. Do all managers in the firm use the information system to make decisions?
2. Is there a chief information officer or director of information systems position in the firm?
3. Are data in the information system updated regularly?
4. Do managers from all functional areas of the firm contribute input to the information system?
5. Are there effective passwords for entry into the firm's information system?
6. Are strategists of the firm familiar with the information systems of rival firms?
7. Is the information system user-friendly?
8. Do all users of the information system understand the competitive advantages that information can provide firms?
9. Are computer training workshops provided for users of the information system?
10. Is the firm's information system continually being improved in content and user-friendliness?

A summary step in conducting an internal strategic-management audit is to construct an IFE Matrix. This strategy-formulation tool summarizes and evaluates the major strengths and weaknesses in the functional areas of a business, and it also provides a basis for identifying and evaluating relationships among those areas. Intuitive judgments are required in developing an IFE Matrix, so the appearance of a scientific approach should not be interpreted to mean this is an all-powerful technique. A thorough understanding of the factors included is more important than the actual numbers. Similar to the EFE Matrix and Competitive Profile Matrix described in Chapter 4, an IFE Matrix can be developed in five steps:

1. List critical success factors as identified in the internal-audit process. Use a total of from ten to twenty internal factors, including both strengths and weaknesses. List strengths first and then weaknesses. Be as specific as possible, using percentages, ratios, and comparative numbers.

2. Assign a weight that ranges from 0.0 (not important) to 1.0 (all-important) to each factor. The weight assigned to a given factor indicates the relative importance of the factor to being successful in the firm's industry. Regardless of whether a key factor is an internal strength or weakness, factors considered to have the greatest effect on organizational performance should be assigned the highest weights. The summation of all weights must total 1.0.

3. Assign a 1 to 4 rating to each factor to indicate whether that factor represents a major weakness (rating = 1), a minor weakness (rating = 2), a minor strength (rating = 3), or a major strength (rating = 4). Ratings are thus company-based, whereas the weights in Step 2 are industry-based.

4. Multiply each factor's weight by its rating to determine a weighted score for each variable.

5. Sum the weighted scores for each variable to determine the total weighted score for the organization.

Regardless of how many factors are included in an IFE Matrix, the total weighted score can range from a low of 1.0 to a high of 4.0, with the average score being 2.5. Total weighted scores well below 2.5 characterize organizations that are weak internally, whereas scores significantly above 2.5 indicate a strong internal position. Like the EFE Matrix, an IFE Matrix should include from ten to twenty key factors. The number of factors has no effect upon the range of total weighted scores because the weights always sum to 1.0.

When a key internal factor is both a strength and a weakness, the factor should be included twice in the IFE Matrix, and a weight and rating should be assigned to each statement. For example, the Playboy logo both helps and hurts Playboy Enterprises; the logo attracts customers to the *Playboy* magazine, but it keeps the Playboy cable channel out of many markets.

An example of IFE Matrix is provided in Table 5–8. Note that the firm's major strengths are its current ratio, profit margin, and employee morale as indicated by the 4 ratings. The major weaknesses are lack of a strategic-management system, rising R & D expenses, and ineffective dealer incentives. The total weighted score of 2.80 indicates that the firm is above average in its overall internal strategic position.

In multidivisional firms each autonomous division or strategic business unit should construct an IFE Matrix. Divisional matrices can then be integrated to develop an overall corporate IFE Matrix.

TABLE 5-8   A Sample Internal Factor Evaluation Matrix

CRITICAL SUCCESS FACTORS	WEIGHT	RATING	WEIGHTED SCORE
STRENGTHS			
1. Current ratio increased to 2.52	.06	4	.24
2. Profit margin increased to 6.94	.16	4	.64
3. Employee morale is high	.18	4	.72
4. New computer information system	.08	3	.24
5. Market share has increased to 24 percent	.12	3	.36
WEAKNESSES			
1. Legal suits have not been resolved	.05	2	.10
2. Plant capacity has fallen to 74 percent	.15	2	.30
3. Lack of a strategic management system	.06	1	.06
4. R & D expenses have increased 31 percent	.08	1	.08
5. Dealer incentives have not been effective	.06	1	.06
Total	1.00		2.80

Note: The ratings values are as follows: 1 = major weakness, 2 = minor weakness, 3 = minor strength, 4 = major strength.

CONCLUSION

Management, marketing, finance/accounting, production/operations, research and development, and computer information systems represent the core operations of most businesses. A strategic-management audit of a firm's internal operations is vital to organizational health. Many companies still prefer to be judged solely on their bottom-line performance. However, an increasing number of successful organizations are using the internal audit to gain competitive advantages over rival firms.

Systematic methodologies for performing strength-weakness assessments are not well developed in the strategic-management literature, but it is clear that strategists must identify and evaluate internal strengths and weaknesses in order to formulate and choose among alternative strategies effectively. The EFE Matrix, Competitive Profile Matrix, IFE Matrix, and a clear statement of mission provide the basic information needed to formulate competitive strategies successfully. The process of performing an internal audit represents an opportunity for managers and employees throughout the organization to participate in determining the future of the firm. Involvement in the process can energize and mobilize managers and employees.

KEY TERMS AND CONCEPTS

Buying
Capital Budgeting
Computer Information Systems
Controlling

Cost/Benefit Analysis
Cultural Products
Customer Analysis
Distribution

Dividend Decision
Financial Ratio Analysis
Financing Decision
Functions of Finance/Accounting
Functions of Management
Functions of Marketing
Functions of Production/Operations
Human Resource Management
Internal Audit
Internal Factor Evaluation (IFE) Matrix
Investment Decision
Marketing Research

Motivating
Opportunity Analysis
Organizational Culture
Organizing
Personnel Management
Planning
Pricing
Social Responsibility
Staffing
Synergy
Test Marketing

ISSUES FOR REVIEW AND DISCUSSION

1. Explain why prioritizing the relative importance of strengths and weaknesses to include in an IFE Matrix is an important strategic-management activity.

2. How can delegation of authority contribute to effective strategic management?

3. Diagram a formal organizational chart that reflects the following positions: a president, two executive officers, four middle managers, and eighteen lower-level managers. Now, diagram three overlapping and hypothetical informal group structures. How can this information be helpful to a strategist in formulating and implementing strategy?

4. How could a strategist's attitude toward social responsibility affect a firm's strategy? What is your attitude toward social responsibility?

5. Which of the three basic functions of finance/accounting do you feel is most important in a small electronics manufacturing concern? Justify your position.

6. Do you think aggregate R & D expenditures for American firms will increase or decrease next year? Why?

7. Explain how you would motivate managers and employees to implement a major new strategy.

8. Why do you think production/operations managers are often not directly involved in strategy-formulation activities? Why can this be a major organizational weakness?

9. Give two examples of staffing strengths and two examples of staffing weaknesses of an organization with which you are familiar.

10. Would you ever pay out dividends when your firm's annual net profit is negative? Why? What effect could this have on a firm's strategies?

11. If a firm has zero debt in its capital structure, is that always an organizational strength? Why or why not?

12. Describe the production/operations system in a police department.

13. After conducting an internal audit, a firm discovers a total of one hundred strengths and one hundred weaknesses. What procedures could then be used to determine the most important of these? Why is it important to reduce the total number of key factors?

14. Select one of the suggested readings at the end of this chapter. Look that article up in your college library. Give a 5-minute oral report to the class summarizing the article and your views on the topic.

15. Why do you believe cultural products affect all the functions of business?

16. Do you think cultural products affect strategy formulation, implementation, or evaluation the most? Why?

17. Identify cultural products at your college or university. Do these products, viewed collectively or separately, represent a strength or weakness for the organization?

18. Describe the computer information system at your college or university.

19. Explain the difference between data and information in terms of each being useful to strategists.

20. What are the most important characteristics of an effective computer information system?

1. Robert Grant, "The Resource-Based Theory of Competitive Advantage: Implications for Strategy Formulation." *California Management Review* (Spring 1991): 116.

2. Reprinted by permission of the publisher from "Integrating Strength-Weakness Analysis into Strategic Planning," by William King, *Journal of Business Research II*, no. 4, p. 481. Copyright 1983 by Elsevier Science Publishing Co., Inc.

3. Igor Ansoff, "Strategic Management of Technology," *Journal of Business Strategy* 7, no. 3 (Winter 1987): 38.

4. Claude George, Jr. *The History of Management Thought*, 2nd ed. (Englewood Cliffs, N.J.: Prentice-Hall, 1972), 174.

5. Edgar Schein, *Organizational Culture and Leadership* (San Francisco: Jossey-Bass, 1985), 9.

6. John Lorsch, "Managing Culture: The Invisible Barrier to Strategic Change," *California Management Review* 28, 2 (1986): 95–109.

7. Y. Allarie and M. Firsirotu, "How to Implement Radical Strategies in Large Organizations," *Sloan Management Review* (Spring 1985): 19.

8. Adam Smith, *Wealth of Nations* (New York: Modern Library, 1937), 3–4.

9. Daft, Richard, *Management*, 3rd ed. (Orlando, Fla.: Dryden Press, 1993), 512.

10. Shelley Kirkpatrick and Edwin Locke, "Leadership: Do Traits Matter?" *Academy of Management Executive* 5, no. 2 (May 1991): 48.

11. Peter Drucker, *Management Tasks, Responsibilities, and Practice* (New York: Harper & Row, 1973), 463.

12. Brian Dumaine, "What the Leaders of Tomorrow Sec," *Fortune* (July 3, 1989): 51.

13. J. M. Bryson and P. Bromiley, "Critical Factors Affecting the Planning and Implementation of Major Products," *Strategic Management Journal* 14, no. 5 (July 1993): 319.

14. Robert Waterman, Jr. "The Renewal Factor," *Business Week* (September 14, 1987): 104.

15. J. Evans and B. Berman, *Marketing* (New York: Macmillan, 1982), 17.

16. Quoted in Robert Waterman, Jr., "The Renewal Factor," *Business Week* (September 14, 1987): 108.

17. J. V. Horne, *Financial Management and Policy* (Englewood Cliffs, N.J.: Prentice-Hall, 1974), 10.

18. W. Boulton and B. Saladin, "Let's Make Production-Operations Management Top Priority for Strategic Planning in the 1980s," *Managerial Planning* 32, no. 1 (July–August 1983): 19.

19. Vida Scarpello, William Boulton, and Charles Hofer, "Reintegrating R & D into Business Strategy," *Journal of Business Strategy* 6, no. 4 (Spring 1986): 50.

20. Philip Rouseel, Kamal Saad, and Tamara Erickson, "The Evolution of Third Generation R&D," *Planning Review* 19, no. 2 (March–April 1991): 18–26.

21. Ibid., 50, 51.

22. Hugh Watson and Kelly Rainer, Jr., "A Manager's Guide to Executive Support Systems," *Business Horizons* (March–April 1991): 49.

23. Gerrit Janssens and Ludo Cuyvers, "EDI—A Strategic Weapon in International Trade," *Long Range Planning* 24, no. 2 (April 1991): 46–52.

24. Robert Mockler, "A Catalog of Commercially Available Software for Strategic Planning," *Planning Review* 19, no. 3 (May/June 1991): 28. John Sterling, "Strategic Management Software Review," *Planning Review* (January–February 1992): 29–33.

Bahrami, Homa. "The Emerging Flexible Organization." *California Management Review* 34, no. 4 (Summer 1992): 33–52.

Bowman, E. H., and H. Singh. "Corporate Restructuring: Reconfiguring the Firm." *Strategic Management Journal* 14, Special Issue (Summer 1993): 5–14.

Boynton, Andrew C. "Achieving Dynamic Stability Through Information Technology." *California Management Review* 35, no. 2 (Winter 1993): 58–77.

Broderick, Renae, and John W. Boudreau. "Human Resource Management, Information Technology and the Competitive Edge." *The Executive* VI, no. 2 (May 1992): 7–17.

Bryson, J. M., and P. Bromiley. "Critical Factors Affecting the Planning and Implementation of Major Products." *Strategic Management Journal* 14, no. 5 (July 1993): 319–338.

Parthasarthy, R., and P. Sethi. "Business Strategy and Organizational Structure." *Academy of Management Review* 17, no. 1 (January 1992): 86–111.

Camuffo, Arnaldo, and Giovanni Costa. "Strategic Human Resource Management—Italian Style." *Sloan Management Review* 34, no. 2 (Winter 1993): 59–68.

Cool, K., and I. Dierickx. "Rivalry, Strategic Groups and Firm Profitability." *Strategic Management Journal* 14, no. 1 (January 1993): 47–60.

Davidson, Alistair. "A Directory of Strategic Management Software Tools." *Planning Review* 22, no. 4 (July–August 1993): 35–37.

Huston, Larry A. "Using Total Quality to Put Strategic Intent into Motion." *Planning Review* 20, no. 5 (September–October 1992): 21–23.

Kennedy, Carol. "Changing the Company Culture at Ciba-Geigy." *Long Range Planning* 26, no. 1 (February 1993): 18–27.

Krackhardt, David, and Jeffrey R. Hanson. "Informal Networks: The Company Behind the Chart." *Harvard Business Review* 71, no. 4 (July–August 1993): 104–113.

Levering, Robert. "Can Companies Trust Their Employees?" *Business and Society Review* 81 (Spring 1992): 8–12.

Levinson, Harry. "Between CO and COO." *Academy of Management Executive* VII, no. 2 (May 1993): 71–83.

Morgan, Malcolm J. "How Corporate Culture Drives Strategy." *Long Range Planning* 26, no. 2 (April 1993): 110–118.

Niven, Daniel. "When Times Get Tough, What Happens to TQM?" *Harvard Business Review* (May–June 1993): 20–37.

Parthasarthy, Raghavan, and S. Prakash Sethi. "The Impact of Flexible Automation on Business Strategy and Organizational Structure." *Academy of Management Review* 17, no. 1 (January 1992): 86–111.

Pearson, Christine M., and Ian I. Mitroff. "From Crisis Prone to Crisis Prepared: A Framework for Crisis Management." *The Executive* VII, no. 1 (February 1993): 48–59.

Reilly, A. H., J. M. Brett, and L. K. Stroh. "The Impact of Corporate Turbulence on Managers' Attitudes." *Strategic Management Journal* 14, Special Issue (Summer 1993): 167–180.

Reilly, William K. "Environment, Inc." *Business Horizons* 35, no. 2 (March–April 1992): 9–11.

Saunier, Fredric, and Susan B. Cohen. "Marketers Aflutter over Advertising Clutter." *Business and Society Review* 80 (Winter 1992): 46–50.

Sheridan, John E. "Organizational Culture and Employee Retention." *Academy of Management Journal* 35, no. 5 (December 1992): 1036–1056.

Spitzer, T. Quinn, and Benjamin Tregoe. "Thinking and Managing Beyond the Boundaries." *Business Horizons* 36, no. 1 (January–February 1993): 36–40.

Starr, Martin K. "Accelerating Innovation." *Business Horizons* 35, no. 4 (July–August 1992): 44–51.

Tenaglia, Mason, and Patrick Noonan. "Scenario-Based Strategic Planning: A Process for Building Top Management Consensus." *Planning Review* 20, no. 2 (March–April 1992): 12–19.

Vandenberg, Robert J., and Charles E. Lance. "Examining the Causal Order of Job Satisfaction and Organizational Commitment." *Journal of Management* 18, no. 1 (March 1992): 153–168.

Wilhelm, Warren R. "Changing Corporate Culture—or Corporate Behavior? How to Change Your Company." *The Executive* VI, no. 4 (November 1992): 72–77.

EXPERIENTIAL EXERCISES

PERFORMING A FINANCIAL RATIO ANALYSIS FOR HERSHEY FOODS

PURPOSE

Financial ratio analysis is one of the best techniques for identifying and evaluating internal strengths and weaknesses. Potential investors and current shareholders look closely at firms' financial ratios, making detailed comparisons to industry averages and to previous periods of time. Financial ratio analyses provide vital input information for developing an IFE Matrix.

INSTRUCTIONS

Step 1   On a separate sheet of paper, number from 1 to 20. Referring to Hershey's income statement and balance sheet (pp. 40–41), calculate twenty 1992 financial ratios for the company. Use Table 5–3 as a reference.

Step 2   Go to your college library and find industry average financial ratios for the confectionery industry. Record the industry average values in a second column on your paper.

Step 3   In a third column, indicate whether you consider each ratio to be a strength, a weakness, or a neutral factor for Hershey.

CONSTRUCTING AN IFE MATRIX FOR HERSHEY FOODS

PURPOSE

This exercise will give you experience developing an IFE Matrix. Identifying and prioritizing factors to include in an IFE Matrix fosters communication among functional and divisional managers. Preparing an IFE Matrix allows human resource, marketing, production/operations, finance/accounting, R & D, and computer information systems managers to vocalize their concerns and thoughts regarding the business condition of the firm. This results in an improved collective understanding of the business.

INSTRUCTIONS

Step 1   Join with two other individuals to form a three-person team. Develop a team IFE Matrix for Hershey Foods.

Step 2   Compare your team's IFE Matrix to other teams' IFE Matrices. Discuss any major differences.

Step 3   What strategies do you think would allow Hershey to capitalize on its major strengths? What strategies would allow Hershey to improve upon its major weaknesses?

CONSTRUCTING AN IFE MATRIX FOR MY UNIVERSITY

PURPOSE

This exercise gives you the opportunity to evaluate your university's major strengths and weaknesses. As will become clearer in the next chapter, an organization's strategies are largely based upon striving to take advantage of strengths and improving upon weaknesses.

INSTRUCTIONS

Step 1   Join with two other individuals to form a three-person team. Develop a team IFE Matrix for your university. You may use the strength/weaknesses determined in Experiential Exercise 1D if you like.

Step 2   Go to the board and diagram your team's IFE Matrix.

Step 3   Compare your team's IFE Matrix to other teams' IFE Matrices. Discuss any major differences.

Step 4   What strategies do you think would allow your university to capitalize on its major strengths? What strategies would allow your university to improve upon its major weaknesses?

USING THE *STRATEGY FORMULATOR* SOFTWARE

PURPOSE

The purpose of this exercise is to enhance your skills using the *Strategy Formulator* software that is available with this text. This software can make it easier for you to develop, revise, update, and print various strategy-formulation analyses.

INSTRUCTIONS

Step 1   Use the *Strategy Formulator* software to develop a list of strengths and weaknesses for your university (Experiential Exercise 5C).

Step 2   Bring a printout of your work to class. Discuss any problems or questions you encountered in using this software.

Chapter 6

STRATEGY ANALYSIS AND CHOICE

OBJECTIVES

After studying this chapter, you should be able to:

■ Describe a three-stage framework for choosing among alternative strategies.

■ Explain how to develop a TOWS Matrix, SPACE Matrix, BCG Matrix, IE Matrix, and QSPM.

■ Identify important behavioral, political, ethical, and social responsibility considerations in strategy analysis and choice.

■ Discuss the role of intuition in strategic analysis and choice.

■ Discuss the role of organizational culture in strategic analysis and choice.

■ Discuss the role of a board of directors in choosing among alternative strategies.

Strategic analysis and choice largely involves making subjective decisions based on objective information. This chapter introduces important concepts that can help strategists generate feasible alternatives, evaluate those alternatives, and choose a specific course of action. Behavioral aspects of strategy formulation are described, including politics, culture, ethics, and social responsibility considerations. Modern tools for formulating strategies are described, and the appropriate role of a board of directors is discussed.

THE NATURE OF STRATEGY ANALYSIS AND CHOICE

As indicated by the shaded portion of Figure 6–1, this chapter focuses on establishing long-term objectives, generating alternative strategies, and selecting strategies to pursue. Strategy analysis and choice seeks to determine alternative courses of action that could best enable the firm to achieve its mission and objectives. The firm's present strategies, objectives, and mission, coupled with the external and internal audit information, provide a basis for generating and evaluating feasible alternative strategies.

Unless a desperate situation faces the firm, alternative strategies will likely represent incremental steps to move the firm from its present position to a desired future position. For example, Kindercare Learning Centers has a strategy to open one hundred new centers per year, thus expanding from current markets into new areas. Alternative strategies do not come out of the wild blue yonder; they are derived from the firm's mission, objectives, external audit, and internal audit; they are consistent with, or build upon, past strategies that have worked well!

The Process of Generating and Selecting Strategies. Strategists never consider all feasible alternatives that could benefit the firm, because there are an infinite number of possible actions and an infinite number of ways to implement those actions. Therefore, a manageable set of the most attractive alternative strategies must be developed. The advantages, disadvantages, trade-offs, costs, and benefits of these strategies should be determined. This section discusses the process that many firms use to determine an appropriate set of alternative strategies.

Identifying and evaluating alternative strategies should involve many of the managers and employees who earlier assembled the organizational mission statement, performed the external audit, and conducted the internal audit. Representatives from each department and division of the firm should be included in this process, as was the case in previous strategy-formulation activities. Recall that involvement provides the best opportunity for managers and employees to gain an understanding of what the firm is doing and why, and to become committed to helping the firm accomplish its objectives.

All participants in the strategy analysis and choice activity should have the firm's external and internal audit information by their sides. This information, coupled with the firm's mission statement, will help participants crystallize in their own minds particular strategies that they believe could benefit the firm most. Creativity should be encouraged in this thought process.

Alternative strategies proposed by participants should be considered and discussed in a meeting or series of meetings. Proposed strategies should be listed in writing. When all feasible strategies identified by participants are given and understood, the strategies should be ranked in order of attractiveness by all participants, with 1 = should not be implemented, 2 = should possibly be implemented, 3 = should proba-

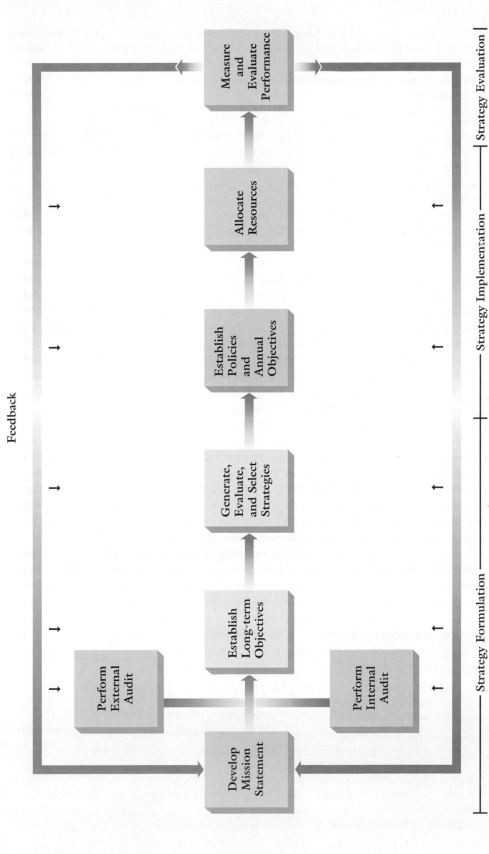

FIGURE 6-1 A Comprehensive Strategic-Management Model

Feedback

Perform External Audit

Develop Mission Statement

Establish Long-term Objectives

Generate, Evaluate, and Select Strategies

Establish Policies and Annual Objectives

Allocate Resources

Measure and Evaluate Performance

Perform Internal Audit

Strategy Formulation — Strategy Implementation — Strategy Evaluation bly be implemented, and 4 = should definitely be implemented. This process will result in a prioritized list of "best" strategies that reflects the collective wisdom of the group.

LONG-TERM OBJECTIVES

Long-term objectives represent the results expected from pursuing certain strategies. Strategies represent the actions to be taken to accomplish long-term objectives. The time frame for objectives and strategies should be consistent, usually from 2 to 5 years.

An increasing number of firms recognize that establishing long-term objectives and strategies must be a give-and-take process. In practice, organizations generally establish objectives and strategies concurrently. The strategic-management model thus illustrates with multidirectional arrows a symbiotic relationship between establishing objectives and establishing strategies. Objectives become crystallized as feasible strategies are formulated and selected.

The Nature of Long-term Objectives. Objectives should be quantitative, measurable, realistic, understandable, challenging, hierarchical, obtainable, and congruent among organizational units. Each objective should also be associated with a time line. Objectives are commonly stated in terms such as growth in assets, growth in sales, profitability, market share, degree and nature of diversification, degree and nature of vertical integration, earnings per share, and social responsibility. Clearly established objectives offer many benefits. They provide direction, allow synergy, aid in evaluation, establish priorities, reduce uncertainty, minimize conflicts, stimulate exertion, and aid in both the allocation of resources and the design of jobs.

Long-term objectives are needed at the corporate, divisional, and functional levels in an organization. They are an important measure of managerial performance. Many practitioners and academicians attribute a significant part of U.S. industry's competitive decline to the short-term, rather than long-term, strategy orientation of managers in the United States. Arthur D. Little argues that bonuses or merit pay for managers today must be based to a greater extent on long-term objectives and strategies. A general framework for relating objectives to performance evaluation is provided in Table 6–1. A particular organization could tailor these guidelines to meet its own needs, but incentives should be attached to both long-term and annual objectives.

Clearly stated and communicated objectives are vital to success for many reasons. First, objectives help stakeholders understand their role in an organization's future.

TABLE 6-1   Varying Performance Measures by Organizational Level

ORGANIZATIONAL LEVEL	BASIS FOR ANNUAL BONUS OR MERIT PAY
Corporate	75% based on long-term objectives 25% based on annual objectives
Divisional	50% based on long-term objectives 50% based on annual objectives
Functional	25% based on long-term objectives 75% based on annual objectives

They also provide a basis for consistent decision making by managers whose values and attitudes differ. By reaching a consensus on objectives during strategy-formulation activities, an organization can minimize potential conflicts later during implementation. Objectives set forth organizational priorities and stimulate exertion and accomplishment. They serve as standards by which individuals, groups, departments, divisions, and entire organizations can be evaluated. Objectives provide the basis for designing jobs and organizing activities to be performed in an organization. They also provide direction and allow for organizational synergy. Without long-term objectives, an organization would drift aimlessly toward some unknown end! It is hard to imagine an organization or individual being successful without clear objectives. Success only rarely occurs by accident; rather, it is the result of hard work directed toward achieving certain objectives.

Not Managing by Objectives. An unknown educator once said, "If you think education is expensive, try ignorance." The idea behind this saying also applies to establishing objectives. Strategists should avoid the following alternative ways to "not managing by objectives."

- Managing by Extrapolation—adheres to the principle "If it ain't broke, don't fix it." The idea is to keep on doing about the same things in the same ways, because things are going well.
- Managing by Crisis—based on the belief that the true measure of a really good strategist is the ability to solve problems. Since there are plenty of crises and problems to go around for every person and every organization, strategists ought to bring their time and creative energy to bear on solving the most pressing problems of the day. Managing by crisis is actually a form of reacting rather than acting and of letting events dictate the whats and whens of management decisions.
- Managing by Subjectives—built on the idea that there is no general plan for which way to go and what to do; just do the best you can to accomplish what you think should be done. In short, "do your own thing, the best way you know how," (sometimes referred to as "the mystery approach to decision making" because subordinates are left to figure out what is happening and why.)
- Managing by Hope—based on the fact that the future is laden with great uncertainty and that if we try and do not succeed, then we hope our second (or third) attempt will succeed. Decisions are predicted on the hope that they will work and that good times are just around the corner, especially if luck and good fortune are on our side.[1]

A COMPREHENSIVE STRATEGY-FORMULATION FRAMEWORK

Important strategy-formulation techniques can be integrated into a three stage decision-making framework, as shown in Figure 6–2. The tools presented in this framework are applicable to all sizes and types of organizations and can help strategists identify, evaluate, and select strategies.

Stage 1 of the formulation framework consists of the EFE Matrix, the IFE Matrix, and the Competitive Profile Matrix. Called the *Input Stage,* Stage 1 summarizes the basic input information needed to formulate strategies. Stage 2, called the *Matching Stage,* focuses upon generating feasible alternative strategies by aligning key external and internal factors. Stage 2 techniques include the Threats-Opportunities-Weaknesses-Strengths (TOWS) Matrix, the Strategic Position and Action Evaluation

(SPACE) Matrix, the Boston Consulting Group (BCG) Matrix, the Internal-External (IE) Matrix, and the Grand Strategy Matrix. Stage 3, called the *Decision Stage,* involves a single technique, the Quantitative Strategic Planning Matrix (QSPM). A QSPM uses input information from Stage 1 to objectively evaluate feasible alternative strategies identified in Stage 2. A QSPM reveals the relative attractiveness of alternative strategies and thus provides an objective basis for selecting specific strategies.

All nine techniques included in the strategy-formulation framework require integration of intuition and analysis. Autonomous divisions in an organization commonly use strategy-formulation techniques to develop strategies and objectives. Divisional analyses provide a basis for identifying, evaluating, and selecting among alternative corporate-level strategies.

Strategists themselves, not analytic tools, are always responsible and accountable for strategic decisions. Lenz emphasizes that the shift from a words-oriented to a numbers-oriented planning process can give rise to a false sense of certainty; it can reduce dialogue, discussion, and argument as a means to explore understandings, test assumptions and foster organizational learning.[2] Strategists therefore must be wary of this possibility and use analytical tools to facilitate, rather than diminish, communication. Without objective information and analysis, personal biases, politics, emotions, personalities, and *halo error* (the tendency to put too much weight on a single factor) unfortunately may play a dominant role in the strategy-formulation process.

THE INPUT STAGE

Procedures for developing an EFE Matrix, an IFE Matrix, and a Competitive Profile Matrix were presented in the previous two chapters. The information derived from these three matrices provides basic input information for the matching and decision stage matrices described later in this chapter.

The input tools require strategists to quantify subjectivity during early stages of the strategy-formulation process. Making "small" decisions in the input matrices regarding the relative importance of external and internal factors allows strategists to gener-

STAGE 1: THE INPUT STAGE				
External Factor Evaluation (EFE) Matrix		Competitive Profile Matrix		Internal Factor Evaluation (IFE) Matrix
STAGE 2: THE MATCHING STAGE				
Threats-Opportunities-Weaknesses-Strengths (TOWS) Matrix	Strategic Position and Action Evaluation (SPACE) Matrix	Boston Consulting Group (BCG) Matrix	Internal-External (IE) Matrix	Grand Strategy Matrix
STAGE 3: THE DECISION STAGE				
Quantitative Strategic Planning Matrix (QSPM)				

FIGURE 6-2 The Strategy-Formulation Analytical Framework

ate and evaluate alternative strategies more effectively. Good intuitive judgment is always needed in determining appropriate weights and ratings.

Strategy is sometimes defined as the "match" an organization makes between its internal resources and skills . . . and the opportunities and risks created by its external factors.[3] The matching stage of the strategy-formulation framework consists of five techniques that can be used in any sequence: the TOWS Matrix, the SPACE Matrix, the BCG Matrix, the IE Matrix, and the Grand Strategy Matrix. These tools rely upon information derived from the input stage to match external opportunities and threats with internal strengths and weaknesses. Matching external and internal critical success factors is the key to effectively generating feasible alternative strategies! For example, a firm with excess working capital (an internal strength) could take advantage of the aerospace industry's 40-percent annual growth rate (an external opportunity) by acquiring a firm in the aerospace industry. This example portrays simple one-to-one matching. In most situations, external and internal relationships are more complex, and the matching requires multiple alignments for each strategy generated. The basic concept of matching is illustrated in Table 6–2.

Any organization, whether military, product-oriented, service-oriented, governmental, or even athletic, must develop and execute good strategies to win. A good offense without a good defense, or vice versa, usually leads to defeat. Developing strategies that use strengths to capitalize on opportunities could be considered an offense, whereas strategies designed to improve upon weaknesses while avoiding threats could be termed defensive. Every organization has some external opportunities and threats and internal strengths and weaknesses that can be aligned to formulate feasible alternative strategies.

The Threats-Opportunities-Weaknesses-Strengths (TOWS) Matrix. The *Threats-Opportunities-Weaknesses-Strengths (TOWS) Matrix* is an important matching tool that helps managers develop four types of strategies: SO Strategies, WO Strategies, ST

TABLE 6-2   Matching Key External and Internal Factors to Formulate Alternative Strategies

KEY INTERNAL FACTOR		KEY EXTERNAL FACTOR		RESULTANT STRATEGY
Excess working capacity (an internal strength)	+	20% annual growth in the cablevision industry (an external opportunity)	=	Acquire Visioncable, Inc.
Insufficient capacity (an internal weakness)	+	Exit of two major foreign competitors from the industry (an external opportunity)	=	Pursue horizontal integration by buying competitors' facilities
Strong R & D expertise (an internal strength)	+	Decreasing numbers of young adults (an external threat)	=	Develop new products for older adults
Poor employee morale (an internal weakness)	+	Strong union activity (an external threat)	=	Develop a new employee-benefits package

Strategies, and WT Strategies.[4] Watching key external and internal factors is the most difficult part of developing a TOWS Matrix and requires good judgment, and there is no one best set of matches. Note in Table 6–2 that the first, second, third, and fourth strategies are SO, WO, ST, and WT Strategies respectively.

SO Strategies use a firm's internal strengths to take advantage of external opportunities. All managers would like their organizations to be in a position where internal strengths can be used to take advantage of external trends and events. Organizations generally will pursue WO, ST, or WT Strategies in order to get into a situation where they can apply SO Strategies. When a firm has major weaknesses, it will strive to overcome them and make them strengths. When an organization faces major threats, it will seek to avoid them in order to concentrate on opportunities.

WO Strategies aim at improving internal weaknesses by taking advantage of external opportunities. Sometimes key external opportunities exist, but a firm has internal weaknesses that prevent it from exploiting those opportunities. For example, there may be a high demand for electronic devices to control the amount and timing of fuel injection in automobile engines (opportunity), but a certain auto parts manufacturer may lack the technology required for producing these devices (weakness). One possible WO Strategy would be to acquire this technology by forming a joint venture with a firm having competency in this area. An alternative WO Strategy would be to hire and train people with the required technical capabilities.

ST Strategies use a firm's strengths to avoid or reduce the impact of external threats. This does not mean that a strong organization should always meet threats in the external environment head-on. A recent example of ST Strategy occurred when Texas Instruments used an excellent legal department (a strength) to collect nearly $700 million in damages and royalties from nine Japanese and Korean firms that infringed on patents for semiconductor memory chips. Rival firms that copy ideas, innovations, and patented products are a major threat in many industries.

WT Strategies are defensive tactics directed at reducing internal weaknesses and avoiding environmental threats. An organization faced with numerous external threats and internal weaknesses may indeed be in a precarious position. In fact, such a firm may have to fight for its survival, merge, retrench, declare bankruptcy, or choose liquidation.

A schematic representation of the TOWS Matrix is provided in Figure 6–3. Note that a TOWS Matrix is composed of nine cells. As shown, there are four key factor cells, four strategy cells, and one cell that is always left blank (the upper left cell). The four strategy cells, labeled SO, WO, ST, and WT, are developed after completing four key factor cells, labeled S, W, O, and T. There are eight steps involved in constructing a TOWS Matrix.

1. List the firm's key external opportunities.
2. List the firm's key external threats.
3. List the firm's key internal strengths.
4. List the firm's key internal weaknesses.
5. Match internal strengths with external opportunities and record the resultant SO Strategies in the appropriate cell.
6. Match internal weaknesses with external opportunities and record the resultant WO Strategies.
7. Match internal strengths with external threats and record the resultant ST Strategies.
8. Match internal weaknesses with external threats and record the resultant WT Strategies.

	STRENGTHS—S	WEAKNESSES—W
Always leave blank	1. 2. 3. 4. 5. List strengths 6. 7. 8. 9. 10.	1. 2. 3. 4. 5. List weaknesses 6. 7. 8. 9. 10.
OPPORTUNITIES—O 1. 2. 3. 4. 5. List opportunities 6. 7. 8. 9. 10.	**SO STRATEGIES** 1. 2. 3. 4. Use strengths to take 5. advantage of opportunities 6. 7. 8. 9. 10.	**WO STRATEGIES** 1. 2. 3. 4. Overcome weaknesses by 5. taking advantage of 6. opportunities 7. 8. 9. 10.
THREATS—T 1. 2. 3. 4. 5. List threats 6. 7. 8. 9. 10.	**ST STRATEGIES** 1. 2. 3. 4. Use strengths to avoid 5. threats 6. 7. 8. 9. 10.	**WT STRATEGIES** 1. 2. 3. 4. Minimize weaknesses and 5. avoid threats 6. 7. 8. 9. 10.

FIGURE 6-3 The TOWS Matrix

The purpose of each Stage 2 matching tool is to generate feasible alternative strategies, not to select or determine which strategies are best! Not all of the strategies developed in the TOWS Matrix, therefore, will be selected for implementation. A sample TOWS Matrix for a food company is provided in Figure 6–4.

The strategy-formulation guidelines provided in Chapter 2 can enhance the process of matching key external and internal factors. For example, when an organization has both the capital and human resources needed to distribute its own products (internal strength) and distributors are unreliable, costly, or incapable of meeting the firm's needs (external threat), then forward integration can be an attractive ST Strategy. When a firm has excess production capacity (internal weakness) and its basic industry is experiencing declining annual sales and profits (external threat), then concentric diversification can be an effective WT Strategy. It is important to use specific, rather than general, strategy terms when developing a TOWS Matrix. In addition, it is important to include the "S1,O2"

FIGURE 6-4 The TOWS Matrix for Campbell Soup Company

	STRENGTHS—S	WEAKNESSES—W
	1. Current ratio increased to 2.52	1. Legal suits have not been resolved
	2. Profit margin increased to 6.94	2. Plant capacity has fallen to 74%
	3. Employee morale is high	3. Lack of a strategic management system
	4. New computer information system	4. R&D expenses have increased 31%
	5. Market share has increased to 24%	5. Dealer incentives have not been effective
OPPORTUNITIES—O	SO STRATEGIES	WO STRATEGIES
1. Western European unification	1. Acquire food company in Europe (S1, S5, O1)	1. Form a joint venture to distribute soup in Europe (W3, O1)
2. Rising health consciousness in selecting foods	2. Build a manufacturing plant in Mexico (S2, S5, O5)	2. Develop new Pepperidge Farm products (W1, O2, O4)
3. Free market economies arising in Asia	3. Develop new healthy soups (S3, O2)	
4. Demand for soups increasing 10% annually	4. Form a joint venture to distribute soup in Asia (S1, S5, O3)	
5. U.S./Mexico Free Trade Agreement		
THREATS—T	ST STRATEGIES	WT STRATEGIES
1. Food revenues increasing only 1% annually	1. Develop new microwave TV dinners (S1, S5, T2)	1. Close unprofitable European operations (W3, T3, T5)
2. ConAgra's Banquet TV dinners lead market with 27.4% share	2. Develop new biodegradable soup containers (S1, T4)	2. Diversify into nonsoup foods (W5, T1)
3. Unstable economies in Asia		
4. Tin cans are not biodegradable		
5. Low value of the dollar		

type notation after each strategy in the TOWS Matrix. This notation reveals the rationale for each alternative strategy.

The Strategic Position and Action Evaluation (SPACE) Matrix. The *Strategic Position and Action Evaluation (SPACE) Matrix,* another important Stage 2 "matching" tool, is illustrated in Figure 6–5. Its four-quadrant framework indicates whether aggressive, conservative, defensive, or competitive strategies are most appropriate for a given organization. The axes of the SPACE Matrix represent two internal dimensions (*financial strength* [FS] and *competitive advantage* [CA]) and two external dimensions (*environmental stability* [ES] and *industry strength* [IS]). These four factors are the most important determinants of an organization's overall strategic position.[5]

Depending upon the type of organization, numerous variables could comprise each of the dimensions represented on the axes of the SPACE Matrix. Some variables commonly included are given in Table 6–3. For example, return on investment, leverage,

FIGURE 6-5 The SPACE Matrix

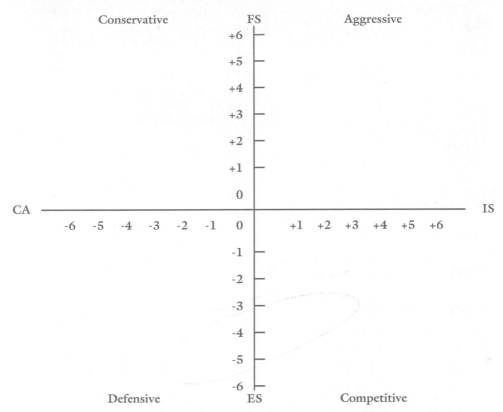

Source: H. Rowe, R. Mason, and K Dickel, *Strategic Management and Business Policy: A Methodological Approach* (Reading, Massachusetts: Addison–Wesley Publishing Co. Inc., © 1982): 155. Reprinted with permission of the publisher.

liquidity, working capital, and cash flow are commonly considered determining factors of an organization's financial strength. Like the TOWS Matrix, the SPACE Matrix should be tailored to the particular organization being studied and based on factual information as much as possible.

The steps required to develop a SPACE Matrix are:

1. Select a set of variables to comprise financial strength (FS), competitive advantage (CA), environmental stability (ES), and industry strength (IS).
2. Assign a numerical value ranging from +1 (worst) to +6 (best) to each of the variables that comprise the FS and IS dimensions. Assign a numerical value ranging from -1 (best) to -6 (worst) to each of the variables that comprise the ES and CA dimensions.
3. Compute an average score for FS, CA, IS, and ES by summing the values given to the variables of each dimension and dividing by the number of variables included in the respective dimension.
4. Plot the average scores for FS, IS, ES, and CA on the appropriate axis in the SPACE Matrix.
5. Add the two scores on the *x*-axis and plot the resultant point on X. Add the two scores on the *y*-axis and plot the resultant point on Y. Plot the intersection of the new *xy* point.

TABLE 6-3   Example Factors that Comprise the SPACE Matrix Axes

INTERNAL STRATEGIC POSITION	EXTERNAL STRATEGIC POSITION
FINANCIAL STRENGTH (FS)	**ENVIRONMENTAL STABILITY (ES)** *
Return on investment	Technological changes
Leverage	Rate of inflation
Liquidity	Demand variability
Working capital	Price range of competing products
Cash flow	Barriers to entry into market
Ease of exit from market	Competitive pressure
Risk involved in business	Price elasticity of demand
COMPETITIVE ADVANTAGE (CA)	**INDUSTRY STRENGTH (IS)**
Market share	Growth potential
Product quality	Profit potential
Product life cycle	Financial stability
Customer loyalty	Technological know-how
Competition's capacity utilization	Resource utilization
Technological know-how	Capital intensity
Control over suppliers and distributors	Ease of entry into market
	Productivity, capacity utilization

Source: H. Rowe, R. Mason, and K. Dickel, *Strategic Management and Business Policy: A Methodological Approach* (Reading, Massachusetts: Addison–Wesley Publishing Co. Inc., 1982): 155–156. Reprinted with permission of the publisher.

*A stable environment represents a better strategic position than an unstable environment.

6. Draw a directional vector from the origin of the SPACE Matrix through the new intersection point. This vector reveals the type of strategies recommended for the organization: aggressive, competitive, defensive, or conservative.

Some examples of strategy profiles that can emerge from a SPACE analysis are shown in Figure 6–6. The directional vector associated with each profile suggests the type of strategies to pursue: aggressive, conservative, defensive, or competitive. When a firm's directional vector is located in the *aggressive quadrant* of the SPACE Matrix, an organization is in an excellent position to use its internal strengths to (1) take advantage of external opportunities, (2) overcome internal weaknesses, and (3) avoid external threats. Therefore, market penetration, market development, product development, backward integration, forward integration, horizontal integration, conglomerate diversification, concentric diversification, horizontal diversification, or a combination strategy can all be feasible, depending on the specific circumstances that face the firm. As indicated in the Global Perspective, the SPACE vector for Coors Brewery points in the aggressive quadrant and the firm is greatly increasing exports as a strategy.

The directional vector may appear in the *conservative quadrant* (upper left quadrant) of the SPACE Matrix, which implies staying close to the firm's basic competencies and not taking excessive risks. Conservative strategies most often include market penetration, market development, product development, and concentric diversification. The

FIGURE 6-6 Example Strategy Profiles

Aggresssive Profiles

A financially strong firm that has achieved major competitive advantages in a growing and stable industry

A firm whose financial strength is a dominating factor in the industry

Conservative Profiles

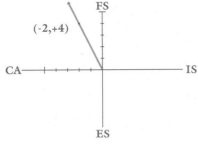

A firm that has achieved financial strength in a stable industry that is not growing; the firm has no major competitive advantages

A firm that suffers from major competitive disadvantages in an industry that is technologically stable but declining in sales

Competitive Profiles

A firm with major competitive advantages in a high-growth industry

An organization that is competing fairly well in an unstable industry

Defensive Profiles

A firm that has a very weak competitive position in a negative growth, stable industry

A financially troubled firm in a very unstable indusrty

Source: H. Rowe, R. Mason, and K Dickel, *Strategic Management and Business Policy: A Methodological Approach* (Reading, Massachuetts: Addison–Wesley Publishing Co. Inc., © 1982): 155. Reprinted with permission of the publisher.

CHAPTER 6: STRATEGY ANALYSIS AND CHOICE   **205**

directional vector may be located in the lower left or *defensive quadrant* of the SPACE Matrix, which suggests that the firm should focus on improving internal weaknesses and avoiding external threats. Defensive strategies include retrenchment, divestiture, liquidation, and concentric diversification. Finally, the directional vector may be located in the lower right or *competitive quadrant* of the SPACE Matrix, indicating competitive strategies. Competitive strategies include backward, forward, and horizonal integration, market penetration, market development, product development, and joint venture.

SPACE Matrix analysis for a bank is provided in Table 6–4.

The Boston Consulting Group (BCG) Matrix. Autonomous divisions (or profit centers) of an organization make up what is called a *business portfolio*. When a firm's

---

TABLE 6-4   A SPACE Matrix for a Bank

FINANCIAL STRENGTH	RATINGS
The bank's primary capital ratio is 7.23 percent, which is 1.23 percent over the generally required ratio of 6 percent.	1.0
The bank's return on assets is negative 0.77, compared to a bank industry average ratio of positive 0.70.	1.0
The bank's net income was $183 million, down 9 percent a year earlier.	3.0
The bank's revenues increased 7 percent to $3.46 billion.	4.0
	9.0

INDUSTRY STRENGTH	
Deregulation provides geographic and product freedom.	4.0
Deregulation increases competition in the banking industry.	2.0
Pennsylvania's interstate banking law allows the bank to acquire other banks in New Jersey, Ohio, Kentucky, The District of Columbia, and West Virginia.	4.0
	10.0

ENVIRONMENTAL STABILITY	
Lesser developed countries are experiencing high inflation and political instability.	-4.0
Headquartered in Pittsburgh, the bank has historically been heavily dependent on the steel, oil, and gas industries. These industries are depressed.	-5.0
Banking deregulation has created instability throughout the industry.	-4.0
	-13.0

COMPETITIVE ADVANTAGE	
The bank provides data processing services for more than 450 institutions in 38 states.	-2.0
Superregional banks, international banks, and non-banks are becoming increasingly competitive.	-5.0
The bank has a large customer base.	-2.0
	-9.0

CONCLUSION

ES Average is -13.0⁄3 =-4.33   IS Average is +10.0⁄3=3.33

CA Average is   -9.0⁄3 =-3.00   FS Average is +9.0⁄4=2.25

Directional Vector Coordinates: x axis: -3.00+(+3.33)= +0.33

y axis: -4.33+(+2.25)= -2.08

The bank should pursue Competitive Type Strategies

divisions compete in different industries, a separate strategy often must be developed for each business. The *Boston Consulting Group (BCG) Matrix* and the *Internal-External (IE) Matrix* are designed specifically to enhance a multidivisional firm's efforts to formulate strategies.

The BCG Matrix graphically portrays differences among divisions in terms of relative market share position and industry growth rate.[6] The BCG Matrix allows a multidivisional organization to manage its portfolio of businesses by examining the relative market share position and the industry growth rate of each division relative to all other divisions in the organization. *Relative market share position* is defined as the ratio of a division's own market share in a particular industry to the market share held by the largest rival firm in that industry. Relative market share position is given on the x-axis of the BCG Matrix. The midpoint on the x-axis is usually set at .50 corresponding to a division that has half the market share of the leading firm in the industry. The y-axis represents the industry growth rate in sales, measured in percentage terms. The growth rate percentages on the y-axis could range from -20 to +20 percent, with 0.0 being the midpoint. These numerical ranges on the x and y axes are often used, but other numerical values could be established as deemed appropriate for particular organizations.

An example of a BCG Matrix appears in Figure 6–7. Each circle represents a separate division. The size of the circle corresponds to the proportion of corporate revenue generated by that business unit, and the pie slice indicates the proportion of corporate profits generated by that division. Divisions located in Quadrant I of the BCG Matrix are called Question Marks, those located in Quadrant II are called Stars, those located in Quadrant III are called Cash Cows, and finally those divisions located in Quadrant IV are called Dogs.

■ Question Marks—Divisions in Quadrant I have a low relative market share position, yet compete in a high-growth industry. Generally, these firms' cash needs are high and their cash generation is low. These businesses are called Question Marks because the organization must decide whether to strengthen them by pursuing an intensive strategy (market penetration, market development, or product development) or to sell them.

- Stars—Quadrant II businesses (often called Stars) represent the organization's best long-run opportunities for growth and profitability. Divisions with a high relative market share and a high industry growth rate should receive substantial investment to maintain or strengthen their dominant positions. Forward, backward, and horizontal integration; market penetration; market development; product development; and joint ventures are all appropriate strategies for these divisions to consider.

- Cash Cows—Divisions positioned in Quadrant III have a high relative market share position but compete in a low-growth industry. Called Cash Cows because they generate cash in excess of their needs, they are often "milked." Many of today's Cash Cows were yesterday's Stars. Cash Cow divisions should be managed to maintain their strong position for as long as possible. Product development or concentric diversification may be attractive strategies for strong Cash Cows. However, as a Cash Cow division becomes weak, retrenchment or divestiture can become more appropriate.

- Dogs—Quadrant IV divisions of the organization have a low relative market share position and compete in a slow-or-no-market-growth industry; they are Dogs in the firm's portfolio. Because of their weak internal and external position, these businesses often are liquidated, divested, or trimmed down through retrenchment. When a division first becomes a Dog, retrenchment can be the best strategy to pursue because many Dogs have bounced back, after strenuous asset and cost reduction, to become viable, profitable divisions.

The major benefit of the BCG Matrix is that it draws attention to the cash flow, investment characteristics, and needs of an organization's various divisions. The divisions of many firms evolve over time: Dogs become Question Marks, Question Marks become Stars, Stars become Cash Cows, and Cash Cows become Dogs, in an ongoing counterclockwise motion. Less frequently, Stars become Question Marks, Question Marks become Dogs, Dogs become Cash Cows, and Cash Cows become Stars (in a clockwise motion). In some organizations, no cyclical motion is apparent. Over time, organizations should strive to achieve a portfolio of divisions that are Stars.

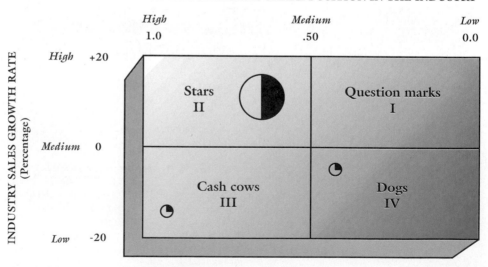

FIGURE 6-7 The BCG Matrix

One example of a BCG Matrix is provided in Figure 6–8, which illustrates an organization composed of five divisions with annual sales ranging from $5,000 to $60,000. Division I has the greatest sales volume, so the circle representing that division is the largest one in the Matrix. The circle corresponding to Division 5 is the smallest since its sales volume ($5,000) is least among all the divisions. The pie slices within the circles reveal the percent of corporate profits contributed by each division. As shown, Division 1 contributes the highest profit percentage, 39 percent. Notice in the diagram that Division 1 is considered a Star, Division 2 is a Question Mark, Division 3 is also a Question Mark, Division 4 is a Cash Cow, and Division 5 is a Dog.

The BCG Matrix, like all analytical techniques, has some limitations. For example, viewing every business as either a Star, Cash Cow, Dog, or Question Mark is an oversimplification; many businesses fall right in the middle of the BCG Matrix and are thus not easily classified. Furthermore, the BCG Matrix does not reflect whether or not various divisions or their industries are growing over time; that is, the matrix has no temporal qualities, but rather is a snapshot of an organization at a given point in time. Finally, other variables besides relative market share position and industry growth rate in sales, such as size of the market and competitive advantages, are important in making strategic decisions about various divisions.

The Internal-External (IE) Matrix. The *Internal-External (IE) Matrix* positions an organization's various divisions in a nine-cell display illustrated in Figure 6–9.[7] The IE Matrix is similar to the BCG Matrix in that both tools involve plotting organization divisions in a schematic diagram; this is why they are both called portfolio matrices. Also, the size of each circle represents the percentage sales contribution

Division	Revenues	Percent revenues	Profits	Percent profits	Percent market share	Percent growth rate
1	$60,000	37	$10,000	39	80	+15
2	40,000	24	5,000	20	40	+10
3	40,000	24	2,000	8	10	1
4	20,000	12	8,000	31	60	-20
5	5,000	3	500	2	5	-10
Total	$165,000	100	$25,500	100		

FIGURE 6-8 An Example BCG Matrix

of each division, and pie slices reveal the percentage profit contribution of each division in both the BCG and IE Matrix.

But there are some important differences between the BCG Matrix and IE Matrix. First, the axes are different. Also, the IE Matrix requires more information about the divisions than the BCG Matrix. Further, the strategic implications of each matrix are different. For these reasons, strategists in multidivisional firms often develop both the BCG Matrix and the IE Matrix in formulating alternative strategies. A common practice is to develop a BCG Matrix and an IE Matrix for the present, and then develop projected matrices to reflect the future. This "before and after" analysis forecasts the expected effect of strategic decisions on an organization's portfolio of divisions.

The IE Matrix is based on two key dimensions: the IFE total weighted scores on the x-axis and the EFE total weighted scores on the y-axis. Recall that each division of an organization should construct an IFE Matrix and an EFE Matrix for its part of the organization. The total weighted scores derived from the divisions allow construction of the corporate-level IE Matrix. On the x-axis of the IE Matrix, an IFE total weighted score of 1.0 to 1.99 represents a weak internal position, a score of 2.0 to 2.99 is considered average, and a score of 3.0 to 4.0 is strong. Similarly, on the y-axis, an EFE total weighted score of 1.0 to 1.99 is considered low, a score of 2.0 to 2.99 is medium, and a score of 3.0 to 4.0 is high.

The IE Matrix can be divided into three major regions that have different strategy implications. First, the prescription for divisions that fall into cells I, II, or IV can be described as "Grow and Build." Intensive (market penetration, market development, and product development) or integrative (backward integration, forward integration, and horizontal integration) strategies can be most appropriate for these divisions. Second, divisions that fall into cells III, V, or VII can best be managed with "Hold

FIGURE 6-9 The Internal-External (IE) Matrix

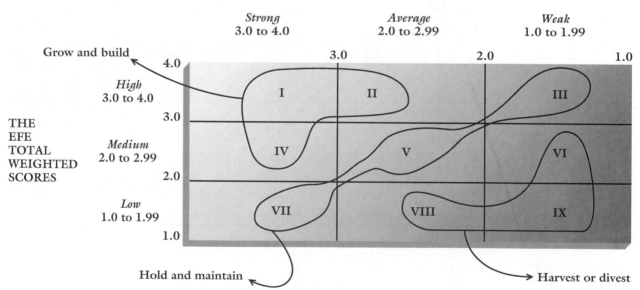

Note: The IE was developed from the General Electric (GE) Business Screen Matrix. For a description of the GE Matrix, see: Michael Allen, "Diagramming GE's Planning for What's WATT," in *Corporate Planning: Techniques and Applications,* eds. R. Allio and M. Pennington (New York: AMACOM, 1979).

and Maintain" strategies; market penetration and product development are two commonly employed strategies for these types of divisions. Third, a common prescription for divisions that fall into cells VI, VIII, or IX is "Harvest or Divest." Successful organizations are able to achieve a portfolio of businesses positioned in or around cell I in the IE Matrix.

An example of a completed IE Matrix is given in Figure 6–10, which depicts an organization composed of four divisions. As indicated by the positioning of the circles, "Grow and Build" strategies are appropriate for Division 1, Division 2, and Division 3. Division 4 is a candidate for "Harvest or Divest." Division 2 contributes the greatest percentage of company sales and thus is represented by the largest circle. Division 1 contributes the greatest proportion of total profits, since it has the largest percentage pie slice.

The Grand Strategy Matrix. In addition to the TOWS Matrix, SPACE Matrix, BCG Matrix, and IE Matrix, the *Grand Strategy Matrix* has become a popular tool for formulating alternative strategies. All organizations can be positioned in one of the Grand Strategy Matrix's four strategy quadrants. A firm's divisions could likewise be positioned. As illustrated in Figure 6–11, the Grand Strategy Matrix is based on two evaluative dimensions: competitive position and market growth. Appropriate strategies for an organization to consider are listed in sequential order of attractiveness in each quadrant of the matrix.

Firms located in Quadrant I of the Grand Strategy Matrix are in an excellent strategic position. For these firms, continued concentration on current markets (market penetration and market development) and products (product development) are appropriate strategies. It is unwise for a Quadrant I firm to shift notably from its

FIGURE 6-10 An Example IE Matrix

Division	Sales	Percent sales	Profits	Percent profits	IFE scores	EFE scores
1	$100	25	10	50	3.6	3.2
2	200	50	5	25	2.1	3.5
3	50	12.5	4	20	3.1	2.1
4	50	12.5	1	5	1.8	2.5
Total	400	100	20	100		

established competitive advantages. When a Quadrant I organization has excessive resources, then backward, forward, or horizontal integration may be effective strategies. When a Quadrant I firm is too heavily committed to a single product, then concentric diversification may reduce the risks associated with a narrow product line. Quadrant I firms can afford to take advantage of external opportunities in many areas: they can aggressively take risks when necessary. As indicated in the Natural Environment Perspective, Quadrant I firms often take the lead in developing "green" products and advocating environmental preservation.

Firms positioned in Quadrant II need to evaluate their present approach to the marketplace seriously. Although their industry is growing, they are unable to compete effectively, and they need to determine why the firm's current approach is ineffectual and how the company can best change to improve its competitiveness. Since Quadrant II firms are in a rapid-market-growth industry, an intensive strategy (as opposed to integrative or diversification) is usually the first option that should be considered. However, if the firm is lacking a distinctive competence or competitive advantage, then horizontal integration is often a desirable alternative. As a last result, divestiture or liquidation should be considered. Divestiture can provide funds needed to acquire other businesses or buy back shares of stock.

Quadrant III organizations compete in slow-growth industries and have weak competitive positions. These firms must make some drastic changes quickly to avoid

FIGURE 6-11 The Grand Strategy Matrix

RAPID MARKET GROWTH

Quadrant II

1. Market development
2. Market penetration
3. Product development
4. Horizontal integration
5. Divestiture
6. Liquidation

Quadrant I

1. Market development
2. Market penetration
3. Product development
4. Forward integration
5. Backward integration
6. Horizontal integration
7. Concentric diversification

WEAK COMPETITIVE POSITION ———————————————— STRONG COMPETITIVE POSITION

Quadrant III

1. Retrenchment
2. Concentric diversification
3. Horizontal diversification
4. Conglomerate diversification
5. Divestiture
6. Liquidation

Quadrant IV

1. Concentric diversification
2. Horizontal diversification
3. Conglomerate diversification
4. Joint ventures

SLOW MARKET GROWTH

Source: Adapted from Roland Christensen, Norman Berg, and Malcolm Salter, *Policy Formulation and Administration* (Homewood, Ill.: Richard D. Irwin, 1976), 16–18.

further demise and possible liquidation. Extensive cost and asset reduction (retrenchment) should be pursued first. An alternative strategy is to shift resources away from the current business into different areas. If all else fails, the final options for Quadrant III businesses are divestiture or liquidation.

Finally, Quadrant IV businesses have a strong competitive position but are in a slow-growth industry. These firms have the strength to launch diversified programs into more promising growth areas. Quadrant IV firms have characteristically high cash flow levels and limited internal growth needs and can often pursue concentric, horizontal, or conglomerate diversification successfully. Quadrant IV firms may also pursue joint ventures.

A NATURAL ENVIRONMENT PERSPECTIVE
A Demographic Profile of Environmental Attitudes

Americans can be grouped into categories based on their attitudes, actions, and concern towards natural environment deterioration and preservation. Note in the table that persons most concerned about the natural environment tend to be more educated, have higher household income, live in the West or Northeast, and live in cities. These persons especially engage in activities such as not purchasing products from companies that are environmentally irresponsible, avoiding purchasing aerosol products, recycling paper and bottles, using biodegradable products, and contributing money to environmental groups. This information can be helpful to companies in formulating strategies such as market development (where to locate new facilities), product development (manufacturing new equipment or developing green products), and market penetration (whom to focus advertising efforts upon).

Characteristics	High Concern for the Natural Environment	Low Concern for the Natural Environment
Sex		
Male	34%	55%
Female	66	45
Education		
Less than high school	11	30
High school graduate	39	39
Some college	22	20
College graduate or more	28	11
Occupation		
Executive/professional	25	11
White collar	18	15
Blue collar	19	36
Marital Status		
Married	69	59
Not married	30	41
Political/Social Ideology		
Conservative	43	36
Middle of the road	26	41
Liberal	28	16
Region		
Northeast	31	17
Midwest	27	22
South	18	48
West	24	13
Median Income (in thousands)	$32.1	$21.2

Source: Adapted from the Roper Organization, 205 East 42nd Street, New York, NY 10017, and also from Joe Schwartz and Thomas Miller, "The Earth's Best Friends," *American Demographics,* February 1991, p. 28.

Analysis and intuition provide a basis for making strategy-formulation decisions. The matching techniques just discussed reveal feasible alternative strategies. Many of these strategies will likely have been proposed by managers and employees participating in the strategy analysis and choice activity. Any additional strategies resulting from the matching analyses could be discussed and added to the list of feasible alternative options. As indicated earlier in this chapter, participants could rate these strategies on a 1 to 4 scale so that a prioritized list of the "best" strategies could be achieved.

The Quantitative Strategic Planning Matrix (QSPM). Other than ranking strategies to achieve the prioritized list, there is only one analytical technique in the literature designed to determine the relative attractiveness of feasible alternative actions. This technique is the *Quantitative Strategic Planning Matrix (QSPM),* which comprises Stage 3 of the strategy-formulation analytical framework.[8] This technique objectively indicates which alternative strategies are best. The QSPM uses input from Stage 1 analyses and matching results from Stage 2 analyses to "decide" objectively among alternative strategies. That is, the EFE Matrix, IFE Matrix, and Competitive Profile Matrix that comprise Stage 1, coupled with the TOWS Matrix, SPACE Analysis, BCG Matrix, IE Matrix, and Grand Strategy Matrix that make up Stage 2, provide the needed information for setting up the QSPM (Stage 3). The QSPM is a tool that allows strategists to evaluate alternative strategies objectively, based on previously identified external and internal critical success factors. Like other strategy-formulation analytical tools, the QSPM requires good intuitive judgment.

The basic format of the QSPM is illustrated in Table 6–5. Note that the left column of a QSPM consists of key external and internal factors (from Stage 1), and the top row consists of feasible alternative strategies (from Stage 2). Specifically, the left

TABLE 6-5   The Quantitative Strategic Planning Matrix—QSPM

		STRATEGIC ALTERNATIVES		
KEY FACTORS	WEIGHT	STRATEGY 1	STRATEGY 2	STRATEGY 3
EXTERNAL FACTORS				
Economy				
Political/Legal/Governmental				
Social/Cultural/Demographic/Environmental				
Technological				
Competitive				
INTERNAL FACTORS				
Management				
Marketing				
Finance/Accounting				
Production/Operations				
Research and Development				
Computer Information Systems				

column of a QSPM consists of information obtained directly from the EFE Matrix and IFE Matrix. In a column adjacent to the critical success factors, the respective weights received by each factor in the EFE Matrix and the IFE Matrix are recorded.

The top row of a QSPM consists of alternative strategies derived from the TOWS Matrix, SPACE Matrix, BCG Matrix, IE Matrix, and Grand Strategy Matrix. These matching tools usually generate similar feasible alternatives. However, not every strategy suggested by the matching techniques has to be evaluated in a QSPM. Strategists should use good intuitive judgment in selecting strategies to include in a QSPM.

Conceptually, the QSPM determines the relative attractiveness of various strategies based on the extent to which key external and internal critical success factors are capitalized upon or improved. The relative attractiveness of each strategy within a set of alternatives is computed by determining the cumulative impact of each external and internal critical success factor. Any number of sets of alternative strategies can be included in the QSPM, and any number of strategies can comprise a given set. But only strategies within a given set are evaluated relative to each other. For example, one set of strategies may include concentric, horizontal, and conglomerate diversification, whereas another set may include issuing stock and selling a division to raise needed capital. These two sets of strategies are totally different, and the QSPM evaluates strategies only within sets. Note in Table 6–5 that three strategies are included and they comprise just one set.

A QSPM for Campbell Soup Company is provided in Table 6–6. This example illustrates all the components of the QSPM: Key Factors, Strategic Alternatives, Weights, Attractiveness Scores, Total Attractiveness Scores, and Sum Total Attractiveness Score. The three new terms just introduced—(1) Attractiveness Scores, (2) Total Attractiveness Scores, and (3) Sum Total Attractiveness Score—are defined and explained below as the six steps required to develop a QSPM are discussed.

Step 1 **List the firm's key external opportunities/threats and internal strengths/weaknesses in the left column of the QSPM**. This information should be taken directly from the EFE Matrix and IFE Matrix. A minimum of ten external critical success factors and ten internal critical success factors should be included in the QSPM.

Step 2 **Assign weights to each external and internal critical success factor**. These Weights are identical to those in the EFE Matrix and the IFE Matrix. The Weights are presented in a straight column just to the right of the external and internal critical success factors.

Step 3 **Examine the Stage 2 (matching) matrices and identify alternative strategies that the organization should consider implementing**. Record these strategies in the top row of the QSPM. Group the strategies into mutually exclusive sets if possible.

Step 4 **Determine the Attractiveness Scores (AS),** defined as numerical values that indicate the relative attractiveness of each strategy in a given set of alternatives. Attractiveness Scores are determined by examining each external or internal critical success factor, one at a time, and asking the question, "Does this factor affect the choice of strategies being made?" If the answer to this question is YES, then the strategies should be compared relative to that key factor. Specifically, Attractiveness Scores should be assigned to each strategy to indicate the relative attractiveness of one strategy over others, considering the particular factor. The range for Attractiveness Scores is 1 = not attractive, 2 =

somewhat attractive, 3 = reasonably attractive, and 4 = highly attractive. If the answer to the above question is NO, indicating that the respective critical success factor has no effect upon the specific choice being made, then do not assign Attractiveness Scores to the strategies in that set.

TABLE 6-6   A QSPM for a Food Company

| CRITICAL SUCCESS FACTORS | WEIGHT | STRATEGIC ALTERNATIVES | | | |
| | | JOINT VENTURE IN EUROPE | | JOINT VENTURE IN ASIA | |
		AS	TAS	AS	TAS
OPPORTUNITIES					
1. Western European unification	.10	4	.40	2	.20
2. Rising health consciousness in selecting foods	.15	3	.45	3.	.45
3. Free market economies arising in Asia	.10	2.	.20	4	.40
4. Demand for soups increasing 10 percent annually	.15	3	.45	3	.60
5. NAFTA	.05	—	—	—	—
THREATS					
1. Food revenues increasing only 1 percent annually	.10	3	.30	3	.30
2. ConAgra's Banquet TV Dinners lead market with 27.4 percent share	.05	—	—	—	—
3. Unstable economies in Asia	.10	4	.40	1	.10
4. Tin cans are not biodegradable	.05	—	—	—	—
5. Low value of the dollar	.15	4	.60	2	.30
STRENGTHS					
1. Profits rose 30 percent	.10	3	.30	3	.30
2. New North American division	.10	—	—	—	—
3. New health conscious soups are successful	.10	4	.40	2	.20
4. Swanson TV dinner's market share has increased to 25.1 percent	.05	3	.15	3	.15
5. One fifth of all managers' bonuses is based on overall corporate performance	.05	—	—	—	—
6. Capacity utilization increased from 60 percent to 80 percent	.15	3	.45	3	.45
WEAKNESSES					
1. Pepperidge Farm sales have declined 7 percent	.05	—	—	—	—
2. Restructuring cost $302 million	.10	—	—	—	—
3. The company's European operation is losing money	.15	2	.30	3	.45
4. The company is slow in globalizing	.15	4	.60	3	.45
5. Pretax profit margin of 8.4 percent is only one half industry average	.10	3	.30	3	.30
TOTAL			5.30		4.65

AS = Attractiveness Score; TAS = Total Attractiveness Score

Attractiveness Score: 1 = not acceptable; 2 = possibly acceptable; 3 = probably acceptable; 4 = most acceptable

Step 5 **Compute the Total Attractiveness Scores.** Total Attractiveness Scores are defined as the product of multiplying the Weights (Step 2) by the Attractiveness Scores (Step 4) in each row. The Total Attractiveness Scores indicate the relative attractiveness of each alternative strategy, considering only the impact of the adjacent external or internal critical success factor. The higher the Total Attractiveness Score, the more attractive the strategic alternative (considering only the adjacent critical success factor).

Step 6 **Compute the Sum Total Attractiveness Score.** Add Total Attractiveness Scores in each strategy column of the QSPM. Sum Total Attractiveness Scores reveal which strategy is most attractive in each set of alternatives. Higher scores indicate more attractive strategies, considering all the relevant external and internal factors that could affect the strategic decisions. The magnitude of the difference between the Sum Total Attractiveness Scores in a given set of strategic alternatives indicates the relative desirability of one strategy over another.

In Table 6–6 two alternative strategies—establishing a joint venture in Europe and establishing a joint venture in Asia—are being considered by a food company.

Note that the NAFTA has no impact on the choice being made between the two Campbell Soup strategies, so slashes (—) appear across that row. Several other factors also have no effect on the choice being made, so slashes are recorded in those rows as well. If a particular factor affects one strategy but not the other, it affects the choice being made, so attractiveness scores should be recorded. The sum total attractiveness score of 5.30 in Table 6–6 indicates that the joint venture in Europe is a more attractive strategy, compared to the joint venture in Asia.

You should have a rationale for each AS score assigned. In Table 6–6, the rationale for the AS scores in the first row is that the unification of Western Europe creates more stable business conditions in Europe than Asia. The AS score of 4 for the joint venture in Europe and 2 for the joint venture in Asia indicates that the European venture is "most acceptable" and the Asian venture is "possibly acceptable," considering only the first critical success factor. AS Scores therefore are not mere guesses; they should be rational, defensible, and reasonable.

Positive Features and Limitations of the QSPM. A positive feature of the QSPM is that sets of strategies can be examined sequentially or simultaneously. For example, corporate-level strategies could be evaluated first, followed by divisional-level strategies, and then functional-level strategies. There is no limit to the number of strategies that can be evaluated or the number of sets of strategies that can be examined at once using the QSPM.

Another positive feature of the QSPM is that it requires strategists to integrate pertinent external and internal factors into the decision process. Developing a QSPM makes it less likely that key factors will be overlooked or weighted inappropriately. A QSPM draws attention to important relationships that affect strategy decisions. Although developing a QSPM requires a number of subjective decisions, making small decisions along the way enhances the probability that the final strategic decisions will be best for the organization. A QSPM can be adapted for use by small and large, for-profit and nonprofit organizations, and can be applied to virtually any type of organization. A QSPM can especially enhance strategic choice in multinational firms because many key factors and strategies can be considered at once. It also has been applied successfully by a number of small businesses.[9]

The QSPM is not without some limitations. First, it always requires intuitive judgments and educated assumptions. The ratings and attractiveness scores require judgmental decisions, even though they should be based on objective information. Discussion among strategists, managers, and employees throughout the strategy-formulation process, including development of a QSPM, is constructive and improves strategic decisions. Constructive discussion during strategy analysis and choice may arise because of genuine differences of interpretation of information and varying opinions. Another limitation of the QSPM is that it can be only as good as the prerequisite information and matching analyses upon which it is based.

CULTURAL ASPECTS OF STRATEGY CHOICE

All organizations have a culture. Culture includes the set of shared values, beliefs, attitudes, customs, norms, personalities, and heroes that describe a firm. Culture is the unique way an organization does business. It is the human dimension that creates solidarity and meaning, and inspires commitment and productivity in an organization when strategy changes are made. All human beings have a basic need to make sense of their world, to feel in control, and to make meaning. When events threaten meaning, individuals react defensively. Managers and employees may even sabotage new strategies in an effort to recapture the status quo.

It is beneficial to view strategic management from a cultural perspective because success often rests upon the degree of support that strategies receive from a firm's culture. If a firm's strategies are supported by cultural products such as values, beliefs, rites, rituals, ceremonies, stories, symbols, language, and heroes, then managers can often implement changes swiftly and easily. However, if a supportive culture does not exist and is not cultivated, then strategy changes may be ineffective or even counterproductive. A firm's culture can become antagonistic to new strategies, and the result of that antagonism may be confusion and disarray.

Strategies that require fewer cultural changes may be more attractive because extensive changes can take considerable time and effort. Whenever two firms merge, culture-strategy linkages become especially important to evaluate and consider. For example, Michael Blumenthal, chairman of the board and chief executive officer of Unisys Corporation (the company formed by the merger of Sperry and Burroughs), describes the culture of Unisys as a conscious distillation of the best customs, mores, symbols, and principles from Sperry and Burroughs; Unisys is not merely a balanced mix of Sperry and Burroughs.

When two or three companies from different countries form a joint venture, such as the recent venture among Honeywell, NEC Corporation of Japan, and Compagnie des Machines Bull of France, merging corporate cultures can be a problem. Jerome Meyer, a Honeywell executive, is president and CEO of the new organization, the first multinational computer company. "We've not had an alliance of these dimensions before, with its geographic diversity and cultural conflict," said Michael Geran, an analyst with E. F. Hutton. "The skill to run it will be a tremendous challenge." He predicted that Meyer would become primarily "a referee."

Culture provides an explanation for the difficulties a firm encounters when it attempts to shift its strategic direction, as the following statement explains:

> Not only has the "right" corporate culture become the essence and foundation of corporate excellence, but success or failure of needed corporate reforms hinges on management's sagacity and ability to change the firm's driving culture in time and in tune with required changes in strategies.[10]

All organizations are political. Unless it is managed, political maneuvering consumes valuable time, subverts organizational objectives, diverts human energy, and results in the loss of some valuable employees.[11] Sometimes political biases and personal preferences get unduly embedded in strategy choice decisions. Internal politics affect the choice of strategies in all organizations. The hierarchy of command in an organization, combined with the career aspirations of different people and the need to allocate scarce resources, guarantees the formation of coalitions of individuals who strive to take care of themselves first and the organization second, third, or fourth. Coalitions of individuals often form around key strategy issues that face an enterprise. A major responsibility of strategists is to guide the development of coalitions, to nurture an overall team concept, and to gain the support of key individuals and groups of individuals.

In the absence of objective analyses, strategy decisions are too often based on the politics of the moment. With development of improved strategy-formation tools, political factors become less important in making strategic decisions. In the absence of objectivity, political factors sometimes dictate strategies, and this is unfortunate. Managing political relationships is an integral part of building enthusiasm and esprit de corps in an organization. Don Beeman and Tom Sharkey offer the following guidelines for minimizing the negative aspects of organizational politics:

1. Make clear the bases and processes for performance evaluation.
2. Differentiate rewards among high and low performers.
3. Make sure rewards are as immediately and directly related to performance as possible.
4. Minimize resource competition among managers.
5. Replace resource competition among managers.
6. Where highly cohesive political empires exist, break them apart by removing or splitting the most dysfunctional subgroups.
7. Be keenly sensitive to managers whose mode of operation is personalization of political patronage. Approach these persons with a directive to "stop political maneuvering." If it continues, remove them from the position and preferably the company.[12]

A classic study of strategic management in nine large corporations examined the political tactics of successful and unsuccessful strategists.[13] Successful strategists were found to let weakly supported ideas and proposals die through inaction and to establish additional hurdles or tests for strongly supported ideas considered unacceptable but not openly opposed. Successful strategists kept a low political profile on unacceptable proposals and strived to let most negative decisions come from subordinates or a group consensus, thereby reserving their personal vetoes for big issues and crucial moments. Successful strategists did a lot of chatting and informal questioning to stay abreast of how things were progressing and to know when to intervene. They led strategy but did not dictate it. They gave few orders, announced few decisions, depended heavily on informal questioning, and sought to probe and clarify until a consensus emerged.

Successful strategists generously and visibly rewarded key thrusts that succeeded. They assigned responsibility for major new thrusts to "champions," the individuals most strongly identified with the idea or product and whose futures were linked to its success. They stayed alert to the symbolic impact of their own actions and statements so as not to send false signals that could stimulate movements in unwanted directions.

Successful strategists ensured that all major power bases within an organization were represented in, or had access to, top management. They interjected new faces and new views into considerations of major changes. (This is important because new employees and managers generally have more enthusiasm and drive than employees who have been with the firm a long time. New employees do not "see the world the same old way" nor act as screens against changes.) Successful strategists minimized their own political exposure on highly controversial issues and in circumstances where major opposition from key power centers was likely. In combination, these findings provide a basis for managing political relationships in an organization.

Since strategies must be effective in the marketplace and capable of gaining internal commitment, the following tactics used by politicians for centuries can aid strategists:

- *Equifinality:* It is often possible to achieve similar results using different means or paths. Strategists should recognize that achieving a successful outcome is more important than imposing the method of achieving it. It may be possible to generate new alternatives that give equal results but with far greater potential for gaining commitment.
- *Satisfying:* Achieving satisfactory results with an acceptable strategy is far better than failing to achieve "optimal" results with an unpopular strategy.
- *Generalization:* Shifting focus from specific issues to more general ones may increase strategists' options for gaining organizational commitment.
- *Focus on Higher-order Issues:* By raising an issue to a higher level, many short-term interests can be postponed in favor of long-term interests. For instance, by focusing on issues of survival, the auto and steel industries were able to persuade unions to make concessions on wage increases.
- *Provide Political Access on Important Issues:* Strategy and policy decisions with significant negative consequences for middle managers will motivate intervention behavior from them. If middle managers do not have an opportunity to take a position on such decisions in appropriate political forums, they are capable of successfully resisting the decisions after they are made. Providing such political access provides strategists with information that might otherwise not be available and that could be useful in managing intervention behavior.[14]

THE ROLE OF A BOARD OF DIRECTORS

The widespread lack of involvement by boards of directors in the strategic-management process is changing in America. Historically, boards of directors have mostly been "insiders" who would not second-guess top executives on strategic issues. It has generally been understood that strategists are responsible and accountable for implementing strategy, so they, not board members, should formulate strategy. Consequently, chief executive officers usually avoided discussions of overall strategy with directors because the results of those discussions often restricted their freedom of action. The judgments of board members were seldom used on acquisitions, divestitures, large capital investments, and other strategic matters. Often the board would meet only annually to fulfill its minimum legal requirements; in many organizations, boards served merely a traditional legitimizing role.

Today, boards of directors are composed mostly of "outsiders" who are becoming more involved in organizations' strategic management. In a recent study of 1,300 large corporations in the United States, nearly 40 percent of the boards of directors reported that they were actively involved in their firms' strategic-management process.[15] The trend in America is towards smaller boards, now averaging 12 members rather than 18 as they did a few years ago. Smaller boards can discuss issues more easily; individuals in small groups take responsibility more personally.

Just as directors are beginning to place more emphasis on staying informed about an organization's health and operations, they are also taking a more active role in assuring that publicly issued documents are accurate representations of a firm's status. It is becoming widely recognized that a board of directors has legal responsibilities to stockholders and society for all company activities, for corporate performance, and for assuring that a firm has an effective strategy. Failure to accept responsibility for auditing or evaluating a firm's strategy is considered a serious breach of a director's duties. Stockholders, government agencies, and customers are filing legal suits against directors for fraud, omissions, inaccurate disclosures, lack of due diligence, and culpable ignorance about a firm's operations with increasing frequency. Liability insurance for directors has become exceptionally expensive and has caused numerous directors to resign.

Two recent rulings have particulary affected the role of boards of directors in the strategy-formulation process. First, the Supreme Court of Delaware ruled that the directors of the Trans Union Corporation violated the interests of shareholders when they hastily accepted a takeover bid from the Marmon Group; that ruling erodes the so-called business judgment rule, which protects directors from liability as long as their decisions represent a good-faith effort to serve the best interests of the corporation. One clear signal from the Trans Union case is that haste can be costly for board members.

In another landmark ruling that illustrates how boards of directors are increasingly being held responsible for the overall performance of organizations, the Federal Deposit Insurance Corporation forced Continental Illinois to accept the resignations of ten of the troubled bank's outside directors. The impact of increasing legal pressures on board members is that directors are demanding greater and more regular access to financial performance information.

Kesner and Johnson recently identified some boardroom reforms that are lessening the likelihood of lawsuits today. These reforms include increasing the percentage of outsiders on the board, separating the positions of CEO and chairperson, requiring directors to hold substantial amounts of stock in the firm, and decreasing the board size.[16] Outsiders now outnumber insiders at 90 percent of all American firms, and the average number of outsiders is three times that of insiders.

A direct response of increased pressure on directors to stay informed and execute their responsibilities is that audit committees are becoming commonplace. Milton Lauenstein proposes that a board of directors should conduct an annual strategy audit in much the same fashion that it reviews the annual financial audit.[17] In performing such an audit, a board could work jointly with operating management and/or seek outside counsel. The questions provided in Table 6–7 illustrate the areas that a strategy audit might encompass, but, of course, not all of these questions apply to every situation and organization.

The trend among corporations toward decreased diversification, increased takeover activity, increased legal pressures, multidivisional structures, and multinational operations augments the problem of keeping directors informed. Boards should play a role beyond that of performing a strategic audit. They should provide greater input and advice in the strategy-formulation process to assure that strategists are providing for the long-term needs of the firm. This is being done through the formation of three particular board committees: nominating committees to propose candidates for the board and senior officers of the firm; compensation committees to evaluate the

TABLE 6-7   A Board of Directors Strategy-Audit Framework

- Is the company adequately informed about its markets? What further information would be worth the cost of getting? How should it be obtained?
- How well informed is the company about its competitors? How well is it able to forecast what competitors will do under various circumstances? Is there a sound basis for such competitive appraisals? Is the company under-estimating or overestimating its competitors?
- Has management adequately explored various ways of segmenting its market? To what extent is it addressing market segments in which the company's strengths provide meaningful advantages?
- Are the products and services the company proposes to sell ones that it can provide more effectively than competitors? What is the basis for such a belief?
- Do the various activities proposed in the strategy provide synergistic advantages? Are they compatible?
- Does the proposed strategy adequately address questions of corporate objectives, financial policy, scope of operations, organization, and integration?
- What specific resources (personnel, skills, information, facilities, technology, finances, relationships) will be needed to execute the strategy? Does the company already possess these resources? Has management established programs for building these resources and overall competence which will provide telling competitive advantages over the long run?
- To what extent does the strategy define a unique and appropriate economic role for the company? How different is it from the competitors' strategy?
- Has the issue of growth rate been raised? Are there good reasons to believe that investment in growth will pay off? Does the company's track record support such a conclusion?
- Does the proposed dividend policy reflect the company's growth policy, based on a demonstrated ability or inability to reinvest cash flow advantageously? Or is it just a "safe" compromise, conforming to what others usually do?
- Is management capable of implementing the strategy effectively? What leads to this conclusion?
- How and to what extent is the strategy to be communicated to the organization? Is it to be distributed in written form? If competitors are aware of the company's strategy, will that help or hurt?
- What provision is to be made for employing the strategy as a guide to operating decisions? To what extent is it to be used by the board? How?
- How is it to be kept up-to-date? Are there to be regular reviews? How often and by whom?
- Has a set of long-range projections of operations following the strategy been prepared? Have the possible results of following alternative strategies been prepared?
- Does the strategy focus on the few really important key issues? Is it too detailed? Does it address genuine business questions (as opposed to "motherhood" statements)?
- In its strategic thinking, has management avoided the lure of simplistic approaches such as:
  Growth for growth's sake?
  Diversification for diversification's sake?
  Aping the industry leader?
  Broadening the scope in order to secure "incremental" earnings?
  Assuming it can execute better than competitors without objective evidence that such is the case?
- Are there other issues, trends, or potential events that should have been taken into account?

Source: Milton Lauenstein, "Boards of Directors: The Strategy Audit," *Journal of Business Strategy* 4, no. 3 (Winter 1984): 90, 91. Reprinted with permission.

performance of top executives and determine the terms and conditions of their employment; and public policy committees to give board-level attention to company policies and performance on subjects of concern such as business ethics, consumer affairs, and political activities.[18]

Nearly 41 percent of all firms that have a board of directors have developed a mission statement for the board.[19] A board of directors' mission statement outlines the purpose and intent of the board and defines to whom, or for what, the board is held accountable. A board mission statement also indicates company expectations about the quality of preparation for and the process for conducting board meetings. Overall, the mission of boards of directors must be expanded in the 1990s. Companies should assign managers to join directors on board committees, rather than limit the board's contact with only a few top managers. Directors must assume a more activist stance in management development, rather than just react to management initiatives.

Powerful boards of directors are associated with high organizational performance.[20] Powerful boards participate in corporate decisions more fully, share their experiences with the CEO regarding certain strategies, and are actively involved in industry analysis. Firms can develop more powerful boards by regularly reviewing board committee activities, evaluating board meetings, and involving the board more extensively in strategic issues. More and more companies are paying board members partly or totally in stock, which gives outside directors more and more reason to identify with the shareholders they represent rather than the CEO they oversee.

CONCLUSION

The essence of strategy formulation is an assessment of whether an organization is doing the right things and how it can be more effective in what it does. Every organization should be wary of becoming a prisoner of its own strategy, because even the best strategies become obsolete sooner or later. Regular reappraisal of strategy helps management avoid complacency. Objectives and strategies should be consciously developed and coordinated and should not merely evolve out of day-to-day operating decisions.

An organization with no sense of direction and no coherent strategy precipitates its own demise. When an organization does not know where it wants to go, it usually ends up some place it does not want to be! Every organization needs to consciously establish and communicate clear objectives and strategies.

Modern strategy-formulation tools and concepts are described in this chapter and integrated into a practical three-stage framework. Tools such as the TOWS Matrix, SPACE Matrix, BCG Matrix, IE Matrix, and QSPM can significantly enhance the quality of strategic decisions, but they should never be used to dictate the choice of strategies. Behavioral, cultural, and political aspects of strategy generation and selection are always important to consider and manage. Due to increased legal pressure from outside groups, boards of directors are assuming a more active role in strategy analysis and choice. This is a positive trend for organizations.

KEY TERMS AND CONCEPTS

Aggressive Quadrant
Attractiveness Scores (AS)
Board of Directors
Boston Consulting Group (BCG) Matrix

Business Portfolio
Cash Cows
Competitive Advantage (CA)
Competitive Quadrant

ISSUES FOR REVIEW AND DISCUSSION

1. How would application of the strategy-formulation framework differ from a small to a large organization?

2. What types of strategies would you recommend for an organization that achieves total weighted scores of 3.6 on the IFE and 1.2 on the EFE Matrix?

3. Given the following information, develop a SPACE Matrix for the XYZ Corporation: FS = +2 ES = −6 CA = −2 IS = +4

4. Given the information in the table below, develop a BCG Matrix and an IE Matrix:

Divisions	1	2	3
Profits	$10	$15	$25
Sales	$100	$50	$100
Relative Market Share	0.2	0.5	0.8
Industry Growth Rate	+.20	+.10	−.10
IFE Total Weighted Scores	1.6	3.1	2.2
EFE Total Weighted Scores	2.5	1.8	3.3

5. Explain the steps involved in developing a QSPM.

6. How would you develop a set of objectives for your school of business?

7. What do you think is the appropriate role of a board of directors in strategic management? Why?

8. Discuss the limitations of various strategy-formulation analytical techniques.

9. Explain why cultural factors should be an important consideration in analyzing and choosing among alternative strategies.

10. How are the TOWS Matrix, SPACE Matrix, BCG Matrix, IE Matrix, and Grand Strategy Matrix similar? How are they different?

11. How would profit and nonprofit organizations differ in their applications of the strategy-formulation framework?

12. Select an article from the suggested readings at the end of this chapter and prepare a report on that article for your class.

NOTES

1. Steven C. Brandt, *Strategic Planning in Emerging Companies* (Reading, Massachusetts: Addison-Wesley, 1981). Reprinted with permission of the publisher.

2. R. T. Lenz, "Managing the Evolution of the Strategic Planning Process," *Business Horizons* 30, no. 1 (January–February 1987): 37.

3. Robert Grant. The Resource-Based Theory of Competitive Advantage: Implications for Strategy Formulation. *California Management Review* (Spring 1991): 114.

4. Heinz Weihrich, "The TOWS Matrix: A Tool for Situational Analysis," *Long Range Planning* 15, no. 2 (April 1982): 61.

5. A. Rowe, R. Mason, and K. Dickel, *Strategic Management and Business Policy: A Methodological Approach* (Reading, Mass.: Addison-Wesley, 1982), 155.

6. Boston Consulting Group, *Perspectives on Experience* (Boston: The Boston Consulting Group, 1974). Also, Barry Hedley, "Strategy and the Business Portfolio," *Long Range Planning* 10, no. 1 (February 1977): 9.

7. This technique is similar to the General Electric Business Screen, but the axes are labeled more clearly and the scoring procedure is improved in this text.

8. Fred David, "The Strategic Planning Matrix—A Quantitative Approach," *Long Range Planning* 19, no. 5 (October 1986): 102. Andre Gib and Robert Margulies, "Making Competitive Intelligence Relevant to the User." *Planning Review* 19, no. 3 (May/June 1991): 21.

9. Fred David, "Computer-Assisted Strategic Planning in Small Businesses," *Journal of Systems Management* 36, no. 7 (July 1985): 24–34.

10. Y. Allarie and M. Firsirotu, "How to Implement Radical Strategies in Large Organizations," *Sloan Management Review* 26, no. 3 (Spring 1985): 19. Another excellent article is P. Shrivastava, "Integrating Strategy Formulation with Organizational Culture," *Journal of Business Strategy* 5, no. 3 (Winter 1985): 103–111.

11. Don Beeman and Thomas Sharkey, "The Use and Abuse of Corporate Politics," *Business Horizons* 30, no. 2 (March–April 1987): 30.

12. Ibid.

13. James Brian Quinn, *Strategies for Change: Logical Incrementalism* (Homewood, Ill.: Richard D. Irwin, 1980), 128–145. These political tactics are listed in A. Thompson and A. Strickland, *Strategic Management: Concepts and Cases* (Plano, Tex.: Business Publications, 1984), 261.

14. William Guth and Ian MacMillan, "Strategy Implementation Versus Middle Management Self-Interest," *Strategic Management Journal* 7, no. 4 (July–August 1986): 321.

15. John Henke, Jr., "Involving the Board of Directors in Strategic Planning," *Journal of Business Strategy* 7, no. 2 (Fall 1986): 89.

16. Idalene Kesner and Roy Johnson. "Crisis in the Boardroom: Fact and Fiction." *Academy of Management Executive* 4, no. 1 (February 1990): 28.

17. Milton Lauenstein, "Boards of Directors: The Strategic Audit," *Journal of Business Strategy* 4, no. 3 (Winter 1984): 87–91.

18. Murray Weidenbaum, "Updating the Corporate Board," *Journal of Business Strategy* 7, no. 1 (Summer 1986): 80.

19. Ada Demb, Danielle Chouet, Tom Lossius, and Fred Neubauer, "Defining the Role of the Board," *Long Range Planning* 22, no. 1 (February 1989): 61–68.

20. John A. Pearce II and Shaker A. Zahra, "The Relative Power of CEOs and Boards of Directors: Associations with Corporate Performance." *Strategic Management Journal* 12 (1991):1 135–153.

CURRENT READINGS

Bogan, Christopher E., and Michael J. English. "Benchmarking: A Wakeup Call for Board Members (and CEOs Too)." *Planning Review* 22, no. 4 (July–August 1993): 28–34.

Cannella, Albert A., Jr., and Michael Lubatkin. "Succession as a Sociopolitical Process: Internal Impediments to Outsider Selection." *Academy of Management Journal* 36, no. 4 (August 1993): 763–793.

Ferris, Gerald R., and K. Michele Kacmar. "Perceptions of Organizational Politics." *Journal of Management* 18, no. 1 (March 1992): 93–116.

Hambrick, Donald C., and Albert A. Cannella, Jr. "Relative Standing: A Framework for Understanding Departures of Acquired Executives." *Academy of Management Journal* 36, no. 4 (August 1993): 733–762.

Johnson, R. A., R. E. Hoskisson, and M. A. Hitt. "Board of Director Involvement in Restructuring: The Effects of Board Versus Managerial Controls and Characteristics." *Strategic Management Journal* 14, Special Issue (Summer 1993): 33–50.

Judge, William Q., Jr., and Carl P. Ziethaml. "Institutional and Strategic Choice Perspectives on Board Involvement in the Strategic Decision Process." *Academy of Management Journal* 35, no. 4 (October 1992): 766–794.

Krachenberg, A. Richard, John W. Henke, Jr., and Thomas F. Lyons. "The Isolation of Upper Management." *Business Horizons* 36, no. 4 (July–August 1993): 41–47.

Mallette, Paul, and Karen L. Fowler. "Effects of Board Composition and Stock Ownership on the Adoption of 'Poison Pills.'" *Academy of Management Journal* 35, no. 5 (December 1992): 1010–1035.

Normann, Richard, and Rafael Ramircz. "From Value Chain to Value Constellation: Designing Interactive

Strategy." *Harvard Business Review* 71, no. 4 (July–August 1993): 65–77.

Rajagopalan, Nandini, Abdul M. A. Rasheed, and Deepak K. Datta. "Strategic Decision Processes: Critical Review and Future Directions." *Journal of Management* 19, no. 2 (Summer 1992): 349–384.

Sadtler, David R. "Brief Case: The Role of Today's Board in Corporate Strategy." *Long Range Planning* 26, no. 4 (August 1993): 112–113.

Salmon, Walter J. "Crisis Prevention: How to Gear up Your Board." *Harvard Business Review* (January–February 1993): 68–75.

Wiersema, Margarethe F., and Karen A. Bantel. "Top Management Team Demography and Corporate Strategic Change." *Academy of Management Journal* 35, no. 1 (March 1992): 91–121.

EXPERIENTIAL EXERCISES

DEVELOPING A TOWS MATRIX FOR HERSHEY FOODS

PURPOSE

The most widely used strategy-formulation technique among American firms is the TOWS Matrix. This exercise requires development of a TOWS Matrix for Hershey. Matching key external and internal factors in a TOWS Matrix requires good intuitive and conceptual skills. You will improve with practice in developing a TOWS Matrix.

INSTRUCTIONS

Recall from Experiential Exercise 1A that you already may have determined Hershey's external opportunities/threats and internal strengths/weaknesses. This information could be used in completing this exercise. Follow the steps outlined below:

Step 1 On a separate sheet of paper, construct a large nine-cell diagram that will represent your TOWS Matrix. Label the cells appropriately.

Step 2 Record Hershey's opportunities/threats and strengths/weaknesses appropriately in your diagram.

Step 3 Match external and internal factors to generate feasible alternative strategies for Hershey. Record SO, WO, ST, and WT Strategies in appropriate cells of the TOWS Matrix. Use the proper notation to indicate the rationale for the strategies. You do not necessarily have to have strategies in all four strategy cells.

Step 4 Compare your TOWS Matrix to another student's TOWS Matrix. Discuss any major differences.

DEVELOPING A SPACE MATRIX FOR HERSHEY FOODS

PURPOSE

Should Hershey pursue aggressive, conservative, competitive, or defensive strategies? Develop a SPACE Matrix for Hershey to answer this question. Elaborate on the strategic implications of your directional vector. Be specific in terms of strategies that could benefit Hershey.

INSTRUCTIONS

Step 1 Join with two other persons in class and develop a joint SPACE Matrix for Hershey.

Step 2 Diagram your SPACE Matrix on the board. Compare your matrix with other teams' matrices.

Step 3 Discuss the implications of your SPACE analysis.

Experiential Exercise 6C

DEVELOPING A BCG MATRIX FOR HERSHEY FOODS

PURPOSE

Portfolio matrices are widely used by multidivisional organizations to help identify and select strategies to pursue. A BCG analysis identifies particular divisions that should receive fewer resources than others. It may identify some divisions to be divested. This exercise can give you practice developing a BCG Matrix.

INSTRUCTIONS

Step 1 Place the following five column headings at the top of a separate sheet of paper: Divisions, Revenues, Profits, Relative Market Share Position, Industry Growth Rate.

Step 2 Complete a BCG Matrix for Hershey.

Step 3 Compare your BCG Matrix to other students' matrices. Discuss any major differences.

Experiential Exercise 6D

DEVELOPING A QSPM FOR HERSHEY FOODS

PURPOSE

This exercise can give you practice developing a Quantitative Strategic Planning Matrix to determine the relative attractiveness of various strategic alternatives.

INSTRUCTIONS

Step 1 Join with two other students in class to develop a joint QSPM for Hershey.

Step 2 Go to the blackboard and record your strategies and their Sum Total Attractiveness Scores. Compare your team's strategies and total attractiveness scores to those of other teams.

Step 3 Discuss any major differences.

FORMULATING INDIVIDUAL STRATEGIES

PURPOSE

Individuals and organizations are alike in many ways. Each has competitors and each should plan for the future. Every individual and organization faces some external opportunities and threats and has some internal strengths and weaknesses. Both individuals and organizations establish objectives and allocate resources. These and other similarities make it possible for individuals to use many strategic-management concepts and tools. This exercise is designed to demonstrate how the TOWS Matrix can be used by individuals to plan their futures. As one nears completion of a college degree and begins interviewing for jobs, planning can be particularly important.

INSTRUCTIONS

On a separate sheet of paper, construct a TOWS Matrix. Include what you consider to be your major external opportunities, your major external threats, your major strengths, and your major weaknesses. An internal weakness may be a low grade point average. An external opportunity may be that your university offers a graduate program that interests you. Match key external and internal factors by recording in the appropriate cell of the matrix alternative strategies or actions that would allow you to capitalize upon your strengths, overcome your weaknesses, take advantage of your external opportunities, and minimize the impact of external threats. Be sure to use the appropriate matching notation in the strategy cells of the matrix. Since every individual (and organization) is unique, there is no one right answer to this exercise.

THE MACH TEST

PURPOSE

The purpose of this exercise is to enhance your understanding and awareness of the impact that behavioral and political factors can have on strategy analysis and choice.

INSTRUCTIONS

Step 1 On a separate sheet of paper, number from 1 to 10. For each of the ten statements given below, record a 1, 2, 3, 4, or 5 to indicate your attitude, where

1 = I disagree a lot.
2 = I disagree a little.
3 = My attitude is neutral.
4 = I agree a little.
5 = I agree a lot.

1. The best way to handle people is to tell them what they want to hear.
2. When you ask someone to do something for you, it is best to give the real reason for wanting it, rather than giving a reason that might carry more weight.
3. Anyone who completely trusts anyone else is asking for trouble.
4. It is hard to get ahead without cutting corners here and there.
5. It is safest to assume that all people have a vicious streak, and it will come out when they are given a chance.
6. One should take action only when it is morally right.
7. Most people are basically good and kind.
8. There is no excuse for lying to someone else.
9. Most people forget more easily the death of their father than the loss of their property.
10. Generally speaking, people won't work hard unless they're forced to do so.

Step 2 Add up the numbers you recorded beside statements 1, 3, 4, 5, 9, and 10. This sum is Subtotal One. For the other four statements, reverse the numbers you recorded, so a 5 becomes a 1, 4 becomes 2, 2 becomes 4, 1 becomes 5, and 3 remains 3. Then add those four numbers to get Subtotal Two. Finally, add Subtotal One and Subtotal Two to get your Final Score.

Your Final Score. Your Final Score is your Machiavellian Score. Machiavellian principles are defined in a dictionary as "manipulative, dishonest, deceiving, and favoring political expediency over morality." These tactics are not desirable, are not ethical, and are not recommended in the strategic-management process! You may, however, encounter some highly Machiavellian individuals in your career, so beware. It is important for strategists not to manipulate others in the pursuit of organizational objectives. Individuals today recognize and resent manipulative tactics more than ever before. J. R. Ewing (on *Dallas*) is a good example of someone who is a high Mach (score over 30). The National Opinion Research Center used this short form in a random sample of American adults and found the national average Final Score to be 25.[1] The higher your score, the more Machiavellian (manipulative) you tend to be. The following scale is descriptive of individual scores on this test:

- below 16: Never uses manipulation as a tool.
- 16 to 20: Rarely uses manipulation as a tool.
- 21 to 25: Sometimes uses manipulation as a tool.
- 26 to 30: Often uses manipulation as a tool.
- over 30: Always uses manipulation as a tool.

Test Development. The Mach (Machiavellian) test was developed by Dr. Richard Christie, whose research suggests the following tendencies:

1. Men are generally more Machiavellian than women.
2. There is no significant difference between high Machs and low Machs on measures of intelligence or ability.
3. Although high Machs are detached from others, they are detached in a pathological sense.
4. Machiavellian scores are not statistically related to authoritarian values.
5. High Machs tend to be in professions that emphasize the control and manipulation of individuals; for example, law, psychiatry, and behavioral science.

6. Machiavellianism is not significantly related to major demographic characteristics, such as educational level or marital status.
7. High Machs tend to come from a city or have urban backgrounds.
8. Older adults tend to have lower Mach scores than younger adults.[2]

A classic book on power relationships, *The Prince,* was written by Niccolo Machiavelli. Several excerpts from *The Prince* are given below:

Men must either be cajoled or crushed, for they will revenge themselves for slight wrongs, while for grave ones they cannot. The injury therefore that you do to a man should be such that you need not fear his revenge.

We must bear in mind . . . that there is nothing more difficult and dangerous, or more doubtful of success, than an attempt to introduce a new order of things in any state. The innovator has for enemies all those who derived advantages from the old order of things, while those who expect to be benefitted by the new institution will be but lukewarm defenders.

A wise prince, therefore, will steadily pursue such a course that the citizens of his state will always and under all circumstances feel the need for his authority, and will therefore always prove faithful to him.

A prince should seem to be merciful, faithful, humane, religious, and upright, and should even be so in reality; but he should have his mind so trained that, when occasion requires it, he may know how to change to the opposite.[3]

NOTES

1. Richard Christie and Florence Geis, *Studies in Machiavellianism* (Academic Press, 1970). Material in this exercise adapted with permission of the authors and the Academic Press.

2. Ibid., 82–83.
3. Niccolo Machiavelli, *The Prince* (New York: The Washington Press, 1963).

Experiential Exercise 6C

DEVELOPING A BCG MATRIX FOR MY UNIVERSITY

PURPOSE

A BCG Matrix is useful to develop for many nonprofit organizations, including colleges and universities. Of course there are no profits for each division or department and in some cases no revenues. However, you can be creative in performing a BCG Matrix. For example, the pie slice in the circles can represent the number of majors receiving jobs upon graduation, or the number of faculty teaching in that area, or some other variable that you believe is important to consider. The size of the circles can represent the number of students majoring in particular departments or areas.

INSTRUCTIONS

Step 1 On a separate sheet of paper, develop a BCG Matrix for your university. Include all academic schools, departments, or colleges.

Step 2 Diagram your BCG Matrix on the blackboard.

Step 3 Discuss differences among the BCG Matrices on the board.

USING THE *STRATEGY FORMULATOR* SOFTWARE

PURPOSE

The purpose of this exercise is to give you practice using the *Strategy Formulator* software to generate and prioritize strategies.

INSTRUCTIONS

Step 1 Gather the work that you have developed for your university in earlier Experiential Exercises.

Step 2 Using the *Strategy Formulator* software, develop the following matrices: TOWS, SPACE, IE, Grand Strategy. Generate and prioritize strategies for your university.

Step 3 Bring a printout of your work to class. Discuss any problems or questions that you encountered.

THE ROLE OF BOARDS OF DIRECTORS

PURPOSE

The widespread lack of involvement by boards of directors in the strategic-management process is changing in America! Historically, boards of directors have mostly been "insiders" who would not second-guess top executives on strategic issues. It has generally been understood that strategists are responsible and accountable for implementing strategy, so they should formulate strategy, not board members. Consequently, chief executive officers usually avoided discussions of overall strategy with directors because the results often restricted their freedom of action. The judgments of board members was seldom used on acquisitions, divestitures, large capital investments, and other strategic matters. Often the board would meet only annually to fulfill its minimum legal requirements. Boards just served a traditional legitimizing role in many organizations.

This exercise will give you a better understanding of the role of boards of directors in formulating, implementing, and evaluating strategies.

INSTRUCTIONS

Identify a person in your community who serves on a board of directors. Make an appointment to interview that person and seek answers to the questions given below. Summarize your findings in a five minute oral report to the class.

On what board are you a member?

How often does the board meet?

How long have you served on the board?

What role does the board play in this company?

How has the role of the board changed in recent years?

What changes would you like to see in the role of the board?

To what extent do you prepare for the board meeting?

To what extent are you involved in strategic management of the firm?

LOCATING COMPANIES IN A GRAND STRATEGY MATRIX

PURPOSE

The Grand Strategy Matrix is a popular tool for formulating alternative strategies. All organizations can be positioned in one of the Grand Strategy Matrix's four strategy quadrants. The divisions of a firm could likewise be positioned. The Grand Strategy Matrix is based on two evaluative dimensions: competitive position and market growth. Appropriate strategies for an organization to consider are listed in sequential order of attractiveness in each quadrant of the matrix. This exercise gives you experience using a Grand Strategy Matrix.

INSTRUCTIONS

Using the year-end 1993 financial information given below, prepare a Grand Strategy Matrix on a separate sheet of paper. Write the respective company names in the appropriate quadrant of the matrix. Based on this analysis, what strategies are recommended for each company?

COMPANY	COMPANY SALES/ PROFIT GROWTH (%)	INDUSTRY	INDUSTRY SALES/ PROFITS GROWTH (%)
Eaton	+8/-23	Automotive Parts	+11/0
Cummins Engine	+13/+78	Automotive Parts	+11/0
Pennzoil	+18/+820	Oil, Gas, & Coal	-3/+12
Chevron	-7/-43	Oil, Gas, & Coal	-3/+12
Microsoft	+26/+24	Computer Software	+14/+4
Lotus Development	+9/-31	Computer Software	+14/+4
Boise Cascade	+7/0	Forest Products	+5/+91
Weyerhaeuser	+3/42	Forest Products	+5/+91

PART · 3

Strategy
Implementation

Chapter 7

IMPLEMENTING STRATEGIES: MANAGEMENT ISSUES

$O\ B\ J\ E\ C\ T\ I\ V\ E\ S$ After studying this chapter, you should be able to:

- Explain why strategy implementation is more difficult than strategy formulation.
- Discuss the importance of annual objectives and policies in achieving organizational commitment for strategies to be implemented.
- Explain why organizational structure is so important in strategy implementation.
- Describe the relationships between production/operations and strategy implementation.
- Explain how a firm can effectively link performance and pay to strategies.
- Discuss Employee Stock Ownership Plans (ESOPs) as a strategic-management concept.
- Describe how to modify an organizational culture to support new strategies.

*T*he strategic-management process does not end when the firm decides what strategy or strategies to pursue. There must be a translation of strategic thought into strategic action. This translation is much easier if managers and employees of the firm understand the business, feel a part of the company, and through involvement in strategy-formulation activities have become committed to helping the organization succeed. Without understanding and commitment, strategy-implementation efforts face major problems.

Implementing strategy affects an organization from top to bottom; it impacts all the functional and divisional areas of a business. It is beyond the purpose and scope of this text to examine all the business administration concepts and tools important in strategy implementation. This chapter focuses on management issues most central to implementing strategies in the 1990s, while Chapter 8 focuses on important marketing, finance/accounting, R & D, and computer information systems issues.

THE NATURE OF STRATEGY IMPLEMENTATION

The strategy-implementation stage of strategic management is represented by the shaded portion of Figure 7–1. Successful strategy formulation does not guarantee successful strategy implementation. It is always more difficult to do something (strategy implementation) than to say you are going to do it (strategy formulation)! Although inextricably linked, strategy implementation is fundamentally different from strategy formulation. Strategy formulation and implementation can be contrasted in the following ways:

- Strategy formulation is positioning forces before the action.
- Strategy implementation is managing forces during the action.
- Strategy formulation focuses on effectiveness.
- Strategy implementation focuses on efficiency.
- Strategy formulation is primarily an intellectual process.
- Strategy implementation is primarily an operational process.
- Strategy formulation requires good intuitive and analytical skills.
- Strategy implementation requires special motivation and leadership skills.
- Strategy formulation requires coordination among a few individuals.
- Strategy implementation requires coordination among many persons.

Strategy-formulation concepts and tools do not differ greatly for small, large, for-profit, or nonprofit organizations. However, strategy implementation varies substantially among different types and sizes of organizations. Implementing strategies requires such actions as altering sales territories, adding new departments, closing facilities, hiring new employees, changing an organization's pricing strategy, developing financial budgets, developing new employee benefits, establishing cost-control procedures, changing advertising strategies, building new facilities, training new employees, transferring managers among divisions, and building a better computer information system. These types of activities obviously differ greatly between manufacturing, service, and governmental organizations.

Management Perspectives. In all but the smallest organizations, the transition from strategy formulation to strategy implementation requires a shift in responsibility from strategists to divisional and functional managers. Implementation problems can

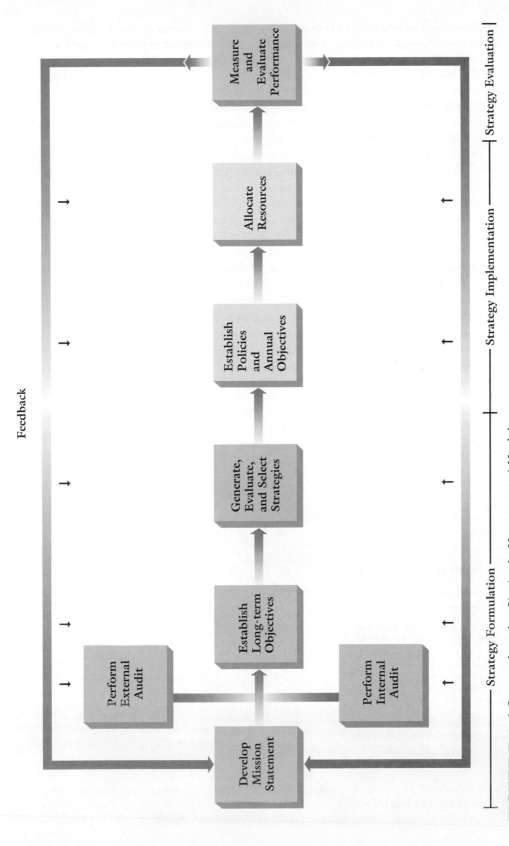

FIGURE 7-1 A Comprehensive Strategic-Management Model

Feedback

Perform External Audit

Develop Mission Statement

Perform Internal Audit

Establish Long-term Objectives

Generate, Evaluate, and Select Strategies

Establish Policies and Annual Objectives

Allocate Resources

Measure and Evaluate Performance

Strategy Formulation ———— Strategy Implementation ———— Strategy Evaluation arise because of this shift in responsibility, especially if strategy-formulation decisions come as a surprise to middle- and lower-level managers. Managers and employees are motivated more by perceived self-interests than by organizational interests, unless the two coincide. Therefore, it is essential that divisional and functional managers be involved as much as possible in strategy-formulation activities. Of equal importance, strategists should be involved as much as possible in strategy-implementation activities. As indicated in the Global Perspective, management styles vary across countries; this magnifies the challenge facing strategists in multinational firms.

Management issues central to strategy implementation include establishing annual objectives, devising policies, allocating resources, altering an existing organizational structure, revising reward and incentive plans, minimizing resistance to change, matching managers with strategy, developing a strategy-supportive culture, adapting production/operations processes, and developing an effective human resource function. Management changes are necessarily more extensive when strategies to be implemented move a firm in a major new direction.

Managers and employees throughout an organization should participate early and directly in strategy-implementation decisions. Their role in strategy implementation should build upon prior involvement in strategy-formulation activities. Strategists' genuine personal commitment to implementation is a necessary and powerful motivational force for managers and employees. Too often, strategists are "too busy" to actively support strategy-implementation efforts, and their lack of interest can be detrimental to organizational success. The rationale for objectives and strategies should be understood and clearly communicated throughout an organization. Major competitors' accomplishments, products, plans, actions, and performance should be apparent to all organizational members. Major external opportunities and threats should be clear, and managers' and employees' questions should be answered. Top-down flow of communication is essential for developing bottom-up support.

A GLOBAL PERSPECTIVE
COMPARING MANAGEMENT STYLES ACROSS COUNTRIES

Management styles vary across countries. Managers in some countries rank high on "conformity," and authoritarian management styles are commonly used in these cultures. Managers in other countries rank high on "individualism"; participative management styles are more common and effective in these countries. Knowledge of these differences can be useful in selecting managers for overseas assignments and for enhancing effectiveness of foreign operations.

The following diagram gives the relative ranking of various countries' beliefs about conformity and individualism.

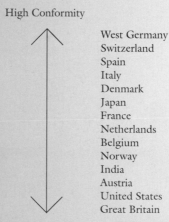

High Conformity

West Germany
Switzerland
Spain
Italy
Denmark
Japan
France
Netherlands
Belgium
Norway
India
Austria
United States
Great Britain

High Individualism

Source: Adapted from R. Klauss and B. M. Bass, "Group Influence on Individual Behavior Across Cultures," *Journal of Cross-Cultural Psychology* 5 (June 1974): 236–46.

Hamel and Prahalad emphasize the need for firms to develop a competitor focus at all hierarchical levels by gathering and widely distributing competitive intelligence; every employee should be able to benchmark her or his efforts against best-in-class competitors so that the challenge becomes personal.[1] This is a challenge for strategists of the firm. Firms should provide training for both managers and employees to ensure they have and maintain the skills necessary to be world-class performers.

ANNUAL OBJECTIVES

Establishing annual objectives is a decentralized activity that directly involves all managers in an organization. Active participation in establishing annual objectives can lead to acceptance and commitment. Annual objectives are essential for strategy implementation because they (1) represent the basis for allocating resources, (2) are a primary mechanism for evaluating managers, (3) are the major instrument for monitoring progress toward achieving long-term objectives, and (4) establish organizational, divisional, and departmental priorities. Considerable time and effort should be devoted to ensuring that annual objectives are well-conceived, consistent with long-term objectives, and supportive of strategies to be implemented. Approving, revising, or rejecting annual objectives is much more than a rubber-stamp activity. The purpose of annual objectives can be summarized as follows:

> Annual objectives serve as guidelines for action, directing and channeling efforts and activities of organization members. They provide a source of legitimacy in an enterprise by justifying activities to stakeholders. They serve as standards of performance. They serve as an important source of employee motivation and identification. They give incentives for managers and employees to perform. They provide a basis for organizational design.[2]

Clearly stated and communicated objectives are critical to success in all types and sizes of firms. Annual objectives, stated in terms of profitability, growth, and market share by business segment, geographic area, customer groups, and product, are common in organizations. Figure 7–2 illustrates how the Stamus Company could establish annual objectives based on long-term objectives. Table 7–1 reveals associated revenue figures that correspond to the objectives outlined in Figure 7–2. Note that, according to plan, the Stamus Company will slightly exceed its long-term objective of doubling company revenues between 1994 and 1996.

TABLE 7-1   The Stamus Company's Revenue Expectations
(in millions of dollars)

	1994	1995	1996
Division I Revenues	1.0	1.400	1.960
Division II Revenues	0.5	0.700	0.980
Division III Revenues	0.5	0.750	1.125
Total Company Revenues	2.0	2.850	4.065

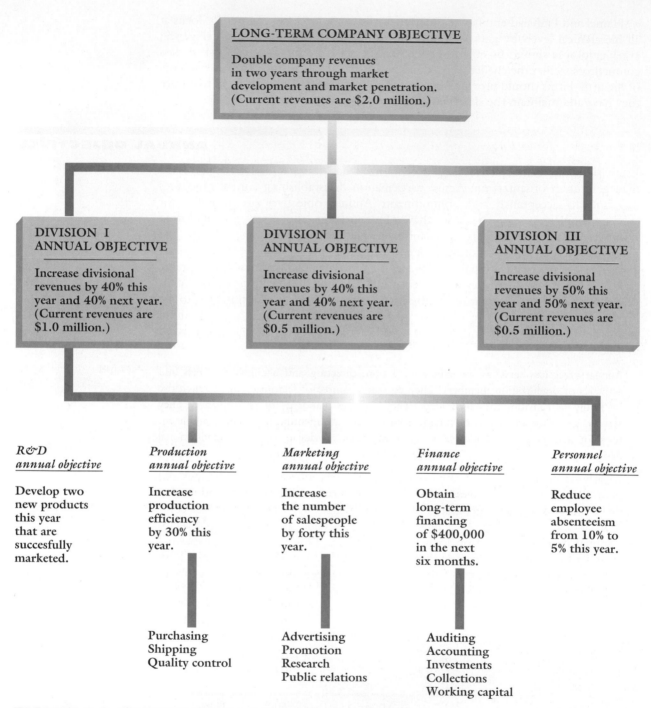

LONG-TERM COMPANY OBJECTIVE

Double company revenues
in two years through market
development and market penetration.
(Current revenues are $2.0 million.)

**DIVISION I
ANNUAL OBJECTIVE**

Increase divisional
revenues by 40% this
year and 40% next year.
(Current revenues are
$1.0 million.)

**DIVISION II
ANNUAL OBJECTIVE**

Increase divisional
revenues by 40% this
year and 40% next year.
(Current revenues are
$0.5 million.)

**DIVISION III
ANNUAL OBJECTIVE**

Increase divisional
revenues by 50% this
year and 50% next year.
(Current revenues are
$0.5 million.)

*R&D
annual objective*

Develop two
new products
this year
that are
succesfully
marketed.

*Production
annual objective*

Increase
production
efficiency
by 30% this
year.

*Marketing
annual objective*

Increase
the number
of salespeople
by forty this
year.

*Finance
annual objective*

Obtain
long-term
financing
of $400,000
in the next
six months.

*Personnel
annual objective*

Reduce
employee
absenteeism
from 10% to
5% this year.

Purchasing
Shipping
Quality control

Advertising
Promotion
Research
Public relations

Auditing
Accounting
Investments
Collections
Working capital

FIGURE 7-2 The Stamus Company's Hierarchy of Aims

Figure 7–2 also reflects how a hierarchy of annual objectives can be established based on an organization's structure. Objectives should be consistent across hierarchical levels and form a network of supportive aims. Horizontal consistency of objectives is as important as vertical consistency. For instance, it would not be effective for manufacturing to achieve more than its annual objective of units produced if marketing could not sell the additional units.

Annual objectives should be measurable, consistent, reasonable, challenging, clear, communicated throughout the organization, characterized by an appropriate time dimension, and accompanied by commensurate rewards and sanctions. Too often, objectives are stated in generalities, with little operational usefulness. Annual objectives such as "to improve communication" or "to improve performance" are not clear, specific, or measurable. Objectives should state quantity, quality, cost, and time and also be verifiable. Terms such as "maximize," "minimize," "as soon as possible," and "adequate" should be avoided.

Annual objectives should be compatible with employees' and managers' values and should be supported by clearly stated policies. More of something is not always better! Improved quality or reduced cost may, for example, be more important than quantity. It is important to tie rewards and sanctions to annual objectives so that employees and managers understand that achieving objectives is critical to successful strategy implementation. Clear annual objectives do not guarantee successful strategy implementation but they do increase the likelihood that personal and organizational aims can be accomplished. Overemphasis on achieving objectives can result in undesirable conduct, such as faking the numbers, distorting the records, and letting objectives become ends in themselves. Managers must be alert to these potential problems.

POLICIES

Changes in a firm's strategic direction do not occur automatically. On a day-to-day basis, policies are needed to make a strategy work. Policies facilitate solving recurring problems and guide the implementation of strategy. Broadly defined, *policy* refers to specific guidelines, methods, procedures, rules, forms, and administrative practices established to support and encourage work toward stated goals.[3] Policies are instruments for strategy implementation. Policies set boundaries, constraints, and limits on the kinds of administrative actions that can be taken to reward and sanction behavior; they clarify what can and cannot be done in pursuit of an organization's objectives.

Policies let both employees and managers know what is expected of them, thereby increasing the likelihood that strategies will be implemented successfully. They provide a basis for management control, allow coordination across organizational units, and reduce the amount of time managers spend making decisions. Policies also clarify what work is to be done by whom. They promote delegation of decision making to appropriate managerial levels where various problems usually arise. Many organizations have a policy manual that serves to guide and direct behavior. About 80 percent of all corporations in the United States have instituted "no smoking" policies.[4]

Policies can apply to all divisions and departments (for example, "We are an equal opportunity employer"). Some policies apply to a single department ("Employees in this department must take at least one training and development course each year"). Whatever their scope and form, policies serve as a mechanism for implementing strategies and obtaining objectives. Policies should be stated in writing whenever possible. They represent the means for carrying out strategic decisions. Examples of policies that support a company strategy, a divisional objective, and a departmental objective are given in Table 7–2.

TABLE 7-2   A Hierarchy of Policies

Company Strategy: Acquire a chain of retail stores to meet our sales growth and profitability objectives.

Supporting policies:

1. "All stores will be open from 8 A.M. to 8 P.M. Monday through Saturday." (This policy could increase retail sales if stores currently are open only 40 hours a week.)

2. "All stores must submit a Monthly Control Data Report." (This policy could reduce expense-to-sales ratios.)

3. "All stores must support company advertising by contributing 5 percent of their total monthly revenues for this purpose." (This policy could allow the company to establish a national reputation.)

4. "All stores must adhere to the uniform pricing guidelines set forth in the Company Handbook." (This policy could help assure customers that the company offers a consistent product in terms of price and quality in all its stores.)

Divisional Objective: Increase the division's revenues from $10 million in 1993 to $15 million in 1994.

Supporting policies:

1. "Beginning in January 1993, this division's salespersons must file a weekly activity report that includes the number of calls made, the number of miles traveled, the number of units sold, the dollar volume sold, and the number of new accounts opened." (This policy could assure that salespersons do not place too great an emphasis in certain areas.)

2. "Beginning in January 1993, this division will return to its employees 5 percent of its gross revenues in the form of a Christmas bonus." (This policy could increase employee productivity.)

3. "Beginning in January 1993, inventory levels carried in warehouses will be decreased by 30 percent in accordance with a Just-in-Time manufacturing approach." (This policy could reduce production expenses and thus free funds for increased marketing efforts.)

Production Department Objective: Increase production from 20,000 units in 1993 to 30,000 units in 1994.

Supporting policies:

1. "Beginning in January 1993, employees will have the option of working up to twenty hours of overtime per week." (This policy could minimize the need to hire additional employees.)

2. "Beginning in January 1993, perfect attendance awards in the amount of $100 will be given to all employees who do not miss a workday in a given year." (This policy could decrease absenteeism and increase productivity.)

3. "Beginning in January 1993, new equipment must be leased rather than purchased." (This policy could reduce tax liabilities and thus allow more funds to be invested in modernizing production processes.)

Some example issues that may require a management policy are as follows:

- To offer extensive or limited management-development workshops and seminars
- To centralize or decentralize employee-training activities
- To recruit through employment agencies, college campuses, and/or newspapers
- To promote from within or hire from the outside
- To promote on the basis of merit or on the basis of seniority
- To tie executive compensation to long-term and/or annual objectives
- To offer numerous or few employee benefits
- To negotiate directly or indirectly with labor unions

- To delegate authority for large expenditures or to retain this authority centrally
- To allow much, some, or no overtime work
- To establish a high- or low-safety stock of inventory
- To use one or more suppliers
- To buy, lease, or rent new production equipment
- To stress quality control greatly or not
- To establish many or only a few production standards
- To operate one, two, or three shifts
- To discourage using insider information for personal gain
- To discourage sexual harassment
- To discourage smoking at work
- To discourage insider trading
- To discourage moonlighting

RESOURCE ALLOCATION

Resource allocation is a central management activity that allows for strategy execution. In organizations that do not use a strategic-management approach to decision making, resource allocation is often based on political or personal factors. Strategic management enables resources to be allocated according to priorities established by annual objectives. Nothing could be more detrimental to strategic management and to organizational success than for resources to be allocated in ways not consistent with priorities indicated by approved annual objectives.

All organizations have at least four types of resources that can be used to achieve desired objectives: financial resources, physical resources, human resources, and technological resources. Allocating resources to particular divisions and departments does not mean that strategies will be successfully implemented. A number of factors commonly prohibit effective resource allocation, including an overprotection of resources, too great an emphasis on short-run financial criteria, organizational politics, vague strategy targets, a reluctance to take risks, and a lack of sufficient knowledge.[5]

Below the corporate level, there often exists an absence of systematic thinking about resources allocated and strategies of the firm. Yavitz and Newman explain why:

> Managers normally have many more tasks than they can do. Managers must allocate time and resources among these tasks. Pressure builds up. Expenses are too high. The CEO wants a good financial report for the third quarter. Strategy formulation and implementation activities often get deferred. Today's problems soak up available energies and resources. Scrambled accounts and budgets fail to reveal the shift in allocation away from strategic needs to currently squeaking wheels.[6]

The real value of any resource-allocation program lies in the resulting accomplishment of an organization's objectives. Effective resource allocation does not guarantee successful strategy implementation because programs, personnel, controls, and commitment must breathe life into the resources provided. Strategic management itself is sometimes referred to as a "resource-allocation process."

MANAGING CONFLICT

Interdependency of objectives and competition for limited resources often leads to conflict. *Conflict* can be defined as a disagreement between two or more parties on one or more issues. Establishing annual objectives can lead to conflict because individuals have different expectations and perceptions, schedules create pressure, personalities are incompatible, and misunderstandings between line and staff occur. For example, a collection manager's objective of reducing bad debts by 50 percent in a given year may conflict with a divisional objective to increase sales by 20 percent.

Establishing objectives can lead to conflict because managers and strategists must make trade-offs, such as whether to emphasize short-term profits or long-term growth, profit margin or market share, market penetration or market development, growth or stability, high risk or low risk, and social responsiveness or profit maximization. Conflict is unavoidable in organizations, so it is important that conflict be managed and resolved before dysfunctional consequences affect organizational performance. Conflict is not always bad. An absence of conflict can signal indifference and apathy. Conflict can serve to energize opposing groups into action and may help managers identify problems.

Various approaches for managing and resolving conflict can be classified into three categories: avoidance, defusion, and confrontation. *Avoidance* includes such actions as ignoring the problem in hopes that the conflict will resolve itself or physically separating the conflicting individuals (or groups). *Defusion* can include playing down differences between conflicting parties while accentuating similarities and common interests, compromising so that there is neither a clear winner nor loser, resorting to majority rule, appealing to a higher authority, or redesigning present positions. *Confrontation* is exemplified by exchanging members of conflicting parties so that each can gain an appreciation of the other's point of view, focusing on superordinate goals such as company survival, or holding a meeting at which conflicting parties present their views and work through their differences.

MATCHING STRUCTURE WITH STRATEGY

Changes in strategy often require changes in the way an organization is structured for two major reasons. First, structure largely dictates how objectives and policies will be established. For example, the format for objectives and policies established under a geographic organizational structure is couched in geographic terms. Objectives and policies are stated largely in terms of products in an organization whose structure is based on product groups. The structural format for developing objectives and policies can significantly impact all other strategy-implementation activities.

The second major reason why changes in strategy often require changes in structure is that structure dictates how resources will be allocated. If an organization is structured based on customer groups, then resources will be allocated in that manner. Similarly, if an organization's structure is set up along functional business lines, then resources are allocated by functional areas. Unless new or revised strategies place emphasis in the same areas as old strategies, structural reorientation commonly becomes a part of strategy implementation.

In a classic study of seventy large American corporations, Alfred Chandler concluded that changes in strategy lead to changes in organizational structure.[7] Structure, he says, should be designed to facilitate the strategic pursuit of a firm and, therefore, follows strategy. Without a strategy or reasons for being (mission), structure is not important. Chandler found a particular structure sequence to be often repeated as organizations grow and change strategy over time; this sequence is depicted in Figure 7–3.

There is no one optimal organizational design or structure for a given strategy or type of organization. What is appropriate for one organization may not be appropriate for a similar firm, although successful firms in a given industry do tend to organize themselves in a similar way. For example, consumer-goods companies tend to emulate the divisional structure-by-product form of organization. Small firms tend to be functionally structured (centralized). Medium-size firms tend to be divisionally structured (decentralized). Large firms tend to use an SBU (strategic business unit) or matrix structure. As organizations grow, their structures generally change from simple to complex as a result of concatenation, or the linking together of several basic strategies.[8]

Numerous external and internal forces affect an organization; no firm could change its structure in response to every one of these forces, because to do so would lead to chaos. However, when a firm changes its strategy, the existing organizational structure may become ineffective. Symptoms of an ineffective organizational structure include too many levels of management, too many meetings attended by too many people, too much attention being directed toward solving interdepartmental conflicts, too large a span of control, and too many unachieved objectives. Changes in structure can facilitate strategy-implementation efforts, but changes in structure should not be expected to make a bad strategy good, or to make bad managers good, or to make bad products sell.

Structure undeniably can and does influence strategy. Strategies formulated must be workable, so if a certain new strategy required massive structural changes it would not be an attractive choice. In this way, structure can shape the choice of strategies. But a more important concern is determining what types of structural changes are needed to implement new strategies and how these changes can best be accomplished. We examine this issue by focusing on seven basic types of organizational structure: functional, divisional by geographic area, divisional by product, divisional by customer, divisional by process, strategic business unit (SBU), and matrix.

The Functional Structure. The most widely used structure is the functional or centralized type, because this structure is the simplest and least expensive of the seven alternatives. A *functional structure* groups tasks and activities by business function

FIGURE 7-3 Chandler's Strategy–Structure Relationship

such as production/operations, marketing, finance/accounting, research and development, and computer information systems. A university may structure its activities by major functions that include academic affairs, student services, alumni relations, athletics, maintenance, and accounting. Besides being simple and inexpensive, a functional structure also promotes specialization of labor, encourages efficiency, minimizes the need for an elaborate control system, and allows rapid decision making. Some disadvantages of a functional structure are that it forces accountability to the top, minimizes career development opportunities, and is sometimes characterized by low employee morale, line/staff conflicts, poor delegation of authority, and inadequate planning for products and markets.

The 1980s and 1990s witnessed most large companies abandoning the functional structure in favor of decentralization and improved accountability. A company that still adheres to a functional design, however, is Food Lion, Inc., as shown in Figure 7–4.

The Divisional Structure. The *divisional* or *decentralized structure* is the second most common type used by American businesses. As a small organization grows, it has more and more difficulty managing different products and services in different markets. Some form of divisional structure generally becomes necessary to motivate employees, control operations, and compete successfully in diverse locations. The divisional structure can be organized in one of four ways: by geographic area, by product or service, by customer, or by process. Within a divisional structure, functional activities are performed both centrally and in each separate division.

A divisional structure has some clear advantages. First and perhaps foremost, accountability is clear. That is, divisional managers can be held responsible for sales and profit levels. Since a divisional structure is based on extensive delegation of authority, managers and employees can easily see the results of their good or bad performances. As a result, employee morale is generally higher in a divisional structure than it is in a centralized structure. Other advantages of the divisional design are that it creates career development opportunities for managers, allows local control of local situations, leads to a competitive climate within an organization, and allows new businesses and products to be added easily. AT&T recently restructured by breaking large businesses into smaller, focused units, totaling twenty-four divisions and nineteen subsidiaries.

The divisional design is not without some limitations, however. Perhaps the most important limitation is that a divisional structure is costly, for a number of reasons. First, each division requires functional specialists who must be paid. Second, there exists some duplication of staff services, facilities, and personnel; for instance, functional specialists are also needed centrally (at headquarters) to coordinate divisional activities. Third, managers must be well-qualified, since the divisional design forces delegation of authority; better-qualified individuals require higher salaries. A divisional structure can also be costly because it requires an elaborate, headquarters-driven control system. Finally, certain regions, products, or customers may sometimes receive special treatment, and it may be difficult to maintain consistent, companywide practices. Nonetheless, for most large organizations and many small firms, the advantages of a divisional structure more than offset the potential limitations.

A *divisional structure by geographic area* is appropriate for organizations whose strategies need to be tailored to fit the particular needs and characteristics of customers in different geographic areas. This type of structure can be most appropriate for organizations that have similar branch facilities located in widely dispersed areas. A divisional structure by geographic area allows local participation in decision making

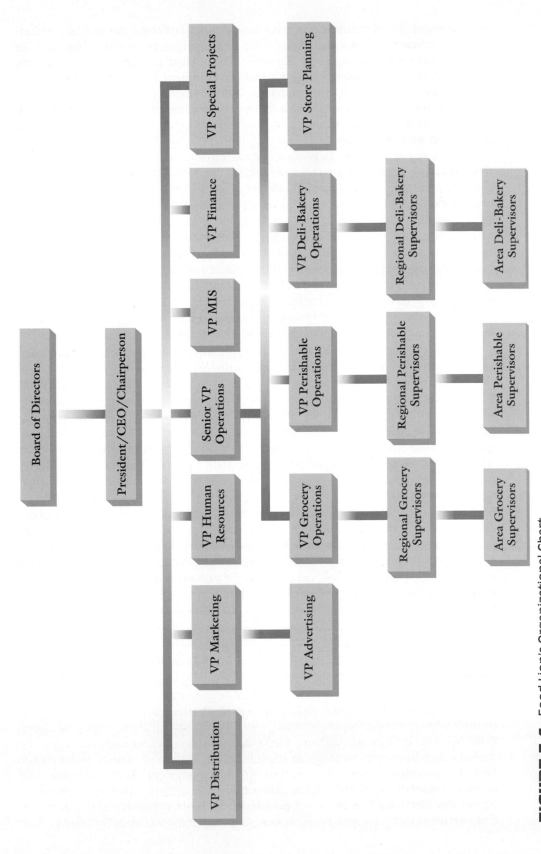

FIGURE 7-4 Food Lion's Organizational Chart

and improved coordination within a region. ABB (Asia Brown Bover Ltd.) reorganized its management structure into three large geographic regions: Europe, the Americas, and Asia-Pacific. Percy Barnevik, ABB's chief executive officer, says the growing unification of Europe requires that the continent be treated as one market, while the opening up of markets under the North American Free Trade Agreement made establishment of one region for the Americas a logical step. Treating the Asia-Pacific region as one division ensures focused attention in the area of the world with the greatest growth potential.

The *divisional structure by product* is most effective for implementing strategies when specific products or services need special emphasis. Also, this type of structure is widely used when an organization offers only a few products or services, or when an organization's products or services differ substantially. The divisional structure allows strict control and attention to product lines, but it may also require a more skilled management force and reduced top-management control. General Motors, Du Pont, and Procter & Gamble use a divisional structure by product to implement strategies. Huffy, the largest bicycle company in the world, is another firm that is highly decentralized based on a divisional-by-product structure. Based in Ohio, Huffy's divisions are the Bicycle division, the Gerry Baby Products division, Huffy Sports division, YLC Enterprises, and Washington Inventory Service. Harry Shaw, Huffy's chairman, believes decentralization is one of the keys to Huffy's success.

When a few major customers are of paramount importance and many different services are provided to these customers, then a *divisional structure by customer* can be the most effective way to implement strategies. This structure allows an organization to cater effectively to the requirements of clearly defined customer groups. For example, book publishing companies often organize their activities around customer groups such as colleges, secondary schools, and private commercial schools. Some airline companies have two major customer divisions: passengers and freight or cargo services. Merrill Lynch is organized into separate divisions that cater to different groups of customers, including wealthy individuals, institutional investors, and small corporations.

A *divisional structure by process* is similar to a functional structure, since activities are organized according to the way work is actually performed. However, a key difference between these two designs is that functional departments are not accountable for profits or revenues, whereas divisional process departments are evaluated on these criteria. An example of a divisional structure by process is a manufacturing business organized into six divisions: electrical work, glass cutting, welding, grinding, painting, and foundry work. In this case, all operations related to these specific processes would be grouped under the separate divisions. Each process (division) would be responsible for generating revenues and profits. The divisional structure by process can be particularly effective in achieving objectives when distinct production processes represent the thrust of competitiveness in an industry.

The Strategic Business Unit (SBU) Structure. As the number, size, and diversity of divisions in an organization increase, controlling and evaluating divisional operations become increasingly difficult for strategists. Increases in sales often are not accompanied by similar increases in profitability. The span of control becomes too large at top levels of the firm. For example, in a large conglomerate organization composed of ninety divisions, the chief executive officer could have difficulty even remembering the first names of divisional presidents. In multidivisional organizations, an SBU structure can greatly facilitate strategy-implementation efforts.

The *SBU structure* groups similar divisions into strategic business units and delegates authority and responsibility for each unit to a senior executive who reports directly to the chief executive officer. This change in structure can facilitate strategy implementation by improving coordination between similar divisions and channeling accountability to distinct business units. In the ninety-division conglomerate just mentioned, the ninety divisions could perhaps be regrouped into ten SBUs according to certain common characteristics such as competing in the same industry, being located in the same area, or having the same customers.

Two disadvantages of an SBU structure are that it requires an additional layer of management, which increases salary expenses, and the role of the group vice-president is often ambiguous. However, these limitations often do not outweigh the advantages of improved coordination and accountability. Atlantic Richfield is a firm that successfully uses an SBU-type structure.

The Matrix Structure. A *matrix structure* is the most complex of all designs because it depends upon both vertical and horizontal flows of authority and communication (hence the term "matrix"). In contrast, functional and divisional structures depend primarily on vertical flows of authority and communication. A matrix structure can result in higher overhead because it creates more management positions. Other characteristics of a matrix structure that contribute to overall complexity include dual lines of budget authority (a violation of the unity-of-command principle), dual sources of reward and punishment, shared authority, dual reporting channels, and a need for an extensive and effective communication system.

Despite its complexity, the matrix structure is widely used in many industries, including construction, health care, research, and defense. Some advantages of a matrix structure are that project objectives are clear, there are many channels of communication, workers can see visible results of their work, and shutting down a project can be accomplished relatively easily.

In order for a matrix structure to be effective, organizations need participative planning, training, clear mutual understanding of roles and responsibilities, excellent internal communication, and mutual trust and confidence. The matrix structure is being used more frequently by American businesses because firms are pursuing strategies that add new products, customer groups, and technology to their range of activities. Out of these changes are coming product managers, functional managers, and geographic-area managers, all of whom have important strategic responsibilities. When several variables, such as product, customer, technology, geography, functional area, and line of business, have roughly equal strategic priorities, a matrix organization can be an effective structural form.

LINKING PERFORMANCE AND PAY TO STRATEGIES

American businesses are aligning strategy, performance, and pay more closely. The *Wall Street Journal* recently reported that 51 percent of companies are practicing some form of pay for performance for employees and managers other than top executives.[9] This percentage was up from 44 percent in 1989 and 47 percent in 1990. The 1991 average employee performance bonus was 6.8 percent of pay for individual performance, 5.5 percent of pay for group productivity, and 6.4 percent of pay for companywide profitability.

Staff control of pay systems, a related problem, often prevents line managers from using financial compensation as a strategic tool. Flexibility regarding managerial and employee compensation is needed to allow short-term shifts in compensation that can stimulate efforts to achieve long-term objectives. NBC recently unveiled a new method for paying its affiliated stations. The compensation formula is 50-percent based on audience viewing of shows from 4 P.M. to 8 P.M., and 50-percent based on how many adults aged 25 to 54 watch NBC over the course of a day.

How can an organization's reward system be more closely linked to strategic performance? How can decisions on salary increases, promotions, merit pay, and bonuses be more closely aligned to support the long-term strategic objectives of the organization? There are no widely accepted answers to these questions, but a dual bonus system based on both annual objectives and long-term objectives is becoming common. The percentage of a manager's annual bonus attributable to short-term versus long-term results should vary by hierarchical level in the organization. A chief executive officer's annual bonus could, for example, be determined on a 75-percent short-term and 25-percent long-term basis. It is important that bonuses not be based solely on short-term results, because such a system ignores long-term company strategies and objectives.

Du Pont Canada has a 16-percent return on equity objective. If this objective is met, the company's 4,000 employees receive a "performance sharing cash award" equal to 4 percent of pay. If return on equity falls below 11 percent, employees get nothing. If return on equity exceeds 28 percent, workers receive a 10-percent bonus.

Profit sharing is another widely used form of incentive compensation. More than 30 percent of American companies have profit-sharing plans, but critics emphasize that too many factors affect profits for this to be a good criterion. Taxes, pricing, or an acquisition would wipe out profits, for example. Also, firms try to minimize profits in a sense to reduce taxes.

Still another criterion widely used to link performance and pay to strategies is gain sharing. *Gain sharing* requires employees or departments to establish performance targets; if actual results exceed objectives, all members get bonuses. Ed Lawler at the University of Southern California reports that 26 percent of American companies use some form of gain sharing; about 75 percent of gain-sharing plans have been adopted since 1980.[10] Carrier, a subsidiary of United Technologies, has had excellent success with gain sharing in its six plants in Syracuse, New York; Firestone's tire plant in Wilson, North Carolina, has experienced similar success with gain sharing.

Criteria such as sales, profit, production efficiency, quality, and safety could also serve as bases for an effective bonus system. If an organization meets certain understood, agreed-upon profit objectives, every member of the enterprise should share in the harvest. A bonus system can be an effective tool for motivating individuals to support strategy-implementation efforts. BankAmerica, for example, recently overhauled its incentive system to link pay to sales of the bank's most profitable products and services. Branch managers receive a base salary plus a bonus based on the number of new customers and on sales of bank products. Every employee in each branch is also eligible for a bonus if the branch exceeds its goals. Thomas Peterson, a top BankAmerica executive, says, "We want to make people responsible for meeting their goals, so we pay incentives on sales, not on controlling costs or on being sure the parking lot is swept."

Five "tests" are often used to determine whether a performance-pay plan will benefit an organization:

1. *Does the plan capture attention?* Are people talking more about their activities and taking pride in early successes under the plan?
2. *Do employees understand the plan?* Can participants explain how it works and what they need to do to earn the incentive?

3. *Is the plan improving communications?* Do employees know more than they used to about the company's mission, plans, and objectives?
4. *Does the plan pay out when it should?* Are incentives being paid for desired results—and being *withheld* when objectives are not met?
5. *Is the company or unit performing better?* Are profits up? Has market share grown? Have gains resulted in part from the incentives?[11]

In addition to a dual bonus system, a combination of reward-strategy incentives such as salary raises, stock options, fringe benefits, promotions, praise, recognition, criticism, fear, increased job autonomy, and awards can be used to encourage managers and employees to push hard for successful strategic implementation. The range of options for getting people, departments, and divisions to actively support strategy-implementation activities in a particular organization is almost limitless. Merck, for example, recently gave each of its 37,000 employees a ten-year option to buy 100 shares of Merck stock at a set price of $127. Steven Darien, Merck's vice president of human resources, says, "We needed to find ways to get everyone in the workforce on board in terms of our goals and objectives. Company executives will begin meeting with all Merck workers to explore ways in which employees can contribute more."

Strategists need to design an effective system for their firm. Motivational incentives can be positive, negative, intrinsic, or extrinsic. In the final analysis, a successful reward/performance system allows for blended fulfillment of both short-term and long-term organizational and personal objectives. *Fortune* recommends the following five guidelines for linking performance and pay to strategies:

1. Start with a clear strategy.
2. Focus on jobs that can be measured.
3. Decentralize incentives.
4. Separate incentive from base pay.
5. Create a "sunset" provision—conditions under which the program will be modified or terminated.[12]

MANAGING RESISTANCE TO CHANGE

No organization or individual can escape change. But the thought of change raises anxieties because people fear economic loss, inconvenience, uncertainty, and a break in normal social patterns. Almost any change in structure, technology, people, or strategies has the potential to disrupt comfortable interaction patterns. For this reason, people resist change. The strategic-management process itself can impose major changes on individuals and processes. Reorienting an organization to get people to think and act strategically is not an easy task.

The level of familiarity with strategic thinking in the U.S. is high, but acceptance is low. U.S. management has to undergo a cultural change, and it's difficult to force people to change their thinking; it's like ordering them to use personal computers. One obstacle is that top executives are often too busy fighting fires to devote time to developing managers who can think strategically. Yet, the best-run companies recognize the need to develop managers who can fashion and implement strategy.[13]

Resistance to change can be considered the single greatest threat to successful strategy implementation. Resistance in the form of sabotaging production machines, absenteeism, filing unfounded grievances, and an unwillingness to cooperate regularly occurs in organizations. People often resist strategy implementation because they do not understand what is happening or why changes are taking place. In that case, employees may simply need accurate information. Successful strategy implementation hinges upon managers' ability to develop an organizational climate conducive to change. Change must be viewed as an opportunity rather than as a threat by managers and employees.

Resistance to change can emerge at any stage or level of the strategy-implementation process. Although there are various approaches for implementing changes, three commonly used strategies are a force change strategy, an educative change strategy, and a rational or self-interest change strategy. A *force change strategy* involves giving orders and enforcing those orders; this strategy has the advantage of being fast, but it is plagued by low commitment and high resistance. The *educative change strategy* is one that presents information to convince people of the need for change; the disadvantage of an educative change strategy is that implementation becomes slow and difficult. However, this type of strategy evokes greater commitment and less resistance than does the force strategy. Finally, a *rational* or *self-interest change strategy* is one that attempts to convince individuals that the change is to their personal advantage. When this appeal is successful, strategy implementation can be relatively easy. However, implementation changes are seldom to everyone's advantage.

The rational change strategy is the most desirable, so this approach is examined a bit further. Managers can improve the likelihood of successfully implementing change by carefully designing change efforts. Jack Duncan describes a rational or self-interest change strategy as consisting of four steps. First, employees are invited to participate in the process of change and the details of transition; participation allows everyone to give opinions, to feel a part of the change process, and to identify their own self-interests regarding the recommended change. Second, some motivation or incentive to change is required; self-interest can be the most important motivator. Third, communication is needed so that people can understand the purpose for the changes. Giving and receiving feedback is the fourth step; everyone enjoys knowing how things are going and how much progress is being made.[14]

Igor Ansoff summarizes the need for strategists to manage resistance to change as follows:

> Observation of the historical transitions from one orientation to another shows that, if left unmanaged, the process becomes conflict-laden, prolonged, and costly in both human and financial terms. Management of resistance involves anticipating the focus of resistance and its intensity. Second, it involves eliminating unnecessary resistance caused by misperceptions and insecurities. Third, it involves mustering the power base necessary to assure support for the change. Fourth, it involves planning the process of change. Finally, it involves monitoring and controlling resistance during the process of change. . . .[15]

Due to diverse external and internal forces, change is a fact of life in organizations. The rate, speed, magnitude, and direction of changes vary over time by industry and organization. Strategists should strive to create a work environment in which change is recognized as necessary and beneficial so that individuals can adapt to change more easily. Adopting a strategic-management approach to decision making can itself require major changes in the philosophy and operations of a firm.

Strategists can take a number of positive actions to minimize managers' and employees' resistance to change. For example, individuals who will be affected by a change should be involved in the decision to make the change and in decisions about how to implement change. Strategists should anticipate changes and develop and offer training and development workshops so managers and employees can adapt to those changes. They also need to communicate the need for changes effectively. The strategic-management process can be described as a process of managing change. Robert Waterman describes how successful (renewal) organizations involve individuals to facilitate change:

> Implementation starts with, not after, the decision. When Ford Motor Company embarked on the program to build the highly successful Taurus, management gave up the usual, sequential design process. Instead they showed the tentative design to the work force and asked their help in devising a car that would be easy to build. Team Taurus came up with no less than 1,401 items suggested by Ford employees. What a contrast from the secrecy that characterized the industry before! When people are treated as the main engine rather than interchangeable parts, motivation, creativity, quality, and commitment to implementation go up.[16]

MANAGING THE NATURAL ENVIRONMENT

Monsanto, a large U.S. chemical company, is an excellent example of a firm that protects the natural environment. Monsanto set a goal in 1988 to reduce its toxic air emissions by 90 percent between 1989 and 1992, and it achieved that aim. Monsanto's motto is "Zero Spills, Zero Releases, Zero Incidents, and Zero Excuses."

The 1990s may well be remembered as the "decade of the environment." Earth itself has become a stakeholder for all business firms. Consumer interest in businesses' preserving nature's ecological balance and fostering a clean, healthy environment is high and growing. Evidence of this growing interest is that circulation of the top three natural environmental magazines, *Audubon, Greenpeace,* and *Sierra,* is soaring. Advertising revenues from these three magazines increased nearly 25 percent annually in the early 1990s, when the magazine industry in general experienced slow or no growth in advertising revenues. This consumer interest is spurring companies to reconcile environmental and economic considerations.

The ecological challenge facing all organizations requires managers to formulate strategies that preserve and conserve natural resources and control pollution. Special natural environmental issues include ozone depletion, global warming, depletion of rain forests, destruction of animal habitats, protecting endangered species, developing biodegradable products and packages, waste management, clean air, clean water, erosion, destruction of natural resources, and pollution control. More and more firms are developing "green" product lines that are biodegradable and/or are made from recycled products. "Green" products sell well.

The Environmental Protection Agency recently reported that U.S. citizens and organizations spend more than about $100 billion annually on pollution abatement, and projected this amount will double by 1995. Environmental concerns touch all aspects of a business's operations, including workplace risk exposures, packaging, waste reduction, energy use, alternative fuels, environmental cost accounting, and recycling practices.[17]

Managing as if the earth matters requires an understanding of how international trade, competitiveness, and global resources are connected. Environmental affairs can no longer be simply a technical function performed by specialists in a firm; more emphasis must be placed on developing an environmental perspective among all employees and managers of the firm. Many companies are moving environmental affairs from the staff side of the organization to the line side, to make the corporate environmental group report directly to the chief operating officer. Some firms are also including environmental factors on their performance appraisal instruments and tying environmental performance directly to raises, bonuses, and promotions. For example, Conoco ties compensation of all its top managers to environmental action plans, and Occidental Chemical includes environmental responsibilities in all job descriptions.[18]

Societies have been plagued by environmental disasters to such an extent recently that firms failing to recognize the importance of environmental issues and challenges could suffer severe consequences. Managing environmental affairs can no longer be an incidental or secondary function of company operations. Hooper and Rocca emphasize that "Product design, manufacturing, transportation, customer use, and ultimate disposal of a product should not merely reflect environmental considerations, but be driven by them. Firms that excel in the management of environmental affairs will benefit from constructive relations with consumers, regulators, vendors, and other industry players—substantially improving their prospects of success."[19]

Starik and Carroll advocate "strategic environmental management" whereby firms formulate and implement strategies from an environmental perspective.[20] Environmental strategies could include developing or acquiring "green businesses," divesting or altering environment-damaging businesses, striving to become a low-cost producer through waste minimization and energy conservation, or pursuing a differentiation strategy through green product features. In addition to creating strategies, firms could include an environmental representative on the board of directors, conduct regular environmental audits, implement bonuses for favorable environmental results, become involved in environmental issues and programs, incorporate environmental values in mission statements, establish environmentally oriented objectives, acquire environmental skills, and provide environmental training programs for company employees and managers.

CREATING A STRATEGY-SUPPORTIVE CULTURE

Strategists should strive to preserve, emphasize, and build upon aspects of an existing culture that support proposed new strategies. Aspects of an existing culture that are antagonistic to a proposed strategy should be identified and changed. Substantial research indicates that new strategies are often market driven and dictated by competitive forces. For this reason, changing a firm's culture to fit a new strategy is usually more effective than changing a strategy to fit an existing culture. Numerous techniques are available to alter an organization's culture, including recruitment, training, transfer, promotion, restructure of an organization's design, role modeling, and positive reinforcement.

In a recent article, Jack Duncan described *triangulation* as an effective, multimethod technique for studying and altering a firm's culture.[21] Triangulation includes the combined use of obtrusive observation, self-administered questionnaires, and personal interviews to determine the nature of a firm's culture. The process of triangulation reveals needed changes in a firm's culture that could benefit strategy.

Schein indicates that the following elements are most useful in linking culture to strategy:

1. Formal statements of organizational philosophy, charters, creeds, materials used for recruitment and selection, and socialization.
2. Designing of physical spaces, facades, buildings.
3. Deliberate role modeling, teaching, and coaching by leaders.
4. Explicit reward and status system, promotion criteria.

5. Stories, legends, myths, and parables about key people and events.

6. What leaders pay attention to, measure, and control.

7. Leader reactions to critical incidents and organizational crises.

8. How the organization is designed and structured.

9. Organizational systems and procedures.

10. Criteria used for recruitment, selection, promotion, leveling off, retirement, and "excommunication" of people.[22]

In the personal and religious side of life, the impact of loss and change is easy to see.[23] Memories of loss and change often haunt individuals and organizations for years. Ibsen says, "Rob the average man of his life illusion and you rob him of his happiness at the same stroke."[24] When attachments to a culture are severed in an organization's attempt to change direction, employees and managers often experience deep feelings of grief. This phenomenon commonly occurs when external conditions dictate the need for a new strategy. Managers and employees often struggle to find meaning in a situation that changed many years before. Some people find comfort in memories; others find solace in the present. Weak linkages between strategic management and organizational culture can jeopardize performance and success. Deal and Kennedy emphasize that making strategic changes in an organization always threatens a culture:

> …people form strong attachments to heroes, legends, the rituals of daily life, the hoopla of extravaganza and ceremonies, and all the symbols of the workplace. Change strips relationships and leaves employees confused, insecure, and often angry. Unless something can be done to provide support for transitions from old to new, the force of a culture can neutralize and emasculate strategy changes.[25]

The "old" corporate culture at AT&T could be described as consisting of lifetime careers, intense loyalty to the company, up-from-the-ranks management succession, dedication to the service ethos, and management by consensus. As AT&T moved from a regulated monopoly to a highly competitive environment in the 1980s, the company made numerous changes to create a culture that supported the new strategy; it redesigned its organizational structure, articulated its value system explicitly, provided management training to modify behavior in support of new values, revised recruiting aims and practices, and modified old symbols. AT&T abandoned its familiar logo, a bell with a circle, and adopted a new logo, a globe encircled by electronic communications, that symbolizes its new strategies to compete with U.S. Sprint and MCI.

PRODUCTION/OPERATIONS CONCERNS WHEN IMPLEMENTING STRATEGIES

Production/operations capabilities, limitations, and policies can significantly enhance or inhibit attainment of objectives. Production processes typically constitute more than 70 percent of a firm's total assets. A major part of the strategy-implementation process takes place at the production site. Production-related decisions such as plant size, plant location, product design, choice of equipment, kind of tooling, size of inventory, inventory control, quality control, cost control, use of standards, job specialization, employee training, equipment and resource utilization, shipping and packaging, and technological innovation can have a dramatic impact on the success or failure of strategy-implementation efforts.

There was a time when people were "factors of production," managed little differently from machines or capital. No more. The best people will not tolerate it. And if that way of managing ever generated productivity, it has the reverse effect today. While capital and machines either are or can be managed toward sameness, people are individuals. They must be managed that way. When companies encourage individual expression, it is difficult for them not to be successful (renew). The only true source of success in a company is the individual.[26]

Examples of adjustments in production systems that could be required to implement various strategies are provided in Table 7–3 for both for-profit and nonprofit organizations. For instance, note that when a bank formulates and selects a strategy to add ten new branches, a production-related implementation concern is site location. As indicated in the Natural Environment Perspective, pollution control can also be an important concern in production decisions.

Just in Time (JIT) production approaches can significantly reduce the costs of implementing strategies. With JIT, parts and materials are delivered to a production site just as they are needed, rather than being stockpiled as a hedge against later deliveries. Harley-Davidson reports that at one plant alone, JIT freed $22 million previously tied up in inventory and greatly reduced reorder lead time. *Industry Week* made the following observation about JIT:

> Most of the nation's 1,000 largest industrial companies are experimenting with, or preparing to implement, "Just in Time" manufacturing schemes. Suppliers who can't, or won't, play by the new rules are finding themselves on the sidelines. "Just in Case" just isn't good enough any more.[27]

Factors that should be studied before locating production facilities include the availability of major resources, the prevailing wage rates in the area, transportation costs related to shipping and receiving, the location of major markets, political risks in the area or country, and the availability of trainable employees.

For high-technology companies, production costs may not be as important as production flexibility, because major product changes can be needed often. Industries such as biogenetics and plastics rely on production systems that must be flexible

A NATURAL ENVIRONMENT PERSPECTIVE
NATURAL ENVIRONMENT LEGISLATION

- Florida has banned nonbiodegradable polystyrene foam and plastic-coated paper products used for food packaging.
- North Carolina has banned polystyrene food packages that are not being recycled at a 25-percent rate.
- Thirty-eight states have implemented product and packaging mandates designed to reduce waste or promote recycling.
- Seven states have instituted "green" labeling programs.
- Recycling is mandatory or being instituted in more than 1,500 U.S. cities.

- Many cities and states have banned disposable diapers; Oregon is considering making possession of disposable diapers a criminal offense.
- The U.S. Clean Air Act and Clean Water Act provide strict regulations for all businesses.
- The Environmental Protection Agency (EPA) regulations fill more than 11,000 pages.
- The EPA requires all U.S. manufacturers to annually report releases of any of nearly 500 toxic chemicals into the air, ground, and water.

Source: Adapted from Lynn Scarlett, "A Guide to Environmental Myths and Realities," *Consumers' Research,* January 1992, p. 14.

TABLE 7-3 Production Management and Strategy Implementation

TYPE OF ORGANIZATION	STRATEGY BEING IMPLEMENTED	PRODUCTION SYSTEM ADJUSTMENTS
Hospital	Adding a cancer center (Product Development)	Purchase specialized equipment and add specialized people.
Bank	Adding ten new branches (Market Development)	Perform site location analysis.
Beer brewery	Purchasing a barley farm operation (Backward Integration)	Revise the inventory control system.
Steel manufacturer	Acquiring a fast-food chain (Conglomerate Diversification)	Improve the quality control system.
Computer company	Purchase a retail distribution chain (Forward Integration)	Alter the shipping, packaging, and transportation systems.

enough to allow frequent changes and rapid introduction of new products. An article in *Harvard Business Review* explains why some organizations get into trouble:

> They too slowly realize that a change in product strategy alters the tasks of a production system. These tasks, which can be stated in terms of requirements for cost, product flexibility, volume flexibility, product performance, and product consistency, determine which manufacturing policies are appropriate. As strategies shift over time, so must production policies covering the location and scale of manufacturing facilities, the choice of manufacturing process, the degree of vertical integration of each manufacturing facility, the use of R & D units, the control of the production system, and the licensing of technology.[28]

A common management practice, cross-training of employees, can facilitate strategy implementation and can yield many benefits. Employees gain a better understanding of the whole business and can contribute better ideas in planning sessions. Production/operations managers need to realize, however, that cross-training employees can create problems related to the following issues:

1. It can thrust managers into roles that emphasize counseling and coaching over directing and enforcing.
2. It can necessitate substantial investments in training and incentives.
3. It can be very time-consuming.
4. Skilled workers may resent unskilled workers who learn their jobs.
5. Older employees may not want to learn new skills.

HUMAN RESOURCE CONCERNS WHEN IMPLEMENTING STRATEGIES

The job of human resource manager is changing rapidly as companies downsize and reorganize in the 1990s. Strategic responsibilities of the human resource manager include assessing the staffing needs and costs for alternative strategies proposed during strategy formulation and developing a manpower plan for effectively implementing strategies. This plan must consider how best to manage spiraling health-care insurance costs. Employers' health-coverage expenses consume an average 26 percent of firms' net profits, even though most companies now require employees to pay part of their health-insurance premiums. The plan must also include how to motivate employees and managers during a time when layoffs are common and work loads are high.

The human resource department must develop performance incentives that clearly link performance and pay to strategies. The process of "empowering" managers and employees through involvement in strategic-management activities yields the greatest benefits when all organizational members understand clearly how they will benefit personally if the firm does well. Linking company and personal benefits is a major new strategic responsibility of human resource managers. Other new responsibilities for human resource managers may include establishing and administering an Employee Stock Ownership Plan (ESOP), instituting an effective child-care policy, and providing leadership for managers and employees to balance work and family.

A well-designed strategic-management system can fail if insufficient attention is given to the human resource dimension. Human resource problems that arise when businesses implement strategies can usually be traced to one of three causes: (1) disruption of social and political structures, (2) failure to match individuals' aptitudes with implementation tasks, and (3) inadequate top management support for implementation activities.[29]

Strategy implementation poses a threat to many managers and employees in an organization. New power and status relationships are anticipated and realized. New formal and informal groups are formed whose values, beliefs, and priorities may be largely unknown. Managers and employees may become engaged in resistance behavior as their roles, prerogatives, and power in the firm change. Disruption of social and political structures that accompany strategy execution must be anticipated and considered during strategy formulation and managed during strategy implementation.

A concern in matching managers with strategy is that jobs have specific and relatively static responsibilities, while people are dynamic in their personal development. Commonly used methods that match managers with strategies to be implemented include transferring managers, developing leadership workshops, offering career development activities, promotions, job enlargement, and job enrichment.

A number of other guidelines can help ensure that human relationships facilitate rather than disrupt strategy-implementation efforts. Specifically, managers should do a lot of chatting and informal questioning to stay abreast of how things are progressing and to know when to intervene. Managers can build support for strategy-implementation efforts by giving few orders, announcing few decisions, depending heavily on informal questioning, and seeking to probe and clarify until a consensus emerges. Key thrusts that succeed should be rewarded generously and visibly. A sense of humor is important, too. According to Adia Personnel Services, 72 percent of personnel executives nationwide say that humor is appropriate in discussions with colleagues; 63 percent say humor is appropriate in job interviews; 58 percent say humor is appropriate in performance reviews; and 53 percent say humor is appropriate in tense meetings.

It is suprising that so often during strategy formulation, individual values, skills, and abilities needed for successful strategy implementation are not considered. It is rare that a firm selecting new strategies or significantly altering existing strategies possesses the right line and staff personnel in the right positions for successful strategy implementation. The need to match individual aptitudes with strategy-implementation tasks should be considered in strategy choice.

Inadequate support from strategists for implementation activities often undermines organizational success. Chief executive officers, small business owners, and government agency heads must be personally committed to strategy implementation and express this commitment in highly visible ways. Strategists' formal statements about the importance of strategic management must be consistent with actual support and rewards given for activities completed and objectives reached. Otherwise, stress created by inconsistency can cause uncertainty among managers and employees at all levels.

Perhaps the best method for preventing and overcoming human resource problems in strategic management is to actively involve as many managers and employees as possible in the process. Although time-consuming, this approach builds understanding, trust, commitment, and ownership and reduces resentment and hostility. The true potential of strategy formulation and implementation resides in people.

Employee Stock Ownership Plans (ESOPs). An ESOP is a tax-qualified, defined-contribution employee-benefit plan whereby employees purchase stock of the company through borrowed money or cash contributions. ESOPs empower employees to work as owners; this is a primary reason why the number of ESOPs grew dramatically throughout the 1980s and 1990s to more than 10,000 plans covering more than 11.5 million employees. ESOPs now control over $60 billion in corporate stock in the United States.

Besides reducing worker alienation and stimulating productivity, ESOPs allow firms other benefits, such as substantial tax savings. Principal, interest, and dividend payments on ESOP-funded debt are tax deductible. Banks lend money to ESOPs at interest rates below prime. This money can be repaid in pretax dollars, lowering the debt service as much as 30 percent in some cases.

If an ESOP owns more than 50 percent of the firm, those who lend money to the ESOP are taxed on only 50 percent of the income received on the loans. ESOPs are not for every firm, however, because the initial legal, accounting, actuarial, and appraisal fees to set up an ESOP are about $50,000 for a small or mid-sized firm, with annual expenses of about $15,000. Analysts say ESOPs also do not work well in firms that have fluctuating payrolls and profits. Human resource managers in many firms conduct preliminary research to determine the desirability of an ESOP, and then facilitate its establishment and administration if benefits outweigh the costs.

To establish an ESOP, a firm sets up a trust fund and purchases shares of its stock, which are allocated to individual employee accounts. All full-time employees over age 21 usually participate in the plan. Allocations of stock to the trust are made on the basis of relative pay, seniority, or some other formula. When an ESOP borrows money to purchase stock, the debt is guaranteed by the company and thus appears on the firm's balance sheet. On average, ESOP employees get $1,300 worth of stock per year, but cannot take physical possession of the shares until they quit, retire, or die. The median level of employee ownership in ESOP plans is 30 to 40 percent, although the range is from about 10 percent to 100 percent.

Research confirms that ESOPs can have a dramatic positive effect on employee motivation and corporate performance, especially if ownership is coupled with expanded employee participation and involvement in decision making. Market surveys indicate that customers prefer to do business with firms that are employee-owned.

Many companies are following the lead of Polaroid, which established an ESOP as a tactic for preventing a hostile takeover. Polaroid's CEO, MacAllister Booth, says, "Twenty years from now we'll find that employees have a sizable stake in every major American corporation." (It is interesting to note here that Polaroid is chartered in the state of Delaware, which requires corporate suitors to acquire 85 percent of a target company's shares to complete a merger; over 50 percent of all American corporations are incorporated in Delaware for this reason.) Wyatt Cafeterias, a Southwestern U.S. operator of 120 cafeterias, also adopted the ESOP concept to prevent a hostile takeover. Employee productivity at Wyatt has greatly increased since the ESOP began, as illustrated in the following quotes:

> The key employee in our entire organization is the person serving the customer on the cafeteria line. In the past, because of high employee turnover and entry-level wages for many line jobs, these employees received far less attention and recognition than managers. We now tell the tea cart server, "You own the place. Don't wait for the manager to tell you how to do your job better or how to provide better service. You take care of it." Sure, we're looking for productivity increases, but since we began pushing decisions down to the level of people who deal directly with customers, we've discovered an awesome side effect—suddenly the work crews have this "happy to be here" attitude that the customers really love.[30]

Companies such as Avis, Procter & Gamble, BellSouth, ITT, Xerox, Delta, Austin Industries, Health Trust, The Parsons Corporation, Dyncorp, and Charter Medical have established ESOPs to assist strategists in divesting divisions, going private, and consummating leveraged buyouts. ESOPs can be found today in all kinds of firms, from small retailers to large manufacturers. Employees can own anywhere from 1 percent to 100 percent of the company. Nearly all ESOPs are established in healthy firms, not failing firms.[31]

Balancing Work Life and Home Life. Doug Hall and Judith Richter emphasize that human resource managers need to foster more effective balancing of professional and private lives, since nearly 50 million people in the United States are now part of two-career families.[32] A corporate objective to become more "lean and mean" must today include consideration for the fact that a good home life contributes immensely to a good work life.

> You can count on baby-boomers to force the issue of family versus work onto the corporate agenda. Fully 73 percent of all women age 25 to 34 now work for pay, as do half of all women with babies under a year old. For them and their husbands, child care, flexible hours, and job sharing are pressing concerns.[33]

The work/family issue is no longer just a "woman's problem." Some specific measures that firms are taking to address this issue are providing spouse relocation assistance as an employee benefit, providing company resources for family recreational and educational use, establishing employee country clubs, such as those at IBM and Bethlehem Steel, and creating family/work interaction opportunities. A recent study by Joseph Pleck of Wheaton College found that in companies that do not offer paternity leave for fathers as a benefit, most men take short informal paternity leaves anyway by combining vacation time and sick days.

Some organizations have developed "family days," when family members are invited into the workplace, taken on plant or office tours, dined by management, and given a chance to see exactly what other family members do each day. "Family days" are inexpensive and increase the employee's pride in working for the organization. Flexible working hours during the week is another human resource response to the need for individuals to balance work life and home life. The work/family topic is being made part of the agenda at meetings and thus is becoming "discussable" in many organizations.

Research indicates that employees who are dissatisfied with child-care arrangements are most likely to be absent or unproductive.[34] Lack of adequate child care in a community can be a deterrent in recruiting and retaining good managers and employees. Some benefits of on-site child-care facilities are improved employee relations, reduced absenteeism and turnover, increased productivity, enhanced recruitment, and improved community relations.

A recent survey of women managers revealed that one-third would leave their present employer for another employer offering child-care assistance. The Conference Board recently reported that over 500 firms in the United States had created on-site or near-site child-care centers for their employees, including Merck, Campbell Soup, Hoffman–La Roche, Stride-Rite, Johnson Wax, CIGNA, Champion International, Walt Disney World, and Playboy Resorts.

Other common child-care service arrangements include employer-sponsored day care, child-care information, and referral services. IBM, Steelcase, Honeywell, Citibank, 3M, and Southland have established contracts with third-party child-care information and referral services.

The nation's largest employer-sponsored day-care center is operated by Intermedics, a Texas-based medical instruments firm. Employee turnover declined 23 percent the first year Intermedics instituted the center. Due to the high cost of child care, numerous firms are forming partnerships to build and manage child-care facilities. The largest collaboration so far is the new $2 million, 194-child day-care center in Charlotte, financed and operated by IBM, American Express, Allstate, Duke Power, and University Research Park. The teacher-child ratio at this center is 50 percent lower than required by North Carolina law. Other large partnership child-care centers have recently been built in Minneapolis, Rochester, Dallas–Fort Worth, and New York City. In Virginia, twenty-two companies recently pooled $100,000 to establish a parent-run child-care cooperative. Other companies that effectively address child-care concerns of managers and employees include Clorox and Nyloncraft. Even small businesses are beginning to offer child-care benefits for employees. Some small firms that now offer an on-site day-care center for employees' children include Bowles Corporation in North Ferrisburg, Vermont; Byrne Electrical Specialists in Rockford, Michigan; Chalet Dental Clinic in Yakima, Washington; and Stackpole Ltd. in Brownsville, Tennessee.

Corporate Fitness Programs. At least 10,000 U.S. employers now offer programs to improve or maintain their employees' health, such as programs to stop smoking, reduce cholesterol, promote regular exercise, and control high blood pressure.[35] Another 1,000 American firms offer on site, fully equipped fitness centers to promote good employee health. Perhaps the leader in this area is Johnson & Johnson, which provides an 11,000-square-foot fitness center, aerobics and other exercise classes, seminars on AIDS and alcohol abuse, and an indoor track. J & J's program is called "Live for Life."

CONCLUSION

Successful strategy formulation does not at all guarantee successful strategy implementation. Although inextricably interdependent, strategy formulation and strategy implementation are characteristically different. In a single word, strategy implementation means "change." It is widely agreed that "the real work begins after strategies are formulated." Successful strategy implementation requires support, discipline, motivation, and hard work from all managers and employees. It is sometimes frightening to think that a single individual can sabotage strategy-implementation efforts irreparably.

Formulating the right strategies is not enough, because managers and employees must be motivated to implement those strategies. Management issues considered central to strategy implementation include matching organizational structure with strategy, linking performance and pay to strategies, creating an organizational climate conducive to change, managing political relationships, creating a strategy-supportive culture, adapting production/operations processes, and managing human resources. Establishing annual objectives, devising policies, and allocating resources are central strategy-implementation activities common to all organizations. Depending on the size and type of organization, other management issues could be equally important to successful strategy implementation.

KEY TERMS AND CONCEPTS

Annual Objectives
Avoidance
Conflict
Confrontation
Culture
Defusion
Devise Policies
Divisional Structure by Geographic Area, Product, Customer, or Process
Educative Change Strategy
Employee Stock Ownership Plans (ESOPs)
Establish Annual Objectives
Force Change Strategy

Functional Structure
Gain Sharing
Horizontal Consistency of Objectives
"Just in Time"
Matrix Structures
Policies
Profit Sharing
Rational Change Strategy
Resistance to Change
Resource Allocation
Strategic Business Unit (SBU) Structure
Vertical Consistency of Objective

ISSUES FOR REVIEW AND DISCUSSION

1. Allocating resources can be a political and an ad hoc activity in firms that do not use strategic management. Why is this true? Does adopting strategic management assure easy resource allocation? Why?

2. Compare strategy formulation with strategy implementation in terms of each being an "art" or a "science."

3. Describe the relationship between annual objectives and policies.

4. Identify a long-term objective and two supporting annual objectives for a familiar organization.

5. Identify and discuss three policies that apply to your present business policy class.

6. Explain the following statement: Horizontal consistency of goals is as important as vertical consistency.

7. Describe several reasons why conflict may occur during objective-setting activities.

8. In your opinion, what approach to conflict resolution would be best for resolving a disagreement between a personnel manager and a sales manager over the firing of a particular salesperson? Why?

9. Describe the organizational culture of your college or university.

10. Explain why organizational structure is so important in strategy implementation.

11. In your opinion, how many separate divisions could an organization reasonably have without using an SBU-type organizational structure? Why?

12. Would you recommend a divisional structure by geographic area, product, customer, or process for a medium-sized bank in your local area? Why?

13. What are the advantages and disadvantages of decentralizing the wage and salary function of an organization? How could this be accomplished?

14. Consider a college organization with which you are familiar. How did management issues affect strategy implementation in that organization?

15. As production manager of a local newspaper, what problems would you anticipate in implementing a strategy to increase the average number of pages in the paper by 40 percent?

16. Select an article from the suggested readings at the end of this chapter. Read the article and give a summary report to the class revealing your thoughts on the topic.

17. Do you believe expenditures for child-care or fitness facilities are warranted from a cost/benefit perspective? Why or why not?

18. Explain why successful strategy implementation often hinges on whether the strategy-formulation process "empowers" managers and employees.

NOTES

1. Gary Hamel and C. K. Prahalad, "Strategic Intent," *Harvard Business Review* (May–June 1989): 67.

2. A. G. Bedeian and W. F. Glueck, *Management,* 3rd. ed. (Chicago: The Dryden Press, 1983), 212.

3. Most authors consider procedures and rules to be policies. Procedures can be defined as chronological steps that must be followed to complete a particular action, such as completing an application form. Rules can be defined as actions that can and cannot be taken, such as "no smoking." Neither a procedure nor a rule provides much latitude in decision making, so some writers do not consider either to be a policy.

4. "No Smoking Sweeps America," *Business Week* (July 27, 1987): 40.

5. Boris Yavits and William Newman, *Strategy in Action: The Execution, Politics, and Payoff of Business Planning* (New York: The Free Press, 1982), 195.

6. Ibid, 200.

7. Alfred Chandler, *Strategy and Structure* (Cambridge, Mass: MIT Press, 1962).

8. Ibid, 14.

9. "Paying Workers to Meet Goals Spreads, But Gauging Performance Proves Tough," *Wall Street Journal* (September 10, 1991): B1.

10. Nancy Perry, "There Comes Richer, Riskier Pay Plans," *Fortune* (December 19, 1988): 54.

11. Ibid, 58.

12. Ibid, 54.

13. Perry Pascarella, "The Toughest Turnaround of All," *Industry Week* (April 2, 1984): 33. Reprinted with permission from *Industry Week*, April 2, 1984. Copyright Renton Publishing Inc., Cleveland, Ohio.

14. Jack Duncan, *Management* (New York: Random House, 1983): 381–390.

15. H. Igor Ansoff, "Strategic Management of Technology," *Journal of Business Strategy* 7, no. 3 (Winter 1987): 38.

16. Robert Waterman, Jr., "How the Best Get Better," *Business Week* (September 14, 1987): 104.

17. James Post, "Managing as if the Earth Mattered," *Business Horizons* (July–August 1991): 32–38.

18. Todd Hooper and Bart Rocca, "Environmental Affairs: Now on the Strategic Agenda," *The Journal of Business Strategy"* (May/June 1991): 26–30.

19. Ibid, p. 30.

20. Mark Starik and Archie Carroll, "Strategic Environmental Management: Business as If the Earth Really Mattered," Presented at the 1991 International Association for Business and Society Meetings, Sundance, Utah, March 22–24, 1991.

21. Jack Duncan, "Organizational Culture: Getting a Fix on an Elusive Concept," *Academy of Management Executives III*, no. 3 (August 1989): 229.

22. E. H. Schein, "The Role of the Founder in Creating Organizational Culture," *Organizational Dynamics* (Summer 1983): 13–28.

23. T. Deal and A. Kennedy, "Culture: A New Look Through Old Lenses," *Journal of Applied Behavioral Science* 19, no. 4 (1983): 498–504.

24. H. Ibsen, "The Wild Duck," in O. G. Brochett and L. Brochett (Eds.), *Plays for the Theater* (New York: Holt, Rinehart & Winston, 1967). Also, R. Pascale, "The Paradox of 'Corporate Culture': Reconciling Ourselves to Socialization," *California Management Review* 28, 2 (1985): 26, 37–40.

25. T. Deal and A. Kennedy, *Corporate Cultures: The Rites and Rituals of Corporate Life* (Reading, Mass: Addison-Wesley, 1982).

26. Robert Waterman, Jr., "The Renewal Factor," *Business Week* (September 14, 1987): 100.

27. "Just in Time: Putting the Squeeze on Suppliers," *Industry Week* (July 9, 1984): 59.

28. Robert Stobaugh and Piero Telesio, "Match Manufacturing Policies and Product Strategy," *Harvard Business Review* 61, no. 2 (March–April 1983): 113.

29. R. T. Lenz and Marjorie Lyles, "Managing Human Resource Problems in Strategy Planning Systems," *Journal of Business Strategy* 60, no. 4 (Spring 1986): 58.

30. J. Warren Henry, "ESOPs with Productivity Payoffs," *Journal of Business Strategy* (July–August 1989): 33.

31. Corey Rosen, "The Growing Appeal of the Leveraged ESOP," *Journal of Business Strategy* (January–February 1989): 17.

32. Douglas Hall and Judith Richter, "Balancing Work Life and Home Life: What Can Organizations Do to Help?" *Academy of Management Executive* II, no. 3 (August 1989): 213.

33. Ronald Henkoff, "Is Greed Dead?" *Fortune* (August 14, 1989): 49.

34. Richard Levine, "Childcare: Inching up the Corporate Agenda," *Management Review* 78, no. 1 (January 1989): 43.

35. Barbara Trenk, "Corporate Fitness Programs Become Hearty Investments," *Management Review* 78, no. 8 (August 1989): 33.

CURRENT READINGS

Bowles, Jerry. "Is Management Committed to Quality?" *Management Review* (April 1992): 42–46.

Barker, Emily. "Du Pont Tries to Clean Up Its Act." *Business and Society Review* 80 (Winter 1992): 36–41.

Berling, Robert J. "The Emerging Approach to Business Strategy: Building a Relationship Advantage." *Business Horizons* 36, no. 4 (July–August 1993): 16–27.

Brache, Alan. "Process Improvement and Management: A Tool for Strategy Implementation." *Planning Review* 20, no. 5 (September–October 1992): 24–26.

Floyd, Steven W., and Bill Wooldridge. "Managing Strategic Consensus: The Foundation of Effective Implementation." *The Executive* VI, no. 4 (November 1992): 27–39.

Friedman, Frank B. "The Changing Role of the Environmental Manager." *Business Horizons* 35, no. 2 (March–April 1992): 25–28.

Haleblian, Jeary, and Sydney Finkelstein. "Top Management Team Size, CEO Dominance, and Firm Performance: The Moderating Roles of Environmental Turbulence and Discretion." *Academy of Management Journal* 36, no. 4 (August 1993): 844–863.

Hambrick, D. C., M. A. Geletkanycz, and J. W. Frederickson. "Top Executive Commitment to the Status Quo: Some Tests of Its Determinants." *Strategic Management Journal* 14, no. 6 (September 1993).

Harrison, Jeffrey S., Ernest H. Hall, Jr., and Rajendra Nargundkar. "Resource Allocation as an Outcropping of Strategic Consistency: Performance Implications." *Academy of Management Journal* 36, no. 5 (October 1993): 1026–1051.

Hatch, Mary Jo. "The Dynamics of Organizational Culture." *Academy of Management Review* 18, no. 4 (October 1993): 657–693.

Kennedy, Carol. "Changing the Company Culture at Ciba-Geigy." *Long Range Planning* 26, no. 1 (February 1993): 18–27.

Kerr, Jeffrey L., and Leslie Kren. "Effect of Relative Decision Monitoring on Chief Executive Compensation." *Academy of Management Journal* 35, no. 2 (June 1992): 370–397.

Krackhardt, David, and Jeffrey R. Hanson. "Informal Networks: The Company Behind the Chart." *Harvard Business Review* 71, no. 4 (July–August 1993): 104–113.

Mainiero, Lisa. "Participation? Nyet: Rewards and Praise? DA!" *Academy of Management Executive* 7, no. 3 (August 1993): 86–88.

Mears, Peter. "How to Stop Talking About, and Begin Progress Toward, Total Quality Management." *Business Horizons* 36, no. 3 (May–June 1993): 11–14.

Michel, John G., and Donald C. Hambrick. "Diversification Posture and Top Management Team Characteristics." *Academy of Management Journal* 35, no. 1 (March 1992): 9–37.

Owen, Crystal L., and William D. Todor. "Attitudes Toward Women as Managers: Still the Same." *Business Horizons* 36, no. 2 (March–April 1993): 12–16.

Price, Michael, and E. Eva Chen. "TQM in a Small, High-Technology Company." *California Management Review* 35, no. 3 (Spring 1993): 96–117.

Schuler, Randall S., Peter J. Dowling, and Helen De Cieri. "An Integrative Framework of Strategic International Human Resource Management." *Journal of Management* 19, no. 2 (Summer 1993): 419–460.

Stearns, Linda Brewster, and Mark S. Mizruchi. "Board Composition and Corporate Financing: The Impact of Financial Institution Representation on Borrowing." *Academy of Management Journal* 36, no. 3 (June 1993): 603–618.

Stiles, Philip. "The Future for Boards: Self-Regulation or Legislation?" *Long Range Planning* 26, no. 2 (April 1993): 119–124.

Trevino, Linda Klebe, and Gail A. Ball. "The Social Implications of Punishing Unethical Behavior: Observers' Cognitive and Affective Reactions." *Journal of Management* 18, no. 4 (December 1992): 717–768.

Tucker, Marvin W., and David A. Davis. "Key Ingredients for Successful Implementation of Just-in-Time: A System for All Business Sizes." *Business Horizons* 36, no. 3 (May–June 1993): 59.

Wright, Patrick M. "An Examination of the Relationships Among Monetary Incentives, Goal Level, Goal Commitment, and Performance." *Journal of Management* 18, no. 4 (December 1992): 677–694.

EXPERIENTIAL EXERCISES

REVISING HERSHEY FOODS' ORGANIZATIONAL CHART

PURPOSE

Developing and altering organizational charts is an important skill for strategists to possess. This exercise can improve your skill in altering an organization's hierarchical structure in response to new strategies being formulated.

INSTRUCTIONS

Step 1 Turn back to Hershey's organizational chart given in the Cohesion Case (following Chapter 1).

Step 2 On a separate sheet of paper, diagram an organizational chart that you believe would best suit Hershey's needs if the company decided to break up the International Division and form six geographic divisions similar to the Hershey Canada Division.

Step 3 Provide as much detail in your chart as possible, including the names of individuals and the titles of positions.

MATCHING MANAGERS WITH STRATEGY

PURPOSE

For many years, strategists believed that good managers could adapt to handle any situation. Consequently, strategists rarely replaced or transferred managers as the need arose to implement new strategies. Today, this situation is changing. Research supports the notion that certain management characteristics are needed for certain strategic situations.[1] Chase Manhattan Bank, Heublein, Texas Instruments, Corning Glass, and General Electric are examples of companies that match managers to strategic requirements.

This exercise can improve your awareness and understanding of particular managerial characteristics that have been found to be most desirable for implementing certain types of strategies. Having the right managers in the right jobs can determine the success or failure of strategy-implementation efforts. This exercise is based on a recently published framework that has proved to be useful in "matching managers to strategy."[2]

INSTRUCTIONS

Your task is to match specific managerial characteristics with particular generic strategies. Four broad types of strategies are examined:

1. Retrenchment/Turnaround
2. Intensive (market penetration, market development, and product development)
3. Liquidation/Divestiture
4. Integration (backward, forward, and horizontal)

Five managerial characteristics have been found to be associated with each of these strategies. On a separate sheet of paper, list the four types of strategies. Beside each strategy, record the appropriate letter of the five managerial characteristics that you believe are most needed to successfully implement those strategies. Each of the managerial characteristics in the following list should be used only once in completing this exercise.

a. Is technically knowledgeable—"knows the business"
b. Is "callous"—tough-minded, determined, willing to be the bad guy
c. Is "take charge"–oriented—strong leader
d. Is a good negotiator
e. Wants to be respected, not necessarily liked
f. Has good analytical ability
g. Is low glory-seeking—willing to do dirty jobs; does not want glamour
h. Has excellent staffing skills
i. Handles pressure well
j. Is a risk taker
k. Has good relationship-building skills
l. Has good organizational and team-building skills
m. Is oriented to getting out the most efficiency, not growth
n. Anticipates problems—"Problem Finder"
o. Has strong analytical and diagnostic skills, especially financial
p. Is an excellent business strategist
q. Has good communication skills
r. Has personal magnetism
s. Is highly analytical—focuses on costs/benefits, does not easily accept current ways of doing things
t. Has good interpersonal influence

NOTES

1. Marc Gerstein and Heather Reisman, "Strategic Selection: Matching Executives to Business Conditions," *Sloan Management Review* 24, no. 2 (Winter 1983): 33–47.

2. Ibid., 37.

DO ORGANIZATIONS REALLY ESTABLISH OBJECTIVES?

PURPOSE

Objectives provide direction, allow synergy, aid in evaluation, establish priorities, reduce uncertainty, minimize conflicts, stimulate exertion, and aid in both the allocation of resources and the design of jobs. This exercise will enhance your understanding of how organizations use or misuse objectives.

INSTRUCTIONS

Step 1 Join with one other person in class to form a two-person team.

Step 2 Contact by telephone the owner or manager of an organization in your city or town. Request a 30-minute personal interview or meeting with that person for the purpose of discussing "business objectives." During your meeting, seek answers to the following questions:

1. Do you believe it is important for a business to establish and clearly communicate long-term and annual objectives? Why or why not?
2. Does your organization establish objectives? If yes, what type and how many? How are the objectives communicated to individuals? Are your firm's objectives in written form or simply communicated orally?
3. To what extent are managers and employees involved in the process of establishing objectives?
4. How often are your business objectives revised and by what process?

Step 3 Take good notes during the interview. Let one person be the note taker and one person do most of the talking. Have your notes typed up and ready to turn in to your professor.

Step 4 Prepare a 5-minute oral presentation for the class, reporting the results of your interview. Turn in your typed report.

UNDERSTANDING MY UNIVERSITY'S CULTURE

PURPOSE

It is something of an art to uncover the basic values and beliefs that are buried deeply in an organization's rich collection of stories, language, heroes, and rituals. Yet culture can be the most important factor in implementing strategies.

INSTRUCTIONS

Step 1 On a separate sheet of paper, list the following terms: hero/heroine, belief, metaphor, language, value, symbol, story, legend, saga, folktale, myth, ceremonial, rite, and ritual.

Step 2 For your college or university, give examples of each term. If necessary, speak with faculty, staff, alumni, administration, or fellow students of the institution to identify examples of each term. Refer back to Chapter 5 for definitions of the terms if needed.

Step 3 Report your findings to the class. Tell the class how you feel regarding cultural products being consciously used to help implement strategies.

Chapter 8

IMPLEMENTING STRATEGIES: Marketing, Finance/Accounting, Research and Development (R & D), and Computer Information Systems (CIS) Issues

NOTABLE QUOTES

The greatest strategy is doomed if it's implemented badly. —Bernard Reimann

Organizations should approach all tasks with the idea that they can be accomplished in a superior fashion. —Thomas Watson, Jr.

There is no "perfect" strategic decision. One always has to pay a price. One always has to balance conflicting objectives, conflicting opinions, and conflicting priorities. The best strategic decision is only an approximation—and a risk. —Peter Drucker

The real question isn't how well you're doing today against your own history, but how you're doing against your competitors. —Donald Kress

Effective organizational responses are retarded not so much by failing to recognize what needs to be done, but by not doing what ought to be done. —John Keane

As market windows open and close more quickly, it is important that R & D be tied more closely to corporate strategy. —William Spenser

Market share matters. The 90th share point isn't as important as the 91st, and nothing is more dangerous than falling to 89. —Bill Saporito

Most of the time, strategists should not be formulating strategy at all; they should be getting on with implementing strategies they already have. —Henry Mintzberg

The best plan is only a plan, that is, good intentions. Unless commitment is made, there are only promises and hopes, but no plan. —Peter Drucker

OBJECTIVES

After studying this chapter, you should be able to:

- Explain market segmentation and product positioning as strategy-implementation tools.

- Discuss procedures for determining the worth of a business.

- Explain why pro forma financial analysis is a central strategy-implementation tool.

- Explain how to evaluate the attractiveness of debt versus stock as a source of capital to implement strategies.

- Discuss the nature and role of research and development in strategy implementation.

- Explain how computer information systems can determine the success of strategy-implementation efforts.

Strategies have no chance of being implemented successfully in organizations that do not market goods and services well, in firms that cannot raise needed working capital, in firms that produce technologically inferior products, or in firms that have a weak information system. This chapter examines marketing, finance/accounting, R & D, and computer information systems issues that are central to effective strategy implementation. Special topics include market segmentation, market positioning, evaluating the worth of a business, determining to what extent debt and/or stock should be used as a source of capital, developing pro forma financial statements, contracting R & D outside the firm, and creating an information support system. Manager and employee involvement and participation are essential for success in marketing, finance/accounting, R & D, and CIS activities.

THE NATURE OF STRATEGY IMPLEMENTATION

The quarterback can call the best play possible in the huddle, but that does not mean the play will go for a touchdown. The team may even lose yardage unless the play is executed (implemented) well. Less than 10 percent of strategies formulated are successfully implemented! There are many reasons for this low success rate, including failing to segment markets appropriately, paying too much for a new acquisition, falling behind competitors in R & D, and not recognizing the benefit of computers in managing information.

Strategy implementation directly affects the lives of plant managers, division managers, department managers, sales managers, product managers, project managers, personnel managers, staff managers, supervisors, and all employees. In some situations, individuals may not have participated in the strategy-formulation process at all and may not appreciate, understand, or even accept the work and thought that went into strategy formulation. There may even be foot-dragging or resistance on their part. Managers and employees who do not understand the business and are not committed to the business may attempt to sabotage strategy-implementation efforts in hopes that the organization will return to its old ways. The strategy-implementation stage of the strategic-management process is shaded in Figure 8–1.

MARKETING ISSUES

Countless marketing variables affect the success or failure of strategy implementation, and the scope of this text does not allow addressing all those issues. However, two variables are of central importance to strategy implementation: market segmentation and product positioning. Ralph Biggadike asserts that market segmentation and product positioning must rank as marketing's most important contributions to strategic management.[1] Some examples of marketing decisions that may require policies are:

1. To use exclusive dealerships or multiple channels of distribution.
2. To use heavy, light, or no TV advertising.
3. To limit (or not) the share of business done with a single customer.
4. To be a price leader or a price follower.
5. To offer a complete or limited warranty.
6. To reward salespeople based on a straight commission or a combination salary/commission.

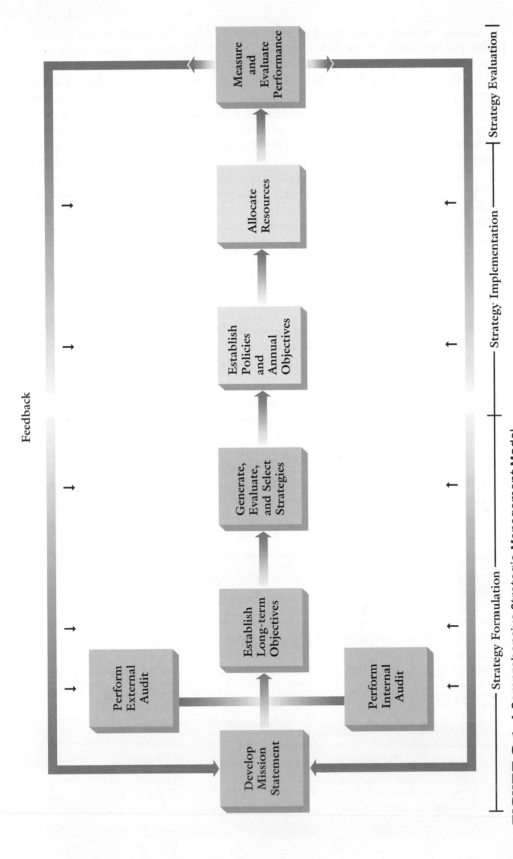

Feedback

Perform
External
Audit

Develop
Mission
Statement

Establish
Long-term
Objectives

Perform
Internal
Audit

Generate,
Evaluate,
and Select
Strategies

Establish
Policies
and
Annual
Objectives

Allocate
Resources

Measure
and
Evaluate
Performance

|— Strategy Formulation —————————|———— Strategy Implementation ————|— Strategy Evaluation —|

FIGURE 8-1 A Comprehensive Strategic-Management Model

Market Segmentation. Market segmentation is widely used in implementing strategies, especially for small and specialized firms. *Marketing segmentation* can be defined as "the subdividing of a market into distinct subsets of customers according to needs and buying habits."[2] Market segmentation is an important variable in strategy implementation for at least three major reasons. First, strategies such as market development, product development, market penetration, and diversification require increased sales through new markets and products. To implement these strategies successfully, new or improved market-segmentation approaches are required. Second, market segmentation allows a firm to operate with limited resources, since mass production, mass distribution, and mass advertising are not required. Market segmentation can enable a small firm to compete successfully with a large firm by maximizing per-unit profits and per-segment sales. Finally, market segmentation decisions directly affect marketing-mix variables: product, place, promotion, and price, as indicated in Table 8–1.

Geographic and demographic bases for segmenting markets are the most commonly employed, as illustrated in Table 8–2. Beer producers, for example, have generally divided the light beer market into three segments:

> The light beer market can be meaningfully separated into three motivation segments: those who are calorie-conscious, those who prefer less alcohol, and those who prefer a lighter taste. In fact, it is possible for one person to consume light beer on three separate occasions for three different reasons. The situation may therefore dictate the segment the consumer falls into.[3]

Evaluating potential market segments requires strategists to determine the characteristics and needs of consumers, analyze consumer similarities and differences, and develop consumer group profiles. Segmenting consumer markets is generally much simpler and easier than segmenting industrial markets, because industrial products, such as electronic circuits and forklifts, have multiple applications and appeal to diverse customer groups. Royal Crown Cola Company recently shifted its market segmentation strategy from teenagers to adults. To make this switch, the company spent

TABLE 8-1   The Marketing Mix Component Factors

PRODUCT	PLACE	PROMOTION	PRICE
Quality	Distribution	Advertising	Level
Features and	channels	Personal selling	Discounts and
options	Distribution	Sales promotion	allowances
Style	coverage	Publicity	Payment terms
Brand name	Outlet location		
Packaging	Sales territories		
Product line	Inventory levels		
Warranty	and locations		
Service level	Transportation		
Other services	carriers		

Source: E. Jerome McCarthy, *Basic Marketing: A Managerial Approach,* 9th ed. (Homewood, Ill: Richard D. Irwin, Inc., 1987), pp. 37–44 (1st ed., 1960.)

TABLE 8-2   Alternative Bases for Market Segmentation

VARIABLE	TYPICAL BREAKDOWNS
GEOGRAPHIC	
Region	Pacific, Mountain, West North Central, West South Central, East North Central, East South Central, South Atlantic, Middle Atlantic, New England
County Size	A, B, C, D
City or SMSA size	Under 5,000; 5,000-20,000; 20,000-50,000; 50,000-100,000; 100,000-250,000; 250,000 500,000; 500,000-1,000,000; 1,000,000-4,000,000; 4,000,000 or over
Density	Urban, suburban, rural
Climate	Northern, southern
DEMOGRAPHIC	
Age	Under 6, 6-11, 12-19, 20-34, 35-49, 50-64, 65+
Sex	Male, female
Family size	1-2, 3-4, 5+
Family life cycle	Young, single; young, married, no children; young, married, youngest child under 6; young, married, youngest child 6 or over; older, married, with children; older, married, no children under 18; older, single; other
Income	Under $2,500; $2,500-$5,000; $5,000-$7,500; $7,500-$10,000; $10,000-$15,000; $15,000-$20,000; $20,000-$30,000; $30,000-$50,000; $50,000 and over
Occupation	Professional and technical; managers, officials, and proprietors; clerical, sales; craftsmen, foremen; operatives; farmers; retired; students; housewives; unemployed
Education	Grade school or less; some high school; high school graduate; some college; college graduate
Religion	Catholic, Protestant, Jewish, other
Race	White, black, Oriental
Nationality	American, British, French, German, Scandinavian, Italian, Latin American, Middle Eastern, Japanese
PSYCHOGRAPHIC	
Social class	Lower lowers, upper lowers, lower middles, upper middles, lower uppers, upper uppers
Lifestyle	Straights, swingers, longhairs
Personality	Compulsive, gregarious, authoritarian, ambitious
BEHAVIORAL	
Use occasion	Regular occasion, special occasion
Benefits sought	Quality, service, economy
User status	Nonuser, ex-user, potential user, first-time user, regular user
Usage rate	Light user, medium user, heavy user
Loyalty status	None, medium, strong, absolute
Readiness stage	Unaware, aware, informed, interested, desirous, intending to buy
Attitude toward product	Enthusiastic, positive, indifferent, negative, hostile

Source: Philip Kotler, *Marketing Management: Analysis, Planning and Control*, © 1984, p. 256. Reprinted by permission of Prentice-Hall, Inc., Englewood Cliffs, New Jersey.

$20 million on a new advertising campaign. RC Cola Company says they have not given up on teens, but will now go after teens through parents.

Market segmentation matrices and decision trees can facilitate implementing strategies effectively. An example of a matrix for segmenting the lawn fertilizer market is provided in Figure 8–2. Similar matrices could be developed for almost any market, product, or service. Market segmentation strategies in the men's fragrance business are described as follows:

> The men's fragrance business breaks into four segments based on price. At the bottom are Mennen's Skin Bracer, Brut 33, and Aqua Velva that are sold mainly in food and drug stores and are priced below $4 for a 3 ounce bottle. The next tier, at about $4 to $5 for 4 ounces, is Old Spice and English Leather. Next, are the mass prestige brands, with twice the amount of scent as after-shaves, led by Chaps and Stetson at $10 and up. Above that are expensive department store brands, such as Obsession for Men, Aramis, Polo, Giorgio, and beyond. Old Spice is the best selling men's fragrance in the world, with sales above $180 million annually.[4]

Segmentation is a key to matching supply and demand, which is one of the thorniest problems in customer service.[5] Segmentation often reveals that "large, random fluctuations in demand" actually consist of several "small, predictable, and manageable" patterns. Matching supply and demand allows factories to produce desirable levels without extra shifts, overtime, and subcontracting. Matching supply and demand also minimizes the number and severity of stockouts. The demand for hotel rooms, for example, can be dependent on foreign tourists, businesspersons, and vacationers. Focusing on these three market segments separately, however, can allow hotel firms to predict overall supply and demand more effectively.

More and more, banks are segmenting markets to increase effectiveness. "You're dead in the water if you aren't segmenting the market," says Anne Moore, president

FIGURE 8-2 Tools for Segmenting the Lawn Fertilizer Market

Heavy users	High income	Central city
		Suburban
		Rural
	Low income	Central city
		Suburban
		Rural
Light users	High income	Central city
		Suburban
		Rural
	Low income	Central city
		Suburban
		Rural
Nonusers	High income	Central city
		Suburban
		Rural
	Low income	Central city
		Suburban
		Rural

Source: Fred Winter, "Market Segmentation: A Tactical Approach," *Business Horizons* (January–February 1984): 60, 61.

of a bank consulting firm in Atlanta. NCNB Corporation recently announced its Financial Connections program for "young adults starting careers." Barnett Banks in Florida offers its Senior Partners Program for different segments of the elderly, based on various lifestyles.

Product Positioning. After segmenting markets so that the firm can target particular customer groups, the next step is to find out what customers want and expect. This takes analysis and research. A severe mistake is to assume the firm knows what customers want and expect. Countless research studies reveal large differences between how customers define service and rank the importance of different service activities and how producers view services.[6] Many firms have become successful by filling the gap between what customers and producers see as good service. What the customer believes is good service is paramount, not what the producer believes service should be.

Identifying target customers upon whom to focus marketing efforts sets the stage for deciding how to meet the needs and wants of particular consumer groups. *Product positioning* is widely used for this purpose. Positioning entails developing schematic representations that reflect how your products or services compare to competitors' on dimensions most important to success in the industry. The following steps are required in product positioning:

1. Select key criteria that effectively differentiate products or services in the industry.
2. Diagram a two-dimensional product positioning map with specified criteria on each axis.
3. Plot major competitors' products or services in the resultant four-quadrant matrix.
4. Identify areas in the positioning map where the company's products or services could be most competitive in the given target market. Look for vacant areas (niches).
5. Develop a marketing plan to position the company's products or services appropriately.

Since just two criteria can be examined on a single product positioning map, multiple maps are often developed to assess various approaches to strategy implementation. Multidimensional scaling could be used to examine three or more criteria simultaneously, but this technique requires computer assistance and is beyond the scope of this text. Some examples of product positioning maps are illustrated in Figure 8–3.

Some rules of thumb for using product positioning as a strategy-implementation tool are:

1. Look for the hole or *vacant niche*. The best strategic opportunity might be an unserved segment.
2. Don't squat between segments. Any advantage from squatting (such as a larger target market) is offset by a failure to satisfy one segment. In decision-theory terms, the intent here is to avoid suboptimization by trying to serve more than one objective function.
3. Don't serve two segments with the same strategy. Usually, a strategy successful with one segment cannot be directly transferred to another segment.
4. Don't position yourself in the middle of the map. The middle usually means a strategy that is not clearly perceived to have any distinguishing characteristics. This rule can vary with the number of competitors. For example, when there are only two competitors, as in U.S. presidential elections, the middle becomes the preferred strategic position.[7]

One firm that uses product positioning effectively is Bristol-Myers Squibb Japan. This pharmaceutical giant recently began marketing Paraplatin, an anti-cancer drug that has few or no side effects, in Japan. Medical doctors in Japan usually conceal knowledge of a cancer diagnosis from a patient; therefore, Paraplatin is a favored cancer drug among the Japanese.

An effective product positioning strategy meets two criteria: (1) it uniquely distinguishes a company from the competition, and (2) it leads customers to expect slightly less service than a company can deliver.[8] Firms should not create expectations that exceed the service the firm can or will deliver. Network Equipment Technology is an example of a company that keeps customer expectations slightly below perceived performance. This is a constant challenge for marketers. Firms need to inform customers about what to expect and then exceed the promise; underpromise and then overdeliver! For multinational firms, this rule of thumb often requires considerable time on the telephone.

A. A PRODUCT POSITIONING MAP FOR BANKS

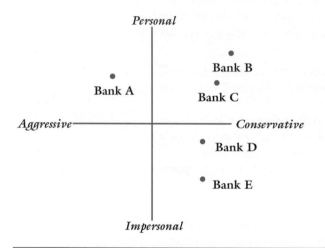

B. A PRODUCT POSITIONING MAP FOR PERSONAL COMPUTERS

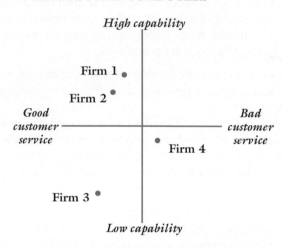

C. A PRODUCT POSITIONING MAP FOR MENSWEAR RETAIL STORES

D. A PRODUCT POSITIONING MAP FOR THE RENTAL CAR MARKET

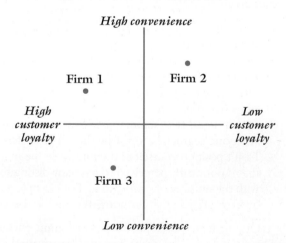

FIGURE 8-3 Examples of Product Positioning Maps

In this section we examine several finance/accounting concepts considered to be central to strategy implementation: acquiring needed capital, developing pro forma financial statements, preparing financial budgets, and evaluating the worth of a business. Some examples of decisions that may require finance/accounting policies are:

1. To raise capital with short-term debt, long-term debt, preferred stock, or common stock.
2. To lease or buy fixed assets.
3. To determine an appropriate dividend payout ratio.
4. To use LIFO, FIFO, or a market-value accounting approach.
5. To extend the time of accounts receivable.
6. To establish a certain percentage discount on accounts paid within a specified period of time.
7. To determine the amount of cash that should be kept on hand.

Acquiring Capital to Implement Strategies. Successful strategy implementation often requires additional capital. Besides net profit from operations and the sale of assets, two basic sources of capital for an organization are debt and equity. Determining an appropriate mix of debt and equity in a firm's capital structure can be vital to successful strategy implementation. An *Earnings Per Share/Earnings Before Interest and Taxes (EPS/EBIT)* analysis is the most widely used technique for determining whether debt, stock, or a combination of debt and stock is the best alternative for raising capital to implement strategies. This technique involves an examina-

A GLOBAL PERSPECTIVE
Downsizing in Europe

More than half of Europe's largest corporations plan to cut their work forces in 1994 and 1995 as global competition and high wage rates force firms to reduce overhead costs.

The downsizing will surpass even that of the United States, where companies have been introducing labor-saving technology for years. The moves could increase overall unemployment, prolonging Europe's recession and adding to pressure on countries to stimulate their economies by lowering interest rates.

Global competition is forcing European firms to produce large quantities of goods in fewer locations. High labor costs in locations such as western Germany are forcing companies to move jobs to East Europe. "It's happening in Europe because the U.S. corporate competitive position is so good," said Stephen Axilrod. He added that the "catch-up" by European companies on downsizing could have a negative impact on U.S. trade if the Europeans do it without lowering interest rates.

Unemployment levels in Europe, which range from 2.7 percent in Luxembourg to 21.3 percent in Spain, will average 12 percent by the end of 1994, up from 11 percent in 1993. That will add over one million people to the current 17 million unemployed, with two million more out of work by the end of 1995. Unemployment in eastern Germany is currently 16.2 percent, while the rate is 11 percent in France, Italy, and Great Britain and 8.4 percent in western Germany.

European countries have laws to protect workers from sudden cutbacks, which makes it more difficult for companies to downsize quickly as compared to U.S. companies.

The anticipated cutbacks in Europe will spur self-employment and entrepreneurial ventures, especially since half of Europe's unemployed have already been out of work for a year or more. Downsizing will also spur the trend toward part-time workers. In the past year, the number of Europe's part-time or self-employed workers has jumped from 8 to 12 percent of the workforce.

Source: Adapted from Fred Bleakley, "Over Half of Europe's Big Firms are Planning Work Force Cuts," *Wall Street Journal*, (September 21, 1993):A-8.

tion of the impact that debt versus stock financing has on earnings per share, under various assumptions as to EBIT.

Theoretically, an enterprise should have enough debt in its capital structure to boost its return on investment by applying debt to products and projects earning more than the cost of the debt. In low earning periods, too much debt in the capital structure of an organization can endanger stockholders' return and jeopardize company survival. Fixed debt obligations generally must be met, regardless of circumstances. This does not mean that stock issuances are always better than debt for raising capital. Some special concerns with stock issuances are dilution of ownership, effect on stock price, and the need to share future earnings with all new shareholders.

In the early 1990s, interest rates were low, yet stock issuances remained very popular for the purpose of paying off corporate debt. Kmart is one firm that issued new stock worth over $1 billion to reduce its debt. Sony Corporation also raised nearly $3 billion by selling new shares of stock to reduce the company's debt. The lingerie maker Warnaco Group, which accounts for 30 percent of the women's bra market in the United States, recently sold six million shares to the public to reduce its debt.

Without going into detail on other institutional and legal issues related to the debt versus stock decision, EPS/EBIT may be best explained by working through an example. Let's say the Brown Company needs to raise $1 million to finance implementation of a market-development strategy. The company's common stock currently sells for $50 per share, and 100,000 shares are outstanding. The prime interest rate is 10 percent, and the company's tax rate is 50 percent. The company's earnings before interest and taxes (EBIT) next year are expected to be $2 million if a recession occurs, $4 million if the economy stays as is, and $8 million if the economy significantly improves. EPS/EBIT analysis can be used to determine if all stock, all debt, or some combination of stock and debt is the best capital financing alternative. The EPS/EBIT analysis for this example is provided in Table 8–3.

TABLE 8-3   EPS/EBIT Analysis for the Brown Company (in millions)

	COMMON STOCK FINANCING			DEBT FINANCING			COMBINATION FINANCING		
	RECESSION	NORMAL	BOOM	RECESSION	NORMAL	BOOM	RECESSION	NORMAL	BOOM
EBIT	$ 2.0	$ 4.0	$ 8.0	$ 2.0	$ 4.0	$ 8.0	$ 2.0	$ 4.0	$ 8.0
Interest[a]	0.0	0.0	0.0	.10	.10	.10	.05	.05	.05
EBT	2.0	4.0	8.0	1.9	3.9	7.9	1.95	3.95	7.95
Taxes	1.0	2.0	4.0	.95	1.95	3.95	.975	1.975	3.975
EAT	1.0	2.0	4.0	.95	1.95	3.95	.975	1.975	3.975
#Shares[b]	.12	.12	.12	.10	.10	.10	.11	.11	.11
EPS[c]	8.33	16.66	33.33	9.5	19.50	39.50	8.86	17.95	36.14

Notes:

[a]The annual interest charge on $1 million at 10% is $100,000 and on $0.5 million is $50,000. This row is in $, not %.

[b]To raise all of the needed $1 million with stock, 20,000 new shares must be issued, raising the total to 120,000 shares outstanding. To raise one half of the needed $1 million with stock, 10,000 new shares must be issued, raising the total to 110,000 shares outstanding.

[c]EPS = Earnings After Taxes (EAT) divided by (Number of shares outstanding)

As indicated by the EPS values of 9.5, 19.50, and 39.50 in Table 8–3, debt is the best financing alternative for the Brown Company if a recession, boom, or normal year is expected. An EPS/EBIT chart can be constructed to determine the break-even point, where one financing alternative becomes more attractive than another. Figure 8–4 indicates that issuing common stock is the least attractive financing alternative for the Brown Company.

EPS/EBIT analysis is a valuable tool for making capital financing decisions needed to implement strategies, but several considerations should be made whenever using this technique. First, profit levels may be higher for stock or debt alternatives when EPS levels are lower. For example, looking only at the earnings after taxes (EAT) values in Table 8–3, the common stock option is the best alternative, regardless of economic conditions. If the Brown Company's mission includes strict profit maximization, as opposed to the maximization of stockholders' wealth or some other criterion, then stock rather than debt is the best choice of financing.

Another consideration when using EPS/EBIT analysis is flexibility. As an organization's capital structure changes, so does its flexibility for considering future capital needs. Using all debt or all stock to raise capital in the present may impose fixed obligations, restrictive covenants, or other constraints that could severely reduce a firm's ability to raise additional capital in the future. Control is also a concern. When additional stock is issued to finance strategy implementation, ownership and control of the enterprise are diluted. This can be a serious concern in today's business environment of hostile takeovers, mergers, and acquisitions. Also, dilution of ownership can be an overriding concern in closely held corporations, where stock issuances affect the decision-making power of majority stockholders. For example, the Smucker family owns 30 percent of the stock in Smucker's, a well-known jam and jelly company. When Smucker's acquired Dickson Family, Inc., the company used mostly debt rather than stock in order not to dilute the family ownership.

When using EPS/EBIT analysis, timing in relation to movements of stock prices, interest rates, and bond prices becomes important. In times of depressed stock prices, debt may prove to be the most suitable alternative from both a cost and a demand standpoint. However, when cost of capital (interest rates) is high, stock issuances become more attractive. In fact, even when interest rates are low, as in 1993, stock

FIGURE 8-4 An EPS/EBIT Chart for the Brown Company

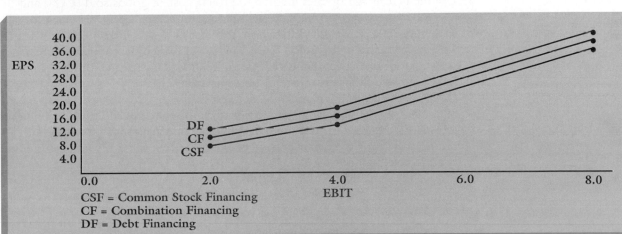

issuances can be very popular. The explosion of new mergers and acquisitions in 1993–1994 was fueled by equity, a time when stock prices were high. Using stock for acquisitions rather than debt enhances a firm's reported earnings because, unlike debt acquirers, stock acquirers do not have to deduct goodwill from their earnings for years to come.

Pro Forma Financial Statements. Pro forma (projected) financial statement analysis is a central strategy-implementation technique because it allows an organization to examine the expected results of various actions and approaches. This type of analysis can be used to forecast the impact of various implementation decisions (for example, to increase promotion expenditures by 50 percent to support a market-development strategy, to increase salaries by 25 percent to support a market-penetration strategy, to increase research and development expenditures by 70 percent to support product development, or to sell $1 million of common stock to raise capital for diversification). Nearly all financial institutions require at least three years of projected financial statements whenever a business seeks capital. A pro forma income statement and balance sheet allow an organization to compute projected financial ratios under various strategy-implementation scenarios. When compared to prior years and to industry averages, financial ratios provide valuable insights into the feasibility of various strategy-implementation approaches.

A 1995 pro forma income statement and balance sheet for the Litten Company are provided in Table 8–4. The pro forma statements for Litten are based on five assumptions: (1) the company needs to raise $45 million to finance expansion into foreign markets, (2) $30 million of this total will be raised through increased debt and $15 million through common stock, (3) sales are expected to increase 50 percent, (4) three new facilities, costing a total of $30 million, will be constructed in foreign markets, and (5) land for the new facilities is already owned by the company. Note in Table 8–4 that Litten's strategies and their implementation are expected to result in a sales increase from $100 million to $150 million and in a net increase in income from $6 million to $9.75 million, in the forecasted year.

There are six steps in performing pro forma financial analysis:

1. Prepare the pro forma income statement before the balance sheet. Start by forecasting sales as accurately as possible.
2. Use the percentage-of-sales method to project cost-of-goods-sold (CGS) and the expense items in the income statement. For example, if CGS is 70 percent of sales in the prior year (as it is in Table 8–4), then use that same percentage to calculate CGS in the future year—unless there is reason to use a different percentage. Items such as interest, dividends, and taxes must be treated independently and cannot be forecasted using the percentage-of-sales method.
3. Calculate the projected net income.
4. Subtract from the net income any dividends to be paid and add the remaining net income to "retained earnings." Reflect the "retained earnings" total on both the income statement and balance sheet, because this item is the key link between the two projected statements.
5. Project the balance sheet items, beginning with retained earnings and then forecasting stockholders' equity, long-term liabilities, current liabilities, total liabilities, total assets, fixed assets, and current assets (in that order). Use the "cash" account as the plug figure; that is, use the cash account to make the assets total the liabilities. Then, make appropriate adjustments. For example, if the "cash" needed to

TABLE 8-4   A Pro Forma Income Statement and Balance Sheet for the Litten Company (in millions)

PRO FORMA INCOME STATEMENT

	Prior Year 1994	Projected Year 1995	Remarks
Sales	100	150.00	50% increase
Cost of goods sold	70	105.00	70% of sales
Gross margin	30	45.00	
Selling expense	10	15.00	10% of sales
Administrative expense	5	7.50	5% of sales
Earnings before interest and taxes	15	22.50	
Interest	3	3.00	
Earnings before taxes	12	19.50	
Taxes	6	9.75	50% rate
Net Income	6	9.75	
Dividends	2	5.00	
Retained earnings	4	4.75	

PRO FORMA BALANCE SHEET

	Prior Year 1994	Projected Year 1995	Remarks
Assets			
Cash	5	7.75	Plug figure
Accounts receivable	2	4.00	Incr. 100%
Inventory	20	45.00	
Total current assets	27	56.75	
Land	15	15.00	
Plant and equipment	50	80.00	Add 3 new at $10 million each
Less: depreciation	10	20.00	
Net plant and equipment	40	60.00	
Total fixed assets	55	75.00	
Total assets	82	131.75	
Liabilities			
Accounts payable	10	10.00	
Notes payable	10	10.00	
Total current liabilities	20	20.00	
Long-term debt	40	70.00	Borrowed $30 million
Common stock	20	35.00	Issued 100,000 shares at $150 each
Retained earnings	2	6.75	2 + 4.75
Total liabilities and new worth	82	131.75	

balance the statements is too small (or too large), make appropriate changes to borrow more (or less) money than planned.

6. List comments (remarks) on the projected statements. Any time a significant change is made in an item from a prior year to the projected year, an explanation (remark) should be provided. Remarks are essential because otherwise pro formas are meaningless.

Financial Budgets. A *financial budget* is a document that details how funds will be obtained and spent for a specified period of time. Annual budgets are most common, although the period of time for a budget can range from a day to over 10 years. Fundamentally, financial budgeting is a method for specifying what must be done to complete strategy implementation successfully. Financial budgeting should not be thought of as a tool for limiting expenditures but rather as a method for obtaining the most productive and profitable use of an organization's resources. Financial budgets can be viewed as the planned allocation of a firm's resources, based on forecasts of the future.

There are almost as many different types of financial budgets as there are types of organizations. Some common types of budgets include cash budgets, operating budgets, sales budgets, profit budgets, factory budgets, capital budgets, expense budgets, divisional budgets, variable budgets, flexible budgets, and fixed budgets. When an organization is experiencing financial difficulties, budgets are especially important in guiding strategy implementation.

Perhaps the most common type of financial budget is the *cash budget*. The Financial Accounting Standards Board has mandated that every publicly held company in the United States must issue an annual cash-flow statement in addition to the usual financial reports. The statement includes all receipts and disbursements of cash in operations, investments, and financing. It supplements the "statement on changes in financial position" formerly included in the annual reports of all publicly held companies. A 1995 cash budget for the Toddler Toy Company is provided in Table 8–5. Note that Toddler is not expecting to have surplus cash until November of 1995.

Financial budgets have some limitations. First, budgetary programs can become so detailed that they are cumbersome and overly expensive. Overbudgeting or underbudgeting can cause problems. Second, financial budgets can become a substitute for objectives. A budget is a tool and not an end in itself. Third, budgets can hide inefficiencies if based solely on precedent rather than periodic evaluation of circumstances and standards. Finally, budgets are sometimes used as instruments of tyranny that result in frustration, resentment, absenteeism, and high turnover. To minimize the effect of this last concern, managers should increase the participation of subordinates in preparing budgets.

Evaluating the Worth of a Business. Evaluating the worth of a business is central to strategy implementation because integrative, intensive, and diversification strategies are often implemented by acquiring other firms. Other strategies, such as retrenchment and divestiture, may result in the sale of a division of an organization, or of the firm itself. Approximately 12,000 transactions occur each year in which businesses are bought or sold in the United States. In all these cases, it is necessary to establish the financial worth or cash value of a business to successfully implement strategies. For example, in 1992 Unisys sold its defense-electronics business for $800 million. Another example is Days Inns of America, which was acquired for $250 million by Blackstone Group while operating under bankruptcy. Of that $250 million,

TABLE 8-5   A Six-month Cash Budget for the Toddler Toy Company in 1995

CASH BUDGET (IN THOUSANDS)	JULY	AUG.	SEPT.	OCT.	NOV.	DEC.	JAN.
Receipts:							
Collections	$12,000	$21,000	$31,000	$35,000	$22,000	$18,000	$11,000
Payments:							
Purchases	14,000	21,000	28,000	14,000	14,000	7,000	
Wages and salaries	1,500	2,000	2,500	1,500	1,500	1,000	
Rent	500	500	500	500	500	500	
Other expenses	200	300	400	200	200	100	
Taxes	—	8,000	—	—	—	—	
Payment on machine	—	—	10,000	—	—		
Total payments	$16,200	$31,800	$41,400	$16,200	$16,200	$8,600	
Net cash gain (loss) during month	-4,200	-10,800	-10,400	18,800	5,800	9,400	
Cash at start of month if no borrowing is done	6,000	1,800	-9,000	-19,400	-600	5,200	
Cumulative cash (cash at start plus gains or minus losses)	1,800	-9,000	-19,400	-600	5,200	14,600	
Less: Desired level of cash	-5,000	-5,000	-5,000	-5,000	-5,000	-5,000	
Total loans outstanding to maintain $5,000 cash balance	$3,200	$14,000	$24,400	$5,600	—	—	
Surplus cash	—	—	—	—	$200	$9,600	

$210 million was comprised of cash and securities, and $40 million was used to repay Days Inns' unsecured debt.

All the various methods for determining a business's worth can be grouped into three main approaches: what a firm owns, what a firm earns, or what a firm will bring in the market. But it is important to realize that valuation is not an exact science. The valuation of a firm's worth is based on financial facts, but common sense and intuitive judgment must enter into the process. It is difficult to assign a monetary value to such factors as a loyal customer base, a history of growth, legal suits pending, dedicated employees, a favorable lease, a bad credit rating, or good patents, which may not be reflected in a firm's financial statements. Also, different valuation methods will yield different totals for a firm's worth, and no prescribed approach is best for a certain situation. Evaluating the worth of a business truly requires both qualitative and quantitative skills.

The first approach in evaluating the worth of a business is determining its net worth or stockholders' equity. Net worth represents the sum of common stock, additional paid-in capital, and retained earnings. After calculating net worth, add or subtract an appropriate amount for goodwill (such as high customer loyalty) and overvalued or undervalued assets. This total provides a reasonable estimate of a firm's monetary value.

The second approach to measuring the value of a firm grows out of the belief that the worth of any business should be based largely on the future benefits its owners may derive through net profits. A conservative rule of thumb is to establish a business's worth as five times the firm's current annual profit. A 5-year average profit level could also be used. When using this approach, remember that firms normally suppress earnings in their financial statements to minimize taxes.

The third approach, letting the market determine a business's worth, involves two methods. First, base the firm's worth on the selling price of a similar company. A potential problem, however, is that sometimes comparable figures are not easy to locate, even though substantial information on firms that buy or sell to other firms is available in major libraries. An alternative approach is called the *price-earnings ratio method*. To use this method, divide the market price of the firm's common stock by the annual earnings per share and multiply this number by the firm's average net income for the past 5 years.

Business evaluations are becoming routine in many situations. Businesses have many strategy-implementation reasons for determining their worth in addition to preparing to be sold or to buy other companies. Employee plans, taxes, retirement, mergers, acquisitions, expansion plans, banking relationships, death of a principal, divorce, partnership agreements, and IRS audits are other reasons for a periodic valuation. It is just good business to have a reasonable understanding of what your firm is worth. This knowledge protects the interests of all parties involved.

Deciding Whether to Go Public. Going public means selling off a percentage of your company to others in order to raise capital; consequently, it dilutes the owners' control of the firm. Going public is not recommended for companies with less than $10 million in sales because the initial costs can be too high for the firm to generate sufficient cash flow to make going public worthwhile. One dollar in four is the average total cost paid to lawyers, accountants, and underwriters when an initial stock issuance is under $1 million; one dollar in twenty will go to cover these costs for issuances over $20 million.[9]

In addition to initial costs involved with a stock offering, there are additional costs and obligations associated with reporting and management in a publicly-held firm. For firms larger than $10 million in sales, going public can provide major advantages; it can allow the firm to raise capital to develop new products, build plants, expand, grow, and market products and services more effectively.

Before going public, a firm must have quality management with a proven track record for achieving quality earnings and positive cash flow. The company also should enjoy growing demand for its products. Sales growth of around 5 or 6 percent a year is good for a private firm, but shareholders expect public companies to grow around 10 to 15 percent per year.

RESEARCH AND DEVELOPMENT (R & D) ISSUES

Research and development (R & D) personnel can play an integral part in strategy implementation. These individuals are generally charged with developing new products and improving old products in a way that will allow effective strategy implementation. R & D employees and managers perform tasks that include transferring complex technology, adjusting processes to local raw materials, adapting processes to local markets, and altering products to particular tastes and specifications. Strategies such as product development, market penetration, and concentric diversification require that new products be successfully developed and that old products be significantly improved. But the level of management support for R & D is often constrained by resource availability:

If U.S. business is to maintain its position in the global business environment, then R & D support will have to become a major U.S. commitment. U.S. managers cannot continue to ignore it or take funds away from it for short-term profits and still have long-term strategic options. If one runs away from more aggressive product and process strategies, one should not be surprised by the fact that competitive advantages are lost to foreign competitors.[10]

Technological improvements that affect consumer and industrial products and services shorten product life cycles. Companies in virtually every industry are relying more and more on the development of new products and services to fuel profitability and growth. Table 8–6 provides a breakdown of R & D expenditures in 1992 for the ten American companies that spent the most on R & D. American companies in 1992 increased their R & D expenditures only 7.1 percent, according to *Business Week*.[11]

U.S. companies spend 3.7 percent of sales on R & D, compared to 5.5 percent for Japanese firms, 5.4 percent for German firms, 5.2 percent for Canadian firms, 6.3 percent for Swiss firms, and 5.8 percent for Swedish firms. Although U.S. R & D expenditures are below those in many other industrialized countries, there are wide variations among companies. IBM, for example, slashed 20 percent or $1 billion from its 1993 R & D budget, but Intel Corporation increased its R & D expenditures 26 percent.

Surveys suggest that "the most successful organizations use an R & D strategy that ties external opportunities to internal strength and is linked with objectives."[12] Well-formulated R & D policies match market opportunities with internal capabilities and provide an initial screen to all ideas generated. R & D policies can enhance strategy-implementation efforts to:

1. Emphasize product or process improvements.
2. Stress basic or applied research.
3. Be leaders or followers in R & D.
4. Develop robotics or manual-type processes.
5. Spend a high, average, or low amount of money on R & D.
6. Perform R & D within the firm or to contract R & D to outside firms.
7. Use university researchers or private-sector researchers.

TABLE 8-6 Ranking the Top Ten American Companies in R & D Spending in 1992

	In Total Dollars (Millions)
1. General Motors	$5,917
2. IBM	5,083
3. Ford Motor	4,332
4. AT&T	2,911
5. Boeing	1,846
6. Digital Equipment	1,754
7. Hewlett-Packard	1,620
8. Eastman Kodak	1,587
9. General Electric	1,353
10. Motorola	1,306

Source: Adapted from *Business Week* (June 28, 1993): 103.

A recent study by Ruekert and Walker stresses the need for effective interactions between R & D departments and other functional departments in implementing different types of generic business strategies.[13] Conflicts between marketing, finance/accounting, R & D, and information systems departments can be minimized with clear policies and objectives. Table 8–7 gives some examples of R & D activities that could be required for successful implementation of various strategies.

Many firms wrestle with the decision to acquire R & D expertise from external firms or to develop R & D expertise internally. The following guidelines can be used to help make this decision:

1. If the rate of technical progress is slow, the rate of market growth is moderate, and there are significant barriers to possible new entrants, then in-house R & D is the preferred solution. The reason is that R & D, if successful, will result in a temporary product or process monopoly that the company can exploit.

2. If technology is changing rapidly and the market is growing slowly, then a major effort in R & D may be very risky, since it may lead to development of an ultimately obsolescent technology or one for which there is no market.

3. If technology is changing slowly but the market is growing fast, there generally is not enough time for in-house development. The prescribed approach is to obtain R & D expertise on an exclusive or nonexclusive basis from an outside firm.

4. If both technical progress and market growth are fast, R & D expertise should be obtained through acquisition of a well-established firm in the industry.[14]

There are at least three major R & D approaches for implementing strategies. The first strategy is to be the first firm to market new technological products. This is a glamorous and exciting strategy but also a dangerous one. Firms such as 3M, Polaroid, and General Electric have been successful with this approach, but many other pioneering firms have fallen, with rival firms seizing the initiative. Two firms also using this first R & D strategy are Global Ozone Solutions and American Thermalfo; these firms manufacture machines that extract ozone-depleting chlorofluorocarbons, or CFCs, from the air. As indicated in

TABLE 8-7   Research and development involvement in selected strategy-implementation situations

TYPE OF ORGANIZATION	STRATEGY BEING IMPLEMENTED	R & D ACTIVITY
Pharmaceutical company	Product development	Develop a procedure for testing the effects of a new drug on different subgroups.
Boat manufacturer	Concentric diversification	Develop a procedure to test the performance of various keel designs under various conditions.
Plastic container manufacturer	Market penetration	Develop a biodegradable container.
Electronics company	Market development	Develop a telecommunications system in a foreign country.

the Natural Environment Perspective, Eastern European cities such as Prague could use these products.

A second R & D approach is to be an innovative imitator of successful products, thus minimizing the risks and costs of start-up. This approach entails allowing a pioneer firm to develop the first version of the new product and to demonstrate that a market exists. Then, laggard firms develop a similar product. This strategy requires excellent R & D personnel and an excellent marketing department.

A third R & D strategy is to be a low-cost producer by mass-producing products similar to but less expensive than products recently introduced. Far Eastern countries used this approach effectively during the 1980s to crush the $8 billion U.S. consumer electronics industry. As a new product is accepted by more and more customers, price becomes increasingly important in the buying decision. Also, mass marketing replaces personal selling as the dominant selling strategy. This R & D strategy requires substantial investment in plant and equipment, but fewer expenditures in R & D than the two approaches described earlier.

R & D activities among American firms need to be more closely aligned to business objectives. There needs to be expanded communication between R & D managers and strategists. Corporations are experimenting with various methods to achieve this improved communication climate, including different roles and reporting arrangements for managers and new methods to reduce the time it takes research ideas to become reality.[15]

NATURAL ENVIRONMENT PERSPECTIVE

DOING BUSINESS IN EASTERN EUROPE AND THE FORMER SOVIET REPUBLICS

The new democratic governments of Eastern Europe and the former Soviet Union recently discovered and reported that decades of atrocities have been committed against the natural environments in their countries. Polluted air and water know no country boundaries, so Western Europe, and indeed the whole earth, has suffered and continues to suffer from environmental destruction in Eastern Europe and Asia.

U.S. firms planning expansion into Eastern Europe and Asia must be careful not to further harm the natural environment in those countries. Firms also must be careful where they locate within these countries because the incidence of diseases such as cancer, typhoid fever, asthma, leukemia, hypertension, pneumonia, bronchitis, and tuberculosis is especially high in some areas.

U.S. firms must make the natural environment a strategic issue and concern when doing business internationally (and domestically). Consider the following facts regarding the natural environment in Eastern Europe and the former Soviet republics:

- Ninety percent of the Black Sea is biologically dead due to industrial wastes pouring in from the Danube and Dnieper rivers.

- Eighty percent of the Baltic Sea is biologically dead due to organic wastes being dumped by Poland, Eastern Germany, and the former Soviet republics.
- The Caspian Sea receives 40 percent of 28.6 cubic kilometers of polluted wastewater annually, most of it from the Volga River.
- Many large cities in the former Soviet republics, including Kaunasin, Lithuania, and Riga, have no sewage treatment facilities at all.
- The largest body of fresh water in the world, Lake Baikal in Asia, is nearly biologically dead after years of industrial pollution and agricultural runoff.
- In Prague, Czechoslovakia, the average annual concentration of sulfur dioxide in the air is 155 micrograms per cubic meter; any level over 40 is dangerous, according to the World Health Organization (WHO); no U.S. city has a level over 20.
- Pesticide poisonings in the former Soviet republics kill 14,000 people annually and cause an additional 700,000 illnesses.
- The Elbe River carries 10 tons of mercury, 24 tons of cadmium, and 142 tons of lead to the North Sea annually.

Source: Adapted from Hilary French, "Green Revolutions: Environmental Reconstruction in Eastern Europe and the Soviet Union," *Columbia Journal of World Business* (Spring 1991): 28–46.

Although no firm would use the same marketing or management approach for 20 years, many companies have 20-year-old information systems that threaten their very existence. Nevertheless, developing new user applications often takes a backseat to keeping an old system running. This unfortunate situation is happening at a time when the quantity and quality of information available to firms and their competitors is increasing exponentially. The Internal Revenue Service is an example of a firm currently revamping its computer information system. The IRS's information system was designed in 1961, overhauled in 1990, and refined in 1994.

Firms that gather, assimilate, and evaluate external and internal information most effectively are gaining competitive advantages over other firms. Recognizing the importance of having an effective computer information system will not be an option in the future; it will be a requirement. Information is the basis for understanding in a firm. Robert Kavner, president of AT&T Data Systems Group, says, "Modern corporations are organizing around information flow. With the growth of communications networks, the barriers of time and place have been breached. By mirroring people's work needs and habits, networked computing systems have made new modes of work possible."

It is estimated that the quantity of human knowledge is doubling every decade. In many industries, information is becoming the most important factor differentiating successful and unsuccessful firms. The process of strategic management is facilitated immensely in firms that have an effective information system. Many companies are establishing a new approach to information systems, one that blends the technical knowledge of the computer experts with the vision of senior management. Some guidelines that allow computer information systems to enhance strategy implementation are as follows:

1. Computer hardware and software should facilitate global information consistency.
2. All component parts should be accessible through a common order-processing system.
3. All divisions should be self-sufficient yet compatible in their information systems capabilities.
4. A basic purpose of information systems is to support cross-functional integration of the business functions.
5. Integration of voice and data communications is a goal of information systems.
6. Data and information obtained within the firm should be available to any department or person in the firm who can demonstrate a need for it, except for reasons of security or integrity of the data base.
7. Information systems design should stress effectiveness in the business environment rather than efficiency in the technical environment.[16]

Information collection, retrieval, and storage can be used to create competitive advantages in ways such as cross-selling to customers, monitoring suppliers, keeping managers and employees informed, coordinating activities among divisions, and managing funds. Like inventory and human resources, information is becoming recognized as a valuable organizational asset that can be controlled and managed. Firms that implement strategies using the best information will reap competitive advantages in the 1990s. John Young, president and CEO of Hewlett-Packard Company, says, "There really isn't any right amount to spend on information systems. Many management teams spend too much time thinking about how to beat down the information system's cost, instead of thinking about how to get more value out of the information they could have available and how to link that to strategic goals of the company."

A good information system can allow a firm to reduce costs. For example, on-line orders from salespersons to production facilities can shorten materials ordering costs and reduce inventory costs. Direct communications between suppliers, manufacturers, marketers, and customers can link elements of the value chain together as though they were one organization. Improved quality and service often result from an improved information system.

Dun & Bradstreet is an example of a company that has an excellent information system. Every D & B customer and client in the world has a separate nine-digit number. The data base of information associated with each number has become so widely used that it is like a business social security number. D & B reaps great competitive advantages from its information system.

CONCLUSION

Successful strategy implementation depends upon cooperation among all functional and divisional managers in an organization. Marketing departments are commonly charged with implementing strategies that require significant increases in sales revenues in new areas and with new or improved products. Finance and accounting managers must devise effective strategy-implementation approaches at low cost and minimum risk to that firm. R & D managers have to transfer complex technologies or develop new technologies to successfully implement strategies. Information systems managers are being called upon more and more to provide leadership and training for all individuals in the firm. The nature and role of marketing, finance/accounting, R & D, and computer information systems activities, coupled with management activities described in Chapter 7, largely determine organizational success.

KEY TERMS AND CONCEPTS

Cash Budget
EPS/EBIT Analysis
Financial Budgets
Information Systems
Market Segmentation
Marketing-Mix Variables
Multidimensional Scaling

Price-Earnings Ratio Method
Pro Forma Financial Statement Analysis
Product Positioning
Research and Development
Retained Earnings
Vacant Niche

ISSUES FOR REVIEW AND DISCUSSION

1. Suppose your company has just acquired a firm that produces battery operated lawn mowers, and strategists want to implement a market-penetration strategy. How would you segment the market for this product? Justify your answer.

2. Explain how you would estimate the total worth of a business.

3. Diagram and label clearly a product positioning map that includes six fast-food restaurants.

4. Explain why EPS/EBIT analysis is a central strategy-implementation technique.

5. How would the R & D role in strategy implementation differ in small versus large organizations?

6. Discuss the limitations of EPS/EBIT analysis.

7. Explain how marketing, finance/accounting, R & D, and computer information systems managers' involvement in strategy formulation can enhance strategy implementation.

8. Is the following statement true or false: "Retained earnings on the balance sheet are not monies available to finance strategy implementation"? Explain.

9. Explain why pro forma financial statement analysis is considered both a strategy-formulation and a strategy-implementation tool.

10. Describe some marketing, finance/accounting, R & D, and computer information system activities that a small restaurant chain might undertake to expand into a neighboring state.

11. Select one of the suggested readings at the end of this chapter, find that article in your college library, and summarize it in a 5-minute oral report for the class.

12. Discuss the computer information system at your college or university.

NOTES

1. Ralph Biggadike, "The Contributions of Marketing to Strategic Management," *Academy of Management Review* 6, no. 4 (October 1981): 624.

2. Philip Kotler, *Marketing Management* (Englewood Cliffs, N.J.: Prentice-Hall, 1976), 144.

3. Fred Winter, "Market Segmentation: A Tactical Approach," *Business Horizons* 27, no. 1 (January–February 1984): 59.

4. Jeff Trachtenberg, "The Sweet Smell of Success," *Forbes* (August 10, 1987): 92.

5. William Davidow and Bro Uttal, "Service Companies: Focus or Falter," *Harvard Business Review* 67, no. 4 (July–August 1989): 80.

6. Ibid., 84.

7. Biggadike, 627.

8. Davidow and Uttal, 85.

9. Philip Taggart, Roy Alexander, Robert Arnold, "Deciding Whether to Go Public," *Nation's Business* (May 1991): 51.

10. Vida Scarpello, William Boulton, and Charles Hofer, "Reintegrating R & D into Business Strategy," *Journal of Business Strategy* 6, no. 4 (Spring 1986): 55.

11. "The Brakes Go in on R & D," *Business Week* (July 1, 1991): 24.

12. T. Kuczmarski and S. Silver, "Strategy: The Key to Successful New Product Development," *Management Review* 71, no. 7 (July 1982): 27.

13. R. Ruekert and O. Walker, "Interactions Between Marketing and R & D Departments in Implementing Different Business Strategies," *Strategic Management Journal* 8, no. 3 (1987): 233–248.

14. Pier Abetti, "Technology: A Key Strategic Resource," *Management Review* 78, no. 2 (February 1989): 38.

15. William Spencer and Deborah Triant, "Strengthening the Link Between R & D and Corporate Strategy," *Journal of Business Strategy* 10, no. 1 (January/February 1989): 42.

16. Thomas Davenport, Michael Hammer, and Tauno Metsisto, "How Executives Can Shape Their Company's Information Systems," *Harvard Business Review* 67, no. 2 (March–April 1989): 131.

CURRENT READINGS

Adriaans, W. "Winning Support for Your Information Strategy." *Long Range Planning* 26, no. 1 (February 1993): 45–53.

Bessen, Jim. "Riding the Marketing Information Wave." *Harvard Business Review* 71, no. 5 (September–October 1993): 150–161.

Boynton, Andrew C. "Achieving Dynamic Stability Through Information Technology." *California Management Review* 35, no. 2 (Winter 1993): 58–77.

Caillouet, Aaron, and Bill Lapeyre. "The Importance of an Accounting Information System in the Strategic Management Process." *SAM Advanced Management Journal* 57, no. 1 (Winter 1992): 21–24.

Davis, Tim R. V. "Linking Quality, Strategy, and Financial Management." *Planning Review* 20, no. 6 (November–December 1992): 36–40.

Hamel, Gary, and C. K. Prahalad. "Strategy as Stretch and Leverage." *Harvard Business Review* (March–April 1993): 75–85.

Hauser, Richard D., Jr., and Frederic J. Hebert. "Managerial Issues in Expert System Implementation."

SAM Advanced Management Journal 57, no. 1 (Winter 1992): 10–15.

Kovacevic, Antonio, and Nicolás Majluf. "Six Stages of IT Strategic Management." *Sloan Management Review* 34, no. 4 (Summer 1993): 77–88.

Lord, M. Alexander. "Implementing Strategy Through Project Management." *Long Range Planning* 26, no. 1 (February 1993): 76–85.

Robertson, Thomas S., and Howard Barich. "A Successful Approach to Segmenting Industrial Markets." *Planning Review* 20, no. 6 (November–December 1992): 4–11.

Zahra, S. A., and J. G. Covin. "Business Strategy, Technology Policy and Firm Performance." *Strategic Management Journal* 14, no. 6 (September 1993): 451–478.

EXPERIENTIAL EXERCISES

DEVELOPING A PRODUCT POSITIONING MAP FOR HERSHEY FOODS

PURPOSE

Organizations continually monitor how their products and services are positioned relative to competitors.[1] This information is especially useful for marketing managers, but is also used by other managers and strategists.

INSTRUCTIONS

Step 1 On a separate sheet of paper, develop a product positioning map for Hershey. Include Nestlé, Mars, and Hershey in your map.

Step 2 Go to the blackboard and diagram your product positioning map.

Step 3 Compare your product positioning map with those diagramed by other students. Discuss any major differences.

PERFORMING AN EPS/EBIT ANALYSIS FOR HERSHEY FOODS

PURPOSE

An EPS/EBIT analysis is one of the most widely used techniques for determining the extent that debt and/or stock should be used to finance strategies to be implemented. This exercise can give you practice performing EPS/EBIT analysis.

INSTRUCTIONS

Let's say Hershey needs to raise $2 billion to introduce Hershey products in twenty new countries around the world in 1993. Determine whether Hershey should use all debt, all stock, or a 50–50 combination of debt and stock to finance this market-development strategy. Assume a 39 percent tax rate and a 5 percent interest rate. Hershey's stock price is $50 per share. Hershey pays an annual dividend of $1.03 per share of common stock. The EBIT range for 1993 is between $300 and $500 million. A total of 90 million shares of common stock are outstanding. Develop an EPS/EBIT chart to reflect your analysis.

USING *CASE ANALYST* TO PREPARE PRO FORMA FINANCIAL STATEMENTS FOR HERSHEY FOODS

PURPOSE

This exercise is designed to give you experience preparing pro forma financial statements. Use the *Case Analyst* software if possible. Pro forma analysis is a central strategy-implementation technique because it allows managers to anticipate and evaluate the expected results of various strategy-implementation approaches. This service will give you practice using the *Case Analyst* software.

INSTRUCTIONS

Step 1 Work with a classmate. Develop a 1993 pro forma income statement and balance sheet for Hershey. Assume that Hershey plans to raise $100 million in 1993 to introduce Hershey products in twenty new countries, and plans to obtain 50 percent financing from a bank and 50 percent financing from a stock issuance. Make other assumptions as needed, and state them clearly in written form.

Step 2 Load the *Case Analyst* software and develop your pro forma analysis.

Step 3 Compute Hershey's current ratio, debt-to-equity ratio, and return-on-investment ratio for 1990, 1991, and 1992. How do your 1993 projected ratios compare to the 1991 and 1992 ratios? Why is it important to make this comparison?

Step 4 Bring your pro forma printout to class and discuss any problems or questions you encountered in using *Case Analyst*.

Step 5 Compare your pro forma statements to the statements of other students. What major differences exist between your analysis and the work of other students?

DETERMINING THE CASH VALUE OF HERSHEY FOODS

PURPOSE

It is simply good business practice to periodically determine the financial worth or cash value of your company. This exercise gives you practice determining the total worth of a company using several methods.

INSTRUCTIONS

Step 1 Calculate the financial worth of Hershey based on three methods: (1) the net worth or stockholders' equity, (2) the future value of Hershey's earnings, and (3) the price-earnings ratio.

Step 2 In a single dollar amount, how much is Hershey worth?

Step 3 Compare your analyses and conclusions with the work of other students.

DEVELOPING A PRODUCT POSITIONING MAP FOR MY UNIVERSITY

PURPOSE

The purpose of this exercise is to give you practice developing product positioning maps. Nonprofit organizations, such as universities, are more and more using product positioning maps to determine effective ways to implement strategies.

INSTRUCTIONS

Step 1 Join with two other persons in class to form a group of three.

Step 2 Jointly prepare a product positioning map that includes your institution and four other colleges or universities in your state.

Step 3 Go to the blackboard and diagram your product positioning map.

Step 4 Discuss differences among the maps diagrammed on the board.

DO BANKS REQUIRE PRO FORMA STATEMENTS?

PURPOSE

The purpose of this exercise is to explore the practical importance and use of projected financial statements in the banking business.

INSTRUCTIONS

Contact two local bankers by phone and seek answers to the questions listed below. Record the answers you receive and report your findings to the class.

1. Does your bank require projected financial statements as part of a business loan application?
2. How does your bank use projected financial statements when they are part of a business loan application?
3. What special advice do you give potential business borrowers in preparing projected financial statements?

PART · 4

Strategy Evaluation

Chapter 9

STRATEGY REVIEW, EVALUATION, AND CONTROL

NOTABLE QUOTES

....

Complicated controls do not work. They confuse. They misdirect attention from what is to be controlled to the mechanics and methodology of the control. —Seymour Tilles

Strategic thinking lives through dialogue or dies through writer's cramp. —David Moore

Although Plan A may be selected as the most realistic . . . the other major alternatives should not be forgotten. They may well serve as contingency plans. —Dale McConkey

Organizations are most vulnerable when they are at the peak of their success.
—R. T. Lenz

As spans of control widen, computers will become even more necessary. —Brian Dumaine

Strategy evaluation must make it as easy as possible for managers to revise their plans and reach quick agreement on the changes. —Dale McConkey

While strategy is a word that is usually associated with the future, its link to the past is no less central. Life is lived forward but understood backward. Managers may live strategy in the future, but they understand it through the past. —Henry Mintzberg

Unless strategy evaluation is performed seriously and systematically, and unless strategists are willing to act on the results, energy will be used up defending yesterday. No one will have the time, resources, or will to work on exploiting today, let alone to work on making tomorrow. —Peter Drucker

I have a duty to the soldiers, their parents, and the country, to remove immediately any commander who does not satisfy the highest performance demands. It is a mistake to put a person in a command that is not the right command. It is therefore my job to think through where that person belongs. —George C. Marshall

OBJECTIVES   After studying this chapter, you should be able to:

- ■ Describe a practical framework for evaluating strategies.
- ■ Explain why strategy evaluation is complex, sensitive, and yet essential for organizational success.
- ■ Discuss the importance of contingency planning in strategy evaluation.
- ■ Discuss the role of auditing in strategy evaluation.
- ■ Explain how computers can aid in evaluating strategies.

*T*he best formulated and implemented strategies become obsolete as a firm's external and internal environments change. It is essential, therefore, that strategists systematically review, evaluate, and control the execution of strategies. This chapter presents a framework that can guide managers' efforts to evaluate strategic-management activities, to make sure they are working, and to make timely changes. Computer information systems being used to evaluate strategies are discussed. Guidelines are presented for formulating, implementing, and evaluating strategies.

THE NATURE OF STRATEGY EVALUATION

The strategic-management process results in decisions that can have significant, long-lasting consequences. Erroneous strategic decisions can inflict severe penalties and can be exceedingly difficult, if not impossible, to reverse. Most strategists agree, therefore, that strategy evaluation is vital to an organization's well-being; timely evaluations can alert management to problems or potential problems before a situation becomes critical. Strategy evaluation includes three basic activities: (1) examining the underlying bases of a firm's strategy, (2) comparing expected results with actual results, and (3) taking corrective actions to ensure that performance conforms to plans. The strategy-evaluation stage of the strategic-management process is illustrated in Figure 9–1.

Adequate and timely feedback is the cornerstone of effective strategy evaluation. Strategy evaluation can be no better than the information on which it operates. Too much pressure from top managers may result in lower managers contriving numbers they think will be satisfactory. Strategists for Boy Scouts of America recently determined, for example, that membership figures coming in from the field had been falsified. The drive to increase membership had motivated people to increase the number of new members reported, but had not motivated them to increase the number of Boy Scouts actually enrolled.[1]

Strategy evaluation can be a complex and sensitive undertaking. Too much emphasis on evaluating strategies may be expensive and counterproductive. No one likes to be evaluated too closely! Dalton and Lawrence emphasize that the more managers attempt to evaluate the behavior of others, the less control they have. Yet, too little or no evaluation can create even worse problems.[2] Strategy evaluation is essential to ensure that stated objectives are being achieved.

In many organizations, strategy evaluation is simply an appraisal of how well an organization has performed. Have the firm's assets increased? Has there been an increase in profitability? Have sales increased? Have productivity levels increased? Have profit margin, return on investment, and earnings-per-share ratios increased? Some firms argue that their strategy must have been correct if the answers to these types of questions are affirmative. Well, the strategy or strategies may have been correct, but this type of reasoning can be misleading, because strategy evaluation must have both a long-run and short-run focus. Strategies often do not affect short-term operating results until it is too late to make needed changes. Braniff Airlines, for example, did not know that its worldwide market development would result in bankruptcy until hundreds of new planes had been purchased and extensive resources committed.

It is impossible to demonstrate conclusively that a particular strategy is optimal or even to guarantee that it will work. One can, however, evaluate it for critical flaws. Richard Rumelt offers four criteria that could be used to evaluate a strategy: consistency, consonance, advantage, and feasibility. Described in Table 9–1, consonance and

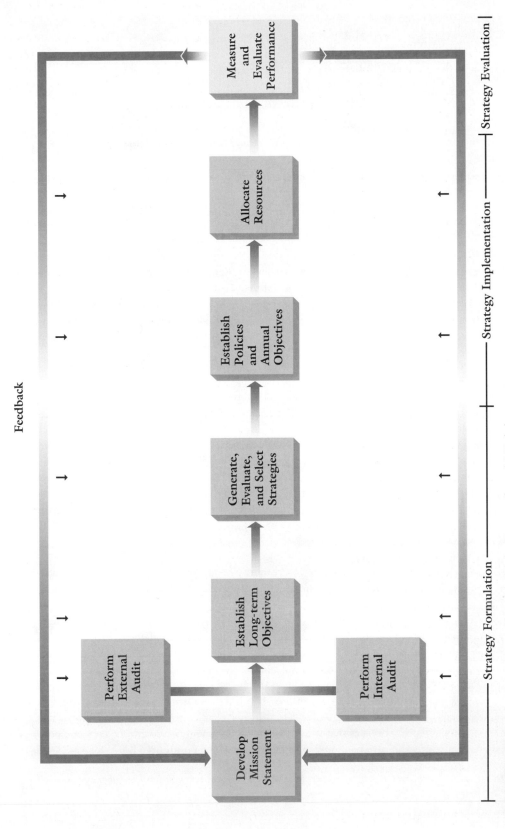

FIGURE 9-1 A Comprehensive Strategic-Management Model

TABLE 9-1   Rumelt's Criteria for Evaluating Strategies

CONSISTENCY

A strategy should not present inconsistent goals and policies. Organizational conflict and interdepartmental bickering are often symptoms of a managerial disorder, but these problems may also be a sign of "strategic inconsistency." Rumelt offers three guidelines to help determine if organizational problems are due to inconsistencies in strategy.

- If managerial problems continue despite changes in personnel, and if they tend to be issue-based rather than people-based, then strategies may be inconsistent.
- If success for one organizational department means, or is interpreted to mean, failure for another department, then strategies may be inconsistent.
- If policy problems and issues continue to be brought to the top for resolution, then strategies may be inconsistent.

CONSONANCE

Consonance refers to the need for strategies to examine *sets of trends* as well as individual trends in evaluating strategies. A strategy must represent an adaptive response to the external environment and to the critical changes occurring within it. One difficulty in matching a firm's key internal and external factors in the formulation of strategy is that most trends are the result of interactions among other trends. For example, the day care explosion came about as a combined result of many trends that included a rise in the average level of education, increased inflation, and an increase in women in the work force. Thus, while single economic or demographic trends might appear steady for many years, there are waves of change going on at the interaction level.

FEASIBILITY

A strategy must neither overtax available resources nor create unsolvable subproblems. The final broad test of strategy is its feasibility; that is, can the strategy be attempted within the physical, human, and financial resources of the enterprise? The financial resources of a business are the easiest to quantify and are normally the first limitation against which strategy is evaluated. It is sometimes forgotten, however, that innovative approaches to financing are often possible. Devices such as captive finance subsidiaries, sale-leaseback arrangements, and tying plant mortgages to long-term contracts have all been used effectively to help win key positions in suddenly expanding industries. A less quantifiable, but actually more rigid, limitation on strategic choice is that imposed by individual and organizational capabilities. In evaluating a strategy, it is important to examine whether an organization has demonstrated in the past that it possesses the abilities, competencies, skills, and talents needed to carry out a given strategy.

ADVANTAGE

A strategy must provide for the creation and/or maintenance of a competitive advantage in a selected area of activity. Competitive advantages normally are the result of superiority in one of three areas: 1) resources, 2) skills, or 3) position. The idea that the positioning of one's resources can enhance their combined effectiveness is familiar to military theorists, chess players, and diplomats. Position can also play a crucial role in an organization's strategy. Once gained, a good position is defensible—meaning so costly to capture that rivals are deterred from full-scale attacks. Positional advantage tends to be self-sustaining, as long as the key internal and environmental factors that underlie it remain stable. This is why entrenched firms can be almost impossible to unseat, even if their raw skill levels are only average. Although not all positional advantages are associated with size, it is true that larger organizations tend to operate in markets and use procedures that turn their size into advantage, while smaller firms seek product/market positions that exploit other types of advantage. The principal characteristics of good position is that it permits the firm to obtain advantage from policies that would not similarly benefit rivals without the same position. Therefore, in evaluating strategy, organizations should examine the nature of positional advantages associated with a given strategy.

Source: Adapted from Richard Rumelt, "The Evaluation of Business Strategy," in W.F. Glueck, ed., *Business Policy and Strategic Management* (New York: McGraw-Hill, 1980), 359–67.

advantage are mostly based on a firm's external assessment, whereas consistency and feasibility are largely based on an internal assessment.

Strategy evaluation is important because organizations face dynamic environments in which key external and internal factors often change quickly and dramatically. Success today is no guarantee for success tomorrow! An organization should never be lulled into complacency with success. Countless firms have thrived one year only to struggle for survival the following year. For example, IBM's profits dropped in 1993 to negative $7.99 billion. Other companies that experienced net profit losses in excess of $1 billion in 1993 were Fort Howard and Eagle-Picher Industries. Organizational demise can come swiftly, as further evidenced by the examples described in Table 9–2.

Strategy evaluation is becoming increasingly difficult with the passage of time, for many reasons. Domestic and world economies were more stable in years past, product life cycles were longer, product development cycles were shorter, technological advancement was slower, change occurred less often, there were fewer competitors, foreign companies were weak, and there were more regulated industries. Other reasons why strategy evaluation is more difficult today include the following trends:

1. A dramatic increase in the environment's complexity
2. The increasing difficulty of predicting the future with accuracy
3. The increasing number of variables
4. The rapid rate of obsolescence of even the best plans

TABLE 9-2   Examples of Organizational Demise

The following companies experienced more than a 20-percent decline in revenues for 1993:

Midlantic	Glendale Federal Bank
Lyondell Petrochemical	Armdahl
Hartmarx	Wang Laboratories
Oryx Energy	Computervision
Alliant Techsystems	Aviall
California Federal Bank	Wheelabrator Technologies

These companies experienced more than a 50-percent decline in profits in 1993:

Michigan National	Federal Paper Board
Ethyl	Bradlees
H. B. Fuller	Filene's Basement
Liz Claiborne	CompUSA
Hechinger	Warner-Lambert
Reliance Electric	Harley-Davidson
ALCOA	Kennametal
Atlantic Richfield	US West
Valero Energy	McGraw-Hill
FMC	Commonwealth Edison
ADVO	Magma Copper
American General	Egghead

5. The increase in the number of both domestic and world events affecting organizations

6. The decreasing time span for which planning can be done with any degree of certainty[3]

The Process of Evaluating Strategies. Strategy evaluation is necessary for all sizes and kinds of organizations. Strategy evaluation should initiate managerial questioning of expectations and assumptions, should trigger a review of objectives and values, and should stimulate creativity in generating alternatives and formulating criteria of evaluation.[4] Regardless of the size of the organization, a certain amount of "management by wandering around" at all levels is essential to effective strategy evaluation. Strategy-evaluation activities should be performed on a continuing basis, rather than at the end of specified periods of time or just after problems occur. Waiting until the end of the year, for example, could result in a firm "closing the barn door after the horses have already escaped."

Evaluating strategies on a continuous rather than a periodic basis allows benchmarks of progress to be established and more effectively monitored. Some strategies take years to implement; consequently, associated results may not become apparent for years. Successful strategists combine patience with a willingness to take corrective actions promptly when necessary. There always comes a time when corrective actions are needed in an organization! Centuries ago, a writer, perhaps Solomon, made these observations about change:

> There is a time for everything,
> a time to be born and a time to die,
> a time to plant and a time to uproot,
> a time to kill and a time to heal,
> a time to tear down and a time to build,
> a time to weep and a time to laugh,
> a time to mourn and a time to dance,
> a time to scatter stones and a time to gather them,
> a time to embrace and a time to refrain,
> a time to search and a time to give up,
> a time to keep and a time to throw away,
> a time to tear and a time to mend,
> a time to be silent and a time to speak,
> a time to love and a time to hate,
> a time for war and a time for peace.[5]

In a study that examined the timing of strategy evaluation in many organizations, Lindsay and Rue hypothesized that strategy-evaluation activities would be conducted more frequently as environmental complexity and instability increased.[6] However, the researchers found a surprising inverse relationship between "planning review frequency" and organizational environment. Top managers in dynamic environments performed strategy-evaluation activities less frequently than those in stable environments. Lindsay and Rue concluded that forecasting is more difficult under complex and unstable environmental conditions, so strategists may see less need for frequent evaluation of their long-range plans. Evidence for this conclusion was stronger for large firms than for small ones.

Managers and employees of the firm should be continually aware of progress being made toward achieving the firm's objectives. As critical success factors change, organizational members should be involved in determining appropriate corrective actions. If assumptions and expectations deviate significantly from forecasts, then the firm should renew strategy-formulation activities, perhaps sooner than planned. In strategy evaluation, like strategy formulation and strategy implementation, people make the difference. Through involvement in the process of evaluating strategies, managers and employees become committed to keeping the firm moving steadily toward achieving objectives.

A STRATEGY-EVALUATION FRAMEWORK

Table 9–3 summarizes strategy-evaluation activities in terms of key questions that should be addressed, alternative answers to those questions, and appropriate actions for an organization to take. Notice that corrective actions are almost always needed except when (1) external and internal factors have not significantly changed and (2) the firm is progressing satisfactorily toward achieving stated objectives. Relationships among strategy-evaluation activities are illustrated in Figure 9–2.

Reviewing Bases of Strategy. As shown in Figure 9–2, reviewing the underlying bases of an organization's strategy could be approached by developing a revised EFE Matrix and IFE Matrix. A revised IFE Matrix should focus on changes in the organization's management, marketing, finance/accounting, production/operations, R & D, and computer information systems strengths and weaknesses. A revised EFE

TABLE 9-3   A Strategy-evaluation Assessment Matrix

HAVE MAJOR CHANGES OCCURRED IN THE FIRM'S INTERNAL STRATEGIC POSITION?	HAVE MAJOR CHANGES OCCURRED IN THE FIRM'S EXTERNAL STRATEGIC POSITION?	HAS THE FIRM PROGRESSED SATISFACTORILY TOWARD ACHIEVING ITS STATED OBJECTIVES?	RESULT
No	No	No	Take corrective actions
Yes	Yes	Yes	Take corrective actions
Yes	Yes	No	Take corrective actions
Yes	No	Yes	Take corrective actions
Yes	No	No	Take corrective actions
No	Yes	Yes	Take corrective actions
No	Yes	No	Take corrective actions
No	No	Yes	Continue present strategic course

FIGURE 9-2 A Strategy-evaluation Framework

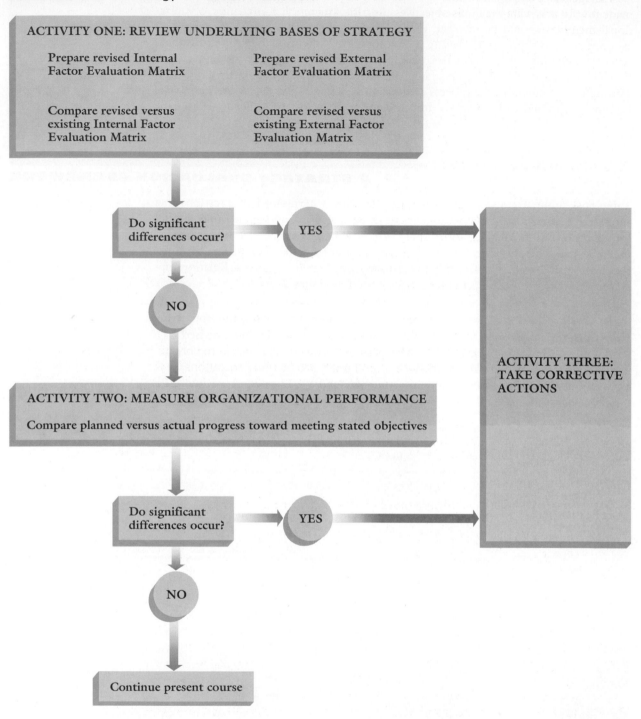

ACTIVITY ONE: REVIEW UNDERLYING BASES OF STRATEGY

Prepare revised Internal
Factor Evaluation Matrix

Prepare revised External
Factor Evaluation Matrix

Compare revised versus
existing Internal Factor
Evaluation Matrix

Compare revised versus
existing External Factor
Evaluation Matrix

Do significant
differences occur?

YES

NO

ACTIVITY THREE:
TAKE CORRECTIVE
ACTIONS

ACTIVITY TWO: MEASURE ORGANIZATIONAL PERFORMANCE

Compare planned versus actual progress toward meeting stated objectives

Do significant
differences occur?

YES

NO

Continue present course

Matrix should indicate how effective a firm's strategies have been in response to key opportunities and threats. This analysis could also address such questions as

1. How have competitors reacted to our strategies?
2. How have competitors' strategies changed?
3. Have major competitors' strengths and weaknesses changed?
4. Why are competitors making certain strategic changes?
5. Why are some competitors' strategies more successful than others?
6. How satisfied are our competitors with their present market positions and profitability?
7. How far can our major competitors be pushed before retaliating?
8. How could we more effectively cooperate with our competitors?

Numerous external and internal factors can prohibit firms from achieving long-term and annual objectives. Externally, actions by competitors, changes in demand, changes in technology, economic changes, demographic shifts, and governmental actions may prohibit objectives from being accomplished. Internally, ineffective strategies may have been chosen, or implementation activities may have been poor. Objectives may have been too optimistic. Thus, failure to achieve objectives may not be the result of unsatisfactory work by managers and employees. All organizational members need to know this to encourage their support for strategy-evaluation activities. Organizations desperately need to know as soon as possible when their strategies are not effective. Sometimes managers and employees on the "front line" discover this well before strategists.

External opportunities and threats and internal strengths and weaknesses that represent the bases of current strategies should continually be monitored for change. It is not really a question of whether these factors will change, but rather when they will change and in what ways. Some key questions to address in evaluating strategies are given here.

1. Are our internal strengths still strengths?
2. Have we added other internal strengths? If so, what are they?
3. Are our internal weaknesses still weaknesses?
4. Do we now have other internal weaknesses? If so, what are they?
5. Are our external opportunities still opportunities?
6. Are there now other external opportunities? If so, what are they?
7. Are our external threats still threats?
8. Are there now other external threats? If so, what are they?
9. Are we vulnerable to a hostile takeover?

Measuring Organizational Performance. Another important strategy-evaluation activity is to measure organizational performance. This activity includes comparing expected results to actual results, investigating deviations from plans, evaluating individual performance, and examining progress being made toward meeting stated objectives. Both long-term and annual objectives are commonly used in this process. Criteria for evaluating strategies should be measurable and easily verifiable. Criteria that predict results may be more important than those that reveal what already has happened. For example, strategists do not want to find out that sales last quarter were 20 percent under what were expectd. More importantly, they need to know that sales next quarter may be 20 percent below standard unless some action is taken to counter the trend. Really effective control requires accurate forecasting.[7]

Failure to make satisfactory progress toward accomplishing long-term or annual objectives signals a need for corrective actions. Many factors, such as unreasonable policies, unexpected turns in the economy, unreliable suppliers or distributors, or ineffective strategies, can result in unsatisfactory progress toward meeting objectives. Problems can result from ineffectiveness (not doing the right things) or inefficiency (doing the right things poorly).

Determining which objectives are most important in the evaluation of strategies can be difficult. Strategy evaluation is based on both quantitative and qualitative criteria. Selecting the exact set of criteria for evaluating strategies depends on a particular organization's size, industry, strategies, and management philosophy. An organization pursuing a retrenchment strategy, for example, could have an entirely different set of evaluative criteria from an organization pursuing a market-development strategy. Quantitative criteria commonly used to evaluate strategies are financial ratios, which strategists use to make three critical comparisons: (1) comparing the firm's performance over different time periods, (2) comparing the firm's performance to competitors', and (3) comparing the firm's performance to industry averages. Some key financial ratios that are particularly useful as criteria for strategy evaluation include:

1. Return on investment
2. Return on equity
3. Profit margin
4. Market share
5. Debt to equity
6. Earnings per share
7. Sales growth
8. Asset growth

But there are some potential problems associated with using quantitative criteria for evaluating strategies. First, most quantitative criteria are geared to annual objectives rather than long-term objectives. Also, different accounting methods can provide different results on many quantitative criteria. Third, intuitive judgments are almost always involved in deriving quantitative criteria. For these and other reasons, qualitative criteria are also important in evaluating strategies. Human factors such as high absenteeism and turnover rates, poor production quality and quantity rates, or low employee satisfaction can be underlying causes of declining performance. Marketing, finance/accounting, R & D, or computer information systems factors can also cause financial problems. Seymour Tilles identifies six qualitative questions that are useful in evaluating strategies:

1. Is the strategy internally consistent?
2. Is the strategy consistent with the environment?
3. Is the strategy appropriate in view of available resources?
4. Does the strategy involve an acceptable degree of risk?
5. Does the strategy have an appropriate time framework?
6. Is the strategy workable?[8]

Some additional key questions that reveal the need for qualitative or intuitive judgments in strategy evaluation are

1. How good is the firm's balance of investments between high-risk and low-risk projects?
2. How good is the firm's balance of investments between long-term and short-term projects?
3. How good is the firm's balance of investments between slow-growing markets and fast-growing markets?
4. How good is the firm's balance of investments among different divisions?
5. To what extent are the firm's alternative strategies socially responsible?
6. What are the relationships among the firm's key internal and external strategic factors?
7. How are major competitors likely to respond to particular strategies?

Taking Corrective Actions. The final strategy-evaluation activity, taking corrective actions, requires making changes to reposition a firm competitively for the future. Some examples of changes that may be needed are altering an organization's structure, replacing one or more key individuals selling a division, or revising a business mission. Other changes could include establishing or revising objectives, devising new policies, issuing stock to raise capital, adding additional salespersons, allocating resources differently, or developing new performance incentives. Taking corrective actions does not necessarily mean that existing strategies will be abandoned or even that new strategies must be formulated.

> The probabilities and possibilities for incorrect or inappropriate actions increase geometrically with an arithmetic increase in personnel. Any person directing an overall undertaking must check on the actions of the participants as well as the results that they have achieved. If either the actions or results do not comply with preconceived or planned achievements, then corrective actions are needed.[9]

No organization can survive as an island; no organization can escape change. Taking corrective actions is necessary to keep an organization on track toward achieving stated objectives. In his thought-provoking books, *Future Shock* and *The Third Wave*, Alvin Toffler argues that business environments are becoming so dynamic and complex that they threaten people and organizations with *future shock*, which occurs when the nature, types, and speed of changes overpower an individual's or organization's ability and capacity to adapt. Strategy evaluation enhances an organization's ability to adapt successfully to changing circumstances. Brown and Agnew refer to this notion as "corporate agility."[10] As indicated in the Natural Environment Perspective, Taiwan is one country that experienced future shock in the 1980s and almost overnight required all of its business firms to use corporate agility to preserve the country's beauty and resources.

Taking corrective actions raises employees' and managers' anxieties. Research suggests that participation in strategy-evaluation activities is one of the best ways to overcome individuals' resistance to change. According to Erez and Kanfer, individuals accept change best when they have a cognitive understanding of the changes, a sense of control over the situation, and an awareness that necessary actions are going to be taken to implement the changes.[11]

Strategy evaluation can lead to strategy-formulation changes, strategy-implementation changes, both formulation and implementation changes, or no changes at all. Strategists cannot escape having to revise strategies and implementation approaches sooner or later. Hussey and Langham offer the following insight on taking corrective actions:

> Resistance to change is often emotionally based and not easily overcome by rational argument. Resistance may be based on such feelings as loss of status, implied criticism of present competence, fear of failure in the new situation, annoyance at not being consulted, lack of understanding of the need for change, or insecurity in changing from well-known and fixed methods. It is necessary, therefore, to overcome such resistance by creating situations of participation and full explanation when changes are envisaged.[12]

Corrective actions should place an organization in a better position to capitalize upon internal strengths; to take advantage of key external opportunities; to avoid, reduce, or mitigate external threats; and to improve internal weaknesses. Corrective actions should have a proper time horizon and an appropriate amount of risk. They should be internally consistent and socially responsible. Perhaps most importantly, corrective actions strengthen an organization's competitive position in its basic indus-

Only a little larger than the state of Maryland, Taiwan has a population of over 21,000,000 people, making it the most densely populated country in the world except for Bangladesh. Manufacturing is Taiwan's principal type of business, and the country was stifling in bad air, awash in contaminated water, and blanketed in its own waste by the mid-1980s.

In late 1988 Taiwan passed the Solid Waste Management Act, which gave the Taiwan Environmental Protection Agency (EPA) strict authority to enforce laws requiring all businesses to manage disposal of their products. Fifteen categories of commercial products and materials became subject to mandatory recycling, and manufacturers were required to take cradle-to-grave responsibility for their products. Soft-drink bottlers funded a collection system and plastics producers funded a processing plant to ensure adequate supplies of postconsumer plastics.

Taiwanese firms are now responsible for retrieving and disposing of their own packages and containers that are non-degradable, not easily reused, or composed of hazardous elements. Firms must collect and recycle or abandon use of their packages distributed in Taiwan.

Taiwan recycles nearly 50 percent of all its soft-drink bottles today through a system that is both efficient and profitable. Primary credit for the "greening" of Taiwan's natural environment goes to Dr. Eugene Chien, who took charge of the country's EPA in 1987 and designed a national solid-waste management policy based on recycling. The EPA's program includes an extensive education program in the nation's grade schools. The Taiwanese today generally do business only with firms that are committed to reversing the decades of natural environment destruction in their country—which the Portuguese sailors in 1590 called *Ilha Formosa*, meaning *beautiful island*.

try. Continuous strategy evaluation keeps strategists close to the pulse of an organization and provides information needed for an effective strategic-management system. Carter Bayles describes the benefits of strategy evaluation as follows:

> Evaluation activities may renew confidence in the current business strategy or point to the need for actions to correct some weaknesses, such as erosion of product superiority or technological edge. In many cases, the benefits of strategy evaluation are much more far-reaching, for the outcome of the process may be a fundamentally new strategy that will lead, even in a business that is already turning a respectable profit, to substantially increased earnings. It is this possibility that justifies strategy evaluation, for the payoff can be very large.[13]

PUBLISHED SOURCES OF STRATEGY-EVALUATION INFORMATION

A number of publications are helpful in evaluating a firm's strategies. For example, in its May and June issue each year, *Fortune* identifies and evaluates the Fortune 1,000 (the largest manufacturers) and the Fortune 50 (the largest retailers, transportation companies, utilities, banks, insurance companies, and diversified financial corporations in the United States). In these issues, *Fortune* also ranks the best and worst performers on various factors such as return on investment, sales volume, and profitability.

In its January issue each year, *Fortune* evaluates organizations in twenty-five industries. Eight key attributes serve as evaluative criteria: quality of management; innovativeness; quality of products or services; long-term investment value; financial soundness; community and environmental responsibility; ability to attract, develop, and keep talented people; and use of corporate assets; *Fortune's* 1993 evaluation reveals the following firms to be best in the respective industries:[14]

Company	Industry
Boeing	Aerospace
United Parcel Service (UPS)	Trucking
Ford Motor	Motor vehicles and parts

Harley-Davidson	Transportation equipment
Deere	Industrial and farm equipment
Motorola	Electronics
Hewlett-Packard	Computers and office equipment
Berkshire Hathaway	Publishing, printing
3M	Scientific and photo equipment
Norfolk Southern	Railroads
Southwest Airlines	Airlines
Walt Disney	Entertainment
Fluor	Engineering and construction
U.S. Healthcare	Health care
Enron	Pipelines
Golden West Financial	Savings institutions
AT&T	Telecommunications
Morgan Stanley Group	Diversified financial
Northwestern Mutual Life	Life insurance
J.P. Morgan	Commercial banking
Herman Miller	Furniture
Procter & Gamble	Soaps, cosmetics
Wal-Mart Stores	General merchandise
Levi Strauss Associates	Apparel
American Brands	Tobacco
Coca-Cola	Beverages
General Mills	Food
Alcoa	Metals
Gillette	Metal products
Corning	Building materials, glass
Rubbermaid	Rubber and plastic products
Kimberly-Clark	Forest products
Shaw Industries	Textiles
Merck	Pharmaceuticals
DuPont	Chemicals
Burlington Resources	Mining, crude oil
Shell Oil	Petroleum refining
Pacific Gas & Electric	Electric and gas utilities
Nike	Wholesalers
Publix Super Markets	Food and drug stores
Home Depot	Specialist retailers

Another excellent evaluation of corporations in America, "The Annual Report on American Industry," is published annually in the January issue of *Forbes*. It provides a detailed and comprehensive evaluation of hundreds of American companies in many different industries. *Business Week*, *Industry Week*, and *Dun's Business Month* also periodically publish detailed evaluations of American businesses and industries. Although published sources of strategy-evaluation information focus primarily on large, publicly held businesses, the comparative ratios and related information are widely used to evaluate small businesses and privately owned firms as well. As indicated in the Global Perspective, the strategies of U.S. firms were recently evaluated in comparison with world competitors. Note that U.S. pharmaceutical firms and forest products firms are excellent world-class competitors.

Strategy evaluation must meet several basic requirements to be effective. First, strategy-evaluation activities must be economical; too much information can be just as bad as too little information, and too many controls can do more harm than good. Strategy-evaluation activities also should be meaningful; they should specifically relate to a firm's objectives. They should provide managers with useful information about tasks over which they have control and influence. Strategy-evaluation activities should provide timely information; on occasion and in some areas, managers may need information daily. For example, when a firm has diversified by acquiring another firm, evaluative information may be needed frequently. However, in an R & D department, daily or even weekly evaluative information could be dysfunctional. Approximate information that is timely is generally more desirable as a basis for strategy evaluation than accurate information that does not depict the present. Frequent measurement and rapid reporting may frustrate control rather than give better control. The time dimension of control must coincide with the time span of the event being measured.

Strategy evaluation should be designed to provide a true picture of what is happening. For example, in a severe economic downturn, productivity and profitability ratios may drop alarmingly, while employees and managers are actually working harder. Strategy evaluations should portray this type of situation fairly. Information derived from the strategy-evaluation process should facilitate action and should be directed to those individuals in the organization who need to take action based on it. Managers commonly ignore evaluative reports that are provided for informational purposes only; not all managers need to receive all reports. Controls need to be action-oriented rather than information-oriented.

The strategy-evaluation process should not dominate decisions; it should foster mutual understanding, trust, and common sense! No department should fail to cooperate with another in evaluating strategies. Strategy evaluations should be simple, not too cumbersome, and not too restrictive. Complex strategy-evaluation systems often confuse people and accomplish little. The test of an effective evaluation system is its usefulness, not its complexity.

Large organizations require a more elaborate and detailed strategy-evaluation system because it is more difficult to coordinate efforts among different divisions and functional areas. Managers in small companies often communicate with each other and their employees daily and do not need extensive evaluative reporting systems. Familiarity with local environments usually makes gathering and evaluating information much easier for small organizations than for large businesses.[15]

But the key to an effective strategy-evaluation system may be the ability to convince participants that failure to accomplish certain objectives within a prescribed time is not necessarily a reflection of their performance.[16]

There is no one ideal strategy-evaluation system. The unique characteristics of an organization, including its size, management style, purpose, problems, and strengths, can determine a strategy-evaluation and control system's final design. Robert Waterman offers the following observation about successful organizations' strategy-evaluation and control systems:

> Successful companies treat facts as friends and controls as liberating. Morgan Guaranty and Wells Fargo not only survive but thrive in the troubled waters of bank deregulation, because their strategy evaluation and control systems are sound, their risk is contained, and they know themselves and the competitive situation so well. Successful companies have a vora-

cious hunger for facts. They see information where others see only data. They love comparisons, rankings, anything that removes decision-making from the realm of mere opinion. Successful companies maintain tight, accurate financial controls. Their people don't regard controls as an imposition of autocracy, but as the benign checks and balances that allow them to be creative and free.[17]

CONTINGENCY PLANNING

A basic premise of good strategic management is that firms plan ways to deal with unfavorable and favorable events before they occur. Too many organizations prepare contingency plans just for unfavorable events; this is a mistake, because both minimizing threats and capitalizing on opportunities can improve a firm's competitive position.

Regardless of how carefully strategies are formulated, implemented, and evaluated, unforeseen events such as strikes, boycotts, natural disasters, arrival of foreign competitors, and government actions can make a strategy obsolete. To minimize the impact of potential threats, organizations should develop contingency plans as part of the strategy-evaluation process. *Contingency plans* can be defined as alternative plans that can be put into effect if certain key events do not occur as expected. Only high-priority areas require the insurance of contingency plans. Strategists cannot and should not try to cover all bases by planning for all possible contingencies. But in any case, contingency plans should be as simple as possible.

Some contingency plans commonly established by firms include the following:

1. If a major competitor withdraws from particular markets as intelligence reports indicate, what actions should our firm take?
2. If our sale objectives are not reached, what actions should our firm take to avoid profit losses?
3. If demand for our new product exceeds plans, what actions should our firm take to meet the higher demand?
4. If certain disasters occur, such as loss of computer capabilities, a hostile takeover attempt, loss of patent protection, or destruction of manufacturing facilities due to earthquakes, tornados, or hurricanes, what actions should our firm take?
5. If a new technological advancement makes our new product obsolete sooner than expected, what actions should our firm take?

Too many organizations discard alternative strategies not selected for implementation, when the work devoted to analyzing these options is valuable information. Alternative strategies not selected for implementation can serve as contingency plans, in case the strategy or strategies selected do not work.

When strategy-evaluation activities reveal the need for a major change quickly, an appropriate contingency plan can be executed in a timely way. Contingency plans can promote a strategist's ability to respond quickly to key changes in the internal and external bases of an organization's current strategy. For example, if underlying assumptions about the economy turn out to be wrong and contingency plans are ready, then managers can make appropriate changes promptly.

In some cases, external or internal conditions present unexpected opportunities. When such opportunities occur, contingency plans could allow an organization to capitalize on them quickly. Linneman and Chandran report that contingency planning gives users such as Du Pont, Dow Chemical, Consolidated Foods, and Emerson Electric three major benefits: it permits quick response to change, it prevents panic in crisis situations and it makes managers more adaptable by encouraging them to appreciate just how variable the future can be. They suggest that effective contingency planning involves a seven-step process as follows:

1. Identify both beneficial and unfavorable events that could possibly derail the strategy or strategies.
2. Specify trigger points. Calculate about when contingent events are likely to occur.
3. Assess the impact of each contingent event. Estimate the potential benefit or harm of each contingent event.
4. Develop contingency plans. Be sure that contingency plans are compatible with current strategy and are economically feasible.
5. Assess the counterimpact of each contingency plan. That is, estimate how much each contingency plan will capitalize on or cancel out its associated contingent event. Doing this will quantify the potential value of each contingency plan.
6. Determine early warning signals for key contingent events. Monitor the early warning signals.
7. For contingent events with reliable early warning signals, develop advance action plans to take advantage of the available lead time.[18]

A frequently used tool in strategy evaluation is the audit. *Auditing* is defined by the American Accounting Association (AAA) as "a systematic process of objectively obtaining and evaluating evidence regarding assertions about economic actions and events to ascertain the degree of correspondence between those assertions and established criteria, and communicating the results to interested users."[19] People who perform audits can be divided into three groups: independent auditors, government auditors, and internal auditors. Independent auditors basically are certified public accountants (CPAs) who provide their services to organizations for a fee; they examine the financial statements of an organization to determine whether they have been prepared according to generally accepted accounting principles (GAAP) and whether they fairly represent the activities of the firm. Independent auditors use a set of standards called generally accepted auditing standards (GAAS). Public accounting firms often have a consulting arm that provides strategy-evaluation services.

Two government agencies, the General Accounting Office (GAO) and the Internal Revenue Service (IRS), employ government auditors responsible for making sure that organizations comply with federal laws, statutes, and policies. GAO and IRS auditors can audit any public or private organization. The third group of auditors are employees within an organization who are responsible for safeguarding company assets, for assessing the efficiency of company operations, and for ensuring that generally accepted business procedures are practiced. To evaluate the effectiveness of an organization's strategic-management system, internal auditors often seek answers to the questions posed in Table 9–4. Aaron Kelly developed the Planning Process Audit (PPA) presented in Table 9–5.

TABLE 9-4   Key Strategy-evaluation Questions

1. Do you feel that the strategic-management system exists to provide service to you in your day-to-day work? How has it helped you in this respect?

2. Has the strategic-management system provided the service that you feel was promised at the start of its design and implementation? In which areas has it failed and exceeded, in your opinion?

3. Do you consider that the strategic-management system has been implemented with due regard to costs and benefits? Are there any areas in which you consider the costs to be excessive?

4. Do you feel comfortable using the system? Could more attention have been paid to matching the output of the system to your needs and, if so, in what areas?

5. Is the system flexible enough in your opinion? If not, where should changes be made?

6. Do you still keep a personal store of information in a notebook or elsewhere? If so, will you share that information with the system? Do you see any benefits in so doing?

7. Is the strategic-management system still evolving? Can you influence this evolution and, if not, why not?

8. Does the system provide timely, relevant, and accurate information? Are there any areas of deficiency ?

9. Do you think that the strategic-management system makes too much use of complex procedures and models? Can you suggest areas in which less complicated techniques might be used to advantage?

10. Do you consider that there has been sufficient attention paid to the confidentiality and security of the information in the system? Can you suggest areas for improvement of these aspects of its operation?

Source: K. J. Radford, *Information Systems for Strategic Decision*. © 1978: 220–21. Reprinted by permission of Prentice-Hall, Inc., Englewood Cliffs, N.J. Also, Lloyd Byars, *Strategic Management* (New York: Harper & Row, 1984), 237.

TABLE 9-5   The Planning Process Audit

1. To what extent do you feel top management has been committed to the pursuit of stated corporate strategy?
2. To what extent do you feel committed to the pursuit of stated corporate strategy?
3. Has top management's decision making been consistent with stated corporate strategy?
4. Has decision making been more or less centralized than anticipated?
5. Do you feel you have received sufficient resource support (financial and human) to pursue your stated plans?
6. Do everyday, operational plans seem to support the overall corporate strategy?
7. How would you rate the extent and quality of the coordination of plans among functional areas/departments/divisions?
8. How would you rate the extent and quality of the communication of plans to lower organizational levels?
9. Does the reward system (pay, promotions, etc.) seem to be tied to your planning efforts?
10. Do the written plans seem to adequately represent the actual goals toward which managers seem to be working?
11. How complex is the present planning process?
12. How formal is the present planning process?
13. Do you feel you have the right types and amounts of external information to fulfill your planning responsibilities?
14. Do you feel you have the right types and amounts of internal information to fulfill your planning responsibilities? If not, what other internal information do you feel you need?
15. Would any other training help you do a better job of planning? If yes, what other specific training would help?
16. What are the major problems of the current planning system?
17. How might the planning process be improved upon?

Source: C. Aaron Kelly, "Auditing the Planning Process," *Managerial Planning* 32, no. 4 (January–February 1984): 13. Used with permission.

The Environmental Audit. For an increasing number of firms, overseeing environmental affairs is no longer a technical function performed by specialists; it rather has become an important strategic-management concern. Product design, manufacturing, transportation, customer use, packaging, product disposal, and corporate rewards and sanctions should reflect environmental considerations. Firms that effectively manage environmental affairs are benefiting from constructive relations with employees, consumers, suppliers, and distributors.

In a recent article, Shimell emphasizes the need for organizations to conduct environmental audits of their operations and to develop a Corporate Environmental Policy (CEP).[20] Shimell contends that an environmental audit should be as rigorous as a financial audit and should include training workshops in which staff can help design and implement the policy. The CEP should be budgeted and requisite funds allocated to ensure that it is not a public relations facade. A Statement of Environmental Policy should be published periodically to inform shareholders and the public of environmental actions taken by the firm.

Instituting an environmental audit can include moving environmental affairs from the staff side of the organization to the line side.[21] Some firms are also introducing environmental criteria and objectives in their performance appraisal instruments and systems. Conoco, for example, ties compensation of all its top managers to environmental action plans. Occidental Chemical includes environmental responsibilities in all its job descriptions for positions.

The usefulness of computers in facilitating strategy evaluation cannot be overestimated. When properly designed, installed, and operated, a computer network can efficiently acquire information promptly and accurately. Computers can allow diverse strategy-evaluation reports to be generated for different levels and types of managers. For example, strategists will want reports concerned with whether the mission, objectives, and strategies of the enterprise are being achieved. Middle managers could require strategy-implementation information, such as whether construction of a new facility is on schedule or a product's development is proceeding as expected. Lower-level managers could need evaluation reports that focus on operational concerns such as absenteeism and turnover rates, productivity rates, and the number and nature of grievances. Computers are being used more and more to integrate reports and enhance strategy evaluation at all levels in organizations.

For over a decade, we have been reading about the senior executive "war room" and what more recently has been termed "the office of the future," a room containing a number of computer terminals with graphic displays. There the chief executive officer of an organization spends most of the day monitoring the firm's internal and external condition and formulating, implementing, and evaluating strategies. The corporate war room may never become a reality, but computers are becoming an integral part of strategic-management systems. Computers now offer strategists integration, uniformity, analysis, and economy in evaluating strategic-management activities.

Business today has become so competitive that strategists are being forced to extend planning horizons and to make decisions under greater and greater degrees of uncertainty. As a result, more information has to be obtained and assimilated to formulate, implement, and evaluate strategic decisions. In any competitive situation, the side with the best intelligence (information) usually wins; computers enable managers to evaluate vast amounts of information quickly and accurately. Xerox president Paul Allaire and Paul Lego, chairman of Westinghouse, are examples of top executives who use a personal computer daily to make faster and better decisions.

A limitation of computer-based systems to evaluate and monitor strategy execution is that personal values, attitudes, morals, preferences, politics, personalities, and emotions are not programmable. This limitation accents the need to view computers as tools, rather than as actual decision-making devices. Computers can significantly enhance the process of effectively integrating intuition and analysis in strategy evaluation. The General Accounting Office of the United States Government offers the following conclusions regarding the appropriate role of computers in strategy evaluation:

> The aim is to enhance and extend judgment. Computers should be looked upon not as a provider of solutions, but rather as a framework which permits science and judgment to be brought together and made explicit. It is the explicitness of this structure, the decision-maker's ability to probe, modify, and examine "What if?" alternatives, that is of value in extending judgment.[22]

Failing to follow certain guidelines in conducting strategic management can foster criticisms of the process and create problems for the organization. An integral part of strategy evaluation must be to evaluate the quality of the strategic-management process.[23] Issues such as "Is strategic management in our firm a people process or paper process?" should be addressed.

> Even the most technically perfect strategic plan will serve little purpose if it is not implemented. Many organizations tend to spend an inordinate amount of time, money, and effort on developing the strategic plan, treating the means and circumstances under which it will be implemented as afterthoughts! Change comes through implementation and evaluation, not through the plan. A technically imperfect plan that is implemented well will achieve more than the perfect plan that never gets off the paper on which it is typed.[24]

Strategic management must not become a self-perpetuating bureaucratic mechanism. Rather, it must be a self-reflective learning process that familiarizes managers and employees in the organization with key strategic issues and feasible alternatives for resolving those issues. Strategic management must not become ritualistic, stilted, orchestrated, or too formal, predictable, and rigid. Words supported by numbers, rather than numbers supported by words, should represent the medium for explaining strategic issues and organizational responses. A key role of strategists is to facilitate continuous organizational learning and change. Robert Waterman emphasizes this, saying:

> Successful companies know how to keep things moving. If they share a habit pattern, it's the habit of habit breaking. Sometimes they seem to like change for its own sake. IBM's chief executive, John Akers, says "IBM never reorganizes except for a good business reason, but if they haven't reorganized in a while, that's a good business reason." Successful companies are deliberate bureaucracy-busters. They delight in smashing pettifogging encumbrances that Harry Quadracci calls "playing office."[25]

R.T. Lenz offers some important guidelines for effective strategic management:

> Keep the strategic-management process as simple and non-routine as possible. Eliminate jargon and arcane planning language. Remember, strategic management is a process for fostering learning and action, not merely a formal system for control. To avoid routinized behavior, vary assignments, team membership, meeting formats, and the planning calendar. The process should not be totally predictable, and settings must be changed to stimulate creativity. Emphasize word-oriented plans with numbers as back-up material. If managers cannot express their strategy in a paragraph or so, they either do not have one or do not understand it. Stimulate thinking and action that challenge the assumptions underlying current corporate strategy. Welcome bad news. If strategy is not working, managers desperately need to know it. Further, no pertinent information should be classified as inadmissable merely because it cannot be quantified. Build a corporate culture in which the role of strategic management and its essential purposes are understood. Do not permit "technicians" to co-opt the process. It is ultimately a process for learning and action. Speak of it in these terms. Attend to psychological, social, and political dimensions, as well as the information infrastructure and administrative procedures supporting it.[26]

An important guideline for effective strategic management is open-mindedness. A willingness and eagerness to consider new information, new viewpoints, new ideas, and new possibilities is essential; all organizational members must share a spirit of inquiry and learning. Strategists such as chief executive officers, presidents, owners of small businesses, and heads of government agencies must commit themselves to listen to and understand managers' positions well enough to be able to restate those positions to the managers' satisfaction. In addition, managers and employees throughout the firm should be able to describe the strategists' positions to the satisfaction of the strategists. This degree of discipline will promote understanding and learning.

No organization has unlimited resources. No firm can take on an unlimited amount of debt or issue an unlimited amount of stock to raise capital. Therefore, no organization can pursue all the strategies that potentially could benefit the firm. Strategic decisions thus always have to be made to eliminate some courses of action and to allocate organizational resources among others. Most organizations can afford to pursue only a few corporate-level strategies at any given time. It is a critical mistake for managers to pursue too many strategies at the same time, thereby spreading the firm's resources so thin that all strategies are jeopardized. Joseph Charyk, CEO of The Communication Satellite Corporation (COMSAT), said, "We have to face the cold fact that Comsat may not be able to do all it wants. We must make hard choices on which ventures to keep and which to fold."[27]

Strategic decisions require trade-offs such a long-range versus short-range considerations or maximizing profits versus increasing shareholders' wealth. There are ethics issues too. Strategy trade-offs require subjective judgments and preferences. In many cases, a lack of objectivity in formulating strategy results in a loss of competitive posture and profitability. Most organizations today recognize that strategic-management concepts and techniques can enhance the effectiveness of decisions. Subjective factors such as attitudes toward risk, concern for social responsibility, and organizational culture will always affect strategy-formulation decisions, but organizations need to be as objective as possible in considering qualitative factors.

CONCLUSION

This chapter presents a strategy-evaluation framework that can facilitate accomplishment of annual and long-term objectives. Effective strategy evaluation allows an organization to capitalize on internal strengths as they develop, to exploit external opportunities as they emerge, to recognize and defend against threats, and to improve internal weaknesses before they become detrimental.

Strategists in successful organizations take the time to formulate, implement, and then evaluate strategies deliberately and systematically. Good strategists move their organization forward with purpose and direction, continually evaluating and improving the firm's external and internal strategic position. Strategy evaluation allows an organization to shape its own future rather than allowing it to be constantly shaped by remote forces that have little or no vested interest in the well-being of the enterprise.

Although not a guarantee for success, strategic management is allowing more and more organizations to make effective long-term decisions, to execute those decisions more efficiently, and to take corrective actions as needed to assure success. Computers are being used increasingly to coordinate strategic-management activities and to assure that decisions are based on good information. A key to effective strategy evaluation and to successful strategic management is an integration of intuition and analysis.

A potentially fatal problem is the tendency for analytical and intuitive issues to polarize. This polarization leads to strategy evaluation that is dominated by either analysis or intuition, or to strategy evaluation that is discontinuous, with a lack of coordination among analytical and intuitive issues.[28]

Strategists in successful organizations realize that strategic management is first and foremost a people process. It is an excellent vehicle for fostering organizational communication. People are what make the difference in organizations.

The real key to effective strategic management is to accept the premise that the planning process is more important than the written plan, that the manager is continuously planning and does not stop planning when the written plan is finished. The written plan is only a snapshot as of the moment it is approved. If the manager is not planning on a continuous basis—planning, measuring, and revising—the written plan can become obsolete the day it is finished. This obsolescence becomes more of a certainty as the increasingly rapid rate of change makes the business environment more uncertain.[29]

KEY TERMS AND CONCEPTS

Advantage

Auditing

Consistency

Consonance

Contingency Planning

Feasibility

Future Shock

Management by Wandering Around

Measuring Organizational Performance

Planning Process Audit (PPA)

Reviewing the Underlying Bases of an Organization's Strategy

Revised IFE Matrix

Revised EFE Matrix

Taking Corrective Actions

ISSUES FOR REVIEW AND DISCUSSION

1. Why has strategy evaluation become so important in business today?

2. BellSouth Services is considering putting divisional EFE and IFE matrices on line for continual updating. How would this affect strategy evaluation?

3. What types of quantitative and qualitative criteria do you think David Glass, CEO of Wal-Mart, uses to evaluate the company's strategy?

4. As owner of a local, independent supermarket, explain how you would evaluate the firm's strategy.

5. Under what conditions are corrective actions not required in the strategy-evaluation process?

6. Identify types of organizations that may need to evaluate strategy more frequently than others. Justify your choices.

7. As executive director of the state forestry commission, in what way and how frequently would you evaluate the organization's strategies?

8. Identify some key financial ratios that would be important in evaluating a bank's strategy.

9. As owner of a chain of hardware stores, describe how you would approach contingency planning.

10. Strategy evaluation allows an organization to take a proactive stance toward shaping its own future. Discuss the meaning of this statement.

11. Select an article listed in the suggested readings for this chapter. Give a 5-minute oral report to the class summarizing the article and your thoughts on the particular topic.

12. Identify guidelines that you think are most important for using strategic management effectively in organizations. Justify your answer.

1. Cortlandt Camman and David Nadler, "Fit Control Systems to Your Managerial Style," *Harvard Business Review* 54, no. 1 (January–February 1976):65.

2. Gene Dalton and Paul Lawrence, *Motivation and Control in Organizations* (Homewood, Ill.: Richard D. Irwin, 1971), 5.

3. Dale McConkey, "Planning in a Changing Environment," *Business Horizons* (September–October 1988): 64.

4. Dale Zand, "Reviewing the Policy Process," *California Management Review* 21, no. 1 (Fall 1978): 37.

5. Eccles. 3: 1–8.

6. W. Lindsay and L. Rue, "Impact of the Organization Environment on the Long-Range Planning Process: A Contingency View," *Academy of Management Journal* 23, no. 3 (September 1980): 402.

7. George Steiner, *Strategic Planning: What Every Manager Must Know* (New York: The Free Press, 1979), 269.

8. Seymour Tilles, "How to Evaluate Corporate Strategy," *Harvard Business Review* 41 (July–August 1963): 111–121.

9. Claude George, Jr., *The History of Management Thought* (Englewood Cliffs, N.J.: Prentice-Hall, 1968), 165–166.

10. John Brown and Neil Agnew, "Corporate Agility," *Business Horizons* 25, no. 2 (March–April 1982): 29.

11. M. Erez and F. Kanfer, "The Role of Goal Acceptance in Goal Setting and Task Performance," *Academy of Management Review* 8, no. 3 (July 1983): 457.

12. D. Hussey and M. Langham, *Corporate Planning: The Human Factor* (Oxford, England: Pergamon Press, 1979), 138.

13. Carter Bayles, "Strategic Control: The President's Paradox," *Business Horizons* 20, no. 4 (August 1977):18.

14. Tricia Welsh, "Best and Worst Corporate Reputations," *Fortune* (February 7, 1994): 58–95.

15. George Rice, Jr., "Strategic Decision Making in Small Business," *Journal of General Management* 9, no. 1 (Autumn 1983): 64.

16. Timothy Brady, "Six Step Method to Long Range Planning for Non-profit Organizations," *Managerial Planning* 32, no. 4 (January–February 1984): 49.

17. Robert Waterman, Jr., "How the Best Get Better," *Business Week* September 14, 1987): 105.

18. Robert Linneman and Rajan Chandran, "Contingency Planning: A Key to Swift Managerial Action in the Uncertain Tomorrow," *Managerial Planning* 29, no. 4 (January–February 1981): 23–27.

19. American Accounting Association, *Report of Committee on Basic Auditing Concepts* (1971), 15–74.

20. Pamela Shimell, "Corporate Environmental Policy in Practice," *Long Range Planning* 24, no. 3 (June 1991): 10.

21. Todd Hooper and Bart Rocca, "Environmental Affairs: Now on the Strategic Agenda," *The Journal of* (June *Business Strategy* (May/June 1991): 28.

22. GAO *Report* PAD–80–21, 17.

23. Bernard Reimann, "Getting Value from Strategic Planning," *Planning Review* 17, no. 3 (May/June): 9.

24. McConkey, 66.

25. Robert H. Waterman, Jr., *The Renewal Factor: How the Best Get and Keep the Competitive Edge* (New York: Bantam, 1987).

26. R.T. Lenz, "Managing the Evolution of the Strategic Planning Process," *Business Horizons* 30, no. 1 (January–February 1987): 39.

27. "COMSAT: Caught in a Cash Crunch that May Ground Some Ventures," *Business Week* (May 21, 1984): 86–87.

28. Michael McGinnis, "The Key to Strategic Planning: Integrating Analysis and Intuition," *Sloan Management Review* 26, no. 1 (Fall 1984): 49.

29. McConkey, 72.

CURRENT READINGS

Bauerschmidt, A. "A Comment on Gilbert's , The Twilight of Corporate Strategy." *Strategic Management Journal* 14, no. 5 (July 1993): 397–409.

Bowman, Edward H., and Dileep Hurry. "Strategy Through the Option Lens: An Integrated View of Resource Investments and the Incremental-Choice Process." *Academy of Management Review* 18, no. 4 (October 1993): 760–782.

Crant, J. Michael, and Thomas S. Bateman. "Assignment of Credit and Blame for Performance Outcomes." *Academy of Management Journal* 36, no. 1 (February 1993): 7–27.

Golden, Brian R. "The Past Is the Past—or Is It? The Use of Retrospective Accounts as Indicators of Past Strategy." *Academy of Management Journal* 35, no. (October 1992): 848–860.

Greenwood, Royston, and C.R. Hinnings. "Understanding Strategic Change: The Contribution of Archetypes." *Academy of Management Journal* 36, no. 5 (October 1993): 1052–1081.

Haveman, Heather A. "Ghosts of Managers Past: Managerial Succession and Organizational Mortality." *Academy of Management Journal* 36, no. 4 (August 1993): 864–881.

Mezias, S. J., and M. A. Glynn. "The Three Faces of Corporate Renewal: Institution, Revolution, and Evolution." *Strategic Management Journal* 14, no. 2 (February 1993): 77–102.

EXPERIENTIAL EXERCISES

PREPARING A STRATEGY-EVALUATION REPORT FOR HERSHEY FOODS

PURPOSE

This exercise can give you experience locating strategy-evaluation information in your college library. Published sources of information can significantly enhance the strategy-evaluation process. Performance information on competitors, for example, can help put into perspective a firm's own performance.

INSTRUCTIONS

Step 1 Use *F & S Index of Corporations and Industries, Business Periodicals Index,* and the *Wall Street Journal Index* in your college library to locate strategy-evaluation information on Hershey, Mars, and Nestlé. List five to ten articles written in the last 6 months that discuss these firms or the confectionery industry.

Step 2 Summarize your research findings by preparing a strategy-evaluation report for your professor. Include in your report a summary of Hershey's strategies and performance in 1994 and a summary of your conclusions regarding the effectiveness of Hershey's strategies.

Step 3 Based on your analysis, do you feel Hershey is pursuing effective strategies? What recommendations would you offer Richard Zimmerman, Hershey's chief executive officer?

EVALUATING MY UNIVERSITY'S STRATEGIES

PURPOSE

An important part of evaluating strategies is determining the nature and extent of changes in an organization's external opportunities/threats and internal strengths/weaknesses. Changes in these underlying critical success factors can indicate a need to change or modify the firm's strategies.

INSTRUCTIONS

As a class, discuss positive and negative changes in your university's external and internal factors during your college career. Begin by listing on the board new or emerging opportunities and threats. Then identify strengths and weaknesses that have changed significantly during your college career. In light of the external and internal changes identified, discuss whether your university's strategies need modifying. Are there any new strategies that you would recommend? Make a list to recommend to your department chairperson, dean, or chancellor.

WHO PREPARES AN ENVIRONMENTAL AUDIT?

PURPOSE

The purpose of this activity is to determine the nature and prevalence of environmental audits among companies in your state.

INSTRUCTIONS

Contact by phone at least five different plant managers or owners of large businesses in your area. Seek answers to the questions listed below. Present your findings in a written report to your professor.

1. Does your company conduct an environmental audit? If yes, please describe the nature and scope of the audit.
2. Are environmental criteria included in the performance evaluation of managers? If yes, please specify the criteria.
3. Are environmental affairs more a technical function or management function in your company?
4. Does your firm offer any environmental workshops for employees? If yes, please describe them.

PART · 5

Global Issues in Strategic Management

Chapter 10

INTERNATIONAL STRATEGIC MANAGEMENT

OBJECTIVES   After studying this chapter, you should be able to:

■ Describe the effects of a world economy and global competitors on strategic management.

■ Discuss the nature and strategic implications of diverse cultures around the world.

■ Discuss ramifications of the North American Free Trade Agreement (NAFTA).

■ Discuss changes in Japan as they affect strategy decisions.

■ Discuss changes in Mexico as they affect strategy decisions.

■ Discuss changes in Russia as they affect strategy decisions.

■ Discuss changes in Europe as they affect strategy decisions.

■ Provide guidelines for firms interested in initiating, continuing, or expanding international operations.

This chapter focuses on international strategic-management issues. Each day more and more U.S. businesses enter global markets and more and more rival foreign firms enter U.S. markets. One-third of all college students in the United States who receive advanced degrees in science, math, and engineering are foreign citizens.

> Recently, I heard a story about George Bush being in a coma for three years and waking to find Dan Quayle standing at his bedside. Upon seeing the Vice President, the President began asking questions. "How long have I been asleep?" The President then inquires about the state of the U.S. economy. To his surprise, Quayle tells him that the budget and the trade deficits have been reduced to zero. Then, the President asks about inflation, which he figures must be at an all-time high. Again, to his surprise, Quayle says that inflation is not a problem. Having his doubts, the President asks for specifics. "How much," he asks "does a first class stamp cost?" "Very reasonable," Quayle responds, "only 30 Yen."[1]

THE NATURE OF GLOBAL COMPETITION

For centuries before Columbus discovered America and surely for centuries to come, businesses have searched and will continue to search for new opportunities beyond their national boundaries. There has never been a more internationalized and economically competitive society than today's. Some American industries, such as textiles, semiconductors, and consumer electronics, are in complete disarray as a result of the international challenge.

Organizations that conduct business operations across national borders are called international firms or multinational corporations (MNCs). The term "parent company" refers to a firm investing in international operations, while "host country" is the country where that business is conducted. As illustrated in Figure 10–1, the strategic-management process is conceptually the same for multinational firms as for purely domestic firms; however, the process is more complex for international firms due to the presence of more variables and relationships. Social, cultural, demographic, environmental, political, governmental, legal, technological, and competitive opportunities and threats that face a multinational corporation are almost limitless, and the number and complexity of these factors increase dramatically with the number of products produced and the number of geographic areas served.

More time and effort are required to identify and evaluate external trends and events in multinational corporations. Geographical distance, cultural and national differences, and variations in business practices often make communication between domestic headquarters and overseas operations difficult. Strategy implementation can be more difficult because different cultures have different norms, values, and work ethics.

The fall of communism and advancements in telecommunications are drawing countries, cultures, and organizations worldwide closer together. Foreign revenue as a percent of total company revenues already exceeds 50 percent in hundreds of U.S. firms, including Exxon, Gillette, Dow Chemical, Citicorp, Colgate-Palmolive, and Texaco. Joint ventures and partnerships between domestic and foreign firms are becoming the rule rather than the exception!

World trade centers are proliferating in the United States and abroad because of growing interest in foreign trade. Trade centers were recently built in Cedar Rapids, Iowa; Santa Ana, California; Hartford, Connecticut; Pomona, California; Long Beach, California; St. Paul, Minnesota; Toledo, Ohio; and Wichita, Kansas. These

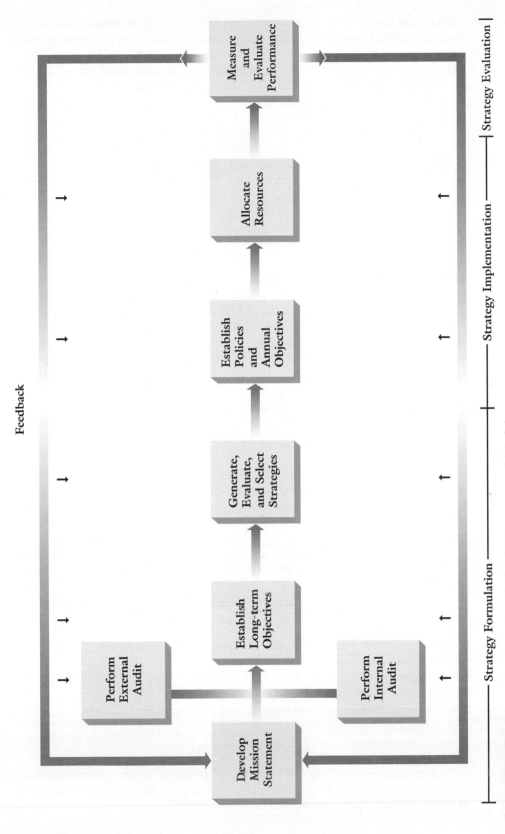

FIGURE 10-1 A Comprehensive Strategic-Management Model

new world trade centers offer many specialized services, such as assisting small businesses in exporting or importing, and housing foreign banks, export firms, and law offices.

Fully 95 percent of the world's population lives outside the United States, and this group is growing 70 percent faster than the American population! The lineup of competitors in virtually all industries today is global. Five of the world's ten largest public companies (in market value) are based in Japan, including Nippon Telegraph & Telephone, the largest corporation in the world. Global competition is more than a management fad. General Motors, Ford, and Chrysler compete with Toyota, Daimler Benz, and Hyundai. General Electric and Westinghouse battle Siemens and Mitsubishi. Caterpillar and Deere compete with Komatsu. Goodyear battles Michelin, Bridgestone, and Pirelli. Boeing and McDonnell Douglas compete with Airbus. Only a few U.S. industries, such as furniture, printing, retailing, consumer packaged goods, and retail banking, are not yet greatly challenged by foreign competitors. But many products and components in these industries too are now manufactured in foreign countries.

International operations can be as simple as exporting a product to a single foreign country, or as complex as operating manufacturing, distribution, and marketing facilities in many countries. More and more U.S. firms are acquiring foreign companies and forming joint ventures with foreign firms, and more and more foreign firms are acquiring U.S. companies and forming joint ventures with U.S. firms. This trend is accelerating dramatically. AT&T's Chief Executive Robert Allen says: "The phrase 'global markets' is not empty rhetoric. Foreign competitors are here. And we must be there." Exporting, however, has seemingly never come naturally to U.S. companies. The United States' exports account for only 5.4 percent of GNP, as compared to 26 percent in Germany, 25 percent in Canada, and 10.5 percent in Japan. Many U.S. firms have been spoiled by the breadth and plenty of home markets and remain ignorant of foreign languages and culture.

Advantages and Disadvantages of International Operations. Firms have numerous reasons to formulate and implement strategies that initiate, continue, or expand involvement in business operations across national borders. Perhaps the greatest advantage is that firms can gain new customers for their products and services, thus increasing revenues. Growth in revenues and profits is a common organizational objective and often an expectation of shareholders, because it is a measure of organizational success.

In addition to seeking growth, firms have the following potentially advantageous reasons to initiate, continue, and expand international operations:

1. Foreign operations can absorb excess capacity, reduce unit costs, and spread economic risks over a wider number of markets.
2. Foreign operations can allow firms to establish low-cost production facilities in locations close to raw materials and/or cheap labor.
3. Competitors in foreign markets may not exist, or competition may be less intense than in domestic markets.
4. Foreign operations may result in reduced tariffs, lower taxes, and more favorable political treatment.
5. Joint ventures can enable firms to learn the technology, culture, and business practices of other people and to make contacts with potential customers, suppliers, creditors, and distributors in foreign countries.

There are also numerous potential disadvantages of initiating, continuing, or expanding business across national borders. One risk is that foreign operations could be seized by nationalistic factions, which occurred in Kuwait during the Gulf War. Other disadvantages include the following:

1. Firms confront different and often little-understood social, cultural, demographic, environmental, political, governmental, legal, technological, economic, and competitive forces when doing business internationally. These forces can make communication difficult between the parent firm and subsidiaries.
2. Weaknesses of competitors in foreign lands are often overestimated, and strengths are often underestimated. Keeping informed about the number and nature of competitors is more difficult when doing business internationally.
3. Language, culture, and value systems differ among countries, and this can create barriers to communication and problems managing people.
4. Gaining an understanding of regional organizations such as the European Economic Community, the Latin American Free Trade Area, the International Bank for Reconstruction and Development, and the International Finance Corporation is difficult and often required in doing business internationally.
5. Dealing with two or more monetary systems can complicate international business operations.

CULTURES AROUND THE WORLD

To successfully compete in world markets, U.S. managers must obtain a better knowledge of historical, cultural, and religious forces that motivate and drive people in other countries. In Japan, for example, business relations operate within the context of "Wa," which stresses group harmony and social cohesion. In China, business behavior revolves around "Guanxi," or personal relations. In Korea, activities involve concern for "Inhwa," or harmony based on respect of hierarchical relationships, including obedience to authority.[2]

In Europe, it is generally true that the farther north on the continent, the more participatory the management style. Most European workers are unionized and enjoy more frequent vacations and holidays than U.S. workers. A 90-minute lunch break and 20-minute morning and afternoon breaks are common in European firms. Guaranteed permanent employment is commonly a part of employment contracts in Europe. In socialist countries like France, Belgium, and the United Kingdom, the only ground for immediate dismissal from work is a criminal offense. A six-month trial period at the beginning of employment is usually part of the contract with a European firm. Many Europeans resent pay-for-performance, commission salaries, and "objective" measurement and reward systems. This is true especially of workers in southern Europe. Many Europeans also find the notion of "team spirit" difficult to grasp, since the unionized environment has dichotomized worker-management relations throughout Europe.

A weakness that U.S. firms have in competing with Pacific Rim firms is a lack of understanding of Far Eastern cultures, including how Asians think and behave. Spoken Chinese, for example, has more in common with spoken English than with spoken Japanese or Korean. Managers around the world face the responsibility of having to exert authority, while at the same time trying to be liked by subordinates. U.S. managers consistently put more weight on being friendly and liked, whereas Asian and European managers exercise authority often without this concern. Americans tend to use first names instantly in business dealings with foreigners, but foreigners find this presumptuous. In Japan, for example, first names are used only among family members and intimate friends; even longtime business associates and co-workers shy away from the use of first names.[3]

American Versus Foreign Cultures. U.S. managers have a low tolerance for silence, whereas Asian managers view extended periods of silence as important for organizing and evaluating one's thoughts. U.S. managers are much more action-oriented than their counterparts around the world; they rush to appointments, conferences, and meetings, and then feel the day has been productive. But for foreign managers, resting, listening, meditating, and thinking is considered productive. Sitting through a conference without talking is unproductive in the United States, but it is viewed as positive in Japan if one's silence helps preserve unity.

U.S. managers also put greater emphasis on short-term results than foreign managers. In marketing, for example, Japanese managers strive to achieve "everlasting customers," whereas many Americans strive to make a one-time sale. Marketing managers in Japan see making a sale as the beginning, not the end, of the selling process. This is an important distinction. Japanese managers often criticize U.S. managers for worrying more about shareholders, whom they do not know, than employees, whom they do know. Americans refer to "hourly employees," whereas Japanese refer to "lifetime employees."

Rose Knotts recently summarized some important cultural differences between U.S. and foreign managers:[4]

1. Americans place an exceptionally high priority on time, viewing time as an asset. Many foreigners place more worth on relationships. This difference results in foreign managers often viewing U.S. managers as "more interested in business than people."

2. Personal touching and distance norms differ around the world. Americans generally stand about 3 feet from each other in carrying on business conversations, but Arabs and Africans stand about 1 foot apart. Touching another person with the left hand in business dealings is taboo in some countries. American managers need to learn the personal space rules of foreign managers with whom they interact in business.

3. People in some cultures do not place the same significance on material wealth as American managers often do. Lists of the "largest corporations" and "highest paid" executives abound in the United States. "More is better" and "bigger is better" in the United States, but not everywhere. This can be a consideration in trying to motivate individuals in other countries.

4. Family roles and relationships vary in different countries. For example, males are valued more than females in some cultures, and peer pressure, work situations, and business interactions reinforce this phenomenon.

5. Language differs dramatically across countries, even countries that speak the same language. Words and expressions commonly used in one country may be greedy or disrespectful in another. For example: "While an American would say that he put some gas in his truck, drove to his girlfriend's apartment, took the elevator to her floor, and rang the doorbell, an Englishman would say that he put some petrol in his lorry, drove to his girlfriend's flat, took the lift to her floor, and then knocked her up."[5]

6. Business and daily life in some societies is governed by religious factors. Prayer times, holidays, daily events, and dietary restrictions, for example, need to be respected by American managers not familiar with these practices in some countries.

7. Time spent with the family and quality of relationships are more important in some cultures than personal achievement and accomplishments, which is espoused by the traditional American manager. For example, where a person is in the hierarchy of a firm's organizational structure, how large the firm is, and where the firm is located are much more important factors to American managers than to many foreign managers.

8. Many cultures around the world value modesty, team spirit, collectivity, and patience much more than competitiveness and individualism, which are so important in America.

9. Punctuality is a valued personal trait when conducting business in America, but it is not revered in many of the world's societies. Eating habits also differ dramatically across cultures. For example, belching is acceptable in many countries as evidence of satisfaction with the food that has been prepared. Chinese cultures consider it good manners to sample a portion of each food served.

10. To prevent social blunders when meeting with managers from other lands, one must learn and respect the rules of etiquette of others. Sitting on a toilet seat is viewed as unsanitary in most countries, but not the United States. Leaving food or drink after dining is considered impolite in some countries. Bowing instead of shaking hands is customary in many countries. Many cultures view Americans as unsanitary for locating toilet and bathing facilities in the same area, while Americans view people of some cultures as unsanitary for not taking a bath or shower every day.

11. Americans often do business with individuals they do not know, but this practice is not accepted in many other cultures. In Mexico and Japan, for example, an amicable relationship is often mandatory before conducting business.

THE GLOBAL CHALLENGE

Foreign competitors are battering U.S. firms in many industries. In its simplest sense, the international challenge faced by U.S. business is twofold: (1) how to gain and maintain exports to other nations and (2) how to defend domestic markets against imported goods. Few companies can afford to ignore the presence of international competition. Firms that seem insulated and comfortable today may be vulnerable tomorrow; for example, foreign banks do not yet compete or operate in most of the United States.

America's economy is becoming much less American. A world economy and monetary system is emerging. Corporations in every corner of the globe are taking advantage of the opportunity to share in the benefits of worldwide economic development. Markets are shifting rapidly and in many cases converging in tastes, trends, and prices. Innovative transport systems are accelerating the transfer of technology, and shifts in the nature and location of production systems are reducing the response time to changing market conditions.

More and more countries around the world are welcoming foreign investment and capital. As a result, labor markets have steadily become more international. East Asian countries have become market leaders in labor-intensive industries, Brazil offers abundant natural resources and rapidly developing markets, and Germany offers skilled labor and technology. The drive to improve the efficiency of global business operations is leading to greater functional specialization. This is not limited to a search for the familiar low-cost labor in Latin America or Asia. Other considerations include the cost of energy, availability of resources, inflation rates, existing tax rates, and the nature of trade regulations. Yang Shangkun insists that China's door is still open to foreign capital and technology, despite the massacre in Tiananmen Square and continued strength of the Communist Party.

The ability to identify and evaluate strategic opportunities and threats in an international environment is a prerequisite competency for strategists. The nuances of competing in international markets are seemingly infinite. Language, culture, politics, attitudes, and economies differ significantly across countries. The availability, depth, and reliability of economic and marketing information in different countries varies extensively, as does industrial structures, business practices, and the number and nature of regional organizations. Differences between domestic and multinational operations that affect strategic management are summarized in Table 10–1.

The Impact of Diverse Industrial Policies. Industrial policies include providing government subsidies, promoting exports, restructuring industries, nationalizing businesses, imposing regulations, changing tax laws, instituting pollution standards, and establishing import quotas. The vicissitudes of foreign affairs make identifying and selecting among alternative strategies more challenging for MNCs than for their domestic counterparts.

> Strategic management has proven to be a valuable tool in the successful firm's repertoire. Firms traveling on the path of international business face more risks than their domestic counterparts, but also may reap greater rewards. Properly done, strategic management offers these firms a map to guide them on their journey through the perilous paths of international business.[6]

Perhaps the greatest threat to domestic firms engaged in international operations is the national and international debt situation. When countries become excessively leveraged, they frequently turn to slashing imports and boosting exports to generate trade surpluses capable of servicing their debt. Faced with these policies, domestic firms producing for export markets can often no longer import essential inputs. When a debtor country is successful in boosting its exports, domestic firms often encounter a protectionist backlash in foreign countries.

Multinational business strategists can contribute to the solution of economic trade problems and improve their firms' competitive positions by maintaining and strengthening communication channels with domestic and foreign governments. Strategists are commonly on the front line of trade and financial crises around the world, so they often have direct knowledge of the gravity and interrelated nature of particular problems. Strategists should relay this knowledge and experience to political leaders. A steady stream of counsel and advice from international business strategists to policymakers and lawmakers is needed.

Strategists in multinational corporations need an understanding of foreign governments' industrial policies. Industrial policies differ from country to country as governments take different actions to develop their own economies. For example, cooperation between business and government in Japan is so good that some experts doubt whether a clear distinction exists there between government and business; some even use the term "Japan, Inc." when referring to the Japanese government and particularly the Ministry for International Trade and Industry (MITI).

Multinational corporations face unique and diverse risks such as expropriation of assets, currency losses through exchange rate fluctuations, unfavorable foreign court interpretations of contracts and agreements, social/political disturbances, import/export restrictions, tariffs, and trade barriers. Strategists in MNCs are often confronted with the need to be globally competitive and nationally responsive at the

TABLE 10-1 Differences Between U.S. and Multinational Operations that Affect Strategic Management.

FACTOR	U.S. OPERATIONS	INTERNATIONAL OPERATIONS
Language	English used almost universally	Local language must be used in many situations
Culture	Relatively homogeneous	Quite diverse, both between countries and within a country
Politics	Stable and relatively unimportant	Often volatile and of decisive importance
Economy	Relatively uniform	Wide variations among countries and between regions within countries
Government interference	Minimal and reasonably predictable	Extensive and subject to rapid change
Labor	Skilled labor available	Skilled labor often scarce, requiring training or redesign of production methods
Financing	Well-developed financial markets	Poorly developed financial markets Capital flows subject to government control
Market research	Data easy to collect	Data difficult and expensive to collect
Advertising	Many media available; few restrictions	Media limited; many restrictions; low literacy rates rule out print media in some countries
Money	U.S. dollar used universally	Must change from one currency to another; changing exchange rates and government restrictions are problems
Transportation/ communication	Among the best in the world	Often inadequate
Control	Always a problem Centralized control will work	A worse problem. Centralized control won't work. Must walk a tightrope between overcentralizing and losing control through too much decentralizing
Contracts	Once signed, are binding on both parties, even if one party makes a bad deal	Can be voided and renegotiated if one party becomes dissatisfied
Labor relations	Collective bargaining; can lay off workers easily	Often cannot lay off workers; may have mandatory worker participation in management; workers may seek change through political process rather than collective bargaining
Trade barriers	Nonexistent	Extensive and very important

Source: R. G. Murdick, R. C. Moor, R. H. Eckhouse, and T. W. Zimmerer, *Business Policy: A Framework for Analysis*, 4th ed. (Columbus, Ohio: Grid Publishing Company, 1984), p. 275.

same time. With the rise in world commerce, government and regulatory bodies are more closely monitoring foreign business practices. The United States Foreign Corrupt Practices Act, for example, defines "corrupt practices" in many areas of business. A sensitive issue is that some MNCs sometimes violate legal and ethical standards of the home country, but not of the host country.

Before entering international markets, firms should scan relevant journals and patent reports, seek the advice of academic and research organizations, participate in international trade fairs, form partnerships, and conduct extensive research to broaden their contacts and diminish the risk of doing business in new markets. Firms can also reduce the risks of doing business internationally by obtaining insurance from the United States government's Overseas Private Investment Corporation (OPIC).

Globalization. Globalization is a process of worldwide integration of strategy formulation, implementation, and evaluation activities.[7] Strategic decisions are made based on their impact upon global profitability of the firm, rather than on just domestic or other individual country considerations. A global strategy seeks to meet the needs of customers worldwide with the highest value at the lowest cost. This may mean locating production in countries with the lowest labor costs or abundant natural resources, locating research and complex engineering where skilled scientists and engineers can be found, and locating marketing activities close to the markets to be served. A global strategy includes designing, producing, and marketing products with global needs in mind, instead of considering individual countries alone. A global strategy integrates actions against competitors into a worldwide plan.

Globalization of industries is occurring for many reasons, including a worldwide trend towards similar consumption patterns, the emergence of global buyers and sellers, and instant transmission of money and information across continents. The European Economic Community (EEC), religions, the Olympics, the World Bank, world trade centers, the Red Cross, environmental conferences, telecommunications, and economic summits all contribute to global interdependencies and the emerging global marketplace.

David Shanks, manager of the Strategic Management Unit of Arthur D. Little, suggests that three major factors are driving many domestic firms into international operations: (1) the maturing economies of industrialized nations, (2) the emergence of new geographic markets and business arenas, and (3) the globalization of financial systems.[8] The typical evolution of a domestic firm into a multinational corporation (MNC) is illustrated in Figure 10–2.

It is clear that different industries become global for different reasons. Convergence of income levels and standardization is what made designer clothing a universal product. The need to amortize massive R & D investments over many markets is a major reason why the aircraft manufacturing industry became global.

FIGURE 10-2 The Typical Evolution of an MNC

| *Begin Export Operations* | *Conduct Licensing Activities* | *Add Foreign Sales Representatives* | *Build Foreign Manufacturing Facilities* | *Establish a Foreign Division of the Firm* | *Establish Several Foreign Business Units* | *An MNC* |

Source: Adapted from C. A. Bartlett, "How Multinational Organizations Evolve." *Journal of Business Strategy* (Summer 1982): 20–32. Also, D. Shanks, "Strategic Planning for Global Competition," *Journal of Business Strategy* (Winter 1985): 83.

Monitoring globalization in one's industry is an important strategic-management activity. Knowing how to use that information for one's competitive advantage is even more important. For example, firms may look around the world for the best technology and select one that has the most promise for the largest number of markets. When firms design a product, they design it to be marketable in as many countries as possible. When firms manufacture a product, they select the lowest cost source, which may be Japan for semiconductors, Sri Lanka for textiles, Malaysia for simple electronics, and Europe for precision machinery. MNCs design manufacturing systems to accommodate world markets. One of the riskiest strategies for a domestic firm is to remain solely a domestic firm in an industry that is rapidly becoming global.

MEXICO

The United States and Mexico share a 2,000-mile-long border that today is bristling with business in response to passage of the North American Free Trade Agreement (NAFTA). Mexico has 92.5 million people hungry for U.S. products and willing to work hard for low wages. More than 80 percent of Mexico's population is under age forty and only 3 percent of all Mexicans have a college degree.

NAFTA allows goods to flow across the U.S.–Mexico border free of duties, just as the U.S.–Canada Free Trade Agreement did in 1989. Many analysts see NAFTA as the first step towards a Western Hemisphere-wide free trade agreement, whereby all of North America, Central America, South America, and the Caribbean would join into a single gigantic free trading zone that could dominate global commerce into the 21st century. Major obstacles still block a hemisphere agreement.

Scores of new Mexican businesses daily are negotiating licensing rights with U.S. companies, as firms on both sides of the border strive to competitively preempt late comers into the expected new market. U.S. exports to Mexico exceed $50 billion annually. Behind Canada and Japan, Mexico is the United States' third-largest export market. Mexican tariffs currently include a 15 to 20 percent levy on consumer goods, a 5 to 10 percent levy on raw materials, a 10 to 15 percent levy on machinery, and a 5 percent levy on most other items. NAFTA reduces if not eliminates these tariffs.

Under provisions of NAFTA, Mexico's comparative advantages of cheaper labor and a more favorable climate enable it to capture large market share in fresh winter vegetables and fruits. The Mexican share of the fresh tomato market is increasing, for example, from 40 percent to 80 percent in a free-trade environment. NAFTA allows lower food prices for U.S. consumers and opens new markets for agricultural machinery and technology. It also reduces the illegal migration problem that currently exists along the border. Mexico's President Salinas says, "The key question is, Where do you want Mexicans to work, in Mexico or in the United States? I would rather export goods than labor."

The big winners are firms manufacturing high-tech products such as autos, computers and telecommunications equipment. American banks, brokerage houses and other financial service firms also benefit as barriers to their entry into the Mexican market are loosened. Apparel manufacturers, shoe companies and other low-tech industries, however, are hurt by increased competition from cheaper Mexican products. U.S. citrus and vegetable farmers also fear increased competition from Mexico. The agreement brings Mexico into the free trade zone between the United States and Canada. It removes tariffs and other barriers to the movement of goods, services, and investment among the three nations over 15 years. The first day the agreement went into effect, tariffs ended on about half of the more than 9,000 products covered.

Tariffs on another 15 percent of the goods will end in five years, and the rest of the products will be duty-free at the end of 15 years. Free trade zones benefit consumers by lowering prices. Manufacturers and workers benefit from expanded markets for their products.

Some groups in the United States opposed NAFTA, including environmentalists who fear that increased industrial activity in Mexico—where pollution-control standards are not as strict as those in the United States—will result in air and water pollution. Some food, agricultural, and manufacturing firms also opposed NAFTA, due to fear that they could not compete with Mexican companies that have access to an abundance of lower-cost labor.

Economic and Political Reforms. Since President Salinas began liberalizing Mexico's economy in 1988, Mexico's federal budget deficit has fallen from about 16 percent of gross national product to 4.3 percent, and inflation has fallen from above 180 percent in 1988 to 12 percent. The maximum tariff on imported goods has been cut from 100 percent in 1982 to 20 percent. Mexico's economy is now growing faster than its population, and more than 75 percent of government industries in Mexico have been privatized.

Mexican minimum wage is 80 cents per hour or $100 monthly. Easier access to Mexico's abundant, low-cost, high-quality labor has spurred U.S. firms to locate manufacturing facilities in Mexico. Jerry Perlman, president and chairman of Zenith Electronics Corporation, says, "If we didn't have support operations in Mexico, our annual operating costs would be $350 million to $400 million higher, and we'd be out of business." Despite low wages in Mexico, Mexicans are acquiring a global reputation for quality workmanship, as evidenced by Ford Motor Company's $1 billion Hermosillo plant, which recently tied the Daimler-Benz plant in Germany for the auto industry's first-place award for lowest production defects.

Mexico is committed to "growing clean" as evidenced by the Salinas government's increasing its environmental budget almost eightfold and shutting down 1,062 polluting plants—82 permanently, including a state-owned refinery in Mexico City that employed 5,000. The U.S. and Mexico are working on a plan for extensive cross-border environmental cooperation, including construction of sewage plants, air pollution, hazardous-waste disposal, pesticides, and other problems. However, immense air and water pollution problems plague Mexico.

New Business Opportunities. Mexico's a good place for business for many reasons, including that Mexicans are a hard-working people; twelve-hour workdays are common. Also, the corporate income tax rate in Mexico is 35 percent, there are no taxes on dividends, local governments do not tax corporate income, there are no constraints on dividend and capital repatriation, and franchisers are allowed unlimited repatriation of royalties. Also, the fisheries, petrochemicals, and trucking industries have been deregulated, corruption is on the wane, and over 100 state businesses from airlines to petrochemicals have been privatized. By law, Mexican children must attend school for 10 years, and 88 percent of the citizenry is literate.

Leading the rush to Mexico are electronics and garment companies, who have established maquiladoras—assembly plants on the U.S.–Mexico border. AT&T, for example, recently moved its cordless-phone repair operation to Mexico from Singapore. Du Pont Company and SCI Systems also are expanding their facilities in Guadalajara. Wal-Mart is opening five warehouse clubs, called Club Aurrera, in a joint venture with Cifra, Mexico's largest retailer. Sears, Roebuck is spending $150 million to open new stores in Mexico. Southwestern Bell Corporation of St. Louis recently acquired Telefonos de Mexico, the state phone monopoly, and PepsiCo acquired Gamesa, the huge snack food firm. Unilever Group acquired part of Conasupo, the Mexican commodities company. Nissan plans a $1 billion expansion of its assembly plant in Aguascalientes. Compaq Computer, Lotus Development Corporation, and Microsoft opened large subsidiaries in Mexico City recently.

Franchising is also beginning to boom in Mexico. Kentucky Fried Chicken, for example, plans to have 180 restaurants operating by 1995. McDonald's has earmarked $500 million to open 250 new restaurants in Mexico by 2000. The tourism industry in Mexico is growing about 11 percent annually as Americans in particular enjoy the combination of reasonable prices, high-quality facilities, political stability, and close proximity.

RUSSIA

The Soviet Union has disintegrated and been replaced by a new confederation of fifteen republics; in terms of population Russia is larger than all the other republics combined and is the fifth-largest country in the world. Russia has more oil reserves than Saudi Arabia, as well as vast quantities of timber and gold and first-rate scientists. Russia spans eleven time zones. Donald Kendall, former CEO of PepsiCo, says the Soviet disintegration "means chaos in the short term but immense business opportunities in the long term. If U.S. companies wait until all the problems are solved, somebody else will get the business."

Money and Politics. Russia now recognizes individual rights, including equality, privacy, freedom of speech, conscience, and religion, and free choice of work. However, these newly won freedoms have contributed to skyrocketing prices and consumer discontent. A major problem facing Russia is economic disarray. The ruble is grossly overvalued at the official exchange rate of $1.79, but the black market rate is three cents. Companies doing business with Russian firms must hedge against the drop of the ruble's dollar value. Many companies will not do business with the former Soviets until the ruble is converted to a gold standard like all major currencies of the world, because the two-tier exchange rate is unwieldy.

Joint Ventures. A joint venture strategy offers an excellent way to enter the Russian market. Joint ventures create a mechanism to generate hard currency, which is important due to problems valuing the ruble. Russia's joint venture law has been revised to allow foreigners to own up to 99 percent of the venture and to allow a foreigner to serve as chief executive officer.

The list of U.S. companies that have active joint ventures with Russia include Archer-Daniels-Midland, Chevron, Combustion Engineering, Dresser Industries, Hewlett-Packard, Honeywell, Johnson & Johnson, MCI, Marriott, McDonald's, Ogilvy & Mather, Radisson, RJR/Nabisco, and Young & Rubicam. In the aerospace industry, Russian firms are cooperating with Germany's Messerschmitt Company; in computers, with IBM; in manufacturing, with Combustion Engineering, Honeywell, and Siemens; in nuclear power, with Asea, Brown Boveri, and Siemens; and in telecommunications, with Nokia. PepsiCo Inc. recently formed a joint venture with Moscow Metropolitan to sell PepsiCo food products in Moscow's subway stations.

Most analysts believe Russia will become a market that many U.S. firms will want to enter in the 1990s. Those firms that start mastering the complexities early and keep informed about the latest developments may likely gain the biggest rewards. Thousands of businesses in Russia have been given financial independence and broad management autonomy. Poor telecommunications equipment, however, often isolates foreign managers in Russia from the parent company. Russia's telephone system is comparable to the U.S. phone system of the 1930s.

Guidelines for Strategic Ventures. The following guidelines are appropriate when considering a strategic venture into Russia. First, avoid regions with ethnic conflicts and violence. Also, make sure the potential partner has a proper charter that has been amended to permit joint venture participation. Be aware that businesspeople in these lands have little knowledge of marketing, contract law, and corporate law, fax machines, voice mail, and other business practices that Westerners take for granted.

Business contracts with Russian firms should address natural environment issues because Westerners often get the blame for air and water pollution problems and habitat destruction. Work out a clear means of converting rubles to dollars before entering a proposed joint venture, because neither Russian banks nor authorities can be counted on to facilitate foreign firms' getting dollar profits out of a business. Recognize that chronic shortages of raw materials hamper business in Russia, so make sure an adequate supply of competitively priced, good-quality raw materials is reliably available. Finally, make sure the business contract limits the circumstances in which expropriation would be legal. Specify a lump sum in dollars should expropriation occur unexpectedly, and obtain expropriation insurance before signing the agreement.

A number of organizations in Russia assist foreign companies interested in initiating, continuing, or expanding business operations there. Some of these organizations are Amtorg, the Consultation Center of the Chamber of Commerce and Industry, Inpred, Interfact, and the U.S. Commercial Office (USCO). Inpred, for example, is a consulting firm in Russia that helps Western managers operate within regulations. Inpred also helps foreign firms locate partners in the republics and develop contracts, and contacts officials to set up meetings between Commonwealth and foreign businesspersons. USCO annually sponsors about twenty-five trade fairs and exhibitions which introduce foreign companies and individuals to the new Commonwealth markets, customers, buyers, and sellers.

Although no larger in size than California, Japan supports a population five times that of California's. Japan is changing rapidly. Masakagu Yamazaki uses the term "flexible individualism" to summarize the changes occurring in Japanese society and business. Workaholic attitudes in Japan are being replaced by greater emphasis on leisure activities and consumption of leisure products and services. Rising incomes, an aging population, and more women in the workforce are increasing the demand for services in all sectors of the Japanese economy. Japanese people save much more of their income than Americans, averaging 17 percent versus 4 percent, but prices in Japan are among the highest in the world. An apple costs $2 and dinner for four can cost $600.

A comparison of educational levels of Japanese and American young people appears in Table 10–2. Teachers in Japan enjoy much more respect, status, job security, and higher pay than their counterparts in America. Japanese teachers visit their students' homes, are available after school to assist students, and supervise learning on vacation days. Education is compulsory for children ages 6 to 15 in Japan, and 95 percent of 5-year-olds and 70 percent of 4-year-olds go to kindergarten. The school year is 240 days and many children spend Sunday and holidays being tutored or studying. Some of the forces behind the educational system in Japan are relative homogeneity in the population, an occupational system in which selection and promotion are based on educational credentials, a relatively equal distribution of educational opportunities across the population, steep competition for entry into prestigious universities, and devotion of families to enhancing the life chances of children.[9] Many analysts contend

TABLE 10-2   The Educational Levels of Young Japanese and Young Americans Compared

	AMERICANS	JAPANESE
Literacy rate	80.0%	99.0%
High school completion rate	72.2%	90.0%
Length of school year	180 days	240 days
High school seniors spending less than five hours per week on homework	76.0%	35.0%
Financing of education:		
national	6.2%	47.3%
state	49.0%	28.1%
local	44.8%	24.6%
Teacher salaries	Determined locally	By national law, teachers are paid 10% more than the top civil servant.

Sources: U.S. Department of Education and Japanese Ministry of Education.

that as we approach the year 2000 and beyond, countries around the world will be as competitive as their underlying education system. U.S. firms could be at a disadvantage compared to Japanese firms if this holds true, because the analysts are primarily referring to secondary education, literacy rates, and average education level of the populace.

More and more Japanese women are pursuing careers outside the home, a practice that was taboo until the mid-1980s. However, women still hold only 1 percent of managerial positions in Japan despite their comprising 40 percent of Japan's workforce. The 1986 Japanese law banning sex discrimination at work established no penalties for violations. Most Japanese men and women still believe that when a woman marries, taking care of her husband and children should be her priority. The Japanese government is encouraging companies to promote more women into managerial positions, but the managerial job in Japan typically requires late hours, after-work drinking sessions with colleagues, and a pledge of allegiance to the company until retirement. Many Japanese women do not cherish that lifestyle, so women on the career track in Japan still remain an oddity.

Research and development has become a basic mission of the Japanese government and nearly all Japanese firms. It is a mission of the whole country. Japan plans to develop a futuristic space shuttle, a colony of space platforms, and an orbiting factory for manufacturing "Made in Space" products. Aerospace companies in the United States and worldwide consider the Japanese market to be a great opportunity and are developing strategies to capitalize on Japan's commitment to commercialize space.

Some U.S. companies have done especially well in Japanese markets, including Coke, Nestlé, Schick, Wella, Vicks, Scott, Del Monte, Kraft, Campbell, Unilever, Twinings, Kellogg, Borden, Ragu, Oscar Mayer, and Hershey. These are all household names in Japan. Schick razor blades have 70 percent of the safety-blade market, McDonald's has 30 percent of the fast-food hamburger market, Coca-Cola has 50 percent of the market for carbonated soft drinks, Pampers has 22 percent of the disposable-diaper market, and Kodak has 15 percent of the amateur color film market. IBM has 40 percent of the market for computers, and Caterpillar has 43 percent of the market for bulldozers.

Japanese Management Style. The Japanese place great importance upon group loyalty and consensus, a concept called *Wa*. Nearly all corporate activities in Japan encourage Wa among managers and employees. Wa requires that all members of a group agree and cooperate; this results in constant discussion and compromise.[10] Japanese managers evaluate the potential attractiveness of alternative business decisions in terms of the long-term effect on the group's Wa. This is why silence, used for pondering alternatives, can be a plus in a formal Japanese meeting. Discussions potentially disruptive to Wa are generally conducted in very informal settings, such as at a bar, so as to minimize harm to the group's Wa. Entertaining is an important business activity in Japan because it strengthens Wa. Formal meetings are often conducted in informal settings. When confronted with disturbing questions or opinions, Japanese managers tend to remain silent, whereas Americans tend to respond directly, defending themselves through explanation and argument.

Most Japanese managers are reserved, quiet, distant, introspective, and others-oriented, whereas most U.S. managers are talkative, insensitive, impulsive, direct, and individual-oriented. Americans often perceive Japanese managers as wasting time and carrying on pointless conversations, whereas U.S. managers often use blunt criticism, ask prying questions, and make quick decisions. These kinds of cultural differences have disrupted many potentially productive Japanese-American business endeavors. Viewing the Japanese communication style as a prototype for all Asian and Oriental cultures is a related stereotype that must be avoided.[11]

Americans have more freedom to control their own fate than do the Japanese. Life is much different in the United States than in Japan; the United States offers more upward mobility to its people. This is a great strength of the United States. Fallows explains:

> America is not like Japan and can never be. America's strength is the opposite: It opens its doors and brings the world's disorder in. It tolerates social change that would tear most other societies apart. This openness encourages Americans to adapt as individuals rather than as a group. Americans go west to California to get a new start; they move east to Manhattan to try to make the big time; they move to Vermont or to a farm to get close to the soil. They break away from their parents' religions or values or class; they rediscover their ethnicity. They go to night school; they change their names.[12]

Global Expansion. Japan is shifting from a strategy of exports to direct investment in the United States and Europe. Japan surpassed the United Kingdom in 1992 as the largest direct investor in the United States. The number of Americans working for Japanese subsidiaries in the United States doubled from 1989 to 1995, to 400,000. The ten largest Japanese employers in the United States in rank order are Matsushita Electric, Sony, Toyota, Honda, Hitachi, Toshiba, Nissan, NEC, Mitsubishi, and Fujitsu. However, over 50 percent of Japanese companies operating in the United States today face worker lawsuits on race, color, religion, age, sex, and equal employment.

In Europe, Toyota completed its first auto plant in 1992, a $1.2 billion facility in Britain. Fujitsu is also building a $690 million manufacturing plant to produce computer chips in northeast England. The Japanese are expected to continue investing heavily in Great Britain because the British welcome the Japanese, while other European countries are divided in their attitudes toward Japan. More than 40 percent of all Japanese investment in Western Europe is in Britain. The Confederation of British Industry predicts that by the year 2000, an astonishing 16 percent of British factory workers will have Japanese bosses.

There are only three major industries—pharmaceuticals, chemicals, and telecommunications equipment—in which European companies are more competitive than Japanese companies. Five of the top ten construction firms in the world are Japanese: Shimizu, Kajima, Jaisei, Takenaka, and Ohbayashi. Until European countries develop a more unified approach towards Japanese investment, England could be "exporting" Japanese products to the Continent in great quantities.

Financial Services. Japan is determined to obtain world leadership and dominance in financial services. The Tokyo Stock Exchange has replaced the New York Stock Exchange as the world's largest, with a market capitalization of over $3 trillion; this is more volume than that of all the exchanges in Europe combined. The Osaka Exchange has surpassed London's as the world's third largest. The world's largest life insurance company, Nippon Life, the world's largest transportation company, NYK, and the world's largest tourism firm, Japan Travel Bureau, are all Japanese. There are only a few areas of financial services where U.S. and European financial institutions still hold a firm lead over their Japanese counterparts. These areas include trust banking, portfolio management, venture capital, mergers and acquisitions, swap arrangements, and engineering complex financial packages.[13] American and European firms must capitalize on these strengths and begin to offer these services worldwide to compete effectively with Japanese financial institutions. The worst enemy of Western financial instititutions is complacency.

Current Developments in Japan. Some current trends that represent opportunities for American firms are:

1. Discount stores in Japan are growing in number at more than twice the rate of department stores. Japanese discount stores are hungry for low-price goods produced anywhere in the world.
2. Shopping malls are being built all over Japan; nearly 1,200 malls are currently under construction or proposed. These malls also crave products from all over the world.
3. Japanese imports of consumer goods are increasing. In 1992, Japanese imports hit $240 billion, more than triple the total in 1987. The traditional mom-and-pop store that has dominated Japan for centuries is giving way to large discount stores and malls.

Japan is clearing barriers, tariffs, and quotas that once discouraged firms from distributing or manufacturing products and services in Japan. This trend presents opportunities for many American firms. Some of Japan's major objectives for the next few years are:

1. To deregulate the economy.
2. To institute aggressive policies to improve residential housing.
3. To increase imports of manufactured goods.
4. To raise agricultural productivity.
5. To reduce the average number of working hours per individual per year to 1,800 (compared to 1,924 in the United States and 1,659 hours in West Germany).
6. To institute a five-day work week for all government offices and financial institutions.
7. To give more foreign aid to underdeveloped countries.[14]

EUROPE

Since World War II, western European countries have comprised distinct national markets where governments protected their own businesses and imposed stiff tariffs on outside firms. Jealousy, regulation, diverse economic conditions, and tensions among nations have characterized Europe for years. Viewed as separate entities, European countries have not represented a sufficiently large customer base to warrant many international companies establishing business operations in Europe. Consequently, Europe has been economically stagnant since World War II, especially compared with the United States and the Far East. For several years during the 1980s, the combined results of the largest 100 companies in Europe, excluding the oil companies, showed a profit level of 0 percent. Unemployment in Europe still remains high and companies generally are not competitive in world markets. The International Monetary Fund reports that between 1983 and 1992, Europe's share of world markets dropped 4.4 percent, to 13.9 percent. In contrast, Asia's fast-growing nations—not even counting Japan—increased their share from 4.6 percent to 8.1 percent.

There are also still wide differences in product tastes across European countries. For example, the French want top-loading washing machines, whereas the British want front-loading washers. The Portuguese eat only 10 kg of beef per capita each year, whereas the French eat 33 kg. Germans eat 9.5 kg of poultry each year, whereas the Spanish eat 22 kg. Electrical outlets in Britain are also different from those in Holland.

With the exception of a few industries such as chemicals, most sectors of the European economy are marked by chronic overcapacity and high fixed costs, such as steel, detergents, pharmaceuticals, transportation, and banking. There is no reason why Europe's $2 billion turbine-generator business should support ten producers. Similar overcapactiy problems plague other industries, such as locomotive manufacturing. European companies are moving quickly, however, to correct the overcapacity problems, and survivors will likely emerge as strong competitors in world markets. Differences among European countries are narrowing due to a massive increase in the flow of people and information across national borders, and European companies are moving rapidly to develop and market products that will be well-received all over Europe. The "Europlug," for example, has recently been developed and marketed in Europe as the electrical plug that "will work everywhere."

Unification. The unification of western Europe created a single market of 320 million people, larger than either the United States' population of 240 million people or Japan's 120 million. Unification of western Europe is perhaps the single most important world event affecting business strategies since the formation of OPEC in the early 1970s. Twelve countries speaking with one voice is more attractive to multinational corporations than twelve countries speaking with twelve voices. A proliferation of cross-border mergers, acquisitions, and alliances in Europe is creating a new generation of European firms large enough to take on U.S. and Japanese companies. In some industries, such as packaging and electric generating equipment, European firms have already replaced American firms as world leaders.

Unification of western Europe brought a reduction or elimination of trade barriers between European countries; people, goods, services, and capital now flow freely across national boundaries. European banks can operate in different countries without prohibitive barriers. Trucks pass freely between national borders, instead of having to wait for hours at places such as the Mount Blanc tunnel between France and Italy, where custom agents used to check documents and cargo. The just-completed Eurotunnel under the English Channel is spurring business between England and the European mainland. The estimated annual savings to European companies from the unification is $75 to $90 billion.

Unification also brought common licensing of food and beverage products in Europe, common radio and television signals, common health and safety standards, elimination of duplication in distribution systems, and standardization of product lines. It has also prompted increased competitor analysis and alliances, decentralization of businesses, new marketing efforts, new strategies, more emphasis on service, improved telecommunications and information flow, and increased momentum for a single monetary system evolving in Europe.

Perhaps the most far-reaching feature of European unification is the planned establishment of a single financial market. Much stronger competitors in Europe have emerged from the 1992 unification, and consumers throughout Europe are benefiting from lower prices and better choices. However, European companies still pay the world's highest wages and generally have trouble offering goods at globally competitive prices. The social welfare system in Europe is especially costly to firms. Most European workers and managers enjoy lifetime employment guarantees. There is a fear throughout Europe that rising unemployment, already at 10.5 percent, may bring back overregulation and protectionism, which would hurt firms' efforts to become more globally competitive.

European industries expected to represent the greatest threat to U.S. firms in the near future are publishing, communications equipment, pharmaceutical, and civilian-aerospace. Representing a lesser but still significant threat to U.S. firms will be European banks and producers of food, beverages, computers, electronics, and autos. U.S. industries that appear for the moment to be least affected by European unification are retailing, trucking, airlines, and insurance.

Mergers and Acquisitions. Since Brussels is the headquarters of the European Economic Community (EEC), significant business and economic activity has shifted there from other national capitals in Europe. A wave of mergers and acquisitions is sweeping Europe as companies try to consolidate strength in core markets. For example, Banco de Bilbao and Banco Vizcaya, Spain's third- and sixth-largest banks, recently combined to form the only Spanish bank to rank among the top thirty in Europe. Consolidations in the paper industry have resulted in strong competitors like Stora Kopparbergs Bergslags and Svanska Cellusosa in Sweden and Finnpap and Kymmene in Finland. Nestlé in Switzerland has acquired a number of other food companies in both Europe and the United States. Two large accounting firms in England, Coopers & Lybrand and Deloitte Haskins & Sells, recently merged, creating the largest accounting firm in Europe. Eurocom S.A., France's largest advertising agency, merged with Roux, Seguela, Cayzac & Goudard, creating by far the largest ad agency in Europe.

Recent examples of European firms that have acquired U.S. firms are Pechiney of France, which acquired Triangle Industries; Grand Metropolitan of Britain, which acquired Pillsbury, Burger King, and Green Giant; Hoechst of Germany, which acquired Celanese; and Nestlé of Switzerland, which acquired Carnation.

Japanese firms are also making large acquisitions in western Europe. For example, Fujitsu acquired Britain's last true computer maker, ICL. Mitsubishi Electric has a stated goal to increase its investment in Europe by as much as 30 percent a year. Olivetti in Italy depends on Canon and Sanyo for office equipment and Fiat depends on Hitachi for construction gear. Nissan, Toyota, and Honda are all building manufacturing plants in Britain and expect to raise overall Japanese market share of automobiles in Britain from 12 percent to 17 percent by 1998.

After Great Britain, the European country receiving the next most extensive Japanese investment is Germany; Germany already imports 40 percent of all Japanese exports to Europe. Dusseldorf, Germany, has Europe's largest number of Japanese residents—over 7,000. Mitusbishi Electric and Toshiba are leading an array of Japanese firms planning investment of over $400 million annually in the Dusseldorf region alone.

GUIDELINES FOR SUCCESS AS A GLOBAL COMPETITOR

Robert Allio offers seven guidelines for winning global battles for customer loyalty and market share:

1. Get to new global markets first. Trying to gain market share from well-entrenched competitors is exceptionally difficult.
2. Counterattack at home. Parent firms often finance expansion into host countries with profits generated at home. Competitor cash flow can be reduced by

attacking them at home. A recent example is the 3M attack on Japanese markets for audiotape and videotape.

3. Invest in new technology. Successful firms in the 1990s are going to utilize the most efficient technology.

4. Consider alternative sourcing. Locate manufacturing facilities in low labor cost areas of the world. A recent example of this is Dominion Textile of Canada's building a denim manufacturing facility in Tunisia.

5. Install the right managerial system. Ensure that managers in foreign markets understand the nuances of culture and language in host countries.

6. Take early losses if necessary. Sacrifice short-term profits for long-term rewards. A recent example is Japanese firms' taking losses for seven years in order to capture the European motorcycle market.

7. Join forces with competitors. Collaborate with competitors who have expertise in other parts of the value chain. Recent examples are Chrysler's deal with Mitsubushi and AT&T's linkup with Olivetti.[15]

Jeremy Main says there is no universal formula for going global, but any company serious about joining the race should do most or all of the following:

1. Make yourself at home in all three of the world's most important markets—North America, Europe, and Asia.

2. Develop new products for the whole world.

3. Replace profit centers based on countries or regions with ones based on product lines.

4. "Glocalize," as the Japanese call it: Make global decisions on strategic questions about products, capital, and research, but let local units decide tactical questions about packaging, marketing, and advertising.

5. Overcome parochial attitudes, such as the "not-invented-here" syndrome. Train people to think internationally, send them off on frequent trips, and give them the latest communications technology, such as teleconferencing.

6. Open the senior ranks to foreign employees.

7. Do whatever seems best wherever it seems best, even if people at home lose jobs or responsibilities.

8. In markets that you cannot penetrate on your own, find allies.[16]

David Garfield, president of Ingersoll-Rand Company, offers three strategy suggestions to make domestic firms more competitive internationally:

1. The best defense is a good offense. Companies need to fight tooth and claw for exports and battle foreign competition on foreign ground wherever possible. This is preferable to competing intensely in domestic markets.

2. Investments that will improve competitive advantage should receive priority attention. Domestic firms should strive to reduce labor costs, lower overhead, compress production cycles, and improve the quality of products and services.

3. Domestic industries and firms need to help one another. They should give preference to American suppliers and distributors; they should encourage one another to take action to improve competitiveness in technology, quality, service, and cost.[17]

CONCLUSION

Success in business more and more depends upon offering products and services that are competitive on a world basis, not just on a local basis. If the price and quality of a firm's products and services are not competitive with those available elsewhere in the world, the firm may soon face extinction. Global markets have become a reality in all but the most remote areas of the world. Certainly throughout the United States, even in small towns, firms feel the pressure of world competitors. Nearly half of all the automobiles sold in the United States, for example, are made in Japan and Germany.

Culture, industrial policies, joint venturing, and exporting are important in the strategic-management process of international firms. As world economies and consumption patterns become increasingly similar and interrelated, political and economic changes represent major opportunities for, and threats to, United States firms. To be successful in the 1990s, businesses must offer products and services that exhibit a price/quality relationship competitive with similar products and services available worldwide.

KEY TERMS AND CONCEPTS

Economic Nationalism
European Economic Community
Glasnost
Guanxi
Host Company
Industrial Policies

Inhwa
Multinational Corporation
Parent Company
Perestroika
Wa

1. Compare and contrast American culture with other cultures worldwide. How do differences in culture affect strategic management?

2. Explain why consumption patterns are becoming more and more similar worldwide. What are the strategic implications of this trend?

3. What are the advantages and disadvantages of beginning export operations in a foreign country?

4. Why do you believe the airline industry is only slowly becoming global?

5. What recommendations do you have for firms wanting to do business with Russia?

6. What strategies are most commonly being pursued by Japanese firms? Why?

7. How does unification of western Europe affect the strategies of U.S. firms?

8. What guidelines for success as a global competitor do you believe are most important?

9. Select one of the readings at the end of this chapter and prepare a 3-minute report to the class on this topic.

10. Do you believe Guanxi, Inhwa, or Wa would help facilitate strategic management in an organization? Why?

NOTES

1. Gephardt, Richard A. "U.S.–Japanese Trade Relations," *Vital Speeches of the Day* Vol. LV, no. 15 (May 15, 1989).

2. Jon Alston, "Wa, Guanxi, and Inhwa: Managerial Principles in Japan, China and Korea," *Business Horizons* 32, no. 2 (March–April 1989): 26.

3. Arthur Whitehall, "American Executives Through Foreign Eyes," *Business Horizons* 32, no. 3 (May–June 1989): 43.

4. Rose Knotts, "Cross-Cultural Management: Transformations and Adaptations," *Business Horizons* (January– February 1989): 29–33.

5. Vern Terpstra and David Kenneth, *The Cultural Environment of International Business* (Cincinnati: South-Western Publishing Company, 1985). Also see: Rose Knotts, "Cross-Cultural Management: Transformations and Adaptations," *Business Horizons* 32, no. 1 (January–February 1989): 31.

6. Ellen Fingerhut and Daryl Hatano, "Principles of Strategic Planning Applied to International Corporations," *Managerial Planning* 31, no. 5 (September–October 1983): 4–14. Also, Narendra Sethi, "Strategic Planning Systems for Multinational Companies," *Long Range Planning* 15, no. 3 (June 1982): 80–89.

7. George Yip and George Coundouriotis. "The World Chocolate Confectionery Industry." *Planning Review* 19, no. 1 (January/February 1991): 6.

8. David Shanks, "Strategic Planning for Global Competition," *Journal of Business Strategy* 5, no. 3 (Winter 1985): 80.

9. Merry White, "Learning and Working in Japan," *Business Horizons* 32, no. 2 (March–April 1989): 42.

10. Alston, 27.

11. Dean Barnlund, "Public and Private Self in Communicating with Japan," *Business Horizons* 32, no. 2 (March–April 1989): 40.

12. Stratford Sherman, "How to Beat the Japanese," *Fortune* (April 10, 1989): 145.

13. Richard Wright and Gunter Pauli, "The Second Wave: Japan's Global Challenge in Financial Services," *Business in the Contemporary World* (Summer 1989): 56.

14. "Japan Goes International," *Business Week* (July 13, 1987): 47.

15. Robert Allio, "Formulating Global Strategy," *Planning Review* 17, no. 2 (March–April 1989): 27.

16. Jeremy Main, "How to Go Global—And Why," *Fortune* (August 28, 1989): 76.

17. David Garfield, "The International Challenge to U.S. Business," *Journal of Business Strategy* 5, no. 4 (Spring 1985): 28, 29.

Babbar, Sunil, and Arun Rai. "Competitive Intelligence for International Business." *Long Range Planning* 26, no. 3 (June 1993): 103–113.

Black, J. Stewart, and Mark Mendenhall. "Resolving Conflicts with the Japanese: Mission Impossible?" *Sloan Management Review* 34, no. 3 (Spring 1993): 49–60.

Boddewyn, Jean J. "Fitting Socially in Fortress Europe: Understanding, Reaching, and Impressing Europeans." *Business Horizons* 35, no. 6 (November–December 1992): 35–43.

Burgers, W. P., C. W. L. Hill, and W. C. Kim. "A Theory of Global Strategic Alliances: The Case of the Global Auto Industry." *Strategic Management Journal* 14, no. 6 (September 1993): 419–432.

Coplin, William D., and Michael K. O'Leary. "The Commercial Prospects for Eastern Europe and the Former Soviet Republics." *Planning Review* 20, no. 6 (November–December 1992): 32–35.

Davis, Edward W. "Global Outsourcing: Have U.S. Managers Thrown the Baby Out with the Bath Water?" *Business Horizons* 35, no. 4 (July–August 1992): 58–65.

Ford, John B., and Earl D. Honeycutt Jr. "Japanese National Culture as a Basis for Understanding Japanese Business Practices." *Business Horizons* 35, no. 6 (November–December 1992): 27–34.

Glynn, Mary. "Strategic Planning in Nigeria versus the U.S.: A Case of Anticipating the (Next) Coup." *Academy of Management Executive* 7, no. 3 (August 1993): 82–85.

Hill, John, and Ronald Dulek. "A Miss Manners Guide to Doing Business in Europe." *Business Horizons* 35, no. 4 (July–August 1993): 48–53.

Hu, Yao-Su. "Global Corporations Are National Firms with International Operations." *California Management Review* 34, no. 2 (Winter 1992): 66–87.

Jacobson, Robert. "The 'Austrian' School of Strategy." *Academy of Management Review* 17, no. 4 (October 1992): 782–807.

Kim, W. Chan, and Renée A. Mauborgne. "Making Global Strategies Work." *Sloan Management Review* 34, no. 3 (Spring 1993): 11–28.

Kim, W. Chan, and Renée A. Mauborgne. "Procedural Justice, Attitudes, and Subsidiary Top Management Compliance with Multinationals' Corporate Strategic Decisions." *Academy of Management Journal* 36, no. 3 (June 1993): 502–526.

Lasserre, Philippe. "Gathering and Interpreting Strategic Intelligence in Asia Pacific." *Long Range Planning* 26, no. 3 (June 1993): 56–66.

Lawrence, Paul, and Charalambos Vlachoutsicos. "Joint Ventures in Russia: Put the Locals in Charge." *Harvard Business Review* (January–February 1993): 44–45.

Lei, David, and John W. Slocum, Jr. "Global Strategy, Competence-Building and Strategic Alliances." *California Management Review* 35, no. 1 (Fall 1992): 81–97.

McLauchlin, James E. "Communicating to a Diverse Europe." *Business Horizons* 36, no. 1 (January–February 1993): 54–56.

Murray, Edwin A., Jr., and John F. Mahon. "Strategic Alliances: Gateway to the New Europe?" *Long Range Planning* 26, no. 4 (August 1993): 102–111.

Roth, Kendall. "Implementing International Strategy at the Business Unit Level: The Role of Managerial Decision-Making Characteristics." *Journal of Management* 18, no. 4 (December 1992): 769–790.

Roth, Kendall, and Allen J. Morrison. "Business-Level Competitive Strategy: A Contingency Link to Internationalization." *Journal of Management* 18, no. 3 (September 1992): 473–488.

Samson, Rene. "Competing with the Japanese—Strategies for European Business." *Long Range Planning* 26, no. 4 (August 1993): 59–65.

Sera, Koh. "Corporate Globalization: A New Trend." *The Executive* VI, no. 1 (February 1992): 89–96.

Shama, Avraham. "Management Under Fire: The Transformation of Managers in the Soviet Union and Eastern Europe." *The Executive* VII, no. 1 (February 1993): 22–35.

Tallman, Stephen B. "A Strategic Management Perspective on Host Country Structure of Multinational Enterprises." *Journal of Management* 18, no. 3 (September 1992): 455–472.

Turpin, Dominique. "Strategic Alliances with Japanese Firms: Myths and Realities." *Long Range Planning* 26, no. 4 (August 1993): 11–15.

EXPERIENTIAL EXERCISES

DETERMINING THE COMPETITIVE ENVIRONMENT FOR HERSHEY'S PRODUCTS IN OTHER COUNTRIES

PURPOSE

Organizations are exploring potential markets in other countries more and more. The purpose of this exercise is to assess the relative attractiveness of various foreign countries for distributing and possibly manufacturing Hershey products.

INSTRUCTIONS

Step 1 Select a European, Asian, African, South American, or Central American country of your choice.

Step 2 Go to your college library. Research your chosen country to identify social, cultural, demographic, geographic, political, legal, governmental, economic, technological, and competitive forces or trends that affect the candy and pasta market there. Decide whether you would recommend Hershey begin or increase export operations or manufacturing operations in that country.

Step 3 Prepare a three-page typed report to Hershey's president of international operations, William F. Christ. Give the results of your research and your specific recommendations.

DETERMINING MY UNIVERSITY'S RECRUITING EFFORTS IN FOREIGN COUNTRIES

PURPOSE

A competitive climate is emerging among colleges and universities around the world. Colleges and universities in Europe and Japan are increasingly recruiting American students to offset declining enrollments. Foreign students already comprise more than one-third of the student body at many American universities. The purpose of this exercise is to identify particular colleges and universities in foreign countries that represent a competitive threat to American institutions of higher learning.

INSTRUCTIONS

Step 1 Select a foreign country. Conduct research to determine the number and nature of colleges and universities in that country. What are the major institutions in that country? What programs are those institutions recognized for offering? What percent of undergraduate and graduate students attending those institutions are American? Do those institutions actively recruit American students?

Step 2 Prepare a report for the president or chancellor of your college or university that summarizes your research findings.

LESSONS IN DOING BUSINESS GLOBALLY

PURPOSE

The purpose of this exercise is to discover some important lessons learned by local businesses who do business internationally.

INSTRUCTIONS

Contact several local business leaders by phone. Find at least three firms that engage in international or export operations. Ask the businessperson to give you several important lessons his or her firm has learned in doing business globally. Record the lessons on paper and report your findings to the class.

PART · 6

Case
Analysis

Case Introduction

HOW TO ANALYZE A BUSINESS POLICY CASE

OUTLINE WHAT IS A BUSINESS POLICY CASE?

GUIDELINES FOR PREPARING CASE ANALYSES

PREPARING A CASE FOR CLASS DISCUSSION

PREPARING A WRITTEN CASE ANALYSIS

MAKING AN ORAL PRESENTATION

FIFTY TIPS FOR SUCCESS IN CASE ANALYSIS

OBJECTIVES After studying this section, you should be able to:

- Describe the case method for learning strategic-management concepts.
- Identify the steps in preparing a comprehensive written case analysis.
- Describe how to give an effective oral case analysis presentation.
- Discuss fifty tips for doing case analysis.

*T*he purpose of this section is to help you analyze business policy cases. Guidelines for preparing written and oral case analyses are given, and suggestions for preparing cases for class discussion are presented. Steps to follow in preparing case analyses are provided. Guidelines for making an oral presentation are described.

WHAT IS A BUSINESS POLICY CASE?

A *business policy case* describes an organization's external and internal condition and raises issues concerning the firm's mission, strategies, objectives, and policies. Most of the information in a business policy case is established fact, but some information may be opinions, judgments, and beliefs. Business policy cases are more comprehensive than those you may have studied in other courses. They generally include a description of related management, marketing, finance/accounting, production/operations, R&D, computer information systems, and environmental issues. A business policy case puts the reader on the scene of the action by describing a firm's situation at some point in time. Business policy cases are written to give you practice applying strategic-management concepts. The case method for studying strategic management is often called *learning by doing*.

GUIDELINES FOR PREPARING CASE ANALYSES

The Need for Practicality. There is no such thing as a complete case, and no case ever gives you all the information you need to conduct analyses and make recommendations. Likewise, in the business world, strategists never have all the information they need to make decisions: information may be unavailable, too costly to obtain, or may take too much time to obtain. So, in preparing business policy cases, do what strategists do every day—make reasonable assumptions about unknowns, state assumptions clearly, perform appropriate analyses, and make decisions. *Be practical.* For example, in performing a pro forma financial analysis, make reasonable assumptions, state them appropriately, and proceed to show what impact your recommendations are expected to have on the organization's financial position. Avoid saying, "I don't have enough information." You can always supplement the information provided in a case with research in your college library. Library research is required in case analyses.

The Need for Justification. The most important part of analyzing cases is not what strategies you recommend, but rather how you support your decisions and how you propose that they be implemented. There is no single best solution or one right answer to a case, so give ample justification for your recommendations. This is important. In the business world, strategists usually do not know if their decisions are "right" until resources have been allocated and consumed. Then it is often too late to reverse the decisions. This cold fact accents the need for careful integration of intuition and analysis in preparing business policy case analyses.

The Need for Realism. Avoid recommending a course of action beyond an organization's means. *Be realistic.* No organization can possibly pursue all the strategies that could potentially benefit the firm. Estimate how much capital will be required to implement what you recommended. Determine whether debt, stock, or a combination of debt and stock could be used to obtain the capital. Make sure your recommendations are feasible. Do not prepare a case analysis that omits all arguments and information not supportive of your recommendations. Rather, present the major advantages and disadvantages of several feasible alternatives. Try not to exaggerate, stereotype, prejudge, or overdramatize. Strive to demonstrate that your interpretation of the evidence is reasonable and objective.

The Need for Specificity. Do not make broad generalizations such as "The company should pursue a market penetration strategy." *Be specific* by telling what, why, when, how, where, and who. Failure to use specifics is the single major shortcoming of most oral and written case analyses. For example, in an internal audit, say, "The firm's current ratio fell from 2.2 in 1993 to 1.3 in 1994, and this is considered to be a major weakness," instead of, "The firm's financial condition is bad." Rather than concluding from a SPACE Matrix that a firm should be defensive, be more specific, saying, "The firm should consider closing three plants, laying off 280 employees, and divesting itself of its chemical division, for a net savings of $20.2 million in 1995." Use ratios, percentages, numbers, and dollar estimates. Businesspeople dislike generalities and vagueness.

The Need for Originality. Do not necessarily recommend the course of action that the firm plans to take or actually undertook, even if those actions resulted in improved revenues and earnings. The aim of case analysis is for you to consider all the facts and information relevant to the organization at the time, generate feasible alternative strategies, choose among those alternatives, and defend your recommendations. Put yourself back in time to the point when strategic decisions were being made by the firm's strategists. Based on information available then, what would you have done? Support your position with charts, graphs, ratios, analyses, and the like—not a revelation from the library. You can become a good strategist by thinking through situations, making management assessments, and proposing plans yourself. *Be original.* Compare and contrast what you recommend versus what the company plans to do or did.

The Need to Contribute. Strategy formulation, implementation, and evaluation decisions are commonly made by a group of individuals rather than by a single person. Therefore, your professor may divide the class into three- or four-person teams to prepare written or oral case analyses. Members of a strategic-management team, in class or in the business world, differ on their aversion to risk, their concern for short-run versus long-run benefits, their attitudes toward social responsibility, and their views concerning globalization. There are no perfect people, so there are no perfect strategists. Be open-minded to others' views. *Be a good listener and a good contributor.*

PREPARING A CASE FOR CLASS DISCUSSION

Your professor may ask you to prepare a case for class discussion. Preparing a case for class discussion means that you need to read the case before class, make notes regarding the organization's external opportunities/threats and internal strengths/weaknesses, perform appropriate analyses, and come to class prepared to offer and defend some specific recommendations.

The Case Method Versus Lecture Approach. The case method of teaching is radically different from the traditional lecture approach, in which little or no preparation is needed by students before class. The *case method* involves a classroom situation in which students do most of the talking; your professor facilitates discussion by asking questions and encouraging student interaction regarding ideas, analyses, and recommendations. Be prepared for a discussion along the lines of "What would you do, why would you do it, when would you do it, and how would you do it?" Prepare answers to the following types of questions:

1. What are the firm's most important external opportunities and threats?
2. What are the organization's major strengths and weaknesses?
3. How would you describe the organization's financial condition?
4. What are the firm's existing strategies and objectives?
5. Who are the firm's competitors and what are their strategies?
6. What objectives and strategies do you recommend for this organization? Explain your reasoning. How does what you recommend compare to what the company plans?
7. How could the organization best implement what you recommend? What implementation problems do you envision? How could the firm avoid or solve those problems?

The Cross-Examination. Do not hesitate to take a stand on the issues and to support your position with objective analyses and outside research. Strive to apply strategic-management concepts and tools in preparing your case for class discussion. Seek defensible arguments and positions. Support opinions and judgments with facts, reasons, and evidence. Crunch the numbers before class! Be willing to describe your recommendations to the class without fear of disapproval. Respect the ideas of others, but be willing to "go against the grain" of majority opinion when you can justify a better position.

Business policy case analysis gives you the opportunity to learn more about yourself, your colleagues, strategic management, and the decision-making process in organizations. The rewards of this experience will depend upon the effort you put forth, so do a good job. Discussing business policy cases in class is exciting and challenging. Expect views counter to those you present. Different students will place emphasis on different aspects of an organization's situation and submit different recommendations for scrutiny and rebuttal. Cross-examination discussions commonly arise, just as they occur in a real business organization. Avoid being a silent observer.

PREPARING A WRITTEN CASE ANALYSIS

In addition to asking you to prepare a case for class discussion, your professor may ask you to prepare a written case analysis. Preparing a written case analysis is similar to preparing a case for class discussion, except written reports are generally more structured and more detailed. There is no ironclad procedure for preparing a written case analysis because cases differ in focus; the type, size, and complexity of the organizations being analyzed also vary.

When writing a strategic-management report or case analysis, avoid jargon, vague words, redundant words, acronyms, abbreviations, sexist language, and ethnic or racial slurs, and watch your spelling. Use short sentences and paragraphs and simple words and phrases. Use quite a few subheadings. Arrange issues and ideas from the most important to the least important. Arrange recommendations from the least controversial to the most controversial. Use the active voice rather than the passive voice for all verbs; for example, say, "Our team recommends the company diversify," rather than, "It is recommended by our team to diversify." Use many examples to add specificity and clarity. Tables, figures, pie charts, bar charts, time lines, and other kinds of exhibits help communicate important points and ideas. Sometimes, a picture *is* worth a thousand words.

The Executive Summary. Your professor may ask you to focus the written case analysis on a particular aspect of the strategic-management process, such as "to identify and evaluate the organization's existing mission, objectives, and strategies," or "to propose and defend specific recommendations for the company," or "to develop an industry analysis by describing the competitors, products, selling techniques, and market conditions in a given industry." These types of written reports are sometimes called *executive summaries.* An executive summary usually ranges from three to five pages of text in length, plus exhibits.

The Comprehensive Written Analysis. Sometimes your professor may ask you to prepare a *comprehensive written analysis.* This assignment requires you to apply the entire strategic-management process to the particular organization. When preparing a comprehensive written analysis, picture yourself as a consultant who has been asked by a company to "conduct a study of our external and internal environment and make specific recommendations for our future." Prepare exhibits to support your recommendations. Highlight exhibits with some discussion in the paper. Comprehensive written analyses usually are about ten pages in length, plus exhibits.

Steps in Preparing a Comprehensive Written Analysis. In preparing a comprehensive written analysis, you could follow the steps outlined here, which follow the stages in the strategic-management process and the chapters in this text.

Step 1 Identify the firm's existing mission, objectives, and strategies.

Step 2 Develop a mission statement for the organization.

Step 3 Identify the organization's external opportunities and threats.

Step 4 Construct a Competitive Profile Matrix.

Step 5 Construct an EFE Matrix.

Step 6 Identify the organization's internal strengths and weaknesses.

Step 7 Construct an IFE Matrix.

Step 8 Prepare a TOWS Matrix, SPACE Matrix, BCG Matrix, IE Matrix, Grand Strategy Matrix, and QSPM as appropriate. Give advantages and disadvantages of alternative strategies.

Step 9 Recommend specific strategies and long-term objectives. Show how much your recommendations will cost. Itemize these costs clearly for each projected year. Compare your recommendations to actual strategies planned by the company.

Step 10 Specify how your recommendations can be implemented and what results you can expect. Prepare forecasted ratios and pro forma financial statements. Present a timetable or agenda for action.

Step 11 Recommend specific annual objectives and policies.

Step 12 Recommend procedures for strategy review and evaluation.

Sometimes your professor will ask you to prepare a business policy case analysis, individually or as a group, and present your analysis to the class. Oral presentations are usually graded on two parts: content and delivery. *Content* refers to the quality, quantity, correctness, and appropriateness of analyses presented, including such dimensions as logical flow through the presentation, coverage of major issues, use of specifics, avoidance of generalities, absence of mistakes, and feasibility of recommendations. *Delivery* includes such dimensions as audience attentiveness, clarity of visual aids, appropriate dress, persuasiveness of arguments, tone of voice, eye contact, and posture. Great ideas are of no value unless others can be convinced of their merit through clear communication. The guidelines presented here can help you make an effective oral presentation.

Organizing the Presentation. Begin your presentation by introducing yourself and giving a clear outline of topics to be covered. If a team is presenting, specify the sequence of speakers and the areas each person will address. At the beginning of an oral presentation, try to capture your audience's interest and attention. You could do this by displaying some products made by the company, telling an interesting short story about the company, or sharing an experience that you had related to the company, its products, or its services. You could develop or obtain a VHS video to show at the beginning of class; you could visit a local distributor of the firm's products and tape a personal interview with the business owner or manager. A light or humorous introduction can be effective at the beginning of a presentation.

Be sure the setting of your presentation is well organized, with chairs, flip charts, a transparency projector, and whatever else you plan to use. Arrive at least 15 minutes early at the classroom to organize the setting, and be sure your materials are ready to go. Make sure everyone can see your visual aids well.

Controlling Your Voice. An effective rate of speaking ranges from 100 to 125 words per minute. Practice your presentation out loud to determine if you are going too fast. Individuals commonly speak too fast when nervous. Breathe deeply before and during the presentation to help yourself slow down. Have a cup of water available; pausing to take a drink will wet your throat, give you time to collect your thoughts, control your nervousness, slow you down, and signal to the audience a change in topic.

Avoid a monotone by placing emphasis on different words or sentences. Speak loudly and clearly, but don't shout. Silence can be used effectively to break a monotone voice. Stop at the end of each sentence, rather than running sentences together with "and" or "uh."

Managing Body Language. Be sure not to fold your arms, lean on the podium, put your hands in your pockets, or put your hands behind you. Keep a straight posture, with one foot slightly in front of the other. Do not turn your back to the audience, which is not only rude but which also prevents your voice from projecting well. Avoid using too many hand gestures. On occasion, leave the podium or table and walk toward your audience, but do not walk around too much. Never block the audience's view of your visual aids.

Maintain good eye contact throughout the presentation. This is the best way to persuade your audience. There is nothing more reassuring to a speaker than to see members of the audience nod in agreement or smile. Try to look everyone in the eye at least once during your presentation, but focus more on individuals who look interested than on persons who seem bored. Use humor and smiles as appropriate throughout your presentation to stay in touch with your audience. A presentation should never be dull!

Speaking from Notes. Be sure not to read to your audience, because reading puts people to sleep. Perhaps worse than reading is memorizing. Do not try to memorize anything. Rather, practice using notes unobtrusively. Make sure your notes are written clearly so you will not flounder trying to read your own writing. Include only main ideas on your note cards. Keep note cards on a podium or table if possible so that you won't drop them or get them out of order; walking with note cards tends to be distracting.

Constructing Visual Aids. Make sure your visual aids are legible to individuals in the back of the room. Use color to highlight special items. Avoid putting complete sentences on visual aids; rather, use short phrases and then elaborate on issues orally as you make your presentation. Generally, there should be no more than four to six lines of text on each visual aid. Use clear headings and subheadings. Be careful about spelling and grammar; use a consistent style of lettering. Use masking tape or an easel for posters—do not hold posters in your hand. Transparencies and handouts are excellent aids; however, be careful not to use too many handouts or your audience may concentrate on them instead of you during the presentation.

Answering Questions. It is best to field questions at the end of your presentation, rather than during the presentation itself. Encourage questions and take your time to respond to each one. Answering questions can be persuasive because it involves you with the audience. If a team is giving the presentation, the audience should direct questions to a specific person. During the question and answer period, be polite, confident, and courteous. Avoid verbose responses. Do not get defensive with your answers, even if a hostile or confrontational question is asked. Staying calm during potentially disruptive situations such as a cross-examination reflects self-confidence, maturity, poise, and command of the particular company and its industry. Stand up throughout the question and answer period.

FIFTY TIPS FOR SUCCESS IN CASE ANALYSIS

Business policy students who have used this text over two editions offer to you the following fifty tips for success in doing case analysis:

1. View your case analysis and presentation as a product that must have some competitive factor to differentiate it favorably from the case analyses of other students.
2. Prepare your case analysis far enough in advance of the due date to allow time for reflection and practice. Do not procrastinate.
3. Develop a mind-set of "why," continually questioning your own and others' assumptions and assertions.
4. The best ideas are lost if not communicated to the reader, so as ideas develop, think of their most appropriate presentation.
5. Maintain a positive attitude about the class, working *with* problems rather than against them.

6. Keep in tune with your professor and understand his or her values and expectations.

7. Since business policy is a capstone course, seek the help of professors in other specialty areas as needed.

8. Other students will have strengths in functional areas that will complement your weaknesses, so develop a cooperative spirit that moderates competitiveness in group work.

9. Read your case frequently as work progresses so you don't overlook details.

10. When preparing a case analysis as a group, divide into separate teams to work on the external analysis and internal analysis. Each team should write its section as if it were to go into the paper; then give each group member a copy.

11. At the end of each group session, assign each member of the group a task to be completed for the next meeting.

12. Have a good sense of humor.

13. Capitalize on the strengths of each member of the group; volunteer your services in your areas of strength.

14. Set goals for yourself and your team; budget your time to attain them.

15. Become friends with the library.

16. Foster attitudes that encourage group participation and interaction. Do not be too hasty to judge group members.

17. Be creative and innovative throughout the case analysis process.

18. Be prepared to work. There will be times when you will have to do more than your share. Accept it, and do what you have to do to move the team forward.

19. Think of your case analysis as if it were really happening; do not reduce case analysis to a mechanical process.

20. To uncover flaws in your analysis and to prepare the group for questions during an oral presentation, assign one person in the group to actively play the devil's advocate.

21. Do not schedule excessively long group meetings; two-hour sessions are about right.

22. A goal of case analysis is to improve your ability to think clearly in ambiguous and confusing situations; do not get frustrated that there is no single best answer.

23. Push your ideas hard enough to get them listened to, but then let up; listen to others and try to follow their lines of thinking; follow the flow of group discussion, recognizing when you need to get back on track; do not repeat yourself or others unless clarity or progress demands repetition.

24. Do not confuse symptoms with causes; do not develop conclusions and solutions prematurely; recognize that information may be misleading, conflicting, or wrong.

25. Work hard to develop the ability to formulate reasonable, consistent, and creative plans; put yourself in the strategist's position.

26. Develop confidence in using quantitative tools for analysis. They are not inherently difficult; it is just practice and familiarity you need.

27. Develop a case-writing style that is direct, assertive, and convincing; be concise, precise, fluent, and correct.

28. Have fun when at all possible. It is frustrating at times, but enjoy it while you can; it may be several years before you are playing CEO again.

29. Acquire a professional typist and proofreader. Do not perform either task alone.

30. Strive for excellence in writing and technical preparation of your case. Prepare nice charts, tables, diagrams, and graphs. Use color and unique pictures. No messy exhibits!

31. In group cases, do not allow personality differences to interfere. When they occur, they must be understood for what they are and put aside.
32. Do not forget that the objective is to learn; explore areas with which you are not familiar.
33. Pay attention to detail.
34. Think through alternative implications fully and realistically. The consequences of decisions are not always apparent. They often affect many different aspects of a firm's operations.
35. Get things written down (drafts) as soon as possible.
36. Read everything that other group members write, and comment on it in writing. This allows group input into all aspects of case preparation.
37. Provide answers to such fundamental questions as what, when, where, why, and how.
38. Adaptation and flexibility are keys to success; be creative and innovative.
39. Do not merely recite ratios or present figures. Rather, develop ideas and conclusions concerning the possible trends. Show the importance of these figures to the corporation.
40. Support reasoning and judgment with factual data whenever possible.
41. Neatness is a real plus; your case analysis should look professional.
42. Your analysis should be as detailed and specific as possible.
43. A picture speaks a thousand words, and a creative picture gets you an A in many classes.
44. Let someone else read and critique your paper several days before you turn it in.
45. Emphasize the "Strategy Selection" and "Strategy Implementation" sections. A common mistake is to spend too much time on the external or internal analysis parts of your paper. Always remember that the "meat" of the paper or presentation is the strategy selection and implementation sections.
46. Make special efforts to get to know your group members. This leads to more openness in the group and allows for more interchange of ideas. Put in the time and effort necessary to develop these relationships.
47. Be constructively critical of your group members' work. Do not dominate group discussions. Be a good listener and contributor.
48. Learn from past mistakes and deficiencies. Improve upon weak aspects of other case presentations.
49. Learn from the positive approaches and accomplishments of classmates.
50. Be considerate, dependable, reliable, and trustworthy.

READINGS

Fielen, John. "Clear Writing Is Not Enough." *Management Review* (April 1989): 49–53.

Holcombe, M., and J. Stein. *Presentations for Decision Makers* (Belmont, Calif.: Lifetime Learning Publications, 1983).

———. *Writing for Decision Makers* (Belmont, Calif.: Lifetime Learning Publications, 1981).

Jeffries, J., and J. Bates. *The Executive's Guide to Meetings, Conferences, and Audiovisual Presentations* (New York: McGraw-Hill, 1983).

Shurter, R., J. P. Williamson, and W. Broehl. *Business Research and Report Writing* (New York: McGraw-Hill, 1965).

Strunk, W., and E. B. White. *The Elements of Style* (New York: Macmillan, 1978).

Zall, P., and L. Franc. *Practical Writing in Business and Industry* (North Scituate, Mass.: Duxbury Press, 1978).

Instructions for Using the *Strategy Formulator* and *Case Analyst* Software

*T*he *Strategy Formulator* and *Case Analyst* software that accompanies this text are user-friendly programs that run on any IBM or IBM-compatible machine with at least one floppy disk drive and 512K (or greater) memory. Step-by-step instructions for using this software are provided in this appendix. *Strategy Formulator* and *Case Analyst* will greatly reduce the time it takes you to prepare quantitative, professional exhibits to support your oral case presentations and written case assignments.

The *Strategy Formulator* program generates strategy-formation matrices that are widely used among organizations. The matrices are described in Chapters 4, 5, and 6 of the text. You will want to use *Strategy Formulator* in analyzing all business policy cases. No prior experience with computers is needed to use this software.

The *Case Analyst* program consists of a set of 33 data files that contain the income statements and balance sheets for nearly all the cases in the text. These data files are presented in Lotus 1-2-3 format (Version 2.2) and can be loaded into any spreadsheet program. *Case Analyst* enables you to generate pro forma financial statements and projected financial ratios. Pro forma analysis is described in Chapter 7 of the text. Generating pro forma financial statements is an important part of analyzing a case because you need to show what impact your recommendations will have on the firm's future.

Making a Backup Copy of the Diskettes. It is a good idea to make a working copy of both the *Strategy Formulator* and *Case Analyst* diskette. Keep the original copies in a safe place as a backup. The operating system manual that came with your computer contains instructions on how to make backup copies. If you are using a computer with a hard disk drive, follow instructions in your DOS manual for creating a subdirectory and copy the original diskette to that subdirectory.

THE *STRATEGY FORMULATOR* SOFTWARE

Strategy Formulator is an innovative program that enables managers and students to formulate strategies for organizations. This personal computer software program incorporates the most modern strategic planning techniques in a simple way. The simplicity of *Strategy Formulator* enables this software to facilitate the "process of strategic planning" by promoting communication, understanding, creativity, and forward thinking among users.

Strategy Formulator is not a spreadsheet or database program; it is a structured brainstorming tool that enhances participation in strategy formulation. The software begins with development of an organizational mission statement as described in Chapter 3. Then, the software guides the user through an internal strategic planning audit of the company, followed by an external audit of the firm as described in Chapters 4 and 5. Next, the software generates alternative strategies for the firm, using analytical tools discussed in Chapter 6.

Strategy Formulator enables students or managers to create an organizational mission statement, identify key internal strengths and weaknesses as well as key external opportunities and threats, and then generate, evaluate, and prioritize alternative strategies that the firm could pursue. Individuals can work through the software independently and then meet to discuss particular strategies.

Strategy Formulator runs on any IBM-compatible personal computer system that has a high density (HD) disk drive. It includes numerous help screens and examples and offers clear printouts. No documentation manual is needed with *Strategy Formulator.* Simply boot DOS, Type SF, and follow directions.

Strategy Formulator gives you hands-on experience using actual strategic planning software and facilitates business policy case analysis. This new software is a derivative of the CheckMATE strategic planning software that is widely used among organizations worldwide. (For additional information about CheckMATE, contact Strategic Planning Systems, P.O. Box 13065, Florence, SC 29504; Phone 803-669-6960; Fax 803-673-9460.)

The Structure and Function of Strategy Formulator. The first and second screens that appear in the *Strategy Formulator* software are given in Figures 1 and 2. Note from the first screen that the F1, F2, and F3 keys are the Save key, Load key, and Print key, respectively. Note that the second screen gives an outline or flowchart of the *Strategy Formulator* program. This second screen is a main menu that returns throughout the program; you simply highlight the particular area you wish to work on and hit Enter to begin that part of the program.

FIGURE 1

THE FIRST SCREEN
STRATEGY FORMULATOR SOFTWARE

The *Strategy Formulator* program provides a systematic approach for managers to devise strategies their organization could pursue. *Strategy Formulator* incorporates the most modern strategic planning techniques in a simple way.

The recommended approach for using *Strategy Formulator* is for managers to work through the software independently, and then meet together to discuss the results and develop a single set of joint recommendations. This approach to strategic planning facilitates communication, forward thinking, understanding, commitment, and performance. The help key (F1) is available at all times throughout the *Formulator* program to give you more information. Press the F1 key now to obtain information about the Save key (F2), Load key (F3), Print key (F4), and Escape key.

Press the return key on the highlighted topic on the menu to activate the various parts of the program.

FIGURE 2

THE SECOND SCREEN

The Structure and Function of *Strategy Formulator*
 I. Create a Mission Statement
 II. Identify Key Internal Strengths and Weaknesses
 III. Identify Key External Opportunities and Threats
 IV. Generate Alternative Strategies Using:
     IE Analysis
     TOWS Analysis
     SPACE Analysis
     GRAND Analysis
 V. Refine Alternative Strategies
 VI. Select Strategies to Pursue
     Other functions:
     Load Data from Disk
     Save Data to Disk
     Print
     Quit Program

Getting Started. Insert the *Strategy Formulator* diskette into any IBM-compatible machine that has a high density (HD) disk drive and, at the prompt, type SF. (You will need to have previously loaded DOS if your system does not have that installed.)

Read the first screen. Hit the F1 key just to get familiar with the Help routine. Hit the Escape key to return to the main menu. Hit Enter to go to the second screen. Note from the second screen that you may simply highlight the "Create a Mission Statement" line and hit Enter to begin work on developing a mission statement— which is the first activity in formulating strategies. Hit Enter again when you are ready to return to the main menu. You may hit the F1 key anytime in the program for help. The Program Mechanics Help, as shown in Figure 3, will (always) appear on the screen if you hit the F1 key twice.

After completing the mission statement, highlight the next line "Identify Key Internal Strengths and Weaknesses." Hit Enter and begin development of a list of the company's key strengths and weaknesses. When you have completed this work, return to the main menu. Continue working sequentially in this manner through the program.

The Save and Load Routines. It is easy to save and load your work in the *Strategy Formulator* program. The Help Screens (F1 key) associated with the Save and Load routines are given in Figures 4 and 5.

The Print Routine. The *Strategy Formulator* software generates nine planning reports that can be printed separately or together, as indicated on a print screen as shown in Figure 6, that appears near the end of the program.

Simply highlight the reports you desire to be printed and hit Enter to begin printing your work. You could highlight the "Print All Reports" to print all of your work. If you press the F1 key, the screen shown in Figure 7 appears.

FIGURE 3

THE PROGRAM MECHANICS HELP SCREEN

- Movement between screens within a module is accomplished by pressing the UP and DOWN arrows. This is true both within the Help facility and within the main program.
- If you wish to delete to the left of the cursor, you should press the BACKSPACE key. If you wish to delete to the right of the cursor, you should press the DELETE key.
- If you wish to insert text, place the cursor where you wish to begin the insertion and press the INSERT key. When the insert mode is in operation, the cursor changes its size and the word "Insert" appears in the bottom right corner of the screen. Insert is turned off again either by pressing the INSERT key or by moving to another answer.
- You can access the HELP facility at any time by pressing the F1 key. From the Help facility, you can return to the screen you were working on by pressing the ESCAPE key.
- You can SAVE all of your work at any time by pressing the F2 key.
- You can LOAD all of your work at any time by pressing the F3 key.
- You can PRINT all or part of your work at any time by pressing the F4 key.
- You can return to the menu at any time by pressing the ESCAPE key.

FIGURE 4

THE SAVE ROUTINE HELP SCREEN

The Save routine is where the information that has been entered into the system is saved for later use.

The Drive is the disk drive where the data is saved.

The Path is the logical place on the drive where the information is saved. You should either read up on this in the DOS manual or go with the default. The default is the drive and path where the program is located.

The File Name is the name that is given to the information that is saved. This name is used later to retrieve the information. It is eight characters long.

The Directory List will give you a list of files that already exist. If you save over a file (use the same name), the contents of that file are lost. It is a good idea to save your files in two places so that there will be a backup if the primary file is lost. To do this, put a floppy disk in the drive and change the disk drive letter to the letter corresponding to the drive you are using. Usually the letter is A; sometimes it is B.

FIGURE 5

THE LOAD ROUTINE HELP SCREEN

The Load routine is where the information that has been saved on the disk is brought back into the system.

The Drive is the disk drive where the data is saved.

The Path is the logical place on the drive where the information is saved. For more information on this, you should read the DOS manual.

The File Name is the name that is given to the information that is saved. This name is used to retrieve the information. It is eight characters long.

The Directory List will give you a list of files that exist on the disk and path that are listed on the screen. The name must show up on the directory in order for the information to be read.

FIGURE 6

STRATEGY FORMULATOR PRINT REPORTS

Print ALL Reports	TOWS Analysis Report
Mission Statement Report	SPACE Analysis Report
Internal Analysis Report	GRAND Analysis Report
External Analysis Report	Alternative Strategies Report
IE Analysis Report	Selected Strategies Report

FIGURE 7

THE PRINT ROUTINE HELP SCREEN

The Print routine is accessed by hitting the F4 key or the print option on the main menu.

Within the print menu, select the report you wish by pressing the up and down arrow keys. You can print all reports or individual ones.

If there is a "printer off line" error, you should locate the on-line button on your printer and press it. This should put your printer on-line.

If there is a "printer paper out" error, you should load paper into your printer. This should correct this problem.

If you wish to bypass the program's printer error detection features for any reason, press the "D" (for disable) key. This is usually not needed, but if the user has nonstandard software or hardware, it may be necessary.

Contents of the Diskette. Income statements and balance sheets for 33 cases are provided in the Lotus 1-2-3 format (Version 2.2) on the *Case Analyst* diskette. The only two cases in the text that do not include financial statements are *W. L. Gore* and *Dave's Pit Stop Cafe.* Spreadsheets saved under Version 2.2 have a WK1 extension attached to their name. Newer versions of Lotus can read these files. Ample space is provided on the diskette for projected income statement and balance sheet information to be entered.

The 33 *Case Analyst* data files are listed below in alphabetical order.

FILE NAME	CORRESPONDING ORGANIZATION
AUDUBON WK1	*The Audubon Zoo*
BANCONE WK1	*Banc One*
BOEING WK1	*Boeing*
BORDEN WK1	*Borden*
CAMPBELL WK1	*Campbell Soup*
CCCA WK1	*Classic Car Club of America*
CIRCUS WK1	*Circus Circus Enterprises*
CITICORP WK1	*Citicorp*
DELL WK1	*Dell Computer*
DMERR WK1	*Dakota, Minnesota, & Eastern Railroad*
GEORGPAC WK1	*Georgia-Pacific*
HARLEY WK1	*Harley-Davidson*
HERSHEY WK1	*Hershey Foods*
IBM WK1	*International Business Machines*
LIMITED WK1	*The Limited*
MCDONNEL WK1	*McDonnell Douglas*
MET WK1	*The Metropolitan Museum of Art*
MHE WK1	*Material Handling Engineering*
NIKE WK1	*Nike*
NORDSTRO WK1	*Nordstrom*
NORWOOD WK1	*Norwood Furniture*
NSP WK1	*NSP Corporate Graphics*
PILGRIM WK1	*Pilgrim's Pride*
PLAYBOY WK1	*Playboy Enterprises*
PROMUS WK1	*Promus Companies*
RYKA WK1	*Rykä*
SPLATTER WK1	*Splatterball Adventure Games*
WALMART WK1	*Wal-Mart Stores*
WALNU WK1	*Walnut Creek Baptist Church*
WEYER WK1	*Weyerhaeuser*
WHIRLPOO WK1	*Whirlpool*
WINNEBAG WK1	*Winnebago Industries*
WTD WK1	*WTD Industries*

Using Case Analyst with Other Spreadsheets. Due to the historic dominance of Lotus in the spreadsheet arena, most popular spreadsheets such as Enable, Excel, and Quattro Pro can work with files created by Lotus. In most cases, the user can manipulate the Lotus file using the other spreadsheet. Once the manipulation is completed, the user has the option of saving the file in the Lotus format or in the format of the other spreadsheet. The details for working with a Lotus file will vary depending on the spreadsheet so users are advised to consult their manuals for details.

Prior Experience with Lotus. To benefit most from this diskette, you should have some prior knowledge and experience with Lotus or a comparable spreadsheet. Minimal prerequisite skills include retrieving and saving a spreadsheet, moving the cursor, using the @SUM function, and using the COPY command. For those who are not familiar with some of the other techniques used in constructing the Hershey case that follows, a brief review is provided below. This review includes details on entering data, formatting cells, editing the spreadsheet, and absolute addressing. A review of the PRINT command is presented in a later section.

Data Entry. Lotus permits users to enter numbers, labels, and formulas. To enter a number, it must begin with a digit, a plus or minus sign, or a decimal. The number should not contain commas, spaces, or a dollar sign. These symbols can be inserted by formatting commands described later. If a number is too wide for a cell, 1-2-3 may display asterisks instead of the number. If this happens, you need to increase the cell-width (/WORKSHEET COLUMN SET-WIDTH).

Labels are used mainly for row and column headings. Labels that are longer than a cell's width are continued across adjacent cells to the right, provided the cells are empty. If the first character of a label is one of those designating a number or formula, a label prefix must be used. Label prefixes determine how to display the label in the cell. The possible label prefixes are the apostrophe (') for left alignment of a label, the quotation mark (") for right alignment, and the caret (^) for centering the label. The default prefix is the apostrophe.

Formatting. The /RANGE FORMAT command can be used to format selected cells in a spreadsheet. This command yields a menu with ten options, but only three are of interest: Currency, Comma (,), and Percent. Before selecting one of the options under Format, you must select the number of decimal places to display. The number of decimals displayed does not change the internal value of the number when it is used in computations. The Currency option places a dollar sign before cell entries, commas between thousands, and negative values appear in parentheses. The , (Comma) option is the same as the Currency option except the dollar sign is suppressed. The Percent option displays the number in a percent format with a fixed number of decimal places.

Editing. Lotus provides users with a number of editing features. First, there are options under the WORKSHEET menu for inserting or deleting rows and columns and for changing the width of a column. Second, striking the F2 key permits you to edit individual cells. While in edit mode, typed characters are inserted immediately to the left of the cursor. The backspace or delete key can be used to delete characters. Third, the Erase option from the RANGE menu can be used to erase entries in a range of cells.

Absolute Addressing. Most of the cells containing assumptions for a pro forma model should be referenced using an absolute address. A cell reference is designated as absolute by preceding each coordinate by a dollar sign (e.g., an absolute address for B5 is $B$5). If a formula like (1+$A$30)*D30 were copied from the D column to the E column, the formula would appear as (1+$A$30)*E30 rather than (1+B30)*E30.

Format of the Spreadsheets on the Case Analyst *Diskette.* The financial data for each case begins in row 20 of column B. Rows 20–26 contain the name of the company and whether this portion of the spreadsheet is an income statement or balance sheet. Columns B–F are used to describe the row entries that will occupy column G and beyond. For nearly all the cases, numeric values for two consecutive years have been entered starting in column G.

Since all of the data will usually not print on one page, the user may have to insert page breaks at appropriate points. In order to accommodate wide lines, the user may have to use a compressed printing mode (i.e., 132 characters per line). To instruct your printer to print in compressed mode, the /PRINT PRINTER OPTIONS menu is used. Select the SETUP option from this menu and enter the appropriate printer code. For example, if you are using an Epson or IBM printer, the proper setup code is \015. If you are using a printer other than an IBM or Epson, you will need to consult your printer manual for the proper code. Before attempting to print in compressed mode, be sure to change the margins to the Left = 4 and Right = 136. Margins can be set by accessing the /PRINT PRINTER OPTIONS menu and selecting Margins. If you are using a printer that is capable of printing 132 characters per line in normal mode, you must access the /PRINT PRINTER OPTIONS menu and delete the code \015.

The Windows version of Lotus makes the printing process much simpler; the user can direct Lotus to fit as much information as possible on a page. In addition, the user has the option of printing in a landscape mode.

Pro Forma Statements. Pro forma (projected) financial statement analysis is an important strategic-management tool because it allows firms to examine the expected results of different strategies. A pro forma income statement and balance sheet allows managers to compute projected financial ratios under different strategy-implementation scenarios. Steps for developing pro forma financial statements are given in Chapter 8.

A Pro Forma Example Using Lotus. Financial statements from the Hershey Foods Cohesion Case on the *Case Analyst* diskette are used as an example. The steps listed below apply generally to other cases as well. A three-year (1994, 1995, and 1996) forecast will be generated from the existing data. However, realize that pro forma statements should reasonably reflect what strategies you recommend the company to pursue in the future. Thus, a constant historical growth or shrink rate may not reasonably show the effect of your strategies on the future financial condition of the firm.

Step 1 Start the Lotus 1-2-3 program. This process may vary depending on the type of computer facilities you are using. Your professor or lab instructor should provide explicit instructions for starting Lotus.

Step 2 Use the /FILE command to retrieve the case of interest. For our example, this will be the file named Hershey.

Step 3 Make sure your printer has been turned on. Use the /PRINT command to generate a paper copy of the case data. This copy of the case will be used as a worksheet.

Step 4 Determine a projected sales growth (decline) rate for Hershey. A reasonable way to determine a value for the projected sales growth (or decline) is to calculate the following ratios:

net sales for 1990/net sales for 1989 (1.12),

net sales for 1991/net sales for 1990 (1.07),

net sales for 1992/net sales for 1991 (1.11), and

net sales for 1993/net sales for 1992 (1.08).

Then use the average of these four ratios as the projected sales growth (decline) rate. This average (1.10) can be computed with Lotus or with a calculator. Now write the average in its decimal form to the left of the "Net Sales" entry on your paper copy.

Step 5 Determine the ratio of the cost-of-goods to net sales. This can be done in the same manner as the calculations for the projected sales growth (decline) rate. In particular, calculate the following ratios:

Cost of Sales 1990/net sales 1990, (.58),

Cost of Sales 1991/net sales 1991 (.58),

Cost of Sales 1992/net sales 1992 (.57), and

Cost of Sales 1993/net sales 1993 (.57).

In the Hershey case, the entries for "Cost of Sales" (row 28) are used for the cost-of-goods. Once these ratios have been determined, calculate the average, and use the decimal value of the average (.58) as the cost-of-goods-sold as a percentage-of-sales figure. On your paper copy, write the average to the left of the "Cost of Sales" entry.

Step 6 Determine percentages for other expense items from the income statement in the same manner, and enter the decimal equivalent to the left of the expense item on your paper copy.

For the next steps you will be using your computer.

Step 7 Prepare columns K, L, and M as follows. First, enter 1994, 1995, and 1996 in cells K23, L23, and M23, respectively. Second, use the Column Width option of the /WORKSHEET menu to increase the width of these columns to 12 or more. Third, to save effort, copy the data in column J to corresponding areas in columns K, L, and M. Fourth, use the /RANGE ERASE command to erase the data in this area; the data will be erased, but the format specifications for cell entries will be retained. Thus, when entries are made in these columns, they will automatically have the same format of the data in columns G–J.

Step 8 Enter your projected sales growth rate (1.10) from Step 4 in cell A25. Enter in column A your estimates for the other expenses in the appropriate row. In the Hershey example, you would enter .58 in cell A28 as the estimate for the ratio for the cost of sales to net sales.

Step 9 Use the spreadsheet to determine projected sales for the next three years. Enter the following formula in cell K25: ($A25) *J25. This represents the projected sales for 1994. Copy the formula in K25 to the range L25. .M25 to generate the projected sales for 1995 and 1996.

Step 10 Use the spreadsheet to determine the estimated "Cost of Sales" for 1994–1996. Enter the following formula in cell K28: +$A28 *J25. This represents the projected cost-of-goods-sold for 1994. For 1995 and 1996, copy the formula from cell K28 to L28 and M28. Continue this process for the remaining expenses. For entries that are totals in the J column, copy the formula stored in the total cell for column J to the corresponding cells in the projected year columns (K, L, and M).

Step 11 To create the pro forma balance sheet, calculate the projected values on your paper copy and then enter these values in the appropriate cell in column A. Use the /COPY command to copy the balance sheet data from column J to the range defined by your projected years. For example, if you are making a three-year projection, then copy column J to columns K, L, and M. After the copy is completed, replace all nonformula entries in column K by your projected values (as was done in the income statement). The value of this procedure is that the existing format specifications for column J will be copied to columns K, L, and M. Thus, the proper number of decimal places, placement of the dollar sign, and positioning of commas will be taken care of automatically. If you want to change the format, select the /RANGE FORMAT menu. Another advantage of copying column J is that all formula entries will also be copied.

Step 12 This step describes how to use the spreadsheet to calculate financial ratios of interest. The financial ratios for a case should be calculated at the bottom of the spreadsheet. Enter the name of the financial ratio as a label in column B. For long names, you may have to put the name in two rows. To calculate the ratio, enter the formula in terms of relative cell addresses in the column of the first projected year. After all ratios have been calculated for the first projected year, copy the cells containing the ratio formulas to the corresponding cells for the other projected years. The value of this procedure is that if the assumptions in column A change, the financial ratios are automatically recalculated.

A Ratio Example. A benefit of having case data on this diskette is the ease with which various financial ratios can be calculated. Recall that a listing of important financial ratios was presented in Chapter 5.

To illustrate how the ratios can be calculated, data from the Hershey case are used. It would be useful if you had a copy of the Hershey example in front of you now. An example from each ratio category is calculated for the year 1993. For each ratio, the appropriate formula in terms of cell references, the numbers used in the calculation, and the results of the calculation are displayed.

Examples of Financial Ratios for Hershey for 1993

CURRENT RATIO
= Current assets/Current liabilities
= +j81/j106
= 888,996/813,845
= 1.09

LONG-TERM-DEBT-TO-
EQUITY RATIO
= Long-term debt/Total stockholders' equity
= +j108/j126
= 165,757/1,412,344
= .12

TOTAL ASSETS
TURNOVER
= Sales/Total assets
= +j25/j90
= 3,488,249/2,855,091
= 1.22

RETURN ON TOTAL
ASSETS (ROA)
= Net income/Total assets
= +j47/j90
= 193,325/2,855,091
= .07

ANNUAL PERCENTAGE
GROWTH IN TOTAL
SALES
= (Total sales$_{1993}$ − Total sales$_{1992}$)/Total sales $_{1992}$
= +(j25 − i25)/i25
= (3,488,249 − 3,219,805)/3,219,805
= 8.34%

The user should note that not all ratios for every case can be calculated since some income statements and balance sheets do not contain the necessary information.

BANKING INDUSTRY NOTE

WRAY O. CANDILIS AND JOHN R. SHUMAN
U.S. Department of Commerce

Federally insured depository institutions held slightly more than $4.9 trillion in assets in 1993, down slightly from 1992. If the interest rates remain low and prices remain steady, however, assets in 1994 are expected to increase 1 percent to approximately $5 trillion.

Commercial banks, savings institutions, and credit unions in 1993 benefited from a widening of spreads between interest rates charged for loans and paid for deposits. Savings institutions reported a record high spread of 4.25 percent between interest earned from mortgage loans and interest paid on deposits.

Depositors in 1993 diverted funds in record volume from banks, thrifts, and credit unions to alternative investments, especially mutual funds and common stock. Commercial banks faced with higher deposit insurance and the need to improve loan quality slowed the growth of deposits and their lending activity.

Despite the slowdown in lending and runoff in deposits, commercial banks and savings institutions continued to increase profits in 1993. Banks in 1994 are expected to report profits for the third consecutive year. Savings institutions are expected to continue to decline in terms of numbers and assets, but should extend a streak of profitable quarters that dates from 1991.

Banks and savings institutions are also expected to continue their evolution into a structure featuring a regional bank-holding company that operates independent depository, commercial and consumer lending, mortgage lending and mortgage servicing, insurance, and securities units. Banks expect securities activities to become a significant growth area.

In 1987 the Federal Reserve Board allowed certain subsidiaries of banks to underwrite and deal in asset-backed securities and municipal revenue bonds. The Fed in 1989 expanded the eligible securities to corporate debt and stock. Revenues from underwriting and dealing in these securities are limited to 10 percent of the subsidiary's total revenues, yet by early 1993 bank subsidiaries accounted for 6.2 percent of the capital of all securities firms. During the 12 months ending June 30, 1993, these subsidiaries underwrote 5.5 percent of all investment-grade corporate debt. Money-center and large regional banks in 1993 also competed aggressively with traditional mutual fund sponsors by retailing mutual funds to their customers, in part as an effort to recapture some of the funds flowing from certificates of deposit to other investment vehicles. Some of these banks have limited their activity to retailing funds sponsored by traditional fund management companies. But more than 110 banks or bank-holding companies offered proprietary mutual funds, primarily to their existing client base. Bank-sponsored mutual funds in 1993 were the fastest growing segment of the mutual-fund industry, accounting for 10.6 percent of total assets, and 30 percent of new sales.

Community development banking also increased in prominence in 1993. Federal banking and savings institution regulators intensified their audits of lending to lower-income communities, and gathered public information on means to increase lending in these neighborhoods. Credit union regulators chartered four new credit unions exclusively to provide services for lower-income members, while another 140 credit unions focused services on lower-income members.

Trends and Forecasts: Commercial Banking (SIC 602) (in billions of dollars except as noted)

| ITEM | 1991 | 1992 | 1993[1] | 1994[2] | PERCENT CHANGE (1990–1994) | | | |
					90–91	91–92	92–93	93–94
Assets	3,545	3,653	3,689	3,763	4.3	3.1	1.0	2.0
Loans	2,288	2,281	2,327	2,420	–0.9	–0.3	2.0	4.0
Investments	706	799	878	966	16.5	13.2	10.0	10.0
Deposits	2,452	2,542	2,593	2,648	3.8	3.7	2.0	2.0
Employment(000)	1,529	1,488	1,473	1,458	–2.3	–2.7	–1.0	–1.0

[1]Estimate

[2]Forecast

Source: Board of Governors of the Federal Reserve System; U.S. Department of Labor, Bureau of Labor Statistics, Estimates and forecasts by U.S. Department of Commerce, International Trade Administration.

COMMERCIAL BANKING

As economic activity maintained its steady, but modest, upward trend, businesses began once again to turn to banks for their short-term capital needs. With low interest rates and steady price levels as a backdrop, bank lending was expected to fare a little better than in the most recent past, rising 2 percent to $2,327 billion in 1993, and 4 percent to $2,420 billion in 1994. Bank lending dropped slightly both in 1991 and 1992. The growth of bank investments, on the other hand, is expected to continue to decelerate from its recent peak increase of 16.5 percent in 1991 to about 10 percent in both 1993 and 1994.

The broad variety of savings and investments instruments marketed by competing depository and nondepository financial institutions is expected to result in a relatively small 3 percent increase in commercial bank deposits in 1993 and 1994. Over the past few years, consumer bank deposits have been especially hit due to the runoff of certificates of deposit, only partly offset by the growth of passbook and money market accounts. Most of the runoff has flowed into mutual funds providing the strength being experienced in the stock and bond markets. This continuous rivalry from competitors has compelled commercial banks to enter the mutual fund business and to keep up the pressure on legislators and regulators in an effort to open up areas, such as the securities market, that previously were off-limits.

Specifically, the Federal Reserve Board has in recent years given approval to a number of banks for broader securities underwriting powers, under "Section 20" of the Glass Steagall Act, which permits banks, through separately capitalized units, to underwrite and deal in corporate debt and equity. These activities, however, can contribute no more than 10 percent of the unit's revenues. Banks have long been able to deal in government securities.

Of the more than 30 banks that have received approval by the Board for securities underwriting privileges under Section 20, about one third are foreign banks while the rest are domestic money-center banks and big regional bank companies. It should be noted that 17 additional foreign banks have used "grandfathered" status under the International Banking Act of 1978 to deal in both commercial banking and securities underwriting activities in the United States.

Profitability of Banks. High net interest-rate margins—the spread between interest income and interest expense—and improved quality of commercial bank assets in 1992, set in a framework of a general economic upturn, resulted in lifting banks out of their 1989–1991 depressed profit picture (Table 1). These trends continued in the first half of 1993.

The average return on assets, measured by income as a percentage of average fully consolidated assets for all size categories of banks went from 0.53 percent in 1991 to 0.92 in 1992. The most progress was experienced by large banks—those with more than $5 billion in assets—and the 10 largest banks, the return on assets of the former going from 0.50 to 1.01 percent, and the latter from 0.21 to 0.65 percent.

The average return on equity, measured by net income as a percentage of average equity capital, also grew substantially for the industry as a whole, going from 7.86 percent in 1991 to 12.80 in 1992. As with the return on assets, the greatest gains were shown by large banks and the ten largest banks, the return on equity of the former increasing from 8.10 to 14.66 percent and the latter from 4.25 to 11.87 percent.

Failures and Problem Banks. The financial health of the commercial banking industry is also evident in the number of failures, which dropped from a peak of 206 in 1989 to 120 in 1992 (Figure 1). Unofficial predictions for 1993 put the number of failures at 50 to 60. The number of banks on the problem list of the Federal Deposit Insurance Corporation (FDIC) also dropped considerably, falling by nearly half from the 1987 peak.

As a consequence of bank failures and the depletion of the Bank Insurance Fund, premium rates have been steadily increasing since 1989 when banks were paying 8.3 cents for every $100 of insured deposits. Beginning in January 1993, the FDIC instituted a risk-based system with premiums ranging from 23 cents for the best-performing banks to 31 cents for the weaker ones. It was at first predicted that by the year 2002 the bank fund would reach the required level of $1.25 for every $100 of insured deposits, at which time premiums would drop to 13.5 cents per $100 of deposits and to 10 cents a year later. More recent predictions, however, based on lower bank-failure projections for the years ahead and a slowing in the growth rate of deposits, estimated that the $1.25 level for every $100 of insured deposits might be reached much

TABLE 1	Profit Rates of Commercial Banks, 1990–92		
ITEM	1990	1991	1992
Return on assets[1]	0.49	0.53	0.92
Return on equity[2]	7.57	7.86	12.80

[1]Net income as a percent of average fully consolidated assets net of loss reserves.
[2]Net income as a percent of average equity capital.
Source: Board of Governors of the Federal Reserve System.

FIGURE 1 Failed and Problem Banks

Number of Banks

Source: Federal Deposit Insurance Corporation.

earlier than 2002, perhaps as early as 1996. Consequently, premiums are now expected to be reduced more quickly than previously predicted.

International Activities. The number of foreign bank offices in the United States rose steadily throughout the past two decades, reaching 747 by the end of 1992, and fell slightly to 720 a year later (Figure 2).

These offices include 8 branches, 224 agencies, 90 subsidiaries more than 25 percent owned by foreign banks, 17 Edge Act and Agreement Corporations, and 11 New York State Investment Companies. Nearly one-half of the offices are in New York, with most of the others in California, Illinois, and Florida. Japan, Canada, France, and the United Kingdom have the largest number of bank offices in the United States. Assets of foreign bank offices in the United States have increased significantly in recent years, rising from $198 billion in 1980 to $865 billion in 1992 or approximately one-fourth of U.S. total banking assets.

In contrast to foreign banks in the United States, U.S. banks abroad have been restructuring and consolidating their activities during the past several years. By the end of 1992, 120 Federal Reserve member banks were operating 774 branches in foreign countries and overseas areas of the United States, a decline from 916 branches at the end of 1985. Of the 120 banks, 88 were national banks operating 660 branches, and 32 were state banks operating the remaining 114 branches.

Technological Developments. Customer use of automated teller machines (ATMs) has been rising significantly over the past few years with the result that branch operating costs have been falling, according to an ATM survey conducted in 1992 by the *American Banker.* Specifically, the annual growth rate for ATMs between 1989 and 1992 has ranged between 17 and 19 percent, with the top five users of teller machines

FIGURE 2 Foreign Bank Offices in the United States

Number of Offices

Source: Board of Governors of the Federal Reserve System.

being Bank of America with 4,500; Citibank 1,900; Wells Fargo 1,687; NationsBank 1,678; and First Interstate 1,332.

Increased ATM usage and the consequent decrease in teller transactions does not necessarily mean the demise of branches. There will always be customers who will prefer a live teller to a machine, but it will be bank officers with their sophisticated personal computers and software that will, with increased efficiency, meet new customers, handle their questions, and sell them new products.

Slower progress than the ATM growth is being shown by the debit card which can be used not only in conjunction with an ATM or the withdrawal of funds, but also in conjunction with a point-of-sale terminal for the transfer of funds from a buyer's account to a seller's account. The development of the debit card also remains quite modest in the United States, although it has had enormous success in other countries.

In the home banking field, it seems that the problems that existed in the 1980s still prevail in the 1990s. It is a relatively expensive service that requires a personal computer, a modem, and the necessary software. However, for the sophisticated customer, it offers the facility of paying bills, transferring funds, and opening new accounts. As the equipment becomes less expensive, however, and as banks offer a broader array of services, home banking could develop into a comprehensive information package that would include such nonbank activities as insurance, entertainment, travel, as well as business and sports news.

Legislative and Regulatory Issues. As a result of the passage of the Federal Deposit Insurance Corporation Improvement Act of 1991 (see *1993 U.S. Industrial Outlook*), with its mandated new disclosure rules and tougher auditing and underwriting standards, commercial bankers have been pressuring legislators and regulators to ease the regulatory burden that might have resulted from the implementation of the act. Consequently, regulators decided to rely on examiners to assure that banks are operating safely rather than to set specific managerial standards. Other examples of regulatory sensitivity to bankers' complaints include a proposal to exempt about 7,500 smaller banks from the act's proposed capital standards for banks facing unusual risk from interest rate swings, loan concentration, and other nontraditional activities; and a proposal to let large banks use their own internal systems, with examiner approval, for measuring interest-rate risk.

The principal banking bills in Congress in 1993 concerned the issues of interstate banking (to authorize nationwide branching subject to restrictions on market share of deposits), community development lending (to establish a fund to support community development by financial institutions), overhauling the Federal Reserve System (to increase accountability of the central bank), Fair Credit Reporting Act Amendments (to make it easier for consumers to obtain copies of their credit reports and correct errors), a secondary market for small business loans (to create such a market by either establishing a federal agency or reducing regulatory impediments to securitization), regulatory relief (to give well-capitalized institutions more favorable treatment, or repeal or modify some of the congressionally mandated regulations), and agency consolidation (to create a single banking oversight agency).

At the state level, legislators aimed at using state law to break down interstate banking barriers. Among the latest states to favorably consider interstate banking reform legislation are North Carolina, Alaska, and Oregon. Several Southeastern states are expected to take up similar legislation in the near future, a move that is necessary to modify the regional banking pact system these states adopted in the mid-1980s. Twenty-two states, including California and New York, require reciprocity as a condition to interstate banking, meaning they will let an out-of-state bank into their state if that bank's home state will let their banks in.

Despite strong banking industry opposition, the Financial Accounting Standards Board (FASB) adopted rules that require banks to assign market value to a broader classification of securities holdings; to value impaired or troubled loans at their current value; and thereafter to reserve against expected loss of interest on such loans. However, in a concession to the industry, FASB gave banks the option of adopting its market-value standard in the fourth quarter of 1993 instead of the first quarter of 1994, as requested by some large banks, and delaying the starting date for a new standard on valuing nonperforming loans and setting loan-loss reserves to the first quarter of 1995.

Judicial Issues. Following many years of debate over the advantages and disadvantages of the separation of commercial banking and insurance, and with billions of dollars at stake, the U.S. Supreme Court in mid-1993 ruled that 1916 law, which authorized national banks with branches in towns of less than 5,000 to sell insurance, remains in force. On demand, the U.S. Circuit Court of Appeals for the District of Columbia also decided that there is no geographic limit on where national banks affected by the Supreme Court ruling may sell insurance. In a related case, the U.S. Supreme Court declined to resolve the issue as to whether the Office of the Comptroller of the Currency may permit national banks to sell title insurance under authority of a federal law that permits national banks to exercise "all such incidental powers as shall be necessary to carry on the business of banking." In refusing to hear this appeal, the Court let stand a decision of the U.S. Court of Appeals for the Second Circuit which barred the sale of such insurance in New York, Vermont, and Connecticut. In yet another insurance case, the U.S. Circuit Court of Appeals for the Fifth Circuit ruled that annuities are insurance products, and thus subject to the so-called town of 5,000 rule. Under the ruling, a national bank could sell annuities by mail in small towns, but it would not be able to offer them from branches in larger cities.

Outlook for 1994. The turnaround in the commercial banking industry during 1992 and 1993 was much stronger than the upturn in the economy as a whole, and will probably remain so during 1994. The industry's liquidity together with its strengthened capital position will provide the means to meet the borrowing requirements of individual and corporate customers, but loan growth is expected to rise no more than 4 percent. Monetary and fiscal authorities will continue to work together to try to prevent any stalling of the economic recovery or any buildup of inflationary pressures.

CITICORP—1994

C A S E

1

RANDY WHITE
Auburn University at
Montgomery
FRED DAVID,
Francis Marion University

Based in New York City, Citicorp (212-559-4822) is a U.S. bank-holding company and sole shareholder of Citibank, N.A. (Citi). Citi has assets exceeding $213 billion and is the largest U.S. bank. However, Citi is in trouble; its 1992 return on assets of 0.23 percent is the lowest of the top ten U.S. banks, as shown in Exhibit 1–1. In the 38 years that *Fortune* has been compiling its annual list of the largest commercial banking companies, Citi has never made as much as 1 percent on assets. In most years, it hasn't even come close. *Fortune* annually evaluates U.S. companies on eight management criteria: quality of management; financial soundness; quality of products or services; ability to attract, develop, and keep talented people; use of corporate asset; value as long-term investment; innovativeness; and, finally, community and environmental responsibility. Citi currently ranks near the bottom of *Fortune's* list, a fact that suggests the bank is poorly managed.[1]

Citi's net income declined steadily from $1.86 billion in 1988 to a loss of $457 million in 1991. Citi's net income rebounded to $722 million in 1992 and $1.9 billion in 1993.

THE BUSINESSES OF CITI

Through a network of 1,389 U.S. offices covering 32 states and the District of Columbia as well as 1,947 offices outside the United States operating in 92 countries, Citi's 81,500 employees (38,500 in the United States and 43,000 outside the United States) market financial services to individuals, businesses, governments, and financial

EXHIBIT 1-1 Top Ten U.S. Banks by Asset Size as of December 31, 1992 (*In millions of dollars except ROE and ROA*)

RANK		ASSETS	RETURN ON ASSET (%)	RETURN ON EQUITY (%)	MARKET VALUE*
1	Citicorp	213,701	.23	6.6	10,811
2	BankAmerica	180,646	.80	12.7	17,517
3	Chemical Bank	139,655	.67	12.4	10,140
4	Nations Bank	118,059	.97	15.8	13,820
5	J. P. Morgan	102,941	1.14	20.8[a]	13,006
6	Chase Manhattan	102,941	.51	11.2	5,444
7	Bankers Trust NY	72,448	.99	23.1	5,925
8	Banc One	61,417	1.31	16.3	13,403
9	Wells Fargo	52,537	.45	7.9	5,995
10	PNC Bank	51,380	1.18	15.5	7,762

*As of March 31, 1993. Market Value is the closing common stock price multiplied by the number of outstanding common shares.

[a]Year-end amounts.

Source: "Bank Scoreboard," *Business Week*, May 3, 1993, p. 150.

institutions. Citi faces intense competition from both bank and nonbank institutions and, in certain of their activities, from government agencies. Its core businesses are shown in Exhibit 1–2.

Global Consumer. The Global Consumer division provides the following broad range of consumer financial services worldwide:

1. Citiphone Banking and Citicard Banking Centers to give customers current account information to manage their money anytime and anywhere. In Japan, Citi has 21 branches and recently introduced several new services, including automatic bill payment, a direct salary payment facility, and an unsecured revolving credit line available via International Citicard which enables customers traveling in other countries to access their home bank accounts;

EXHIBIT 1-2 The Businesses of Citicorp by Net Income (Loss) as of December 31, 1993 (*In millions of dollars*)

BUSINESS FOCUS	NET INCOME (LOSS) $ MILLIONS		AVERAGE ASSETS $ BILLIONS		RETURN ON ASSETS	
	1993	1992[1]	1993	1992[1]	1993	1992[1]
Global consumer[2]						
North America, Europe and Japan	$ 665	$ 439	$ 75	$ 85	.89%	.52%
Developing economies	556	448	25	21	2.22%	2.13%
Global finance[3]						
North America, Europe and Japan	909	490	73	64	1.25%	.77%
Developing economies	761	643	36	32	2.11%	2.01%
North America commercial real estate	(621)	(1,316)	12	14	(5.18)%	(9.40)%
Cross-border refinancing portfolio	92	403	3	4	3.07%	10.08%
Corporate items[4]	(443)	(385)	4	6	(11.08)%	(6.42)%
	$ 1,919	$ 722	$ 228	$ 226	.84%	.32%
Cumulative effect of accounting change[5]	300	—	—	—	—	—
Total Citicorp	$ 2,219	$ 722	$ 228	$ 226	.97%	.32%

(1) Reclassified to conform to current year's presentation.

(2) Global Consumer results reflect after-tax restructuring charges of $143 million in 1993 and $82 million in 1992. Of these amounts, Global Consumer North America, Europe and Japan included $139 million and $74 million, respectively.

(3) Global Finance results reflect after-tax restructuring charges of $95 million in 1993 and $49 million in 1992. Of these amounts, Global Finance North America, Europe and Japan included $83 million and $31 million, respectively.

(4) Corporate Items includes the effects of asset sales, as well as business write-downs. Results for 1993 also reflect after-tax restructuring charges of $16 million, compared with $(8) million in 1992.

(5) Represents cumulative effect of adopting Statement of Financial Accounting Standards No. 109, "Accounting for Income Taxes," as of January 1, 1993.

Source: *Annual Report*, 1993.

2. A National Banking System (NBS) that enables all U.S. branches to access a customer's total banking relationship upon presentation of his/her Citicard; NBS was completed by year-end 1993;

3. Card products such as *Citigold* for affluent customers; Visa and MasterCard accounts, 29 million domestic and 8 million foreign accounts. New card brands appealing to different customer segments such as CHOICE (the price sensitive), Preferred (the upscale), Classic (security, quality, and value appeals), and affinity cards such as Citibank AAdvantage (a frequent-flier mileage reward program based on card activity). Citi's Diners Club travel and entertainment card produces more than $21 billion in worldwide sales in over 175 countries; U.S. sales have climbed to $9 billion.

4. Citibank Private Bank, the world's largest non-Swiss private bank, focuses on management services tailored to wealthy individuals, their families, and their businesses. The average level of client assets managed totaled $1 million in 1993, with locations in 31 countries.

As shown in Exhibit 1–2, Global Consumer includes two subdivisions: (1) Japan, Europe, and North America (JENA), which showed an increase in net income from $455 million in 1992 to $665 million in 1993, and (2) Developing Economies (primarily Latin America and Asia), which earned a record $556 million in 1993, up from $486 million in 1992. This increase was due primarily to solid loan demand and account growth in Argentina, Hong Kong, and Taiwan. At year-end 1993, $23.9 billion of securitized credit-card receivables were outstanding as compared to $25.6 billion in 1992.

Exhibit 1–3 reflects an increase in Global Consumer's net income from $887 million in 1992 to $1,221 million in 1993. Exhibit 1–4 describes Citi's consumer credit-loss history based on its credit-loss ratio (i.e., annual credit losses as a percent of

EXHIBIT 1-3 Global Consumer as of Years Ended December 31
(*In millions of dollars*)

	1993	1992	INC./ (DEC.)	%
Total revenue	$ 9,600	$ 9,285	$ 315	3
Restructuring charges	$ 233	$ 130	$ 103	79
Other operating expense	5,965	5,789	176	3
Total operating expense	$ 6,198	$ 5,919	$ 279	5
Provision for credit losses	$ 1,686	$ 2,134	$(448)	(21)
Income before taxes	$ 1,716	$ 1,232	$ 484	39
Income taxes	495	345	150	43
Net income	$ 1,221	$ 887	$ 334	38
Average assets (In billions)	$ 100	$ 106	$ (6)	(6)
Return on assets	1.22%	.84%	.38%	—

Source: *Annual Report*, 1993.

EXHIBIT 1-4 Consumer Portfolio Loss Ratios as of Years Ended December 31

	AVERAGE LOANS[1] ($ BILLIONS)	NET CREDIT LOSSES ($ MILLIONS)	1993 CREDIT LOSS RATIO	1992 CREDIT LOSS RATIO	1991 CREDIT LOSS RATIO
U.S.					
Mortgages[2]	$19.1	$ 267	1.40%	1.61%	.46%
Credit cards	8.5	440	5.18%	6.28%	5.84%
Other	16.9	331	1.96%	2.47%	2.65%
Total U.S.	$44.5	$1,038	2.33%	2.89%	2.46%
Outside the U.S.	36.9	372	1.01%	1.04%	1.05%
Total	$81.4	$1,410	1.73%	2.16%	1.97%

(1) Loan amounts are net of unearned income.
(2) Includes first and second residential mortgages.
Source: *Annual Report*, 1993.

average consumer loans). The falling credit-loss ratios are due to fewer bankruptcies and an improved housing market. Similarly, loans outside the United States also experienced lower credit loss ratios.

Exhibit 1–5 displays Citi's loss ratios for commercial loans. Regarding the U.S. portfolio, net credit losses declined to $379 million, down from $1.8 billion in 1992; the credit-loss ratio fell to 1.67 percent in 1993 from 4.54 percent in 1992, a 63 percent fall. In offices outside the United States, credit-loss ratios declined 62 percent from 1.74 percent in 1992 to 0.65 percent in 1993; net credit loss also dropped to $209 million in 1992 as compared to $511 million in 1993. Exhibit 1–6 gives the allowances for credit loss.

Global Finance. The global finance sector provides worldwide financial services to corporations, financial institutions, governments, and capital markets. Net income increased markedly from $1.13 billion in 1992 to $1.67 billion in 1993, as shown in Exhibit 1–7.

North America Commercial Real Estate. Consisting of real estate operations in the United States and Canada, the North America Commercial Real Estate division incurred a net loss of $621 million in 1993 compared to a loss of $1.3 billion in 1992, as shown in Exhibit 1–8. Increasing write-offs and write-downs affected this business, and projections indicated continuing unfavorable results. Citi is trying to restructure loans to insure repayment and recoup its losses. Citi's tactics also include continued collection efforts by a staff of 600 experienced real estate professionals in 12 offices in the United States and Canada. Exposure in this division is diversified by office, resi-

EXHIBIT 1-5 Commercial Portfolio Loss Ratios as of Years Ended December 31
(*In millions of dollars*)

	Average Loans ($ Billions)	Net Credit Losses ($ Millions)	1993 Credit Loss Ratio	1992 Credit Loss Ratio	1991 Credit Loss Ratio
In U.S. offices					
Commercial real estate loans[1]	$ 8.4	$285	3.38%	7.80%	4.06%
Other commercial loans and leases[2]	14.3	94	.66%	2.38%	2.58%
	$22.7	$379	1.67%	4.54%	3.21%
In offices outside the U.S.					
Commercial real estate loans[1]	$ 2.5	$124	4.94%	7.75%	7.18%
Other commercial loans and leases[2]	29.6	85	.29%	1.01%	1.00%
	$32.1	$209	.65%	1.74%	2.03%
			2.15%	(.89)%	26.14%
Refinancing country loans	2.8	61	.77%	1.44%	6.89%
	$34.9	$270	1.13%	2.80%	5.13%
Total	$57.6	$649			

(1) Includes mortgage and real estate loans.

(2) Includes net write-offs of real estate-related loans of $24 million, $123 million, and $51 million in U.S. offices in 1993, 1992, and 1991 respectively, with $173 million in offices outside the U.S. in 1992.

Source: *Annual Report*, 1993.

EXHIBIT 1-6 Allowance for Credit Losses as of Years Ended December 31
(*In millions of dollars or as noted*)

	Loans ($ Billions)	1993 Allowance	1992 Allowance	1991 Allowance
Global consumer ratio	$ 84.4	$1,596	$1,338	$1,137
		1.89%	1.60%	1.24%
Commercial ratio	52.1	2,545	2,221	1,650
		4.88%	4.19%	2.97%
Cross-border refinancing portfolio[1]	2.5	238	300	521
Total	$139.0	$4,379	$3,859	$3,308
Ratio		3.15%	2.76%	2.19%
Reserve for Global Consumer Sold Portfolios		$ 527	$ 544	$ 412

(1) The allowance attributable to the cross-border refinancing portfolio represented 8% of medium- and long-term loans and placements at December 31, 1993. When adjusted to add back $2.8 billion of cumulative country write-offs previously charged off, the allowance at December 31, 1993 was equivalent to 53% of similarly adjusted medium- and long-term claims, compared with 51% at year-end 1992 and 54% at year-end 1991.

Source: *Annual Report*, 1993.

EXHIBIT 1-7 Global Finance as of Years Ended December 31 (*In millions of dollars*)

	1993	1992	INC./ (DEC.)	%
Total revenue	$6,108	$5,406	$ 702	13
Restructuring charges	$ 156	$ 76	$ 80	N/M
Other operating expense	3,279	3,137	142	5
Total operating expense	$3,435	$3,213	$ 222	7
Provision for credit losses	$ 305	$ 644	$(339)	(53)
Income before taxes	$2,368	$1,549	$ 819	53
Income taxes	698	416	282	68
Net income	$1,670	$1,133	$ 537	47
Average assets (In billions)	$ 109	$ 96	$ 13	14
Return on assets	1.53%	1.18%	.35%	—

Source: *Annual Report*, 1993.

EXHIBIT 1-8 North America Commercial Real Estate as of Years Ended December 31 (*In millions of dollars*)

	1993	1992[1]	INC./ (DEC.)	%
Total revenue	$ (11)	$ (45)	$ 34	76
Operating expense	377	424	(47)	(11)
Provision for credit losses	610	1,622	(1,012)	(62)
(Loss) before taxes	$(998)	$(2,091)	$(1,093)	(52)
Income taxes	(377)	(775)	(398)	(51)
Net (loss)	$(621)	$(1,316)	$ (695)	(53)
Average assets (in billions)	$ 12	$ 14	$ (2)	(14)
Adjusted for credit-related items:				
Total revenue[2]	$ 173	$ 252	$ (79)	(31)
Operating expense[3]	150	148	2	1
Credit costs[4]	842	1,719	(877)	(51)

(1) Reclassified to conform to current year's presentation.

(2) After adding back the net cost to carry cash-basis loans and OREO.

(3) Excludes net write-downs and direct revenues and expenses related to OREO.

(4) Principally net write-offs, the net cost to carry cash-basis loans and OREO, as well as net write-downs and direct revenues and expenses related to OREO.

Source: *Annual Report*, 1993.

dential, and retail types—36 percent, 23 percent, and 20 percent, respectively. The largest geographic regions are located in the West and Mid-Atlantic—32 percent and 18 percent, respectively; total western exposure was nearly $5.0 billion, with California accounting for approximately 64 percent, whereas total mid-Atlantic exposure was $2.4 billion, with New York responsible for nearly $2 billion or 50 percent.

Cross-Border Refinancing Portfolio. As shown in Exhibit 1–9, net income fell to $92 million, a 77 percent decline. Included in the $402 million for 1992 was the collection of Brazil's past-due interest payments of $74 million for 1992 and $116 million for 1991. Medium- and long-term cross-border claims dropped markedly from $3.3 billion in 1992 to $2.9 billion in 1993, an 18 percent fall. Of the $3.3 billion, approximately $1.0 billion was placed on a cash basis. (A loan put on a cash basis indicates doubtful collection of either principal or interest.) Brazil accounted for $0.9 billion on a cash basis.

Citi anticipated that its share of remaining unpaid interest for 1991 and 1992 would be satisfied through issuance of a $220 million 12-year bond and $44 million cash payment. The $2.9 billion medium and long-term loans consisted approximately of $1.1 billion to South Africa and Venezuela, $0.4 billion to the Philippines, $0.3 billion to Uruguay, and $0.2 billion to 11 other countries. Medium- and long-term loans to 11 other countries totaled $0.2 billion. Trade and short-term obligations of $2.7 billion consisted of $0.9 billion to Argentina, $0.9 billion to Brazil, $0.1 billion to the Philippines, Uruguay, and Venezuela.

Risk Management at Citicorp. The process of risk management is central to Citicorp's continuing efforts to contain loan problems as well as improve its ability to correct present and potential deficiencies. At the core of this credit process are four groups established to coordinate and execute the bank's credit-operating process. One group is the Management Committee, whose responsibility is to allocate key corporate resources, formalize the bank's overall risk capacity, and examine individual credit decisions that could pose future problems.

A second group is the Credit Policy Committee, which insures that credit policies and standards cited in Citi's manual, *Core Credit Policies,* are adhered to. The Committee also maintains contact with both the Management Committee and the Board of Directors regarding portfolio quality, risk profile, loan problems, and credit policy issues. Depending on the severity of the problem, Citi's line managers may turn problem loans over to Institutional Recovery Management, a team organized to control and monitor difficult loan problems.

The Business Risk Review (BRR) group's responsibilities include independent and periodic reviews of both the credit process and portfolio quality so as quickly to identify problem loans. BRR members are senior line officers on rotation for approximately two to three years. BRR reports to the Audit Committee of the Board of Directors.

With regard to its North American Commercial Real Estate portfolio, Citi's strategy is to restructure existing loans through loan-collection efforts, asset sales, asset management, and appraisals. This sector includes over 600 experienced real estate personnel and staff located in 12 offices in the United States and Canada.

As a major part of the risk management process, Citi is required to adhere to capital guidelines issued by the Federal Reserve Board (FRB). For example, quali-

EXHIBIT 1-9 Cross-Border Refinancing Portfolio as of Years Ended December 31
(In millions of dollars)

	1993	1992[1]	INC./ (DEC.)	
Total revenue	$126	$ 196	$ (70)	(36)
Operating expense	28	29	(1)	(3)
Provision for credit losses	(1)	(254)	(253)	N/M
Income before taxes	$ 99	$ 421	$(322)	(76)
Income taxes	7	18	(11)	(61)
Net income	$ 92	$ 403	$(311)	(77)
Average assets (In billions)	$ 3	$ 4	$ (1)	(25)

(1) Reclassified to conform to current year's presentation.
N/M Not meaningful as percentage equals or exceeds 100%.
Source: *Annual Report*, 1993.

fying capital includes two parts: Tier 1 Capital is common stockholders' equity, qualifying perpetual preferred stock and minority interest in consolidated subsidiaries less goodwill and certain other deductions; Tier 2 Capital consists of perpetual preferred stock not included in Tier 1 capital and, subject to% limitations, the allowance for credit losses, qualifying senior and subordinated debt and limited-life preferred stock less certain deductions. FRB ratio guidelines are shown in Table 1–1.

Note in Table 1 that a leverage ratio of 3 percent for the highest rated banks and 4–5 percent for other banks is required. This ratio is Tier 1 capital divided by adjusted average assets. Citi's goal is to attain a 7–7.5 percent Tier 1 capital in 1994.

Strategies of the Chairman. For a number of years, as net income has declined, Chairman John Reed has felt considerable foreign pressure. Coupled with the relative improvement in net income for year-end 1992, Reed embarked on several cost-cutting measures. Table 1–2 compares Citi's facilities and staffing in 1992 with those in 1993. Note in Table 1–2 that Citi's overseas offices declined 1.6 percent, yet staffing increased 7.5 percent.

TABLE 1-1   Regulatory Ratio Guidelines as of December 31, 1993

RATIOS	REQUIRED	1993	1992	1991
Common Stockholders' Equity		4.65%	3.73%	3.39%
Tier 1 Capital	4.00%	6.62%	4.90%	3.73%
Tier 1 & Tier 2 Capital	8.00%	11.45%	9.60%	7.46%
Leverage	3.00%+	6.15%	4.74%	3.94%

Tier 1 Capital and Tier 1 & Tier 2 Capital requirements effective as of year-end 1993.

The elimination of stock dividends in 1991 was an attempt to improve its capital position. Reed himself was affected, as "almost all his net worth is tied up in Citi stock." Based on data published by *Fortune,* among the 200 top-paid CEOs in the United States Reed ranks 38th at over $4.2 million, a figure that includes salary ($1.15 million), bonus ($1.0 million), value of long-term incentives and stock grants ($1.9 million), and other items ($69,000) such as insurance, club memberships, and so on. Yet Reed ranks 138th of 200 CEOs in terms of the five-year total return to shareholders.

Reed has implemented a number of top management changes. He established a leaner management structure, reducing senior management from 95 executives in 1990 to 29 in 1992. Reed made a key decision in hiring Christopher Steffen, a 51-year-old executive who had suddenly resigned as Eastman Kodak's Chief Financial Officer after 11 weeks on the job. Before joining Kodak, Steffen had built a solid reputation as a cost-cutter and generator of profits at several companies such as Chrysler (1981–1989) and Honeywell (1989–1993). However, despite his keen intellect and financial skills, Steffen's management style was regarded as confrontational; moreover, he focused too heavily on numbers, according to some critics. It appeared that Steffen needed better skills in dealing with people.

With Steffen's hiring, Reed apparently felt that the revamping he undertook in 1991 and 1992 was crucial for implementing his desire to reengineer Citi's credit and data processes—that is, to emphasize not individual tasks but rather the delivery of the service (i.e., credit). Reed was favorably impressed after a tour of several companies—Ford Motor, Cummins Engine, and General Electric—studying their reengineering successes dealing with the work process. He reasoned that Citicorp could cut about $1 billion in costs via reengineering .

Reed felt that Steffen would be just the person to carry out the difficult but necessary cost-cutting and productivity programs. As Senior Executive Vice President, Steffen was one of Citicorp's top six officers with responsibilities covering auditing, financial controls, and productivity programs. Yet, the abrasive Steffen might be hampered by the culture of Citicorp, which had traditionally been a decentralized bank acting like a global confederation of fiefdoms. Each major division had its own legal, financial control and human-resources staff with over 100 communications networks, some of which could not converse with others.

TABLE 1-2   Offices and Staff in Domestic and Overseas Locations, Years Ended December 31, 1993, and December 31, 1992

OFFICES	1993	1992	VAR.
U.S.	1,389	1,528	33.0%
Overseas	1,947	1,979	−8.7%
Total	3,336	3,507	6.9%
STAFF			
U.S.	38,500	41,000	−18.0%
Overseas	43,000	40,000	2.6%
Total	81,500	81,000	−8.9%

Source: *Annual Report,* 1993.

Citi rebounded in 1993 with earnings of $2.2 billion and reserves standing at $4.4 billion. These reserves cover 30 percent of non-lesser developed countries' nonperforming assets. However, this level of reserves is still low by industry standards. Citi must continue improving its reserves.

Fortune in 1994 rated Citi's management very poorly. What recommendations could you offer to CEO Reed to improve Citi's effectiveness and efficiency? Citi declared no dividends in 1993 despite having a successful year. Would you recommend that Citi pay dividends for 1994? Remember that 1994 interest rates are rising slowly.

Citi does not have a mission statement, but does have a vision statement as given below. What advice would you offer CEO Reed regarding Citi's vision statement and lack of a mission statement?

Citi currently operates in 90 foreign countries. How can the firm best capitalize on being the most globally oriented commercial bank in the United States? Should other foreign countries be added to Citi's portfolio? Citi's revenue growth in developing countries in Asia and Latin America is averaging 15 percent annually compared to 1 percent growth in revenues from operations in the rest of the world. Should Citi acquire competing commercial banks to strengthen its presence in the developed world?

Prepare a three-year strategic plan for Citi. Include specific recommendations and associated costs as well as projected financial statements to show the expected impact of your suggestions.

CITICORP'S VISION

To be a global bank, unique in worldwide presence . . . dedicated to our customers . . . financially strong . . . consistent . . . committed to our staff and its development . . . delivering sustained superior performance to investors.

UNIQUE, GLOBAL
Unique in being global, operating both locally and collectively around the world in delivering financial services for the benefit of both individual and corporate customers; unique also in spirit.

CUSTOMER DEDICATION
Dedicated to serving the financial needs of our customers. Our success depends upon our importance to them. Customer needs define position, product and service offerings. We seek to build sustained relationships and recognize the importance of continuity of people. We are committed to competitive excellence, delivering customer satisfaction, and investing in the business, people and technology required to meet our customer needs.

FINANCIALLY STRONG
Our balance sheet and earnings will be a source of strength; recognized internally, by customers, investors, competitors, rating agencies, and regulators. Control, executional excellence and productivity improvements are acknowledged objectives.

CONSISTENT
Consistent and dependable: in our commitment to our people, with our customers, in the development and execution of our strategy, and in our risk profile.

STAFF AND ITS DEVELOPMENT
We seek to recruit, develop and retain the most talented people from around the world. We will reward people based on merit, teamwork, results, and shared values. We are accountable: We will take responsibility for our actions and the exercise of judgment. We treat people with trust, openness and respect, and maintain the highest ethical standards in dealing with customers, the community and each other.

DELIVERING SUSTAINED SUPERIOR PERFORMANCE TO OUR INVESTORS
Our objective is to achieve superior return on shareholders' equity. We seek the reality and reputation of being well-managed, being consistently sound in our risk-taking judgments, and being seen as one of the most respected financial institutions in the world; a unique global bank.

1. Welsh, Trish, "Best and Worst Corporate Reputations," *Fortune,* February 7, 1994, p. 8

EXHIBIT 1-10 Citicorp in Brief as of Years Ended December 31 (*In millions of dollars except per share amounts*)

	1993	1992	1991	1990	1989
Net income (loss)					
Before accounting changes	$ 1,919	$ 722	$ (914)	$ 318	$ 498
After accounting changes[1]	$ 2,219	$ 722	$ (457)	$ 458	$ 498
Net income (loss) per share[2]					
On common and common equivalent shares					
Before accounting changes	$ 3.82	$ 1.35	$ (3.22)	$ 0.57	$ 1.16
After accounting changes[1]	$ 4.50	$ 1.35	$ (1.89)	$ 0.99	$ 1.16
Assuming full dilution					
Before accounting changes	$ 3.53	$ 1.35	$ (3.22)	$ 0.57	$ 1.16
After accounting changes[1]	$ 4.11	$ 1.35	$ (1.89)	$ 0.99	$ 1.16
Return on assets and equity					
Return on total assets[3]					
Before accounting changes	.84%	.32%	(.41)%	.14%	.23%
After accounting changes[1]	.97%	.32%	(.21)%	.20%	.23%
Return on common stockholders' equity[4]					
Before accounting changes	17.7%	6.5%	(14.3)%	2.1%	4.3%
After accounting changes[1]	21.1%	6.5%	(7.9)%	3.7%	4.3%
Return on total stockholders' equity[5]					
Before accounting changes	15.3%	7.2%	(9.4)%	3.1%	4.7%
After accounting changes[1]	17.7%	7.2%	(4.5)%	4.4%	4.7%
Capital					
Tier 1 capital	$13,388	$10,262	$ 8,540	$ 7,999	$ 7,974
Tier 1 + tier 2 capital	$23,152	$20,111	$17,080	$15,998	$ 15,948
Tier 1 capital ratio	6.62%	4.90%	3.73%	3.26%	3.22%
Tier 1 + tier 2 capital ratio	11.45%	9.60%	7.46%	6.52%	6.44%
Common stockholders' equity as a percentage of total assets	4.65%	3.73%	3.39%	3.77%	3.57%
Total stockholders' equity as a percentage of total assets	6.44%	5.23%	4.37%	4.48%	4.37%
Common stockholders' equity per share	$ 26.04	$ 21.74	$ 21.23	$ 24.34	$ 25.36

(1) Refers to adoption of Statement of Financial Accounting Standards No. 109, "Accounting for Income Taxes," as of January 1, 1993; accounting change for venture capital subsidiaries in 1991; and accounting change for certain derivative products in 1990.

(2) Based on net income (loss) less preferred stock dividends, except where conversion is assumed.

(3) Net income (loss) as a percentage of average total assets.

(4) Earnings (loss) applicable to common stock as a percentage of average common stockholders' equity.

(5) Net income (loss) less redeemable preferred dividends as a percentage of average total stockholders' equity.

Source: *Annual Report,* 1993.

EXHIBIT 1-11 Citicorp Consolidated Statement of Operations as of Years Ended December 31 (*In millions of dollars except per share amounts*)

	1993	CITICORP AND SUBSIDIARIES 1992[1]	1991[1]
Interest revenue			
Interest and fees on loans	$16,408	$18,476	$20,440
Interest on deposits with banks	1,106	1,029	886
Interest on federal funds sold and securities			
purchased under resale agreements	2,952	1,393	637
Interest and dividends on investment securities	950	875	1,081
Interest on trading account assets	2,485	2,010	1,310
	$23,811	$23,783	$24,354
Interest expense			
Interest on deposits	$ 9,797	$10,458	$11,116
Interest on securities sold, not yet purchased	195	175	315
Interest on other borrowed money	4,155	3,414	3,438
Interest on long-term debt and subordinated capital notes	1,974	2,280	2,220
	$16,121	$16,327	$17,089
Net interest revenue	$ 7,690	$ 7,456	$ 7,265
Provision for credit losses	$ 2,600	$ 4,146	$ 3,890
Net interest revenue after provision for credit losses	$ 5,090	$ 3,310	$ 3,375
Fees, commissions, and other revenue			
Fees and commissions	$ 5,057	$ 5,084	$ 4,815
Trading account	939	326	457
Foreign exchange	995	1,005	709
Investment securities transactions	94	12	330
Other revenue	1,300	1,738	1,174
	$ 8,385	$ 8,165	$ 7,485
Other operating expense			
Salaries	$ 3,817	$ 3,683	$ 3,873
Employee benefits	1,028	965	938
Total employee expense	$ 4,845	$ 4,648	$ 4,811
Net premises and equipment expense	1,601	1,680	1,807
Restructuring charges	425	227	750
Other expense	3,744	3,502	3,729
	$10,615	$10,057	$11,097
Income (loss) before taxes and cumulative effects			
of accounting changes	$ 2,860	$ 1,418	$ (237)
Income taxes	941	696	677
Income (loss) before cumulative effects of accounting changes	$ 1,919	$ 722	$ (914)
Cumulative effects of accounting changes:			
Accounting for income taxes	300	–	–
Venture capital[2]	–	–	457
Net income (loss)	$ 2,219	$ 722	$ (457)

EXHIBIT 1-11 *Continued*

	1993	CITICORP AND SUBSIDIARIES 1992[1]	1991[1]
Income (loss) applicable to common stock	$ 1,900	$ 497	$ (649)
Earnings (loss) per share on common and common equivalent shares			
Income (loss) before cumulative effects of accounting changes	$ 3.82	$ 1.35	$ (3.22)
Cumulative effects of accounting changes:			
Accounting for income taxes	0.68	–	–
Venture capital[2]	–	–	1.33
Net income (loss)	$ 4.50	$ 1.35	$ (1.89)
Assuming full dilution			
Income (loss) before cumulative effects of accounting changes	$ 3.53	$ 1.35	$ (3.22)
Cumulative effects of accounting changes:			
Accounting for income taxes	0.58	–	–
Venture Capital[2]	–	–	1.33
Net income (loss)	$ 4.11	$ 1.35	$ (1.89)

(1) Reclassified to conform to current year's presentation.

(2) In addition to the cumulative effect adjustment, the venture capital accounting change had the effect of reducing the 1991 net loss by $125 million ($0.37 per share).

Source: *Annual Report,* 1993.

EXHIBIT 1-12 Citicorp Consolidated Balance Sheet As of Years Ended December 31

	CITICORP AND SUBSIDARIES	
	1993	1992
Assets		
Cash and due from banks	$ 4,836	$ 5,138
Deposits at interest with banks	6,749	6,550
Investment securities		
At cost (market value $5,666 in 1993 and $6,504 in 1992)	5,637	6,515
At lower of aggregate cost or market value		
(market value $9,088 in 1993 and $7,574 in 1992)	8,705	7,213
At fair value	1,489	1,328
Trading account assets	18,117	17,085
Federal funds sold and securities purchased		
under resale agreements	7,339	6,381
Loans, net		
Consumer	$ 84,354	$ 83,453
Commercial	54,613	56,257
Loans, net of unearned income	$138,967	$139,710
Allowance for credit losses	(4,379)	(3,859)
Total loans, net	$134,588	$135,851
Customers' acceptance liability	1,512	1,802
Premises and equipment, net	3,842	3,819
Interest and fees receivable	2,552	2,721
Other assets	21,208	19,298
Total	$216,574	$213,701
Liabilities		
Non-interest-bearing deposits in U.S. offices	$ 13,442	$ 13,572
Interest-bearing deposits in U.S. offices	38,347	44,175
Non-interest-bearing deposits in offices outside the U.S.	6,644	5,243
Interest-bearing deposits in offices outside the U.S.	86,656	81,185
Total deposits	$145,089	$144,175
Securities sold, not yet purchased	2,352	1,894
Purchased funds and other borrowings	16,777	18,120
Acceptances outstanding	1,531	1,866
Accrued taxes and other expenses	6,452	5,049
Other liabilities	12,260	11,244
Long-term debt (note 1)	15,983	16,886
Subordinated capital notes	2,150	3,250
Redeemable preferred stock	27	36
Stockholders' equity		
Preferred stock	$ 3,887	$ 3,212
Common stock ($1.00 par value)	412	392
Issued shares: 412,017,300 in 1993 and 391,888,124 in 1992		

EXHIBIT 1-12 *Continued*

	1993	CITICORP AND SUBSIDIARIES 1992
Surplus	3,898	3,598
Retained earnings	6,149	4,368
Common stock in treasury, at cost	(393)	(389)
Shares: 25,527,133 in 1993 and 25,399,438 in 1992		
Total stockholders' equity	$ 13,953	$ 11,181
Total	$216,574	$213,701

Source: *Annual Report*, 1993.

EXHIBIT 1-13 Citicorp Consolidated Statement of Cash Flows as of Years Ended December 31 (*In millions of dollars*)

		CITICORP AND SUBSIDIARIES	
	1993	1992	1991
Cash flows from operating activities			
Net income (loss)	$ 2,219	$ 722	$ (457)
Adjustments to reconcile net income (loss) to net cash provided by (used in) operating activities:			
Provision for credit losses	$ 2,600	$ 4,146	$ 3,890
Depreciation and amortization of premises and equipment	568	587	652
Amortization of goodwill	55	60	72
Restructuring charges	425	227	750
Business write-downs	179	–	–
Provision for deferred taxes	(612)	4	249
Cumulative effects of accounting changes	(300)	–	(457)
Venture capital activity	(161)	249	(144)
Net (gain) on sale of investment securities	(94)	(12)	(330)
Net (gain) on the sale of subsidiaries and affiliates	(77)	(417)	(168)
Changes in accruals and other, net	(1,244)	(1,648)	(1,810)
Net (increase) in trading account assets	(1,032)	(5,021)	(4,546)
Net increase (decrease) in securities sold, not yet purchased	458	162	(962)
Total adjustments	$ 765	$ (1,663)	$ (2,804)
NET CASH PROVIDED BY (USED IN) OPERATING ACTIVITIES	$ 2,984	$ (941)	$ (3,261)

EXHIBIT 1-13   *Continued*

	1993	CITICORP AND SUBSIDIARIES **1992**	**1991**
Cash flows from investing activities			
Net (increase) decrease in deposits at interest with banks	$ (199)	$ 137	$ 854
Purchases of investment securities	(31,017)	(27,734)	(38,447)
Proceeds from sale of investment securities	7,886	5,100	8,144
Maturities of investment securities	21,599	21,604	28,882
Net (increase) in federal funds sold and securities purchased under resale agreements	(958)	(1,831)	(479)
Net (increase) in loans	(86,698)	(78,426)	(94,904)
Proceeds from sales of loans and credit card receivables	82,961	82,746	92,519
Capital expenditures on premises and equipment	(829)	(1,252)	(929)
Proceeds from sales of premises and equipment	175	342	394
Proceeds from sales of subsidiaries and affiliates	230	1,453	926
Proceeds from sales of other real estate owned (OREO)	1,740	1,052	617
NET CASH PROVIDED BY (USED IN) INVESTING ACTIVITIES	$ (5,110)	$ 3,191	$ (2,423)
Cash flows from financing activities			
Net increase (decrease) in deposits	$ 2,816	$ (2,200)	$ 4,023
Net increase (decrease) in federal funds purchased and securities sold under repurchase agreements	(1,336)	2,633	136
Proceeds from issuance of commercial paper and funds borrowed with original maturities of less than one year	335,235	360,550	424,475
Repayment of commercial paper and funds borrowed with original maturities of less than one year	(333,417)	(361,403)	(424,626)
Proceeds from issuance of long-term debt	4,682	3,460	4,783
Repayment of long-term debt and retirement of redeemable preferred stock	(6,444)	(6,365)	(4,703)
Proceeds from issuance of preferred stock	654	1,275	1,222
Redemption and repurchase of preferred stock	–	–	(650)
Proceeds from issuance of common stock	302	119	81
Dividends paid	(313)	(216)	(435)
NET CASH PROVIDED BY (USED IN) FINANCING ACTIVITIES	$ 2,179	$ (2,147)	$ 4,306
Effect of exchange rate changes on cash and due from banks	$ (355)	$ (293)	$ (392)
Net (decrease) in cash and due from banks	$ (302)	$ (190)	$ (1,770)
Cash and due from banks at beginning of year	5,138	5,328	7,098
CASH AND DUE FROM BANKS AT END OF YEAR	$ 4,836	$ 5,138	$ 5,328
Supplemental disclosure of cash flow information			
Cash paid during the year for:			
Interest	$ 14,481	$ 14,493	$ 15,379
Income taxes	$ 1,197	$ 473	$ 484
Non-cash investing activities			
Transfers from loans to OREO	$ 1,644	$ 3,761	$ 2,039

Source: *Annual Report,* 1993.

EXHIBIT 1-14 Citicorp Geographic Distribution of Revenue, Earnings (Loss), and Assets as of Years Ended December 31 (*In millions of dollars*)

	Total Revenue[1]			Income (Loss) Before Taxes and Cumulative Effects of Accounting Changes			Net Income (Loss)			Average Total Assets		
	1993	1992	1991	1993	1992	1991	1993	1992	1991	1993	1992	1991
North America[2]	$ 8,198	$ 8,309	$ 8,736	$ 247[3]	$(1,008)[3]	$(1,250)[3]	$ 556	$(379)	$(885)	$117,075	$124,795	$131,416
Central and South America	1,913	2,080	1,335	819	1,346	555	519	924	317	22,238	19,005	15,988
Europe, Middle East, and Africa	3,628	3,287	2,993	1,100	475	218	677	218	132	47,820	45,653	41,462
Asia/Pacific	2,336	1,945	1,686	694	605	240	467	319	(21)	41,107	36,348	33,031
Total	$16,075	$15,621	$14,750	$2,860	$ 1,418	$ (237)	$2,219[4]	$ 722	$(457)[5]	$228,240	$225,801	$221,897

(1) Includes net interest revenue and fees, commissions, and other revenue.

(2) Includes amounts attributed to United States operations (in 1993, 1992, and 1991 respectively) as follows: total revenue, $8,100 million, $8,180 million, and $8,552 million; income (loss) before taxes and cumulative effects of accounting changes, $405 million, $(722) million, and $(1,285) million; net income (loss), $659 million, $(544) million, and $(894) million; and average total assets, $111,117 million, $120,237 million, and $125,970 million.

(3) Includes approximately $22 million in 1993, $35 million in 1992, and $71 million in 1991 of tax-exempt income, reducing the federal income tax provision attributed to the United States.

(4) The 1993 results include the $300 million cumulative effect of adopting Statement of Financial Accounting Standards No. 109, "Accounting for Income Taxes."

(5) The 1991 results include the $457 million cumulative effect of the accounting change for venture capital, all of which is attributed to U.S. operations.

Source: *Annual Report,* 1993.

EXHIBIT 1-15   Citicorp Loans Outstanding as of Years Ended December 31 (In millions of dollars at year end)

CONSUMER LOANS OUTSTANDING	1993	1992
In U.S. offices		
Mortgage and real estate[1][2][3]	$22,719	$26,140
Installment, revolving credit and other		
consumer loans	22,490	21509
Lease financing	152	353
	$45,361	$48,002
In offices outside the U.S.		
Mortgage and real estate[1][4]	$13,908	$12,863
Installment, revolving credit and other		
consumer loans	25,355	23,011
Lease financing	672	746
	$39,935	$36,620
	$85,296	$84,622
Unearned income	(942)	(1,169)
Consumer loans—net	$84,354	$83,453

COMMERCIAL LOANS OUTSTANDING	1993	1992
In U.S. Offices		
Commercial and industrial[5]	$ 8,969	$10,168
Mortgage and real estate[6]	7,440	9,194
Loans to financial institutions	269	271
Lease financing	3,541	3,547
	$20,219	$23,180
In offices outside the U.S.		
Commercial and industrial[5]	$23,624	$21,332
Mortgage and real estate[6]	2,201	2,657
Loans to financial institutions	3,123	3,300
Governments and official institutions	4,807	5,055
Lease financing	800	927
	$34,555	$33,271
	$54,774	$56,451
Unearned income	(161)	(194)
Commercial loans—net	$54,613	$56,257

(1) Loans secured primarily by real estate.

(2) Includes $4.2 billion and $4.3 billion of commercial real estate loans related to community banking and private banking activities at December 31, 1993 and 1992, respectively.

(3) Includes $6.3 billion and $6.6 billion of residential mortgage loans held for sale and carried at the lower of aggregate cost or market value at December 31, 1993 and 1992, respectively.

(4) Includes approximately $1.4 billion and $1.0 billion of loans secured by commercial real estate at December 31, 1993 and 1992, respectively.

(5) Includes loans not otherwise separately categorized.

(6) Loans secured primarily by real estate.

Source: *Annual Report*, 1993.

BANC ONE CORPORATION—1993

C A S E

2

RANDY WHITE
Auburn University at
Montgomery

Headquartered in Columbus, Ohio, Banc One (614-248-5944) is a bank-holding corporation for 61 affiliate banks. The corporation uses the spelling "Banc" because Ohio and several other states forbid using the word "bank" in a bank-holding company's name. Banc One operates affiliate banks in Colorado, Illinois, Kentucky, Michigan, Texas, and Wisconsin. It also operates several additional corporations that engage in data processing, venture capital, merchant banking, trust, brokerage, equipment leasing, mortgage banking, and insurance.

Banc One ranks eighth among the top 100 U.S. banks in asset size (see Exhibit 2–1). Banc One's return on assets of 1.31 percent and its return on equity of 16.3 percent are outstanding. *Euromoney* magazine recently ranked Banc One as number six among the world's 100 best banks. There was only one other U.S. bank in the top ten—J. P. Morgan, which ranked number one.

As shown in Exhibits 2–2 and 2–3 Banc One made numerous acquisitions in 1992, expanding from its home base in Ohio into Illinois, Indiana, Michigan, Wisconsin, West Virginia, Kentucky, Texas, Arizona, Colorado, Utah. As of March 31, 1993, Banc One's assets exceeded $70 billion, with 1,277 offices in 12 states. Banc One recently entered California with its $1.2 billion acquisition of Arizona's Valley National and moved into Nebraska by acquiring FirsTier Financial, the second largest Nebraska bank, with assets of $3 billion. Banc One recently expanded into Oklahoma by acquiring the seventh-largest bank there, Central Banking Group. Overall, Banc One acquired seven bank

EXHIBIT 2-1 Top Ten U.S. Banks by Asset Size as of December 31, 1992 (in millions of dollars except ROA, ROE, and NPA)

RANK	ASSETS	ROA (%)[a]	ROE (%)[b]	NPA (%)[c]	MARKET VALUE[d]
1 Citicorp	213,701	.23	6.6	4.9	10,811
2 BankAmerica	189,646	.80	12.7	3.4	17,517
3 Chemical Bank	139,655	.67	12.4	4.4	10,140
4 Nations Bank	118,059	.97	15.8	1.7	13,820
5 J. P. Morgan	102,941	1.14	20.8[e]	0.5	13,006
6 Chase Manhattan	102,941	.51	11.2	5.3	5,444
7 Bankers Trust NY	72,448	.99	23.1	2.5	5,925
8 Banc One	61,417	1.31	16.3	1.0	13,403
9 Wells Fargo	52,537	.45	7.9	5.1	5,995
10 PNC Bank	51,380	1.18	15.5	1.6	7,762

[a]Return on Asset
[b]Return on Equity
[c]Nonperforming Asset
[d]As of March 31, 1993. Market Value is the closing common stock price multiplied by the number of outstanding common shares.
[e]Year-end amounts
Source: "Bank Scoreboard," *Business Week*, May 3, 1993, p. 150.

companies with $13.3 billion in assets and two thrifts with $700 million in assets during 1992.

Bank One celebrated its 25th anniversary in 1993 as a multibank-holding company. The corporation's net income increased from $493 million in 1990 to over $781 million in 1992, while earnings per share climbed from $2.33 to $3.28. Banc One's foreign loans of $237 million were less than .7 percent of total loans, with the United Kingdom accounting for $105 million or 44 percent of total foreign loans; Mexico had $15 million outstanding in 1992 compared to $16 million in 1991. Banc One provides technological assistance in retail banking and card processing through a joint agreement with Banco Nacional de Mexico, whose headquarters are in Mexico City.

MANAGEMENT CONTROL

Chairman John B. McCoy is the third member of the McCoy family to lead Banc One. John H. McCoy, his grandfather, served as president and guided the corporation during its early years. John G. McCoy, his father, joined the bank in 1937 and did much to build Banc One, then called City National Bank. After John H.'s death in 1958, John G. became president and CEO; upon John G.'s retirement in 1984, John B. became president and eventually chairman in 1987.

John B. had been a major driving force for Banc One's growth through implementation of the corporate culture known as the "uncommon partnership." Each affiliate bank is viewed as a partner within the corporate structure and has responsibilities to formulate its own business plan, control all personnel and lending functions, and determine all product pricing and marketing, based on local market conditions. In essence, this uncommon partnership allows local banks to set prices and decide on their own which of Banc One's family of 120 financial products to use. Banks also

EXHIBIT 2-2 Bank Affiliations Completed and Savings and Loan Assets Purchased as of December 31, 1992 (in billions of dollars)

BANK AFFILIATIONS COMPLETED IN 1992	CITY, STATE	ASSETS ($ BILLIONS)	OFFICES
TB Marine Corporation	Springfield, IL	$1.2	19
First Illinois Corporation	Evanston, IL	1.7	19
First Security Corporation	Lexington, KY	1.6	13
Bedford National Bank	Bedford, IN	.2	2
Jefferson Bancorp, Inc.	Peoria, IL	.3	5
Team Bancshares, Inc.	Dallas, TX	5.5	56
Affiliated Bankshares of Colorado, Inc.	Denver, CO	2.8	43

SAVINGS AND LOAN ASSETS PURCHASED		DEPOSITS ($ BILLIONS)	
Diamond Savings and Loan Company	Findlay, OH	$ .6	18
Savings of America	Cincinnati, OH	.1	4

Source: *Annual Report*, 1992.

develop their own marketing programs, make their own hires, and set their own salaries.

McCoy views himself as people-oriented and interested in watching them grow. However, when queried about his thoughts regarding people who made mistakes, the outspoken McCoy bluntly responded: "You learn from mistakes, not from successes, so hold up your hand and tell us. . . . But if you have a problem, and don't tell, and it's a disaster, it's your ass. . . ."

Career opportunities at Banc One abound as individuals move from the presidency of smaller affiliates up to a larger affiliate. The depth and quality of management experience CEOs exceeds 18 years. Banc One fills almost all CEO positions internally. The structure and culture of the corporation motivate both managers and employees. The fact that "80 percent of the officers and over two-thirds of all employees own stock in the company" further motivates employees and, to a large extent, reinforces the business culture. McCoy's reported annual compensation in 1992 totalled over $2.8 million—salary $907,000; bonus $980,000; other sources such as insurance and club memberships, $93,000; value of long-term incentives and stock grants, $825,000. McCoy ranked 77 of the 200 top-paid U.S. executives in 1992. Banc One's organizational chart is given in Figure 2–1.

A key to Banc One's ability to control and evaluate its decentralized operation is through a Management Information and Control System (MICS). Whenever an affiliate is brought into Banc One's structure, MICS is installed to gather and evaluate data and report the data in the same manner to each entity. Individual and comparative financial results are provided. To insure that information is timely, monthly updates and forecasts are prepared by local staff. In essence, affiliates share and compare data. The ultimate objective is "to be able to measure every aspect of our business across the company in exactly the same way for comparison purposes."

With many firms attempting to cut costs by outsourcing some of their operational activities, McCoy continues to improve and develop new technologies

EXHIBIT 2-3 Banc One Market Share[a] as of December 31, 1992 (in billions of dollars)

	ASSETS	STATE RANK
Arizona	9.8	2 nd
Colorado	2.8	3 rd
Illinois	3.9	8 th
Indiana	7.5	2 nd
Kentucky	1.7	4 th
Michigan	.6	11 th
Ohio	19.3	2 nd
Texas	18.8	3 rd
Utah	.9	4 th
West Virginia	3.0	1 st
Wisconsin	6.7	3 rd

[a]Assumes "all remaining announced affiliations are completed." (*Annual Report*, 1992, p. 5.)

Source: *Annual Report*, 1992.

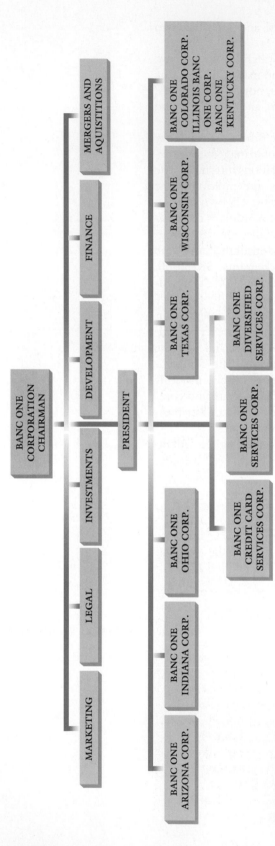

FIGURE 2-1 Banc One Corporation

within the Banc One system. For example, through a six-year alliance with Electronic Data Systems (EDS) in Dallas, Banc One began to install parts of its Strategic Banking System (SBS) in its affiliates. SBS is a state-of-the-art, total-bank-operating system keyed to the customer, thus providing to each affiliate bank a total financial picture of customer relationships. SBS integrates Banc One's product profitability and household demographic systems and gives Banc One personnel (e.g., customer service representatives, loan officers, and new account managers) immediate access to relevant information for additional sales. McCoy recently described an example of building a loyal customer base: "If Mrs. Smith walks into a branch to make a checking deposit, a message will come up on the screen that prompts our service rep to offer her a credit card with a $5,000 limit. Since she's a longtime customer, a message will appear with an offer to waive the service fee for three years." Development costs for SBS have exceeded $100 million, but EDS has incurred the greatest part of the cost and risk in developing SBS. EDS, however, retains the right to sell the system to other banks when completed.

Another joint venture was recently established with Andersen Consulting to set up a new credit and debit card-processing system called TRIUMPH. Rights to the system remain with Banc One. Banc One is the third-largest credit-card processor in the United States, providing services to some 3,000 "commercial bank, savings and loan, credit union and broker clients with 14 million cardholder accounts."

In another arrangement with three other regional banks, a new company called Electronic Payment Services (EPS) has been established "to provide automated teller machine and electronic point-of-sale systems and processing. . . ." About 13,000 ATMs could be linked to process annually 650 million point-of-sale transactions. Perhaps most telling is Banc One's commitment over the past 25 years to allocate annually 3 percent of its profits to technology research and development. Banc One is known as the technology bank. As a Kidder Peabody vice president commented, "I've never heard a bank say they were determined to spend a certain amount of their income stream on R&D and have it turn out to such advantage."

McCoy works at keeping things simple and predictable. Among his rules are to keep management in place when a bank is taken over, because those managers know the market better than anyone else; consolidate back-office functions; and never buy a bank more than one-third the size of the corporation. "That way if the deal turns out to be a bust, it won't drag down the entire bank." Banc One's mission statement and precepts are given in Figure 2–2.

RISK MANAGEMENT

Although credit decisions are made on a local basis, Banc One insures necessary remedial action for all present and potential problem loans, which are quickly identified through monthly analyses of delinquencies and nonperforming assets. Analyses have been carried out by such in-house groups as affiliate bank management, state holding company loan-review personnel, and corporate credit officers. Additionally, continuing efforts are maintained to refine credit policies dealing with appraisals, borrower's financial condition, lending outside of well-defined geographical areas, and loan concentrations to any single industry or borrower. The firm maintains that only five borrowing relationships exceed $100 million and there are only twenty other relationships which exceed $50 million. Of these only seven had more than $50 million outstanding at year end with the largest being $83 million.

FIGURE 2-2

BANC ONE CORPORATION
MISSION STATEMENT

WE BELIEVE

Enterprise and the opportunities created by individual choice are cornerstones of our "Uncommon Partnership." They produce the greatest value for the customer and the greatest stimulant to business. Those core values provide the best plan for delivering true satisfaction for every customer and the most desirable return for investors.

PRECEPTS

Based on this belief, the Board of Directors of BANC ONE CORPORATION adopted these precepts as the official guideline for the commitment and performance of our people.

One We believe in creating an atmosphere in which our people working together:
- care about what they do
- utilize their own abilities to make the right decisions
- focus on customers and uncover innovative ways to service their changing financial needs
- promptly respond to problems and customer concerns in a professional sensitive manner.

Two We believe in conducting our business:
- with uncompromising honesty, fairness and integrity
- to achieve superior financial performance for our shareholders
- to identify, develop, retain, and provide equal opportunity for all people who demonstrate the willingness and ability to perform and grow
- with an unflinching focus on providing a quality of services that ensures customer satisfaction.

Three We believe management should base decisions on:
- maintaining a balance between the needs of our customers, employees and shareholders
- the need to support the social, cultural, and economical programs which enhance the quality of life in our communities
- providing creative leadership to the direction and success of the financial industry
- expanding the geographic influence and customer service opportunities of the organization as enterprise and prudence permits.

We believe commitment to performance and a focus on the quality of customer service are essential to success. We believe in the everlasting process of building a great bank.

In 1992 Banc One instituted "a corporate credit development group and charged it with development of a systemwide credit training program." Thus, formal credit training for all lending employees in addition to a continuing education program for commercial credit employees was set up.

Banc One has well-defined programs to resolve and dispose of foreclosed properties through management centralization of problem assets. For example, commercial loans are placed in a nonaccrual basis after 90 days past due or if collection of the debt is doubtful. For loans put on a nonaccrual basis, all previously accrued and unpaid interest is charged against income. If recovery appears certain, interest received is included in income for future periods. Residential real estate loans are put in a nonaccrual status when 120 days past due or if deemed uncollectible. In the case of installment loans, accrued interest and the remaining principal balance are charged off at the earlier of when the loan was 120 days past due or if collection was uncertain. Average balance on installment loans is over $8,700. Credit card loans are written off when 180 days past due or collection is questionable. There are approximately 8.3 million credit card accounts, with an average balance of $581.

Banc One's expansion into 14 states with different economic, political, and regional conditions carries increased risk. Major financial institutions already exist in those states. Asked whether he felt the "empire building" should continue, McCoy responded, "If there isn't change, then I'm not going to be here, because it wouldn't be fun anymore."

Banc One's plans for 1993 include purchase of Valley National Corporation of Arizona for $11.4 billion and Key Centurion Bancshares of West Virginia for $1.6 billion. The company has an eye on Liberty National BanCorp of Kentucky for $4.7 billion and FirsTier Financial Corporation of Nebraska for $3.0 billion. Banc One strives to be the first, second, or third largest bank in each state it operates. This policy suggests further acquisitions are needed in Illinois, Utah, and Michigan, where Banc One's market share is only 2%, 6%, and 1%, respectively. Banc One also has a policy never to acquire a bank more than one-third its own combined size.

Despite the large amount of consolidation that has already taken place among financial institutions, the U.S. banking landscape remains fragmented. As of June 30, 1993, there were still 11,198 insured commercial banks and 1,825 insured thrift institutions in the country, with total domestic office deposits of $2.94 trillion. Banc One's total deposits of $59.0 billion at June 30 represented just 2.0% of total U.S. domestic deposits—and this is a banking organization that ranks fourth in the country in market share. Consolidation of the U.S. banking industry will continue and Banc One should be able to find ongoing opportunities to expand its presence.

Prepare a three-year strategic plan for Banc One. Include specific recommendations regarding whether Banc One should enter the securities business which it has avoided to date. Also, do you feel Banc One's mission statement and organizational chart are adequate? Include an acquisition plan in your recommendations for CEO McCoy.

EXHIBIT 2-4 Members of Banc One Corporation

BANC ONE OHIO CORPORATION

Ohio

Akron
Athens
Cambridge
Cincinnati
Cleveland
Columbus
Coshocton
Dayton
Dover
Fremont
Lima
Mansfield
Marietta
Marion
Portsmouth
Sidney
Steubenville
Youngstown
Bank One Ohio
   Trust Company,
   NA

Michigan

East Lansing
Fenton
Sturgis
Ypsilanti

BANC ONE DIVERSIFIED SERVICES CORPORATION

Banc One Financial Services, Inc.
Banc One Insurance Group
Banc One Investment Advisors Corporation
Banc One Leasing Corporation
Banc One Mortgage Corporation
Banc One Securities Corporation

NON-BANK AFFILIATES

Banc One Capital Corporation
Banc One Credit Card Services Company
Banc One Management and Consulting
   Corporation
Banc One Services Corporation

BANC ONE ARIZONA CORPORATION

Serving markets in:
Arizona

Utah

BANC ONE INDIANA CORPORATION

Indiana

Bloomington
Crawfordsville
Indianapolis
Lafayette
Marion
Merrillville
Rensselaer
Richmond

BANC ONE REGIONAL AFFILIATE GROUP

Colorado

BANC ONE COLORADO CORPORATION

Boulder
Colorado Springs
Denver
Greeley
Fort Collins/
   Loveland
Western Colorado

Illinois

BANC ONE ILLINOIS CORPORATION

Bloomington-
   Normal
Champaign-Urbana
Chicago
Elgin
Evanston
La Grange
Peoria
Springfield
Wilmette

Kentucky

Lexington

BANC ONE WISCONSIN CORPORATION

Wisconsin

Antigo
Appleton
Beaver Dam
Elkhorn
Fond du Lac
Green Bay
Janesville
Madison
Milwaukee
Monroe
Oshkosh
Racine
Stevens Point
West Bend
Bank One
   Wisconsin Trust
   Company, NA

BANK ONE, TEXAS, NA AND TEAM BANCSHARES, INC.

Serving markets in:
Texas

Abilene
Amarillo
Arlington
Austin
Beaumont/Orang/
   Port Arthur
Brenham
Corsicana
Dallas
Denison
Denton
Fort Worth
Fredericksburg
Greenville
Houston
Levelland
Longview
Marshall
Midland
Odessa
San Antonio
Sherman
Temple
Tyler
Waco
Wichita Falls

PENDING AFFILIATES

Key Centurion Bancshares, Inc., Charleston, West Virginia
First Community Bancorp, Inc., Rockford, Illinois
United National Bank, Denton, Texas
Parkdale Bank, Beaumont, Texas
First Financial Associates, Inc., Kenosha, Wisconsin
Colorado Western Bancorp, Inc., Montrose, Colorado

(Certain pending affiliates are subject to shareholder and regulatory approval.)

Source: Provided by Banc One Corporation (April, 1993).

EXHIBIT 2-5 Banc One Consolidated Balance Sheet as of Years Ended December 31
(in thousands of dollars except share data)

$ (THOUSANDS, EXCEPT SHARE DATA)	DECEMBER 31, 1993	DECEMBER 31, 1992
Assets:		
Cash and due from banks	$ 4,757,475	$ 5,186,870
Short-term investments (including Eurodollar placements and foreign negotiable certificates of deposit of $4,492 and $299,578 at December 31, 1993 and 1992)	931,959	2,267,310
Securities:		
Securities held for investment (market value approximates $16,903,201 and $16,575,168 at December 31, 1993 and 1992)	16,591,970	16,349,280
Securities held for sale (market value approximates $860,897 and $1,722,954 at December 31, 1993 and 1992)	815,941	1,658,735
Total securities	17,407,911	18,008,015
Loans and leases (net of unearned income of $676,980 and $655,983 at December 31, 1993 and 1992)	53,845,620	47,809,448
Reserve for loan and lease losses	918,153	909,896
Net loans and leases	52,927,467	46,899,552
Collection pools	22,302	420,220
Other assets:		
Bank premises and equipment, net	1,387,218	1,313,044
Interest earned not collected	624,185	598,119
Other real estate owned	193,158	288,252
Excess of cost over net assets of affiliates purchased	227,312	265,003
Other	1,439,574	1,492,734
Total other assets	3,871,447	3,957,152
Total assets	$79,918,561	$76,739,119
Liabilities:		
Deposits:		
Non-interest bearing	$13,674,976	$13,158,961
Interest bearing	47,268,205	48,595,644
Total deposits	60,943,181	61,754,605
Federal funds purchased and repurchase agreements	6,744,437	4,631,394
Other short-term borrowings	2,020,176	1,383,927
Long-term borrowings	1,701,662	1,357,462
Accrued interest payable	222,946	258,671
Other liabilities	1,252,521	1,111,474
Total liabilities	72,884,923	70,497,533

EXHIBIT 2-5 *Continued*

$ (THOUSANDS, EXCEPT SHARE DATA)	DECEMBER 31,	
	1993	1992
Commitments and contingencies (Notes 14 and 17)		
Stockholders' equity:		
Preferred stock, 35,000,000 shares authorized:		
Class B convertible, no par value, 373,076 shares issued and		
outstanding, at December 31, 1992		9,700
Series C convertible, no par value, 4,998,000 and 5,000,000 shares		
issued and outstanding, at December 31, 1993 and 1992	249,900	250,000
Common stockholders' equity:		
Common stock, no par value, $5 stated value, 600,000,000 shares		
authorized, 380,687,187 and 272,246,801 shares issued and		
outstanding, at December 31, 1993 and 1992, respectively		
(December 31, 1993 shares reflect the 10% stock dividend		
effective February 10, 1994 and the five-shares-for-four-shares		
stock split effective August 31, 1993)	1,903,436	1,361,234
Capital in excess of aggregate stated value of common stock	3,833,611	3,009,221
Retained earnings	1,046,691	1,611,431
Total stockholders' equity	7,033,638	6,241,586
Total liabilities and stockholders' equity	$79,918,561	$76,739,119

Source: *Annual Report*, 1993.

EXHIBIT 2-6 Banc One Consolidated Statement of Income as of Years Ended December 31 (in thousands of dollars)

$ (THOUSANDS, EXCEPT PER SHARE AMOUNTS)	1993	1992	1991
Interest income:			
Interest and fees on loans and leases	$4,759,498	$4,638,246	$4,197,706
Interest and dividends on:			
Taxable securities	812,899	994,065	874,578
Tax exempt securities	118,426	132,178	162,546
Other interest income, (including interest on Eurodollar placements and foreign negotiable certificates of deposi of $2,415, $17,161, and $22,316 in 1993, 1992, and 1991)	37,255	116,470	184,105
Interest on Collection pools	7,053	36,965	52,295
Interest on Note receivable from FDIC			18,808
Total interest income	5,735,131	5,917,924	5,490,038
Interest expense:			
Interest on deposits:			
Demand and savings deposits	599,432	737,056	884,035
Time deposits	763,713	1,121,195	1,484,089
Other borrowings	281,903	261,853	354,326
Total interest expense	1,645,048	2,120,104	2,722,450
Net interest income	4,090,083	3,797,820	2,767,588
Provision for loan and lease losses	368,507	604,131	586,239
Net interest income after provision for loan and lease losses	3,721,576	3,193,689	2,181,349
Other income:			
Income from fiduciary activities	211,796	205,120	184,506
Service charges on deposit accounts	432,296	413,494	308,937
Loan processing and service income	451,786	434,417	380,945
Securities gains	16,016	24,677	53,121
Income from management of Collection pools, net	22,777	28,226	59,301
Equity in earnings of Bank One, Texas, NA, net of income tax			57,012
Other	356,988	334,535	294,467
Total other income	1,491,659	1,440,469	1,338,289
Other expenses:			
Salaries and related costs	1,618,342	1,511,310	1,209,872
Net occupancy expense, exclusive of depreciation	151,521	174,605	124,953
Equipment expense	106,754	97,103	87,149
Taxes other than income and payroll	76,514	70,290	60,054
Depreciation and amortization	262,759	216,331	149,486
Outside services and processing	489,646	469,366	287,265
Marketing and development	148,401	119,810	94,570
Communication and transportation	224,921	196,044	160,312
Other	435,258	498,077	466,202
Total other expenses	3,514,116	3,352,936	2,639,863

EXHIBIT 2-6 *Continued*

$ (THOUSANDS, EXCEPT PER SHARE AMOUNTS)	1993	1992	1991
Income before income taxes and change in accounting principle	1,699,119	1,281,222	879,775
Income tax provision:			
Income excluding securities transactions	(572,924)	(396,244)	(197,426)
Securities transactions	(5,606)	(8,390)	(18,061)
Provision for income taxes	(578,530)	(404,634)	(215,487)
Income before cumulative effect of change in accounting principle	1,120,589	876,588	664,288
Cumulative effect of change in method of accounting for income taxes	19,391		
Net income	$1,139,980	$ 876,588	$ 664,288
Net income per common share (amounts reflect the 10% common stock dividend effective February 10, 1994 and the five-shares-for-four-shares stock split effective August 31, 1993)			
Income before cumulative effect of change in accounting principle	$ 2.93	$ 2.29	$ 1.82
Cumulative effect of change in method of accounting for income taxes	.05		
Net income per common share	$ 2.98	$ 2.29	$ 1.82
Weighted average common shares outstanding (000)	376,828	373,699	356,102

Source: *Annual Report*, 1993.

$ (THOUSANDS)	1993	1992	1991
Cash provided by (used in) operating activities:			
Net income	$ 1,139,980	$ 876,588	$ 664,288
Adjustments:			
Provision for loan and lease losses	368,507	604,131	586,239
Depreciation and amortization	331,969	272,338	153,532
Net (increase) decrease in trading account portfolio	(14,754)	52,411	(182,222)
Net increase in warehoused mortgage loans	(428,617)	(406,340)	(221,337)
Net change in deferred loan fees and costs	(8,835)	(3,075)	6,581
Gain on sale of other assets	(21,197)	(28,845)	(79,895)
Gain on sale of loans	(1,960)	(14,536)	(25,768)
Gain on sale of investment securities	(16,016)	(24,677)	(53,121)
Net decrease in other assets	243,551	114,159	193,847
Net (decrease) increase in other liabilities	(131,480)	(13,947)	21,697
Net change in deferred income taxes	42,849	(40,366)	(11,097)
Cumulative effect of change in accounting principle	(19,391)		
Equity in earnings of Bank One, Texas, NA			(57,012)
Net cash provided by operating activities	1,484,606	1,387,841	995,732
Cash provided by (used in) investing activities:			
Purchase of securities held for sale	(350,000)		
Purchases of investment securities	(6,010,067)	(10,682,930)	(7,022,627)
Maturities of securities held for sale	476,242		
Maturities of investment securities	6,068,254	6,929,321	3,572,611
Proceeds from the sale of securities held for sale	716,764		
Proceeds from the sales of investment securities	83,525	1,369,257	3,092,568
Net increase in loans, excluding sales and purchases	(4,745,355)	(2,784,492)	(2,847,880)
Proceeds from the sales of loans	76,721	694,499	643,902
Purchases of loans and related premiums	(768,264)	(747,056)	(369,410)
Net decrease in short-term investments	1,410,165	2,430,144	336,252
Additions to bank premises and equipment	(274,836)	(268,364)	(214,452)
Disposals of bank premises and equipment	38,643	38,529	40,450
Payments received on Collection pools	398,742	885,186	718,838
Net decrease in note receivable from FDIC			321,502
Cash acquired less purchase price of final 61% interest in Bank One, Texas, NA			544,710
Net cash acquired in other acquisitions	36,148	247,327	307,082
Net decrease (increase) in mortgage servicing rights	12,283	(53,819)	(2,672)
All other investing activities, net		(8,347)	(3,520)
Net cash used in investing activities	(2,831,035)	(1,950,745)	(882,616)

EXHIBIT 2-7 *Continued*

$ (THOUSANDS)	1993	1992	1991
Cash provided by (used in) financing activities:			
Net increase in demand deposit, money market and savings accounts	588,636	4,614,205	3,099,252
Net decrease in certificates of deposits	(2,317,125)	(4,949,369)	(2,092,622)
Net increase (decrease) in short-term borrowings	2,715,250	991,844	(379,426)
Proceeds from the issuance of long-term borrowings	395,887	493,912	34,578
Repayment of long-term borrowings	(51,687)	(80,266)	(99,952)
Proceeds from issuance of stock			563,740
Cash dividends paid	(379,418)	(202,155)	(234,230)
All other financing activities, net	(34,509)	36,000	23,255
Net cash provided by financing activities	917,034	904,171	914,595
Increase (decrease) in cash and cash equivalents	(429,395)	341,267	1,027,711
Cash and cash equivalents at January 1,	5,186,870	4,845,603	3,817,892
Cash and cash equivalents at December 31,	$4,757,475	$5,186,870	$4,845,603

Source: *Annual Report*, 1993.

EXHIBIT 2-8 Banc One Loan and Lease Analysis as of Years Ended December 31 (in thousands of dollars)

	1992	1991	1990	1989	1988
Ending loan and lease balances:					
Commercial, financial, and agricultural	$12,724,081	$12,466,118	$10,136,768	$ 9,362,356	$ 9,241,961
Real estate	11,844,359	10,895,716	7,447,742	5,998,965	5,148,821
Installment, net	8,530,834	7,720,043	5,557,322	4,700,312	4,483,519
Credit card	4,813,183	4,372,938	2,386,267	1,690,260	1,878,830
Leases, net	809,976	809,872	793,167	745,229	698,191
Total loans and leases	$38,722,433	$36,264,687	$26,321,266	$22,497,122	$21,451,322
Nonperforming assets and delinquencies:					
Non-accrual loans	$ 380,474	$ 485,054	$ 440,245	$ 289,115	$ 294,776
Renegotiated loans	26,179	19,931	22,303	47,025	46,024
Other real estate owned	222,711	265,695	155,341	112,137	87,472
Total nonperforming assets	$ 629,364	$ 770,680	$ 617,889	$ 448,277	$ 428,272
Loans delinquent 90 days or more (not included in non-accrual)	$ 179,661	$ 234,594	$ 142,043	$ 92,973	$ 88,406
Loans classified as doubtful[a]	45,128	124,575	75,204	74,634	87,938
Interest foregone on nonperforming loans (after tax)[b]	$ 25,316	$ 26,913	$ 27,180	$ 20,092	$ 16,727
Reserve and loss ratios:					
Ending reserve to ending balances:					
Commercial, financial, and agricultural	1.74%	1.56%	1.45%	1.41%	1.20%
Real estate	.73	1.12	.87	.75	.80
Installment, net	1.44	1.46	1.29	1.31	1.24
Credit card	3.17	3.50	3.14	3.67	3.63
Leases, net	1.69	.98	.83	1.11	1.24
Total loans and leases	1.88	1.87	1.65	1.56	1.54
Net charge-offs to average balances:					
Commercial, financial, and agricultural	.70	1.13	1.18	.87	.74
Real estate	.38	.52	.24	.35	.66
Installment, net	1.48	1.57	1.33	1.25	1.05
Credit card	4.82	4.94	4.49	3.92	4.35
Leases, net	1.00	1.23	1.13	1.64	1.83
Total loans and leases	1.25	1.43	1.20	1.08	1.14
Recoveries to gross charge-offs	22.38	19.38	22.19	24.42	22.52
To ending loans and leases:					
Nonperforming assets	1.63	2.13	2.35	1.99	2.00
Loans delinquent 90 days or more	.46%	.65%	.54%	.41%	.41%

[a]Defined as loans with a high loss possibility after collateral liquidation based on existing facts, market conditions, and value. These loans are provided for in the reserve for loan losses, as appropriate. Any interest income recognized on these loans is immaterial.

[b]The amount of gross interest on nonperforming loans that would have been recorded during 1992 and 1991 if the loans had been current throughout the year totaled $58 million and $62 million, respectively. Of this amount, $19 million and $22 million of interest was actually recorded on nonperforming loans during 1992 and 1991, respectively. Texas is included in these amounts for the whole year of 1991 even though it was consolidated beginning October 1, 1991.

*unaudited

Source: *Annual Report*, 1992.

EXHIBIT 2-9 Banc One Loan and Lease Reserves[a] as of Year Ended December 31 (in thousands of dollars)

	Commercial, Financial and Agricultural	Real Estate	Installment	Credit Card	Leases	Unallocated	Total Reserves
Balance, December 31, 1987	$123,098	$20,162	$49,516	$62,081	$12,166	$19,500	$286,523
Reserves of entities acquired and sold, net	24,816	17,599	2,821	(543)	(48)	3,885	48,530
Provision, 1988	28,162	36,117	46,644	87,617	7,725	22,691	228,956
Gross losses	(88,217)	(34,267)	(68,628)	(96,602)	(13,818)		(301,532)
Recoveries	22,738	1,583	25,238	15,724	2,623		67,906
Net losses	(65,479)	(32,684)	(43,390)	(80,878)	(11,195)		(233,626)
Balance, December 31, 1988	110,597	41,194	55,591	68,277	8,648	46,076	330,383
Reserves of entities acquired and sold, net	6,207	10,003	1,251	8	4	266	17,739
Provision, 1989	95,614	13,516	62,464	62,645	11,196	(3,238)	242,197
Gross losses	(102,212)	(22,822)	(86,635)	(88,589)	(15,267)		(315,525)
Recoveries	22,032	2,906	28,820	19,627	3,654		77,039
Net losses	(80,180)	(19,916)	(57,815)	(68,962)	(11,613)		(238,486)
Balance, December 31, 1989	132,238	44,797	61,491	61,968	8,235	43,104	351,833
Allowance applicable to loans transferred to the Collection pool	(820)	(1,845)	(77)				(2,742)
Reserves of entities acquired and sold, net	5,556	8,476	4,843	13,926		2,897	35,698
Provision, 1990	128,341	30,195	77,434	86,085	6,683	22,047	350,785
Gross losses	(145,391)	(19,288)	(102,838)	(108,275)	(12,663)		(388,455)
Recoveries	27,451	2,625	30,608	21,220	4,291		86,195
Net losses	(117,940)	(16,663)	(72,230)	(87,055)	(8,372)		(302,260)
Balance, December 31, 1990	147,375	64,960	71,461	74,924	6,546	68,048	433,314
Allowance applicable to loans transferred to the Collection pool	(1,168)	(681)	(32)				(1,881)
Reserves of entities acquired and sold, net	51,873	36,178	30,327	32,411	900	11,231	162,920
Provision, 1991	116,433	66,894	107,632	193,992	10,212	7,566	502,729

EXHIBIT 2-9 *Continued*

	COMMERCIAL, FINANCIAL AND AGRICULTURAL	REAL ESTATE	INSTALLMENT	CREDIT CARD	LEASES	UNALLOCATED	TOTAL RESERVES
Gross losses	(146,070)	(49,977)	(138,468)	(171,818)	(14,721)		(521,054)
Recoveries	25,463	4,823	41,992	23,663	5,016		100,957
Net losses	(120,607)	(45,154)	(96,476)	(148,155)	(9,705)		(420,097)
Balance, December 31, 1991	193,906	122,197	112,912	153,172	7,953	86,845	676,985
Allowance applicable to loans transferred from the Collection pool	652	36	1				689
Reserves of entities acquired and sold, net	2,020	1,843	885	75			4,823
Provision, 1992	113,238	4,187	128,779	205,984	13,982	44,309	510,479
Gross losses	(129,428)	(50,697)	(172,906)	(233,108)	(14,189)		(600,328)
Recoveries	40,401	8,417	52,992	26,589	5,947		134,346
Net losses	(89,027)	(42,280)	(119,914)	(206,519)	(8,242)		465,982
Balance, December 31, 1992[a]	$220,789	$85,983	$122,663	$152,712	$13,693	$131,154	$726,994

[a]unaudited

Source: *Annual Report*, 1992.

EXHIBIT 2-10 Banc One Consolidated Statement of Changes in Stockholders' Equity as of Year Ended December 31 (in thousands of dollars)

$ (THOUSANDS, EXCEPT PER SHARE AMOUNTS)	PREFERRED STOCK	COMMON STOCK SHARES	COMMON STOCK STATED VALUE	CAPITAL IN EXCESS OF AGGREGATE STATED VALUE OF COMMON STOCK	RETAINED EARNINGS	TOTAL STOCKHOLDERS' EQUITY
Balance, December 31, 1990	$ 23,156	238,701,770	$1,193,508	$1,854,143	$1,443,846	$4,514,653
Net income					664,288	664,288
Cash dividends:						
Corporation:						
Common ($.76 per share)[1]					(186,968)	(186,968)
Class B Preferred ($3.00 per share)					(2,421)	(2,421)
Series C Preferred ($2.54 per share)					(12,639)	(12,639)
Pooled affiliates					(43,434)	(43,434)
Shares issued in acquisitions		1,019,632	5,098	20,702		25,800
Preferred stock offering, net of issuance costs	250,000			(5,350)		244,650
Common stock offering, net of issuance costs		7,625,000	38,125	280,965		319,090
Conversion of preferred into common	(3,742)	351,749	1,759	1,983		
Exercise of stock options, net of shares purchased		(57)	(1)	(2,792)		(2,793)
Pooled affiliate stock issuance and other		1,455,658	7,280	19,726	12,138	39,144
10% common stock dividend at fair market value		17,330,839	86,654	773,389	(860,043)	
Balance, December 31, 1991	269,414	266,484,591	1,332,423	2,942,766	1,014,767	5,559,370
Net income					876,588	876,588
Cash dividends:						
Corporation:						
Common ($.89 per share)[a]					(257,101)	(257,101)
Class B Preferred ($3.00 per share)					(1,486)	(1,486)
Series C Preferred ($3.50 per share)					(17,500)	(17,500)
Pooled affiliates					(25,748)	(25,748)
Shares issued in acquisitions		1,254,000	6,270	6,371	20,049	32,690
Conversion of preferred into common	(9,714)	995,789	4,979	4,735		
Exercise of stock options, net of shares purchased		569,311	2,847	(22,486)		(19,639)
Pooled affiliate stock issuance and other		2,943,110	14,715	77,835	1,862	94,412
Balance, December 31, 1992	259,700	272,246,801	1,361,234	3,009,221	1,611,431	6,241,586

EXHIBIT 2-10 *Continued*

$ (THOUSANDS, EXCEPT PER SHARE AMOUNTS)	PREFERRED STOCK	COMMON STOCK		CAPITAL IN EXCESS OF AGGREGATE STATED VALUE OF COMMON STOCK	RETAINED EARNINGS	TOTAL STOCKHOLDERS' EQUITY
		SHARES	STATED VALUE			
Net income					1,139,980	1,139,980
Cash dividends:						
Corporation:						
Common ($1.07 per share)[1]					(388,245)	(388,245)
Class B Preferred ($.75 per share)					(216)	(216)
Series C Preferred ($3.50 per share)					(17,498)	(17,498)
Pooled affiliates					(4,987)	(4,987)
Shares issued in acquisitions		4,907,702	24,539	12,269	59,409	96,217
Conversion of preferred into common	(9,800)	1,005,825	5,029	4,771		
Exercise of stock options, net of shares purchased		(575,147)	(2,876)	(44,758)		(47,634)
Pooled affiliate stock issuance and other		304,452	1,521	12,062	852	14,435
Common stock split five-for-four, effective August 31, 1993		68,189,628	340,949	(340,949)		
10% common stock dividend at fair market value		34,607,926	173,040	1,180,995	(1,354,035)	
Balance, December 31, 1993	$249,900	380,687,187	$1,903,436	$3,833,611	$1,046,691	$7,033,638

[a]Amounts reflect the effect of the 10% common stock dividends effective February 14, 1992 and February 10, 1994, and the five-shares-for-four-shares stock split effective August 31, 1993.

Source: *Annual Report, 1993.*

RETAILING INDUSTRY NOTE
JAMES WALSH
U.S. Department of Commerce

The retail trade sector (SIC 52 59) is one of the major sources of jobs in the U.S. economy, consistently accounting for about 21 percent of all nonfarm jobs in the private sector. Retail establishments are primarily engaged in selling merchandise for personal or household consumption.

Retail merchandise lines are divided into the following categories: building materials, hardware, garden supplies, and mobile home dealers (SIC 52); general merchandise stores (SIC 53); food stores (SIC 54); automobile dealers and gasoline service stations (SIC 55); apparel and accessory stores (SIC 56); home furniture, furnishings, and equipment stores (SIC 57); eating and drinking places (SIC 58); and miscellaneous retail stores (SIC 59).

In general, sales of retail establishments in SIC groups 52, 55, 57, and 59 are mostly from durable goods and sales of retail establishments in SIC groups 53, 54, 56, and 58 are mostly from nondurable goods.

Year-to-year changes in sales of retail stores concentrating on nondurable merchandise lines, such as food and clothing, tend to mirror changes in general business conditions as indicated by the gross domestic product (GDP), which is forecast to grow about 3 percent in 1994. In contrast, year-to-year changes in sales of retail stores concentrating in durable goods, such as furniture and major household appli-

Trends and Forecasts: Retail Sales (SIC 52–59) (in billions of dollars except as noted)

| | | | | | PERCENT CHANGE (1991–1994) | | |
ITEM	1991	1992	1993[1]	1994[2]	91–92	92–93	93–94
All stores	1,866	1,962	2,086	2,232	5.1	6.3	7.0
Total nondurables	1,212	1,257	1,329	1,411	3.7	5.7	6.2
General merchandise	228	247	280	320	8.3	13.4	14.3
Apparel	97	105	108	112	8.2	2.9	3.7
Restaurants	197	202	207	216	2.5	2.5	4.4
Drugs	76	77	78	80	1.3	1.3	2.6
Food	377	384	387	399	1.9	0.8	3.1
Other	237	242	269	284	2.1	11.2	5.6
Total durables	654	705	757	821	7.8	7.4	8.5
Employment (millions)	19.3	19.1	19.3	NA	–1.0	1.1	NA
Average hourly earnings ($)	6.95	7.14	7.26	NA	2.7	1.7	NA

[1]Estimate.

[2]Forecast.

Source: U.S. Department of Commerce: Bureau of the Census, International Trade Administration (ITA); U.S. Department of Labor, Bureau of Labor Statistics. Estimates and forecasts by ITA.

ances, tend to exaggerate changes in business conditions by increasing more than the GDP during good years and declining more than the GDP during slowdowns. In addition to overall business conditions, retail sales reflect changes in prices, merchandise mix, and shifts to alternative channels of distribution.

This industry note focuses on the trends that influence the current and near-term demand for nondurable retail merchandise.

Industry Sales. In 1993 total retail sales reached nearly $2.1 trillion, a gain of more than 6 percent in current dollars. A major portion of the increase was due to price hikes. It is difficult to measure the precise increase in "real dollars" because of the incompatibility of retail sales data and the Consumer Price Index, which measures inflation.

Stores selling mostly nondurables accounted for nearly 64 percent of total retail sales, with 1993 revenues topping $1.3 trillion, up 5.7 percent over 1992. Sales of durable goods totaled $757 billion in current dollars, up more than 7 percent from 1992, and accounted for 36 percent of the total.

However, these year-to-year gains should be taken as only a rough approximation of the direction of change for the sales value of all consumer durables or nondurables because of the way Census Bureau data is reported. For example, Kmart reported furniture sales totaling $364 million in 1991. The Census Bureau reported all of these sales as retail sales of nondurables because Kmart's principal merchandise lines are nondurable.

Retail stores selling primarily nondurable goods, for which Census Bureau data are available, include general merchandise stores, department stores, food stores, variety stores, apparel stores, restaurants, and drug stores. Other retailers for which Census data are not available include discount stores, warehouse clubs, convenience stores, and catalog and video sales firms.

A list of the top 100 retailing firms compiled by *Chain Store Age Executive* magazine combined the sales data for the top 100 retailing firms in 1992, including data for types of retailers not collected by Census. The results indicated that discount stores accounted for 21 percent of all sales by the top retail stores selling nondurable goods, second only to supermarkets, which represented 35 percent of total sales. Warehouse clubs, a relatively recent entrant into the retail market, accounted for 6 percent of nondurable sales in 1992. (See Table 1.)

According to the *Chain Store Age Executive,* discount stores and warehouse clubs achieved their current market position mainly by underpricing department stores, variety stores, and drug stores. Supermarkets also increased their market share at the expense of drug stores, and specialty apparel stores captured markets formerly claimed by department stores. A new category of retailer—"G" stores, operated by the major gasoline companies—encroached on the market share of traditional convenience stores.

New Strategies for the 1990s. In response to increased competition from new market participants, retailers are exercising a full array of strategies, including downsizing and restructuring, changing their merchandise mix, adding services, and adapting the "quick response system" for controlling inventory management costs. Over the past decade, these strategies, singly or in combination, helped retailers faced with declining market shares and falling profit margins to prevent further erosion of their market positions and improve their overall revenues.

But these competitive strategies may not be enough for the 1990s. David Glass, president and chief executive officer of Wal-Mart, told the 1993 National Retail

TABLE 1 1992 Retail Sales of Nondurable Products (by type of store, ranked by total sales*)

ITEM	MARKET SHARE (IN PERCENT)
Supermarkets	35.0
Discount stores	21.0
Department stores	13.0
General merchandise	8.0
Specialty apparel	7.0
Warehouse clubs	6.0
Drug stores	5.0
Convenience stores	3.0
Variety stores	2.0
Total	100.0

*Based on total sales of the top 100 retailers of nondurable merchandise in 1992. Excludes revenues of catalogs and video sales channels, estimated at $2 billion.

Source: *Chain Store Age Executive*, April 1993.

Federation convention that "all concepts of doing business are changing." He pointed out that the customer of the 1990s is looking for genuine value, coupled with superior and different customer services. Others have made similar observations. P. R. Trimmer, in his book *50 Powerful Ideas You Can Use to Keep Your Customer*, called customer service "the competitive battleground for the 1990's."

The retail customer of the 1990s is significantly different from the retail customer of a decade ago, and retail strategies need to be reassessed in view of the changing demographics and new buying patterns.

The most significant demographic change is in the declining importance of households composed of married couples, dropping from 60.8 percent in 1980 to 55.3 percent in 1991. At the same time, the number of people living alone increased, influencing the consumer buying habits and forcing retailers to respond with appropriate packaging and marketing, as evidenced by the increase in "single serving" products.

Some retailers depend on groups other than households for their target markets. For instance, men between the ages of 18 and 34 are the mainstay customers of convenience stores. But the number of men in this age group is expected to decline during the 1990s, portending a difficult period for convenience stores.

Another demographic change is the projected surge in the number of teenagers and young adults in the next five years. This group will be more inclined to embrace electronic shopping channels and interactive television, sometimes referred to as "storeless" shopping.

Changing buying patterns projected for the 1990s reflect new priorities for households composed of married couples and a different life-style for single-person households.

Many married couples consisting of maturing baby boomers have changed their priorities to emphasize more leisure time. Increasingly they have rejected the day-long shopping trips of the past in favor of quick "buy and go" patterns. These changing attitudes toward shopping appear to have had an effect on the retailing scene. Sales at super regional malls—those with at least three anchor stores—dropped 7.3 percent between 1990 and 1992, after increasing 18 percent during the previous three years. During the same period, retail sales at smaller community shopping centers increased 15 percent and sales at neighborhood strip centers increased nearly 7 percent.

Consequently, superstores are being downsized to attract the 1990s consumer. In the 1980s the superstores had 220,000–260,000 square feet. In the 1990s the superstores will cover 116,000–188,000 square feet.

Retailers also have altered strategies to appeal to the increased number of people living alone. This group follows a different life-style from that of the traditional retail customer. According to Barbara Caplan, Vice President of Yankelovich, Clancy Shulman, people living alone "no longer feel that they have to do what society says, but feel that they have permission to do as they please." This group of customers tends to shun traditional buying patterns and look for unusual items and wider assortments of merchandise.

As Michael Wellman, Vice President for Marketing at Kmart, told retailers at the 1993 National Demographic and Lifestyle annual conference, "The successful retailer of the 1990's must change his operation to meet the needs of the 1990's customer." These changes will include new marketing vehicles such as "electronic retailing."

Electronic retailing, as defined by Carl Steidtmann, Director of Management Horizons, a division of Price Waterhouse, includes interactive communications via faxes, electronic data interchanges, and other interactive media. Here are some examples of electronic retailing already in place:

- An upstate New York supermarket allows its customers to electronically check out and pay for their purchases without the aid of a check-out person.
- A discount store in Maryland allows its customers to fax their orders to the store for immediate assembly and delivery to the ordering customer.
- Several "G" stores are experimenting with interactive electronic menus at the gasoline pump that list the merchandise carried in the store. The customer electronically indicates the merchandise to be purchased, pays for the gasoline and other merchandise at the pump with a credit card, and picks up the bagged selections at the store's drive-in window.

Competitive Measures. Shifts in market position during the last five years prompted retailers to adopt competitive countermeasures, including downsizing and consolidation, merchandise mix changes, more consumer services, and greater use of advanced technologies, such as quick-response systems, to control inventory costs and increase productivity.

A quick-response system usually involves a strategic alliance between a retailer and manufacturer, coupled with an Electronic Data Interchange (EDI) system, which includes sharing sales, marketing, and inventory data with vendors; bar coding on packaging to track sales and inventory; and point-of-sale scanners to track sales and implement an automated stock replenishment system. It is also essential that an EDI system be able to issue invoices and payments electronically and track consumer buyer patterns.

The most frequently cited benefits of a quick response system include increased inventory turnover and reduced inventory levels, operating costs, and frequency of out-of-stock items. A recent Garr Consulting Group survey of a cross section of retailers conducted for *Chain Store Age Executive* magazine found that 61 percent of those surveyed had entered into strategic alliances with vendors to take advantage of the benefits of a quick-response system.

The various competitive strategies undertaken by major types of retailers during the last few years are reviewed in the next section.

Department Stores. Department store sales increased from nearly $153 billion in 1988 to $183 billion in 1993, a five-year increase of nearly 20 percent, according to Census Bureau data. Despite the growth in sales volume, department stores lost market share to discount stores, warehouse clubs, and specialty apparel shops, dropping from nearly 15 percent of the market for nondurable retailers in 1988 to slightly less than 14 percent in 1993.

To adjust to the competitive pressures from other types of retailers, several department stores, including R. H. Macy and Federated Stores, filed Chapter 11 bankruptcy actions while they downsized and restructured their operations. Other department stores have changed their merchandise mix to deemphasize their durable lines and highlight their fashion apparel, gifts, and designer household items.

The Garr Consulting Group survey showed 78 percent of the department store managers interviewed reported they had entered into strategic alliances with their vendors to implement the quick-response system. In terms of sales, the top five department stores are Mays, J. C. Penny, Federated, R. H. Macy, and Dillard.

Supermarkets. Food retailers increased their sales but accounted for a smaller share of nondurable goods purchased during the 1988–1993 period. Sales rose from $326 billion in 1988 to $387 billion in 1992, a gain of nearly 19 percent, according to the Census Bureau. In terms of market share, food stores claimed more than 29 percent of the total market for nondurable retailers in 1993, down from the nearly 32 percent claimed in 1988. Supermarkets have consistently accounted for about 80 percent of all food store sales.

During the last several years, supermarkets lost sales to drugstores, discount stores, and warehouse clubs. To meet these competitive challenges, supermarkets changed their merchandise mix by dropping duplicated product lines and allocating more shelf space to fast-moving nonfood items and promotional items. Some supermarkets also have revised their marketing strategy, shifting some of their advertising dollars from weekly newspaper inserts to direct mail circulars.

According to the Garr Consulting Group survey, 46 percent of the supermarket managers surveyed said that they have entered into strategic alliances with their vendors to implement the quick-response system. In addition, a few supermarkets have expanded their consumer services, such as accepting telephone orders of groceries for home delivery.

The top five supermarkets are Kroger, American Stores, Safeway, A&P, and Winn-Dixie.

Warehouse Clubs. The number of warehouse clubs increased from 15 in 1983 to 577 in 1992, experiencing double-digit growth in sales and earnings until the early 1990s. Since then, warehouse club sales and earnings have declined.

Part of this deterioration in sales and earnings is due to competitive challenges from other types of retailers such as supermarkets. In response, warehouse clubs are downsizing and restructuring, changing their mix of merchandise, adding more services, and opening new markets. Kmart's recent sale of Pace Club to Sam's Club and Costco's merger with Price Club are examples of the new competitive strategies. Price Club and Sam's Club also entered new markets by forming joint ventures with retailers in Mexico.

The top warehouse clubs include Price Club, Sam's Club, and Waban.

Discount Stores. Sales of the big ten discount stores grew at a robust average annual rate of 11.5 percent from 1987 to 1991, according to *Chain Store Age*

Executive magazine. But discount stores' sales have begun to slow, increasing only 10.3 percent from 1990 to 1991—the latest period for which revenue figures are available. A closer look at the individual sales changes from 1990 to 1991, compared to the full 1987–1991 period, reveals a significant slowdown in the revenue of several discounters, including Hills, Ames, and Rose's. As a result, discount stores have implemented strategies to maintain their market standing, including downsizing and restructuring, changing their merchandise mix, adding services, and intensifying the use of their quick-response systems.

The Garr Consulting Group report revealed that 50 percent of the discount store managers responding to the survey said they have entered into strategic alliances with their vendors to implement their quick-response systems.

Discount stores also are changing their merchandise mix by adding groceries to their product lines. Others are adding more services, such as beauty shops and in-store opticians. A few discount stores also are expanding into new markets by forming joint ventures with retailers in Mexico.

The major discount stores include Wal-Mart, Kmart, Stop-N-Shop, Pacific Enterprises, and Ames.

Apparel Stores. Apparel and accessory stores posted sales of $108 billion in 1993, up 27 percent from the $85 billion recorded for 1988. In terms of market position, apparel and accessory stores have maintained a fairly stable 8 percent of total sales of all retailers of nondurable merchandise. Apparel and accessory stores have been effective in maintaining their market position by emphasizing fashion and value, thereby capturing consumer clothing sales previously claimed by department stores.

According to the Garr Consulting Group survey, 59 percent of the apparel store managers surveyed reported that they have entered into strategic alliances with their vendors to implement quick-response systems.

The top retail firms selling mostly apparel and accessories are Melville, The Limited, TJX Co., U.S. Shoe, and Gap.

Catalog and Video Retailers. The top six catalog retailers show an average annual increase in sales of 13.8 percent during the period 1987–1991 compared to the 5.7 percent increase registered from 1990 to 1991, the latest year for which revenue figures are available. *Chain Store Age Executive* magazine attributed the 1990–1991 slowdown to the recession, rather than competitive pressures from other direct sales channels.

Catalog retailers are maintaining their competitive edge in part by expanding into foreign markets. For example, L. L. Bean has formed four joint ventures in Japan; Lands' End is developing the British market and plans to test the market in France; and J. Crew recently hired a vice president for international development to guide their expansion into foreign markets.

Video retailers were given a boost recently by the merger of QVC and Home Shopping Network. These two video retailers claim to cover about 99 percent of the total $2.2 billion market for video sales. Some industry analysts view current video retailers as rivals for the catalog retail customer, but about half of all video retail sales —$1.1 billion—are from repeat customers. The greater competitive threat for both catalog and video retailers appears to be from general merchandise stores, such as Dillard, that are planning their own shopping channels with interactive electronic arrangements that would allow the at-home customer to make direct purchases.

The top catalog retailers are Fingerhut, Spiegel, Lands' End, and L. L. Bean. The top video retailers are QVC, Home Shopping Network, and the Fashion Channel.

Until recently, few retailers attempted to expand into foreign markets. But the easing of investment restrictions in some foreign countries, and the emerging trend of establishing affiliated firms abroad, has launched a new era in retailing.

The precise volume of exports and imports attributable to retailers is not known because merchandise trade flows are identified by type of product (e.g., manufactured, agricultural, metals, and minerals, etc.) rather than type of organization. The only export data identified by type of organization are listed in the *U.S. Direct Investment Abroad* (DIA) reports published every five years. The latest, the 1989 benchmark survey, shows the 50 U.S. retailers, with 211 foreign affiliates, exported merchandise valued at $200 million to affiliated firms in foreign markets. They included retailers of general merchandise, food, clothing, autos, garden supplies, hardware, as well as discount stores and catalog retailers. In addition, U.S. retailers reported $500 million in direct sales to foreign customers.

In 1989 major stores with at least one affiliated firm in a foreign market included Sears, J. C. Penney, Woolworth, and Carter-Hawley. The foreign affiliates of these retail parent firms were either wholly owned or majority owned by the U.S. firm. Since then, several other major U.S. retailers have established affiliated firms in foreign countries, including Toys-R-Us, Sam's Club, Kmart, Price Club, Blockbuster, and Dillard.

Most recent investments in foreign affiliates have been in Mexico because of the easing of government restrictions on joint ventures and other business activities that had previously been imposed on foreign investors. Further expansions are expected as a result of the North American Free Trade Agreement.

Foreign governments often impose restrictions on how or where foreign firms may operate or limit foreign investment to certain sectors or organizational arrangements. These constraints discourage U.S. retailers from expanding into new markets through affiliated firms in foreign countries. A major objective of the Uruguay Round of multilateral trade negotiations, as well as separate bilateral consultations, is to reduce or eliminate restrictions on investment. If the negotiations are successful, more U.S. retailers will be encouraged to expand to new foreign markets. For example, bilateral consultations with Japan have resulted in an easing of restrictions on the size of foreign retail stores, prompting Toys-R-Us and Blockbuster Video to establish affiliated firms there.

Additional U.S. investment in retail affiliates abroad may increase the demand for American exports from U.S. parent retail firms to their foreign affiliates.

Outlook for 1994. Total retail sales should reach $2.2 trillion in 1994, up 7 percent from 1993. Total revenue earned by stores concentrating in nondurable product lines will exceed $1.4 trillion, an increase of more than 6 percent over 1993, largely reflecting higher prices. These projected increases reflect the general view of business forecasters that consumer spending in 1994 will provide the underlying strength for the 3 percent growth rate in the GDP forecast for the 1993–1994 period. During 1993 consumer spending, reflecting uneasiness about the future, was projected to remain flat as consumers continued to reduce their debt burden. However, low interest rates and diminished inflationary pressures should encourage business investment and induce consumers to spend more in 1994.

THE LIMITED, INC.—1994

Based in Columbus, Ohio, the Limited (614-479-7000) continues to exploit opportunities for growth. Net sales from 1991 to 1992 increased 13 percent to almost $7 billion. New income increased in 1992 by 12.9 percent to $455 million. An additional 2.5 million square feet of selling space was added during 1992 for a total of 22.9 million square feet of selling space for all Limited stores. Stores now number 4,425. The Limited, Inc., has become the largest women's apparel specialty store and mail-order retailer in the United States.

Leslie Wexner, chairman of The Limited, believes that creativity and innovation are the essential ingredients for his company's success in the highly competitive specialty retailing industry. "I think specialty retailing is as valid, and perhaps more valid, than twenty years ago," Wexner says.

> In a world that's changing faster, the intensity of your efforts and your knowledge is obsolete faster; and it becomes increasingly difficult to be knowledgeable and/or competitive if you have a broad-based business. . . . The fashion business is a business of change, with fashion cycles on a short and long term basis always moving.

For over thirty years, Wexner's Limited stores have achieved success by "breaking the rules" in the specialty retailing industry. Instead of offering a wide variety of types of clothing, the stores offer a limited assortment of women's sportswear in large quantities and a variety of colors. The company emphasizes rapid turnover of inventory so only the newest in fashion is in the stores at all times. The Limited, Inc. has 12 retail store divisions targeted to specific groups of shoppers: The Limited, Express, Henri Bendel, Victoria's Secret Stores, Abercrombie & Fitch, Lerner New York, Lane Bryant, Structure, The Limited Too, Cacique, Bath & Body Works, and Penhaligon's.

The operations of these 12 divisions are independent so that division presidents can make needed changes very quickly. Wexner does not believe that centralized control works in the fashion industry. "Every time somebody says 'economy of scale' somebody else should jump up and say 'what about diminishing returns?'" The decentralization of operations at The Limited provides the company a distinct advantage in the turbulent retail apparel industry. Wexner believes that his company's performance suggests that The Limited has been successful in its attempt to "reinvent the large specialty store."

HISTORY

Leslie Wexner's mother and father both worked in retailing—his father for the Miller Wall specialty chain and his mother as a buyer for Lazarus. When Wexner was fourteen, his parents opened their own specialty apparel store in Columbus, Ohio. After college and one year in law school, Wexner returned to work in his parents' store until he decided what he wanted to do with his life. He planned that his work in retail would be temporary, but he says he "got hooked."

In 1963 Leslie Wexner borrowed $10,000 from an aunt and a bank to open The Limited's first store. During its first year in operation, this store achieved sales of $157,000. His strategy was to provide a "limited" assortment of quality, fashionable sportswear at medium prices. The "limited" concept worked well, and by the late

1970s Wexner began a twofold strategy of market development and product development. New stores were opened and acquired to appeal to women of different ages, different sizes, and different budget limits.

Since 1984 Wexner has tried to acquire department store chains such as Federated Department Stores, R. H. Macy, and Carter Hawley Hale (CHH). Probably the greatest disappointment in Wexner's acquisition attempts was his failed attempt to acquire CHH for $1.1 billion. At the time he submitted the offer, CHH consisted of 124 department stores, 117 specialty stores, and 841 bookstores. Some of the store names associated with CHH at the time included Thalhimers, Neiman-Marcus, Broadway, and Bergdorf Goodman. The Limited acquired about 700,000 shares of CHH stock at the time of its offer. In response to The Limited's takeover attempt, General Cinema acquired $300 million of CHH stock and CHH began buying its own stock. The Securities and Exchange Commission stepped in to stop both The Limited and CHH from unfairly attempting to control the takeover situation. These legal developments stalled Wexner's takeover attempt. After the CHH takeover attempt failed in 1986, Wexner began thinking more about internal growth than about new acquisitions. CHH recently filed for Chapter 11 bankruptcy. Wexner now says about CHH, "we wouldn't take it for free."

Throughout the 1980s Wexner acquired a variety of businesses including Lane Bryant, Victoria's Secret, Sizes Unlimited, Lerner, Henri Bendel, and Abercrombie & Fitch, each of which was in financial trouble when Wexner acquired it. He also started several store divisions during the 1980s, including Express, Structure, Limited Too, and Cacique. During the 1990s the number of acquisitions and business startups has continued to grow, but at a slower pace. The growth of The Limited, Inc. is shown in Exhibit 3–1.

OPERATIONS

Despite the industry slump during the late 1980s, The Limited, Inc., has continued to perform well. During 1992, 231 new stores were opened. Net sales increased 13 percent and net income increased by 13 percent to $455 million in 1992. The largest revenue generator for The Limited during 1992 was Express. Structure doubled its sales in 1991 and almost did it again in 1992 to approximately $348 million. Victoria's Secret Stores and Victoria's Secret Catalogue also had a successful 1992.

Wexner has been disappointed in the performance of two of The Limited's divisions since 1990. A portion of the decrease in profits for these two divisions during 1990 were explained by renovation costs. The Limited Stores were upgraded with high-tech lighting, marble floors, chrome, mirrors, and so forth, and the size of many stores was doubled. In addition, the former division president of The Limited Stores, Verna Gibson, phased out the popular Forenza private label. In its place, Gibson introduced a higher-priced line called Paul et Duffier that did not sell well. Lerner also incurred significant renovation expenses. Although some industry observers believe that Lerner's new richer-looking design, featuring piano players, overstuffed furniture, and large dressing rooms, provides a pleasant shopping environment, it did not help to increase Lerner's sales.

During 1992, The Limited flagship store continued to have merchandising problems. Estimates are that Limited sales for 1992 were $1.3 billion, a decrease of 5 percent from 1991 sales. At the beginning of the 1990s, consumers became more value-conscious and demanded higher-quality clothing than The Limited offered. Howard Gross, president of The Limited, hopes that better-quality merchandise will

EXHIBIT 3-1 Growth of The Limited, Inc.

OPERATING RESULTS (THOUSANDS EXCEPT PER SHARE AMOUNTS)

	1993	1992	% CHANGE
Net Sales	$7,245,088	$6,944,296	4%
Operating Income	$701,556	$788,698	(11%)
Net Income	$390,999	$455,497	(14%)
Net Income as a Percentage of Sales	5.4%	6.6%	
Net income Per Share	$1.08	$1.25	(14%)
Dividends Per Share	$.36	$.28	29%

YEAR-END POSITION (THOUSANDS EXCEPT FINANCIAL RATIOS)

	1993	1992	% CHANGE
Total Assets	$4,135,105	$3,846,450	8%
Working Capital	$1,513,181	$1,063,352	42%
Current Ratio	3.1	2.5	
Long-Term Debt	$650,000	$541,639	20%
Debt-to-Equity Ratio	27%	24%	
Shareholders' Equity	$2,441,293	$2,267,617	8%
Return on Average Shareholders' Equity	17%	22%	

STORES OPEN AT END OF YEAR (RANKED BY SALES)

	1993	1992
Express	673	640
Lerner New York	877	915
The Limited	746	759
Victoria's Secret Stores	570	545
Lane Bryant	817	809
Structure	394	330
The Limited Too	184	185
Bath & Body Works	194	121
Abercrombie & Fitch Co.	49	40
Henri Bendel	4	4
Cacique	108	71
Penhaligon's	7	6
Total Number of Stores	4,623	4,425
Selling Square Feet	24,426,000	22,863,000
Number Of Associates		97,500

Source: The Limited *Annual Report*, 1993.

lure its customers back to Limited stores. Lerner New York's former budget-conscience customers now spend their money at Wal-Mart, Kmart and other discount stores. In response, Lerner New York decided to move upscale and began selling moderately priced clothing. This is a risky strategy because it may take some time for potential customers to understand that Lerner provides a higher-quality product and is no longer a budget-priced store.

Business Structure. The Limited, Inc. is presently organized into 20 major operating divisions that include 12 different store types, two mail-order divisions, and six facilitating-type operations. The 20 divisions are described briefly here.

Limited Stores. This is the flagship division of the organization. Originally, merchandise in these stores was targeted to women between the ages of 16 and 25. Limited Stores has now shifted its orientation to women in the "thirtysomething" age group. These stores focus on the sale of medium-priced fashion clothing and accessories. Fifteen larger-format Limited stores called International Fashion Stores were opened in 1990, and many older stores are presently being renovated to provide additional selling space. Most of the 759 Limited stores are located in regional shopping centers or malls across the United States.

Express. The Express was recently redesigned to have a more sophisticated image instead of the neon-lit, high-tech store of the mid-1980s. Merchandise includes a unique assortment of popular-priced sportswear in the latest American and international styles. A private label brand created for Express is called Compagnie Internationale. The 640 Express stores in operation are located mostly in shopping malls.

Lerner New York. This division sells conventional women's sportswear. The Lerner stores have begun a transition from a budget-priced store to a moderately priced store. The Limited purchased the Lerner chain in 1985 for $297 million. Presently there are 915 Lerner stores in operation in malls and shopping centers across the United States.

Victoria's Secret. Victoria's Secret stores are the dominant intimate-apparel store in the world, presently selling more lingerie than industry competitors Vanity Fair and Maidenform. These stores specialize in high-quality European and American designer lingerie, with prices ranging from $5 to $2,000. In 1988 Victoria's Secret stores began selling toiletries, bath products, and fragrances. This division focuses on women aged 25 to 45, but gifts purchased by men account for a significant portion of the total sales. The stores had been decorated in a "Victorian Parlor" style, and the recently updated store design is an English-influence decor called "Bond Street." There are 545 Victoria's Secret stores in the United States.

Victoria's Secret Catalogue. This division is one the fastest-growing mail-order operations in the United States. Since its purchase by The Limited in 1982, the catalogue has steadily increased its operations. Now Victoria's Secret Catalogue is the dominant catalogue for lingerie in the world.

Lane Bryant. Lane Bryant had been in operation for 80 years; it was actually larger than The Limited, Inc., at the time it was purchased by The Limited in 1982. Lane

Bryant's market is primarily women between 30 and 50. The store specializes in the sale of medium-priced clothing, intimate apparel, and accessories for the "special-sized woman" (sizes 14 and up). Nearly all Lane Bryant stores were originally located in regional shopping centers, but Wexner has shifted Lane Bryant stores to mall locations near the other Limited stores. Because about 40 percent of American women are size 14 or larger, much growth is expected for Lane Bryant. There are presently 809 Lane Bryant stores.

Brylane. This division is the nation's largest catalogue retailer. Brylane sells women's special-sized apparel and misses sizes in their Lane Bryant Direct, Lerner Direct, and Roaman's catalogues. This division maintains a distribution center in Indianapolis, Indiana, where all orders are shipped and received.

Henri Bendel. In 1985 The Limited purchased this upscale fashion store. The store offers the best in clothing and accessories from international designers. Prices are designed for the fashion-conscious but not the budget-conscious shopper. This is the only high-priced store owned by The Limited. The first Henri Bendel store is located in New York City, and three more stores have been opened in major cities in the United States.

Abercrombie & Fitch. The Limited purchased Abercrombie & Fitch in 1988 from Oshman's Sporting Goods for $45 million in cash. The company sells traditional sportswear and outdoor sporting apparel and related gift items for younger men and women. The Limited operates 40 Abercrombie & Fitch stores.

Structure. The Limited, Inc., began testing the market for men's fashions by offering "Express for Men" in Express stores beginning in 1987. Sixty-nine Structure stores were opened in 1989, and by the end of 1992 there were 330 stores. They carry good-quality, affordable clothing in the latest styles. The store design mixes Palladian and modern architectural styles to appeal to men who "have a good sense of fine design." Structure stores generally open into Express stores so that customers can shop in both stores without having to exit to the mall area.

Limited Too. The market for girls' clothing (sizes 6–14) was tested by The Limited in the late 1980s when the Limited Too brand was offered in The Limited's flagship store. Sixty-two stores were opened during 1989, and by the end of 1992 there were 185 Limited Too Stores. Clothing sold in Limited Too stores is stylish–the newest in colors, prints, and fabrics—and moderately priced.

Bath & Body Works. In response to demand by consumers for natural personal-care products, The Limited opened six Bath & Body Works stores in 1990. These stores have a natural-market, open-air design and sell a variety of personal care products. There are now 121 Bath & Body Works stores.

Cacique. Select lingerie presented as Parisian in style is sold in 71 Cacique stores. Lingerie is made of high-quality fabrics in sophisticated designs.

Penhaligon's. The Limited purchased Penhaligon's in 1990 from Laura Ashley Holdings for approximately $11 million. The six stores, located in England, offer high-quality personal care products including perfumes, shaving accessories, soaps, and bath salts. Penhaligon products are also sold in some of the finest department stores around the world.

Mast Industries. The business of this division is to arrange for the manufacture and import of women's clothing from around the world, and to wholesale this merchandise to The Limited stores and to other companies.

Limited Distribution Services. The Limited's distribution center is located in Columbus, Ohio, with seven buildings and about 4.2 million square feet. This includes a 760,000-square-foot fulfillment center and office complex for Victoria's Secret Catalogue that was completed in 1992. The Limited also owns a mail-order center of approximately 750,000 square feet in Indianapolis, Indiana.

Limited Store Planning. This division designs store layout and develops merchandising techniques for all of The Limited's retail divisions.

Limited Real Estate. This division handles store leases for the 13 retail divisions. In 1991 the Real Estate division began a process of remodeling many stores and opening new larger-format stores (6 million square feet of selling space) for a total selling space at the end of 1991 of 20.3 million square feet. By the end of 1992, the total selling space of Limited Stores was almost 23 million square feet.

Limited Credit Services. This division handles consumer credit for both the retail and mail-order divisions. Activities of Limited Credit Services include billing, credit assessment, and credit collection. World Financial Network, Inc., a company-owned subsidiary, finances the company's private credit-card receivables.

Gryphon Development L.P.. This division, acquired by The Limited in 1992, develops and supplies fragrances for Bath & Body Works and Victoria's Secret.

COMPETITION

The retail sale of women's clothing is a very competitive business. Competitors of The Limited include nationally, regionally, and locally owned department stores, specialty stores, and mail-order catalogue businesses. Some of The Limited's major competitors are The Gap, Petrie Stores, Casual Corner, Marshall Fields, Carson Pirie Scott, Dayton-Hudson, Dillard's, May Department Stores, Charming Shoppes, Nordstrom, Sears, and J. C. Penney.

The years 1987 through 1990 were not good ones for the women's fashion industry. Many clothing retailers were purchased by debt-heavy corporations. Other retailers have gone out of business, including B. Altman, Garfinckel's, and Bonwit Teller. Leaders in the apparel retail industry have begun rethinking their strategies in hopes of improving the industry outlook for the 1990s. For example, some companies have chosen to concentrate on selling separates, whereas other companies promote collections and branded labels such as Liz Claiborne, J. G. Hook, and J. H. Collectibles. Improved customer service, including seminars and fashion shows, is a strategy adopted by many companies in the industry. Other companies have chosen to update displays, concentrate on private labels, emphasize career clothes, or to offer a mix of casual and career clothing.

According to *Stores,* The Limited, Inc. was the number one apparel chain in the United States during both 1991 and 1992. (The top ten apparel chains are shown in Exhibit 3–2.) Other specialty retailers who were in the top ten for sales volume in 1991 and 1992 include Melville Apparel, Nordstrom, TJX Cos., The Gap, Petrie Stores, Saks Fifth Avenue, U. S. Shoe, Charming Shoppes, and Kohls.

Two of The Limited's major competitors are described here.

The Gap, Inc. At the end of January 1993, The Gap had 1,307 apparel stores in operation. Several of its divisions compete directly with The Limited stores. The Gap, Inc. (885 stores), sells casual sportswear items for both men and women. GapKids (262 stores) sells children's sportswear. Banana Republic (160 stores) sells travel and outdoor sporting apparel. The Gap, Inc. also operates 22 GapKids in the United Kingdom and 24 in Canada. Financial information for The Gap, Inc., is shown in Exhibit 3–3.

EXHIBIT 3-2 Top Ten Apparel Chains (in millions of dollars)

CHAIN	1991 SALES	1992 SALES	PERCENT CHANGE
The Limited	$6,149.2	$6,944.3	12.9
Melville Apparel	3,243.2	3,486.1	7.5
Nordstrom	3,179.8	3,422.0	7.6
TJX Cos.	2,757.7	3,261.2	18.3
The Gap	2,518.9	2,960.4	17.2
Petrie Stores	1,354.5	1,438.2	6.2
Saks Fifth Avenue	1,300.0	1,350.0	3.8
U.S. Shoe Apparel	1,364.0	1,262.2	(7.5)
Charming Shoppes	1,020.7	1,178.7	15.5
Kohls	930.5	1,096.9	17.8

Source: "Top 100 Retailers," *Stores,* July 1993.

EXHIBIT 3-3 Financial Information for the Gap, Inc. (in millions of dollars except per share amount)

	1989	1990	1991	1992
Gross Revenue	1586.6	1933.8	2518.9	2960.2
Net Income	104.1	144.5	229.9	210.2
Long-Term Debt	17.5	5.0	77.5	75.0
Net Worth	338.0	465.7	677.8	887.8
Earnings Per Share	.74	1.02	1.62	1.47

Source: *Value Line.*

The Gap, Inc., is experimenting with larger-format stores that sell a complete line of merchandise including jeans, sweatsuits, shirts, sweaters, slacks, skirts, and accessories. The Gap has reduced its promotion budget because of its good location in malls and its high name recognition among young adults. During 1993 The Gap began switching 48 of its lowest performing Gap stores into discount centers called Gap Warehouse, which sell the same kinds of merchandise as do Gap stores but of lesser quality and at lower prices.

Petrie Stores Corporation. Petrie Stores sells women's clothing for teens, juniors, young misses, and larger-sized women. Some of the store names for the 1,720 Petrie chain include Petrie's, David's, Marianne, G & G, Rave, Winkelman's, Jean Nicole, Stuarts, and Plus. In 1992 the company added 36 Plus stores and 64 Combo units. The Combo units sell both large-size and junior clothing and allow the company to save in overhead costs by combining the two store types. Plans for 1993 call for 30 more Plus stores and 80 more Combo stores. Petrie Stores also owns approximately 14 percent of Toys R Us and 18 percent of Deb Shops. The majority of Petrie's apparel stores are located in shopping centers. Selected financial information for Petrie Stores is shown in Exhibit 3–4.

DEMOGRAPHIC AND SOCIETAL TRENDS

Some analysts suggest that as the baby boomers reach their late thirties, retailers and manufacturers of women's apparel have not provided for this group's needs. This large market group for women's apparel has found only youthful fashions and fads available for purchase. As a result, large numbers of customers have begun staying away from the stores entirely or purchasing fewer clothing items. Also, older shoppers (the fastest-growing demographic group) are complaining that retailers cater to younger tastes.

Many baby-boomer women, who make up about half of all U.S. working women, have little time for shopping. When they do have free time, they do not equate shopping with pleasure and prefer to relax at home. However, men are becoming much more fashion-conscious. They do more of their own shopping and make more clothing purchases on impulse than in the past.

EXHIBIT 3-4 Financial Information for Petrie Stores Corporation (in millions of dollars except per share amount)

	1989	1990	1991	1992
Gross Revenue	1257.5	1281.9	1354.5	1438.2
Net Income	32.3	13.6	16.0	14.8
Long-Term Debt	125.0	125.0	125.0	125.0
Net Worth	644.2	638.0	644.3	650.1
Earnings Per Share	.69	.29	.34	.32

Source: *Value Line.*

Currently, there is a mini baby boom, many of the new parents are older and have more disposable income than did new parents in the past. Also, the grandparents of these children are more likely to be affluent. Even though these trends would ordinarily indicate a good future for apparel retailing, there is a strong simultaneous trend away from the conspicuous consumption days of the 1980s. Retailers in the apparel industry are thus likely to struggle.

ECONOMIC CONDITIONS

The individual shopper's economic situation is not improving. The gap between rich and poor is increasing. It is estimated that by the year 2000, the number of house holds with annual incomes of $15,000 or less (in 1984 dollars) will increase to about 36 percent of U.S. families, or about 40 million families. The number of "downscale" shoppers is increasing. Many adults owe significant debt for cars and homes and are unable to spend much money for apparel, so they often purchase clothing at outlet malls or discount stores. Many of the women in the baby-boom group spend their disposable income on items for their children and not clothing for themselves. Occasionally, however, the downscale shopper may want to indulge himself or herself by purchasing fashion items from specialty stores.

Apparel retailers also have economic concerns. The top 30 retailers owe more than $60 billion to creditors. Several major retail chains have filed for reorganization under Chapter 11 bankruptcy. It is difficult for retail chains to predict consumer spending patterns. In 1987 spending was slow, but it improved in late 1988. However, by January 1989 spending slowed again, and 1991 was likewise a sluggish year for apparel overall. There was some consumer optimism after the presidential election in 1992, and the 1992 holiday season was a pleasant surprise for retailers. However, industry observers believe that consumers will remain cautious until they see how changes in the federal tax code and health-care reform will affect them.

If the economy continues to be weak, specialty retailers will have to take more gambles. Specialty retailers have gained a competitive advantage in the past by guessing a fashion trend early and purchasing inventory to provide that trend to customers. If a specialty retailer purchases inventory for a fashion trend but cannot turn over the inventory, the store loses profit and cannot afford to take more risks. However, if they do not gamble by trying to keep up with fashion trends, it is impossible to make a profit when the economy turns around because the merchandise will be out-of-date.

INTERNAL FACTORS FOR THE LIMITED, INC.

Marketing. Wexner believes that his company is "reinventing the specialty store business." Since the 12 Limited retail store divisions offer different price ranges and styles of clothing and related goods, Wexner has created the impact of a department store in many malls. In addition, the chain has begun an ambitious expansion. Limited executives believe that expanded-format stores are the success factor for the future. Larger stores can carry wider merchandise selections and offer better merchandise presentation. Wexner believes that "customers now want one-stop shopping and greater individuality, so they feel more secure when they see a broader assortment in one place." Many of these remodeled stores are located near each other in the malls to create the feeling of a department store for the customer. The increased size of these stores is shown in Exhibit 3–5.

EXHIBIT 3-5 Size Increases for Larger-Format Limited Stores

	Goal-1994	1993	1992	Change From	
				1994-1993	1993-1992
Express					
Stores	751	673	640	78	33
Selling Sq. Ft.	4,746,000	3,902,000	3,470,000	844,000	432,000
Lerner New York					
Stores	848	877	915	(29)	(38)
Selling Sq. Ft.	6,542,000	6,802,000	6,963,000	(260,000)	(161,000)
The Limited					
Stores	716	746	759	(30)	(13)
Selling Sq. Ft.	4,402,000	4,482,000	4,257,000	(80,000)	225,000
Victoria's Secret Stores					
Stores	610	570	545	40	25
Selling Sq. Ft.	2,676,000	2,346,000	2,029,000	330,000	317,000
Lane Bryant					
Stores	827	817	809	10	8
Selling Sq. Ft.	3,954,000	3,852,000	3,755,000	102,000	97,000
Structure					
Stores	499	394	330	105	64
Selling Sq. Ft.	1,942,000	1,409,000	1,076,000	533,000	333,000
The Limited Too					
Stores	234	184	185	50	(1)
Selling Sq. Ft.	747,000	566,000	567,000	181,000	(1,000)
Bath & Body Works					
Stores	319	194	121	125	73
Selling Sq. Ft.	496,000	248,000	132,000	248,000	116,000
Abercrombie & Fitch Co.					
Stores	72	49	40	23	9
Selling Sq. Ft.	581,000	405,000	332,000	176,000	73,000
Henri Bendel					
Stores	4	4	4	0	0
Selling Sq. Ft.	93,000	93,000	93,000	0	0
Cacique					
Stores	115	108	71	7	37
Selling Sq. Ft.	344,000	318,000	186,000	26,000	132,000
Penhaligon's					
Stores	7	7	6	0	1
Selling Sq. Ft.	3,000	3,000	3,000	0	0
Total Retail Divisions					
Stores	5,002	4,623	4,425	379	198
Selling Sq. Ft.	26,526,000	24,426,000	22,863,000	2,100,000	1,563,000

Source: The Limited *Annual Report*, 1993.

The Limited is experimenting with a new concept it calls "superstores." In 1991 the company opened its first mall anchor store at the Dadeland Mall in Miami, Florida. The 80,000-square-foot superstore contains six specialty stores—Limited, Limited Too, Express, Bath & Body Works, Structure, and Cacique. The entrance to The Limited also serves as a mall entrance. During the first year of the superstore operation, mall traffic at Dadeland increased and sales per square foot increased more than 20 percent for the total mall. In 1992 a 63,000-square-foot superstore opened at the mall at St. Matthews in Louisville, Kentucky.

In the past, The Limited has spent very little on advertising campaigns, relying instead on walk-in traffic in malls to sell their products. Wexner says that the company actually spends a significant amount of money on advertising because they send out hundreds of millions of catalogues per year and have nearly 4,500 storefronts where three million potential customer pass each day. Occasionally in the past the company included small advertisements in "mall shopper" magazines. In November 1989 national advertising for The Limited appeared in *Vogue, Vanity Fair,* and other women's magazines. The $10 million campaign was an attempt to increase brand recognition for the company's private labels.

The Limited's distribution center is located in Columbus, Ohio. Over 60 percent of the U.S. population is located within a 500-mile radius of Columbus, so Wexner feels this is an ideal location for a distribution center. Another advantage of the Columbus location is its nearness to New York City, the port where incoming merchandise produced in foreign countries is received by Mast Industries. All merchandise arriving in New York is shipped directly to the distribution center for allocation among The Limited's stores. A computerized distribution system aids distributors in their selections for each store's inventory. This system allows The Limited to monitor inventory levels, the merchandise mix, and the sales pattern at each store so that appropriate adjustments can be made as needed.

Production. The Limited, Inc. does not produce its own clothing, but it does have a division that contracts for the manufacture of clothing. Mast Industries specializes in contracting for production of high-quality, low-cost products. Much of the merchandise imported by Mast is marked with one of The Limited's own labels: The Limited, Compagnie Internationale, Cacique Lingerie, Structure, Victoria's Secret, and Limited Too. Leslie Wexner believes that having private label brands allows The Limited to keep merchandise inventory current and unique. Approximately 85 percent of The Limited's clothing is produced through Mast Industries.

The Limited can also maintain control over its clothing supply through Mast Industries. Mast is able to make copies of new trends in apparel and have these products on store shelves before the original design is produced for sale. Company managers try to maintain a 1,000-hour turnaround time between recognizing new style and delivering the merchandise to stores. Mast can send high-resolution, computer images of clothing designs by satellite to Far Eastern manufacturers. In addition, computer information that is collected from all individual stores is used to determine what needs to be produced in the Far East the next day. The newly produced items arrive in a few days at the Columbus distribution center and are sent to the stores.

In 1992 Mast purchased merchandise from approximately 4,800 different suppliers/factories, but no more than 4 percent of The Limited's inventory was purchased from any single manufacturer. About half of The Limited's inventory is produced outside the United States.

Finance. The Limited's income statements and balance sheets are provided in Exhibit 3–6 and Exhibit 3–7, respectively. These statements reveal increasing levels for sales, income, assets, and shareholder's equity. A consolidated statement of The Limited's shareholders' equity is given in Exhibit 3–8.

OUTLOOK

According to Leslie Wexner, "the key is our ability to change." However, while the company moves quickly to deal with immediate realities, long-range vision is never forgotten. Growth continues to be a primary objective for the future. By the mid-1990s the company plans for sales volume to be above $10 billion, with after-tax profit of about 10 percent. By the middle of the decade, Wexner expects the company's new divisions (those begun in the period 1988–1991) to account for $2 billion in sales and have more selling space than the company had in 1991. According to Kenneth Gilman, the chief financial officer:

> Some of our larger, older businesses are growing through repositioning, and others by remodeling their stores into larger-size formats. Both approaches will help the businesses achieve higher sales per square foot and sales per store. And of course the newer businesses are increasing their numbers of stores and their sales per square foot. The bottom line is that each of our businesses has a different growth profile, and each has the potential for significant and continued growth.

EXHIBIT 3-6 Income Statements for The Limited, Inc.
(in thousands of dollars per share amounts)

	1993	1992	1991
Net Sales	$7,245,088	$6,944,296	$6,149,218
Cost of Goods Sold, Occupancy and Buying Costs	(5,286,253)	(4,953,556)	(4,355,675)
Gross Income	1,958,835	1,990,740	1,793,543
General, Administrative and Store Operating Expenses	(1,259,896)	(1,202,042)	(1,080,843)
Special and Nonrecurring Items, Net	2,617	–	–
Operating Income	701,556	788,698	712,700
Interest Expense	(63,865)	(62,398)	(63,927)
Other Income, net	7,308	10,080	11,529
Gain on Issuance of United Retail Group Stock	–	9,117	–
Income Before Income Taxes	644,999	745,497	660,302
Provision for Income Taxes	254,000	290,000	257,000
Net Income	$390,999	$455,497	$403,302
Net Income Per Share	$1.08	$1.25	$1.11

Source: The Limited *Annual Report,* 1993.

Growth plans for 1993 include the following:

1. The company expects sales of $8 billion and after-tax profits of 8 percent.
2. Selling space will increase 2.5 million square feet (11 percent increase over 1992).
3. Limited Too will continue its double-digit growth from the existing base of stores.
4. 350 new stores will be opened and 290 others will be renovated.
5. Substantial gains will be made in financial performance at both Lerner New York and The Limited flagship store.

EXHIBIT 3-7 Balance Sheet for The Limited, Inc. (in thousands of dollars)

	JAN. 29, 1994	JAN. 30, 1993		
Assets				
Current Assets				
Cash and Equivalents	$ 320,558	$ 41,235		
Accounts Receivable	1,056,911	837,377		
Inventories	733,700	803,707		
Other	109,456	101,811		
Total Current Assets	2,220,625	1,784,130		
Property and Equipment, net	1,666,588	1,813,948		
Other Assets	247,892	248,372		
Total Assets	$4,135,105	$3,846,450		
Liabilities and Shareholders' Equity				
Current Liabilities				
Accounts Payable	$ 250,363	$ 309,092		
Accrued Expenses	347,892	274,220		
Certificates of Deposit	15,700	–		
Income Taxes	93,489	137,466		
Total Current Liabilities	707,444	720,778		
Long-Term Debt	650,000	541,639		
Deferred Income Taxes	275,101	274,844		
Other Long-Term Liabilities	61,267	41,572		
Shareholders' Equity				
Common Stock	189,727	189,727		
Paid-in Capital	128,906	127,776		
Retained Earnings	2,397,112	2,136,794		
	2,715,745	2,454,297		
Less: Treasury Stock, at cost	(274,452)	(186,680)		
Total Shareholders' Equity	2,441,293	2,267,617		
Total Liabilities and Shareholders' Equity	$4,135,105	$3,846,450		
Total Shareholders' Equity	1240.5	1560.1	1876.8	2267.6
Total Liabilities and Shareholder's Equity	2418.5	2872.0	3418.9	3846.4

Source: The Limited *Annual Report*, 1993.

6. The Limited will continue to build on the successes of the newer stores such as Express, Victoria's Secret, Structure, Cacique, and Panhaligon's. In addition to growth, other strategies include rebuilding and remodeling older stores, improving the merchandise mix and quality, and continuing to take advantage of company name recognition and the supplier advantages provided by Mast Industries. Wexner hopes these plans will allow The Limited to continue improving its position in the specialty retailing industry.

However, the potential for serious problems exists for Wexner. Some of these include: (1) the possibility of failure of the new, larger format stores or superstores, (2) another downturn in the women's apparel industry, (3) financial instability, especially due to expansion and remodeling debt, (4) investor disenchantment because of Wexner's risk-taking attitude, (5) a saturation of Limited stores in the U.S. malls and (6) difficulty in finding reliable foreign suppliers.

Wexner is philosophical about the ability of The Limited to compete in the women's apparel industry of the future:

> The key challenge facing us in the 90s is the same one that faces us every day: to keep taking the risk of change. Sometimes when you're trying to improve, you break something that is already fixed. Bus unless you change, and take the risk of failure, you limit your opportunities for success. That's why questioning, probing and reinventing are so important. This is how we redefined the specialty store business several times . . . and how we will continue to reinvent ourselves in the future.

EXHIBIT 3-8 Consolidated Statement of Shareholder's Equity (in thousands of dollars)

	COMMON STOCK	
	SHARES OUTSTANDING	PAR VALUE
Balance, February 2, 1991	360,598	$189,727
Net Income	–	–
Cash Dividends	–	–
Exercise of Stock Options & Other	1,188	–
Balance, February 1, 1992	361,786	189,727
Net Income	–	–
Cash Dividends	–	–
Exercise of Stock Options & Other	862	–
Warrants Issued for Acquisition	–	–
Balance, January 30 , 1993	362,648	189,727
Net Income	–	–
Cash Dividends	–	–
Purchase of Treasury Stock	(5,288)	–
Exercise of Stock Options & Other	441	–
Balance, January 29, 1994	357,801	$189,727

Source: The Limited *Annual Report*, 1993.

The following list presents some of the concerns that Wexner—and—you, might consider:

1. Is The Limited expanding too rapidly and becoming too diversified?
2. How could The Limited improve its market segmentation strategies?
3. Is the expanded format store a good idea for The Limited? What about the super-store concept?
4. Should The Limited spend more money on print and television advertising?
5. What is the likelihood of another downturn in the women's apparel industry?
6. Should The Limited attempt a takeover of a department store such as Petrie Stores or continue to grow internally?
7. How serious are the potential problems The Limited could face in the future?

C A S E
4
STEVE BARNDT
Pacific Lutheran University

NORDSTROM, INC.—1994

Headquartered in Seattle, Washington, Nordstrom (206-628-2111) is a fashion specialty retail chain that operates 52 apparel and shoe department stores, 16 clearance clothing stores, and four youth-oriented clothing stores in Alaska, Arizona, California, Illinois, Maryland, Minnesota, New Jersey, Oregon, Utah, Virginia, and Washington. Nordstrom has attained a position of leadership and an outstanding reputation for service. Salesperson attention to the customer, selection of goods, product return policy, and amenities to make shopping an enjoyable experience are acknowledged to be extraordinary in the industry.

After many years as a regional retail chain servicing the Northwest states, expansion into California was steady through the 1980s. In 1988 the company became a national retailer with the opening of a store in Virginia. Company sales in fiscal year 1993 were $3.42 billion, whereas net earnings were $1.36 million.

HISTORY

John W. Nordstrom immigrated to the United States from Sweden in 1887 at the age of 16 and worked for a number of years as a logger, miner, and laborer. After earning $13,000 by gold mining in the Klondike, he settled in Seattle where he opened a shoe store in partnership with shoemaker Carl Wallin in 1901. In 1923 Wallin and Nordstrom opened a second store in Seattle. John Nordstrom's three sons bought his interest in the store in 1928 and Carl Wallin's in 1929, establishing the family owner ship and management that has continued to the present.

In the early years under John Nordstrom, two basic philosophies were developed that have since guided business practice. The first is a customer orientation according to which the company emphasizes outstanding service, selection, quality, and value. The second is a policy of selection of managers from among employees who have experience on the sales floor. All of the Nordstrom family members who attained management positions started their careers as salesmen.

Rapid growth did not begin until after World War II. Starting with an expansion in 1950, with the opening of two new stores, growth continued so that by 1961 there were eight shoe stores and thirteen leased shoe departments in Washington, Oregon, and California. In 1963 Nordstrom diversified into women's fashion apparel with the acquisition of Best's Apparel and its stores in Seattle and Portland. Before the 1960s ended, five new Nordstrom Best stores offered clothes, shoes, and accessories had been opened.

The 1970s saw additional changes and rapid, steady growth. Management was passed to the third generation of Nordstroms in 1970, and the company went public in 1971, accompanied by a change in name to Nordstrom, Inc. Continued growth in the Northwest provided the company with 24 stores by 1978. Geographical expansion to California began in 1978 and has continued. By 1987 Nordstrom's Southern California presence was reflected in its position of first or second in market share for women's suits, women's blazers, men's tailored pants, women's dresses, women's coats, women's shoes, and men's shoes in the Los Angeles market. In early 1993, Nordstrom operated 31 stores in California including six Nordstrom Rack discount stores. The Rack line of stores was started in 1983 and by 1992 has grown to 15 in the Western states. Exhibit 4–1 shows the growth in Nordstrom, Nordstrom Rack, Place Two (youth fashion), and Last Chance (clearance) stores during the recent years ended January 31, 1993.

STRATEGIES

The Nordstrom strategy emphasizes merchandise and service tailored to appeal to the affluent and fashion-conscious shopper without losing its middle-class customers. The large Nordstrom specialty department stores cater to their target market with an unparalleled attention to the customers, guaranteed service, and a wide and deep line of merchandise. The success of this strategy has made the company one that competitors fear and attempt to follow. As has been noted, "Nordstrom is sometimes known as the 'Black Hole,' into which shoppers disappear, never to enter nearby stores."

In addition to its mainline stores, Nordstrom also operates four smaller Place Two specialty stores specializing in youth fashions, one Last Chance cut-price clearance store, and 15 Nordstrom Rack stores. The Racks serve as discount outlets offering clearance merchandise from the main stores plus some merchandise purchased directly from manufacturers. They cater to bargain shoppers who value Nordstrom quality.

EXHIBIT 4-1 Nordstrom Growth 1977–1993

YEAR ENDED JANUARY 31	COMPANY OPERATED STORES	TOTAL SQUARE FOOTAGE
1985	44	3,924,000
1986	52	4,727,000
1987	53	5,098,000
1988	56	5,527,000
1989	58	6,374,000
1990	59	6,898,000
1991	63	7,655,000
1992	68	8,590,000
1993	72	9,224,000

Source: Nordstrom *Annual Report,* 1985, 1986, 1987, 1989, and 1992.

Store architecture and merchandise differ from store to store. Each is designed to fit life-styles prevailing in the local geographic and economic environment. For example, the downtown San Francisco and Seattle stores provide their mainstay clientele, the upscale professionals, with extensive men's clothing and accessories selections. In every location merchandise selection, local tastes, and customer preferences help shape the store's interior. Approximately 70 percent of the merchandise featured is available at all Nordstrom stores, while the other 30 percent is unique to each store or region.

Product Lines. Nordstrom's specialty department stores carry focused lines of classically styled, relatively conservative merchandise. The merchandise has been described as "primarily classic and not trendy, the selection limited to styles with broad appeal." Women's fashions account for the largest share of the Nordstrom product line. However, menswear appears to be gaining in emphasis in some locations. For example, menswear comprised 18 percent of the inventory and 21 to 22 percent of total sales in the downtown San Francisco store. This is contrasted with a 16 percent share of sales from menswear company-wide. Exhibit 4–2 shows the company-wide sales breakdown by merchandise category.

Nordstrom carries both designer and private-label merchandise. In the past, private labels have been carried on 15 percent of the merchandise. Men's apparel and men's and women's shoes were the largest private-label lines where approximately 50 percent of men's clothes and 25 percent of shoes carried the Nordstrom name. Designer lines have made up the bulk of the merchandise. In its various stores Nordstrom has featured apparel lines by Claude Montana, Gianfranco Ferre, Christian Lacroix, Carolina Herrera, Carolyne Roehm, Calvin Klein, Anne Klein, Donna Karan, and Gianni Versace, among others. The Facconnable line of menswear is sold throughout the chain. Selection of lines and styles is largely based on wants indicated in direct customer feedback.

The company keeps alert to changes in both taste for and profitability of its product offerings. It has a history of change. If a new line of merchandise appears to better serve customers than an existing one, Nordstrom does not hesitate to make the switch. For example, recently the company closed out its fur salons and converted the space into departments carrying more profitable merchandise such as large-size women's apparel. The volume of its orders has allowed Nordstrom to develop a broad supplier base. No one supplier has significant bargaining power.

EXHIBIT 4-2 Merchandise Sales by Category

MERCHANDISE CATEGORY	SHARE OF 1992 SALES
Women's Apparel	39 percent
Women's Accessories	20 percent
Shoes	19 percent
Men's Apparel and Furnishings	16 percent
Children's Apparel and Accessories	4 percent
Other	2 percent

Source: Nordstrom *Annual Report,* 1992.

Merchandising. Nordstrom's merchandising is noted for its extensive inventories and dedicated, helpful sales force. However, Nordstrom also differs from rivals in several other ways. The typical store has 50 percent more salespeople on the floor than similar-sized competitors. The salesforce uses its product knowledge to show appropriate merchandise to customers, assist them in their selections, and suggest accessories. Salespeople keep track of their regular customers' fashion tastes and sizes and then call them or send notes about new merchandise in which they may have an interest. The company carries a very large inventory, providing an unusually wide selection of colors and sizes. With an inventory almost twice as large per square foot as its department store competitors, Nordstrom has a depth of inventory almost comparable to smaller specialty stores while offering a more complete line. As an indication of the inventory intensity, the San Francisco Center (downtown) store had $100 million invested in opening day inventory, including 100,000 pairs of shoes, 10,000 men's suits, and 20,000 neckties.

Nordstrom is one of the industry leaders in dividing its stores into small boutiques featuring targeted merchandise mixes. Rather than featuring a single type of merchandise, departments offer a variety of items (e.g., coats, suits, dresses, etc.) all of which are keyed to a particular lifestyle. Departments are added or changed to serve evolving customer needs. For instance, in response to growth in the number of women in higher-level management positions, women's tailored clothing departments were added. Though designer fashions are generally not given special treatment in display, the company has introduced special departments to display some of its higher-priced designer apparel.

Luxurious settings of polished wood and marble are used in place of the chrome and bright colors common in competing stores. Merchandise is arranged in departments according to life-styles. Stores feature clusters of antiques and open displays of merchandise usually arranged at right angles to each other. Mannequins are used sparingly; a piece of antique furniture is a more common display prop. Merchandise is displayed without bulky antitheft tags. In addition, there is no closed-circuit television, presenting a less intimidating atmosphere to customers. Instead, Nordstrom relies on the presence of its large sales force to discourage theft.

Nordstrom spends less than 2 percent of sales on advertising, half as much as is commonly spent. The company relies heavily on word-of-mouth to attract customers. The advertising that is used emphasizes styles and breadth of merchandise selection rather than price.

Pricing. Prices are competitive with comparable merchandise, and Nordstrom follows the same mark-up practices common to retail fashion stores. But because of the company's selectivity in providing high-quality merchandise, prices tend to be high. However, the company is committed to providing value and will not be undersold on its merchandise. If a customer finds an item carried by Nordstrom for sale at a lower price at another store, Nordstrom will match that lower price.

Consumer caution in spending during the recession that started at the end of the 1980s placed downward pressure on prices in the industry. Nordstrom responded with a shift to a greater share of value-priced merchandise. A major means of providing lower-priced, quality merchandise has been the substitution of Nordstrom-label goods for branded goods.

Customer Service. Under recent conditions of lower inflation and higher incomes, the public has raised its expectations of service. Many Americans have become tired of self-service or inattentive sales help. Two-income households and busy professionals have become hooked on convenience and are willing to pay for it. At the same time, retailers who shifted to lower levels of customer service are having difficulty in upgrading service. Understaffing in sales positions and overwork coupled with low pay and lack of a career path do not provide the conditions necessary to motivate employees to improve service.

Nordstrom has never cut service and therefore does not have to overcome structural, motivational, or cultural barriers to provide satisfying service. The company is already there—it is the undisputed leader in customer service. Nordstrom's excellent service is centered in the sales force and supported by company policy and investment in facilities and personnel. At Nordstrom a customer can expect to be in a department no longer than two minutes before a salesperson is in attendance to answer questions, explain merchandise, and make suggestions. This salesperson might lead the customer to merchandise in other departments to help the shopper find what he or she wants.

Sales clerks routinely attend customers in dressing rooms, bringing them alternate items of apparel or sizes to try on. They also routinely send thank-you notes and announcements of sales and arrival of merchandise that should be of interest to the customer. Other examples of such extraordinary out-of-the-way service by Nordstrom sales personnel include warming up customer's cars on cold days, paying parking tickets for customers who couldn't find legal parking, personal delivery of items to the customer's home, and ironing a newly bought item of apparel so the customer could wear it back to work.

Extraordinary service stems from several mutually supportive factors. First, the number of salespeople on the floor is high—50 percent higher than is common. This means the sales clerks are less rushed when waiting on customers. Second, the sales force is carefully recruited. Third, pay is higher than in comparable positions elsewhere and, in addition, is partly based on performance (volume of sales). This means that the sales clerk who satisfies customers earns more. In addition, there is a kind of peer pressure to sell more (satisfy more customers) because those who earn more are seen as role models. Last, Nordstrom has a powerful corporate culture that stresses attentiveness to the customer. This culture is well established, having been instituted under John W. Nordstrom and reinforced ever since. The company has been successful at transferring this culture to its new stores at their start-up. A key practice in establishing the Nordstrom culture in new stores is to open them under the leadership of a cadre of experienced Nordstrom managers and salespeople who provide guidance and training to the locally hired personnel. For example, when Nordstrom opens its new store in Indianapolis, about 10 percent of its employees will be moved from other Nordstrom stores.

In keeping with the feeling that the customer is king and always right, Nordstrom has a no-questions-asked merchandise return policy. The company willingly replaces or refunds the price of any item of merchandise whether new or used, with or without a sales receipt. Probably the best known of many refund tales is that of an individual who bought a pair of tires from the same store when it was under other ownership and returned them to Nordstrom for a refund. The purchase price of the pair of tires was refunded even though Nordstrom does not and never has sold tires.

Luxurious settings and furnishings make the shopper feel special. Standard extras in many of the stores include a pianist playing enjoyable music on a baby grand piano, free coat and package checking, play areas for children, extra-large dressing rooms, free gift wrap at the cash register, and tea for weary customers as they try on apparel in the dressing rooms. Newer, larger stores feature even more extras. For example, to help differentiate itself from competition the San Francisco Center store has a beauty treatment spa, four restaurants, a pub in the men's department, and valet parking.

Location. Nordstrom targets growing affluent communities for its stores. Although the majority of its stores are located in suburban shopping centers, others are located in the central business districts of large and small cities. In either type of location, Nordstrom chooses to locate close to other retailers because of the drawing power of a concentration of shopping facilities. Exhibit 4–3 shows the locations and size of Nordstrom and Nordstrom Rack stores in 1993.

As a late entrant in many regions—for example, the East, the Midwest, and Southern and Northern California—Nordstrom has had an advantage in its selection of store sites in growing high-income areas. Early entrant chains often find themselves doing business in outdated stores in older, less economically attractive areas. However, the industry is mature, with most attractive shopping districts saturated with retailers. Finding locations attractive for growth with adequate available square footage requires buying out competitors or engaging in a geographically extended search. Following its coverage of virtually all major Pacific Northwest markets in the 1970s and very early 1980s, Nordstrom channeled its growth to California. By the late 1980s Nordstrom had covered most of the attractive California markets, limiting its further growth there. This forced the company to search for expansion opportunities in several other, slower-growing geographical regions. Nordstrom currently plans to open stores in a number of selected locations spread across the East, Northeast, Southcentral, and Midwest regions, and is considering opening stores in the Southeast and Intermountain West. Such growth is opportunistic, involving new shopping-mall space in growth areas or occupancy of vacated space in older shopping centers. An example of the latter is Nordstrom's entry into the Paramus, New Jersey, market in a store vacated when May Department Stores closed its Hahne's chain. Seven distribution centers are located in regions to serve stores. These include recently opened distribution centers in Maryland and Iowa that serve the growing number of stores in surrounding states.

MANAGEMENT AND ORGANIZATION

Strategic and significant financial decisions are made at the top level in the organization, and operational decisions at the region and store level. Managers in each region, store, and department have responsibility and accountability for profit and autonomy and authority to make decisions regarding their area. This decentralized management allows managers to be entrepreneurially creative in tailoring each store's merchandise and layout to its customers. Free of decision making for regional and store operations, top management has been able to concentrate on future expansion.

The company structure can be described in terms of three levels of management responsibility—top or executive level, midlevel, and store level. The top level consists of four cochairmen of the board: brothers James F. Nordstrom, 53, and John N. Nordstrom, 55, and cousin Bruce A. Nordstrom, 59, often referred to as the "family"; plus John A. McMillan, 61, who is married to a Nordstrom. The cochairmen retain strategic management responsibility, concentrating on setting the strategic direction and making expansion location decisions. The "family" is deeply involved in providing the overall guidance to the company and exercises effective control with about 40 percent ownership. When a new store opens, one or more of the Nordstroms will be there on the selling floor. During a downturn in 1987, family

EXHIBIT 4-3 Retail Store Facilities

The following table sets forth certain information with respect to each of the stores operated by the Company. The Company also operates leased shoe departments in 11 department stores in Hawaii. In addition, the Company operates seven distribution centers and leases other space for administrative functions.

Location	Year Opened or Acquired	Present Total Store Area/Sq. Ft.	Location	Year Opened or Acquired	Present Total Store Area/Sq. Ft.
Washington Group			Northern California Group		
Downtown Seattle[a]	1963	245,000	Hillsdale Shopping Center	1982	149,000
Northgate Mall	1965	122,000	Broadway Plaza	1984	193,000
Tacoma Mall	1966	132,000	Stanford Shopping Center	1984	187,000
Bellevue Square	1967	184,000	The Village of Corte Madera	1985	115,000
Southcenter Mall	1968	170,000	Oakridge Mall	1985	150,000
Yakima	1972	44,000	Valley Fair	1987	165,000
Spokane	1974	121,000	280 Metro Center Rack	1987	31,000
Alderwood Mall	1979	125,000	Stonestown Galleria	1988	174,000
Pavilion Rack	1985	39,000	Downtown San Francisco	1988	350,000
Alderwood Rack	1985	25,000	Arden Fair	1989	190,000
Downtown Seattle Rack	1987	42,000	Stoneridge Mall	1990	173,000
			Marina Square Rack	1990	44,000
Oregon Group					
Lloyd Center	1963	150,000	Alaska Group		
Downtown Portland	1966	174,000	Anchorage	1975	97,000
Washington Square	1974	108,000			
Vancouver Mall	1977	71,000	Utah Group		
Salem Centre	1980	71,000	Crossroads Plaza	1980	140,000
Clackamas Town Center	1981	121,000	Fashion Place Mall	1981	110,000
Clackamas Rack	1983	28,000	Ogden City Mall	1982	76,000
Downtown Portland Rack	1986	19,000	Sugarhouse Center Rack	1991	31,000
Southern California Group			Capital Group		
South Coast Plaza	1978	235,000	Tysons Corner Center	1988	238,000
Brea Mall	1979	195,000	The Fashion Centre at		
Los Cerritos Center	1981	122,000	Pentagon City	1989	241,000
Fashion Valley Mall	1981	156,000	Potomac Mills Rack	1990	46,000
Glendale Galleria	1983	147,000	Montgomery Mall	1991	225,000
Santa Ana Rack	1983	21,000	City Place Rack	1992	37,000
Topanga Plaza	1984	154,000	Towson Town Center	1992	205,000
University Towne Centre	1984	130,000	Towson Rack	1992	31,000
Woodland Hills Rack	1984	48,000			
The Galleria at South Bay	1985	161,000	Northeast Group		
Westside Pavilion	1985	150,000	Garden State Plaza	1990	272,000
Horton Plaza	1985	151,000	Menlo Park Mall	1991	266,000
Mission Valley Rack	1985	27,000	Freehold Raceway Mall	1992	174,000
Montclair Plaza	1986	133,000			
North County Fair	1986	156,000	Midwest Group		
MainPlace Mall	1987	169,000	Oakbrook Center	1991	249,000
Chino Town Square Rack	1987	30,000	Mall of America	1992	240,000
Paseo Nuevo	1990	186,000	Place Two and Clearance		
The Galleria at Tyler	1991	164,000	Stores[b]		
			Washington and Arizona		99,000

[a]Excludes approximately 23,000 square feet of corporate and administrative offices.

[b]Includes four Place Two stores and one clearance store.

Source: Nordstrom *Annual Report*, 1993.

members returned to the floor for stints of selling and visible leadership to help motivate meeting goals. They are visible leaders and approachable by employees and customers, but they remain reticent about themselves and the company.

While the cochairmen share strategic management, operational management is delegated to an "office of the president." In 1991 the cochairmen appointed four copresidents to manage the day-to-day operations. These four share the office by focusing on different aspects of the business. Raymond Johnson, 51, handles accessories, lingerie, children's clothes, personnel, and legal matters; Darrel Hume, 45, is in charge of store planning, finance, and men's apparel; Galen Jefferson, 43, handles women's wear and merchandise systems; and John Whitacre, 40, concentrates on shoes, restaurants, and budgeting. Each has authority to make decisions that clearly fall in their respective areas. They meet formally once a week and informally communicate with one another throughout the week as necessary. Disagreements that arise among the copresidents are usually resolved by choosing the view or course of action that best serves the customer.

The midmanagement level is comprised of the corporate treasurer; geographical group general managers for the Northern California, Southern California, Oregon, Washington and Alaska, Utah, Northeast, Midwest, and capital groups of stores; region managers responsible for smaller groups of stores in several of the geographical store groups; and various managers in charge of merchandise categories and staff support areas such as public relations, legal affairs, and sales promotion.

Operational management of the stores is the responsibility of store managers with the assistance of their staff and department managers. Stores and departments have their own buyers. Exhibit 4–4 shows the general chain of command at Nordstrom.

Throughout the company, idea generation and operational decision making are encouraged, expected, and supported at the lowest levels where the individual has the appropriate information. Managers in the sales departments routinely make decisions on what inventory to carry and whether to accept checks, set lower prices to stay competitive, and accept returned merchandise without consulting higher-level managers or staff specialists.

Units and the individuals in them are goal-driven. As one writer has put it, "the life of a Nordstrom salesperson is defined by goals. Departmental, storewide, and company goals. Qualitative and quantitative goals." Store goals are set for the year and both reflect and influence department goals. Department goals influence salesperson goals. Yearly goals are translated into monthly goals. Daily goals are more changeable and reflect pro rata accomplishment of monthly goals as well as historical performance. On a daily basis, departments aim to surpass sales of the same day last year by a set level and individual goals are adjusted accordingly. If the department is behind in reaching its monthly goal, daily goals of the department and each sales clerk are likely to be pegged higher to get back on track.

Salespeople and departments are kept aware of the level of their goal accomplishment and are provided rewards for goal achievement. Salespeople are reminded of the day's goal and may be asked during the day how they are doing. Reaching goals is praised and when longer-term goals, such as annual personal goals, are achieved, recognition is public, often in the form of an announcement or letter from a Nordstrom. Top-performing salespeople are admitted to the Pacesetters' Club. Pacesetters receive a certificate, a Pacesetter business card, a 33 percent discount on Nordstrom merchandise (rather than the standard 20 percent), and a night on the town.

The company also promotes performance and conformity to it standards of customer service through the widespread use of heroics. The exploits of employees who make

EXHIBIT 4-4 Nordstrom Management Structure

Darrel Hume
Raymond Johnson
Galen Jefferson
John Whitacre
Co-Presidents

Cynthia Paur, Ex. VP
Sales Promotion

Jack Irving, Ex. VP
Men's Wear Mer. Mang.

Gail Cottle, Ex. VP
Prod Development

John Goesling, Ex. VP
Treasurer

Martha Wikstrom, VP
Capital Gen. Mang.

Karen Purpur
Secretary

David Lindsey, VP
Store Planning

David Mackie, VP
Legal and RE

Charles Dudley, VP
Human Resources

Joseph Demarte, VP
Personnel

Robert Nunn, Ex. VP
Shoe Division Mer. Mang.

Jammie Baugh, Ex. VP
S. Calif. Gen Mang.

Blake Nordstrom, VP
WA & AS Gen. Mang.

Cody Kondo, VP
NE Gen. Mang.

James Nordstrom, VP
N. Calif. Gen. Mang.

Paul Hunter, VP
Rack Div. Gen. Mang.

Dale Crichton, VP
Cosmetics and Gift
Mer. Mang.

Barbara Kanaya, VP
Accessories Mer. Mang.

unusual or extraordinary efforts to please customers or who have specially noteworthy levels of sales are communicated through the organization, formally and informally, so that they may serve as role models. This technique, along with the use of goals, serves as a powerful indicator of the kinds of behavior the company wants and rewards.

HUMAN RESOURCES

Nordstrom has about 33,000 year-long employees plus seasonal hires. The company likes to hire young people who have not learned behaviors inconsistent with the Nordstrom customer-service values and then start them in sales positions. The actual decision of whom to hire is left to the sales department managers rather than to a staff personnel department. The company's hiring practice, in conjunction with its major expansion in recent years, has left the company with a work force that is relatively young and often college educated. Even its mid- and top-level managers are young. Top managers are in their early forties to midfifties. Midlevel vice presidents range in age from low thirties to midfifties, with most less than 45 years of age.

The company follows a promote-from-within policy. Because the company is growing fast, this serves as a motivator to those who aspire to rapid advancement. Promotions to line management positions are made from among employees with sales and customer contact experience. Those who are promoted to higher-level positions are encouraged and expected to keep in contact with customers. For example, the company's buyers, who all started in sales positions, spend a large amount of their time on the sales floor to learn what customers want.

Other expectations are transmitted in various ways and will bring on corrective actions if violated. One of these is dress. Employees are expected to wear neat business attire. Further, it is understood that the attire should be acquired from Nordstrom. Personal business, including telephone calls, is not to be conducted in a customer area. Abuse of employee discount privileges, violation of criminal law, rudeness to a customer, and unacceptable personal conduct are grounds for immediate dismissal. Underperforming employees usually leave on their own as do those who are uncomfortable with constant pressure to meet goals and accommodate the customer no matter what the customer does or how he or she behaves. Those who remain are loyal to the company and accepting of its cultural values.

High pay is important in attracting, retaining, and motivating employees. Pay ranges from about $6 to $9 per hour plus commissions of 6.5 to 10 percent. Combined hourly and commission pay for first-year salespeople averages $20,000 to $22,000 per year, and after three years, about $50,000 per year. Top salespeople can earn $80,000 to $100,000 per year. With these kind of earnings, Nordstrom's sales employees' compensation is high relative to the rest of the industry.

Commission pay ties rewards directly to sales and customer service performance. The higher the sales to satisfied customers, the greater the reward. Since returned merchandise is subtracted from the sales clerk's sales and therefore decreases commission income, selling for the sake of a sale alone is discouraged. Monetary rewards and public recognition are supplemented with motivational speeches and skits, along with pep-talk meetings. The objectives of these techniques are in general to build employees' confidence in their ability to perform to higher limits, and in particular to get them worked up to capitalize on the selling opportunities associated with one of the four major annual sales.

IMAGE AND PUBLIC RELATIONS

Nordstrom is well known as a premium service retailer. Its reputation for service and selection of merchandise provides the company with a mystique. As a result, Nordstrom receives a great deal of favorable free publicity. New store openings are preceded by numerous articles in the local press that help create the perception that Nordstrom offers a superior shopping experience. Continuing favorable reports in the media reinforce that perception. For example, the press recently reported the results of a nationwide survey that ranked Nordstrom first among the top 70 U.S. retail department and discount store chains in overall customer satisfaction.

Although much publicity has been favorable, a number of unfavorable charges and accusations have surfaced in recent years. These include allegations by labor unions of wrongdoing and charges by black interest groups of discrimination. In late 1989 the United Food & Commercial Workers Union charged that Nordstrom encouraged its salespeople to work off-the-clock taking inventory, writing thank-you notes, making home deliveries, or tracking down hard-to-find garments over the phone—in other words, to do work for the company for which they were not compensated. The Washington State Department of Labor and Industries subsequently found Nordstrom in violation of state wage laws and directed the company to reimburse workers for work performed without pay. The union followed up with a class action lawsuit on behalf of 50,000 past and present Nordstrom employees in Washington, Oregon, California, Utah, Alaska, and Virginia seeking compensatory damages and penalties. Without admitting guilt, the company has agreed to pay back wages and legal fees to qualifying present and former employees. Total cost to the company has been estimated at $15 to $30 million. Earlier the company established a $15 million contingency liability reserve for retroactive wage claims.

The union also engaged in an attempt to discredit Nordstrom's image with customers. The union alleged the company requires its employees to wear garments it is promoting during work hours, then allows them to replace the merchandise back on the rack, sometimes without a cleaning. Subsequently, Oregon sued Nordstrom for selling used lipstick, shoes, and other merchandise at its Oregon stores. Without admitting any wrongdoing, Nordstrom settled the suit with Oregon, paying the state $25,000. The company claims its employees are encouraged but not required to wear Nordstrom clothing. The Nordstrom clothing they wear must be purchased and employees can buy at a discount.

In an unrelated incident a sales clerk in a California Nordstrom store filed a lawsuit alleging that Nordstrom invaded her privacy through the use of a hidden video camera in a small room used by some employees as a restroom and a place in which to change clothes. Nordstrom contended that the room was not an employee lounge and the camera was there to monitor a safe containing high value merchandise.

In 1992 seven blacks filed a class action lawsuit claiming discrimination against blacks in recruitment, hiring, and promotion. Subsequently a group calling itself People Against Racism at Nordstrom (PARAN) targeted the company for a national boycott based on allegations of discrimination. Later, another six plaintiffs entered the lawsuit. However, by late 1992, 12 had withdrawn.

In spite of the charges described here, Nordstrom is generally considered to be a good community citizen. It has a record of supporting benefits for social-program fund raising in its communities. For example, in its hometown it recently provided the Seattle Housing Group with $4.7 million, more than half the cost of building a 100-unit low-income housing project.

Nordstrom started a free program called "Healthy Beginnings" to help expectant mothers avoid risks to themselves and their pregnancies. Under the program, they receive educational materials, pregnancy risk screenings, access to a toll-free hot line, and a Nordstrom gift certificate. Within the company, Nordstrom introduced a family leave program in 1991, allowing up to 12 weeks of unpaid leave to care for newborn or newly adopted children or seriously ill family members.

Nordstrom has been a leader in catering to people with disabilities. In 1992 the company was awarded an "Excellence in Access Award" for making its stores accessible to disabled customers and providing special services to them. Also in 1992 Nordstrom received an EDI (Equality/Dignity/Independence) award from the National Easter Seal Society for featuring models with disabilities in its catalogs.

Support for minorities includes a minority vendor program started in 1989 that, into 1992, had awarded $20 million in contracts to minority-owned businesses. The company committed $220,000 for advertising in West Coast African-American newspapers over ten months and contributed $10,000 to the United Negro College Fund. Within the company, 27 percent of the workforce is composed of members of minorities, as is 16 percent of its management. Further, Nordstrom claims it employs a greater percentage of African-Americans in every region where it does business than that minority's share of the population. Many special and minority interest groups support and praise Nordstrom for its efforts.

FINANCIAL POSITION

Over the ten-year period from February 1983 to January 1993, Nordstrom enjoyed continuous growth in sales. Net earnings grew each year except fiscal years 1989 and 1990. Exhibit 4–5 reveals the company's recent sales and earnings information. As shown in Exhibit 4–6, earnings per store in fiscal years 1989 to 1992 failed to continue an upward climb started in 1986.

Nordstrom is a leader in sales per square foot, a key measure of efficiency in the industry. In 1989 the department store industry averaged $173 in sales per square foot. Although Nordstrom is not directly comparable to general department stores in that it sells only apparel, shoes, and accessories that can be densely stocked, it can be compared to specialty stores. In 1988 and 1989 specialty stores averaged $248 and $243 in sales per square foot, respectively. As shown in Exhibit 4–7, Nordstrom stores averaged $398 in fiscal year 1989 and $381 in fiscal year 1992. Many of the company's new stores exceed $400 per square foot in their first year. The company's best sales record, of $600 per square foot, was reached at the South Coast Plaza store in 1987. Nordstrom stores also get off to a quicker start than is common. "On the average, it takes a Nordstrom store between one and two years before it reaches chainwide sales per square foot performance. This compares to an industry average of about three years." Note in Exhibit 4–7 that Nordstrom's per foot sales decreased in 1991, 1992 and 1993.

EXHIBIT 4–5 Consolidated Statements of Earnings (dollars in thousands except per share amount)

Year ended January 31,	1993	% OF SALES	1992	% OF SALES	1991	% OF SALES
Net sales	$3,421,979	100.0	$3,179,820	100.0	$2,893,904	100.0
Costs and expenses:						
Cost of sales and related buying and occupancy costs	2,339,107	68.3	2,169,437	68.2	2,000,250	69.1
Selling, general and administrative	902,083	26.4	831,505	26.2	747,770	25.8
Interest, net	44,810	1.3	49,106	1.5	52,228	1.8
Service charge income and other, net	(86,140)	(2.5)	(87,443)	(2.7)	(84,660)	(2.9)
Total costs and expenses	3,199,860	93.5	2,962,605	93.2	2,715,588	93.8
Earnings before income taxes	222,119	6.5	217,215	6.8	178,316	6.2
Income taxes	85,500	2.5	81,400	2.5	62,500	2.2
Net earnings	$ 136,619	4.0	$ 135,815	4.3	$ 115,816	4.0
Net earnings per share	$ 1.67		$ 1.66		$ 1.42	
Cash dividends paid per share	$ .32		$ .31		$ .30	

Source: Company reports.

EXHIBIT 4-6 Average Per-Store Performance (in thousands of dollars)

FISCAL YEAR	NUMBER OF STORES	NET SALES PER STORE	NET EARNINGS PER STORE
1983	39	19,710	1,032
1984	44	21,788	925
1985	52	25,036	963
1986	53	30,753	1,376
1987	56	34,290	1,656
1988	58	40,137	2,126
1989	59	45,273	1,948
1990	63	45,935	1,938
1991	68	46,762	1,997
1992	72	47,527	1,897

Source: Nordstrom *Annual Report*, 1987–1992.

EXHIBIT 4-7 Nordstrom Sales Per Square Foot

YEAR ENDED JANUARY 31	SALES PER SQUARE FOOT ($)	CONSUMER PRICE INDEX OF RETAIL APPAREL AND UPKEEP		SALES PER SQUARE FOOT
		Year	Index	
1981	184	1980	90.9	202
1982	200	1981	95.3	210
1983	205	1982	97.8	210
1984	243	1983	100.2	243
1985	267	1984	102.1	262
1986	293	1985	105.0	279
1987	322	1986	105.9	304
1988	349	1987	110.6	316
1989	380	1988	115.4	329
1990	398	1989	118.6	336
1991	391	1990	124.1	315
1992	388	1991	128.7	301
1993	381	1992	131.9	289

Note: Retail apparel price index is a composite including men's and boys' apparel, women's and girls' apparel, infants' and toddlers' apparel, footwear, other apparel, and apparel services.

Sources: Nordstrom *Annual Report*, 1988, 1991; U.S. Department of Commerce, *Statistical Abstract of the United States 1992*; and U.S. Labor Department, *Monthly Labor Review*, March 1993, p. 87.

Efforts to improve profitability have included both cost cutting and revenue enhancement. A continuing pressure to reduce costs was initiated in September 1990, when management directed all stores to cut expenses by 3 to 12 percent depending on store performance. The exact nature of cost reductions, whether in personnel, inventories, or advertising, was at the discretion of each store manager. The company has undertaken a systematic attack on inventory costs through information transfer. Nordstrom has instituted an improved management information system to improve its inventory ordering and vendor service. Its Vendor Information Partnership lets suppliers and Nordstrom buyers communicate and obtain updated information about inventories, status of orders, and payments. Buyers can initiate reorders through the system. The company is also evaluating a personal computer–based system that can be used to track sales demand by item by store, identify the level and location of inventories, and initiate transfer of inventory between locations.

Nordstrom spends considerably less on advertising than is common among competitors. As compared to an industry average of 4 percent of sales, Nordstrom spends less than 2 percent on advertising. Total company advertising expenditures amounted to only $58,424,000; $55,320,000; $50,412,000; $47,150,000; and $41,556,000 in fiscal years 1992, 1991, 1990, 1989, and 1988 respectively. The low level of advertising expenditures allows the company to pay more in salesperson compensation without eroding profit margins. As has been noted, Nordstrom can get by with less advertising in part by capitalizing on the mystique created by the media.

In order to boost sales in an otherwise depressed market, the company has recently increased its volume of lower-priced merchandise. This has largely been carried out by replacing nationally branded merchandise with goods produced for the company to its specifications and bearing the Nordstrom label. This has allowed selling at lower prices without major reductions in margins. Another move to boost revenues involved establishing the Nordstrom National Credit Bank in Colorado to issue and service its credit card operations. With a federally chartered national bank, Nordstrom can charge its cardholders in any state the maximum interest allowed in the state where chartered. The bank does not engage in any checking or savings and loans operations—it handles only credit card operations.

The company has used internally generated operating earnings, debt, and proceeds from the sale of common stock to finance its growth. Currently, debt is preferred over equity as a source of capital. However, Nordstrom has avoided the high level of debt that plagues many of its competitors. Incremental, store-by-store growth has been managed so that only relatively modest increases in debt have been needed to supplement operating earnings in financing growth. In fact, Exhibit 4–8 shows a decline in relative use of debt over the last five years. Capital expenditures in the near future will not require any major increase in debt. Opening new stores and modernizing present stores is expected to require the expenditure of approximately $550,000,000 through 1995. Exhibit 4–9 presents the company's recent balance sheets.

COMPANY PLANS

Growth is planned to continue at the approximate rate of three to four new large specialty department stores per year. These large stores will range in size from about 150,000 to 250,000 square feet. In addition, the Nordstrom Racks will continue their steady expansion. Distribution centers will be established to serve the stores that are in geographical areas new to Nordstrom.

EXHIBIT 4-8 Nordstrom Liquidity and Debt Ratios, Fiscal Years 1989–1993

	YEAR ENDED JANUARY 31				
	1993	1992	1991	1990	1989
Current Ratio	2.28	2.13	1.98	2.06	2.04
Quick Ratio	1.34	1.21	1.16	1.21	1.14
Long Term Debt/Equity	.42	.54	.59	.64	.61
Long Term Debt/Total Assets	.21	.25	.26	.27	.26
Total Debt/Total Assets	.49	.53	.57	.57	.58

Note: Total debt is calculated as total liabilities and equity less equity

Source: Nordstrom *Annual Report,* 1991, 1992.

EXHIBIT 4-9 Consolidated Balance Sheets (Dollars in thousands)

JANUARY 31,	1993	1992
Assets		
Current assets:		
Cash and cash equivalents	$ 29,136	$ 14,651
Accounts receivable, net	603,198	608,227
Merchandise inventories	536,739	506,632
Prepaid expenses	50,771	48,128
Total current assets	1,219,844	1,177,638
Property, buildings and equipment, net	824,142	856,404
Other assets	9,184	7,833
Total assets	$2,053,170	$2,041,875
Liabilities and Shareholders' Equity		
Current liabilities:		
Notes payable	$ 38,319	$ 134,735
Accounts payable	220,176	216,432
Accrued salaries, wages and taxes	158,028	145,792
Accrued expenses	31,141	31,741
Accrued income taxes	22,216	16,402
Current portion of long-term debt	41,316	8,801
Total current liabilities	511,196	553,903
Long-term debt	440,629	502,199
Deferred income taxes	49,314	46,542
Contingent liabilities		
Shareholders' equity	1,052,031	939,231
Total liabilities and shareholders' equity	$2,053,170	$2,041,875

Source: Nordstrom *Annual Report,* 1992.

Nordstrom has no plans to expand its operations to foreign nations. At least initially, national expansion will be targeted at the Washington-to-Boston corridor, the Southeast, the Midwest, and South-central regions. When the company enters a new area it will open several stores within a very few years to make more efficient use of the required supporting distribution center and the regional staff. The company will open its new stores under the leadership of experienced employees relocated or promoted from other Nordstrom stores. As in the past, this cadre will be relied on to anchor and communicate the Nordstrom culture.

Nordstrom's pace of expansion was slowed for 1993 when two large stores originally scheduled for opening were postponed until 1994 because of construction and environmental-impact slowdowns. In 1993 only one Rack and an outlet store opened. However, plans call for opening ten new large specialty stores between 1994 and 1996 (see Exhibit 4–10). The schedule reflects an emphasis on gaining a critical mass of stores between Washington and New York City and in the upper Midwest. The Dallas store is the first in the Texas (South-central) region. Additional stores will follow. Houston, Austin, and San Antonio are being considered. The company is also actively considering or seeking store sites in Connecticut and the Atlanta, Boston, Phoenix, Detroit, Las Vegas, and Denver areas. Nordstrom particularly likes to enter areas where competitors are not very profitable and where it can woo previously neglected customer segments with its outstanding service.

The growth of off-price clothing sales at 15 percent recently compared to 6 percent for general merchandise has prompted Nordstrom to enter that market on an experimental basis. Nordstrom planned to try two different cut-price discount store concepts specifically to cater to the low-priced, branded-goods market. One of these trial stores, the Last Chance outlet store, is similar to the Rack discount stores but carries non-Nordstrom goods. The second discount-type store was to bear the Nordstrom name and open in Philadelphia in 1993. This Nordstrom Factory Direct outlet store was to offer quality Nordstrom-label merchandise.

Prepare a strategic plan for Nordstrom as it enters the mid-1990s. Include specific recommendations for growth and improved efficiency. Do you feel Nordstrom should

EXHIBIT 4–10 Planned Additions to Large Specialty Store Chain

LOCATION	YEAR
Annapolis Mall, MD	1994
Circle Centre Mall, Indianapolis, IN	1994
Old Orchard Mall, Skokie, IL	1994
Santa Anita Mall, Arcadia, CA	1994
Washington Square, Portland, OR	1994
White Plains (Westchester Co.), NY	1994
Dallas Galleria, TX	1995
Mall at Short Hills, NJ	1995
Woodfield Mall, Schaumberg, IL	1995
King of Prussia Plaza, PA	1996

Source: Nordstrom *Annual Report*, 1992.

consider offering a catalog with women's apparel, accessories, and shoes? What rate of expansion would you recommend for Nordstrom Factory Direct stores Last Chance stores, Nordstrom Rack stores, as well as the mainstream Nordstrom stores? Is the Nordstrom organizational strategy effective?

NOTES

1. This brief history of Nordstrom, Inc., draws heavily on the Nordstrom 1987 *Report*, pp. 5–12.
2. "Nordstrom's Expansion Blitz," *Chain Store Age Executive*, December 1988, pp. 49–50, 53.
3. Jan Shaw, "Executives Catch Nordstrom Fever in Opening Week," *San Francisco Business Times*, October 10, 1988, p. 10.
4. Richard W. Stevenson, "Watch Out Macy's, Here Comes Nordstrom," *New York Times Magazine*, August 27, 1989, p. 35.
5. Robert Sharoff, "Chicago Seen as Good Move for Nordstrom," *Daily News Record*, January 6, 1989, pp. 2, 11.
6. "Nordstrom's Gang of Four," *Business Week*, June 15, 1992, pp. 122–123.
7. Stevenson, "Watch Out Macy's," p. 39.
8. Melinda Wilson, "Upscale Nordstrom's May Land in Detroit," *Crain's Detroit Business*, May 23, 1989.
9. Pat Baldwin, "You Can Get Satisfaction: Nationwide Survey Ranks Nordstrom's No. 1," *Dallas Morning News*, January 9, 1993, p. 2F.
10. "Nordstrom Labor Suit is Settled," *Los Angeles Times*, January 12, 1993, pp. D1 and 2.
11. Debra Prinzing, "Nordstrom and Minorities," *Puget Sound Business Journal*, May 29, 1992, p. 12.
12. "Nordstrom Receives Easter Seal Award for Innovative Catalogs," *PR Newswire*, September 23, 1992.
13. Prinzing, "Nordstrom and Minorities," p. 12.
14. *Standard and Poor's Industry Surveys*, January 1993, p. R81.
15. "Nordstrom's Expansion Blitz," p. 50.

EXHIBIT 4-11 Consolidated Statements of Shareholders' Equity (Dollars in thousands except per share amounts)

Year ended January 31,	1993	1992	1991
Common Stock			
Authorized 250,000,000 shares; issued and outstanding 81,974,797, 81,844,227 and 81,737,910 shares			
Balance at beginning of year	$ 153,055	$150,699	$148,857
Issuance of common stock	2,384	2,356	1,842
Balance at end of year	155,439	153,055	150,699
Retained Earnings			
Balance at beginning of year	786,176	675,711	584,393
Net earnings	136,619	135,815	115,816
Cash dividends paid ($.32, $.31 and $.30 per share)	(26,203)	(25,350)	(24,498)
Balance at end of year	896,592	786,176	675,711
Total shareholders' equity	$1,052,031	$939,231	$826,410

Source: Nordstrom *Annual Report*, 1992.

EXHIBIT 4-12 Consolidated Statements of Cash Flows (Dollars in thousands)

Year ended January 31,	1993	1992	1991
Operating Activities			
Net earnings	$136,619	$135,815	$115,816
*Adjustments to reconcile net earnings to net cash provided by operating activities:			
Depreciation and amortization	102,763	96,034	85,615
Change in:			
Accounts receivable, net	5,029	(32,719)	(39,234)
Merchandise inventories	(30,107)	(58,288)	(28,368)
Prepaid expenses	(2,643)	(6,263)	(20,018)
Accounts payable	3,744	12,166	8,928
Accrued salaries, wages and taxes	12,236	17,095	6,090
Accrued expenses	(600)	(2,927)	5,588
Income tax liabilities	8,586	(6,926)	13,710
Net cash provided by operating activities	235,627	153,987	148,127
Investing Activities			
Additions to property, buildings and equipment, net	(69,982)	(145,761)	(199,407)
Other, net	(1,870)	(1,393)	(1,277)
Net cash used in investing activities	(71,852)	(147,154)	(200,684)
Financing Activities			
(Decrease) increase in notes payable	(96,416)	(14,771)	46,933
Principal payments on long-term debt	(29,055)	(85,647)	(79,240)
Proceeds from issuance of common stock	2,384	2,356	1,842
Cash dividends paid	(26,203)	(25,350)	(24,498)
Proceeds from issuance of long-term debt, net	—	106,568	99,131
Net cash (used in) provided by financing activities	(149,290)	(16,844)	44,168
Net increase (decrease) in cash and cash equivalents	14,485	(10,011)	(8,389)
Cash and cash equivalents at beginning of year	14,651	24,662	33,051
Cash and cash equivalents at end of year	$ 29,136	$ 14,651	$ 24,662

Source: Nordstrom *Annual Report,* 1992.

WAL★MART STORES, INC—1994

Headquartered in Bentonville, Arkansas, Wal★Mart (501—273-4000) does not have a formal mission statement. When asked about Wal★Mart's lack of a mission, Public Relations Coordinator Kim Ellis recently replied: "We believe that our customers are most interested in other aspects of our business, and we are focused on meeting their basic consumer needs. If in fact we did have a formal mission statement, it would be something like this: 'to provide quality products at an everyday low price and with extended customer service . . . always.' "

Hawaii, Rhode Island, and Washington each received its first Wal★Mart store in 1993. Only two other states, Alaska and Vermont, do not yet have a Wal★Mart. Some towns do not want a Wal★Mart, such as Greenfield, Massachusetts, which rejected a proposed store in October 1993. The town of 18,000 was afraid a Wal★Mart outside of town would destroy downtown.

Wal★Mart has not yet entered foreign countries. With the exception of Mexico. David Glass, President and CEO of Wal★Mart, plans continued rapid expansion of the company. The major question facing Wal★Mart is where to expand and at what rate.

Wal★Mart is composed of four major divisions: Sam's Club, Wal★Mart Stores, Wal★Mart Supercenters, and McLane & Western Merchandisers. Forty-eight new Sam's Clubs were opened in fiscal year 1993 while 40 other Sam's were remodeled. Wal★Mart opened 161 new Wal★Mart stores in fiscal 1993 and remodeled another 170 stores. Wal★Mart is a company on the move.

McLane & Western, Wal★Mart's specialty distribution subsidiary, experienced record sales and earnings in 1993. McLane serves over 30,000 convenience stores and independent grocers. McLane's sales increased 16 percent to nearly $3 million in fiscal 1993. McLane recently acquired two distribution and food-processing facilities of The Southland Corporation, enhancing McLane's nationwide distribution network. McLane has entered into a service agreement with Southland that opens up a number of new supply opportunities with convenience stores across the United States. Clarksville, Arkansas, is the home of McLane's first full-line grocery distribution center. This 705,000-square-foot center opened in 1993 and serves Wal★Mart Supercenters. A second center recently open in Temple, Texas.

HISTORY

No word better describes Wal★Mart than *growth*. Wal★Mart Stores, Inc. began as a small-town variety store business in 1945, when Sam Walton opened his first Ben Franklin franchises in Newport, Arkansas. Based in rural Bentonville, Arkansas, Walton, his wife Helen, and his brother Bud operated the nation's most successful Ben Franklin franchises. "We were a small chain," said Walton of his 16-store operation. "Things were running so smoothly we even had time for our families." What more could a man want? A great deal, as it turned out.

Walton could see that the variety store was gradually dying because supermarkets and discounters were developing. Far from being secure, Walton knew that he was under siege. He decided to counterattack. He first tried to convince the top management of Ben Franklin to enter discounting. After their refusal, Walton made a quick trip around the country in search of ideas. He then began opening his own discount stores in small Arkansas towns like Bentonville and Rogers.

The company opened its first discount department store (Wal★Mart) in November 1962. The early stores has bare tile floors and pipe racks. Wal★Mart did not begin to revamp its image significantly until the mid-1970's and growth in the early years was slow. However, once the company went public in 1970, sales began to increase rapidly. If one had purchased 100 shares of the stock in 1970, they would have been worth $350,000 in 1985.

Such retailers as Target, Venture, and Kmart provided the examples that Wal★Mart sought to emulate in its growth. The old Wal★Mart store colors, dark blue and white (too harsh), were dumped in favor of a three-tone combination of light beige, soft blue, and burnt orange. Carpeting, which had long been discarded on apparel sales floors, was put back. New racks were put into use that displayed the entire garment instead of only an edge.

Wal★Mart began to expand by taking over falling chains and "Waltonizing" them. In July 1981 Walton picked up ailing Kuhn's Big-K stores—one warehouse and 92 locations—in effect acquiring cheap leases at a discount price. Wal★Mart assumed $19 million in debt and issued $7.5 million worth of preferred stock. Now Kuhn's has a new management team and $60 million in cash for a major facelift. Profits may pour in, as they did after Wal★Mart's only previous acquisition, the 1977 purchase of Mohr Value Stores. "We fixed them up and retrained the people, and now they're our best group," said Walton.

In 1987 Wal★Mart implemented two new concepts: hypermarkets, 200,000-square-foot stores that sell everything including food, and supercenters, scaled-down supermarkets. Also in 1987 Walton named David Glass as the new chief executive officer (CEO) while he remained chairman of the board.

In 1990 Wal★Mart completed the acquisition of 14 centers of McLane Company, a national distribution system in 11 states providing over 12,500 types of grocery and nongrocery products. Also in 1990 Wal★Mart sold its 14 Dot Discount Drug Stores. Sam's Clubs, in 1991, merged the twenty-eight wholesale clubs of The Whole Club, Inc., of Indianapolis, Indiana into its operations.

At the end of its 1992 fiscal year (January 31, 1993), Wal★Mart had 1,880 discount stores (including 30 supercenter stores) in 45 states and Puerto Rico, 148 Sam's Wholesale Clubs in 41 states, 3 hypermarkets, 14 McLane's distribution centers, and 13 distribution centers (see Exhibit 5–1).

OPERATIONS

Most of the 1,880 Wal★Mart stores are located in towns of 5,000 to 25,000. There are still smaller stores for communities of less than 5,000. Wal★Mart's expense structure, measured as a percentage of sales, continues to be among the lowest in the industry. Although Walton watched expenses, he rewarded sales managers handsomely. Sales figures are available to every employee at Wal★Mart. Monthly figures for each department are ranked and made available throughout the organization. Employees who do better than average get rewarded with raises, bonuses, and a pat on the back. Poor performers are only rarely fired, although demotions are possible.

All employees (called "associates") have a stake in the financial performance of the company. Store managers earn as much as $100,000 to $150,000 per year. Even part-time clerks qualify for profit sharing and stock-purchase plans. Millionaires among Wal★Mart's middle managers are not uncommon. Executives frequently solicit ideas for improving the organization from employees and often put them into use.

	WALMART	SAM'S
Alabama	74	7
Arizona	28	4
Arkansas	77	3
California	43	3
Colorado	32	1
Connecticut	1	1
Delaware	2	
Florida	122	23
Georgia	83	9
Idaho	5	1
Illinois	97	18
Indiana	65	12
Iowa	43	3
Kansas	43	3
Kentucky	66	4
Louisiana	74	9
Maine	6	2
Maryland	7	2
Massachusettes	2	2
Michigan	22	6
Minnesota	27	7
Mississippi	57	3
Missouri	105	9
Montana	2	1
Nebraska	16	1
Nevada	5	2
New Hampshire	7	2
New Jersey	3	2
New Mexico	19	1
New York	16	3
North Carolina	74	8
North Dakota	8	2
Ohio	42	16
Oklahoma	81	6
Oregon	12	
Pennsylvania	26	5
Puerto Rico	2	
South Carolina	49	5
South Dakota	8	1
Tennessee	86	7
Texas	229	44
Utah	11	
Virginia	37	6
West Virginia	10	3
Wisconsin	47	9
Wyoming	9	
	1,880	256

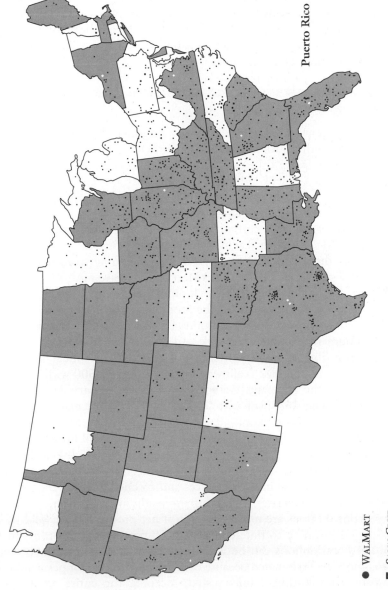

- ● WALMART
- ■ SAM'S CLUB
- ▲ DISTRIBUTION CENTER
- ★ SUPER CENTER
- ✪ WALMART HOME OFFICE AND THREE WALMART DISTRIBUTION CENTERS
- ◆ McLANE DISTRIBUTION CENTER
- ✳ WESTERN MERCHANDISERS HOME OFFICE

EXHIBIT 5-1 Trade Territory Map

With Wal★Mart stock selling at 20 to 30 times earnings—an almost incredible price—Walton presided over a sizable fortune before his death in 1992. Wal★Mart stock is still 39 percent held by the Walton family. Family holdings are worth nearly $8 billion.

Continuing a Walton tradition, Wal★Mart invites over 100 analysts and institutional investors to the fieldhouse at the University of Arkansas for its annual meeting in mid-June. During the day-and-a-half session, investors meet top executives, as well as Wal★Mart district managers, buyers, and 200,000 hourly salespeople. Investors see a give-and-take meeting between buyers and district managers.

Wal★Mart unveiled in mid-1993 its first environmental demonstration store, a 121,294-square-foot facility in Lawrence, Kansas. This store is designed so that a second floor could be added if Wal★Mart vacates to allow conversion to apartments. The store is exceptionally energy efficient but costs 20 percent more than the average Wal★Mart, which costs about $2.4 million or $20 a square foot. The environmental store features on-site recycling, native plants that make up the landscaping, and solar-powered lights. Planning for this store began in 1990 when Hillary Rodham Clinton served on Wal★Mart's board of directors.

EMPLOYEE BENEFITS

Wal★Mart management takes pride in the ongoing development of its people. Training is seen as critical to outstanding performance, and new programs are implemented often in all areas of the company. The combination of grass-roots meetings, the open-door policy, videos, printed material, classroom and home study, year-end management meetings, and on-the -job training has enabled employees to prepare themselves for advancement and added responsibilities.

Wal★Mart managers stay current with new developments and needed changes. Executives spend one week per year in hourly jobs in various stores. Walton himself once traveled at least three days per week, visiting competitors' stores and attending the opening of new stores, leading the Wal★Mart cheer, "Give me a W, give me a A . . ."

Wal★Mart encourages employee stock purchases; about 8 percent of Wal★Mart stock is owned by employees. Under the Stock Purchase Plan, stock may be bought by two different methods. First, an amount is deducted from each employee's check with a maximum of $62.50 per check. An additional 15 percent of the amount deducted is contributed by Wal★Mart (up to $1,800 of annual stock purchases). Second, a lump-sum purchase is allowed in April up to $1,500 with an additional 15 percent added by the company. Wal★Mart also as of January 31, 1993 offered an associate stock ownership plan with approximately 4,000 management associates granted stock options.

Wal★Mart has a corporate profit-sharing plan with contributions of $98,327,000 as of January 31, 1991, $129,653,000 in 1992, and $166,035,000 in 1993. The purposes of the profit-sharing plan is to furnish an incentive for increased efficiency, to provide progressive recognition of service, and to encourage careers with the company by Wal★Mart associates. This is a trustee-administered plan, which means the company's contributions are made only out of net profits and are held by a trustee. The company from time to time contributes 10 percent of net profits to the trust.

Company contributions can be withdrawn only on termination. If employment with the company is terminated because of retirement, death, or permanent disability, the company contribution if fully vested, meaning the entire amount is nonforfeitable. If termination of employment occurs for any other reason, the amount that is nonforfeitable depends on the number of years of service with the company. After completion of the third year of service with the company, 20 percent of each participant's account is nonforfeitable for each subsequent year of service. After seven years of service, a participant's account is 100 percent vested.

Walton was admittedly old-fashioned in many respects. Wal★Mart store policies reflect many of his values. For example, store policies forbid employees from dating other employees without prior approval of the executive committee. Also, women are rare in management positions. Annual manager meetings include sessions for wives to speak out on the problems of living with a Wal★Mart manager. No women were in the ranks of Wal★Mart's top management. Walton also resisted placing women on the board of directors. Only 12 women have made it to the ranks of buyers (12 percent of all buyers). Wal★Mart is an EEOC/AA employer but has managed to get away with "apparent" discriminatory policies, perhaps because most Wal★Marts are located in small rural towns in the Sun Belt states.

MARKETING

The discount retailing business is seasonal to a certain extent. Generally, the highest volume of sales and net income occurs in the fourth fiscal quarter and the lowest volume occurs during the first fiscal quarter. Wal★Mart draws customers into the store by radio and television advertising, monthly circulars, and weekly newspaper adds. Television advertising is used to convey an image of everyday low prices and quality merchandise. Radio is used to a lesser degree to promote specific products that are usually in high demand. Newspaper and monthly circulars are major contributors to the program, emphasizing deeply discounted items, and are effective at luring customers into the store.

Efforts are also made to discount corporate overhead. Visitors often mistake corporate headquarters for a warehouse owing to its limited decorating and "show." Wal★Mart executives share hotel rooms when traveling to reduce expenses. The company avoids spending money on consultants and marketing experts. Instead, decisions are made based on intuitive judgments of managers and employees and on the assessment of strategies of other retail chains.

Wal★Mart advertises a "Buy American" policy in an effort to keep production at home. Consequently, Wal★Mart buyers are constantly seeking vendors in grass-roots America. For example, Wal★Mart dropped Fuji film for 3M. In addition, Wal★Mart censors products that are not conservative. The company has banned recordings and removed magazines based on lyrics and graphics, as well as stopped marketing teen rock magazines.

GROWTH IN DISTRIBUTION CENTERS

During the 1993 fiscal year, close to 77 percent of Wal★Mart's merchandise passed through one of 22 distribution warehouses, an amount greater than Kmart's or Sear's. Wal★Mart Distribution Centers are located as follows: three in Bentonville, Arkansas; two each in Searcy, Arkansas, and Laurens, South Carolina; and one each in Ft. Smith, Arkansas; Palestine, Texas; Cullman, Alabama; Mt. Pleasant, Iowa; Brookhaven, Mississippi; Douglas, Georgia; Plainview, Texas; New Braunfels, Texas; Loveland, Colorado; Seymour, Indiana; Poterville, California; Sutherland, Virginia; Greencastle, Indiana; Brooksville, Florida; and Grove City, Ohio. Wal★Mart has a total of 20,381,727 square feet of storage space. Sam's, unlike Wal★Mart stores, receive the majority of its merchandise by direct shipments from suppliers, rather than from the company's distribution centers.

Wal★Mart maintains warehouse space in Oklahoma, Arkansas, and Georgia that is utilized for seasonal merchandise. The McLane distribution centers primarily buy, sell, and distribute merchandise to the convenience store industry with an aggregate square footage of 4,213,430 square feet, including two distribution centers in San Bernardino, California, and Fredericksburg, Virginia.

Wal★Mart's distribution operations were highly automated. Terminals at each store wire merchandise requests to warehouses, which in turn either ship immediately or place a reorder. Wal★Mart computers are linked directly with over 200 vendors, making deliveries faster. Wal★Mart has one of the world's largest private satellite communication systems to control distribution. In addition, Wal★Mart has installed point-of-sale bar-code scanning in all of its stores.

Wal★Mart owns a fleet of truck-tractors that can deliver goods to any store in 38 to 48 hours from the time the order is placed. After trucks drop off merchandise, they frequently pick up merchandise from manufacturers on the way back to the distribution center. This back-haul rate averages over 60 percent and is yet another way Wal★Mart cuts costs.

MERCHANDISE

Wal★Mart stores generally have 36 departments and offer a wide variety of merchandise, including apparel for women, girls, men, boys, and infants. Each store also carries curtains, fabrics and notions, shoes, housewares, hardware, electronics, home supplies, sporting goods, toys, cameras and supplies, health and beauty aids, pharmaceuticals, and jewelry. Nationally advertised merchandise accounts for a majority of sales of the stores. Wal★Mart has begun marketing limited lines of merchandise under the brand name "Sams's American Choice." The merchandise is carefully selected to insure quality and must be made in the United States.

During the fiscal year ended January 31, 1993, sales at Wal★Mart stores by product category were as follows:

CATEGORY	PERCENTAGE OF SALES
Softgoods	28%
Hardgoods (hardware, housewares, auto supplies and small appliances)	26
Stationery and candy	11
Sporting goods and toys	10
Health and beauty aids	8
Pharmaceuticals	7
Gifts, records, and electronics	6
Shoes	2
Jewelry	2
	100%

Sales in pharmaceuticals above are a combination of owned and licensed departments. These pharmaceutical percentages includes sales of licensed departments, but Wal★Mart records as revenues only rentals received from such departments.

Sam's offers bulk displays of name-brand hardgood merchandise, some softgoods, and institutional-size grocery items. Each Sam's also carries jewelry, sporting goods, toys, tires, stationery, and books. During fiscal year 1992 Sam's began experimenting with fresh bakery, meat, and produce departments. Sam's has 131 clubs with fresh-food departments.

McLane's offers a wide variety of grocery and nongrocery products, including per-ishable and nonperishable items. The nongrocery products consist primarily of tobacco products, hardgood merchandise, health and beauty aids, toys, and stationery. Western Merchandisers offers a wide variety of prerecorded music, videos, and books. Both McLane and Western Merchandisers are wholesale distributors that sell their merchan-dise to a variety of retailers, including the Wal★Mart stores and Sam's Clubs.

OPERATIONS

Except for extended hours during certain holiday seasons, most Wal★Mart stores are open from 9:00 a.m. to 9:00 p.m. six days a week, and from 12:30 p.m. to 5:30 p.m. on Sundays, with the remainder of the stores closed on Sunday. Some Wal★Mart stores and most of the Supercenter stores are open 24 hours each day. Wal★Mart tries to meet or undersell local competition but maintains uniform prices, except where lower prices are necessary to meet local competition. Wal★Mart stores maintain a "satisfaction guaranteed" program to promote cus-tomer goodwill and acceptance.

Sam's are membership only, cash-and-carry operations. However, a financial ser-vice credit-card program (Discover Card) is available in all clubs. Qualified members include businesses and those individuals who are members of certain qualifying orga-nizations, such as government and state employees and credit union members. Both business and individual members have an annual membership fee of $25 for the pri-mary membership card.

Operating hours vary among Sam's, but generally are Monday through Friday from 10:00 a.m. to 8:30 p.m. Most Sam's are open on the weekend from 9:30 a.m. to 7:00 p.m. on Saturday and 12:00 noon to 6:00 p.m. on Sunday. Sam's attempts to maximize sales volume and inventory turnover while minimizing expenses.

STRATEGIES TODAY

Europe is nearly void of mass discount retailing companies, and analysts view Europe as a goldmine for Wal★Mart or Kmart. Thousands of small European retailers are worried. In Germany and France, for example, established merchants are fiercely opposing proposals to legalize late-evening and seven-day-a-week retailing, the hall-mark of American discounters. In England, small retailers are trying to persuade the government to limit the spread of big discounters. Napoleon once called England "a nation of shopkeepers" and this description still applies to most of Europe. "It's like America in the 1950s" says Moulton of Lostco Wholesale Corporation in Seattle.

Wal★Mart recently entered into a joint venture interest with CIFRA, Mexico's largest retailer. The joint venture operates three Club Aurreras, four Bodegas discount stores, and one Aurrera combination store. This joint venture plans to add a large number of units during the coming years.

In fiscal 1994 Wal★Mart plans to open approximately 150 new Wal★Mart stores and 65 Sam's Clubs. The company also plans to expand or relocate approximately 100 older Wal★Mart stores and 25 Sam's Clubs, including relocation or expansion of 40 Wal★Mart Supercenters. Also planned is the construction of two new full-line distribution centers, two grocery distribution centers, a distribution center to process clothing, and a storage center.

1. What strategies would you recommend to CEO David Glass, as Wal★Mart has become the largest retailing firm in the United States?
2. Should Wal★Mart get a foothold in Europe before competitors such as Kmart seize the initiative?
3. Should Wal★Mart expand further in Mexico? expand in the United States? expand into Canada?
4. Should Wal★Mart make further acquisitions?

EXHIBIT 5-2 Ten-Year Financial Summary (dollar amounts in thousands except per share data)

WAL★MART STORES, INC. AND SUBSIDIARIES	1993	1992
OPERATING RESULTS		
Net sales	$55,483,771	$43,886,902
Net sales increase	26%	35%
Comparative store sales increase	11%	10%
Rentals from licensed departments and other income-net	500,793	402,521
Cost of sales	44,174,685	34,786,119
Operating, selling, and general and administrative expenses	8,320,842	6,684,304
Interest costs:		
Debt	142,649	113,305
Capital leases	180,049	152,558
Provision for federal and state income taxes	1,171,545	944,661
Net income	1,994,794	1,608,476
Per share of common stock[a]		
Net income	.87	.70
Dividends	.11	.09
FINANCIAL POSITION		
Current assets	$10,197,590	$ 8,575,423
Inventories at replacement cost	9,779,981	7,856,871
Less LIFO reserve	511,672	472,572
Inventories at LIFO cost	9,268,309	7,384,299
Net property, plant, equipment and capital leases	9,792,881	6,433,801
Total assets	20,565,087	15,443,389
Current liabilities	6,754,286	5,003,775
Long-term debt	3,072,835	1,722,022
Long-term obligations under capital leases	1,772,152	1,555,875
Preferred stock with mandatory redemption provisions	—	—
Shareholders' equity	8,759,180	6,989,710
FINANCIAL RATIOS		
Current ratio	1.5	1.7
Inventories/working capital	2.7	2.1
Return on assets	12.9%	14.1%
Return on shareholders' equity[b]	28.5%	30.0%
OTHER YEAR-END DATA		
Number of Wal*Mart Stores	1,880	1,720
Number of Sam's Clubs	256	208
Average Wal*Mart Store size	81,200	75,000
Number of Associates	434,000	371,000
Number of Shareholders	180,584	150,242

[a]Restated to reflect the two-for-one stock split announced January 22, 1993.

[b]On beginning of year balances.

Source:Wal*Mart *Annual Report,* 1993.

EXHIBIT 5-3 Consolidated Statements of Income (amounts in thousands except per share data)

WAL★MART STORES, INC. AND SUBSIDIARIES	FISCAL YEAR ENDED JANUARY 31		
	1993	**1992**	**1991**
REVENUES			
Net sales	$55,483,771	$43,886,902	$32,601,594
Rentals from licensed departments	36,035	28,659	22,362
Other income-net	464,758	373,862	239,452
	55,984,564	44,289,423	32,863,408
COSTS AND EXPENSES			
Cost of sales	44,174,685	34,786,119	25,499,834
Operating, selling, and general and administrative expenses	8,320,842	6,684,304	5,152,178
INTEREST COSTS			
Debt	142,649	113,305	42,716
Capital leases	180,049	152,558	125,920
	52,818,225	41,736,286	30,820,648
INCOME BEFORE INCOME TAXES			
	3,166,339	2,553,137	2,042,760
PROVISION FOR FEDERAL AND STATE INCOME TAXES			
Current	1,136,918	906,183	737,020
Deferred	34,627	38,478	14,716
	1,171,545	944,661	751,736
Net income	$ 1,994,794	$ 1,608,476	$ 1,291,024
Net Income per share	$ .87	$ .70	$ .57

Source: Wal*Mart *Annual Report*, 1993.

Net Income (millions of dollars)

1984	1985	1986	1987	1988	1989	1990	1991	1992	1993
196.2	270.8	327.5	450.1	627.6	837.2	1075.9	1291.0	1608.5	1994.8

EXHIBIT 5-4 Consolidated Balance Sheets (amounts in thousands)

WAL★MART STORES, INC. AND SUBSIDIARIES	JANUARY 31	
	1993	1992

ASSETS

	1993	1992
CURRENT ASSETS:		
Cash and cash equivalents	$12,363	$30,649
Receivables	524,555	418,867
Recoverable costs for sale/leaseback	312,016	681,387
Inventories:		
At replacement cost	9,779,981	7,856,871
Less LIFO reserve	511,672	472,572
LIFO	9,268,309	7,384,299
Prepaid expenses	80,347	60,221
Total Current Assets	10,197,590	8,575,423
PROPERTY, PLANT, AND EQUIPMENT, AT COST:		
Land	1,692,510	1,077,658
Buildings and improvements	4,641,009	2,569,095
Fixtures and equipment	3,417,230	2,683,481
Transportation equipment	111,151	86,491
	9,861,900	6,416,725
Less accumulated depreciation	1,607,623	1,338,151
Net property, plant, and equipment	8,254,277	5,078,574
Property under capital leases	1,986,104	1,724,123
Less accumulated amortization	447,500	368,896
Net property under capital leases	1,538,604	1,355,227
OTHER ASSETS AND DEFERRED CHARGES	574,616	434,165
Total Assets	$20,565,087	$15,443,389

LIABILITIES AND SHAREHOLDERS' EQUITY

	1993	1992
CURRENT LIABILITIES:		
Commercial paper	$ 1,588,825	$453,964
Accounts payable	3,873,331	3,453,529
Accrued liabilities	1,042,108	829,381
Accrued federal and state income taxes	190,620	226,828
Long–term debt due within one year	13,849	5,156
Obligations under capital leases due within one year	45,553	34,917
Total Current Liabilities	6,754,286	5,003,775
LONG–TERM DEBT	3,072,835	1,722,022
LONG–TERM OBLIGATIONS UNDER CAPITAL LEASES	1,772,152	1,555,875
DEFERRED INCOME TAXES	206,634	172,007

TABLE 5-4 *Continued*

WAL★MART STORES, INC. AND SUBSIDIARIES (AMOUNT IN THOUSANDS)	JANUARY 31	
	1993	1992
SHAREHOLDERS' EQUITY:		
Preferred stock ($.10 par value; 100,000 shares authorized, none issued)		
Common stock ($.10 par value; 5,500,000 shares authorized, 2,299,638 and 1,149,028 issued and outstanding in 1993 and 1992 respectively)	229,964	114,903
Capital in excess of par value	526,647	625,669
Retained earnings	8,002,569	6,249,138
Total Shareholders' Equity	8,759,180	6,989,710
Total Liabilities and Shareholders' Equity	$20,565,087	$15,443,389

Source: Wal★Mart *Annual Report*, 1993.

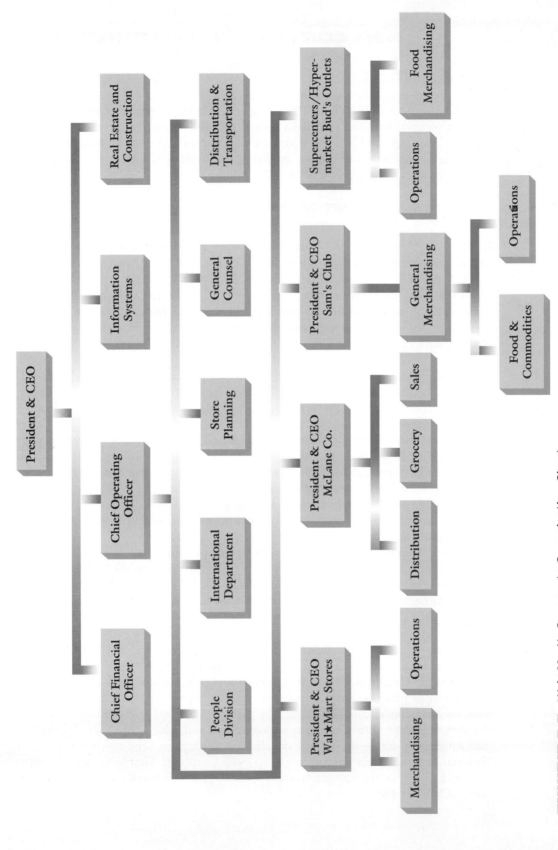

EXHIBIT 5-5 Wal★Mart's Corporate Organization Chart

NSP CORPORATE GRAPHICS—1993

NSP Corporate Graphics (205-821-0050) is based in Auburn, Alabama. In his third year as president of NSP Corporate Graphics (NSP), Michael Plumb has seen annual sales increase from $700,000 in 1982 to approximately $5.5 million in 1992. NSP's sales are on their way to a record $6 million in 1993. Product turnaround time has been cut drastically and NSP has become a leader in the screen-printing industry. Yet, numerous competitors are taking market share from NSP and are trying to put Plumb's business out of business.

NSP'S HISTORY

C. H. "Babe" McGehee and Tom Edwards became friends in the fifth grade after McGehee's family moved to the small town of Auburn, Alabama. As McGehee recalled, the early days were trying. As a "preacher's kid," he had to fight all of the boys in his class just to be accepted. After he beat up Edwards, one of the larger boys in his class, he never had further problems. Instead, the two became best friends, a friendship that was to last a lifetime. Their friendship grew in college where they pledged with the same fraternity at Auburn University. They lost touch for a while during World War II but were reunited later.

McGehee was working in construction in Mobile, Alabama, and Edwards was back in Auburn building houses with his father. Edwards convinced McGehee to join him in the construction business in Auburn. A very enterprising team, they were always in search of new opportunities. Edwards found a plant for sale that produced wooden ammunition boxes for use in the Korean conflict. The two partners bought the plant and moved it from Columbus, Missouri, to Auburn in 1952. The end of the conflict brought a significant decrease in the demand for ammunition boxes, so the partners modified the business to produce returnable wooden soft-drink containers. By 1962, the returnable glass bottle business was losing ground, and the future for a container company looked grim. When NSP's container plant was closed in 1990, it was the last remaining plant of its type in the United States.

Edwards became interested in the screen-printing business and began looking for viable prospects. Screen printing is an old form of printing on silk. Areas of silk are blocked out to make an impression on material, and ink is deposited through a screen mesh. Photographic and chemical agents are used to screen out color. Screen printing is superior to some other forms of printing because it allows heavier deposits of ink onto a surface and results in a more vibrant, longer-lasting finish.

Edwards identified Dixie Printing in nearby Opelika as their next business opportunity. Screen printing was a natural choice because the company's skill in cutting special angles for wooden soft-drink containers was readily transferred to Dixie Printing's production of plywood shapes for highway traffic signs. After cutting the plywood base, the firm applied the sign front. The partners bought Dixie Printing, convinced the former owner, Jim Crawford, to join them and move their new business to Auburn directly across the street from the container plant. The newly formed firm, National ScreenPrinters (later changed to NSP Corporate Graphics, Inc.), incorporated as a closely held corporation in 1962 with 30,000 shares of stock selling at a par value of $10 per share.

The first meeting of NSP's board of directors was held on February 2, 1962. The company had approximately sixty original stockholders then, primarily from the Auburn/Opelika area. Less than two-thirds of the stock was sold with the rest retained by the company. Within three years, NSP reached its goal of profitability. In 1985, NSP declared its first dividends at $.50 per share.

SUCCESSION OF MANAGEMENT

During the early years, McGehee spent most of his time running the container factory, while Edwards took over the operations of the screen-printing business. While Edwards was overseeing manufacturing, McGehee handled most of the personnel issues. The two occupied a single office at NSP that was equipped with two desks and a manual Royal typewriter.

Edwards was the driving leader of the new corporation. His expertise in machinery and equipment created the spirit of strong manufacturing and commitment to quality for which NSP became recognized. NSP is one of the few companies in the industry that is almost entirely automated, a tribute to the solid foundation established by Edwards. In 1979 Edwards died unexpectedly, and McGehee became president of the firm. A portrait of the two in the lobby of NSP signified Edwards's continued presence in the company.

As president, McGehee was a laissez-faire administrator who believed in the talents and capabilities of his employees and, therefore, did not interfere with their work. McGehee attributed the success of NSP to the theme of one of his favorite sayings: "No amount of planning will replace dumb luck." He admitted that during the 1970s NSP did no strategic planning.

In 1982, Michael Plumb joined NSP as sales manager, working out of his home in Atlanta, Georgia. Plumb had a degree in history from the University of Vermont. His northeastern work ethic was considered by fellow employees to be quite foreign to the NSP style, and he was often described by others as an "aggressive Yankee." Plumb's previous experience and training at 3M, Creatist, and Kux Manufacturing, along with his "slick" appearance, natural gift of gab, and knowledge of the product, made him an accomplished salesman. In 1987 his position was upgraded in title to vice president of sales.

Moving to Auburn, Plumb became a good corporate citizen, a member of Rotary, and an active member, along with his family, in the Presbyterian church. He also became a crisis center telephone volunteer. The crisis center not only taught Plumb to listen effectively (through forty hours of intense training), but also made him more aware of the problems that could be affecting his employees.

In 1989, on his seventieth birthday, McGehee stepped down as president of the corporation but remained involved as chairman of the board of directors. He envisioned another in-house candidate as his heir apparent, but in one of the few instances of disagreement with McGehee, the board of directors chose Plumb who they felt better fit the image they wanted to project as the company's chief executive. The board wanted someone with new visions, someone with a well-rounded background in the screen-printing industry. Plumb best met that need. He had experience in all three levels of screen printing: he sold to screen-printing companies, he worked for an installation company, and he sold screen printing.

In 1992, NSP was ranked in the top 15 percent (in terms of size) of all screen-printing firms in the country. Although still involved in fleet graphics, NSP has expanded its services to include all aspects of corporate graphics, signage, and design.

Michael Plumb. As CEO of NSP, Plumb's management philosophy parallels Alvin Toffler's: "Dare to image the future." Toffler suggested that managers look for "big chances," be willing to work toward specific goals, and dare to differ from conventional wisdom. Plumb believes in this philosophy without taking it to extremes. For example, when he became president of NSP, Plumb surprised employees when he did not move to the largest office but instead stayed in a smaller inner office.

Another of Plumb's personal philosophies is to "do what you do well and do it often." His special talent is sales, so he spends at least one-quarter of his time making new contacts and servicing old accounts, particularly the Federal Express account, and another quarter of his time managing sales. With competition in the industry being so fierce, Plumb spends considerable time on the road. He has his eyes set on obtaining business related to the 1996 Olympics since NSP is located only 100 miles from Atlanta. Plumb also spends time working in the plant because he feels the only way to keep current on the business is to do the job. The remainder of his time is spent in new market development and performing the normal duties of a corporate executive.

Plumb has his own philosophy of Total Quality Management which begins with employee training. He believes that a greater understanding of the total business process by all NSP employees will enhance the overall productivity and competitiveness of the firm. His plans are to train his total workforce to know and appreciate every aspect of the business.

Plumb is considered to be a challenging person, very demanding of his employees. He sets high standards for himself and expects others to have equally high goals for themselves. He is a tried-and-true person and allows no obstacles to stand in the way of his accomplishments. As a result, he seldom takes time to relax. Although he is very family-oriented and concerned about spending quality time with his family, he often finds himself thinking of business during family vacations or other outings. One of his greatest obsessions is a determination to be fair. In both his work and home life, Plumb is careful to look at all situations in terms of the fairness of the outcome.

Plumb keeps NSP's employees fully apprised of the firm's position in the industry. He takes every available moment to update the employees on NSP progress. On one occasion when the city was under a tornado alert and all employees were gathered in the basement for safety, Plumb announced the previous quarter's earnings and updated all employees on new accounts. Plumb holds quarterly meetings with all employees. Seldom, if ever, is there a written, preestablished agenda. His meetings are informal and light-hearted, yet he is always in control. Still, he is quick to compliment employees for their part in any financial or productivity improvements or to answer any question pertaining to company operations. His monthly meetings with management personnel are also informal. Although ideas for new ventures surface for discussion, the direction that the company will take is usually predetermined by Plumb.

THE SCREEN-PRINTING INDUSTRY

Large-format screen printing in the United States is about a $750 million industry. In 1990, the two largest competitors—Ariston and Screen Art—merged, which placed the new company in a position of dominance. Despite the merger, the screen-printing industry is primarily comprised of many small to mid-sized firms. Very little capital is required (about $10,000) to get started in screen printing; the industry is, consequently, flooded with mom-and-pop operations. The screen-printing business is largely regionalized, with few national firms.

The fragmented market and steep competition results in characteristically low operating margins and low switching costs to the buyer of screen-printing services. This is compounded by the fact that most larger screen-printing clients use more than one vendor, which makes it difficult for any one company to solely maintain a major corporate account. Competition is so intense that an exclusive account today could be subdivided or retracted tomorrow. Survival in the industry depends on a firm's ability to diversify its business among a large number of companies.

Generally, two types of screen-printing businesses exist: (1) Firms that specialize in fleet and large graphics, and (2) silk-screen shops that concentrate on T-shirts and specialty advertising items, such as coffee cups. NSP is considered an industrial screen printer specializing in fleet graphics. However, NSP is attempting to make the switch to a niche strategy specializing in art and graphics, while still performing screen-printing functions services to existing clients.

Without reliance on the existing fleet graphics business, NSP could not survive. As a company evolving toward specialization in art and graphics, NSP has added advertising agencies to its list of customers. Plumb feels that the technical ability NSP provides can benefit advertising agencies who often contract out graphics and screen printing work.

Fleet Graphics. Fleet graphics is a successful means of corporate exposure. A 1977 study conducted by the American Trucking Association showed that an over-the-road tractor-trailer combination makes 101 visual impressions per mile during daylight hours. Assuming an average annual mileage of 100,000, this totals 10.1 million impressions. The study further measured the visual impact of local delivery vans, for a total of 16 million visual impressions per year. Nighttime use of trucks adds another 37.5 percent to the previous numbers. Statistics show that over two-thirds of motorists favor the use of fleet graphics as a means of advertising.

In response to the positive appeal of fleet graphics, much of the industry has focused on "spicing up" the distribution fleets. One company, Eastern Foods, Inc., changed its trucks and tractors for their Naturally Fresh salad dressings from brown and white with yellow stripes to an elaborately produced rolling billboard of full-color vegetables and salad dressings.

The fleet graphics business is dependent on the truck-trailer market which is considered by some to be in a state of crisis. Trailer manufacturers are cutting capacity, consolidating production into fewer manufacturing plants, and finding ways to create long-term business partnerships with motor-carrier customers. The financial demands on the industry have heightened as a result of leveraged buy-outs on the part of major trailer manufacturers. Typically, the trucking industry has been restrictive in the amount of money companies allocate toward advertising, and this has become more pronounced in recent years. Improvements to the trailer business are dependent on the U.S. economy improving.

Advertising Agencies. Advertising agencies can be classified as international, national, regional, or local. Some agencies have hundreds of employees and service scores of large clients. Saatchi & Saatchi is one of the largest firms and has billings in excess of $11 billion. With increasing frequency, large companies are taking advertising activities inhouse. Some companies are doing a combination of inhouse and agency, while others "farm out" work to independents.

All advertising agencies are not full-service companies. A full-service agency generally employs account representatives, creative people, and media buyers. The firms are generally responsible for developing the creative strategy, analyzing market data, and buying media time. Advertising agencies usually work on a 15 percent commission. Creative boutiques, on the other hand, usually are responsible for writing and creating advertisements, but do not get involved in formulating advertising strategies.

Strategic Planning. Prior to Plumb's arrival, NSP did no formal strategic planning. Planning was always "seat of the pants" or whatever seemed right at the time. For example, the decision to get into interior design graphics came with the addition of a former staff member who had previous experience in the field—no market research was conducted.

Formal planning has been on the horizon for NSP for several years. Prior to 1990, the company's one attempt at formal planning came quite by accident. At a scheduled meeting between key management personnel and a major supplier, the supplier failed to show up. Consequently, the managers found themselves at loose ends and began talking about future directions. On reflection, Plumb believes those were the best two hours they had ever spent. He believes planning is a necessary evil. In 1990, Plumb developed a mission statement and long-term objectives for NSP as presented in Exhibits 6–1 and 6–2, respectively. No strides have been made toward formalized strategic planning since 1990. Of the long-term objectives presented to the management team in 1991, only one objective, "Increase ColorFX" was added to the list and none were removed.

EXHIBIT 6-1 NSP Corporate Graphics, Inc., Mission Statement

NSP will provide our customers with high quality products and service to enhance corporate image. Long-term enduring relationships will be developed with our customers and suppliers. A consistent, caring, and conscientious posture with all our contacts will be maintained through motivated co-owners in our ESOP company. NSPeople will keep a clear focus to provide integrity and responsiveness to our customers. A reasonable profit will be reinvested equally to our shareholders and employees, knowing that NSPeople are the driving force behind our product and service.

EXHIBIT 6-2 NSP Corporate Graphics, Inc., Long-term Objectives

1. Establish market niches(s), areas of diversification
2. Strive for 100 percent UV printing, if possible
3. Establish the art department as a profit center
4. Expand the CAMGraphix (computerized graphics)
5. Expand ColorFX
6. Purchase a new die cut machine or a TA 41 machine
7. Determine the feasibility of establishing an in-house advertising agency
8. Provide a computer station for each artist
9. Perfect the accounting system to trace costs
10. Establish a positive working environment
11. Examine the employee benefits program

Source: NSP Corporate Graphics, Inc.

In 1991, Plumb decided NSP would be everything to 300 top customers. "Everything" meant doing all corporate graphics for the client—from letterhead design to interior signage to fleet graphics. There was no magic associated with the number 300, no break-even point, no market research. Plumb's only rationale for this number was to take an average of his 5.5 salespeople (including himself) and multiply that times servicing the needs of about fifty to sixty accounts each.

Today, about 30 industrial accounts are the mainstay of NSP's revenue. The company services about 200 other accounts. While his plan of 300 has not been fully realized, Plumb feels NSP will meet this goal. He has been successful in spreading revenue dependence over more than one or two firms. A few years previously, Federal Express was NSP's primary account. NSP's new focus, however, is to capitalize on the art and graphics portion of their business.

The Federal Express Account. When Plumb joined NSP, he brought the Federal Express account with him, having first called on them in 1978. After fifteen years of a close working relationship, which is uncharacteristic of the industry, Plumb still feels the need to nurture Federal Express as if the company were a new account. Federal Express comprises 18 percent of NSP's annual business, although that percentage may increase in 1993. Of the six staff artists at NSP, one is fully devoted to the Federal Express account. NSP has received Federal Express's fleet graphics business and its entire corporate identity program.

Organizational Structure. The organizational structure of NSP is depicted in Exhibit 6–3. McGehee serves as chairman of the board and Plumb is president. Jim Davis is plant manager. Davis has been with NSP about sixteen years. Betty Stallings, comptroller and business manager, has been with NSP about fourteen years.

Neil McGee, who joined NSP in 1989 as a member of the art department, serves as marketing manager. Ken Roberts also joined NSP in 1990 as sales manager. A position of multi-media director was added to the staff in August 1993 and is held by Patrick Smith.

Bobbie Griggs came to the job of personnel specialist from the production area with no previous personnel experience. In selecting someone for this position, Plumb wanted a person with intelligence and initiative, and Bobbie seemed to fit that description. She has been with the company for approximately six years.

Employee Stock Ownership Program (ESOP). Getting employees involved in the profitability of the company was an idea that McGehee and Edwards shared from the early days of operation. In early 1981, McGehee became interested in a simplified employee pension (SEP) plan and operationalized it in 1983, the same year the company's net profit first broke $100,000, and dividends of $2 per share were declared. McGehee was not completely satisfied with the SEP because he wanted employees to feel more a part of the company. He soon became convinced that an ESOP was what his company needed. If employees were given the opportunity to buy into their own company, he believed they would take a greater interest in the business and the company would benefit. In 1985 NSP became one of the first small firms in America to bring the ESOP concept to its employees.

NSP is about 30 percent employee owned. No stockholder has a controlling interest in NSP. McGehee is the largest stockholder and maintains about 12 percent of the stock. This is apparent by the slogan on each employees' name tag: "If it has to be, it is up to me." The importance of the ESOP program is even proudly displayed in all

EXHIBIT 6-3 Organizational Structure of NSP Corporate Graphics, Inc.

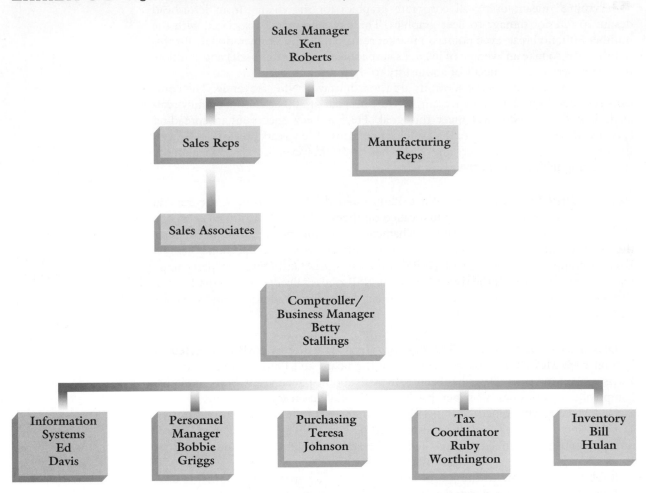

advertisements about NSP. Under terms of the plan, employees become eligible to participate after reaching age eighteen and after completing twelve consecutive months of employment. Contributions to the plan are based on a percentage of the salaries of participants, and the rate is set by the board of directors annually. Vesting in the program takes five years.

Employees annually receive a record of their ownership, and each year a distribution is made, even in years when NSP does poorly. McGehee feels the ESOP encourages quality and service because it motivates employees to work harder. As a result, craftsmanship, delivery, and installation are superior because they, as owners of the company, care about the products that are produced.

Pension Plan. The primary investment to the ESOP, according to the terms of the plan, is NSP stock. The contribution rates for 1992 and 1991 amounted to $36,940 and $54,731, respectively. During 1991, the ESOP purchased 183 shares of the Company's common stock that had been held as treasury stock. During 1989 the ESOP's purchase of 3,531 shares of the Company's common stock was financed with borrowed funds; the Company guaranteed to the lender that NSP would make contributions to the ESOP which were adequate to fund the debt service requirements of the loan.

EXHIBIT 6-3 *Continued*

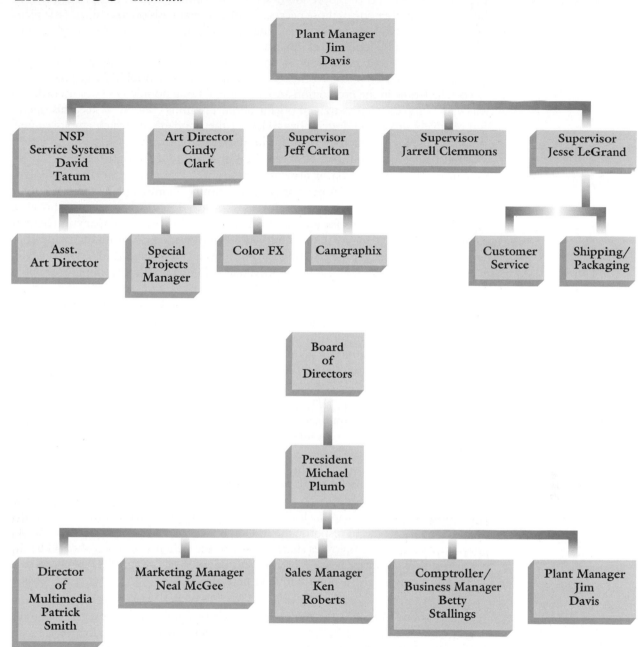

Personnel. The soul of NSP's operations is its 75 full-time employees. But no one in the company reflects the friendly, warm attitude of the NSPeople (as they fondly refer to themselves) more than Ruby Worthington. Known to employees and clients alike as "Miss Ruby," she had been receptionist and tax coordinator for fifteen years. Miss Ruby, according to Plumb, keeps the "southern warmth" in the business, something that NSP strives to retain.

Personnel activities, like most other aspects of NSP, are not formalized. Until recently, there was no employee job descriptions. Although job descriptions seem to Plumb to be another one of those necessary evils, his emphasis on formalizing the planning procedure extended to the development of descriptions for all NSP jobs to coincide with a merit system of performance evaluation. Plumb believes every employee should be able to do many jobs; cross training is the key to successful operations. This belief has been carried into the office. For example, in 1991 Bobbie Griggs continued to work half-time in the production area, and Larry Long doubled in sales. In order to achieve a completely cross-trained organization, Plumb is content to keep his operation relatively small. Job descriptions today set the standards by which employee performance is judged, something that previously was nonexistent at NSP.

Almost since its beginning, NSP operated one ten-hour shift four days per week. No one, with the exception of management and the office staff, worked on Friday. The company ran about 20 percent overtime hours. Plumb's philosophy is to pay overtime rather than hiring new employees. A team of graduate students who were analyzing NSP operations for a class project suggested that the company implement staggered shifts. Staggered shifts would allow employees to continue working four days, while at the same time covering the entire week. Staggered shifts began at NSP in November 1990. Concurrently, approximately 70 percent of the employees opted to work five eight-hour days.

Employees are on the honor system in regard to time worked. There are no time cards. The use of time cards, however, has become an issue among employees who feel that implementation of time cards are needed because too many employees are taking advantage of the honor system. Most employees do not find time cards to be an invasion of privacy, but do consider wearing uniforms problematic.

An area where Plumb has problems dealing with the honor system is in relation to sick days. Plumb is seldom sick; he has little tolerance for sickness and believes sick days are often used for extra time off. As a result, NSP's sick leave policy requires anyone who misses work due to illness on a Friday or Monday to submit a doctor's excuse.

NSP is not unionized and Plumb wants it to stay that way. Quarterly meetings are one way of allowing employees to voice concerns before problems get out of hand. Plumb noted some dissatisfaction among his staff in adjusting to his new niche strategy. Plumb feels that perhaps he is pushing his employees too hard without rewarding them for their efforts. In response, he has implemented a before-taxes profit-sharing program whereby all employees share equally in the benefits — from Michael to the people on the shop floor. Since establishment of the program, profits have been paid every quarter, averaging around $400 per person

Sales Force. Plumb is aware of the importance of a good sales force. "It used to be that if you were ethical and a nice guy you could keep a job. This is no longer the case. Today you have to be all that and good," he explained. "Today the three Ps of selling are price, product, and personality." Three sales representatives and two sales associates report to Ken Roberts. One of the sales representatives, Brad Hugall, operates out of the Auburn office, while the others operate primarily out of Georgia and Mississippi. The three manufacturer representatives extend the business into New York, Florida, and Texas. Much of their day-to-day selling is conducted by telephone.

Financial constraints are the reason for keeping the sales force small and relatively immobile. It is too costly to "go out and drum up business." Instead, Plumb elects to further develop existing accounts to provide all the corporate graphics — concentrating on exceptional art — for his accounts. This goal could be met without increasing the current size of the sales force. "If you develop a unique enough relationship with the customer, you can differentiate yourself from the masses."

NSP sales representatives operate in designated territories. The sales goal for all representatives is $1 million annually. Most are meeting that goal for 1993. Commissions are generally not affected by the profit margin on the specific sales. Compensation is based on a commission of 5 percent after a base level of $30,000 in sales is met. According to Plumb, while manufacturer representatives have added to the business, the company could not survive without full-time sales people. "It's the nature of the business—you can only count on your internal sales force," he explained.

Performance. NSP's balance sheet, statement of income and retained earnings, and statement of cash flows are displayed in Exhibits 6–4 — 6–6, respectively. In a comparison to 1990, cost of goods sold increased by 34.37 percent, operating expenses increased by 11.76 percent, and gross profits increased by a total of $660,694 in 1992. However, Comptroller Betty Stallings said 1993 will be the best year ever—"a dream year for us." "We have managed to implement controls that have finally gotten our cost of goods sold down and our profits up. We are finally headed in the right direction." Stallings added that an unexplained increase in original equipment business from existing customers like Federal Express will add to the expected increased profits in 1993. "I can't really put my finger on what we are doing right this year, but we are pleased with the results."

When Plumb took over the presidency, NSP began to take a better look at where the true costs of the business exist. NSP has implemented a "Covalent System" used for cost recovery, cost estimating, cost tracking, and cost inventory. The focus of this system is to make NSP more efficient. Maintaining good vendor relations has become as important as increasing sales. The Covalent System has also helped NSP identify product lines and markets where the company is not showing an adequate return. For example, the system indicated a poor return on its metal plate-printing operations which was then discontinued and sold. Inefficiencies in machine operations have also been identified through the Covalent System, as well as duplication of efforts. The latter became apparent in the supervision of four-color printing. Formerly, during the printing of four-color jobs an employee from the art department and the printing department would supervise the work. This unnecessary duplication increased job costs. The Covalent System allows NSP employees to know exactly where jobs are in the production process in order to keep clients more adequately informed as to a project's status. One downside of the Covalent System has been the response from employees. "I think many of our employees think we forced the system on them," Stallings said. NSP is in the process of changing the Covalent System through employee interview process.

Services Provided. NSP is a company dedicated to superior corporate art and graphics; however, the firm still does fleet graphic work. Services provided by NSP can be divided into eight categories:

1. *Truckgraphix®*. Truckagraphix® is the trademark name for NSP's larger-than-life decals for the side of company vehicles. The decals offer a more cost-effective method of identification than paint and is used by more than 85 percent of trucks on the road today. Additionally, the decals last almost four times longer than painting. NSP's capabilities span from a simple one-color mark to full-color photographic reproductions, which are light-reflective for easy visibility at night.

EXHIBIT 6-4 NSP Corporate Graphics, Inc., Schedules of Cost of Goods Sold for Years Ended December 31

	1992	1991	1990
Assets			
Current Assets			
Cash	$ 25,070	$ 102,359	$ 32,327
Trade accounts receivable (net)	1,114,853	1,072,378	981,550
Receivable from employees	4,019	1,993	—
Income tax refunds receivables	—	16,001	—
Other receivables	1,613	113	5,221
Inventories	572,532	788,288	790,665
Prepaid expenses	44,834	27,481	43,190
Total current assets	1,762,921	2,008,613	1,852,953
Property, Plant, and Equipment			
Land	10,613	10,613	10,613
Land improvements	38,197	32,212	6,031
Buildings and improvements	676,086	635,803	645,242
Furniture, fixtures, and equipment	1,535,781	1,165,500	1,112,099
Vehicles	36,858	36,858	36,492
	2,297,535	1,880,986	1,810,477
Less accumulated depreciation			
Net Property, plant, and equipment	1,057,770	881,769	764,356
	1,239,765	999,217	1,046,121
Other Assets			
Deposits	—	—	—
Total Assets	$3,002,686	$3,007,830	$2,899,134
Liabilities and Stockholders' Equity			
Current Liabilities			
Line of credit	—	291,034	268,035
Bank overdraft	—	—	—
Current portion of notes, capital			
Leases payable	100,850	41,527	62,013
Current portion ESOP note payable	—	—	—
Accounts payable	208,262	359,470	235,677
Accrued salaries and wages	37,509	41,888	32,256
Accrued interest	4,403	5,285	5,953
Accrued income tax	33,891	—	—
Deferred income tax	—	—	11,875
Payroll, sales taxes payable	14,494	17,238	66,062
Pension plan contribution payable	3,358	—	—
Total current liabilities	402,767	756,442	681,871
Long-term Liabilities			
Notes and capital leases payable net of			
current portion	289,848	37,051	59,293
ESOP note payable	195,736	223,575	307,947
Deferred income taxes	115,982	113,744	95,780
Total long-term liabilities	601,566	374,370	463,020
			(62,013)
Total Liabilities	$1,004,333	$1,130,812	$1,082,878

Source: NSP Corporate Graphics, Inc.

EXHIBIT 6-5 NSP Corporate Graphics, Inc., Balance Sheets for Years Ended December 31

	1992	1991	1990
Inventory, beginning of year	$ 788,288	$ 790,664	$ 168,740
Production department			
Purchases	2,091,337	2,042,837	1,869,483
Salaries	625,643	616,033	612,266
Scotchprint	48,146	—	—
Professional services	4,581	—	—
Application labor expenses	1,497	6,735	1,878
Depreciation	160,222	132,360	126,272
Freight	12,085	7,172	3,133
Insurance	149,088	107,450	112,428
Taxes	56,445	51,823	49,626
Supplies	99,567	95,000	91,353
Repairs and maintenance	45,564	26,460	30,819
Utilities	46,992	48,112	45,855
Contract labor	96,684	136,612	52,529
Uniforms	9,402	9,744	9,355
Rent	8,043	6,721	6,000
Refunds	—	—	140
Travel	5,557	7,604	7,176
Miscellaneous	6,906	5,034	107,997
Total costs—production	3,467,699	3,299,697	3,126,310
Art department			
Salaries	170,809	165,553	136,310
Supplies	10,465	10,194	12,440
Contract labor	47,606	26,600	20,010
Insurance	10,224	16,691	11,215
Taxes	13,682	13,429	10,900
Repairs and maintenance	8,452	2,442	3,176
Miscellaneous	3,720	1,401	5,055
Total costs—art	264,958	236,310	198,991
Application department			
Salaries	58,057	53,042	61,898
Supplies	615	988	1,899
Contract labor	2,968	5,510	361
Taxes	4,709	4,326	5,069
Travel	11,203	15,256	16,568
Repairs and maintenance	851	695	4,999
Insurance	7,293	7,223	14,681
Depreciation	3,072	3,072	3,072
Miscellaneous	239	242	7,244
Total costs—application	89,007	90,354	115,791
Goods available for sale	4,609,952	4,417,025	3,440,092
Less inventory, end of year	572,532	788,288	790,664
Costs of goods sold	$4,037,420	$3,628,737	$2,649,428

EXHIBIT 6-5 *Continued*

	1992	1991	1990
Stockholders' Equity			
Common stock—authorized 30,000 shares; $10 par value per share; issued 27,134 shares at December 31, 1989 and 22,665 shares at December 31, 1988	271,344	271,344	271,334
Additional paid in capital	602,167	602,168	575,324
Retained earnings	1,377,068	1,285,115	1,285,115
Less			
Treasury stock at cost, 3,163 shares at December 31, 1989 and 1988	(28,393)	(28,393)	(12,529)
ESOP contra account	(223,833)	(253,215)	(303,090)
Dividends paid	—	—	—
Total stockholders' equity	1,998,353	1,877,018	1,816,256
Total Liabilities and Stockholders' Equity	$3,002,686	$3,007,830	$2,899,134

Source: NSP Corporate Graphics, Inc.

EXHIBIT 6-6 NSP Corporate Graphics, Inc., Income Statement for December 31

	1992	1991	1990
Sales	$5,211,588	$4,647,779	$4,484,290
Cost of Goods Sold	4,037,420	3,628,737	2,649,428
Gross profit	1,174,168	1,019,042	1,834,862
Operating expenses			
General and administrative	388,280	335,139	304,724
Sales	544,704	522,335	518,511
	932,984	857,474	823,235
Income from operations	241,184	161,568	1,011,672
ESOP contribution	—	—	—
Other income and (expenses)	(73,046)	(97,104)	(50,797)
Net income (loss)	$ 168,138	$ 64,464	$ 960,830

Source: NSP Corporate Graphics, Inc.

Truckgraphix® is used by such customers as Eastern Foods (Naturally Fresh), Food World, and Delta Airlines (ground equipment).

2. *Creative design systems.* The company has professionally trained graphic designers who can revise and update an existing logo or create a total corporate identity program.

3. *Durabanners®.* Durabanners® is the registered name of NSP's posters and banners of the business. Made with state-of-the-art equipment, the pressure-sensitive vinyl banners are created to last up to seven years.

4. *Architectural and environmental graphics.* A new service offered by NSP, architectural and environmental graphics includes design services for both internal and external reimaging. This group includes signage, color bars, geometric shapes and symbols, and worded messages, that can be used to modernize a facility.

5. *Decor.* The decor group deals with internal signage for supermarkets, drug and soft goods retailers, hardware and auto parts stores, and convenience and department stores. This group includes such things as banners, aisle markers, shelf talkers, and displays.

6. *Corporate graphics.* A diversified venture for NSP is corporate graphics. For interested customers, NSP will design a complete graphics package for a company that includes logos and letterhead paper.

7. *Original equipment manufacturers.* NSP produces decals for installation by the manufacturer on such products as lawn mowers, ladders, boats, trailers, and snowmobiles. This market is a difficult market to break into because manufacturers rarely change this type of graphics from current suppliers.

8. *ColorFX.* A new venture for NSP is ColorFX. ColorFX is a 4-color process achieved by computerized electrostatic printing. This process allows NSP to do color processing on a small scale for customers.

9. *Service systems.* Installation is a final step to NSP's graphics. The company provides customers with either personal installation or a detailed how-to book for easy application.

Plumb believes that it is important to service NSP accounts completely. So, if a client needs something that NSP cannot provide, NSP should find someone who could. An example of this is storefront awnings. NSP had the screen-printing capabilities but did not supply awnings. Management, therefore, found a small mom-and-pop operation that could supply awnings, and the job went to NSP.

While most of NSP's graphics work is done by computer, the art department is capable of producing work far beyond computer graphics—whatever the client wants.

NEW VENTURES

For about $350 million NSP recently purchased 3M's Scotchprint machine. This new investment is "ColorFX," a take off on the *FX* and *FX2* special effects movies. ColorFX is designed to enhance NSP's art capabilities and shifts the company away from the fleet industry. At the time of the purchase, only nine companies in the U.S., six in Europe, and two in the Orient owned a Scotchprint machine. ColorFX allows NSP to do 4-color processing without color separations. With the addition of ColorFX, color processing can be done on any scale—large or small. With the change in strategy, Plumb sees the need to change attitudes. No longer will his sales force tell the customer what NSP can do, instead they will ask "what are your needs?" Thus far, the sale of ColorFX has been slower than anticipated. Customers needing ColorFX are different from fleet graphics customers, something to which the salesforce is still adjusting. Target customers for the new product are advertising agencies, outdoor advertisers, and the retail point-of-purchase market. "We are still on the learning curve," admitted Stallings. "But, we are trying to tap into the grocery business—if we can do that, we will be on our way to profitability. Right now, however, our fleet business is keeping us operating."

As might be expected, Plumb has *never* been afraid to try new ventures. He "lives on the edge" in his business—always wanting to be the first out of the starting blocks. One venture that Plumb previously entertained was the production and sales of a lighted table. Plumb commissioned two engineering professors at Auburn University to design and build a table for their use. Because the resulting table was perfectly suited for NSP's large-scale graphic work, Plumb considered producing and selling the table to competitors. "Someone is going to eventually build such a table and market it. Why shouldn't it be us?" he asked. However, members of his management staff convinced him that their time would be better served concentrating on their primary business. As a result, NSP is investigating obtaining and then selling a patent for the table.

Back-lighted signs were the last NSP venture, prior to ColorFX. Through a working agreement with the 3M Corporation, NSP has implemented a "roll 'n' ship" program that allows them to design signage on one of 3M's translucent films that can be rolled into easily transportable tubes for damage-free shipping. This program allows firms with multilocation backlighted signs to portray a consistent image.

CONCLUSION

Plumb is an aggressive entrepreneur. He spends much of his time in day-to-day operations trying to better NSP. He does not move conservatively. He is a risk taker, full of new ideas for NSP. He is convinced the only way to survive is through his niche strategy. Only two years previously, he felt the only way to survive was to diversify, to concentrate on his chosen 300 accounts and provide any service that they requested. He sees many new opportunities on the horizon including the Olympics in 1996. With NSP's close proximity to Atlanta, he feels his company is a natural to capitalize on any available business. Plumb is going to be there—and he plans to be at the forefront.

Plumb believes in NSP, and he believes in the concept of ESOP. With employees in command of the company, he feels the company can only get better. As he puts it, "We control our own destiny because we own our own destiny."

CASE 7

SPLATTERBALL ADVENTURE GAMES, INC.—1993

BETH JACK AND
MARILYN M. HELMS
The University of
Tennessee at Chattanooga

Splatterball Adventure Games, Inc., (615-842-8766), based in Chattanooga, Tennessee, conducts paintball or "simulation war" games. The company also maintains a store located in East Ridge, Tennessee, approximately five miles outside of Chattanooga. The playing field location for the game is Apison, Tennessee, approximately twenty miles from Chattanooga. The company has one principal, Mr. Doug Gray, who monitors games, conducts sales, and repairs guns. He has outside help for accounting services and hires part-time help on the field when necessary. The company has not made a profit during the past two years.

Paintball became popular on a national level in the early 1980s and includes both amateur and professional players in the sport. The development of the professional player occurred in the late 1980s. Like other sports, professional status is obtained when players earn money for playing paintball. In the case of paintball, money is earned by winning tournaments. Some of these tournaments have first place prizes as high as $30,000 for a ten member team. For a team to be designated as a professional team, three-fifths of the members must be professional players.

Paintball is played mainly in the United States. As of October 9, 1993, the periodical *Paintball News* listed 250 different paintball playing fields in 44 states in their directory. Another 14 fields in Canada and Mexico are also represented. At least 23 fields exist in California alone. It is difficult to know exactly how many fields do exist outside the United States because many are located in countries that consider the guns used in paintball illegal.

The American Paintball League (APL) was established in mid-1992 and includes more than 200 member fields. According to Mike Fugarino of APL, the sport appears to be growing steadily, but very little empirical data exists to support this hypothesis. Paintball groups are a loose coalition, with no definitive national representation beyond national periodicals. According to the September 11, 1993, issue of *Paintball News,* more than 800 people competed in the 1993 International Amateur Paintball Open in Cranberry, Pennsylvania, held in August. More than $50,000 in prize money was awarded.

Development of the sport has led to standard governing. Several different governing organizations do exist, but the most prevalent is the International Paintball Players' Associations (IPPA). This organization organizes tournaments, establishes guidelines, monitors pending legislation that may be harmful to the industry, and attempts to bring together the participants in paintball.

There are several variations in the way paintball is played depending on location of field, type of field, and field operator. Tournaments usually follow IPPA rules.

Standard equipment for all players include comfortable clothing and shoes for running through obstacles. Many people choose to wear camouflage although it is not necessary. All players must wear protective eye goggles whenever on the field. Also required are guns, carbon-dioxide tanks, and paintballs. All of the equipment, with the exception of the clothing, can be bought or rented from the field operator.

Additional equipment used by regular players includes semi-automatic guns, gun cleaners, replacement parts for guns, vests, and speedloaders. This equipment is allowed in tournament play and is used to increase the performance and ability of the players. Supplies can be ordered from vendors across the country or purchased from paintball specialty stores. Most advertise in *Paintball News,* a industry trade publication.

Games are usually played in densely wooded areas. This gives players obstacles to hide behind and adds to the difficulty of the game. The games can be played in large backyards, however there are usually not enough obstacles for effective play. Paintball is not played in parks unless prior approval is received from park managers or area officials. The paint used in the paintball is water-based and environmentally safe, but it still leaves marks on trees and other obstacles until there is enough rain to wash the paint away. Also, the plastic casing around the paintball will be left behind.

The object of paintball is to capture the opponent team's flag and return it to your own flag station. Flags remain at stations until a member of the opposing team captures it. Flag stations are simply a small area from which a flag is hung from a tree or from a pole placed in a clearing.

The area around a flag station varies from field to field. In some cases, there will be a natural barrier from which a player can defend the station. In other cases, the area is wide and open and must be defended from its perimeter. If a person who has captured the flag is shot while carrying the flag, the flag is considered "dead." It cannot simply be transferred to another teammate. That individual must return the flag to its original station to be recaptured by another team member.

There are two main differences in tournament play and casual play. In casual play, the team returning the captured flag to its own station wins the game. However, in tournament play, teams advance through round-robin brackets in a point system. Points are awarded for the number of opposing players shot, first flag pulled, and returning the flag to one's own flag station. There are point penalties for safety violations, foul or abusive language, and physical contact during a game. The maximum number of points awarded is one hundred.

Each member of a team carries a carbon-dioxide based gun that shoots the paintball. The original guns were pressed plastic with few moving parts. The carbon-dioxide came in small metal tubes that were pierced when inserted into the gun and would shoot approximately twenty to thirty rounds of paintballs. The guns now used have become more complicated with more moving parts. These guns are made of metal and often more closely resemble real guns. Manufacturers have begun to introduce new types of guns such as semi-automatics. Carbon-dioxide used in the guns can be obtained in refillable tanks and used for an entire game.

Paintballs are about the size of a large marble. They were originally made of oil-based paint enclosed in a thin plastic shell. This quickly changed because once this paint dried onto clothing, it was extremely difficult to remove. The paintballs are now water–based and come in a wide variety of colors. Most fields avoid using red so injuries are not mistaken for paint. The manufacturing process for paintballs is constantly being improved so that a more uniform ball can be made for better accuracy.

Professional teams have been reduced from fifteen member teams to either ten or five member teams. This development has occurred so that games could be played under a forty-five minute time limit. Amateur games, usually played on weekends, are not as strict about time limits and the number of members on a team. Usually the field operator will instruct individuals to form two to four teams, depending on the number of people at the field. They try not to allow more than twenty-five players on a team, if possible. Games are usually limited to one hour, although amateur games tend to end within thirty minutes. Tournament events can have an average of 20 teams participating.

The typical paintball player is male. Only three percent are women, and they tend to play primarily at the amateur level. The average professional player is between 22 and 35 years old, while the average casual player is between 18 and 30 years old. Players come from a wide variety of backgrounds, including professional managers, physicians, blue-collar workers, and students.

Tournaments are sponsored year round in the United States. For the month of October 1993, for example, 31 paintball tournaments throughout the United States were listed and 29 were listed for November 1993. More than 2,000 individuals per month participate in U.S. tournaments. The most prestigious tournament takes place every October in Nashville, Tennessee. This tournament, the International Masters

Tournament, is the biggest of its kind with a sixty-four team field and a $30,000 first prize. This tournament lasts five days and includes both five-member and ten-member team competitions. This tournament usually includes at least two British teams every year. The top eight finishers of this tournament are able to obtain sponsorship from manufacturers of paintball equipment. This tournament is also a chance for vendors to display their new products and innovations to players.

HISTORY OF SPLATTERBALL ADVENTURE GAMES, INC.

Splatterball Adventure Games, Inc. in Chattanooga, Tennessee runs local paintball games and maintains a retail store that sells paintball supplies and repairs guns. It is through this store that many games are scheduled.

The owner, Doug Gray, began his involvement with the sport of paintball in 1981 as a member of a small team based in Chattanooga. Many of the players lived in Nashville so the group decided to open a field there. Mr. Gray is still an active member of the Nashville Ridgerunners Professional Paintball Team. The field in Nashville is very successful at organizing paintball tournaments and bringing in teams from the entire Southeast region.

There is no longer a field in Chattanooga, so Mr. Gray drives two hours to Nashville almost every weekend to play the sport. Mr. Gray gets his friends and acquaintances to go to Nashville with him in order to play. During a recent trip, Mr. Gray considered opening a field of his own in Chattanooga so he could practice closer to home. Eventually, he was able to generate enough local interest in paintball to support his field in Chattanooga.

Mr. Gray leased a parcel of land approximately 20 miles southeast of Chattanooga. According to Mr. Gray, "since this was more of a hobby than business, I decided to run the operations from my home." He bought some of the plastic guns to use for rentals so he could continue to bring new players to his field.

Mr. Gray worked closely with the Nashville field in setting up his own field. His close ties enabled him to obtain many of his supplies at volume discount prices, as well as gain other advantages that would otherwise have been denied to him as an independent.

Mr. Gray's business continued to grow as paintball began to receive national attention. Businesses and groups began to schedule games for their members. As his business expanded, Mr. Gray began to carry more rental equipment and supplies for the part-time player.

Eventually the business grew so large it became difficult to manage from his home. The rental equipment took up so much room that he decided it was time to establish a center of operations. However, in order to make this feasible, Mr. Gray needed an infusion of capital for the store lease, furniture lease, and additional equipment. He estimated the total cost to be $7,500. It was at this time he took in one partner and the business incorporated with each partner owning five hundred shares of stock.

Unfortunately, the partnership was not successful. Both partners had differing ideas on how the income should be distributed. Mr. Gray wanted most of the money reinvested into the business for further growth. However, his partner decided he wanted his capital infusion paid back immediately. After one year the partnership was dissolved through Mr. Gray's purchase of his partner's five hundred shares of stock for $11,000. The original investment was $10,000, and his partner had received approximately $1,200 in capital withdrawals when the repurchase was made.

The Situation in 1993. Today, Mr. Gray is the sole stockholder of Splatterball and has decided to reevaluate what he is trying to accomplish. What is the future of Splatterball? Where is he trying to go with the business? How does he get there?

The business is quickly becoming a full-time operation. Hours of operation of the store are 11 A.M. to 3 P.M. Monday through Friday. The store is only open on weekends if no games are being played at the field. Mr. Gray would like to increase the hours of operation but is not currently in the position to do so. He has a full time job as a computer programmer, and he works from 4 P.M. to 12:15 A.M. during the week. Eventually, he would like to leave this position and have the paintball business as his primary source of income.

The store generates some walk-in business, often from people who play the game on their own property. Mr. Gray offers gun repair services and sells guns, supplies, and trade magazines. Most of Splatterball's income, however, is derived from the games. The field is available year-round but games are scheduled in advance, especially during winter months. With scheduling, necessary supplies can be ordered, and the appropriate number of field judges can be obtained. Splatterball only keeps one hundred rental guns in stock, so if extremely large groups play, Mr. Gray has to borrow guns from other fields. He has worked out an agreement with a field in Atlanta in which each field makes guns available to the other at no charge.

Since 1990, Splatterball has had its own professional and amateur teams that play regularly at the field and in national tournaments. These teams have no sponsorship, and there is no fee to become a member. Each member is responsible for all tournament entry fees and their own supplies. Mr. Gray relies heavily on his professional team members to give their support in running the store and in officiating games when they are not playing. Their compensation is in the form of discounts on supplies and gun repairs. Individuals playing the game with a group who decide that they would like to play on a regular basis are recruited as new members. These individuals will generally play with the team for six months before becoming a team member.

Currently, almost all games are scheduled on Saturdays and Sundays. Groups may schedule the field for an entire day. It is also possible for Mr. Gray to run games during the week before 2 P.M. Splatterball continues to sponsor walk-on games on weekends, enabling individuals to try paintball without having to find other players to make up two teams. In addition to the typical player, Mr. Gray has some school groups that regularly rent the field for an entire day.

Mr. Gray's business background includes several years of college courses in addition to his own trial and error experience gained since he first started Splatterball in 1981. He has taken a small business management course at a local junior college, but feels that he learned the most about management from starting the business. When asked about his management style, Mr. Gray says, "I am a doer out of necessity, but a delegator by nature. I am great at long-range planning and need to be careful not to forget the small daily details that keep me in business."

COMPETITION

Splatterball's competition is primarily from the amusement industry in general and specifically from other paintball fields. Movies, music, and sport hunting are just a few examples of the broad range of amusement competition from the leisure-time industries. Because of the great deal of physical activity involved, Mr. Gray feels he competes for the physical fitness dollar as well.

Competition between paintball fields is very friendly. The closest fields to Chattanooga are in Atlanta, Knoxville, and Nashville. A directly competing field opened in Chattanooga during 1992 but remained in business only a few months. Each of these fields are approximately a two-hour drive from Chattanooga so Gray does not compete directly with them for local players. Instead, he has worked out arrangements enabling each field to host participating regional teams in league play. This league has eight teams from Chattanooga, Nashville, Atlanta, Kentucky, and Birmingham. The teams play eight times on the first Sunday of each month from March through October at different field locations. This arrangement gives each team a chance to play at various fields on a competitive level. Although a trophy is awarded to the team accumulating the most points at the end of the tournament year, the main purpose of the league is to provide practice opportunities to prepare for major tournaments.

Most fields in this league are about the same size as the Chattanooga field, with the exception of Nashville. The Nashville field is four times the size of the Splatterball field and has an agreement with a local campground to use the campground area for major tournaments in the Spring and Fall. As it is privately held, the exact earnings of the Nashville operation is unknown but is estimated by Mr. Gray to be around $1,000,000 annually, including field operations, specialty store operations, and tournaments.

In the physical fitness area, Splatterball has been able to work in cooperation with different programs. The game has been included as an activity in an intensive six week fitness program in Chattanooga and has been used to build self-confidence as well as physical fitness. Unfortunately, the executive games segment of the paintball market has not grown as expected. There are a few small businesses that use the games for team-building exercises and require employees to participate. Their best group is the McCallie School, a local boys private preparatory high school that plays once every couple of months. Splatterball also competes with the hobby/entertainment industry in general. Often it can be heard around the field that someone played that weekend instead of hunting or buying some personal item.

COSTS

The cost of playing Splatterball depends on the experience level of the player. Novice players have lower costs, because they usually rent all their equipment. Mr. Gray charges a $22.52 flat field fee which includes a $12 gun rental, forty rounds of paint, and one small tank of carbon-dioxide. Novice players generally shoot less than more experienced players and often to not have to purchase extra paint. The typical charge is $1.08 for one tube of paint (eight rounds).

An experienced player tends to incur higher costs since most purchase their own guns which start at $150 each. Also, there is the purchase of camouflage gear and extra supplies and accessories to maintain the performance of their equipment. It is not uncommon for an experienced player to shoot thirty tubes of paint per game. Since most play a minimum of three, forty-five minute games, costs can be high.

Players that are part of a team often have higher expenses than those incurred by the experienced player. Many own several backup guns in case of gun failure. These failures are usually due to wear on parts and do not occur regularly, but if a gun fails during a tournament, the team will be short a player. Also, there are entrance fees for tournaments which can be as much as $200 per member. The July 31, 1993, issue of *Paintball News* indicated that professional tournaments are charging as much as $1,850 in entry fees and awarding up to $40,000 in prize money.

Splatterball Adventure Games, Inc. has a very "loose" accounting system. Mr. Gray has recently taken advantage of an offer of free accounting services in exchange for 100 shares of stock. Mr. Gray now owns 900 shares of the 1,500 shares with 500 shares retained by the business. Bill, the accountant, often works on weekends but does not get involved with the operation of the games.

Exhibits 7–1 and 7–2 show the current financial statements for 1991 and 1992. The largest debt is Mr. Gray's repayment of $7,500 of the original $11,000 loan used to repurchase the stock from his former partner. Other expenses, such as supplies, can usually be directly matched to sales since most supplies are received within two days of use to eliminate spoilage. Paintballs have a shelf-life of several months, but tend to become soft. Thus, the sooner they are used, the better they perform.

Mr. Gray has had an offer from two of his team members to work in the business for 150 shares of stock each. One is a computer programmer with a college degree, and the other assists in the management of his family's convenience store. These two players have helped Mr. Gray run Splatterball for four years. Neither would invest any money, but instead would reinvest their share of the profits plus provide free services. They have offered to assist in running games and working in the store to increase the hours of store operations. Both are experienced in gun repair and would be able to assist in this aspect of the business as well. Both individuals would be able to work during the hours Mr. Gray is at his full-time job. Mr. Gray has considered this offer for several years and has consulted with an attorney as to the fair value and distribution of future income either through dividends or salaries. Currently, no changes have been made and Mr. Gray continues to pay these two individuals to work in the store and assist on the field when necessary.

LEGAL ISSUES

The current legal environment is of great concern to Splatterball. Although every player signs a waiver form (See Exhibit 7–3) each time they play, these waivers have not been tested through a lawsuit. Mr. Gray has had several attorneys review his form and has always received approval.

Injuries are one of the main concerns for Mr. Gray. Two years ago a new player was hit in the eye with a paintball and lost his vision. This player had taken his goggles off even though he had been instructed not to and had signed a waiver stating he would wear the goggles at all times. In this particular instance, Splatterball was very lucky as a spectator had taken a picture of the injured player not wearing the required safety goggles. This picture prevented a negligence lawsuit. However, the potential legal problems were brought to the forefront by this incident.

The entire paintball industry has worked hard to promote safe usage practices both on and off the field. *Paintball Sports Magazine* has published several articles regarding safe usage of guns. Tournaments impose penalties against teams whenever a players is found not wearing goggles. Off the field, gun barrels are required to have plugs so if accidentally discharged, the paintball will break in the gun. Field operators monitor how hard guns are shooting the paintball. They calibrate, or chronograph, guns to ensure they do not shoot so hard as to injure a player. Even though the guns are carefully monitored, being hit by a paintball hurts. If shot from close range, the paintball leaves a bruise and occasionally a small welt. Welts, although painful, disappear within one to two days with no special attention required.

Most fields, including Splatterball, and all tournaments discourage shooting other players in the head. They have simply ruled that head shots do not count as "kills" or points. If a player is hit in the head, he or she may call a judge over to help him or her

EXHIBIT 7-1 Splatterball Adventure Games, Inc. Income Statement for the Years Ended 1991 and 1992

	1991	1992
INCOME		
Sales	$7,107.00	$11,742.00
Net Sales	7,107.00	11,742.00
COST OF GOODS SOLD		
Total Cost of Goods Sold	0.00	0.00
Gross Profit	7,107.00	11,742.00
EXPENSES		
Advertising	2,195.00	800.00
Auto Expense	15.22	
Bank Service Charges	22.50	48.00
Bank Wire Transfer Fees	18.00	
Casual Labor	175.00	300.00
Dues & Subscriptions	58.00	58.00
Entertainment	173.28	60.00
Entry Fees	278.00	180.00
Miscellaneous Expense	190.10	163.12
Office Expense	377.69	233.01
Paint & CO2 Supplies	6,280.71	8,004.73
Postage	10.24	26.68
Rent	100.00	750.00
Field Supplies	1,204.97	1,621.11
Telephone	111.88	367.48
Uniforms	128.56	
Total Expenses	11,339.15	12,612.13
Net Operating Income	(4,232.15)	(870.13)
OTHER INCOME		
Interest Income	13.00	0.00
Total Other Income	13.00	0.00
OTHER EXPENSES		
Total Other Expenses	0.00	0.00
Income Before Taxes	(4,219.15)	(870.13)

Source: Splatterball Adventure Games, Inc.

wipe off the paint. The judge will declare the player neutral until the paint is removed, and the player is put back into the game.

Whenever new players come to the field, they are given instructions before the game begins. The field operator walks over the field with new players to point out boundaries, the flag station location, and any areas players need to avoid because of potential injury.

The entire splatterball industry has worked together in regards to concerns regarding equipment. There have been attempts in several states, most notably California where there are several major fields, to ban the sale of toys that closely resemble guns.

EXHIBIT 7-2 Splatterball Adventure Games, Inc., Balance Sheet for the Years Ended 1991 and 1992

ASSETS	1991	1992
CURRENT ASSETS		
Cash	(1,777.58)	216.12
Inventory	260.99	318.00
Total Current Assets	(1,516.59)	534.12
FIXED ASSETS		
Office Equipment	189.95	149.28
Paint Guns	8,539.10	8,740.63
Field Equipment	2,592.25	2,038.44
Total Fixed Assets	11,321.30	10,928.35
OTHER ASSETS		
Total Other Assets	0.00	0.00
TOTAL ASSETS	9,804.71	11,462.47
Liabilities & Equity		
CURRENT LIABILITIES		
Accounts Payable	1,145.00	2,953.40
Notes Payable	11,363.26	7,680.42
Sales Tax Payable	515.60	698.78
Total Current Liabilities	13,023.86	11,332.60
LONG TERM LIABILITIES		
Total Long Term Liabilities	0.00	0.00
Total Liabilities	13,023.86	11,332.60
STOCKHOLDERS EQUITY		
Common Stock	1,000.00	1,000.00
Current Earnings	(4,219.15)	(870.13)
TOTAL EQUITY	(3,219.15)	129.87
TOTAL LIABILITIES AND CAPITAL	9,804.71	11,462.47

Source: Splatterball Adventure Games, Inc.

EXHIBIT 7-3 Splatterball Adventure Games, Inc., Application to Play

WAIVER OF LIABILITY AND ASSUMPTION OF RISK

1. I, the undersigned wish to play the Splatterball Adventure game. I recognize and understand that playing the game involves running certain risks. Those risks include, but are not limited to, the risk of injury relating from the impact of the paint pellets used in the Game. Injuries resulting from possible malfunction of equipment used in the Game and injuries resulting from tripping or falling over obstacles in the Game playing field. In addition, I recognize that the exertion of playing the game could result in injury or death.

2. Despite these and other risks, and fully understanding such risks, I wish to play the Game and hereby assume the risks of playing the Game. I also hereby hold harmless Splatterball Adventure Game, Inc., hereafter called the Sponsors, and John Felts (landowner) and indemnify them against any and all claims, actions, suits, procedures, costs, expenses (including attorney's fees and expenses), damages and liabilities arising out of, connected with, or resulting from my playing the Game, including without limitation, those resulting from the manufacture, selection, delivery, possession, use or operation of such equipment. I hereby release the Sponsors from any and all such liability, and I understand that this release shall be binding upon my estate, my heirs, my representatives and assigns. I hereby certify to the Sponsors that I am in good health and do not suffer from a heart condition or other ailment which could be exacerbated by the exertion involved in playing the Game.

3. I hereby promise to play the Game only in accordance with the rules of the Game as set forth by the Sponsors. In particular, I agree:
   a. to wear safety goggles at all times when I am on the playing field or at the target area, even after I have been marked with paint or the game is over and to keep the goggles snug by pulling the straps tight; I understand that serious eye injury, including loss of eyesight, could occur if the safety goggles are not on when marking pistols may be discharged anywhere near me. Should my safety goggles fog up or for any reason be such that I cannot see through them properly, I will ask someone near me, on the playing field or in the target area, to lead me out of the area I am into to one where all marking pistols are on "SAFETY". Only then will I remove my safety goggles to clean them. I understand that any "safety goggle" is subject to fogging up or getting dirty and that if I am anywhere near a marking pistol as it discharges, and my "safety goggles" are not properly on, I may get seriously and permanently injured;
   b. to avoid any physical contact of fighting with other players;
   c. to stay within the boundaries of the playing field and not to chase or run after anyone over ledges or mountainous terrain; and
   d. to keep the marking pistol I am using on "safety" (the no-shoot position) in the staging area at all times, in the target area while not shooting and on the playing field before and after each game, to aim or point the pistol at another person ONLY during an active game and never to wave or brandish the pistol about in the staging area or the target area.
   e. to avoid pointing at or shooting at the head of any player at any time.

4. For safety reasons I agree to use only equipment and/or supplies provided to me by the Sponsors while playing the game or in the target area. Written permission of the Sponsors is necessary should I elect to use other equipment or supplies. If I have chosen not to use the goggles or marking pistol available from the Sponsors, I hereby certify that the goggles or marking pistol, which I have chosen to use, are at least as safe as the Sponsor's form claims arising out of any additional risk resulting from my use of goggles or marking pistol other than those available from the Sponsors.

5. I agree to ask the Sponsor for clarification of any rule or safety procedure, for further instruction as regard anything that I don't understand about the equipment and supplies as regards anything else that may effect the safety of or playing of the Game.

6. I have read this waiver of liability and assumption of risk carefully, and understand that by signing below, I am agreeing, on behalf of myself, my estate, my heirs, representatives and assigns not to sue the Splatterball Adventure Games, Inc. or to hold them or their insurors liable for any injury including death, resulting from my playing the Game, I intend to be fully bound by this Agreement.

By virtue of my signature, I acknowledge and agree to all terms and conditions set forth on this form.

X Signature _____

Date signed _____

Is this your first visit to our field?   YES ( ) NO ( )

Source: Splatterball Adventure Games, Inc.

This is due to the publicity surrounding some shootings of children because someone thought they had real guns. Because the newer guns resemble real guns, the industry is notably concerned.

Teams, field operators, and suppliers try to keep paintball games as safe as possible. Because of the nature of the sport, there are sometimes injuries, but most injuries can be avoided. These same people have also worked hard to keep the sport legal in all states through letter writing campaigns and lobbying.

THE FUTURE

Mr. Gray would eventually like to turn Splatterball into his full time job. "If I could create a larger demand in the off-season, I could depend on Splatterball as my sole source of income," he states. The addition of shareholders to ease the financial burden of expansion is another consideration of Mr. Gray's. It would enable Splatterball to run more games, especially during the week.

There is no real marketing strategy in place for Splatterball although Mr. Gray feels one is needed. He has some informational brochures available for distribution, but the main source of new business comes from word of mouth. Mr. Gray would like to implement a strategy that will not deplete too much of his personal financial resources, yet still enable him to work full time in his hobby.

Prepare a strategic plan for Mr. Gray that you feel will turn the company into a profitable business.

EXHIBIT 7-4   Slatterball Adventure Games, Inc., Marketing Brochure

SPLATTERBALL
Adventure Games, Inc.

**5725 Ringgold Road, Suite D
East Ridge, TN 37412**

One of the best ways to play Splatterball is with a group of your co-workers. Intra-corporate games are fast-becoming one of the country's most enjoyable ways to increase productivity, camaraderie and competitive drive within business groups.

Photo above shows W.U.S.Y.-US101. Southeast Tennessee's top-rated country music radio station. US101 is the current reigning champion of the Chattanooga "media league."

Please call us for more information as well as group rates and lodging information for out-of-town guests.

"Your heart is beating fast. Adrenalin races through your body, sharpening your senses to a degree you never thought possible."

EXHIBIT 7-4 *Continued*

Field Fee...$10
Equipment Rental...$15

The above rate insures you of an entire day of play. The only limitation is your own endurance and desire.

(Group rates are available. Call our information line at 499-1151 for details.)

The day rate includes:

1 Spitfire, pump action rifle.

An initial supply of paintballs(40) and a day's supply of CO_2.

Safety certified J.T. competition goggles.

(Although paint is water soluble, players are advised to wear only old clothing! Standard brush or treebark camouflage gets best results.)

5725 RINGGOLD ROAD SUITE D
EAST RIDGE, TN 37412
(615) 499-1151

The description on the opposing page can only pale in comparison to the real experience of playing Chattanooga's oldest and best known survival game.

Splatterball Adventure Games Inc. wants to introduce you to the excitement of a day in the field with friends and foes.

Paintball is one of the country's fastest growing sports...it's easy, it's exciting, it's affordable, and can be played solo or with a team. A single fee includes all the equipment, instructions, N.A.P.R.A. certified referees and even a picnic lunch depending on the size of your group.

We offer over 25 acres of various topography as a playing field, set in beautiful, woodsy hills only 20 minutes from downtown Chattanooga. Anyone in reasonable health can play...some groups may even be designed by age bracket.

"Beside you, your comrades, glancing right and left. The sound of your movement through the woods seems like thunder...your muscles taut, finger on the trigger of your weapon...the only object that will get you through the next several minutes alive. Then, a sharp retort in the creekbed ahead of you. Your breath quickens. You race for the cover of a grove of young saplings and sage brush...firing as you go. One of your buddies goes down.. In a flash, you see the enemy. Without thinking your hand swings up. By gut instinct you react. CRACK. You see the impact...and breathe easier, a smile on your lips, as the enemy stalks off the field, hand raised above his head, the sign of his own defeat in battle."

NORWOOD FURNITURE COMPANY—1993

The Spring of 1993 brought a great deal of change to Norwood Furniture. In fact, so much has changed that Jess and Jan feel as though they have just gone through a time warp.* Business today is so different than what it was just a few years ago, but their original objective still is to operate a profitable family owned business selling quality furniture at above average prices to customers in and around their two store locations. Norwood Furniture's SIC code is 3970.

HISTORY

Nineteen years ago, Jess and Jan Norwood needed a recliner to replace their 20-year-old chair. Their search for a recliner proved unsuccessful. However, while at King Furniture, Jan found an antique rocker that could be used in one of their children's bedrooms. As Jess loaded the rocker into the car, Joe King, the owner, remarked, "I would like to sell this business." As they drove home, the Norwoods wondered how much Joe King really wanted for the business. They returned to the store to ask and he said, "$30,000 plus the inventory." Within months, the Norwoods purchased the business from King, who financed the capital needed by the Norwoods.

The Norwoods bought the furniture business in September 1974. Jess decided that it would be worthwhile to stay at his current job as a machinist for a year while Jan ran the business. This would provide at least one secure income. Sales kept steadily increasing and, with the increase in sales, Jess planned to enter the business full-time by June 1. However, a sudden sales decline frightened him enough that he decided to remain in his factory. Three months later, one year after the purchase, Jess had his first full-time day at the store.

By 1980, the Norwoods began to observe their business drawing customers from Wilkes-Barre (40,000) a city twenty-five miles north of Hazleton, with a population two-thirds that of Hazleton. Convinced that a market existed in Wilkes-Barre, they rented, for $400 a month, a 2,700 square feet store on Main Street.

In 1982, the Norwoods rented a store near Allentown, some sixty miles south of Hazleton. The store had space for unloading in the back area, a parking lot next door, and the rent was only $500 per month. However, according to Jess, "Business absolutely died, we couldn't believe going into such a huge community (125,000) and doing such a small amount of business." In March 1984, the Norwoods moved the store to another location on a major access route to Allentown.

In July 1986, Norwood Furniture had just completed its worst month in 4 years at its Allentown Store. Jess Norwood was reflecting on why this store, located in a city with 125,000 people, was doing less business than either of his two other stores. The location of the other stores were in cities with less than 60,000 people. Jess really felt it would be unwise, after 12 years, to change the operation drastically. Yet, he knew changes were necessary to survive. Jess and Jan finally decided to liquidate the Allentown operation and bring its manager back to the Hazleton store.

*Store locations and family member names are disguised.

In 1991, the Norwood Furniture store at Wilkes-Barre, which had been located in the downtown business district, relocated just two miles outside of Wilkes-Barre. The location is close to Nanticoke, approximately twenty miles from Scranton, and only seventy interstate miles from Binghamton, New York.

Store Locations. The store in Hazleton has about 9,800 square feet and is located on à side street, just off the main street shopping area. Parking in the downtown area is ample, with a 30 car public off-street parking area directly across the street from the store. Within the last three years, a corner store location became available, and the Norwoods purchased this space. The corner provided the missing entrance to the main street sales district and needed expansion of the sales area. This new area became the carpet display and sales area. The cut up floor design of the Hazleton store, however, makes it difficult to track customers as they move about. Generally, a sales person must stay right with the customer as they shop. For security and alerting salespeople, each entry door has an indicator bell. The Hazleton store location is illustrated in Exhibit 8–1.

The Wilkes-Barre store was originally located on the city's main business street. The extent of the furniture display areas consisted of two 20 × 60 foot areas. Walk-in customers found the store's access convenient with sufficient street and garage parking in the area. However, while at the downtown location, the Norwoods felt the impact as fellow merchants considered several alternatives to Friday night shopping which resulted in frustrated customers. Several merchants tried Thursday night, others stayed with Friday night. This factor, coupled with space constraints of their downtown store, prompted Jess, Jan, and their son John to find another store site. For several years, they had been aware of a shopping district developing just south of Wilkes-Barre. A good site was located next to a busy highway and surrounded by a

EXHIBIT 8-1 Hazleton Store Location

number of other businesses including Kmart, several banks, and a grocery store. The Norwoods purchased the land and obtained a bank loan.

Construction of the new Wilkes-Barre store started during the fall of 1990 and was completed in February 1991. The building has a pole construction on a concrete slab. There is track lighting throughout the store which consists of 9,000 square feet of gallery type displays of furniture and accessories. The openness of the store allows one salesperson to effectively work three customers at one time. Sales results have pleasantly surprised the Norwoods as sales have more than met their break-even level. The new Wilkes-Barre store layout is illustrated in Exhibit 8–2.

There is a two-lane highway in front of the Wilkes-Barre store. Due to development of businesses in the area, the county has begun construction of a three-lane highway less than one-half mile from the store.

COMPETITION

Surrounding the Hazleton store is a variety of stores that sell furniture. One major competitor is the Farnsworth Furniture store which features a wider price range of furniture and uses a quantity display concept.

When the Norwood's location was in the downtown business district, the major competitor was Newton's, a large general merchandise store, which sells some furniture. With the stores new location, there are no competitors within the immediate business area. Other stores in Wilkes-Barre carry only a limited number of furniture lines and have few or no waterbeds. There is only one retailer and installer of carpet within the city limits. Jan and Jess believe their operation is on the edge of becoming the number one furniture and carpet retailer in the Wilkes-Barre area.

EXHIBIT 8-2   Norwood Furniture Wilkes-Barre Store Layout

During the growth period from 1976 to 1982, the Norwoods and their two sons, John and Robert, were always the key employees. As Jess and Jan recalled, there were times when they felt the boys were too young to be doing the type of physical work needed. After spending some time away from the area, both of the sons, decided to return to the family business.

John, Jess, Jan, and one salesperson currently operate the Wilkes-Barre store seven days a week. The store hours are 9:30 A.M. to 8 P.M. Monday through Friday, 9 A.M. to 5 P.M. Saturday, and 12 P.M. to 4 P.M. Sunday. Whoever works the weekday evening shift does not have to work the weekend hours. John, however, is the principle manager of this location and spends five full days each week at the store.

Jess, Jan, Robert, and a bookkeeper are at the Hazleton store five days a week. John spends a day per week at this location, when his father or mother are at the Wilkes-Barre store. Robert moves between the two stores as need arises. By 1993, there were six people outside the family who worked at the two store locations. Although the six jobs are involved with both stores, all six employees operate out of the Hazleton store. Their responsibilities include cleaning displays, assembling furniture, delivering customer's orders, laying carpet, and performing various carpentry functions necessary for display changes. The most recent person to join the business is the new bookkeeper/accountant. The business retains a full-time (CPA) accounting firm to handle the year end audit and filing of Federal income taxes.

THE FAMILY

Jess Norwood was 37 years old when he entered the furniture sales business. He had some experience during high school working for a drugstore and feels that this experience was an excellent basis for learning the retail business. When he graduated from high school in 1957, he could not find a factory job, so he became a car salesman. Jess jokes about the empty suitcase Jan brought over one day, announcing, "If you want to live there selling cars, then here are your clothes." Soon, Jess began studying in an apprentice program for machinists. After the apprentice training program, he left to work as a machinist for a larger firm. This lasted for 10 years during which Norwood Furniture became a reality. Jess is now the full-time owner/manager for the overall operation of the two stores. He is responsible for the accounting records, including receivables and payables, purchasing, and overall functional decision making for both stores.

In 1976, Jan left being a housewife and became a manager, owner, and partner of the furniture store. Jan spent her early years working with her parents running a hotel and sporting good store. She commented that the job included "a little bit of buying, but I also spent nights in a creek catching bait for the sporting goods store." She continued this job until their first son (John) was born. Though never having had any formal business training, Jan did quite a bit of reading about operating a business and many of the ideas for their current stores originated with her. For instance, it was her idea to remodel the basement of the Hazleton store into a display area.

The oldest son, John, went to college, completed a Business Degree and to the surprise of his parents, informed them that he wanted to come back and join the furniture business. At the time, the current business did not have the income to cover his salary. However, John's interest and enthusiasm allowed a plan to be developed to expand the business's product line and eventually to enter the carpet sales market. John apprenticed as a carpet mechanic for a year before Jess decided he was ready to go out on his own. His first solo job proved the value of his training. "It was the most cut up mess you ever saw in your life," said Jess, and Jan agreed, adding "it got done and it was a good job when it was done— in fact, those customers just recently came back and bought another carpet." John is manager of the Wilkes-Barre store. His one day a week at the Hazleton store provides him the opportunity to better understand the total business operation.

Robert, the younger son, is married and has a family. Robert is manager of the Allentown location. He now works full time laying carpet, assembling furniture, and helping with sales at both the Wilkes-Barre and Hazleton stores.

Ann, their daughter, became involved in the business when she was 16 years old. She has been invaluable to her parents in providing a young woman's perspective on products and displays. Ann's interest in the area of interior decorating lead her to go to college with a major in interior design. As her father noted, "Ann's awareness of color, style, and integration of the various furniture units has added a needed dimension to our business." Ann has completed college, married, and is now working part time at the Wilkes-Barre store. In addition to helping in the store's layout and decoration, she assists customers with questions concerning interior design and during off hours does some private consulting for home decoration.

MARKETING

When the Norwoods bought the business in 1974, their main product lines were sofas and chairs. In 1981, while shopping in the Shoppingtown Mall in Albany, they noticed a store called Waterbed World. Its display was a bedroom suite called the Vintage Suite from Burlington Furniture, the same manufacturer that supplied conventional bedroom suites to the Norwoods. They contacted the Burlington salesperson and arranged to begin selling waterbeds. As Jess recalls, "when we got that waterbed suite in the store, we practically had to give it away—it didn't sell."

The first profitable load of waterbeds followed soon after when Jess and Jan took their van and 12-foot trailer to Alabama and picked up 27 waterbeds from Schwagert, Inc. Schwagert manufactured less expensive, but high quality waterbeds. Jan remembers stopping over in Atlanta, Georgia, at the Liberty Warehouse to get the mattresses. "We went in and said we had no cash, I don't even know if we have a check. Jan told them who we were, and who they could check with and we left there with, I think, about $4,000 worth of products." On the other hand, we did get a call off to John immediately, and he put a check, for the correct amount, into the mail that day. Once back to Hazleton, Jess no sooner had the headboard set down when a young man came in and said if we could deliver it tomorrow, he'd buy it. That first sale was about $400.

In the fall of 1983, a competitor in Hazleton that carried the La-Z Boy line of recliners went bankrupt. A salesperson came into our store and announced "that he was going to place the La-Z-Boy product line in one of the three stores in the area." He then asked for an "interview." After several meetings, he asked the Norwoods if they would like to place an order. Jess and Jan agreed and purchased the minimum initial order for 25 chairs with a 150 day, 2 percent discount. These chairs sold quickly even though the Norwoods carried other well-known recliners such as Kroehler, Berkline, Futuristic, and Pontiac. The majority of their customers preferred the La-Z-Boy rocker recliner.

After the initial success, energy devoted to selling the La-Z-Boy line declined and sales declined substantially. Jess commented, "The decline was our own fault because we were so active in doing other things, we weren't paying attention to the chairs. It's hard to handle multiple stores and concentrate on everything all the time. You don't have the advertising budget for it, and you just pick on the things that are important to you and the things that are working and that are profitable. That's probably what we did, and there again, it was probably waterbeds—if you look at our books, it's probably waterbeds."

The Norwood furniture business is shifting from being a waterbed store marketing to lower end customers, to being a total furniture and furnishings store targeting middle to upper level income customers. Advertising the business now covers the entire range of media. Newspaper and radio continue to be their most effective forms with television a distant third. The Norwoods have a mobile lighted sign with removable letters in front of the Wilkes-Barre store. This lighted billboard is not the most beautiful, but it is a very effective device to attract the customer's attention.

ACCOUNTING AND FINANCE

During the first 16 years, Jess did all of the accounting, even though it was a task he did not enjoy. Jess would rather be out on the floor selling, but the $200 monthly fee an outside firm would charge, was just too much. In 1990, Jess did hire a full time bookkeeper/accountant to handle the stores' books. This person also does other jobs at the Hazelton store's location. What had appeared to be a continuous problem bothering Jess: "the yearly statements never being completed until several months after the year end closing" now seemed rectified with the addition of the new bookkeeper. The bookkeeper keeps running records of each stores operation and prepares the year-end financial tax return that summarizes each year's results for the total operation. Jess occasionally goes through the ledger to analyze how well various aspects of the business are performing. The financial statements for 1990, 1991, and 1992 are given at the end of this case (Exhibits 8–3, 8–4, and 8–5).

As 1992 was drawing to a close, Jess and Jan set two primary goals for their business. First, they want to get to a million dollar sales level; and second, they want to become the number one store in Wilkes-Barre. They feel that each goal is possible since, during the recent recession, the business has remained profitable. A concern in Jess's mind however is the, approximately, $500,000 debt load that the stores are carrying.

THE FUTURE

The Norwood store operations are running smoothly and each member of the family is participating in each store. Up-to-date records and other decision-making information has been developed by the bookkeeper. The Norwood customer base has remained stable and their policy of standing behind their products even after the manufacturer's warranty has expired is still a major selling point for people. The competition, formerly only stores selling furniture, has now become furniture stores that sell other lines of household goods such as kitchen appliances. Jess and Jan have noticed that Norwood's customers are now looking for a wide range of goods that extend beyond furniture. Jess is thinking about introducing a line of appliances to compliment the furniture and carpet business. Several customers have recently asked whether Norwoods carries kitchen appliances such as microwaves, stoves, and refrigerators.

EXHIBIT 8-3 Norwood Furniture Balance Sheet (Unaudited) December 31, 1990

	1990	1991	1992
ASSETS			
Current Assets			
Cash			
Accounts Receivable	$ 35,736	$ 31,171	$ 48,089
Inventory	14,639	22,638	30,329
	145,926	201,747	203,400
Total Current Assets	196,301	255,556	281,818
Property, Plant and Equipment:			
Land	85,000	85,000	85,000
Building	181,178	309,282	309,282
Building Improvements	78,511	69,264	69,264
Furniture and Fixtures	10,125	10,125	10,125
Delivery Equipment and Tools	49,469	49,469	80,205
Total Assets	404,283	523,140	553,876
Less: Accumulated Depreciation	95,629	107,093	124,067
Total Property, Plant and Equipment	308,654	416,047	429,809
TOTAL ASSETS	504,955	671,603	711,627
LIABILITIES AND PROPRIETOR'S CAPITAL			
Current Liabilities:			
Accounts Payable	20,249	15,858	36,905
Building Construction Cost Payable	57,380	0	0
Taxes Payable	9,338	7,022	9,429
Current Portion of Debt	8,813	316,011	62,439
Total Current Liabilities	95,780	338,891	108,773
Long-Term Liabilities:			
Note Payable—Bank Loans (Note B)	178,033	114,161	338,494
Total Long-Term Liabilities	178,033	114,161	338,494
TOTAL LIABILITIES	273,813	453,052	447,267
Owners' Equity	231,142	218,551	264,360
TOTAL LIABILITIES AND OWNERS' EQUITY	$504,955	$671,603	$711,627

Source: Norwood Furniture Company.

EXHIBIT 8-4 Norwood Furniture—Income Statement

	1990	1991	1992
SALES	$743,036	$791,629	$880,236
Less: Returns & Allowances	1,858	0	
Net Sales	741,178	791,629	880,236
Cost of Goods Sold	432,488	452,900	515,520
Gross Operating Profit	308,690	338,729	364,716
Operating Expenses			
Advertising	41,695		37,966
Car & Truck Expense	10,074		7,160
Depreciation and			
Section 179 Deduction	8,483		0
Dues and Subscriptions	0		873
Insurance	21,064		18,431
Interest—Mortgage	10,778		0
—Other	0		0
Legal and Professional Service	1,071		1,070
Office Expense	3,371		4,535
Rent or Lease:			
Machinery and Equipment	0		900
Other Business Property	10,400		0
Repairs and Maintenance	9,408		7,165
Supplies	59		1,384
Taxes and Licenses	4,046		20,606
Travel Meals & Entertainment:			
Travel	0		2,481
Meals & Entertainment	100		569
20% of (meals & entertainment) subject to limitation	20		0
Difference	80		0
Utilities	21,508		22,597
Wages	96,624		127,482
Other Expenses	13,639		4,427
Total Operating Expenses	252,420	244,137	257,646
NET OPERATING PROFIT (LOSS)	56,270	94,592	107,070
Other Expenses:			
Depreciation		11,464	16,974
Interest		37,745	29,773
Total Other Expenses		49,209	46,747
NET INCOME	56,270	45,383	60,323
Owner's Equity at Beginning of Year		231,142	218,551
Less: Owners' Withdrawals—Net		57,974	14,514
OWNERS' EQUITY AT END OF YEAR	$231,142	$218,551	$264,360

Source: Norwood Furniture Company.

EXHIBIT 8-5 Norwood Furniture 1992 Statement of Cash Flows (Unaudited)

Cash received from customers	$872,545	
Cash Paid to Suppliers	(496,126)	
Cash Paid for Expenses	(237,040)	
Cash Paid for Taxes	(18,199)	
Cash Paid for Interest	(29,773)	
Net Cash Provided by Operating Activities		$91,407
Cash Flows from Investing Activities:		
Purchase of Property, Plant & Equipment	(30,736)	
Net Cash Used by Investing Activities		(30,736)
Cash Flows from Financing Activity:		
Proceeds from issuance of Debt	273,198	
Payment of Debt	(302,437)	
Owner Withdrawals	(14,514)	
Net Cash Provided by Financing Activity		(43,753)
Net Increase (Decrease) in Cash		16,918
Cash at Beginning of Year		31,171
Cash at End of Year		48,089

Reconciliation of Net Income to Net Cash

Provided by Operating Activity

Net Income	$60,323
Add (deduct) items not using (providing) cash	16,974
(Increase) Decrease in Accts. Receivable	(7,691)
(Increase) Decrease in Inventory	(1,653)
Increase (Decrease) in Accts. Payable	21,047
Increase (Decrease) in Taxes Payable	$2,407
Net Cash Flows from Operating Activities	$91,407

Note A - Summary of Significant Accounting Policies
  Basis of Acctg.

    (Norwood) Furniture (a proprietorship) is engaged in the retail furniture business with stores in Pennsylvania. The financial statements are presented on an accrual basis of accounting. Inventory is valued using the lower of cost or market (FIFO) method.

    As a way to expand their product line, Jess is thinking about carrying used furniture. He and Jan agree that used furniture would be quite a departure from their original business objectives: "giving their customers quality at an above average margin of profit." However, just two months ago the Norwood's had a trade-in sale. Customers could trade in an old couch, sofa, or chair toward a new price of furniture. The result was a sale that far exceeded their wildest hopes and resulted in an entirely new market, people interested in buying the trade-ins. Many of the trade-ins were still excellent

EXHIBIT 8-5 *Continued*

Property, Plant and Equipment:

Depreciation of plant and equipment is provided on an accelerated depreciation method. Expenditures for maintenance and repairs are charged against operations, Renewals and betterments that materially extend the life of an asset are capitalized.

Federal Income Taxes:

The proprietorship itself is not a taxpaying entity for purposes of federal and state income taxes. Federal and state income taxes of the proprietor are computed on his total income from all sources, accordingly, no provision for income tax is made in this statement.

Note B - Long Term Debt

Note payable in equal monthly installments of $1,041 (int.=6%) collateralized by property and equipment.	$69,875	$8,527	$61,346
Mortgage payable in variable monthly installment (currently $2,517,73, including interest currently 8.875%). Amount and rate is adjusted annually in March.	242,872	12,725	230,147
Note payable in equal monthly installment of $555.10 (int.=6%).	43,599	4,158	39,441
Bank line of credit payable at Prime +1 (current int.=7%).	26,147	26,147	0
Note payable in equal monthly installments of $350 (int. at 9.25%).	10,884	3,324	7,560
Note payable in equal monthly installments of $349.61 (int. at 8.9%).	7,556	7,556	0
TOTAL	$400,933	$62,439	$338,494

Source: Norwood Furniture Company.

quality and had several years of good use left. Jess was able to set the trade-in price such that he made a good profit, and the buyer got a fair price. The trade-in sale involved delivery but did not involve guarantees, service agreements, or other contracts that linger on with the seller long after a new sale has been completed.

Jess is concerned about the closing of a clothing store located directly across the main street from their Hazleton store. Over the years, Jess has found that women coming into town for clothes shopping will often shop other stores close by.

Jess and Jan are interested in letting their sons take over the total operation. There are now grand children to enjoy, and Jess and Jan both have some health problems. Jess and Jan are unsure how to best step aside and allow their children to run the business. Develop a strategic plan for Jess and Jan to guide the Norwood Furniture Company to continued growth and profitability in the mid-to-late 1990s.

DAVE'S PIT STOP CAFE—1993*

Dave's Pit Stop Cafe (517-269-5945) is located in the center of Bad Axe, Michigan, a small town surrounded by rich agricultural land that serves as the county seat for Huron County. Huron County's two major industries are agriculture (it has long been a major producer of corn, sugar beets, and soy beans) and, during the summer months, tourism. The main road through Bad Axe is M-53, which originates in Detroit a hundred miles due south and terminates seventeen miles north of Bad Axe at the village of Port Austin on the shore of Lake Huron. M-53 makes a right angle turn to the east shortly before it enters Bad Axe, as shown in Exhibit 9–1. It turns north again at the stoplight at the center of town.

EXHIBIT 9–1 Location of Dave's Pit Stop Cafe and Selected Other Businesses, Bad Axe, MI

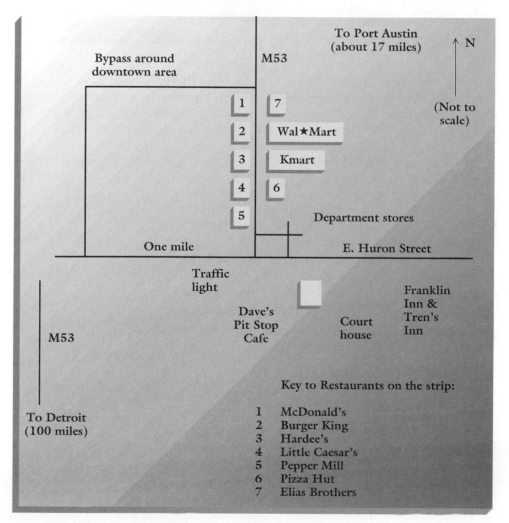

* Copyright 1993 by Henry H. Beam

EXHIBIT 9-2   Dave's Pit Stop Cafe

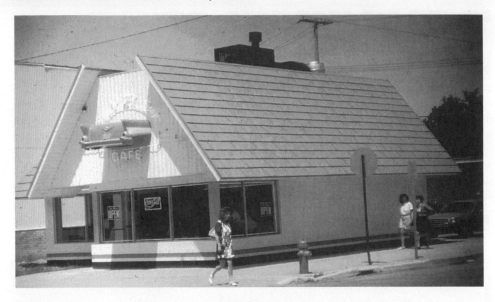

A block to the east, on the northwest corner, is Dave's Pit Stop Cafe. The court house and the offices of ten lawyers, several real estate and insurance agencies, and a two-person architectural firm are within a block of the cafe. According to the 1990 census, the population of Bad Axe, 3,484, has changed little for over fifty years.

In the summer of 1992, visitors to Dave's Pit Stop Cafe could not miss the rear of a 1957 Chevy sticking out of the second floor. The owner, Dave Schemansky, had wanted to do something creative to make people take a second look. Thus, he bought an original 1957 Chevrolet, tail fins and all, and had the vehicle cut in two. Then he had the rear half bolted to the exterior above the building's entrance (Exhibit 9–2). The interior walls were decorated with framed posters of automobiles and a classic pop poster of Marlon Brando on a motorcycle as he appeared in the 1954 movie, *The Wild One*. Michigan license plates dating from the 1950s were displayed on the walls, adding to the vintage automobile theme.

HOW THE PIT STOP CAME INTO BEING

"I like cars. I've always been around them and I really like them." That's what Dave Schemansky, 34, told a *Huron Daily Tribune* reporter shortly after he opened his restaurant in December, 1991. The menu, as well as the rear of the '57 Chevy mounted over the entrance, reflect this interest. All the deli sandwiches are named after automobiles of the 1950s and 1960s, such as the Cadillac Eldorado (a corned beef and swiss cheese triple decker) and the Ford Galaxie (turkey, ham, tomato, lettuce, and mayonnaise). The summer 1992 menu is shown in Exhibit 9–3. Dave's specialty is chili. Over fifteen gallons are sold daily during the winter months. In 1991, Dave won second place with his recipe at the Huron County chili cookoffs.

Dave graduated from high school in Royal Oak, a northern suburb of Detroit. His interest in cars comes naturally, since his father worked for Ford Motor Company for over forty years. Dave worked as a design technician first for General Motors, then for

EXHIBIT 9-3 The Summer 1992 Menu

"Coney Island"

1-C	Hot Dog..	1.25
2-C	Coney Island Hot Dog....................	1.40
	Hot dog served with chili, mustard and onions	
3-C	Dave's Special.............................	2.15
	Hot dog served with chili, mustard, onion, ground beef and cheese	
4-C	Loose Hamburger........................	1.75
	Served with chili, mustard and onions	
5-C	Hotdog with Saurerkraut................	1.70

"Chili"

6-C	Dave's Famous Chili......................	1.60

"Hamburgers"

(All our burgers start with 1/3 lb. all beef served with lettuce, tomato, onion, pickle and mayo on a toasted bun.)

7-C	Hamburger................................	2.35
8-C	Hamburger Deluxe......................	3.35
	with fries and coleslaw	
9-C	Cheeseburger............................	2.60
10-C	Cheeseburger Deluxe..................	3.60
	with fries and coleslaw	
11-C	Bacon Cheeseburger....................	2.85
12-C	Patty Melt................................	2.80
	1/3 lb beef with cheese and onion grilled together on rye	
13-C	Deli Burger..............................	4.85
	1/3 lb. hamburger, pastrami, swiss cheese, lettuce, tomato and onion, topped with Russian dressing	
14-C	Double Cheese Burger.................	5.00
15-C	Chili Cheese Burger....................	3.10

21-D	Woody....................................	4.30
	Pastrami, swiss cheese and Russian dressing	
22-D	Biscayne................................	4.65
	Corned beef, swiss, cheese, cole slaw and Russian dressing	
23-D	Plymouth Sport Fury...................	5.95
	Hot pastrami, corned beef, swiss cheese, dipped in Russian dressing	
24-D	Rueben..................................	4.65
	(Guaranteed to please the most discriminating) Corned beef, swiss cheese and sauerkraut on three thin slices of rye and grilled............. Half 3.05	
25-D	Buick Special...........................	4.70
	Triple Decker-Roast beef, tomato, egg, lettuce and Russian dressing............. Half 3.00	
26-D	Dave's Limousine.......................	6.40
	A bit of everything on large (white or rye)	

"Meat on Rye"

Corned Beef..................................	3.95
Hot Pastrami.................................	4.95
Roast Beef....................................	4.05

"Just Plain Good"

Sliced Turkey................................	3.65
Chicken Salad................................	3.00
Tunafish Salad...............................	2.75
Grilled Cheese...............................	1.25
Egg Salad.....................................	1.50
Ham..	3.25
Tuna Melt.....................................	3.75
Tuna on grilled rye bread with American cheese	

	Grilled Ham & Cheese....................	2.50
16-C	Mushroom Burger........................	4.00
	Sauteed mushroom & swiss cheese	
17-C	Pitstop Burger...........................	3.75
	Hamburger, ham & swiss cheese	
18-C	Philly Burger............................	3.50
	Hamburger, grilled green peppers/onions and swiss cheese	
19-C	Olive Burger.............................	4.00
	Hamburger smothered with olives	
20-C	Garbage Burger..........................	4.75
	Hamburger with ham, cheese, bacon, onions, mushrooms & green peppers	
21-C	Fire Pit Burger..........................	4.75
	Hamburger, salsa sauce, refried beans, jalopena peppers and sour cream	

"Dave's Deli Delights"

(All sandwiches served with chips and a pickle)

1-D	Chevrolet Bel-Air........................	4.40
	Triple decker-corned beef, lettuce, tomato and Russian dressing...........Half 2.85	
2-D	Buick Skylark............................	4.65
	Triple decker-corned beef, egg, lettuce, tomato and Russian dressing.........Half 3.00	
3-D	Chevrolet Corvette......................	4.50
	Pastrami, egg coleslaw and Russian dressing.......................Half 2.90	
4-D	Cadillac Eldorado.......................	4.80
	Triple decker-corned beef, swiss cheese, lettuce, tomato and Russian dressing........Half 3.12	
5-D	Packard..................................	4.30
	Triple Decker-chicken salad, lettuce and tomato.......................Half 2.80	
6-D	T-Bird....................................	4.70
	Triple decker-turkey, bacon, lettuce, tomato and mayonnaise.................Half 3.05	

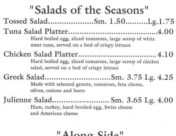

"Salads of the Seasons"

Tossed Salad................Sm. 1.50.........Lg.1.75	
Tuna Salad Platter........................4.00	
Hard boiled egg, sliced tomatoes, large scoop of white meat tuna, served on a bed of crispy lettuce	
Chicken Salad Platter.....................4.10	
Hard boiled egg, sliced tomatoes, large scoop of chicken salad, served on a bed of crispy lettuce	
Greek Salad.........................Sm. 3.75 Lg. 4.25	
Made with selected greens, tomatoes, feta cheese, olives, onions and beets	
Julienne Salad.......................Sm. 3.65 Lg. 4.00	
Ham, turkey, hard broiled egg, Swiss cheese and American cheese	

"Along Side"

French Fries...1.00 Chili Fries...............1.50	
Cheese Fries..1.30 Cole Slaw...................30	
Onion Chips..1.50	
Chili/Cheese Fries 1.75	

"Children's Menu"

(12 Years and Under)

Hamburger.................................2.60	
Served with fries, pop or milk	
Grilled Cheese Sandwich..................2.05	
Served with fries, pop or milk	
Hot Dog....................................2.05	
Served with fries, pop or milk	

"Beverages"

Soft Drinks......................Sm. 65 Lg.75	
Milk (white)....................Sm. 70 Lg.85	
Coffee..............50 ....Decaf.........50	
Hot Chocolate..............................60	

7-D	Chevrolet Impala........................	3.95
	Triple decker-bacon, tomato, lettuce and mayonnaise................Half 2.60	
8-D	Studebaker Hawk........................	4.50
	Triple decker-sliced turkey, lettuce, tomato and mayonnaise...............Half 2.90	
9-D	Mercury.................................	4.65
	Triple decker-ham, lettuce, tomato, swiss cheese and mayonnaise...............Half 3.00	
11-D	Buick Electra............................	4.40
	Triple decker-pastrami, coleslaw and Russian dressing.................Half 2.85	
12-D	Corvette Sting Ray......................	4.60
	Triple decker-roast beef, onion, lettuce, tomato, american cheese and mayonnaise............Half 2.85	
13-D	Ford Mustang 2+2.......................	5.95
	4 decker-corned beef, pastrami, lettuce, tomato and Russian dressing...............Half 3.85	
14-D	Dodge Coronet Super Bee..............	4.30
	Hot corned beef, swiss cheese and lettuce	
15-D	Pontiac GTO.............................	4.25
	Hot pastrami, coleslaw, and Russian dressing	
16-D	Pontiac Firebird.........................	4.40
	Hot corned beef, coleslaw and Russian dressing	
17-D	Plymouth Road Runner..................	4.50
	Turkey, coleslaw and Russian dressing	
18-D	Ford Galaxie.............................	4.70
	Turkey, ham, tomato, lettuce, and mayonnaise	
19-D	Tucker....................................	5.70
	Sliced turkey, pastrami, swiss cheese and Russian Dressing	
20-D	Pontiac Catalina.........................	3.65
	Swiss cheese, lettuce, tomato and mayonnaise	

Free Delivery
with $15.00 Purchase

181 E. Huron

Bad Axe

269-2760

Ford Motor Company. However, during the difficult times in the automobile industry in the late 1980s, he was laid off, which gave him the incentive to open the restaurant. "I'd seen this building here for a long time, and I always said it had potential, if it just had atmosphere." Thus Dave leased the building, formerly used as a Dairy Queen, gutted it, and installed new plumbing, wiring, and kitchen equipment. He was assisted in the renovation by his girlfriend, Patty Bowen, who also did the bookkeeping. For seating, there were eight tables with four chairs each. All 955 square feet of space on the main level was used for the restaurant, while the 650 square feet of space on the second floor was divided between storage and a small office.

Initially, the Pit Stop opened at 6 A.M. for breakfast, but there were few customers. After a few months of operation, Dave settled on the following hours:

Monday through Wednesday	9:30 A.M. to 7:00 P.M.
Thursday and Friday	9:30 A.M. to 8:00 P.M.
Saturday	9:30 A.M. to 6:00 P.M.
Sunday	Closed

The slowest part of the day is from opening until 11:00 A.M. The busiest day is usually Friday, which is also payday for many local workers.

LARGE HELPINGS AND SERVICE

Dave takes pride in the large helpings served to customers. As he puts it, "We serve the biggest sandwiches in town—everybody gets a to-go box!" One customer who ate lunch at the cafe in June 1992, ordered the Hamburger Deluxe with french fried potatoes, coleslaw, and coffee. He was able to eat the hamburger, but, true to Dave's word, he took most of the french fries home in a to-go box. Others who eat at Dave's cafe agree that the food is good but the portions are too large for most people.

All food is prepared to order and only fresh meat is used. Dave does most of the cooking, an activity he enjoys. During busy periods, such as lunch time, two or three waitresses seat customers, take orders, and serve the food. Otherwise, there is usually only one waitress. Waitresses are paid minimum wage ($4.25 per hour in 1992).

Most people who eat at Dave's are not in a hurry. Nevertheless, there are occasional complaints about slow service or unavailability of some items on the menu. For example, at a time when the cafe was not busy, one customer waited five minutes for a waitress to bring him a menu after he was seated, and an additional fifteen minutes for the waitress to bring him his order. Another customer, who had brought his family to the cafe for lunch, was disappointed to find that Dave was out of chili, his specialty. His children ordered milk, but Dave was out of that, too, so they had soft drinks instead. Other than that, their food was fine.

COMMERCIAL DEVELOPMENT AND COMPETITION

During the 1980s, most commercial development in Bad Axe took place along a two mile section of M-53 on the northern edge of the town. Both Kmart and Wal★Mart built stores along this "strip". This strip also features two hardware stores, three medium sized supermarkets, and several gas stations with mini-marts in them. Burger King, Hardee's, and McDonald's each have a fast food franchise along this strip. Pizza is available from Little Caesar's and Pizza Hut. The Elias Brothers Big Boy restaurant at the north end and the Pepper Mill at the south end feature family style meals served by a waitress. It is a little over a mile from Dave's Pit Stop Cafe to the Pepper Mill, where the strip begins.

Dave's cafe is located in the center of town. Two small, family-owned restaurants are located nearby. Two motels, the Franklin Inn and Tren's Inn, are located less than a mile to the east of M-53. Each has a restaurant and a lounge. A large department store building in the block to the east of Dave's has been vacant for over a year. It is for sale for $125,000. For many years, it housed the Polewach store, Bad Axe's largest merchandiser prior to the arrival of Kmart. Another longtime downtown business, the D & C Variety Store, closed in December 1992. Exhibit 9–4 gives some economic data on Huron County.

FINANCIAL ASPECTS

Dave leases the building for his Pit Stop Cafe from Willet O'Dell. Willet's permanent residence had been in New Jersey, but since retiring in 1988, he and his wife spend the summer months at their cottage near Port Austin and travel most of the rest of the year. Willet has long-standing family ties to Bad Axe. The lot on which the cafe is located had belonged to Willet's grandfather at a time when it was considered the best commercial location in Bad Axe. His grandfather had operated a general merchandise store on the site until a fire destroyed it in 1920. In 1950, Willet's father leased the lot to a local businessman who built a cinder-block structure that served as a Dairy Queen during summer months. However, the lease contained no provision for the owner of the Dairy Queen building to buy the lot.

Willet inherited the lot and the lease in 1986 after the death of his mother. Tired of years of sporadic lease payments by the tenant, Willet took ownership of the Dairy Queen building in 1990 in return for forgiveness of all unpaid rent. The building and a small parking area each occupied about half the 44 foot by 100 foot lot. Additional parking (at no charge) was readily available along the streets adjacent to the restaurant.

In September 1991, a real estate consultant prepared a report for Willet which estimated the market value of the land at $27,600 and the property (land, unoccupied building, and equipment) at about $57,550. According to the tax assessment, the value of the property was $70,400. The consultant suggested a selling price for the property of $69,000. Rather than sell the property, Willet opted to lease the land and building.

Dave Schemansky was one of two individuals who expressed an interest in leasing the building for use as a restaurant. He developed a business plan which showed an estimated monthly pre-tax profit of $2,257 on estimated monthly sales of $12,500. In November 1991, Dave signed a one-year lease with monthly payments of $725. The lease contained an option, exercisable anytime during the life of the lease, for Dave to buy the lot and building for $75,000 on a land contract. (A land contract is an agreement between a buyer and a seller of real estate, with no financial institution involved. The seller holds title to the property until the final payment is made. If the buyer defaults (i.e., fails to make payments as specified in the agreement), the land contract is void and the seller keeps the property, the down payment and any payments made.) Terms were at $15,000 down payment with 9.5 percent interest on the unpaid balance for ten years. The lease also contained a clause which stated, "Tenant's failure to pay rent when due or to perform any of his obligations hereunder shall constitute a default." Once the lease had been signed, Willet spent about $7,000 to have a new roof put on the building and to have the exterior painted in bright art deco colors.

Business at the restaurant generally is brisk, with sales highest, as expected, during the summer months. Sales for August 1992 were unusually low because the city of Bad

EXHIBIT 9-4 Economic Data on Huron County

County Seat: Bad Axe

PROFILE OF HURON COUNTY, MICHIGAN
January, 1992

LOCATION SERVICES
Huron County Economic Development Corporation
250 East Huron, Room 302
Bad Axe, MI 48413

Contact: Carl Osentoski
Phone: 517/269-6431

POPULATION

1970 Census	34083
1980 Census	36459
1990 Census	34951
Median Age (as of 1990)	35.8 years

LABOR FORCE (1990 average)

Total Labor Force	16475
Employed	14800
Total Unemployment	1675
Unemployment Rate	10.1%
3-Year Average	9.8%

PRINCIPAL ECONOMIC BASE EMPLOYERS

Active Industries, Elkton	887	Metal stamping
Michigan Sugar, Sebewaing	380	Beet sugar
Sebewaing Industries, Sebewaing	369	Automotive stampings
NutraSweet, Harbor Beach	128	Medicinal/Botanical
U.S. Mfg., Bad Axe	120	Steering gears & boxes
Gemini Plastics	105	Plastic profile extrusions
Arjay Mfg., Bad Axe	94	Custom molding/thermoplastics
Nortec, Bad Axe	94	Custom plastic molding
Walbro Precision Plastics	94	Molded thermoplastic parts
Pigeon Mfg., Pigeon	88	Metal stamping
Thumb Tool & Engineering, Bad Axe	78	Extrusion dies
Huron Tool	70	Automotive
Hercules, Harbor Beach	69	Food seasonings
Acme Roll Forming, Sebewaing	60	Sheet metal
Derek Tool, Owendale	50	Carbide tools
Vultron, Bad Axe	50	Electronic signs
Cel-Star, Port Austin	40	Rubber products
Spartan Carbide, Bad Axe	40	Carbide tools
Port Austin Level, Port Austin	35	Levels
Lyntex Mfg., Ubly	30	Cut & sew of webbings, elastic
Total Employees:	2881	

Source: Michigan Department of Commerce, County Profiles.

Axe had the downtown streets, including the one in front of Dave's cafe, blocked off for over a week to install new sidewalks. Exhibit 9–5 gives some data on sales for the months of May 1992 through September 1992. Exhibit 9–6 shows the estimated

EXHIBIT 9-5 Data on May – September Monthly Sales

Month	Sales	Highest Daily Sales	Day	Lowest Daily Sales	Day	Days Open
May	$9,004.57	$649.63	Friday	$ 96.14	Monday	26
June	8,494.75	——	not available	——		
July	8,894.37	$488.58	Friday	$192.40	Tuesday	26
August	4,824.00	——	not available	——		
September (estimated)	7,500.00	——	not available	——		

Source: Dave's Pit Stop Cafe.

EXHIBIT 9-6 Expenses for the Month of July, 1992

NON-FOOD EXPENSES:

Rent	$ 725.00
Gas	65.00
Electric	310.00
Water	50.00
Phone	95.00
Waste Removal	86.00
Coke Machine	30.00
Towels	40.00
Bookkeeping	150.00
Health Insurance	287.52
Restaurant Insurance	167.00
Advertising (local radio station)	45.00
Part time help (waitresses)	1,400.00
Load repayment	685.00
Subtotal	$4,135.52
FOOD EXPENSES (ESTIMATED):	$1,600.00
Total expenses	$5,735.52

Source: Dave's Pit Stop Cafe.

expenses for operation Dave's Pit Stop Cafe for the month of July 1992. Nevertheless, Dave has struggled to make his monthly rent payments to Willet almost from the start. Failure to pay rent on time is costly, since the lease contains a clause which requires Dave to pay a penalty of five dollars per day for each day the rent is late. In June 1992, after repeated prodding from Willet, Dave paid three of the five months of back rent he owed. He also asked for a reduction in the rent to $500 a month, noting that commercial property in downtown Bad Axe rented for between 28 and 32 cents per square foot per month. Dave also claimed that he had spent $27,000, considerably more than he had anticipated, to make the improvements that resulted in his cafe.

As of August 1, 1992, Dave owed Willet $1,975 in back rent and $1,530 in late fees. He also owed about $1,400 to various contractors for work done renovating the building's interior. After some haggling about payment of the back rent, Willet and Dave agreed to modify the lease, effective August 14, 1992. The rent was reduced to $550 per month and was due on the 14th of the month rather than the 1st. Willet also waived all late payments up to August 14, 1992, and reduced future late payments from $5 to $2 per day. Dave brought his rental payments up to date as of October 14, 1992. However, he failed to make the November payment.

DAVE'S SITUATION IN DECEMBER 1992

As December 14th approached, Dave needed to make a major decision. If he did not make his December rental payment on time, he would fall two months behind in his payments. If this happened, Willet, who had grown increasingly impatient with Dave's failure to pay rent on time, would probably enforce the default provision. Dave would no longer be able to operate his Pit Stop Cafe at its present location. Willet would have to find another tenant for the building or sell it. On the other hand, if Dave wanted to exercise his option to buy the land and the building, he would need to make both the November and December rental payments by December 14th. He would then have to come up with $15,000 for the down payment by August 1993. This would be difficult, since Dave had little personal property and he had already borrowed a substantial amount from his father to start the Pit Stop Cafe.

Conduct a strategic analysis for Dave's Pit Stop Cafe. Do you feel Dave can stay in business? Should he stay in business? Prepare a strategic plan for Dave giving specific recommendations and your justifications.

CASE 10

AUDUBON ZOO—1994

CLAIRE ANDERSON
Old Dominion University
CAROLINE FISHER
Loyola University

The Audubon Zoo (504-861-2537) is located in New Orleans, Louisiana. The ancient business of making money on wild animals has become exceptionally competitive. More and more money is spent every year to build, expand, and improve zoos and aquariums in the United States, reaching over $1.2 billion in 1992. The building of mega-aquariums, known in the business as the "blue wave," cost nearly $100 million each and may feature acrylic tunnels that let you walk beneath sharks. Zoos are fighting back with multimillion-dollar exhibits with real animal sounds and exotic surroundings.

More people today go to zoos and aquariums than attend professional football, basketball, and baseball games combined; 105 million in 1992. However, the animal industry is on the defensive as never before. Animal rights groups have stepped up criticism of zoos and aquariums. The popularity of *Free Willy*, a movie about a boy and a sadly caged whale, fueled critics' attacks. Zoo attendance is increasing only slightly and governments are slashing budgets for nonprofit zoos. Zoo biologists are giving way to zoo marketers who are looking for unique ways to increase revenues, such as hosting corporate meetings, regional sales meetings, cocktail parties, weddings, and even conventions. At Zoo Atlanta, for example, 75 after-hour events brought in $200,000 in 1992, up from zero four years ago. Zoo Atlanta allows you to reserve the zoo for five hours for $6,000 and touch some of the animals. Zoo Atlanta is now taking reservations for 1996 Olympic corporate parties.

The Fort Worth Zoo caters dinner parties and business meetings. The Aquarium of the Americas in New Orleans lets you reserve an evening meeting for $4,000 for three hours, with cocktails and food costing extra. The four Sea Worlds host business after-hours events for $22 a person, park admission included, food and beverages extra.

Zoo and aquarium managers know that animal rights activists are persistent. *Free Willy* ends with a toll-free telephone number for people who want to learn more about protecting whales. "People are starting to see these places as a-*buse*-ment parks," Dan Matthews of People for the Ethical Treatment of Animals says. All zoos, aquariums, and marine theme parks are animal prisons and in the greed business, he says. Marketing campaigns strive to position zoos as protectors of species not as cagers of animals. Both zoos and aquariums are run mostly by not-for-profit foundations that constantly remind society that their income goes toward fighting animal extinction. Some zoos even change their name, such as the Bronx Zoo, which now is called the International Wildlife Conservation Park.

For-profit Sea World constantly battles an image problem, annually spending more than $1 million rescuing and rehabilitating animals. Although more than 90 percent of Anheuser-Busch's operating income comes from beer, the company's 1991 *Annual Report* is entitled "A Century of Environmental Responsibility." The *Annual Report* is devoted to the company's commitment to animal welfare.

Although activists probably will not win the release of zoo and marine animals, they could cause a whale of a problem if corporate sponsors decline. Few doubt that the industry, which goes back at least 3,000 years to China, will survive, but innovative strategies will be needed.

HISTORY

The Audubon Zoo was the focus of national concern in the early 1970s, with well-documented stories of animals kept in conditions that were variously termed an "animal ghetto," "the New Orleans antiquarium," and even "an animal concentration camp." In 1971, the Bureau of Governmental Research recommended a $5.6 million zoo improvement plan to the Audubon Park Commission and the City Council of New Orleans. The local *Times Picayune* commented on the new zoo: "It's not going to be quite like the 'Planet of the Apes' situation in which the apes caged and studied human beings but something along those broad general lines." The new zoo confines people to bridges and walkways while the animals roam amid grass, shrubs, trees, pools, and fake rocks. The gracefully curving pathways, generously lined with luxuriant plantings, give the visitor a sense of being alone in a wilderness, although crowds of visitors may be only a few yards away.

A chronology of major events in the life of the Audubon Zoo is presented in Exhibit 10–1. One of the first significant changes made was the institution of an admission charge in 1972. Admission to the zoo had been free to anyone prior to the adoption of the renovation plan. Ostensibly, the initial purpose behind instituting the admission charge was to prevent vandalism, but the need for additional income was also apparent. Despite the establishment of and increases in admission charges, admission charges have increased dramatically. Exhibit 10–4 reveals that attendance also is seasonal, with July and August being the busiest months and December and January being the slowest months.

The Audubon Park Commission launched a $5.6 million developmental program based on the Bureau of Governmental Research plan for the zoo in March

1972. A bond issue and a property tax dedicated to the zoo were put before the voters on November 7, 1972. When it passed by an overwhelming majority, serious discussions began about what should be done. The New Orleans City Planning Commission finally approved the master plan for the Audubon Park Zoo in September 1973. But the institution of the master plan was far from smooth.

Over two dozen special interests were ultimately involved in choosing whether to renovate and expand the existing facilities or move to another site. Expansion became a major community controversy. Some residents opposed the zoo expansion, fearing that "loss of green space" would affect the secluded character of the neighborhood. Others opposed the loss of what they saw as an attractive and educational facility.

Most of the opposition came from the zoo's affluent neighbors. Zoo director John Moore ascribed the criticism to "a select few people who have the money and power to make a lot of noise." He went on to say, "The real basis behind the problem is that the neighbors who live around the edge of the park have a selfish concern because they want the park as their private back yard." Legal battles over the expansion plans continued until early 1976. At that time, the Fourth Circuit Court of Appeals ruled that the expansion was legal. An out-of-court agreement with the zoo's neighbors (the Upper Audubon Association) followed shortly.

The expansion of the Audubon Zoo took it from 14 to 58 acres. The zoo was laid out in geographical sections: the Asian Domain, World of Primates, World's Grasslands, Savannah, North American Prairie, South American Pampas, and Louisiana Swamp, according to the master plan developed by the Bureau of

EXHIBIT 10-1 Chronology of Events for the New Zoo

1972	Voters approved a referendum to provide tax dollars to renovate and expand the Zoo. The first Zoo-To-Do was held. An admission charge was instituted.
1973	The City Planning Commission approved a master plan for the Audubon Park Zoo calling for $3.4 million for upgrading. Later phases called for an additional $2.1 million to be completed by 1978.
1974	Friends of the Zoo formed with 400 members to increase support and awareness of the Zoo.
1975	Renovations began—$25 million public and private funds—14 acres to be expanded to 58 acres.
1976	The Friends of the Zoo assumed responsibility for concessions.
1977	John Moore went to Albuquerque, Ron Forman took over as Park and Zoo director.
1980	First full time education staff assumed duties at the Zoo.
1980	Last animal removed from antiquated cage—a turning point in Zoo history.
1981	Contract signed allowing New Orleans Steamboat Company to bring passengers from downtown to the Park.
1981	Delegates from the American Association of Zoological Parks Aquariums ranked the Audubon Zoo as one of the top three zoos of its size in America.
1981	Zoo accredited.
1982	The Audubon Park Commission reorganized under Act 352, which required the Commission to contract with a non-profit organization for the daily management of the Park.
1985	The Zoo was designated as a Rescue Center for Endangered and Threatened Plants.
1986	Voters approved a $25 million bond issue for the Aquarium.
1988	The Friends of the Zoo became The Audubon Institute.
1990	The Aquarium of the Americas opened in September.
1993	Freeport-McMoran Audubon Species Survival Center opened.
1995	Audubon Center for Research on Endangered Species scheduled to open.
1995	Audubon Insectarium scheduled to open.

Source: The Audubon Institute.

Governmental Research. Additional exhibits included the Wisner Discovery Zoo, Sea Lion exhibit, and Flight Cage. See Exhibit 10–2 for a map of the new zoo.

The Audubon Zoo currently employs 625 people and has a local economic impact of $100 million annually. More than 80,000 households and 200,000 individuals are members of the Zoo. The Zoo plans to open the Freeport-McMoran Audubon

EXHIBIT 10-2 A Map of the Audubon Park Zoo

Source: The Audubon Institute. Used with permission.

Species Survival Center in 1993, the Audubon Center for Research on Endangered Species in 1995, and the Audubon Insectarium in 1995.

PURPOSE

The main outward purpose of the Audubon Zoo is entertainment. Many of the zoo's promotional efforts are aimed at creating an image of the zoo as an entertaining place to go. Obviously, such a campaign is necessary to attract visitors to the zoo. Behind the scenes, the zoo also preserves and breeds many animal species, conducts research, and educates the public. The mission statement of the Audubon Institute, which encompasses the zoo, is given in Exhibit 10–3.

OPERATIONS

Friends of the Zoo. Friends of the Zoo was formed in 1974 and incorporated in 1975 with 400 original members. The group's stated purpose is to increase support and awareness of the Audubon Zoo. Initially, Friends of the Zoo tried to raise interest and commitment to the zoo, but its activities have increased dramatically over the years to include funding, operating, and governing the zoo. Friends of the Zoo has a 24-member governing board. Yearly elections are held for six members of the board who serve four-year terms. The board oversees the policies of the zoo and sets guidelines for memberships, concessions, fund-raising, and marketing. Actual policy making and operations are controlled by the Audubon Park Commission, however, which sets zoo hours, admission prices, and so forth.

Through its volunteer programs, Friends of the Zoo staffs many of the zoo's programs. Volunteers from members of the Friends of the Zoo served as "edZOOcators," education volunteers who are specially trained to conduct interpretive education programs, and "Zoo Area Patrollers," who provide general informa-

---

EXHIBIT 10-3 Audubon Institute Mission Statement

The mission of the Audubon Institute is to cultivate awareness and appreciation of life and the earth's resources and to help conserve and enrich our natural world. The Institute's primary objectives toward this are:

Conservation: To participate in the global effort to conserve natural resources by developing and maintaining captive stocks of endangered plants, animals, and marine life, and by cooperating with related projects in the wild.

Education: To impart knowledge and understanding of the interaction of nature and man through programs, exhibits, and publications and to encourage public participation in global conservation efforts.

Research: To foster the collection and dissemination of scientific information that will enhance the conservation and educational objectives of the facilities of the Audubon Institute.

Economics: To insure long–range financial security by sound fiscal management and continued development, funding through creative means that encourage corporate, foundation, and individual support.

Leadership: To serve as a model in the civic and professional communities. To foster a spirit of cooperation, participation, and pride.
Source: The Audubon Institute.

tion about a geographic area of the zoo and help with crowd control. Other volunteers assist in the Commissary, Animal Health Care Center, and Wild Bird Rehabilitation Center or help with membership, public relations, graphics, clerical work, research, or horticulture.

In 1988, the name of the Friends of the Zoo was changed to the Audubon Institute to reflect its growing interest in activities beyond the zoo alone. It planned to promote the development of other facilities and manage these facilities once they were a reality.

Fund-Raising. The Audubon Zoo and the Audubon Institute raise funds through five major types of activities: Friends of the Zoo membership, concessions, Adopt an Animal, Zoo-to-Do, and capital fund drives. Zoo managers from around the country come to the Audubon Zoo for tips on fund-raising.

Membership. Membership in the Audubon Institute is open to anyone. Admission prices and membership fees have increased over the years, as summarized in Exhibits 10–4 and 10–5. The number of members also increased steadily, from the original 400 members in 1974 to 38,000 members in 1990, but decreased to 28,000 in 1992.

EXHIBIT 10-4   Audubon Zoo Admission Data

YEAR	SENIOR/ ADULT	CHILD
1972	$0.75	$0.25
1978	1.00	0.50
1979	1.50	0.75
1980	2.00	1.00
1981	2.50	1.25
1982	3.00	1.50
1983	3.50	1.75
1984	4.00	2.00
1985	4.50	2.00
1986	5.00	2.50
1987	5.50	2.50
1988	5.50	2.50
1989	6.00	3.00
1990	6.50	3.00
1991	7.00	3.25
1992	7.00	3.25
1993	7.50	3.50

EXHIBIT 10-4 *Continued*

ADMISSIONS FOR 1990–1993

AUDUBON ZOO

MONTH	1990	1991	1992	1993
January	38,091	18,710	27,139	35,797
February	49,881	38,296	47,411	38,878
March	125,551	99,217	104,906	87,959
April	129,408	92,776	109,825	136,157
May	126,881	89,881	119,948	132,685
June	88,600	83,655	79,607	80,636
July	95,923	81,746	77,279	90,232
August	101,309	94,022	99,724	84,118
September	57,105	51,180	39,380	51,485
October	77,948	87,642	90,131	
November	63,940	56,882	50,960	
December	26,856	32,178	30,498	
Total	981,493	826,167	876,708	737,947

AQUARIUM OF THE AMERICAS

MONTH	1990	1991	1992	1993
January		128,894	79,786	71,041
February		127,718	82,761	66,619
March		206,931	142,383	117,290
April		182,614	135,815	116,437
May		199,232	145,879	139,975
June		191,603	136,262	135,232
July		235,093	182,461	177,725
August		207,544	157,969	143,152
September	247,875	112,574	90,965	88,778
October	220,498	101,583	94,301	
November	201,021	109,766	85,670	
December	162,334	98,561	72,889	
Total	831,728	1,902,113	1,407,061	1,056,249

Source: The Audubon Institute.

Membership allows free entry to the Audubon Zoo and many other zoos around the United States. Participation in Zoobilation (annual-members-only evenings at the zoo) and the many volunteer programs described earlier are other benefits of membership.

Increasing membership required a special approach to marketing the zoo. Chip Weigand, director of marketing for the zoo, says:

> In marketing memberships, we try to encourage repeat visitations, the feeling that one can visit as often as one wants, the idea that the zoo changes from visit to visit and that there are

EXHIBIT 10-5 Audubon Zoo Membership Fees and Membership

YEAR	FAMILY MEMBERSHIP FEES	INDIVIDUAL MEMBERSHIP FEES	NUMBER OF MEMBERSHIPS
1979	$20	$10	1,000
1980	20	10	7,000
1981	20	10	11,000
1982	25	15	18,000
1983	30	15	22,000
1984	35	20	26,000
1985	40	20	27,000
1986	45	25	28,616
1987	45	25	29,318
1988	45	25	33,314
1989	49	29	35,935
1990	49	29	38,154
1991	49	30	30,171
1992	49	30	28,422

Source: The Audubon Institute.

good reasons to make one large payment or donation for a membership card, rather than paying for each visit. . . . The overwhelming factor is a good zoo that people want to visit often, so that a membership makes good economical sense.

Results of research conducted on visitors to the zoo are contained in Exhibits 10–6 and 10–7.

The zoo has a membership designed for businesses, the Audubon Zoo Curator Club, with four categories of membership: Bronze, $250; Silver, $500; Gold, $1,000; and Platinum, $2,500 and more.

Concessions. The Audubon Zoo concessions for refreshments and gifts are run by volunteer members of the Audubon Institute, and all profits go directly to the zoo. Profits from operation of the concession brought in $400,000 a year by 1980 and over $1 million in profits in 1990. In 1993, the Audubon Institute was considering leasing the concessions to a third party vendor.

Adopt an Animal. Zoo Parents pay a fee to "adopt" an animal, the fee varying with the animal chosen. Zoo Parents' names are listed on a large sign inside the zoo. They also have their own celebration, Zoo Parents Day, held at the zoo yearly.

Zoo-to-Do. Zoo-to-Do is a black-tie fund-raiser held annually with live music, food and drink, and original, high-class souvenirs such as posters or ceramic necklaces. Admission tickets, limited to 3,000 annually, are priced starting at $100 per person. A raffle is conducted in conjunction with the Zoo-to-Do, with raffle items varying from an opportunity to be zoo curator for the day to the use of a Mercedes Benz for a year. Despite the rather stiff price, the Zoo-to-Do is a popular sellout every year. Local

EXHIBIT 10-6 Respondent Characteristics of Zoo Visitors According to Visitation Frequency (in percent)

RESPONDENT CHARACTERISTIC	NUMBER OF ZOO VISITS OVER PAST TWO YEARS			
	FOUR OR MORE	TWO OR THREE	ONE OR NONE	NEVER VISITED ZOO
AGE				
Under 27	26	35	31	9
27 to 35	55	27	15	3
36 to 45	48	32	11	9
46 to 55	18	20	37	25
Over 55	27	29	30	14
MARITAL STATUS				
Married	41	28	20	11
Not Married	30	34	24	13
CHILDREN AT HOME				
Yes	46	30	15	9
No	34	28	27	12
INTERESTED IN VISITING NEW ORLEANS AQUARIUM				
Very, with Emphasis	47	26	18	9
Very, without Emphasis	45	24	23	12
Somewhat	28	37	14	11
Not Too	19	32	27	22
MEMBER OF FRIENDS OF THE ZOO				
Yes	67	24	5	4
No, but Heard of It	35	30	24	12
Never Heard of It	25	28	35	13
WOULD YOU BE INTERESTED IN JOINING FOTZ (NON-MEMBERS ONLY)				
Very/Somewhat	50	28	14	8
No/Don't Know	33	29	26	12

Source: The Audubon Institute.

restaurants and other businesses donate most of the necessary supplies, which decreases the cost of the affair. In 1985 the Zoo-to-Do raised about $500,000 in one night, more money than any other nonmedical fund-raiser in the country.

Marketing. The American Association of Zoological Parks and Aquariums report that most zoos find the majority of their visitors live within a single population center in close proximity to the park. Thus, in order to sustain attendance over the years,

EXHIBIT 10-7 Relative Importance of Seven Reasons as to Why Respondent Does Not Visit the Zoo More Often (in percent)

REASON (CLOSE ENDED)	VERY IMPORTANT WITH EMPHASIS	VERY IMPORTANT WITHOUT EMPHASIS	SOMEWHAT IMPORTANT	UNIMPORTANT
The distance of the Zoo's location from where you live	7	11	21	60
The cost of a Zoo visit	4	8	22	66
Not being all that interested in Zoo animals	2	12	18	67
The parking problem on weekends	7	11	19	62
The idea that you get tired of seeing the same exhibits over and over	5	18	28	49
It's too hot during the summer months	25	23	22	30
Just not having the idea occur to you	8	19	26	48

Source: The Audubon Institute.

zoos must attract the same visitors repeatedly. A large number of the Audubon Zoo's promotional programs and special events are aimed at just that.

Marketing goals for the Audubon Institute are to position the institute as a world leader in species preservation and resource conservation and to reinforce and maintain Audubon Zoo's position as a world-class facility. For 1991 the Audubon Institute wanted to increase attendance at the zoo by 10 percent to 1.1 million visitors. Another major objective is to raise the level of awareness of the Audubon Institute and its mission 50 percent in a three-state region.

The zoo's marketing budget is over $800,000 per year, excluding salaries. This budget includes group sales, public relations, advertising, and special events but does not include developmental fund-raising or membership. Breakdowns of the marketing budget for 1993 can be found in Exhibit 10–8.

The Audubon Zoo and the Audubon Institute conduct a multitude of very successful promotional programs. The effect is to have continual parties and celebrations going on that attract a variety of people to the zoo and raise additional revenue. Exhibit 10–9 lists the major annual promotional programs that the zoo conducts. The zoo also schedules concerts of well-known musicians, such as Irma Thomas, Pete Fountain, the Monkees, and Manhattan Transfer, and other special events throughout the year. As a result, a variety of events occur each month.

Many educational activities are held all year long: (1) a Junior Zoo Keeper program for seventh- and eighth-graders, (2) a student intern program for high school and college students, and (3) a ZOOmobile that takes live animals to such locations as special education classes, hospitals, and old-age homes.

EXHIBIT 10-8 1993 Marketing Budget

MARKETING

Administrative	$319,200
Sales	159,700
Public Relations	99,950
Concerts/Events	166,000
Special Events	74,500
TOTAL	$819,350
Revenues from Special Events	160,000
NET BUDGET	$659,305

PUBLIC RELATIONS

Education, Travel, and Subscriptions	5%
Printing and Duplicating	58
Professional Services	14
Delivery and Postage	3
Telephone	1
Entertainment	2
Supplies	15
Miscellaneous	2

SPECIAL EVENTS

General and Administrative	18%
LA Swamp Fest	22
Earthfest	16
Ninja Turtle Breakfast	13
Jazz Search	9
Fiesta Latina	6
Crescent City Cats	6
Other Events	10

Source: The Audubon Institute.

Riverboat. A riverboat ride on the romantic paddle-wheeled *Cotton Blossom* takes visitors from downtown to the zoo. Originally, the trip began at a dock in the French Quarter, but it was later moved to a dock immediately adjacent to New Orleans' newest attraction, the Riverwalk, a Rouse development, on the site of the 1984 Louisiana World Exposition. Not only is the riverboat ride great fun, it also lures tourists and conventioneers from the downtown attractions of the French Quarter and the new Riverwalk to the zoo some 6 miles upstream. A further allure of the riverboat ride is a return trip to downtown on the New Orleans streetcar, one of the few remaining trolley cars in the United States. The Zoo Cruise not only draws more visitors but has generated additional revenue through landing fees paid by the New Orleans Steamboat Company, and it helps keep traffic out of uptown New Orleans.

The zoo's ability to generate operating funds has been ascribed to the dedication of the Audubon Institute, continuing increases in attendance, and creative special events and programs. A history of adequate operating funds allows the zoo to guar-

EXHIBIT 10-9 Selected Audubon Park Zoo Promotional Programs

MONTH	ACTIVITY
March	Louisiana Black Heritage Festival. A two-day celebration of Louisiana's Black history and its native contributions through food, music, and arts and crafts.
March	Earth Fest. The environment and our planet are the focus of this fun-filled and educational event. Recycling, conservation displays, and puppet shows.
April	Jazz Search. This entertainment series is aimed at finding the best new talent in the area with the winners to be featured at the New Orleans' Jazz & Heritage Festival.
April	Zoo-To-Do for Kids. At this "pint-sized" version of the Zoo-To-Do, fun and games abound for kids.
May	Zoo To-Do. Annual black tie fund-raiser featuring over 100 of New Orleans' finest restaurants and three music stages.
May	Irma Thomas Mother's Day Concert. The annual celebration of Mother's Day with a buffet.
August	Lego Invitational. Architectural firms turn thousands upon thousands of Lego pieces into their own original creations.
September	Fiesta Latina. Experience the best the Hispanic community has to offer through music, cuisine, and arts and crafts.
October	Louisiana Swamp Festival. Cajun food, music, and crafts highlight this four-day salute to Louisiana's bayou country; features hands-on contact with live swamp animals.
October	Boo at the Zoo. This annual Halloween extravaganza features games, special entertainment, trick or treat, a haunted house, and the Zoo's Spook Train.

Source: The Audubon Institute.

antee capital donors that their gifts will be used to build and maintain top-notch exhibits. A comparison of the 1990 and 1991 statements of operating income and expense for the Audubon Institute is in Exhibit 10–10.

Fund Drives. The Audubon Zoo Development Fund was established in 1973. Corporate-industrial support of the zoo has been very strong—many corporations underwrote construction of zoo displays and facilities. A partial list of major corporate sponsors is in Exhibit 10–11. A sponsorship is considered to be for the life of the exhibit. The developmental department operates on a 12 percent overhead rate, which means that $.88 of every dollar raised goes toward the projects. By 1989 the master plan for development was 75 percent complete; the fund-raising goal was $1.5 million.

Zoo Director. L. Ron Forman, Audubon Zoo Director, is called a "zoomaster extraordinaire" and is described by the press as a "cross between Doctor Doolittle and the Wizard of Oz," as a "practical visionary," and as "serious, but with a sense of humor." A native New Orleanian, Forman quit an MBA program to join the city government as an administrative assistant and found himself doing a business analysis project on the Audubon Park. Once the city was committed to a new zoo, Forman was placed on board as an assistant to the zoo director, John Moore. In early 1977,

EXHIBIT 10-10 The Audubon Institute, Inc. Operating Income and Expenses

	1990 Zoo	1990 Aquarium	1990 Total	1991 Zoo	1991 Aquarium	1991 Total	1992 Zoo	1992 Aquarium	1992 Total
OPERATING INCOME (IN THOUSANDS)									
Admissions	3,587	3,664	7,251	2,908	8,900	11,808	2,763	7,953	10,716
Food and Gift Operations	3,496	711	4,207	2,565	2,600	5,165	2,663	2,397	5,060
Membership	1,932	2,318	4,250	1,658	1,290	2,948	1,957	646	2,603
Recreational Program	396	0	396	366	130	496	647	143	790
Visitor Services	218	0	218	198	650	848	144	315	459
Other	32	650	682	129	7	136	436	6	442
Total Income	9,660	7,343	17,003	7,824	13,577	21,401	8,610	11,460	20,070
OPERATING EXPENSES (IN THOUSANDS)									
Maintenance	1,444	1,316	2,760	1,220	2,470	3,690	1,582	2,330	3,912
Educational/Curatorial	2,526	2,783	5,311	2,117	3,500	5,617	2,197	1,808	4,005
Food and Gift Operations	2,375	483	2,858	2,010	920	2,930	1,805	1,383	3,188
Membership	840	631	1,471	528	540	1,068	612	361	973
Recreational	358	362	720	231	400	631	276	100	376
Marketing	633	593	1,226	479	1,500	1,979	492	1,569	2,061
Visitor Services	373	125	498	205	650	855	230	366	596
Administration	1,110	1,050	2,160	1,034	3,597	4,631	1,416	2,289	3,705
Construction Expenses	0	0	0	0	0	0	0	1,254	1,254
Total Expenses	9661	7,343	17,004	7,824	13,577	21,401	8,610	11,460	20,070
Net Profit	0	0	0	0	0	0	0	0	0
OPERATING INCOME									
Admissions	49%	51%	100%	25%	75%	100%	26%	74%	100%
Food and Gift Operations	83	17	100	50	50	100	53	47	100
Membership	45	55	100	56	44	100	75	25	100
Recreational Program	100	0	100	74	26	100	82	18	100
Visitor Services	100	0	100	23	77	100	31	69	100
Other	5	95	100	95	5	100	99	1	100
Total Income	57	43	100	37	63	100	43	57	100
OPERATING EXPENSES									
Maintenance	52%	48%	100%	33%	67%	100%	40%	60%	100%
Educational /Curatorial	48	52	100	38	62	100	55	45	100
Food and Gift Operations	83	17	100	69	31	100	57	43	100
Membership	57	43	100	49	51	100	63	37	100
Recreational	50	50	100	37	63	100	73	27	100
Marketing	52	48	100	24	76	100	24	76	100
Visitor Services	75	25	100	24	76	100	39	61	100
Administration	51	49	100	22	78	100	38	62	100
Construction Expenses	0	0	0	0	0	0	0	100	100
Total Expenses	57	43	100	37	63	100	43	57	100

Source: The Audubon Institute.

EXHIBIT 10-11 Audubon Zoo Major Corporate Sponsors

Amoco Foundation
American Express
Anheuser-Busch, Inc.
Arthur Anderson and Company
J. Aron Charitable Foundation, Inc.
BellSouth Corporation
BP America
Chevron USA, Inc.
Conoco, Inc.
Consolidated Natural Gas Corporation
D. H. Holmes, Ltd.
Entergy Corporation
Exxon Company, USA
Freeport-McMoran, Inc.
Host International, Inc.
Kentwood Spring Water
Louisiana Coca-Cola Bottling Company, Ltd.
Louisiana Land and Exploration Company
Martin Marietta Manned Space Systems
McDonald's Operators of New Orleans
Mobil Foundation, Inc.
National Endowment for the Arts
National Science Foundation
Ozone Spring Water
Pan American Life Insurance Company
Phillip Morris Companies, Inc.
Shell Companies Foundation, Inc.
Tenneco, Inc.
Texaco USA
USF&G Corporation
Wendy's of New Orleans, Inc.

Source: The Audubon Institute.

Moore gave up the battle between the "animal people" and the "people-people," and Forman took over as park and zoo director.

Forman was said to bring an MBA-meets-menagerie style to the zoo that was responsible for transforming it from a public burden into an almost completely self-sustaining operation. The result has not only benefitted the citizens of the city but has also added a major tourist attraction to the economically troubled city of the 1980s.

Staffing. The zoo uses two classes of employees, civil service, through the Audubon Park Commission, and noncivil service. The civil service employees include the curators and zookeepers. They fall under the jurisdiction of the city civil service system but are paid out of the budget of the Friends of the Zoo. Employees who work in public relations, advertising, concessions, fund-raising, and so on, are hired through the Friends of the Zoo and are not part of the civil service system. See Exhibit 10–12 for further data on staffing patterns.

A visitor to the new Audubon Zoo can quickly see why New Orleanians are so proud of their zoo. In a city called one of the dirtiest in the nation, the zoo is virtually spotless. This is a result of adequate staffing and the clear pride of both those who work at and those who visit the zoo. One of the first points made by volunteers guiding school groups is that anyone seeing a piece of trash on the ground must pick it up. A 1986 city poll showed that 93 percent of the citizens surveyed gave the zoo a high approval rating—an extremely high rating for any public facility.

Kudos came from groups outside the local area as well. Delegates from the American Association of Zoological Parks and Aquariums ranked the Audubon Zoo as one of the three top zoos of its size in America. In 1982 the American Association of Nurserymen gave the zoo a Special Judges Award for its use of plant materials. In 1985 the Audubon Zoo received the Phoenix Award from the Society of American Travel Writers for its achievements in conservation, preservation, and beautification.

By 1987, the zoo was virtually self-sufficient. The small amount of money received from government grants amounted to less than 10 percent of the budget. The master plan for the development of the zoo was 75 percent complete, and the reptile exhibit

EXHIBIT 10-12   Audubon Zoo Employee Structure

YEAR	NUMBER OF PAID EMPLOYEES	NUMBER OF VOLUNTEERS	ANNUAL TOTALS
1972	36	0	36
1973	49	0	49
1974	69	0	69
1975	90	0	90
1976	143	0	143
1977	193	0	193
1978	184	0	184
1979	189	0	189
1980	198	0	198
1981	245	0	245
1982	305	0	305
1983	302	56	358
1984	419	120	539
1985	454	126	580
1986	426	250	676
1987	431	300	731
1988	462	310	772
1989	300	270	570
1990	450	350	800
1991	266	325	591
1992	245	374	619
			7,937

Source: The Audubon Institute.

was scheduled for completion in the fall. The organization had expanded with a full complement of professionals and managers. (See Exhibit 10–13 for the organizational structure of the zoo.)

Although the zoo had made great progress in fifteen years, all was not quiet on the political front. In a court battle, the city won over the state on the issue of who wielded ultimate authority over Audubon Park and Zoo. Indeed, the zoo has benefitted from three friendly mayors in a row, starting with Moon Landrieu, who championed the new zoo, to Ernest "Dutch" Morial, to Sidney Barthelemy who threw his support to both the zoo and the aquarium proposal championed by Forman.

The Aquarium. In 1986, Forman and a group of supporters proposed the development of an aquarium and riverfront park to the New Orleans City Council. In November 1986, the electorate voted to fund an aquarium and a riverfront park by a 70 percent margin, one of the largest margins the city had ever given to any tax proposal. Forman hailed this as a vote of confidence from the citizens and a mandate to build a world-class aquarium that would produce new jobs, stimulate the local economy, and create an educational resource for the children of the city.

The Aquarium of the Americas opened in September 1990. The $40 million project is located adjacent to the Riverwalk, providing a logical pedestrian link for visitors between New Orleans major attractions of the Riverwalk and the Jax Brewery, a shopping center in the French Quarter. Management of the aquarium was placed under the Audubon Institute, the same organization that ran the Audubon Zoo. A feasibility study prepared by Harrison Price Company projected a probable 868,000 visitors during the first year of operation, with 75 percent of the visitors coming from outside the metropolitan area. These attendance figures were reached in only four months and six days from the grand opening. Attendance remained strong through 1992 after dropping off a little from the grand opening numbers.

Zoo director Forman has demonstrated that zoos have almost unlimited potential. A 1980 *New Orleans* magazine article cited some of Forman's ideas, ranging from a safari train to a breeding center for rare animals. The latter has an added attraction as a potential money maker since an Asiatic lion cub, for example, sells for around $10,000. This wealth of ideas was important because expanded facilities and programs are required to maintain attendance at any public attraction.

THE FUTURE

Although the zoo and aquarium enjoyed political support in 1992, New Orleans is still suffering from high unemployment and a generally depressed economy resulting from the depression in the oil industry. A few facts about New Orleans are given in Exhibit 10–14. The zoo operates in a city where many attractions compete for the leisure dollar of citizens and visitors. The Audubon Zoo must vie with the French Quarter, Dixieland jazz, the Superdome, and Mardi Gras.

The Audubon Institute has a strategic plan for the 1990s as outlined below. Evaluate the effectiveness of this plan and offer additions, changes, and deletions based on a thorough strategic analysis.

The components of the Institute's plan include:

Wilderness Park, a 300-acre preserve located on the 1,200-acre campus of the Freeport-McMoran Audubon Species Survival Center, providing a wilderness recreational area within a hardwood forest, complete with an abundance of native fauna. (Opening: Spring 1994, estimated cost $1 million)

EXHIBIT 10-13 Organizational Chart for the Audubon Park Commission

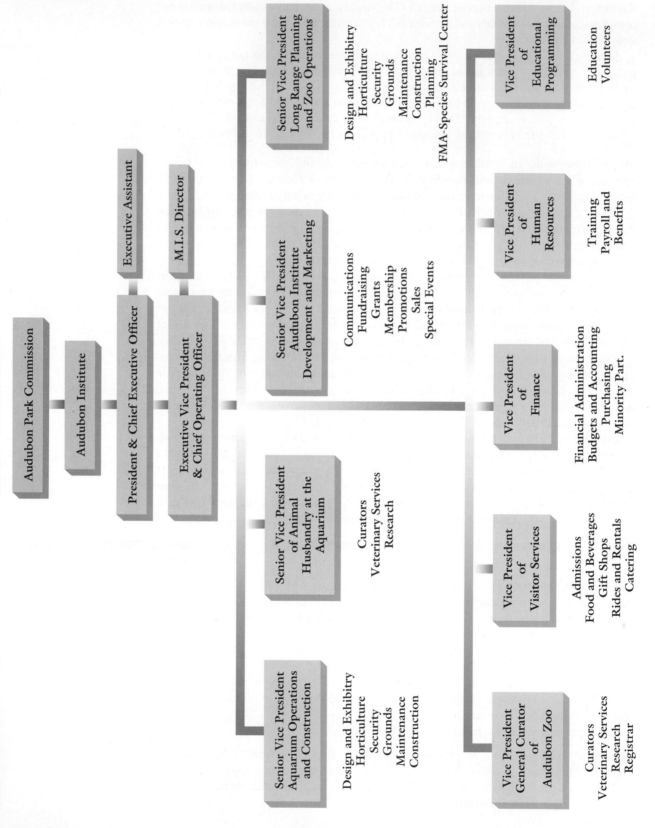

Audubon Park Commission

Audubon Institute

President & Chief Executive Officer

Executive Assistant

M.I.S. Director

Executive Vice President & Chief Operating Officer

Senior Vice President Aquarium Operations and Construction

Design and Exhibitry
Horticulture
Security
Grounds
Maintenance
Construction

Senior Vice President of Animal Husbandry at the Aquarium

Curators
Veterinary Services
Research

Senior Vice President Audubon Institute Development and Marketing

Communications
Fundraising
Grants
Membership
Promotions
Sales
Special Events

Senior Vice President Long Range Planning and Zoo Operations

Design and Exhibitry
Horticulture
Security
Grounds
Maintenance
Construction
Planning
FMA-Species Survival Center

Vice President of Educational Programming

Education
Volunteers

Vice President of Human Resources

Training
Payroll and Benefits

Vice President of Finance

Financial Administration
Budgets and Accounting
Purchasing
Minority Part.

Vice President of Visitor Services

Admissions
Food and Beverages
Gift Shops
Rides and Rentals
Catering

Vice President General Curator of Audubon Zoo

Curators
Veterinary Services
Research
Registrar

Audubon Center for Research of Endangered Species (Acres), where studies on the procreation and successful rearing of animals in captivity will take place. (opening: Fall 1995, estimated cost $15 million Federal Grant)

Insectarium and Butterfly Pavillion, a unique facility exclusively dedicated to the insect world, featuring "hands-on" exhibitry to encourage the visitor—young and old—to explore the realm of these fascinating creatures. (opening: June 1996, estimated cost $2 million)

Expansion of the Woldenberg Riverfront Park, 16 acres located downriver from the Aquarium, continuing the pattern of beautiful plantings, water features, and gracious green space already developed on the banks of the Mississippi River. (completion: June 1996, estimated cost $1 million)

Phase II of the Aquarium of the Americas, a 60,000-square-foot addition, including a 350-seat Imax theater (opening: Fall 1995) and a changing exhibits gallery. (opening: Spring 1996, estimated cost of both $10 million)

Zoo 2000, a new master plan focusing on increasing and enhancing the participatory conservation and environmental education experience of the Audubon Zoological Garden. (completion: 1997, estimated cost $17 million)

Total Estimated Cost: $46 million

EXHIBIT 10-14   A Few Facts About the New Orleans MSA

Population	1,324,400
Households	489,900
Median Age	30.8 years
Median Household EBI	$29,130
Average Temperature	70 degrees Fahrenheit
Average Annual Rainfall	63 inches
Average Elevation	5 feet below sea level
Area	363.5 square miles
	199.4 square miles of land

MAJOR ECONOMIC ACTIVITIES

Tourism (5 million visitors per year)
Oil and Gas Industry
The Port of New Orleans (170 million tons of cargo/year)

TAXES

State Sales Tax	4.0%
Parish (County) Sales Tax	5.0% (Orleans)
	4.0% (Jefferson)
State Income Tax	2.1-2.6% on first $20,000
	3.0-3.5% on next $30,000
	6.0% on $51,000 & over

Parish Property Tax of 126.15 mills (Orleans) is based on 10% of appraised value over $75,000 homestead exemption.

Sources: *Sales and Marketing Management* and South Central Bell *Yellow Pages*, 1991.

THE CLASSIC CAR CLUB OF AMERICA—1994

Headquartered in Des Plaines, Illinois (708-390-0443), the Classic Car Club of America, Inc. (CCCA) was formed in 1952 by a small group of enthusiasts interested in luxury cars of the late 1920s and 1930s. A listing of certain high-priced, high-quality, and limited-production cars were designated as "Classic Cars," and the period of 1925–1942 was chosen as the limits of the "Classic Era." It was felt that cars built prior to 1925 had not yet reached technical maturity, and that after World War II the quality of most so-called luxury cars had succumbed to the economic pressures of mass production. Some pictures of Classic Cars are provided in Figure 11–1.

Over the years, the list of CCCA recognized Classics was modified and expanded, and the time period was extended to 1948 to include certain pre-World War II models that continued in production for a few years after the war. While all cars included on the list were of considerably higher price and quality than the mass-production cars of this era, there was also a wide variance in original prices and quality of these recognized Classics. For example, in 1930 a new Ford Model A (*not* a Classic) cost about $450. In comparison, two of the many CCCA-recognized Classics of that year are the Auburn Eight, which was priced as low as $1,195, and the Duesenberg Model J, which sold new in the $12,000–$14,000 range. The Auburn, although a car of middle price and quality, is considered a Classic because its styling was exceptional at the time while the Duesenberg was the highest priced and most exotic American car of the era, carrying custom-built bodies and bought by an exclusive clientele of movie stars, playboys, and other superrich personalities. Most Classics fell somewhere between these two extremes, with original prices in the $2,000–$5,000 range (a considerable amount of money at that time). Exhibit 11–1 lists those cars recognized as Classics by the CCCA in 1993.

THE COLLECTOR CAR HOBBY

The "collector car" hobby in the United States is a broad and wide-reaching activity involving a large number of Americans. Basically, a "collector car" is any automobile owned for purposes other than normal transportation. The most widely-read collector car hobby magazine, *Hemmings Motor News*, had a circulation of about 265,000 in December 1993. Another magazine, *Car Collector*, estimates that nearly one million Americans are engaged in the old car hobby. However, a figure of 350,000–500,000 would probably be a more conservative estimate of the number of Americans engaged in this hobby.

"Collector car" is a loose term, ranging from turn-of-the-century "horseless carriages" to currently-built but limited-production cars, such as Italian super-sports cars. Naturally, owners of collector cars enjoy the company of other persons with similar interests, and thus a wide variety of car clubs exist, to suit almost any particular segment of this vast hobby. The largest of these clubs, the Antique Automobile Club of America, caters to owners of virtually all cars twenty-five years old or older, and has a membership of more than 55,000.

FIGURE 11-1 Classic Cars: 1941 Packard (top left); 1934 Rolls Royce (top right); 1926 Duesenburg (bottom).

CCCA ORGANIZATION AND ACTIVITIES

When the club's 1993 fiscal year ended on October 31, 1993, the club had 5,447 members, as indicated below. (Exhibit 11–2 gives a comparison of membership figures for recent years.)

Active (regular membership—1993 dues at $30 a year)	4179
Associate (for spouses, no publications—$5 a year)	1005
Life (after ten years, one-time fee of $420)	199
Life Associate (spouse of Life— $42)	59
Honorary (famous car designers, etc.)	5
	5,447

CCCA members receive a variety of benefits from their membership including a magazine, *The Classic Car*, which is published four times a year. The magazine, which is highly respected by automotive historians, features color photos of Classics on the front and back covers, as well as forty-eight pages or more of articles and black-and-white photos of Classics. A CCCA *Bulletin* is also published eight times a year, and contains club and hobby news, technical columns, and members' and commercial ads for Classic cars, parts, and related items. A further publication is the club's *Handbook and Directory*, published annually. It contains the CCCA bylaws, judging rules, requirements for regions, etc., as well as a current listing of members and the Classic cars they own. Commercial car-related advertisements are solicited for this *Handbook and Directory*, and its cost is largely paid for by these advertisements.

The CCCA sponsors three types of national events each year. The annual meeting in January includes business meetings and a car judging meet, and is held in a different location in the United States each year. In April and July, a series of "Grand Classic" judging meets are held in ten to twelve locations around the country, with a

EXHIBIT 11-1 CCCA-recognized Classic Cars

A.C.	Farman*	N.A.G.*
Adler*	Fiat*	Nash*
Alfa Romeo	FN*	Packard*
Alvis*	Franklin*	Peerless
Amilcar*	Frazer-Nash*	Peugot*
Armstrong-Siddeley*	Hispano-Suiza*	Pierce-Arrow
Aston Martin*	Horch	Railton*
Auburn*	Hotchkiss*	Raymond Mays*
Austro-Daimler	Hudson*	Renault*
Ballot*	Humber*	Reo*
Bentley	Invicta	Revere
Benz*	Isotta-Fraschini	Riley*
Blackhawk	Itala	Roamer*
B.M.W.*	Jaguar*	Rochet Schneider*
Brewster*	Jensen*	Rohr*
Brough Superior*	Jordan*	Rolls-Royce
Bucciali*	Julian*	Ruxton
Bugatti	Kissell*	Squire
Buick*	Lagonda*	S.S. and S.S. Jaguar*
Cadillac*	Lanchester*	Stearns-Knight
Chenard-Walcker*	Lancia*	Stevens-Duryea
Chrysler*	La Salle*	Steyr*
Cord	Lincoln*	Studebaker*
Cunningham	Lincoln Continental	Stutz
Dagmar*	Locomobile*	Sunbeam*
Daimler*	Marmon*	Talbot*
Darracq*	Maserati*	Talbot-Lago*
Delage*	Maybach	Tatra*
Delahaye*	McFarlan	Triumph*
Delaunay Belleville*	Mercedes	Vauxhall*
Doble	Mercedes-Benz*	Voisin
Dorris	Mercer	Wills Ste Claire
Duesenberg	M.G.*	Willys-Knight*
du Pont	Minerva*	
Excelsior*		

* Indicates that only certain models of this make are considered Classic. Some other
   1925–1948 custom-bodied cars not listed above may be approved as Classic upon
   individual application.
Source: The CCCA.

total of 400 to 600 Classics being exhibited and judged. At CCCA judging meets,
cars are rated by a point system which takes into account the quality and authenticity
of restoration and the general condition of the car, both mechanically and cosmeti-
cally. CCCA judging meets are not publicized to the general public and access to view
the cars is restricted to club members and their guests only.

EXHIBIT 11-2   Selected CCCA Membership Data (for October 31 fiscal year end)

	1993	1992	1991	1990	1989	1988	1987	1986
Active Members	4179	4184	4156	4188	4170	4118	3935	3885
Associate Members	1005	1012	977	893	928	914	828	773
Life Members	199	195	188	185	175	170	163	160
Life Associate Members	59	60	59	56	53	50	48	45
Honorary Members	5	5	6	6	7	6	7	6
Total	5447	5456	5386	5328	5333	5258	4981	4869

Source: The CCCA.

Each year, the club sponsors several "Classic CARavans" in various parts of the United States and Canada. The "CARavan" is a tour in which members in as many as 100 Classic cars join together in a week-long planned itinerary.

The Annual Meeting, Grand Classics, and CARavans are designed to be financially self-supporting, with attending members paying fees that cover the costs of the events.

The CCCA also has members who have volunteered to be technical advisors available to assist other members. Furthermore, the club makes available for sale to members certain club-related products, such as ties and umbrellas with a Classic Car design.

The club is managed by a fifteen-member Board of Directors, with a President, Vice Presidents, Treasurer, Secretary, etc. All are club member volunteers (from all over the United States) who have shown a willingness and ability to help run the CCCA and have been elected by the total membership to three-year terms of office. They are not reimbursed for their expenses, which include attending eight Board meetings each year, most of which are held at headquarters offices which are rented in Des Plaines, Illinois (a location chosen because of its central location within the United States and its close proximity to Chicago's main airport). Another member volunteers as "Executive Administrator" and oversees the club's secretary and its daily operations. The only paid employees of the club are the full-time office secretary and the publications editor, who is a free-lance editor doing other work besides that for the CCCA. An organization chart of the CCCA is shown in Exhibit 11–3.

In addition to belonging to the national CCCA, the majority of members also pay dues and belong to a local CCCA region. In 1994 there were twenty-eight regions throughout the United States. (See Figure 11–2.) Each region sponsors a variety of local activities for members and their Classics and publishes its own magazine or newsletter. Many of the regions also derive revenues from the sale of classic car replacement parts or service items, offered to all members of the national club.

Legally separate from the CCCA and its regions, a Classic Car Club of America Museum also exists. It occupies space as part of a larger old-car museum in Hickory Corners, Michigan, and displays a variety of Classic cars that have been donated to it. The CCCA Museum, unlike the CCCA itself, is eligible to receive tax-deductible gifts of money and property (such as cars). Although the CCCA has granted the museum the right to use the "CCCA" name, the museum has a separate Board of Trustees and is run totally separate from the club.

EXHIBIT 11-3 CCCA Organizational Chart

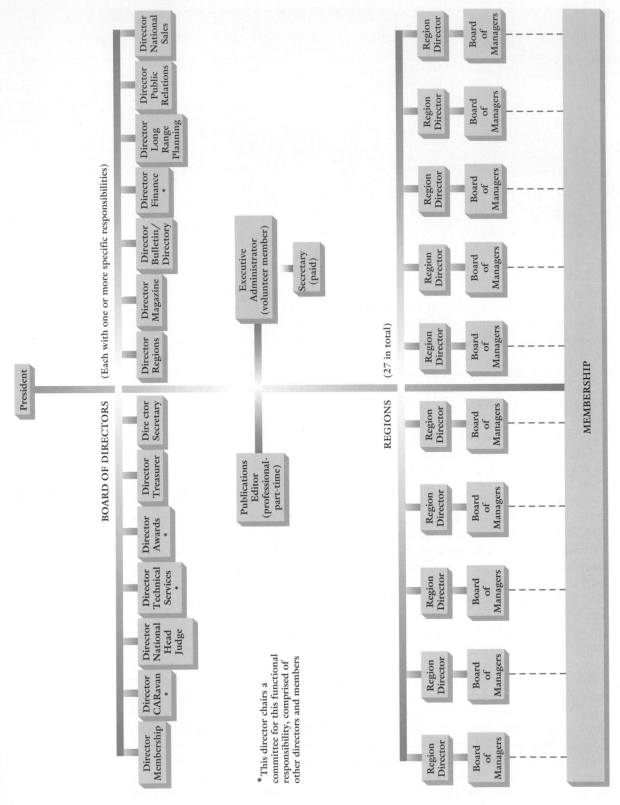

President

BOARD OF DIRECTORS

(Each with one or more specific responsibilities)

Director Membership

Director CARavan *

Director National Head Judge

Director Technical Services *

Director Awards *

Director Treasurer

Dire ctor Secretary

Director Regions

Director Magazine

Director Bulletin/ Directory

Director Finance *

Director Long Range Planning

Director Public Relations

Director National Sales

Publications Editor (professional- part-time)

Executive Administrator (volunteer member)

Secretary (paid)

*This director chairs a committee for this functional responsibility, comprised of other directors and members

REGIONS

(27 in total)

Region Director — Board of Managers (×12)

MEMBERSHIP

FIGURE 11-2 Map Showing Boundaries of Regions of Classic CAr club of America

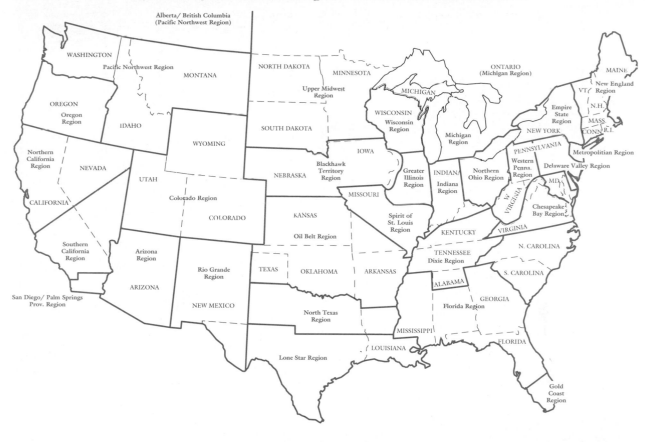

CURRENT CONCERNS THAT FACE THE CCCA

While the officers and directors of the CCCA believe the club to be strong, both financially and in its value to its members, a variety of concerns about the future exist.

Of primary concern is the continuing effect of inflation upon the club's ability to maintain its current level of services and benefits to the membership. In particular, the cost of publications, and headquarters office administration and rent have risen considerably over the years. The board of directors has responded by both watching costs carefully and by raising annual dues several times (from $10 in the 1960s to the current $30 per year), but it recognizes that certain cost increases are unavoidable, and that raising dues too high may result in a loss of members. (Financial statements are provided in Exhibit 11–4.)

One way to overcome this problem is to increase the number of members and thus create greater revenues for the club. (The number of members who pay full dues has only increased moderately over the years. See Exhibit 11–2.) The directors know that many Classic owners do not belong to the CCCA. While CCCA members owned about 8000 Classics in 1994, no one really knows how many Classic owners are not in the club. Club efforts in recent years to increase membership have been targeted at these Classic-owning non-CCCA members. Letters have been sent to past members who failed to renew their CCCA membership (about 5–10 percent each year), region officers have contacted local non-CCCA members known to own Classics, mailings

EXHIBIT 11-4 CCCA Financial Statements (cash-flow basis)

	FY 1993	FY 1992	FY 1991	FY 1990	FY 1989	FY 1988	FY 1987	FY 1986	FY 1985	FY 1984	FY 1983
RECEIPTS											
Active Dues (dues received for current fiscal year)	$46,879	$50,168	$49,627	$101,009	$121,998	$59,067	$56,709	$58,926	$78,663	$39,999	$47,950
Prepaid Active Dues (dues received for next fiscal year- See Note)	87,382	79,860	77,760	76,722	26,170	3,809	65,509	61,560	55,079	17,350	54,975
Associate Dues	1,960	2,210	1,925	3,560	4,503	2,329	2,005	2,061	3,279	931	972
Prepaid Associate Dues	3,540	3,105	2,945	2,970	1,005	130	2,275	2,165	1,851	685	1,227
Life Membership	1,260	4,320	3,990	4,830	4,333	3,066	2,730	1,799	840	2,975	7,310
Publications Sales	2,683	1,972	2,053	4,393	2,285	3,004	3,082	2,987	2,661	3,665	3,429
Bulletin Advertising	11,176	9,583	9,884	9,924	10,919	9,747	8,986	8,618	3,318	4,992	3,662
Magazine Advertising	1,815	2,526	2,100	3,850	4,510	2,400	1,975	3,329	750	1,900	3,567
Directory Advertising	10,010	11,100	14,500	9,625	14,050	9,900	8,500	0	0	0	0
Awards (member registration fees for meets, etc.)	15,975	11,328	14,509	10,860	10,3331	6,653	6,481	5,234	5,779	5,439	5,240
CARavan	32,400	26,300	27,837	30,000	26,485	27,135	11,610	12,160	51,919	25,441	11,660
National Sales Items (badges, jewelry, ties, etc.)	4,358	4,952	4,397	8,495	6,417	6,298	4,722	5,002	5,136	6,155	5,235
Interest Earned	12,531	15,889	16,707	15,179	13,881	9,983	5,543	5,466	2,588	11,772	10,416
Regional Insurance (reimbursement from regions)	2,100	4,119	2,278	3,250	270	2,530	3,210	2,280	1,845	1,780	1,110
Miscellaneous & Foreign Exchange	941	584	3,008	3,792	2,695	2,768	1,580	931	9,725	3,071	877
Total Receipts	$235,010	$228,016	$233,520	$288,459	$249,852	$148,819	$184,916	$172,518	$223,433	$126,155	$157,630
ASSETS											
Bank Balance	$25,890	$76,035	$18,626	$34,188	$8,324	$7,728	$31,438	$36,605	$18,466	$11,296	$5,356
Investments (at cost: Money market funds, CDs, etc.) [includes life membership fund]	339,235	262,705	291,880	177,409	149,360	117,099	101,827	71,148	59,885	27,296	96,966
	(66,393)	(66,600)	(62,830)	(57,034)	(51,834)	(48,021)	(44,577)	(42,962)	(37,325)	(36,845)	(37,245)

EXHIBIT 11-4 *Continued*

	FY 1993	FY 1992	FY 1991	FY 1990	FY 1989	FY 1988	FY 1987	FY 1986	FY 1985	FY 1984	FY 1983
LIABILITIES:											
None											
DISBURSEMENTS											
Bulletin	$42,225	$25,658	$33,675	$21,510	$25,343	$23,224	$18,389	$22,651	$19,538	$20,734	$16,828
Magazine	53,219	46,277	43,788	41,019	45,724	39,031	39,091	44,697	47,972	45,788	46,598
Directory	15,447	15,985	19,150	16,225	14,776	11,085	12,925	11,647	1,784	11,739	16,181
Awards (judging, meetings, trophies, etc.)	9,805	14,386	36,474	21,588	22,619	11,662	4,094	3,386	4,038	20,378	8,888
General Administration	9,776	10,110	9,736	7,777	9,916	13,268	11,983	12,658	11,801	14,664	8,786
Office (salaries, rent, etc.)	35,483	30,996	32,239	30,030	29,049	27,186	27,190	29,431	27,750	27,326	28,573
CARavan	24,206	16,679	16,074	20,025	16,025	15,741	5,247	6,323	46,924	29,777	5,069
National Sales Items	3,340	343	2,917	3,629	7,574	2,041	6,007	2,204	2,623	2,784	1,710
Membership (recruitment)	15,641	4,802	14,181	14,289	10,053	5,836	6,341	4,872	7,246	2,950	5,670
Regional Insurance	4,447	7,284	2,279	2,788	744	2,759	6,032	2,250	2,800	1,924	1,600
Regional Relations	0	0	0	0	0	0	0	0	27	302	454
Computer Services	4,661	21,171	0	7,695	6,789	33	9,064	8,137	9,339	4,493	3,678
Miscellaneous	5,490	8,018	9,584	3,112	2,786	3,869	7,931	861	456	426	2,562
Taxes	6,952	7,404	3,122	5,515	4,002	1,523	4,709	470	1,377	6,599	0
Total Disbursements	$230,692	$209,113	$223,218	$195,201	$195,401	$157,258	$159,004	$149,587	$183,675	$189,884	$146,597
Excess Receipts over Disbursements	$4,288	$18,903	$10,302	$93,258	54,451	[8,439]	25,912	22,931	39,758	[63,729]	11,033

Source: CCCA reports.

have been made to Classic-owning persons found in directories of other old-car clubs, articles about CCCA activities as well as a few paid advertisements have been placed in various old car hobby magazines, and membership ads have been placed in single-marque car clubs (such as the Packard club) in return for allowing those clubs to place their membership ads in the CCCA's publications.

Furthermore, while some CCCA members do not own Classics, most do, for much of the pleasure of belonging to the club derives from participating in the various activities with a Classic car. Thus, while Classic enthusiasts who do not own a Classic might also be an appropriate target for CCCA new membership recruitment efforts, the primary focus has been on persons currently owning a Classic.

The club's membership recruitment efforts have only been moderately successful. While new members have offset the annual five to ten percent attrition rate, total membership has risen only slightly in recent years. Yet, unless the listing of recognized Classics is expanded, the number of Classic cars in existence is fixed, and with it, by and large, is the number of Classic owners.

There are varying opinions within the CCCA with regard to expanding the current listing of Classic cars. While there is some debate over adding further makes and models within the current 1925–1948 year limits, the main controversy concerns whether or not to add cars built after 1948.

A minority of members favor this post–1948 expansion and make several arguments. They say that some high-quality cars were built after 1948 and these should also be considered "Classic." Furthermore, they argue that the club is currently not attracting young members (only 13 percent of CCCA members are less than 45 years old), and this is because younger people are less able to afford the cost of a Classic and are also unable to "identify" with a 1925–1948 car as they can with a car of the 1950s or 1960s. Although current prices of Classics vary greatly depending on the make of car, its condition, and type of body, all prices rose significantly in the 1970s and 1980s. Also, it is true that many current CCCA members own classics because of nostalgia for cars of their youth.

On the other hand, most members of the Board of Directors, along with a clear majority of the membership, argue against the expansion of the list of Classics past 1948. The primary argument is that a Classic car is more than just a high quality luxury car. Rather, it is the product of a "Classic Era," when the truly wealthy lived a separate lifestyle from the rest of the population, and when an elite group of auto makers and custom-body craftsmen were willing and able to produce cars to meet this upper-class lifestyle. By the end of World War II, it is argued, social upheavals ended this lifestyle, and economic pressures closed down the custom-body builders and most of the independent luxury car makers, with the remaining luxury cars generally becoming simply bigger, heavier, and better-appointed versions of other cars made by multiline manufacturers. Thus, expanding beyond 1948 would alter the basic focus and philosophy of the club, and it is this narrow focus that differentiates the CCCA from other clubs and thus makes it so attractive and important to its members.

Furthermore, it is argued, while a few truly special car models were made after 1948, the quantities produced were very small, and the addition of these cars to the CCCA listing would bring in few new members to the club.

Beyond the Board's concerns about the future financial strength of the club, there is also a concern about the use of members' Classics and the nature of CCCA activities. As previously mentioned, the values of Classics has risen significantly over the years. In 1952, when the club was founded, most people viewed Classics as simply "old cars," and they could generally be bought for a few hundred to a few thousand dollars.

Today, many view Classics as major investment items, with professional dealers and auctions a significant factor in the marketplace. While some less exotic and unrestored Classic models can be found for under $15,000, most sell for $20,000 to $75,000, and the most desirable Classics, (convertible models with custom bodies, twelve- and sixteen-cylinder engines, etc.) can sell for $100,000 and more. (A very small number of especially exotic and desirable Classics have recently sold in the $500,000 to $1,500,000 range, and a 1929 Bugatti Royale reportedly sold in 1987 for over $9.8 million!) Furthermore, judging meets have become very serious events, with high scores adding significantly to a Classic's sales value. Thus, many highly desirable and/or top scoring Classics are now hardly driven at all and are transported in enclosed trailers to and from judging meets. While most Classic owners still enjoy driving their cars, and the CCCA CARavans continue to be highly popular among club members, some members yearn for the "old days" when there was less emphasis on judging and on a car's value and CCCA members would drive and park their Classics anywhere.

Still another concern of some members involves the possibility of a greater stress in future years on the conservation of gasoline in this country. If the country did focus more seriously on its high usage of gasoline, how would the public view Classic cars and the collector car hobby in general? Would the ownership and driving of cars for nontransportation purposes be considered unpatriotic or wasteful?

MEMBERSHIP SURVEY

In response to these various concerns, the CCCA board of directors established a Long-Range Planning Committee to study issues about the future of the club and to make recommendations to the Board. In 1983 and again in 1991, a membership questionnaire was sent to all members along with their membership renewal material. The response rate was excellent. Exhibit 11–5 presents the 1991 questionnaire and a tabulation of those responses which were quantifiable, along with a comparison to the 1983 survey responses.

FUTURE DIRECTION OF THE CCCA

As the club's 1994 fiscal year began, the CCCA board of directors was studying these issues. The board members knew that they could not ignore the problem of rising costs, and that their response must go beyond raising dues. While the survey clarified some of the opinions of the membership, the board did not view this survey as a ballot, with the board obligated to follow the majority preference in every question area.

Together for their regular board of directors meeting, the fifteen officers and directors of the CCCA asked themselves the following questions:

1. How should we deal with rising costs to the club?
2. What should be our policy with regard to future dues increases?
3. Should we consider the reduction of CCCA services to our membership in the future?
4. Is expansion of the listing of recognized Classics desirable?
5. What are the alternative ways to increase membership?
6. How can younger people be attracted to the CCCA?
7. Are there other possible sources of revenue to the club?
8. Were important questions not included in the previous membership surveys that should be included in a future survey?
9. Are there other long range issues or concerns that the club has not yet addressed?

1. I have been a member of the CCCA:
   1991   8% less than 2 years   19% 2-5 years   20% 5-10 years   53% more than 10 years
   (1983) 11% less than 2 years   20% 2-5 years   18% 5-10 years   51% more than 10 years

2. May age is:
   1991   0% under 25   3% 25-34   10% 35-44   24% 45-54   32% 55-64   31% 65 or over
   (1983) 1% under 25   3% 25-34   17% 35-44   30% 45-54   28% 55-64   22% 65 or over

3. My age when joining CCCA was:
   1991   7% under 25   19% 25-34   26% 35-44   26% 45-54   17% 55-64   5% 65 or over
   (1983) not asked

4. I live in the _____ Region. (Not tabulated in this summary.)

5. I am a member of a CCCA region:
   1991   76% yes   24% no
   (1983) 69% yes   31% no
   If yes, which region: 15% Michigan, 13% So. Cal., 6.4% Pac. NW, others less than 6%.
   If not, why not? Of those responding here (54% of those who answered "no"): 30% indicated distance, 21% no time, 13% no classic or not running, 8% not invited or didn't know about it, 9% not interested, 3% lack of activities, and 16% miscellaneous of less than 2% each.

6. I have attended:

1991	(1983)	
74%	(64%)	One or more Grand Classics
27%	(19%)	One or more National CCCA CARavans
34%	(24%)	One or more Annual Meetings
65%	(52%)	One or more Regional events
13%	—	None of the above

7. I belong to how many other car clubs:

	Average	0	1	2	3	4	5	6-10	10 or more
1991	3	8%	18%	22%	19%	12%	9%	11%	2%
(1983)	3	9%	19%	23%	17%	12%	7%	11%	2%

   I am more active in some of these clubs than I am in CCCA:
   1991   42% yes   58% no
   (1983)   44% yes   56% no
   If yes, why? Of those responding here (84% of those who answered "yes"): 22% prefer a one marque club, 21% indicated distance, 16% interest in other clubs, 10% also interested in nonclassics, 10% want more activities, 8% don't own classic or not running, and 13% miscellaneous of 3% or less.

8. Compared to other clubs, the CCCA is:
   1991   32% the best   47% better than most   20% average   1% poor
   (1983) 31% the best   47% better than most   21% average   1% poor

9. Compared to other clubs, the value I receive for my CCCA dues is:
   1991   29% the best   42% better than most   28% average   1% poor
   (1983) 27% the best   40% better than most   31% average   3% poor

EXHIBIT 11-5 *Continued*

10. Overall, I rate *The Classic Car Magazine*:

1991	74% excellent	23% good	3% fair	0% poor	
(1983)	74% excellent	24% good	1% fair	0% poor	

11. Overall, I rate the *CCCA Bulletin*:

1991	55% excellent	39% good	6% fair	0% poor	
(1993)	35% excellent	51% good	13% fair	1% poor	

12. With regard to the CCA listing of recognized Classic cars:

1991	(1983)	
63%	(69%)	I basically think the current listing is good.
32%	(28%)	I think the listing should be expanded.
5%	(3%)	I think the listing should be reduced.

    Of those commenting (31%) and desiring change: 26% accept newer cars, 18% accept others in Classic era, 7% accept older cars, 11% eliminate some current Classics, 7% 1925–1948 year span, and 31% other of less than 5% each.

13. With regard to the scoring currently used at Grand Classics and Annual Meetings:

*1991	(1983)	
82%	(86%)	I basically think the current system is good.
18%	(14%)	I think the system could be improved. If so, how?

    Of those commenting (only 10%): 19% judging/scoring, 10% more points, 10% drive cars before judging, 8% recognize original cars, 11% better judges, etc., and 42% misc. of 5% or less. (*Without "don't know" so as to compare with 1983.)

14. Overall I would rate the Grand Classics as:

1991	46% excellent	32% good	3% fair	1% poor	18% don't know
(1983)	50% excellent	30% good	2% fair	1% poor	17% don't know

    or 100% basis without "dont' know"

1991	56% excellent	39% good	4% fair	1% poor	———
(1983)	61% excellent	36% good	2% fair	1% poor	———

15. Overall I would rate the Annual Meetings as:

1991	21% excellent	23% good	2% fair	0% poor	54% don't know
(1983)	15% excellent	22% good	5% fair	0% poor	59% don't know

    or 100% basis without "don't know"

1991	46% excellent	50% good	4% fair	0% poor	———
(1983)	35% excellent	53% good	12% fair	0% poor	———

16. Overall I would rate the CARavans as:

1991	32% excellent	11% good	1% fair	0% poor	56% don't know
(1983)	28% excellent	16% good	2% fair	0% poor	54% don't know

    or 100% basis without "don't know"

1991	73% excellent	25% good	2% fair	0% poor	———
(1983)	61% excellent	35% good	3% fair	1% poor	———

EXHIBIT 11-5 *Continued*

17. The CCCA has not associated itself with automobile auctions. How do you feel about this policy?
    [1991]   62% strongly agree   21% agree   4% disagree   3% strongly disagree   9% don't know
    or 100% basis without "don't know"
    [1991]   69% strongly agree   23% agree   4% disagree   3% strongly disagree
    This question was not asked in 1983.

18. I completed the previous CCCA questionnaire sent to members in 1983:
    23% yes   37% no   40% don't know
       or 100% basis without "don't know"
    38% yes   62% no

19. If there is one thing I'd recommend the CCA *not change*, it would be:
    Of those commenting (24%): 26% 1925–48 year span, 20% publications, 9% quality of cars considered
       classic, 8% CARavans, 6% happy with club, 5% Grand Classics, 4% judging\scoring, and 22% other of
       3% or less.

20. If there is one thing I'd recommend the CCCA change, it would be:
    Of those commenting (25%): 13% accept newer cars, 7% judging/scoring, 6% accept other cars in the
       classic era, 4% encourage younger people, 4% CARavans, and 66% miscellaneous 3% or less.

21. I think the CCCA could be improved by: (only 15% commenting)
    An emphasis on encouraging younger members. A desire to see newer cars accepted, and general
       "happiness" with the Club. Many miscellaneous comments too numerous to list.

22. Other comments: (only 18% responding)
    Principally a general satisfaction with the Club.
    Encourage younger people.
    Many miscellaneous comments too numerous to list.

Source: The CCCA. Used with permission.

WALNUT CREEK BAPTIST CHURCH—1993*

TED W. LEGATSKI
Texas A&M University
PAUL R. REED
Sam Houston State
University
R. DEAN LEWIS
Sam Houston State
University

Reverend Dean Earl glanced out of his office window hardly noticing the workmen, barely 15 feet from his desk, putting the finishing touches on the east access road of Interstate 45. His thoughts were on his two-year effort to convince his staff and the church's board of deacons of the merits of strategic planning.

For some time, he had been concerned about the direction of Walnut Creek Baptist Church. Although so much was happening that was encouraging, there remained in his mind some lingering doubts. Was the church doing all that it could to meet the needs of the community? Was the church using its resources efficiently as well as effectively? Was the church growing at a rate that would allow it to continue its present programs and add much needed new ones? Were the church's physical facilities and grounds adequate for future growth? Was the church in control at all?

The church had an excellent professional staff with appropriate religious and theological training and a supportive board, but, as was common in many not-for-profit organizations, they lacked business administrative expertise. Reverend Earl had recognized these deficiencies and had initiated a personal investigation into strategic issues.

The pile of documents on his desk contained a Southern Baptist publication describing strategic analysis for church development, a borrowed 1992 edition of a popular strategic management textbook, plus a myriad of memos and discussion notes tracing the history of the many meetings on the subject. Last week, to his surprise, the Deacons gave him the go ahead to conduct a strategic audit of the church. The July 1994 deadline, some 12 months away, made him wonder about their degree of enthusiasm. In any event, there was nothing to say he couldn't finish earlier. Reverend Earl found his pad of lined paper in the center of the pile and began moving things around looking for his pencil. It was time to get serious, he thought!

THE EXTERNAL ENVIRONMENT

Walnut Creek Baptist Church was established in 1969 in the southern part of Montgomery County, Texas, approximately 30 miles north of downtown Houston. The church is near an exit on Interstate 45, 10 miles south of Conroe, the county seat.

The area has undergone tremendous changes since the church was started, especially since the late 1970s. The oil boom brought rapid growth to the Houston metropolitan area, including Montgomery County, which was one of the fastest-growing counties in the nation during the early 1980s. The mid-1980s brought serious recession to the area. Home prices fell by as much as 50 percent, and many residential and commercial properties fell into foreclosure. There was also a dramatic increase in small-business failures in the immediate area. By the late 1980s, many believed that the recession had hit bottom. Indeed, economic conditions, although considerably lower than before, had stabilized, and southern Montgomery County was growing once again. By December 1992 the population of southern Montgomery County was estimated at 60,000, an increase of approximately 30 percent over 1985 estimates.

Besides growth, a number of other basic changes had taken place. In 1969 most residents worked either in the immediate area or in Conroe. By the early-1990s, many area residents worked in downtown Houston or even farther from home. Average commuting time to downtown Houston was in excess of one hour each way; peak periods could take twice that long. It was not at all uncommon for people to leave home at 5 A.M. and not return until 7 P.M.

Another fundamental change that had occurred was a shift in basic values. Southern Montgomery County was viewed by many, especially its northern neighbors, as a "yuppie" haven. Recreational and social activities were a high priority with many residents, and the availability of these attractions was often cited by real estate salespeople. A wide variety of youth sport activities were also available. Unfortunately, there was also high alcohol and recreational drug usage in the area. Less than 25 percent of the residents were members of a local church.

While current median age data were not available at the time, local experts agreed that the area age levels were likely considerably below that of surrounding areas. The ethnic breakdown of the area population then was approximately 80 percent white, 15 percent Hispanic, and 5 percent black and other. The area is serviced by the seven Southern Baptist churches as shown in Exhibit 12–1. Selected demographics for these churches are listed in Exhibits 12–2 through 12–6.

In 1990 the Texas Department of Highways and Public Transportation had announced plans to widen Interstate 45 and its service roads. These plans would have placed the northbound service road right through the middle of the church sanctuary. There had been some speculation about whether the highway would be willing to purchase the entire 3.81-acre church property and, if so, at what price.

More recently, the highway department announced that the expansion plans had been revised. The highway department decided to shift the majority of the new right of way needed to the west side of Interstate 45 where only one building would need to be removed. Ongoing construction had moved the new service road to within three feet of the church's sign pylon and 12 feet from the church's sanctuary or main auditorium. This would soon be very disruptive to church activities, particularly Sunday services.

THE INTERNAL ENVIRONMENT

Walnut Creek Baptist Church was incorporated under the state laws of Texas and operates under a constitution and bylaws. It closely follows Southern Baptist doctrine.

Walnut Creek Baptist employs three full-time ministers in addition to Revered Earl: associate pastor/minister to adults, minister of music, and minister of youth. The Little Learners program (Mother's Day Out) also has a full-time director and one other paid staff position. In addition, there are five full-time support staff people.

Actions taken by the church are governed by a committee system. The church has established policy guidelines for thirty-one standing committees.

As with most nonprofit organizations, Walnut Creek Baptist relies heavily on volunteer workers. Workers may be true volunteers or actively recruited to perform specific roles. Training is provided when deemed necessary. A personnel policy manual for paid staff includes job descriptions and standards as well as procedures for periodic formal performance appraisals. There are formal guidelines for committees, but no similar guidelines for other volunteer positions, such as Sunday school teacher. There are no written job descriptions or procedures for performance reviews.

EXHIBIT 12-1 Southern Baptist Church Locations

A. Walnut Creek Baptist
B. Gateway Baptist
C. First Baptist of Tamina
D. Sring Creek Baptist
E. First Baptist of
      The Woodlands
F. Sawdust Road Baptist
G. Woodlands Parkway Baptist

A staff member is assigned to each committee in order to coordinate its activities. The staff member assists the lay volunteers in performing the committee's duties and communicates the committee's activities to the rest of the staff during the weekly staff meetings. The chairman of each committee (normally a lay member) presents committee recommendations that require a vote of church members during congregational business meetings.

Each committee is responsible for its own long-range planning as its membership deems necessary for such planning. For example, the Little Learners Committee has been working on plans to expand the program from its present preschool status to a full elementary curriculum. Reverend Earl feels that long-range planning in the church is probably the exception rather than the rule.

The committee system includes a long-range planning committee, which historically has concerned itself exclusively with planning for new buildings and facilities. The church has no written goals that extend beyond one year and has adopted no formal long-range objectives or strategies. The church leadership does not consider this to be a problem since they believe that a clear consensus exists as to the direction that the church is and should be taking.

The pastor is responsible to the board of deacons for general policy guidance, but in actuality he receives great latitude in exercising control over church affairs. Reverend Earl's philosophy is for the church body to vote on as few matters as possible. He also believes in delegating considerable authority to the other staff members. He firmly believes that his main duties are to be engrossed in the Scriptures and to keep himself mentally, physically, and spiritually prepared to meet the needs of the church.

The church's membership is primarily middle-class, white-collar working families, with a small percentage in the higher income brackets. There are also a substantial number of single-parent families. Reverend Earl believes that these people need a stable base on which to build their lives. He believes that they are looking for relationships where they know that people care, they can find help in managing their children, and they can develop wholesome personal friendships.

Walnut Creek Baptist has sought to meet these needs by teaching and preaching basic biblical doctrine, offering programs directed toward the needs of children and youth, and presenting special seminars and other training opportunities. Extensive counseling is also available, including special programs for drug and alcohol abuse.

Reverend Earl was rather proud of Walnut Creek's marketing efforts: A 15-foot sign pylon, next to the church, supported a theater type marquee which could display messages of 10 to 12 words. The lettering was large enough to be read by travelers as they raced along I–45 at speeds well in excess of the posted 55 mph. A map showing

EXHIBIT 12-2 Southern Montgomery County Baptist Churches, Membership

		RESIDENT MEMBERSHIP		
CHURCH	YEAR ESTABLISHED	1985	1990	1992
First Baptist of Tamina	1947	146	158	158
First Baptist of the Woodlands	1978	1,003	975	1,168
Gateway Baptist	1986[a]	—	149	225
Walnut Creek Baptist	1969	2,589	2,178	2,345[b]
Sawdust Road Baptist	1979	408	510	245
Spring Creek Baptist	1967	406	150	230[b]
Woodlands Parkway Baptist	1984[c]	—	190	331

Source: Texas Baptist Annual.

[a] Gateway Baptist was formed in 1986 when approximately half the membership of Spring Creek Baptist left to form a new church.

[b] Corrected figure obtained from individual churches.

[c] Woodlands Parkway Baptist is located closest to new residential developments.

EXHIBIT 12-3 Southern Montgomery County Baptist churches, Sunday school attendance

CHURCH	1985	1990	1992
First Baptist of Tamina	27	61	90
First Baptist of the Woodlands	467	549	535
Gateway Baptist	—	65	101
Walnut Creek Baptist	1,064	950	995
Sawdust Road Baptist	149	181	151
Spring Creek Baptist	171	40	68
Woodlands Parkway Baptist	—	167	257

Source: Texas Baptist Annual.

EXHIBIT 12-4 Southern Montgomery County Baptist churches, revenues

CHURCH	1985	1990	1992
First Baptist of Tamina	$29,575	$61,438	n/a
First Baptist of the Woodlands	615,915	1,070,014	1,098,580
Gateway Baptist	—	103,780	156,210
Walnut Creek Baptist	1,370,165	1,399,769	1,386,231
Sawdust Road Baptist	115,035	148,067	164,840
Spring Creek Baptist	231,515	70,700	86,520
Woodlands Parkway Baptist	—	253,663	445,690

Source: Texas Baptist Annual.

EXHIBIT 12-5 Southern Montgomery County Baptist churches, property and debt, 1992

CHURCH	PROPERTY	DEBT
First Baptist of Tamina	n/a	n/a
First Baptist of the Woodlands	$5,000,000	$1,500,000
Gateway Baptist	30,000	0
Walnut Creek Baptist	4,127,770	615,587
Sawdust Road Baptist	450,000	88,000
Spring Creek Baptist	n/a	n/a
Woodlands Parkway Baptist	650,000	244,555

Source: Tryon Evergreen Association.

EXHIBIT 12-6 Southern Montgomery County Baptist Churches, Staff Salaries and Debt Retirement Expenditures, 1992

CHURCH	SALARIES	DEBT RETIREMENT
First Baptist of Tamina	n/a	n/a
First Baptist of the Woodlands	$287,534	$394,615
Gateway Baptist	95,887	0
Walnut Creek Baptist	341,206	236,451
Sawdust Road Baptist	64,257	41,600
Spring Creek Baptist	33,382	0
Woodlands Parkway Baptist	132,980	25,263

Source: Tryon Evergreen Association

the church's location and schedule of services had been run in the suburban edition of the yellow pages for several years. The church also locally distributed flyers three or four times a year publicizing various youth-oriented programs.

Walnut Creek Baptist is located on 3.81 acres fronting Interstate 45. No undeveloped land adjoins the property. The physical plant consists of five buildings and parking spaces for 471 cars. Three of the buildings, with a total of 18,866 square feet, are used exclusively for educational space. The Family Center contains a full-sized gymnasium, commercial kitchen, and educational space. The building has a total of 24,175 square feet, of which approximately 16,000 is available for education. The auditorium, completed in 1981, seats 1,700 people, although close to 2,000 have been accommodated with temporary seating. The building also contains the church offices and educational space. The total square footage is 51,000, with 40 percent available for educational use. Exhibit 12–7 provides a physical layout of the church property.

Southern Baptists have long held to the strategy of growing through the Sunday school. Therefore, great emphasis is usually placed in properly designing and utilizing educational space. Two rules of thumb are normally used in planning educational space. The first is to provide approximately 45 square feet of floor space per person. The second is that a church will not maintain an average Sunday school attendance in excess of 80 percent of its design capacity.

In site planning, two rules of thumb are to have two acres of land per 300 attendees and one parking space for each three people.

The church's financial affairs are directed by the treasurer and the finance/budget committee. The budget for each year is established through a process in which the various committees and ministry heads present their budget requests for the coming year. An attempt is then made to predict revenues by extrapolating figures from the previous year as adjusted by an informal assessment of current economic trends. Revenue projections are also adjusted for attendance trends.

In the last ten years, the church has never reached its revenue projection. As a result, expenditures are tightly controlled, even though funds have been authorized through the budget. A staff member authorizes all expenditures. All checks require two signatures, and the treasurer is supposed to certify that funds are available before checks are issued. There are no formal limits on the amount of an expenditure that a staff member can authorize,

EXHIBIT 12-7 Walnut Creek Baptist Church Site Elevation

The image labels include:

- Unused
- 471 Parking Spaces
- Family Life Center
- Education
- Future Education
- Education
- Education
- Worship Center / Education / Offices
- Sign Pylon
- Service Road for Interstate Highway

although informal constraints are acknowledged. The church does not use a cash flow budget. An income statement and balance sheet are presented in Exhibits 12–8 and 12–9.

TOPICS FOR CONSIDERATION

Address the following questions regarding the status of Walnut Creek Baptist Church:

1. Is the church doing all that it can to meet the needs of the community?
2. Is the church using its resources efficiently and effectively?
3. Is the church growing at a rate that will allow it to continue its present programs as well as add new ones?
4. Is the church in control of its situation?
5. Are the churches current control systems appropriate?
6. Does the church have adequate physical facilities and grounds for future growth?

BIBLIOGRAPHY

Anderton, T. Lee. *Church Property/Building Guidebook. Rev.* Nashville: Convention Press, n.d.

Texas Baptist Annual, 1986. Dallas: Baptist General Convention of Texas, 1986.

Texas Baptist Annual, 1991. Dallas: Baptist General Convention of Texas, 1992.

Tryon Evergreen Baptist Association, Conroe, TX, 1992.

Walnut Creek Baptist Church. *Constitution and Bylaws. Author, n.d.*

Walnut Creek Baptist Church. Policy Manual. *Author, n.d.*

EXHIBIT 12-8 Walnut Creek Baptist Church Income Statement for Years Ending December 31

	1989	1990	1991	1992
Revenues				
Tithes/offerings	$ 867,725	$ 884,328	$ 914,092	$ 922,701
Designated gifts	116,807	159,247	180,376	163,428
Restricted funds	325,165	277,900	224,766	195,667
Little Learners	51,557	69,380	95,246	100,357
Interest & bonds	12,622	8,914	7,629	4,078
Total	$1,373,876	$1,399,769	$1,422,109	$1,386,231
EXPENSES				
Missions	75,718	77,205	85,708	94,986
Activities/education	26,081	33,551	36,624	54,769
Administrative	261,724	291,335	322,880	396,189
Counseling/discipleship/evangelism	21,648	15,669	19,299	20,143
Preschool/children/youth	72,951	100,373	92,486	89,312
Wages/salaries	280,735	345,450	341,206	316,966
Debt service	452,548	387,538	234,643	291,318
Noncash Expenses	104,869	87,031	85,411	47,621
Total	$1,296,274	$1,338,152	$1,218,257	$1,311,304
Operating Income	77,602	61,617	203,852	74,927
Fees/expenses	0	0	(75)	0
Net	$ 77,602	$ 61,617	$ 203,777	$ 74,927

Source: Walnut Creek Baptist Church documents, as adjusted.

	1989	1990	1991	1992
ASSETS				
Current Assets				
Petty Cash	$ 55	$ 55	$ 500	$ 500
Checking	3,875	(12,047)	31,976	26,894
Savings	49,682	61,826	47,632	27,192
Restricted Savings	145,672	116,317	203,621	100,000
Bonds	1,743	0	0	1,620
Total	$ 201,027	$ 166,151	$ 283,729	$ 156,204
Fixed Assets				
Land	295,349	295,349	295,349	295,349
Improvements	2,691,165	2,703,169	2,701,660	2,691,877
Depreciation	(1,007,143)	(1,081,974)	(1,158,086)	(1,140,544)
Total	1,979,371	1,916,544	1,838,923	1,846,682
Other Assets				
Deferred Charges	56,575	53,475	54,898	13,140
Total	56,575	53,475	54,898	13,140
Total Assets	$ 2,236,973	$ 2,136,170	$ 2,177,550	$ 2,016,026
LIABILITIES				
Current Liabilities				
Accounts Payable	$ 16,845	$ 13,451	$ 0	$ 0
Bonds	48,766	54,733	187,957	863
Matured Bonds	6,003	2,867	1,124	1,124
Payroll	(69)	(95)	(56)	0
Total	71,545	70,956	189,025	1,987
Long-term Liabilities				
"B" bonds	12,250	0	0	0
1986 bonds	1,065,000	945,000	665,000	0
Bank Note Payable	0	0	0	615,587
Accrued interest	29,579	0	0	0
Total	1,106,829	945,000	665,000	615,587
Total Liabilities	1,178,374	1,015,956	854,025	617,574
GENERAL FUND				
Fund Balance	1,058,599	1,120,214	1,323,525	1,398,452
Total	$ 2,236,973	$ 2,136,170	$ 2,177,550	$ 2,016,026

Source: Walnut Creek Baptist Church documents, as adjusted.

THE METROPOLITAN MUSEUM OF ART—1994

MARILYN M. HELMS,
PAULA J. HAYNES, AND
TAMMY L. SWENSON
The University of
Tennessee at Chattanooga

Based in New York City, the Metropolitan Museum of Art, or the Met (212-535-7710), ended its 1992–93 fiscal year with an operating deficit of $1.15 million. The deficit occurred in part because of decreases in admissions income and increases in operating expenses. Although the museum suffered a decline in per-capita visitor contributions and weaker merchandise sales in 1992–93, support from endowments increased substantially. The museum also enjoyed strong gains on its investment fund, reporting a 15 percent return from the previous period.

In the 1990s, many non-profit organizations are facing decreased support from patrons, government, and corporate and private philanthropy. These issues were challenging for strategic management. In 1993, admissions income represented only 10 percent of total revenue for the year; operations depend greatly upon endowment support, both from individuals and government sources. After having cut a large portion of its support to the Metropolitan Museum of Art in 1991–92, New York City increased its operating support by $595,000 in 1992–93, thus helping to partially restore previous funding levels.

The Met depends on external sources of revenue including interest on endowments, gifts, governmental appropriations, and grants as well as internal sources of revenue from merchandising operations, auditorium rental, parking garage fees, restaurants, admissions, memberships, royalties, and fees. Operating expenses include curatorial departments, educational programs and libraries, providing public information, marketing research, stocking inventories for auxiliary operations, and administrative costs. Total expenditures are rising at a faster rate than total revenues, and management of the Museum needs to find ways to sustain financial stability.

HISTORY

The State of New York granted a charter to a group forming a corporation in the name of the Metropolitan Museum of Art on April 13, 1870. The corporation was formed for the purpose of establishing and maintaining a museum and library of art, of encouraging and developing study of fine arts and the application of arts to manufacture and practical life, of advancing the general knowledge of kindred subjects, and, to that end, of furnishing popular instruction and recreation. This mission remains unchanged through 1993 with one exception; the word "recreation" is no longer part of the mission. The museum is a nonprofit tax-exempt [501(c)(3)] organization.

CITY SUPPORT

New York City owns the museum building but collections are the property of the corporation operating the Met. The city appropriates funds to the museum for maintaining the building as well as providing utilities at no charge. In 1993, allocations totaled $14,884,799, which was 8.1 percent of the total 1993 operating revenue; these allocations represented a partial, though somewhat sluggish, recovery of city support to previous years' levels. A history of support from the City of New York is included in the Five Year Summary shown in Exhibits 13–1 to 13–4. According to Bradford Kelleher, head of the Met's merchandising and publishing activities, "people think we

EXHIBIT 13-1 The Metropolitan Museum of Art Five Year Summary

	1993	1992*	1991*	1990*	1989*†
OPERATING FUND					
Revenue and Support					
Total income from endowment including The Cloisters, less or plus endowment income stabilization reserves as noted below	$18,217,436	$15,253,879	$14,169,461	$12,815,529	$10,838,371
City of New York:					
Funds for guardianship and maintenance	7,841,471	6,853,617	9,645,657	10,193,481	9,892,601
Value of utilities provided	7,043,328	5,941,552	6,068,111	5,398,227	5,489,227
Memberships	11,588,899	11,434,836	11,723,453	10,809,726	10,557,710
Gifts and grants:					
Education, community affairs, and special exhibitions	6,941,903	6,774,915	5,784,889	5,921,025	4,419,936
General purpose contributions	18,634,992	17,885,118	15,864,740	14,126,525	11,492,125
Income for specified funds utilized	2,258,308	721,037	439,330	539,539	403,308
Admissions	8,733,207	9,115,457	8,621,001	7,304,343	10,032,361
Royalties and fees	1,260,152	1,646,293	1,814,579	1,222,951	1,438,572
Other	3,689,999	3,620,855	3,817,124	4,941,078	4,393,423
Income before auxiliary activities	86,209,695	79,247,559	77,948,345	73,272,424	68,957,634
Revenue of auxiliary activities	98,762,341	92,977,194	90,154,977	79,565,366	78,480,090
TOTAL REVENUE AND SUPPORT	184,972,036	172,224,753	168,103,322	152,837,790	147,437,724
Expenses					
Curatorial:					
Curatorial departments, conservation, cataloguing, and scholarly publications	20,477,337	21,019,361	21,470,368	19,845,456	18,219,950
Operation of The Cloisters	3,568,841	3,216,458	3,253,558	2,913,132	2,801,680
Special exhibitions	8,371,094	6,985,200	5,789,990	6,242,448	5,061,807
Education, community programs, and libraries	4,910,108	4,587,853	5,300,858	5,104,734	5,700,470
Financial, legal, and other administrative functions	6,602,448	6,175,840	6,084,069	5,542,451	5,046,463
Communications, development, and membership services	5,582,308	4,745,585	5,431,390	6,649,179	5,398,638
Operations:					
Guardianship	16,067,186	14,548,710	15,404,915	14,981,129	13,497,933
Maintenance	9,027,426	9,911,716	9,994,162	8,460,979	8,075,233
Operating services	5,982,392	5,388,269	5,359,190	4,870,045	4,572,179
Value of utilities provided by the City of New York	7,043,328	5,941,552	6,068,111	5,398,227	5,489,227
Nonexhibition capital construction and renovation	3,135,992	3,179,204	2,088,713	2,530,557	1,163,930
Expenses before auxiliary activities	90,768,460	85,699,748	86,245,324	82,538,337	75,027,510

EXHIBIT 13-1 *Continued*

OPERATING FUND	1993	1992*	1991*	1990*	1989*†
Cost of sales and expenses of auxiliary activities	95,353,942	88,809,318	83,818,862	72,894,246	68,924,676
TOTAL EXPENSES	186,122,402	174,509,066	170,064,186	155,432,583	143,952,186
Net (Decrease) Increase in Operating Fund Balance	($1,150,366)	($2,284,313)	($1,960,864)	($2,594,793)	($3,485,538)
Additional information:					
Endowment funds balance	$535,073,452	$487,930,208	$450,890,594	$425,725,761	$396,149,106
Capital Construction expenditures	$ 30,110,406	$ 33,111,821	$ 22,978,339	$ 20,434,301	$ 15,476,598
Acquisitions of art	$ 85,169,652	$ 21,242,915	$ 16,945,340	$ 18,259,644	$ 17,107,754
Income (from) to endowment income stabilization reserves	($3,398,905)	$109,932	$2,378,908	$2,123,180	$2,903,502
Full-time employees	1,673	1,607	1,627	1,659	1,568
Visitors to the Main Building and The Cloisters	4,615,588	4,667,884	4,702,078	4,558,560	4,816,388

*Fiscal years 1989–1992 have been reclassified to conform with the fiscal 1993 presentation of scholarly publications expenses.

†Fiscal 1989 amounts have not been restated to apply Financial Accounting Standard No. 93.

Source: The Metropolitan Museum of Art.

are rich because we are custodians of a treasure house, but we are not. The museum has operated at or near a deficit for 10 years."

New York City's budget problems included cuts of 36 percent in 1991–92, or a total of $3.5 million, in the city's annual support for the Met. The Met's total annual budget is $186 million. Given the cuts, William Luers, President of the Met, did not open the Museum for the 13th Annual Museum Mile Festival. It was the first time the Met did not participate in the annual three-hour event staged by the 10 museums that line the upper 5th Avenue. According to Luers, "We have always been involved in the festival but it costs between $25,000 to $30,000 to open for the one night celebration. We felt bad about not staying open, but we're cutting a lot of other things as well, including window washing, which costs $120,000 a year." As a result of the city's cuts, The Met implemented a rotating gallery closing schedule in September 1991, closing roughly half of their galleries on Tuesdays through Thursdays as a means of cutting operating costs. As of November 1993, the rotating schedule remains in effect.

COLLECTIONS AND ACTIVITIES

Located on the east side of Central Park, the Met's collections include ancient and modern art from Egypt, Greece, Rome, the Near and Far East, pre-Columbian cultures and the United States. The Cloisters, a branch museum, located in Fort Tryon Park on the far northern tip of Manhattan Island, houses the European medieval art

EXHIBIT 13-2 The Metropolitan Museum of Art Balance Sheet June 30, 1993 with Comparative Totals as of June 30, 1992

	1993 Operating Fund	1993 Funds for Specified Purposes	1993 Endowment Funds	1993 Elimination of Interfund Receivables and Payables	1993 Total	1992 Total
ASSETS						
Cash	$1,552,054	$117,112			$1,669,166	$798,773
Investments, at market (Notes A, B, and I)	3,414,384	121,048,321	$537,712,825		662,175,530	593,124,807
Receivables (Notes A and C)	5,964,032	15,513,585	106,372,604		127,850,221	67,761,692
Interfund receivables, net (Note D)				(44,664,441)	(44,664,441)	—
Merchandise inventories (Notes A and E)	22,296,507				22,296,507	21,308,804
Fixed assets, at cost, net (Notes A and F)	22,034,859	12,698,535			34,733,394	26,757,614
Deferred charges, prepaid expenses and other assets	4,020,910	55,913	1,045,590		5,122,413	5,776,913
TOTAL ASSETS	$59,282,746	$149,433,466	$689,795,460	($44,664,441)	$853,847,231	$715,528,603
LIABILITIES AND FUND BALANCES						
Accounts payable	$8,810,593	$7,468,050	$102,169,384		$118,448,027	$67,093,060
Accrued expenses, primarily payroll, annual leave, and pension (Note G)	13,234,030				13,234,030	
Interfund payables, net (Note D)	28,687,382	15,977,059		($44,664,441)	—	12,370,775
Deferred income, principally memberships, gifts, and grants	10,030,381				10,030,381	12,508,355
Notes payable (Note H)	2,672,376		7,227,624		9,900,000	25,200,000
Loan payable (Note I)	—		45,325,000		45,325,000	46,140,000
TOTAL LIABILITIES	63,434,762	23,445,109	154,722,008	(44,664,441)	196,937,438	163,312,190
Fund (deficit) balance (Notes J and K)	(4,152,016)	125,988,357	535,073,452		656,909,793	552,216,413
TOTAL LIABILITIES AND FUND BALANCES	$59,282,746	$149,433,466	$689,795,460	($44,664,441)	$853,847,231	$715,528,603

Source: The Metropolitan Museum of Art.

EXHIBIT 13-3 Statements of Activity of the Operating Fund for the Years Ended June 30, 1993 and 1992

	1993	1992
REVENUE AND SUPPORT		
Return from endowment funds, including $3,398,905 allocated from and $109,932 allocated to income stabilization reserves in 1993 and 1992, respectively	$ 16,403,379	$ 13,616,046
Appropriation from the City of New York		
Funds for guardianship and maintenance	7,841,471	6,853,617
Value of utilities provided	7,043,328	5,941,552
Admissions at Main Building	8,183,991	8,572,125
Memberships	11,588,899	11,434,836
Gifts and grants:		
General purposes and education	19,054,598	18,362,940
Special exhibitions	6,522,298	6,297,094
The Cloisters:		
Return from endowment funds used in operations	1,814,057	1,637,833
Admissions and other	884,417	809,284
Royalties and fees	1,260,153	1,646,293
Other income	5,613,104	4,075,939
Revenue and support before auxiliary activities	86,209,695	79,247,559
Revenue of auxiliary activities:		
Merchandise operations	86,261,137	82,388,036
Restaurant, parking garage, auditorium, and other	12,501,204	10,589,158
TOTAL REVENUE AND SUPPORT	184,972,036	172,224,753
EXPENSES		
Curatorial:		
Curatorial departments, conservation, cataloguing and scholarly publications	20,477,337	20,829,434
Operation of The Cloisters	3,568,841	3,216,458
Special exhibitions	8,371,094	6,985,200
Education, community programs, and libraries	4,910,108	4,587,853
Membership services	2,810,876	2,510,180
Communications	449,927	189,927
Financial, legal, and other administrative functions	6,602,448	6,175,840
Development	2,321,506	2,235,405
Operations:		
Guardianship (Note A)	16,067,186	14,548,710
Maintenance (Note A)	9,027,426	9,911,716
Operating services	5,982,391	5,388,269
Value of utilities provided by the City of New York	7,043,328	5,941,552
Nonexhibition capital construction and renovation	3,135,992	3,179,204
Expenses before auxiliary activities	90,768,460	85,699,748

EXHIBIT 13-3 *Continued*

	1993	1992
Cost of sales and other expenses of auxiliary activities		
Merchandise operations	83,974,789	79,068,100
Restaurant, parking garage, auditorium, and other	11,379,153	9,741,218
TOTAL EXPENSES	186,122,402	174,509,066
EXPENSES IN EXCESS OF REVENUE AND SUPPORT	($1,150,366)	($2,284,313)

Source: The Metropolitan Museum of Art.

collection. The structure was constructed from parts of five European monasteries. Opened in 1938, the land and building were donated to the City of New York and much of the art within was donated by John D. Rockefeller, Jr. With almost 2 million square feet of space, the Met is really 21 different museums or galleries with separate curatorial departments.

The Met calls itself the largest art museum in the Western Hemisphere. They have more than two thousand employees. More than a million works of art from all over the world, ranging from the prehistoric to the contemporary, are on display. According to Kathleen Mary Arffmann, Manager of Visitor Services for the Met, when planned expansions are completed by the end of the 1990s, the Met will be the world's largest museum.

In addition to the many gallery wings, the Museum has a 250,000 volume library of art and reference materials used by graduate students in accordance with the Museum's affiliation with New York University. This Thomas J. Watson Library has a computerized online public access catalog that was initiated in November 1992. The Met has a 708 and a 246 seat auditorium; 3 classrooms; a restaurant and cafeteria; a parking garage; and a 10,000 square foot museum store. Twelve other retail stores operated by the Met exist in New York City, Connecticut, California, Ohio, New Jersey, Georgia, and Texas. The Met also has a mail order catalog with 1,500 items sent 6 times a year to almost 3 million people.

Activities at the museum include guided tours, lectures, gallery talks, concerts, formally organized educational programs for children, inter museum loans, and permanent, temporary, and travelling exhibitions.

MANAGEMENT

The Met operates by a dual management system as shown in Exhibit 13–5. The president and director report directly to the Board of Trustees. The dual management system was started in 1978, when the board decided the Museum was too complex and large for one person to manage. Prior to the board's action in 1978, Thomas Hoving had been chief executive at the Museum since 1967. Hoving's acquisitions and expansion projects included addition of the Lehman Wing, a glass-covered garden court, in 1975; the Sackler Wing, a climate-controlled glass-roofed room housing the Temple

	1993			1992		
	Operating Fund	Funds for Specified Purposes	Endowment Funds	Operating Fund	Funds for Specified Purposes	Endowment Funds
FUND BALANCE BEGINNING OF YEAR	($3,001,650)	$ 67,287,855	$487,930,208	($ 717,337)	$56,944,626	$450,890,594
ADDITIONS						
Return from endowment funds		6,953,917			7,135,851	
Return to endowment fund income for stabilization reserves				109,932		
Investment income		2,525,740			3,104,298	
Increase in net investment appreciation		9,101,116	48,615,847		10,554,735	30,367,885
Gifts, bequests, and grants		127,952,990	24,700,641		35,911,012	8,698,786
Proceeds from sales of art		830,016			712,095	
Return from invested loan proceeds		457,407			560,395	
		147,821,186	73,316,488	109,932	57,978,386	39,066,671
DEDUCTIONS						
Expenses in excess of revenue and support	1,150,366			2,284,313		
Return from endowment fund income stabilization reserves	3,398,905					
Acquisitions of art		85,169,651			21,242,915	
Construction, renovation, and other capital expenditures		19,579,475			21,251,219	
Fellowships, reference books, and other		3,042,919			3,219,958	
Interest and other loan-related expenses		3,457,902			3,495,845	
Depreciation and amortization		645,076			562,209	
	4,549,271	111,895,023		2,284,313	49,772,146	
INTERFUND TRANSFERS						
Transfer of income stabilization reserves from (to) endowment	3,398,905	4,057,677	(7,456,582)	(109,932)	2,079,754	(1,969,822)
Other		18,716,662	(18,716,662)		57,235	(57,235)
FUND (DEFICIT) BALANCE, END OF YEAR (NOTES J AND K)	($4,152,016)	$125,988,357	$535,073,452	($3,001,650)	$67,287,855	$487,930,208

Source: The Metropolitan Museum of Art.

of Dendur, in 1978; and the American Wing in 1980. Major renovations of the Great Hall and Costume Institute were completed in 1970 and 1971.

Most of the controversy that surrounded Hoving's tenure was due to his role in institutionalizing the "blockbuster", or special event, at the Metropolitan as an answer to the financial crisis. According to Hoving, "the public is most attracted to temporary events and attendance figures were high at the large scale ticketed events." Examples of these types of events were the "Treasures of Tutankhamen" show in 1978 and 1979, during which 1.2 million tickets were sold. Other examples of large scale ticketed events include "The Great Age of Fresco," "Mexico: Splendors of Thirty Centuries," and "Harlem on My Mind." The "blockbuster" issue was a very questionable one, however. According to supporters, "the attraction of new audiences will diminish the elitist image of museums." People against such exhibitions, such as Sherman Lee, Director of the Cleveland Museum, say "the values of the marketplace, if applied carelessly, may undermine public confidence in the Museum's integrity."

As of 1993, de Montebello and William H. Luers, the president, share the responsibility of managing the Met. Philippe de Montebello, born in France and a graduate of Harvard and New York University, is primarily responsible for all curatorial functions, conservation departments, libraries, and educational activities. William H. Luers, a past United States Ambassador to Czechoslovakia, is responsible for the business side of the Metropolitan. His responsibilities include daily operations, merchandising, development, human resources, internal auditing, and all financial matters including budgeting. Even though the president is responsible for development of the Metropolitan including fund-raising, de Montebello is involved in development, as well as in acquiring donations of works of art and money. Mr. Luers stated "Philippe should be perceived as the man who gives aesthetic and artistic vision to the Museum. And I am the manager, diplomat, executive, fund-raiser and basically a communicator."

De Montebello's career in art has been pursued at the Met—initially as an associate curator and in 1977 as acting director and the following year he became director. In addition to his duties as director, he continues to write articles for art publications.

Revenues earned from additional attendees have helped support Museum's activities from 1980 to 1993. Since Lee's retirement from the Cleveland Museum, Philippe de Montebello, the current Director of the Metropolitan and Hoving's successor, has taken on responsibility of the "anti-blockbuster" cause. Mr. de Montebello's position is to "lament the cost-effective mentality that places any Museum activity that does not generate attendance or immediate income in jeopardy." For the year ended June 30, 1990, there were no large-scale exhibition events at the Metropolitan, and the total revenue from admissions decreased by 27 percent. However, during 1991 the Museum's increased admission prices and large-scale exhibition offerings increased total admission revenues. By 1993, a strategic shift was clearly taking place with the reopening of the Nineteenth Century Paintings and Sculpture Galleries in September. After spending two years and nearly $13 million on renovations, the Metropolitan Museum opened with an impressive collection of Impressionist and Post-Impressionist masterpieces. The highlight of this exhibit, Van Gogh's *Wheat Field with Cypresses,* seems to contradict earlier "anti-blockbuster" sentiments.

De Montebello feels a number of things are essential in being a top-notch director of a great museum: knowledge of your own field and, in the case of an art museum, a very broad knowledge of art and a genuine desire to communicate it. Beyond that, you have to be diplomatic, forceful, and well situated, because you have to be able to raise money. You have to be able to express yourself in order to set policy with the

EXHIBIT 13-5 The Metropolitan Museum of Art Organizational Chart

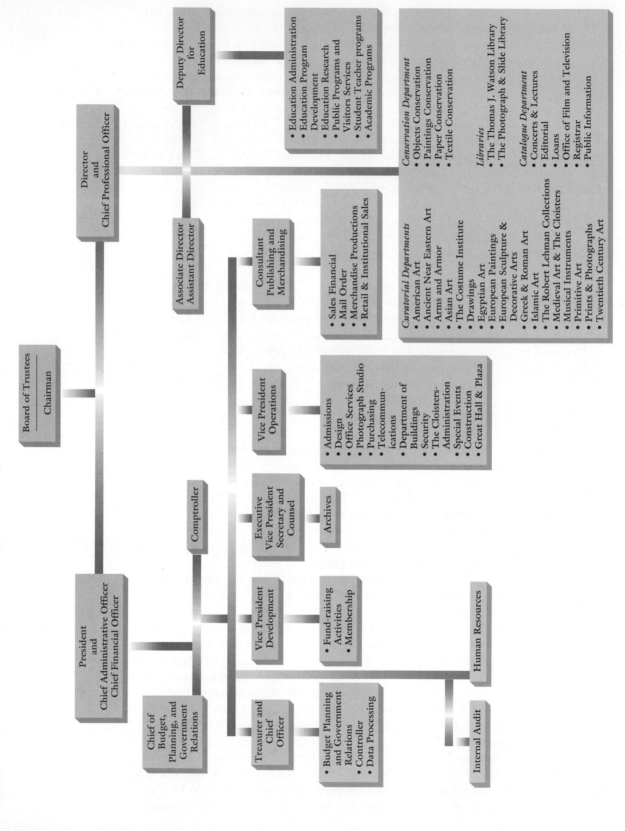

board of trustees, to work with very large staff of experts in their fields, and to arbitrate. You have to be decisive. Obviously, you must be able to be a lot of things at once.

COMPETITORS AND SPECIAL EXHIBITIONS

The Museum of Modern Art in New York, whose membership of 45,000 is off 20 percent from its 1987 peak, received a flood of new art devotees lured by a blockbuster exhibit, the Henri Matisse retrospective. According to the Museum of Modern Art (MOMA), such shows pack a box office wallop because the art is drawn from many collections. But they are getting scarcer as funding slows and insurance costs rise. To capitalize, the MOMA is boosting its direct-mail appeals and is installing a special recruitment desk in its lobby.

The MOMA saw a 15 percent increase in membership during the exhibition show's four-month run in 1991. The Philadelphia Museum of Art sent special mailings tied to their Picasso exhibition show. But such members are poor renewal candidates, warns Bonnie Coulter of the Philadelphia Museum. With fewer blockbusters in the offing, the Museum of Fine Arts in Boston focuses on upgrading membership. Washington's National Gallery of Art uses numerous special exhibitions.

When asked about the main function of a great museum, de Montebello feels the purpose is to furnish both instruction and pleasure to the general public. To do so, they collect and preserve great art, put the art on display, and conduct research. The strength of the Met is its remarkable comprehensiveness in representing the history of mankind in visual terms at a high level of quality.

According to de Montebello, all important art institutions are trying to do great things with a limited currency, which is works of art or the subjects of exhibitions. The key players are the French museums, the National Gallery in Washington, D.C., the Royal Academy in London, and the Met. Then there are other American museums that have very active programs—Los Angeles, Chicago, Boston, and Philadelphia.

FUND-RAISING AT THE MET

In 1982, the Met began a campaign to raise $150 million to offset operating deficits and enhance their endowment. Even though large gifts had been solicited for specific projects on several occasions, this campaign was the first formal, public fund-raising drive ever conducted by the Met. These funds were supposed to help the Metropolitan Museum achieve financial stability, to allow all galleries to stay open when the Museum is open, and to finance the existing educational programs, the work of curatorship, and the conservation library. The five-year drive, completed in 1987, was successful in meeting the $150 million goal; however, the Metropolitan experienced an operating deficit of $2.6 million for the 1989–90 fiscal year and a $1.9 million deficit for 1990–91. The 1992 deficit increased to $2.3 million but by 1993 had dropped back to $1.15 million, the lowest deficit in four years. The development staff implemented the following fund-raising techniques in an attempt to offset deficits. Philippe de Montebello says "there is no ministry of culture in the United States. We don't receive a check from Washington, so we have to seek ways to provide revenues."

Endowed Chairs. An effective fund-raising technique, borrowed from universities and hospitals, has been soliciting funds for existing curatorship in the form of endowed chairs. All major art dealers in New York, as well as industry leaders are approached regularly to solicit the endowments. These chairs carry the name of the donor who would add to the endowment indefinitely. The purpose of this drive is to raise the salaries of curators so the Metropolitan can be competitive within the job market by attracting the best people and retain the people they already have by increasing their existing salaries. Raises of this type would not have otherwise been possible due to the operating fund shortfalls.

Corporate Sponsorship. As governmental funding decreases, corporations have come under increasing pressure to take the lead in funding social and community programs. Based on a 1991 study performed by *American Demographics,* the largest share of corporate support goes to education (38 percent) with health and human services (34 percent) following. The study does not present a promising future for corporate sponsorship of the arts because most corporations practice "strategic philanthropy" focusing philanthropic efforts to maximize their returns. At the Metropolitan, great effort is given to matching the 30 annual special exhibits to corporations' activities to entice them to fund the exhibit, otherwise the exhibit might not be shown. One example of matching a corporation's activities to an exhibit was a gift of $500,000 from the Hunting World Group of Companies to maintain a gallery displaying American Arms.

The corporate patron program requires an annual donation of $30,000. This membership allows companies to have one party a year, at their own expense, in the Temple of Dendur, the American Wing, or the Medieval Sculpture Hall. Proceeds cover a portion of the Met's operating costs. Even though private use of public space is a controversial issue, it has proven to be a successful way to generate revenue.

Memberships. The Museum has various levels of membership and councils. The Chair's council members donate $25,000 annually and are included in governance of the Museum. Membership in this council is by invitation only. The Real Estate Council is responsible for raising money for special showings not fully financed. Each member is given 15 invitations to a special showing.

Many memberships are available to the general public. Members enjoy free admission and receive the quarterly *Bulletin* magazine and the bimonthly *Calendar.* Also they receive mail order Museum catalogues and are given 10 percent off all merchandise purchased in the Museum shop. In 1993, the Metropolitan Museum's membership was almost 100,000. Contribution levels required for all categories of membership were increased in 1991. Exhibits 13–6 and 13–7 provide a comparison of the number of members by category for 1987 through 1993.

Government Grants. For the year ended June 30, 1993, the Met received funding from local, state, and federal governments. The City of New York provided the building that houses the Museum, the utilities, and appropriated funds for maintaining the building. The State of New York provided an annual allocation from the New York State Council on the Arts for general operating and program support. Special capital funds from the Natural Heritage Trust were received to support the special exhibitions program.

Federal agencies such as the National Endowment for the Arts and the Institute of Museum Services provide support for specific projects and general operations. Funds provided from all governmental sources amounted to more than $15 million for the year

EXHIBIT 13-6 Number of Annual Members by Category

CURRENT PRICES	1993	1992	1991	1990	1989
Student ($30)	1,478	1,590	1,557	1,575	1,517
Individual ($70)	29,362	30,260	29,175	33,054	34,548
Dual ($125)*	19,268	20,187	21,261	23,299	24,485
Sustaining ($300)	7,242	6,186	6,539	7,329	7,729
Supporting					
Contributing ($600)	1,011	1,076	1,547	1,671	1,885
Donor ($900)	428	448	555	611	634
Sponsor ($2,000)	518	461	507	521	541
Patron ($4,000)	132	136	156	182	175
Upper Patron ($6,000)	26	25	51	62	51
National Association ($35)***	40,287	36,876	32,848	31,555	29,777
National Friend ($200)**	60				
Total	99,812	97,245	94,196	99,859	101,342

  *Includes Life Members.
  **New category for 1993.
***Nonresident Membership.
Note: Rates for all membership categories were increased an average of 21% in 1991.
Source: The Metropolitan Museum of Art.

ended June 30, 1993; only $250,000, or less than 2 percent of government funding, came from the federal government. Most government support is appropriated on an annual basis; therefore, during recessionary periods, this external funding is uncertain.

Gifts. The 1986 Tax Reform Act discouraged donations of works of art to the Metropolitan and other museums. The change in the tax law reduced the tax deduction donors could take for appreciated art objects. As a result many art objects were sold to the highest bidder at auction houses. A survey conducted by *American Demographics* found that charitable giving by corporations fell 12 percent after the 1986 Tax Reform Act became effective. In March 1991, the Metropolitan received the largest gift it had received in over 50 years, probably due to a temporary "tax window," a one year restoration of tax deductions for the full market value of art donated in 1991. Valued at $1 billion, the paintings donated by Walter Annenberg will not become the property of the Metropolitan until Mr. Annenberg's death. According to the Tax Reform Act of 1986, people who donate appreciable property, like a painting that has become more valuable, can deduct only what they paid and not the current market value if they are subject to the alternative minimum tax. This was repealed by the 1993 Tax Reform Act which reinstated the deduction for art object donations.

In 1992, a bill was passed creating a procedure to value property before a donor gives it to charity. Backers of the bill, including the Met, say their goal is to keep costly audit disputes from arising years after donors take big deductions for gifts of major artwork. The bill would allow a process for donors and the Internal Revenue Service (IRS) to agree in advance on appraisals of artwork and collectibles valued at over $50,000. While donors may inflate their charitable deduction estates, they tend to

EXHIBIT 13-7   Members of the Corporation

	1993	1992	1991	1990	1989
Honorary Fellows for Life	3	3	3	3	3
Fellows for Life	820	843	873	901	911
Fellows in Perpetuity	318	323	329	336	342
Benefactors	302	305	355	389	372
Total Corporation Members	1,443	1,474	1,560	1,629	1,628
Total Annual Members	99,812	97,245	94,196	99,859	101,342
Grand Total	101,255	98,719	95,756	101,488	102,970

Source: The Metropolitan Museum of Art.

undervalue their taxable bequests of art. The IRS has an Art Advisory Panel of outside experts to review these works of art.

Donations to 250 museums surveyed by the American Association of Museums soared 541 percent in 1991 when an eighteen-month window went into effect on June 30 for donors to get a full tax break. (In contrast, donations had fallen 50 percent from 1987 through 1990.) A 1993 provision extended the tax break indefinitely. Contributions were expected to remain strong because of this ruling, although historical data has suggested that the economy, and not the tax code, has the greatest effect on charitable giving.

According to the Business Committee for the Arts, business giving to the arts reportedly fell by 2 percent in 1992. A survey of 419 arts organization directors cited numerous challenges in soliciting corporate donations: business does not understand the benefits of art sponsorship; business is only interested in projects that draw big crowds; business wants a large return for a small contribution; business wants quantifiable results that aren't always available; and business wants more lead time than the arts organizations can provide.

ADMISSIONS

For the year ended June 30, 1993, 4.6 million people visited the Museum and the Cloisters making the Met the number one tourist attraction in New York City. Attendance decreased in 1993 due in part to the rotating gallery closings. Revenue from admissions decreased by $382,000 (4.2 percent) from the previous year. Management of the Museum has veered away from ticketing exhibitions in an effort to make special exhibitions more spontaneous and more rewarding for the frequent visitor.

HOURS OF OPERATION

Evening hours were added on Friday and Saturday nights in 1991 in place of opening on Tuesday evening in an attempt to increase attendance. Attendance on Tuesday evening averaged 2,500, while attendance on Friday and Saturday evenings ranged from 3,500 to 5,000 visitors in 1991. The trend continued through 1993. Exhibit 13–8 reveals the hours of operation and donations for admission to the Museum.

TARGET CUSTOMER

Surveys are conducted by the Metropolitan each year to determine the key demographics of their visitors. Exhibit 13–9 reveals demographics of the average visitor to the Met which is used to effectively market the Museum's services. Of the 1,357 surveyed, 48 percent were New York City residents, 39.6 percent were residents in other United States areas, and 12.4 percent were foreign visitors.

VOLUNTEERS

Approximately 800 volunteers work at the Metropolitan Museum. Three hundred of these are volunteers, who lead tours. Mostly women volunteers are now employed. As women continue to enter the work force, nonprofit organizations may have difficulty finding volunteers to work during daytime hours.

AUXILIARY OPERATIONS

A growing number of business executives serve on the board because the Museum has evolved into a big business with an investment portfolio, reproduction studio, and retail outlets. Because external funds are uncertain, greater emphasis is placed on generation of internal sources of revenue.

Museum Shops. The Met sells a wide range of goods, from expensive reproductions of statues to coffee mugs and poster art. The Met relies on such merchandise to support its operations.

Profits from merchandising has been rising faster than income from endowments, as a percent of total operating income, since 1967. Retail shops are operated within the Museum, at the Cloisters, and in twelve offsite locations. Met's sales are largely made in the museum itself, where the Met has run an expanded 10,000 square foot store since 1979. The majority of the Met's retail sales come from the onsite store. Four satellite shops are in New York: Rockefeller Center, New York Public Library, The Americana at Manhasset, and Macy's. Two are in Connecticut: Stamford Town

EXHIBIT 13-9 Customer Demographics

DEMOGRAPHICS	AVERAGE	PERCENT
Number of visits within 1 year	1–3 visits	32.8
Time spent in Museum	2 hours	36.0
Primary reason for visiting Museum	special exhibition	51.1
Median age of visitors	age 38	
Sex of visitors	female	57.0
Education of visitors	baccalaureate	33.5
Occupation of visitors	teachers/other professionals	47.5
Ethnicity of visitors	caucasian	76.1
Museum membership	member	15.5

Source: The Metropolitan Museum of Art.

Center and Westfarms Mall. Two are in California: Century City Shopping Center in Los Angeles and Southcoast Plaza in Costa Mesa. One is in Ohio at Columbus City Center, and one is in New Jersey at the Mall at Shorthills. The two most recent additions include Lenox Mall in Atlanta and the Galleria in Houston. The Met does most of the original modeling and design work in manufacturing the art reproductions in its own studio, then subcontracts the actual production to small factories and artisans around the world. Final approval of reproductions for resale rests with the original's curator, who wields an absolute veto over each potential reproduction.

Because the Met is a tax-exempt nonprofit organization, it pays no taxes on profits realized from retail operations; therefore, some retailers feel the Met has an unfair advantage over businesses selling similar goods. The Museum is only required to pay sales taxes on retail items unrelated to its mission of art education, in accordance with section 511 (imposition of tax on unrelated business income of charitable organizations) of the *Internal Revenue Code*. The only regular sales activity the Met pays income tax for is rental of its membership list to other businesses. The Met is a leader in opposing changes that would increase tax burdens on nonprofit institutions.

The purpose of the unrelated business income tax is to prevent tax-exempt organizations from competing unfairly with businesses whose earnings are taxed. Unrelated business income is any income derived from any unrelated trade or business. The term is defined in section 513 of the *Internal Revenue Code* as "the case of any organization subject to the tax imposed by section 511, any trade or business the conduct of which is not substantially related (aside from the need of such organization for income or funds or the use it makes of the profits derived) to the exercise or performance by such organization of its charitable, educational, or other purpose or function constituting the basis for its exemption under section 501."

The Met's stores sell greeting cards, posters, calendars, scarves, art reproductions, postcards, sculptures, glass, and jewelry. Nearly all items offered are reproductions or adaptations from the Museum's collections. These items are not available for sale at any other retail location; they are sold only in the Museum shops or through mail order. According to Museum management, "the sale of items in the shops falls within the mission of the Museum because sale of an item makes people think about the Museum outside its walls and serves as an extension of their visit."

The Metropolitan's merchandising activities resemble those of commercial businesses in some ways but are unique in others. Differences include the requirement that all merchandise sold in the Museum must reflect the permanent (not blockbuster) collection to preclude assessment of taxes on the earnings. Therefore, the decision on the types of items to sell do not necessarily reflect customer wants. Marketing research consists of showing pictures of items in the permanent collection to randomly selected customers in the Museum shop to determine if the items should be reproduced for sale.

The Met in late 1992 installed a Fujitsu Atrium 9000 point of sale (POS) system at its largest satellite gift shop and has continued plans to begin rolling out the personal computer (PC)-based system to other stores. The system installed at the Rockefeller Center store consists of a controller terminal with 8 intelligent primary terminals and 5 satellites. The system provides full sales transaction processing, credit check authorization, manager workstation functions, and host communications capabilities. Its interactive help function and user-friendly interface have made training sales associates easy. The Met also uses two of Fujitsu's host software packages—online host communications and host sales audit.

Groups who represent small businesses are lobbying for changes in the tax code because some commercial ventures undertaken by nonprofit institutions compete unfairly with private companies who are selling nearly the same merchandise. These groups want the tax code rewritten detailing specifically which items would be considered tax exempt.

Vagueness of the tax laws allow museums to make unfair profits from everyday items like napkins, neckties, and mugs. The museum's profit margin from shops and mail order is triple that of some department stores. The Met's inventories of gifts and merchandise is more than $22 million.

Mail Order. More than half of the Met's merchandise sales comes from a booming mail-order business operated out of a warehouse in Queens, New York. The average order of $45 is low by mail order standards but the response rate is higher than average as nine percent of those who received Christmas catalogues placed orders.

The Museum rarely advertises except to invite people to join their catalog mailing list. Six catalogs per year, containing 1,500 different items, are mailed to members and other customers. The Christmas catalog is mailed to 3 million people; the other catalogs are mailed to a smaller group. Some of the Met's merchandising policies, such as buying large quantities of an item to get it at a lower price, have led to inventory storage problems. It is not unusual for an item to remain in inventory for up to two years. The Museum manufactures molds to make copies of art in its own reproduction studio.

In 1993, the Met's mail-order operation, gift shops, and royalty agreements had sales of over $86 million and net income of about $3.5 million. Sources of merchandising revenue included 23.5 percent from sculpture, silverware, glassware, and jewelry; 21.0 percent from art books; 18.4 percent from paper goods; 16.1 percent from prints; 6.4 percent from children's products; 5.7 percent from textiles; 5.7 percent from royalties from retailers and other museums that sold products based on the Met's collection; 1.7 percent from postcards; and 1.5 percent from other products. Those not receiving a Met Christmas catalogue can order a copy of the 144-page catalogue for $1.00. Advertisements for the catalogue appear in popular magazines like *Vogue*.

The Museum leases space for offsite retail stores and for the warehouse that serves as headquarters and storage for the mail-order business. Lease costs for all rented space used for the retail operation amounted to $2,322,044 and $2,014,727 for the years ended June 30, 1993 and 1992, respectively.

Mail order competition is from other museum shops who, like the Met, have catalogues as well. For-profit catalogues like those from the Museum Company, the Nature Company, Lillian Vernon, Harriette Carter, and Walter Drake, among others, can be viewed as competitors.

The Met's catalog is also featured on the Prodigy interactive home computer information system. Prodigy customers can view and order merchandise from a variety of catalogs. Ed Sessler, Prodigy's director of merchandise marketing says Prodigy wants to become more focused and work with larger first-tier catalogers, like the Met. The Met catalog has been pleased with Prodigy. Although business started slowly, Metropolitan marketing analyst Philip Fertick says sales have increased and surpassed expectations.

Restaurants. The Museum operates a restaurant, cafeteria, and bar. The restaurant and bar are open to accommodate the evening hours on Fridays and Saturdays. In 1990, the Museum received approval from the City of New York to open a new restaurant to replace the current restaurant and cafeteria so the space could be used for additional galleries.

Other Auxiliaries. Other auxiliary operations at the Met are the parking garage and auditoriums. The parking garage, located adjacent to the Museum, is used by patrons at the rate of $8.50 for the first hour, $1.00 for each additional hour up to the fifth, $17.50 for five to ten hours, and $19.50 beyond ten hours. Included in these rates is New York City's 18.25 percent parking and sales tax.

Results of Auxiliary Operations. Net income from merchandising operations was $2,286,348 for the year ended June 30, 1993. Though total retail sales increased by 7.9 percent, mail-order sales declined by 4.5 percent, consistent with recent industry trends. The net contribution to the Museum's operations from auxiliaries totaled $3.41 million in 1993. Exhibit 13–2 gives the Met's Balance Sheet while Exhibit 13–1 provides a five year summary.

FUTURE OUTLOOK

Recession and Museum Attendance. The future financial stability of the Met is a key concern of management as 1994 begins. Fiscal instability of the City of New York could lessen future city support and declining federal funding might have an adverse affect on the Museum's operations.

According to the book *Megatrends 2000* by Naisbitt and Aburdene, researchers predict the arts will begin to replace sporting events as society's primary leisure activity. The authors cite a 1988 report by the National Endowment of the Arts which calculated that Americans spend $28 billion on sports events compared to $3.7 billion on art events. A reversal of these numbers by the year 2000 could yield substantial additional revenue for the Met. More than 500 million people visited American museums in 1991, far more than attended professional sporting events.

In 1992, charitable contributions decreased for the first time in modern history. One nationwide survey of shareholders showed that top priorities for spending money are for such things as cleaning corporate facilities and stopping environmental pollution. Contributing more money to charities ranks 8 out of 10 items. Statistics from

The Economist, show that while the French government spends approximately $30 per capita on the arts and the British $9, the United States Federal and State Governments together spend only about $2.

Museum Gift Shop Competition. Patrons want to support local culture and are spending generously on books, maps, models, posters, replicas, and other Museum shop items. In 1993, the Metropolitan ranked first of all other museum shops in sales and remained the only museum manufacturing its own line of merchandise. Second in sales was the Smithsonian Institution in Washington, D.C., with their nine Museum shops and a catalog business. As of 1993, other shops with a minimum of $1 million in annual sales included the Museum of Modern Art and Whitney Museum of American Art in New York, Boston's Museum of Fine Arts, San Francisco Museum of Modern Art, the Art Institute of Chicago, Los Angeles County Museum of Art, Philadelphia Museum of Art, and San Diego Museum of Art.

Competition for Museum shops is not solely limited to museum locations. The Museum Company, a retailer based in East Rutherford, New Jersey, operates stores in seven states and sells merchandise from the Louvre in Paris, the British Museum, and other art institutions. The Museum Company pays royalties to museums, and its 1993 revenues topped $10 million. Will Edwards, a partner in the chain of 21 Museum Company stores based in New York, objects to museums running their own retail stores in malls because they have an unfair tax advantage. The Museum Company is an entrepreneurial venture. Its first-year revenues topped $10 million. Stores are located mostly in malls. Edwards is a member of the coalition for Fair Business Practices, a group that voiced their objections to the nonprofits operating in the retail world.

Other Museum Competition. Direct competitors, or other museums, are plentiful in the New York area, including the American Museum of Natural History, the Museum of Modern Art, the Whitney Museum, and the Museum of the City of New York.

Because there are multiple demands for the free time of Museum visitors, many activities, outings, and other forms of recreation and leisure are potential substitutes. Other activities and forms of available recreation range from sporting events to theatrical presentations. The New York metropolitan area was the home of two National Basketball Association teams; three National Hockey League teams; two National Football League teams; two baseball teams; and two race tracks. Broadway, the most celebrated street in America, offers daily productions in forty theaters and numerous off-Broadway shows for both the tourist and resident of New York.

In addition, each of the five New York boroughs have many attractions from which to choose, including the Statue of Liberty, the Bronx Zoo, and the National Historic Landmark district on Staten Island. Central Park and the World Trade Center are easily accessible to all visitors via the New York City subway.

SUMMARY

Both Philippe de Montebello and William Luers are faced with having to generate additional donations externally and deciding whether to use large scale ticketed "blockbuster" exhibits. They also would like to expand the Met's retail operations and attract additional visitors to the Met in the increasingly crowded leisure markets. Developing a strategic plan for the future that would address these issues is an immediate priority for the management team to present to the Board of Trustees.

GAMING INDUSTRY NOTE

JOHN K. ROSS, III, MIKE KEEFFE, AND BILL MIDDLEBROOK
Southwest Texas State University

The gaming industry has captured a large amount of the vacation/leisure-time dollars spent in the United States. Gamblers lose over $30 billion annually on legal wagering, including wagers at racetracks and bingo parlors and in lotteries and casinos. This figure does not include dollars spent on lodging, food, transportation, and other related expenditures associated with visits to gaming facilities. Casino gambling accounts for 79 percent of all legal gambling expenditures, far surpassing second-place lotteries at 6.8 percent. The popularity of casino gambling may be credited to more frequent and somewhat higher payout as compared to lotteries and racetracks; however, as winnings are recycled, the multiplier effect restores a high return to casino operators.

Marketing research reveals that the U.S. casino player is slightly older, more affluent, and less educated than the average American. Casino players average age 49, with median household income of $39,500, and about one-half have never attended college. The average age and household income of all Americans is 47 and $27,900, respectively. More than 10 percent of all U.S households made at least one trip to a casino in 1993.

Gaming is becoming widely accepted in the United States as a form of entertainment. Nineteen states now have legalized gambling. Marketing research reveals that 55 percent of all Americans say gambling is "perfectly acceptable for anyone," 35 percent say gambling is "acceptable for others, but not for me," and 10 percent say gambling is "not acceptable for anyone." Many of the 31 states that have not yet legalized gambling have lotteries and video poker, and view gaming as a viable source of revenue that can lower the tax burden on the general population.

The state of Nevada and Atlantic City, New Jersey, dominate the gaming industry, being the established areas allowing full-fledged casino gambling. Nevada accounts for over $6 billion annually in casino revenues as compared to Atlantic City's $3.5 billion. It is believed that Nevada generates more revenue and higher profitability because of lower interest expense from old debt and lower regulatory and labor costs. Limited gaming activity (such as floating casinos, bingo, poker parlors, video gambling, lotteries, and pari-mutuel betting) is allowed in other states, but because of legal constraints in these states significant expansion beyond Nevada and Atlantic City is expected to be slow.

Besides geographical location, the primary differences in the two markets reflect the different types of consumers frequenting these markets. Whereas Las Vegas attracts overnight resort-seeking vacationers, Atlantic City's clientele are predominantly day-trippers traveling by automobile or bus. According to the Las Vegas Convention and Visitor Authority, Las Vegas is a destination market, with most visitors planning their trip more than a week in advance (81 percent), arriving by car (47 percent) or airplane (42 percent), and staying in a hotel (72 percent). Gamblers are typically return visitors (77 percent), averaging 2.2 trips per year, and like playing the slots (65 percent).

Development of new and existing markets will determine the industry's future. New theme resorts are being introduced to differentiate the market and are expected to capture most of the increase in gaming revenues. Atlantic City is expanding transportation and lodging accommodations to better enable it to attract resort and convention-related business, but it will be some time, if ever, before it can compare with Nevada.

The gaming industry is led by nine companies that account for more than 70 percent of total gaming revenues. Hilton Hotels, Promus, Caesars World, and Circus Circus are the leaders in gaming. Other revenue leaders are Bally Manufacturing, Mirage, Resorts International, Trump, Showboat, and Aztar.

MARKETPLACES

Laughlin. The city of Laughlin, Nevada, represents a market quite distinct from those of Las Vegas and Reno. Its population is 4,791 as compared to 741,459 for Las Vegas and 139,900 for Reno. Laughlin caters to the day travelers from nearby Arizona and Southern California population centers and annually attracts more than four million visitors. Ten casinos opened in Laughlin between 1986 and 1993, and some expansion of the current 9,000 hotel rooms is now under way. Such construction activities have been, at times, a disruptive factor to the tourism business because of the strain placed on the city's housing, schools, and water supplies. Laughlin has been described as the industry's fastest-growing market, with gaming revenues of about $507 million in 1993 compared to $40 million in 1985. Its future, however, depends on the extent to which it becomes a destination resort rather than a day-trip resort. Although Circus's facilities must compete with eight major casinos, they are able to maintain a 95 percent occupancy rate.

Las Vegas. Las Vegas is a more established gambling market, although growth has recently been quite explosive. More than 70 casinos operate in the Las Vegas area and collect over $5 billion annually. On the "strip," well-known casinos such as Caesar's World, Harrah's, and the Golden Nugget brought in about 80 percent of the strip's winnings and more than one-third of the statewide totals. Many cater to the upscale gambler, offering big-name entertainment, free drinks for gamblers, easy credit, and glamorous surroundings. Las Vegas draws clientele largely from Southern California and the rest of the southwestern United States. It ranks as one of the most popular convention locations in the nation and is becoming more popular for tours from Asia and Europe.

From 1989 to 1993 several new casino-hotels opened in Las Vegas, such as the Mirage, Excalibur, Luxor, Grand Slam Canyon, and O'Sheas. Additionally, MGM has begun development of the MGM Grand Hotel and Theme Park, scheduled to open in 1994. This rapid growth in Las Vegas has some observers worried; however, most expect it to be readily absorbed by the current market and increased tourism. The expected increase in family vacationers may end up exerting pressures on the more traditional gambling-only casino operations, forcing them to compete with the theme resorts.

Reno. In Reno recent growth has been much more modest, with total gambling revenues about $700 million annually. Like Las Vegas, Reno is a relatively established gaming market, with 12 major casinos catering to the upscale gambler. It draws clientele largely from Northern California and the rest of the northwestern United States.

MAJOR INDUSTRY PLAYERS

Bally Manufacturing Corporation. Bally Manufacturing Corporation is a diversified organization that operates casinos and fitness centers and produces and distributes gaming products. Bally is currently enjoying a recovery in its casino operations in both Atlantic City and Nevada. Through the first half of 1993, both the Park Place and Bally Grand saw increased revenue through winnings, with the Park Place reestablishing its position in the upper tier of Atlantic casinos. Bally has acquired 40 percent of the stock of Bally's Grand in Nevada through bankruptcy proceedings.

In addition to casinos, Bally's Scientific Games offers gaming equipment and services. They produce German wall machines and coin-operated gaming equipment; recently they were the first to sell slot machines to the former Soviet Union. Producing and selling paper-ticket lottery games is another of Bally's gaming segments, with customers in the United States as well as Costa Rica, Guatemala, and Venezuela. Finally, Bally operates 315 fitness centers and manufactures exercise bicycles, among other items, for the health club market.

Caesar's World, Inc. Caesar's World is one of the top revenue–producing casino operators in the United States. Caesar's owns and operates three casino/hotels: Caesar's Palace in Las Vegas, Caesar's Tahoe, and Caesar's Atlantic City. Altogether these properties offer 223,000 square feet of casino space and 2,600 rooms, with an average 84 percent occupancy (86 percent in Las Vegas). Caesar's probably will experience an adverse impact from the opening of the new theme park/casinos/hotels in Las Vegas and Trump's Taj Mahal in Atlantic City. Caesar's reacted to competitive pressures by renovating and adding to its properties in all three locations. In addition, it began operation of its first cruise casino called Caesar's Palace at Sea aboard a Japanese-owned luxury cruise liner. Another cruise casino is already under construction and should be operating in the near future.

Capitalizing on the Caesar's name are two other subsidiaries, Caesar's World Resorts and Caesar's World Merchandising. Caesar's World Resorts owns and operates four nongaming resorts in the Pocono Mountains of Pennsylvania. In addition, Caesar's has an agreement with a Japanese firm to manage a new noncasino resort to open in 1992 in Henderson, Nevada. Caesar's World Merchandising, Inc. markets private-label apparel, accessories, gifts, and fragrances.

Mirage Resorts (formerly Golden Nugget, Inc.). All of Mirage's gaming operations are located in Nevada. It owns and operates the Golden Nugget-Downtown, Las Vegas (which may be spun off), the Mirage on the strip in Las Vegas, and the Golden Nugget-Laughlin. The Mirage, an extremely ambitious resort venture with 3,056 hotel rooms and 95,000 square feet of casino space, became Vegas's top attraction when it opened in 1989. Constructed around a tropical theme, it offers a 20,000-gallon aquarium, a 54-foot-high volcano that erupts with pina-colada scented fumes every 15 minutes, rare white tigers in a jungle scene, tropical gardens, a multitude of restaurants, bars and shops, and an adjacent 16,000-seat outdoor sports arena. The Mirage was the first of the tourist- and family-oriented theme resorts in Las Vegas. The project cost more than $615 million and was largely financed with borrowed money.

Mirage's latest venture is Treasure Island, a pirate-theme casino/resort, which opened in October 1993. Adding 3,000 rooms to the Las Vegas market, the project cost an estimated $430 million. Its visitors will have the opportunity to watch a ship sink during a pirate battle in front of the resort and are expected to add significantly to Mirage's profit during 1994.

Hilton Hotels Corporation. The Hilton family name is well known around the world for fine hotels. Hilton owns five casino/hotels: the Las Vegas Hilton and Flamingo Hiltons in Las Vegas, two in Reno, and one in Laughlin. These casino-hotels have 12,557 guest rooms with an 85 percent average occupancy rate. Hilton gaming revenues exceed $700 million annually. Total Hilton revenues in 1993 were $1.39 billion, while profits were $103 million.

Producing slightly less revenue are the 243 other hotels and inns owned, managed, or franchised by Hilton. Although Hilton experienced a slight improvement in occupancy rate in 1993, almost all of its earnings growth occurred in the gaming operations. The company is moving rapidly into the riverboat gaming venue, with boats operating out of New Orleans and Kansas City.

Promus Companies, Inc. A relatively new company, Promus is a spin-off of Holiday Corporation (the transaction occurred in February 1990). Promus has both casino-hotel and hotel-only operations. It operates Harrah's casino/hotels in Reno, Lake Tahoe, and Laughlin; Bill's Lake Tahoe; Holiday Casino and Holiday Inn Hotel in Las Vegas; and Harrah's in Atlantic City. Promus has also ventured into the riverboat gambling market, with boats operating out of Joliet, Illinois, Vicksburg, Mississippi, and Tunica, Mississippi, and has won the rights to co-operate the only land-based casino complex in New Orleans, Louisiana. Plans call for a 120,000-square-foot casino to be completed by the end of 1994. Gaming operations contribute 80 percent to revenues and 81 percent to operating income. The Promus gaming facilities are illustrated on the U.S. map given in Figure 13–1. Note that 19 states today have legalized gambling, up from only two (New Jersey, Nevada) in 1989.

Promus's hotel segment develops real estate for the purpose of selling it while retaining franchise and management contracts. It operates over 500 hotels under the names of Embassy Suites, Hampton Inn, and Homewood Suites and is the ninth largest hotel chain in the world. Promus's 1993 revenues were a record $1.25 billion, a 12.5 percent increase over 1992, while net income rose 31.5 percent to $304 million.

MGM Grand, Inc. MGM Grand, Inc. has undergone numerous changes in recent months to prepare for the opening of its largest and potentially most profitable gamble. Although the MGM Grand Air, Inc. subsidiary has been a drain on the corporation, MGM Grand has been able to sell off its MGM Sands and Desert Inn holdings, purchase and close the Marina Hotel and Casino and the Tropicana Country Club in Las Vegas, and finance the construction of the MGM Grand Hotel and Theme Park. Situated on 115 acres directly across from the Excalibur, the MGM Grand Hotel and Theme Park has been erected at an estimated cost of over $1 billion. This complex will be the world's largest hotel, with 5,011 rooms and a 170,000-square-foot casino, and will feature a 35-acre theme park, its theme being the Wizard of Oz. Visitors will walk under a 109-foot-tall gold lion and up the yellow brick road into Emerald City, an entertainment area. Staged performances on three levels will entertain visitors riding the 50-passenger elevator.

Showboat, Inc. Showboat owns and operates one casino/hotel in Las Vegas and one in Atlantic City. The company plans to expand geographically, but debt accounting for 69 percent of Showboat's capitalization restrains growth.

Circus Circus Enterprises. Circus Circus owns and operates five casino/hotels in Nevada, two in Las Vegas and Laughlin, and one in Reno. Circus recently opened its $370 million pyramid-shaped Luxor Resort in Las Vegas to overflowing crowds. Also in 1993, Circus opened its Grand Slam Theme Park in Las Vegas. Circus's 1993 revenues grew 4 percent to $873 million, whereas its profits fell 8 percent to $110 million.

Circus Circus's plans for 1994 and 1995 include opening a huge Spanish-style casino/hotel in Reno and other casino/hotels in Sydney, Australia, and Windsor, Ontario. In addition, Circus will be opening two riverboats, one in Tunica County, Mississippi, and one in Chalmette, Louisiana.

FIGURE 13-1 Nineteen States with Legalized Gambling in the United States in 1993 (Promus casinos are highlighted)

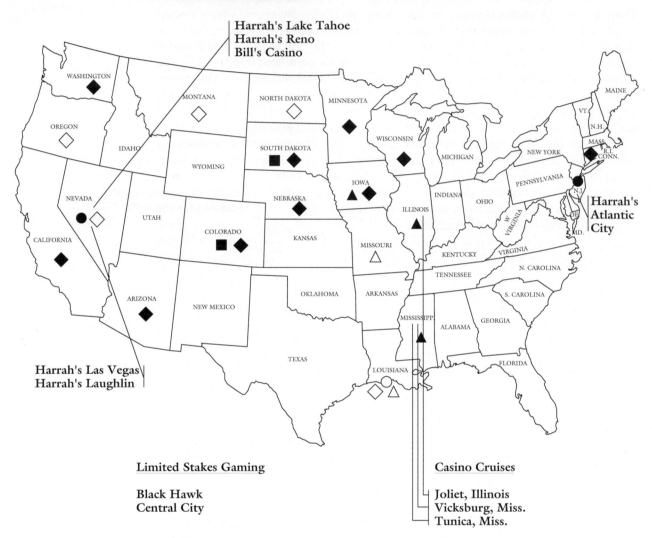

Limited Stakes Gaming

Black Hawk
Central City

Casino Cruises

Joliet, Illinois
Vicksburg, Miss.
Tunica, Miss.

▲ Riverboat or dockside casinos open
△ Riverboat or dockside casinos legal, none open
◆ Indian casinos open
◇ Indian casinos approved, none open
● Traditional land-based casinos open
○ Traditional land-based casino approved, none open
■ Limited-stakes casinos open

PROMUS COMPANIES, INC.—1993

FRED R. DAVID
Francis Marion University

Headquartered in Memphis, Tennessee, Promus (901-762-8600) is one of the leading casino entertainment and hotel companies in the United States. Promus's hotel division operates the Embassy Suites, Hampton Inn, and Homewood Suites hotel brands. Its stock soared 150 percent in 1992, from $22 to $55 a share—18th-best on the New York Stock Exchange. About 80 percent of Promus's revenues and net income comes from gaming. Its Harrah's casino entertainment division operates seven casino properties and is expanding into riverboat and Indian gaming. Harrah's Dockside Casino in Tunica County, Mississippi, approximately 20 miles south of Memphis, is a $49 million facility featuring 32,100 square feet of casino entertainment space, with 1,460 slot machines and 54 table games. In addition to the dockside building, a 30,000-square-foot shoreside facility features a 255-seat restaurant, retail space, and a lounge. Parking for approximately 1,300 cars is adjacent to the casino. The casino maintains its own self-contained power and sewage plants. Promus is building Louisiana's first land-based casino, a 120,000-square-foot facility with 4,800 slot machines and 200 gambling tables. When completed, this casino will be the largest in the world.

CASINO ENTERTAINMENT

Gambling is on the rise in the United States, and casino entertainment is becoming more widely accepted. Nearly 30 million households in the United States have one or more gamblers, and, according to *The Harrah's Survey of U.S. Casino Gaming Entertainment*, 55 percent of the population now say they feel gambling "is perfectly acceptable for anyone" (based on research by an independent market research firm). The survey also indicates that 50 percent of the American adult population has gamed at a casino at some point in their lifetime. The survey reported a four-percentage-point increase annually in people who had visited a casino. This increase translates to an additional 4.4 million gamers and a 20 percent increase in annual trips. The survey further determined that the most rapid growth in gaming in the United States is taking place in newer jurisdictions such as riverboat and Indian reservation gaming.

Here's how the states line up on lotteries and casinos: South Dakota, Colorado, Louisiana, and New Jersey have lotteries and casinos. Nevada has casinos but no lottery. Thirty-two states—Georgia, Florida, Texas, Washington, Oregon, Montana, Idaho, California, Arizona, Nebraska, Kansas, Minnesota, Wisconsin, Iowa, Illinois, Missouri, Indiana, Kentucky, Michigan, Ohio, West Virginia, Virginia, Delaware, Maryland, Pennsylvania, New York, Rhode Island, Connecticut, Massachusetts, New Hampshire, Vermont, and Maine—and the District of Columbia have lotteries but no casinos. Some of these 32 states—Florida, Rhode Island, and New York, for example—also have other forms of parimutuel wagering, such as horse racing, greyhound racing, and jai-alai. Thirteen states—North Dakota, Wyoming, Utah, New Mexico, Oklahoma, Arkansas, Mississippi, Alabama, Tennessee, North Carolina, South Carolina, Alaska, and Hawaii—have neither lotteries nor casinos. Iowa, Illinois, Mississippi, Missouri, Louisiana, and Indiana have legalized riverboat gambling.

Harrah's operates casino hotels in all major U.S. gaming markets, including Reno, Lake Tahoe, Las Vegas, and Laughlin, Nevada; and Atlantic City, New Jersey. Harrah's casino properties comprise over 460,000 square feet of casino space, 11,000 slot machines, 500 table games, 6,000 hotel rooms or suites, approximately 80,000 square feet of convention space, 40 restaurants, three showrooms, and three cabarets. Promus's strategy is to impress upon customers that they will receive the same quality experience at any Harrah's property regardless of location. Over the last five years, Promus has invested more than $354 million in maintaining and upgrading its existing Harrah's casino hotels.

Competitors within the casino entertainment industry compete on the basis of facility features such as theme and decor, location within a market, service, and promotional activity. Harrah's competes by providing high-quality entertainment value principally through its services to guests and the interaction among employees and customers. Every Harrah's operation aims to provide comfortable and enjoyable surroundings. Harrah's targets the broad middle-market gaming customer segment and does not actively seek to attract the very high-end or the very low-end segment. Its Nevada properties account for approximately 7.5 percent of the total gaming revenue in Nevada, and Harrah's Atlantic City accounts for approximately 8.9 percent of the total gaming revenue in New Jersey.

Atlantic City. The Harrah's Atlantic City casino hotel opened in Atlantic City, New Jersey, in 1980. With approximately 61,200 square feet of casino space, it has the highest gaming revenues and operating profit of the Promus casinos. Harrah's Atlantic City is situated on 21.4 acres in the Marina area of Atlantic City and consists of dual 16-story hotel towers with 268 suites and 492 regular rooms and adjoining low-rise buildings that house the casino and a 23,000-square-foot convention center. The hotel has nine restaurants, an 850-seat showroom, a pool, a health club, a teen center with video games, child care facilities, and parking for 2,678 cars. The property also has a 107-slip marina. Occupancy at the hotel has averaged over 88 percent for the past five years. Most of the casino's customers arrive by car from within a 150-mile radius which includes Philadelphia, New York, and northern New Jersey. Harrah's Atlantic City gears its advertising and promotional campaigns to the "drive-in" market, which makes this market especially susceptible to gasoline prices and adverse weather.

Harrah's Atlantic City competes directly with 11 other casinos in Atlantic City and to a lesser degree with a casino on an Indian reservation in Ledyard, Connecticut. The casino in Ledyard opened in 1992, with slot-machine play being first offered by the Ledyard casino in early 1993. The soft regional economy continued to make it difficult for Atlantic City operators to maintain operating margins as competition for revenues increased. Note from the statistics in Table 14–1 that Promus's net income in Atlantic City has been declining.

TABLE 14-1 Promus's Net Income, Atlantic City

	1992	1991	1990	PERCENTAGE INCREASE/(DECREASE) '92 vs '91	'91 vs '90
Revenues	$312.1	$310.3	$313.9	0.6%	(1.1)%
Operating income	$ 66.2	$ 65.7	$ 74.2	0.8%	(11.5)%
Operating margin	21.2%	21.2%	23.6%	—	(2.4) pts.

Reno. Harrah's Reno, situated on approximately 3.5 acres, consists of a casino-hotel complex with a 24-story structure, a 14,500-square-foot convention center, and 64,400 square feet of casino floor space. The hotel, with seven suites and 558 rooms, has six restaurants, a 420-seat Sammy's Showroom, a pool, a health club, and an arcade. The complex can accommodate 383 cars in a valet parking garage and another 377 cars in a self-park garage. In addition to this on-site parking, Harrah's Reno also leases approximately 850 spaces nearby that are available for overflow valet parking. Occupancy at the hotel has averaged approximately 91 percent for the past five years.

Harrah's Reno caters primarily to middle- and upper-income customers. The casino's marketing programs include a club for slot-machine players that gives complimentaries based on levels of play, a showroom guest program that invites valued customers to the casino to see a show, and a limited bus program that provides subsidized transportation to the casino. The primary markets for Harrah's Reno are Northern California, the Pacific Northwest, and Canada.

Promus competes with seven major casinos in the Reno area and with five major casinos in the Lake Tahoe area. No major additions to casinos or rooms are in progress in Northern Nevada and none were anticipated for 1993 through 1995.

Lake Tahoe. Harrah's Lake Tahoe is situated on 22.9 acres near Lake Tahoe and consists of an 18-story tower and adjoining low-rise building that house a 16,500-square-foot convention center and approximately 63,200 square feet of casino space. The casino hotel, with 62 suites and 472 luxury rooms, has seven restaurants, an 800-seat South Shore Showroom, a 197-seat cabaret, a health club, a retail shop, a heated pool, and an arcade. The facility has customer parking for 791 cars in a garage and 1,161 additional spaces in an adjoining lot. Occupancy at the hotel has averaged over 81 percent for the past five years. A 400-suite Embassy Suites hotel provides an additional supply of high-quality guest rooms, conveniently located adjacent to Harrah's Lake Tahoe.

Harrah's also operates Bill's Lake Tahoe Casino, which is located on a 2.1-acre site adjacent to Harrah's Lake Tahoe casino hotel. The casino includes approximately 18,000 square feet of casino space and two casual on-premise restaurants, Bennigan's and McDonald's, operated by nonaffiliated restaurant companies. Bill's Casino appeals to those customers who enjoy a more casual atmosphere. The primary markets for the casinos are California and the Pacific Northwest. Note from the statistics given in Table 14–2 that Promus's net income has been increasing from its Reno and Lake Tahoe operations.

TABLE 14-2   Promus's Net Income, Northern Nevada Division

	1992	1991	1990	PERCENTAGE INCREASE (DECREASE) '92 vs '91	'91 vs '90
Revenues	$310.5	$304.5	$312.0	2.0%	(2.4)%
Operating income	$ 67.3	$ 56.5	$ 52.2	19.1%	8.2%
Operating margin	21.7%	18.6%	16.7%	3.1 pts.	1.9 pts.

Las Vegas. Is Las Vegas becoming Disney on the desert? The answer seems to be yes, as Vegas has become a year-round family resort. Four family attractions opened in 1993 alone: Grand Slam Canyon, Luxor, Treasure Island, and MGM Grand Adventures. All four of these theme parks are owned by competitors of Promus.

Harrah's Las Vegas is located on approximately 16.4 acres of the strip in Las Vegas and consists of a 15-floor hotel tower with 500 rooms, a 23-floor hotel tower with 491 rooms, a 32-floor hotel tower with 734 rooms, and adjacent low-rise buildings that house the 15,000-square-foot convention center and the casino. The hotel has 1,725 total rooms with 22 suites. The size and location of the property permits Promus to expand its facilities if needed.

The Harrah's Las Vegas complex has approximately 79,300 square feet of casino space, five restaurants, a 525-seat Commander's Theater, a health club, and a heated pool. There are 3,087 parking spaces available, including a substantial portion in a self-park garage. Occupancy at the hotel has averaged over 91 percent for the past five years.

Harrah's Las Vegas caters to middle-income customers. The casino has marketing programs, such as a low-priced, high-volume buffet, coupons, and merchandise give-aways, which are less expensive than the marketing programs at Promus's other casino hotels. The casino's primary markets are the Midwest, California, and Canada.

Harrah's Las Vegas is in direct competition with numerous Las Vegas strip properties. The Las Vegas market has seen a significant increase in the number of rooms and casino space during the last three years. This expansion resulted from completion of two of the largest casino hotels in the world along with major expansions by existing casinos, which added over 10,000 rooms to the market. Despite this influx of rooms and casino space, Promus's Las Vegas properties have increased revenues annually. Three major competitors are currently developing new casino facilities in Las Vegas, adding an additional 10,500 rooms to the market. Table 14–3 shows that Promus's revenues have been increasing recently in Las Vegas.

Laughlin. Harrah's Laughlin opened in August 1988 in Laughlin, Nevada. It is located on a 44.9-acre site in a natural cove on the Colorado River and features a hotel with 1,658 rooms (including 23 suites), five restaurants, and a 90-seat cabaret, all with a south-of-the-border theme. It is the only property in Laughlin with a developed beachfront on the river. Harrah's Laughlin has approximately 47,000 square feet of casino space and approximately 7,000 square feet of convention center space. The facility has customer parking for 2,789 cars and vans, including a covered parking garage, and a park for recreational vehicles. Since opening, occupancy at Harrah's

TABLE 14-3   Promus's Net Income, Southern Nevada Division

	1992	1991	1990	PERCENTAGE INCREASE/(DECREASE) '92 vs '91	'91 vs '90
Revenues	$266.3	$242.0	$239.3	10.0%	1.1%
Operating income	$ 65.8	$ 55.6	$ 57.4	18.3%	(3.1)%
Operating margin	24.7%	23.0%	24.0%	1.7 pts.	(1.0) pts.

Laughlin has averaged over 91 percent. Harrah's Laughlin caters primarily to middle-income customers and targets its advertising and promotional campaigns to the drive-in market. It is located within a four-hour drive from both the Los Angeles and Phoenix metropolitan areas, whose combined populations total approximately 15 million people.

Harrah's Laughlin completed construction in September 1992 of a $37 million expansion that included a new 701-room hotel tower and additional parking facilities, restaurant seating, and meeting space. The Laughlin gaming market has changed significantly over the past three years with the virtual doubling of available rooms and increasing casino space. Harrah's competes with nine other casinos in Laughlin. Most competitors in Laughlin are planning to expand room capacity in the next few years. The Laughlin market has been served primarily by road (car, bus, and recreational vehicle) travel from Arizona and California residents.

Riverboat Casinos. Legalization of gaming in states beyond Nevada and New Jersey created the opportunity for Harrah's to expand into new casino entertainment markets. Harrah's first riverboat in Joliet, Illinois (Harrah's Casino Cruises Joliet), opened in 1993, and other Harrah's riverboat projects are under way in Vicksburg, Mississippi, Shreveport, Louisiana, and North Kansas City, Missouri. Riverboat cruises are limited to a duration of four hours, and no gaming may be conducted while the boat is docked. Minimum and maximum wagers on games are set by the licensee and wagering may not be conducted with money or other negotiable currency. No person under the age of 21 is permitted to wager, and wagers may only be taken from a person present on a licensed riverboat. With respect to electronic gaming devices, the payout percentage may not be less than 80 percent or more than 100 percent.

Legalization of riverboat gambling in Illinois imposes a 20 percent wagering tax on adjusted receipts from gambling games. The tax imposed is to be paid by the licensed owner to the Illinois Gaming Board on the day after the day when the wagers were made. Of the proceeds of that tax, 25 percent goes to the local government where the home dock is located, a small portion to the Illinois Gaming Board for administration and enforcement expenses, and the remainder to the state education-assistance fund.

Legalization also requires that licensees pay a $2.00 admission tax for each person admitted to a gaming cruise. Of this admission tax the host municipality or county receives $1.00. The licensed owner is required to maintain public books and records clearly showing amounts received from admission fees, the total amount of gross receipts, and the total amount of adjusted gross receipts.

Joliet. Harrah's operates a riverboat gaming entertainment complex in Joliet, Illinois. The Empress is a 210-foot riverboat with 17,900 square feet of casino space, 42 table games, 569 slot machines, and a pavilion and related parking facilities on shore. A second riverboat, with 12,600 square feet of casino space, began operating in 1994 at Joliet. Revenues from the Empress in 1993 were about $75 million.

Vicksburg. Promus operates a dockside casino entertainment complex in Vicksburg, Mississippi. The project costs approximately $35.6 million and includes a 250-foot stationary riverboat with approximately 20,000 square feet of casino space, 600 slot machines, 43 table games, and a 120-room Harrah's hotel.

North Kansas City. Promus operates a riverboat casino entertainment center in North Kansas City, Missouri. Promus spent $69 million to develop the casino, which includes a 300-foot riverboat with 30,000 square feet of casino entertainment space, 1,100 slot machines, 55 table games, and related shoreside facilities.

Shreveport. Promus operates a casino entertainment complex in Shreveport, Louisiana, that features a 210-foot riverboat with 19,600 square feet of casino entertainment space, an anticipated 700 slot machines and 40 table games, and dockside facilities. Promus spent $41.3 million on this project.

For 1994, analysts expect Promus's total riverboat revenues to be about $405 million —$250 million from the two boats in Joliet, $55 million from the full-year operation of Vicksburg, and partial-year contributions from Shreveport and North Kansas City.

Indian Gaming. Promus purchased a 20 percent ownership interest in Sodak Gaming Supplies, Inc. ("Sodak") in 1992. Under terms of an agreement with International Game Technology ("IGT") expiring in 1997, Sodak is the exclusive distributor for IGT of its gaming equipment in the states of North Dakota, South Dakota, and Wyoming, and on Indian reservations within the 48 contiguous states, excluding Nevada and New Jersey. The distribution agreement may be extended beyond the current five-year term by IGT at its option.

Promus has been selected by the Ak-Chin Indian Community to negotiate an exclusive management and development agreement for a planned $18.5 million casino on the Community's land approximately 25 miles south of Phoenix, Arizona. Proceeding with the project is subject to various regulatory approvals and the resolution of uncertainties relative to gaming on Indian reservations in Arizona.

Abroad. Promus has applied for a license to operate a casino entertainment facility in Auckland, New Zealand. If the application is successful, Promus anticipates making an investment of up to $15 million in a joint venture to develop and construct the proposed casino, which would be managed by Promus.

HOTELS

Promus's hotel business consists of the Embassy Suites, Hampton Inn, and Homewood Suites brands. Each brand is targeted to a specific market segment. Although the U.S. economy appears to be recovering, it could take the hotel industry several years to absorb the current supply of rooms. But because very few new hotels are being built, demand is rising faster than supply. Hotel occupancy rates for 1993 averaged 64 percent, the highest in a decade and up from 62 percent in 1992. The average room rate edged up 2 percent to $61 in 1993 as demand grew 5.1 percent, while supply grew only 1.2 percent. Average hotel rates in key cities are as follows:

CITY	OCCUPANCY RATE	AVERAGE DAILY RATE
New York	69%	$135
Boston	72	119
Washington	65	115
San Francisco	69	111
Honolulu	81	99
Miami	84	90
Chicago	63	89
Philadelphia	62	84
San Diego	66	81

Atlanta	60	79
Los Angeles	60	76
Tampa	68	72
Houston	60	70
Dallas	63	68
Orlando	72	68
Phoenix	64	68
San Antonio–Austin	67	63
Memphis	63	62
Denver	63	61

Intense competition exists in the sale of hotel franchises and in obtaining management contracts. Promus's hotel brands are in vigorous competition with a wide range of facilities offering various types of lodging options and related services to the public. All of Promus's hotel brands outperform their respective competitive segment in terms of both revenue-per-available-room (RevPAR) and occupancy.

The more than 100 Embassy Suites hotels appeal to the traveler who has a need or desire for greater space and more focused services than are available in traditional upscale hotels. Embassy Suites hotels comprise the largest all-suite hotel system in the Unites States by number of suites and system revenues.

Hampton Inn hotels are moderately priced hotels designed to attract the business and leisure traveler desiring quality accommodations at affordable prices. Since 1984 when the brand was introduced, Hampton has grown to more than 350 hotels.

The 24 Homewood Suites hotels represent Promus's entry in the extended-stay market and target the traveler who stays five or more consecutive nights, as well as the traditional business and leisure traveler.

At the beginning of 1993, Promus's three hotel brands included 350 properties that are licensed by Promus, 66 properties that are managed by Promus, and 39 properties that are owned and operated by Promus. These properties total 68,276 rooms and suites.

Promus pursues a strategy of growth for its hotel brands by minimizing its ownership of hotel real estate and concentrating on obtaining new franchise or management contracts. As a part of this strategy, owned or leased hotels are sold and operated either by Promus under a management contract or by the purchaser under license from Promus. In recent years the declining real estate and financial markets have constrained Promus's ability to sell hotel assets, although Promus intends to continue this strategy. No major projects to construct additional company-owned hotels are currently planned.

Each of Promus's hotel brands uses a centralized business system, which includes access to reservation services and also to performance support or training, operations management, and revenue management. This network of business systems is one of the most sophisticated systems in the hotel industry. The Embassy Suites, Hampton Inn, and Homewood Suites business systems' reservation module receives reservation requests entered on terminals located at all of their respective hotels and reservation center, and major domestic airlines. The systems immediately confirm reservations or indicate accommodations available at alternate system hotels. Confirmations are transmitted automatically to the hotel for which the reservation is made. Promus's computer center in Memphis, Tennessee, houses the computers and satellite communications equipment necessary for its commercial, reservations, and property management systems.

Promus offers an unconditional money-back guarantee of service satisfaction at all three of its hotel brands. The Hampton Inn "100 Percent Satisfaction" guarantee and

Homewood Suites "Suite Assurance" guarantee have been in place since 1989; the "Embassy Suites Way" guarantee was initiated at Embassy Suites in 1991 and was expanded system-wide in the second quarter of 1992. All of Promus's hotel brands offer suites/rooms exclusively for nonsmoking guests.

To facilitate international growth, Promus has acquired a minority interest in a Hong Kong–based hotel-management and development company in order to expand Promus's hotel brands into the Asia Pacific region. Promus's participation in this venture will not require it to make substantial investments of capital. One result of the venture is a franchised Embassy Suites hotel currently under construction in Bangkok, Thailand.

Embassy Suites Hotels. Embassy Suites hotels are all-suite hotels targeted to the traveler who has a need or desire for greater space and more focused services than are available in most traditional hotels. Exhibit 14–1 sets forth information regarding all Embassy Suites hotels, including company-owned hotels, hotels operated by Embassy under management contracts or joint venture arrangements, and hotels operated by licensees. As the year 1993 began, three hotels were under construction, all of which will be licensee-operated. Embassy Suites hotels are located in 30 states and Washington, D.C. One hotel is located in Canada and another, as mentioned, is under construction in Thailand. Embassy Suites hotels generally have between 142 and 460 suites. Each guest suite has a separate living room and dining/work area, with a color television, refrigerator, and wet bar, as well as a traditional bedroom where most fea-

EXHIBIT 14-1 Embassy Suites Hotels

	LICENSED		OWNED		MANAGEMENT CONTRACTS/ JOINT VENTURES	
	NUMBER OF HOTELS	NUMBER OF SUITES	NUMBER OF HOTELS	NUMBER OF SUITES	NUMBER OF HOTELS	NUMBER OF SUITES
Fiscal Year-End 1989	40	9,470	7	1,455	51	13,032
1990 Activity:						
Additions	5	1,135	1	261	7	1,870
Conversions, net	8	2,114	—	—	(8)	(2,114)
Sales/Terminations	(11)	(2,895)	—	—	—	—
Fiscal Year-End 1990	42	9,824	8	1,716	50	12,788
1991 Activity:						
Additions	2	476	6	1,519	4	1,254
Conversions, net	2	677	1	215	(3)	(892)
Sales/Terminations	(4)	(1,171)	—	—	(7)	(1,698)
Fiscal Year-End 1991	42	9,806	15	3,450	44	11,452
1992 Activity:						
Additions	2	685	—	—	—	(3)
Conversions, net	1	221	—	—	(1)	(221)
Fiscal Year-End 1992	45	10,712	15	3,450	43	11,228

Source: Promus *Annual Report.*

ture a remote-controlled television. Most Embassy Suites hotels are built around an atrium lobby. All hotels offer a free breakfast and complimentary evening cocktails.

The following table sets forth information concerning system occupancy, average daily rate per occupied suite, and revenue per available suite for all Embassy Suites hotels:

FISCAL YEAR	OCCUPANCY RATE	AVERAGE DAILY RATE PER OCCUPIED SUITE	REVENUE PER AVAILABLE SUITE
1992	71.7%	$90.97	$65.26
1991	69.4	88.19	61.19
1990	69.8	86.73	60.56

Hampton Inn Hotels. Hampton Inn hotels are moderately priced hotels designed to attract the business and leisure traveler desiring quality accommodations at affordable prices. Exhibit 14–2 sets forth information regarding all Hampton Inn hotels, including company-owned hotels, hotels operated by Hampton Inns under management contracts or joint venture arrangements, and hotels operated by licensees. As 1993 began 26 hotels were under construction, all of which will be licensee-operated.

EXHIBIT 14-2 Hampton Inn Hotels

	LICENSED		OWNED		MANAGEMENT CONTRACTS/ JOINT VENTURES	
	NUMBER OF HOTELS	NUMBER OF ROOMS	NUMBER OF HOTELS	NUMBER OF ROOMS	NUMBER OF HOTELS	NUMBER OF ROOMS
Fiscal Year-End 1989	183	22,962	10	1,353	19	2,376
1990 Activity:						
Additions	36	4,598	3	403	—	—
Terminations	(3)	(380)	—	—	—	—
Fiscal Year-End 1990	216	27,180	13	1,756	19	2,376
1991 Activity:						
Additions	45	5,362	2	293	2	242
Terminations	(2)	(239)	—	—	—	—
Fiscal Year-End 1991	259	32,303	15	2,049	21	2,618
1992 Activity:						
Additions	32	3,216	—	(1)	2	292
Terminations	(2)	(277)	—	—	—	—
Fiscal Year-End 1992	289	35,242	15	2,048	23	2,910

Source: Promus *Annual Report.*

Hampton Inn hotels are located in 41 states in the United States and one is under construction in Canada. An average Hampton Inn hotel has from 100 to 150 rooms. The Hampton Inn hotel's standardized concept provides a guest room featuring a color television, free in-room movies, free local telephone calls, and complimentary continental breakfast. Hampton Inn hotels also offer an electronic communications alerting system and reservations system for deaf and hearing-impaired guests. Unlike full-service hotels, Hampton Inn hotels do not feature restaurants, lounges, or large public spaces. Room rates typically are below those of traditional midscale hotels.

Hampton Inns also has a modified lodging property for use in communities supporting hotels of fewer than 100 rooms. The building design for these smaller communities has the same features as a standard Hampton Inn hotel but with fewer rooms and a smaller lobby. Hampton Inn hotels compete in the segment of the lodging market that is directed primarily to business and leisure travelers desiring quality accommodations at reasonable prices. The following table sets forth information concerning system occupancy, average daily rate per occupied room, and revenue per available room for all Hampton Inn hotels:

Fiscal Year	Occupancy Rate	Average Daily Rate per Occupied Room	Revenue per Available Room
1992	71.2%	$48.91	$34.82
1991	68.6	47.22	32.39
1990	69.3	45.71	31.69

Homewood Suites Hotels. The Homewood Suites brand represents Promus's entry in the extended-stay market and is targeted for the traveler who stays five or more consecutive nights, but is a unique alternative to traditional business and leisure travelers. Exhibit 14–3 sets forth information regarding all Homewood Suites hotels, including company-owned hotels and hotels operated by licensees. As 1993 began one Homewood Suites hotel was under construction and will be licensee-operated. Homewood Suites hotels are located in 16 states and a hotel is under construction in one additional state. Homewood Suites hotels feature residential-style accommodations, including a living-room area (some with fireplaces), separate bedroom (with a king-size bed) and bath, and a fully equipped kitchen. The hotel buildings, generally two or three stories, are centered around a central community building, called the Lodge, which affords guests a high level of social interaction. Amenities include a limited complimentary breakfast and a complimentary evening social hour, a convenience store, shopping service, business center, outdoor pool, exercise center, and limited meeting facilities.

Homewood Suites recently designed a smaller, modified prototype of its standard hotel for use in suburban areas of major cities, as well as secondary cities with active industrial or commercial areas. The modified prototype reflects the signature design and amenities of a traditional Homewood Suites hotel, but with fewer suites, a smaller Lodge, and other construction modifications that will require less land.

The following table sets forth information concerning system occupancy, average daily rate per occupied suite, and revenue per available suite for all Homewood Suites hotels:

Fiscal Year	Occupancy Rate	Average Daily Rate per Occupied Suite	Revenue per Available Suite
1992	71.9%	$69.65	$50.10
1991	65.2	66.84	43.56
1990	59.3	64.49	38.34

Results of Operations. Promus's casino entertainment and hotel segments both achieved record operating results during 1992. These operating results, coupled with the lower overall cost of debt, were the primary contributors to a 75 percent increase in net income. The casino entertainment segment contributed approximately 80 percent of Promus's 1992 consolidated revenues and operating income. A summary of the performance of Promus's operating segments for three recent years is presented in Exhibit 14–4. Promus's most recent balance sheets, income statement, statements of stockholders' equity, and statement of cash flows are given in Exhibits 14–5, 14–6, 14–7, and 14–8.

CONCLUSION

Hilton Hotels, Mirage Resorts, and Circus Circus Enterprises are battling Promus for riverboat and gambling licenses and management contracts. Municipalities are becoming savvier in dealing with gaming companies by demanding more shoreline development with restaurants and hotel rooms. The net result is lower profit margins

EXHIBIT 14-3   Homewood Suites Hotels

	Licensed		Owned	
	Number of Hotels	Number of Rooms	Number of Hotels	Number of Rooms
Fiscal Year-End 1989	2	127	1	30
1990 Activity:				
Additions	7	724	6	790
Fiscal Year-End 1990	9	851	7	820
1991 Activity:				
Additions	5	653	1	120
Fiscal Year-End 1991	14	1,504	8	940
1992 Activity:				
Additions	2	250	—	(8)
Fiscal Year-End 1992	16	1,754	8	932

Source: Promus *Annual Report.*

for gaming companies such as Promus. Yet, opportunities abound in gaming. The state of Texas and the city of Chicago are expected to legalize riverboat gambling soon, and Promus must act quickly to get prime locations and contracts.

Promus has formed a separate division to seek new opportunities in the Indian reservation gaming market. Although Harrah's is doing well in the land-based casinos, new theme parks such as the Luxor and Treasure Island are pressuring Harrah's.

Promus's hotel operating income rose 43 percent in 1992 and hotel demand is increasing more than supply, but the hotel business is still characterized by discounting and low occupancy rates. Perhaps the greatest constraint on Promus's strategies today is the firm's debt situation. Debt at year-end 1992 exceeded $800 million, or about twice the firm's equity. A 2-to-1 debt-to-equity ratio restrains investment options. Promus may need an equity offering to finance expansion during the mid-1990s.

Should Promus expand its Hampton Inn, Embassy Suites, and/or Homewood Suites hotels? Develop a three-year strategic plan for CEO Michael Rose that will enable Promus to fulfill its Vision Statement:

> Our vision is to provide the best experience to our gaming and hotel customers by having the best people trained, empowered, and pledged to excellence, delivering the best service, quality and value to every customer, every time ... guaranteed.

EXHIBIT 14-4 Operating Results by Segment

| | FISCAL YEAR ENDED | | | PERCENTAGE INCREASE (DECREASE) | |
	DECEMBER 31, 1992	JANUARY 3, 1992	DECEMBER 28, 1990	'92 vs '91	'91 vs '90
CASINO ENTERTAINMENT					
Revenues					
Casino	$711,777	$686,177	$689,789	3.7%	(0.5)%
Food and beverage	133,485	129,147	134,779	3.4%	(4.2)%
Rooms	94,092	88,749	91,653	6.0%	(3.2)%
Other	43,901	39,620	35,728	10.8%	10.9%
Less: casino promotional allowances	(92,151)	(84,750)	(84,503)	8.7%	0.3%
Total revenues	891,104	858,943	867,446	3.7%	(1.0)%
Operating expenses					
Departmental direct costs					
Casino	334,702	338,529	331,412	(1.1)%	2.1%
Food and beverage	71,551	69,702	74,225	2.7%	(6.1)%
Rooms	31,958	31,346	32,314	2.0%	(3.0)%
Other	265,683	248,571	254,006	6.9%	(2.1)%
Total operating expenses	703,894	688,148	691,957	2.3%	(0.6)%
	187,210	170,795	175,489	9.6%	(2.7)%
Property transactions	(327)	168	9	N/M	N/M
Operating income	$186,883	$170,963	$175,498	9.3%	(2.6)%
Operating income before property transactions margin	21.0%	19.9%	20.2%	1.1 pts	(0.3)pts

EXHIBIT 14-4 *Continued*

	FISCAL YEAR ENDED			PERCENTAGE INCREASE (DECREASE)	
	DECEMBER 31, 1992	JANUARY 3, 1992	DECEMBER 28, 1990	'92 vs '91	'91 vs '90
HOTEL					
Revenues					
Rooms	$124,192	$ 88,109	$ 54,415	41.0%	61.9%
Food and beverage	8,310	6,436	3,580	29.1%	79.8%
Franchise and management fees	51,719	45,320	48,881	14.1%	(7.3)%
Other	33,993	27,126	22,571	25.3%	20.2%
Total revenues	218,214	166,991	129,447	30.7%	29.0%
Operating expenses					
Departmental direct costs					
Rooms	71,191	51,256	32,121	38.9%	59.6%
Food and beverage	8,696	6,127	3,520	41.9%	74.1%
Other	89,252	75,358	79,369	18.4%	(5.1)%
Total operating expenses	169,139	132,741	115,010	27.4%	15.4%
	49,075	34,250	14,437	43.3%	137.2%
Property transactions	(5,713)	(1,354)	6,305	N/M	N/M
Operating income	$ 43,362	$ 32,896	$ 20,742	31.8%	58.6%
Operating income before property transactions margin	22.5%	20.5%	11.2%	2.0 pts	9.3pts
OTHER					
Revenues	$ 3,748	$ 5,178	$ 7,313	(27.6)%	(29.2)%
Operating expenses	2,577	6,056	10,075	(57.4)%	(39.9)%
Operating income (loss)	$ 1,171	$ (878)	$ (2,762)	N/M	68.2%

N/M = not measurable.

Source: Promus *Annual Reports.*

EXHIBIT 14-5 Consolidated Balance Sheets (in thousands, except per share amounts)

	December 31,	
	1993	1992
ASSETS		
Current assets		
Cash and cash equivalents	$ 61,962	$ 43,756
Receivables, including notes receivable of $2,197 and $9,831, less allowance for doubtful accounts of $10,864 and $11,598	47,448	53,283
Deferred income taxes	21,024	15,196
Prepayments	18,063	11,697
Supplies	12,996	11,296
Other	2,065	1,919
Total current assets	163,558	137,147
Land, buildings, riverboats and equipment		
Land	245,846	243,678
Buildings, riverboats and improvements	1,143,356	1,064,363
Furniture, fixtures and equipment	435,231	375,489
	1,824,433	1,683,530
Less: accumulated depreciation	(486,231)	(435,039)
	1,338,202	1,248,491
Investments in and advances to nonconsolidated affiliates	70,050	50,985
Deferred costs and other	221,308	159,914
	$1,793,118	$1,596,537
LIABILITIES AND STOCKHOLDERS' EQUITY		
Current liabilities		
Accounts payable	$ 60,530	$ 50,669
Construction payables	26,345	—
Accrued expenses	162,969	102,716
Current portion of long-term debt	2,160	3,898
Total current liabilities	252,004	157,283
Long-term debt	839,804	877,427
Deferred credits and other	86,829	83,606
Deferred income taxes	63,460	46,623
	1,242,097	1,164,939
Minority interest	14,984	3,668
Commitments and contingencies		
Stockholders' equity		
Common stock, $1.50 par value, authorized—120,000,000 shares, outstanding—102,258,442 and 101,882,082 shares (net of 25,251 and 44,442 shares held in treasury)	153,388	152,823
Capital surplus	201,035	178,972
Retained earnings	187,203	100,857
Deferred compensation related to restricted stock	(5,589)	(4,722)
	536,037	427,930
	$1,793,118	$1,596,537

Source: Promus *Annual Report.*

EXHIBIT 14-6 Consolidated Statements of Income (in thousands, except per share amounts)

	FISCAL YEAR ENDED		
	DECEMBER 31, 1993	DECEMBER 31, 1992	JANUARY 3, 1992
Revenues			
Casino	$ 812,081	$ 711,777	$ 686,177
Rooms	223,129	218,284	176,858
Food and beverage	147,616	141,795	135,583
Franchise and management fees	60,359	51,719	45,320
Other	109,390	81,642	71,924
Less: casino promotional allowances	(100,720)	(92,151)	(84,750)
Total revenues	1,251,855	1,113,066	1,031,112
Operating expenses			
Departmental direct costs			
Casino	369,335	334,702	338,529
Rooms	98,653	103,149	82,602
Food and beverage	84,733	80,247	75,829
Depreciation of buildings, riverboats and equipment	77,590	69,575	63,857
Other	318,669	287,937	266,128
Total operating expenses	948,980	875,610	826,945
	302,875	237,456	204,167
Property transactions	1,345	(6,040)	(1,186)
Operating income	304,220	231,416	202,981
Corporate expense	(27,136)	(28,450)	(26,825)
Interest expense, net of interest capitalized	(106,561)	(118,282)	(133,992)
Other (expense) income, including interest income	(714)	3,615	10,030
Income before income taxes and minority interest	169,809	88,299	52,194
Provision for income taxes	(73,262)	(36,881)	(22,183)
Minority interest	(4,754)	—	—
Income before extraordinary items	91,793	51,418	30,011
Extraordinary items, net of tax benefit (provision) of $3,415 and $(753)	(5,447)	1,074	—
Net income	$ 86,346	$ 52,492	$ 30,011
Earnings per share before extraordinary items	$ 0.89	$ 0.51	$ 0.33
Extraordinary items, net	(0.05)	0.01	—
Earnings per share	$ 0.84	$ 0.52	$ 0.33
Average common shares outstanding	102,562	101,116	90,480

Source: Promus *Annual Report*.

EXHIBIT 14-7 Consolidated Statements of Stockholders' Equity

	Common Stock		Capital Surplus	Retained Earnings	Deferred Compensation Related to Restricted Stock	Total
	Shares Outstanding	Amount				
Balance - December 28, 1990	$ 79,959	$119,938	$ 77,660	$ 18,354	$(12,203)	$203,749
Net income				30,011		30,011
Public offering of common stock, net of issue costs of $6,920	21,000	31,500	94,580			126,080
Net shares issued under incentive compensation plans, less income tax provision of $1,600	409	614	(61)		5,102	5,655
Balance - January 3, 1992	101,368	152,052	172,179	48,365	(7,101)	365,495
Net income				52,492		52,492
Net shares issued under incentive compensation plans, including income tax benefit of $3,726	514	771	6,793		2,379	9,943
Balance - December 31, 1992	101,882	152,823	178,972	100,857	(4,722)	427,930
Net income				86,346		86,346
Pro-rata share of proceeds from equity investee's initial public offering, less income tax provision of $2,662			3,752			3,752
Net shares issued under incentive compensation plans, including income tax benefit of $10,467	376	565	18,311		(867)	18,009
Balance - December 31, 1993	102,258	$153,388	$201,035	$187,203	$ (5,589)	$536,037

Source: Promus *Annual Report.*

EXHIBIT 14-8 Consolidated Statements of Cash Flows

	FISCAL YEAR ENDED		
	DECEMBER 31, 1993	DECEMBER 31, 1992	JANUARY 3, 1992
Cash flows from operating activities			
Net income	$ 86,346	$ 52,492	$ 30,011
Adjustments to reconcile net income			
to cash flows from operating activities			
Extraordinary items	8,862	(1,827)	—
Depreciation and amortization	98,095	92,342	88,073
Other noncash items	27,356	25,678	21,779
Minority interest share of net income	4,754	—	—
Equity in earnings of and distributions from			
nonconsolidated affiliates	2,782	6,452	13,431
Net (gains) losses from property transactions	(1,481)	972	(5,405)
Net change in long-term accounts	2,239	(11,451)	(12,288)
Net change in working capital accounts	33,929	2,437	7,386
Tax indemnification payments to Bass	(8,459)	(13,238)	(32,186)
Cash flows provided by operating activities	254,423	153,857	110,801
Cash flows from investing activities			
Land, buildings, riverboats and equipment additions	(235,766)	(117,771)	(118,266)
Increase in construction payables	26,345	—	—
Proceeds from sales of equity investments	—	3,733	12,026
Proceeds from property transactions	25,169	3,585	6,459
Investments in and advances to nonconsolidated			
affiliates	(15,431)	(13,487)	(3,986)
Other	(27,954)	(8,334)	(13,371)
Cash flows used in investing activities	(227,637)	(132,274)	(117,138)
Cash flows from financing activities			
Debt retirements	(358,762)	(189,219)	(82,406)
Proceeds from issuance of senior subordinated			
notes, net of issue costs of $3,819 and $5,687	196,181	194,313	—
Net borrowings under Revolving Credit Facility,			
net of issue costs of $11,547	158,453	—	—
Net repayments under retired revolving credit facility	(9,000)	(16,000)	(43,000)
Minority interest contributions, net of distributions	4,548	2,908	—
Proceeds from issuance of common stock, net of issue			
costs of $6,920	—	—	126,080
Premiums paid on early extinguishment of debt	—	(4,426)	—
Cash flows (used in) provided by financing activities	(8,580)	(12,424)	674
Net increase (decrease) in cash and cash equivalents	18,206	9,159	(5,663)
Cash and cash equivalents, beginning of period	43,756	34,597	40,260
Cash and cash equivalents, end of period	$ 61,962	$ 43,756	$ 34,597

Source: Promus *Annual Report.*

JOHN K. ROSS, III,
MIKE KEEFFE, and
BILL MIDDLEBROOK
Southwest Texas State
University

CASE 15

CIRCUS CIRCUS ENTERPRISES, INC.—1994

The sun bears down as you travel across the desert searching for your destination. The heat causes the air to rise in waves toward the sky as you carefully examine the horizon. At last, above the sand dunes shimmering in the heat, you see the top of the fabled pyramid. Even at this distance you can tell it is bigger than anything you imagined. The closer you get to the desert oasis where the pyramid is located, the bigger it seems in this land of dreams. Finally you stand at the base of the pyramid, at the foot of the great sphinx, anxious to explore the huge complex before you. Then the sphinx flashes its eyes at you—and you enter. Flashes its eyes? Yes, for this is Las Vegas—and you have entered the land of Circus Circus Enterprises, Inc. (702-734-0410).

Although Circus Circus Enterprises, Inc. (hereafter Circus) describes itself as a merchant and compares its stores to supermarkets and shopping malls, its products are hardly those one would find on typical store shelves. The "merchandise" of Circus is entertainment and the "stores" are huge pink-and-white-striped concrete circus tents, a 600-foot-long riverboat replica, a giant castle, and the latest addition—a great pyramid. Circus's areas of operation are the glitzy vacation and convention meccas of Las Vegas, Reno, and Laughlin, Nevada, and, if plans work out, other locations in the United States and abroad. The company's marketing of it products has been called "right out of the bargain basement," and has catered to "low rollers," although Circus now aims more at the middle-income gambler and family-oriented vacationers wanting more than a conventional gambling-oriented vacation.

Circus was purchased in 1974 for $50,000 as a small and unprofitable casino operation by partners William G. Bennett, an aggressive cost-cutter who ran furniture stores before entering the gaming industry in 1965, and William N. Pennington (see Exhibit 15–1 for Board of Directors and top managers). The partners were able to rejuvenate Circus back to profitability, went public with a stock offering in October 1983, and in the last five years had an average growth rate in earnings per share of more than 22.6 percent per year. Today, Circus is the largest casino-hotel operator in both the Las Vegas and Laughlin markets in terms of square footage of casino space and number of hotel rooms—this, despite the incredible growth in both markets. For instance although Laughlin has experienced over 100 percent growth in total hotel rooms, Circus operates nearly 30 percent of that total. Casino gaming operations provide over half of total revenue for Circus (see Exhibit 15–2), and in 1993 they reported a net income of more than $120 million and employed more than 13,600 people.

CIRCUS CIRCUS OPERATIONS

Circus defines entertainment as pure play and fun, and it goes out of the way to see that customers have plenty of opportunity for both. Each of Circus's "stores" has a distinctive personality. Circus Circus–Las Vegas is the world of the Big Top, where live circus acts perform for free every 30 minutes. Kids may cluster around video games while the adults migrate to nickel slot machines and dollar game tables. The latest addition to the original casino is the $90 million Grand Slam Canyon Adventuredome, a five-acre, glass-enclosed theme park including a four-loop roller coaster. Recent soft results at the Las Vegas property have induced management to include more rides costing an additional $5 to $8 million.

EXHIBIT 15-1 Circus Circus Enterprises, Inc.

I. DIRECTORS

Name	Age	Title
William G. Bennett	68	Chairman of the Board and CEO, Circus Circus Enterprises
William P. Pennington	70	Cofounder, Circus Circus Enterprises
Clyde T. Turner	55	President and CEO, Circus Circus Enterprises
Fred W. Smith	59	President and CEO, Donrey Media Group
James Cashman III	44	President, Cashman Equipment and Vice President, Cashman Cadillac, Inc.
Tony Coelho	na	Managing Director, Wertheim Schroder & Co., Inc.
Carl F. Dodge	77	Former Chairman, Nevada Gaming Commission, retired
Arthur M. Smith, Jr.	71	Chairman of the Board, retired, First Interstate Bank of Nevada

II. TOP MANAGEMENT

Name	Title
William G. Bennett	Chairman of the Board and CEO, Circus Circus Enterprises
Clyde T. Turner	President and CFO, Circus Circus Enterprises
William J. Paulos	Senior Vice President
Terry L. Caudill	Vice President, Chief Accounting Officer and Treasurer
Mike Sloan	General Counsel and Secretary

Source: *Annual Report*, 1993.

EXHIBIT 15-2 Circus Circus Enterprises, Inc. Sources of Revenue

Casinos	56.8%
Food and Beverage	15.6%
Hotel	16.9%
Other	10.6%

Source: Company reports.

Luxor, the newest Circus property, opened on October 15, 1993, when 10,000 people entered to play the 2,525 slot and video poker games and 82 table games in the 100,000-square-foot casino in the hotel atrium (reported to be the world's largest). By the end of the opening weekend 40,000 people per day were visiting the 36-story bronze pyramid that encases the hotel and entertainment facilities. Circus management is gambling that over 11 million visitors will tour the Luxor in the first year. In the Luxor you can take a cruise on one of 11 barges down an 18,000-foot River Nile past an obelisk and a sphinx, see a show in the 1,100-seat dinner theater, dine in one of the seven restaurants, exercise in the state-of-the-art health spa, or play the slots.

Circus operates nine properties in all (see Exhibit 15–3). At one end of the Vegas strip is Circus Circus–Las Vegas, a circus big-top that covers 795 hotel rooms, shopping areas, two specialty restaurants, a buffet with seating for 1,100, fast-food shops, cocktail lounges, video arcades, 110,000 square feet of casino, live circus acts, and the Grand Slam Canyon. Guests who stay in the facility's other 1,998 rooms travel by elevated monorail from the adjacent Circus Skyrise and Circus Manor, or from the nearby Circusland RV Park.

Located next to the Luxor, Excalibur is one of the first sights travelers see as they exit Interstate Highway 15. (Management was confident that the sight of a giant, colorful medieval castle would make a lasting impression on mainstream tourists and vacationing families arriving in Las Vegas.) Guests cross a drawbridge over a moat onto a cobblestone walkway where multicolored spires, turrets, and battlements loom above. The castle walls are four 28-story hotel towers containing a total of 4,032 rooms. Inside is a medieval world complete with a Fantasy Faire inhabited by strolling jugglers, fire eaters, and acrobats as well as a Royal Village complete with peasants, serfs, and ladies-in-waiting around medieval theme shops. The 100,000-square-foot casino encloses 2,600 slot machines, more than 100 game tables, a sports book, and a poker and keno area. There are 12 restaurants, capable of feeding more than 20,000 people daily, and a 900-seat amphitheater. Excalibur, which opened in June 1990, was built for $294 million, primarily financed with internally generated funds, and contributed 33 percent of the organization's revenues in the year ending January 31, 1993.

Situated between the two anchors on the Las Vegas strip are two smaller casinos operated by Circus. The Silver City Casino and Slots-A-Fun primarily depend on the foot traffic along the strip for their gambling patrons.

All of Circus's operations do well in the city of Las Vegas. However, Circus Circus 1993 operational earnings have remained relatively flat, reflecting the general economic downturn. Circus's hotel room occupancy rates in Las Vegas are typically 98 to 100 percent, due in part to low room rates ($30 to $50 at Circus Circus–Las Vegas)

EXHIBIT 15-3 Circus Circus Enterprises, Inc. Properties and Revenues by Market

	PROPERTIES	PERCENT REVENUES
Las Vegas	Circus Circus–Las Vegas	49.9
	Luxor	
	Excalibur	
	Grand Slam Canyon	
	Silver City Casino	
	Slots-A-Fun	
Laughlin	The Colorado Belle	29.6
	The Edgewater	
Reno	Circus Circus–Reno	20.5

Source: Company reports.

and popular buffets. Seating over 3,000, the restaurants at Excalibur alone are able to offer the most meals per day of any single-site commercial establishment in the world. Although Circus loses 50 cents on each meal it serves, the popular buffets generate enough cash flow each year to cover debt obligations nearly six times.

The company's other big-top facility is Circus Circus–Reno. With the addition of Skyway Tower in 1985, this big top now offers a total of 1,625 hotel rooms, 60,600 square feet of casino, a buffet that can seat 700 people, shops, video arcades, cocktail lounges, midway games, and circus acts. As a project, Circus Circus–Reno had several marginal years, but nevertheless has become one of the leaders in that market.

The Colorado Belle and the Edgewater Hotel are located in Laughlin, Nevada, a city 90 miles south of Las Vegas on the banks of the Colorado River. The Colorado Belle, opened in 1987, features a huge paddle-wheel riverboat replica, buffet, cocktail lounges, and shops. The Edgewater, acquired in 1983, has a southwestern motif, a 57,000-square-foot casino, a bowling center, a buffet, and cocktail lounges. Combined, these two properties contain 2,700 rooms and over 120,000 square feet of casino; and together, these two operations contributed 23 percent of the company's revenues in the year ended January 31, 1993.

Circus has achieved success through an aggressive growth strategy and a corporate structure designed to enhance that growth (see Exhibit 15–4). Since 1984 Circus has increased its available hotel rooms from approximately 2,500 to more than 13,000. Casino space has increased from 165,000 square feet to more than 536,000 square feet during the same period. A strong cash position, innovative ideas, and attention to cost control has allowed Circus to satisfy the bottom line during a period when competitors were typically taking on large debt obligations to finance new projects (see Exhibits 15–1, 15–2, 15–3, 15–4). Yet the market is changing.

New Ventures. Gambling of all kinds has spread across the country. No longer does the average individual need to go to Las Vegas or New Jersey. Instead, gambling can be found at the local quick market (lottery), at the bingo hall, at many Indian reservations, and along the Mississippi river. In order to maintain a competitive edge, Circus has recently announced several projects that will take it beyond the bounds of Nevada.

EXHIBIT 15-4 Circus Circus Organizational Chart

Circus has decided to join the Mississippi River gambling development by creating a riverboat casino site less than 20 miles from Memphis. Subject to licensing, Circus will own and operate one of three dockside casinos at the site. As an additional river operation, Circus is attempting to secure a riverboat license from the Indiana Gaming Commission for the town of Portage, Indiana. Located 35 miles east of Chicago, the proposed development would include a riverboat, an entertainment facility, and a small hotel. The estimated cost for this project is $80 to $100 million. Gambling is, of course, not limited to the United States and Circus is attempting to expand internationally by joining with Press Holdings Limited and Nine Network Australia to bid on a proposed casino license in Sydney, Australia. If the bid is successful, circus would own 50 percent of the casino.

Closer to home, Circus has also announced plans to bid on a casino project in Windsor, Canada. This would be a joint arrangement with Caesar's World, Inc. and Hilton Hotels to build a 75,000-square-foot casino, a 1,000-seat showroom, three dining areas, and a 300-room hotel.

Even closer to home, in May 1993 Circus formed a joint partnership with Eldorado Hotel/Casino to develop and operate Project C in downtown Reno. This will be a theme project depicting a 16th-century Spanish port on the island of Atlantis, with 1,800 rooms and 60,000 square feet of casino space at an estimated cost of $270 million.

Circus's projects are being tailored to attract mainstream tourists and family vacationers. Prices and credit limits are low, while the diversity of potential entertainment activities is substantial.

THE LEGAL ENVIRONMENT

Within the gaming industry all current operators must consider compliance with extensive gaming regulations as a primary concern. Gambling operations are subject to regulatory control by the Nevada State Gaming Control Board, the Clark County Nevada Gaming and Liquor Licensing Board, and by city governments. Gaming companies must submit detailed operating and financial reports to authorities. Nearly all financial transactions, including loans, leases, and the sale of securities, must be reported. Some financial activities are subject to approval by regulatory agencies. As Circus moves into other locations outside of Nevada, it will need to adhere to local regulations.

Although Circus can expect to exert only limited influence on regulatory matters, it took a step in 1989 to strengthen its ability to deal with regulatory concerns by electing Carl F. Dodge, a former chairman of the Nevada Gaming Commission, to its board of directors.

THE FUTURE FOR CIRCUS CIRCUS

Circus has done well by introducing theme-oriented entertainment "megastores" and can be expected to innovate more on that concept. Likewise, its focus on serving middle-income tourists by delivering family entertainment at relatively low prices (room rates range from $39) has been effective in capturing market share. Excalibur and Luxor represent a move upscale in the clientele income target, and it is not yet clear whether future projects will cater to the lower-or upper-middle-class tourists. Circus believes that customer loyalty in the gaming industry is closely tied to the merchant's ingenuity, and management believes that the philosophy that brought them this far can be expected to carry them into the future. Circus is considering ventures outside Las Vegas and Nevada as they arise. It has set aggressive performance targets for itself, including exceeding 20 percent in both the average annual growth rate in earnings per share and in return on equity, as well as sustaining its industry-leading profit margin and return on invested capital.

Circus intends to continue its growth in the Nevada markets by way of further innovation in theme oriented entertainment. It is also expanding to other gambling locations, including Sydney, Australia, and Windsor, Ontario, with a casino and riverboats in Chalmette, Louisiana, Michigan City, Indiana, and Tunica County, Mississippi. Develop a three-year strategic plan for CEO Bennett that will fulfill Circus's mission statement, which follows.

MISSION STATEMENT

Circus, Circus is dedicated to providing a total entertainment package, including gaming, for family vacationers. Our tremendous success is based on a simple framework of innovation, expansion, and value.

Bold architecture, state-of-the-art special-effects attractions, and an emphasis on high-tech, "latest and greatest" entertainment concepts make our "megastores" the most innovative in the gaming industry. Our customers expect and receive value as well as a broad, intense entertainment experience.

We believe that our concepts of value and leading-edge entertainment will be the "heartstone" of the expansion of gaming across the country and beyond. We stand ready with both the ability and the willingness to expand into other geographic regions here and abroad.

While innovation, expansion, and value are watchwords for success, we are ultimately dependent upon people—our customers and our employees. With Circus, the customer is always king, as we constantly strive to meet rising expectations and deliver more value. Our employees, who serve those customers so well, are an integral part of our success.

Circus Circus, in partnership with our customers, is doing its share to conserve the natural environment.

EXHIBIT 15-5 Selected Financial Information

	1993	1992	1991	1990	1989	1988
Earnings Per Share*	2.05	1.84	1.39	1.30	1.29	.74
Current Ratio	.90	1.14	.88	.66	1.12	2.34
Total Liability/Total Assets	.48	.58	.77	.76	.72	.47
Operating Profit Margin	24.4%	24.9%	22.9%	28.7%	28.6%	27.6%

* Adjusted to reflect 2-for-1 stock split effective July 1991. In June 1993 the Board of Directors declared a 3-for-2 stock split.
Source: Company reports.

EXHIBIT 15-6 Eight-Year Summary

	SALES (000)	NET INCOME
FY 93	$843,025	$117,322
FY 92	806,023	103,348
FY 91	692,052	76,292
FY 90	522,376	76,064
FY 89	511,960	81,714
FY 88	458,856	55,900
FY 87	373,967	28,198
FY 86	306,993	37,375

Source: Company reports.

EXHIBIT 15-7 Circus Circus Enterprises, Inc. Annual Income (000) Fiscal Year Ended January 31

	1993	1992	1991	1990	1989	1988
Net Sales	843,025	806,023	692,052	522,376	511,960	458,856
Cost of Goods	386,971	346,663	313,269	227,942	217,891	200,005
Gross Profit	456,054	441,360	378,783	294,434	294,069	258,851
Selling, General, and Administrative Expenses	204,022	193,584	179,309	124,228	125,380	113,361
Income Before Depreciation and Amortization	252,032	247,776	199,474	170,206	168,689	145,490
Depreciation and Amortization	46,550	47,385	40,998	31,216	31,800	29,134
Nonoperating Income	820	245	(570)	1,030	1,493	4,113
Interest Expense	22,989	43,632	42,048	26,818	28,425	19,733
Income Before Tax	183,313	157,004	115,858	113,202	109,957	100,736
Provision for Income Taxes	62,330	53,656	39,566	38,138	37,478	38,809
Net Income Before Extraordinary Items	120,983	103,348	76,292	75,064	72,479	61,927
Extraordinary Items and Discontinued Operations	(-3,661)	0	0	0	9,235	(6,027)
Net Income	117,322	103,348	76,292	75,064	81,714	55,900
Outstanding Shares	58,167	56,600	54,977	62,572	57,814	75,814

Source: Company reports.

EXHIBIT 15-8 Circus Circus Enterprises Inc., Balance Sheet

			ANNUAL ASSETS (000)			
FISCAL YEAR ENDED JANUARY 31,	**1993**	**1992**	**1991**	**1990**	**1989**	**1988**
Cash	43,415	34,158	18,134	19,411	20,667	14,212
Marketable Securities	0	0	0	0	0	60,097
Receivables	3,977	4,171	5,977	2,156	3,197	3,319
Inventories	16,565	15,894	16,573	9,337	15,714	10,861
Other Current Assets	14,478	13,687	13,601	10,323	8,212	8,734
Total Current Assets	78,435	695,154	717,466	41,227	47,790	97,223
Property, Plant and Equipment	851,463	695,154	717,466	612,905	455,074	413,745
Deferred Charges	9,997	9,080	9,438	9,252	0	0
Intangibles	10,563	10,927	11,290	11,654	12,328	11,198
Deposits and Other Assets	0	0	0	0	8,920	6,891
Total Assets	950,458	783,071	792,479	675,038	524,112	529,057

			ANNUAL LIABILITIES (000)			
FISCAL YEAR ENDED JANUARY 31,	**1993**	**1992**	**1991**	**1990**	**1989**	**1988**
Accounts Payable	11,473	11,814	16,048	23,690	9,578	7,177
Current Long-term Debt	154	941	938	935	1,485	2,053
Accrued Expenses	47,397	45,558	43,652	35,104	29,326	30,822
Income Taxes	708	1,185	818	2,345	2,168	1,420
Total Current Liability	87,494	59,498	48,750	62,074	42,557	41,472
Deferred Charges/Increases	64,123	58,830	48,209	42,586	38,933	39,529
Long-term Debt	308,092	337,680	496,750	408,314	296,316	168,339
Noncurrent Capital Leases	0	0	0	0	0	485
Other Long-term Liability	740	867	1,221	1,340	1,394	1,174
Total Liabilities	460,449	326,196	184,843	514,314	379,200	250,999
Common Stock Net	1,599	1,590	1,571	1,912	1,907	1,903
Capital Surplus	111,516	84,026	52,302	47,376	43,273	42,035
Retained Earnings	502,257	384,935	281,587	205,295	130,370	237,290
Treasury Stock	125,353	144,355	150,617	93,859	30,638	3,170
Shareholder Equity	490,009	326,196	184,843	160,724	144,912	278,058
Total Liability and Net Worth	950,458	783,071	792,479	675,038	524,112	529,057

Source: Company reports.

EXHIBIT 15-9 Consolidated Statements of Income, Fiscal Year Ended January 31
(In thousands, except share data)

	1993	1992	1991
Revenues			
Casino	$495,012	$471,823	$414,688
Rooms	147,115	141,716	109,869
Food and beverage	135,786	129,951	112,274
Other	92,500	89,652	78,956
	870,413	833,142	715,787
Less—complimentary allowances	(27,388)	(27,119)	(23,735)
	843,025	806,023	692,052
Costs and expenses			
Casino	189,499	175,771	155,809
Rooms	68,783	64,799	52,289
Food and beverage	128,689	124,093	105,171
Other operating expenses	58,917	56,565	51,283
General and administrative	130,152	124,313	105,805
Depreciation and amortization	46,550	47,385	40,998
Preopening expense	—	—	11,177
	622,590	592,926	522,532
Operating profit before corporate expense	220,435	213,097	169,520
Corporate expense	14,953	12,706	11,044
Income from operations	205,482	200,391	158,476
Other income (expense)			
Interest, dividends and other income (loss)	820	245	(570)
Interest expense	(22,989)	(43,632)	(42,048)
	(22,169)	(43,387)	(42,618)
Income before provision for income tax	183,313	157,004	115,858
Provision for income tax	62,330	53,656	39,566
Income before extraordinary loss	120,983	103,348	76,292
Extraordinary loss on early extinguishment of debt, net of income tax benefit of $1,885	(3,661)	—	—
Net income	$117,332	$103,348	$ 76,292
Earnings per share			
Income before extraordinary loss	$ 2.11	$ 1.84	$ 1.39
Extraordinary loss on early extinguishment of debt	(0.06)	—	—
Net Income	$ 2.05	$ 1.84	$ 1.39

Source: *Annual Report*, 1993.

EXHIBIT 15-10 Consolidated Statements of Cash Flows

	YEAR ENDED JANUARY 31, INCREASE (DECREASE) IN CASH AND CASH EQUIVALENTS (IN THOUSANDS)		
	1993	1992	1991
Cash flows from operating activities:			
Net income before extraordinary loss	$120,983	$103,348	$76,292
Adjustments to reconcile net income before extraordinary loss to net cash provided by operating activities:			
Depreciation and amortization	48,182	48,870	42,395
Increase in deferred income tax	5,293	10,621	5,623
Increase (decrease) in interest payable	(4,100)	(1,668)	435
Increase (decrease) in income tax payable	(477)	367	(1,527)
(Gain) loss on sale of fixed assets	(41)	(93)	1,389
(Increase) decrease in other current assets	(1,268)	2,412	(14,335)
Increase in other current liabilities	5,598	3,415	13,678
(Increase) decrease in other noncurrent assets	(2,368)	531	(71)
Decrease in other noncurrent liabilities	(65)	(65)	(65)
Total adjustments	50,754	64,390	47,522
Net cash provided by operating activities	171,737	167,738	123,814
Cash flows from investing activities:			
Capital expenditures	(208,586)	(26,569)	(148,519)
Increase (decrease) in construction payables	27,762	(4,075)	(13,207)
Proceeds from sale of equipment and other assets	4,510	527	663
Net cash used in investing activities	(176,314)	(30,117)	(161,063)
Cash flows from financing activities:			
Net effect on cash of issuances and payments of debt with initial maturities of three months or less	69,957	(138,993)	(23,382)
Issuances of debt with original maturities in excess of three months	—	—	51,014
Principal payments of debt with original maturities in excess of three months	(100,397)	(20,320)	(39,309)
Exercise of stock options and warrants	46,491	50,806	4,585
Effect on cash of extraordinary loss	(2,155)	—	—
Purchases of treasury stock	—	(12,801)	(56,758)
Proceeds from inssuance of senior subordinated notes	—	—	99,875
Other	(62)	(289)	(53)
Net cash provided by (used in) financing activities	13,834	(121,597)	35,972
Net increase (decrease) in cash and cash equivalents	9,257	16,024	(1,277)
Cash and cash equivalents at beginning of year	34,158	18,134	19,411
Cash and cash equivalents at end of year	$ 43,415	$ 34,158	$18,134
Supplemental Cash Flow Disclosures:			
Interest paid (net of amount capitalized)	$ 26,104	$ 43,727	$40,330
Income tax paid	$ 41,500	$ 30,350	$34,400

Source: *Annual Report*, 1993.

RAILROADING INDUSTRY NOTE
JOEL PALLEY

The railroad freight industry generated nearly $32 billion in operating revenues in 1993. The 12 major freight railroads accounted for almost $29 billion of that total. Amtrak, the quasi-government rail passenger corporation serving 45 states, had estimated revenues of $1.4 billion in 1993, up from $1.3 billion in 1993.

FREIGHT SERVICE

In 1993, for the seventh consecutive year, the railroad industry recorded a new high for freight traffic, which increased by nearly 2 percent as measured by revenue ton-miles (a measure than incorporates both weight and distance). Shipments (as measured by carloads) of motor vehicles and parts continued their rebound from 1991, increasing by nearly 10 percent from 1992, and metals rose by an estimated 9 percent. Intermodal traffic (trailer-on-flatcar and container-on-flatcar) grew an estimated 7 percent. Coal, the largest rail commodity, declined an estimated 3 percent because of a coal strike, reduced coal exports, and inventory reductions by electric utilities. Among other top rail commodities, chemicals increased 1 percent, while grain shipments rose 2 percent.

For the 12 months ending June 30, 1993, the freight railroad industry earned an average 7.2 percent return on its net investment base (excluding special charges). Since 1980, the year the Staggers Rail Act partially deregulated rail rates and services, the railroads have invested nearly $160 billion in track and equipment. Freight rates declined by 1.5 percent per year in real terms between 1990 and 1993, roughly the same annual rate of decline since the passage of the Staggers Act, compared to an increase of 2.9 percent per year in the five years prior to 1980.

Intermodal and Technology Issues. Railroad productivity measured by revenue ton-miles per employee continues to increase at a faster rate than that of almost any other industry, doubling between 1983 and 1992. Rail intermodal traffic has risen from 3.1 million trailers and containers in 1980 to 6.7 million in 1992. The increase is due largely to the introduction in 1984 of specialized railcars with depressed platforms that carry containers stacked two high (double-stack containers). Containers from the Far East move through West Coast ports to inland destinations under expedited schedules on such double-stack trains, carrying export and domestic traffic on the backhaul. Roughly 130 double-stack trains depart the West Coast weekly. Double-stack cars now account for approximately 40 percent of total intermodal capacity and 80 percent of containers.

Technological Innovation. The rail industry is developing an Automatic Train Control System (ATCS), which utilizes microelectronics and telecommunications to control train operations. It will be implemented in four areas—work order reporting, locomotive performance monitoring, track force equipment management, and positive train separation and control. The Department of Transportation's Federal Railroad Administration (FRA), in cooperation with the industry, will conduct a safety inquiry into this new technology and report to the Congress on the feasibility of implementing ATCS in a way that will enhance railroad's safety, efficiency, productivity, and customer service capabilities.

Safety Issues. The FRA regulates rail safety in the United States. In 1992–1993, FRA issued final rules covering bridge worker safety standards, state safety participation regulations, and the use of event recorders. FRA is continuing research for proposed rules on grade crossing warning devices, alcohol and drug testing improvements, power brakes, tank car improvements, and tank car shell thickness.

Cooperation with Mexico. Cooperative efforts between the United States and Mexico have increased the efficiency and safety of rail transportation between the two countries. Rail transportation is an important factor in supporting the increasing trade between the United States and Mexico. In anticipation of congressional approval of the North American Free Trade Agreement (NAFTA), and in response to burgeoning trade between the two countries, U.S. railroads and the Mexican National Railway (Ferrocarriles Nacionales de Mexico, or FNM) introduced innovative management and operating practices and worked together to streamline border-crossing procedures.

Under NAFTA proposals, U.S. and Canadian railroads will be able to market their own services in Mexico and use their own locomotives to carry run-through trains under agreements with FNM. Railroads and other private investors, such as shippers or steamship lines, may build and own terminals and spur lines, and finance construction of rail infrastructure. The NAFTA-member countries will also continue consultations to make their rail safety standards compatible.

Some of these concepts are being put into practice through new cooperative ventures between U.S. and Mexican railroads. The FNM has purchased Union Pacific Railroad's Transportation Control System, which provides computerized monitoring and management of yard operations, inventory, billing, scheduling, and planning functions. The system has been installed in Mexico City and is expected to be in place in Monterrey and Nuevo Laredo in 1993, with full implementation by 1994.

The Santa Fe Railway, the FNM, and Concarril, a Mexican rail car builder, have entered into an agreement to provide rail cars to Santa Fe. The Southern Pacific has invested in a Mexican company, Ferropuertos, that is building distribution centers to handle imported grain, mineral exports, and intermodal traffic moving both to and from the United States.

Some U.S. railroads that have no direct connections with the FNM in Mexico are forging new connections by utilizing the sea lanes of the Gulf of Mexico. Burlington Northern (BN) and the Mexican corporation Grupo Protexa have formed a joint transportation venture to integrate rail and barge services between interior points in Mexico and the United States. In April 1993 BN started moving trains southbound to Galveston, Texas, where the rail cars are transported on Protexa's oceangoing barges to the Mexican ports of Coatzacoalcos, Veracruz, and Altamira. From there, they are distributed by FNM to the interior of Mexico.

Eastern railroads are considering similar rail-barge links to Mexican ports from U.S. ports in the Gulf of Mexico. Such cooperative efforts will increase the competitiveness of both countries' rail industries, opening new markets for both trade and the railroads.

Rail plays a major role in moving products between the United States and Mexico. According to the USDA's 1992 report entitled *U.S.-Mexico Bilateral Trade: Estimated Modal Shares,* in 1991 the United States exported 15.8 million tons of freight by rail to Mexico, led by farm products (3.9 million tons), food and kindred products (1.9 million tons), waste or scrap materials (1.5 million tons), and primary metal products (1.5 million tons). In the same year 4.7 million tons of freight were

Trends and Forecasts: Class I Railroads (SIC 4011)

ITEM	1991	1992	1993[1]	1994[2]	PERCENT CHANGE (1991–1994)		
					91–92	92–93	93–94
Operating revenue (billion $)	27.7	28.3	28.7	29.4	2.2	1.4	2.4
Revenue ton-miles (billions)	1,036	1,064	1,080	1,110	2.7	1.5	2.8
Average employment (000)	231	222	215	208	−3.9	−3.2	−3.3

[1] Estimate.
[2] Forecast.
Source: Association of American Railroads, U.S. Department of Labor, Bureau of Labor Statistics; Railroad Retirement Board. Estimates and forecasts by the Federal Railroad Administration.

imported by rail from Mexico, including transportation equipment (1.0 million tons); miscellaneous mixed shipments of TOFC/COFC (0.8 million tons); clay, concrete, glass, and stone products (0.5 million tons); and primary metal products (0.5 million tons).

Labor Issues. Wages and other labor-related expenses are the largest component of railroad operating costs. Nationwide collective bargaining disputes over wages, work rules, and health care resulted in a one-day strike in 1991 and a two-day strike in 1992, after administrative procedures had been exhausted. Both times, Congress passed legislation ending the strike (for more information see the *1993 U.S. Industrial Outlook*, pages 40–47). All major national railroad labor contracts are in force until January 1, 1995.

Railroads are realizing greater efficiencies through reduced train crew size. The standard crew on through freight trains now consists generally of an engineer and a conductor. This standard was affirmed by the arbitration process established under the legislation which ended the 1991 dispute.

Industry Structure and Regulatory Environment. The 12 Class I freight railroad systems (defined in 1992 as systems with operating revenues of more than $250 million) and Amtrak employed an estimated 215,000 persons in 1993, down from 222,000 in 1992. In addition, in 1992 there were 33 regional railroads with 12,338 employees; 278 independently owned local railroads (not part of Class I systems) with 6,055 employees; and 192 switching and terminal railroads with 7,322 employees.

Although the pace of mergers among major railroads has slowed since the early 1980s, sales of line segments by Class I railroads to smaller operators continue. In cases where traffic volumes have declined on branch lines, Class I railroads have sold their lines to smaller, lower-cost operators. These short-line operators have improved service to local shippers while continuing to feed traffic to the major railroads.

The Staggers Act did not completely deregulate the freight railroads, but it did reduce ICC authority in areas where competition served to limit rail rates. Now more than three-quarters of freight traffic is not subject to maximum rate regulation, either because competition has kept rates at levels below the threshold for ICC authority, or because the ICC exempted the traffic altogether. The ICC has explicitly exempted traffic moving in boxcars and trailers-on-flatcars. In addition, the Commission has exempted many agricultural and manufactured commodities (including most lumber and wood products, and transportation equipment), regardless of car type, after determining that competition was sufficient to protect shippers.

During the last few years, an average of less than a dozen new rate complaints and protests have been filed per year, down sharply from an annual average of nearly 300 rate complaints or protests before the Staggers Act went into effect. (For additional background on the Staggers Rail Act, see the *1990 U.S. Industrial Outlook,* chapter 42.) Railroad-shipper contracts, legalized by the Act, have had a significant impact on the industry. Now more than 60 percent of all rail traffic moves under contract. The terms of these agreements, although filed at the ICC, are confidential; only a very general summary is released to the public. (For additional information on railroad-shipper contracts, see the *1993 U.S. Industrial Outlook,* Chapter 40, pp. 6–7).

In January 1993 the FRA released a report entitled *Small Railroad Investment Goals and Financial Options: A Report to Congress.* The study surveyed regional and shortline railroads concerning their capital needs and their interest in possible federal loan guarantees. Of 339 respondents, 76 percent filed abbreviated surveys, which were requested of those carriers not interested in, or not foreseeing a need for, a federal loan guarantee. The remaining 24 percent indicated interest in obtaining loan guarantees for track rehabilitation, financing locomotives and rolling stock, and refinancing existing loans. The study found that these carriers could not meet their goals with financing from traditional sources. Collectively, these railroads indicated that they would need to spend $1.77 billion through 1995 to maintain and upgrade their systems. They also expect to finance or fund internally $1.33 billion of these requirements, but would be unable to raise the remaining $440 million, mostly for track rehabilitation. An additional $290 million would be needed for refinancing existing loans.

Outlook for 1994. In 1994 rail traffic volume is forecast to continue the modest recovery of 1993, with revenue ton-miles increasing 3 percent. Coal traffic, the top commodity carried by the railroads, is expected to grow by 2 to 3 percent in 1994 after its 1993 decline, in line with industry and government forecasts of increased coal production. Because of the increasing importance of container and double-stack service, intermodal traffic is expected to continue to be the fastest growing area, increasing by 3 to 5 percent. Traffic in chemicals, lumber and wood products, paper, metallic ores, primary metal products, motor vehicles and parts, stone, clay, and glass, and other industrial commodities, are expected to increase as a consequence of expanding industrial production. Growth in grain traffic will depend largely on export demand, such as whether larger grain shipments are made to the former Soviet Union. Class I railroad employment is forecast to decline by approximately 3 percent to 208,000— in part with early retirements—as the railroads continue to increase their operating efficiencies.

DAKOTA, MINNESOTA & EASTERN RAILROAD—1994

PAUL REED
Sam Houston State
University
CAROL CUMBER
South Dakota State
University

The Dakota, Minnesota & Eastern (DM&E) Railroad (605-697-2400) is headquartered in Brookings, South Dakota, and operates mainly in South Dakota and Minnesota* but also has a 69-mile branch line serving Mason City, Iowa. DM&E's location in the upper Midwest is always subject to weather extremes such as floods. On July 21, 1993, Minnesota had over three million acres underwater with crop damage estimated at $1 billion. In South Dakota alone, 25 percent of all farmland was flooded and farmer losses exceeded $500 million. Corn and soybean losses would reduce DM&E revenues for the next 18 months by $1.5 to $2 million. Flood-related reduction in the construction industry had already severely hurt DM&E cement shipments. One bright spot was that wheat production was expected to be 25 percent above average in South Dakota.

Railroads of today are far different from the traditional railroads of yesterday. In essence, railroads were once responsible for hauling almost everything and everybody into and out of every city and village; in 1929 they accounted for 75 percent of all United States intercity freight ton-miles. The volume of freight handled by today's railroads is 238 percent of that of 1929, but huge market share has been lost to trucks, river carriers, and pipelines. Railroads today handle about 37 percent of all freight ton-miles and have evolved from general freight carriers to specialized freight carriers primarily handling large-volume bulk commodities, oversized or bulky loads, and general products and merchandise when combined into container- or trailer-sized lots.

The DM&E has struggled since its inception in 1986, primarily because of problems with the Chicago and North Western (C&NW) Railroad, DM&E's major customer and supplier. President John C. "Pete" McIntyre has led DM&E from start-up and is basically pleased with its progress. Revenues have continued to climb, net income has improved, and the debt-to-equity ratio has been halved. New customers have been found and many older customers increasingly have switched from truck to rail. Yet McIntyre feels DM&E will never reach its potential until it is freed from C&NW dominance and new markets are found. So on April 14, 1993, DM&E placed a request to the Interstate Commerce Commission (ICC) for relief from certain C&NW restrictions. Repair costs for the 1993 flood approximate $2 million and have put a severe strain on the DM&E budget, although federal grants may assist in the rebuilding effort.

THE DM&E'S BEGINNINGS

The Chicago and North Western (C&NW) is one of seven railroads that connect Chicago with the states of the upper Midwest. It is a conservative company with many lightly traveled lines and only marginal profits even in the best of times. The route system is directed west and northwest of Chicago, and its many rail lines crisscross northern Illinois, Iowa, Nebraska, Wisconsin, Minnesota, and South Dakota. Trackage also serves small portions of Wyoming and the Upper Peninsula of Michigan.

The mid-1970s saw many rail lines, including C&NW, suffering heavy losses or facing bankruptcy. This general malaise coupled with new legislation and more flexible regulatory agencies contributed to a massive industry restructuring. Many lines

*This case is intended for classroom discussion only, not to depict effective or ineffective handling of administrative situations. All rights reserved to the authors and the Southwest Case Research Association.

merged, were severely downsized, or disappeared with bits and pieces purchased by former competitors or entrepreneurs. C&NW was particularly active during the 1970s, purchasing and then abandoning major portions of competitors, such as Chicago GreatWestern (1,450 miles) and Minneapolis and Saint Louis (1,300 miles), plus acquiring the Minneapolis–Kansas City line of the Rock Island (600 miles). By the late 1980s, C&NW had also sold or abandoned some 4,500 miles of its own trackage, including the vast majority of its lines in Minnesota and South Dakota.

Most of the trackage of what is now the DM&E (Exhibit 16–1) had been unprofitable for C&NW for several years. In 1983 and again in 1985, C&NW petitioned to abandon the line from five miles west of Pierre to Rapid City. This action would leave South Dakota with no centrally located east-west rail transportation. C&NW's requests were met with unusually strong opposition from the State and U.S. Senator Larry Pressler, R-South Dakota. Realizing that abandonment was no longer a wise move, C&NW was faced with either continued operations or sale. All parties agreed that the former was not feasible, and therefore the C&NW initiated actions that ultimately led to the formation of the DM&E.

The C&NW contracted with a subunit of L. B. Foster, Inc., a railroad supply firm, to negotiate the sale of the line. It was obvious that the Pierre–Rapid City (PRC) section could not stand alone, so the sale package was gradually expanded eastward to Winona, Minnesota, with several north-south branch lines included. It was felt that these approximately 965 miles of railroad would generate enough traffic to adequately service the debt associated with its purchase plus provide a satisfactory return to the owner.

As discussion continued, L. B. Foster itself became interested in the proposed rail package. The company eventually developed business plans that included all operating aspects of the railroad plus pro forma financial statements, and negotiated the purchase price with C&NW. Final closing took place on September 4, 1986. The $26 million agreement was heavily leveraged with Westinghouse Credit Corporation, the primary lender, and with C&NW assuming a $4 million subordinated note. Foster provided a small portion of the equity financing along with TXL Corporation, Lombard Investments, and DM&E top management.

The buyers acquired 826 miles of track and rights to operate on an additional 139 miles. Included were 18 C&NW locomotives, averaging 35 years old, and maintenance and repair equipment. C&NW retained ownership of the tracks at DM&E's main interchanges at Winona and Mankato, Minnesota, Mason City, Iowa, and Rapid City, South Dakota. It also could exercise veto power over DM&E's rates and route proposals or any changes in existing financing. The new line also had to agree to pay substantial monetary penalties unless 89 percent of DM&E's originated traffic was loaded in C&NW freight cars.

Lack of funds coupled with the C&NW equipment agreement precluded the DM&E purchase or lease of freight cars. Additional locomotive needs were satisfied by the purchase of 22 vintage diesels from the Soo Line and Norfolk Southern railroads. Recruiting a trained workforce was a major item on the agenda. DM&E was not bound by C&NW labor union agreements and was therefore not required to have a union workforce. Beginning salaries were pegged approximately 15 percent below comparable jobs on unionized railroads but were well above the average South Dakota and Minnesota wage earners' income. A profit sharing plan offset the wage differential to some degree. Work rules were designed to permit far more flexibility than was the case with C&NW.

DM&E hiring gave initial priority to local C&NW employees because of their experience and familiarity with the lines purchased. DM&E filled approximately 60

EXHIBIT 16-1 Dakota, Minnesota and Eastern Railroad

percent of its 130 positions from this source and the remaining hires came from other rail lines or had no prior railroad experience.

DM&E's early years of operation contained more than the average number of problems. Integration of new people, procedures, policies, communication channels, and the like took weeks. A concern to the newly hired president McIntyre was the purchase agreement itself. Traffic projections had been overstated and physical condition of track was far worse than estimated. Revenue projections had been based on an unrealistic level of business, and DM&E was seriously undercapitalized with no working capital available on the first day of operations. C&NW had been paid far too much for the property and by agreeing to the aforementioned C&NW restrictions, the negotiators had in effect severely limited McIntyre and his subordinates' ability to operate the road efficiently. Other problems included a serious drought that ruined crops, heavy rains that washed out miles of track, blizzards that stopped traffic, burned-out locomotive engines, and a plant explosion at the railroad's largest customer.

This almost continuous series of problems pushed DM&E to the brink of insolvency. On the positive side, misfortune seemed to bond management and workers together. By 1991 hard work had overcome many of the inherited problems, and it was apparent that the railroad had turned the corner.

ASPECTS OF DM&E

Exhibit 16–2 shows that the Winona–Rapid City main line and the track to Mason City carry the greatest freight tonnages and most traffic is eastbound. Track conditions on most of the line prevent freight train speeds in excess of 25 mph, and approximately 30 percent of the line can support only 10 mph.

DM&E serves the main line with a minimum five-day-per-week scheduled train service between Rapid City and Winona. A similar schedule handles freight between Waseca, Minnesota, and Mason City, Iowa. During peak months (June–October), two trains per seven-day week are often scheduled. Extra trains also originate at points between Pierre and Waseca to handle grain and other tonnage. Branch lines use trains on an as-needed basis. Local freights at Rochester and New Ulm, Minnesota, serve all on-line customers in Minnesota, thus relieving scheduled trains from making numerous stops.

Freight cars are sorted and blocked at the division points at Waseca and Huron, South Dakota. DM&E must turn over almost all traffic to C&NW at its four principal gateways. This forces DM&E to pay C&NW switching charges in excess of $100 per car or share revenue on all through traffic. Exhibit 16–3 gives populations of the largest cities (1990 Census) along the DM&E route and reveals ownership of the tracks.

DM&E owns and operates car and locomotive repair shops at Huron. Major repairs and overhauls are performed on locomotives. Similar services are provided on an as-needed basis to freight cars of other railroads. All active locomotives have been rebuilt or received major overhaul since start-up. The availability rate for locomotives is over 90 percent and approaches 100 percent during winter months, when many units are stored because of lower traffic requirements. During the summer–fall season, DM&E leases approximately a dozen locomotives to handle increased traffic.

Grain and grain-derived products make up 50 percent of DM&E's carloads. Grain shipments include wheat, corn, and soybeans from eastern South Dakota and the western two-thirds of Minnesota. The second major item of traffic is bentonite clay (used in foundry operations, oil drilling, iron-ore pelletizing, and cat litter), which is turned over by C&NW at Rapid City to DM&E for delivery farther east.

EXHIBIT 16-2 Dakota, Minnesota & Eastern Railroad Corporation: 1992 Freight density map (Shown in million gross tons per mile)

//////////// Trackage rights

▬▬▬▬▬▬ Owned

Other major traffic sources include industrial sand, cement, wood chips, lumber, and kaolin clay (manufacturing of cement). Exhibit 16–4 shows the traffic mix since start-up.

Corporate Philosophy. In the words of Pete McIntyre, the DM&E's mission is "to provide rail users in the upper Midwest with consistent, damage-free, on time, wholesale and retail transportation service with the intent of moderate growth and profitability, recognizing its employees as valuable assets and with the aim of being customer driven." The railroad has made a long-term commitment to provide reliable freight services and not to diversify into nonrail businesses. The credo of moderate traffic growth is supported by McIntyre's emphasis on "growing the business we already have" and receiving more through traffic from connections. In 1992 DM&E had the following traffic mix: forwarded (originated and delivered on-line or to connections), 47.6 percent; overhead (received from and delivered to other railroads), 45.1 percent; and received (received from other lines for delivery to DM&E customers), 7.4 percent of total carloads. Total carloads increased from 43,000 in 1987 to over 55,000 in 1992.

DM&E strives to strengthen its position as a rail freight carrier in the upper Midwest by making its existing system more efficient. Accordingly, DM&E increased its carloadings and revenues by enlarging its market share of freight shipped by existing customers, by regaining customers who had shifted to trucks when the railroad was operated by previous owners, by serving new shippers in its territory, and by improving relations with other railroads. DM&E historically has employed a strategy

EXHIBIT 16-3 Largest Cities and Track Ownership

STATE	CITY	SIZE	TRACK OWNERSHIP
Minnesota	Winona	47,828	C&NW
	Rochester	70,745	DM&E
	Owatonna	19,386	C&NW
	Waseca	18,079	DM&E
	Mankato	31,477	C&NW
Iowa	Mason City	29,040	C&NW
South Dakota	Brookings	16,270	DM&E
	Huron	12,448	DM&E and BN
	Watertown	17,592	BN and DM&E
	Aberdeen	24,927	BN and DM&E
	Pierre	12,906	DM&E
	Rapid City	54,523	C&NW

Source: U.S. Bureau of the Census, 1990.

EXHIBIT 16-4 Historical Carloadings by Category (1987–1992)

CATEGORIES OF TRAFFIC	1987	1988	1989	1990	1991	1992
Wheat	10,888	8,919	6,664	8,949	10,532	9,883
Bentonite Clay	0	0	740	6,756	9,054	9,666
Woodchips	2,827	3,413	3,450	3,768	3,232	3,353
Corn	5,082	7,031	8,436	10,443	8,045	8,469
Cement	2,893	3,572	3,132	1,976	2,171	2,853
Industrial Sand	3,115	2,733	4,055	5,040	2,369	3,407
Lumber/Boards	165	145	109	825	656	546
Soybeans	3,090	4,061	1,902	2,915	2,766	2,973
Kaolin Clay	0	0	0	663	1,036	1,295
Soybean Oil	2,636	2,011	1,458	1,566	1,969	1,971
Wheat Flour	760	598	434	966	974	930
All Others	11,623	10,260	9,644	8,721	8,658	9,814
Total	43,079	42,743	40,024	52,588	51,462	55,160

Source: Company records.

of strengthening its existing traffic base and increasing its market share within the territory it serves rather than expanding beyond South Dakota and Minnesota. Recent activities, however, indicate that DM&E desires to acquire additional trackage owned by C&NW.

DM&E has aggressively gone after traffic from both large and small shippers. It has initiated long-term agreements with large shippers to stabilize its traffic base; given 8 to 10 percent discounts to grain shippers who make unit train shipments of 25 cars or more; and initiated pricing and service packages to provide South Dakota and Minnesota farmers' markets in Texas, the eastern United States, the Pacific coast, and the Gulf coast via the Mississippi River. DM&E continues to streamline operations and facilities through upgrading its locomotive fleet, continually improving and repairing unsatisfactory track and roadbed inherited from C&NW, adding or rescheduling train service, and opening a computerized Customer Service Center to improve rail-customer interface.

Marketing. DM&E has done considerable research and planning to identify and satisfy customer needs. Marketing vice president Lynn Anderson stresses that DM&E "must determine what our customers' expectations are: in terms of car supply, transit times, loss or damage, billing, communications, switching, car tracing, and response time. What does the customer expect from us? With this knowledge, we can expedite the action needed to provide customers with superior service." Although DM&E's innovative ideas affect shippers and receivers of all categories of traffic, the marketing of grain is of particular interest. DM&E took advantage of the Winona end of track on the Mississippi River by developing a rail-barge service that opened up new markets to shippers and receivers at prices that took advantage of cheaper barge rates. This traffic has grown from 750 carloads of grain and grain products in 1987 to nearly 9,000 in 1992. Elevators from as far west as Pierre have found this option attractive. When the Mississippi freezes in the winter DM&E has organized trains for delivery of grain to the Pacific Northwest and Texas.

Lynn Anderson's department also faces many challenges: the limited size and nature of the railroad's target markets, determined by demographics of the DM&E service area; freight car shortages, particularly during peak demand; difficulty in interchanging traffic with C&NW; prior agreements that preclude car interchange with the Soo Line at Owatonna and Winona; and the impact of weather on shippers, receivers, and DM&E itself.

Transportation Conditions. Providing safe, timely service that meets customer needs is a never-ending challenge to DM&E. Poor track, a lethargic C&NW, and intermittent locomotive shortages have too often translated into high operating costs and dissatisfied customers. A great portion of the DM&E line west of Huron is the original 72-pound (per yard) rail laid in the early 1900s. Eighty-odd years of pounding have made the track and the supporting grade increasingly unable to support 100-ton railcars moving at speeds much above 10 mph.

DM&E tracks end short of the yards at Mason City, Rapid City, and Winona, and as a result, entry, car switching, and exit are controlled by C&NW. DM&E trains are often forced to idle for several hours while waiting for C&NW yard crews to put outgoing trains together or clear tracks for incoming cars. Getting entry onto C&NW tracks through Mankato can be equally exasperating, and several-hour waits for passage of C&NW through trains or yard switching are common. These impediments are particularly irritating because DM&E pays C&NW over $2 million a year for switching services. Also, increased traffic occasionally overloads available locomotive supply, causing slow underpowered trains or tonnage being left behind for later pickup. Exhibit 16–5 shows the seasonality of DM&E traffic.

Poor track conditions have increased the average Rapid City–Winona passage from 69 to more than 80 hours and have been largely responsible for 89 derailments in

1992 at a cost of $2.2 million. Derailments through May 1993 numbered 26 at a cost of $857,000. Train crew costs have also skyrocketed, with most crews going beyond the standard eight hours and sometimes stopping their trains in place because of the federally mandated 12-hour crew maximum. Slower trains and crews "dying out" on the line require overnight motel and meal expenses or cab fares to pick up old crews and deliver fresh ones.

Crews. DM&E has 45 conductors and 43 engineers plus a management and administrative staff of 15. DM&E has been training its own conductors for the last few years and has begun a 70-day cross-training program, in conjunction with the Santa Fe railroad, where senior conductors are qualified as engineers. This dual qualification has added job stability by permitting conductors to serve as engineers during peak season and return to their former duties during slack time. Temporary conductors are used as needed.

Modern communications link train crew, home office, and customers via locomotive-mounted radio, fax machines at each railroad station, and the recently opened Customer Service Center. Crews are able to communicate instantaneously about changes in car requirements for on-line customers, schedule status, train meets, and so on and to act upon changes with dispatch.

Engineering. The DM&E engineering department maintains track, bridges, and other physical plant in a safe condition. This task includes cross-tie replacement, rail replacement, rock ballasting, surfacing (cleaning, leveling, and smoothing of track), subgrade and bridge improvements. DM&E inherited a poorly maintained railroad with 40 percent unsatisfactory cross ties, 10 defective rails per mile, and at least 50 per-

EXHIBIT 16-5 Dakota, Minnesota & Eastern Railroad (1987–1993): Carloads by Month

	1987	1988	1989	1990	1991	1992	1993
January	2,483	2,814	2,000	3.640	2,870	3.644	3,227
February	2,471	2,854	2,072	3,130	2,579	3,404	3,552
March	2,965	3,807	2,437	2,954	3,337	3,709	4,362
April	3,522	3,874	3,175	3,550	3,883	5,250	4,245
May	3,574	3,811	3,319	4,272	4,211	4,476	4,178
June	4,012	4,394	3,146	4,636	4,431	5,202	4,415
Subtotal	19,027	21,554	16,149	22,182	21,311	25,685	23,979
July	4,991	3,898	3,766	5,751	5,872	5,716	
August	4,544	3,782	4,502	6,369	5,642	5,251	
September	3,942	4,018	3,663	4,787	5,057	5,384	
October	3,919	4,310	5,118	6,329	6,149	5,778	
November	3,347	2,662	3,515	4,526	3,714	3,887	
December	3,309	2,519	3,311	2,644	3,717	3,459	
Total	43,079	42,743	40,024	52,588	51,462	55,160	

Source: Company records.

cent of the track unsafe for speeds greater than 10 mph. Added to these woes was discovery that the native clay (Pierre shale) subgrade on the PRC section was unstable during periods of heavy rains. The frequent end result is that water, clay, and ballast are squeezed to both sides of the railbed, thus causing the track to sink. Some of these soft-spot areas extend for 500 feet.

The weather is unkind to DM&E. Blizzards and cold weather block track, freeze switches, and cause rail failures. A wildfire in October 1992 raced down seven miles of track in western South Dakota, burning out or severely damaging 89 timber spans and ultimately costing DM&E $500,000. Unseasonably wet weather has played havoc on the PRC section and by late July 1993 had washed out roadbed in eastern South Dakota and at many places across Minnesota.

DM&E has spent over $34 million on track and bridge-related capital projects. More than half of this amount was from cash generated from operations, and the remainder came from federal and state loans and grants plus loans from customers. DM&E also performs normal maintenance and maintenance-support activities that are not included in capital expenditures. Exhibit 16–6 shows capital expenditures by year. Budgeted capital track expenditures for 1993 approximate $8.3 million, with $3 million spent in South Dakota and $5.3 million in Minnesota.

Through 1992, capitalized expenditures include 488,000 cross ties; 639,000 tons of rock ballast (8,520 car loads); surfacing of approximately 650 miles of track; replacement of 30 miles of rail and 1.5 miles of bridging with culvert and earthen fill; strengthening of 12 steel bridges; installation of 4,000 feet of cross-drain plastic pipe and 2,700 feet of longitudinal-drain plastic pipe; and extension of several rail sidings.

DM&E has long recognized that a targeted main-line average speed of 25 mph will never be attained until a solution to the PRC subgrade problems is found and the lightweight rail between Wolsey and Pierre, South Dakota, is replaced. DM&E estimates the "Big Fix" will cost an estimated $37 million. The project includes replacement of 104 miles of 72-pound rail, 85 miles of ditching, surfacing of the entire 170-mile PRC subdivision, with a total of 6,800 cars of ballast and installation of 35 miles of waterproof fabric between ballast and clay. Also, over 4,500 feet of perforated lateral drain pipe and 20 miles of perforated longitudinal piping will be used to remove trapped pockets of water.

The DM&E engineering department is staffed with 27 section personnel who are spread out at regular intervals along the nine sections of 850-mile owned rail. Each three-man section is responsible for maintaining a safe railroad across its section. The department's other 37 nonmanagement personnel install and maintain signals, repair bridges, inspect track, and operate a variety of equipment. This 64-man base workforce is augmented by temporary hires in the spring and summer. DM&E uses contractors for all major capital projects. This department is highly respected by the train crews.

Mechanical. The DM&E mechanical department has to maintain the locomotive fleet, repair all foreign on line railcars, and provide service to nearly 300 newly leased covered hoppers. James Appleman's 36-member department has the equipment and expertise to perform almost any type of maintenance or repair requirement. The fact that locomotive availability remains 90 percent or higher, with units manufactured between 1952 and 1974 and averaging 39 years old, speaks for itself. The department covers 80 percent of its entire budget from foreign railcar repairs.

Human Resources. Human Resources Management (HRM) is not centrally administered. Hiring and training are done at the department level, whereas pay, benefits, performance appraisal, and administrative record-keeping are performed by the Finance and Accounting Department. DM&E recently began interviewing candidates for the newly created position of HRM director. It is assumed that HRM functions will be increasingly consolidated under this person's watch.

No function of the DM&E has higher priority than human resources, however. Pete McIntyre continually stresses the importance of all employees both as people and as the real reason for DM&E's success. Most key managers seem to embrace this attitude, though some seem to have difficulty adjusting from the confrontational leadership style too typical of the railroad industry.

DM&E schedules "employee appreciation dinners" in the summer and during the holiday season at major locations. Employees enjoy the give and take during these festivities and feel free to express their views. McIntyre and other rail officials get out on the line as often as possible but acknowledge that their hectic jobs keep them from getting needed feedback. Face-to-face communication is supplemented by a quarterly newsletter, *DM&E Enroute*, which keeps employees, customers, and supporters informed of current operations and future plans. One innovation is an open invitation for employees to phone McIntyre direct, or in his absence, leave a message. Overall,

EXHIBIT 16-6 Dakota, Minnesota & Eastern Railroad Corporation Capital Expenditures (In thousands of dollars)

	1987	1988	1989	1990	1991	1992	TOTAL
Capital Expenditures							
SD Track—West of Pierre	$2,156	$ 464	$3,099	$ 2,614	$ 955	$2,221	$11,509
SD Track—East of Pierre	2,362	713	2,768	3,429	219	1,120	10,611
Total SD Track	$4,518	$1,177	$5,867	$ 6,043	$1,174	$3,341	$22,120
MN Track	837	4,721	692	2,969	1,374	1,713	12,306
Total All Track	$5,355	$5,898	$6,559	$ 9,012	$2,548	$5,054	$34,426
Locomotive & All Other	47	1,043	1,528	1,410	1,267	1,454	6,749
Total	$5,402	$6,941	$8,087	$10,422	$3,815	$6,508	41,175
Funded by:							
SD Grant (FRA Funds)[a]	626	0	0	0	0	89	715
SD Grant (State Funds)	452	676	374	345	278	567	2,692
SD State Loan	0	0	0	0	75	0	75
SD Industry	0	296	50	0	48	76	470
SD FRA Loan	0	0	4,870	2,720	60	0	7,650
MN Grant (FRA Funds)	0	209	19	70	21	49	368
MN Grant (State Funds)	357	709	235	408	334	509	2,552
MN State Loan	0	2,898	263	967	5	0	4,133
MN Industry	0	336	129	210	0	40	715
DM&E Cash	3,967	1,817	2,147	5,702	2,994	5,178	21,805
Total	$5,402	$6,941	$8,087	$10,422	$3,815	$6,508	$41,175

[a]FRA=Federal Rail Administration.
Source: Company records.

employees have a positive attitude toward these efforts, although some feel they need more one-on-one contact. Total employment has gradually increased from 130 at start-up to 233 by April 1993. DM&E wages for its craft, clerical, and nonunion employees are shown in Exhibit 16–7. These wages are considered to be very competitive versus local rates.

DM&E remained nonunion until June 1990 when train crew, railcar repairmen, and electricians began to be represented by the United Transportation Union (UTU). One of the major complaints against DM&E was its failure to improve wages as compared to major railroads. Exhibit 16–8 shows the current DM&E and UTU wage scale agreement. Exhibit 16–9 gives a sample comparison of benefits offered by the DM&E and the Unionized National Railroad Plan.

The American Train Dispatchers Association attempted to organize DM&E dispatchers in 1989 but failed. The UTU attempted to organize DM&E engineering employees in 1991 but was rejected by a vote margin of 2 to 1. In August 1992 DM&E's car repairmen voted to decertify the UTU and form their own local union.

EXHIBIT 16-7 Craft, Clerical, and Nonunion Employees' Salary Ranges

GRADE	JOB TITLE(S)	GRADE	JOB TITLE(S)
1	Part-time or Temporary Nonexempt Employee	6	Assistant Track/B&B Foreman Machine Operator A Machine Operator B Road & Equipment Repairman
2	Administrative Assistant Accounting Clerk Operating Clerk Secretary	8	Track Inspector Track B&B Foreman Welder Signalman Mechanical Mechanic
4	Track/B&B Laborer Welder Helper Mechanical Laborer Clerk/Yard Clerk	10	Mechanical Foreman, Weekend Mechanical Foreman, Regular Mechanical Leadman

SALARY RANGES

GRADE	MINIMUM	25TH	MIDPOINT	75TH	MAXIMUM
1	5.20	5.85	6.45	7.10	7.70
2	7.15	7.75	8.40	9.00	9.65
4	9.05	9.80	10.65	11.40	12.25
6	9.55	10.35	11.20	12.00	12.90
8	10.05	10.90	11.85	12.70	13.65
10	10.80	11.70	12.70	13.60	14.60

Note: DM&E has admitted from the beginning that it could not match the train crew pay of unionized Class I railroads. Rates of pay are 15 to 25 percent below comparable wages on the C&NW. Extensive overtime on DM&E plus profit sharing and year-round employment (Class I railroads often have winter layoffs) undoubtedly narrows this gap.

Source: *DM&E Policy and Procedure Manual.*

EXHIBIT 16-8 Wage Scale Agreement, Rates of Pay

I. Regular assignments (straightaway and through freight runs). Overtime will begin at the expiration of eight (8) hours on runs of 100 miles or less.

| | PER DAY | | | | | PER MILE OVER |
	1/1/93	9/1/93	9/1/94	9/1/95	9/1/96	100 MILES
Conductor	$ 89.88	$ 93.48	$ 98.15	$102.57	$107.18	79.17¢
Engineer	$103.79	$107.94	$113.34	$118.44	$123.77	91.66¢
Brakeman	$ 83.56	$ 86.90	$ 91.25	$ 95.36	$ 99.65	74.07¢

II. Work trains and assignments that ordinarily do not leave terminal, or that operate out to points within 35 miles of the terminal.

| | PER DAY | | | | |
	1/1/93	9/1/93	9/1/94	9/1/95	9/1/96
Conductor	$100.01	$104.01	$109.21	$114.13	$119.26
Engineer	$107.67	$111.98	$117.58	$122.87	$128.40
Brakeman	$ 95.71	$ 99.54	$104.52	$109.22	$114.14

Note: DM&E uses bonus and merit pay to further reward employees. Bonuses for all nonmanagerial employees averaged $1,700 in 1990, $2,200 in 1991, and $2,700 in 1993. All but operating UTU nonmanagerial employees are eligible to receive performance appraisal–based merit pay. This incentive averaged 3 percent in 1990, 2 percent in 1991, and 3 percent in 1992. In addition, this category of employees received 3 percent across-the-board increases in 1990 and 1992.

The benefit package offered to DM&E employees equals or exceeds those provided by the major union railroads.

Source: DM&E and UTU Contract Agreement.

EXHIBIT 16-9 Sample Benefit Comparison

BENEFIT	DM&E	UNIONIZED NATIONAL RAILROAD PLAN
Life Insurance	$50,000	$10,000
Accidental D&D	$50,000	$8,000
401 (K)	Yes	Not Provided
Profit Sharing	Yes	Not Provided
Maximum Medical	$500,000	$500,000
Deductible	$100 each individual	$100 each individual
Maximum out-of-pocket	$500 individual, $1,000 family	$2,000 each person covered

Source: DM&E Benefit Brochures.

In November 1992 the International Association of Machinists failed in their attempt to organize the DM&E's mechanical employees.

Finance. DM&E has improved its financial condition since start-up. Operating revenues for 1991 were $37.9 million and traffic volume 51.4 thousand carloads, a 6.3 percent increase in revenues and a 2.2 percent decline in carloads. In 1992 operating revenue was $40.1 million with traffic volume of 55.1 thousand carloads, an increase of 5.8 and 7.2 percent respectively. During the first six months of 1993, operating revenues were $19.61 million compared to a nearly identical $19.62 million for the same period in 1992. At the same time, carloadings dropped from 25.6 thousand to 23.9 thousand, a decrease of 7.1 percent. Net income for the six-month period was 48 percent below last year. Exhibit 16–10 presents income statement data for the years 1990–1992.

Traffic volume from 1987 to 1992 increased in 7 of 12 commodity groups, with an overall increase of 22 percent. The largest increases were in bentonite clay, corn, woodchips, and kaolin clay. Major decreases in wheat and soybean oil were attributable to weather and market conditions rather than loss to other transportation modes. Increases in gross revenues were due to increased traffic and higher per car charges. (See Exhibit 16–11.)

Operating expenses rose 10.6 percent between 1990 and 1992. Increased traffic coupled with roadbed problems increased expenses in four of six categories. Decline in net income during the first six months of 1993 was attributable to increased car hire, derailment, and crew costs associated with repairing track.

Cash generated from operations is DM&E's primary source of funds for debt service, capital expenditures, and working capital. DM&E was highly leveraged at start-up and has been forced continually to ask for federal, state, and local financing to assist in roadbed maintenance. Governmental loans are at approximately 3 percent and have a delayed principle payment feature. Westinghouse Credit Corporation and C&NW loans average around 12.5 percent interest. DM&E continues to pay down its senior debt and has reduced its debt-to-equity ratio to 2.8 to 1. The ideal railroad debt-to-equity ratio is 1 to 1; 2 to 1 is considered highly leveraged in banking circles. In the May 1993 issue of *DM&E Enroute*, CFO Kurt Feaster stated that DM&E could be below 2 to 1 in two years. See Exhibit 16–12 for balance sheet information for 1990–1992.

C&NW

One of the most unusual twists in the DM&E–C&NW saga occurred in July 1992 when the C&NW unexpectedly backed out of their 1989 agreement to sell the Colony Line for $6.3 million (see Exhibit 16–13). Their excuse was that DM&E lacked financing, but McIntyre denied this charge and commented that "after months of negotiations and coming this far, we couldn't believe they would renege on their agreement." DM&E had hoped, by purchase of the Colony Line, to acquire the originating points of the 20,000 cars a year that are generated on this trackage, which would have permitted the DM&E to control subsequent routing of these cars and also increase their share of car revenues. Colony Line shippers and local and state authorities also expressed their concern about the change of events.

In August 1992 the Union Pacific Railroad (UP) requested ICC approval to acquire the majority, or even 100 percent, ownership of C&NW. Addition of

EXHIBIT 16-10 Dakota, Minnesota & Eastern Railroad Income Statements 1990–1992

	1990	1991	1992
REVENUES			
Freight	34,909	36,941	40,377
Other	660	976	577
Net Revenue	35,569	37,917	40,954
OPERATING EXPENSES			
Car Hire and Car Leases	4,927	5,332	5,723
Fuel	3,581	3,393	3,381
Accident Expense + Insurance	3,649	2,987	3,831
Transportation	5,900	6,848	7,288
Maintenance of Way (includes property tax)	3,177	3,673	3,515
Maintenance of Equipment	1,974	2,038	1,952
Total Operating Expenses	23,208	24,271	25,690
Gross Profit	12,361	13,646	15,264
GENERAL AND ADMINISTRATIVE EXPENSES			
Wages and Benefits	1,678	1,723	2,049
Professional Fees (includes audit)	830	432	599
Other	115	360	382
Other Expenses (Income)	(413)	(92)	(164)
EBITDA	10,151	11,223	12,398
Adjustments	0	0	(1,029)
ADJUSTED EBITDA	10,151	11,223	11,369
Depreciation and Amortization	2,689	2,947	3,314
EBIT	7,462	8,276	8,055
Interest—Revolver (net of interest income)	221	66	(10)
Interest—Westinghouse	2,975	2,725	2,319
Interest—CNW	697	810	991
Interest—Government Loans	235	266	249
Interest—First Bank/Tifco/etc.	117	124	148
Interest—New Debt	0	0	0
EBT	3,217	4,285	4,358
Income Tax	993	1,471	895
NET INCOME	2,224	2,814	3,463
Less Preferred Dividends—Reg.	186	186	186
Net Income Available to Common	2,038	2,628	3,277

Source: Company records.

EXHIBIT 16-11 Dakota, Minnesota & Eastern Railroad Corporation Top Eleven Commodities (1987–1992)

Commodity	Gross Freight Revenue						Revenue Per Carload					
	1987	1988	1989	1990	1991	1992	1987	1988	1989	1990	1991	1992
Wheat	$ 9,687,565	$ 9,367,530	$ 7,131,587	$ 9,570,644	$11,809,116	$11,134,529	$890	$1,050	$1,070	$1,069	$1,121	$1,127
Bentonite Clay	0	0	745,517	7,913,920	9,651,590	10,806,305	—	—	1,007	1,171	1,066	1,118
Woodchips	2,781,150	3,821,725	3,755,085	4,274,558	3,544,238	3,888,649	984	1,120	1,088	1,134	1,097	1,160
Corn	1,270,934	1,830,224	2,673,626	3,803,260	2,969,148	3,278,697	250	360	317	364	369	387
Cement	2,383,082	2,931,008	2,588,389	1,602,287	1,613,215	2,219,796	824	821	826	811	743	778
Industrial Sand	509,150	510,321	746,693	971,763	462,578	684,565	164	187	184	193	195	201
Lumber/Boards	74,893	81,599	92,333	852,319	626,959	534,014	454	563	847	1,033	956	978
Soybeans	734,869	1,261,295	726,857	1,099,612	1,042,046	1,149,938	238	311	382	377	377	387
Kaolin Clay	0	0	0	311,610	497,087	621,341	—	—	—	470	480	480
Soybean Oil	480,580	432,282	300,320	345,404	428,920	420,660	182	215	206	221	218	213
Wheat Flour	109,846	99,499	89,262	433,464	511,697	591,264	145	166	206	449	525	636
All Others	4,849,217	4,609,784	4,306,748	4,533,120	4,821,565	4,856,336	417	449	447	520	557	495
Total	$22,881,286	$24,945,267	$23,156,417	$35,711,961	$37,978,159	$40,186,094	$ 531	$ 589	$ 579	$ 679	$ 738	$ 729

Source: Company records.

the most powerful railroad in the United States to the C&NW equation, in the DM&E's opinion, would have severely restricted its already limited operational freedom. As a result, the DM&E intervened in the ICC proceedings requesting:

EXHIBIT 16-12 Dakota, Minnesota & Eastern Railroad Balance Sheets 1990–1992

	1990	1991	1992
ASSETS			
Cash	1,821	2,789	1,231
Accounts Receivable	5,061	6,937	6,555
Materials and Supplies Inventory	419	421	417
Prepaid Expenses	607	514	574
Total Current Assets	7,908	10,661	8,777
PP&E—Net	51,384	51,866	53,369
Capitalized Leases—Net	0	0	0
Deferred Finances & Other Assets	476	450	1,062
Total Assets	59,768	62,977	63,208
LIABILITIES AND STOCKHOLDERS' EQUITY			
Accounts Payable—Trade	2,963	2,400	1,834
Accounts Payable—International + Contract Allowance	1,351	1,670	1,158
Car Hire Payable	420	730	591
Notes Payable	284	283	286
Wages and Benefits Payable	1,598	1,548	1,519
Interest Payable	316	296	495
Other Accrued Liability	2,291	3,320	2,858
Total Current Liabilities	9,223	10,247	8,741
Deferred Income Tax Liability	3,050	4,427	4,784
Revolving Loan	1,616	2,000	2,000
Westinghouse Term Loans	22,071	18,959	16,105
CNW Term Loan	5,490	6,180	7,388
Government Loans—Net	10,969	10,778	10,652
First Bank	424	516	313
New Debt	0	0	0
Other Liabilities	683	876	874
Total Liabilities	53,526	53,983	50,857
Preferred Stock	1,651	1,838	2,025
Senior Preferred Stock	0	0	0
Common Stock	3,290	3,290	3,290
Retained Earnings	1,300	3,927	7,203
Treasury Stock	0	(61)	(167)
Total Stockholders' Equity	6,241	8,994	12,351
Total Liability & Stockholders' Equity	59,767	62,977	63,208

Source: Company records.

1. Enforcement of the sale of the Colony Line with trackage rights from Dakota Junction to Crawford, Nebraska, for an unrestricted connection with Burlington Northern, or trackage rights over both lines.
2. Removal of interchange restrictions at Winona, Mankato, Owatonna, and Mason City.
3. Allowing direct service to shippers at Winona and access to shippers via reciprocal switching agreement at the other three cities.
4. Modifying the car supply agreement, which requires the DM&E to use C&NW cars while at the same time not requiring the C&NW to furnish them. The DM&E could use cars from any source without C&NW penalty.

As of mid-July 1993 the entire matter remained under ICC study.

COMPETITION

DM&E's operations are subject to competition from railroads and trucks. There are several local and three major railroads that have lines in or near the DM&E service area. Aside from the C&NW, the 23,000-mile Burlington Northern (BN) trackage could prove to be a serious threat. Because of its size and resources, BN offers highly competitive rates and provides direct access to the Gulf, the Pacific Northwest, and the Midwest.

As major carriers continue selling off ancillary lines, opportunities remain for smaller railroads to pick up complementary trackage. C&NW's Minneapolis–Sioux City, Iowa, branch (277 miles), the Soo's corn lines across southern Minnesota (112

EXHIBIT 16-13 DM&E's North/South Trackage from Rapid City miles) and northern Iowa to the Mississippi River (253 miles), and BN's Sioux City to Aberdeen, South Dakota, route (265 miles), may fit this category for DM&E.

Trucks carry a greater share of intercity traffic than do railroads. Their innate flexibility, relatively low capital requirements, and huge network of tax-supported highways give them great advantage in smaller-volume and under-500-mile shipments. Railroads are very competitive in bulk shipments over long distances. Intermodal shipments (truck or container on rail flatcar) often offer the advantages of both modes to shippers. The DM&E faces the strongest truck competition in Minnesota.

CONCLUSION

Develop a three-year strategic plan for DM&E. Include ten major recommendations with associated costs or savings and pro forma financial statements. Prepare projected ratios to show the expected impact of your proposed strategies.

MOTORCYCLES AND MOTOR VEHICLES INDUSTRY NOTE
JOHN VANDERWOLF
Office of Consumer Goods

Constant-dollar product shipments of motorcycles and parts increased an estimated 5 percent in 1993. Imports of motorcycles were about 19 percent higher, while exports increased less than 1 percent. With domestic shipments and imports up, apparent consumption jumped 19 percent (Table 1).

The U.S. motorcycle market may have finally turned around. Since its peak in 1980 during the last oil crisis, the demand for motorcycles has slowly decreased. However, in 1992 new motorcycle registrations increased by almost 4 percent. New registrations for 1993 also are expected to be up; they were more than 5 percent higher during the first five months of the year.

The excess supply that had built up in the 1980s began to diminish in the early 1990s, as owners began looking for larger, newer motorcycles. The average age and income of motorcycle owners increased as baby boomers matured, so they began purchasing newer, bigger, more comfortable, and more expensive motorcycles. In 1980 the average age of the motorcycle owner was 24 years; in 1990 it was 31. The 26-to-35 age group generally makes more money ($34,032) than those under 25 ($14,319), according to the 1991 Consumer Expenditure Survey prepared by the Bureau of Labor Statistics. Therefore, many motorcycle owners have upgraded to a heavyweight motorcycle (an engine exceeding 750cc). The market for these motorcycles has been growing since 1987.

Table 1: Motorcycles and Parts: Domestic Shipments and Trade, 1988–94 (in millions of dollars except as noted)

ITEM	1991	1992[1]	1993[2]	1994[3]	PERCENT CHANGE (1991–1994)[4] 91–92	92–93	93–94
Product shipments	776.1	865.0	945.9		11.5	9.4	
Product shipments (1987$)	694.8	733.1	769.0	788.0	5.5	4.9	2.5
Apparent consumptions[5]	919.0	1,171.0	1,398.5		27.4	19.4	
Imports	583.9	802.7	952.6	1,025.0	37.5	18.7	7.6
Imports to apparent consumption (%)	63.5	68.5	68.1		7.9	–0.6	
Exports	441.0	496.7	500.0	525.0	12.6	0.7	5.0
Exports to shipments (%)	56.8	57.4	52.9		1.1	–7.9	

1. Estimated product shipments.

2. Estimated trade and product shipments.

3. Forecast.

4. Percent changes are calculated on more detailed data.

5. Apparent consumption = product shipments – exports + imports.

Source: U.S. Department of Commerce: Bureau of the Census; International Trade Administration (ITA). Estimates and forecasts by ITA.

The U.S. industry has benefited from this trend, as all three domestic manufacturers produce primarily large-engine class motorcycles. The two Japanese-owned manufacturing facilities in the United States produce most of their companies' heavyweight motorcycles sold in this country. However, the biggest beneficiary has been the sole U.S.-owned manufacturer, Harley-Davidson. Having saved itself from going out of business in the early 1980s, the company has rebounded to become the dominant supplier (67 percent) of heavyweight motorcycles in the U.S. market. Harley-Davidson's products have a unique style and appeal that have attracted many of the motorcycle owners in the baby boom generation.

Consumers' perceptions of motorcycle safety have been a negative force affecting demand. They often think that motorcycling is a dangerous hobby and one to avoid. However, this trend has abated to some degree. Easing consumers' safety concerns has been the decrease in accident rates of the last several years. In 1992 the rate of motorcycle accidents dropped 12 percent from 1991, to 206 accidents per 10,000 registered motorcycles. The Motorcycle Safety Foundation rider education programs have promoted the safe use of motorcycles, and the industry believes these programs have been effective.

Lessening concern about motorcycle safety and a decreasing supply of used motorcycles may explain the growth in sales of some other motorcycles, such as off-road, dual-purpose, and small-engine street motorcycles. These segments grew an estimated 10 percent in 1993.

U.S. Trade Patterns in 1992 Motorcycles, Bicycles, and Parts (SIC 3751) (in millions of dollars, percent)

	EXPORTS			IMPORTS	
	Value	Share		Value	Share
Canada and Mexico	90	13.4	Canada and Mexico	18	1.1
European Community	306	45.5	European Community	94	6.1
Japan	81	12.0	Japan	804	52.3
East Asia NICs	28	4.2	East Asia NICs	599	39.0
South America	78	11.6	South America	3	0.2
Other	89	13.2	Other	20	1.3
World Total	671	100.0	World Total	1,537	100.0

TOP FIVE COUNTRIES					
	Value	Share		Value	Share
Germany	110	16.3	Japan	804	52.3
Netherlands	88	13.2	Taiwan	476	31.0
Japan	81	12.0	China	87	5.7
Canada	62	9.3	Italy	43	2.8
Argentina	54	8.1	Germany	32	2.1

Source: U.S. Department of Commerce: Bureau of the Census; International Trade Administration.

U.S. exports have become a more important factor in domestic production. The exports-to-shipments ratio reached a high of 57 percent in 1992, before dropping to 53 percent in 1993. As a result of the growth of U.S. experts, the industry's trade balance in general has improved significantly. In 1986 the trade deficit was $812 million; in 1993 it was an estimated $453 million. (The deficit reached a low of $143 million in 1991.)

Three major factors likely contributed to the 1993 slowdown in exports following 3 years of double-digit growth. First, overall economic growth in the major motorcycle markets has diminished. Second, Harley-Davidson decided to maintain 1993 production near 350 units per day, most of which is aimed to meet domestic market demand. Harley-Davidson has had difficulty meeting foreign demand for the last several years, preferring not to increase production at the expense of product quality. Therefore, many entrepreneurs stepped in and began exporting used Harleys, which is the likely reason that the exports-to-shipments ratio was so high in 1991 and 1992. However, it may be possible that the supply of used Harleys in

Trends and Forecasts: Motorcycles, Bicycles, and Parts (SIC 3751) (in millions of dollars except as noted)

ITEM	1991	1992[1]	1993[2]	1994[3]	PERCENT CHANGE (1991–1994)		
					91–92	92–93	93–94
INDUSTRY DATA							
Value of shipments[4]	1,914	2,100	2,226	—	9.7	6.0	—
Value of shipments (1987$)	1,701	1,784	1,858	1,906	4.9	4.1	2.6
Total employment (000)	10.8	11.4	12.0	—	5.6	5.3	—
Production workers (000)	8.5	9.0	9.5	—	5.9	5.6	—
Average hourly earnings ($)	11.69	11.10	11.45	—	–5.0	3.2	—
Capital expenditures	61.5	—	—	—	—	—	—
PRODUCT DATA							
Value of shipments[5]	2,112	2,300	2,449	—	8.9	6.5	—
Value of shipments (1987$)	1,877	1,954	2,044	2,087	4.1	4.6	2.1
TRADE DATA							
Value of imports	1,329	1,537	1,732	1,840	15.7	12.7	6.2
Value of exports	615	671	704	750	9.1	4.9	6.5

1. Estimate, except exports and imports.
2. Estimate.
3. Forecast.
4. Value of all products and services sold by establishments in the motorcycles, bicycles, and parts industry.
5. Value of products classified in the motorcycles, bicycles, and parts industry produced by all industries.

Source: U.S. Department of Commerce: Bureau of the Census; International Trade Administration (ITA). Estimates and forecasts by ITA.

the United States now has dried up to a degree, slowing export sales by these entrepreneurs.

The European Community (EC) is by far the largest foreign market for U.S. motorcycle exports, totaling an estimated $347 million in 1993, or 69 percent of exports. However, the market share of U.S. companies could be even greater if it were not for stringent noise emission standards in the EC—the third factor in slowing export growth. Meeting current noise regulations has forced reductions in the performance of U.S. motorcycles exported to the EC. Harley-Davidson has stated that standards proposed for 1997 cannot be met without design changes likely to be unacceptable to a majority of its customers.

U.S. manufacturers exported an estimated $93 million to Germany in 1993, down 4 percent from 1992. Germany was the largest individual country export market for U.S. motorcycles. The second-largest market was Canada at an estimated $90 million, up 24 percent from 1992. Japan was the third-largest foreign market—about $60 million, as U.S. exports there increased 10 percent.

In Japan several rules and regulations severely limit the potential export market for large U.S.-built motorcycles, including the extremely difficult operator license test for large motorcycles and the ban on carrying passengers on highways. According to the available evidence, these regulations do not contribute to safety or to other public purposes. Careful analysis of accident data demonstrates that larger motorcycles are less likely to be involved in accidents than smaller ones.

In 1993 U.S. imports of motorcycles grew an estimated 19 percent to $953 million. Japan is the largest foreign supplier of motorcycles, accounting for 86 percent of total U.S. imports. Taiwan, Germany, and Italy were the other major suppliers of motorcycles, accounting for 4 percent, 3.4 percent, and 2.6 percent of U.S. imports, respectively, in 1993.

Outlook for 1994. Constant-dollar product shipments of motorcycles and parts are forecast to increase 3 percent. Exports will be up about 5 percent and should benefit from improving economic growth in the major markets for motorcycles. Imports are expected to rise by about 8 percent in 1994. Apparent consumption will continue to grow but at a slower annual rate, estimated at 7 percent. Slower increases in personal disposable income will likely reduce the growth of personal consumption expenditures on motorcycles.

Long-term Prospects. Real domestic product shipments are expected to grow at an annual rate of 2 to 3 percent between 1993 and 1998, as both the export sector and the domestic market grow. The latter should stabilize or slightly increase. Demographic influences and safety concerns will continue to affect the domestic demand for motorcycles.

Foreign demand for motorcycles is expected to remain strong. Germany and Japan should continue to be the largest foreign markets for U.S. motorcycles. The economies of the Organization for Economic Cooperation and Development countries (major industrial nations) are expected to grow about 3 percent annually over the next four years. Growth in the U.S. share of the EC motorcycle markets will likely hinge on how effectively U.S. manufacturers are able to adapt to the new noise emission standards there.

The North American Free Trade Agreement will provide U.S. manufacturers with additional opportunities. Mexican tariffs for motorcycles, currently at 20 percent, are scheduled to be phased out over the next five years under NAFTA. Mexican tariffs for motorcycle parts, currently at 15 percent, were eliminated immediately upon implementation of the agreement. Furthermore, U.S. producers will likely benefit from increases in the Mexican standard of living, giving more consumers the chance to purchase a motorcycle.

The average age of a motorcycle owner is expected to continue to increase over the next five years, to at least 35 years. Consumers in the 35-to-54 age group generally reach their maximum earning potential. The 1992 Consumer Expenditures Survey reported that new motorcycle expenditures were the highest among these consumers.

The perception of danger associated with motorcycle riding may continue to affect sales. However, if accident rates continue to decline, any negative effects on sales should be minimized. The trend toward large touring motorcycles will contribute to lower accident rates. In general, motorcycle manufacturers should expect much better results in the next five years than they experienced in the last ten years.

HARLEY-DAVIDSON—1994

C A S E

17

FRED R. DAVID
Francis Marion University
CHARLES SHRADER
Iowa State University

Over the last decade, Harley-Davidson took itself from the brink of destruction to its current status as one of the most admired companies in the world. Headquartered in Milwaukee, Wisconsin, Harley (414-342-4680) is now winning the battle among the heavyweight motorcycle competitors—Honda, Kawasaki, Suzuki, and Yamaha. Harley has gained a 60 percent share of the heavyweight motorcycle market-share in the United States and 15 percent internationally. However, the company has an unusual—and big—problem: Because of a lack of plant capacity, Harley cannot meet demand for its motorcycles. Customers worldwide who order a new Harley must wait at least a year for delivery. Dealers are upset; they have no inventory. Consumers are upset. Harley plans to increase motorcycle production from 76,000 units in 1992 to over 100,000 units annually by 1996, but analysts contend this planned increase is still far below demand.

The Harley-Davidson corporate vision is given as follows:

> Harley-Davidson is an action-oriented, international company—a leader in its commitment to continuously improve the quality of profitable relationships with stakeholders (customers, employees, suppliers, shareholders, governments, and society). Harley-Davidson believes the key to success is to balance stakeholders' interests through the empowerment of all employers to focus on value-added activities.

HISTORY

The Harley-Davidson story began in 1903 when William Harley, aged 21 and a draftsman at a Milwaukee manufacturing firm, designed and built a motorcycle with the help of three Davidson brothers: Arthur, a pattern maker; Walter, a railroad mechanic; and William, a tool maker. At first, the brothers tinkered with ideas, motors, and old bicycle frames. Legend has it that their first carburetor was fashioned from a tin can. They were able to make a 3-horsepower, 25-cubic-inch engine and successfully road tested the first motored cycle.

Operating out of a shed in the Davidson family's backyard, the men built and sold three motorcycles. Production was expanded to eight in 1904 and in 1906 the company's first building was erected on the current site of the main offices in Milwaukee, Wisconsin. Harley-Davidson Motor Company was incorporated in 1907, and Arthur set off to recruit dealers in New England and the South. William completed a degree in engineering, specializing in internal combustion engines, and quickly applied his expertise in the company; he developed the first V-twin engine in 1909. He followed this with a major breakthrough in 1912—the first commercially successful motorcycle clutch. This made possible the use of a roller chain to power the motorcycle. The first three-speed transmission was offered in 1915.

During the early 1900s the United States experienced rapid growth in the motorcycle industry, with firms such as Excelsior, Indian, Merkel, Thor, and Yale growing and competing. Most of the early U.S. motorcycle companies turned out shoddy, unreliable products. But this was not considered to be true of Harley-Davidson and Indian cycles. Early continued success in racing and endurance made Harley a favorite among motorcyclists. The company's V-twin engines became known for power and reliability.

During World War I, Harley-Davidson supplied the military with motorcycles and became the largest motorcycle company in the world in 1918. The company built a 300,000-square-foot plant in Milwaukee in 1922. In 1949 Harley first faced international competition from British motorcycles, such as Nortons and Triumphs, which handled better and were cheaper, lighter, and just as fast, even though they had smaller engines. To counter the British threat, Harley-Davidson improved the design of their engines and increased the horsepower of their heavier cycles. The result, in 1957, was the first modern superbike: the Harley Sportster. It was also during the 1950s that Harley developed the styling that is famous to this day.

In an attempt to expand production capacity and raise capital, Harley went public in 1965 and then merged with the conglomerate AMF, Inc. (American Machine and Foundry) in 1969. Known for its leisure and industrial products, AMF expanded Harley's production capacity from 15,000 units to 40,000 units in 1974. With the expanded capacity, AMF pursued a milking strategy, favoring short-term profits rather than investment in research and development and retooling. Japanese motorcycle manufacturers, however, continued to improve, whereas Harley began to turn out heavy, noisy, vibrating, laboriously handling, poorly finished machines.

In 1975 Honda Motor Company introduced the Gold Wing, which quickly became the standard for large touring motorcycles, a segment that Harley had owned. At the time, Harley's top-of-the-line touring bike sold for almost $9,000, while the comparable Honda Gold Wing was approximately $7,000. Not only were Japanese cycles priced less than similar Harleys, but Japanese manufacturing techniques yielded operating costs that were 30 percent lower than Harley.

Motorcycle enthusiasts more than ever began to go with Japanese products because of their price and performance advantages. Even some loyal Harley owners and police department contracts were lost. The company was rapidly losing ground in both technological advances and the market. Starting in 1975 and continuing through the mid-1980s, Japanese companies penetrated the big-bore, custom motorcycle market with Harley look-alikes sporting V-twin engines. The Honda Magna and Shadow, the Suzuki Intruder, and the Yamaha Virago were representative of the Japanese imitations. The Japanese captured a significant share of the large cycle segment and controlled nearly 90 percent of the total motorcycle market.

Vaughn L. Beals, Jr., served as the Harley-Davidson manager during its six years under AMF control. Beals was uncomfortable with AMF's short-term orientation and unwillingness to confront the problems caused by imports. Consequently, in June 1981 a subgroup of Harley management, including Beals, completed a leveraged buyout of Harley-Davidson from AMF. To celebrate, Beals and the management team made a Pennsylvania-to-Wisconsin motorcycle ride, proclaiming as their slogan, "the eagle soars alone."

Beals himself was an engineer who simply loved motorcycles. He surrounded himself with a team that loved motorcycles as well. No longer was the company run by AFM's "finance guys." It was now run by a group of motorcycle riders. Under the management of Beals, Richard Teerlink, and Thomas Gelb, Harley-Davidson adopted a very efficient approach to manufacturing. Three major programs comprise the manufacturing approach: materials as needed (MAN) or just-in-time inventory, statistical operator control (SOC), and employee involvement.

Under the MAN system, Harley suppliers must comply with the company's quality requirements. Harley offers long-term contracts to suppliers who do comply and who deliver only the exact quantity needed for a given period of time. Harley also transports materials from suppliers. When the Harley transportation company makes scheduled pickups from suppliers, Harley has greater control over the shipments and is thereby able to cut costs.

Harley invests heavily in research and development. One payoff of this investment is a computer-aided design (CAD) system that allows management to make changes in the entire product line while maintaining elements of the traditional styling. Harley is recognized as an industry leader in many aspects of production, including belt driven technology, vibration isolation, and steering geometry.

Employee involvement at Harley means the full participation of all employees in the continuous improvement process. Decisions made in quality circles are a major source of input for quality improvement. Employees participate in meetings and have a stake in the success of the company through bonus programs that share financial rewards and the Employee Stock Purchase Program. The employee involvement practices at Harley ensure high morale, low absenteeism, and few grievances.

Harley's purchasing strategy includes working with suppliers that are close to Harley's own facilities. Nearly 80 percent of the company's suppliers are located within 180 miles of Milwaukee. Proximity to suppliers means that the MAN system and just-in-time inventory practices are easier to implement. Plant productivity has continued to improve in the 1990s. For example, the York plant produced approximately 160 motorcycles a day in 1987 and 285 a day in 1990, and currently produces over 300 motorcycles a day. The concern for quality is transmitted to dealers as well. Harley mechanics at dealerships are expected to take a series of qualifying examinations dealing with 24 motorcycle repair categories. Exam questions deal with categories such as transmission, suspension, and electronics repair. Mechanics receive factory training and support, and dealers keep their customers apprised of how well the local mechanics are doing.

HARLEY DIVISIONS

Harley operates in two segments: (1) Motorcycles and Related Products and (2) Transportation Vehicles. Harley's Motorcycles and Related Products segment designs, manufactures, and sells superheavyweight (engine displacement of 851cc or above) touring and custom motorcycles and a broad range of related products. Harley is the only major American motorcycle manufacturer. The company's bike sales abroad exceeded $285 million in 1993, or 24 percent of their $1.2 billion total.

The Transportation Vehicles segment consists entirely of Holiday Rambler Corporation and its subsidiaries. Holiday Rambler is a wholly owned subsidiary that manufactures recreational vehicles, principally motorhomes and travel trailers, and specialized commercial vehicles. Holiday Rambler began manufacturing recreational vehicles in 1953 and was acquired by Harley in 1986. Holiday Rambler's recreational vehicle sales declined 12 percent in 1993 to about $65 million. Holiday Rambler's commercial vehicles (marketed under the Utilimaster brand name), which include walk-in vans and parcel delivery trucks, are built for a diverse range of specialized commercial uses.

Revenue, operating profit (loss), and identifiable assets attributable to each of Harley's segments are as follows (in thousands):

	MOTORCYCLES AND RELATED	TRANSPORTATION VEHICLES	CORPORATE
1992			
Revenue	$822,929	$282,355	$ —
Operating Income (loss)	102,300	2,137	(7,240)
Identifiable Assets	341,940	178,252	1,972
1991			
Revenue	$701,969	$237,894	$ —
Operating Income (loss)	89,551	(13,427)	(7,479)
Identifiable Assets	281,790	189,326	3,117
1990			
Revenue	$624,027	$240,573	$ —
Operating Income (loss)	90,219	825	(7,669)
Identifiable Assets	227,819	177,498	2,150

During 1992 the recreational vehicle industry reported volume increases for the first time in three years. Most of the increase was realized in the middle-to-low price segment of the market. The Recreational Vehicle division generally targets its products toward the middle-to-upper price segment of the market.

Motorcycles and Related Products. Harley's motorcycle products emphasize traditional styling, design simplicity, durability, ease of service and evolutionary change. Studies indicate that the typical Harley motorcycle owner is a male in his late thirties with a household income of approximately $53,000, who purchases a motorcycle for recreational rather than transportational purposes, and who is an experienced motorcycle rider. Approximately two-thirds of Harley's sales are to buyers with at least one year of higher education.

The superheavyweight class of motorcycles comprises four types: standard, which emphasizes simplicity and cost; performance, which emphasizes racing and speed; touring, which emphasizes comfort and amenities for long-distance travel; and custom, which emphasizes styling and individual owner customization. Touring and custom models are the only class of superheavyweight motorcycle that Harley manufactures. Harley sells 20 models of touring and custom superheavyweight motorcycles, with suggested retail prices ranging from approximately $5,000 to $16,000. The touring segment of the superheavyweight market was pioneered by Harley and includes motorcycles equipped for long-distance touring, with fairings, windshields, saddlebags, and Tour Pak. The custom segment of the market includes motorcycles featuring the distinctive styling associated with certain classic Harley-Davidson motorcycles. These motorcycles are highly customized through the use of trim and accessories. Harley's motorcycles are based on variations of five basic chassis designs and are powered by three air-cooled, twin-cylinder engines of "V" configuration that have displacement of 883 cc, 120 cc, and 1,340 cc. Harley manufactures its own engines and frames.

The top of Harley's custom product line is typically priced at approximately twice that of its competitors' custom motorcycles. The custom portion of the Harley product line represents the highest unit volumes and continues to command a price premium because of its features, styling, and high resale value. Harley's smallest displacement custom motorcycle (the 883 cc Sportster) is directly price competitive with competitors' comparable motorcycles. Surveys of retail purchasers indicate that, historically, over 80 percent of the purchasers of this Sportster model have come from competitive-brand motorcycles or are people new to the sport of motorcycling. Domestically, motorcycle sales generated 52.8 percent, 50.6 percent, and 50.7 percent of revenues in the Motorcycles and Related Products segment during 1992, 1991, and 1990 respectively.

Harley's Motorcycle Products business consists primarily of parts and accessories and rider apparel. The major product categories for motorcycle parts are replacement parts, mechanical accessories, rider accessories (MotorClothes), and specially formulated oil and other lubricants. Harley's replacement parts include original equipment parts, generally made in the United States, and a less expensive line of imported parts introduced to compete against foreign-sourced aftermarket suppliers. Harley provides a variety of services to its dealers and retail customers, including optional extended-service contracts, insurance programs, service training schools, delivery of its motorcycles, motorcycling vacations, memberships in an owners club, and customized software packages. Harley has had recent success under a program emphasizing modern store design and display techniques in the merchandising of parts and accessories by its dealers. Currently more than 370 domestic and 90 international dealerships have completed, or are in the process of, store design renovation projects. Domestic motorcycle parts and accessories sales comprised 15.3 percent, 14.9 percent, and 14.8 percent of net sales in the Motorcycles and Related Products segment in 1992, 1991, and 1990, respectively. Net sales from motorcycle parts and accessories have grown 71.2 percent over the last three years (since 1989).

Licensing. In recent years, Harley has endeavored to create an awareness of the brand among the nonriding public by licensing the trademark "Harley-Davidson" through production and sales of a broad range of consumer items, including t-shirts and other clothing, trading cards, jewelry, small leather goods, and toys. Although the majority of licensing activity occurs in the United States, Harley has expanded into international markets.

This licensing activity provides Harley with a valuable source of advertising. Licensing also has proven to be an effective means for enhancing Harley's image with consumers and provides an important tool for policing the unauthorized use of Harley's trademarks. Royalty revenues from licensing accounted for approximately 1 percent of the net sales from the Motorcycles and Related Products segment during each of the three years in the period ended December 31, 1992. Though net sales from licensing activities are small, the profitability of this business is relatively high.

Marketing and Distribution. Harley's basic channel of United States distribution for its motorcycles and related products is approximately 600 independently owned full-service dealerships. With respect to sales of new motorcycles, approximately 75 percent of the dealerships sell Harley motorcycles exclusively. All dealerships carry Harley's replacement parts and aftermarket accessories and perform servicing of Harley motorcycle products.

Harley's marketing efforts are divided among dealer promotions, customer events, magazine and direct-mail advertising, public relations, and cooperative programs with dealers. Harley also sponsors racing activities and special promotional events and participates in all major motorcycle consumer shows and rallies. In an effort to encourage Harley owners to become more actively involved in the sport of motorcycling, Harley formed a riders club in 1983. The Harley Owners Group (HOG) currently has in excess of 192,000 members worldwide and is the industry's largest company-sponsored enthusiast organization. In addition, Harley is a national sponsor of the Muscular Dystrophy Association. Harley's expenditures on domestic marketing and advertising were approximately $4.52 million, $36.1 million, and $34.7 million during 1992, 1991, and 1990, respectively.

International Sales. International sales were $240 million, $205 million, and $176 million, accounting for approximately 29 percent, 29 percent, and 28 percent of net sales of the Motorcycles and Related Products segment during 1992, 1991, and 1990, respectively. Harley believes that the international heavyweight market (engine displacements of 751cc and above) is growing and is significantly larger than the U.S. heavyweight market. Harley has wholly owned subsidiaries located in Germany, Japan, and the United Kingdom. The German subsidiary also serves Austria and France. The combined foreign subsidiaries have a network of 118 dealers, of which approximately 43 percent sell Harley motorcycles exclusively. Elsewhere, sales are managed through 17 distributors in 14 countries. These distributors service approximately 280 additional countries who primarily seek fleet sales and parts orders. Germany, Japan, Canada, and France, in descending order, represent Harley's largest export sales.

Competition. The United States and international superheavyweight/heavyweight motorcycle markets are highly competitive. Harley's competitors, Yamaha, Honda, Suzuki, and Kawasaki, have financial and marketing resources greater than Harley's as well as larger overall sales volumes and a more diversified product line. During 1992 the superheavyweight segment represented 32 percent of the total United States motorcycle market in terms of units registered. The touring and custom segments of the superheavyweight motorcycle market together accounted for 73 percent, 72 percent, and 77 percent of total superheavyweight segment retail unit sales in the United States during 1992, 1991, and 1990, respectively. Custom and touring motorcycles are generally the most expensive and most profitable vehicles in the market. Resale prices of Harley-Davidson motorcycles, as a percentage of price when new, are significantly higher than resale prices of motorcycles sold by the competitors. The primary reason for this is that production of Harley bikes is more than a year behind demand.

Harley estimates its worldwide competitive position to be as follows:

751+ cc Motorcycles Registration Data (Units in thousands)

	1992	1991	1990
North America:			
Total registrations	92.3	80.7	84.2
Harley-Davidson registrations	56.0	48.3	50.2
Harley-Davidson market share percentage	60.6%	59.9%	59.6%
Europe:			
Total registrations	128.0	104.9	96.1
Harley-Davidson registrations	12.5	10.7	8.7
Harley-Davidson market share percentage	9.7%	10.2%	9.0%
Japan/Australia:			
Total registrations	28.2	24.6	26.1
Harley-Davidson registrations	5.2	5.2	4.8
Harley-Davidson market share percentage	18.4%	21.1%	18.4%

1. Includes the United States and Canada.

2. Includes Austria, Belgium, France, Germany, Italy, Netherlands, Spain, Switzerland, and United Kingdom.

3. Data for Queensland, Northern Territory, and South Australia not available.

Employees. As of December 31, 1992, the Motorcycles and Related Products segment had approximately 4,000 employees. Production workers at the motorcycle manufacturing facilities in Wauwatosa and Tomahawk, Wisconsin, are represented principally by the Allied Industrial Workers (AIW) of the AFL-CIO, as well as the International Association of Machinist and Aerospace Workers (IAM). Production workers at the motorcycle manufacturing facility in York, Pennsylvania, are represented principally by the IAM. The collective bargaining agreements with the AIW and the Wisconsin-IAM expired March 27, 1994, and the collective bargaining agreement with the Pennsylvania-IAM expired February 2, 1994.

Transportation Vehicles.

Recreational Vehicles. The Recreational Vehicle division's motorhomes and travel trailers are designed to appeal to people interested in travel and outdoor recreational activities. These recreational vehicles are distinct from mobile homes, which are manufactured housing designed for permanent and semipermanent dwelling.

Principal types of recreational vehicles produced by the Recreational Vehicle division include Class A or "conventional" motorhomes, Class C or "mini" motorhomes, and travel trailers. Recreational vehicle classifications are based on standards established by the Recreation Vehicle Industry Association (RVIA). A motorhome is a self-powered vehicle built on a motor vehicle chassis. The interior typically includes a driver's area, kitchen, bathroom, and dining and sleeping areas. Motorhomes are self-contained, with their own lighting, heating, cooking, refrigeration, sewage-holding and water-storage facilities, so that they can be lived in without being attached to utilities. As such, they generally qualify as second homes for income-tax purposes. Although they generally are not designed to provide complete facilities for permanent or semipermanent living, motorhomes do provide comfortable living facilities for short periods of time.

Class A motorhomes are constructed of medium-duty truck chassis, which are purchased with engine and drive-train components. The living area and driver's compartment are designed, manufactured, and installed by the Recreational Vehicle Division. Class C motorhomes are built on a van or small truck chassis, which are purchased with engine and drive-train components and a finished access to the driver's compartment.

Travel trailers are nonmotorized vehicles designed to be towed by passenger automobiles, pick-up trucks, sport utility vehicles, or vans. They are otherwise similar to motorhomes in features and use. Harley produces both "conventional" and "fifth-wheel" travel trailers. Conventional travel trailers are towed by means of a bumper or frame hitch attached to the towing vehicle. Fifth-wheel trailers, designed to be towed by pick-up trucks, are constructed with a raised forward section that is attached to the bed area of the pick-up truck. This design allows a bilevel floor plan and additional living space.

Harley's premium lines of recreational vehicles are marketed under the Navigator and Imperial brand names. Models in these lines are manufactured with high-quality materials and components, including entertainment centers, solid-oak cabinetry, and brass fixtures, and may be equipped with luxury features such as microwave convection ovens, washer/dryers, and built-in vacuum cleaner systems. These models are generally purchased by people who previously have owned recreational vehicles. The Navigator is a bus-style motorhome that carries a suggested retail price of $193,000 to $220,000. In Harley's Imperial line, suggested retail prices of motorhomes generally range between $105,000 and $125,000, and of travel trailers between $37,000 and $64,000.

Harley also produces motorhomes and travel trailers for the midrange market under the Aluma-Lite brand name. These models are produced with fewer standard features than the Imperial. Suggested retail prices for the Aluma-Lite line range between $48,000 and $95,000 for motorhomes and between $18,000 and $54,000 for travel trailers. Also in the midrange market, Harley produces the Endeavor and the Vacationer motorhome models. Suggested retail prices in these lines range between $47,000 and $76,000.

The following table presents information regarding wholesale sales of Harley's recreational vehicles during the periods indicated:

Wholesale Sales Sales, Year Ended December 31, (in thousands)

	1992	1991	1990
Premium lines	$ 71,643	$ 41,246	$ 37,561
Midrange lines	76,418	79,788	76,202
Other	—	—	2,553
Total	$148,061	$121,034	$116,316

In addition to wholesale sales of the Recreational Vehicle division's products shown above, sales by the Recreational Vehicle division also include retail sales by wholly owned Holiday World stores. The Recreational Vehicle division's sales (including retail, wholesale, and other sales) were $202.1 million, $170.6 million, and $166.5 million in 1992, 1991, and 1990, respectively. Sales of the Recreational Vehicle division accounted for 71.6 percent, 71.7 percent, and 69.2 percent of the Transportation Vehicle segment's revenues for the years ended December 31, 1992, 1991, and 1990, respectively.

Competition and Other Business Considerations. The recreational vehicle market is highly competitive among a number of manufacturers. Competition is based on price, design, quality, and service. The primary external factors affecting the recreational vehicle industry are the consumer's perception of health of the economy, interest rates, availability of retail financing, and the availability of gasoline. Harley believes that all of these items have played significant roles during the recent, three-year downcycle in the recreational vehicle industry.

Fifteen manufacturers account for approximately 87 percent of total units sold in the recreational vehicle market classifications in which the Recreational Vehicle division competes. The remaining units include products manufactured by approximately 50 additional manufacturers. Fleetwood Enterprises, Inc. accounts for approximately 37 percent and 28 percent of the Class A and travel trailer markets, respectively. Harley's share of the Class A and travel trailer markets is 5.3 percent and 2.6 percent, respectively. Harley ranks fourth in Class A market share and ninth in travel trailer market share. Coachmen and Winnebago are two other large competitors in this market.

Marketing and Distributing. The Recreational Vehicle division markets its recreational vehicle products through a network of approximately 140 dealers located throughout the continental United States, including 12 company-owned Holiday World dealers. Holiday World dealers also stock previously owned vehicles and new recreational vehicles manufactured by certain of Holiday Rambler's competitors. Holiday World dealers provide Holiday Rambler with valuable knowledge regarding consumer preferences and information regarding products of its competitors, as well as other marketing information. Holiday Rambler's sales and service agreements require dealers to maintain a service department and a supply of recreational vehicle parts, supplies, and accessories. These agreements are subject to renewal on an annual basis.

Holiday Rambler is gearing its marketing effort to be more responsive to its customers' needs. Holiday Rambler has redesigned a number of its stores, expanded its roster of dealers, and continues the development of new product offerings.

Holiday Rambler's new owner questionnaires indicate that approximately 68 percent of purchasers of Holiday Rambler's new recreational vehicles are 56 years or older, a growing segment of the U.S. population. Customer loyalty is reinforced by Holiday Rambler's sponsorship of the Holiday Ramblers Recreational Vehicle Club, Inc., a not-for-profit corporation. The club is open only to owners of Holiday Rambler's recreational vehicles and has approximately 12,500 members. The club holds 34 club-sponsored rallies and caravans each year and is provided with administrative and promotional assistance by Holiday Rambler. Holiday Rambler receives valuable feedback from its customers at these events.

COMMERCIAL VEHICLES

Through its Utilimaster Corporation subsidiary, Harley builds truck bodies for specialized commercial uses. Sales of Harley's commercial vehicles and truck bodies accounted for 24.0 percent, 23.4 percent, and 25.7 percent of the Transportation Vehicle segment's revenues in 1992, 1991, and 1990, respectively.

Utilimaster currently installs truck bodies on chassis of various sizes supplied by third parties. The truck bodies are offered in aluminum or fiberglass-reinforced plywood (FRP) construction and are available in lengths of 9 to 28 feet. Harley's products (excluding chassis) range in price from $2,300 to $34,000 although special service vehicles can sell as high as $55,000.

The principal types of commercial bodies are as follows:

Parcel Delivery Vans. Aluminum or FRP parcel delivery van bodies are installed on chopped van chassis supplied by major Detroit truck manufacturers. These parcel delivery van bodies that are manufactured by Harley range in length from 10 to 16 feet and are primarily used for local delivery of parcels, freight, and perishables.

Standard Walk-In Vans. Utilimaster manufactures its standard walk-in vans (step-vans) on a truck chassis supplied with engine and drive-train components, but without a cab. Harley fabricates the driver's compartment and body using aluminum panels. Uses for these vans include the distribution of food products and small packages.

Truck Bodies. Utilimaster's truck bodies are typically up to 28 feet in length with pre-painted aluminum or FRP panels, aerodynamic front and side corners, hardwood floors, and various door configurations to accommodate end-user loading and unloading requirements. These products are used for diversified dry freight transportation. Harley installs its truck bodies on chassis supplied with a finished cab.

Mobile Rescue and Special Use Emergency Vehicles. Utilimaster builds a variety of specialty use vehicles for the fire and rescue industry. These vehicles range in length from 10 to 22 feet and usually require extensive customization to meet the needs of the local emergency agencies.

Aeromate. The Aeromate was developed for customers needing a midsize delivery vehicle that offered maneuverability, front-wheel drive, fuel efficiency, a large cargo area, and driver comfort, features not available from production vans and larger delivery vans. Its six-cylinder engine, automatic transmission, and drive train are purchased from a third party in the automotive industry and retrofitted to the Harley-built chassis. The all-aluminum truck body can hold 317 cubic feet of cargo, weighing up to one ton.

Marketing and Distribution. Utilimaster markets its commercial vehicles and bodies directly to 450 fleet accounts and to single commercial vehicles purchasers through a network of 900 automobile and truck dealers. This network is distinct from Harley's recreational-vehicle dealer network. Harley does not provide financing to these dealers or fleet accounts.

Competition. Though the Commercial Vehicle division experiences some competition from the large automotive manufacturers, which traditionally have offered a narrow selection of standardized commercial-vehicle body options for their truck chassis, its principle competition is from a small number of manufacturers with the resources to satisfy the volume requirements and specialized needs of commercial-vehicle fleet customers. These manufacturers include Grumman Corporation, Union City Body Company, Inc., and Supreme Corporation. Competition among manufacturers is based on price, quality, and responsiveness to customer requirements both in design and timing of delivery.

PROPERTIES

The following is a summary of the principle properties of the company's Motorcycles and Related Products segment:

TYPE OF FACILITY	LOCATION	SQUARE FEET	STATUS
Executive Offices, Engineering, and Warehouse	Milwaukee, WI	502,720	Owned
Manufacturing	Wauwatosa, WI	317,734	Owned
Manufacturing	Tomahawk, WI	70,327	Owned
Manufacturing	York, PA	949,380	Owned
Motorcycle Testing	Talladega, AL	11,500	Lease expiring 1996
Office and Warehouse	Morfelden-Walldorf, Germany	50,880	Lease expiring 2001
Office	Tokyo, Japan	3,090	Lease expiring 1993
Warehouse	Tokyo, Japan	6,282	Lease expiring 1993
Office	Brackley, England	2,845	Lease expiring 1995
Warehouse	Brackley, England	1,122	Lease expiring 1995

The Motorcycles and Related Products segment has three facilities that perform manufacturing operations: Wauwatosa, Wisconsin, a suburb of Milwaukee (motorcycle power train production); Tomahawk, Wisconsin (fiberglass parts production and painting); and York, Pennsylvania (motorcycle parts fabrication, painting, and assembly). Harley completed the transition to a new paint facility at its York, Pennsylvania, location during 1992.

Harley anticipates that the size of the existing facilities should be adequate to meet its current goal of being able to produce 100,000 motorcycles annually by 1996.

The principal properties of the Transportation Vehicle segment are as follows:

TYPE OF FACILITY	LOCATION	SQUARE FEET	STATUS
Executive Offices	Wakarusa, IN	51,178	Owned
Manufacturing and Warehouse	Wakarusa, IN	842,367	Owned
Factory Service Center	Wakarusa, IN	41,138	Owned
Purchasing and Quality Cont.	Wakarusa, IN	23,850	Owned
Research and Development	Wakarusa, IN	38,120	Owned
Sales Facilities	Various	8,290	Leased
Manufacturing and Offices	Nappanee, IN	169,711	Owned
Manufacturing	Mishawaka, IN	16,180	Owned
Retail Dealership Facilities	Various	201,900	Owned
Retail Dealership Facilities	Various	2,724	Leased

The Transportation Vehicles segment's units are manufactured in approximately 30 separate buildings. Additionally, the segment owns 20 buildings used for administrative, storage, and other purposes. Substantially all of the facilities are located on three sites at or near the Transportation Vehicles segment's corporate headquarters in Wakarusa, Indiana. Harley owns all of the production facilities and the underlying parcels of land. Because recreational and commercial vehicles are produced largely through a labor-intensive assembly process, the facilities do not house extensive capital equipment. The Transportation Vehicle segment's present facilities are generally adequate for their current intended use. Capacity increases may be achieved at a relatively low cost, largely by adding production employees.

FINANCIAL PERFORMANCE

Harley's financial performance improved steadily from 1988 to 1992. Harley has been able to reduce its long-term debt from $168 million in 1988 to $19 million in 1992. Harley reported worldwide net sales during 1992 of $1.1 billion. Worldwide motorcycle demand continues to outpace production, and dealers throughout the world remain on an allocation program that limits the number of motorcycles that may be ordered. Harley expects worldwide motorcycle demand to outpace production through 1996.

Harley held approximately 63 percent of the superheavyweight segment (engine displacement of 851 cc and above) of the domestic motorcycle market during 1992 and 1991. United States registrations of superheavyweight motorcycles increased by 10,637 units (14.9 percent) during 1992. Although definitive market share information does not exist for many of the smaller foreign markets, Harley estimates that it holds an average market share of approximately 13 percent in the heavyweight segment (751 cc and above) of the foreign markets in which it competes. Outside of the United States, registration data are generally not available for the superheavyweight classification.

Total international revenues in the Motorcycles and Related Products segment increased 16.6 percent to $239.5 million during 1992. Revenue from international motorcycle sales and parts and accessories sales increased 17.1 percent and 13.5 percent, respectively, during 1992, despite reported consumer concerns regarding worldwide economic conditions. Over the past three years approximately 31 percent of all motorcycle unit production has been allocated and shipped to international markets.

Worldwide, the motorcycle parts and accessories business reported a 19.5 percent revenue increase over 1991. The MotorClothes line of rider accessories increased $15.3 million (approximately 45 percent) during the same period. The MotorClothes line has begun to attract "nontraditional" customers and is increasing floor traffic at dealerships. Margins on the MotorClothes line are slightly lower than the margins generated by the other major parts and accessories lines.

The Transportation Vehicles segment reported a $44.5 million (18.7 percent) revenue increase compared to 1991. The Recreational Vehicle division provided the majority of the increase. Improvements in market conditions, as well as introductions of several new products during the year, contributed to the Recreational Vehicle division's revenue increase. The division began shipping the new "bus style" Navigator motorhome at the end of the second quarter, which generated the division's largest single source of revenue increase during 1992. Revenue also benefited from a $16.6 million increase in total sales at the division's 12 retail Holiday World stores. Approximately $9.4 million of this increase was the result of two new retail Holiday World stores, in California, which opened at the beginning of 1992.

The Motorcycles and Related Products segment reported a $48.8 million (24.4 percent) increase in gross profit compared to 1991. Motorcycle volume increases accounted for approximately one-half of the change. Improvements in the gross profit percentage were primarily the result of a shift in motorcycle mix toward higher-margin custom units. The shift in product mix accounted for approximately one-third of the segment's increase in gross profit. The Motorcycle division's focus during 1993 was on identifying and eliminating manufacturing waste and inefficiencies and improving product quality rather than expanding capacity.

The Transportation Vehicles segment reported a $13.9 million (42.8 percent) increase in gross profit compared to 1991. The gross profit percentage for the segment improved to 16.4 percent during 1992 from 13.6 percent in 1991. Gross profit in the Recreational Vehicle division showed improvement due, in part, to the introduction of the Navigator motorhome. The division also benefited from a shift in product mix within the towable lines toward higher-margin, fifth-wheel products. The gross profit percentage at the Commercial Vehicle division increased during 1992, due to higher sales volume and lower warranty costs.

THE HARLEY IMAGE

Few motorcycle companies can elicit the name recognition and brand loyalty of Harley-Davidson. Harley's appeal is based on the thrill and prestige of owning and riding the king of big bikes. Harleys are known as sturdy, powerful, macho bikes that are not for wimps and kids—true bikes for the open road.

Part of the Harley image is built on an appreciation of tradition. Harley bikes are considered to be of classic design. The teardrop gas tanks, the "soft-tail" suspensions, and the low, uneven rumble of Harley engines are believed to be the substance of fundamental motorcycling. The company has a knack for combining the old and the new. For example, Harley recently offered a bike with a "springer" front-end fork. The spring fork had not been offered on Harley motorcycles since 1949. Harley made major technological improvements in the fork but maintained the original look and offered it on a limited-edition model. The springer fork was made to appeal to someone who wanted traditional style and custom design as well as modern advancements.

A worrisome problem with the Harley image, on the other hand, is the perceived connection between Harleys and "outlaw" groups. The negative image associated with the Road Warrior films affected sales in some areas to such a degree that the company has initiated a public relations campaign. The campaign gently attacks the biker image by directing the majority of advertising at young professionals. The message is that Harley-Davidson represents fun, recreation, and reliability. The company trumpets the fact that famous professionals such as the former baseball star Reggie Jackson ride Harleys, and advertisements picturing these celebrities atop their "hogs" further help the company's image. The campaign seems to work. More doctors, lawyers, and dentists have begun to purchase Harleys.

Harley also put tighter controls on licensing its name, ensuring it is not used in obscene ways. Harley is careful not to alienate their loyal "biker" customers, however. And the company continues to promulgate—even enhance—its tough image through advertising in motorcycle magazines. For example, one ad pictures a group of rather tough-looking bikers with the caption "Would you sell an unreliable bike to these guys? We don't!" Another ad shows a junkyard filled with scrapped Japanese bikes. The caption is, "Can you find a Harley in here?"

A related image problem for Harley is that it cannot attract very many women customers. Harleys are very big and heavy. The Harley low-rider series attracts some women customers because the bikes are lower and easier to get on. Notwithstanding this partial success, some Japanese companies introduced smaller, lighter, low-riding, inexpensive Harley look-alikes in a straightforward attempt to attract women buyers. Honda's Rebel (250 cc) and Yamaha's Route 66 (V-twin, 250 cc) are two such bikes that have become fairly successful with women.

Perhaps the most objective indicator of the strength of the image came from an unlikely source—Japan itself. The Japanese have made numerous attempts to copy Milwaukee designs. For example, Suzuki's Intruder (1,400 cc) went to great lengths to hide the radiator, because Harleys were air cooled. Yamaha's Virago (1,100 cc) and Kawasaki's Vulcan (1,500 cc) were V-twin street bikes conspicuously styled in the Harley tradition. Nevertheless, some analysts feel that Japanese imitations only serve to strengthen the mystique of the original. The more the Japanese try to make look-alike bikes, the more the real thing increases in value.

HARLEY'S FUTURE

During 1992 Harley shipped 3,000 motorcycles to Japan and could have sold many more. Harley is one of only a few firms actively apologizing to its dealers for not being able to meet demand. Virtually no Harley dealers in the United States or overseas have any retail inventory of Harley bikes. Consumers must get on a one- to two-year waiting list even to purchase a new Harley. Harley must expand capacity. The major questions are where, how, and when. Harley's top management plans to reach their 100,000 annual motorcycle output goal in 1996 by boosting production at existing facilities, rather than by hiring additional employees or building any new facilities. Some analysts believe that is impossible.

Divestiture of Holiday Rambler is another strategic issue being considered by Harley's management. Potential revenues from this sale could be used to finance plant expansion. Winnebago and Coachmen likely would be interested in Holiday Rambler. Proceeds could be used to build another manufacturing facility, perhaps in Europe.

Another strategic issue concerns Harley's 49 percent–owned Eagle Credit subsidiary. Eagle is attempting to provide "one-stop" financial services to Harley dealers and customers, including a credit card, floor-plan financing, consumer loans, and insurance. Formed in January 1993, Eagle Credit has become very successful in the $700 million motorcycle loan business. The Harley credit card, introduced in 1993, has over 20,000 cards approved. Should Harley diversify further into the consumer finance market?

Develop a strategic plan for Richard Teerlink, Harley's president and chief executive officer.

EXHIBIT 17-1 Harley-Davidson, Inc. Selected Financial Data *(In thousands, except per share amounts)*

	1993	1992	1991	1990	1989
Income statement data:					
Net sales	$1,217,428	$1,105,284	$939,863	$864,600	$790,967
Cost of goods sold	880,269	808,871	706,140	635,551	596,940
Gross profit	337,159	296,413	233,723	229,049	194,027
Selling, administrative, and engineering	267,353*	199,216	165,078	145,674	127,606
Income from operations	69,806	97,197	68,645	83,375	66,421
Other income (expense):					
Interest expense, net	(831)	(4,912)	(7,312)	(9,701)	(14,322)
Lawsuit judgment	—	2,200	—	(7,200)	—
Other	(2,460)	(5,676)	(3,239)	(3,857)	910
	(3,291)	(8,388)	(10,551)	(20,758)	(13,412)
Income from continuing operations before income taxes, extraordinary items, and accounting changes	66,515	88,809	58,094	62,617	53,009
Provision for income taxes	48,072	34,636	21,122	24,309	20,399
Income from continuing operations before extraordinary items and accounting changes	18,443	54,173	36,972	38,308	32,610
Discontinued operation, net of tax	—	—	—	—	3,590
Income before extraordinary items and accounting changes	18,443	54,173	36,972	38,308	36,200
Extraordinary items, net of tax	—	(388)	—	(478)	(3,258)
Income before accounting changes	18,443	53,785	36,972	37,830	32,942
Accounting changes, net of tax	(30,328)	—	—	—	—
Net income (loss)	$ (11,885)	$ 53,785	$ 36,972	$ 37,830	$ 32,942
Weighted average common shares assuming no dilution	37,950	35,889	35,580	35,576	34,548
Per common share:					

EXHIBIT 17-1 *Continued*

	1993	1992	1991	1990	1989
Per common share:					
Income from continuing operations	$.49	$1.51	$1.04	$1.08	$.94
Discontinued operation	—	—	—	—	.10
Extraordinary items, net of tax	—	(.01)	—	(.02)	(.09)
Accounting changes, net of tax	(.80)	—	—	—	—
Net Income (loss)	$(.31)	$1.50	$1.04	$1.06	$.95
Dividends declared	$.12	—	—	—	—
Balance sheet data:					
Working capital	$142,996	$ 96,232	$ 64,212	$ 50,152	$ 51,313
Total assets	583,285	522,164	474,233	407,467	378,929
Short-term debt, including current					
maturities of long-term debt	21,369	16,965	41,089	23,859	26,932
Long-term debt, less current maturities	3,429	2,360	46,906	48,339	74,795
Total debt	24,789	19,325	87,995	72,198	101,727
Stockholders' equity	324,912	335,380	238,000	198,775	156,247

*Includes $57.0 million charge related primarily to the write-off of goodwill at the Transportation Vehicles segment (Holiday Rambler).

Source: *Annual Report*, 1993.

EXHIBIT 17-2 Motorcycle Unit Shipments and Consolidated Net Sales 1993 Compared to 1992

	1993	1992	CHANGE	% CHANGE
Motorcylce unit shipments	81,696	76,495	5,201	6.8%
Net Sales (in millions):				
Motorcycles	$ 734.3	$ 667.2	$ 67.1	10.0%
Motorcycle Parts and Accessories	199.0	155.7	43.3	27.8
Total Motorcycles and Related Products	933.3	822.9	110.4	13.4
Recreational Vehicles	192.7	202.1	(9.4)	(4.6)
Commercial Vehicles	78.9	67.9	11.0	16.2
Other	12.5	12.4	0.1	1.1
Total Transportation Vehicles	284.1	282.4	1.7	0.6
Consolidated Harley-Davidson, Inc.	$1,217.4	$1,105.3	$112.1	10.1%

Source: *Annual Report*, 1993.

EXHIBIT 17-3 Consolidated Gross Profit 1993 Compared to 1992 *(Dollars in millions)*

	1993	1992	CHANGE	PERCENT OF SALES 1993	PERCENT OF SALES 1992
Motorcycles and Related Products	$292.0	$250.0	$42.0	$31.3%	30.4%
Transportation Vehicles	45.2	46.4	(1.2)	15.9	16.4
Consolidated Harley-Davidson, Inc.	$337.2	$296.4	$40.8	27.7%	26.8%

Source: *Annual Report*, 1993.

EXHIBIT 17-4 Harley-Davidson, Inc. Consolidated Statements of Income
(In thousands, except per share amounts)

	YEARS ENDED DECEMBER 31		
	1992	1991	1990
Net sales	$1,105,284	$939,863	$864,600
Cost of goods sold	808,871	706,140	635,551
Gross profit	296,413	233,723	229,049
Selling, administrative, and engineering	199,216	165,078	145,674
Income from operations	97,197	68,645	83,375
Interest income	956	950	1,736
Interest expense	(5,868)	(8,262)	(11,437)
Lawsuit judgment	2,200	—	(7,200)
Other-net	(5,676)	(3,239)	(3,857)
Income before provision for income taxes and extraordinary item	88,809	58,094	62,617
Provision for income taxes	34,636	21,122	24,309
Income before extraordinary item	54,173	36,972	38,308
Extraordinary item, loss on debt repurchases, net of tax	(388)	—	(478)
Net income	$ 53,785	$ 36,972	$ 37,830
Earnings per common share assuming no dilution:			
Income before extraordinary item	$1.51	$1.04	$1.08
Extraordinary item	(.01)	—	(.02)
Net income	$1.50	$1.04	$1.06
Earnings per income share assuming full dilution:			
Income before extraordinary item	$1.46	$1.04	$1.08
Extraordinary item	(.01)	—	(.02)
Net income	$1.45	$1.04	$1.06

Source: *Annual Report*, 1992.

EXHIBIT 17-5 Harley-Davidson, Inc. Consolidated Balance Sheets
(In thousands, except share amounts)

DECEMBER 31,	1993	1992
ASSETS		
Current assets:		
Cash and cash equivalents	$ 77,709	$ 44,122
Accounts receivable, net of allowance for		
doubtful accounts	86,031	93,178
Inventories	140,151	94,428
Deferred income taxes	20,290	24,120
Prepaid expenses	9,571	9,617
Total current assets	333,758	265,465
Property, plant, and equipment, net	205,768	183,787
Goodwill, net	—	56,710
Deferred income taxes	11,676	—
Other assets	32,083	16,202
	583,285	522,164
LIABILITIES AND STOCKHOLDERS' EQUITY		
Current liabilities:		
Notes payable	$ 20,580	$ 15,933
Accounts payable	56,350	58,004
Accrued expenses and other liabilities	113,043	94,264
Current maturities of long-term debt	789	1,032
Total current liabilities	190,762	169,233
Long-term liabilities	12,612	7,224
Deferred income taxes	—	10,327
Postretirement health-care benefits	54,999	—
Commitments and contingencies (Note 7)		
Stockholders' equity:		
Series A Junior Participating preferred stock,		
none issued	—	—
Common stock, 38,452,490 shares issued in		
1993 and 1992	385	385
Additional paid-in capital	137,150	131,053
Retained earnings	189,410	205,850
Cumulative foreign currency translation		
adjustment	186	757
	327,131	338,045
Less:		
Treasury stock (456,464 and 567,284 shares		
in 1993 and 1992, respectively), at cost	(1,583)	(1,028)
Unearned compensation	(636)	(1,637)
Total stockholders' equity	324,912	335,380
	$583,285	$522,164

Source: *Annual Report*, 1993.

EXHIBIT 17-6 Harley-Davidson, Inc Consolidated Statements of Cash Flows *(in thousands)*

YEARS ENDED DECEMBER 31,	1993	1992	1991
Cash flows from operating activities:			
Net income (loss)	$(11,885)	$53,785	$36,972
Adjustments to reconcile net income (loss) to net cash provided by operating activities:			
Goodwill and restructuring charges	57,024	—	—
Depreciation and amortization	33,272	29,410	22,603
Deferred income taxes	(25,922)	(993)	(2,981)
Lawsuit:			
Reversal	—	(2,200)	—
Settlement paid	—	(5,000)	—
Long-term employee benefits	57,386	1,369	1,258
Loss on disposal of long-term assets	626	1,164	1,346
Equity in net loss of joint ventures	1,427	—	—
Net changes in other current assets and current liabilities	(15,756)	10,380	(9,772)
Total adjustments	108,057	34,130	12,454
Net cash provided by operating activities	96,172	87,915	49,426
Cash flows from investing activities:			
Net capital expenditures	(55,202)	(47,229)	(47,766)
Investment in joint ventures	(10,350)	—	—
Other-net	(1,484)	(2,727)	(766)
Net cash used in investing activities	(67,036)	(49,956)	(48,532)
Cash flows from financing activities:			
Net increase (decrease) in notes payable	4,647	(23,593)	17,175
Payments on long-term debt	(1,183)	(9,420)	(1,771)
Dividends paid	(4,555)	—	—
Issuance of stock under employee stock plans	5,542	8,257	620
Net cash provided by (used in) financing activities	4,451	(24,756)	16,024
Net increase in cash and cash equivalents	33,587	13,203	16,918
Cash and cash equivalents:			
At beginning of year	44,122	30,919	14,001
At end of year	$ 77,709	$44,122	$30,919

Source: *Annual Report*, 1993.

EXHIBIT 17-7 Harley-Davidson, Inc. Consolidated Statements of Changes in Stockholders' Equity
(In thousands, except share amounts)

	Common Stock		Additional Paid-In Capital	Retained Earnings	Cumulative Foreign Currency Translation Adjustment	Treasury Stock	Unearned Compensation
	Issued Shares	Balance					
Balance December 31, 1990	$18,310,000	$183	$ 87,115	$115,093	$ 995	$(771)	$(3,840)
Net income	—	—	—	36,972	—	—	—
Amortization of unearned compensation, net of cancellations	—	—	—	—	—	(218)	(1,280)
Exercise of stock options	—	—	615	—	—	5	—
Foreign currency translation adjustment	—	—	—	—	571	—	—
Balance December 31, 1991	18,310,000	183	87,730	152,065	1,566	(984)	(2,560)
Two-for-one common stock split	18,310,000	183	(183)	—	—	—	—
Net income	—	—	—	53,785	—	—	—
Amortization of unearned compensation, net of cancellations	—	—	—	—	—	(73)	923
Exercise of stock options	—	—	2,757	—	—	29	—
Tax benefit of restricted shares and stock options	—	—	5,471	—	—	—	—

EXHIBIT 17-7 *Continued*

	Common Stock		Additional Paid-in Capital	Retained Earnings	Cumulative Foreign Currency Translation Adjustment	Treasury Stock	Unearned Compensation
	Issued Shares	Balance					
Conversions of subordinated debentures	1,832,490	19	35,278	—	—	—	—
Foreign currency translation adjustment	—	—	—	—	(809)	—	—
Balance December 31, 1992	38,452,490	385	131,053	205,850	757	(1,028)	(1,637)
Net loss	—	—	—	(11,885)	—	—	—
Dividends declared	—	—	—	(4,555)	—	—	—
Amortization of unearned compensation, net of cancellations	—	—	—	—	—	(566)	1,001
Exercise of stock options	—	—	2,044	—	—	11	—
Tax benefit of restricted shares and stock options	—	—	4,053	—	—	—	—
Foreign currency translation adjustment	—	—	—	—	(571)	—	—
Balance December 31, 1993	$38,452,490	$385	$137,150	$189,410	$ 186	$(1,583)	$ (636)

Source: *Annual Report,* 1993.

EXHIBIT 17-8 Business Segments

The Company operates in two business segments: Motorcycles and Related Products and Transportation Vehicles. Information by industry segment is set forth below (in thousands):

	1993	1992	1991
Net Sales:			
Motorcycles and Related Products	$ 933,262	$ 822,929	$701,969
Transportation Vehicles	284,166	282,355	237,894
	$1,217,428	$1,105,284	$939,863
Income (loss) from operations:			
Motorcycles and Related Products	$ 136,217	$ 102,300	$ 89,551
Transportation Vehicles[a]	(59,533)	2,137	(13,427)
General corporate expenses	(6,878)	(7,240)	(7,479)
	69,806	97,197	68,645
Interest expense, net	(831)	(4,912)	(7,312)
Other:			
Motorcycles and Related Products:			
Lawsuit judgment reversal	—	2,200	—
Other	(3,249)	(3,811)	(1,355)
Transportation Vehicles	789	(1,865)	(1,884)
	(2,460)	(3,476)	(3,239)
Income before provision for income taxes, extraordinary item and accounting changes	$ 66,515	$ 88,809	$ 58,094

[a]Includes a $57.0 million charge related primarily to a write-off of goodwill in 1993.

	MOTORCYCLES AND RELATED PRODUCTS	TRANSPORTATION VEHICLES	CORPORATE	CONSOLIDATED
1993				
Identifiable assets	$437,813	$134,699	$10,773	$583,285
Depreciation and amortization	27,225	5,813	234	33,272
Net capital expenditures	52,324	2,766	112	55,202
1992				
Identifiable assets	$341,940	$178,252	$1,972	$522,164
Depreciation and amortization	22,630	6,639	141	29,410
Net capital expenditures	12,276	4,754	199	47,229
1991				
Identifiable assets	$281,790	$189,326	$3,117	$474,233
Depreciation and amortization	15,404	7,058	141	22,603
Net capital expenditures	43,621	2,987	1,158	47,766

There were no sales between business segments for the years ended December 31, 1993, 1992 or 1991.

(b)Foreign operations

EXHIBIT 17-8 *Continued*

Included in the consolidated financial statements are the following amounts relating to foreign affiliates:
(In thousands)

	1993	1992	1991
Assets	$ 49,109	$ 37,962	$ 31,081
Liabilities	40,769	27,716	15,882
Net sales	144,639	132,557	99,441
Net income	5,113	5,315	5,558

Export sales of domestic subsidiaries to nonaffiliated customers were $117.6 million, $106.9 million and $105.7 million in 1993, 1992 and 1991, respectively.

Source: *Annual Report*, 1993.

CASE 18

WINNEBAGO INDUSTRIES—1994

FRED R. DAVID
Francis Marion University

What has six feet of stand-up head room, kitchen, dinette, shower, toilet, and closet; sleeps four; and gets 22 miles per gallon on the highway? It's called LeSharo, a motor home made by Winnebago. Saving money is nice, but it is not the real reason people travel in a motor home. Motor homing is just plain fun. Motor homers are an adventurous lot—they like to go, see, and do. Florida residents have replaced Californians as the most active motor home campers. New Yorkers are third on the "most on the go" list. Recreational vehicle (RV) owners say that they not only save money when camping but can avoid the bother of having to stop for restaurants and bathrooms.

According to a recent study, motor home traveling is much less expensive than traveling by car or plane and staying in a motel. Motor homers stop when there is something to see and do. They often spend summers where it is cool and winters where it is warm.

The name *Winnebago* is considered synonymous with the term *motor home*. However, Winnebago—headquartered in Forest City, Iowa (515-582-3535)—today has fallen behind Fleetwood Enterprises of Riverside, California, the industry's recognized front-runner. Winnebago's fiscal year 1993 ended August 28, with a net income of $9.28 million, following four consecutive yearly losses totaling more than $62 million.

EARLY MOTOR HOMING

Motor homing has a rich history. Native Americans were the first Americans to engage in traveling with their home hundreds of years ago. They did so for both practical and recreational reasons. For them survival depended on staying close to sources of food, so as herds moved and the weather changed, Native Americans picked up their lightweight homes and traveled.

The first motor home was built in 1915 to take persons from the Atlantic Coast to San Francisco. It had wooden wheels and hard rubber tires. It was promoted as having all the comforts of an ocean cruiser. By the 1920s the house car had become a fixture in the United States and a symbol of freedom. All kinds of house cars could be seen traveling across America's dirt roads. They ranged from what looked like large moving cigars to two-story houses with porches on wheels. But these house cars featured poor weight distribution, poor insulation, and poor economy. From the 1930s to the 1950s they gave way in popularity to the trailer.

In the mid-1950s motor homes were called motorized trailers. They were overweight, underpowered, and poorly insulated, but still a vast improvement over the house cars of the 1920s. In the 1960s motor homing became much more popular, largely as a result of the innovations of Winnebago. From Forest City, Iowa, where the company was founded in 1958, Winnebago set the pace for new development of motor homes. The Winnebago name became a household word. Buyers of motor homes were asked, "When will your Winnebago be delivered?"

WINNEBAGO: 1958 TO 1992

Winnebago's phenomenal growth during the 1960s came to an end in 1970. That year was marked by a recession, and Winnebago's stock plunged nearly 60 percent before recovering. The OPEC oil embargoes of 1973 and 1974 had disastrous effects on Winnebago because gas was either unavailable or unaffordable. The company's net income averaged less than 1 percent of sales between 1973 and 1978. From a level of $229 million in 1978, Winnebago's sales dropped to $92 million in 1979.

A troubled board of directors called John Hanson, founder of the company, out of retirement in March 1979, reelecting him chairman of the board and president of Winnebago. To resolve Winnebago's problems, Hanson reduced the number of employees from 4,000 to 800 in less than nine months. He initiated the development of a propane conversion system for motor homes. This system allows users to power their vehicles with less costly propane, which eliminates worries about the supply and cost of gasoline. Hanson also pioneered the development of a lightweight, fuel-efficient motor home powered by a revolutionary heavy-duty diesel engine.

Winnebago was nearly forced into bankruptcy in 1980 when the company lost $13.5 million. But conditions improved. Employment at Winnebago increased from 800 in 1980 to 1,400 by May 1981. The company introduced a fuel-efficient, lightweight, aerodynamically designed line of motor homes. In 1982 Winnebago entered into an agreement with five manufacturers to allow use of the Winnebago name on products ranging from camping equipment to outdoor clothing. Winnebago declared its first cash dividend on common stock in October 1982: 10¢ per share. In 1983 Winnebago introduced a new family of front-wheel-drive vehicles powered by Renault diesel engines. Sales of $239 million in 1983 set a company record, and the number of Winnebago employees increased to 2,200. On August 10, 1983, Hanson was inducted into the Recreational Vehicle/Motor Home Hall of Fame in South Bend, Indiana. In 1984 Winnebago Industries won an award for the outstanding company turnaround in 1983.

In the mid-1980s, Winnebago's choice of Renault as supplier of its diesel engine for front-wheel-drive RVs came back to haunt them. The diesel engines were unreliable, and significant damage was done to Winnebago's reputation as a premier motor home manufacturer. The diesels were discontinued in 1988. However, the sad saga has not ended. In 1991 the Federal Trade Commission (FTC) decided to investigate whether Winnebago engaged in deceptive practices in selling the line of diesel-powered motor homes (1983–1986) under the names Winnebago LeSharo and Itaska

Phasar and van conversions called Centauri. Although the number of vehicles involved is small by industry standards, the problems represent one of the biggest cases of vehicle failure in terms of the percentage that failed. Apparently, the FTC is concerned about Winnebago's reluctance to deal with owners' problems effectively and take positive (reasonable) steps in resolving them.

In 1985 Winnebago's motor home sales were $395 million, up from $376 million in 1984. However, sales of other RVs and equipment, including van conversions and vans, declined to $19.3 million in 1985 from $21.2 million in 1984. Gross profits as a percentage of sales decreased in 1985 to 13.7 percent from 15.9 percent in 1984. The Winnebago Acceptance Corporation (WAC) provides financing for Winnebago dealers; its net income in 1985 was $456,000, down from $3.1 million in 1984. Overall, Winnebago's net income declined to $18 million in 1985 from $27 million in 1984.

Financial disappointments in fiscal year 1985 led to the formation of a new management team in 1986. Gerald Gilbert was elected chief executive officer and president. He had previously been president of a joint-venture company between Control Data Corporation and Honeywell, Inc. Clyde Church was elected to the newly created position of vice president of product planning and engineering. Richard Berreth was elected vice president of operations, and Bryan Hays was elected vice president of sales and marketing. Winnebago made its first appearance on the *Fortune* 500 list of the largest U.S. manufacturers in April 1986. In October Winnebago celebrated the production of its 200,000th motor home in 20 years. John Hanson (then 73) served as chairman of the board of directors.

Fiscal year 1987 was good for Winnebago, but fiscal year 1988 was bad. Net earnings declined from $19.9 million in 1987 to $2.7 million in 1988, although sales for 1988 increased to $425 million compared to $406 million in 1987. In April 1988 Winnebago signed an agreement to begin selling Winnebago products in 14 European countries. Dealerships were established in Sweden, Norway, Germany, Austria, and France. In August 1988 Winnebago signed an agreement with the Mitsubishi Corporation of Japan to sell Winnebago and Itasca motor homes in Japan. Winnebago also has an agreement with firms in Taiwan and Great Britain to begin selling its motor homes.

Fiscal 1988 was the first full year of operation of Cycle-Sat, a television advertising broadcast distribution company acquired by Winnebago. More that 500 television stations signed agreements to use the Cyclecypher system for receiving spot television commercials via satellite, and 320 stations completed installation of the equipment.

Winnebago's performance in fiscal year 1989 was disappointing. The company's share of the $2 billion U.S. motor home industry market declined to 21 percent from 22 percent the previous year, and the company lost $4.675 million.

Fiscal 1990 brought further bad news for the firm as revenues declined 25 percent, losses increased fourfold to $17.8 million, and dividends were reduced to 10¢ per share versus 40¢ in 1989.

Winnebago incurred record losses of $29.3 million in 1991, with sales declining 33 percent. This year was disastrous and brought Winnebago to its knees. Winnebago was not the lone firm in the motor home industry experiencing problems; revenues in the industry declined 10 percent to $2.98 billion, while unit sales sank 16 percent to 61,200 units. Winnebago's share of the market deteriorated to 18 percent from 20 percent.

John K. Hanson, age 80, is the active chairman of the board and CEO of Winnebago. He and his family control 47 percent of Winnebago's common stock, which hit a dismal low of $2.125 per share in 1991. Hanson is the recognized monarch of Winnebago and often acts the part. He is not the least bit hesitant in firing anyone who he believes is not performing, including CEOs. He even "coaxed" his son John to resign as deputy chairman. The youngest son, Paul, was at one time associated with the firm as a financial advisor. However, he is alleged to have lost a personal fortune of $4 million in less than a five-year period. There appears to be no family member in the wings prepared to take the ship's help from Hanson.

In 1992 Winnebago's sales increased 32 percent, but net income was a negative $10.6 million. Several new products were introduced in 1992, including the new bus-styled Vectra. The company created a new subsidiary in 1992, Winnebago Industries Europe, headquartered in Cologne, Germany, to expand operations internationally. Also in 1992 the company introduced the Winnebago Brave, Winnebago Warrior, Itasca Passage, and Itasca Sunrise. In the March–April 1992 issue of *Consumers Digest* magazine, Winnebago received the "Best Buy" ratings on several of its 1992 motor homes. Winnebago's Original Equipment Manufacturer (OEM) division, which sells component parts to outside manufacturers, increased 30 percent in 1992 to a record $17.4 million. Winnebago's Cycle-Sat subsidiary, which distributes radio and television commercials, grew in 1992 with 93 new television stations joining the Cycle-Sat network.

WINNEBAGO—1993

Winnebago rebounded in fiscal 1993 as revenues increased 30.2 percent and net income was a positive $9.7 million. The company's motor home shipments increased 22.9 percent for the year, with industry market share surpassing 19 percent. Fiscal 1993 revenues for Cycle-Sat increased 45 percent to $14.8 million as the network's client base rose 65 percent. Winnebago's OEM sales increased 12 percent in fiscal 1993 while sales of customized vans and trucks increased 25 percent. Winnebago moved its European headquarters location in fiscal 1993 to Saarbucken, Germany. European sales increased, especially in the United Kingdom. Sales in Japan were stagnant partly because of the depressed Japanese economy.

Winnebago manufactures three principal kinds of recreational vehicles: Type A motor homes, Type C motor homes, and van conversions. Type A motor homes are constructed on a chassis that already has the engine and drive components. They range in length from 22 to 37 feet and in price from $28,500 to over $103,000. An example of the Type A motor home is the luxurious Elante, which offers leather seating, central air, a double-door refrigerator, a water purification system, a four-burner range, a water heater with electronic ignition, a powered range hood with deluxe monitor panel and digital clock, a shower, and carpeting throughout. Other Type A motor homes include the Chieftain, Windcruiser, Itasca, and the new Vectra. The Winnebago Brave and Itasca Sunrise models are the company's top-selling vehicles, although the Winnebago Adventurer and Itasco Suncruiser are popular. Sales of Winnebago's Type A motor homes have increased three years in a row to a high of 6,095 vehicles in 1993.

Type C motor homes are constructed on a van chassis; the driver's compartment is accessible to the living area. Type C motor homes are compact and easy to drive. They range from 21 to 29 feet in length and have five popular floor plans. Typical options of a Type C vehicle include six feet of head room, shower, stove, sink, refrigerator, and two double beds. Winnebago's Minnie Winnie vehicle is the most popular Type C motor home in the country. The company's Itasca Sundancer, Winnebago Warrior, and Itasca Spirit also are popular. Sales of Winnebago's Type C motor homes have fallen four years in a row to a low of 1,998 vehicles in 1993.

The third type of RV manufactured by Winnebago is the van conversion. These vehicles are conventional vans manufactured by Ford, General Motors, and Chrysler that are custom tailored by Winnebago with special interiors, exteriors, windows, and vents. An example is the 19-foot Centauri, the largest van conversion available. On a recent 3,000-mile test trip, the Centauri averaged 24.11 miles per gallon. In many American households, van conversions are replacing the family car as the vehicle of choice. These vehicles can turn a long family trip from an ordeal into a pleasant adventure.

Marketing. The peak selling season for RVs has historically been spring and summer. Type A and Type C motor homes are marketed under the Winnebago and Itasca brand names and are sold through a network of 310 dealers, down from 340 in 1992, in the United States and to a limited extent in Canada and other foreign countries. Thirteen of these dealers accounted for more than 25 percent of Winnebago's motor home sales; one dealer accounted for 3.5 percent of motor home sales. Most Winnebago dealers also are dealers for automobiles and other motor home lines, but all dealers must provide complete service for RVs. Sales agreements with dealers are renewed on an annual or biannual basis.

Foreign sales by Winnebago are less that 10 percent of net sales. Foreign sales opportunities in Canada, Europe, and Japan are a priority at Winnebago. The largest international distributor is Mitsubishi Corporation, with a network of 21 authorized dealers in 46 locations throughout Japan.

Winnebago has 29 field sales and service personnel to aid its dealers. The company promotes its products through advertisements in national RV magazines, cable television, radio, newspapers, and trade shows. A substantial portion of Winnebago's sales of RVs to dealers is made on cash terms. Most dealers are financed on a "floor plan" basis under which a bank or finance company lends the dealer all of the purchase price, collateralized by a lien, or title to, the merchandise purchased. Winnebago, on request of the lending institution, will execute a repurchase agreement. These agreements provide that in the event of dealer default Winnebago will repurchase the financed merchandise.

Numerous Winnebago caravans are arranged each year to travel across the United States, Mexico, and Canada. With over 60,000 members since 1972, the Winnebago International Travelers' Club is one of the world's largest motor home associations. They organize national, state, and local Winnebago rallies, have a monthly newspaper, and offer discounts at KOA campsites nationwide.

The Winnebago Logo. Eighty percent of all Americans recognize the Winnebago name. Nine licensees currently pay royalties to Winnebago for using the company's name on products ranging from camping equipment to clothing. Presently, 2,000 retail outlets carry one or more products bearing the Winnebago logo.

Although licensing of the Winnebago name began in 1982, revenues to date have not been significant. There are now Winnebago bass and fishing boats, marine flotation devices, backpacks, sports bags, travel bags, slacks, shorts, shirts, vests, jackets, gloves, socks, hats, stoves, lanterns, grills, sleeping bags, air mattresses, tents, screenhouses, and suitcases. Winnebago's Scout 1 sleeping bag, Chieftain IV tent, Double Diamond air mattress, and other products have been advertised in many magazines.

Production Facilities. Winnebago has major production facilities in Forest City, Iowa. These facilities comprise over 1.4 million square feet and contain the company's manufacturing, maintenance, and service operations. The company also has 698,000 square feet of warehouse and executive office space in Forest City. Winnebago leases one manufacturing facility and one storage facility in Hampton, Iowa (74,000 square feet and 10,000 square feet), a manufacturing facility in Lorimor, Iowa (17,200 square feet), and a manufacturing facility in Garner, Iowa, which is subleased to Northern Iowa Electronics (NIE) (40,000 square feet). Winnebago owns a 14,400-square-foot facility in Forest City that is leased to Cycle-Sat. All corporate facilities in Forest City are located on approximately 784 acres of land owned by Winnebago. The company's European subsidiary recently purchased a 16,700-square-foot distribution and service facility in Kirkel, Germany.

Winnebago purchases its Type A and Type C chassis and engines from the Chevrolet Division of the General Motors Corporation, Ford Motor Company, Oshkosh Truck Corporation, and Toyota. General Motors is Winnebago's largest vendor for vans.

Winnebago has four 1,000-foot assembly lines for producing motor homes. Statistical process control is practiced at Winnebago and has enhanced the quality of its van products. As a motor home flows down the assembly line, quality control is carefully monitored. Units are randomly taken from the line for a thorough examination. The performance of every RV is tested before it is delivered to a dealer's lot. The company makes sure that all of its motor home components meet or exceed federal and durability standards. Some of the tests routinely performed include lamination strength, appliance performance, chip resistance, vibration, drop, salt spray, and crash tests.

Research and Development. Winnebago spent approximately $1.08 million, $1.82 million, and $1.63 million on research and development during fiscal 1993, 1992, and 1991, respectively. These activities employed 17, 34, and 28 full-time employees, respectively, during these years.

Winnebago uses computer technology to design its motor homes. The company has a state-of-the-art, computer-aided design/computer-aided manufacturing (CAD/CAM) system. This system aids in producing low-cost sheet metal parts, new paint lines for steel and aluminum parts, and modifications of assembly equipment.

Winnebago has had a 40,000-square-foot product-testing facility at Forest City since 1989. This facility houses some of the most sophisticated technology being used in the RV industry, such as a high- and low-temperature chamber for subjecting parts to extreme temperatures and high stress.

Cycle-Sat. Cycle-Sat is in the satellite courier and tape duplication business, specializing in the satellite transmission of commercials to television stations. Fiscal year 1993 was its sixth full year of operation. Cycle-Sat continues to expand its automated distribution system. Cycle-Sat has a patent for its cyclecypher and its network distribution process.

Until fiscal 1993 Cycle-Sat had been losing money annually since it began operations. Cycle-Sat has a satellite-supported duplication and distribution center in Memphis, Tennessee, and additional offices in Los Angeles, New York City, and Chicago.

WINNEBAGO'S EXTERNAL ENVIRONMENT

Winnebago's motor homes can attract a low-frills buyer desiring the most stripped-down RV, the person with expensive tastes desiring the ultimate in RV luxury, and everyone in between. RVs can be purchased or rented. Many families unable to buy a mobile home rent one to take on vacation. As the baby boomers age and approach retirement, many of them will consider selling their primary residence, purchasing and moving into a motor home, and traveling to any point they desire in North America.

The motel and hotel industries have been experiencing an oversupply of available rooms, which has resulted in extremely low room rates. Compared to the cost of owning/renting and operating an RV, the costs of staying in a motor home versus a motel are about the same if not a bit lower in favor of the motel. Motor home sales historically increase whenever travel, tourism, and vacationing gain in popularity. The converse is also true.

Lower fuel prices, interest rates, inflation rates, and a robust, fully employed economy spur motor home sales. Conversely, when the economy is stagnant or receding, and fuel prices are high along with inflation and interest rates, motor home sales suffer. In 1993, interest rates, gas prices, and inflation rates were low, so Winnebago prospered.

There are about 122,000 campsites in U.S. state parks, including 4,500 maintained by the U.S. Forest Service and 100 in the National Parks System. In addition, there are more than 15,000 private campgrounds and over 1,620 county parks. Winnebagos can access nearly all of these sites.

COMPETITORS

Twelve firms account for 80 percent of the RV industry's volume. Among the largest publicly held are Fleetwood Enterprises, Winnebago Industries, Coachmen Industries, Rexhall Industries, Mallard Coach, Kit Manufacturing, Harley-Davidson, and Skyline Corporation. Of all the competitors, Fleetwood Enterprises is first in sales, followed by Coachman and then Winnebago. The following is a list of major motor home competitors:

COMPANY	1993 REVENUES	NUMBER OF EMPLOYEES	LOCATION
Fleetwood Enterprises, Inc.	$1,589.3 M	12,000	Riverside, CA
Coachman Industries, Inc.	292.8 M	1,854	Elkhart, IN
Mark III Industries, Inc.	750.0 M	2,165	Ocala, FL
Jayco, Inc.	160.0 M	975	Middlebury, IN
Glaval Corp.	130.0 M	850	Elkhart, IN
Newmar Corp.	65.0 M	350	Nappanee, IN
Monaco Coach Corp.	65.0 M	260	Junction City, OR
Tiffin Motor Homes, Inc.	80.0 M	200	Red Bay, AL

Fleetwood. Fleetwood Enterprises is the nation's largest producer of both RVs and manufactured housing. It holds 30 percent of the RV market. The RV line includes conventional Type A motor homes, chopped-van Type C motor homes, travel trailers, fifth-wheel travel trailers, folding camping trailers, and truck campers. Motor homes represent 62 percent of Fleetwood's sales while mobile home sales comprise 38 percent of revenues.

Fleetwood stayed profitable through the recession of 1990–1991. Two factors enhance Fleetwood's RV sales performance: (1) concentration on ringing up sales even when margins must be slashed and (2) innovative marketing. Its products, even virtually identical ones, are sold under a number of names. Folding campers sell under the name Coleman (the famous brand that it acquired in 1989); motor homes sell under the names Pace Arrow, Southwind, Cambria, Limited, Flair, Jamboree, and Tioga; and travel trailers are sold as Avion, Prowler, Terry, and Wilderness brands. For Fleetwood, the payoff is more presence and enhanced sales.

Fleetwood recently acquired a Germany-based luxury-priced motorhome manufacturer named Nielsmen and Bischoff. This acquisition paves the way for expanded distribution of Fleetwood recreational vehicles in Europe. Fleetwood is adding 20 percent more production capacity to its base of 27 plants in order to meet rising demand in both its motor homes and mobile homes.

FUTURE PLANS, PROBLEMS, AND CONCERNS

Recreational vehicle demand tends to be robust in the earlier stages of an economic recovery. This phenomenon held true in 1993 in the United States and may also characterize Europe and Japan in 1994 and 1995.

Winnebago Industries, Inc. has started converting Chevrolet half-ton two-wheel-drive and four-wheel-drive pickups and Suburban sport utility vehicles featuring walnut interior wood accents and customized exteriors with fiberglass running boards, tailgate protectors, and bug screens. The pickup conversion packages will retail from $3,500 to $4,225 while the Suburban conversions will cost $5,065 to $6,500.

Winnebago Industries, Inc. plans to double its van conversion sales as part of a long-range strategy to play a major role in the market. Winnebago has previously concentrated on the motor home market. Not interested in the price wars in the entry-level van conversion segment, Winnebago is focusing instead on the mid- to high-priced models. The company's wholesale base price for a conversion is from $5,500 to $5,800. A Special Edition could range from $10,000 to $12,000. Projected van conversion sales were from 1,600 to 1,800 in FY 1993.

Fleetwood is a major manufacturer of mobile homes, including both single-wide and double-wide versions. Should Winnebago consider widening the scope of its business beyond motor homes?

Winnebago appears to suffer from management instability. Hanson has hired and fired four presidents in five years. This type of environment does not enhance the morale of management. Members of management tend to hold back innovativeness, free thinking, and the willingness to take risks for fear that such qualities could lead to their demise. Hanson is over 80 years old. Should he be encouraged to retire?

How does the opening of markets in Eastern Europe and the countries that comprise the former Soviet Union affect Winnebago? Are these the types of markets in which Winnebago should invest some of its limited capital? What emphasis should the firm place on international operation in the future? Would Mexico be a good area to target now that NAFTA is a reality?

EXHIBIT 18-1 Net Revenues by Major Product Class (Dollars in thousands)

YEAR ENDED (1)	AUGUST 28, 1993	AUGUST 29, 1992	AUGUST 31, 1991	AUGUST 25, 1990	AUGUST 26, 1989
Motor Homes	$ 326,861	$ 245,908	$ 180,878	$286,713	$389,224
	85.1%	83.4%	81.2%	86.2%	89.0%
Other Recreation Vehicle Revenues (2)	17,655	17,126	15,586	22,039	22,455
	4.6%	5.8%	7.0%	6.6%	5.1%
Other Manufactured Products Revenues (3)	20,344	18,090	13,974	11,423	10,744
	5.3%	6.1%	6.3%	3.4%	2.5%
Total Manufactured Products Revenues	364,860	281,124	210,438	320,175	422,423
	95.0%	95.3%	94.5%	96.2%	96.6%
Service Revenues (4)	19,223	13,870	12,210	12,658	15,077
	5.0%	4.7%	5.5%	3.8%	3.4%
Total Revenues	$ 384,083	$ 294,994	$ 222,648	$332,833	$437,500
	100.0%	100.0%	100.0%	100.0%	100.0%

(1) The fiscal year ended August 31, 1991 contained 53 weeks; all other fiscal years in the table contained 52 weeks.

(2) Primarily recreation vehicle–related parts and service and van conversions.

(3) Principally sales of extruded aluminum and component products for other manufacturers.

(4) Principally Cycle-Sat revenues from satellite courier and tape duplication services, NIE revenues from contract assembly of a variety of electronic products, and in years ended August 28, 1993, August 25, 1990 and August 26, 1989, WAC revenues from dealer financing.

Source: Company reports, 1993.

EXHIBIT 18-2 Unit Sales of Recreation Vehicles

YEAR ENDED [a]	AUGUST 28, 1993	AUGUST 29, 1992	AUGUST 31, 1991	AUGUST 25, 1990	AUGUST 26, 1989
Motor Homes					
Class A	6,095	4,161	2,814	4,613	7,367
Class C	1,998	2,425	2,647	3,820	3,401
Total	8,093	6,586	5,461	8,433	10,768
Van Conversions	1,103	876	842	1,789	1,801

[a]The fiscal year ended August 31, 1991 ontained 53 weeks; all other fiscal years in the table contained 52 weeks.

Source: Company reports, 1993.

EXHIBIT 18-3 Interim Financial Information (unaudited) (Dollars in thousands except per share data)

YEAR ENDED AUGUST 28, 1993	NOVEMBER 28, 1992	QUARTER ENDED FEBRUARY 27, 1993	MAY 29, 1993	AUGUST 28, 1993
Net revenues	$83,416	$77,462	$115,915	$107,290
Operating income	939	(717)	4,562	3,503
Net income	1,117	407	4,579	3,175
Net income per share	.04	.02	.18	.13

YEAR ENDED AUGUST 29, 1992	NOVEMBER 30, 1991	QUARTER ENDED FEBRUARY 29, 1992	MAY 30, 1992	AUGUST 29, 1992
Net revenues	$60,175	$ 59,987	$ 88,883	$85,949
Operating (loss) income from continuing operations	(1,672)	(5,491)	3,142	2,933
(Loss) income from continuing operations[a]	(1,840)	(5,492)	2,830	2,733
Net (loss) income	(9,614)	(5,492)	2,220	2,317
Net (loss) income per share from continuing operations	(.07)	(.22)	.11	.11

In the fourth quarter ended August 28, 1993 the company recorded expense of $1,555,000 as a result of the Spectrum motor home recall.

[a]Before cumulative effect of change in accounting principle.

Source: Company reports, 1993.

EXHIBIT 18-4 Consolidated Balance Sheets (Dollars in thousands)

ASSETS	AUGUST 28, 1993	AUGUST 29, 1992
Current Assets		
Cash and cash equivalents	$ 11,238	$ 13,286
Marketable securities	2,309	1,215
Receivables, less allowance for doubtful accounts ($2,798 and $829, respectively)	29,239	27,515
Dealer financing receivables less allowance for doubtful accounts ($290 and $317, respectively)	6,742	102
Inventories	40,610	35,702
Prepaid expenses	3,636	3,999
Deferred income taxes	511	—
Total current assets	94,285	81,819
Property and Equipment, at cost		
Land	2,153	1,273
Buildings	38,373	38,591
Machinery and equipment	72,505	70,257
Transportation equipment	5,609	5,525
	118,640	115,646
Less accumulated depreciation	81,012	77,591
Total property and equipment, net	37,628	38,055
Long-Term Notes Receivable, less allowances ($1,362 and $1,427, respectively)	4,203	2,910
Investment in Life Insurance	11,853	8,906
Deferred Income Taxes	2,652	1,544
Other Assets	6,429	6,527
Total Assets	$157,050	$139,761

EXHIBIT 18-4 *Continued*

LIABILITIES AND STOCKHOLDERS' EQUITY	AUGUST 28, 1993	AUGUST 29, 1992
Current Liabilities		
Current maturities of long-term debt	$ 1,719	1,223
Accounts payable, trade	19,462	18,408
Accrued expenses:		
Insurance	6,445	7,143
Vacation liability	2,864	2,512
Promotional	4,636	4,405
Other	10,399	8,329
Liability on product warranties	4,091	2,375
Total current liabilities	49,616	44,395
Long-term Debt and Obligations		
Under Capital Lease	3,183	3,113
Deferred Compensation	18,766	16,157
Deferred Income Taxes	1,823	1,544
Minority Interest in Consolidated Subsidiary	1,969	2,474
Contingent Liabilities and Commitments		
Stockholder s' Equity		
Capital stock, common, par value $.50; authorized		
60,000,000 shares	12,908	12,903
Additional paid-in capital	24,811	25,157
Reinvested earnings	52,245	42,967
	89,964	81,027
Less treasury stock, at cost	8,271	8,949
Total Stockholders' Equity	81,693	72,078
Total Liabilities and Stockholders' Equity	$157,050	$139,761

Source: Company reports, 1993.

YEAR ENDED	AUGUST 28, 1993	AUGUST 29, 1992	AUGUST 31, 1991
Revenues			
Manufactured products	$364,860	$281,124	$210,438
Service	19,223	13,870	12,210
Total net revenues	384,083	294,994	222,648
Costs and expenses			
Cost of manufactured products	316,230	249,498	196,584
Cost of services	14,620	13,165	12,623
Selling and delivery	21,875	18,691	20,342
General and administrative	23,388	16,853	14,791
Other expense (income)	188	(952)	403
Minority interest in net loss of consolidated subsidiary	(505)	(1,173)	(766)
Total costs and expenses	375,796	296,082	243,977
Operating income (loss)	8,287	(1,088)	(21,329)
Financial expense	(96)	(585)	(340)
Income (loss) from continuing operations before income taxes	8,191	(1,673)	(21,669)
(Credit) provision for taxes	(1,087)	96	(5,398)
Income (loss) from continuing operations	9,278	(1,769)	(16,271)
Loss from discontinued operations	—	(1,026)	(13,110)
Cumulative effect of change in accounting principle (Note 1)	—	(7,774)	—
Net income (loss)	$ 9,278	$ (10,569)	$ (29,381)
Income (loss) per share:			
Continuing operations	$ .37	$ (.07)	$ (.65)
Discontinued operations	—	(.04)	(.53)
Cumulative effect of change in accounting principle	—	(.31)	—
Net income (loss)	$ .37	$ (.42)	$ (1.18)
Weighted average number of shares of stock (in thousands)	25,042	25,016	24,986

Source: Company reports, 1993.

EXHIBIT 18-6 Consolidated Statements of Changes in Stockholders' Equity
(Amounts in thousands)

	COMMON SHARES		PAID-IN CAPITAL	ADDITIONAL REINVESTED EARNINGS	TREASURY STOCK	
	NUMBER	AMOUNT			NUMBER	AMOUNT
Balance, August 25, 1990	25,777	$12,888	$ 26,959	$ 82,917	1,017	$11,602
Proceeds from the sale of common stock to employees	17	9	38		(1)	(15)
Contribution of treasury stock to employee stock bonus plan	—	—	(1,856)	—	(228)	(2,597)
Net loss	—	—	—	(29,381)	—	—
Balance, August 31, 1991	25,794	12,897	25,141	53,536	788	8,990
Proceeds from the sale of common stock to employees	12	6	16	—	(3)	(41)
Net loss	—	—	—	(10,569)	—	—
Balance, August 29, 1992	25,806	12,903	25,157	42,967	785	8,949
Proceeds from the sale of common stock to employees	9	5	(346)	—	(60)	(678)
Net income	—	—	—	9,278	—	—
Balance, August 28, 1993	25,815	$ 12,908	$ 24,811	$ 52,245	725	$ 8,271

Source: Company reports, 1993.

EXHIBIT 18-7 Consolidated Statements of Cash Flows (Dollars in thousands)

YEAR ENDED	AUGUST 28, 1993	AUGUST 29, 1992	AUGUST 31, 1991
Cash flows from operating activities:			
Net income (loss)	$ 9,278	$ (10,569)	$ (29,381)
Adjustments to reconcile net income (loss) to net cash from operating activities:			
Cumulative effect of change in accounting principle	—	7,774	—
Provision for disposal of Commercial Vehicle Division	—	416	8,118
Depreciation and amortization	7,961	8,195	11,070
Deferred income taxes	(1,340)	—	645
Loss (gain) on disposal of property, leases and other assets	630	507	(779)
Provision for doubtful receivables	1,496	916	(1,563)
Provision for lease residual reserve	—	—	733
Earned income on lease residuals	—	—	(128)
Deferred compensation and employee stock bonus plan	2,609	2,031	213
Realized and unrealized (gains) and losses on investments, net	(305)	625	(330)
Minority interest in net loss of consolidated subsidiary	(505)	(1,173)	(766)
Other	339	(68)	61
Change in assets and liabilities:			
(Increase) decrease in receivables and other assets	(1,186)	(4,853)	1,105
(Increase) decrease in inventories	(5,390)	(3,417)	17,380
Decrease in income tax refund receivables	—	6,339	3,847
Increase (decrease) in accounts payable and accrued expenses	3,227	5,063	(16,403)
Increase (decrease) in income taxes payable	1,106	—	(3,363)
Net cash provided (used) by operating activities	17,920	11,786	(9,541)
Cash flows from investing activities:			
Investments in marketable securities	(7,922)	(18,639)	(11,735)
Proceeds from sale of marketable securities	7,133	18,094	12,229
Purchases of property and equipment	(7,671)	(3,040)	(3,807)
Proceeds from sale of property and equipment	101	252	183
Investments in dealer receivables	(28,424)	—	—
Collections of dealer receivables	21,671	—	—
Investments in long-term notes receivable and other assets	(5,893)	(3,599)	(2,835)
Proceeds from long-term notes receivable and other assets	294	229	877
Proceeds from the sale of equipment under direct financing and operating leases	—	—	1,738
Net cash used by investing activities	(20,711)	(6,703)	(3,350)

EXHIBIT 18-7 *Continued*

YEAR ENDED	AUGUST 28, 1993	AUGUST 29, 1992	AUGUST 31, 1991
Cash flows from financing activities and capital transactions:			
Payments of long-term debt	(1,528)	(1,064)	(3,971)
Proceeds from issuance of long-term debt	1,934	55	1,289
Proceeds from issuance of Cycle-Sat common stock	—	2,500	—
Proceeds from issuance of common and treasury stock	337	63	62
Net cash provided (used) by financing activities and capital transactions	743	1,554	(2,620)
Net (decrease) increase in cash and cash equivalents	(2,048)	6,637	(15,511)
Cash and cash equivalents at beginning of year	13,286	6,649	22,160
Cash and cash equivalents at end of year	$ 11,238	$ 13,286	$ 6,649

Source: Company reports, 1993.

EXHIBIT 18-8 Winnebago Organizational Chart

John K. Hanson, 80
Chairman of the Board
and Chief Executive Officer

Fred G. Dohrmann, 61
President and Chief Operating Officer

Edwin F. Barker, 46
Vice President, Controller
and Chief Financial Officer

Sharon L. Hansen, 56
Vice President, Administration

Jerome V. Clouse, 50
Vice President, Treasurer
and International Development

Gregory M. Boman, 33
Vice President, Sales and Marketing

Raymond M. Beebe, 51
Vice President, General Counsel
and Secretary

Bruce D. Hertzke, 42
Vice President, Operations

Paul D. Hanson, 47
Vice President, Strategic Planning

Source: Company reports, 1993.

AEROSPACE INDUSTRY NOTE
CLAYTON MOWRY
RONALD GREEN

The U.S. aerospace industry, one of America's most successful industries, is facing some difficult challenges. The three key issues confronting the aerospace sector are continuing defense cuts, increasing international competition, and a weak global economy.

Still a global leader, the U.S. aerospace industry is a critical part of the country's domestic and export economies. The aerospace industry is the nation's leading net exporter of manufactured goods, selling products worth $40 billion in 1993, and produces the largest trade surplus of any U.S. manufacturing industry (approximately $28 billion in 1993). Aerospace is also a leading technology driver, utilizing a number of the technologies identified as critical by the White House Office of Science and Technology Policy, the Department of Defense (DOD), and the Department of Commerce. The industry accounts for more than 25 percent of all the nation's research and development expenditures, making it the country's leader in R&D spending on new technologies.

INDUSTRY SALES

The aerospace industry is facing serious challenges. As a result of continued defense cuts, a weak global economy, and increased international competition, industry shipments will decline in 1994 for the third year in a row. The value of aerospace industry shipments, unadjusted for inflation, peaked in 1992 at $134 billion. Shipments in 1993 fell 11 percent, in real terms, and shipments in 1994 are expected to be 11 percent lower than 1993. Historically, at least half of the industry's revenues were derived from the military sector. Cuts in the defense budgets for aerospace products, both in the United States and in other developed countries, have reduced requirements for military aircraft, missiles, and related equipment from U.S. suppliers. Total U.S. defense spending peaked in 1985, and current budget requests indicate an annual average decline of overall spending of more than 5 percent per year through 1997. The major impact will be from procurement cuts, estimated to be down 47 percent from the peak years of the 1980s build up. Increased emphasis on dual-use technology combined with funding for defense conversion should focus future attention on research and development. Rather than canceling ongoing projects, the 1994 defense budget recommends continuing development. By contrast, the defense industry's production will continue to fall (Figure 1).

In the past, significant growth in the civil sector sustained the aerospace industry during periodic downturns in defense spending. Between 1985 and 1991, when defense aerospace shipments were declining at a rate of approximately 2 percent per year, commercial aerospace shipments increased more than 11 percent per year. This counter-cyclical characteristic of the industry has disappeared. In 1992 civil orders represented 62 percent of the industry's total order backlog—down from 65 percent in 1991. The civil sector is facing the cumulative effect of the worldwide economic downturn and a decline in global airline passenger traffic. Airline traffic reached its peak of 466 million passengers in 1990. Thereafter, a series of events began that severely damaged the economic underpinning of the industry. The Persian Gulf crisis and the worldwide recession caused the airlines'

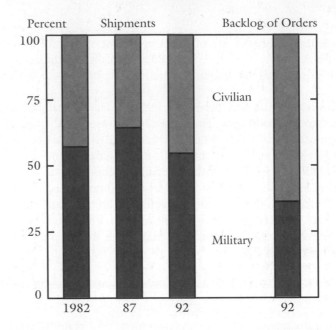

FIGURE 1 Military Share of Aerospace Shipments and Backlog Shrinks

Source: U.S. Department of Commerce, Bureau of the Census, *Current Industrial Reports* #MA37D, 1983–92.

loss of $13 billion between 1990 and 1993. This weak financial performance of the airline industry has, in turn, affected aerospace equipment orders and shipments during 1992 and into 1993.

The downturn in the industry is reflected in a severe decline in employment. Between 1989 and 1993 total aerospace industry employment fell from 912,000 to 615,000 according to Bureau of Labor statistics. Total aerospace employment declined between December 1989 and June 1993 at an average rate of almost 6,000 jobs per month. Layoffs have occurred in both the commercial and military sectors. Capacity utilization for the industry, as calculated by the Federal Reserve, fell from 85 percent in mid-1990 to only 69 percent by May 1993. As long as capacity utilization remains low, prospects for reversing or stabilizing employment trends remain poor.

International Competitiveness. The U.S. aerospace industry faces increasing international challenges as well. Although the United States retains both market and technology leadership within the global aerospace industry, its position has eroded. In 1970 the United States led the global aerospace market with a share of almost 80 percent (excluding the former members of the Council for Mutual Economic Assistance, or COMECON, a group of nations led by the former Soviet Union). In 1993 U.S. aerospace shipments still led the world, but had shrunk to less than 60 percent of the worldwide market. This decline reflects the success of other countries in their efforts to foster the development and growth of their national aerospace industries, particularly Europe. Many foreign governments have ambitious plans for developing competitive aerospace industries and support the growth of these industries with subsidies for product development and production. Foreign governments have required U.S. aerospace companies to provide offsets and technology transfers and made sales con-

Trends and Forecasts: Aerospace (SIC 372, 376) (In millions of dollars except as noted)

ITEM	1991	1992[1]	1993[2]	1994[3]	PERCENT CHANGE (1991–1994)		
					91–92	92–93	93–94
Industry Data							
Value of shipments[4]	131,345	133,613	120,742	101,962	1.7	–9.6	–15.6
Value of shipments (1987$)	116,911	116,287	103,510	92,313	–0.5	–11.0	–10.8
Total employment (000)	746	674	587	542	–9.7	–12.9	–7.7
Production workers (000)	362	323	279	267	–10.8	–13.6	–4.3
Average hourly earnings ($)	16.73	17.56	18.37	—	5.0	4.6	—
Capital expenditures	3,407	—	—	—	—	—	—
Product Data							
Value of shipments[5]	124,109	126,800	112,244	93,921	2.2	–11.5	–16.3
Value of shipments (1987$)	109,742	110,349	96,230	80,760	0.6	–12.8	–16.1
Trade Data							
Value of imports	12,422	12,914	11,277	10,973	4.0	–12.7	–2.7
Value of exports	42,343	43,562	39,560	33,745	2.9	–9.2	–14.7

[1] Estimate, except exports and imports.
[2] Estimate.
[3] Forecast.
[4] Value of all products and services sold by establishments in the aerospace industry.
[5] Value of products classified in the aerospace industry produced by all industries.

Source: U.S. Department of Commerce: Bureau of the Census; International Trade Administration (ITA). Estimates and forecasts by ITA.

tingent upon their own firms' supplying some of the components. In addition, some governments have encouraged consolidation and cooperation among domestic companies to reduce competition within their borders, enabling their firms to compete more effectively with established U.S. companies (Figure 2).

Europe provides the most formidable competition to the U.S. aerospace industry. According to European Community (EC) statistics, the EC aerospace industry grew almost twice as fast as the U.S. industry during the period 1978–1989. In 1990 the EC industry was nearly half the size of the U.S. industry. The emergence of the Airbus Industrie consortium, composed of the member governments of France, the United Kingdom, Germany, and Spain, is primarily responsible for the erosion of global U.S. market share. Since its inception, Airbus has received an estimated $26 billion, including interest, in direct government supports to assist in the development of its fleet of aircraft. Historically, U.S. companies have not received government assistance. European governments also support their commercial space, smaller aircraft, rotorcraft, engine, and parts industries.

Most individual EC governments have encouraged concentration in their aerospace industries, leading to diversified, national monoliths such as Deutsche Aerospace (Germany), Aerospatiale (France), Alenia (Italy), Fokker (Netherlands), and British Aerospace (U.K.). Even though Deutsche Aerospace privatized its operations in 1992 and Aerospatiale has been offered by the French government as a candidate for future privatization, the trend toward intra–EC ventures will continue

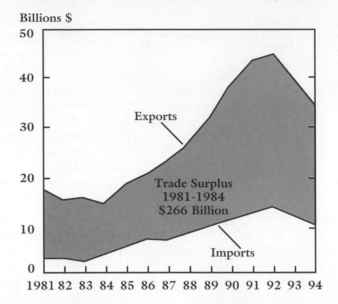

FIGURE 2 U.S. Aerospace Trade Surplus Narrows*

*Estimate.

Source: U.S. Department of Commerce: Bureau of the Census; International Trade Administration, Technology and Aerospace Industries Division.

to lead to even larger industry consortiums as the EC governments work to integrate their economies. An example is the recent takeover of Fokker by Deutsche Aerospace, with a possible further consolidation with Aerospatiale and Alenia's regional jet programs, the ATR-42 and the ATR-72.

In the future Japan will become a more significant competitor in several segments of the industry. Small by global standards, the Japanese aerospace industry production totaled only $8.5 billion in 1991, but the industry has grown at a rate of 9 percent a year since 1984. Targeted by the Japanese government, aerospace research and development efforts have focused on aircraft fuelage and systems components, electronics, high-speed propulsion systems, and space launch vehicles. Japan's growth in the aerospace industry stems from its partnerships and cooperative ventures with Western aerospace companies, most notably Boeing. These partnerships enabled Japanese aerospace output to grow from less than $1 billion in 1970 to more than $8.5 billion by 1991. Japan, a "program partner" in the new Boeing 777 aircraft, already possesses much of the expertise needed to produce a world-class aircraft of its own design in the future. In fact, discussions are underway for Boeing to assist its Japanese suppliers in building an 80-seat jetliner, the YSX.

China also has become a major market for U.S. aerospace products. In 1992, U.S. aerospace exports to China totaled over $2 billion. More than 40,000 U.S. aerospace jobs are estimated to have been created as a result of trade with China. It is estimated that China will need more than $40 billion in new aircraft over the next 20 years, making China one of the brighter spots in today's aerospace market. China's market remains fragile, as does its foreign relations with the United States, but the market potential is promising. China also plans to build an indigenous aerospace industry and will become both a growing subcontractor and competitor in segments of the aerospace industry, especially in lower-cost military and commuter aircraft.

The new spirit of international cooperation prevalent in the Russian aerospace industry presents both opportunities and challenges for the U.S. industry. A market that contains the world's largest airline, largest space industry, and greatest pent-up consumer demand certainly provides new long-term opportunities for U.S. aerospace companies. It is estimated that the former Soviet market will require 2,000 new aircraft for domestic service and 250 aircraft for international routes during the next 18 years. Yet it also presents the challenge of new competition. An example is the 1993 roll-out and first flight of the IL-96M, a four-engine, long-range aircraft. While the IL-96M will be powered by U.S.-built Pratt & Whitney engines and fitted with U.S. advanced avionics, it will compete with the McDonnell Douglas's MD-11 and Boeing's future 777 twin-engine aircraft. Another recent product of Russian aero space collaboration with the West is Tupolev's TU-204, a midrange, 200-seater twin jet airliner with Rolls-Royce engines designed to compete against the Boeing 757. Prior to the dissolution of the Soviet Union, Soviet aerospace factories produced at least as many aircraft, missiles, and spacecraft as the United States. Today, most of these facilities are operating at less than 30 percent capacity. Desire for new orders for those factories, for technology, and for hard currency will force the industries of the former Soviet republics to both collaborate and compete in the international market. These factors play a key role in Russia's future participation in the Space Station. In September 1993 Vice President Gore and Russian Prime Minister Chernomyrdin agreed to the construction of a space station blending elements from the U.S. Freedom and Russian Mir projects.

Other countries also seek larger shares of the global aerospace industry, including Canada, Brazil, Indonesia, Sweden, South Korea, Israel, and Australia.

Environmental Profile. The aerospace industry has made great strides in addressing environmental problems that are aircraft related. Today, on take-off and landing, a jetliner produces less than one-quarter of the pollutants produced by a 1960s transport. Noise abatement also has been a major concern. By the year 2000, most of the commercial jet aircraft will meet stringent Stage 3 noise standards even though this will mean the retirement of many aircraft before the end of their functional lifespan. Hughes Aircraft has developed partnerships with local governments in Southern California, working to reduce the region's problem with smog. Boeing, Hughes, IBM, Autoclave Engineers Group, and five national laboratories are leading a large research and development cooperative to find more environmentally sound processing techniques for aerospace materials, including reducing the volatile organic compounds used in paints, coatings, and solvents. Environmental concerns now are considered at the earliest stages of designing an aircraft.

Pratt & Whitney, General Dynamics, Hercules, and many others have major campaigns to eliminate wastes produced in the production of aircraft parts and aircraft engines. In many cases, wastes have been reduced 60 to 90 percent. Aerospace companies have recognized that they have valuable technologies to supply to the global environmental marketplace. Several companies have formed environmental subsidiaries, such as General Dynamic's Environmental Sciences and Technologies, Lockheed's Environmental Systems & Technology Company, and Hughes' Environmental Systems, to develop and market environmental products worldwide. As traditional markets shrink, aerospace companies are expected to diversify further into the environmental technology industry.

U.S. Trade Patterns in 1992 Aerospace SIC 37A (In millions of dollars, percent)

EXPORTS	Value	Share	IMPORTS	Value	Share
Canada and Mexico	3,027	6.9	Canada and Mexico	2,309	17.9
European Community	14,782	33.9	European Community	8,911	69.0
Japan	4,442	10.2	Japan	593	4.6
East Asia NICs	9,140	21.0	East Asia NICs	258	2.0
South America	2,205	5.1	South America	168	1.3
Other	9,966	22.9	Other	674	5.2
World Total	43,562	100.0	World Total	12,914	100.0

TOP FIVE COUNTRIES

	Value	Share		Value	Share
Japan	4,442	10.2	France	4,098	31.7
France	3,714	8.5	United Kingdom	2,617	20.3
United Kingdom	3,353	7.7	Canada	2,241	17.4
Germany	2,967	6.8	Netherlands	909	7.0
China	2,112	4.8	Japan	593	4.6

See "Getting the Most Out of *Outlook '94*" for definitions of the country groupings.
Source: U.S. Department of Commerce: Bureau of the Census; International Trade Administration.

The cost of environment requirements is becoming a competitive concern. McDonnell Douglas estimates that costs related to safety, health, and environmental requirements in California alone have more than doubled since 1986. Business planning has become more difficult and time consuming in order to meet constantly changing environmental regulations. In addition to increasing production costs resulting from U.S. regulations, disparity in costs related to international environmental standards among nations could place U.S. manufacturers at a competitive disadvantage in the near future. The U.S. aerospace industry is urging negotiated international standards.

Outlook for 1994. U.S. aerospace sales should continue to decline in 1994. From January through June 1993, new aerospace orders were 24 percent lower than orders during the same period of 1992. Although the aerospace manufacturers' backlog remains quite large ($202 million), it has gradually declined since its peak in March 1991. Between the end of 1991 and the end of 1992, the backlog declined nearly 9 percent. Between January and June 1993, the backlog declined by more than 4 percent. As a result, aircraft manufacturers have been forced to reduce their production rates. For example, Boeing will cut its production of jetliners by one-third from January 1993 to mid-1994—a reduction of almost 50 percent from peak production levels of early 1992. Defense spending as a share of U.S. gross domestic product will be about 3 percent, the lowest level of the post–World War II period and half of what it was in the mid-1980s. With economic uncertainty restricting aftermarket purchases of spares, engine and parts suppliers in both military and civil segments of the industry will decline as well. Defense cutbacks have curtailed demand in the missile segment. U.S. space vehicle manufacturers will see an increase in commercial launches in 1994 due in part to long delays in launch schedules during 1993.

U.S. aerospace industry shipments will total about $102 billion in 1994. Aircraft production will continue to lead the industry with shipments of $42 billion. Shipments of engines and engine parts (SIC 3724) will fall to $17 billion, and shipments of aircraft parts (SIC 3728) will decline to $16 billion. Shipments of guided missiles and space vehicles (SIC 376) will increase 2 percent to $22 billion. Employment in that sector will decline 4 percent.

U.S. aerospace export sales, including avionics and flight simulators, are forecast to decline to about $35 billion in 1994, but will remain stronger than domestic sales (Table 1). More than 40 percent of the existing aerospace backlog is from foreign customers. Imports will also decline in 1994 to about $11 billion (Table 2). Imports will be driven primarily by increased shipments of Airbus Industrie aircraft to U.S. airlines. Aerospace companies will continue to cut back on employment as military programs are delayed or terminated.

The large civil transport sector includes all passenger and cargo aircraft weighing more than 15,000 kilograms, typically two- and four-engine jetliners. In contrast to the booming production rates and bursting order books of the late 1980s, the large transport industry is adjusting itself to lower demand and declining orders from the airline industry, reduced production of narrow-body and wide-body aircraft, and fierce competition from Europe.

Large Transport Sector Restructuring. The future prospects for the large civil aircraft sector are mixed. Defense cuts continue to have a significant impact. U.S. military aircraft shipments, which long comprised a significant share of U.S. aircraft manufacturing, declined after reaching a record of $24 billion in 1987. Military aircraft shipments dropped to $8.4 billion in 1993 (Table 3). Boeing sells 20 percent of its products, by value, and McDonnell Douglas sells 60 percent of its products to the U.S. Government, almost all of it to the Department of Defense and the National Aeronautics and Space Administration (NASA). Exports are crucial to both companies. Boeing exports 55 percent of its aircraft and McDonnell Douglas exports approximately 25 percent of its products. Therefore, the significant reductions in DOD and foreign government military aircraft procurements, as well as the global recession, have affected the two U.S. aircraft manufacturers.

In the past, business on the commercial side has compensated for the cuts in defense. However, the 1991 conflict in the Persian Gulf, combined with the worldwide recession, stymied growth in airline traffic. Although international traffic recovered during 1992, and U.S. domestic traffic was stimulated by significant price discounting, the airline industry remained in dire financial straits. From 1990 to 1993, the U.S. airline industry lost $13 billion and is only now showing signs of partial, fitful, and inadequate recovery. After a decade of growth in the 1980s, these recent losses contributed to large-scale layoffs by airlines, aircraft manufacturers, and suppliers. Although deregulation fostered increased price competition among airlines, the economic downturn and slowdown in traffic reduced or even eliminated profit margins in the short term for many carriers, with some companies declaring bankruptcy. Braniff, Eastern, and Pan Am went out of business. Numerous smaller airlines

TABLE 1   U.S. Total Exports of Aerospace Vehicles and Equipment, 1992–1994 (Values in millions of dollars)

ITEMS	1992[1] UNITS	1992[1] VALUE	1993[2] UNITS	1993[2] VALUE	1994[3] UNITS	1994[3] VALUE
Aerospace vehicles and equipment, total	—	45,030	—	40,118	—	34,777
Civilian aircraft	2,086	24,337	1,808	21,077	1,735	15,489
Under 4,536 kg. unladen weight, new	586	297	500	187	510	191
4,536–15,000 kg. unladen weight, new	60	295	48	254	50	260
Over 15,000 kg. unladen weight, new	387	22,379	275	19,500	195	13,900
Rotocraft, new	212	118	190	106	180	100
Nonpowered aircraft, new	—	7	—	12	—	13
Used or rebuilt	841	1,241	795	1,018	800	1,025
Military aircraft	428	2,083	500	1,311	500	1,384
New	331	1,909	370	1,250	380	1,284
Used	97	174	130	61	120	100
Aircraft engines and parts	—	6,699	—	6,361	—	6,394
Piston engines and parts	—	315	—	291	—	294
Complete engines, new and used	7,278	104	7,170	108	7,200	109
Engine parts	—	211	—	183	—	185
Turbine engines and parts[4]	—	6,384	—	6,070	—	6,100
Complete engines, new and used	18,540	2,484	27,150	2,580	26,000	2,600
Engine parts	—	3,900	—	3,490	—	3,500
Propellers, rotors, and parts	—	289	—	296	—	300
Landing gear and parts	—	362	—	310	—	320
Aircraft parts and accessories, n.e.c.	—	8,496	—	8,321	—	8,400
Avionics	—	795	—	663	—	700
Flight simulators	—	205	—	200	—	210
Guided missiles and parts	—	1,428	—	1,200	—	1,210
Space vehicles and parts	—	336	—	379	—	370

[1]Revised.

[2]Estimate.

[3]Forecast.

[4]Category changed to include reaction engines, other than turbojets—except missile and rocket—and their parts.

Source: U.S. Department of Commerce: International Trade Administration (ITA), Bureau of the Census. Estimates and forecasts by ITA.

such as Air Florida, People Express, and Ozark have merged or disappeared; others, such as TWA, Northwest, and Continental, are close to emerging or have recently emerged from Chapter 11 bankruptcy.

To help address these problems, President Clinton created the National commission to Ensure a Strong Competitive Airline Industry on April 7, 1993. The Commission's mandate was to investigate, study, and make policy recommendations about the financial health and future competitiveness of the U.S. airline and aerospace industries. The report summarizing the Commission's findings was released on August 19, 1993. Key recommendations contained in this report include: 1) cre-

TABLE 2   U.S. Total Imports of Aerospace Vehicles and Equipment, 1992–1994 (Values in millions of dollars)

ITEMS	1992[1] UNITS	1992[1] VALUE	1993[2] UNITS	1993[2] VALUE	1994[3] UNITS	1994[3] VALUE
Aerospace vehicles and equipment, total	—	14,473	—	13,154	—	11,463
Civilian Aircraft	620	3,866	664	3,442	649	3,474
Under 4,536 kg. unladen weight, new	118	104	122	60	125	62
4,536–15,000 kg. unladen weight, new	126	1,272	130	1,154	132	1,170
Over 15,000 kg. unladen weight, new	64	2,007	52	1,775	50	1,800
Rotocraft, new	148	179	140	192	142	195
Nonpowered aircraft, new	—	3	—	1	—	2
Used or rebuilt	164	301	220	260	200	245
Military aircraft	77	55	70	16	65	16
New (quantity of powered aircraft only)	26	50	32	14	30	13
Used	51	5	38	2	35	3
Aircraft engines and parts	—	6,124	—	5,344	—	4,116
Piston engines and parts	—	100	—	94	—	96
Complete engines, new and used	2,987	43	2,400	41	2,500	42
Engine parts	—	57	—	53	—	54
Turbine engines and parts[4]	—	6,204	—	5,250	—	4,020
Complete engines, new and used	2,849	3,017	2,480	2,630	2,158	2,020
Engine parts	—	3,007	—	2,620	—	2,000
Propellers, rotors, and parts	—	26	—	22	—	23
Landing gear and parts	—	78	—	61	—	53
Aircraft parts and accessories, n.e.c.	—	3,284	—	3,347	—	2,920
Avionics	—	511	—	478	—	435
Flight simulators	—	205	—	75	—	80
Guided missiles and parts	—	108	—	103	—	96
Space vehicles and parts	—	216	—	266	—	250

[1]Revised.

[2]Estimate.

[3]Forecast.

[4]Category changed to include reaction engines, other than turbojets—except missile and rocket—and their parts.

Source: U.S. Department of Commerce: International Trade Administration (ITA), Bureau of the Census. Estimates and forecasts by ITA.

ation of an independent Federal corporate entity within the Department of Transportation (DOT) to manage air traffic control and related functions; 2) establishment of a financial advisory committee to review the financial condition of individual airlines; 3) negotiation of multilateral agreements for passenger and cargo services, replacing the current system of bilateral agreements; 4) permitting foreign

TABLE 3   Shipments of Complete U.S. Aircraft, 1990–1994 (Values in millions of dollars)

| | AIRCRAFT TOTAL | | CIVIL | | | | | | | | MILITARY TOTAL | |
| | | | TOTAL | | LARGE TRANSPORTS | | GENERAL AVIATION[1] | | ROTOCRAFT | | | |
YEAR	UNITS	VALUE	UNITS	VALUE	UNITS	VALUE	UNITS	VALUE	UNITS	VALUE	UNITS	VALUE
1990	3,486	39,206	2,268	24,476	521	22,215	1,144	2,007	603	254	1,218	14,730
1991	2,934	40,776	2,181	29,035	589	26,856	1,021	1,968	571	211	753	11,741
1992[1]	2,465	41,828	1,833	32,246	610	30,268	899	1,836	324	142	632	9,582
1993[2]	2,079	36,483	1,429	28,097	429	26,310	710	1,660	290	127	650	8,386
1994[3]	1,851	28,475	1,311	20,555	306	18,715	730	1,720	275	120	540	7,920

1. Revised.

2. Estimate.

3. Forecast.

Source: U.S. Department of Commerce; International Trade Administration (ITA); general aviation (through first half 1993), General Aviation Manufacturers Association; rotorcraft (through first half 1993); Aerospace Industries Association. Estimates and forecasts by ITA.

investors to hold up to 49 percent voting equity in U.S. airlines; 5) increasing Export-Import Bank funding levels for large and small aircraft; and 6) enactment of a statute of repose for general aviation aircraft that would limit the liability of manufacturers of these aircraft to 15 years from the date of manufacture. The Commission made over 60 specific recommendations, but its omissions were equally significant. The Commission did *not* recommend major revisions to the present deregulated structure or suggest increased U.S. government supports or loan guarantees for the purchase or retrofitting of aircraft to meet Stage 3 aircraft noise standards. The Commission reasoned that although the U.S. International Airline Transport Association projected U.S. airline losses of $2 billion in 1993, airline over-expansion and aircraft over-capacity need to be addressed through market forces.

In addition to U.S. airline losses, international airlines are facing the difficulties of both a sluggish world economy and the competitive challenges derived from increased deregulation and international competition. This combination of events has led to restructuring policies by airlines, a slowdown in aircraft orders, and order deferrals. As a result, aircraft manufacturers have had to cut production rates of most models and are often confronted with unsold or "white tail" aircraft produced without a firm customer. These disruptions have undercut manufacturers' efforts to adjust to the defense cuts by transferring employees from defense to commercial product lines. At this time, both segments of the industry remain in a recession. Even significant international customers, such as the leasing company Guinness Peat Aviation Group of Ireland, have been forced to restructure in order to avoid bankruptcy and are canceling or rescheduling orders.

Strong competition from the European-based Airbus Industrie is further exacerbating the effects of lower demand. While U.S. aircraft manufacturers maintain 65 percent of the current world backlog of firm orders for large aircraft (Boeing with 56 percent and McDonnell Douglas with 9 percent), Airbus has established a firm control of the number two position with 34 percent and other European manufacturers with 1 per-

Trends and Forecasts: Aircraft (SIC 3721) (In millions of dollars except as noted)

Item	1991	1992[1]	1993[2]	1994[3]	PERCENT CHANGE (1991–1994)		
					91–92	92–93	93–94
Industry Data							
Value of shipments[4]	58,090	58,900	53,000	41,500	1.4	−10.0	−21.7
Value of shipments (1987$)	48,449	47,045	41,309	36,630	−2.9	−12.2	−11.3
Total employment (000)	258	241	219	200	−6.6	−9.1	−8.7
Production workers (000)	125	114	102	95.0	−8.8	−10.5	−6.9
Average hourly earnings ($)	17.82	18.78	19.63	20.45	5.4	4.5	4.2
Capital expenditures	1,046	—	—	—	—	—	—
Product Data							
Value of shipments[5]	52,514	53,870	47,000	36,425	2.6	−12.8	−22.5
Value of shipments (1987$)	43,798	43,027	36,633	27,765	−1.8	−14.9	−24.2
Trade Data							
Value of imports	3,438	3,921	3,458	3,490	14.0	−11.8	0.9
Value of exports	24,173	26,419	23,414	16,900	9.3	−11.4	−27.8

[1] Estimate, except exports and imports.

[2] Estimate.

[3] Forecast.

[4] Value of all products and services sold by establishments in the aircraft industry.

[5] Value of products classified in the aircraft industry produced by all industries.

Source: U.S. Department of Commerce: Bureau of the Census; International Trade Administration (ITA). Estimates and forecasts by ITA.

cent. Helping to increase the pressure on the U.S. companies, Airbus introduced several new aircraft models over the last few years: the A340 in October 1991, the A330 in October 1992, and the A321 in May 1993. Airbus launched a 130-seat derivative of the A320—the A319—in 1993. Boeing and McDonnell Douglas have introduced their own new aircraft models: Boeing will deliver its first 777 aircraft, a twin-engine long-range jet, in May 1995, and has announced its intention to upgrade the line of 737 aircraft; McDonnell Douglas will deliver its first MD-90, a narrow-body, low-noise-level aircraft, in October 1994. During 1993 Boeing and McDonnell Douglas exported 275 large transport aircraft valued at $19.5 billion, and were the most significant contributors to the trade performance of the U.S. aerospace industry. The value of large civil transport exports are expected to fall 29 percent in 1994; imports will rise 1 percent.

All of these factors have affected the two U.S. producers. Both McDonnell Douglas and Boeing have announced reduced production rates for their aircraft and have had to resort to layoffs. Boeing announced planned layoffs of 28,000 workers for 1993 and the first half of 1994. By June 1993 McDonnell Douglas had trimmed its workforce by almost 59,000 or 44 percent below the peak levels of June 1990.

Foreign Markets. To help stem the tide of this declining demand and overcapacity, U.S. manufacturers are looking to Asia to provide future growth markets and partnerships for increasing their competitiveness. McDonnell Douglas has increased its ties with the People's Republic of China (PRC). In 1992 McDonnell Douglas successfully concluded a contract with the PRC to produce 40 narrow-body aircraft as part of their "trunkliner" program—35 were previously coproduced with the PRC. Boeing has made their three major Japanese suppliers "program partners" on the 777, and is also expanding its relationships with smaller Asian countries like Taiwan. This region of the world is attracting U.S. aircraft manufacturers with access to inexpensive capital, high-quality manufacturing, and lower production costs.

Over the long term, this segment of the aerospace industry should see increased growth. Demand in world commercial markets, particularly the expanding economies of Asia and the Pacific Rim, is expected to show increases over the next 10 to 15 years. In fact, the larger share of the commercial transport market is now overseas. The U.S. share, as a percentage of the world market, will shrink. Airline traffic, especially international traffic, is expected to show strong growth throughout the rest of the decade and the industry expects to deliver more than 14,000 aircraft over the next 20 years. Many new commercial sales are expected to come from the replacement of older, less fuel-efficient aircraft that will not meet airlines' requirements or federal and international noise and emissions standards.

Wide-body, longe-range aircraft, those targeted for the fast-growing international markets in Asia, will experience the most growth. Industry forecasts predict annual deliveries of about 225 long-range aircraft in 2011, compared with only 129 per year in 1992. In this product segment, the U.S.-made aircraft, the Boeing 747 and the Douglas MD-11, are competing against the A340, which is Airbus's first entrant into the long-range market.

The U.S. industry will continue to confront fierce competition from Airbus Industrie. However, there are indications that the U.S. and EC aerospace industries may be able to cooperate in the future. One example is the joint feasibility study being conducted by Boeing and the four major European aircraft manufacturers (Aerospatiale, Deutsche Aerospace, British Aerospace, and CASA) to determine the potential market for a Very Large Commercial Transport (VLCT) that would carry more than 600 passengers over long-range routes. A second example is the bilateral and multilateral negotiations to reduce the level of government supports provided to the aerospace industry. On July 17, 1992, the U.S. government and the European Commission signed a bilateral agreement that restricts government supports provided to the large civil aircraft sector. Specifically, the agreement prohibits all production supports and sets limits of 33 percent on the level of permissible government funding for new aircraft programs (down from 70 to 90 percent of existing Airbus aircraft). This agreement is viewed by the U.S. government and the domestic aerospace industry as a critical step in leveling the competitive playing field for U.S. large transport manufacturers who have suffered significantly from the competition of government-supported Airbus. Multilateral negotiations, which are focusing on broadening the product and country coverage of the bilateral agreement, began in July 1992 and continued through 1993. As part of these negotiations, the United States is seeking to strengthen the disciplines in the bilateral agreement by further reducing the level of government support allowed on new aircraft programs and adopting a stronger dispute settlement mechanism. The U.S. Government and the European Commission are also holding consultations to monitor and enforce each party's adherence to the 1992 bilateral agreement.

Aircraft Engine Manufacturing. The aircraft engine (SIC 3724) and aircraft parts (3728) industries face the same challenges confronting the U.S. large aircraft manufacturers. In 1993 U.S. manufacturers of aircraft engines, engine parts, and aircraft parts shipped an estimated $41 billion of products and employed 236,400 workers. This is down from shipments of $47.4 billion and employment of 276,000 in 1992. Shipments for this sector are expected to fall 18 percent in 1994 to $33.4 billion.

The recent deferrals and cancellations of aircraft orders by the airlines have directly affected the engine orders associated with those aircraft. The worldwide backlog of orders for civil turbofan engines stood at 5,800 at the beginning of 1992, but declining production rates at Boeing an McDonnell Douglas will stretch that backlog out several years. Therefore, the engine companies have been forced to restructure while they continue to invest heavily in the development of new products and technologies to take advantage of the recovery when it finally comes. All three major engine companies—General Electric (GE) and United Technologies' Pratt & Whitney (P&W) division in the United States, and Rolls Royce in the United Kingdom—are in the midst of costly programs to develop new engines to power the next generation of wide-body aircraft. GE is investing in the GE90, Rolls Royce is working on the Trent and P&W on the PW4000.

Aerospace suppliers of aircraft structures, systems, and components also face the same problems and are undergoing unprecedented consolidation, with many companies destined to exit the industry ranks for good. Boeing and McDonnell Douglas

Trends and Forecasts: Aircraft Engines and Engine Parts (SIC 3724) (In millions of dollars except as noted)

ITEM	1991	1992[1]	1993[2]	1994[3]	PERCENT CHANGE (1991–1994)		
					91–92	92–93	93–94
Industry Data							
Value of shipments[4]	22,746	24,075	21,000	17,250	5.8	−12.8	−17.9
Value of shipments (1987$)	19,211	19,621	16,680	13,350	2.1	−15.0	−20.0
Total employment (000)	122	109	95.4	90.0	−10.7	−12.5	−5.7
Production workers (000)	67.3	59.5	50.5	47.5	−11.6	−15.1	−5.9
Average hourly earnings ($)	15.56	15.80	16.20	16.35	1.5	2.5	0.9
Capital expenditures	771	—	—	—	—	—	—
Product Data							
Value of shipments[5]	21,315	22,561	19,450	15,752	5.8	−13.8	−19.0
Value of shipments (1987$)	18,002	18,387	15,450	12,190	2.1	−16.0	−21.1
Trade Data							
Value of imports	4,990	5,752	5,403	5,350	15.3	−6.1	−1.0
Value of exports	6,994	6,642	6,528	6,600	−5.0	−1.7	1.1

[1] Estimate, except exports and imports.

[2] Estimate.

[3] Forecast.

[4] Value of all products and services sold by establishments in the aircraft engines and engine parts industry.

[5] Value of products classified in the aircraft engines and engine parts industry produced by all industries.

Source: U.S. Department of Commerce: Bureau of the Census; International Trade Administration (ITA). Estimates and forecasts by ITA.

have concentrated their purchases on a smaller number of high-quality suppliers. In 1992 the number of aerospace/defense suppliers dwindled to about 30,000 companies, down from 120,000 in the mid-1980s. More than 60 percent of the value of each U.S. aircraft is produced by subcontractors. Fuselage, wing, and empennage structures, hydraulic, electrical, pneumatic, and environmental systems, avionics, composite structures, and assorted other parts are manufactured by thousands of other U.S. and foreign suppliers to the prime aircraft manufacturers.

These consolidations translate into job losses. All three of the big aircraft engine manufacturers have announced workforce reductions. P&W is cutting its peak 1991 workforce of 44,000 down to 30,000, while GE is reducing its payroll from 36,000 to 30,000. Rolls Royce is shrinking its workforce by 10 percent. Similar reductions are expected from the large suppliers of aircraft systems, such as Raytheon, GM-Hughes, Martin Marietta, Allied Signal, and TRW. Employment in the U.S. aircraft engines and engine parts (SIC 3724) and aircraft parts (SIC 3728) sectors fell 16 percent between 1990 and 1992. Long-term prospects are for continued declines on the military side and stabilizing employment on the commercial side.

In spite of the reduced demand, the U.S. engine segment is maintaining its global market position in the face of difficult economic conditions and foreign competition. Profit margins for new engines have been squeezed by the present perilous state of airline finances. In addition, since airlines fly less and require fewer spare engines in a recession, the engine manufacturers' lucrative spare parts business has been adversely affected.

Aircraft parts suppliers face the additional challenge of further globalization of large transport aircraft. Boeing and McDonnell Douglas gradually have increased the foreign content of their aircraft. For example, the percentage of foreign products (excluding the engines) installed on the Boeing 727, launched in 1959, was approximately 2 percent. Foreign products (excluding the engines) installed on the 767, launched in 1978, represent closer to 15 percent, and on the 777, launched in 1990, it may be almost 30 percent. For McDonnell Douglas, foreign products (excluding the engines) range from 15 to 20 percent of the aircraft value on the MD-11 and MD80/90, up significantly from the content on the older DC-9 and DC-10.

Military Aircraft Sector. U.S. military aircraft manufacturers shipped only $8.4 billion in complete aircraft in 1993 and are downsizing to adapt to the worldwide decline in defense spending for aircraft. U.S. manufacturers expect to ship only 540 aircraft or $7.9 billion in sales in 1994, less than half the number shipped in 1987. Historically, the U.S. government accounted for 80 percent of military aircraft sales. DOD's Foreign Military Sales program and direct exports of military aircraft have accounted for the remaining 20 percent. The reduced threat from the former Soviet Union has made defense spending a significant target for budget cuts. Although the United States has become the world's largest arms exporter with the collapse of the Soviet Union, the international market for aircraft has decreased as well. The latest Pentagon budget request indicated a cumulative real decline in DOD budget authority of more than 40 percent since 1985. The 1994 budget request also projects a 7 percent reduction in procurement funds. While procurement of aircraft has declined significantly, research, development, testing, and evaluation funding has remained stable, providing some haven for U.S. providers of advanced military aircraft technologies.

The budget cuts have hit all military aircraft: fixed-wing and helicopter, combat and transport, as well as production and development programs, resulting in cancellations and delays. DOD canceled the Navy A-12 attack fighter in 1991 after sched-

Trends and Forecasts: Aircraft Parts and Equipment, NEC (SIC 3728) (In millions of dollars except as noted)

ITEM	1991	1992[1]	1993[2]	1994[3]	PERCENT CHANGE (1991–1994)		
					91–92	92–93	93–94
Industry Data							
Value of shipments[4]	21,544	23,286	20,030	16,220	8.1	−14.0	−19.0
Value of shipments (1987$)	18,865	19,735	16,580	12,555	4.6	−16.0	−24.3
Total employment (000)	187	167	141	125	−10.7	−15.6	−11.3
Production workers (000)	108	96.3	79.8	78.3	−10.8	−17.1	−1.9
Average hourly earnings ($)	15.05	16.00	16.80	17.47	6.3	5.0	4.0
Capital expenditures	1,006	—	—	—	—	—	—
Product Data							
Value of shipments[5]	25,288	26,766	23,020	18,645	5.8	−14.0	−19.0
Value of shipments (1987$)	22,144	22,683	19,060	15,120	2.4	−16.0	−20.7
Trade Data							
Value of imports	3,888	3,132	2,325	2,030	−19.4	−25.8	−12.7
Value of exports	9,953	9,050	8,703	9,020	−9.1	−3.8	3.6

[1] Estimate, except exports and imports.

[2] Estimate.

[3] Forecast.

[4] Value of all products and services sold by establishments in the aircraft parts and equipment, NEC industry.

[5] Value of products classified in the aircraft parts and equipment, NEC industry produced by all industries.

Source: U.S. Department of Commerce: Bureau of the Census; International Trade Administration (ITA). Estimates and forecasts by ITA.

ule delays, cost overruns, and technical problems. Programs such as the Army's RAH-66 light helicopter and the Air Force's F-22 fighter, B-2 strategic bomber, and C-17 transport have been funded at levels lower than originally planned. Total C-17 procurement may be cut or procurement schedules stretched out. Although the C-17 program has suffered from cost overruns and technical problems in the past, 1993 was a turning point for the program. The C-17 survived heavy Congressional scrutiny and a successful resolution of the technical problems is expected.

Lost jobs are the ultimate price of defense cuts. Defense firms have cut hundreds of thousands of jobs over the past 5 years, and military aircraft companies are no exception. During 1992 alone, the prime military aircraft manufacturers, McDonnell Douglas, General Dynamics, Northrop, Lockheed, Rockwell, and Grumman, cut more than 29,000 jobs. These same companies have announced plans to cut another 20,000 jobs during 1993–1994. In the first half of 1993, aerospace employment declined at a 15 percent rate with commercial employment declining faster than military. Unlike past business cycles, the commercial sector is not able to absorb job losses in the military aircraft sector. As the restructuring winds down, the rate of job loss is expected to slow to between 5 and 10 percent in 1994. Increases in employment may not occur until the second half of this decade.

Exports provide little buffer from domestic spending cuts. Global defense spending is on the decline everywhere. U.S. manufacturers are finding it more difficult to compete in the European defense market as Europe's own military aircraft industry has been consolidated in an attempt to hold on to a larger share of declining local markets and to maintain a viable European defense industrial base.

Overcapacity resulting from years of Cold War production is intensifying competition worldwide. In 1990 U.S. manufacturers produced only about one-third of the world's military aircraft. Russia, the Ukraine, and other newly independent states produced thousands of military aircraft. Now operating at production rates less than one-third of capacity, these facilities in the former Soviet Union are scrambling for international sales. Both new and used MIG aircraft are being offered in aircraft competitions around the world. Other major competitors, such as France and the United Kingdom, are struggling to find international customers for their aircraft. China, Brazil, Italy, Taiwan, and Sweden are developing or producing fighters for international sales. Sales that are being made are often at break-even prices and require substantial concessions such as offsets and technology transfer. Most of the 1994 U.S. military exports will be helicopters as the need for sophisticated, front-line fighters decreases. The recent arms build-up in the Persian Gulf region is coming to an end, and the latest reduction in tensions between Israel and its neighbors will continue to reduce the need for new front-line fighters.

MISSILES AND SPACE LAUNCH VEHICLES

Shipments of U.S. missile systems, space launch vehicles, and related equipment are forecast to increase at a real rate of nearly 3 percent in 1994. Defense cutbacks and continued decline in the aerospace industry have curtailed demand in the missile segment, which is forecast to increase by only 2 percent. The space launch industry will increase commercial launches in 1994 due in part to long delays in launch schedules during 1993.

Missile Systems. In the wake of the cold war, Pentagon officials are shifting priorities away from nuclear weaponry and toward missile systems that will provide enhanced strategic conventional capability. New weapons programs in missiles and space will focus on U.S. ability to deter or win regional, non-nuclear conflicts. The president's budget request for fiscal year (FY) 1994 includes procurement of 24 Trident II nuclear missiles at a cost of more than $1.1 billion.

Improvements to the U.S. missile and space arsenal will highlight capabilities for precision strikes on command and control centers and knocking down enemy tactical ballistic missiles. Smarter and more lethal systems that increase standoff attack capabilities, such as the Tri-Service Stand-Off Attack Missile (TSSAM), will also take priority. Requested FY94 funding for initial procurement of the TSSAM was $195 million, while research and test outlays for the program are $433 million.

The Army and Navy are seeking to develop deep-strike missile systems to engage enemy targets quickly and improve reaction times. The Army Tactical Missile System (ATACMS) is a ground-based, deep-strike system that would coincide with Air Force attack capabilities. The Pentagon requested $144 million in the FY94 budget to procure 255 ATACMs. The Navy relies on its Tomahawk cruise missile for precision strikes against targets deep in enemy territory. The Navy plans to procure 216 Tomahawks in FY94 at a cost of $248 million.

On the defensive side of missile procurement, high priority will be given to the ground-based Anti-Tactical Ballistic Missiles (ATBM) and theater missile defensive systems over space-based interceptors. The FY94 budget request for the Strategic Defense Initiative Organization (SDIO) remained at the same $3.8 billion funding level of 1993. Funding for Theater High-Altitude Area Defense Missile (THAAD) and the Patriot/ERNT programs will receive priority under the new plan, while the Brilliant Pebbles program will be scaled back from $219 million in FY93 to $73 million in FY94, mainly for research and development.

Overall, 1994 DOD missile outlays are expected to increase by 2 percent, followed by cuts of 2 percent and 3 percent in 1995 and 1996, respectively.

The export market will become increasingly competitive in 1994 as European and Russian manufacturers compete with U.S. companies for shrinking defense spending overseas. Sales of U.S. missile systems (SIC 3761) through Foreign Military Sales programs reached an estimated $338 million in 1993, down significantly from $599 million in 1992. Air-to-air missiles represent the majority of this market. The United States has led this market in the past as foreign buyers looked to equip American-made fighters with U.S. missiles. The French MICA and Russian built AS-12 air-to-air missiles now pose a challenge to U.S. AIM-120 AMRAAM as well as the popular

Trends and Forecasts: Guided Missiles and Space Vehicles (SIC 3761) (In millions of dollars except as noted)

ITEM	1991	1992[1]	1993[2]	1994[3]	PERCENT CHANGE (1991–1994)		
					91–92	92–93	93–94
Industry Data							
Value of shipments[4]	23,399	22,089	21,625	22,035	–5.6	–2.1	1.9
Value of shipments (1987$)	24,787	23,599	22,956	24,081	–4.8	–2.7	4.9
Total employment (000)	136	119	97.1	93.0	–12.5	–18.4	–4.2
Production workers (000)	45.0	37.6	31.5	31.2	–16.4	–16.2	–1.0
Average hourly earnings ($)	19.07	20.05	20.85	21.50	5.1	4.0	3.1
Capital expenditures	450	—	—	—	—	—	—
Product Data							
Value of shipments[5]	16,075	15,400	14,846	15,306	–4.2	–3.6	3.1
Value of shipments (1987$)	17,028	16,452	15,760	16,728	3.1	4.2	6.1
Trade Data							
Value of imports	1.8	4.1	12.6	6.3	127.8	207.3	–50.0
Value of exports	318	599	338	523	88.4	–43.6	54.7

[1] Estimate, except exports and imports.

[2] Estimate.

[3] Forecast.

[4] Value of all products and services sold by establishments in the guided missiles and space vehicles industry.

[5] Value of products classified in the guided missiles and space vehicles industry produced by all industries.

Source: U.S. Department of Commerce: Bureau of the Census; International Trade Administration (ITA). Estimates and forecasts by ITA.

Sidewinder and Sparrow missiles. Unfortunately for U.S. suppliers, Israel has decided not to purchase the AIM-120 Advanced Medium Range Air-to-Air Missile (AMRAAM) in 1994, fearing similar escalating purchases by Saudi Arabia and other Arab states. Israel will rely on upgrades to the existing AIM-7 Sparrow and AIM-9 Sidewinder missiles.

Several European missile manufacturers are expected to merge in 1994–1995 to compete with larger and already consolidated U.S. companies. Shrinking defense budgets in Europe are expected to result in the consolidation of missile manufactures to benefit from joint R&D and economies of scale in production for European, U.S., and export market sales. Paris-based Matra-Hachette and the U.K.'s British Aerospace are contemplating the first move. British Aerospace was selected in 1992 to build the European Advanced Short Range Air-to-Air Missile (ASRAAM).

Space Launch Vehicles. The international market for commercial launch services for medium and large geosynchronous communications satellites declined from 14 launches in 1992 to 9 launches in 1993 because of delays in launch schedules. Geosynchronous, also known as geostationary, refers to satellites that travel at the same speed as the earth's rotation so the satellite appears to remain in the same place. The market is forecast to double in 1994 with 18 commercial launches scheduled. The actual number may be less if launch service companies are again unable to meet their aggressive schedules.

After five years of competing for commercial launch services, U.S. providers General Dynamics and McDonnell Douglas are holding on to a 36 percent share of the international market. The French/European consortium, Arianespace, had seven launches on its manifest for 1993 and plans ten launches in 1994. Arianespace controlled 62 percent of the large geosynchronous (GEO) commercial market in 1993. Arianespace currently has a launch backlog of 39 satellites worth approximately $3 billion. China's Long March Industry Corporation launched two commercial payloads in 1993 and has two launches on its manifest in 1994.

Commercial launch manifests for 1994 are crowded due to several launch failures in 1993. The failures caused long delays in international launch schedules as investigators determined causes and rockets lay idle awaiting green lights or modifications. Although expected launch rates may double in 1994, U.S. commercial launch providers still face another year of flat demand for satellite launch services. The demand for commercial launches of medium and large communications satellites leveled off at about 10 to 14 per year and is projected to remain that way for the next five years. The initial surge in demand for Expendable Launch Vehicles (ELVs) caused by the 1986 Challenger disaster, and aided by the U.S. government policy shift to dedicated launch vehicles, has subsided. Commercial launch service providers have since caught up with the backlog of commercial and military launches. Launch capacity will continue to exceed demand over the next five years as more international players enter the already crowded market for commercial launch services.

The U.S. Department of Transportation (DOT) licensed four large vehicle launches for geosynchronous communications satellites in 1993 and one launch for a Strategic Defense Initiative Organization (SDIO) experimental satellite. The communications satellite launches include two UHF satellites, the NATO IVB satellite, and the Telestar 401 satellite. Four of the five GEO launches were set for December 1993.

The government remains the largest consumer of U.S. space launch services, albeit a declining one. DOD, NASA, and the National Oceanic and Atmospheric Administration (NOAA) have had a joint requirement for about a dozen expendable launch vehicles per year, two or three of which are procured commercially, plus another three to four small orbital or suborbital launches. However, the declining strategic military threat and concomitant decline in defense spending has resulted in a downward revision in DOD's launch plans. Previously, the U.S. government used refurbished strategic missiles to meet some of its medium- and large-capacity launch requirements. A DOD directive now prohibits this practice because it unfairly competed with private U.S. launch services.

The United States lofted 14 expendable launch vehicles (ELVs) and eight Space Shuttle missions from Cape Canaveral, Florida, and four ELVs from Vandenberg Air Force Base in California in 1992. The French company Arianespace launched seven Ariane-4 boosters from Kourou in French Guiana. Russia conducted 33 launches from Plesetsk and 21 from the Baikanour Cosmodrome in Kazakhstan. The People's Republic of China conducted two launches out of Jiquan in addition to two flights of the Long March ELV from Xichang. Japan and India each launched one rocket.

U.S. commercial launch service providers will face increasingly fierce foreign competition in 1994. The European Space Agency is testing its next generation of the Ariane booster, the Ariane V, which will be able to put three medium-size satellites or several small satellites into orbit with a single launch at a reduced cost. In

Trends and Forecasts: Space Propulsion Units and Parts (SIC 3764) (In millions of dollars except as noted)

ITEM	1991	1992[1]	1993[2]	1994[3]	PERCENT CHANGE (1991–1994)		
					91–92	92–93	93–94
Industry Data							
Value of shipments[4]	3,658	3,453	3,336	3,234	–5.6	–3.4	–3.1
Value of shipments (1987$)	3,867	4,125	3,925	3,717	6.7	–4.8	–5.3
Total employment (000)	27.7	25.6	23.1	22.8	–7.6	–9.8	–1.3
Production workers (000)	9.5	8.3	8.1	7.9	–12.6	–2.4	–2.5
Average hourly earnings ($)	19.05	—	—	—	—	—	—
Capital expenditures	102	—	—	—	—	—	—
Product Data							
Value of shipments[5]	4,530	4,299	4,188	4,092	–5.1	–2.6	–2.3
Value of shipments (1987$)	1,789	5,136	4,927	4,703	7.2	–4.1	–4.5
Trade Data							
Value of imports	0.5	0.4	0.4	0.2	–20.0	0.0	–50.0
Value of exports	6.7	12.6	0.7	9.1	88.1	–94.4	530.0

[1] Estimate, except exports and imports.

[2] Estimate.

[3] Forecast.

[4] Value of all products and services sold by establishments in the space propulsion units and parts industry.

[5] Value of products classified in the space propulsion units and parts industry produced by all industries.

Source: U.S. Department of Commerce; Bureau of the Census; International Trade Administration (ITA). Estimates and forecasts by ITA.

January 1993 the U.S. Government approved Lockheed Corporation's request to enter into a joint venture with Russia's Khrunichev Enterprise, maker of the Proton launch vehicle. The new company, called Lockheed Khrunichev Energiya or LKE, will provide marketing and integration support for the Russian-made Proton. Negotiations to allow the launch of Western communications satellites on the Proton were completed in 1993 allowing Russia eight GEO launches through the year 2000. Launch prices for Russian ELVs are required to meet a 7.5 percent threshold below the lowest Western bid for a given contract. Proton launches to low earth orbit (LEO) will be considered on a case-by-case basis. Russia has already received U.S. permission to launch a satellite for the international consortium INMARSAT. The Proton is currently the most powerful commercial ELV in the world, with the ability to loft several small communications satellites to low earth orbit or two large satellites to geosychronous orbit. The PRC, originally expected to capture a limited share of the market, has had difficulties winning launch contracts. China's 1989 Memorandum of Agreement (MOA) with the United States allowing the Chinese to launch nine satellites over six years expires at the end of 1994. Negotiations are expected to resume in 1994 to renegotiate a follow-up agreement to the 1989 MOA.

Trends and Forecasts: Space Vehicle Equipment, NEC (SIC 3769) (In millions of dollars except as noted)

ITEM	1991	1992[1]	1993[2]	1994[3]	PERCENT CHANGE (1991–1994) 91–92	92–93	93–94
Industry Data							
Value of shipments[4]	1,907	1,810	1,751	1,723	–5.1	–3.3	–1.6
Value of shipments (1987$)	1,731	2,162	2,060	1,980	24.9	–4.7	–3.9
Total employment (000)	14.2	12.9	11.8	11.6	–9.2	–8.5	–1.7
Production workers (000)	7.7	7.6	7.4	7.1	–1.3	–2.6	–4.1
Average hourly earnings ($)	18.36	—	—	—	—	—	—
Capital expenditures	31.4	—	—	—	—	—	—
Product Data							
Value of shipments[5]	4,387	3,904	3,740	3,701	–11.0	–4.2	–1.0
Value of shipments (1987$)	3,981	4,664	4,400	4,254	17.2	–5.7	–3.3
Trade Data							
Value of imports	103	104	78.2	96.4	1.0	–24.8	23.3
Value of exports	899	839	577	693	–6.7	–31.2	20.1

[1] Estimate, except exports and imports.

[2] Estimate.

[3] Forecast.

[4] Value of all products and services sold by establishments in the space vehicle equipment, NEC industry.

[5] Value of products classified in the space vehicle equipment, NEC industry produced by all industries.

Source: U.S. Department of Commerce: Bureau of the Census; International Trade Administration (ITA). Estimates and forecasts by ITA.

The trend towards larger vehicles, with dramatically increased lift capabilities such as the Proton and Ariane V launch vehicles, is expected to curtail the number of commercial launches in coming years. The ability to launch multiple satellites on a single rocket could reduce demand for launch vehicles even in a growing market for satellite-based telecommunications, remote sensing, and direct broadcast services. Currently, the ability to "multiple-manifest" commercial launches for different customers remains largely unproven. Delivery lead times and changing launch schedules cause problems for customers and launch service providers. The ability to efficiently schedule and launch two GEO telecommunications satellites for different customers could prove to be a determining factor in lowering the cost per pound to orbit.

Developing the next Pc-265   c-265generation U.S. launch vehicle remains a low funding priority in FY94. The president's budget proposal scales back funding for the Spacelifter program, delaying yet again the development of a new rocket to replace the nation's current stable of ELVs. The National Aerospace Plane (NASP) program was also the victim of tighter budgets. In FY94 the United States will reduce funding for research and development in space transportation technologies. Lack of support for developing a new vehicle was reflected in the Senate Armed Services Committee suggestion that DOD investigate the possibility of launching payloads on non-U.S. launch vehicles. The House version of the budget retained the requested $53.9 million for spacelifter and added $36.74 million to the NASP program.

Strides toward developing a new single-stage-to-orbit (SSTO) technology highlighted industry R&D efforts last year and work continues in 1994. On August 18, 1993, the McDonnell Douglas Delta Clipper Experimental (DC-X) SSTO vehicle made a successful hover test, rising 150 feet in the air, moving laterally 350 feet, and landing. The DC-X will test the SSTO concept to demonstrate the viability of leapfrogging ahead of foreign competition in the international launch services industry. The House Armed Services Committee requested $75 million in additional funding in FY94 to continue the DC-X program and build a larger version of the experimental vehicle. The House committee also recommended that the SSTO program be shifted from the Ballistic Missile Defense Organization (BMDO) to the Advanced Research Projects Agency (ARPA).

NASA announced initial funding in both FY93 and FY94 for a four-phase study on developing new launch vehicles to meet expected demand in nonmilitary launch markets. The work will be conducted by a consortium of five aerospace companies including Boeing, Martin Marietta, Lockheed, General Dynamics, and Rockwell International.

Although funding for the next generation of launch vehicles has not increased, the Department of Defense announced a winner in the hotly contested Medium Launch Vehicle–3 competition (MLV-3). In April of 1993 the McDonnell Douglas Delta II ELV was awarded the contract to launch replacement satellites for the NAVSTAR Global Positioning System (GPS). Under the new contract, the Air Force has options for 36 launches valued at over $1 billion. The contract calls for McDonnell Douglas to "launch on demand" within 40 days of an Air Force notice.

In 1994 the new and growing segment of the space transportation industry continues to be the small and medium-launch vehicle industry. Small launch vehicles serve the market for lightweight payloads (from a few hundred to 2,000 pounds) launched to low earth orbit or suborbital microgravity applications. These payloads consist primarily of suborbital scientific microgravity experiments as well as small telecommunications satellites, commonly known as microsats or lightsats. Medium vehicles serve the small communications and remote sensing markets with lift capabilities from 3,000 to 6,000 pounds to low earth orbit.

Lockheed Corporation announced it will enter the market for launch vehicles capable of placing payloads into low earth orbit (LEO) with a family of rockets to debut in 1995. The French company, Aerospatiale, is also considering the small vehicle market using Russian propulsion units to develop new lightweight vehicles capable of carrying single or multiple LEO payloads. These new vehicles would compete with Orbital Sciences Taurus ELV on the low end of lift capacity at approximately 3,200 pounds to LEO. McDonnell Douglas has also proposed a new launcher called the Delta-Lite, which would compete in the high-end of the market at 5,000 pounds to LEO. EER's Conestoga rocket was scheduled to carry NASA's COMET reentry vehicle in the summer of 1993, but funding problems caused a delay and the launch date is undetermined.

In the long term, the U.S. launch industry is working to focus efforts on lowering the cost per pound to orbit for commercial payloads. Three options—upgrading the existing fleet of vehicles, developing a new vehicle with off-the-shelf technology, and investing in new leap-frog technology—are at the center of the debate. Over the past three years, Congress has watched the National Launch System (NLS), Spacelifter, and a host of new single-stage-to-orbit and two-stage-to-orbit vehicles claim the next generation mantel. Projected costs for a completely new launch system are $8 to $10 billion over ten years. Marshaling these billions of dollars under increasingly tighter budgets will continue to be the major challenge facing U.S. launch service companies and policy makers over the next several years.

CASE 19

MCDONNELL DOUGLAS CORPORATION—1994

FRED R. DAVID
Francis Marion University

Our shared vision is to become the preeminent team of customer-focused people, creating the highest quality aerospace products and services which contribute to world peace, understanding and achievement. (John McDonnell, CEO, McDonnell Douglas Annual Report, 1992.)

Headquartered in St. Louis, Missouri, McDonnell Douglas Corporation (MDC) 314-232-0232 is the nation's largest defense contractor, the world's largest builder of military aircraft, the world's third largest commercial aircraft maker, and the third largest NASA contractor. However, MDC's earnings fell from $423 million in 1991 to $161 million in 1992. Company debt increased 19 percent to $2.8 billion. MDC's stock price fell from $73 to $48 per share during 1992.

MDC's 1992 earnings were substantially below 1991's as a result of three factors. First, there were $383 million of pretax charges in the C-17 program as a result of exceeding a fixed-price ceiling on development and initial production. Second, operating earnings of MDC's commercial aircraft business fell by $182 million. Third, the new accounting rule for retiree health benefits reduced 1992 earnings by $133 million.

MDC closed three fabrications plants in the United States during 1992 in order to raise average plant utilization to more than 75 percent by 1994, when in-house fabrication work will be consolidated at remaining plants. MDC reduced employment by 32 percent during 1990–1992, while industry employment fell 24 percent in the same period. Demand for both commercial aircraft and military aircraft is declining, so MDC may be in serious trouble. The company needs a clear strategic plan for the mid-1990s.

Operating earnings for MDC's military aircraft segment were $19 million in 1992, $404 million in 1991, and negative $48 million in 1990. Excluding the C-17, MDC's ten biggest government aerospace programs as a group (F/A-18, F-15, AV-8B, T-45 trainer aircraft, AH-64 Apache helicopter, Tomahawk and Harpoon missiles, Advanced Cruise Missile, Delta Launch vehicle, and Space Station) had 1992 earnings equal to nearly 10 percent of revenues. That is a fair return by industry standards and is up from 9 percent in 1991 and 8 percent in 1990. Seven of the ten projects had improved margins in 1992.

MDC is the prime contractor for three major military aircraft programs that are likely to remain in production into the next decade; although total U.S. government purchases of aerospace products—the F/A-18 Hornet, the C-17 Globemaster III, and the T-45 Goshawk—are declining, MDC expects positive earnings from the C-17 program in 1993 with delivery of the final aircraft in the development program. Flight and ground testing of the new military transport will continue into 1994.

With a larger wing, a lengthened fuselage, and higher thrust engines, the F/A-18 E/F will have the range and payload capabilities to perform the bulk of the U.S. Navy's strike and fighter missions well into the next century. The next-generation Hornet is central to the U.S. Navy's new "From the Sea" war-fighting doctrine, which shifts its focus from open-ocean warfare to regional and coastal operations. The advanced Hornet will have up to 40 percent more range than earlier versions, combined with greater weapons-carrying capacity, improved survivability, and capacity for future growth. The first flight of the F/A-18 E/F is scheduled for late 1995.

MDC's most important achievement in 1992 was the award of a $3.7 billion contract from the U.S. Navy to begin development of a major upgrade of the Hornet, called F/A-18 E/F. Coupled with continuing purchases by the Navy of F/A-18 C/D models, this development program firmly establishes the Hornet as the cornerstone of U.S. naval aviation well into the next century. MDC expects to remain the nation's largest defense contractor in 1993, measured by prime Department of Defense contract awards. However, Lockheed and Martin Marietta, which have enlarged their defense businesses through major acquisitions, are challenging MDC for the number one position in total sales to the government.

Internationally, the Hornet program now has been selected as the front-line fighter of six countries outside the United States: Finland, Switzerland, Kuwait, Canada, Australia, and Spain. Deliveries to the Finnish air force will begin in 1995 and continue through 2000. In Switzerland selection of the F/A-18 over the F-16 and several European-made fighters was reaffirmed by the Swiss Federal Council in 1991 and approved by the Swiss parliament in 1992. However, the Swiss order is subject to a positive outcome on a national referendum in 1993. The Israeli air force is evaluating several advanced combat aircraft, including the F/A-18. By year-end 1992, 1,150 Hornets had been delivered to the U.S. Navy and Marine Corps and to other nations.

MDC won a $3 billion order for the F/A-18 Hornet from Finland in the most fiercely contested international fighter plane competition in 1992. MDC also won a $5 billion order for 72 F-15 Eagles from Saudi Arabia and a $400 million order for 13 AV-8B Harrier II Plus aircraft from Italy. The Saudi Arabian F-15 sale was a great example of teamwork at a grassroots level. Thousands of people at MDC and its suppliers joined together in rallying U.S. congressional and presidential support for the sale. The sale extends F-15 production into 1998, preserving 7,000 jobs at MDC.

The C-17 Globemaster III is a central element in the U.S. Air Force's post–cold war strategy of "global reach, global power." The giant aircraft will provide large cargo airlift capability from U.S. bases to austere airfields anywhere in the world. Air Force plans call for production and delivery of 120 Globemaster IIIs for that mission. During 1992 MDC delivered four initial production C-17s to the Air Force for the flight test program. In the first half of 1993, MDC delivered the fifth and sixth production aircraft, which were the last aircraft covered in the development and initial production contract.

MDC expects the C-17 to be profitable in 1993. However, with 75 percent of flight testing still to go, additional problems may be identified during testing. MDC is under firm contract for 10 production C-17s, and Congress has approved funding for ten more aircraft. Production of an additional eight aircraft was authorized in the 1993 defense bill.

The sale of 72 F-15 Eagles to Saudi Arabia extends production of the F-15 into 1998. Additionally, the Saudi order will permit MDC to compete with the F-15 for other international orders in coming years. Saudi F-15 deliveries are expected to begin in 1995.

MDC is supporting U.S. Navy and Marine Corps efforts, which could lead to remanufacturing of existing AV-8B Harrier day attack aircraft to the Harrier II Plus radar/night attack configuration—providing an aircraft with greatly improved capabilities and a new service life at approximately two-thirds the cost of a new Harrier II Plus.

The first production aircraft deliveries of the T-45A Goshawk to the U.S. Naval Air Station in Kingsville, Texas, began in early 1992. By midyear, Kingsville formed the first T-45 training squadron. Current Navy plans call for 268 aircraft to be delivered through the year 2003. The program suffered a setback recently, however, when its first test aircraft veered from the runway and sustained major damage after landing at Edwards Air Force Base, California. Test flights resumed after the cause of the accident was established. Nine St. Louis–assembled T-45s were delivered to the Navy in 1992.

The majority of the U.S. Army's procurement of AH-64 Apache helicopters are expected to be delivered by late 1993. However, orders from the United Arab Emirates, Greece, and other countries have extended Apache deliveries into mid-1995 and hold open the door for additional foreign military sales. Projected international orders would sustain the production line into 1996, when the U.S. Army plans to begin a modernization program to remanufacture its Apache fleet into a new and more capable AH-64 C/D configuration. The first two AH-64D Longbow prototypes flew for the first time in 1992, each ahead of contract schedule. The MD Explorer, the first all-new commercial helicopter in the 1990s, featuring the NOTAR system, celebrated its first year of service in October. To date, more than 30 MD 520Ns have been delivered worldwide. In 1992 MDC delivered 57 MD 500 Series helicopters.

COMMERCIAL AIRCRAFT

MDC's commercial aircraft business continued to make a profit in 1992, operating in a cyclical market that has gone from boom to bust as a result of three consecutive years of heavy losses by U.S. and world airlines. As a result of weak market conditions, MDC delivered only 84 MD-80 twin jets in 1992, compared with 138 in 1991. Even so, the program generated sufficient earnings to more than offset a small losss in the new MD-11 trijet line. There will be a further decrease in twin jet deliveries in 1993. The ability of airlines to pay for MD-80 and MD-11 deliveries scheduled in 1993 is a major concern. Projections of positive cash flow for the MD-11 and the commercial transport business as a whole in 1993 are based on scheduled deliveries and payment of aircraft as ordered. MDC is working closely with some airline customers to help financial arrangements to complete deliveries on time.

In 1992 the world's airlines and leasing companies placed firm orders for fewer than 325 new jetliners, net of cancellations. By contrast, airlines and leasing companies placed net firm orders for more than 1,600 aircraft in 1989. With the large number of orders received from 1987 to 1990, MDC faced the challenge of increasing production rapidly to satisfy customer requirements for new aircraft with near-term delivery schedules. In adjusting to fewer new orders and the cancellation of a number of existing orders since then, MDC has faced the radically different challenge of reducing cost structures and scaling back production while continuing to make on-time deliveries of quality products and continuing to work on new models or new-generation aircraft.

Development and production milestones were met in preparing the MD-90—an advanced derivative of the MD-80—for its rollout and first flight in 1993 and entry into its flight test and certification program. The MD-90 will be the quietest and most environmentally clean aircraft in the 150-seat aircraft class when it enters airline service in 1994. The MD-11 jetliner reached a key milestone in 1993. The unit cost of a newly delivered MD-11 fell below the sales price on a consistent basis for the first time. Although the MD-11 did not achieve improved earnings in 1993, it generated positive cash flow. The MD-11 trijet was the biggest single consumer of cash of all MDC programs in 1992.

MDC delivered 42 MD-11 trijets in 1992—11 more than in 1991, the first full year of production. At year end, 76 MD-11s were in service, with 14 operators, carrying more than one-half million passengers and traveling more than 10 million miles each month. As of December 31, 1992, the MD-11 program status included 97 firm orders, 127 options and reserves, and 76 deliveries, for a total of 300 aircraft. On the same date, the MD80/90 program included 186 firm orders, 227 options and reserves, and 1,047 deliveries, for a total of 1,460 aircraft. MDC is scheduled to deliver more than 30 trijets and more than 40 twin jets in 1993. However, the ability of some airlines to pay for deliveries scheduled in 1993 is a major concern. Increased MD-11 trijet deliveries in 1992 offset reduced MD-80 twin jet deliveries. MDC delivered 84 MD-80 twin jets in 1992, as compared with 138 in 1991 and 139 in 1990. The decreased MD-80 deliveries in 1992 reflect the overall softness in the commercial aircraft market. MDC delivered 42 MD-11 trijets in 1992, compared with 31 in 1991 and 3 in 1990.

MDC was almost even with Airbus Industrie in total seats delivered in 1992—each with about 19 percent of the industry total. MDC was also close to matching Airbus in new firm orders, net of cancellations, with 11 percent of the industry total for 1992 compared with 13 percent for Airbus. Swissair, Delta, Altitalia, Martinair, and International Lease Finance Corporation all placed firm orders for MD-11s in 1992. SAS, a Scandinavian airline, became the first airline in Europe to order the MD-90. In a modification of an existing order, SAS added six MD-90s while reducing their MD-80 orders by seven.

In MDC's biggest commercial win in 1992, MDC and the People's Republic of China reached agreement on a major aircraft purchase and coproduction program. In a competition with the Boeing 737, MDC twin jets were selected by the PRC for its Trunkliner program. Final assembly of 40 twin jets (a combination of MD-80s and MD-90s) will be performed in China. The agreement with China calls for discussions by 1995 that could lead to orders for up to 130 additional MD-90s.

Operating revenues in the commercial aircraft segment decreased 2 percent after increasing 72 percent in 1991. The commercial aircraft segment reported operating earnings of $109 million in 1992 and $291 million in 1991, and operating losses of

$83 million in 1990. Factors contributing to lower 1992 earnings for the segment were reduced margins on the MD-11 trijet and higher research and development expenditures. Research and development costs, which were lower in 1992 for the MD-11 trijet, increased on the MD-90. In addition, research and development costs were incurred in 1992 on the MD-12, a proposed four-engine jumbo airliner.

Despite higher deliveries and revenues, the MD-11 program incurred operating losses in 1992 after recording a small operating profit in 1991. Contributing to the 1991 operating profit was the retention of $40 million of advance payments made by commercial airline customers that defaulted in their contracts in 1991. Because costs on the MD-11 program did not decline as rapidly as planned, MDC has raised its cost estimate for the total program.

MISSILES, SPACE, AND ELECTRONIC SYSTEMS

The missiles, space, and electronic systems division had record earnings in 1992. Revenues increased by 6 percent, mostly as a result of increased work on Space Station Freedom, the largest single program in this division. Revenues had decreased by 6 percent in 1991. Space Station Freedom will provide participants with new opportunities for research in life sciences, materials and earth sciences, and astrophysics.

Operating earnings of the missiles, space, and electronic systems segment were $197 million in 1992 as compared to $168 million in 1991 and $167 million in 1990. Increased 1992 operating earnings reflect improved margins on the Harpoon, Tomahawk, ACM, and Delta programs, partially offset by a decrease in earnings on electronic systems programs.

MDC is responsible for the largest part of the Space Station Freedom program: building the initial segments that are first launched into space. In 1992 MDC and NASA took several important steps toward making Space Station Freedom ready for first element launch in 1996. In preparation for the integration and testing of elements that will be sent into space, MDC has substantially completed construction of a 178,000-square-foot office tower and a high bay assembly and test building at the space station's Clear Lake Development Facility in Houston, Texas.

An important milestone was reached when 21 detailed design reviews of space station elements and systems were completed in preparation for a critical design review in 1993. Space Station Freedom accounted for about 40 percent of 1992 revenues in MDC's space systems business. The decision to "restructure" the program, announced by President Clinton's administration in 1993, raises uncertainties as to the configuration and schedule of the program, including the portion of the program for which MDC is responsible.

During 1992 MDC's Delta launch program continued to enhance its record as the world's most reliable launch system. There were 11 Delta launches in 1992, bringing the total number of successful consecutive launches to 39. The Delta program has strongly improved earnings, partly as a result of reduced manufacturing costs at the Delta assembly plant in Pueblo, Colorado, and improved cycle time for launch processing at the Cape Canaveral Air Force Station in Florida.

MDC is working on a contract won in 1991 for a single-stage rocket technology (SSRT) experiment for the Strategic Defense Initiative Organization to demonstrate technology readiness for a single stage-to-orbit reusable launch vehicle. Integration, assembly, and test activities are already under way, and test firings and demonstration flights were completed in 1993.

MDC's missiles business led the way for its segment in improved financial performance in 1992. The Tomahawk and Harpoon/SLAM missile programs had an outstanding year in terms of winning new business, driving down costs, and improving profitability. The Tomahawk meets the need for weapon systems that enable the United States to project power quickly—and convincingly. In the eight years since MDC entered the program as a dual-source producer, the inflation-adjusted price of the Tomahawk missile has dropped by more than two-thirds, and overall program savings for the U.S. government have been estimated at $3.5 billion.

MDC has won the majority production share in the last two annual dual-source competitions to build Navy Tomahawks. MDC is currently working under a $179 million contract to build 114 Tomahawks, which represented 65 percent of the Navy's 1992 procurement. In January 1993 MDC received a $201.6 million contract to build another 120 Tomahawks and to remanufacture an additional 120 missiles in inventory into upgraded Block III Tomahawks. That contract represents 60 percent of total Tomahawk procurement for 1993.

Overseas customers ordered 122 Harpoon anti-ship missiles in 1992, which was ten fewer than in 1991. Over 40 percent of the 5,919 Harpoons produced since the program began 21 years ago have been delivered to a total of 20 overseas customers. U.S. orders for the basic Harpoon missile stopped in 1989.

MDC's electronic systems business lost money in 1992 as a result of $38 million in loss provisions in the laser crosslink program. The laser crosslink is an advanced product that enables satellites to communicate directly with one another in orbit, reducing dependency on ground stations. Under a fixed-price development contract, MDC has incurred losses totaling $119 million in this program since its inception in 1980. TRW, the program's prime contractor, expects MDC to deliver five additional units in 1993 and 1994.

Most of the other parts of MDC's electronic systems business continued to operate profitably in 1992. Work performed in complex software, microprocessors, and lasers contributes to many MDC products. MDC is a leader in the military command, control, communications, and intelligence (C^3I) field. For 1993 Congress approved 36 Mast Mounted Sights, an electro-optical system that enables helicopter pilots and ships' crews to detect and designate targets for attack helicopters, by day or night or in inclement weather.

OTHER MCDONNELL DOUGLAS OPERATIONS

McDonnell Douglas Finance Corporation (MDFC). MDFC reduced its total assets by 22 percent to $2 billion as it disposed of a number of businesses in 1992 and continued to sharpen its focus on core markets of aircraft and commercial equipment leasing. During the year MDFC reduced its exposure in noncore lending and leasing operations by more than one-half. The disposition of several of the finance company's operations and portfolios was the principal factor in causing a substantial reduction in MDC's 1992 revenues for businesses grouped under "financial services and other."

MDFC's aircraft financing and commercial equipment leasing were solidly profitable. The aircraft financing operation provided $255 million in financing for MDC commercial aircraft customers. Aircraft transactions completed in 1992 varied in type from bridge notes on an MD-88 aircraft for Aerolineas Argentinas, to predelivery notes on eight MD-82s for USAir, and to lease financing of a new MD-83 for Reno Air, a recently formed carrier. MDFC also helped arrange the financing of two MD-11 aircraft for Varig and another three for China Eastern. At year end the aircraft-leasing operation portfolio totaled $1 billion, with MDC-built aircraft accounting for 76 percent of the value. The commercial equipment leasing operation wrote $51 million in new leases in 1992 and ended the year with a portfolio worth $557 million. Included in its business is the lease of corporate aircraft and other large equipment items.

McDonnell Douglas Realty Company (MDRC). MDRC manages a 4.6-million-square-foot portfolio valued in excess of $500 million. In 1992 the company provided increased consulting services to MDC by negotiating rental reductions, auditing existing lease arrangements, and consolidating lease facilities to utilize space more efficiently. MDRC's revenue and the total asset value of its portfolio increased approximately 7 percent in 1992, and its commercial portfolio continued to perform above average, with less than 12 percent vacancy rates. MDRC in 1992 continued to work on the development of two new MDC facilities near Houston, Texas, that will serve the space station program.

McDonnell Douglas Travel Company (MDTC). In a poor year for the travel industry MDTC generated $152 million in business travel sales, almost matching 1991 business volume. MDTC was established in 1986 and is a travel agency serving MDC and all its divisions, as well as external customers.

McDonnell Douglas Technical Services Company (MDTSC). MDTSC was established in 1989 to provide MDC and other employers with a pool of experienced and skilled workers (including retirees) to fill specific needs on short notice. MDTSC's business increased by 60 percent in 1992 as its five branch offices placed professionals in over 2,000 contract assignments within MDC and at commercial clients. MDTSC has further increased its capabilities by developing a resource pool instantly accessible from its online computer database of more than 50,000 potential employees.

CONCLUSION

The sale of McDonnell Douglas Information Systems International (MDISI) in the first quarter of 1993 completed a four-year program to divest all MDC businesses in the information systems field. In total, including MDISI, divestitures in the information systems field resulted in pretax gains of about $375 million on proceeds of more than $900 million.

MDC's long-term strategy is to obtain partners around the world interested in sharing in the risks and rewards of the commercial aircraft business. MDC was not able to bring an international alliance together in 1992. MDC also plans to divest of its laser systems business and portions or all of McDonnell Douglas Helicopter Company.

MDC must reverse recent declines in earnings. Should the company diversify into nonaircraft-related businesses? Should MDC acquire an ailing U.S. airline? Should MDC seek a merger with Boeing in an attempt to compete more effectively with Airbus? Prepare a strategic plan for CEO McDonnell that will best assure prosperity for MDC in the mid- to late 1990s.

EXHIBIT 19-1 Selected Financial Data

MILLIONS OF DOLLARS	REVENUES			EARNINGS			FIRM BACKLOG (UNAUDITED)[†]		
	1993	1992	1991	1993	1992	1991	1993	1992	1991
Military aircraft	$ 6,852	$ 7,238	$ 7,795	$ 83	$ 8	$ 394	$ 7,997	$ 7,619	$ 9,540
Commercial aircraft	4,760	6,595	6,752	40	102	283	9,172	13,364	17,913
Missiles, space and electronic systems	2,575	3,169	2,979	338	191	163	2,210	3,069	2,995
Financial services and other	287	352	519	31	20	26			
Operating revenues/earnings	14,474	17,354	18,045	492	321	866			
Non-operating income/net	13	11	16	(5)	(4)	(13)			
Discontinued operations				37	57	66			
General corporate expenses				(9)	(12)	(6)			
Postretirement benefit curtailment				70	1,090				
Interest expense				(89)	(309)	(232)			
Income taxes				(100)	(388)	(258)			
Cumulative effect of accounting change					(1,536)				
	$14,487	$17,365	$18,061	$ 396	$ (781)	$ 423	$19,379	$24,052	$30,448

MILLIONS OF DOLLARS	ASSETS[†]			PROPERTY, PLANT AND EQUIPMENT ACQUIRED			DEPRECIATION AND AMORTIZATION		
	1993	1992	1991	1993	1992	1991	1993	1992	1991
Military aircraft	$ 3,715	$ 3,960	$ 4,328	$23	$ 70	$ 49	$149	$191	$212
Commercial aircraft	4,561	5,850	5,529	1	29	51	70	89	79
Missiles, space and electronic systems	1,330	1,524	1,741	38	116	70	48	102	102
Financial services and other	2,340	2,222	2,793		2		49	71	102
Continuing operations	11,946	13,556	14,391	62	217	170	316	453	495
Corporate	80	133	133	2		1	7	12	4
Discontinued operations		92	77						
	$12,026	$13,781	$14,601	$64	$217	$171	$323	$465	$499

[†]Amounts as of December 31.

Source: McDonnell Douglas *Annual Report*, 1993.

EXHIBIT 19-2 Consolidated Statement of Operations

YEARS ENDED DECEMBER 31 (MILLIONS OF DOLLARS, EXCEPT SHARE DATA)	1993	1992	1991
Revenues	$14,487	$17,365	$18,061
Costs and expenses:			
Cost of Products, services and rentals	12,822	15,567	15,561
General and administrative expenses	720	825	1,003
Research and development	341	509	429
Postretirement benefit curtailment	(70)	(1,090)	
Interest expense:			
Aerospace segments	89	309	232
Financial services and other segment	126	159	221
Total Costs and Expenses	14,028	16,279	17,446
Earnings from Continuing Operations Before Income Taxes and Cumulative Effect of Accounting Change	459	1,086	615
Income taxes	100	388	258
Earnings from Continuing Operations Before Cumulative Effect of Accounting Change	359	698	357
Discontinued operations:			
Earnings from operations, net of income taxes		20	(8)
Gain on disposals, net of income taxes	37	37	74
	37	57	66
Earnings Before Cumulative Effect of Accounting Change	396	755	423
Cumulative effect of initial application of new accounting standard for postretirement benefits		(1,536)	
Net Earnings (Loss)	$ 396	$ (781)	$ 423
Earnings (Loss) Per Share:			
Continuing operations	$ 9.17	$ 17.97	$ 9.32
Discontinued operations:			
Earnings from operations		.50	(.22)
Gain on disposals	.93	.96	1.93
Cumulative effect of accounting change		(39.53)	
	$ 10.10	$ (20.10)	$ 11.03
Dividends Declared Per Share	$ 1.40	$ 1.40	$ 1.40

Source: McDonnell Douglas *Annual Report*, 1993.

EXHIBIT 19-3 Consolidated Balance Sheet

DECEMBER 31 (MILLIONS OF DOLLARS AND SHARES)	1993	1992
Assets		
Cash and cash equivalents	$86	$82
Accounts receivable	555	604
Finance receivables and property on lease	2,357	2,262
Contracts in process and inventories	5,774	7,230
Property, plant and equipment	1,750	1,991
Other assets	1,504	1,612
Total Assets	$12,026	$13,781
Liabilities and Shareholders' Equity		
Liabilities:		
Accounts payable and accrued expenses	$2,190	$3,018
Accrued retiree benefits	$1,388	1,544
Income taxes	574	572
Advances and billings in excess of related costs	1,251	1,384
Notes payable and long-term debt:		
Aerospace segments	1,625	2,767
Financial services and other segment	1,513	1,474
	8,541	10,759
Minority Interest	72	
Shareholders' Equity:		
Preferred Stock—none issued		
Common Stock—issued and outstanding:		
1993, 39.3 shares; 1992, 39.2 shares	39	39
Additional capital	335	327
Retained earnings	3,043	2,702
Translation of foreign currency statements	(4)	(10)
Unearned ESOP compensation		(36)
	3,413	3,022
Total Liabilities and Shareholders' Equity	$12,026	$13,781

Source: McDonnell Douglas *Annual Report,* 1993.

EXHIBIT 19-4 Consolidated Statement of Shareholders' Equity

YEARS ENDED DECEMBER 31 (MILLIONS OF DOLLARS)	1993	1992	1991
Common Stock			
Beginning balance	$ 39	$ 38	$ 38
Shares issued to employee savings plans		1	
	39	39	38
Additional Capital			
Beginning balance	327	287	283
Employee stock awards and options	6	2	4
Shares issued to employee savings plans	2	38	
	335	327	287
Retained Earnings			
Beginning balance	2,702	3,538	3,168
Net earnings (loss)	396	(781)	423
Cash dividends declared	(55)	(55)	(53)
	3,043	2,702	3,538
Translation of Foreign Currency Statements	(4)	(10)	14
Unearned ESOP Compensation			
Beginning balance	(36)		
Prepayment of future employee benefits		(50)	
Shares allocated to employees	36	14	
		(36)	
Shareholders' Equity	$3,413	$3,022	$3,877

Source: McDonnell Douglas *Annual Report,* 1993.

EXHIBIT 19-5 Consolidated Statement of Cash Flows

YEARS ENDED DECEMBER 31 (MILLIONS OF DOLLARS)	1993	1992	1991
Operating Activities			
Earnings from continuing operations			
before cumulative effect of accounting change	$ 359	$ 698	$ 357
Adjustments to reconcile earnings from continuing operations			
before cumulative effect of accounting change			
to net cash provided (used) by operating activities:			
Depreciation of property, plant and equipment	258	353	370
Depreciation of rental equipment	50	58	89
Amortization of intangible and other assets	15	54	40
Gain on sale of assets	(44)		
Pension income	(138)	(107)	(55)
Postretirement benefit curtailment	(70)	(1,090)	
Non-cash retiree health care costs	20	133	
Change in operating assets and liabilities:			
Accounts receivable	40	97	2
Finance receivables and property on lease	(521)	(316)	111
Contracts in process and inventories	1,445	43	(1,098)
Accounts payable and accrued expenses	(822)	(22)	612
Income taxes	(5)	217	240
Advances and billings in excess of related costs	(112)	(703)	38
Discontinued operations		(2)	(26)
Net Cash Provided (Used) by Operating Activities	475	(587)	680
Investing Activities			
Property, plant and equipment acquired	(64)	(217)	(171)
Proceeds from sale of property, plant and equipment		173	
Finance receivables and property on lease	414	529	706
Proceeds from sale of discontinued businesses	181	70	200
Proceeds from sale of assets	32		
Other, including discontinued operations	11	(51)	(2)
Net Cash Provided by Investing Activities	574	504	733
Financing Activities			
Net change in borrowings (maturities 90 days or less)	(830)	574	(1,087)
Debt having maturities more than 90 days:			
New borrowings	681	1,461	487
Repayments	(954)	(2,009)	(743)
Minority interest	72		
Payments from (to) ESOP—net	36	(36)	
Proceeds of stock options exercised	5		
Dividends paid	(55)	(54)	(67)
Net Cash Used by Financing Activities	(1,045)	(64)	(1,410)
Increase (Decrease) in Cash and Cash Equivalents	4	(147)	3
Cash and cash equivalents at beginning of year	82	229	226
Cash and cash equivalents at end of year	$ 86	$ 82	$ 229

Source: McDonnell Douglas *Annual Report*, 1993.

The Boeing Company (206-655-2121), headquartered in Seattle, Washington, is the largest aerospace firm in the United States, as measured by total sales, and the world's leading manufacturer of commercial aircraft. For the past three years, Boeing has also had the distinction of being the nation's largest exporter. Jetliners currently in production include the 737, 747, 757, and 767—with the new 777 model scheduled for delivery in 1995. Boeing manufactures helicopter, military aircraft, electronic systems, and missiles.

The year 1992 was difficult for most airline carriers, which are Boeing's primary customer. While world passenger traffic recovered from the decline in 1991, stiff competition among carriers drove down fares and depressed yields. As a result, many airlines recorded substantial losses. The market for new aircraft was correspondingly down in 1992, with Boeing announcing new orders valued at $17.8 billion, compared with $20.6 billion the year before.

Because of lower demand and the growing number of requests by airlines to defer orders, Boeing cut production rates on Boeing 737, 747, 757, and 767 jetliners. By mid-1994, Boeing will be producing 21 jetliners per month, compared with 32.5 at year-end 1992. Development of the new Boeing 777 wide-body aircraft is on schedule, however, with the first delivery scheduled in 1995.

In defense and space Boeing recorded an operating profit of $204 million on sales of $5.4 billion in 1992. The tight federal budget climate, the change of administration, falling defense expenditures, and the end of the cold war raise many questions over the prospects for the defense business. Boeing is therefore in a precarious position, facing falling demand for both its commercial aircraft and defense products. The company needs a clear strategic plan for the future.

COMMERCIAL AIRCRAFT

Airline demand for new aircraft has declined, so Boeing has reduced production rates on the 737, 747, 757, and 767 models. In 1993 production of the 757 decreased to five per month, production of 737s fell to ten per month, and 767 monthly production decreased to three. In the second quarter of 1994, 747 production will be cut from five to three aircraft per month.

Boeing has about a 60 percent share of the world market for commercial jets, with announced orders valued at $17.8 billion. Approximately 80 percent of Boeing's airline orders are from non-U.S. carriers. Boeing's recent aircraft deliveries are as follows:

MODEL	1992	1991	1990
737	218	215	174
747	61	64	70*
757	99	80	77
767	63	62	60
Total commercial	441	421	381
707 military derivatives	5	14	4
Total jet transports	446	435	385
Commuter aircraft**	6	59	64

*Includes two Air Force One units.
**The de Havilland commuter aircraft division was sold in March 1992.

Development of Boeing's new 777 twinjet is proceeding on schedule. More than 80 percent of the engineering requirements have been released to manufacturing; major assembly has begun; flight testing of the first 777 will start in June 1994; and the first delivery is scheduled for May 1995. Sized to fit the market segment between the company's 767 and 747 aircraft, the 777 will carry 375–400 passengers in a two-class configuration and will be the widest, most spacious airplane in its class. The 777 represents a major step forward in customer-oriented design, offering many improvements in interior flexibility, passenger comfort, and flight-deck design.

In developing the 777, Boeing worked more closely with its airline customers than ever before. Customers were invited to play an integral part in the design process to ensure that every feature of the new aircraft was configured to meet their needs. Since the 777 program was launched in October 1990, Boeing has received 118 orders from 11 customers, with options for 95 more.

The smallest member of the Boeing jetliner family is the 737 series. The Boeing 737 is the world's best selling commercial aircraft, with more than 3,000 planes ordered since the first 737 flew in 1967. Customers now have three 737 models to choose from, with seating configurations ranging from 100 to 172 seats. Boeing received 114 orders for 737s in 1992.

The Boeing 757 and 767 are medium-capacity, fuel-efficient twinjets that meet FAA requirements for extended-range operations. The 757 can carry 186 passengers in mixed-class seating as far as 4,600 nautical miles. The 767 is larger, carrying about 260 passengers in mixed class, with a range on some versions in excess of 6,000 nautical miles. Boeing announced 38 orders for 757s and 21 orders for 767s in 1992.

The United Parcel Service has become a major customer for the 767 freighter, with an order for 30 aircraft and an option for 30 more. The order is the largest ever received by Boeing for an all-cargo airplane. Design engineering for the new freighter has begun, with certification and delivery scheduled in October 1995. The 767 freighter will be capable of carrying 56 tons of payload as far as 3,000 nautical miles, or 45 tons as far as 4,000 nautical miles.

The flagship of the Boeing airplane family, the 747-400, can carry 400 passengers more than 7,000 nautical miles, and offers airline customers the lowest seat-mile costs of any aircraft in the world. In 1992 Boeing received 28 new orders for the 747-400.

A new freighter version of the 747-400 was delivered in late 1993. The 747-400F gives Boeing's airline customers the capability of carrying 20 tons more payload on the routes they can fly compared to 747-200 freighters, or carrying the same payload 800 nautical miles farther.

For several years Boeing has been researching the market and optimum configuration for an aircraft even larger than the current 747-400. Boeing has signed an agreement with four European aerospace companies to study the feasibility of developing a new 550-800 seat jetliner. Participating in the one-year study are Germany's Deutsche Aerospace, France's Aerospatiale, British Aerospace, and CASA of Spain. The companies bring four different perspectives to the study, as well as considerable engineering and production resources.

Boeing believes that the cost, resource requirements, and risk associated with a large new airplane are so great that no single company could undertake the program alone. Moreover, preliminary research indicates that the market for such an airplane would be limited and could sustain only one product of the size being studied.

Boeing has also joined forces with a number of other companies to study the prospects for the next-generation supersonic transport, known as the High Speed Civil Transport (HSCT). Many technical barriers remain to producing an HSCT that would be environmentally acceptable and offer operating efficiencies that would keep ticket prices reasonably competitive with subsonic fares.

The European Airbus consortium remains Boeing's most formidable competitor in the commercial aircraft industry. Although the United States and the European community reached an agreement in 1992 that limits direct subsidies to 33 percent of development costs for new models, Airbus still receives hundreds of millions of dollars in government aid to launch new products. Boeing supports the current agreement as a step forward, but continues to urge U.S. trade representatives to negotiate an end to all direct subsidies.

In the highly competitive market for commercial aircraft, Boeing's reputation for customer service is an effective marketing tool. In mid-1993 the company opened a new spare parts distribution center adjacent to the Seattle-Tacoma airport. The 720,000-square-foot facility consolidated three existing spares operations and provided capacity to meet requirements into the next century. Boeing receives nearly 3,000 orders for spare parts each day. Another important part of customer service is training for pilots, mechanics, and maintenance people. Boeing trains about 2,100 pilots and 4,600 mechanics annually for airline customers around the world. Construction of a new $100 million customer services training center began in 1993.

A number of new Boeing manufacturing facilities recently started operations. A 937,000-square-foot skin and spar mill near Tacoma, Washington, produces parts. The plant houses 14 milling machines with beds over 100 feet long, including several 270-foot mills that are the largest machines of their type in the world. These mills allow for two 105-foot wing skins to be machined at once. Upper and lower wing-skin panels and stringers for the 777 and all wide-body models are produced at the plant, which is designed to significantly reduce flowtime on parts. In-process time is expected to fall from an 80-day average to ten days or less.

Boeing's new 518,000-square-foot Integrated Aircraft Systems Laboratory allows for the integrated testing of new airplane systems before they are installed in the airplane. One of the first important goals of the new facility is thorough testing of the 777 systems to ensure the new aircraft will be service-ready from the day it is first delivered.

Construction of the expanded factory and office facilities in Everett, Washington, where the new 777 is produced, has been completed. By mid-1993 about 6,500 employees of the 777 Division had relocated to the new facilities. In March 1992 Boeing completed the sale of Boeing of Canada de Havilland Commuter Aircraft Division to Bombardier, Inc. and the province of Ontario for $50 million.

In Wichita, Kansas, at Boeing's new 1,000,000-square-foot manufacturing plant, improvements to chemical milling and processing minimize the effects on air quality and ground water. The facility has the largest chemical milling recycling system in the world, recovering aluminum and other chemicals for commercial use. Environmental considerations have played a big part in the design and development of the 777. In the 777's interior cabin, water-based inks—rather than traditional solvent-based inks—are being used to silk-screen the wall coverings with colors and patterns. The environmental benefit is the elimination of certain solvents that are considered smog formers.

Other environmental innovations in the 777 program include remotely controlled paint booths that capture and prevent emissions; filtered vacuum units for removing dust during the drilling and grinding of composite materials; and the elimination or reduction of numerous toxic chemicals used in manufacturing aircraft parts.

Defense and space segment revenues were $5.4 billion for 1992, down from the $5.8 billion level for the prior two years. The company's defense and space business is broadly diversified, and no single program accounted for more than 16 percent of total 1990–1992 defense and space business revenues.

The defense and space segment, after incurring substantial operating losses in 1989 and 1990 aggregating nearly $900 million, regained profitability by the fourth quarter of 1991 through organizational consolidation and restructuring, termination of certain fixed-price development contracts, and better technical, cost, and schedule performance. This improved performance trend continued in 1992, resulting in an operating profit of $204 million for 1992 compared to an operating loss of $102 million for the year 1991.

The company has discontinued the separation of its defense and space operations for industry-segment reporting to better reflect the integrated nature of the market and internal operations of the previously segregated military transportation products and related systems segment and the missiles and space segment. The organizational consolidation of the company's various defense and space divisions into the Defense & Space Group reflects the singular nature of this business segment within the company. Because of common market and product and process characteristics, continued segmentation under the previous classifications would not be meaningful.

The principal defense and space programs, based on 1992 revenues, included B-2 bomber subcontract work, Space Station Freedom work packages, CH-47 helicopter, F-22 Advanced Tactical Fighter, E-3 AWACS, KC-135 tanker update modifications, V-22 Osprey tiltrotor transport, RAH-66 Comanche helicopter, E-6 submarine communications aircraft, Avenger air defense system, A-6 re-wing, B-1B bomber avionics, Inertial Upper Stage rocket booster, and Minuteman and Peacekeeper support. U.S. government classified projects also continue to contribute to defense and space segment revenues. Based on current programs and schedules, Boeing projects total 1993 sales to be in the $26 billion range.

Early in 1992 Boeing delivered the final E-3 Airborne Warning and Control System (AWACS) aircraft built for the French and United Kingdom air forces. The AWACS system is now being offered on the military derivative 767 airplane, and the company is actively pursuing foreign sales. The Japanese government has announced that it intends to place an initial order for two 767 AWACS in 1993. The U.S. government is expected to support sales to other overseas customers as well. The Defense & Space Group is continuing its modernization of the existing U.S. and NATO AWACS fleet.

The U.S. Navy, citing its changing role in the post–cold war environment, issued a termination for the P-3 Update IV program, under which Boeing was developing an advanced avionics system for the submarine-hunting fleet of aircraft. Despite the P-3 cancellation, Boeing is optimistic about opportunities for this product in the international marketplace.

The V-22 Osprey helicopter program entered the engineering and manufacturing development (EMD) phase in 1992, during which four new V-22s were built and two existing aircraft modified to the production-representative configuration. EMD is valued at $2 billion, which is shared by the Osprey's codevelopers, Boeing and Bell Helicopter Textron. Boeing delivered 40 remanufactured CH-47D Chinook helicopters, 35 to the U.S. Army, and 5 to the Spanish army in 1992. The company also delivered two new CH-47Ds to an Asian customer.

In December 1992 the U.S. Army and a Boeing/Sikorsky team finalized the restructuring of demonstration-validation phases of the new RAH-66 Comanche armed-reconnaissance helicopter. This prototyping and flight-test phase is valued at nearly $2 billion through 1997. Boeing has a contract to replace components in all U.S. Navy and Marine Corps H-46 helicopters. Kit production is valued at about $350 million.

In 1992 Congress voted to cap B-2 bomber production at 20 aircraft. Boeing produces the outboard wing and aft center sections of the bomber, as well as the fuel system and critical elements of the mission-management systems. Boeing completed delivery of major B-2 components in 1993 and continued to support the B-2 program through flight testing and the operational phase for several years.

The first prototype hardware for NASA's Space Station Freedom was produced in 1992 and tested at the Marshall Space Flight Center in Huntsville, Alabama. Boeing is NASA's prime contractor for the station's living and laboratory modules.

Production of the original order for 325 Avenger air defense missile fire units for the U.S. Army was completed in 1992, with the assembly line continuing work on a $436 million order for 679 more Avenger units. Boeing is continuing tests to integrate missiles other than the U.S.-built Stinger on the Avenger units as part of an aggressive foreign sales effort in 1993.

The Inertial Upper Stage (IUS) space booster celebrated its tenth anniversary by deploying a Defense Support Program surveillance satellite in 1992 and a NASA Tracking and Data Relay Satellite in 1993. Boeing has delivered 23 IUS vehicles, the most reliable upper-stage booster rocket in the U.S. inventory, and has a long-lead contract to build three more for the U.S. Air Force.

BOEING COMPUTER SERVICES

Boeing Computer Services supplies the company's need for advanced computing and telecommunications. The division also develops and manages large, complex information systems for the Department of Defense, NASA, and other federal government agencies. In 1992 one of the division's major responsibilities was to provide computer-aided design, computer-aided manufacturing, and systems integration for the 777 program. One of the major goals of the 777 program is to achieve 100 percent digital product definition, digital preassembly, and digital data exchange. In support of this goal, Computer Services electronically interconnected all Boeing facilities involved in the 777 program as well as key suppliers and partners worldwide, thereby improving the cost-efficiency of 777 development and production.

Recent development and delivery of enhanced solid-model viewing of 777 design data enhances the ability of engineers to detect and correct design errors prior to the manufacturing process. Implementing the principles of Continuous Quality Improvement as a management tool has improved efficiency of operations and reduced the cost of information systems. This division has consolidated and streamlined its organization to provide better support to all internal and external customers.

OTHER BOEING CONCERNS

Labor Contracts. Three-year labor agreements were reached in the fourth quarter of 1992 with the International Association of Machinists and Aerospace Workers and the United Auto Workers, representing approximately 50,000 employees and 98 percent of all hourly employees. Labor contract negotiations with the Seattle Professional

Engineering Employees Association (SPEEA), representing approximately 28,000 engineering and technical employees, reached an impasse in December after union members rejected the company's offer. Boeing implemented certain provisions of its final contract proposals to SPEEA prior to year end. In February 1993 SPEEA members voted to accept the company's offer.

Backlog. Total firm backlog of unfilled orders at December 31, 1992, was $87.9 billion, compared with $97.9 billion at the end of 1991. Of the total December 31 backlog, $82.6 billion or 94 percent was for commercial customers (including foreign governments) and $5.3 billion or 6 percent was for the U.S. government. Comparable figures at the end of 1991 were $92.8 billion or 95 percent commercial, and $5.1 billion or 5 percent U.S. government.

In evaluating the company's firm backlog for commercial customers, certain risk factors should be considered. Approximately 55 percent of the firm backlog for commercial jet airplanes is scheduled to be delivered after 1994, including all 777 aircraft. Deliveries of 777s begin in 1995. A continuation of the weak economic environment in many areas of the world could result in additional customer requests to negotiate the rescheduling or possible cancellation of firm orders.

CONCLUSION

As indicated in Exhibits 20–1 to 20–5, Boeing's net income fell 60 percent in 1992 while long-term debt increased 35 percent. Revenues dropped 16 percent in 1993. Further U.S. defense cuts are expected and more of Boeing's airline customers are facing demise. In the face of these odds, prepare a strategic plan for CEO John Fery. Keep in mind Boeing's current mission statement (from its *Annual Report*): "To be the number one aerospace company in the world and among the premier industrial concerns in terms of quality, profitability, and growth."

EXHIBIT 20-1 Boeing Company Corporate Headquarters, August 1, 1993

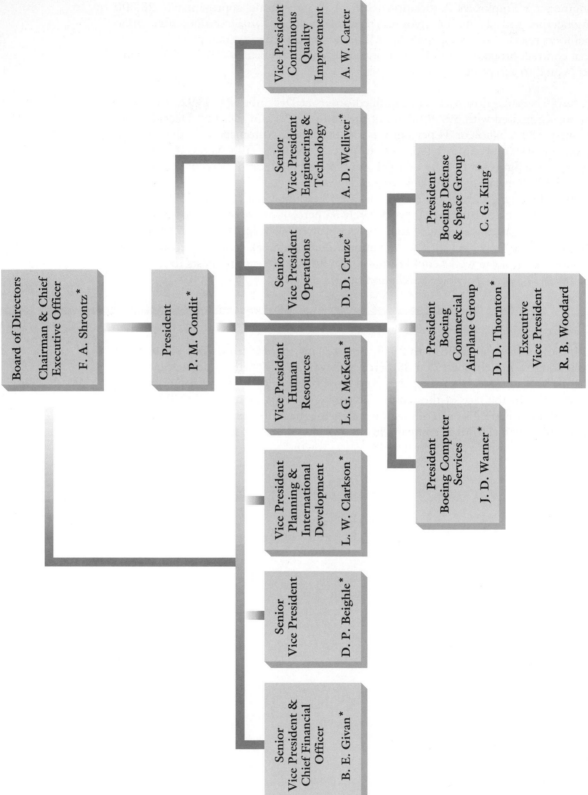

*Member, Executive Council.

Source: Company report.

EXHIBIT 20-2 Consolidated Statements of Net Earnings (Dollars in millions except per share data)

YEAR ENDED DECEMBER 31	1993	1992	1991
Sales and other operating revenues	$25,438	$30,184	$29,314
Costs and expenses	23,747	28,144	27,360
Earnings from operations	1,691	2,040	1,954
Other income, principally interest	169	230	263
Interest and debt expense	(39)	(14)	(13)
Earnings before federal taxes on income and cumulative effect on change in accounting	1,821	2,256	2,204
Federal taxes on income	577	702	637
Earnings before cumulative effect of change in accounting	1,244	1,554	1,567
Cumulative effect to January 1, 1992, of change in accounting for postretirement benefits other than pensions		(1,002)	
Net earnings	$ 1,244	$ 552	$ 1,567
Earnings per share:			
Before cumulative effect of change in accounting	$ 3.66	$ 4.57	$ 4.56
Cumulative effect to January 1, 1992, of change in accounting for postretirement benefits other than pensions		(2.95)	
	$ 3.66	$ 1.62	$ 4.56
Cash dividends per share	$ 1.00	$ 1.00	$ 1.00

Source: *Annual Report*, 1993.

EXHIBIT 20-3 Consolidated Statements of Financial Position (Dollars in millions except per share data)

DECEMBER 31,	1993	1992
ASSETS		
Cash and cash equivalents	$ 2,342	$ 2,711
Short-term investments	766	903
Accounts receivable	1,615	1,428
Current portion of customer financing	218	229
Deferred income taxes	800	115
Inventories	10,485	11,073
Less advances and progress billings	(7,051)	(8,372)
Total current assets	9,175	8,087
Customer financing	2,959	2,066
Property, plants and equipment, at cost	13,232	12,293
Less accumulated depreciation	(6,144)	(5,569)
Deferred income taxes	63	212
Other assets	1,165	1,058
	$20,450	$18,147
LIABILITIES AND SHAREHOLDERS' EQUITY		
Accounts payable and other liabilities	$ 5,854	$ 5,248
Advances in excess of related costs	226	639
Income taxes payable	434	232
Current portion of long-term debt	17	21
Total current liabilities	6,531	6,140
Accrued retiree health care	2,148	2,004
Long-term debt	2,613	1,772
Contingent stock repurchase commitment	175	175
Shareholder's equity:		
Common shares, par value $5.00—		
600,000,000 shares authorized;		
349,256,792 shares issued	1,746	1,746
Additional paid-in capital	413	418
Retained earnings	7,180	6,276
Less treasury shares, at cost—		
1993—9,118,995; 1992—9,836,313	(356)	(384)
Total shareholders' equity	8,983	8,056
	$20,450	$18,147

Source: *Annual Report*, 1993.

EXHIBIT 20-4 Consolidated Statements of Cash Flows (Dollars in millions)

YEAR ENDED DECEMBER 31,	1993	1992	1991
CASH FLOWS—OPERATING ACTIVITIES:			
Net earnings	$1,244	$552	$1,567
Adjustments to reconcile net earnings to net cash			
provided by operating activities:			
Effect of cumulative change in accounting			
for postretirement benefits other than pensions		1,002	
Depreciation and amortization—			
Plant and equipment	953	870	768
Leased aircraft, other	72	91	58
Deferred income taxes	(536)	(26)	95
Gain/undistributed earnings—affiliates	(1)	(13)	1
Changes in operating assets and liabilities—			
Accounts receivable	(187)	635	(41)
Inventories, net of advances and progress billings	(733)	(138)	458
Accounts payable and other liabilities	606	229	(140)
Advances in excess of related costs	(413)	(28)	(416)
Federal taxes on income	202	206	(453)
Change in prepaid pension expense	(134)	(202)	(403)
Change in accrued retiree health care	144	184	40
Net cash provided by operating activities	1,217	3,362	1,534
CASH FLOWS—INVESTING ACTIVITIES:			
Short-term investments	137	(388)	623
Customer financing additions	(1,560)	(1,156)	(223)
Customer financing reductions	626	16	123
Plant and equipment, net additions	(1,317)	(2,160)	(1,850)
Proceeds from sale of affiliate		50	
Other	8	(19)	(3)
Net cash used by investing activities	(2,106)	3,657)	(1,330)
CASH FLOWS—FINANCING ACTIVITIES:			
Debt financing	837	482	993
Shareholders' equity—			
Cash dividends paid	(340)	(340)	(343)
Treasury shares acquired		(109)	(127)
Stock options exercised, other	23	35	23
Net cash provided by financing activities	520	68	546
Net increase (decrease) in cash and cash equivalents	(369)	(277)	750
Cash and cash equivalents at beginning of year	2,711	2,938	2,188
Cash and cash equivalents at end of year	$2,342	$2,711	$2,938

Source: *Annual Report*, 1993.

EXHIBIT 20-5   Foreign sales by geographic area consisted of the following:

The Company operates in two principal industries: Commercial Aircraft, and Defense and Space. Commercial Aircraft operations principally involve development, production, and marketing of commercial jet transports and providing related support services, principally to the commercial airline industry. Defense and Space operations involve research, development, production, modification, and support of military aircraft and related systems, space systems, and missile systems. No single product line in the Defense and Space segment represented more than 10 percent of consolidated revenues, operating profits, or identifiable assets.

YEAR ENDED DECEMBER 31,	1993	1992	1991
Asia	$ 8,870	$ 7,108	$ 5,458
Europe	4,698	7,165	8,745
Oceania	635	1,911	1,659
Africa	264	430	558
Western Hemisphere	149	872	1,436
	$14,616	$17,486	$17,856

Defense sales were approximately 6 percent, 3 percent, and 5 percent of total sales in Europe for 1993, 1992, and 1991, respectively. Defense sales were approximately 2 percent, 5 percent, and 5 percent of total sales in Asia for 1993, 1992, and 1991, respectively. Exclusive of these amounts, Defense and Space sales were principally to the U.S. government.

Corporate income consists principally of interest income from corporate investments. Corporate expense consists of noncapitalized interest on debt and other general corporate expenses. Corporate assets consist principally of cash, cash equivalents, short-term investments, and deferred income taxes.

YEAR ENDED DECEMBER 31,	1993	1992	1991
REVENUES			
Commercial Aircraft	$20,568	$24,133	$22,970
Defense and Space	4,407	5,429	5,846
Other industries	463	622	498
Operating revenues	25,438	30,184	29,314
Corporate income	169	230	263
Total revenues	$25,607	$30,414	$29,577
OPERATING PROFIT			
Commercial Aircraft	$ 1,646	$ 1,990	$ 2,246
Defense and Space	219	204	(102)
Other industries	16	27	(2)
Operating profit	1,881	2,221	2,142
Corporate income	169	230	263
Corporate expense	(229)	(195)	(201)
Earnings before taxes	$ 1,821	$ 2,256	$ 2,204

EXHIBIT 20-5 *Continued*

IDENTIFIABLE ASSETS AT DECEMBER 31

Commercial Aircraft	$12,686	$10,178	$ 7,806
Defense and Space	3,525	3,687	4,262
Other industries	202	264	196
	16,413	14,129	12,264
Corporate	4,037	4,018	3,660
Consolidated assets	$20,450	$18,147	$15,924

DEPRECIATION

Commercial Aircraft	$710	$ 598	$ 484
Defense and Space	230	241	269
Other industries	67	73	51
Total depreciation	$ 1,007	$ 912	$ 804

CAPITAL EXPENDITURES, NET

Commercial Aircraft	$ 1,120	$ 1,890	$ 1,445
Defense and Space	164	212	317
Other industries	33	58	88
Total capital expenditures, net	$ 1,317	$ 2,160	$ 1,850

Source: *Annual Report*, 1993.

FOREST PRODUCTS INDUSTRY NOTE

KATHLEEN RICE, GARY STANLEY, AND BARBARA WISE

I. WOOD PRODUCTS

Fifteen manufacturing sectors make up SIC 24 (Lumber and Wood Products). Most of the lumber and wood products industry is concentrated in the Pacific Northwest and the Southeast. Secondary concentrations are found across the Midwest, Northeast, and in Appalachia. Establishments classified in SIC 24 engage in the cutting and subsequent processing of timber into other products.

The construction sector is the main end-use market for most of the industry's products. Other end-use markets include furniture, cabinets and fixtures, wood chips, and pallets and skids. The furniture and cabinets sectors of the construction industry are particularly important to producers of nonstructural panel products (particleboard, medium-density fiberboard, hardboard, and plywood). Other value-added products consist of hardwood and softwood plywood, millwork, and reconstituted panel products. More than 80 percent of the softwood lumber, 65 percent of structural panels (softwood plywood and oriented strand board [OSB]), and the majority of all millwork are used in construction-related activities.

Residential construction grew about 4 percent in 1993, with more than 1 million new-single family units added. This level of single-family housing construction will probably be maintained over the next several years.

Construction activity in Florida, Louisiana, and Hawaii picked up in 1993 in large part to rebuild following Hurricane Andrew, which hit southern Florida and Louisiana in September 1992, and Hurricane Iniki, which struck Hawaii less than two weeks later, causing more than $1 billion of damage on the island of Kauai. Only about 60 percent of the required rebuilding of residential and business property has occurred during 1993. The extreme flooding in the Midwest along the Mississippi, Missouri, and Illinois rivers during the summer of 1993 has also created a demand for new housing and farmland structures. This demand for reconstruction coupled with the shortage of domestic timber will increase the level of imports of softwoods from Canada.

Lumber and wood products shipments increased less than 1 percent (in constant dollars) in 1993, to an estimated $78.1 billion. Production remained flat or declined in most product sectors, with the value-added sectors, such as millwork and paneling, registering minor gains.

Since 1988 sales by the U.S. Forest Service (USFS) and the Bureau of Land Management (BLM) of timber from the Pacific Northwest declined by almost 80 percent (from about 26 million cubic meters in 1988 to about 7 million cubic meters in 1992). According to industry sources, more than 125 lumber and panel products mills in the Pacific Northwest have closed in the past three years partly as a result of the inadequate log supplies from federal and state lands.

Environmental Profile. Since the U.S. Fish and Wildlife Service (FWS) listed the northern spotted owl as a threatened species in June 1990, about 7 million acres of previously available federal and state timberlands can no longer be harvested. In response, President Clinton proposed a Forest Plan in July 1993 aimed at providing a "sustainable economy and a sustainable environment in the Pacific Northwest." The program is not expected to be implemented before late 1994. Industry estimates put the lands removed from harvest at about 25 percent of the total in the Pacific Northwest, and at about 11 percent of the national total.

Timber harvesting has been severely restricted or curtailed completely within the approximately 2 million hectares of the Pacific Northwest that have been designated as the habitat of the endangered owl. The USFS and BLM have been enjoined by federal courts from allowing any further timber sales—regardless of their location—until management plans are adopted and cleared by the FWS.

Preservationists will continue efforts to curtail or restrict logging on national forest lands not only in the Pacific Northwest but in other timberlands, including the Southeast and Midwest. The Endangered Species Act will be reevaluated by Congress in 1994.

International Competitiveness. Despite slow to moderate growth in many foreign markets, exports of wood products rose in 1993 to $7.1 billion, an increase of more than 15 percent over 1992. Almost all of the increase was the result of higher prices. The volume of exports was essentially flat. The relatively weak U.S. dollar and intense marketing efforts by the industry were major factors in the rise in exports.

Japan, Canada, and Mexico were again the major markets for U.S. exports, accounting for about two-thirds of shipments. Other significant markets were South Korea, Germany, and the United Kingdom. Softwood logs and softwood lumber remained by far the largest export commodities.

U.S. imports of solid wood products also increased in 1993, to about $7.7 billion. The major supplier of solid wood products is Canada, with softwood lumber the main commodity. Increases in softwood lumber imports, which were needed to make up for tight domestic supplies, accounted for most of the import increase of more than

U.S. Trade Patterns in 1992: Wood, Excluding Buildings SIC 241-244,249 (In millions of dollars, percent)

EXPORTS	Value	Share	IMPORTS	Value	Share
Canada and Mexico	1,553	23.0	Canada and Mexico	4,815	71.5
European Community	1,271	18.9	European Community	272	4.0
Japan	2,710	40.2	Japan	9	0.1
East Asia NICs	698	10.4	East Asia NICs	1,153	17.1
South America	23	0.3	South America	267	4.0
Other	483	7.2	Other	223	3.3
World Total	6.737	100.0	World Total	6,739	100.0

TOP FIVE COUNTRIES	Value	Share		Value	Share
Japan	2,710	40.2	Canada	4,520	67.1
Canada	1,040	15.4	Indonesia	404	6.0
Mexico	513	7.6	Mexico	295	4.4
South Korea	319	4.7	Taiwan	239	3.5
Germany	302	4.5	China	238	3.5

Source: U.S. Department of Commerce: Bureau of the Census; International Trade Administration.

14 percent from the year-earlier level. Other principal suppliers to the U.S. market were Indonesia, Taiwan, Mexico, China, Brazil, and Malaysia.

Outlook for 1994. Shipments of solid wood products should increase in 1994, as the U.S. economy and the economies of most trading partners improve. Solid, if not spectacular, growth in U.S. residential construction and household furniture should bring about an increase of more than 1 percent in domestic wood products shipments.

Imports and exports will increase modestly in 1994; both are expected to increase by about 2 percent, thus remaining about equal. Tight supply conditions in the U.S. market will lead to another increase in softwood lumber imports from Canada.

LOGGING

Commercial forest land, capable of growing 20 cubic feet per acre each year, covers about 195 million hectares, or one-fifth of the U.S. land base; a high proportion (70 percent) is privately owned. The U.S. Forest Service (USFS) estimates that commercial timberlands in the United States contain more than 23 billion cubic meters of timber. Currently, net annual growth exceeds removals (harvests) by more than 30 percent. More than 1 million hectares of U.S. forest land are replanted or seeded each year.

Trends and Forecasts: Logging (SIC 2411) (In millions of dollars except as noted)

ITEM	1991	1992[1]	1993[2]	1994[3]	PERCENT CHANGE (1991–1994) 91–92	92–93	93–94
Industry Data							
Value of shipments[4]	11,434	13,149	16,516	—	15.0	25.6	—
Value of shipments (1987$)	8,912	9,534	9,438	9,627	7.0	-1.0	2.0
Total employment (000)	78.1	—	—	—	—	—	—
Production workers (000)	65.4	—	—	—	—	—	—
Average hourly earnings ($)	9.80	—	—	—	—	—	—
Capital expenditures	293	—	—	—	—	—	—
Product Data							
Value of shipments[5]	10,728	12,337	15,612	—	15.0	26.5	—
Value of shipments (1987$)	8,362	9,011	8,921	9,099	7.8	-1.0	2.0
Trade Data							
Value of imports	199	219	252	284	10.1	15.1	12.6
Value of export	2,715	2,749	3,374	3,711	1.3	22.7	10.0

[1] Estimate, except exports and imports.

[2] Estimate.

[3] Forecast.

[4] Value of all products and services sold by establishments in the logging industry.

[5] Value of products classified in the logging industry produced by all industries.

Source: U.S. Department of Commerce: Bureau of the Census; International Trade Administration (ITA). Estimates and forecasts by ITA.

Notwithstanding the large domestic resource base, tight log supplies prevailed in 1993 throughout the Pacific Northwest. The volume of USFS and Bureau of Land Management (BLM) timber sales continued to decline in 1992 and 1993. Harvesting in the Pacific Northwest has fallen by more than 75 percent since 1989 (about 7 million cubic meters in 1992, compared with more than 26 million cubic meters in 1989). This is a result of forest management constraints imposed after the northern spotted owl was listed as a threatened species under the Endangered Species Act. Environmental litigation also was a factor.

The logging industry harvested an estimated 465 million cubic meters of sawlogs, veneer logs, pulpwood, and related wood products in 1993, valued at $15.6 billion. Softwood logs, followed by pulpwood and hardwood logs, were the industry's leading commodities, accounting for more than three-fourths of total shipments.

Softwood log production was estimated at 178 million cubic meters in 1993, down about 1 percent from 1992. Lower harvests in the Pacific Northwest accounted for the decline. Harvest levels in the South increased, but not enough to offset the decline in the Pacific Northwest. Hardwood log production in 1993 is estimated at 44 million cubic meters. Stumpage prices for both softwood and hardwood logs were sharply higher in 1993, a factor of regional availability of timber and the market for wood building products.

The volume of uncut federal timber under contract in the Pacific Northwest fell to a historical low in 1992–1993. Again, President Clinton's announced Forest Plan will have an unknown impact on the industry.

International Competitiveness. Exports of sawlogs, veneer logs, pulpwood, and related wood products were valued at $2.7 billion in 1992 and were expected to reach almost $3.4 billion in 1993, an increase of about 23 percent. The volume of exports declined slightly, however.

Japan, South Korea, and China were the leading export markets for softwood logs in 1993, accounting for more than 95 percent of total sales overseas. The volume of log exports to South Korea and China were significantly lower in 1993 because of restrictions on the export of U.S. logs from the Pacific Northwest and increased competition from New Zealand.

The value of hardwood log exports was expected to increase by less than 2 percent in 1993, while the volume of shipments declined by an estimated 3 percent. U.S. hardwood log exports were about 1.1 million cubic meters and were valued at $302 million. Canada and Japan were the industry's leading export markets, accounting for almost 48 percent of total export sales, with each market accounting for about one-fourth of the total. Other foreign markets included Germany, Italy, and Taiwan.

Outlook for 1994. Shipments of sawlogs, veneer logs, pulpwood, and related wood products are expected to increase by about 2 percent in 1994. This forecast is dependent upon lifting of court injunctions that have halted sales from the Pacific Northwest, higher demand in the nations to which the United States exports, and congressional review of how the Fish and Wildlife Service selects threatened and endangered species.

LUMBER

Industry shipments declined by 1 percent (in constant dollars) in 1993, to an estimated $25 billion. Prices continued to increase during 1992 and 1993, with softwood lumber reaching an all-time high of almost $500 per thousand board feet in March 1993. Prices have since leveled off to an average of about $340 per thousand board feet.

The sawmills and planing mills industry (SIC 2421) primarily produces lumber, which accounts for about 70 percent of the industry's total value of shipments. Softwood lumber accounts for about three-quarters of total lumber production, and hardwood lumber makes up the rest. The remaining 30 percent consists of wood chips, softwood flooring, furniture stock, and other general sawmill products, including untreated railway ties.

Since 1990 softwood lumber production in the Pacific Northwest has steadily declined, from 9.8 billion board feet in 1989 to less than 7.5 billion board feet in 1993. Softwood lumber production also declined in the Inland Region (Rocky Mountain States), from 11.3 billion board feet in 1989 to about 9 billion board feet in 1993. Southern yellow pine lumber production increased from 12.5 billion feet to more than 14 billion board feet in 1993.

Residential construction—particularly single-family homes—is the principal softwood lumber market. In 1993 single-family housing starts increased about 4 percent. Higher housing starts combined with the slight decline in lumber production resulted in higher lumber prices. The additional demand was met by higher softwood lumber imports, primarily from Canada.

Trends and Forecasts: Sawmills and Planing Mills, General (SIC 2421) (In millions of dollars except as noted)

ITEM	1991	1992[1]	1993[2]	1994[3]	PERCENT CHANGE (1991–1994)		
					91–92	92–93	93–94
Industry Data							
Value of shipments[4]	17,485	20,111	24,929	—	15.0	24.0	—
Value of shipments (1987$)	16,341	16,900	16,731	17,066	3.4	-1.0	2.0
Total employment (000)	130	126	122	—	-3.1	-3.2	—
Production workers (000)	116	113	109	—	-2.6	-3.5	—
Average hourly earnings ($)	9.33	—	—	—	—	—	—
Capital expenditures	464	—	—	—	—	—	—
Product Data							
Value of shipments[5]	17,515	20,043	24,846	—	14.4	24.0	—
Value of shipments (1987$)	16,369	16,843	16,675	17,008	2.9	-1.0	2.0
Trade Data							
Value of imports	2,638	3,472	4,956	5,501	31.6	42.7	11.0
Value of exports	2,203	2,322	2,573	2,702	5.4	10.8	5.0

[1] Estimate, except exports and imports.

[2] Estimate.

[3] Forecast.

[4] Value of all products and services sold by establishments in the sawmills and planing mills, general industry.

[5] Value of products classified in the sawmills and planing mills, general industry produced by all industries.

Source: U.S. Department of Commerce: Bureau of the Census; International Trade Administration (ITA). Estimates and forecasts by ITA.

Repair and remodeling of residential and nonresidential structures is another major market for the sawmills and planing industry. In 1993 home improvement spending rose 5 percent in constant dollars, from $51.3 billion to $53.9 billion. This further helped to inflate the price of lumber.

Employment in the industry has declined steadily since 1988 and was down another 3 percent in 1993, from 126,000 the previous year to 122,000. The decline occurred mostly in the Pacific Northwest where, over the past six years, more than 125 sawmills have closed or curtailed operations because of the shortage of timber.

The court-imposed restrictions on logging in the Pacific Northwest have spurred the lumber industry to conduct research into new processes and alternative materials. Recyclable products and greater sawmill efficiency, including energy-saving techniques, continue to be important industry goals.

International Competitiveness. The value of the U.S. lumber industry's exports has increased by almost 27 percent from 1989 to 1993, rising from a little more than $2 billion to almost $2.6 billion. In 1993 alone exports increased by 11 percent. The value of exports of softwood lumber (the major product of this industry) was up more than 7 percent, while actual volume was down about 2 percent in 1993. All softwood lumber exports for 1992 were valued at more than $1.3 billion, the same as in 1991, while the volume of exports was down by more than 14 percent.

Japan is the largest foreign market for softwood lumber, importing more than 36 percent of the total value of U.S. exports. Mexico, with 15 percent, follows, and Canada is third, importing about 11 percent.

Hardwood lumber exports exceeded $974 million in 1993, a 13 percent increase over the previous year. Major export markets for U.S. hardwood lumber are Canada, Japan, Italy, Taiwan, the United Kingdom, and Germany. Exports to Canada were about $200 million in 1992, an increase of more than 16 percent over 1991. Exports to Japan were about $133 million in 1992; exports in 1993 are expected to increase by more than 10 percent.

In 1993 additional softwood lumber imports from Canada helped to offset declines in domestic shipments. Canada provides about 98 percent of all softwood lumber imports and accounts for about 32 percent of domestic consumption. The value of imports from Canada increased 32 percent in 1992, to $3.2 billion, and are expected to increase in 1993 by about 42 percent, increasing Canada's share of domestic consumption substantially.

Outlook for 1994. Industry shipments are expected to increase in 1994 by about 2 percent (in constant dollars). Prices leveled off in 1993 to an average of about $340 per thousand board feet. Continued price volatility can be expected in 1994.

The 4- and 5-percent increases in single-family housing starts and repair and remodeling predicted for 1994 are major incentives for the industry to increase production and remain competitive with foreign lumber imports.

MILLWORK

Aided by an increase in housing starts and by a continuing high level of expenditures for residential repair, remodeling, and home improvement (RRHI) projects, the millwork industry experienced increased demand for its primary commodities in recent years.

New residential construction continues to be the leading end-use market for millwork products, accounting for about 55 percent of demand. The RRHI end-user segment is becoming increasingly important to the millwork industry. The reason is that despite reduced mortgage interest rates, the slow U.S. economy continues to dissuade many consumers from purchasing new houses or moving up to larger ones.

The millwork industry manufactures a wide range of fabricated millwork products. These include wood millwork commodities with metal, vinyl, and other plastic overlays. Doors are the industry's sales leader, accounting for about 30 percent of total shipments. Next come wooden windows (including aluminum, metal, and vinyl clad) and sashes (26 percent), standard and prefinished moldings (12 percent), and wooden frames for doors and windows (more than 3 percent).

The remaining 28 percent of the industry's annual sales are made up of various millwork products, including wooden blinds, shutters, screens, shades, folding and stationary stairwork, porch columns and rails, trellises, carvings, ornaments, and similar products.

International Competitiveness. The U.S. millwork industry continued to run a trade deficit in both 1991 and 1992. Aided by a weak dollar and strong foreign demand (especially from Canada and Mexico), exports reached $207 million in 1991 compared to $143 million in imports the previous year. In 1992 the pattern was

Trends and Forecasts: Millwork (SIC 2431) (In millions of dollars except as noted)

Item	1991	1992[1]	1993[2]	1994[3]	Percent Change (1991–1994)		
					91–92	92–93	93–94
Industry Data							
Value of shipments[4]	8,969	9,837	10,789	—	9.7	9.7	—
Value of shipments (1987$)	7,868	8,065	8,226	8,473	2.5	2.0	3.0
Total employment (000)	84.9	86.6	86.0	—	2.0	-0.7	—
Production workers (000)	66.7	68.8	67.9	—	3.1	-1.3	—
Average hourly earnings ($)	9.96	10.26	10.47	—	3.0	2.0	—
Capital expenditures	141	—	—	—	—	—	—
Product Data							
Value of shipments[5]	8,464	9,283	10,181	—	9.7	9.7	—
Value of shipments (1987$)	7,424	7,610	7,762	7,995	2.5	2.0	3.0
Trade Data							
Value of imports	225	306	350	395	36.0	25.8	—
Value of exports	207	272	325	320	31.4	-4.4	—

[1] Estimate, except exports and imports.

[2] Estimate.

[3] Forecast.

[4] Value of all products and services sold by establishments in the millwork industry.

[5] Value of products classified in the millwork industry produced by all industries.

Source: U.S. Department of Commerce: Bureau of the Census; International Trade Administration (ITA). Estimates and forecasts by ITA.

repeated: exports rose strongly but were unable to catch up with the volume of imports. As of May 1993 exports were trailing imports by $24 million.

The major customers for U.S. exports over the last four years have been Canada (55 percent), Mexico (more than 17 percent), Japan (7 percent), and the United Kingdom (6 percent).

Mexico is by far the leading exporter to the United States, accounting for almost 49 percent of U.S. imports of millwork. Canada is a distant second with only 14 percent of the dollar volume. Thailand is in third place with 9 percent.

Outlook for 1994. The U.S. millwork industry should experience higher sales in 1994 with the expected increase in residential construction and RRHI activity. Millwork product shipments are forecast to increase by more than 3 percent in constant dollars.

HARDWOOD VENEER AND PLYWOOD

Shipments of hardwood veneer and plywood increased about 3 percent in 1993 (in constant dollars) to $2 billion. Both domestic and overseas markets were generally stronger, reflecting the modest U.S. recovery and growth in some foreign markets. The market for hardwood plywood, especially paneling, which is used extensively in mobile-home construction, experienced a surge in demand following Hurricane Andrew in September 1992.

Establishments classified in the hardwood veneer and plywood industry (SIC 2435) produce hardwood plywood, hardwood veneer (face and technical veneers), hardwood-type products (such as laminated veneer lumber), and prefinished hardwood plywood paneling. These products are used in a wide range of applications, including residential and nonresidential construction, repair and remodeling, manufactured housing, furniture, and cabinets and fixtures.

Hardwood plywood shipments accounted for an estimated 45 percent of total product shipments in 1993, followed by hardwood veneer (25 percent), hardwood plywood-type products (20 percent), and prefinished hardwood plywood paneling (10 percent). Prefinished hardwood plywood paneling's share of total product shipments has declined steadily over the past decade, largely because of changing consumer tastes. Prefinished hardwood plywood paneling was long the product of choice, but in the 1980s gypsum board became the top choice.

Production of stock hardwood plywood (4 by 6 to 10 feet) increased for the ninth year in a row in 1993, to an estimated 78 million square meters, compared with 42 million square meters in 1985. Stock hardwood plywood comes in a wide range of thicknesses (the most common is 3/4 inch, or 19.05 mm). Production is fairly evenly divided between the East and West. While output was rising in both regions in 1992, tight raw material supplies in the West resulted in a much smaller gain in that region.

Stock hardwood plywood production makes up almost 50 percent of total hardwood plywood production. The hardwood plywood industry also produces three other types of panels—architectural or decorative panels, made-to-size panels, and cut-to-size panels. There are no production estimates available, but indications are that output rose to accommodate key end-use sectors (construction, furniture, and cabinet and fixtures).

Hardwood plywood producers use both veneer and other types of core material in the manufacturing process. Other types of core include not only lumber, but also reconstituted panel products, such as particleboard, medium density fiberboard

(MDF), and oriented strand board (OSB). About three-fourths of the industry's production is manufactured with veneer cores. On a percentage basis, the use of MDF lumber cores has increased substantially over the past decade; however, it still accounts for less than 15 percent of total hardwood plywood production. More than a dozen species of wood are used as face veneers in the production of hardwood plywood, but birch-faced (much of it imported from Canada) and oak-faced (primarily red oak) hardwood plywood account for more than three-fourths of the total. Use of these two species has increased over the past decade because of increased use of light-colored woods for furniture.

International Competitiveness. U.S. hardwood veneer and plywood exports increased to a record $303 million in 1993, marking the sixth consecutive annual increase. The largest overseas markets were Germany, Canada, Mexico, and Japan. Hardwood veneer exports amounted to 76 percent of the industry's exports, with Germany and Canada the leading foreign markets (accounting for 30 percent and 14 percent, respectively). Japan took 7 percent, followed by the United Kingdom (5 percent), and Spain and Belgium (between 4 and 5 percent each). Hardwood plywood exports increased nearly 47 percent in 1993, to an estimated $72.5 million.

Trends and Forecasts: Hardwood Veneer and Plywood (SIC 2435) (In millions of dollars except as noted)

ITEM	1991	1992[1]	1993[2]	1994[3]	PERCENT CHANGE (1991–1994)		
					91–92	92–93	93–94
Industry Data							
Value of shipments[4]	1,897	1,997	2,092	—	5.3	4.8	—
Value of shipments (1987$)	1,727	1,934	1,998	2,048	12.0	3.3	2.5
Total employment (000)	17.3	17.4	17.9	—	0.6	2.9	—
Production workers (000)	14.8	14.8	15.3	—	0.0	3.4	—
Average hourly earnings ($)	8.03	8.28	8.53	—	3.1	3.0	—
Capital expenditures	45.5	—	—	—	—	—	—
Product Data							
Value of shipments[5]	1,743	1,837	1,917	—	5.4	4.4	—
Value of shipments (1987$)	1,587	1,778	1,831	1,877	12.0	3.0	2.5
Trade Data							
Value of imports	588	729	758	792	24.0	4.0	4.5
Value of exports	248	278	303	333	12.1	9.0	9.9

[1] Estimate, except exports and imports.

[2] Estimate.

[3] Forecast.

[4] Value of all products and services sold by establishments in the hardwood veneer and plywood industry.

[5] Value of products classified in the hardwood veneer and plywood industry produced by all industries.

Source: U.S. Department of Commerce: Bureau of the Census; International Trade Administration (ITA). Estimates and forecasts by ITA.

The largest markets were Canada (41 percent), Mexico (23 percent), and Japan (11 percent).

Hardwood veneer and plywood imports increased by 4 percent in 1993, to an estimated $758 million. Most of this increase came as temperate hardwood plywood and veneer from Canada, as well as new sources such as Russia and Paraguay. Indonesia is the largest supplier of tropical and temperate hardwood plywood to the United States, supplying more than 40 percent of total imports. Indonesia purchases U.S. veneer-grade hardwood logs, which are processed into veneer and then overlaid on lauan plywood cores for export to the United States. Imports of tropical hardwood plywood and veneer fell about 11 percent in 1993, in part because of increased concerns over the effects of logging in tropical forests.

Outlook for 1994. Moderate growth in the furniture and construction sectors should lead to higher production levels in 1994. All sectors of the industry should experience some increase, even producers of prefinished hardwood plywood paneling, whose production dropped substantially over the past decade.

Exports are projected to increase for the seventh straight year because of increased worldwide demand for temperate veneer and hardwood plywood. Exports to Japan, which increased about 27 percent in 1993, are expected to rise again. Japan, one of the world's largest consumers of tropical wood products, is increasingly coming under fire because of growing concern even within the country itself about tropical deforestation. Imports are forecast to increase 4 to 5 percent to meet rising demand in the residential construction and furniture industries.

SOFTWOOD PLYWOOD AND VENEER

Shipments for the softwood plywood and veneer industry declined slightly in 1993. However, prices were significantly higher so that the value of industry shipments increased to an estimated $5.7 billion. Softwood plywood production decreased to 17 million cubic meters, compared with 17.1 billion cubic meters in 1992. Higher prices resulted in large part from higher raw material costs and increased demand in traditional end-use markets, such as housing and repair and remodeling.

There were 117 softwood plywood mills operating in 1993, down from 121 in 1992. Mills closed were located in Oregon and Washington. Mills in the Pacific Northwest, many of which are heavily dependent on timber from federal lands, now account for less than one-fourth of softwood plywood production, down from nearly 40 percent in 1985. At the same time, plywood mills in the South have increased production. Southern plywood mills now account for about 65 percent of softwood plywood production.

Residential construction is the biggest end-use market for softwood plywood and veneer, accounting for nearly one-third of demand. In addition to single-family housing, repair and remodeling, industrial applications and nonresidential construction are important markets. New housing starts were up 4 percent in 1993, and the value of home improvement projects increased 5 percent during the same period. The market for private nonresidential building construction fell in 1993 because of overbuilding in earlier years.

Although these factors suggest strong demand for plywood products, supply difficulties in the Pacific Northwest and increased incursions by substitute products such as oriented strand board (OSB) in traditional markets have dampened growth of plywood shipments. OSB, a structural panel, has been gaining popularity in the construction industry since the mid-1980s. It is estimated that OSB now makes up about 30 percent of structural panel shipments in the United States.

In addition, increased acceptance of laminated veneer lumber in the construction industry has created an additional end-use market for softwood veneer, which formerly was sold exclusively to the plywood industry. Separate shipment data are not available for softwood veneer, but many plywood mills have reported increased competition for veneer supplies from laminated veneer lumber mills, with resulting increases in prices.

International Competitiveness. Exports of softwood plywood and veneer continued to grow in 1993, to an estimated $340 million. EC countries (particularly the United Kingdom, Netherlands, Germany, and Belgium) constituted the major export market. Exports to EC countries remained steady or declined slightly. Exports to Mexico and Japan increased substantially.

Resolution of issues relating to performance standards for softwood plywood in construction applications allowed implementation in 1993 of previously agree tariff reductions on softwood plywood under the U.S.-Canada Free Trade Agreement. Under the agreement, plywood tariffs were reduced by 50 percent effective January 1, 1993, to be followed by a staged reduction to zero over the next five years. Exports

Trends and Forecasts: Softwood Veneer and Plywood (SIC 2436) (In millions of dollars except as noted)

ITEM	1991	1992[1]	1993[2]	1994[3]	PERCENT CHANGE (1991–1994) 91–92	92–93	93–94
Industry Data							
Value of shipments[4]	4,592	5,380	5,653	—	17.2	5.1	—
Value of shipments (1987$)	4,320	4,475	4,457	4,524	3.6	-0.4	1.5
Total employment (000)	31.7	31.2	30.8	—	-1.6	-1.3	—
Production workers (000)	28.6	28.3	28.0	—	-1.0	-1.1	—
Average hourly earnings ($)	10.78	10.89	10.99	—	1.0	0.9	—
Capital expenditures	86.7	—	—	—	—	—	—
Product Data							
Value of shipments[5]	3,972	4,654	4,892	—	17.2	5.1	—
Value of shipments (1987$)	3,737	3,872	3,857	3,914	3.6	-0.4	1.5
Trade Data							
Value of imports	35.5	59.0	74.4	93.7	66.2	26.1	25.9
Value of exports	275	336	340	357	22.2	1.2	5.0

[1] Estimate, except exports and imports.

[2] Estimate.

[3] Forecast.

[4] Value of all products and services sold by establishments in the softwood veneer and plywood industry.

[5] Value of products classified in the softwood veneer and plywood industry produced by all industries.

Source: U.S. Department of Commerce: Bureau of the Census; International Trade Administration (ITA).

to Canada rebounded in 1993 and constituted nearly 15 percent of all plywood exported.

Outlook for 1994. The availability of timber in the Western United States will continue to be the biggest concern for the softwood plywood industry in 1994. In addition, engineered wood products such as OSB will continue to make inroads into construction, plywood's largest end-use market.

In constant dollars, shipments of softwood plywood and veneer are projected to increase 1 to 2 percent in 1994, driven by an expected 4 percent increase in housing starts, a 5 percent increase in the home repair and remodeling sector, and improved exports. Demand should also increase marginally as homes in the Midwest are repaired and rebuilt following the summer floods of 1993.

Exports should continue to grow, as the economies in the U.K., Canada, and Mexico (each a major export market) are expected to experience modest growth in 1994. At the same time, imports should grow substantially as tight domestic supplies make this market attractive to overseas producers.

Under the North American Free Trade Agreement (NAFTA), the construction market in Mexico should offer opportunities for plywood exporters. Mexican tariffs on veneer will drop to zero immediately, and tariffs on plywood products will be phased out over a ten-year period. Currently, consumption of softwood plywood greatly exceeds production in Mexico. Because of inadequate reforestation programs in the past, this situation is likely to offer opportunities for plywood exporters for some time to come.

II. PAPER PRODUCTS

The United States paper and allied products industry is recognized worldwide as a high-quality, high-volume, low-cost producer that benefits from a large consumer base, a modern technical infrastructure, adequate raw materials, and a highly skilled labor force. The industry ranks eighth among U.S. manufacturing industries in the value of its shipments, and third among the nondurables sectors in sales. It ranks second in capital expenditures, according to the most recent Bureau of the Census data. Although the paper industry is one of the largest U.S. consumers of energy, ranking third behind metals and chemicals, it also has the highest rate of self-generated energy, totaling over 56 percent in 1992–1993.

The primary-products sector encompasses pulp, paper, and paperboard manufacturing (SIC 261, 262, and 263). These capital-intensive industries obtain cellulose fibers from timberlands, or from purchased virgin and recycled fibers. They produce commodity grades of wood pulp, printing and writing papers, sanitary tissue, industrial-type papers, containerboard, and boxboard. According to a reliable industry survey, this sector operated 544 paper and paperboard mills and 207 pulp mills in 1992, with total employment of 196,700.

The more labor-intensive converting sector, with 68 percent of the industry's employees, consists of 14 fairly distinct industries that use primary products, such as paper and paperboard, in the manufacture of coated papers, bags, boxes, and envelopes. Some companies in this sector are integrated with primary manufacturers, especially in the production of sanitary tissue products, corrugating shipping containers, folding cartons, flexible packaging, and envelopes. Other converters purchase paper, paperboard, and plastic film from the primary sector, and transform those materials into finished products. Most converters are fully independent operations,

Trends and Forecasts: Paper and Allied Products (SIC 26) (In millions of dollars except as noted)

ITEM	1991	1992[1]	1993[2]	1994[3]	PERCENT CHANGE (1991–1994)		
					91–92	92–93	93–94
Industry Data							
Value of shipments[4]	128,824	131,282	130,000	135,797	1.9	-1.0	4.5
Value of shipments (1987$)	113,395	114,529	115,146	118,600	1.0	0.5	3.0
Total employment (000)	621	622	620	623	0.2	-0.3	0.5
Production workers (000)	477	478	477	479	0.2	-0.2	0.4
Average hourly earnings ($)	13.34	13.71	13.92	—	2.8	1.5	—
Capital expenditures	9,009	—	—	—	—	—	—
Product Data							
Value of shipments[5]	124,658	127,102	125,891	131,505	2.0	-1.0	4.5
Value of shipments (1987$)	109,811	110,909	111,507	114,852	1.0	0.5	3.0
Trade Data							
Value of imports	10,473	10,424	11,361	11,823	-0.5	9.0	4.1
Value of exports	9,332	10,122	9,827	10,416	8.5	-2.9	6.0

[1] Estimate, except exports and imports.

[2] Estimate.

[3] Forecast.

[4] Value of all products and services sold by establishments in the paper and allied products industry.

[5] Value of products classified in the paper and allied products industry produced by all industries.

Source: U.S. Department of Commerce: Bureau of the Census; International Trade Administration (ITA).Estimates and Forecast by ITA.

but those linked with primary-product producers account for the lion's share of industry sales.

INDUSTRY PERFORMANCE

Aggregate shipments of the U.S. paper and allied products industry were estimated at $130 billion in current dollars in 1993, down less than 1 percent from 1992. The small decline was directly attributable to continued depressed prices that affected some leading grades of pulp, paper, and board, and to deep regional discounting, which significantly lowered the actual unit prices of many delivered products. Nevertheless, volume of shipments was up for many primary products, including some principal grades of paper and paperboard, in both domestic and foreign markets. Several segments of the converting sector also achieved moderate growth, including production of corrugated box, sanitary paper products, and some printing and writing paper.

The pulp, paper, and paperboard sectors (SIC 261, 262, 263) accounted for about 40 percent of the value of the industry's total shipments in 1993.The sector made significant real growth in output and in sales of some printing and writing papers and of boxboard, but shipments of market pulp and containerboard declined.

The larger, more labor-intensive converting sector, which accounted for the remaining 60 percent of paper industry shipments, also achieved significant real growth in certain sectors in 1993, particularly corrugated and folding-carton shipping containers and boxes, sanitary paper products, and envelopes. This sector is concentrated largely in populous metropolitan areas—especially in the Northeast, the Southeast, the Great Lakes region, and California—where end-user markets are accessible and transportation costs can be minimized.

Poised for Growth. By controlling operating rates and improving sales and distribution methods, manufacturers have drawn down inventories of paper and paperboard to near-normal levels, in contrast to the levels during previous business downturns. For the first time in recent years, improvements and rebuilds of existing machinery and equipment were reported to have exceeded the installation of new machines—a significant savings to the industry at a time of reduced profitability. Additions to plant capacity in 1993 were only about 2 percent more than those made in 1992, keeping operating rates high—92 percent for primary paper production and 95 percent for paperboard manufacture—without leading to price reductions for most grades. As a result, the industry was in a relatively strong economic position through 1993 amid growing indications of increased business activity, and should be able to maintain it well into 1994 at least.

In the three years through 1994, a survey in mid-1993 found, U.S. companies planned to spend a total of $13.4 billion on mill improvements, 4 percent less than indicated in the survey a year earlier, following declines of 8 percent in 1992 and 11 percent in 1991. The latest survey suggested that the trend would turn positive as the global economy improved.

With the industry's expansion winding down from the record pace of 1987–1990, environmental improvements have replaced capacity additions as the driving force behind capital spending plans. Environmental programs account for nearly 15 percent of total spending plans, up from 14 percent in 1992. Stricter state environmental standards have prompted projects to add secondary treatment plants, control odorous emissions, and reduce the use of elemental chlorine.

Earnings and Jobs Decline. Earnings declined more sharply than sales through the first half of 1993. A few companies' profits improved slightly in the second quarter, but the industry experienced a 23 percent drop from the second quarter of 1992 and 15 percent from the first quarter of 1993, when surging prices of its wood products buoyed the industry's earnings from sales of those products. Cash flow was held down by depressed prices, especially for containerboard, market wood pulp, and certain printing and writing paper grades.

Employment in the paper industry was about 620,000 in 1993, down slightly from 1992 and 2 percent below the record of 630,000 in 1989. Principal causes of the declines were mergers, acquisitions, consolidations, and the phasing out of older, less-efficient machinery and operations.

Strikes dropped off dramatically, from 19 in 1983 to only one in 1992–1993. The United Paper Workers International Union, which represents a large majority of employees, has agreed to contracts as long as five and six years. Wage increases averaged less than 3 percent in 1993, than in 1992. U.S. companies also have been able to cut labor costs by eliminating Sunday premium pay and redesigning work practices and job descriptions.

Perhaps the most serious friction between labor and management is over health care. As in other industries, rapidly escalating insurance costs threaten the viability of many companies. With health-insurance premiums estimated to equal almost half of operating profits, negotiations will center on the extent of employee health coverage and the dollar amount of medical cost-sharing.

Corporate restructuring continued, especially among large companies, both in the United States and abroad. Although mergers and takeovers declined in 1993 because of the uncertain economy and poor cash flows, some major acquisitions were followed by divestitures, consolidations, and closings of less-profitable operations.

International Competitiveness. After narrowing for four straight years, to $302 million in 1992, the U.S. paper industry's trade deficit quadrupled in 1993 to $1.5 billion. When one factors in trade of recovered paper (not included in SIC data), where U.S. exports of $560 million far exceeded imports of $26 million, the 1993 trade deficit falls to $1 billion.

Although U.S. export tonnage was essentially unchanged from the 1992 level, the value of exports decreased about 3 percent in 1993, following a 9 percent rise in 1992, further reflecting softness in prices for U.S. paper and allied products. Because of poor economic conditions in Asia and Europe, the U.S. industry was unable to take advantage of the dollar's lowest international value in years. Exports of kraft linerboard, the industry's single largest export, were hit especially hard by a decline in foreign demand. Despite low prices and the dollar's low value, exports of this commodity, used in the construction of corrugated shipping containers, fell 8 percent in value in 1993, primarily as a result of lower sales to the European Community and Japan. Other regions that reduced purchases of U.S. paper and allied products included Scandinavia, the Caribbean, Taiwan, South Korea, and China. A few countries substantially increased purchases from the U.S., however: Mexico, up 11 percent; Canada, up 8 percent; and Thailand, up 18 percent.

Canada remained the largest market with 21 percent of the total, followed by the EC with 19 percent, Mexico with 15 percent, and Japan with 12 percent.

The continued growth of U.S. exports of paper and allied products to Canada in 1993, despite Canada's economic difficulties, was due largely to the U.S.-Canada Free Trade Agreement. By eliminating all paper-industry tariffs between the nations on January 1, 1993, it made U.S. paper and allied products very competitive in Canada, especially converted paper and paperboard packaging.

With the North American Free Trade Agreement (NAFTA), U.S. paper exports to Mexico will accelerate as well. U.S. exports to Mexico increased 70 percent over the past five years, to $1.4 billion in 1993 from $841 million in 1988. NAFTA phases out market barriers to the majority of primary pulp, paper, and paperboard grades over a five-year period. It eliminates corrugated-box tariffs and nontariff barriers over seven years, and tariffs on most converted products over ten years.

In the General Agreement on Tariffs and Trade (GATT), the paper industry continues to press U.S. and foreign government and industry officials to eliminate all barriers to the import and export of paper and allied products.

The U.S. and Japanese governments met several times during 1993 to assess the effectiveness and status of the Paper Agreement they had signed in April 1992. Its primary objective was to open Japan's $60 billion paper market to foreign suppliers. The agreement requires the Japanese government to encourage Japanese paper distributors, converters, printers, and corporate users to increase imports, develop long-term relationships with foreign suppliers, establish nondiscriminatory purchasing practices, and adopt specific purchasing guidelines that are applicable to both domestic and foreign suppliers. Under the agreement the Japanese government must focus its efforts on important local users of paper products, including 164 major companies that are participants in the Ministry of International Trade and Industry's import expansion program.

Exports and Imports Increase. Exports have played an increasingly important role in the U.S. paper industry, accounting for nearly 8 percent of U.S. paper goods shipments in 1993, or about $9.8 billion. Exports' share of total shipments has increased since 1990, when they constituted less than 7 percent all shipments.

Imports of paper and allied products surged 9 percent in 1993 and accounted for almost 9 percent of the total U.S. consumption of those products, or $11.4 billion. The principal supplier to the United States in 1993 was Canada, with 78 percent of all U.S. imports. Other principal suppliers included Finland, Germany, Japan, the United Kingdom, and Brazil.

The jump in imports was led by Canadian newsprint, up 17 percent; printing and writing paper, up 12 percent; and wood pulp, up 12 percent. The increase in imports of Canadian newsprint in 1993 reversed a five-year decline. Canadian newsprint, which until the early 1980s supplied about 60 percent of total annual U.S. consumption, has become significantly less competitive with U.S. virgin and recycled newsprint in recent years, because of higher production costs, U.S. requirements for high-quality recycled newsprint, and major additions to U.S. production capacity. Canadian-supplied newsprint now accounts for slightly more than 48 percent of U.S. newsprint consumption, compared with about 52 percent in 1991.

U.S. Trade Patterns in 1992 Paper and Allied Products SIC 26 (in millions of dollars, percent)

EXPORTS			IMPORTS		
	Value	Share		Value	Share
Canada and Mexico	3,119	30.8	Canada and Mexico	8,016	76.9
European Community	2,436	24.1	European Community	841	8.1
Japan	1,189	11.7	Japan	222	2.1
East Asia NICs	1,534	15.2	East Asia NICs	376	3.6
South America	466	4.6	South America	270	2.6
Other	1,377	13.6	Other	698	6.7
World Total	10,122	100.0	World Total	10,424	100.0

TOP FIVE COUNTRIES					
	Value	Share		Value	Share
Canada	1,836	18.1	Canada	7,870	75.5
Mexico	1,283	12.7	Finland	381	3.7
Japan	1,189	11.7	Germany	243	2.3
Germany	493	4.9	Brazil	238	2.3
South Korea	486	4.8	Japan	222	2.1

Source: U.S. Department of Commerce: Bureau of the Census; International Trade Administration.

Environmental Profile. In 1993 the domestic industry attained a wastepaper recovery rate of 41 to 42 percent, surpassing its 1995 goal of 40 percent. Recycled paper constituted nearly 31 percent of fiber used at domestic paper and paperboard mills in 1993, up from 29 percent in 1992. Almost half of the recovered paper and paperboard consisted of old corrugated scrap and recovered boxes and containers; old newsprint was the second-largest recovery component. About one-third of the primary paper and board mills in operation during 1993 used wastepaper as their principal fiber component, and at another 50 percent, waste materials constituted up to half of the fiber mix. Most mill additions in 1993 were planned to use recycled fibers as a significant portion of their papermaking materials.

The U.S. government tightened its requirements in 1993 for recycled fiber content in the large quantity of printing and writing papers it purchases. About 95 percent of the bulk paper bought by the Government Printing Office in 1993 reportedly consisted of recycled fibers. The Environmental Protection Agency (EPA) began in 1993 to revise its 1988 minimum-content guidelines for paper products the government buys. These guidelines specify minimum secondary fiber and post-consumer content. In addition to national efforts, many states and local jurisdictions continued to press in 1993 for tougher recycling and packaging legislation. EPA continued to revise water-effluent and air-emission limitations and standards for the industry under the Clean Water Act and the Clean Air Act.

The guidelines, due out early in 1994 for promulgation in the second half of 1995, are expected to address dioxins and other substances, with potential implications for bleached pulp mills. Amendments to the Clean Air Act, signed into law at the end of 1990, provide extensive changes to existing regulations regarding sources of ozone, carbon monoxide, and particulate matter, which could have a profound effect on pulp and paper mills in regions where ambient air quality does not meet health-based national standards. Paper companies will be required to demonstrate, on a case-by-case basis, that they are in compliance with all existing air standards, or that the benefits of a mill significantly outweigh the costs of complying with antipollution regulations.

Because the European Community is the U.S. paper industry's largest regional export market, the EC's recent draft legislation on packaging and packaging waste, precipitated by the restrictive actions of Germany and other member countries, is of growing concern in the United States and other paper-trading countries. The objectives are to reduce the amount of packaging waste produced, require the recovery of packaging waste, and minimize the volume of such waste that goes into final disposal. With ten years, 90 percent of packaging waste would have to be recovered and 60 percent recycled. Other proposals include an EC packaging tax to ensure collection of waste and to fund recycling projects. Strict provisions are included to ensure that member states do not use these levies as barriers to trade. Nevertheless, an EC packaging tax, and the imposition of packaging-waste-recovery requirements on manufacturers, retailers, and distributors, could add to the costs of U.S. paper exports and reduce general product competitiveness.

Outlook for 1994. Supported by stronger domestic demand for packaging and industrial-type paper grades and by strengthening export markets, real growth of 3 percent is expected in shipments of paper and allied products in 1994. Successful conclusion of the NAFTA and GATT agreements could bring a substantial rise in U.S. exports.

U.S. exports should increase at least 6 percent in 1994, and the gain could be significantly higher if trade barriers are lowered in Japan, Mexico, and the EC. Imports will continue to expand in 1994, especially newsprint, pulp, and printing and writing paper from Canada. Shipments of paper and allied products to the EC should expand because of the U.S. paper industry's largely successful efforts to meet the new EC guidelines and product standards.

The U.S. industry already has a significant presence in Western Europe, and will attempt further to strengthen its EC market share through joint ventures or acquisitions of local papermaking operations, especially in the more lucrative sectors of printing and writing papers and of sanitary tissue manufacture.

Commodities in this sector (SIC 2611) include a number of chemical and mechanical paper-grade pulps and special alpha and dissolving pulps, which are sold on the open market rather than used in integrated manufacture. The various grades of pulp can be made from softwoods, hardwoods, or other fibrous raw material sources that include recovered secondary fiber, rags, or agricultural products including cotton linters, kenaf, bagasse, or straw. Shipments by this industry, both export and domestic, constitute 12 to 16 percent of total U.S. production and do not include domestic transfer shipments to affiliated paper and board mills.

Following a record-breaking 1992, U.S. market pulp shipments declined more than 2 percent in 1993 to less than 9 million metric tons (t). Causes included depressed foreign sales in key markets, sluggish domestic demand, falling prices, continued global overcapacity, and significant increases in consumption of recovered paper in the United States and abroad. The one bright spot for the domestic industry was an increase of nearly 10 percent in the volume of domestic shipments, reversing a downward slide since 1988. Exports represented two-thirds of the volume of all U.S. shipments in 1993, slightly smaller than the 70 percent market share that exports held in 1992.

Industry Developments. The domestic market pulp industry's dominant product is paper-grade pulp, accounting for nearly 95 percent of total domestic sales, or 8 million t, in 1993. Bleached softwood kraft pulp constituted 58 percent of production, but bleached hardwood kraft pulp continued to increase its fiber market share to 38 percent. Higher domestic production of coated and uncoated free sheet papers, which contain at least 90 percent bleached chemical wood pulp by fiber weight, increased the demand for U.S. virgin papermaking fibers from domestic paper and board manufacturers. In 1993 the remaining sales in SIC 2611 consisted primarily of bleached and unbleached sulfite pulp (nearly 3 percent) and unbleached kraft pulp (2 percent).

The consumer market for global pulp is going through a transition, driven largely by changes in Europe. The European Community, representing more than 40 percent of total pulp demand, obtains 20 percent of its pulp from the United States and 11 percent from Japan. Tremendous interest and investment brought about by environmental and public pressures (especially in Europe), have been directed in the past several years to the development and production of totally chlorine-free (TCF) market pulps, made without the use of chlorine compounds in the bleaching process. Chlorine (primarily elemental chlorine gas) had been identified as the main cause of toxic dioxin compounds in pulp-mill effluents.

Chemical paper-grade market pulp, used primarily in the manufacture of printing and writing papers, is produced in about 37 countries. About 63 percent, or 22.8 million t, of world output came from the NORSCAN countries (United States, Canada, Sweden, Finland, and Norway) in 1993. In recent years, the market share of NORSCAN producers has come under increased pressure from low-cost, state-of-the-art pulp mills in Latin America, Western Europe, and Africa. These countries not only enjoy abundant, fast-growing solid wood resources (especially eucalyptus and tropical pine species), but also have lower costs for labor, environmental protection, and basic operations.

Prices Continue to Decline. Prices for market pulp continued a four-year decline in 1993 as a result of excess global supply and inventories, increased use of secondary fiber, and soft world demand for virgin papermaking fibers. From the 1990 record price of $840 per metric ton for northern bleached softwood kraft, which is the global benchmark pulp grade, prices fell to $440 per metric ton in 1993, their lowest level since the price collapse of 1985. Other pulp grades, including southern bleached softwood kraft, experienced similar price declines.

Extensive downtime and production curtailments at pulp mills, designed to remove excess pulp from the consumer market, sharply reduced the U.S. market pulp sector's operating rates for 1993. In June 1993 the market pulp sector operated at 85 percent of capacity, down from 93 percent in the same period in 1992. One of the few positive trends for U.S. market pulp producers in 1993 was inventory reduction. From 882,000 t (a 41-day supply) at the end of 1992, producers' inventory levels declined to 769,000 (a 32-day supply) by mid-1993.

Trends and Forecasts: Pulp Mills (SIC 2611) (In millions of dollars except as noted)

ITEM	1991	1992[1]	1993[2]	1994[3]	PERCENT CHANGE (1991–1994) 91–92	92–93	93–94
Industry Data							
Value of shipments[4]	5,329	5,612	5,200	5,619	5.3	-7.3	8.1
Value of shipments (1987$)	4,898	5,265	5,133	5,251	7.5	-2.5	2.3
Total employment (000)	16.8	16.5	16.7	16.9	-1.8	1.2	1.2
Production workers (000)	12.8	12.7	12.9	13.0	-0.8	1.6	0.8
Average hourly earnings ($)	18.36	18.73	19.15	—	2.0	2.2	—
Capital expenditures	991	—	—	—	—	—	—
Product Data							
Value of shipments[5]	5,741	6,047	5,603	6,054	5.3	-7.3	8.0
Value of shipments (1987$)	5,277	5,673	5,531	5,658	7.5	-2.5	2.3
Trade Data							
Value of imports	2,142	2,104	2,073	2,114	-1.8	-1.5	2.0
Value of exports	2,920	3,236	2,709	2,844	10.8	-16.3	5.0

[1] Estimate, except exports and imports.

[2] Estimate.

[3] Forecast.

[4] Value of all products and services sold by establishments in the pulp mills industry.

[5] Value of products classified in the pulp mills industry produced by all industries.

Source: U.S. Department of Commerce: Bureau of the Census; International Trade Administration (ITA). Estimates and forecasts by ITA.

Recovered-paper consumption by U.S. paper and board mills continued to increase in 1993, causing a decrease in demand for virgin papermaking fibers. In 1993 U.S. paper and board mills consumed approximately 81 million t. Of that total, 57 million t (or 70 percent) was virgin wood pulp and 24 million t (or 30 percent) was recovered paper and paperboard. The quantity of wood pulp consumed in 1993 was unchanged from the previous year while the quantity of recovered paper and board consumed was up more than 8 percent.

Continued capacity increases by North American market pulp producers, combined with essentially flat world demand, contributed to sluggish market conditions in 1993. U.S. market pulp capacity surged nearly 4 percent and Canadian capacity rose 3 percent in 1993. These start ups, along with the completion of other projects in Western Europe and Asia, added more than 1.5 million t of market pulp capacity during 1992–1993.

International Competitiveness. The United States trades large quantities of pulp annually, and has enjoyed a positive trade balance in this commodity grouping since 1987. A surge in imports of Canadian wood pulp, however, sharply narrowed the trade surplus in 1993. The principal grade of market pulp traded by the United States is bleached and semi-bleached kraft pulp, accounting for nearly 80 percent of pulp exports and 86 percent of imports in 1993.

In 1993 the volume of U.S. exports of pulp decreased about 8 percent to 5.6 million t. Because prices fell as well, the value of exports plunged more than 16 percent. U.S. exporters shipped pulp to 74 countries in 1993, but the major importers were Japan with 18 percent of total U.S. exports; South Korea, 12 percent; Mexico, 10 percent; and Italy, 7 percent.

Although U.S. pulp imports increased nearly 10 percent in 1993, to 5.5 million t, and accounted for almost 10 percent of total U.S. wood pulp consumption, declining prices caused the value of pulp imports to drop nearly 2 percent. The only significant suppliers of pulp imports were Canada, 86 percent, and Brazil, 10 percent of U.S. imports.

Outlook for 1994. A turnaround in the world economy should result in higher sales of U.S. market pulp in 1994. Domestic and foreign market shipments should increase 2 percent to nearly 9 million t. Higher demand by European and Asian producers of printing and writing paper should contribute to the expansion.

The volume of U.S. exports of pulp should increase more than 8 percent to 6 million t, widening their market share to nearly 70 percent of all U.S. market pulp shipments. U.S. imports are also expected to increase in 1994, as Canadian pulp exports to the large U.S. market increase by 6 percent. As the world's largest paper and board manufacturer, the United States will continue to be the target of many countries pulp export efforts. U.S. pulp producers will need to monitor their own capacity utilization rates, consumer and producer inventory levels around the world, and relationships with worldwide paper and board production to prevent further significant increases in surplus pulp in the market.

PAPER AND PAPERBOARD MILLS

U.S. primary paper and paperboard (SIC 262, 263) production rose more than 2 percent to 76 million metric tons (t) in 1993, primarily because of increased domestic demand for printing-and writing-paper grades. The value of sales declined slightly, however, to just over $46 billion, because of lower prices for most grades of paper and paperboard, resulting in operating losses for most U.S. paper and board companies. The price declines were due to a continuing oversupply around the world.

Operating rates remained about as high in 1993 as in 1992, with paper mills operating around 92 percent and paperboard mills operating at 95 percent. Despite a record-low U.S. dollar, export volumes of paper and board showed only marginal growth, reflecting decreased demand in principal export markets, including Europe and most of Asia. Domestic sales of primary paper were boosted by higher demand from leading users of printing and writing papers, especially from advertisers, printers, magazine and catalog publishers, and business forms and office and personal stationery. The domestic paperboard sector, in contrast, experienced a year of inventory drawdowns, reduced prices, sluggish domestic demand, and lower foreign demand for U.S. casemaking materials, resulting in minimal growth in 1993 shipments.

In 1993 the paperboard sector produced 38.6 million t of containerboard, boxboard, and related products, and the paper sector generated 37.8 million t of output. In 1993 shipments of paper commodities, which have a higher per unit value than paperboard, were valued at $30.8 billion, down nearly 4 percent from 1992, and paperboard shipments were valued at $15.2 billion, down more than 10 percent.

Domestic Paper Mills. The industry (SIC 262) produces four principal commodities: Printing and writing paper, newsprint, tissue, and packaging and industrial papers. The largest sector, printing and writing paper, accounted for 22 million t, or nearly 58 percent of all production by the paper industry in 1993. Shipments by domestic paper mills rose 3 percent in 1993, driven by higher demand from the value-added, high-end advertising, commercial printing and publishing end-user segments. The growth in shipments of printing and writing paper was paced by higher sales of uncoated free sheet, coated groundwood, and coated free sheet.

Uncoated free sheet is the single largest paper grade produced by the domestic industry, accounting for 52 percent of total printing and writing paper shipments and 30 percent of all paper commodities. Shipments of this grade increased nearly 4 percent in 1993. The higher demand allowed the industry to sustain several price increases during the year. Operating rates remained in the 90–93 percent range, but additional capacity added during the year makes a similar performance unlikely in 1994.

Shipments of uncoated groundwood increased more than 7 percent in 1993, to more than 4 million t. This grade represents more than 18 percent of domestic shipments of printing and writing paper. Increases in magazine startups and in advertising strengthened demand for coated groundwood papers, which represent more than two-thirds of the total magazine paper used in 1993.

After several years of strong growth, shipments of newsprint increased only 1 percent in 1993, to 6 million t, accounting for nearly 17 percent of total U.S. paper shipments. Despite a 1 percent increase in U.S. newspaper publishers' consumption of newsprint, overall sales were somewhat disappointing because newsprint exports declined more than 10 percent. Demand for newsprint was sluggish and capacity additions were minimal, so that operating rates for the industry were in the 95–97 percent range and prices were stable.

Paperboard Mills. After several years of strong growth, U.S. production of paperboard (SIC 263) increased less than 2 percent in 1993. Exports, a strong market for several years, declined moderately in 1993, reflecting the world economic slowdown, especially in Europe and much of Asia.

Trends and Forecasts: Paper and Paperboard Mills (SIC 262, 263) (In millions of dollars except as noted)

Item	1991	1992[1]	1993[2]	1994[3]	Percent Change (1991–1994) 91–92	92–93	93–94
Industry Data							
Value of shipments[4]	48,357	47,830	47,156	48,692	-1.1	-1.4	3.3
Value of shipments (1987$)	43,135	43,324	43,582	44,672	0.4	0.6	2.5
Total employment (000)	181	180	180	182	-0.6	0.0	1.1
Production workers (000)	138	137	137	138	-0.7	0.0	0.7
Average hourly earnings ($)	17.55	17.99	18.10	—	2.5	0.6	—
Capital expenditures	5,790	—	—	—	—	—	—
Product Data							
Value of shipments[5]	47,148	46,679	46,024	47,523	-1.0	-1.4	3.3
Value of shipments (1987$)	42,072	42,282	42,536	43,599	0.5	0.6	2.5
Trade Data							
Value of imports	6,949	6,774	7,316	7,535	-2.5	8.0	3.0
Value of exports	4,135	4,349	4,393	4,613	5.2	1.0	5.0

[1] Estimate, except exports and imports.

[2] Estimate.

[3] Forecast.

[4] Value of all products and services sold by establishments in the paper and paperboard mills industry.

[5] Value of products classified in the paper and paperboard mills industry produced by all industries.

Source: U.S. Department of Commerce: Bureau of the Census, International Trade Administration (ITA). Estimates and forecasts by ITA.

U.S. production of paperboard is essentially split into two product lines: containerboard and boxboard. Containerboard sales, representing 69 percent of all paperboard production in 1993, totaled 26.7 million t, an increase of only 1 percent. Boxboard production came to 11.9 million t.

Production of containerboard for domestic use, representing 61 percent of all U.S. production, increased less than 2 percent in 1993 to 24 million t.

Containerboard primarily consists of linerboard and corrugating medium, which are the base components used to manufacture corrugated shipping containers and other corrugated products. Domestic linerboard production in 1993 totaled 16.4 million t, about 61 percent of total containerboard output and about 42 percent of all U.S. paperboard production. Unbleached kraft linerboard accounts for more than 92 percent of U.S. linerboard production, but white-surface, high-performance, and recycled linerboard grades have shown the strongest growth in recent years. In 1993 U.S. production of recycled linerboard more than doubled, to more than 1 million t. Total domestic production of corrugating medium gained less than 1 percent, however, to 7 million t. This product represents 30 percent of U.S. containerboard production and just under 19 percent of U.S. paperboard production.

Domestic boxboard production, continuing its recent strong performance, increased more than 4 percent in 1993, driven by higher domestic demand for packaging end-uses (which increased nearly 4 percent) and nonpackaging boxboard grades (up more than 6 percent). The latter includes fiber cans, tubes, and drums; construction-related gypsum wallboard; and panelboard used in automobile production. Boxboard for domestic packaging uses saw its strongest performance in several years, spurred in part by slightly higher consumer spending on nondurable goods.

International Competitiveness. U.S. exports of primary paper and board were essentially unchanged in 1993 as paper-related exports rose slightly and paperboard products fell a bit. Despite a lower-valued U.S. dollar and lower unit values on most paper and board grades, total paper and board exports increased only 1 percent to nearly 7 million t.

Exports of the various printing and writing paper grades increased 11 percent in 1993 to more than 1 million t, following a 24 percent surge in 1992. Two printing- and writing-paper commodities, uncoated free sheet and coated groundwood, were responsible for most of the increase, with export increases of 14 percent (to 465,300 t) 23 percent (to 191,000 t) respectively. Principal U.S. export markets for uncoated free sheet in 1993 were Canada, 54 percent, and Mexico, 14 percent. For coated groundwood, the leading U.S. export markets were Canada, 35 percent; Mexico, 19 percent; Japan, 18 percent; and the Netherlands, 13 percent.

The economic downturns in Europe and Asia in 1993 were characterized by a reduction in those U.S. export markets' shipments of nondurable goods, a principal end-use for corrugated boxes. Overall, U.S. paperboard exports declined nearly 3 percent to 4 million t. Exports of unbleached kraft linerboard, accounting for 60 percent of all paperboard exports, fell 8 percent to less than 3 million t as foreign demand for U.S. containerboard fell. One paperboard grade whose exports did expand vigorously was recycled paperboard. Foreign demand for this folding carton board expanded 16 percent in 1993 to 256,820 t.

U.S. paper and board imports surged more than 15 percent to 12 million t in 1993, driven by a moderate turnaround in the U.S. economy. The largest import gains were in newsprint, up more than 18 percent to 7 million t, almost all from Canada. Because most prices remained flat or fell slightly, the value of newsprint imports increased only 8 percent to $7.3 billion. The wide range of paper grades, including newsprint and printing and writing paper, accounted for 11 million t, or about 92 percent of total U.S. imports of paper and board.

U.S. imports of printing and writing paper, which made up 26 percent of total imports, increased nearly 14 percent to 3.1 million t in 1993. This growth was attributable to large increases in U.S. imports of coated groundwood (more than 24 percent) and uncoated free sheet printing and writing papers (17 percent). U.S. printing- and writing-paper imports come primarily from Canada, Scandinavia, and the European Community.

U.S. imports of the paperboard grades, although still relatively small, increased 10 percent in 1993, to 907,000 t. The United States imported significantly larger quantities of kraft containerboard and virgin and recycled boxboard, primarily because of strong demand by U.S. corrugated box plants and folding carton plants. The leading supplier of paperboard to the United States was Canada, accounting for 90 percent of total imports.

Outlook for 1994. U.S. paper and paperboard shipments will increase more than 3 percent in value in 1994 as domestic demand remains strong and U.S. producers enjoy higher sales overseas. Exports of paper and board should increase 5 percent, and imports, buoyed by a stronger U.S. economy, should increase at least 3 percent.

The U.S. industry will continue to direct most of its additional output overseas, especially to printers, publishers, and boxmakers in Asia, Latin America, and the EC. But the domestic market will continue to claim about 90 percent of domestic output.

Domestic paper and board producers are expected to add 1.5 million t of capacity in 1994, adding to the overcapacity that prevailed in 1993, especially in printing and writing paper. If the global economy improves enough in 1994, the additional output could be easily absorbed by foreign converters and packagers. If not, operating rates in domestic paper and board mils will probably be flat or slightly lower, and pressure on domestic producers to schedule extended periods of mill downtime will increase.

WEYERHAEUSER COMPANY—1994

MICHELLE R. GREENE
AND FRED R. DAVID
Francis Marion University

Headquartered in Tacoma, Washington, Weyerhaeuser's (206-924-2058) sales and net income increased 7.4 percent and 55.7 percent in 1993.

Weyerhaeuser's vision statement is to be "the best forest products company in the world." Their strategies for realizing this vision are: "making total quality the Weyerhaeuser way of doing business. Relentless pursuit of full customer satisfaction. Empowering Weyerhaeuser people. Leading the industry in forest management and manufacturing excellence. Producing superior returns for our shareholders."

THE PAST

The name Weyerhaeuser originally became identified with forest products in 1858 when a young German immigrant named Frederick Weyerhaeuser acquired a lumberyard and sawmill in western Illinois. The success of his first venture led Weyerhaeuser to purchase timberland in Wisconsin and Minnesota. Weyerhaeuser wanted to control other forests but soon realized he needed financial assistance to realize his goal. He began to seek partners in his timber business. Weyerhaeuser and his associates soon became a major force in the American timber and lumber industries.

In 1900 Weyerhaeuser organized a group of midwestern investors to buy forest land in the Pacific Northwest. The venture became one of the largest private land transactions in American history. Weyerhaeuser and 15 partners purchased 900,000 acres of timberland from the Northern Pacific Railway for $6 per acre. Then 65 years old, Weyerhaeuser could scarcely have dreamed that his enterprise would become a giant in American industry. The investors' group named the company for Weyerhaeuser and opened its first office in Tacoma. The company was incorporated in 1900 as the Weyerhaeuser Timber Company.

In addition to acquiring a sawmill, buying timber, and selling wood products, the new company kept harvested lands for reforestation. Weyerhaeuser was always determined to plant and care for more trees than his company harvested each year. The company's high-yield forestry today is a scientific forest-management program designed to produce more timber than is cut while protecting fish and wildlife. The program includes planting seedlings within a year after harvest, fertilizing heavily, and rehabilitating brushlands.

Weyerhaeuser Company earnings increased soundly in 1993 to $579 million on $8.3 billion in sales, up from $372 million and $7.7 billion in 1992. Weyerhaeuser in 1993 sold its baby diaper business—a successful but noncore operation—for $44 million and also divested its tax-deferred annuities and mutual fund business (GNA Corporation) for $36 million. This sale is the largest divestiture ever made by Weyerhaeuser. GNA also was a profitable investment for Weyerhaeuser over its nine years of ownership.

Weyerhaeuser recently completed the purchase from Procter & Gamble Company of two pulp mills, three sawmills, timberlands in Georgia, and a forest-management license in Alberta. Weyerhaeuser has strengthened its engineered fiber products business with another acquisition, an oriented strand board mill at Slave Lake, Alberta. The formerly idle mill provided needed additional capacity and flexibility to meet the growing demand for Weyerhaeuser's oriented strand products.

Weyerhaeuser is modernizing its pulp and paper complexes in Plymouth, North Carolina ($500 million); Longview, Washington ($400 million); and Kamloops, British Columbia ($80 million). The projects are part of one of the largest modernization programs in company history. Installation of state-of-the-art systems at all three facilities will allow for the elimination of elemental chlorine from the pulp-manufacturing process, improve product quality to meet ever-increasing customer demands, reduce energy and chemical costs, and significantly enhance air and water quality. Another benefit will be the use of additional recycled paper for increased production at Plymouth. Scheduled completion of the projects is late 1994 to mid-1995.

Weyerhaeuser recently celebrated the 25th anniversary of its high-yield forestry strategy that brought the company to leadership in forestry management. In the international arena, Weyerhaeuser celebrated the 20th anniversary of its business relationship with the People's Republic of China. Weyerhaeuser was the first U.S. forest products company to ship an industrial product to China through contacts made at the 1972 Guangzhou Trade Fair. Weyerhaeuser, now the leading U.S. exporter of forest products, provides China with corrugating medium, linerboard, logs, lumber, paper and pulp. In 1993 Weyerhaeuser celebrated the 30th anniversary of establishing a Weyerhaeuser office in Tokyo.

Weyerhaeuser and Svenska Cellulosa of Sweden have entered into an agreement that will enable the corrugated packaging business of both of the companies to better satisfy the increasing requirements of international customers. One of Weyerhaeuser's greatest achievements was earning registration from the International Organization for Standardization (ISO) for quality of both products and processes at four of the company's pulp and paper facilities.

THE COMPANY STRUCTURE

Weyerhaeuser has 37,000 employees, of which 34,200 are employed in its timber-based businesses. Approximately 17,000 employees are covered by collective bargaining agreements. Approximately 2,800 of the company's employees are involved in the activities of its real estate and financial services subsidiaries. In 1993 the company's sales to customers outside the United States totaled $2.2 billion, which included $1.8 billion of exports from the United States and Canada. The company's other two large subsidiaries are timberlands/wood products and pulp/paper/packaging.

Timberlands/Wood Products. Weyerhaeuser's wood products businesses produce and sell softwood lumber, plywood, and veneer; composite panels; oriented strand board; hardboard; hardwood lumber and plywood; doors; treated products; logs; chips; and timber. These products are sold primarily through the company's own sales organizations. Building materials are sold to wholesalers, retailers, and industrial users.

Weyerhaeuser owns approximately 5.5 million acres of commercial forest land in the United States, of which 50 percent is located in the South and 50 percent in the Pacific Northwest. The company also has long-term license agreements in Canada covering approximately 17.8 million acres, of which 14 million acres are considered to be productive forest land. Weyerhaeuser's combined total timber inventory on U.S. and Canadian lands is approximately 245 million cunits (a cunit is 100 cubic feet of solid wood) of which approximately 75 percent is softwood species. The company is engaged in extensive planting, suppression of nonmerchantable species, precommercial and commercial thinning and fertilization, all of which increase the yield from its fee timberland acreage.

Timberlands and Wood Products reported strong 1993 earnings—the highest since 1980—with plywood, engineered fiber products, and building materials distribution businesses posting record profits for the year. Timber supply restrictions in the public forests of the Pacific Northwest have reduced West Coast raw material availability and caused significant price increases, while reductions in international timber supply translated into stronger business results in Japan and China. Plans to protect the northern spotted owl led to reduced harvest on company-owned lands.

Weyerhaeuser has had a serious challenge with the new forest practice rules in Washington. The new rules are some of the most comprehensive in the United States and address such issues as size and timing of harvest acres, wetlands and streamside management zones, use of chemicals and critical habitat reserves. Weyerhaeuser participates actively in the regulatory process and supports its goals.

Annual production levels for Weyerhaeuser's different lumber products are given in Exhibit 21–1. Note that demand for all lumber products increased. Southern lumber prices attained record levels in several product lines because the Western harvest

EXHIBIT 21-1 Weyerhaeuser Annual Production Levels for Wood Products (Millions of dollars)

NET SALES	1993	1992	1991	1990	1989
Raw materials					
(logs, chips and timber)	$1,021	$ 872	$ 843	$ 834	$ 893
Softwood lumber	1,669	1,097	938	1,016	1,229
Softwood plywood and veneer	567	498	412	411	490
Oriented strand board, composite					
and other panels	623	495	383	381	424
Hardwood lumber	154	127	118	117	119
Hardwood plywood and doors	141	116	117	135	236
Treated products	84	67	65	80	95
Miscellaneous products	209	145	72	99	180
	$4,468	$3,417	$2,948	$3,073	$3,666

Source: Weyerhaeuser *Annual Report,* 1993.

reduction resulted in more pressure on the South to make up the shortfall. Production for the year was hampered by an unusually wet spring, which slowed log supplies to the mills and mill startups. The southern lumber business has expanded its product mix by adding the Barnesville, Georgia, mill, which was part of an acquisition from Procter & Gamble. Weyerhaeuser today has 56 manufacturing facilities within its Timberlands and Wood Products division, as shown in Exhibit 21–2. Note in Exhibit 21–3 that Weyerhaeuser is operating at over 90 percent capacity in all categories except hardwood lumber.

Pulp, Paper, and Packaging. Weyerhaeuser's pulp, paper, and packaging revenues decreased in 1993, as shown in Exhibit 21–4. There were declines in all categories except pulp and chemicals. Note that the 1993 composite sales figures show a 12.9 percent decrease. For the year market pulp demand showed a modest improvement. Domestic newsprint prices continue to deteriorate with very slow growth in the domestic market and negative growth in the Japanese market. Substantial overcapacity in printing and writing papers has resulted in continued low industry-operating

EXHIBIT 21-2 Weyerhaeuser Principal Manufacturing Facilities—
Timberlands and Wood Products.

Softwood lumber, plywood and veneer	35
Composite panels	6
Oriented strand board	5
Hardboard	1
Hardwood lumber	8
Hardwood doors	1

Source: Weyerhaeuser *Annual Report*, 1993.

EXHIBIT 21-3 Weyerhaeuser Timberlands and Wood Products—Annual Production
(Millions)

	CAPACITY	1993	1992	1991	1990	1989
Logs—cubic feet	—	673	749	782	817	839
Softwood lumber—board feet	3,215	3,135	2,782	2,687	2,719	2,759
Softwood plywood and veneer— square feet (3/8")	1,246	1,188	1,125	966	1,076	1,069
Composite panels—square feet (3/4")	609	564	540	493	505	587
Oriented strand board—square feet (3/8")	1,440	1,443	1,234	1,208	1,156	1,121
Hardboard—square feet (7/16")	130	120	118	90	119	131
Hardwood lumber—board feet	255	221	210	196	202	212
Hardwood doors (thousands)	561	522	469	448	556	833

Source: Weyerhaeuser *Annual Report*, 1993.

rates and price reductions of 40 percent on high-volume grades. Note in Exhibit 21–5 that Weyerhaueser is operating at nearly 100 percent capacity in all its pulp, paper, and packaging categories, except MSF packaging. Recycled paper usage continues to be an important part of the raw material for the company's products. More than 23 percent of the raw material for the company's pulp and papermaking operations is recycled fiber, up from 15 percent in 1989.

Weyerhaeuser recently strengthened its pulp and paper businesses by acquiring a softwood kraft papergrade mill in Grande Prairie, Alberta, and a fluff pulp mill in Oglethorpe, Georgia, both from Procter & Gamble Company. The two newly acquired pulp mills increased market pulp capacity by 40 percent and further strengthened Weyerhaeuser's world leadership in fluff and softwood papergrade.

In containerboard packaging, the $105 million modernization of the No. 1 paper

EXHIBIT 21-4 Weyerhaeuser Pulp, Paper, and Packaging Sales (Millions of dollars)

NET SALES	1993	1992	1991	1990	1989
Pulp	$ 823	$ 711	$ 803	$ 865	$ 917
Newsprint	322	326	288	293	321
Paper	648	673	655	751	733
Paperboard and containerboard	255	321	361	366	373
Container and packaging products	1,302	1,323	1,175	1,183	1,261
Recycling	77	93	90	88	85
Chemicals	32	31	34	28	31
Personal care products	—	514	450	338	347
Miscellaneous products	120	117	147	140	147
	$3,579	$4,109	$4,003	$4,052	$4,215

Source: Weyerhaeuser *Annual Report*, 1993.

EXHIBIT 21-5 Weyerhaeuser Pulp, Paper, and Packaging—Annual Production (Thousands)

	CAPACITY	1993	1992	1991	1990	1989
Pulp—air-dry metric tons	2,130	2,096	1,506	1,527	1,386	1,275
Newsprint—metric tons	675	618	588	461	459	486
Paper—tons	1,015	1,007	971	889	900	919
Paperboard—tons	220	217	229	238	217	221
Containerboard—tons	2,360	2,269	2,240	2,224	2,171	2,168
Packaging—MSF	36,800	32,795	31,040	27,583	26,146	25,764
Recycling—tons	—	1,847	1,692	1,415	1,204	1,163
Personal care products—standard cases	—	—	16,743	14,902	11,471	12,019

Source: Weyerhaeuser *Annual Report*, 1993.

machine at Valliant, Oklahoma, has been completed and producing high-performance linerboard. Weyerhaeuser is converting the linerboard machine at Plymouth, North Carolina, to produce a 100 percent recycled product. The company expects corrugated packaging demand to rise with improvement in general economic conditions and export containerboard shipments to grow with the later pickup in the European economies and economic recovery in the Far East.

The newsprint business in 1993 was unable to increase its domestic and export market shares during a difficult period of oversupply in the marketplace. Slow growth in the domestic market and negative growth in the Japanese market hampered sales of the large incremental volumes associated with the start-up of North Pacific Paper Corporation's (NORPAC) new newsprint machine. The business has achieved full operation of the expanded facility and successfully developed and introduced two new product grades into the Japanese market. Overall, Weyerhaeuser operated 84 pulp, paper, and packaging manufacturing plants in 1993, as shown in Exhibit 21–6.

Real Estate and Financial Services. Through its financial services subsidiary, Weyerhaeuser is involved in a broad range of financial services. The principal operating groups of Weyerhaeuser Financial Services (WFS) are Weyerhaeuser Mortgage Company and Mortgage Securities Corporation. Weyerhaeuser Mortgage Company has offices in 12 states, with a serving portfolio of $8.4 billion covering more than 112,000 loans throughout the country. Earnings for 1993 were $76.4 million, up 13 percent from 1992. However, as shown in Exhibit 21–7, total revenues of WFS fell 51.8 percent in 1993. Mortgages are resold in the secondary market through mortgage-backed securities to financial institutions and investors.

Weyerhaeuser Real Estate Company (WRECO) earned $18.3 million in 1993, up 42 percent from 1992. The 1993 low interest rates and improving consumer confidence resulted in revenues increasing to $829 million as housing starts increased in all regions of the nation except California and the Pacific Northwest. WRECO's total revenues for 1993 are given in Exhibit 21–8. Note that all categories increased.

Foreign Operations and Export Sales. Weyerhaeuser exports logs to China and Korea; pulp, containerboard, lumber, and plywood to Europe; and pulp, newsprint, paperboard, containerboard, logs, lumber, and wood chips to Japan. Exhibit 21-9

EXHIBIT 21-6 Weyerhaeuser Pulp, Paper, and Packaging—Principal Manufacturing Facilities

Pulp	8
Newsprint	1
Paper	5
Paperboard	1
Containerboard	5
Packaging	36
Recycling	21
Chemicals	7

Source: Weyerhaeuser *Annual Report,* 1993.

gives the company's recent export sales to Japan versus other foreign countries. Note that the company's total export sales declined 3 percent in 1993, but exports to Japan increased 4 percent.

Finance. Weyerhaeuser's consolidated financial information is given in Exhibits 21–10 through 21–13. A list of Weyerhaeuser's top managers appears in Exhibit 21–14.

Weyerhaeuser is facing fierce competition among lenders for loan-origination volume, spurred by continuing lower mortgage interest rates and continued refinance activity. Strategic expansion of the current origination system of 40 retail branches and seven wholesale branches is planned for the coming year. Continued focus is on responding to customer needs, improving processes, and enhancing efficiency and quality throughout the business.

THE WEYERHAEUSER FUTURE

Because of environmental concerns and new regulations in the Pacific Northwest, Weyerhaeuser perhaps should acquire timberlands elsewhere in the United States and the world. The majority of its current timber is located in the Pacific Northwest. Should Weyerhaeuser purchase timber in South America, Asia, or the northeastern United States?

Weyerhaeuser's sales to customers outside the United States fell 3.7 percent in 1993. With passage of the North American Free Trade Act on November 17, 1993, trade barriers between the United States and Mexico have been lifted. The Latin American region in general is an area where Weyerhaeuser could prosper. Should Weyerhaeuser focus on producing and marketing its products in Mexico? Prepare a strategic plan for CEO John W. Creighton, Jr., that will guide Weyerhaeuser to continued prosperity in the remaining years of this decade.

EXHIBIT 21-7 Net Sales and Revenues—WFS (Millions of dollars)

	1993	1992	1991	1990	1989
Interest	$110	$144	$209	$278	$383
Investment income	116	452	454	369	314
Loan origination and servicing fees	127	103	98	89	92
Premiums	14	21	19	23	21
Other revenues	34	112	82	49	41
	$401	$832	$862	$808	$851

Source: Weyerhaeuser *Annual Report*, 1993.

EXHIBIT 21-8 Net Sales and Revenues—WRECO (Millions of dollars)

	1993	1992	1991	1990	1989
Single-family units	$615	$569	$591	$644	$718
Multi-family units	30	4	16	15	12
Residential lots	43	39	25	35	44
Commercial lots	41	6	17	10	27
Commercial buildings	3	5	30	23	66
Acreage	27	20	16	31	55
Other	70	47	49	53	53
	$829	$690	$744	$811	$975

Source: Weyerhaeuser *Annual Report*, 1993.

EXHIBIT 21-9 Weyerhaeuser's Export Sales

	1993	1992	1991
Export sales:			
Customers in Japan	$ 952,000	$ 912,000	$ 887,000
Customers outside Japan	493,000	589,000	663,000
Total export sales	$1,445,000	$1,501,000	$1,550,000
Total net sales and revenues	$9,545,000	$9,266,000	$8,773,000

Source: Weyerhaeuser *Annual Report*, 1993.

EXHIBIT 21-10 Weyerhaeuser Operations by Division

Business Segments	Sales to and Revenue from Unaffiliated Customers	Intersegment Sales and Revenue	Total Sales and Revenue	Approximate Contribution to Earnings	Depreciation, Amortization and Fee Stumpage	Capital Expenditures	Assets
1993:							
Timberlands and wood products	$4,467,751	$ 352,314	$4,820,065	$ 891,431	$161,903	$ 240,760	$ 2,582,832
Pulp and paper products	3,579,042	6,189	3,585,231	60,854	263,961	652,092	5,731,965
Real estate	828,713	—	828,713	18,326	9,123	15,007	1,863,615
Financial services	401,711	—	401,711	76,437	33,976	4,737	1,892,180
Corporate and other	269,181	28,409	297,590	(46,961)	17,968	54,885	1,274,185
	9,546,398	386,912	9,933,310	1,000,087	486,931	967,481	13,344,777
Eliminations	(1,606)	(386,912)	(388,518)	—	—	—	(706,324)
Interest expense		—	—	(292,459)	—	—	—
Less: capitalized interest		—	—	100,825	—	—	—
Income before income taxes and extraordinary item		—	—	808,453	—	—	—
Income taxes		—	—	(281,168)	—	—	—
Extraordinary item		—	—	52,052	—	—	—
	$9,544,792	—	$9,544,792	$ 579,337	$486,931	$ 967,481	$12,638,453
1992:							
Timberlands and wood products	$3,416,832	$ 340,368	$3,757,200	$ 515,394	$149,504	$ 246,096	$ 2,374,152
Pulp and paper products	4,109,080	28,822	4,137,902	251,091	254,956	931,913	5,614,490
Real estate	690,342	—	690,342	12,897	7,310	7,869	1,693,741
Financial services	832,389	—	832,389	67,633	48,685	2,646	8,148,285
Corporate and other	220,032	29,907	249,939	(106,863)	42,291	16,990	1,201,418
	9,268,675	399,097	9,667,772	740,152	502,746	1,205,514	19,032,086

EXHIBIT 21-10 *Continued*

Business Segments	Sales to and Revenue from Unaffiliated Customers	Intersegment Sales and Revenue	Total Sales and Revenue	Approximate Contribution to Earnings	Depreciation, Amortization and Fee Stumpage	Capital Expenditures	Assets
Eliminations	(2,206)	(399,097)	(401,303)	—	—	—	(873,683)
Interest expense	—	—	—	(262,209)	—	—	—
Less: capitalized interest	—	—	—	85,406	—	—	—
Income before income taxes	—	—	—	563,349	—	—	—
Income taxes	—	—	—	(191,300)	—	—	—
	$9,266,469	—	$9,266,469	$ 372,049	$502,746	$1,205,514	$18,158,403
1991:							
Timberlands and wood products	$2,948,358	$ 366,988	$3,315,346	$ 155,386	$157,506	$ 161,589	$ 2,223,886
Pulp and paper products	4,002,738	19,685	4,022,423	108,287	245,533	472,412	4,928,239
Real estate	744,366	—	744,366	(175,331)	8,197	7,485	1,500,250
Financial services	862,403	—	862,403	60,409	46,843	3,518	7,956,631
Corporate and other	215,501	29,062	244,563	(148,212)	43,243	18,367	1,186,906
	8,773,366	415,735	9,189,101	539	501,322	663,371	17,795,912
Eliminations	(753)	(415,735)	(416,488)	—	—	—	(810,038)
Interest expense	—	—	—	(265,240)	—	—	—
Less: capitalized interest	—	—	—	86,853	—	—	—
Income (loss) before income taxes and effect of accounting changes	—	—	—	(177,848)	—	—	—
Income taxes	—	—	—	76,900	—	—	—
Effect of accounting changes	—	—	—	(61,000)	—	—	—
changes	$8,772,613	—	$8,772,613	$(161,948)	$501,322	$ 663,371	$16,985,874

Interest expense of $95,309, $151,519 and $219,441 before the elimination of intercompany interest of $0, $3,403 and $6,455 in 1993, 1992, and 1991, respectively, is included in the determination of "approximate contribution to earnings" for financial services.
Certain reclassifications have been made to conform prior years' data to the current format.
Source: Weyerhaeuser *Annual Report*, 1993.

EXHIBIT 21-11 Weyerhaeuser Consolidated Statement of Earnings For the Three Years in the Period Ended December 26, 1993 (Dollar amounts in thousands except per share figures)

	1993	1992	1991
Net sales and revenues:			
Weyerhaeuser:	$8,314,368	$7,743,738	$7,165,844
Real estate and financial services	1,230,424	1,522,731	1,606,769
Net sales and revenues	9,544,792	9,266,469	8,772,613
Costs and expenses:			
Weyerhaeuser:			
Costs of products sold	6,251,612	5,919,199	5,581,388
Depreciation, amortization and fee stumpage	443,832	446,751	446,282
Selling, general and administrative expenses	592,586	591,845	572,605
Research and development expenses	44,456	42,981	56,257
Taxes other than payroll and income taxes	136,897	121,793	120,283
Restructuring and other charges	—	—	290,000
	7,469,383	7,122,569	7,066,815
Real estate and financial services:			
Costs and operating expenses	835,400	979,478	1,026,546
Depreciation and amortization	43,099	55,995	55,040
Selling, general and administrative expenses	206,174	252,337	232,055
Taxes other than payroll and income taxes	9,191	11,700	9,838
Restructuring and other charges	—	—	155,000
	1,093,864	1,299,510	1,478,479
Total costs and expenses	8,563,247	8,422,079	8,545,294
Operating income	981,545	844,390	227,319
Interest expense and other:			
Weyerhaeuser:			
Interest expense incurred	214,813	189,648	197,337
Less interest capitalized	23,179	12,845	18,950
Other income (expense), net	60,339	35,050	9,977
Real estate and financial services:			
Interest expense incurred	172,955	220,677	280,889
Less interest capitalized	77,646	72,561	67,903
Other income (expense), net	53,512	8,828	(23,771)
Earnings (loss) before income taxes, extraordinary item and effect of accounting changes	808,453	563,349	(177,848)
Income taxes before extraordinary item and effect of accounting changes	281,168	191,300	(76,900)
Earnings (loss) before extraordinary item and effect of accounting changes	527,285	372,049	(100,948)
Extraordinary item, net of applicable taxes of $33,732	52,052	—	—
Effect of accounting changes	—	—	(61,000)
Net earnings (loss)	$579,337	$372,049	$(161,948)
Per common share:			
Earnings (loss) before extraordinary item and effect of accounting changes	$2.58	$1.83	$(.50)
Extraordinary item	.25	—	—
Effect of accounting changes	—	—	(.30)
Net earnings (loss)	$2.83	$1.83	$(.80)
Dividends paid	$1.20	$1.20	$1.20

Source: Weyerhaeuser *Annual Report*, 1993.

EXHIBIT 21-12 Weyerhaueser Consolidated Balance Sheet (Dollar amounts in thousands)

	DECEMBER 26, 1993	DECEMBER 27, 1992
Assets		
Weyerhaeuser		
Current assets:		
Cash and short-term investments, including		
restricted deposits of $14,351 and $23,706	$ 73,257	$ 40,985
Receivables, less allowances of $9,798 and $9,614	782,507	769,910
Inventories	762,471	723,904
Prepaid expenses	280,511	168,079
Total current assets	1,898,746	1,702,878
Property and equipment	5,606,072	5,612,220
Construction in progress	666,177	322,376
Timber and timberlands at cost, less fee stumpage		
charged to disposals	604,773	591,610
Other assets and deferred charges	191,946	208,948
Total assets	8,967,714	8,438,032
Real estate and financial services		
Cash and short-term investments, including restricted		
deposits of $34,042 and $38,432	86,598	483,340
Receivables, less discounts and allowances of $6,589		
and $5,868	135,347	172,897
Mortgage and construction notes and mortgage loans		
receivable	830,569	857,963
Investments	60,355	5,232,428
Mortgage-backed certificates and restricted		
deposits	349,757	614,252
Real estate being processed for development, less reserves of		
$29,783 and $76,920	738,597	617,087
Land being processed for development, less reserves of		
$19,132 and $28,053	699,611	711,129
Deferred acquisition costs	39,751	295,314
Other assets	730,154	735,961
Total assets	3,670,739	9,720,371
	$12,638,453	$18,158,403

Source: Weyerhaeuser *Annual Report,* 1993.

EXHIBIT 21-12 *Continued*

	DECEMBER 26, 1993	DECEMBER 27, 1992
Liabilities and shareholders' interest		
Weyerhaeuser		
Current liabilities:		
Notes payable	$ 4,624	$ 14,684
Current maturities of senior long-term debt	14,522	113,607
Accounts payable	492,040	386,561
Accrued liabilities	565,002	623,163
Total current liabilities	1,076,188	1,138,015
Senior long-term debt	2,997,890	2,658,867
Convertible subordinated debentures	—	193,035
Limited recourse income debenture	—	187,963
Deferred income taxes	904,332	760,876
Deferred pension and other liabilities	535,162	511,839
Minority interest in subsidiaries	109,314	93,476
Commitments		
Total liabilities	5,622,886	5,544,071
Real estate and financial services		
Notes and commercial paper	289,038	280,351
Future annuity and contract reserves	—	5,529,700
Collateralized mortgage obligation bonds	307,416	543,157
Long-term debt	1,997,146	2,195,715
Other liabilities	455,871	419,420
Commitments		
Total liabilities	3,049,471	8,968,343
Shareholders' interest		
Common shares: authorized 400,000,000 shares, issued 206,072,890 shares, $1.25 par value	257,591	257,591
Other capital	411,096	404,250
Cumulative translation adjustment	(73,363)	(36,481)
Retained earnings	3,391,217	3,057,702
Treasury common shares, at cost: 983,952 and 1,795,595	(20,445)	(37,073)
Total shareholders' interest	3,966,096	3,645,989
	$12,638,453	$18,158,403

Source: Weyerhaeuser *Annual Report*, 1993.

EXHIBIT 21-13 Weyerhaeuser Consolidated Statement of Cash Flows (*Dollar amounts in thousands*)

For the Three Years in the Period Ended December 26, 1993	Consolidated			Weyerhaeuser Company			Real Estate and Financial Services		
	1993	1992	1991	1993	1992	1991	1993	1992	1991
Cash flows provided by operations:									
Net earnings (loss)	$ 579,337	$ 372,049	$ (161,948)	$ 511,594	$ 332,043	$ (89,185)	$ 67,743	$ 40,006	$ (72,763)
Non-cash charges to income:									
Depreciation, amortization and fee stumpage	486,931	502,746	501,322	443,832	446,751	446,282	43,099	55,995	55,040
Deferred income taxes, net	93,033	125,300	(43,000)	107,591	97,192	(6,530)	(14,558)	28,108	(36,470)
Contributions to employee investment plans	2,462	31,577	25,420	2,462	31,577	25,420	—	—	—
Extraordinary item, including current tax benefit	(90,419)	—	—	(90,419)	—	—	—	—	—
Deferred income taxes on extraordinary item	38,367	—	—	38,367	—	—	—	—	—
Effect of accounting charge	—	—	198,000	—	—	187,000	—	—	11,000
Effect of accounting changes — deferred taxes	—	—	(137,000)	—	—	(122,505)	—	—	(14,495)
Restructuring and other charges	—	—	445,000	—	—	290,000	—	—	155,000
Changes in working capital:									
Receivables	(93,196)	(191,078)	20,060	(55,155)	(120,186)	5,606	(38,041)	(70,892)	14,454
Inventories, prepaid expenses, real estate and land	(246,356)	(174,519)	3,183	(164,475)	(31,551)	(30,341)	(81,881)	(142,968)	33,524
Mortgages held for sale	22,758	164,686	168,875	—	—	—	22,758	164,686	168,875
Other liabilities	177,629	289,041	372,262	61,971	(78,407)	66,676	115,658	367,448	305,586
(Gain) loss on disposition of assets	(16,352)	9,868	7,776	(2,741)	9,509	8,476	(13,611)	359	(700)
Gain on sales of businesses	(111,750)	(2,742)	—	(70,199)	—	—	(41,551)	(2,742)	—
Other	18,826	(17,222)	(67,451)	34,325	7,789	27,514	(15,499)	(25,011)	(94,965)
Net cash provided by operations	861,270	1,109,706	1,332,499	817,153	694,717	808,413	44,117	414,989	524,086
Cash flows from investing in the business:									
Property and equipment	(926,899)	(574,715)	(647,887)	(907,155)	(564,200)	(636,884)	(19,744)	(10,515)	(11,003)
Timber and timberlands	(40,582)	(41,436)	(15,484)	(40,582)	(41,436)	(15,484)	—	—	—
Mortgage and investment securities acquired	(776,424)	(4,556,619)	(1,765,701)	—	—	—	(776,424)	(4,556,619)	(1,765,701)

EXHIBIT 21-13 *Continued*

Acquisition of businesses	—	(589,363)	—	—	(589,363)	—	—	—	—
Proceeds from sale of:									
Property and equipment	53,710	55,362	51,259	26,954	52,034	47,703	26,756	3,328	3,556
Businesses	615,784	—	22,668	204,100	—	22,668	411,684	—	—
Mortgage and investment securities	509,982	4,276,056	1,280,131	—	—	—	509,982	4,276,056	1,280,131
Other	(25,393)	(18,215)	(50,227)	(5,675)	58,942	(6,460)	(19,718)	(77,157)	(43,767)
Net cash flows from investing in the business	(589,822)	(1,448,930)	(1,125,241)	(722,358)	(1,084,023)	(588,457)	132,536	(364,907)	(536,784)
Cash flows from financing activities: Sale of debentures, notes and CMO bonds	1,290,889	782,116	847,002	930,882	117,451	633,755	360,007	664,665	213,247
Sale of industrial revenue bonds	135,400	151,840	40,900	135,400	151,840	40,900	—	—	—
Savings deposits, net	—	(618,467)	(142,465)	—	—	—	(618,467)	(618,467)	(142,465)
Notes and commercial paper borrowings, net	(659,939)	421,435	(445,004)	(519,837)	503,813	(585,773)	(140,102)	(82,378)	140,769
Sales of receivables	—	—	64,417	—	64,417	64,417	—	—	—
Proceeds from issuance of investment contracts	60,943	430,566	566,469	566,469	—	—	60,943	430,566	566,469
Cash dividends on common shares	(245,822)	(243,965)	(241,814)	(245,822)	(243,965)	(241,814)	—	—	—
Intercompany cash dividends on common shares	—	—	—	435,000	22,300	23,000	(435,000)	(22,300)	(23,000)
Payments on debentures, notes, bank credit agreements, income debenture, capital leases and CMO bonds	(1,243,094)	(692,725)	(502,554)	(823,851)	(222,783)	(78,654)	(419,243)	(469,942)	(423,900)
Exercise of stock options	20,571	27,060	4,438	20,571	27,060	4,438	—	—	—
Other	5,134	(10,231)	2,003	5,134	(10,231)	(675)	—	(97,856)	2,678
Net cash flows from financing activities	(635,918)	247,629	193,392	(62,523)	345,485	(140,406)	(573,395)	333,798	333,798
Net increase (decrease) in cash and short-term investments	(364,470)	(91,595)	400,650	2,272	(43,821)	79,550	(396,742)	(47,774)	321,100
Cash and short-term investments at beginning of year	524,325	615,920	215,270	40,985	84,806	5,256	483,340	531,114	210,014
Cash and short-term investments at end of year	$ 159,855	$ 524,325	$ 615,920	$ 73,257	$ 40,985	$ 84,806	$ 86,598	$ 483,340	$ 531,114
Cash paid (received) during the year for:									
Interest, net of amount capitalized	$ 306,050	$ 331,832	$ 376,154	$ 203,618	$ 181,630	$ 160,157	$ 102,432	$ 150,202	$ 215,997
Income taxes	$ 158,002	$ (17,900)	$ 73,250	$ 161,236	$ (10,138)	$ 26,056	$ (3,234)	$ (7,762)	$ 47,194

Source: Weyerhaeuser *Annual Report*, 1993.

EXHIBIT 21-14 Top Managers at Weyerhaeuser

DIRECTORS

William H. Clapp
John W. Creighton, Jr.
W. John Driscoll
Don C. Frisbee
Philip M. Hawley
E. Bronson Ingram
John I. Kieckhefer
William D. Ruckelshaus
Richard H. Sinkfield
George H. Weyerhaeuser

SENIOR OFFICERS

John W. Creighton, Jr.
President and
Chief Executive Officer

Charles W. Bingham
Executive Vice President,
Timberlands, Raw Materials
and External Affairs

William R. Corbin
Executive Vice President,
Wood Products

Steven R. Hill
Senior Vice President,
Human Resources

Norman E. Johnson
Senior Vice President,
Technology

William C. Stivers
Senior Vice President and
Chief Financial Officer

CORPORATION

John S. Coates
Vice President and
Managing Director,
Pension Fund Investments

David R. Edwards
Vice President and Treasurer

Clifford R. Hall
Vice President,
Information Technology

Mack L. Hogans
Vice President,
Government Affairs

Robert C. Lane
Vice President and
General Counsel

John S. Larsen
Vice President,
Office of the Environment

Richard K. Long
Vice President,
Corporate Communications

Sandy D. McDade
Secretary

Susan M. Mersereau
Vice President, Quality,
Corporate Region Services
and Aviation

Larry W. Pollock
Vice President and
Director of Taxes

Darien E. Roseen
Vice President,
Strategic Planning

Edward L. Soule
Vice President,
Corporate R&D

Kenneth J. Stancato
Vice President and
Controller

Marvin E. Waters
Vice President,
Labor Relations

TIMBERLANDS

Conor W. Boyd
Vice President, Washington

J. Carl Jessup
Vice President, South

Scott R. Marshall
Vice President, Policy,
Finance and Strategic Planning

Rex McCullough
Vice President,
Forestry Research

John P. McMahon
Vice President, Timberlands,
External and Regulatory Affairs

Edward P. Rogel
Vice President,
Human Resources

John H. Wilkinson
Vice President, Oregon

WOOD PRODUCTS

Arnold B. Curtis
Vice President,
Hardwood Business Group

Lynn E. Endicott
Vice President;
Purchasing and Transportation

Thomas M. Luthy
Vice President,
Engineered Fiber Products

John N. Purcell
Vice President,
Western Lumber

John D. Selig
Vice President,
Southern Lumber

Steven J. Sery
Vice President,
Canadian Lumber

David T. Still
Vice President, Building
Materials Distribution

D.J. Young
Vice President, Plywood

PULP, PAPER AND PACKAGING

Peter G. Belluschi
Vice President, Newsprint and
Bleached Paperboard

Michael J. Cordry
Vice President, Quality

R.L. Erickson
Vice President,
Manufacturing and
Technology

Carl W. Geist, Jr.
Vice President,
Pulp and Recycling

Ronald J. Glick
Vice President,
Counterboard Packaging

George D. Henson
Vice President, Recycling

Richard E. Lodmill
Vice President, Chemicals

Robert F. Meyer
Vice President, Fine Paper

WEYERHAEUSER REAL ESTATE COMPANY

C. Stephen Lewis
President and Chief Executive
Officer

WEYERHAEUSER FAR EAST

William E. Franklin
President

WEYERHAEUSER FINANACIAL SERVICE, INC.

Donald E. Lange
President and Chief Executive
Officer, Weyerhaeuser
Mortgage Company

WESTWOOD SHIPPING LINES

Arnfinn Giske
President and Chief Executive
Officer

WEYERHAEUSER CANADA LTD.

George H. Weyerhaeuser, Jr.
President and Chief Executive
Officer

U.S. NATIONAL AFFAIRS OFFICE

Frederick S. Brown
Vice President, Federal
Relations

WTD INDUSTRIES—1994

MICHELLE R. GREENE
and Fred R. David
Francis Marion University
STEVE BARNDT
Pacific Lutheran University

For the fiscal year ending April 30, 1993, WTD Industries, Inc. (503–246–3440), reported net income of $23.11 million compared to $2.99 million for fiscal 1992. Emerging from Chapter 11 bankruptcy in November 1992, WTD may be over the worst of its failed strategies in the early 1990s. Headquartered in Portland, Oregon, WTD operates twelve lumber mills in the Pacific Northwest.

HISTORY

WTD Industries was founded by Bruce L. Engel, a Portland, Oregon, lawyer, educated at Reed College and the University of Chicago School of Law. In 1981 Engel became involved in an effort to save a client's financially troubled sawmill business in Glide, Oregon. Ultimately, Engel and a partner acquired the bankrupt mill in exchange for assuming $2 million in debts. His original idea was to make changes necessary to achieve profitability, operate it until industry conditions improved, and then sell the mill. Subsequently, success with the first sawmill and other opportunities for bargain acquisitions in a depressed industry caused Engel to shift to objectives of growth and profitable operation of wood-products-converting facilities. A second mill at Silverton, Oregon, was acquired in 1982. In 1983 sawmills located at Philomath, Oregon, were acquired, and the business was incorporated as WTD Industries. Through it all, Engel has not revealed what the letters WTD stand for, even to managers and employees of the company.

In 1984 WTD added another softwood sawmill operation, this one near Corvallis, Oregon, and its first hardwood sawmill at Philomath, Oregon. The next year WTD started operations in Washington with newly acquired softwood and hardwood mills at Sedro Woolley, Olympia, and South Bend. Three more mills were added in 1986—Valley and Aberdeen in Washington and Tillamook in Oregon. Late in 1986 WTD went public with 1,850,000 shares of common stock. Net proceeds in excess of $15 million fueled a major expansion in 1987.

Thirteen companies were acquired in 1987—seven in Oregon, five in Washington, and one in Montana. In addition to WTD's first geographic expansion outside of the Pacific Northwest, 1987 also marked the company's growth into nonsawmill production operations. Five of the 1987 acquisitions were plants producing veneer, and one was a plywood plant. Although it is contrary to company strategy to invest in timberlands, WTD purchased 17,000 acres in 1987 near the Philomath mills. By mid-1991, most of the timber in this land had been harvested.

Growth in 1988 was modest by comparison to 1987 with only three acquisitions—sawmills in Washington and Oregon and a plywood plant in New York. Seven softwood lumber sawmills located at Alturas, California; Custer, South Dakota; West Burke, Vermont; Judith Gap, Montana; and Portland, Cottage Grove, and Central Point, Oregon, were acquired in 1989 and 1990. In addition, the conversion of a hardwood mill at Tillamook, Oregon, to a higher-capacity softwood mill was completed in 1990. Partially offsetting acquisitions, four lumber or veneer mills were sold or otherwise liquidated in the period 1989–1991.

The cutback in home building in 1990 with its consequent reduction in demand for lumber resulted in lumber prices that were 15 percent lower than average. At the same time, log costs increased 7 percent because of export log demand and cutbacks in the harvest of timber from public lands. Even with reductions in operating costs by way of curtailing of operations in selected locations and a reduction of overhead, WTD's poor financial performance precluded its meeting all the covenants associated with debt agreements. WTD had $221 million in assets and $460 million in sales in 1990, but experienced a severe downturn in 1991 as sales declined to $244 million and assets dropped to $106 million. When its bank line of credit was declared in default, WTD and each of its subsidiaries filed for Chapter 11 bankruptcy on January 30, 1991, and emerged from bankruptcy on November 22, 1992.

Net sales for fiscal 1993 increased 15.4 percent to $246 million while net income increased 694 percent to $23 million. WTD's long-term debt, however, is a staggering $64 million, up from $519 thousand in 1992.

WTD'S OPERATIONS

WTD produces and sells a variety of wood products, including softwood lumber, hardwood lumber, softwood veneer, and wood chips. Softwood lumber, consisting of studs and other dimension lumber in a wide range of widths, lengths, and thicknesses, is the major product, accounting for 72 percent of sales. The predominant species that are converted into softwood lumber are Douglas fir, hemlock, white fir, lodgepole pine, ponderosa pine, spruce, and larch. Although softwood lumber, along with all other products, is branded with the name of WTD's marketing organization and its logo, these products are basically commodities competing against similar, substitute products.

The second-highest source of sales, accounting for 13 percent of the total, is chips, a residual product made from the parts of logs not suitable for conversion into lumber or veneer. Chips are used to make pulp for later conversion into paper products. Less important products include veneer, hardwood lumber, and plywood. Veneer, a thin layer of wood peeled from logs, is used in the lay-up of plywood. Hardwood lumber is produced in sizes appropriate for cabinet and furniture manufacturers. The major species is alder, although some maple is also cut. Plywood plants use veneers to produce sheathing, underlayment, and sanded and marine plywood in standard sizes. The company's plywood and veneer plants were closed during 1991.

With the minor exception of a few specialty or highly finished products such as special cuts of wood for furniture, WTD is a producer of undifferentiated products. The company aims to produce and move these commodity-like products in volume, relying on high per-worker output. Labor productivity improvements in the company's existing mills are responsible for boosting aggregate lumber production by about 50 percent.

On a quarter-to-quarter basis, WTD's financial results have varied widely and will continue to vary as a result of seasonal fluctuations and market factors affecting the demand for logs, lumber, and other wood products. The industry is subject to fluctuations in sales and earnings as a result of such factors as industry production in relation to product demand and variations in interest rates and housing starts. Currency fluctuations affect the forest products industry when exchange rates spur log exports and drive up domestic log prices.

The industry is also affected by weather conditions and changing timber management policies. Fire danger and excessively dry or wet conditions temporarily reduce logging activity and may increase open-market log prices. Timber management policies of various governmental agencies change from time to time, periodically causing actual or feared shortages in some areas. These policies change because of environmental concerns, public-agency budget issues, and a variety of other reasons. Therefore, past results for any given year or quarter are not necessarily indicative of future results.

It is the company's practice to curtail production at facilities from time to time because of adverse weather or other conditions that impair log flow, imbalances between log costs and product prices, or other factors that cause the cost of operation to exceed the cost of shutdown. Management may also permanently close facilities when their future profit-making ability under expected operating conditions is not deemed promising. Management believes its labor practices and compensation systems, as well as relatively low capital cost in relation to production capacity, give it the flexibility to curtail operations and resume production as conditions warrant.

Raw materials comprise the majority of the cost of products sold by the company. Historically, a strong correlation has existed between log costs and lumber prices. However, endangered-species litigation, increased log export demand, and erratic demand for lumber and plywood altered this relationship in recent years. Since that time the relationship between lumber prices and log costs has generally been more favorable, allowing for improved results. There can be no assurance that a favorable relationship between log costs and lumber prices will exist in the future.

Over the last two years, harvests of federal timber have declined markedly because of preservationist litigation and court rulings associated with the northern spotted owl. Although WTD relies primarily on open-market logs to source its mills, log costs have risen substantially as a result of reduced raw material availability. There can be no assurance that the company will be able to obtain sufficient raw materials at prices that allow production to remain at or exceed current levels.

WTD has sold eighteen mills and is today focusing on twelve "core mills" located in Washington, Oregon, and Vermont, as illustrated in Figure 22–1.

FINANCES

Gross profit for fiscal 1993 was 8.0 percent of sales, compared to 8.6 percent for fiscal 1992. While prices increased about 15 percent and log costs increased about 13 percent in 1993 over 1992, the costs of manufacturing lumber (excluding log cost) rose 9 percent. This cost increase was primarily the result of a 4 percent decrease in production. Selling, general, and administration expenses for 1993 were 5.1 percent of sales compared to 5.6 percent of sales in 1992.

Working capital decreased by $6.9 million for fiscal 1993, to $39.2 million. This was the result of working capital provided by operations and the sale of idle facilities, offset by capital spending, the costs of holding and disposing of idle facilities, and principal payments and reclassifications made in connection with the company's reorganization plan. Substantially all of the company's assets are pledged as security for its various debt instruments.

INVENTORY STRATEGY

Inventories of logs influence profitability in two ways. The first is that assured and continuous availability is necessary for an efficient conversion process and the satisfaction of customer's order delivery requirements. The second is that logs are a costly resource and can represent a substantial tie-up of working capital as well as a major factor in determining profit margin. Although lumber prices tend slightly to lead log

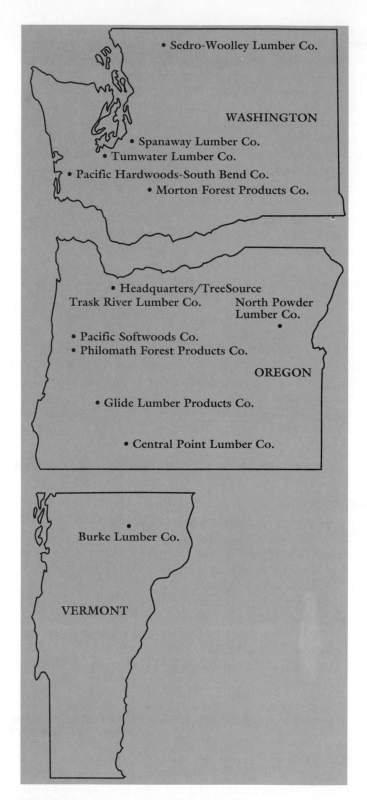

FIGURE 22-1 WTD Plant Locations

prices, moving in the same direction and maintaining a more or less constant relationship over the long term, short-term variations can and do occur. For example, increased foreign demand for logs, activities by environmental interest groups to restrict sales of government timber, and weather conditions unfavorable for logging have all decreased log supply and raised prices independent of domestic demand for lumber. With the cost of purchased logs at delivery accounting for two-thirds of finished product costs at WTD, such a shortage-induced rise in log prices without a rise in lumber prices can turn a profitable operation into an unprofitable one.

From 1987 to 1990 shortages of logs at reasonable prices led to the closing of 46 Northwest sawmills that were less well managed or positioned. Since then the imbalance has intensified because of the continued high demand for high-quality export logs and severe cutbacks in government sales of timber harvest contracts associated with protecting the spotted owl.

Traditional industry response among its larger competitors to lessen risks associated with uncertain availability and the potential of high open-market log prices has been to line up inventories of standing timber sufficient for two years or more of production and stockpile substantial inventories of logs at the mills. These firms typically secure control over timberlands either through ownership or harvest rights. The timber-owning competitors are in a position either (1) to buy on the open market or through harvest contracts when log prices are low and to harvest owned timber (presumably on the books at a lower, historical cost) when log prices are high or (2) to give priority to filling their needs from owned timber on a continuing basis. In either strategy there is a potential to sustain higher operating margins.

Competitors who lack their own timberlands usually contract with timberland owners or the government for the right to harvest timber over a number of years. Such contracts are subject to competitive bidding, and bid prices reflect the near-term profit potential of lumber-manufacturing operations and availability of timber. Companies that own timber contracts can be expected to do well during periods of rising lumber prices and poorly when lumber prices fall. In fact, WTD owes its start to the fact that in the late 1970s many sawmill owners committed themselves to high-priced timber contracts prior to an industry downturn. When lumber prices fell, they found themselves faced with bankruptcy.

WTD purposely avoids owning large inventories of logs, preferring to buy in the open market at prices that closely follow lumber market prices. WTD's strategy has always been to buy logs and convert them into lumber within a matter of weeks, before the profit margin can be eroded. The ability to follow this strategy provided consistent, although modest, profits. WTD today owns a small amount of fee timberlands in the vicinity of various mills. The following table shows the percentages of logs supplied by open-market purchases, timber contracts and fee timberlands, and total log footage required:

Year Ended April 30,	Open Market	Timber Contracts	Fee Timber	Log Requirements
1988	73%	20%	7%	616,000 MBF
1989	70	21	9	680,000
1990	69	25	6	766,000
1991	75	19	6	408,000
1992	88	8	4	338,000
1993	90	6	4	306,000

MBF = thousand board feet.

In support of its inventory strategy, WTD aims to maintain log inventories equal to approximately three weeks' operating requirements. Larger inventories are carried only when it is necessary to collect selected materials for specialty orders, when weather or seasonal factors prevent regular deliveries, or when open-market buying is not possible, necessitating the purchasing of timber-cutting contracts. The latter are sold primarily by government agencies and ordinarily require the cutting and removal of public timber within three years. WTD attempts to harvest timber under these contracts within one year, preferably within three to four months to minimize the risk of a reduced margin from falling lumber prices. In keeping with WTD's acceptance of variable costs in place of fixed costs, all forest operations are contracted to logging companies. This includes road building, cutting, and delivery to the mills.

Reliance on a supply of reasonably priced logs has left the company vulnerable to imbalances between log supply and demand. Problems first arose in late 1987 when two softwood sawmills, both of which normally rely on timber-harvesting contracts with government agencies, were faced with a shortage of logs and unprofitably high prices created by foreign demand and forest fires. The company was forced to shut the two mills down temporarily until a supply of acceptably priced logs could be assured. In calendar years 1988 and 1989, several mills were temporarily closed from time to time because of log shortages. Unprofitable operations caused by shortage-induced high costs of raw materials became more widespread in 1990 and resulted in the closure of 21 lumber and plywood mills in 1990 and 1991. In the first half of 1991, log costs and lumber prices came back into a more normal relationship but not before the cost-revenue imbalance had precipitated WTD's bankruptcy. The following table gives WTD's inventory of logs, lumber, veneer, and supplies for 1993:

| | APRIL 30, | |
	1993	1992
Logs	$ 7,569	$10,913
Lumber and veneer	9,515	8,958
Supplies	1,238	1,457
	$18,322	$21,328

Growing government recognition that the Northwest is experiencing a timber shortage had spurred governmental action. At one time, pressure from organized environmentalist special interest groups seeking to protect the habitat of the spotted owl had virtually stopped the sale of old-growth timber from federal lands in the West. In response to the spotted owl's endangered species status and environmentalist and forestry pleas, the government reached a compromise that has reopened the sale of federal timber but at drastically reduced levels. The extent to which logging on federal, state, and private lands will be restricted to preserve the spotted owl at the expense of jobs has become a hotly contested political issue on the West Coast. Further compromises are possible. For example, the federal government is considering use of its authority to place temporary bans on the export of logs from state land in order to increase the supply of logs to domestic sawmills.

Major competitors such as Weyerhaeuser have invested in new technologies, some using computers and lasers, to increase the yield of higher-value products. Other technologies are commonly being incorporated to reduce labor content and increase capacity. However, WTD has focused on employee productivity incentives rather then investing in expensive automated machinery to increase production. Although the company purposely avoids investing in costly automated plants and machinery, it does invest in projects offering major savings or immediate production improvements that have paybacks of three years or less. For the most part this has meant modest capital expenditures, approximating annual depreciation costs, to replace and upgrade worn and inefficient equipment. As an example of the difference in WTD's approach to investment in technology, WTD invested $1 million to replace old parts at its Glide, Oregon, mill, while International Paper invested $90 million in a computer-driven mill process at its competing mill in Gardiner, Oregon.

All marketing, sales, and distribution of WTD's products are the responsibility of Treesource, Inc. (503–246–8600), a wholly owned subsidiary in Portland, Oregon. Through this centralized sales and marketing unit, WTD gains economies of scale not available to independent mills. Treesource is able to coordinate production at various mills to satisfy customer orders, arrange lowest-cost transportation, and fill orders for an assortment of products beyond the capability of any single mill. In addition, centralized credit management offers economies in credit checking, monitoring, and collecting. Since each salesperson is responsible for the marketing and sales for one or two of the company's mills, fewer salespeople are needed than if each mill were responsible for its own sales.

Treesource has targeted the construction, industrial, and remodel-and-replace (do-it-yourself) segments. Of these, the construction segment is the most active. Most sales are to distributors and wholesalers, industrial users, and retailers. Products sold to distributors and wholesalers, the largest customer segment, include softwood lumber for the residential construction, commercial construction, and remodel-and-replace segments plus hardwood boards for the construction and remodel-and-replace segments. Major customers include such large distributors as Georgia-Pacific, Weyerhaeuser, and Dixieline. The second-largest channel, sales to retailers including chain merchandisers, provides softwood and hardwood lumber for the remodel-and-replace user. Sales to industrial buyers, the third-largest segment, includes hardwood for furniture and cabinet manufacturers. Direct sales of intermediate materials, including veneer plus products that are immediately usable by the customer (e.g., railroad ties), are a minor market. The majority of WTD's sales are to buyers in the United States. Exports, primarily to Canada but also to Europe, Australia, and the Far East, are expanding. WTD's 1993 target market mix is

1. Stocking distributors 53%
2. Office wholesale 30%
3. Retail 9%
4. Remanufacturers 5%
5. Other 3%

Most sales are arranged through telephone contact between salesperson and buyer. The company offers competitive delivered prices, a variety of products, availability of products, and reliability as competitive advantages. WTD also offers a 1 percent discount if an account is paid within ten days, providing an effective incentive for prompt payment. In addition, WTD attempts to create a name familiarity by identifying all product lots with the Treesource trademark and name of the producing mill after they are packaged or strapped. WTD's ten largest customers in 1993 are

Georgia-Pacific Corporation

San Diego Wholesale

Weyerhaeuser Company

North Pacific Lumber Co.

Furman Lumber, Inc.

BMC West Corporation

Reliable Wholesale Lumber, Inc.

Timber Products Sales Co.

Mid-Pac Lumber Co.

Boise Cascade Corporation

Transportation is the third-highest cost component of a delivered product, exceeded only by logs and labor. Treesource arranges for the transportation of products from all WTD mills and as a result is able to secure volume discounts that help WTD to lower costs and be price competitive. Shipments of products are normally made direct from the mill to the buyer's destination via rail, truck, or barge.

Activities that benefit or apply to more than one mill are performed at a centralized location in order to gain advantages of functional specialization and scale. Sales, market development, engineering, finance, and legal services are the key activities that are centralized. Log-buying specialists are located at the individual mills because of their need to be familiar with and responsive to local conditions, suppliers, and mill needs. However, a vice president position is responsible for developing and overseeing log procurement strategies. With most support functions performed elsewhere by others, local mill managers can concentrate on operations. In May 1993 WTD employed approximately 1,100 employees, down from over 2,600 a few years earlier.

ENVIRONMENTAL REGULATION

WTD is subject to federal, state, and local waste, disposal, and pollution control regulations, including air, water, and noise pollution; these regulations have required, and are expected to continue to require, additional operating and capital expenditures. During 1992 WTD incurred expenditures of approximately $250,000 for waste disposal and pollution control.

During fiscal 1993 WTD spent approximately $400,000 for cleanup of discontinued facilities, although actual costs may exceed this amount depending on the possible presence of pollutants discovered in the cleanup process. With respect to ongoing facilities, WTD incurred expenses in fiscal 1993 in complying with various state and federal environmental programs, such as developing Spill Prevention Control Countermeasure plans, applying for stormwater discharge permits under the National Pollutant Discharge Elimination System, and complying with federal underground storage tank regulations.

WTD is also formulating plans to manage log-yard waste (bark and other debris) at each operating facility. WTD spend approximately $650,000 for fiscal 1993 with respect to these matters and other routine environmental compliance.

CONCLUSION

WTD is in need of a clear strategic plan to remain profitable. Prepare a strategic plan for CEO Bruce Engel. Should WTD acquire timberlands outside of the Pacific Northwest? Should WTD focus on softwood rather than on hardwood processing? Is it time for WTD to put itself for sale on the market? How much is the company worth?

EXHIBIT 22-1 WTD Industries, Inc. and Subsidiaries Consolidated Statements of Operations (In thousands, except per share data)

YEAR ENDED APRIL 30,	1993	1992	1991
Net sales	$246,887	$213,896	$ 243,931
Cost of sales	227,040	195,386	250,468
Gross profit (loss)	19,847	18,510	(6,537)
Selling, general and administrative expenses	12,615	12,047	20,957
Reorganization charges	563	3,272	58,000
Operating income (loss)	6,669	3,191	(85,494)
Other income (expense)			
Interest expense	(2,864)	(235)	(10,197)
Miscellaneous	151	36	589
	(2,713)	(199)	(9,608)
Income (loss) before income taxes	3,956	2,992	(95,102)
Provision for income taxes (benefit)	1,543	1,167	(9,950)
Income (loss) before extraordinary items	2,413	1,825	(85,152)
Extraordinary items			
Gain on debt restructure, net of tax provision of $7,700	12,102	—	—
Tax benefit to NOL carryforward	9,243	1,167	—
	21,345	1,167	—
Net income (loss)	23,758	2,992	(85,152)
Accumulated preferred dividends	647	—	—
Net income (loss) applicable to common shareholders	$ 23,111	$ 2,992	$ (85,152)
Net income (loss) per common share—primary			
income (loss) before extraordinary items	$ 0.29	$ 0.73	$ (34.17)
Extraordinary items	3.46	0.47	—
	$ 3.75	$ 1.20	$ (34.17)
Net income (loss) per common share—fully diluted			
income (loss) before extraordinary items	$ 0.28	$ 0.73	$ (34.17)
Extraordinary items	3.43	0.47	—
	$ 3.71	$ 1.20	$ (34.17)

Source: WTD *Annual Report*, 1993.

EXHIBIT 22-2 Consolidated Balance Sheets (In thousands)

APRIL 30,	1993	1992
Assets		
Current assets		
Cash and cash equivalents	$ 2,124	$ 4,738
Accounts receivable, net	19,583	14,788
Inventories	18,322	21,328
Restricted cash	—	7,606
Prepaid expenses	2,399	2,416
Timber, timberlands and timber-related assets	18,998	17,530
Total current assets	61,426	68,406
Notes and accounts receivable	161	224
Timber and timberlands	847	716
Property, plant and equipment, at cost		
Land	2,572	2,732
Buildings and improvements	9,953	9,008
Machinery and equipment	59,553	56,473
	72,078	68,213
Less accumulated depreciation	37,839	32,211
	34,239	36,002
Construction in progress	493	1,538
	34,732	37,540
Idle assets	974	4,979
Less costs of disposal	574	2,077
	400	2,902
Other assets	2,473	3,773
	$100,039	$113,561

Source: *Annual Report*, 1993.

EXHIBIT 22-3 Consolidated Balance Sheets (In thousands, except share information)

APRIL 30,	1993	1992
Liabilities and stockholders' equity (deficit)		
Current liabilities		
Accounts payable	$ 7,390	$ 8,524
Accrued expenses	8,549	7,546
Reserve for disputed and unallowed		
prepetition claims	1,204	—
Timber contracts payable	2,695	4,750
Current maturities of long-term debt	2,333	1,424
Total current liabilities	22,171	22,244
Long-term debt, less current maturities	64,184	519
Liabilities subject to compromise	—	134,351
Commitments and contingencies		
Stockholders' equity (deficit)		
Preferred stock, no par value; 10,000,000		
shares authorized:		
Series A	20,581	—
Series B	5,756	—
Common stock, no par value	23,123	15,205
Additional paid-in capital	15	15
Retained earnings (deficit)	(35,791)	(58,773)
	13,684	(43,553)
	$100,039	$113,561

Source: *Annual Report,* 1993.

EXHIBIT 22-4 WTD Industries, Inc. and Subsidiaries Consolidated Statements of Cash Flows (In thousands)

YEAR ENDED APRIL 30,	1993	1992	1991
Cash provided by (used for) operating activities:			
Net income (loss)	$23,758	$ 2,992	$(85,152)
Adjustments to reconcile net income (loss) to cash provided by (used for) operations:			
Depreciation, depletion and amortization	13,124	8,178	11,968
Deferred income tax	—	—	(3,187)
Gain on sale of marketable securities	—	—	(239)
Reorganization charges	563	898	58,000
Gain on debt restructure, before income tax provision	(19,802)	—	—
Accounts receivable	(4,795)	(5,404)	17,291
Inventories	2,974	(8,963)	24,667
Prepaid expenses	208	1,285	(2,212)
Income tax refund receivable	—	6,317	—
Timber, timberlands and timber-related assets, current	(7,975)	(3,472)	—
Accruals and payables	(6,449)	6,409	(9,651)
Income taxes payable	—	—	(301)
Cash provided by operating activities	1,606	8,240	11,184
Cash provided by (used for) investing activities:			
Notes and accounts receivable	63	10	70
Net reductions of (additions to) timber and timberlands	(155)	(1,137)	3,944
Acquisition of property, plant and equipment	(5,319)	(3,410)	(2,781)
Proceeds from sale of securities	—	8	1,431
Cost of holding idle facilities	(996)	(2,860)	(979)
Proceeds from sale of idle facilities	4,819	5,324	—
Other investing activities	207	552	2,398
Cash provided by (used for) investing activities	(1,381)	(1,513)	4,083
Cash provided by (used for) financing activities:			
Notes and acceptances payable	—	—	(8,414)
Proceeds from long-term borrowings	—	142	95
Principal payments on long-term debt	(9,646)	(369)	(2,497)
Other assets	(33)	(696)	161
Restricted cash	7,606	(5,453)	(2,153)
Dividends paid on preferred stock	(776)	—	—
Issuance of common stock	10	—	—
Cash used for financing activities	(2,839)	(6,376)	(12,808)
Increase (decrease) in cash and cash equivalents	(2,614)	351	2,459
Cash balance at beginning of year	4,738	4,387	1,928
Cash balance at end of year	$ 2,124	$ 4,738	$ 4,387
Cash paid (refunded) during the year for:			
Interest	$ 2,628	$ 87	$ 11,590
Income taxes	$ —	$(6,317)	$ (6,612)

Source: *Annual Report*, 1993.

EXHIBIT 22-5 Consolidated Statement of Changes in Stockholders' Equity (deficit) (in thousands)

	Series A Preferred Stock		Series B Preferred Stock		Common Stock		Paid-in Capital	Retained Earnings (Loss)	Stockholders' Equity (Deficit)
	Shares	Amount	Shares	Amount	Shares	Amount			
Balance at April 30, 1990	—	—	—	—	6,229	$15,205	$15	$23,387	$ 38,607
Net loss	—	—	—	—	—	—	—	(85,152)	(85,152)
Balance at April 30, 1991	—	—	—	—	6,229	15,205	15	(61,765)	(46,545)
Net income	—	—	—	—	—	—	—	2,992	2,992
Balance at April 30, 1992	—	—	—	—	6,229	15,205	15	(58,773)	(43,553)
Four-for-ten reverse split	—	—	—	—	(3,737)	—	—	—	—
Shares issued pursuant to reorganization plan	269	$20,581	197	$10,730	1,869	2,934	—	—	34,245
Shares converted	—	—	(91)	(4,974)	3,176	4,974	—	—	—
Stock options exercised	—	—	—	—	11	10	—	—	10
Dividends paid	—	—	—	—	—	—	—	(776)	(776)
Net income	—	—	—	—	—	—	—	23,758	23,758
Balance at April 30, 1993	269	$20,581	106	$5,756	7,548	$23,123	$15	$(35,791)	$ 13,684

Source: *Annual Report*, 1993.

MICHELLE R. GREENE
AND FRED R. DAVID
Francis Marion University

GEORGIA-PACIFIC CORPORATION—1994

In 1993 Georgia-Pacific (404-521-4000) headed in a new direction. The company's chief executive officer and chairman of the board, T. Marshall Hahn, Jr., who had been the company's leader for ten years, retired as CEO on May 3. Later in the year he also retired as chairman of the board, but continued to serve on the board of directors. Hahn was replaced by A. D. Correll, who previously was the company's president and chief operating officer. Georgia-Pacific's sales increased 4 percent in 1993 to $12.3 billion, but net income declined to negative $18 million.

HISTORY

Although his grandfather had advised against entering the timber business, in 1927 Owen R. Cheatham bought a wholesale lumber and timber yard in Augusta, Georgia. Cheatham had only half the money needed to buy the company, so he went to the man for which his old prep school had been named, J. Hunt Hargrave. Hargrave agreed to loan Cheatham a quarter of the sum needed if the president of the Planters Bank, J. Hurt Whitehead, would match it. His new company, the Georgia Hardwood Lumber Company, was incorporated in Georgia on September 26.

The Great Depression of 1929 ruined many businesses, but Cheatham was innovative. He went to Europe and discovered the Depression was ending more quickly there than in the United States. A building boom was under way in Europe and lumber was needed. His company could buy lumber at depressed prices in the United States, ship it abroad, and sell it for increased prices in Europe.

The export business to Europe enabled Cheatham to expand his company in the United States. After World War II, five mills were in operation in Georgia, Alabama, Arkansas, Mississippi, and South Carolina. The company also had an office in New York and was opening one in Portland, Oregon.

The reason for opening an office in Portland was a new product called plywood. At the time, people believed plywood could only be made successfully from Douglas fir, which grew in the Pacific Northwest. Cheatham, who was a pioneer in the plywood business when most competitors thought plywood could not be made profitably, found that plywood would bring three times the return of lumber. Upon this knowledge, the company acquired Bellingham Plywood Corporation, a large plywood plant in Bellingham, Washington, and acquired the Washington Veneer Company in 1948. Three other plywood manufacturing operations were also purchased in Olympia, Washington; Springfield, Oregon; and Savannah, Georgia.

On April 2, 1951, the company name was changed to Georgia-Pacific Plywood Company. The concept of dynamic conservation was introduced that year with the purchase of a new sawmill and related timberlands in Toledo, Oregon. Dynamic conservation was based on the fact that timber is the only natural resource that continually replaces itself. The primary element of dynamic conservation was scientific forestry, which made trees grow faster and stronger, and produced new and better seed stock from the healthiest trees in the forest. Because of the rate of cutting by former owners of the sawmill, there was only enough timber in the area to last another nine years. Georgia-Pacific wanted to modernize the plant and close the sawmill. Enough adjacent timberland was acquired so that all the reserves were put on the dynamic conservation schedule. Georgia-Pacific invested more than $60 million in building a new plywood mill, paper mill, and pulp mill. By 1960, the year Toledo was supposed to disappear, employment was up 50 percent, payrolls were up 100 percent, purchases of services and supplies from local merchants were up 65 percent, and the population of Toledo was up 33 percent.

By 1966 Georgia-Pacific had completed construction of its fourth and fifth pine plywood plants in Louisville, Mississippi, and Emporia, Virginia. Georgia-Pacific entered into Latin America for the first time with the purchase of Companhia Amazones in 1965 at the price of $2.145 million. That acquisition brought in more than 600,000 acres of timber and timberland, along with a veneer plant, in Brazil near the mouth of the Amazon. Georgia-Pacific enhanced its position in the chemicals business in 1966 by acquiring National Polychemicals, Inc. in Conway, North Carolina, and Lufkin, Texas. These facilities operated production of phenol and urea formaldehyde resin.

GEORGIA-PACIFIC TODAY

Georgia-Pacific does not maintain a central research laboratory for the development of new wood and paper products. Instead, research and development activities take place at the individual plants and other decentralized laboratories. Georgia-Pacific feels that employees are best acquainted with the potential of new products at decentralized laboratories.

Forestry research, aimed at improving seedling growth rate and quality, is conducted extensively throughout the United States and Canada. The research usually takes place where Georgia-Pacific owns and operates fee timberland. Forest research employees are continually seeking to improve reforestation methods and timber management techniques. The company's containerboard and packaging division opened a new research facility in Atlanta, Georgia, in 1992.

Georgia-Pacific employs approximately 52,000 people, most of whom are members of unions; the company considers its relationship with its employees to be good. Seventy-seven union contracts were renewed in 1993, including five at large paper facilities. Georgia-Pacific has 253 manufacturing facilities in the United States, one recycled-paper mill in Canada, and two wood-moulding manufacturing facilities in Mexico. The company has two major operating divisions: the Building Products Divisions and the Pulp and Paper Division.

Building Products Division. Georgia-Pacific is the leading manufacturer and distributor of building products in the United States. The company produces plywood, oriented strand board and other wood panels, lumber, gypsum wallboard, chemicals, and other products. Georgia-Pacific is the leading wholesaler of building products in the United States, with 139 distribution centers located in 46 states. The centers serve traditional lumberyards, consumer-oriented home centers, makers of mobile homes, and other manufacturers. Eleven centers are millwork and specialty centers that primarily sell wood mouldings, doors, and windows. In order to offer a broader line of products and to supplement Georgia-Pacific's product lines, the distribution centers also purchase products from other manufacturers. In 1992 these purchases were approximately $2.1 billion, which was up from $1.7 billion in 1991. Outside purchases comprise almost half of all materials sold at the centers. Purchased products include wood panels, lumber and roofing, doors, insulation, vinyl siding, and adhesives, as well as product lines that they do not manufacture, such as nails and other metal products.

The building products division had net sales of $6.112 billion in 1992, a 13.1 percent increase from 1991. Sales of this division accounted for 52 percent of Georgia-Pacific's total sales in 1992. Georgia-Pacific exports consisted of $141 million in 1992. Georgia-Pacific ships building products to 60 countries and has building products sales offices in Europe and Mexico. Although Georgia-Pacific's largest export markets are in the Caribbean and Europe, Mexico has been the company's fastest-growing market since 1990.

The building products division's business is affected by the number of housing starts, the level of home repairs, remodeling, additions, commercial building activity, the availability and cost of mortgage funds, and changes in the industry's capacity. In 1992 the economy was sluggish but lower mortgage interest rates helped to support an increase in housing construction. Prices for structural panels and lumber rose to record high levels in 1992 as logging restrictions on government lands resulted in more mill closures in the West and a tightening supply and demand balance.

Wood Panels. Georgia-Pacific is the industry's largest producer of structural wood panels and accounts for about 20 percent of domestic structural panel capacity. There are 43 wood panel plants located primarily in the southern United States that produce 9.7 billion square feet of panels per year. In 1992 Georgia-Pacific's wood panel division had total sales of $2.543 billion, a 21.3 percent increase in sales from 1991. The wood panel division accounts for 22 percent of the company's total sales.

Georgia-Pacific operates 24 plywood and oriented strand board plants. Specialty applications of plywood account for 60 percent of its plywood production. These specialty applications include decorative siding, sanded plywood, and concrete form. Many other wood panel applications are produced at 19 mills, primarily for industrial and construction applications. Items such as hardboard, particleboard, panelboard, softboard, and fiberboard are made from logs, sawdust, shavings, and chips. These types of wood panels are used in the production of furniture, housing, shelving, fixtures, toys, automotive parts, and siding panels. A breakdown of Georgia-Pacific's annual production in the wood panel division follows:

	NUMBER OF FACILITIES	ANNUAL CAPACITY
Soft plywood (3/8″)	18	5,019
Hardwood plywood (sm)	2	495
Hardboard (1/8″)	8	1,395
Particleboard (3/4″)	8	1,148
Oriented strand board (3/8″)	4	952
Panelboard (1/8″)	1	379
Softboard (1/2″)	1	250
Fiberboard (3/4″)	1	100
	43	9,738

Georgia-Pacific operates four oriented strand board plants. Oriented strand board (OSB) is a nonveneered sheathing grade product made from strands of wood that are arranged in perpendicular layers and bonded into a panel by a resin. Like the uses of plywood, OSB is used for roof decking, sidewall sheathing, and floor underlayment. Georgia-Pacific's newest OSB plant is located in Mt. Hope, West Virginia, and has an annual capacity of 325 million square feet.

Lumber. Georgia-Pacific is the second-largest producer of lumber in the United States, accounting for about 5 percent of domestic lumber production. Approximately 2.6 billion board feet of lumber is produced annually. Georgia-Pacific had total lumber sales of $2.055 billion in 1992, an increase of 13 percent from 1991. Lumber sales for 1992 accounted for 17 percent of the company's total sales. The company operates 43 lumber mills located primarily in the South. Several types of wood are produced by these mills including southern pine, a variety of Appalachian and southern hardwoods, cypress, redwood, cedar, spruce, western pine, Douglas fir, and pressure-treated southern pine. Georgia-Pacific recently purchased a softwood lumber mill in Philomath, Oregon, to process Douglas fir and western hemlock logs from company-owned timberlands. The 43 mills account for 2.739 billion board feet of production.

Gypsum. Georgia-Pacific is the third largest producer of gypsum products in the United States. The company operates ten gypsum board plants with an annual capacity of 3.1 billion square feet of gypsum board. The company owns gypsum reserves of about 125 recoverable tons. Some of its gypsum products are wallboard, fire-door cores, plaster, and joint compound, all primarily used in residential and commercial construction. In 1992 the company's gypsum product sales totaled $216 million, a decrease of 2.7 percent from 1991. These sales figures have been declining since 1986. Sales from the gypsum products account for only 2 percent of Georgia-Pacific's total sales. Although the company's sales of gypsum products went down in 1992, the production of gypsum had a 45 percent increase from 1991, which had a production level of 1.955 billion square feet. Georgia-Pacific conducts gypsum research at its gypsum research and development center in Decatur, Georgia.

Chemicals. Georgia-Pacific is one of the forest industry's leading suppliers of resins, adhesives, and paper chemicals. The company operates 16 plants with a production of 2.962 billion pounds of thermosetting resins. The chemicals division accounted for $240 million of sales in 1992, a 7.6 percent increase from 1991, and overall accounts for 2 percent of total sales. More than 2 billion pounds of thermosetting resins are shipped annually to Georgia-Pacific mills and outside customers. Georgia-Pacific recently purchased a phenolic resins coatings business that produces highly specialized resins used in marine varnishes, metal cans and tanks, food containers, and other products. The company conducts chemical research in its Tacoma, Washington, facility.

Timber and Timberlands. Georgia-Pacific owns more than 6 million acres of timber and timberlands in the United States and Canada. The lumber is primarily near the company's lumber mills. Georgia-Pacific controlled 927,000 acres of timberland in 1992, which was a slight increase from 1991. Timberlands owned in fee consisted of 5.722 million acres in 1992, a decrease of 4.1 percent from 1991. Geographically, 70 percent of Georgia-Pacific's timber is located in the South, 20 percent is located in the East, and 10 percent is in the West. Georgia-Pacific's timber includes southern pines and hardwoods; Douglas fir, hemlock, and other species from the Pacific Northwest; redwood, Douglas fir, true firs, and western pines in Northern California; and numerous species of hardwoods and softwoods in Maine, West Virginia, and Wisconsin, and New Brunswick, Canada.

Georgia-Pacific owns the underlying mineral rights on the majority of its fee lands in the United States. Mining of metallurgical coal and production of oil and gas generates royalty income for Georgia-Pacific that is not material in amount. The company does not expect to realize any material income from these operations in the foreseeable future.

Pulp and Paper Division. Georgia-Pacific pulp and paper division produces a variety of items including containerboard and packaging, communication papers, market pulp, tissue, and envelopes. The company operates 103 facilities in the United States and one in Canada. Annual capacity of pulp, paper, and paperboard includes 8.6 million tons, which accounts for 8 percent of the total annual capacity in the United States. The pulp and paper division had total sales of $5.711 billion in 1992, a 6.2 percent decrease from 1991. This decrease in sales changed the balance between the building products division and the pulp and paper division. The pulp and paper division had operated as the leading sales contributor for Georgia-Pacific for the past two years.

The pulp and paper division's products are affected primarily by changes in industry capacity. The level of economic growth in the United States, currency exchange rates, and foreign market conditions also influence pulp and paper demand. In 1992 sluggish demand in the United States and export markets and excess capacity and inventories in the industry combined to keep prices and profits depressed in the pulp and paper division.

Containerboard and Packaging. Georgia-Pacific produces containerboard, corrugated containers and packaging, bleached board, and kraft paper. The company operates four containerboard mills and 37 corrugated packaging plants. With an annual capacity of 3.9 million tons of containerboard and packaging, Georgia-Pacific is the nation's second-largest producer of containerboard, accounting for about 12 percent of the United States capacity. The containerboard and packaging division had $2.001 billion of sales in 1992, a .3 percent decrease from 1991. These sales accounted for 17 percent of Georgia-Pacific's total sales in 1992.

After the containerboard is processed, about 50 percent of the production is transferred to a corrugated packaging plant. The remainder is sold to independent converters. In addition to making corrugated packaging with the containerboard, Georgia-Pacific's corrugated packaging plants manufacture double- and triple-wall containers and packaging, bulk bins, water-resistant packaging, and high-finish and preprinted packaging for point-of-sale displays. Georgia-Pacific exports about 15 percent of its containerboard, primarily to Central America, Western Europe, and the Far East.

Georgia-Pacific produces about 364,000 tons of bleached paperboard annually. The bleached paperboard is used primarily in frozen food containers, food service items, and other products. The company in its two plants annually produces 350,000 tons of kraft paper, which is used in the production of grocery bags and multiwall bags.

Communication Papers. Georgia-Pacific is the largest producer of uncoated free-sheet paper in the United States. Eight paper mills are in production with an annual capacity of 2.2 million tons, accounting for approximately 16 percent of annual capacity in the United States. Such communication paper items include office reprographics and commercial printing, business forms, stationery, tablets, envelopes, and checks. In 1992 Georgia-Pacific produced 2.223 billion tons of communication papers, an 11 percent increase from 1991.

A 1992 study of buying criteria and brand familiarities of merchants, printers, and other end-users convinced Georgia-Pacific to consolidate its communication papers product lines. To heighten its brand recognition, Georgia-Pacific is now marketing its business and printing paper products under the brand name of Georgia-Pacific Papers. Text and specialty papers are marketed under the name Nekoosa, which is operated by the company's Hopper Paper Division.

Market Pulp. Georgia-Pacific is the world's second-largest producer of market pulp. The company's seven pulp mills produce approximately 1.9 million tons of pulp annually. In 1992 Georgia-Pacific produced 1.891 million tons of market pulp, a 3.3 percent increase from 1991 production. This production level accounted for approximately 20 percent of the domestic capacity. The company produces southern softwood, southern hardwood, and northern hardwood pulps for use in the manufacture of many paper grades. The company is also a major supplier of fluff pulp and other specialty pulps.

Georgia-Pacific recently converted its Brunswick, Georgia, pulp mill to fluff pulp, which now represents 550,000 tons of company output per year. Fluff pulp is used primarily in disposable diapers and other sanitary items. These types of products are currently experiencing growing demand, particularly in developing countries.

Because of the increasing use of recycled fiber in the United States, the company is expected to have limited growth in domestic demand. However, increased paper consumption in export markets is expected to boost total market pulp demand. Georgia-Pacific exports approximately 65 percent of its market pulp, employing its direct sales force at offices in France, Germany, Italy, Japan, Switzerland, Taiwan, and the United Kingdom.

Tissue. Georgia-Pacific is the fifth-largest producer of tissue in the United States. The company operates five tissue mills with an annual capacity of over 500,000 tons of tissue. In 1992 these mills produced 578,000 tons of tissue, a 10.9 percent increase from 1991's production level of 521,000 tons. Georgia-Pacific's 1992 sales of tissue was $682 million, an increase of 2.7 percent from 1991.

The company operates six converting facilities that produce consumer and commercial tissue products such as paper towels, napkins, and bath tissue. Most of Georgia-Pacific's consumer tissue products are sold under the brand names Angel Soft, Sparkle, Coronet, MD, and Delta. The commercial tissue products are produced for industrial, food-service, office, hotel, motel, and hospital markets.

Paper Distribution and Tissue. Georgia-Pacific operates 80 distribution centers in 31 states under the name Butler Paper Company. Customers include commercial printers, in-plant printers, copy centers, and major corporations. Butler sells printing, writing, and industrial papers obtained from many manufacturers, including their own mills. The company's envelope production is handled by the Mail-Well Envelope Division, which operates 17 plants. In 1992 Mail-Well produced 15 billion envelopes, a 15.4 percent increase from 1991 production levels. The envelope division, along with the paper distribution division, had total sales of $1.208 billion in 1992, a 1 percent decrease from 1991. These sales figures have continually decreased since its beginning in 1990, prompting Georgia-Pacific in March 1993 to announce plans to sell the Butler Paper Company to Alco Standard Corporation.

Georgia Pacific and the Natural Environment. Georgia-Pacific is committed to responsible forest practices and conservation methods. The company supports regulations that benefit the environment, human health, and safety based on sound science and prudent economic analysis. Georgia-Pacific is dedicated to operating all of its facilities in compliance with applicable environmental laws, regulations, and permits. Through an environmental audit program, the company monitors compliance with this policy.

With the hiring of Lee M. Thomas as senior vice-president of environmental and government affairs in March 1993, Georgia-Pacific aims to insure compliance with environmental laws and regulations. Thomas, a former administrator of the United States Environmental Protection Agency, will also be chairman of the company's Environmental Policy Committee, which will have direct access to Georgia-Pacific's board of directors and will regularly provide the board with environmental reports.

Georgia-Pacific is always trying to protect the environment as evidenced on April 18, 1993, when the company signed an agreement with Interior Secretary Bruce Babbitt to protect the endangered red-cockaded woodpecker. The woodpecker is primarily located in the southern United States.

GEORGIA-PACIFIC'S FUTURE

At the April 2, 1993 timber summit in Seattle, Washington, Georgia-Pacific and other major forest products companies agreed with President Bill Clinton to provide more environmental protection of the Pacific Northwest. Since the Pacific Northwest is a controversial timber-cutting area of the country, should Georgia-Pacific focus on other areas of the country? Should the company seek expanded operations in foreign markets? Economies of scale are becoming more and more important in being a successful forest products company. Should Georgia-Pacific acquire a major competitor, supplier, or distributor?

The production of paper from recycled materials is becoming increasingly important, driven by user needs and environmental concerns. Georgia-Pacific leads in the recycling effort with over 100 products on the market. However, other companies are catching up to and exceeding Georgia-Pacific in the recycling effort. Should Georgia-Pacific invest more time and money in producing recycled materials?

Prepare a strategic plan for CEO Correll that could enable Georgia-Pacific to return to profitability. Note that, as shown in the attached exhibits, the company's net income was negative in 1991, 1992, and 1993, while company debt further increased. The trend in earnings must be reversed for Georgia-Pacific to remain competitive in the forest products industry.

EXHIBIT 23-1 Statements of Income—Georgia-Pacific Corporation and Subsidiaries (Millions, except per share amounts)

| | YEAR ENDED DECEMBER 31 | | |
	1993	1992	1991
Net sales	$12,330	$11,847	$11,524
Costs and expenses			
Cost of sales	9,814	9,397	9,164
Selling, general and administrative	1,190	1,170	1,137
Depreciation and depletion	764	789	724
Interest	513	565	584
Other (income) loss	26	—	(344)
Total costs and expenses	12,307	11,921	11,265
Income (loss) before income taxes, extraordinary item and accounting changes	23	(74)	259
Provision (benefit) for income taxes	41	(14)	293
(Loss) before extraordinary item and accounting changes	(18)	(60)	(34)
Extraordinary item—loss from early retirement of debt, net of taxes	(16)	(9)	(45)
Cumulative effect of accounting changes, net of taxes	—	(55)	(63)
Net (loss)	$ (34)	$ (124)	$ (142)
Per share			
(Loss) before extraordinary item and accounting changes	$ (.21)	$ (.69)	$ (.40)
Extraordinary item—loss from early retirement of debt, net of taxes	(.18)	(.10)	(.52)
Cumulative effect of accounting changes, net of taxes	—	(.64)	(.73)
Net (loss)	$ (.39)	$ (1.43)	$ (1.65)
Average number of shares outstanding	87.7	86.4	85.8

Source: Georgia-Pacific *Annual Report*, 1993.

EXHIBIT 23-2 Statements of Cash Flows—Georgia-Pacific Corporation and Subsidiaries (*Millions*)

	YEAR ENDED DECEMBER 31		
	1993	1992	1991
Cash provided by (used for) operations			
Net (loss)	$ (34)	$ (124)	$ (142)
Adjustments to reconcile net (loss) to cash provided by operations:			
Depreciation	711	747	673
Depletion	53	42	51
Deferred tax benefit	(125)	(133)	(25)
Amortization of goodwill	59	59	60
Stock compensation programs	53	42	67
Gain on sales of assets	(32)	(33)	(38)
Amortization of debt issue costs, discounts and premiums	7	6	35
Other (income) loss	26	—	(344)
Extraordinary item, net of taxes	—	—	45
Cumulative effect of accounting changes, net of taxes	—	55	63
(Increase) decrease in receivables	(174)	(87)	92
(Increase) decrease in inventories	(93)	61	(43)
Change in other working capital	40	193	45
Increase (decrease) in taxes payable	(158)	13	(2)
Change in other assets and other long-term liabilities	56	27	43
Cash provided by operations	389	868	580
Cash provided by (used for) investment activities			
Capital expenditures			
Property, plant and equipment	(421)	(347)	(490)
Timber and timberlands	(46)	(37)	(38)
Total capital expenditures	(467)	(384)	(528)
Proceeds from sales of assets	260	55	1,251
Other	5	(4)	23
Cash provided by (used for) investment activities	(202)	(333)	746
Cash provided by (used for) financing activities			
Repayments of long-term debt	(576)	(566)	(2,055)
Additions to long-term debt	511	754	610
Fees paid to issue debt	(5)	(7)	(4)
Increase (decrease) in bank overdrafts	52	(50)	27
Increase (decrease) in commercial paper and other short-term notes	(41)	(519)	226
Cash dividends paid	(142)	(140)	(140)
Cash (used for) financing activities	(201)	(528)	(1,336)
Increase (decrease) in cash	(14)	7	(10)
Balance at beginning of year	55	48	58
Balance at end of year	$ 41	$ 55	$ 48

Source: Georgia-Pacific *Annual Report,* 1993.

EXHIBIT 23-3 Balance Sheets—Georgia-Pacific Corporation and Subsidiaries (*Millions, except shares and per share amounts*)

	DECEMBER 31 1993	DECEMBER 31 1992
Assets		
Current assets		
Cash	$ 41	$ 55
Receivables, less allowances of $32 and $35	377	331
Inventories		
Raw materials	367	321
Finished goods	786	792
Supplies	262	282
LIFO reserve	(213)	(203)
Total inventories	1,202	1,192
Other current assets	26	29
Total current assets	1,646	1,607
Timber and timberlands, net	1,381	1,402
Property, plant and equipment		
Land and improvements	237	247
Buildings	1,074	1,101
Machinery and equipment	9,550	9,420
Construction in progress	125	64
Total property, plant and equipment, at cost	10,986	10,832
Accumulated depreciation	(5,538)	(5,001)
Property, plant and equipment, net	5,448	5,831
Goodwill	1,832	1,891
Other assets	238	181
Total assets	$10,545	$10,912

EXHIBIT 23-3 *Continued*

	DECEMBER 31	
	1993	1992
Liabilities and shareholders' equity		
Current liabilities		
Bank overdrafts, net	$ 173	$ 121
Commercial paper and other short-term notes	650	691
Current portion of long-term debt	57	257
Taxes payable	35	193
Accounts payable	582	563
Accrued compensation	184	179
Accrued interest	114	132
Other current liabilities	269	316
Total current liabilities	2,064	2,452
Long-term debt, excluding current portion	4,157	4,019
Other long-term liabilities	827	731
Deferred income taxes	1,095	1,202
Commitments and contingencies		
Shareholders' equity		
Common stock, par value $.80; authorized 150,000,000 shares; 90,269,000 and 88, 111,000 shares issued	71	70
Additional paid-in capital	1,202	1,094
Retained earnings	1,217	1,393
Long-term incentive plan deferred compensation	(56)	(39)
Other	(32)	(10)
Total shareholders' capacity	2,404	2,508
Total liabilities and shareholders' equity	$10,545	$10,912

Source: Georgia-Pacific *Annual Report,* 1993.

EXHIBIT 23-4 Statements of Shareholders' Equity—Georgia-Pacific Corporation and Subsidiaries (*Millions, except shares*)

Common Stock Shares Issued		Total	Comman Stock	Additional Paid-In Capital	Retained Earnings	Long-term Incentive Plan Deferred Compensation	Other
86,704,000	Balance at December 31, 1990	$2,975	$69	$ 995	$1,939	$(30)	$ 2
	Net loss	(142)	–	–	(142)	–	–
	Cash dividends declared-$1.60 per common share	(140)	–	–	(140)	–	–
	Common stock issued:						
145,000	Stock option plan	8	–	8	–	–	–
580,000	Employee stock purchase plans	20	1	19	–	–	–
(8,000)	Long-term incentive plan	25	–	23	–	2	–
	Other	(10)	–	–	–	–	(10)
87,421,000	Balance at December 31, 1991	2,736	70	1,045	1,657	(28)	(8)
	Net loss	(124)	–	–	(124)	–	–
	Cash dividends declared—$1.60 per common share	(140)	–	–	(140)	–	–
	Common stock issued:						
186,000	Stock option plan	12	–	12	–	–	–
112,000	Employee stock purchase plan	4	–	4	–	–	–
392,000	Long-term incentive plan	22	–	33	–	(11)	–
	Other	(2)	–	–	–	–	(2)

EXHIBIT 23-4 *Continued*

Common Stock Shares Issued		Total	Common Stock	Additional Paid-in Capital	Retained Earnings	Long-term Incentive Plan Deferred Compensation	Other
88,111,000	Balance at December 31, 1992	2,508	70	1,094	1,393	(39)	(10)
	Net loss	(34)	–	–	(34)	–	–
	Cash dividends declared—$1.60 per common share	(142)	–	–	(142)	–	–
	Common stock issued:						
107,000	Stock option plans	7	–	7	–	–	–
1,575,000	Employee stock purchase plans	55	1	54	–	–	–
476,000	Long-term incentive plan	26	–	43	–	(17)	–
	Other	(18)	–	4	–	–	(22)
90,269,000	Balance at December 31, 1993	$2,402	$71	$1,202	$1,217	$(56)	$(32)

Source: Georgia-Pacific *Annual Report*, 1993.

EXHIBIT 23-5 Georgia-Pacific Corporation and Subsidiaries (Millions)

(MILLIONS)	YEAR ENDED DECEMBER 31					
	1993		1992		1991	
Net sales						
Building products	$ 7,067	58%	$ 6,112	52%	$ 5,405	47%
Pulp and paper	5,231	42	5,711	48	6,089	53
Other operations	32	–	24	–	30	–
Total net sales	$12,330	100%	$11,847	100%	$11,524	100%
Net (loss)						
Building products	$973	126%	$ 691	100%	$344	32%
Pulp and paper	(187)	(24)	(8)	(1)	362	34
Other operations	10	1	9	1	17	2
Other income (loss)ª	(26)	(3)	–	–	344	32
Total operating profits	770	100%	692	100%	1,067	100%
General corporate	(205)		(166)		(165)	
Interest expense	(513)		(565)		(584)	
Cost of accounts receivable sale program	(29)		(35)		(59)	
(Provision) benefit for income taxes	(41)		14		(293)	
(Loss) before extraordinary item and accounting changes	(18)		(60)	(34)		
Extraordinary item-loss from early retirement of debt, net of taxes	(16)	(9)	(45)			
Cumulative effect of accounting changes, net of taxes	–		(55)		(63)	
Net (loss)	$ (34)		$ (124)		$ (142)	

EXHIBIT 23-5 *Continued*

(MILLIONS)	YEAR ENDED DECEMBER 31					
	1993		1992		1991	
Depreciation, depletion and goodwill amortization						
Building products	$ 215	26%	$ 206	24%	$ 232	30%
Pulp and paper	595	72	626	74	537	68
Other and general corporate	13	2	16	2	15	2
Total depreciation and goodwill amortization	$ 823	100%	$ 848	100%	$ 784	100%
Capital expenditures[b]						
Building products	$ 146	31%	111	29%	$43	8%
Pulp and paper	261	56	217	56	436	83
Timber and timberlands	46	10	37	10	38	7
Other and general corporate	14	3	19	5	11	2
Total capital expenditures	$ 467	100%	$ 384	100%	$ 528	100%
Assets						
Building products	$ 1,726	16%	$ 1,634	15%	$ 1,681	16%
Pulp and paper	6,909	66	7,414	68	7,208	68
Timber and timberlands	1,380	13	1,402	13	1,377	13
Other and general corporate	530	5	462	4	363	3
Total assets	$10,545	100%	$10,912	100%	$10,629	100%

[a] Other income represents the results of various asset divestitures. If theses amounts had been included in segment operating profits, pulp and paper operating profits would have been $(213) million in 1993 and $546 million in 1991 and building products operating profits would have been $504 million in 1991.
[b] The capital expenditure amounts reported above represent additions, at cost, to property, plant and equipment and timber and timberlands.
Source: Georgia-Pacific *Annual Report,* 1993.

EXHIBIT 23-6 Selected Financial Data Financial Position, End of Year (*Dollar amounts, except per share, are in millions*)

	1993	1992	1991
Financial position, end of year			
Current assets	$ 1,646	$ 1,607	$ 1,562
Timber and timberlands, net	1,381	1,402	1,377
Property, plant and equipment, net	5,448	5,831	5,567
Net assets of discontinued operations	–	–	–
Goodwill	1,832	1,891	1,949
Other assets	238	181	174
Total assets	10,545	10,912	10,629
Current liabilities	2,064	2,452	2,722
Long-term debt	4,157	4,019	3,743
Other long-term liabilities	827	731	633
Deferred income taxes	1,095	1,202	795
Redeemable preferred stock	–	–	–
Shareholders' equity	$ 2,402	$ 2,508	$ 2,736
Working capital	$ (418)	$ (845)	$ (1,160)
Other statistical data			
Capital expenditures (including acquisitions)	$ 467	$ 384	$ 528
Capital expenditures (excluding acquisitions)	467	384	528
Per common share			
Market price: High	75.00	72.00	60.25
Low	55.00	48.25	36.25
Year-end	68.75	62.38	53.63
Book value	26.60	28.47	31.30
Total debt to capital	57.0%	57.0%	60.1%
Current ratio	.8	.7	.6

Source: Georgia-Pacific *Annual Report*, 1993.

EXHIBIT 23-7 Sales and Operating Profits by Industry Segment—Georgia-Pacific Corporation and Subsidiaries (*Millions*)

	1993		1992		1991		1990***	
Net sales								
Building products								
Wood panels	$ 2,913	24%	$ 2,543	22%	$ 2,097	18%	$ 2,296	18%
Lumber	2,672	22	2,055	17	1,819	16	1,966	16
Chemicals	267	2	240	2	223	2	247	2
Gypsum products	236	2	216	2	222	2	270	2
Roofing	180	1	185	2	183	2	192	2
Other	799	7	873	7	861	7	952	7
	7,067	58	6,112	52	5,405	47	5,923	47
Pulp and paper								
Containerboard and packaging	1,902	15	2,001	17	2,008	17	2,440	19
Communication papers	1,195	10	1,070	9	1,134	10	1,360	11
Tissue	713	6	682	6	664	6	719	6
Market pulp	622	5	681	6	645	6	779	6
Paper distribution and envelopes	748	6	1,208	10	1,218	10	1,027	8
Other	51	–	69	–	420	4	377	3
	5,231	42	5,711	48	6,089	53	6,702	53
Other operations	32	–	24	–	30	–	40	–
Continuing operations	$12,330	100%	$11,847	100%	$11,524	100%	$12,665	100%
Operating results*								
Building products	$ 973	126%	$ 691	100%	$ 344	32%	$ 423	29%
Pulp and paper	(187)	(24)	(8)	(1)	362	34	979	67
Other operations	10	1	9	1	17	2	17	1
Other income (expense)**	(26)	(3)	–	–	344	32	48	3
Continuing operations	$ 770	100%	$ 692	100%	$ 1,067	100%	$ 1,467	100%

*Operating results are before income taxes, interest, cost of accounts receivable sale program, general corporate expenses, unusual items, extraordinary items and accounting changes.

**Other income (expense) includes a net $26 million pretax loss in 1993, a net $344 million pretax gain in 1991 and a net $48 million pretax gain in 1990 resulting from asset divestitures and pretax restructuring charges of $135 million in 1983. If these amounts had been included in segment operating profits, pulp and paper operating profits would have been $(213) million in 1993, $546 million in 1991, $939 million in 1990 and $13 million in 1983; building products operating profits would have been $504 million in 1991, $511 million in 1990 and $277 million in 1983; and other operations operating profits would have been $13 million in 1983.

***Sales and operating profits of Great Northern Nekoosa Corporation and its subsidiaries have been included beginning on March 9, 1990.

Source: Georgia-Pacific *Annual Report*, 1993.

EXHIBIT 23-8 Operating Statistics—Georgia-Pacific Corporation and Subsidiaries

| | AS OF DECEMBER 31, 1993 | |
	NUMBER OF FACILITIES	ANNUAL CAPACITY
Pulp and paper		
Paper (t.tons)		
Containerboard and packaging		
Linerboard and medium	4	2,941
Other paperboard	5	664
Kraft paper	2	342
Communication papers	8	2,223
Tissue	5	573
Groundwood papers	–	–
Market pulp (t.tons)	6	1,880
Total paper and market pulp	30	8,623
Converting		
Corrugated packaging (m.sq.ft.)	37	27,963
Tissue (t.tons)	6	610
Envelopes (billion envelopes)	17	15
Other	12	
Total paper, market pulp and converting	102	
Distribution centers	0**	
Building products		
Wood panels		
Softwood plywood (3⁄8") (m.sq.ft.)	17	5,019
Hardwood plywood (sm) (m.sq.ft.)	2	600
Hardboard (1⁄8") (m.sq.ft.)	8	1,395
Particleboard (3⁄4") (m.sq.ft.)	8	1,210
Oriented strand board (3⁄8") (m.sq.ft.)	4	952
Panelboard (1⁄8") (m.sq.ft.)	1	379
Softboard (1⁄2") (m.sq.ft.)	1	250
Medium-density fiberboard (3⁄4") (m.sq.ft.)	1	100
Lumber (m.bd.ft.)	40	2,732
Moulding (m.bd.ft.)	2	21
Gypsum board (m.sq.ft.)	10	3,063
Roofing-shingles (t.squares)	5	9,484
Formaldehyde (m.lbs.)	13	1,891
Thermosetting resins (m.lbs.)	16	3,014
Other	19	
Total building products	147	
Distribution centers	137	
Other operations	2	
Resources (as of December 31)		
North American timberlands (t.acres)		
Owned		
Controlled		

The Corporation has 248 manufacturing facilities in the United States, one recycled-paper mill in Canada, and 2 wood moulding manufacturing facilities in Mexico.

*The production of Great Northern Nekoosa facilities has been included beginning on March 9, 1990.

**Butler Paper assets were sold in July, 1993.

***Excludes 540,000 fee acres and 98,000 controlled acres of timberland sold in January 1991.

Source: Georgia–Pacific *Annual Report,* 1993

EXHIBIT 23-8 *Continued*

					PRODUCTION					
1993	1992	1991	1990*	1989	1988	1987	1986	1985	1984	1983
3,030	2,889	2,936	3,139	1,419	1,297	1,318	1,146	976	740	452
567	526	522	544	555	458	393	368	368	374	377
343	377	358	354	350	356	348	394	452	529	541
2,119	2,002	1,994	1,780	1,161	970	868	731	552	574	518
594	576	556	553	519	511	490	496	476	486	487
–	–	603	531	–	–	–	–	–	–	–
1,940	1,829	1,793	1,667	1,194	870	718	611	587	629	601
8,593	8,199	8,762	8,568	5,198	4,462	4,135	3,746	3,411	3,332	2,976
29,998	25,411	24,010	31,356	16,640	16,577	15,750	14,572	13,703	11,880	8,427
543	521	491	497	467	462	446	437	432	422	422
13	13	13	12	–	–	–	–	–	–	–
5,462	5,133	4,968	5,395	5,341	5,545	5,050	4,706	4,414	4,443	4,430
477	458	424	437	420	456	357	335	311	343	442
1,388	1,330	1,202	1,203	1,203	1,198	1,159	349	368	361	346
1,089	977	932	984	1,062	1,004	695	425	410	381	400
1,045	1,011	851	969	873	793	652	525	173	96	51
366	365	332	344	318	330	295	248	290	311	299
247	234	237	252	242	238	231	241	239	243	241
98	92	79	88	74	62	59	75	76	69	77
2,580	2,568	2,570	2,674	2,426	2,324	1,956	1,784	1,684	1,650	1,603
21	23	22	36	29	30	30	8	–	–	–
2,409	2,112	1,955	2,309	2,403	2,406	2,620	2,473	2,495	2,412	2,242
7,274	7,447	7,775	7,674	8,106	7,155	6,976	7,361	7,789	7,539	5,973
1,809	1,614	1,540	1,547	1,454	1,394	1,309	1,233	1,188	1,169	1,081
2,761	2,571	2,377	2,470	2,372	2,362	2,136	1,805	1,650	1,527	1,451
5,821	5,942	5,969	8,203***	5,430	5,480	4,910	4,700	4,760	4,920	4,630
681	707	922	1,047***	670	1,010	670	530	480	480	530

sm = surface measure basis

t = thousands

m = millions

Source: Georgia–Pacific *Annual Report*, 1993.

EXHIBIT 23-9 Georgia–Pacific Corporation Officers

A.D. Correll
Chairman and Chief Executive Officer

James C. Van Meter[1]
Vice Chairman and Chief Financial Officer

W.E. Babin
Executive Vice President-Pulp and Paper

Davis K. Mortensen
Executive Vice President-Building Products

Donald L. Glass
Senior Vice President-Building Products
Manufacturing and Sales

James F. Kelley
Senior Vice President-Law and General
Counsel

Maurice W. Kring
Senior Vice President-Containerboard and
Packaging

George A. MacConnell
Senior Vice President-Distribution and
Millwork

John F. McGovern[2]
Senior Vice President-Finance

David W. Reynolds
Senior Vice President-Human Resources and
Administration

Lee M. Thomas
Senior Vice President-Environmental,
Government Affairs and Communications

James E. Bostic, Jr.
Group Vice President-Communication Papers

Gerard R. Brandt
Group Vice President-Packaged Products

Willie L. Duke
Group Vice President-Softwood Lumber

Duncan B. Facey
Group Vice President-Distribution Division

Clint M. Kennedy
Group Vice President-Pulp and Bleached Board

John F. Rasor
Group Vice President-Forest Resources

J. Wayne Amy
Vice-President-Metal Products

Joseph J. Armetta
Vice-President-Distribution Division Midwest
Region

Jerry P. Collier
Vice President-Millwork

Rebecca M. Crockford
Vice President-Compensation and Benefits

David S. Dimling
Vice President-Sales and Marketing
Communication Papers

David R. Fleiner
Vice-President-Structural Panels

[1] Resigned February 28, 1994
[2] Named Chief Financial Officer February 28, 1994

EXHIBIT 23-9 *Continued*

William C. Howard
Vice President-Environmental Engineering and
Technical Support

Stephen K. Jackson
Vice President-Distribution Division Northeast
Region

Jerry L. Kincaid
Vice President-Manufacturing Communication
Papers

William A. Mamrack
Vice President-Taxes

John E. Masaschi
Vice President-Industrial Wood Products
Division

Charles H. McElrea
Vice President-Pulp and Paper Logistics and
Purchasing

Robert J. Millikan
Vice President-Engineering and Technology
Pulp and Paper

Dewey L. Mobley
Vice President-Western Wood Products
Manufacturing Division

William B. Nagle, Jr.
Vice President-Lumber Distribution

Source: Georgia-Pacific *Annual Report*, 1993.

Kelly E. Powell, Jr.
Vice President-Distribution Division Western
Region

William D. Rose
Vice President-Specialty Manufacturing and
Sales

Robert A. Starling
Vice President-Distribution Division Southern
Region

James R. Taylor
Vice President-Chemical Division

James E. Terrell
Vice President and Controller

Douglas A. Thom
Vice President-Packaging

Michael A. Vidan
Vice President-Gypsum and Roofing Division

Carl Wilson
Vice President-Information Resources

James T. Wright
Vice President-Human Resources

Kenneth F. Khoury
Secretary

Danny W. Huff
Treasurer

SHOES AND APPAREL INDUSTRY NOTE

JOANNE TUCKER
AND JAMES BYRON

The nonrubber footwear industry (SIC 314) produces all types of footwear except rubber protective and rubber-soled fabric-upper (the traditional "sneakers") footwear, both of which are classified in SIC 3021 (Table 1). Nonrubber footwear is constructed with leather, vinyl, plastic, or textile uppers or combinations of these materials for both genders and all ages. In 1993, industry shipments increased about 4 percent to an estimated $3.9 billion, from $3.8 billion in 1992. In constant dollars, the increase was more than 1 percent. Unit shipments increased less than 1 percent to 172 million pairs in 1993, from 171 million pairs in 1992. By quantity, the rate of change varied among the industry's four major sectors: house slippers (SIC 3142) were down 5 percent; men's footwear, except athletic (SIC 3143) increased 1 percent; and women's footwear, except athletic (SIC 3144) and footwear, except rubber, NEC(SIC 3149) were up between 3 and 4 percent each.

Production Up. In 1993, production of nonrubber footwear increased almost 1 percent to more than 165 million pairs, from more than 164 million pairs in 1992. This marked the first annual increase since 1988 and only the fourth since 1968, when production peaked at about 642.4 million pairs. Over the subsequent 25-year period, U.S. production has declined at a compound annual rate of about 5 percent. In 1993, production, by quantity, was up for three sectors and down only for slippers.

House Slippers. Shipments of house slippers declined about 5 percent to more than 45 million pairs in 1993. Their product value dropped to an estimated $268 million. Slippers accounted for 26 percent of the quantity but only 7.5 percent of the value of total nonrubber footwear product shipments, primarily because most slippers are produced from lower-cost vinyls and textiles. The ratio of imports to apparent consumption for slippers was about 28 percent by quantity, the lowest of the four sectors.

Men's Footwear, Except Athletic. Men's nonathletic footwear includes dress and casual shoes, work shoes, and boots. Shipments of men's footwear increased about 1 percent, to 43.3 million pairs in 1993 from 42.8 million pairs in 1992. Value increased about 3 percent in 1993 to an estimated $1.84 billion. Men's footwear accounted for 25 percent by quantity and 51 percent by value of nonrubber footwear shipments in 1993. More than 90 percent of men's footwear was made with leather uppers. By quantity, imports as a percentage of total consumption of men's footwear were an estimated 76 percent in 1993.

Women's Footwear, Except Athletic. Shipments of women's footwear increased more than 3 percent to 58 million pairs in 1993. Value increased about 6 percent to an estimated $1.3 billion. Women's footwear accounted for 34 percent by quantity and 35 percent by value. Import penetration for women's footwear was an estimated 90 percent.

Footwear, Except Rubber, NEC. Shipments of footwear for youths and boys, misses, children, infants and babies, and athletic and other miscellaneous types of

TABLE 1   Trends and Forecasts: Footwear, except Rubber (SIC 314) (*In Millions of Dollars except as noted*) 1991-1994

ITEM	1991	1992[1]	1993[2]	1994[3]	PERCENT CHANGE 91–92	92–93	93–94
INDUSTRY DATA							
Value of shipments[4]	3,775	3,778	3,918	4,134	0.1	3.7	5.5
3142 House slippers	277	295	290	293	6.5	−1.7	1.0
3143 Men's footwear	2,064	2,093	2,158	2,287	1.4	3.1	6.0
3144 Women's footwear	1,154	1,158	1,228	1,302	0.3	6.0	6.0
3149 Footwear NEC	280	232	242	252	−17.1	4.3	4.1
Value of shipments (1987$)	3,199	3,126	3,174	3,236	−2.3	1.5	2.0
3142 House slippers	251	274	261	256	9.2	−4.7	−1.9
3143 Men's footwear	1,686	1,665	1,685	1,719	−1.2	1.2	2.0
3144 Women's footwear	1,028	997	1,032	1,063	−3.0	3.5	3.0
3149 Footwear NEC	233	190	196	198	−18.5	3.2	1.0
Total employment (000)	53.1	50.3	48.2	48.2	−5.3	−4.2	0.0
Production workers (000)	46.0	43.2	41.0	41.4	−6.1	−5.1	1.0
Average hourly earnings ($)	6.83	7.17	7.53	7.83	5.0	5.0	4.0
Capital expenditures	31.5	—	—	—	—	—	—
3142 House slippers	2.4	—	—	—	—	—	—
3143 Men's footwear	18.1	—	—	—	—	—	—
144 Women's footwear	9.1	—	—	—	—	—	—
3149 Footwear NEC	1.9	—	—	—	—	—	—
PRODUCT DATA							
Value of shipments[5]	3,495	3,491	3,622	3,822	-0.1	3.8	5.5
3142 House slippers	256	273	268	271	6.6	−1.8	1.1
3143 Men's footwear	1,763	1,788	1,843	1,954	1.4	3.1	6.0
3144 Women's footwear	1,186	1,190	1,261	1,337	0.3	6.0	6.0
3149 Footwear NEC	289	240	250	260	−17.0	4.2	4.0
Value of shipments (1987$)	2,971	2,896	2,943	3,001	−2.5	1.6	2.0
3142 House slippers	232	253	241	236	9.1	−4.7	−2.1
3143 Men's footwear	1,441	1,422	1,439	1,468	−1.3	1.2	2.0
3144 Women's footwear	1,057	1,025	1,060	1,092	−3.0	3.4	3.0
3149 Footwear NEC	241	196	203	205	−18.7	3.6	1.0
TRADE DATA							
Value of imports	8,315	8,590	9,385	10,042	3.3	9.3	7.0
Value of exports	306	342	329	368	11.8	−3.8	11.9

1. Estimate, except exports and imports.

2. Estimate.

3. Forecast.

4. Value of all products and services sold by establishments in the footwear, except rubber industry.

5. Value of products classified in the footwear, except rubber industry produced by all industries.

Source: U.S. Department of Commerce: Bureau of the Census; International Trade Administration (ITA). Estimates and forecasts by ITA.

footwear increased about 3 percent to an estimated 25 million pairs in 1993. Value increased about 4 percent to $250 million. Shipments of footwear in this group accounted for 15 percent by quantity and 7 percent by value. Production of misses' and athletic footwear increased in 1993, but children's and infants' and babies' footwear declined.

Consumption of athletic footwear, including imports and domestic production of rubber-fabric "sneakers," reached a high of about 565 million pairs in 1992 but declined about 1 percent in 1993. Athletic footwear represented about 38 percent of combined nonrubber and rubber-fabric footwear consumption of about 1.5 billion pairs in 1993. Imports of juvenile footwear were up about 7 percent in the first half of 1993 from the same period in 1992, but imports of athletic nonrubber footwear declined.

Footwear Consumption Up. Apparent consumption of nonrubber footwear increased about 2 percent in 1993 to an estimated 1.1 billion pairs. Per capita consumption also increased for the third consecutive year by about 1 percent, to 4.43 pairs. Driven by demand for imported nonrubber athletic footwear, per capita consumption increased sharply during the early 1980s, peaking at 4.8 pairs in 1986. Per capita consumption declined to 4.3 pairs in 1990 and has increased only slightly since then. Per capita consumption of combined nonrubber and rubber/canvas footwear was 5.65 pairs in 1993, down from 1992 because of a drop in "sneaker" consumption of about 6 percent.

Personal consumption expenditures (PCE) on both rubber and nonrubber footwear were up only 0.4 percent in 1993 to an estimated $32.4 billion. However, PCE on footwear in constant (1987) dollars were down almost 2 percent. Inventories at all levels of distribution increased during the year, as both sales and prices at the retail level weakened.

Retailers' outdoor business was good throughout 1993. Lightweight hikers, waterproof boots, outdoor crosstrainers, and sport sandals were in demand and consumption of these types is expected to grow in 1994. Styles shifted away from the athletic look to an outdoor look but incorporated the same comfort technology, such as padded linings, collars, and insoles that made athletic shoes so popular. Water-resistant leather uppers, including suedes, predominated, especially in boots.

Factory Prices, Profits Up. The average factory price for nonrubber footwear increased about 2 percent to an estimated $21.16 per pair in 1993. This was the smallest annual increase in three years and reflected the intense pressure on prices from imported footwear. The producer price index (PPI) for nonrubber footwear was up almost 2 percent for January–June 1993, compared with the same period in 1992.

According to an analysis of publicly held footwear companies, six producers that manufactured athletic footwear overseas earned the most profits in 1992. The entire group of 31 companies saw total sales increase 7 percent and profits rise 22 percent over 1991. Six athletic footwear companies accounted for 60 percent of the group's sales and 80 percent of its profits. Nike was among the top five performers in seven financial ratios and Reebok was similarly ranked in four ratios. But with slower growth in athletic footwear, composite performances for the group were not as solid as they have been. The financial performance of individual companies, particularly among the small and medium-sized manufacturers, was much improved in 1992 over 1991. Median return on sales for the group grew from nearly 3 percent in 1991 to more than 4 percent in 1992, and median return on equity rose from more than 7 percent to slightly more than 11 percent over the same period.

An article in *Footwear News* (July 1993) indicated that consumers' footwear buying habits had shifted to form, function, and comfort and away from brands. Many were seeking lower-priced goods in strip shopping centers and outlet stores instead of in shopping malls. The same article found that, as a group, 18 publicly held U.S. footwear resource companies (companies that either produce domestically or source abroad) reported a 4.8 percent increase in sales in 1992 over 1991, but a 19.5 percent decline in profits. However, 94 percent of the group's total profits came from the two largest athletic footwear producers. Four companies, including the third largest athletic producer, recorded losses in 1992. The new profit-to-sales ratio for the group was 4.1 percent in 1992, down from 5.4 percent in 1991. In 1992, the profit-to-equity ratio was 14.1 percent, down from 18.7 percent in 1991. For a group of five footwear retailers, the same survey showed that sales increased 7.8 percent in 1992 over 1991, and profits were up 9 percent.

Plants, Employment Down. The *Census of Manufacturers for 1987* lists 379 companies operating 471 establishments in the nonrubber footwear industry. In 1966, about 990 plants were in operation. Based on published reports of plant closings, these declines have continued since 1987. Ten closings were recorded in 1992. Many of the plants recently closed were owned by the largest manufacturing and retailing companies, which chose to source more footwear from lower-cost producers overseas. In 1993, total employment declined about 4 percent to an estimated 48,200. Production employment declined also by about 5 percent.

About 47.5 percent of nonrubber footwear produced in 1992 had leather uppers, down from 51 percent in 1991. About 15 percent had leather outsoles. Leather upper use was highest in men's footwear (95 percent) and women's footwear (65 percent). Juvenile types averaged about 31 percent and athletics 75 percent.

New Technology. The industry considers new technology essential to increase productivity and lower costs. Increased use of computers has already integrated design, management, manufacturing, and marketing functions, emphasizing such nonprice factors as quality and quick delivery in competition with imports. Emphasis has been placed on linking computer-aided design (CAD) and computer-aided manufacturing (CAM) systems and software. As a result, tooling can be produced from CAD data and linked to auto-stitchers, milling, and turning machines. There has been a resurgence of interest in three-dimensional CAD, which produces more accurate shoe patterns and reduces the number of prototypes required.

Computers also enable manufacturers to combine several operations or machines under fewer operators, reducing handling time and improving quality. Computerized robots have also been developed for handling and transferring operations within and between these production modules. Much of this new technology has been developed and used in Europe and, depending on the availability of capital, can be readily transferred to Far Eastern producers. However, the labor-saving benefits of such technology would not be as great for producers with low unit labor costs. The net effect of such technology would be to reduce the costs of U.S. production relative to Far Eastern production, although the latter will continue to maintain a competitive advantage for most footwear.

Nonrubber footwear imports rose almost 3 percent in 1993 to an estimated 1 billion pairs, from 974 million pairs in 1992. The customs value increased more than 9 percent to $9.4 billion. The unit value of nonrubber footwear imports in 1993 was about $9.39, up from 1992, but still almost 60 percent below the unit value of domestic production (Table 2).

Imports increased from 175 million pairs in 1968 to 405 million pairs in 1979, when they stabilized during a four-year period of Orderly Marketing Agreements (OMAs) with South Korea and Taiwan. Following expiration of these OMAs in June 1981, imports increased by more than 100 million pairs a year until 1986, reaching 941 million pairs. Following a decline to less than 900 million pairs in 1989, nonrubber footwear imports rose to the record level of 1 billion pairs in 1993. Over the 25-year period since 1968, imports have increased at a compound annual rate of about 7 percent.

During the first six months of 1993, the five largest suppliers, by quantity, of nonrubber footwear to the United States were China (56 percent), Brazil (12 percent), Indonesia (8 percent), Taiwan (almost 6 percent), and the Republic of Korea (4 percent). These five countries accounted for nearly 85 percent of all U.S. nonrubber footwear imports for the six-month period. Although the United States imported nonrubber footwear from more than 90 countries during this period, only four other countries—Italy, Thailand, Spain, and Hong Kong—captured more than 1 percent of U.S. nonrubber footwear imports.

TABLE 2 U.S. Trade Patterns in 1992 Footwear, Except Rubber SIC 314 (*In millions of dollars, percent*)

EXPORTS			IMPORTS		
	VALUE	SHARE		VALUE	SHARE
Canada and Mexico	65	19.1	Canada and Mexico	145	1.7
European Community	115	33.5	European Community	1,292	15.0
Japan	39	11.3	Japan	3	0.0
East Asia NICs	15	4.3	East Asia NICs	5,715	66.5
South America	21	6.2	South America	1,166	13.6
Other	87	25.6	Other	269	3.1
World Total	342	100.0		8,590	100.0

TOP FIVE COUNTRIES					
	VALUE	SHARE		VALUE	SHARE
Canada	46	13.4	China	2,970	34.6
Japan	39	11.3	Brazil	1,099	12.8
United Kingdom	25	7.2	South Korea	1,074	12.5
France	24	7.1	Italy	772	9.0
Italy	23	6.8	Taiwan	696	8.1

Source: U.S. Department of Commerce: Bureau of the Census; International Trade Administration.

U.S. imports of nonrubber footwear were up nearly 10 percent for the first six months in 1993 compared with the same period in 1992. Imports from China rose 28 percent and were expected to increase by 140 million pairs in 1993 to almost 650 million pairs. More production continued to shift to China from Taiwan and Korea, formerly the two major exporters, because of lower costs. A large measure of technological and financial support for mainland China's rapidly expanding footwear operations comes from Taiwanese manufacturers. Indonesia, up 23 percent, and Brazil, up 16 percent, both recorded substantial export growth to the United States during the period January–June 1993 compared with the same period in 1992. Korea's exports to the United States dropped 45 percent and Taiwan's declined 37 percent.

China accounted for more than 35 percent of U.S. imports of nonrubber footwear with leather uppers during January–June, 1993. In addition, Brazil (23 percent), Indonesia (9 percent), Korea (8 percent), and Italy (6 percent) ranked in the top five suppliers, accounting for more than 80 percent of the total. China and Brazil were the largest suppliers of men's leather footwear. Brazil, China, and Italy were the largest suppliers of women's leather footwear, and China and Brazil were the largest suppliers of juvenile footwear. China (40 percent) and Indonesia (25 percent) were the largest suppliers of leather athletic footwear. China was the largest supplier to the United States in all 19 major gender or material subcategories of nonrubber footwear imports except women's leather footwear, where it ranked second behind Brazil.

U.S. leather footwear imports accounted for 53 percent of all nonrubber footwear imports during January–June 1993, unchanged from the same period in 1992. The import share of footwear with vinyl or plastic uppers for January–June 1993 was 44 percent, and of items with textile uppers 3 percent. The import share with leather uppers has dropped from a high of 59 percent in 1990 due to the substitution of cheaper vinyl, plastic, and other materials for more expensive leather. For January–June 1993, leather's share was highest for athletic and men's nonrubber footwear imports and lowest for juvenile and slipper types.

U.S. manufacturers export ever larger quantities of cut footwear parts to developing countries, where they are assembled and re-exported to the United States as finished or partly finished footwear. Under the U.S. Harmonized Tariff Schedule (Heading No. 9802), duties are assessed only on the value-added content. Moreover, U.S. duties on partially finished but unlasted nonrubber footwear are less than 5 percent, compared with 8.5 percent or more for completed leather footwear. Frequently, final manufacturing operations that require less labor, such as bottoming, finishing, and packing are performed in the United States. For January–June 1993, such partially completed leather footwear imports totaled more than 13 million pairs, up about 12 percent over the same period in 1992. The largest suppliers were the Dominican Republic, Mexico, Thailand, India, and China.

Exports Down. U.S. exports of nonrubber footwear declined about 4 percent in 1993 to more than 20 million pairs. Value declined more than 1 percent to an estimated $337 million. The average unit price was about $16.44, up from $15.98 in 1992. U.S. producers compete effectively in high-cost developed country markets, including all of the European Community countries. European demand was steady for U.S. branded men's moccasins, boat shoes, hiking boots, Western boots, and work boots.

The United States exported 10 million parts of nonrubber footwear valued at $156 million during the first half of 1993. Mexico took more than 16 percent of the total, by quantity, followed by Canada (9 percent), Russia (8 percent), Poland (8 percent), Japan (7 percent), France (5 percent), and the United Kingdom (4 percent).

U.S. exports of nonrubber footwear to Mexico were made up largely of low-priced juvenile types with vinyl uppers. For the first half of 1993, U.S. footwear exports to Russia were up 20 percent over the same period in 1992 by quantity, and included mostly men's and women's leather footwear.

U.S. exports of nonrubber footwear to Japan were unchanged in the first half of 1993 compared with 1992. About 24 percent of these exports were men's leather types, and 43 percent were athletic types. The latter are exempt from Japan's stringent global tariff-rate quotas on leather nonathletic footwear. These quotas and required licensing procedures restrict Japan's leather footwear imports and discourage U.S. manufacturers from developing the Japanese market. Japan's quota of about 7 million pairs annually in 1993 represents only a small fraction of its leather footwear market, which is estimated to exceed 180 million pairs a year.

Trade Legislation. Several attempts by Congress to pass footwear import quota legislation since 1985 failed to survive presidential vetoes, and it is very unlikely that further attempts will be made. Legislation extending the Caribbean Basin Initiative (CBI) passed in late 1990, and continues to exempt footwear and leather products, among others, from duty-free status. Footwear is statutorily exempt from duty-free treatment accorded beneficiary developing countries under the Generalized System of Preferences (GSP) program.

Most U.S. producers were concerned about increased imports from Mexico following the removal of duties on footwear under the North American Free Trade Agreement (NAFTA). NAFTA provides for a 15-year staged reduction of U.S. duties on rubber footwear, including rubber-fabric types. These U.S. duties range from 37 to 67 percent. Most nonrubber footwear, including leather types which are dutiable at 8.5 to 12 percent, would receive a shorter phaseout period of 10 years. NAFTA rules of origin for footwear would require that non-North American parts undergo a tariff shift at the tariff heading level and that footwear meet a regional content requirement of 55 percent. These strict rules are intended to ensure that third countries could not use Mexico as an export platform or transhipment site to gain duty-free access to the U.S. market. U.S. footwear imports from other Central and South American countries could also increase significantly if accorded duty-free status under Administration-proposed trade initiatives with these countries.

OUTLOOK FOR 1994

Shipments of nonrubber footwear are expected to increase about 1 percent in 1994, to 174 million pairs. Shipments will increase in three sectors: men's footwear by 2 percent to 44 million pairs; women's footwear by 3 percent to 60 million pairs; and footwear, except rubber NEC, by 1 percent to 25.5 million pairs. Shipments of slippers will decline about 2 percent to 45 million pairs. Imports, by quantity, are expected to increase 1 percent and exports by 7 percent. Consequently, apparent consumption will increase only 1 percent and per capita consumption will remain unchanged. Import penetration will remain unchanged from 1993 at 87 percent of apparent consumption.

II. APPAREL

The apparel products industry (SIC 23), also known as the sewn products industry, consists primarily of firms that produce wearing apparel, both cut and sewn and knit to shape, for all population groups. Apparel accounted for 74 percent of total SIC 23 shipments in 1992.

The apparel products industry increased its shipments by 2 percent in 1993, about the same growth as in the previous year. Shipments were nearly 1 percent higher, following a small decline in 1992, because price increases for apparel products decelerated. The shipment gains have occurred in response to sharp increases in consumer spending for clothing, although imports also have benefited from higher spending (Table 3). Some of the increased production, however, reflected inventory buildup in late 1992 and early 1993, similar to what occurred in the overall economy. This inventory rise probably will hold down production to some extent until stocks are worked down.

Total employment in the apparel products industry was about 939,000 workers in 1993. Employment has been declining since 1977, and this is reflected in all product lines, particularly outerwear. In 1992, the number of production workers increased slightly, although total employment registered a small decline, reflecting cost-saving cuts in management positions. Production workers constituted 84 percent of the work force in 1993, compared with 68 percent for all U.S. manufacturing. The aver-

TABLE 3	Trends and forecasts: Apparel and Other Textile Products (SIC 23) *(In millions of dollars except as noted)* 1991-1993				

				PERCENT CHANGE	
ITEM	1991	1992[1]	1993[2]	91-92	92-93
INDUSTRY DATA					
Value of shipments[3]	65,345	66,652	68,052	2.0	2.1
Value of shipments (1987$)	59,021	58,790	59,391	−0.4	1.0
Total employment (000)	960	959	939	−0.1	−2.1
Production workers (000)	815	816	799	0.1	−2.1
Average hourly earnings ($)	6.73	6.91	7.06	2.7	2.2
PRODUCT DATA					
Value of shipments[4]	62,649	64,115	65,461	2.3	2.1
Value of shipments (1987$)	56,634	56,552	57,130	−0.1	1.0
TRADE DATA					
Value of imports	27,230	32,462	35,449	19.2	9.2
Value of exports	3,708	4,625	5,556	24.7	20.1

1. Estimate, except exports and imports.

2. Estimate.

3. Value of all products and services sold by establishments in the apparel and other textile products industry.

4. Value of products classified in the apparel and other textile products industry produced by all industries.

Source: U.S. Department of Commerce: Bureau of the Census; International Trade Administration (ITA). Estimates and forecasts by ITA.

age number of hours worked weekly by production workers grew to 37.2 in 1992, the highest level in at least 20 years. This growth indicates not only the industry's increased activity, but also its hesitancy in hiring permanent workers until the economy is in a solid recovery. Average hours may increase marginally in 1993.

Despite improvements in technology, manufacturing processes in this industry are still quite labor-intensive. Wages and profit margins are low relative to other manufacturing industries. In 1993, the hourly earnings of production workers averaged $7.10, 2 percent above 1992. Employees making men's coats and suits averaged the highest hourly wages, while children's wear workers earned the least. Earnings of apparel and fabricated textile product workers were about 40 percent below the average for all U.S. manufacturing employees and about 35 percent below workers in nondurable goods industries in 1993.

Apparel. Inflationary pressures in the apparel industry continued to ease in 1993, with the rate of price increases slowing for the third year in a row. A slowdown in inflation in the overall economy, little pressure from raw materials costs, and continuing declines in employment due to productivity gains all contributed to keep inflation in check.

Personal consumption expenditures on clothing expanded sharply at the end of 1992 and the beginning of 1993, following declines the two prior years, but then tapered off somewhat around mid-year. Despite the second-half slowdown, constant-dollar personal consumption expenditures for clothing expanded at a faster rate than total consumption expenditures and at a much faster pace than other nondurable spending. (Usually, toward the beginning of an economic recovery, nondurable spending lags behind purchases of durable goods, such as autos and appliances, that had been postponed during the recession.)

Retail sales of apparel and accessory stores in mid-1993 were running about 5 percent higher than in 1992. This was slightly less than the previous year's increase but well ahead of the 1991 pace. Retail inventories increased in 1992 and, at mid-year 1993, were about 9 percent above mid-year 1992. Weather disasters may have contributed to the inventory buildup in 1993. The ratio of inventories to sales in 1993 rose for the first time in 6 years.

Because labor is such a significant cost component in apparel manufacturing, producers in low-wage developing countries enjoy a significant cost advantage over U.S. producers, creating intense competition and downward pressure on profits. In addition, consumers persisted in searching for value, buying more sale merchandise in department stores and shifting some purchasing to discount and factory outlet stores. Apparel manufacturers continued to shift sourcing out of the country, most recently to the Caribbean, Central America, or South America. Major companies produced an estimated 70 percent of their sales in U.S. plants in 1993.

Structurally, the domestic industry is made up of a few large companies and many small and medium-size firms. According to one study, in 1993, the larger apparel firms appear to have become more diversified, accounting for 75 percent of apparel sales and all of the growth in volume. The divergence between the performance of the larger firms and many of the smaller companies widened, as profits of the latter group declined in 1992. As a result, the larger companies had most of the funds needed for reinvestment in the industry.

Men's and Boys' Apparel. Shipments of men's and boys' clothing, which outperformed the apparel industry in 1992, slowed somewhat in 1993, although boys' wear was still strong. Production of suits and coats continued the uptrend begun in 1992, following years of decline, helped by a move toward European styling, industry consolidation, and the general absence of inflation in this sector. Production of men's and boys' shorts, sweatshirts, knit sport shirts, and jeans also showed significant increases. Dress shirts, ties, and slacks recorded only slight gains. Dress shirt purchases were mainly for replenishment. Underwear shipments grew only slightly in value as a result of overproduction and price competition. Shipments of both men's and boys' sweaters continued to decline. In terms of sales, brand-name apparel recorded an above-average performance, but consumers generally looked for value.

Employment in men's and boys' outerwear fell in 1993, following the first increase in several years in 1992. Employment in the underwear segment, however, continued to expand. Hourly earnings grew faster than the industry average. Sharply expanding exports in both outwear and underwear accounted for a large portion of the growth in shipments.

Women's, Girl's, and Children's Apparel. Women's outerwear shipments outperformed the industry average in 1992 and 1993, partially because of a strong showing in exports. European women recently began buying more U.S. clothing, and now markets are opening up for high-status designer apparel in the Far East, including China. Employment in the women's outerwear sector continued to decline sharply, and earnings increases were below average, largely because of the heavy impact of imports on the women's apparel industry. Women's and children's underwear showed little change in shipments between 1992 and 1993.

Retail sales of women's apparel slowed somewhat in 1993, following a reasonable performance in 1992. The lackluster economic picture, coupled with a lack of significant fashion change, had a negative impact on sales. Designer apparel has been particularly hard hit as consumers turned more toward value in apparel purchases and discount pricing. Women's activewear, jeans, and skirts are the brightest spots in this segment of the apparel industry. Sweaters sales have been slow.

Girls' wear sales showed considerable strength in the beginning of 1993, following a good year in 1992. As with boys' wear, demographic trends have had a major impact on this segment of the market. More children have been born in recent years to older, better educated, and more affluent parents who tend to spend more money on them. Imports of girls' wear had little growth in 1993, but exports continued to make gains. Employment in girls' and children's wear manufacturers continued to decline steeply, while average hourly earnings increased modestly.

Environmental Issues. Apparel companies and their suppliers are embracing the "green" movement. Companies address environmental issues for a number of reasons, including concern for the earth, winning over those consumers who buy only environment-friendly products, or simply taking advantage of a popular movement. Among the rising trends in the industry are the use of organic cotton that is grown without pesticides; new low-impact dyeing methods and vegetable-based, nontoxic dyes; the use of cotton grown in natural shades of tan, brown, and green that needs no dyeing; and the use of respun fibers made from waste trimmings of textile mills or from old clothing that has been cleaned, shredded, and spun into new yarn.

INTERNATIONAL COMPETITIVENESS

The trade deficit in apparel products has been growing in recent years (Figure 1). It increased from $28 billion in 1992 to an estimated $30 billion in 1993, despite a 20 percent gain in exports and import growth of 9 percent, half the rate in 1992. The increase in the value of imports overwhelmed the export advance because imports continue to be substantially larger than exports in value terms.

Although the sewn products industry (SIC 23) is historically not export-oriented, manufacturers have increasingly turned their attention to overseas markets in recent years, rather than depend solely on the slow-growing U.S. market. Exports accounted for about 9 percent of product shipments in 1993, up from 4 percent in 1989. The depreciation in the exchange rate value of the dollar and the growing demand abroad for quality apparel and fabricated textile products contributed to the surge in exports the past several years. In 1993, exports, which were affected by depressed economic conditions in all the major apparel markets abroad, grew at the slowest rate in more than 4 years, but still managed a 20 percent gain. Some of the export growth consisted of shipments of garment parts for assembly abroad and subsequent reimport, but exports of finished apparel for sale in foreign markets increased sharply as well. Apparel components that are shipped to other countries for assembly and eventual return to the U.S. market under the HTSUS 9802 (previously 807) program receive preferential duty treatment. (The importer pays duty only on the value added abroad under this program.)

U.S. manufacturers have taken advantage of their reputation for high quality, U.S. Government-sponsored foreign trade fairs and export seminars, and long-term export strategies to expand their shipments abroad. Occasionally, modifications in design and fit are necessary to sell in foreign markets, but many customers are looking for the American look and ease of care and wearing. In addition to direct exports, greater numbers of U.S. retailers and catalog houses have established sales outlets in other countries to sell U.S. apparel products. Men's outerwear and home furnishings remain the largest export categories. Men's and boys trousers are the most important products exported to Japan, Canada, and the European Community (EC), followed

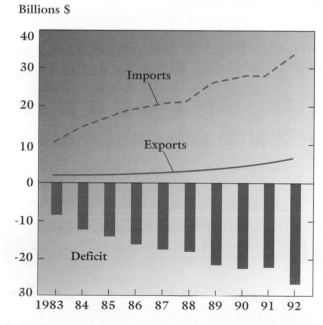

FIGURE 1 U.S. Trade Deficit Grows in Apparel and Fabricated Textile Products

Source: U.S. Department of Commerce, Bureau of the Census.

by men's and boys' knit shirts. Menswear and women's outwear exports recorded particularly steep increases in 1993. Children's wear and women's and children's underwear continue to make strong export gains.

Japan, the EC countries, and Canada are the largest customers for U.S. apparel, with steep gains in shipments the past few years. Sales of completed garments to Mexico also grew sharply. After the United States and Canada implemented a free trade agreement in 1989, the U.S. share of the Canadian apparel market grew sharply. During the same period, however, the U.S. share of the Mexican market dropped following liberalization of Mexican import barriers (Figure 2). If the recently negotiated North American Free Trade Agreement (NAFTA) is implemented, U.S. exports are expected to regain some of their lost share in the Mexican market. Under the agreement, virtually all trade restrictions would be eliminated within 10 years, some much sooner. The expected benefit to the Mexican economy resulting from implementation of the agreement should boost demand for U.S. exports there.

Although small in value, exports of U.S. clothing have been growing rapidly to Eastern Europe and China, where demand is increasing for upscale goods, status symbols, and Western looks. U.S. manufacturers that are able to take advantage of opportunities in these countries should experience a surge in their exports. Exports of cut apparel parts to the Caribbean Basin countries have advanced sharply in recent years, particularly to the Dominican Republic and Costa Rica, which are the leading participants in HTSUS 9802 garment assembly operations.

The largest suppliers of imports of apparel products to the U.S. market in 1993 were China, Hong Kong, South Korea, and Taiwan, but only China increased its shipments of sewn products to the United States. These four countries accounted for nearly half of U.S. imports of all apparel and fabricated textile products. In 1993, the largest import increases, in addition to those from China, were from countries with

FIGURE 2 United States Share of Canadian and Mexican Apparel Imports

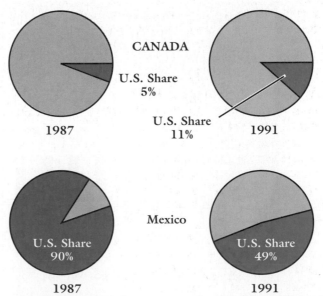

Source: U.S. Department of Commerce, Office of Textiles and Apparel.

large HTSUS 9802 operations, namely Mexico, the Dominican Republic, and the Philippines. Arrivals of HTSUS 9802 goods now account for 15 percent of all apparel imports, up from 9 percent as recently as 1990. Apparel imports in 1993 grew at less than half the 19 percent rate in 1992 (Tables 4 and 5).

LONG-TERM PROSPECTS

Factors contributing to a favorable long-term outlook for the industry include the growing recovery in economic activity and consumer spending, and continuing growth in exports and investment. Environmental and health issues and the need for further technological advancement and quality improvement are among the challenges facing the industry.

The continuing recovery of the economy should lead to a pickup in consumer confidence. The decline in consumer debt is expected to level off, while new housing starts should gain momentum. These factors should lead to increases in consumer spending on apparel and fabricated textile products. Favorable demographic and technological trends also should help boost shipments.

During the next several years, the U.S. apparel marketplace will become even more competitive, with more overseas producers vying with U.S. manufacturers for shares of the market. More U.S. companies also are shifting assembly operations to other countries to lower their production costs. U.S. producers can use new technology to strengthen the industry's productivity, quality, flexibility,

TABLE 4 U.S. Trade Patterns in 1992 Apparel and Other Textile Products SIC 23 (*In millions of dollars, percent*)

EXPORTS	VALUE	SHARE	IMPORTS	VALUE	SHARE
Canada and Mexico	1,427	30.9	Canada and Mexico	2,436	7.5
European Community	493	10.6	European Community	1,600	4.9
Japan	521	11.3	Japan	210	0.6
East Asia NICs	103	2.2	East Asia NICs	17,942	55.3
South America	198	4.3	South America	656	2.0
Other	1,883	40.7	Other	9,619	29.6
World Total	4,625	100.0	World Total	32,462	100.0

TOP FIVE COUNTRIES	VALUE	SHARE		VALUE	SHARE
Mexico	943	20.4	China	5,447	16.8
Dominican Republic	570	12.3	Hong Kong	4,336	13.4
Japan	521	11.3	South Korea	2,728	8.4
Canada	484	10.5	Taiwan	2,539	7.8
Costa Rica	277	6.0	Mexico	1,945	6.0

Source: U.S. Department of Commerce: Bureau of the Census; International Trade Administration.

TABLE 5   U.S. Trade Patterns in 1992 Apparel SIC 231, 232, 233, 234, 235, 236, 237, 238
(*In millions of dollars, percent*)

EXPORTS			IMPORTS		
	VALUE	SHARE		VALUE	SHARE
Canada and Mexico	909	24.4	Canada and Mexico	1,529	5.1
European Community	415	11.1	European Community	1,418	4.8
Japan	490	13.2	Japan	101	0.3
East Asia NICs	56	1.5	East Asia NICs	16,870	56.7
South America	153	4.1	South America	612	2.1
Other	1,701	45.7	Other	9,235	31.0
World Total	3,723	100.0	World Total	29,765	100.0

TOP FIVE COUNTRIES					
	VALUE	SHARE		VALUE	SHARE
Mexico	662	17.8	China	4,823	16.2
Dominican Republic	556	14.9	Hong Kong	4,301	14.4
Japan	490	13.2	South Korea	2,619	8.8
Costa Rica	275	7.4	Taiwan	2,302	7.7
Canada	247	6.6	Dominican Republican	1,233	4.1

Source: U.S. Department of Commerce: Bureau of the Census; International Trade Administration.

and response time, thereby becoming stronger competitors in the international area.

Exports will continue to provide a significant share of the growth in shipments of apparel products, even though U.S. firms will still encounter stiff challenges from foreign competitors. When major industrialized economies expand more rapidly, the favorably valued U.S. dollar should help companies increase sales abroad of quality U.S. goods. U.S. manufacturers should continue to take advantage of export opportunities in countries such as Japan, Canada, and Mexico, where trade barriers have been reduced. A successful conclusion to the NAFTA agreement should lead to increased opportunities south of the border, and may serve as a model for similar agreements with other Latin American countries. The increased economic integration of the European market is expected to benefit U.S. exporters by eliminating national barriers to trade. In addition, the economic and political reforms in Eastern Europe and the newly independent states of the former Soviet Union may create additional opportunities for U.S. exports and investment in the apparel sector.

W. L. GORE & ASSOCIATES, INC.—1994

FRANK SHIPPER
Salisbury State University
CHARLES MANZ
Arizona State University

On July 26, 1976, Jack Dougherty, a newly minted MBA from the College of William and Mary was bursting with resolve and dressed in a dark blue suit. This was his first day of work at W. L. Gore & Associates. He presented himself to Bill Gore, shook hands firmly, looked him in the eye, and said he was ready for anything. What happened next was one thing for which Jack was not ready. Gore replied, "That's fine, Jack, fine. Why don't you look around and find something you'd like to do." Three frustrating weeks later he found that something, a machine that laminates the company's patented GORE-TEX membrane to fabric. By 1982, Jack had become responsible for all advertising and marketing in the fabrics group. This story is part of the folklore that is heard over and over about Gore, a well-known company based in Newark, Delaware.

In 1994, the orientation process for new employees at Gore (302-738-4880) is slightly more structured. New Associates (employees) take a journey through the business as they settle into their positions, regardless of the specific position for which they are hired. (In this case, the word Associate is used and capitalized because in W. L. Gore & Associates' literature the word is always used instead of employees and is capitalized. In fact, the case writers were told that Gore "never had 'employees'—always 'Associates.' ") A new sales Associate in the Fabric Division may spend six weeks rotating through different areas before beginning to concentrate on sales and marketing. Among other things the new hire may learn is how GORE-TEX fabric is made, what it can and cannot do; how Gore handles customer complaints; and how it makes investment decisions.

Anita McBride related her first on-the-job experience at W. L. Gore & Associates in a similar way. She had previously worked for a structured organization. When she came to Phoenix, her sponsor said, "Well, here's your office—it's a wonderful office—and Here's your desk," and walked away. Anita thought, "Now what do I do."

> She continues: you know? I was waiting for a memo or something, or job description. Finally, after another month, I was so frustrated, I felt, "What have I gotten myself into?" And so I went to my sponsor and said "What the heck do you want from me? I need something from you." And he said, "If you don't know what you're supposed to do, examine your commitment and opportunities."

W. L. Gore is a loosely structured, privately-held company, with worldwide sales of about $950 million. Sales are derived from four divisions: 1) Gore-Tex Consumer and Technical Fabrics, 2) Electronic Products, 3) Medical Products, and 4) Industrial Products.

HISTORY

W. L. Gore & Associates is a company that evolved from the late Wilbert L. Gore's experiences personally, organizationally, and technically. He was born in Meridian, Idaho, near Boise in 1912. By age six, he had become an avid hiker in the Wasatch Mountain Range in Utah. In those mountains, at a church camp, he met Genevieve, his future wife. She is called Vieve by everyone. In 1935, they got married and became partners. He would make breakfast and she would make lunch. The partnership lasted a lifetime.

Wilbert, called Bill by everyone, received a bachelor of science degree in chemical engineering in 1933 and a masters of science in Physical Chemistry in 1935 from the University of Utah. He began his professional career at American Smelting and Refining in 1936. He moved to Remington Arms Company in 1941. He moved once again to E. I. DuPont de Nemours in 1945. He held positions as research supervisor and head of operations research. While at DuPont, he worked on a team to develop applications for polytetrafluoroethylene, frequently referred to as PTFE in the scientific community and known as "Teflon" by DuPont's consumers (it is known by consumers under other names from other companies). On this team, Bill felt a sense of excited commitment, personal fulfillment, and self-direction. He followed the development of computers and transistors and felt that PTFE had the ideal insulating characteristics for use with such equipment.

Bill tried a number of ways to make a PTFE-coated ribbon cable without success. A breakthrough came in his home basement laboratory. He was explaining the problem to his son, Bob. Bob saw some PTFE sealant tape made by 3M and asked his father, "Why don't you try this tape?" His father then explained to his son that everyone knows you cannot bond PTFE to itself. Bob went on to bed.

Bill Gore remained in his basement lab and proceeded to try what everyone knew would not work. At about 4 A.M., he woke up his son waving a small piece of cable around saying excitedly, "It works, it works." The following night, father and son returned to the basement lab to make ribbon cable coated with PTFE.

For the next four months, Bill Gore tried to persuade DuPont to make a new product—PTFE coated ribbon cable. After talking to a number of key decision-makers, it became clear that DuPont wanted to remain a supplier of raw materials and not a fabricator.

Bill began to discuss with his wife, Vieve, the possibility of starting their own insulated wire and cable business. On January 1, 1958, their wedding anniversary, they founded W. L. Gore & Associates, Inc. The basement of their home served as their first facility. After finishing dinner on their anniversary, Vieve turned to her husband of 23 years and said, "Well, let's clear up the dishes, go downstairs, and get to work." They viewed this as another partnership.

Bill Gore was 45 years old with five children to support when he left DuPont. He left behind a career of 17 years, and a good and secure salary. To finance the first two years of the business, the Gores mortgaged their house and took $4,000 from savings. All of their friends told them not to do it.

The first few years were rough. In lieu of salary, some of their employees accepted room and board in the Gore home. At one point, 11 Associates were living and working under one roof. The order, which was almost lost, that put the company on a profitable footing came from the City of Denver's water department. One afternoon, Vieve answered a phone call while sifting PTFE powder. The caller indicated that he was interested in the ribbon cable, but wanted to ask some technical questions. Bill was out running some errands. The caller asked for the product manager. Vieve explained that he was out at the moment. Next he asked for the sales manager and finally, the president. Vieve explained that they were also out. The caller became outraged and hollered, "What kind of company is this anyway?" With a little diplomacy, the Gores were able eventually to secure an order for $100,000. This order put the company over the hump and it began to take off.

W. L. Gore & Associates has continued to grow and develop new products primarily derived from PTFE, including their best known product, GORE-TEX fabric. GORE-TEX is a registered trademark of W. L. Gore & Associates. In 1986, Bill Gore died while backpacking in the Wind River Mountains of Wyoming. Until the time of his death, he had functioned as chairman. His son, Bob, assumed the presidency, a position he continues to occupy. Vieve remains as the only other officer, secretary-treasurer.

THE OPERATING COMPANY

W. L. Gore & Associates is a company without titles, hierarchy, or any of the conventional structures associated with enterprises of its size. The titles of president and secretary-treasurer are used only because they are required by the laws of incorporation. In addition, Gore's corporate mission is simply stated as "make money and have fun." When questioned about the absence of formal policies and a code of ethics typical of other corporations, an Associate states, "The company belief is that its four basic operating principles cover ethical practices required of people in business, and Gore will not tolerate illegal practices." Gore's management style has been referred to as un-management. The organization has been guided by Bill's experiences on teams at DuPont and has evolved through his study of how people view their full potential.

In 1965, W. L. Gore & Associates was a thriving and growing company with a facility on Paper Mill Road in Newark, Delaware, and about 200 Associates. One warm Monday morning in the summer, Bill Gore was taking his usual walk through the plant. All of a sudden, he realized that he did not know everyone in the plant. The team had become too big. As a result, the company instituted a policy that no facility will have over 150–200 Associates. Gore's expansion policy is "Get big by staying small." The purpose of maintaining small plants is to accentuate a close-knit and interpersonal atmosphere.

Today, W. L. Gore & Associates consists of 44 plants worldwide with over 5,860 Associates. In some cases, the plants are clustered together on the same site as in Flagstaff, Arizona, where four plants are located on the same site. Twenty-seven Gore plants are in the United States and 17 are overseas. Gore's overseas plants, located in Scotland, Germany, France, and Japan manufacture electronics, medical, industrial, and fabric products.

Gore electronic products are found in unconventional places where conventional products will not do. In space shuttles, for example, Gore microwave assemblies withstand the heat of ignition and the cold of space. In addition, Gore's signal transmission products are found in the world's fastest companies. Gore cables are underground, in oil drilling operations, and undersea, on submarines that require superior microwave signal equipment and no-fail cables that can survive high pressure. The Gore Electronic Products Division has a history of anticipating future customer needs with innovative products. Gore electronic products are well known in industries such as oil exploration and robotics for their ability to last under adverse conditions.

In the medical arena, GORE-TEX expanded PTFE is considered an ideal replacement for human tissue in many situations. In patients suffering from cardiovascular disease, the diseased portion of arteries is often replaced by tubes of expanded PTFE that are strong, biocompatible, and able to carry blood at arterial pressures. Gore has a dominant share in this market. Other Gore medical products include patches for soft tissue repairs such as aneurysms and hernias. GORE-TEX sutures allow for tissue attachment and offer the surgeon silklike handling coupled with extreme strength. In 1985, W. L. Gore & Associates, Inc., won Britain's Prince Philip Award for Polymers in the Service of Mankind. The award recognized especially the life-saving achievements of the Gore medical products team.

The industrial products division produces a number of products including sealants, filter bags, cartridges, clothes, and coatings. These products tend to have specialized and critical applications. Gore's reputation for quality appears to influence the industrial purchasers of these products.

The Gore Fabrics Division supplies laminates to licensed manufacturers of ski wear; running suits; footwear; gloves; hunting, fishing, golfing, and cycling garments; and foul-weather gear. Firefighters and U.S. Navy pilots wear GORE-TEX fabric gear as do some Olympic athletes. The U.S. Army has adopted a total garment system built around a GORE-TEX fabric component.

GORE-TEX membrane for fabric application has 9 billion pores randomly dotting each square inch and is feather light. Each pore is 700 times larger than a water vapor molecule, yet thousands of times smaller than a water droplet. Wind and water cannot penetrate the pores, but perspiration can escape. As a result, fabrics bonded with GORE-TEX membrane are waterproof, windproof, and breathable. The laminated fabrics bring protection from the elements to a variety of products—from survival gear to high-fashion rain wear. Recently, other manufacturers, including 3M, have brought out products to compete with GORE-TEX fabrics. Gore, however, continues to have a commanding share of this market.

Bill Gore knew that products alone do not make a company. He wanted to avoid smothering the company in thick layers of formal "management." He felt that they stifled individual creativity. As the company grew, he devised an innovative way to assist new Associates to get started and to guide their progress. This was seen as particularly important when it came to compensation. W. L. Gore & Associates has developed what they call their "sponsor" program to meet these needs. When people apply to Gore, they are initially screened by personnel specialists as in most companies. For those who meet the basic criteria, there are interviews with other Associates. Before anyone is hired, an Associate must agree to be their sponsor. The sponsor is to take a personal interest in the new Associate's contributions, problems, and goals. The sponsor is both a coach and an advocate. The sponsor guides the new associate's progress, helping and encouraging, dealing with weaknesses and concentrating on strengths. Sponsoring is not a short-term commitment. All Associates have sponsors and many have more than one. When individuals are hired initially, they will have a sponsor in their immediate work area. If they move to another area, they will have a sponsor in that work area.

Because the sponsoring program looks beyond conventional views of what makes a good Associate, some anomalies occur in the hiring practices. Bill Gore has proudly told the story of "a very young man" of 84 who walked in, applied, and spent five very good years with the company. The individual had 30 years of experience in the industry before joining Gore. His other Associates had no problems accepting him, but the personnel computer did. It insisted that his age was 48. The individual success stories at Gore come from diverse backgrounds.

An internal memo by Bill Gore described three kinds of sponsorship expected and how they might work as follows:

1. The sponsor who helps a new Associate *get started* on his job. Also, the sponsor who helps a present Associate get started on a new job (starting sponsor).

2. The sponsor who sees to it that the Associate being sponsored *gets credit* and recognition for contributions and accomplishments (advocate sponsor).

3. The sponsor who sees to it that the Associate being sponsored is *fairly paid* for contributions to the success of the enterprise (compensation sponsor).

A single sponsor can perform any one or all three kinds of sponsorship. A sponsor is a friend and an Associate. All the supportive aspects of the friendship are also present. Typically, two Associates advocate for each other.

In addition to the sponsor program, Gore Associates are asked to follow four guiding principles:

1. Try to be fair.
2. Use your freedom to grow.
3. Make your own commitments, and keep them.
4. Consult with other Associates prior to any action that may adversely affect the reputation or financial stability of the company.

The four principles are often referred to as fairness, freedom, commitment and waterline. The waterline terminology is drawn from an analogy to ships. If someone pokes a hole in a boat above the waterline, the boat will be in relatively little real danger. If someone, however, pokes a hole below the waterline, the boat is in immediate danger of sinking.

The operating principles were put to a test in 1978. By this time the word about the qualities of GORE-TEX fabric were being spread throughout the recreational and outdoor markets. Production and shipment had begun in volume. At first a few complaints were heard. Next, some of the clothing started coming back. Finally, much of the clothing was being returned. The trouble was that the GORE-TEX fabric was leaking. Waterproof was one of the two major properties responsible for GORE-TEX fabric's success. The company's reputation and credibility were on the line.

Peter W. Gilson who led Gore's fabric division says, "It was an incredible crisis for us at that point. We were really starting to attract attention; we were taking off—and then this." Peter and a number of his Associates in the next few months made a number of those below the waterline decisions.

First, the researchers determined that oils in human sweat were responsible for clogging the pores in the GORE-TEX fabric and altering the surface tension of the membrane. Thus, water could pass through. They also discovered that a good washing could restore the waterproof property. At first this solution known as the "Ivory Snow Solution" was accepted.

A single letter from "Butch," a mountain guide in the Sierras, changed the company's position. Butch wrote how he had been leading a group and, "My parka leaked and my life was in danger." As Gilson says, "That scared the hell out of us. Clearly our solution was no solution at all to someone on a mountain top." All of the products were recalled. As Gilson says, "We bought back, at our own expense, a fortune in pipeline material. Anything that was in the stores, at the manufacturers, or anywhere else in the pipeline."

In the meantime, Bob Gore and other Associates set out to develop a permanent fix. One month later, a second-generation GORE-TEX fabric had been developed. Gilson, furthermore, told dealers that if at any time a customer returned a leaky parka, they should replace it and bill the company. The replacement program alone cost Gore roughly $4 million.

ORGANIZATIONAL STRUCTURE

Bill Gore refers to the structure as a lattice organization, as portrayed in Exhibit 24–1. The characteristics of this structure are:

1. Direct lines of communication—person to person—with no intermediary
2. No fixed or assigned authority
3. Sponsors, not bosses

EXHIBIT 24-1 W. L. Gore's Lattice Structure

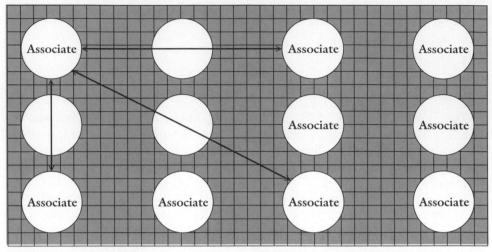

Source: W. L. Gore Associates.

4. Natural leadership defined by followership
5. Objectives set by those who must "make them happen"
6. Tasks and functions organized through commitments.

The structure within the lattice is described by the people at Gore as complex and evolves from interpersonal interactions, self-commitment to group-known responsibilities, natural leadership, and group-imposed discipline.

Bill Gore once explained this structure by saying, "Every successful organization has an underground lattice. It's where the news spreads like lightning, where people can go around the organization to get things done." Another description of what is occurring within the lattice structure is constant cross-area teams—the equivalent of quality circles going on all the time. When a puzzled interviewer told Bill that he was having trouble understanding how planning and accountability worked, Bill replied with a grin, "So am I. You ask me how it works—every which way."

One thing that might strike an outsider in the meetings and the other places in the Gore organization is the informality and amount of humor. Meetings tend to be only as long as necessary. Words such as "responsibilities" and "commitments," are, however, commonly heard. This in an organization that seems to take what it does very seriously, but its members do not take themselves too seriously.

Gore, for a company of its size, may have the shortest organizational pyramid. The pyramid consists of Bob Gore, son of co-founders Bill and Vieve Gore, as president and CEO and Vieve, Bill Gore's widow, as secretary-treasurer. All the other members of the Gore organization are referred to as Associates. Words such as "employees," "subordinates," and "managers" are taboo in the Gore culture.

Gore does not have managers, it has leaders. Bill Gore described in an internal memo the kinds of leadership and the role of leadership as follows:

1. The Associate who is recognized by a team as having a special knowledge, or experience (for example, this could be a chemist, computer expert, machine operator, salesman, engineer, lawyer). This kind of leader gives the team *guidance in a special area*.

2. The Associate the team looks to for coordination of individual activities in order to

achieve the agreed upon objectives of the team. The role of this leader is to persuade team members to *make the commitments* necessary for success (commitment seeker).

3. The Associate who proposes necessary objectives and activities and seeks agreement and team *consensus on objectives.* This leader is perceived by the team members as having a good grasp of how the objectives of the team fit in with the broad objective of the enterprise. This kind of leader is often also the "commitment seeking" leader in 2. above.

4. The leader who evaluates relative contribution of team members (in consultation with other sponsors), and reports these contribution evaluations to a compensation committee. This leader may also participate in the compensation committee on a relative contribution and pay and *reports changes in compensation* to individual Associates. This leader is then also a compensation sponsor.

5. The leader who coordinates the research, manufacturing, and marketing of one product type within a business, interacting with team leaders and individual Associates who have commitments regarding the product type. These leaders are usually called *product specialists.* They are respected for their knowledge and dedication to their product.

6. *Plant leaders* who help coordinate activities of people within a plant.

7. *Business leaders* who help coordinate activities of people in a business.

8. *Functional leaders* who help coordinate activities of people in a "functional" area.

9. *Corporate leaders* who help coordinate activities of people in different businesses and functions and who try to promote communication and cooperation among all Associates.

10. *Intrapreneuring Associates* who *organize new teams* for new businesses, new products, new processes, new devices, new marketing efforts, new or better methods of all kinds. These leaders invite other Associates to "sign up" for their project.

It is clear that leadership is widespread in our lattice organization and is continually changing and evolving. The fact that leaders are frequently *also* sponsors should not confuse the different activities and responsibilities.

Leaders are not authoritarians, managers of people, or supervisors who tell us what to do or forbid us doing things; nor are they "parents" to whom we transfer our own self-responsibility. However, they do often advise us of the consequences of actions we have done or propose to do. Our actions result in contributions, or lack of contributions, to the success of our enterprise. Our pay depends on the magnitude of our contributions. This is the basic discipline of our lattice organization.

Many other aspects of the company are arranged along egalitarian lines. The parking lot does not have reserved parking spaces except for customers and the handicapped. There is only one area in each plant in which to eat. The lunchroom in each new plant is designed to be a focal point for Associate interaction. As Dave McCarter of Phoenix explains, "The design is no accident. A lunchroom in Flagstaff has a fireplace in the middle. We want people to like being here." The locations of the plants are also no accident. Sites are selected based on transportation access, a nearby university, beautiful surroundings, and climate appeal. Land cost is never a primary consideration. McCarter justifies the selection by stating, "Expanding is not costly in the long-run. The loss of money occurs by stymieing people into a box."

Not all people function well under such a system, especially initially. For those accustomed to a more structured work environment, there are adjustment problems. As Bill Gore said, "All our lives, most of us have been told what to do, and some people don't know how to respond when asked to do something—and have the very real option of saying no—on their job. It's the new Associate's responsibility to find out what he or she can do for the good of the operation." The vast majority of the new Associates, after some initial floundering, adapt quickly.

For those who require more structured working conditions and cannot adapt, Gore's flexible work place is not for them. According to Bill, for those few, "It's an unhappy situation, both for the Associate and the sponsor. If there is no contribution, there is no paycheck."

As Anita McBride, an Associate in Arizona, says, "It's not for everybody. People ask me do we have turnover, and yes we do have turnover. What you're seeing looks like utopia, but it also looks extreme. If you finally figure the system, it can be real exciting. If you can't handle it, you gotta go. Probably by your own choice, because you're going to be so frustrated."

In rare cases, an Associate "is trying to be unfair," in Bill's own words. In one case, the problem was chronic absenteeism and in the other, the individual was caught stealing. "When that happens, all hell breaks loose," said Bill Gore. "We can get damned authoritarian when we have to."

In the early years, Gore & Associates has faced a number of unionization drives. The company neither tries to dissuade an Associate from attending an organizational meeting nor retaliate when flyers are passed out. Each attempt has been unsuccessful. None of the plants has been organized to date. Bill believed that no need existed for third-party representation under the lattice structure. He asked the question, "Why would Associates join a union when they own the company? It seems rather absurd." Overall, Associates appear to have responded positively to the Gore system of un-management and un-structure. Bill estimated the year before he died, 1985, that "The profit per Associate is double" that of DuPont.

The lattice structure is not without its critics. As Bill Gore stated, "I'm told from time to time that a lattice organization can't meet a crisis well because it takes too long to reach a consensus when there are no bosses. But this isn't true. Actually, a lattice, by its very nature works particularly well in a crises. A lot of useless effort is avoided because there is no rigid management hierarchy to conquer before you can attack a problem."

The lattice has been put to the test on a number of occasions. For example, in 1975, Dr. Charles Campbell, the University of Pittsburgh's senior resident, reported that a GORE-TEX arterial graft had developed an aneurysm. An aneurysm is a bubblelike protrusion that is life-threatening. If it continues to expand, it will explode. Obviously, this kind of problem has to be solved quickly and permanently.

Within only a few days of Dr. Campbell's first report, he flew to Newark to present his findings to Bill and Bob Gore and a few other Associates. The meeting lasted two hours. Dan Hubis, a former policeman, who had joined Gore to develop new production methods, had an idea before the meeting was over. He returned to his work area to try some different production techniques. After only three hours, a potentially damaging problem to both patients and the company was resolved. Furthermore, Hubis's redesigned graft has gone on to win widespread acceptance in the medical community. Today there are more than 3 million implants worldwide.

Other critics have been outsiders who had problems with the idea of no titles. Sarah Clifton, an Associate at the Flagstaff facility, was being pressed by some outsiders as to what her title was. She made one up and had it printed on some business cards—SUPREME COMMANDER. When Bill Gore learned what she did, he loved it and recounted the story to others.

Another critic, Eric Reynolds, founder of Marmot Mountain Works, Ltd., of Grand Junction, Colorado, and a major Gore customer, said "I think the lattice has its problems with the day-to-day nitty-gritty of getting things done on time and out the door. I don't think Bill realizes how the lattice system affects customers. I mean after you've established a relationship with someone about product quality, you can call up one day and suddenly find that someone new to you is handling your problem. It's frustrating to find a lack of continuity." He goes on to say, "But I have to admit that I've personally seen at Gore remarkable examples of people coming out of nowhere and excelling."

Bill Gore was asked a number of times if the lattice structure could be used by other companies. His answer was, "No. For example, established companies would find it very difficult to use the lattice. Too many hierarchies would be destroyed. When you remove titles and positions and allow people to follow who they want, it may very well be someone other than the person who has been in charge. The lattice works for us, but it's always evolving. You have to expect problems." He maintained that the lattice system works best when put in place in start-up companies by dynamic entrepreneurs.

RESEARCH AND DEVELOPMENT

Research and development, (R & D), like everything else at Gore, is unstructured. R & D takes place in teams in every business throughout the company. The company holds hundreds of patents, although most inventions are held as proprietary or trade secrets. Innovations come from Associates throughout the organization—managment, sales, R & D teams, and so forth. Bill Gore believed that all people had it within themselves to be creative.

The best way to understand how research and development works is to see how innovation has previously occurred at Gore. In 1969, the wire and cable division was facing increased competition. Bill Gore began to look for a way to straighten out the PTFE molecules. As he said, "I figured out that if we ever unfold those molecules, get them to stretch out straight, we'd have a tremendous new kind of material." He thought that if PTFE could be stretched, air could be introduced into its molecular structure. The result would be greater volume per pound of raw material without affecting performance. Thus, fabricating costs would be reduced and the profit margins would be increased. Going about this search in a scientific manner with his son, Bob, the Gores heated rods of PTFE to various temperatures and then slowly stretched them. Regardless of the temperature or how carefully they were stretched, the rods broke.

Working alone late one night in 1969 after countless failures, Bob, in frustration, yanked at one of the rods violently. To his surprise, it did not break. He tried it again and again with the same results.

The next morning Bob demonstrated his breakthrough to his father, but not without some drama. As Bill Gore recalled, "Bob wanted to surprise me, so he took a rod and stretched it slowly. Naturally, it broke. Then he pretended to get mad. He grabbed another rod and said, 'Oh the hell with this,' and gave it a pull. It didn't break—he'd done it." The new arrangement of molecules changed not only the wire and cable division, but led to the development of GORE-TEX fabric and what is now the largest division at Gore, plus a host of other products for medical, industrial, and electronic applications.

Initial field-testing of GORE-TEX fabric was conducted by Bill and Vieve in the summer of 1970. Vieve made a hand-sewn tent out of patches of GORE-TEX fabric. They took it on their annual camping trip to the Wind River Mountains in Wyoming. The very first night in the wilderness, they encountered a hail storm. The hail tore holes in the top of the tent, but the bottom filled up like a bathtub from the rain. As

Bill Gore stated, "At least we knew from all the water that the tent was waterproof. We just needed to make it stronger, so it could withstand hail."

The second largest division began on the ski slopes of Colorado. Bill was skiing with his friend Dr. Ben Eiseman of the Denver General Hospital. As Bill Gore told the story, "We were just to start a run when I absentmindedly pulled a small tubular section of GORE-TEX out of my pocket and looked at it. 'What is that stuff?' 'Got no idea.' I said. 'Well give it to me,' he said, 'and I'll try it in a vascular graft on a pig.' Two weeks later, he called me up. Ben was pretty excited. 'Bill,' he said 'I put it in a pig and it works. What do I do now?' I told him to get together with Pete Cooper in our Flagstaff plant and let them figure it out." Now hundreds of thousands of people throughout the world walk around with GORE-TEX vascular grafts.

Every Associate is encouraged to think, experiment, and follow a potentially profitable idea to its conclusion. For example, at a plant in Newark, Delaware, a machine that wraps thousands of feet of wire a day was designed by Fred L. Eldreth, an Associate with a third-grade education. The design was done over a weekend. Many other Associates have contributed their ideas through both product and process breakthroughs.

Without a research and development department, innovations and creativity work very well at Gore & Associates. The year before he died, Bill Gore claimed that "The creativity, the number of patent applications and innovative products is triple" that of DuPont.

ASSOCIATE DEVELOPMENT

As Ron Hill, an Associate in Newark, said, Gore "will work with Associates who want to advance themselves." Associates are offered many in-house training opportunities. They do tend to be technical and engineering focused because of the type of organization Gore is, but the company also offers in-house programs in leadership development. In addition, the company has cooperative programs with Associates to obtain training through universities and other outside providers. Gore will pick up most of the costs for the Associates. The emphasis in Associate development as in many parts of Gore is that the Associate must take the initiative.

PRODUCTS

Associates in four divisions organize themselves around opportunities in electronics, medical, industrial, and fabrics, as stated earlier. The Electronic Products Division produces cable assemblies and advanced materials for various demanding applications in aerospace, defense, computers, and telecommunications. Gore electronic and industrial application products have earned a reputation for unequaled reliability. Most of the wire and cable is used where conventional cables cannot operate. For example, Gore wire and cable assemblies were used in the space shuttle *Columbia* because they would stand the heat of ignition and the cold of space. Gore wire was used in the moon vehicle shuttle that scooped up samples of moon rocks and Gore's microwave coaxial assemblies have opened new horizons in microwave technology. Back on earth, the electronic wire products help make the world's fastest computers possible because electrical signals can travel through them at up to 93 percent of the speed of light. Because of the physical properties of the GORE-TEX material used in their construction, the electronic products are used extensively in defense systems, electronic switching for telephone systems, scientific and industrial instrumentation, microwave communications, and industrial robotics. Reliability is a watchword for all Gore products.

In medical products, reliability is literally a matter of life and death. GORE-TEX expanded PTFE is an ideal material used to repair the damage caused by cardiovascular disease. When human arteries are seriously damaged or plugged with deposits that interrupt the flow of blood, the diseased portions can often be replaced with GORE-TEX grafts. GORE-TEX vascular grafts and patches are not rejected by the body because the patient's own tissues grow into the graft's open porous spaces. GORE-TEX vascular grafts come in many sizes to restore circulation in nearly all areas of the body. They have saved limbs from amputation and saved lives. Some of the tiniest grafts relieve pulmonary problems in newborns. GORE-TEX expanded PTFE is also used to help people with kidney disease. Associates have developed a variety of surgical reinforcing membranes, known as GORE-TEX cardiovascular patches. Another medical product developed by Gore is a nonshredding dental floss.

Through the waterproof, breathable GORE-TEX fabrics division, Gore technology has traveled to the roof of the world on the backs of renowned mountaineers. GORE-TEX fabric is waterproof and windproof, yet breathable. Those features have qualified GORE-TEX fabric as essential gear for mountaineers and adventurers facing extremely harsh environments. The PTFE membrane blocks wind and water, but allows sweat to escape. That makes GORE-TEX fabric ideal for anyone who works or plays hard. Backpackers have discovered that a single lightweight GORE-TEX fabric shell will replace a poplin jacket and a rain suit, and dramatically out perform both. Skiers, sailors, runners, golfers, bicyclists, hunters, fishermen, and other outdoor enthusiasts have also become big customers of garments made of GORE-TEX fabric. General sportswear, as well as women's fashion footwear and handwear of GORE-TEX fabric, are as functional as they are beautiful. Boots and gloves, both for work and recreation, are waterproof and breathable thanks to GORE-TEX liners. GORE-TEX garments are even becoming standard items issued to many military personnel. Wetsuits, parkas, pants, headgear, gloves, and boots, keep the troops warm and dry in foul weather missions. Other demanding jobs also require the protection of GORE-TEX fabric because of its unique combination of chemical and physical properties.

The GORE-TEX fibers products, like the fabrics, end up in some pretty tough places. The outer protective layer of the NASA's spacesuit is woven from GORE-TEX fibers. They are impervious to sunlight, chemicals, heat, and cold. They are strong and uniquely resistant to abrasion.

Industrial filtration products, such as GORE-TEX filter bags, reduce air pollution and recover valuable solids from gases and liquids more completely than alternatives; they also do it more economically. They could make coal-burning plants virtually smoke free, contributing to a cleaner environment.

The Industrial Products Division also produces joint sealant, a flexible cord of porous PTFE that can be applied as a gasket to the harshest industrial applications, sealing them to prevent leakage of corrosive chemicals, even at extreme temperature and pressure. Steam valves packed with GORE-TEX valve stem packing are guaranteed for the life of the valve when used properly.

GORE-TEX microfiltration products are used in medical devices, pharmaceutical manufacturing, and chemical processing. These membranes remove bacteria and other microorganisms from air or liquids, making them sterile and bacteria free.

COMPENSATION

Compensation at W. L. Gore & Associates takes three forms—salary, profit-sharing, and an Associates' Stock Ownership Program (ASOP). Gore's ASOP is similar legally to an ESOP (Employee Stock Ownership Plan). Gore simply does not use the word "employee" in any of its documentation. Entry-level salary is in the middle for comparable jobs. According to Sally Gore, daughter-in-law of the founder, "We do not feel we need to be the highest paid. We never try to steal people away from other companies with salary. We want them to come here because of the opportunities for growth and the unique work environment." Associates' salaries are reviewed at least once a year and more commonly twice a year. The reviews are conducted by a compensation team for most workers in the facility in which they work. Their pay is proportional to their contributions to Gore's success. Positions do not have designated pay levels. Associates are ranked in relation to each other within similar job areas. The sponsors for all Associates act as their advocate during this review process. Prior to meeting with the compensation committee, the sponsor checks with customers or whoever uses the results of the person's work to find out what contribution has been made. In addition, the evaluation team will consider the Associate's leadership ability, willingness to help others to develop to their fullest.

Besides salaries, W. L. Gore & Associates has profit-sharing and ASOP plans for all Associates. Profit sharing typically occurs twice a year, but is dependent on profitability. The amount is also dependent on time in service and annual rate of pay. In addition, the firm buys company stock equivalent to 15 percent of the Associates' annual income and places it in an (ASOP) retirement fund. Thus, an Associate becomes a stockholder after being at Gore for one year. Bill wanted every Associate to feel that they themselves are the owners.

The principle of commitment is seen as a two-way street. W. L. Gore & Associates tries to avoid layoffs. The company uses a system of transfers as attrition within a plant or cluster of plants when faced with downsizing.

MARKETING STRATEGY

Gore's marketing strategy is based on making the determination that it can offer the best valued products to a marketplace, that people in that marketplace appreciate what it manufactures, and that Gore can become a leader in that area of expertise. The operating procedures used to implement the strategy follow the same principles as other functions at Gore.

First, the marketing of a product revolves around a leader who is referred to as a "product champion." According to Dave McCarter, "You marry your technology with the interests of your champions as you've got to have champions for all these things no matter what. And that's the key element within our company. Without a product champion you can't do much anyway, so it is individually driven. If you get a person interested in a particular market or a particular product for the marketplace, then there is no stopping them."

Second, a product champion is responsible for marketing the product through commitments with sales representatives. Again, according to Dave McCarter, "We have no quota system. Our marketing and our sales people make their own commitments as to what their forecasts are. There is no person sitting around telling them that that is not high enough, you have to increase it by 10 percent, or whatever somebody feels is necessary. You are expected to meet your commitment, which is your forecast, but nobody is going to tell you to change it. . . . There is no order of command, no chain involved. These are groups of independent people who come together to make unified commitments to do something and sometimes when they can't make those agreements . . . you may pass up a market place, but that's OK because there's much more advantage when the team decides to do something. . . ."

Third, the sales representatives are on salary. They are not on commission. They participate in the profit-sharing and ASOP plans in which all other Associates participate.

In the implementation of its marketing strategy, Gore relies on cooperative and word-of-mouth advertising. Cooperative advertising is especially used to promote GORE-TEX fabric products. Those products are sold through a number of clothing manufacturers and distributors, including Apparel Technologies, Lands End, Austin Reed, Timberland, Woolrich, North Face, Grandoe, and Michelle Jaffe. Gore engages in cooperative advertising because the Associates believe positive experiences with any one product will carry over to purchases of other and more GORE-TEX fabric products. Apparently, this strategy is paying off. Richard Zuckerwar, President of The Grandoe Corporation, said about his company's introduction of GORE-TEX gloves, "Sports activists have had the benefit of GORE-TEX gloves to protect their hands from the elements. . . . With this handsome collection of gloves . . . you can have warm, dry hands without sacrificing style."

The power of informal marketing techniques extends beyond consumer products. According to Dave McCarter, "In the technical end of the business, company reputation probably is most important. You have to have a good reputation with your company." He went on to say that without a good reputation, a company's products would not be considered seriously by many industrial customers. In other words, the sale is often made before the representative calls. Using its marketing strategies, Gore has been very successful in securing a market leadership position in a number of areas ranging from waterproof outdoor clothing to vascular grafts.

FINANCIAL INFORMATION

Gore is a closely held private corporation. Financial information is as closely guarded as proprietary information of products and processes.

According to Shanti Mehta, an Associate, Gore's return on assets and sales rank it among the top 10 percent of the Fortune 500 companies. According to another source, W. L. Gore & Associates is working just fine by any financial measure. It has had 33 straight years of profitability and positive return on equity. The compounded growth rate for revenues at W. L. Gore & Associates from 1969 to 1989 was over 18 percent discounted for inflation. In 1969, total sales were about $6 million and in 1989, $600 million. As illustrated in Exhibit 24–2, Gore's total sales for 1992 climbed to over $740 million. This growth has been financed without any debt.

CONCLUSION

Gore was founded on the principles of self-management, empowerment, and smallness. The principle that leaders are defined only by the presence of followers is observed whenever possible. Gore's culture allows leaders who have not been successful to be reabsorbed into the team with relatively little pain.

EXHIBIT 24-2 Growth of Gore's Sales vs. Growth of Gross Domestic Product

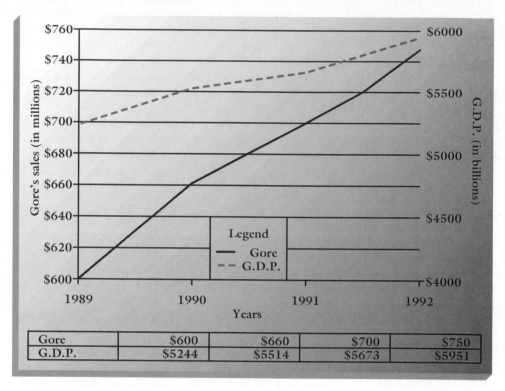

Gore	$600	$660	$700	$750
G.D.P.	$5244	$5514	$5673	$5951

Gore is unique in many ways. To what extent could their uniqueness work effectively in other organizations? Which elements of Gore's uniqueness do you feel should be adopted by other companies?

BIBLIOGRAPHY

Aburdene, Patricia, and John Nasbitt. *Re-inventing the Corporation*. New York: Warner Books, 1985.

Angrist, S. W. "Classless Capitalist." *Forbes,* May 9, 1983, pp. 123–4.

Franlesca, L. "Dry and Cool." *Forbes,* August 27, 1984, p. 126.

Hoerr, J. "A company where everybody is the boss." *Business Week,* April 15, 1985, p. 98.

Levering, Robert. *The 100 Best Companies to Work for in America,* Chapter on W. L. Gore & Associates, Inc. Reading, MA: Addison-Wesley, 1984.

McKendrick, Joseph. "The Employees as Entrepreneur. " *Management World,* January 1985, pp. 12–13.

Milne, M. J. "The Gorey Details." *Management Review,* March 1985, pp. 16–17.

Posner, B. G. "The first day on the job." *Inc.,* June 1986, pp. 73–75.

Price, Kathy. "Firm Thrives Without Boss." *AZ Republic,* February 2, 1986.

Rhodes, Lucien. "The Un-manager." *Inc.,* August 1982, p. 34.

Simmons, J. "People Managing Themselves: Un-management at W. L. Gore Inc." *The Journal for Quality and Participation,* December 1987, pp. 14–19.

"The Future Workplace." *Management Review,* July 1986, p.22–23.

Trachtenberg, J. A. "Give Them Stormy Weather." *Forbes,* March 24, 1986, Vol. 137, No. 6, pp.172–174.

Ward, Alex. "An All-Weather Idea." *The New York Times Magazine,* November 10, 1985, Sec. 6.

Weber, Joseph. "No Bosses. And Even 'Leaders' Can't Give Orders." *Business Week,* December 10, 1990, pp. 196–197.

"Wilbert L. Gore." *Industry Week,* October 17, 1983, pp. 48–49.

NIKE INC.—1994

The athletic shoe industry has grown dramatically in the last several years, but experts predict that athletic shoe sales will increase only slightly in the next few years. Consumer trend watchers believe that the youth market now demands brands such as Tiva sandals and Doc Marten's work boots instead of branded athletic shoes. In addition, there is some evidence that consumers are purchasing casual shoes and moderately priced athletic shoes instead of branded athletic shoes. As a result, competition in an already competitive industry will become more intense. Headquartered in Beaverton, Oregon, Nike's (503-641-6453) CEO Philip Knight says media experts have tried to explain the athletic shoe industry in oversimplified terms:

> Although to some it may appear to be a simple industry, success within it is complicated by the huge human factor. The industry defies automation. It is not a single product model, nor a single manager, nor one ad, nor a single celebrity, not even a single innovation that is the key to Nike. It is the people and their unique and creative way of working together, that has brought our shareholders earnings increases of over $140 million during the last two years.

For the fiscal year 1993, revenues at Nike increased by 15 percent to $3.9 billion, and net income increased by 11 percent to $365 million. Philip Knight hopes to maintain his company's competitive advantage through the 1990s by marketing athletic shoes, clothing, and accessories around the world and by making a few acquisitions that will strengthen the company's core businesses. If Nike is to live up to its namesake "the goddess of victory," Knight and his team of workers will have to stay ahead of competitors in the marathon race for dominance in the athletic shoe industry.

HISTORY

Philip Knight, a dedicated long-distance runner, developed a plan to make low-cost running shoes in Japan and to sell them in the United States as part of his work toward an MBA degree at Stanford University. After graduation, Knight teamed up with Bill Bowerman, his former track coach at the University of Oregon to make his plan a reality. Since Bowerman's hobby was making handcrafted lightweight running shoes, his expertise was very valuable to entrepreneur Knight. In 1964, Bowerman and Knight each contributed $500 and started Blue Ribbon Sports. Knight negotiated with a Japanese athletic shoe manufacturer, Onitsuka Tiger Company, to manufacture the shoes that Bowerman had designed. Blue Ribbon Sports shoes gained a cult following among serious runners because Knight distributed the shoes, called Tigers, at track meets.

In 1971, Blue Ribbon Sports received a trademark on its Swoosh logo, and they introduced the brand name Nike that same year. Blue Ribbon Sports parted ways with Onitsuka Tiger in 1972 and contracted with other Asian manufacturers to produce the company's shoes. Blue Ribbon Sports officially changed its name to Nike in 1978. During the late 1970s and early 1980s, Nike researchers used their technological expertise to develop several types of athletic shoes that revolutionized the industry. The company became more and more successful every year with profits increasing steadily during this time.

In 1984, after five years of 44 percent annual growth, Nike missed the emerging market for aerobic shoes. The company had concentrated its efforts on an unsuccessful line of casual shoes. Reebok took the lead in the athletic shoe industry when it began selling large numbers of its fashion-oriented aerobic shoes to women.

Nike stock prices decreased by 60 percent in 1984 and between 1983 and 1985 profits declined by 80 percent. Some analysts suggested that the decreases in stock prices and profits were the fault of managers who became complacent after the firm's early success. During the early 1980s, Philip Knight focused his attention on international operations and left daily decision making to other managers. Other top managers switched from job to job and this led to poor coordination between the design, marketing, and production efforts of the company. An excess inventory of 22 million pairs of shoes in 1985 forced Nike to cut prices to reduce the inventory. This excess in inventory also caused Nike to release some of its manufacturing capability in the Far East. Much of this capacity was picked up by Reebok. After Nike lost the top spot in the industry, it had to lay off 350 employees in 1986.

Knight took several steps to try to reestablish Nike's dominance in the industry. He created small management teams to focus on narrow markets. He also put a stop to the job changing of top executives. New advertising campaigns were developed that stressed the technology of the shoes. Focus groups were used to determine customers' athletic shoe needs. The company also began to add touches of fashion, including color, to its many new products. All of these changes helped Nike regain a slight leadership position in the industry in 1988.

In 1988, Nike purchased New Hampshire-based Cole-Haan for $64 million. The subsidiary has several brand names including Country, Sporting, Classic, Bragano, and Cole-Haan. A new footwear category, Tensile Air was introduced in 1990. The Tensile Air is a dress shoe with the Nike air-cushioning system. Nike's casual footwear business grew 16 percent the following year, lead by Cole-Haan. Nike also acquired the Cole-Haan Accessories Company in 1990, a distributor of premium quality belts, braces, and small leather goods.

PRESENT CONDITIONS

Nike sells athletic shoes, accessories, and clothing for men, women, and children. The company's products are sold to approximately 15,000 retail accounts in the United States including department stores, footwear stores, and sporting goods stores. Nike also sells its products through independent distributors, licensees, and subsidiaries in 80 countries around the world. Nike passed the $1 billion sales mark in Europe in 1993 and had sales of $178 million in the Asia/Pacific Region in 1993. Distribution rights for Australia and New Zealand were acquired by Nike in 1992. Nike is also moving aggressively into Latin American countries. Domestic and international revenues for Nike are shown in Exhibit 25–1.

Nike has diversified its operations in several different ways in recent years. In 1990, Nike opened a retail store called NikeTown in Portland, Oregon. A second NikeTown was opened in 1992 in Chicago. Nike does not plan to become a major retail force, but believes that these stores help educate consumers about the breadth of Nike products. In addition, Nike began experimenting with the store-in-a-store concept when it opened its first Nike Concept Shop in Macy's Union Square in San Francisco in 1992. Nike acquired Tetra Plastics, the manufacturer of the plastic film in Nike's air sole shoes, in 1991 for $37.5 million. In 1993, Nike purchased a cap making company called Sports Specialties.

EXHIBIT 25-1 Nike, Inc., domestic and international revenue (In thousands of dollars)

	1992	PERCENT CHANGE	1991	PERCENT CHANGE	1990	PERCENT CHANGE
			YEAR ENDED MAY 31			
Domestic footwear	$1,747,600	4	$1,676,400	22	$1,368,900	29
Domestic apparel	361,400	11	325,700	22	266,100	28
Other brands	161,900	16	139,400	16	120,500	26
Total United States	2,270,900	6	2,141,500	22	1,755,500	29
International footwear	867,500	33	651,700	76	369,400	32
International apparel	266,800	27	210,400	91	110,300	58
Total International	1,134,300	32	862,100	80	479,700	38
Total Nike	$3,405,200	13	$3,003,600	34	$2,235,200	31

Source: Nike, Inc., Form 10–k, 1993.

COMPETITION

The athletic shoe industry has grown from $2 billion to almost $10 billion at wholesale from 1985 to 1993. Nike, Reebok, Keds, and L.A. Gear are the top four sellers of athletic shoes in the United States. (See Exhibit 25–2.)

Some of the other two dozen competitors in the industry include Adidas, Puma, New Balance, K-Swiss, Kangaroo, Converse, and British Knights. The most intense competition has been among three of the industry leaders: Nike, L.A. Gear, and Reebok. The secret to success for these three competitors is that they contract for the manufacture of shoes to low-wage factories in Far East countries. This strategy allows each company to concentrate on marketing, image, and research and development.

Reebok International, Ltd. Reebok designs and develops athletic shoes and clothing worldwide. Reebok sells 175 models of shoes in 450 different color combinations for aerobics, tennis, fitness, running, basketball, cycling, volleyball, and walking. The company also owns Avia, a line of high performance athletic shoes. The company has diversified its offerings recently to include more types of casual shoes, sports clothing, and other types of athletic shoes. Some examples of these new products include Reebok Outdoor shoes, City Trails (women's hiking-style shoes), F-16 (men's leather casual shoes), BlackTop basketball shoes, and the Shaquille O'Neal shoe. In 1992, Reebok discontinued its Rockport, Boston Whaler, and Ellesse brands.

In the early 1980s, Reebok sold aerobic shoes primarily to women, but by the mid-1980s large numbers of men were buying Reebok shoes. Men now account for 45 percent of Reebok sales. The company's shoes are designed to make a fashion statement and are marketed to build on this image. Reebok CEO Paul Fireman believes that "Reebok is basically about freedom of expression." During 1992 Reebok opened three retail stores called Reebok Station with locations in Boston, Santa Monica, and New York City. Reebok has been successful in selling its

EXHIBIT 25-2 U.S. Branded Athletic Footwear Industry—Market Share

	1991	1992	1993(E)	1994(E)
Nike	29%	30%	32%	32%
Reebok	23	24	24	25
Keds	6	6	6	5
L.A. Gear	9	5	5	6
ASICS	3	4	5	6
Converse	3	4	4	5
Fila	1	3	3	3
Adidas	3	3	3	3
Avia	2	2	2	2
K-Swiss	2	2	2	2
Others (a)	19	17	14	11
Total U.S. Revenue (millions)	$5,789	$6,048	$6,050	$6,100
Percent change	4.8%	4.5%	0.0%	0.8%

(E) Estimate.

(a) Category includes over 15 companies with the largest single share equaling 1.9% in 1991 and 1.7% in 1992.

Source: Sporting Goods Intelligence (12/92); Kidder, Peabody & Co. Inc. estimates.

products to international markets. In 1992, foreign operations were 34 percent of total sales and 38 percent of net income. Selected financial information for Reebok is shown in Exhibit 25–3.

L.A. Gear, Inc. L.A. Gear markets athletic shoes, leisure shoes, casual clothing, and accessories (sport bags, hats, watches). The company was formed in 1983 and went public in 1986. The company's products are marketed on fashion, but they are manufactured to look like they offer technology. In just five years of operation, the company became the number three seller of athletic shoes in the United States. (Presently, L.A. Gear is the number four seller of athletic shoes in the United States.) Selected financial information for L.A. Gear is included in Exhibit 25–4.

International Competition. Competition is increasing in Europe. Adidas, a German company, is the number one seller of athletic shoes in Europe. Nike and Reebok are second and third, respectively. Nike had a 21 percent share and Reebok a 16 percent share of the international market in 1992. Analysts believe that doing well in the European market is crucial to the continued success of companies in the athletic shoe industry. Nike sales in the European, Asian, and Latin American markets increased 24 percent to about $1.4 billion in 1992 (36 percent of Nike's worldwide revenue). Reebok's total international revenues were about $1 billion. Both Nike and Reebok hope to continue increasing their revenues in the international retail market. Adidas and Puma, the two top European-owned competitors, will be fighting to maintain their share of the competitive market for athletic shoes.

EXHIBIT 25-3 Reebok selected financial information (In millions of dollars except per-share amounts)

	1989	1990	1991	1992	1993
Gross Revenues	1,822.1	2,159.2	2,734.5	3,943.5	2,915.2
Net Income	175.0	176.6	234.7	249.4	224.4
Long-term Debt	111.3	105.8	170.4	116.0	111.0
Return on Equity (%)	20.7	17.7	28.5	30.0	26.7
Net Profit Margin (%)	9.6	8.1	8.6	8.4	7.6
Earnings Per Share	1.53	1.54	2.37	2.69	2.55

Note: Reebok International (617-341-5000) is based in Stoughton, Massachusetts.

EXHIBIT 25-4 L.A. Gear selected financial information (In millions of dollars except per-share amounts)

	1990	1991	1992	1993
Gross Revenues	819.6	619.2	430.2	410.1
Net Income	25.6	(46.6)	(56.6)	(30.9)
Long-term Debt	0.0	0.0	0.0	0.0
Return on Equity (%)	12.4	(35.3)	(64.7)	(45.4)
Net Profit Margin (%)	3.1	(7.5)	(13.1)	(7.5)
Earnings Per Share	1.28	(2.40)	(2.67)	(1.34)

Note: L.A. Gear (310-822-1995) is based in Los Angeles, California.

CHANGES IN THE ATHLETIC SHOE INDUSTRY

The athletic shoe industry has changed tremendously since "sneakers" were invented. In 1873, the "sneaker" was developed from India rubber and canvas material. Dunlop became the dominant seller of sneakers in 1938. Keds and PF Fliers dominated the children's market in the 1960s. Adult standard brands such as Adidas and Converse were well accepted by sports enthusiasts for years. When Nike entered the market in the late 1960s, the industry changed forever. In addition to new competition, life-styles began to change and companies began to contract manufacturing rather than invest in plant and equipment to manufacture their own products.

Changes in Life-style. The primary buyers of athletic shoes are between the ages of fifteen and thirty-four. Since the late 1970s, these buyers have become much more brand conscious. In addition, athletic shoes have replaced other casual shoes as the primary street shoe for many consumers. Less than 10 percent of the people who wear athletic shoes buy them for the sport for which they were intended. Some trend watchers believe that athletic shoe companies will have some difficulty selling their products to the youth market in the next few years because of the youth demand shift to work boots and sandals.

Large numbers of baby boomers are interested in staying fit and healthy and have changed their diet and increased their physical activity. However, only one adult in five (aged 25–55) exercises as much as twice a week. In the 1980s, people became obsessed with fitness, and by 1991 sales in the fitness equipment industry exceeded $30 billion. Presently only 10 percent of the U.S. adult population gets the surgeon general's recommended amount of exercise (twenty minutes of vigorous exercise, three times per week).

The number of people aged forty-five and older is expected to increase by 18 million during the 1990s. The years forty-five to fifty-four are generally the peak earning and spending years for adults. As the baby boomers move into this age group, they will demand more attention from consumer goods companies.

Contract Manufacturing. Many athletic shoe companies contract with manufacturing companies in the Far East to produce their shoes. Some of the countries that manufacture shoes for Nike, L.A. Gear, and Reebok include South Korea, Taiwan, China, Thailand, Malaysia, and Indonesia. The athletic shoe companies develop design specifications and new technology for the shoes in the United States and then send these to the factory to be produced.

Even with recent changes in exchange rates in these countries and tariffs of 8.5 percent to 37.5 percent, it is still very cost effective to have shoes made overseas. A shoe that costs approximately $14 to make will be sold wholesale for $25 to $30.

The primary advantage of foreign contract manufacturing is that no capital investment is required and the athletic shoe companies can operate with very little long-term debt. There are also several disadvantages to contract manufacturing. Some countries, such as Korea, that have produced large numbers of athletic shoes in the past are developing the expertise and contacts to begin producing more sophisticated electronics products and do not have the available capacity to continue producing athletic shoes. Some additional disadvantages of overseas production include labor unrest, political unrest, delays caused by shipping, and unreliability of quota systems (embargos).

NIKE INTERNAL FACTORS

Four primary internal factors for Nike include: superior research and development efforts for the company's products, marketing expertise, social responsibility, and financial returns.

Nike Research and Development. Nike spent approximately $20 million on product research, development, and evaluation in 1992. This surprisingly low figure allows Nike to keep on the cutting edge in technology because R and D in the athletic shoe industry is largely design innovation and does not require a large investment in equipment.

In 1980, the company formed the Nike Sport Research Laboratory (NSRL), which uses video cameras and traction testing devices to research several types of concerns including children's foot morphology, "turf toe," and apparel aerodynamics. In addition, NSRL evaluates ideas that have been developed by the Advanced Product Engineering (APE) group. APE is involved in long-term product development. Shoes arc created for five years in the future. This group developed cross-training shoes, the Nike Footbridge stability device, inflatable fit systems, and the Nike 180 air-cushioning system. Researchers make shoe molds in the model shop and evaluate the shoe tension and adhesion in the testing lab.

Nike continues to rely on superior technological developments to differentiate its products from competitors. The company presently sells approximately 300 models of athletic shoes in 900 styles for 24 different sports including basketball, tennis, cross-training, baseball, hiking, cycling, cheerleading, and windsurfing. Exhibit 25–5 indicates the major developments of Nike technology from 1964 to present.

Marketing. Since Nike does not actually produce shoes, the main focus of the company is creating and marketing the products. Nike positions its products as high-performance shoes designed with high-technology features. The general target market for Nike athletic shoes is males and females between eighteen and thirty-four years old.

Nike advertises its products in a variety of ways and targets its ads to specific groups or types of people. In 1992 Nike targeted women in its advertising for the first time since 1988. The "Instant Karma" ad campaign for women cost Nike approximately $12 million. Nike began a $20 million advertising campaign in Europe in 1993. The com-

EXHIBIT 25-5   Nike, Inc., Technological Developments

DATE	DEVELOPMENT	PURPOSE
1964	Lightweight shoe	Reduces weight for better performance
1975	"Waffle" sole shoe	High traction, lightweight
1979	Nike Air Sole	Air-cushioning system lessens the impact of the heel on pavement to prevent injuries
1987	Visible Air line (10 shoe models)	Gas-cushioning system prevents injury (window allows consumer to see the air bag)
	Cross-training shoe	Suitable for several different types of sports including running, baseball, and aerobics
1989	Air Pressure	Provides a tighter fit (pump shoe with a separate device to pump up the shoe)
1990	Air 180	Provides air-cushioning in heel and front of the shoe; heel cushion is 50 percent larger than previous models (consumer has a 180-degree view of the heel air bag)
	Built-in pump shoe	Provides a tighter fit, with the convenience of a built-in pump
1991	Huarache Fit Technology	Combination of neoprene and lycra spandex provides runners with a form-fitting, supportive, and lightweight shoe
1993	Air Max Cushioning technology	Provides 30 percent more cushioning

pany continues to spend advertising dollars on TV ads during professional and college sports events, prime time programs, and late night programs. Prime time ads are intended to reach a broad range of adults and late-night TV advertising is geared toward younger adults. Print media such as *Sports Illustrated, People, Runner's World, Glamour, Self, Tennis, Money, Bicycling,* and *Weight Watchers* are also very important in advertising Nike products. Nike has been successful in its attempts to build loyalty by licensing Nike gear to college sports teams. Some of the universities that made agreements to wear Nike gear during 1993 and 1994 include the University of Miami, Pennsylvania State University, University of Southern California, Florida State University, Duke University, University of Michigan, and University of Nevada-Las Vegas.

Some of the celebrity spokespersons for Nike include Michael Jordan, Andre Agassi, and Bo Jackson. Michael Jordan's Nike contract, to market the Air Jordan basketball shoe, is the most lucrative endorsement contract in sports. Agassi receives $2 million per year to endorse Nike athletic shoes and apparel, including the Challenge Court tennis shoe. Jackson is featured in Nike's cross-training advertisements. Several popular advertising campaigns are listed in Exhibit 25–6.

Nike opened a new 630,000 square foot apparel distribution center in Memphis in 1992 that is called Nike Next Day. Footwear is distributed from centers in Greenland, New Hampshire; Beaverton, Oregon; Wilsonville, Oregon; Yarmouth, Maine; and Memphis, Tennessee. The company operates a "Futures" ordering program that allows retailers to order up to six months in advance with a guarantee to receive their orders within a certain time period and at a certain price. However, retailers can receive apparel orders the next day if they place their orders by 7 PM the day before.

EXHIBIT 25-6   Nike, Inc., Advertisements

THEME	VISUAL IMAGE
"Hangtime"	Air Jordan basketball shoe is promoted featuring Michael Jordan and Spike Lee.
"Bo Knows"	The range of Nike shoes (20 different sport categories) is illustrated.
"Just Do It"	People from many walks of life are shown exercising in Nike shoes.
"Multiple Bo's"	Bo Jackson meets Sonny Bono and fourteen other Bo Jacksons who represent different sports.
"Announcers"	TV sports announcers discuss Nike shoe performance and breadth of product line. (Super Bowl XXIV)
"Rock and Roll Tennis"	Andre Agassi shows his tennis skills in rock-video format.
"Instant Karma"	Print campaign targets women.
"I am not a role model"	Charles Barkley says sports stars are not role models, but parents should be role models.
"Aerospace Jordan"	Cartoon character Bugs Bunny, Looney Tunes bad guy Marvin Martin, and Michael Jordan travel to Mars. (Super Bowl XXVII)
"Running," "Go Slow," "Aerobics"	A series of three TV ads for women stressing comfort and developing a sense of self.

Social Responsibility. Nike has received some criticism in the past few years regarding the contracting of the manufacturing of its shoes. Some consumers are concerned about the exploitive practices of managers in some Asian countries. A reporter for the *Portland Oregonian* stated that 6,700 Indonesian employees work in a plant where the temperature is 100 degrees and paint and glue smells are suffocating. To emphasize their concerns about companies that manufacture products overseas, the Made in America Foundation urged consumers to send their "old, dirty, smelly, worn-out Nikes" to Philip Knight, the Nike CEO. Operation PUSH (a Chicago civil rights organization) organized a boycott of Nike in 1990 in an attempt to force the company to increase its hiring of minorities.

Nike has developed several programs that show the company's concern about social responsibility issues. For example, Nike and the Boys and Girls Clubs of America began a program called the Kids Movement in 1993 to promote fitness among young people. Nike also provides funds for the Children's Television Workshop program *Ghostwriter,* a show that promotes literacy. The "Just Do It" corporate giving program provides funding for programs for young people who live in the inner-city. In addition to these programs, Nike demonstrates its concern for the environment by using recycled materials in the soles of its Air Escape outdoor shoe and plans to expand the technology to its entire shoe line.

Finance/Accounting. Nike, Inc., income statements and balance sheets for 1991 to 1993 are provided in Exhibits 25–7 and 25–8, respectively. These statements reveal increases for sales, income, assets, and shareholders' equity. Consolidated statements

EXHIBIT 25-7 NIKE, Inc., Consolidated Statement of Income *(In thousands, except per-share data)*

	YEAR ENDED MAY 31,		
	1993	1992	1991
Revenues	$3,930,984	$3,405,211	$3,003,610
Costs and expenses:			
Cost of sales	2,386,993	2,089,089	1,850,530
Selling and administrative	922,261	761,498	664,061
Interest	25,739	30,665	27,316
Other expense (income)	1,475	2,141	(43)
	3,336,468	2,883,393	2,541,864
Income before income taxes	594,516	521,818	461,746
Income taxes	229,500	192,600	174,700
Net income	$ 365,016	$ 329,218	$ 287,046
Net income per common share	$ 4.74	$ 4.30	$ 3.77
Average number of common and common equivalent shares	77,063	76,602	76,067

Source: Nike, Inc., *Annual Report,* 1993.

EXHIBIT 25-8 Nike, Inc., Consolidated Balance Sheet *(In thousands of dollars)*

	YEAR ENDED MAY 31,		
	1993	1992	1991
ASSETS			
Current Assets:			
Cash and equivalents	$ 291,284	$ 260,050	$ 119,804
Accounts receivable, less allowance for doubtful accounts of $19,447, $20,046 and $14,288	667,547	596,018	521,588
Inventories	592,986	471,202	586,594
Deferred income taxes	26,378	27,511	25,536
Prepaid expenses	42,452	32,977	26,738
Total current assets	1,620,647	1,387,758	1,280,260
Property, plant and equipment	571,032	497,795	397,601
Less accumulated depreciation	193,037	151,758	105,138
	377,995	346,037	292,463
Goodwill	157,894	110,363	114,710
Other assets	30,927	28,703	20,997
	$2,187,463	$1,872,861	$1,708,430
LIABILITIES AND SHAREHOLDERS' EQUITY			
Current Liabilities:			
Current portion of long-term debt	$ 52,985	$ 3,652	$ 580
Notes payable	108,165	105,696	300,364
Accounts payable	135,701	134,729	165,912
Accrued liabilities	138,563	134,089	102,088
Income taxes payable	17,150	42,422	45,792
Total current liabilities	452,564	420,588	614,736
Long-term debt	15,033	69,476	29,992
Non-current deferred income taxes	29,965	27,074	30,613
Other non-current liabilities	43,575	23,728	
Commitments and contingencies	—	—	—
Redeemable Preferred Stock	300	300	300
Shareholders' equity:			
Common Stock at stated value:			
Class A convertible—26,691, 26,919 and 27,438 shares outstanding	159	161	164
Class B—49,161, 48,591 and 47,858 shares outstanding	2,720	2,716	2,712
Capital in excess of stated value	108,451	93,799	84,681
Foreign currency translation adjustment	(7,790)	686	(4,428)
Retained earnings	1,542,486	1,234,333	949,660
	1,646,026	1,331,695	1,032,789
	$2,187,463	$1,872,861	$1,708,430

Source: Nike, Inc. *Annual Report*, 1992, 1993.

of Nike shareholders' equity and cash flow are shown in Exhibits 25–9 and 25–10 respectively; Exhibit 25–11 presents revenue data for 1991 to 1993.

FUTURE OUTLOOK

Even with limited growth and intense competition in the U.S. athletic shoe market, Nike is expected to perform well in the future. With its innovative marketing and advertising, it should remain a force in the industry. However, there is concern in the industry that consumers will become less brand loyal and begin purchasing moderately priced athletic shoes at discount stores instead of the higher priced Nike products. According to Philip Knight,

> Brands are powerful when they communicate underlying value. In our industry, and probably in other consumer products, consumers will not trade down if there is value and quality in the high end.

There is a tremendous opportunity in the international market for Nike. "In the United States, there are four people for every pair of Nikes; France has 11, Japan 50, and China 11,821. That's a lot of Air Jordans waiting to be sold."[1] The greatest potential growth area for Nike is in the overseas market. It seems that Nike truly lives by the credo they created—"Just Do It."

Consider the following questions regarding Nike's future:

1. Should Nike narrow its product line in athletic shoes?
2. What types of acquisitions would you suggest to Philip Knight for Nike?
3. Should Nike begin producing some of its own products?
4. How should Nike market its shoes internationally? Where?
5. What changes in product and advertising should the company pursue to appeal to the aging baby boomers?
6. How can Nike maintain a competitive advantage over L.A. Gear, Reebok, and Keds?

NOTES

1. Yang, Dori Jones, "Nike's New Trends," *Business Week*, p. 38.

BIBLIOGRAPHY

Arthur, Charles. "Fashions's Fancy Footwork." *Business*, July, 1990, pp. 86–88.

Benoit, Ellen. "Lost Youth." *Financial World*, September 20, 1988, pp. 28–31.

Clay, Bobby. "It is the Shoes." *Black Enterprise*, March 1993, pp. 82–86.

Gill, Penny. "Stores Let Shoes Shine." *Stores*, August 1992, p. 48.

Gould, Les. "How Nike Guarantees Next-Day Delivery to All Its Customers." *Modern Materials Management*, September 1992, pp. 53–55.

Lippert, Barbara. "Defining Women." *Adweek*, March 1, 1993, p. 28.

Lippert, Barbara. "Speed Freaks." *Adweek*, February, 1, 1993, p. 22.

"Nike." *Business and Society Review*, Winter 1993, p. 77.

Ostroff, Jeff. "Targeting the Prime-Life." *American Demographics*, January 1991, pp. 30–52.

Schnorbus, Paula. "Running On Air." *Marketing & Media Decisions*, March 1988, pp. 55–58.

"Where Nike and Reebok Have Plenty of Running Room." *Business Week*, March 11, 1991, pp. 56–60.

Yang, Dori Jones. "Nike's New Trends." *Business Week*, October 4, 1993, p. 38.

EXHIBIT 25-9 Nike, Inc., Consolidated Statement of Shareholders' Equity *(In thousands of dollars)*

	Common Stock				Capital In Excess Of Stated Value	Foreign Currency Translation Adjustment	Retained Earnings	Total
	Class A		Class B					
	Shares	Amount	Shares	Amount				
Balance at May 31, 1990	14,051	$168	23,435	$2,706	$78,582	$ 1,035	$701,728	$784,219
Stock options exercised			276	2	6,099			6,101
Conversion to Class B Common Stock	(393)	(4)	393	4				—
Two-for-one Stock Split October 5, 1990	13,780	—	23,754	—				—
Translation of statements of foreign operations						(5,463)		(5,463)
Net income							287,046	287,046
Dividends on Redeemable Preferred Stock							(30)	(30)
Dividends on Common Stock							(39,084)	(39,084)
Balance at May 31, 1991	27,438	164	47,858	2,712	84,681	(4,428)	949,660	1,032,789
Stock options exercised	214	1			9,118			9,119
Conversion to Class B Common Stock	(519)	(3)	519	3				—

EXHIBIT 25-9 *Continued*

| | Common Stock | | | | Capital In Excess Of | Foreign Currency | | |
| | Class A | | Class B | | Stated | Translation | Retained | |
	Shares	Amount	Shares	Amount	Value	Adjustment	Earnings	Total
Translation of statements of foreign operations						5,114		5,114
Net income							329,218	329,218
Dividends on Redeemable Preferred Stock							(30)	(30)
Dividends on Common Stock						(44,515)	44,515	
Balance at May 31, 1992	26,919	161	48,591	2,716	93,799	686	1,234,333	1,331,695
Stock options exercised			342	2	14,652			14,654
Conversion to Class B Common Stock	(228)	(2)	228	2				—
Translation of statements of foreign operations						(8,476)		(8,476)
Net income							365,016	365,016
Dividends on Redeemable Preferred Stock							(30)	(30)
Dividends on Common Stock						(7,790)	(56,833)	(56,833)
Balance at May 31, 1993	26,691	$159	49,161	$2,720	$108,451		$1,542,486	$1,646,026

Source: Nike, Inc., *Annual Report*, 1993.

EXHIBIT 25-10 Nike, Inc., Consolidated Statement of Cash Flows *(In thousands of dollars)*

YEAR ENDED MAY 31,	1993	1992	1991
Cash provided (used) by operations:			
Net income	$365,016	$329,218	$287,046
Income charges (credits) not affecting cash:			
Depreciation	60,393	47,665	34,473
Deferred income taxes and purchased tax benefits	4,310	8,222	(2,668)
Other non-current liabilities	19,847	9,992	4,769
Other, including amortization	12,951	9,355	5,626
Changes in certain working capital components:			
(Increase) decrease in inventory	(97,471)	115,392	(274,966)
Increase in accounts receivable	(62,538)	(74,430)	(119,958)
Increase in other current assets	(5,133)	(6,239)	(6,261)
(Decrease) increase in accounts payable,			
accrued liabilities and income taxes payable	(32,083)	(3,337)	83,061
Cash provided by operations	265,292	435,838	11,122
Cash provided (used) by investing activities:			
Additions to property; plant and equipment	(97,041)	(106,492)	(164,843)
Disposals of property, plant and equipment	5,006	4,065	1,730
Acquisition of subsidiaries:			
Goodwill	(52,003)	—	(31,482)
Net assets acquired	(25,858)	—	(6,081)
Additions to other non-current assets	(3,036)	(7,494)	(10,511)
Cash used by investing activities	(172,932)	(109,921)	(211,187)
Cash provided (used) by financing activities:			
Additions to long-term debt	1,536	45,901	5,149
Reductions in long-term debt including current portion	(5,817)	(3,467)	(9,974)
(Decrease) increase in notes payable	(2,017)	(194,668)	269,262
Proceeds from exercise of options	7,055	4,159	3,211
Dividends—common and preferred	(53,017)	(43,760)	(36,070)
Cash (used) provided by financing activities	(52,260)	(191,835)	231,578
Effect of exchange rate changes on cash	(8,866)	6,164	(2,158)
Net increase in cash and equivalents	31,234	140,246	29,355
Cash and equivalents, beginning of year	260,050	119,804	90,449
Cash and equivalents, end of year	$291,284	$260,050	$119,804
Supplemental disclosure of cash flow information:			
Cash paid during the year for:			
Interest (net of amount capitalized)	$ 20,800	$29,200	$ 27,200
Income taxes	235,200	184,100	159,900

Source: Nike, Inc., *Annual Report*, 1993.

EXHIBIT 25-11 Nike, Inc., Revenue and Assets by Geographic Areas *(In thousands of dollars)*

YEAR ENDED MAY 31,	1993	1992	1991
Revenues from unrelated entities:			
United States	$2,528,848	$2,270,880	$2,141,461
Europe	1,085,683	919,763	664,747
Other international	316,453	214,568	197,402
	$3,930,984	$3,405,211	$3,003,610
Inter-geographic revenues:			
United States	$ 3,583	$ 7,265	$ 9,111
Europe	—	—	—
Other international	9,350	9,076	11,892
	$ 12,933	$ 16,341	$ 21,003
Total revenues:			
United States	$2,532,431	$2,278,145	$2,150,572
Europe	1,085,683	919,763	664,747
Other international	325,803	223,644	209,294
Less inter-geographic revenues	(12,933)	(16,341)	(21,003)
	$3,930,984	$3,405,211	$3,003,610
Operating income:			
United States	$ 401,096	$ 356,589	$ 325,257
Europe	177,716	173,175	134,069
Other international	65,236	51,602	51,745
Less corporate, interest and other income (expense) and eliminations	(49,532)	(59,548)	(49,325)
	$ 594,516	$521,818	$ 461,746
Assets:			
United States	$1,347,507	$1,095,180	$1,156,091
Europe	429,660	453,794	370,104
Other international	128,080	79,862	94,212
Total identifiable assets	1,905,247	1,628,836	1,620,407
Corporate cash and eliminations	282,216	244,025	88,023
Total assets	$2,187,463	$1,872,861	$1,708,430

Source: Nike, Inc., *Annual Report,* 1993.

VALERIE PORIELLO,
ALLAN HOFFMAN,
BARBARA GOTTFRIED
Bentley College

"Rykä has a great story to tell. We are the only athletic footwear company that is exclusively for women, by women, and now supporting women."—Sheri Poe

It was the day after Christmas 1990 when Sheri Poe, president and chief executive officer of Rykä Inc. (617-762-9900), knew she was on the verge of the marketing break she'd been waiting for. Poe had sent several free pairs of Rykä athletic shoes to Oprah Winfrey. Now Poe was going to be featured as a successful female entrepreneur on Winfrey's popular talk-show, with a television viewing audience numbering in the tens of millions—almost entirely women. Rykä's new line of Ultra-Lite aerobic shoes had just begun to penetrate the retail market. Poe could not have planned for a better advertising spot than Winfrey tossing pairs of Rykä shoes into the studio audience exclaiming, "Can you believe how light these are?"

After the "Oprah" broadcast, the Ultra-Lite line became an overnight success. Lady Footlocker immediately put the Ultra-Lite shoe line in 200 stores, up from the 50 that had been carrying Rykä's regular line of athletic shoes. Retailers were swamped by consumer requests for Rykä products, and the sharp upturn in consumer demand quickly exhausted their inventories. It took Poe over three months to catch up with the orders. Many industry analysts believe that the shot in the arm provided by the Ultra-Lite sales literally saved the company.

Based in Norwood, Massachusetts, Rykä Inc. designs, develops, and markets athletic footwear for women, including aerobic, aerobic/step, cross-training, walk-run, and walking shoes. The company's products are sold all over the world in sporting goods, athletic footwear specialty, and department stores. As a new entrant in the highly competitive athletic footwear industry, the fledgling Rykä Corporation had no choice but to rely on low-budget "guerrilla marketing" tactics such as the "Oprah" show appearance. Since that time, however, Rykä has turned to more traditional marketing techniques such as radio and glossy magazine advertising. Rykä print ads appear regularly in *City Sports, Shape, American Fitness, Elle,* and *IDEA Today;* magazines that particularly target women aged 21-35, who care not just about how they look, but are serious about physical fitness.

Rykä today is a company in financial trouble. Net profits have been negative for the last several years. Perhaps a new mission is needed. Rykä's current mission statement is given below:

Rykä shoes are made for top performance. You'll find that Rykä shoes will help you look good and feel great, no matter how demanding your fitness program.

Rykä shoes are designed, engineered, and manufactured by women for women. Because a woman's needs in a comfortable, attractive, high-performance athletic shoe are different from a man's.

As you lace up for your first workout in your new Rykä shoes, you'll feel the difference. With every pair of Rykä shoes goes the positive energy of women who believe in other women.

Step forward with confidence, and be your best.

Rykä was organized in 1987, when it commenced operations. The company was cofounded by Martin P. Birrittella and his wife, Sheri Poe. Prior to founding Rykä, Birrittella had worked at Matrix International Industries as a vice president of sales and marketing from 1980 to 1986. At Matrix, he was responsible for developing and marketing footwear and health and fitness products, and has two patents pending for shoe designs that have been assigned to Matrix. From 1982 to 1985, Sheri Poe was national sales manager for Matrix. She then moved to TMC Group, a $15-million giftware maker based in New Hampshire, where she was national accounts manager from May 1986 to June 1987.

Sheri Poe is one of only two women CEOs in the state of Massachusetts. Poe admits being an exercise fanatic who really knew nothing about making athletic shoes when she cofounded Rykä. In 1986, Poe had injured her back in an aerobics class and was convinced that the injury had been caused by her shoes, which had never fit properly. After an exhaustive search for footwear that would not stress her body, Poe realized that many other women were probably having the same trouble as she was finding a shoe that really fit and decided to start her own women's athletic footwear company. She believed that rather than adapting men's athletic shoes for women, Rykä should design athletic shoes especially suited for women's feet and bodies. Rykä introduced its first two styles of athletic shoes in 1987 and began shipping the shoes a year later.

Poe had considerable difficulty obtaining venture capital to start a women's athletic shoe company. Potential investors questioned her ability to compete with industry leaders such as Nike and Reebok, given that she had no money and no retail experience—then turned down her requests for loans. Ironically, some of those same venture capitalists now call Poe to ask how they can get in on her $8 million business.

Since she couldn't get anything out of the venture capitalists, Poe leveraged her own house, then turned to family and friends to help finance the company. She also continued to search for more open-minded commercial investors and eventually discovered a Denver investment banker who was willing to do an initial public offering. Poe got a $250,000 bridge loan before the initial public offering—which happened to be about the time the stock market crashed in October 1987. Nevertheless, Rykä went public on April 15, 1988, and despite the unstable market, four million shares in the company were sold at one dollar each in less than a week. The Denver firm completed a second offering before failing. Poe then turned to Paulson Capital Corporation in Oregon for a third offering in 1990.

Sheri Poe believes that by having a woman president Rykä inspires other women to buy the company's products. As she points out, "we're the only company that can tell women that the person running the company is a woman who works out every day." Even Nike doesn't have a woman making all of its product decisions. Poe's image and profile is the most critical component in Rykä's marketing strategy. Rather than using professional models, Rykä's print advertisements feature Poe working out; and in the company's recent venture into television advertising spots, Poe is the company spokesperson. The caption on a recent ad for Rykä's 900-series aerobic shoes reads, "Our president knows that if you huff and puff, jump up and down, and throw your weight around you eventually get what you want," cleverly referring to Poe's own determination to succeed, and including her audience as coconspirators who know how hard it is for a woman to make it in the business world because they have "been there" themselves.

As part of Rykä's unique marketing strategy, Poe appears on regional television and radio shows throughout the country and has been interviewed by numerous magazines and newspapers. Feature articles on Poe and Rykä have appeared in *Entrepreneurial Woman, Executive Female,* and *Working Woman.* Poe has successfully worked the woman angle: she particularly appeals to today's working women because although she has become something of a celebrity, she considers herself a down-to-earth woman who also happens to be a successful executive, and a (divorced, and now remarried) mother. A *Boston Business Journal* article describes her as a CEO whose title "does not cramp [her] style. . . she eschews power suits for miniskirts and jeans, drives herself to work, and lets calls from her kids interrupt her meetings."

THE ATHLETIC FOOTWEAR INDUSTRY

The $11 billion athletic footwear industry is highly competitive. Three major firms control the market: Nike, Reebok, and L.A. Gear. Second string competitors include Adidas, Avia, Asics, and Converse. All of these companies have greater financial strength and more resources than Rykä. While Rykä's sales were $12.1 million in 1992, Nike's were $3.4 billion, Reebok's $3.0 billion, and L.A. Gear's $430 million.

Annual growth in the athletic footwear market has shrunk to approximately 4 percent and it is considered a mature market. Despite the subdued growth characteristics of the overall industry, however, a number of its submarkets are expanding via high specialization, technological innovation, and image and fashion appeal.

Product Specialization. The athletic footwear industry is divided into various submarkets by specialization. Product use categories include: basketball, tennis, running, aerobic, cross-training, walking, etc. Rykä competes only in the latter three markets: aerobic, walking, and cross-training shoes.

Aerobic Segment. The aerobic segment of the athletic shoe industry accounts for approximately $500 million in annual sales. Reebok pioneered the segment and continues to be the industry leader. The market is made up primarily of women and has grown rapidly in recent years. Rykä's number one market is aerobics; 80 percent of Rykä's sales are from the Ultra-Lite and step aerobic lines.

Walking Segment. The second major market Rykä competes in is the walking segment. This high-growth market is now the fourth largest product category in the athletic shoe industry. More than 70 million people walk for exercise and spend $2 billion annually on footwear. Reebok leads this market and is concentrating its marketing efforts on young women. Nevertheless, while the male and younger female walking markets have experienced some growth, the walking segment is primarily focused on women 45–55 years old. Ten percent of Rykä's sales are derived from its Series 500 walking shoe and the company expects the walking shoe segment to be its greatest growth category.

Cross-Training Segment. Rykä also competes in the cross-training segment of the athletic shoe market. Cross-training shoes are popular because they can be used for a variety of activities. Nike created this segment and maintains the lead in market share. Overall sales for the segment are currently at $1.2 billion, and growth is strong. Rykä earns 10 percent of its revenues from its cross-training shoes.

Technological Innovation. Reebok and Nike are fast moving toward the goal of identifying themselves as the most technologically advanced producers of performance shoes. Rykä understands that it must keep up with research and development to survive. Rykä has introduced its nitrogen footwear system, Nitrogen/ES—the "ES" stands for Energy Spheres. The system was developed over a two-year period by a design team with over 35 patents in shoe design and state-of-the-art composite plastics. The idea is that the ES ambient air compression spheres contain nitrogen microballoons that provide significantly more energy return than the systems of any of Rykä's major competitors. Consumer response to the Nitrogen/ES shoe was overwhelming, so Rykä has discontinued sales of a number of models that did not include this special feature.

Two patents were filed for the Nitrogen/ES System. One has been granted; the other is pending. Although patents are intended to provide legal protection, the cost of defending patents can be quite high. With the vast resources available to Rykä's competition, it would be easy for Reebok or Nike to adopt Rykä's technology at little or no risk of an infringement suit. Rykä's limited financial resources would disable them from enforcing their rights in an infringement action.

Fashion. Rykä has focused on performance rather than fashion because Poe believes that fashion-athletic footwear is susceptible to trends and the economy, but performance shoes will not be affected because women always need to protect their bodies. Nevertheless, a large segment of athletic footwear consumers purchase products based on looks rather than function. In fact, the fashion market is a mainstay of Rykä's major competitors, especially Reebok, the originators of the fashion aerobic shoe market; 80 to 90 percent of fashion aerobic shoe buyers do not participate in the sport.

Although Rykä shoes are as technologically advanced as Reebok, Nike or L.A. Gear's, they are often overlooked by fashion-conscious consumers unfamiliar with the Rykä name. Despite the fact that Rykä's sales have grown even during these recessionary times, retailers haven't always carried Rykä shoes because they prefer to stock only those brands which are easily recognizable. The lack of a nationally recognized name is a serious concern for any company; thus for Rykä, as for its competitors, expensive, leading edge advertising campaigns have played an essential part in its marketing initiatives.

A ROCKY START

Given the saturation of the athletic footwear market, athletic shoe companies need more than a good product to stay alive; they need powerful marketing and advertising. Rykä concentrates much of its energies on marketing. As a new manufacturer in an already crowded industry, Poe understands the possibility of being marketed right out of business by big competitors with deep pockets like Nike and Reebok. Rykä's approach is to offer similar products, but focus on the most cost-effective ways to reach a target market, thus carving out a niche that the industry giants have overlooked.

To protect a niche, it is critical to stay one step ahead of the competition. Unfortunately for Rykä, Poe had to learn this lesson the hard way. When the company was first founded, it tried unsuccessfully to challenge the brand name manufacturers in all product categories, including running, tennis, aerobics, walking, and cross-training shoes. However, given its limited capital and the huge advertising budgets of Reebok, Nike, and L.A. Gear, Rykä could not compete in all of these different markets at once. Instead, Rykä cut back and chose to focus on aerobic shoes, and, secondarily, on their walking shoe line. Thus, in addition to limiting product line breadth, Rykä has designed its marketing approach to attract a specific set of customers rather than a broad audience. Poe does not believe that Rykä has to be a giant to succeed. Rather, she contends that Rykä needs to maximize its ability to perform in a particular niche within a large industry.

A NEW DIRECTION

In the already-crowded athletic footwear industry, the various competitors are continually jockeying for a better market position and competitive edge. Currently, women are, and will probably continue to be, the fastest growing segment of the athletic footwear market. Women's athletic footwear accounts for 55 percent of Reebok's sales, 60 percent of Avia's, 45 percent of L.A. Gear's, and 17 percent of Nike's $2.2 billion in domestic sales. In recent years, Reebok and Nike have fought for the number one spot in the women's market, and Reebok initially prevailed; but in each of the past two years, Nike has posted a 30% growth in the market. This unparalleled growth in the women's athletic footwear market is the most important trend in the sporting goods industry today, and it is on this niche that Rykä is staking its future.

An important part of the Rykä mission stems from the fact that their shoes are specifically made for women. While the big name shoe companies were merely making smaller sizes of men's shoes made on men's lasts, Rykä developed a fitness shoe built specifically for women with a patented design for better shock absorption and durability. Rykä had a first mover advantage in this segment and had a sustained competitive advantage in that none of the other companies in the athletic shoe industry can boast having a business strategy focused on women. All other contenders have other lines or are concentrated in other niches. Ultimately, however, it is the Ultra-Lite midsole, Rykä's most significant and successful product advancement, that keeps Rykä up with its competition in its market. The Rykä Ultra-Lite aerobics shoe weighs 7.7 ounces or roughly 30 percent of the weight of a regular aerobic shoe. Within two months of its introduction in December 1990, the company had sold all of its Ultra-Lites at a unit price of $70 a pair (retail). It took three months before additional shoe orders could be filled. Some investment firms were concerned that Rykä might not be able to capitalize on the success of its new line given its difficulty keeping retailers supplied with sufficient quantities. Eventually, Rykä did lose some ground to Nike and Reebok—both of which quickly jumped into the lightweight aerobic shoe market. Despite the competition, however, Rykä's Ultra Lite lines are a success, accounting for close to 90 percent of its total sales today.

After establishing a solid foundation in the aerobics category, Rykä again turned its attention to product differentiation. Its current product line includes the Series 900 Aerobic/Step shoes, the Series 700 Aerobic shoes, the Series 800/Cross-Training shoes, and the Series 500 Walking shoes. To make sure its shoes were not perceived as "too specialized," Rykä designed the Aerobic Step 50/50 and a lightweight version of it, the Step-Lite 50/50, each of which can be worn for both high-impact and step aerobics.

Rykä also designed a dual purpose walk/run shoe, the 570, for women who complement their walking routine with running, but don't want to own shoes for every activity. Rykä is now considering entering the medical footwear market because an increasing number of podiatrists and chiropractors are recommending Rykä walking shoes to their patients.

THE RYKÄ ROSE FOUNDATION

The Rykä ROSE (Regaining One's Self Esteem) Foundation is a not-for-profit organization created by Sheri Poe to help women who have been the victims of violent crimes. The foundation was launched in 1992, and Poe herself personally pledged $250,000. Poe founded the ROSE Foundation because she was raped at age 19. The trauma resulting from the rape led to further suffering from bulimia. She sees herself as a survivor who needed to do something to help fellow victims, "For me, having a company that just made a product was not enough. I wanted to do something more."

Rykä has made a commitment to donate 7 percent of its pretax profits to the foundation and to sponsor special fund-raising events to help strengthen community prevention and treatment programs for women who are the victims of violent crimes. Rykä includes information on the foundation in brochures that are packaged with each box of shoes in the hope that its social conscience may favorably influence some consumers. But for Poe, it is more than a marketing ploy. She considers Rykä's financial commitment to the ROSE Foundation a natural extension of the company's commitment to women.

The foundation has created alliances with health clubs, nonprofit organizations, and corporations, in an effort to reach women directly with educational materials and programs. In addition, the ROSE Foundation funds a $25,000 grants program to encourage organizations to develop creative solutions to the widespread problem of violence against women. One of the foundation's beneficiaries, the National Victim Center, received an award of $10,000 to set up a toll-free (800) telephone number for victims and their families through which they can obtain immediate information, referrals, and other types of assistance.

Poe hopes that the foundation will act as a catalyst for coalition-building to help stop violence against women. But she also envisions the foundation as a means of involving retailers in marketing socially-responsible programs directly to women. Lady Foot Locker has taken advantage of this opportunity and became the first retailer to join forces with the ROSE Foundation. In October 1993, Lady Foot Locker conducted a two-week promotional campaign in their 550 United States stores in conjunction with the ROSE Foundation. The retailer distributed free education brochures and held a special sweepstakes contest to raise awareness about the issue of violence against women. Customer response was overwhelmingly positive, and Lady Foot Locker is considering a future partnership with the ROSE Foundation. Foot Locker, Champs and Athletic X-press have also expressed interest in the foundation.

MVP Sports, a New England retailer, has also participated in Rykä's activities to help stop violence against women. The company, which operates eight stores in the New England area, sponsored a two-week information-based campaign featuring Sheri Poe that included radio, TV, and newspaper advertisements. In addition, Doug Barron, president of MVP Sports, was so impressed with the concept and progressive thinking of the Rykä ROSE Foundation that he decided his company would donate $2 to the foundation for each pair of Rykä athletic shoes sold during the 1992 holiday season. Poe sees MVP Sports' support as an important first step toward actively involving retailers in Rykä's efforts to help prevent violence against women and is reaching out to other retailers who, she hopes, will follow suit.

Poe considers Rykä and its foundation unique. As she sees it, the company has a great story to tell. It is the only athletic footwear company that is exclusively for women, by women, and now supporting women—"the first athletic shoe with a 'soul.'" And Poe is banking on her hunch that the foundation will appeal to Rykä customers who appreciate the idea that their buying power is helping women less fortunate than they are.

Nevertheless, Poe's choice to make Rykä a socially responsible company right from the beginning, rather than waiting until the company is fully established, has had consequences for its financial status. Some industry analysts have suggested that Rykä would be better off funneling any extra cash back into the company until it is completely solvent, and its product lines and their name recognition are automatic. But others argue that the reputation Rykä has garnered as an ethical company, as concerned about social issues as about the "bottom line," effectively appeals to kind-hearted women consumers. For them, the ROSE Foundation is worth in "good press" whatever it has cost the company in terms of actual investment dollars, because the company has effectively carved out a niche that speaks on many different levels to women's ethical and consumer concerns.

MARKETING

Rykä's promotional strategy is aimed at creating both brand awareness and sales at the retail level. By garnering the support of professional sports organizations early on, Rykä acquired instant name recognition in a variety of key audiences. Rykä entered into a six-figure, eight-year licensing agreement with the U.S. Ski Team which permitted Rykä to market its products as the official training shoes of the Team. In addition, the American Aerobics Association International boosted Rykä's brand name recognition when it replaced Avia with Rykä as the association's preferred aerobics shoes. *Shape* magazine labeled Rykä number one in its aerobic shoe category.

Rykä has also begun sponsoring both aerobics teams and aerobics competitions. In 1992, twenty-five countries competed in the World Aerobic championships in Las Vegas, Nevada. The Canadian Team was sponsored by Rykä Athletic Footwear. Rykä was the premier sponsor and the official shoe of the Canadian National Aerobic championship held in Vancouver, BC. To ensure the success of the event and build awareness for the sport of competitive aerobics, Rykä successfully promoted the nationals through retailers, athletic clubs, and individuals. Given that virtually every previous aerobics competition worldwide had been sponsored by Reebok, Canada's selection of Rykä as their official sponsor marked a significant milestone for Rykä, as well as marking Rykä's international recognition as a core brand in the women's athletic market.

The Rykä Training Body. Early on, Sheri Poe determined that the most effective way to reach Rykä's female aerobic niche would be through marketing to aerobics instructors and targeted Rykä's advertising accordingly. In fact, Rykä spends almost as much as industry leaders on print advertisements in aerobics instructors' magazines and very little on print advertising elsewhere. On the other hand, unlike its big competitors, Rykä does not use celebrity endorsements to sell its products, because the company markets on the theory that women will care more about what feels good on their feet than about what any particular celebrity has to say.

Beyond advertising in aerobics magazines, Rykä has successfully used direct mail marketing techniques to target aerobics instructors. The Rykä Training Body is comprised of more than 40,000 women employed as fitness instructors and personal trainers throughout the country. They receive product information four to six times per year, as well as discounts on shoes. Rykä also has a group of its instructors tied to specific local retailers. The instructors direct their students to those retailers, who then offer discounts to the students. Finally, Rykä-affiliated instructors offer demonstrations to educate consumers about what to look for in an aerobics shoe.

In addition to increasing sales, the relationship between Rykä and the aerobics profession has led to significant product design innovations. Aerobic instructors' suggestions, based on their own experience, as well as on feedback from students in their classes, has led to improvements such as more effective cushioning and better arch support in the shoes. Poe considers these teachers as the link to Rykä's customers. In fact, as a direct result of instructor feedback, Rykä was the first manufacturer to respond to the new step-aerobics trend by developing and marketing lightweight shoes specifically designed to support up and down step motions.

Salespeople. Rykä's marketing efforts are also aimed at the people who sell Rykä products. In Rykä's early days, Poe and her advertising manager, Laurie Ruddy, personally visited retail stores to meet salespeople and "sell" them on Rykä products. Now, the vice president of sales and marketing maintains contact with retailers using incentive programs, giveaways, and small monetary bonuses to keep salespeople excited. The company also provides premiums, such as fanny packs or water bottles for customers.

Advertising Budget. Given the highly competitive nature of the athletic footwear industry, effective advertising is crucial in distinguishing among brands and creating brand preference. Back in 1989, Rykä was particularly capital-intensive, given that it was trying to penetrate the athletic shoe market. Its $3.5 million loss that year is largely attributable to advertising spending of approximately $2.5 million, but that amount was nothing compared to Nike, Reebok, and L.A. Gear who, combined, spent more than $100 million on advertising during the same period. At that time, Rykä advertised only in trade publications, so recognition among consumers was lagging.

More recently, Rykä ads have appeared in *Shape, City Sports, American Fitness, ELLE,* and *Idea Today* magazines. Rykä's brand recognition has grown dramatically, even though Rykä's advertising and marketing budget is only about 9 percent of sales. Poe attributes Rykä's marketing success to its direct marketing techniques, especially its targeting of certified aerobic instructors to wear Rykä shoes.

In October 1992, after three successive quarters of record sales and little profitability, Poe announced that Rykä was going to expand its direct marketing to consumers, even if it required increased spending to penetrate the marketplace beyond aerobics instructors. But Rykä is still in another league compared to industry giants when it comes to budgets. Rykä's total advertising budget is approximately $1.5 million, while Nike spent about $20 million recently on a 1991 pan-European campaign to launch a single product, and Reebok is currently spending $28 million on its "I Believe . . ." ad campaign which specifically targets women.

OPERATIONS

As is common in the athletic-footwear industry, Rykä shoes are made by independent manufacturers in Europe and the Far East, including south Korea and Taiwan, according to Rykä product specifications. Rykä's first three years were rough, in large part because of the poor quality of the products provided by its manufacturer in

Taiwan. Now, however, the shoes are made in Korea with strict quality-control measures in effect. The company relies on a Far Eastern buying agent, under Rykä's direction, for the selection of suppliers, inspection of goods prior to shipment, and shipment of finished goods.

Rykä's management believes that this sourcing of footwear products minimizes company investment in fixed assets as well as reducing cost and risk. Given the extent of the underutilized factory manufacturing capacity in countries outside of South Korea and Taiwan, Rykä's management believes that alternative sources of product manufacturing are readily available, should the company have need of them. Because of the volatility of international and economic relations in today's global marketplace, and in order to protect itself from complete dependence on one supplier, Rykä has resolved to keep itself free of any long-term contract with manufacturers beyond the terms of purchase orders issued. Orders are placed on a volume basis through its agent and Rykä receives finished products within 120 days of an order. If necessary, Rykä may pay a premium to reduce the time required to deliver finished goods from the factory to meet customer demand.

The principal raw materials in Rykä shoes are leather, rubber, ethylvinyl acetate, polyurethane, cambrelle, and pigskin, all of which are readily available both in the United States and abroad. Nevertheless, even though Rykä could locate new sources of raw materials within a relatively short period of time if it needed to for its overseas manufacturers, its business could be devastated by any interruption in operations, whereas Reebok and Nike have large stockpiles of inventory and would be less affected by any difficulties with suppliers.

Distribution. Rykä products are sold in sporting-goods stores, athletic-footwear stores, selected high-end department stores, and sport-specialty retailers including Foot Locker, Lady Foot Locker, Athlete's Foot Store, Foot Action, US Athletics, Oshman's, and Nordstroms. Rykä's major distribution relationship is with the 476 Lady Foot Locker stores in the United States and 250 Lady Foot Locker stores in Canada. Today, 400 Lady Foot Locker stores display permanent Rykä signage, identifying Rykä as a brand especially promoted by Lady Foot Locker. Both Sheri Poe and Amy Schecter, vice president of retail marketing for Lady Foot Locker, agree that Rykä shoes have seen solid sales in Lady Foot Locker stores, and the Lady Foot Locker's display of permanent Rykä signage expresses the confidence Lady Foot Locker has in Rykä's future success.

FOOTACTION USA, a division of the Melville Corporation and the second largest specialty footwear retailer in the country, recently began selling Rykä athletic shoes on a trial basis in 40 stores. The trial was so successful, FOOTACTION agreed to purchase five styles of Rykä shoes for its stores, and today 150 FOOTACTION stores carry Rykä products nationally.

Rykä has received orders from three large retail sporting goods chains, adding well over 200 store outlets to its distribution network. The twelfth largest sporting goods retailer in the country, MC Sporting Goods, based in Grand Rapids, Michigan, now carries five styles of Rykä athletic shoes in each of its 73 stores. In addition, Rykä has received orders from the Tampa, Florida-based Sports and Recreation, which will sell four styles of Rykä athletic shoes in all of its 23 sporting goods stores. Charlie Burks, head footwear buyer for Sports and Recreation, based his decision to stock Rykä shoes on his sense that the chain's customers are looking for new, exciting styles of athletic shoes at affordable prices, and that Rykä delivers on performance, fashion, and value. Rykä shoes are also carried in more than 135 Athletic Express stores.

In the competitive athletic footwear industry, distributors and retailers have considerable clout. Lady Foot Locker and Foot Locker retailers accounted for 13 percent of Rykä's net sales several years ago, but today, no single customer or group under common control accounts for more than 10 percent of its total revenue.

Human Resources. When Rykä was in its early stages, Poe set out to gain credibility through human resources. The company offered industry-standard salaries, stock options, and the opportunity for significant input into the day-to-day operations of the company. In addition, Poe attracted four top executives from Reebok for positions in sales, advertising, and public relations. This high-powered team performed so effectively that sales doubled between Rykä's first and second years. But, total executive compensation was too much for the young company. Poe realized that a change in strategy was necessary, and three of the four Reebok veterans have since left.

Rykä now employs 22 people at its Norwood headquarters, as well as 35 sales representatives across the country. Rykä's small size gives it a certain flexibility, enabling the company to concentrate on continual streamlining and improvement, so that new ideas and adjustments can be implemented and in the stores within 120 days.

Rykä recently appointed Roy S. Kelvin as vice president and chief financial officer to reinforce its commitment to the financial community. Poe sees Kelvin, a former New York investment banker, as instrumental to helping the company grow, but there is also a sense in which Poe's appointment of Kelvin is her acknowledgment of the fact that she's competing for funds in an "old-boy's" network, so it is extremely valuable to have an "old-boy" to help build up her list of contacts. Kelvin's main priorities are helping to secure domestic financing, reduce operating expenses, and improve profit margins.

FINANCIALS

Rykä originally financed its operations principally through public stock offerings, warrant exercises, and other private sales of its common stock, netting an aggregate of approximately $7.2 million. In July, 1990 Rykä completed its public stock offering, which raised net proceeds of $3.5 million, allowing the company to market its products aggressively. Rykä has sold shares to private investors who control 65 percent of the shares.

Rykä's product costs are higher than those of the industry leaders for several reasons. First, because Rykä is significantly smaller than the industry leaders, it cannot take advantage of volume production discounts. Second, the company has opted to pay somewhat higher prices for its products than would be charged by alternate suppliers in order to achieve and maintain higher quality. Finally, higher production costs have resulted from Rykä's inventory financing arrangement with its Korean Trading company, which includes financing costs, commissions, and fees as part of cost of sales.

Rykä has taken on some formidable competition in the form of Nike and Reebok. For Rykä to prosper, Sheri Poe must successfully carve out a niche in the women's athletic shoe market before they run out of money. Time is becoming increasingly scarce. As indicated on Rykä's financial statements (Exhibits 26–1 through 26–6), the company lost nearly $500,000 in 1991 and $300,000 in 1992. Sales are increasing, but profits are nonexistent. Prepare a strategic plan that will enable CEO Poe to guide Rykä to prosperity in the mid-to-late 1990s.

EXHIBIT 26-1 Rykä Inc. and Subsidiary Consolidated Balance Sheets—Assets

	DECEMBER 31,	
	1993	1992
Assets		
Current assets		
Cash and cash equivalents	$ 83,753	$1,029,161
Accounts receivable, net of allowance for doubtful accounts of $665,605 in 1993 and $446,034 in 1992	2,789,728	2,958,629
Inventory	3,280,648	3,260,617
Prepaid advertising	0	723,460
Prepaid expenses and other current assets	160,916	240,511
Total current assets	6,315,045	8,212,378
Security deposits and other assets	28,253	21,485
Equipment, furniture and fixtures, net	87,514	85,366
Total assets	$6,430,812	$8,319,229

Source: Rykä Inc. *Annual Report,* 1993.

EXHIBIT 26-2 Rykä Inc. and Subsidiary Consolidated Balance Sheets—Liabilities and Stockholders' Equity

	DECEMBER 31,	
	1993	1992
Liabilities and stockholders' equity		
Current liabilities		
Accounts payable (including $1,028,150 in 1993 payable to factories)	$ 1,324,603	$ 497,179
Payable to Lender	2,627,493	3,100,000
Payable to Factor	500,000	0
Accrued expenses	525,724	145,000
Notes payable to stockholder	125,000	375,000
Current portion of capital lease obligations	10,405	17,795
Total current liabilities	5,113,225	4,134,974
Obligations under capital leases, less current portion	7,473	17,878

EXHIBIT 26-2 *Continued*

	DECEMBER 31,	
	1993	1992
Commitments and contingencies		
Stockholders' equity		
Preferred Stock, $0.01 par value, 1,000,000 shares authorized; none issued or outstanding		
Common Stock, $0.01 par value, 30,000,000 shares authorized; 23,721,356 and 23,101,948 shares issued and outstanding at December 31, 1993 and 1992, respectively	237,213	231,019
Additional paid-in capital	14,780,493	14,214,459
Accumulated deficit	(13,707,592)	(10,279,101)
Total stockholders' equity	1,310,114	4,166,377
Total liabilities and stockholders' equity	$ 6,430,812	$ 8,319,229

Source: Rykä Inc. *Annual Report*, 1993.

EXHIBIT 26-3 Rykä Inc. and Subsidiary Consolidated Statements of Operations

	YEAR ENDED DECEMBER 31,		
	1993	1992	1991
Net sales	$ 14,350,282	$12,193,643	$7,977,925
Cost of goods sold	11,199,119	8,867,375	5,231,346
Gross profit	3,151,163	3,326,268	2,746,579
Operating expenses:			
General and administrative	1,645,553	1,042,211	1,098,925
Provision for losses on doubtful accounts	631,835	197,034	189,000
Sales and marketing	2,085,077	1,526,299	1,098,080
Advertising costs	1,162,825	196,319	298,689
Research and development	361,780	148,958	155,576
Total operating expenses	5,887,070	3,110,821	2,840,270
Operating income (loss)	(2,735,907)	215,447	(93,691)
Other (income) expense:			
Interest expense	699,231	516,455	418,469
Interest income	(6,647)	(4,195)	(12,648)
Total other expense	692,584	512,260	405,821
Net loss	$ (3,428,491)	$ (296,813)	$ (499,512)
Net loss per share	$ (0.15)	$ (0.01)	$ (0.03)
Weighted average shares outstanding	23,573,316	19,847,283	18,110,923

Source: Rykä Inc. *Annual Report*, 1993.

EXHIBIT 26-4 Rykä Inc. and Subsidiary Consolidated Statements of Stockholders' Equity

| | COMMON STOCK | | ADDTIONAL PAID-IN | ACCUMULATED | |
	SHARES	AMOUNT	CAPITAL	DEFICIT	TOTAL
Balance at January 1, 1990	13,242,500	$132,425	$7,109,898	$(5,394,264)	$1,848,059
Issuance of shares for cash in July 1990, in connection with public offering	4,700,000	47,000	4,653,000		4,700,000
Registration costs related to public offering			(1,182,834)		(1,182,834)
Exercise of stock options	62,642	626	21,925		22,551
Net loss				(4,088,512)	(4,088,512)
Balance at December 31, 1990	18,005,142	180,051	10,601,989	(9,482,776)	1,299,264
Issuance of shares for services	30,000	300	9,600		9,900
Exercise of stock options	101,000	1,010	24,240		25,250
Net loss				(499,512)	(499,512)
Balance at December 31, 1991	18,136,142	181,361	10,635,829	(9,982,288)	834,902
Issuance of shares for cash in September 1992, in connection with warrant call	4,021,046	40,210	3,980,836		4,021,046
Redemption of unexercised warrants in September 1992			(169,739)		(169,739)
Registration costs related to warrant call			(644,046)		(644,046)
Exercise of stock options	944,760	9,448	411,579		421,027
Net loss				(296,813)	(296,813)
Balance at December 31, 1992	23,101,948	$231,019	$14,214,459	$(10,279,101)	$4,166,377

Source: Rykä Inc. *Annual Report*, 1992.

EXHIBIT 26-5 Rykä Inc. and Subsidiary Consolidated Statements of Cash Flows

	YEAR ENDED DECEMBER 31,		
	1993	1992	1991
Cash flows from operating activities			
Net loss	$(3,428,491)	$(296,813)	$ (499,512)
Adjustments to reconcile net loss to cash used for operating activities:			
Depreciation and amortization	51,142	62,711	52,034
Provision for losses on doubtful accounts	631,835	197,034	189,000
Advertising credits	614,217		
Issuance of Common Stock for services	31,050		9,900
Changes in operating assets and liabilities:			
Accounts receivable	(462,934)	(1,395,354)	(1,152,403)
Inventory	(20,031)	(1,016,458)	(1,293,102)
Prepaid advertising	109,243	(604,099)	
Prepaid expenses other current assets	79,595	(163,115)	39,043
Accounts payable and accrued expenses	1,208,148	(52,684)	(31,437)
Net cash used for operating activities	(1,186,226)	(3,268,778)	(2,686,477)
Cash flows from investing activities			
Purchase of equipment, furniture and fixtures, net of capital leases	(53,290)	(33,398)	(6,227)
(Increase) decrease in security deposits and other assets	(6,768)	(5,398)	91,310
Net cash provided by (used for) investing activities	(60,058)	(38,796)	85,083

EXHIBIT 26-5 *Continued*

	YEAR ENDED DECEMBER 31,		
	1993	1992	1991
Cash flows from financing activities			
Payable to Lender, net	(472,507)	200,000	2,300,000
Advances from Factor, net	500,000		
Proceeds from notes payable to stockholder	125,000	375,000	
Repayment of notes payable to stockholder	(375,000)		
Repayments of capital lease obligations (32,591)	(17,795)	(32,583)	
Proceeds from exercise of stock options and warrants (net of redemptions)	541,178	4,272,334	25,250
Payment for registration costs		(644,046)	
Net cash provided by financing activities	300,876	4,170,705	2,292,659
Net increase (decrease) in cash and cash equivalents (308,735)	(945,408)	863,131	
Cash and cash equivalents, beginning of year	1,029,161	166,030	474,765
Cash and cash equivalents, end of year	$83,753	$1,029,161	$166,030
Supplemental disclosures of cash flow information:			
Cash paid during the year for interest	$370,945	$548,455	$318,469
Cash paid during the year for income taxes	—	—	—
Supplemental disclosure of noncash activity:			
Footwear sold in exchange for prepaid advertising	—	$494,856	—
Equipment, furniture and fixtures capitalized under capital leases	—	—	$14,698

Source: Rykä Inc. *Annual Report*, 1993.

EXHIBIT 26-6 Rykä Inc. Percentage of Net Sales by Category for the Years Ended December 31, 1993, 1992, and 1991

CATEGORY	1993	1992	1991
Aerobic	65%	80%	80%
Cross-Training	19	5	10
Walking and Walk/Run; Hikers	16	15	10

Source: Rykä Inc. *Annual Report*, 1993.

EXHIBIT 26-7   Rykä Inc., 1993 representatives

Territory #1 (WA, OR, MT, ID, AK)
  *Peggy Finnigan 714-252-0240
  same (fax)

Territory #2 (Northern California)
  *Pat Miller 707-746-5784
  707-746-5785 (fax)
  P.O. Box 215 and/or 342 East 2nd St.
  Benicia, CA 94510

Territory #3 (TX, LA, MS, AR, OK)
  *Richard Hart 717-792-5774
  717-792-5196 (fax)

Territory #4 (Southern California)
(AZ, NV, CO, WY, UT, NM)
  *Peggy Finnigan 714-252-0240
  same (fax)
  86 Almador
  Irvine, CA 92714

  Jeanne Northrop 303-296-0980
  303-431-1865
  451 E 58th Avenue #3367
  Denver, CO 80216

  Mindy Jaffe (HI) 808-922-4222
  same (fax)
  Cellular 808-285-2855
  234 Ohua Avenue #118
  Honolulu, HI 96815

Territory #5 (FL, Puerto Rico)
  *Pat Best (West Coast)
  813-864-4624
  Sunshine Sports
  3000 34th Street South
  St. Petersburg, FL 33715

  *Al Maduro (East Coast, Puerto Rico)
  305-382-3877
  305-387-9446 (fax)
  Sunshine Sports
  11785 S.W. 134th Ct.
  Miami, FL 33186

  Representatives:
  Dave Jenkins 407-779-1737
  133 North East 1st Street
  Satellite Beach, FL 32927

Territory #6 (OH, MI, IN, KY)
  *Dave Phillips 513-459-0121
  same (fax)
  3478 Cutter Lane
  Maineville, OH 45039

  Frank Karr 502-425-6502
  502-429-6668 (fax)
  9013 Cardiff Road
  Louisville, KY 40242

  Chris Karr 317-257-2260
  317-257-4066 (fax)
  6242 N Rural Street
  Indianapolis, IN 46220

Territory #7 (ME, NH, VT, MA, RI,
CT)
  *Bob Morgan 617-383-6346
  617-383-1955 (fax)
  698 Jerusalem Road
  Cohasset, MA 02025

  Tom O'Brien 617-471-2472
  617-471-2855
  189 Everett Street No. 5
  Quincy, MA 02169

Territory #8 (NJ, NY, PA, MD, DE, VA)
  *Richard Hart 717-792-5774
  717-792-5196 (fax)
  111 Weldon Drive
  York, PA 17404

  (MD, VA)
  Keith Jones 301-663-8605
  same (fax)
  5967 Grove Hill Road
  Frederick, MD 21702

  Hank Mason 315-652-7416
  315-652-1570 (fax)
  115 Glenwood Drive
  Liverpool, NY 13090

  Mike Elison 215-874-4418
  same (fax)
  422 Camelot Drive
  Brookhaven, PA 19015

EXHIBIT 26-7 *Continued*

Territory #9 NYC, NJ
 *Thad Budzinski 609-588-9698
 609-588-0019 (fax)
 38 Willow Court
 Mercerville, NJ 08619

Territory #10 (KS, MO, IA, NE, ND, SD, WI, MN, IL)
 *Gene Wayenberg 314-997-4696
 314-997-6963 (fax)
 Great Athletic Wear
 1702 Robin Knoll Lane
 St. Louis, MO 63146

Representatives:
((Northern) IL, (Southern) WI)
Rich Neuffer 815-337-0131
9804 Autum Lane
Woodstock, IL 60098

(MN, SD, ND, WI)
Dennis Fitzpatrick 612-641-1417
612-646-5876 (fax)
2095 Shelby Avenue
St. Paul, MN 55104

(KS, MO)
 Denny Hobson 913-648-0111
 916-648-0669 (fax)
 Hobson & Associates
 7208 West 80th
 Suite 206
 Overland Park, KS 66204

Territory #11 (NC, SC)
 *Mark Diehl 704-365-9482
 704-366-1139 (fax)
 5012 Crooked Oak Lane
 Charlotte, NC 28226

Territory #14 (GA, TN, AL)
 *Lissy Cowdery 404-257-0775
 same (fax)
 470 River Valley Road
 Atlanta, GA 30328

Canadian Distributor
 Myke & Christine Penfold
 416-738-5291
 416-738-4818 (fax)
 333 Confederation Parkway
 Concord, Ontario, Canada L4K 4S1

*Head representative
Source: Rykä Inc. *Annual Report*, 1993.

COMPUTERS INDUSTRY NOTE
TIM MILES
JONATHAN STREETER
HEIDI HOFFMANN

Industry shipments of equipment by the U.S. computer industry will be more than $66 billion in 1994, an increase of 6 percent following 8 percent growth in 1993. Imports will rise faster than exports, resulting in a higher computer trade deficit of about $17 billion in 1994. U.S. manufacturers will continue to restructure their operations and reduce employment, while they face significant challenges in the complex "infotainment" market during the next 5 years.

The computer-equipment sector encompasses electronic computers (SIC 3571), storage devices (SIC 3572), computer terminals (SIC 3575), and computer peripheral equipment, NEC (SIC 3577). Electronic computers include digital computers of all sizes, as well as computer kits assembled by the purchaser. Computer storage devices are such equipment as magnetic and optical disk drives and tape storage units. The category of computer terminals covers teleprinters. Computer peripherals are printers, plotters, graphics displays, and other input/output equipment. Parts and

TABLE 1 Trends and Forecasts: Computers and Peripherals (SIC 3571, 3572, 3575, 3577) (in millions of dollars except as noted)

					PERCENT CHANGE (1991–1994)		
ITEM	1991	1992[1]	1993[2]	1994[3]	91–92	92–93	93–94
Industry Data							
Value of shipments[4]	54,703	58,000	62,500	66,200	6.0	7.8	5.9
Total employment (000)	227	215	200	190	−5.3	−7.0	−5.0
Production workers (000)	76.2	72.5	69.1	66.4	−4.9	−4.7	−3.9
Average hourly earnings ($)	12.52	12.72	12.81	—	1.6	0.7	—
Capital expenditures	1,813	—	—	—	—	—	—
Product Data							
Value of shipments[5]	49,144	52,100	56,300	59,700	6.0	8.1	6.0
Trade Data							
Value of imports	26,424	32,137	40,170	46,196	21.6	25.5	14.5
Value of exports	25,182	26,304	27,066	29,231	4.5	3.1	7.8

[1]Estimate, except exports and imports.

[2]Estimate.

[3]Forecast.

[4]Value of all products and services sold by establishments in the computers and peripherals industry.

[5]Value of products classified in the computers and peripherals industry produced by all industries.

Note: Census reclassified some parts for electronic computers (3571) to component industries (367) for 1988-1990.

Source: U.S. Department of Commerce: Bureau of the Census, International Trade Administration (ITA). Estimates and forecasts by ITA.

components for computers and peripherals are included, as appropriate, in each of these industries. However, since 1988, the U.S. Bureau of the Census has reclassified some parts, such as printed circuit boards and integrated microcircuits, originally reported in electronic computers, in their respective component industries.

In 1993, the U.S. computer industry experienced its second straight year of recovery from the 1990–91 recession, led by an increase in domestic computer demand of 20 percent to an estimated $69.4 billion (Figure 1). During the first half of 1993, shipments rose at a much higher rate than they did in the same period in 1992; new orders showed their strongest annual growth in 9 years; and inventories were at a relatively low level. Despite some uncertainty about the economy, U.S. business purchases of computer systems and peripherals increased substantially, reflecting the efforts of many corporations to reduce costs and boost productivity through the use of this equipment. These purchases helped the industry offset a decline in Federal computer hardware spending and slower growth in exports.

Product shipments of U.S.-based manufacturers were up an estimated 8 percent (in current dollars) in 1993, to $56.3 billion. Computer systems grew faster than peripheral equipment deliveries and represented more than 50 percent of total shipments (Figure 2). The mix of systems shipments was toward cheaper and increasingly more powerful workstations and personal computers, as users continued to shift many of their applications from mainframes and minicomputers to these smaller platforms. Peripheral shipments were largely storage devices and input/output equipment such as printers.

Computer manufacturers were concerned about the effect that mid-1993 shortages of dynamic random access memory (DRAM) chips, flash memory devices, and flat panel display screens would have on the production and pricing of their systems. Regarding DRAM supply, companies reported lead times for 1- and 4-megabit chip

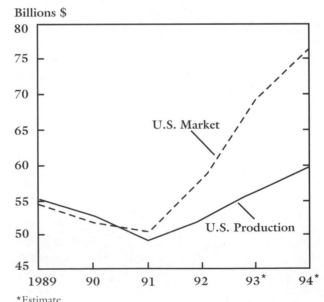

FIGURE 1 Computers: U.S. Market Grows
Faster Than U.S. Production

Billions $

U.S. Market

U.S. Production

*Estimate

Source: U.S. Department of Commerce: Bureau of the Census; International Trade Administration, Office of Computers and Business Equipment.

deliveries of up to 14 weeks and significant price increases for these devices. Many of the smaller U.S. computer systems firms were in a vulnerable position compared with the larger vendors, which were insulated to some extent by long-term contracts with DRAM suppliers. Debate arose within the industry over whether the explosion of a Japanese epoxy resin plant in July 1993 would further exacerbate the imbalance between DRAM supply and demand by late 1993. Some industry observers speculated in August that personal computer prices might rise as much as $150 per system by year end.

Faced with financial losses stemming from declining demand for some products and fierce price competition across a broad spectrum of computer equipment, several U.S. computer manufacturers continued to restructure their domestic and foreign operations and reduce the number of positions during 1993. Total industry employment in the United States fell 7 percent to 200,000 workers (Figure 3). The bulk of the 15,000 jobs lost came from administrative, technical, sales, and support personnel. Layoffs were greater among systems firms than peripheral equipment suppliers. IBM and Digital Equipment Corporation (DEC) announced cutbacks totaling about 70,000 employees worldwide. Many smaller U.S. firms and some subsidiaries of foreign companies in the United States also trimmed their work forces. U.S. production worker employment was once again adversely affected by plant closings. The number of factory workers declined nearly 5 percent to 69,100, but remained a little more than one-third of the industry's labor force.

The U.S. computer equipment industry has used automation as a competitive tool to raise productivity, lower costs, and bring products to market quickly. A 1992 sur-

FIGURE 2 Composition of U.S. Computer Production, 1993*

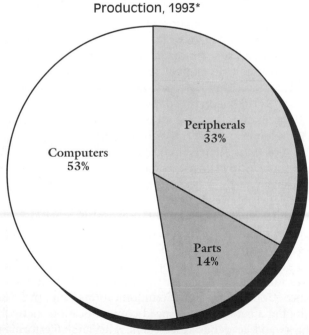

Total = $56.3 Billion

*Estimate

Source: U.S. Department of Commerce: Bureau of Census; International Trade Administration, Office of Computers and Business Equipment.

FIGURE 3 Declining Employment in the U.S. Computer Industry, 1987–94

*Estimate

Source: U.S. Department of Commerce: Bureau of Census; International Trade Administration, Office of Computers and Business Equipment.

vey by the Automation Forum showed that the industry's investment in automation reached $2.1 billion in 1991, a 23 percent increase over the 1989 level. Most of this investment was in production automation software (28 percent of the total) and computer-aided product design and engineering hardware and software (25 percent). The industry was the fifth-largest spender on automation in the United States, but actually led all other U.S. industries in investment per production worker at $20,220. In terms of the demand for computers to automate design, engineering, and manufacturing, U.S. industries spent $11.6 billion on computer equipment during 1991. Among the major users were the automotive, aircraft and aerospace, and electronics industries.

Research and development (R&D) has always been critical to this industry's ability to maintain its technological leadership. Data compiled by *Business Week* in its annual R&D Scoreboard survey shows that a combined sample of 87 U.S. computer firms raised their R&D spending by 4 percent, to $14.2 billion, in 1992 (Table 2). This growth was low relative to the 7 percent average increase for all U.S. industries. However, the computer equipment industry surpassed all other U.S. electronics industries and industrial sectors in absolute spending and only lagged behind health care in the percentage of sales devoted to R&D. Three U.S. computer firms—IBM, DEC, and Hewlett-Packard—ranked among the top 10 R&D spenders in the United States.

Legislation was introduced in Congress in mid-1993 to upgrade the 3-year old High Performance Computing and Communications Initiative (HPCCI), which focuses on developing a national high-speed communications network, primarily for the use of scientists and academic researchers. The High Performance Computing and High Speed Networking Applications Act of 1993 (H.R. 1757), if passed, will allocate $1 billion over 5 years to develop applications that allow broader use of this network in health care, public education, and manufacturing. It also will boost Federal funding of research on supercomputers, advanced networking technologies,

TABLE 2   U.S. R&D spending, 1992 (In billions of dollars, percent)

INDUSTRY	R&D SPENDING	PERCENT OF SALES
Computer equipment	14.2	8.3
Automotive	12.3	4.0
Health care	11.8	9.7
Electrical and electronics	8.0	6.0
Chemicals	5.6	4.3
Aerospace	4.6	4.4
Telecommunications	3.7	3.1

Source: *Business Week,* Aug. 9, 1993.

and software. The European Commission is considering a proposal for a similar 5-year, large-scale, $4.5 billion project on high-performance computing and networking research.

INTERNATIONAL COMPETITIVENESS

The top 100 computer companies worldwide account for a majority share of the international market for information equipment and services. Their sales expanded at a healthy rate of almost 10 percent, to $318 billion in 1992, according to *Datamation* magazine's annual survey of these companies. The U.S. suppliers' share of this group's total remained steady at 61 percent, while the Japanese share fell two percentage points to 25 percent. Major factors behind this share loss may have been the downturn in Japanese computer demand during 1992 and increased competition from U.S. firms in Japan, particularly in the personal computer segment of that market.

Many of the leading U.S. computer equipment suppliers have continued to move aggressively into software and computer services as price competition in hardware has intensified and their profits have dwindled. In 1991 (the latest year available for purposes of comparison), U.S. computer systems and peripheral sales were only slightly more than half of their total revenues (Table 3). European companies were even more involved in computer software and services. In contrast, their competitors in Japan and other Asian nations still derived most of their revenues from computer equipment.

The U.S. computer industry appeared to have ceded its position as the world's leading computer-equipment producer to European Community (EC) manufacturers by 1992 (Figure 4). However, because EC statistics include business machines, such as typewriters and electronic cash registers, the EC industry's computer production is overstated somewhat. Digital Equipment, Hewlett-Packard, IBM, and other U.S. firms also contribute substantially to this industry's output through their European subsidiaries. The production of the Japanese computer industry has risen at a rapid pace, 13 percent annually since 1982, and may surpass that of U.S.-based suppliers by the middle of this decade. Like their U.S. counterparts, both EC and Japanese computer-equipment manufacturers have suffered from recession in their domestic and key overseas markets during the early 1990s. They have reacted in much the same way to losses by restructuring their operations and by instituting hiring freezes or signifi-

TABLE 3 Revenues of Information Equipment and Services Firms, 1991

| | PERCENT | | TOTAL REVENUES |
ITEM	HARDWARE	SOFTWARE	(IN BILLION DOLLARS)
United States	54	46	174
Europe	42	58	29
Japan	69	31	78
Other Asia	93	7	3

Source: *Datamation.*

FIGURE 4 U.S., EC, and Japanese Computer Production, 1982–92 (In billions of dollars)

Note: European Community (EC) production includes a relatively small amount of business equipment.

Source: U.S. Department of Commerce, Bureau of the Census; JEIDA; EC Commission.

cantly cutting back their work forces. The European computer industry reduced employment, for example, by nearly 21,000 workers during 1992–93.

Although it has remained the top exporter of computers, the U.S. industry has lost considerable ground to the Japanese since 1982 (Figure 5). Japanese computer exports have risen 21 percent annually over the past 10 years, nearly twice the rate of the United States and the EC. Peripherals have accounted for almost half of the value of these exports, followed by parts (more than a 30 percent share). Computer systems have played only a minimal role. The Japanese also have increased the amount of computer

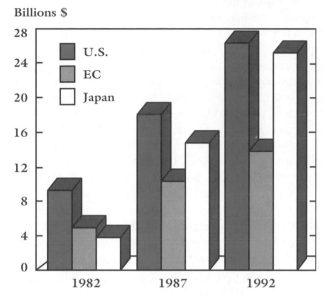

FIGURE 5 U.S., EC, and Japanese Computer Exports, 1982–92 (In billions of dollars)

Note: European Community (EC) exports include a relatively small amount of business equipment.

Source. U.S. Department of Commerce, Bureau of the Census; JEIDA; EC Commission.

TABLE 4 U.S. Computer Trade by Product, 1993* (in millions of dollars except as noted)

PRODUCT	EXPORTS	PERCENT CHANGE 1992–93	IMPORTS	PERCENT CHANGE 1992–1993	TRADE BALANCE
Computer systems	8,390	−2.3	6,427	33.1	1,963
Peripherals	6,767	8.3	20,888	21.6	−14,121
Parts	11,909	3.8	12,854	27.4	−945
Total	27,066	2.9	40,170	25.3	−13,104

*Estimate by ITA.

Note Detail may not sum to total due to rounding.

Source: U.S. Department of Commerce: International Trade Administration (ITA).

production that is exported from 28 percent to more than 50 percent during this period and have a computer trade surplus that currently exceeds $15 billion. In contrast, the EC industry has traditionally exported no more than 20 percent of its production outside the region, concentrating its efforts within the 12 EC member countries. The EC's trade deficit has more than quadrupled in 10 years to more than $20 billion. Imports from non-EC countries have accounted for one-third of European computer consumption, with the United States and Japan as the leading suppliers.

Higher U.S. Trade Deficit. The U.S. computer trade deficit was expected to more than double to an estimated $13 billion in 1993, if trends in U.S. exports and imports through the first 5 months of the year continue (Table 4). Most of this deficit will result from a substantial imbalance in peripherals trade. Japan alone may account for two-thirds of the deficit. Roughly 58 percent of U.S. computer demand will be served by imports.

Computer exports rose only 3 percent to $27 billion during 1993, hurt by weak demand in key overseas markets. The growth was led by peripherals and parts, which together represented nearly 70 percent of export value. Systems exports were down slightly. Exports to Canada and Latin America were up 11 percent and 24 percent, respectively, but were offset by relatively flat shipments to Asia and Europe. Europe has traditionally been the largest regional market, receiving about half of U.S. computer equipment exports (Tables 5 and 6). Canada has emerged as the leading single country market.

Spurred on by a strong upturn in U.S. demand, U.S. computer imports increased 26 percent over their 1992 level, to $40 billion. Asia supplied the bulk of this import value, mainly from Japan, Singapore, Taiwan, and South Korea. Japanese firms were major sources of U.S. imports of peripherals and parts. However, other Asian manufacturers and U.S. subsidiary operations in this region have become significant providers to the U.S. market of personal computers, disk drives, printers, monitors, and components such as motherboards and power supplies.

Cumulative foreign direct investment in the U.S. computer industry fell nearly 18 percent, to $2.4 billion, in 1992, reflecting the sluggish economies of many of the major investing nations. Reduced EC investment was largely responsible for this

TABLE 5 U.S. Trade Patterns in 1992 Computers and Peripherals SIC 3571, 3572, 3575, 3577 (in millions of dollars, percent)

EXPORTS			IMPORTS		
	Value	Share		Value	Share
Canada and Mexico	4,673	17.8	Canada and Mexico	3,168	9.9
European Community	10,410	39.6	European Community	2,673	8.3
Japan	3,308	12.6	Japan	11,226	34.9
East Asia NICs	3,226	12.3	East Asia NICs	14,298	44.5
South America	1,389	5.3	South America	114	0.4
Other	3,297	12.5	Other	658	2.0
World Total	26,304	100.0	World Total	32,137	100.0

TOP FIVE COUNTRIES					
	Value	Share		Value	Share
Canada	3,603	13.7	Japan	11,226	34.9
Japan	3,308	12.6	Singapore	5,488	17.1
United Kingdom	2,811	10.7	Taiwan	4,418	13.7
Germany	2,606	9.9	Canada	2,218	6.9
Netherlands	1,679	6.4	South Korea	1,394	4.3

Source: U.S. Department of Commerce: Bureau of the Census; International Trade Administration.

TABLE 6 U.S. trade patterns, 1993* computers and peripherals SIC 3571, 3572, 3575, 3577 (in millions of dollars, percent)

	EXPORTS			IMPORTS	
	Value	Share		Value	Share
Canada	3,789	14.0	Canada	5,222	13.0
Latin America	2,977	11.0	Latin America	803	2.0
Europe	11,909	44.0	Europe	6,026	15.0
Asia/Pacific	8,120	30.0	Asia/Pacific	28,119	70.0
Africa	271	1.0	Africa	—	—
World Total	27,066	100.0	World Total	40,170	100.0

	TOP FIVE COUNTRIES				
	Value	Share		Value	Share
Canada	3,789	14.0	Japan	11,649	29.0
United Kingdom	3,248	12.0	Singapore	7,632	19.0
Japan	2,977	11.0	Canada	5,222	13.0
Germany	2,707	10.0	Taiwan	4,419	11.0
Netherlands	2,165	8.0	United Kingdom	3,615	9.0

*Estimate by ITA based on January to May 1993 data.

Source: U.S. Department of Commerce: Bureau of the Census; International Trade Administration.

FIGURE 6 Foreign Direct Investment in the U.S. Computer Industry, 1992 (in millions of dollars)

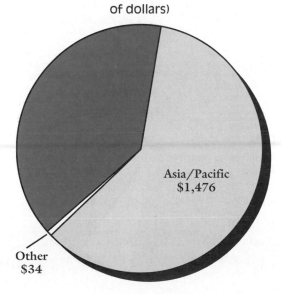

Asia/Pacific $1,476

Other $34

Total = $2.4 Billion

Source: Department of Commerce, Bureau of Economic Analysis.

decline. Japan continued to be the principal investor nation, accounting for 60 percent of the total (Figure 6).

The overseas investment of U.S. computer firms dropped by 11 percent to $20.4 billion, as spending was cut back appreciably in Europe and, to a lesser extent, in Canada (Figure 7). However, their investment buildup in Asia continued with Singapore as the major beneficiary. Spending by U.S. suppliers to expand their personal computer and peripheral equipment manufacturing operations in Singapore rose 70 percent to $1.3 billion. Although investment data are unavailable, trade journal sources indicate that China was an important area of joint-venture activity for U.S. PC and workstation suppliers during 1992.

A debate over the relative contributions of U.S. multinational firms and the affiliates of foreign companies to the U.S. economy has raged in academic circles for several years. The issue has assumed importance more recently in the new Administration's efforts to shape its own distinctive trade policy. At the computer- and business-equipment level, data compiled by the U.S. Department of Commerce's Bureau of Economic Analysis reveal that the U.S. parents of these multinationals have played a much more critical and positive role in the U.S.-based computer industry and the economy than U.S. affiliates of foreign firms. U.S. parent firms' total assets, sales of goods and services, employment, new plant and equipment expenditures, U.S. income tax payments, and R&D spending and intensity were many times greater in 1991 than their foreign counterparts. The parents' U.S. value-added content and employee compensation were also substantially higher. More significantly, these parents have consistently recorded trade surpluses since 1987, while the U.S. affiliates of foreign computer companies have experienced a growing deficit ($2 billion by 1991) and have become a major contributor to the worsening U.S. trade position. The import dependence of the parent firms has been much lower.

FIGURE 7 Overseas Investment of the U.S. Computer Industry, 1992 (in billions of dollars)

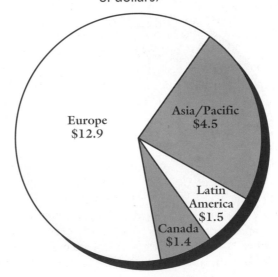

Europe
$12.9

Asia/Pacific
$4.5

Latin
America
$1.5

Canada
$1.4

Total = $20.4 Billion

Source: U.S. Department of Commerce, Bureau of Economic Analysis.

The Computer Systems Policy Project (CSPP), a coalition of chief executive officers from 13 major U.S. computer firms, released a study in mid-1993 that provided additional perspectives on this issue. The CSPP companies had combined worldwide revenues totaling more than $123 billion in 1991, devoted 12 percent of their revenues to R&D, employed more than 400,000 Americans directly, and created 2 million more jobs indirectly in such fields as software design, computer programming, and services. Roughly 80 percent of their R&D jobs and 60 percent of their production workers remain in the United States. Spending to educate, train, and retrain their work forces and customers amounted to $2.3 billion during 1991. These and other firms in the U.S. computer industry also have supplied users with the world's most technologically advanced products. The real price performance (improvement in performance in relation to real prices) of these products has increased 25 percent annually over the past 40 years.

ENVIRONMENTAL PROFILE

SEMATECH and the Microelectronics and Computer Technology Corp. (MCC), along with the Department of Energy (DOE) and the Environmental Protection Agency (EPA), released in early 1993 a study entitled *A Workstation Life Cycle Environmental Study,* which urged U.S. electronics companies and those in other industries to become more environmentally conscious. One of the study's recommendations called for U.S. firms to improve their competitiveness by implementing programs to recycle products more efficiently and reduce pollution substantially. Its R&D-related recommendations included proposals supporting joint industry/government research efforts on environmental technology, and asked Federal laboratories to redirect their relevant resources toward conducting R&D in this area. Congress has been considering environmental legislation addressing several of the issues raised in the study.

Computer-equipment use accounts for 5 percent of the U.S. commercial-energy consumption and may reach 10 percent by the year 2000, according to EPA estimates. Personal computers, for example, consume between 150 and 240 watts when turned on and are the biggest energy consumers among the computer and business equipment used in the U.S. Government (Figure 8). In an effort to reduce this power consumption, the President issued an Executive Order in April 1993 directing Federal agencies to purchase only computer equipment that meets the criteria of the EPA's Energy Star program beginning in October 1993. The criteria require each part of a computer system—central processing unit, monitor, and printer—to enter a standby mode when it is not in use and to consume no more than 30 watts of power.

About 70 computer manufacturers had agreed to develop energy-efficient products by mid-1993. Many of them also made a commitment to convert their existing product lines to conform to the Energy Star criteria. Estimates of the program's cost savings vary. The U.S. government expects that Energy Star will slash at least $40 million from its annual electricity bill. The EPA believes "green" personal computers (PCs) could reduce the average U.S. user's electricity bill by $80 per year. On a national scale, EPA also predicts that the use of these PCs could cut electricity consumption by 25 billion kilowatt hours annually by the year 2000, thereby eliminating the need for 10 coal-fired power plants and reducing carbon-dioxide emissions by nearly 20 million tons.

During 1991, the U.S. computer industry raised its spending to control air and water pollution by 27 percent, to more than $14 million, through changes in production processes and end-of-line techniques. It also incurred $59 million in pollution abatement operating costs, including payments to government for public sewerage services and solid waste management.

FIGURE 8 Share of U.S. Government Power Consumption in Computers and Business Equipment, 1992

Faxes 1%
Typewriters 4%
Mainframes 4%
Copiers 9%
Minicomputers 10%
Personal Computers 48%
Printers 24%

Source: General Services Administration.

Recycling has assumed greater importance as an issue within the industry. Carnegie Mellon University has estimated that approximately 15 million used computers could end up in U.S. landfills by 2005 at a cost to the taxpayer that could approach $1 billion. Several U.S. computer firms have started to recycle processor boards and power supplies along with other reusable components such as batteries and printer toner cartridges. They also are reprocessing parts to recover sheetsteel, plastics, and precious metals.

OUTLOOK FOR 1994

Product shipments by the U.S. computer-equipment industry should rise by 6 percent in current dollars to nearly $60 billion, assuming slower growth in the U.S. market and an expected resurgence in exports. The U.S. market should expand at only half its 1993 rate as domestic business spending on computer systems and peripherals begins to subside after 2 years of substantial growth. Intense price competition, particularly in low-end systems and peripherals, may continue, and exports should benefit from a long-awaited recovery in overseas demand, if key foreign economies emerge from recession and the dollar remains relatively stable. Imports should moderate in response to lower U.S. demand, but will still increase faster than exports. As a result, the U.S. computer trade deficit should increase to about $17 billion in 1994. Imports may total 60 percent of the U.S. market.

SUPERCOMPUTERS

Supercomputer systems are distinguished from other computers by their high processing speeds and their ability to handle numerically intensive problems which are too large for conventional computers. Many of the features which have historically distinguished supercomputers from other types of computer hardware have become more widespread in the computer industry, with the advent of high-speed networking, increasingly advanced mainframes, and powerful workstation clusters. One remaining distinction, however, is that supercomputers are an "enabling" technology. This means that the definition of supercomputers has more to do with applications (software) than hardware. Although advancements in hardware technology and networking have led vendors of mainframes and workstations to call their products "supercomputers," true supercomputers are those systems which are capable of processing the most advanced scientific and commercial applications such as weather forecasting.

Supercomputers now are divided into two main categories: those with one or more high-powered processors and those with many low-powered processors. The former are often referred to as "traditional" or "vector" supercomputers because they were designed to process scientific vector calculations. These systems are physically large, often require liquid cooling systems, and are expensive to acquire and operate. Computers in the latter category are often referred to as scalable parallel systems because the number of processors for an individual model can scale from a few to very many, while using the same software and operating system. These computers are smaller and less expensive than traditional systems, are air-cooled, and account for the vast majority of shipments of supercomputer "nodes" (processing units). The ability to process data using more than one processor (parallel processing) is a characteristic common to both classes of supercomputers.

Initially, scalable systems were considerably less expensive than vector supercomputers, but price distinctions between the two have rapidly begun to disappear. Traditional supercomputers are now available in less expensive, less powerful air-cooled versions. Scalable systems can be configured to have so many processing units that they can become physically larger than many mainframe systems. Supercomputers in both classes now range in price from $350,000 to $35 million. Vector supercomputers continue to account for the majority of manufacturers' annual revenues.

INTERNATIONAL COMPETITIVENESS

The export market has been an area of incremental growth for U.S. supercomputer manufacturers, allowing them to remain competitive in an increasingly saturated domestic market. Most supercomputer vendors ship more than 50 percent of their units overseas, although higher-end, higher-revenue systems tend to find their largest market in the United States. Europe is the single largest export market for U.S. firms, with Germany, France, and the United Kingdom accounting for most sales. The European Community's keen interest in supercomputing has resulted in demand for systems rather than the creation of domestic competition. European users in government, industry, and academia also have contributed significantly to the software base in the high-performance computing arena.

The hardware efforts of European suppliers have been restricted to the scalable parallel field, and their sales of these systems tend to be greatest in their home markets. The increasing competitiveness of European high-performance technology, and the firms' movement away from specialty processors, such as transputers, means that U.S. vendors now begin to see some signs of local competition in Europe.

Overall, European supercomputer sales fell slightly, to less than $500 million in 1993. The majority of revenues came from vector sales, although most units shipped were scalable systems. Despite increased Japanese competition at the high end, U.S. supercomputers accounted for upwards of 80 percent of all such installations in Europe, and about 85 percent of all public-sector, research-facility, and university sites. U.S. vendors also have the lion's share of the European market for scalable systems, despite competition from Parsytec in Germany, Telmat in France, and Meiko in the United Kingdom.

Japan. The Japanese supercomputer market is the second-largest individual market after the United States, but is marked by a more difficult sales environment for U.S. firms. Japanese government efforts to foster a domestic industry are partially to blame, but Japanese industry's inclination to purchase from domestic sources also makes it unusually difficult for foreign firms to enter that market. The private sector accounts for close to 70 percent of all supercomputer sales in Japan; U.S. supercomputers account for only about 25 percent of that market. Japanese computer users have traditionally looked to single-vendor solutions for their hardware needs, which favors such vertically integrated giants as NEC, Fujitsu, and Hitachi.

OUTLOOK FOR 1994

The global market for all types of supercomputers is expected to remain stable, at nearly $1.7 billion. There should be a reduction in sales of traditional supercomputers, by nearly 5 percent, to about $800 million, as manufacturers of those systems move into the scalable market. There is little likelihood that any new firms will enter the field because of rising prices of scalable, parallel computers, and distributed computing.

Lower system prices for newly introduced low-end vector supercomputers have reduced dollar-value sales of traditional supercomputers. However, the market should grow marginally in unit sales.

The outlook for parallel systems also is relatively weak, compared with their rapid growth from 1988 to 1992. Overall, scalable systems will account for approximately 30 percent of worldwide supercomputer revenues in 1994. The industry may well have hit at least a temporary plateau, as researchers and scientists around the world determine how they will switch from traditional supercomputers to new platforms.

MAINFRAMES

Mainframe computers, once the workhorses of the business computing world, are being challenged by a rising tide of new, competitive technologies. On the one hand, the strong demand for cheaper, less powerful systems, which are inexpensive to operate and can be placed directly under the control of individual users, has resulted in the rapid rise of personal computers and workstations. Supercomputers have become the dominant systems at the opposite end of the user spectrum, since mainframes generally have not been capable of providing the advanced scientific operations that many researchers and scientists need.

Mainframe firms have responded by making computers more available to individuals via networks and more capable of advanced scientific uses through the attachment of vector processors. At the same time, companies have continued to make rapid advances in disk-storage capacity and processing performance. Today, mainframe computers range in price from approximately $3 million for low-end systems to as high as $30 million for systems with supercomputer-like capabilities. Nevertheless, a major displacement of mainframe computers by other products has already taken place, and the future market for such large systems will reflect a significant, although diminished, position in the computing world.

The performance of mainframes is generally rated by their ability to process millions of instructions per second (MIPS). Low-end, single-processor mainframes now have processing speeds of about 50 MIPS, while the fastest multiple-processor systems are capable of more than 350 MIPS. As logic and memory-chip technology advances, however, through the use of high-density packaging and very large scale integration (VLSI), the performance parameters defining the mainframe computer will continue to rise. At the same time, the cost per unit of increased performance will fall further. Although the cost per MIPS performance in 1983 was approximately $200,000, by 1993 it had dropped to less than $50,000 and is predicted to decline again in 1994 to less than $40,000. The cost of disk storage also has fallen to about $10 per million bytes (megabytes), while capacity has dramatically risen, so that high-end storage units can store up to 90 billion bytes (gigabytes) of information.

The value of U.S.-based mainframe shipments, which stagnated in 1992 at about $12.4 billion, dropped by more than 8 percent (in current dollars) to about $11.3 billion in 1993, because of substantial price competition and lower-than-expected sales due to downsizing. Unit shipments, which dropped sharply in 1992, fell again in 1993, but only by 4 percent. General concerns about the state of the economy convinced some large-scale users to hold off on new equipment upgrades, despite the advent of new-generation systems with attractive performance characteristics and pricing. Substantial price reductions in 1993 by such industry leaders as IBM and Amdahl, as well as the Japanese firms Fujitsu and Hitachi, also lowered revenues. Nevertheless, the worst of the decline in demand for mainframes may have taken place by mid-1993, as caution by core customers has been increasingly balanced by their need to maintain essential computing capabilities.

Mainframe installations in the United States declined from about 27,000 in 1989 to about 24,000 in 1993. Enhanced performance of large-scale systems has spurred the consolidation of mainframe sites into smaller, centralized units.

INTERNATIONAL COMPETITIVENESS

Japanese firms in the late 1980s severely eroded U.S. dominance in the mainframe industry, and have continued to make inroads into the world's $25 billion market through both corporate acquisition and increased sales. By 1993, Japanese manufacturers accounted for 30 percent of world revenues in an essentially stagnant mainframe market, reducing the U.S. share to 63 percent and that of European-made systems to 7 percent. A weak European market and recession in Japan also have been obstacles for U.S. firms, which are traditionally export-oriented. An interesting side effect of the worldwide slowdown was IBM's shift of some mainframe production work from Japan back to the United States in 1993, due to the markedly increased value of the Japanese yen against the U.S. dollar. As European currencies, and especially the French franc, lost value against the dollar, however, U.S. firms were faced with the prospect of increasing prices in an already depressed and competitive European market.

OUTLOOK FOR 1994

Mainframe manufacturers in the United States will be faced with continuing stagnation and severe price competition, with revenues expected to fall another 3 percent to almost $11 billion. Unit shipments, however, are expected to stabilize to some degree. Domestic sales will continue to be the strongest market for mainframe makers, while the Japanese and European economies begin their struggle toward recovery. Unfortunately, the large layoffs resulting from reduced business and wholesale restructuring over the past two years at several firms will likely be repeated in 1994, as the effects of downsizing and competitive pricing continue. On the other hand, deeply reduced prices for increasingly sophisticated mainframe systems should convince reluctant consumers to begin investing in new computing equipment, despite the continued difficult economic environment.

MIDRANGE

The midrange segment of the computer industry consists of those systems which serve multiple numbers of networked users, either locally or remotely. Computers falling into this segment of the market are generally less expensive and less powerful than mainframes, and are distinguished from high-end workstations in that they serve from two to several hundred users. Prices of midrange systems have ranged between $20,000 and $1million. This category of computers is diverse and complex, consisting of everything from manufacturing-oriented systems, where factory workers enter and receive production data, to processors handling networked, department store, sales terminals that capture sales data and make inventory calculations. The diversity of products and customers in the midrange market makes it difficult to pinpoint technology trends and specific economic factors that characterize the segment as a whole. Nevertheless, the wide use of midrange computers as business tools makes them subject to the same economic factors that broadly affect the manufacturing, retail, and service sectors.

The midrange computer market showed continued signs of weakness in 1993, with total revenues falling about 3 percent (in current dollars) to $25.2 billion. Cumulative discounting in 1992 and 1993 by industry leaders facing eroded market shares has forced unit values to historically low levels. Other major factors driving prices down include the weak world economy, increased competitiveness as vendors move to open systems, and technological changes that enable reductions in manufacturing costs. Despite lower overall industry revenues in 1993, unit shipments increased by almost 2 percent.

INTERNATIONAL COMPETITIVENESS

U.S. midrange vendors are leading suppliers in most foreign countries, other than Japan, reaping fully 50 percent of their revenues outside of the United States. In most major foreign markets, U.S. firms are represented by wholly-owned subsidiaries, whereas in other regions they employ distributors and agents. The strongest U.S. export markets are Canada and Europe, where the United States has at least a 50-percent share. Although U.S. firms are well positioned there, economic difficulties in those markets have had a major dampening effect on midrange revenues in recent years. Nevertheless, while the European recession appeared to deepen in 1993, overall computer exports to Canada increased slightly.

In Japan, the large domestic firms have more than two-thirds of the midrange market and enjoy a significant advantage in terms of brand loyalty and exposure to potential users. U.S. firms which do well selling in heterogeneous computing environments have had difficulty in convincing the Japanese to give up their one-brand (mainframe-to-PC) operating environment. Even though U.S. midrange computers offer more advanced systems software and applications, Japanese users are reluctant to switch to open systems if the cost of converting proprietary software becomes prohibitive.

In the developing world, U.S. firms maintain a competitive advantage in terms of technology, but may lose out in pricing competition with the less costly products of Asian competitors. Promising markets in South America, such as Argentina and Chile, are still relatively small, but are the focus of some attention as markets stagnate elsewhere.

OUTLOOK FOR 1994

Advances in component technology and software, especially in the open-systems area, will spur activity in the midrange market, although little growth is expected in 1994. There will be continued confusion as the distinction between various types and capabilities of midrange systems blurs, and the marketing efforts of suppliers crossover, with mainframes at the high end and workstations at the low end. A moderate recovery in the U.S. economy will probably not make up for the slack demand in Canada and the European Community. Sales in the Japanese market also may be affected by businesses' cautious approach to investment there. Increased competitive pressures will again depress the value of sales, although low to moderate unit growth is expected. The long, steep decline in midrange unit prices, however, may slow significantly as manufacturers assess the extent to which they can make further cuts in costs, without affecting their ability to meet demand. Large-scale layoffs, which made headlines in 1992 and 1993, have brought midrange producers to higher levels of productivity. Thus, even in a relatively flat market, their refocus on core businesses should allow them to operate in 1994 without additional losses in revenues or employment.

WORKSTATIONS

Workstations are single and multiuser computers that make use of high-speed microprocessors to provide technical and business users with superior performance. On the low end, they compete with high-end personal computers, a distinction that has been blurred by the introduction of more powerful, mainstream microprocessors, such as Intel's Pentium. On the high end, they compete with mini-supercomputers in raw performance, and with midrange computers as network servers. Workstations have been sold to the scientific and engineering community since their introduction in the early 1980s, but have more recently become popular in the mainstream business markets, where they are used for electronic publishing, business graphics, financial services, mapping, and office automation.

The most significant feature of workstations is their high-performance, 32-bit reduced instruction set computing (RISC) microprocessors. U.S. shipments of RISC workstations are growing rapidly (Figure 9). Based upon the RISC philosophy of keeping the number of primary instructions for the system's operation small, designers have been steadily increasing workstation performance. More than 90 percent of RISC systems run some version of the UNIX operating system, which provides strong software development, communications, multitasking, and network support capabilities. Although UNIX is ostensibly an "open" system, most vendors have offered a proprietary version to tie customers to their specific hardware platform. Even though UNIX has enabled workstation companies to push the performance of their hardware, software developers have been hesitant to provide applications software for some versions. This situation contrasts sharply with the enormous number of applications that have been written for the DOS- and Windows-based personal computers (PCs).

Workstation unit shipments in the United States grew more than 6 percent, to 227,772 systems, in 1993, according to Dataquest, Inc. The U.S. industry is highly concentrated with five companies holding more than 85 percent of the market. The traditional computer vendor's workstation product lines have provided welcome profits, as demand has declined for mainframe and midrange systems and the substantial support they required. Various industry experts agree that workstation vendors have established strong management, technology, and marketing skills, and will realize above-average profitability and continued market-share gain in the technical-computing sector. The number of vendors in the industry has remained fairly constant, with the exception of the withdrawal of NeXT from the hardware workstation market. That company will maintain a presence in the software market with its NeXTStep operating system.

FIGURE 9 U.S. RISC Workstations Shipments

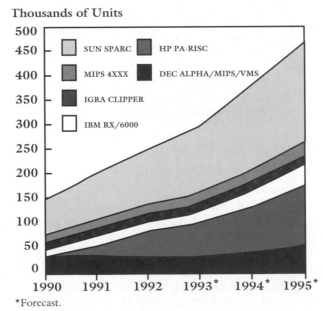

*Forecast.

Note: RISC = reduced instruction set computing.

Source: InfoCorp.

Workstation companies are aggressive in their releases of new products and existing product enhancements. Product upgrades are announced on the average of every 6 to 9 months; major product announcements come every 18 to 24 months, thereby deterring new market entrants. Clone vendors, a powerful force in the PC market, have had relatively little success in winning workstation market share, probably due to this sector's relatively strong emphasis upon performance rather than price, where the clone vendors have a marketing advantage. Average system prices are falling as workstations move into more commercial applications. In the server market, workstations are dramatically less expensive than other server options, such as midrange and mainframe computers.

INTERNATIONAL COMPETITIVENESS

The European workstation market consumed 180,117 units in 1993, according to Dataquest. Datapro International estimates that workstation unit shipments there will increase at a compound annual growth rate of about 21 percent through 1995. Demand for workstations used as servers in commercial applications will grow faster than those used in technical and graphical applications. Prices vary widely across Europe, although the differences are diminishing. The general industrial sector accounted for nearly two-thirds of European workstation shipments, mainly to technical and scientific users. The financial sector and other nontechnical users accounted for the rest.

The European workstation market is controlled by the same five U.S. companies that dominate the U.S. market. These companies sell primarily through direct sales forces and value-added resellers in Europe. Since workstations are a relatively new market segment, these companies are likely to further develop dealer and distributor networks over the next few years. Some of the major vendors have standard European pricing, while others allow their resellers to determine the price of the system and service. Local taxes, such as the value-added tax in the United Kingdom, also influence the price of the product. U.S. workstation vendors have entered into several OEM (original equipment manufacturer) relationships with European computer companies, none of which have become significant competitors to U.S. vendors in their home market.

Japanese workstation vendors, on the other hand, have been successful at turning technology licensing agreements with U.S. workstation vendors into products for their home market. Several Japanese vendors have licensed the right to manufacture the RISC processors designed by U.S. workstation vendors. The majority of systems sold in Japan are based on these microprocessors. Japanese vendors have developed systems for both the high- and low-end workstation markets.

OUTLOOK FOR 1994

Workstation shipments are expected to continue their strong growth, led by systems shipped to former mainframe and midrange users. More users are expected to downsize from large, proprietary systems to smaller, open environments, primarily based on UNIX workstations and servers. Workstations will continue to be the system of choice for scientific and technical users.

As workstation vendors focus their attention on selling to the mainstream business markets, their greatest challenge will lie in weaning DOS/Windows-based PC users away from their familiar operating systems environments by showing the advantages of the high-performance UNIX-based RISC systems. If the new technology promised by DOS/Windows software vendors stumbles in the marketplace, UNIX workstations will look more attractive to business users for their high-end needs and create a new market for workstation vendors. Some RISC vendors are already adjusting their strategy and pricing to capitalize on this potentially large market.

Competition within the workstation market will continue to be driven by lower prices, higher volumes, and better technology. The dominant workstation vendors will each continue on aggressive growth paths, announcing upgrades at least once in 1994, and introducing new, complementary product lines that will provide advanced multiprocessing and multitasking capabilities. Current users will have an impressive upgrade path as vendors begin to introduce 64-bit architectures.

The U.S. market will remain the largest single-country market, with more than 250,000 units shipped in 1994, a 10 percent increase. Japan and Europe will consume nearly 200,000 units each. By the end of 1994, the world's installed base of workstations should total more than 4 million units.

PERSONAL COMPUTERS

Personal computers (PCs) are general application computers based on microprocessor chips with a resident operating system and local programming capability. They are mainly oriented toward single users, but an increasing number are in multiuser settings or employed as network and file servers. There is a growing array of types and sizes grouped into two broad categories—stationary and portables. Stationary systems include desktop and deskside or "tower" configurations. Portables, comprising about 20 percent of the U.S. market, are divided into transportables, A/C and battery-powered laptops, notebooks, sub-notebooks, handheld, and pen-based models. Typical units with a monitor sell for $1,000 to $2,000, although prices range from below $500 for used or older computers to more than $25,000 for the most sophisticated, fully configured systems.

Although performance distinctions are blurring, PCs are differentiated from more powerful workstations, historically used in engineering and scientific applications, by slower microprocessors, less graphics capabilities, and lower display resolutions. Workstations generally run on a UNIX operating system, rather than PC operating systems, such as DOS, OS/2, and Macintosh OS.

The industry expansion of the 1980s, fed by a proliferation of suppliers, has slowed considerably, allowing the major suppliers to stabilize their positions and to retain or regain market share. The share of the top 10 vendors has remained between 50 and 60 percent over the last several years, but could increase due to escalating company acquisitions. The top three PC suppliers (IBM, Apple, and Compaq) continued to dominate the industry, although their market share has dropped from more than 50 percent in 1987 to approximately 30 percent in 1993.

Shipments of personal computers (desktops, desksides, and portables) to the U.S. market in 1993 were 13.2 million units, up 15 percent, according to IDC. (This marks a return to the double-digit growth rates enjoyed by the industry during most of the 1980s, after the bearish markets of 1990 and 1991.) The 1993 estimates include computers manufactured and assembled in the United States by domestic firms and foreign subsidiaries, and imported systems produced offshore by either U.S. or foreign-owned companies.

The value of the U.S. market in 1993 increased slightly to approximately $25 billion according to industry sources. Since 1991, market value has been growing slower than unit shipments and exhibited negative growth in 1991 due to significant price reductions. This is yet another sign of a maturing market with relative product saturation in the largest buying segments—government and business. The U.S.-installed base of PCs exceeded 70 million units compared to half that many in Europe. With heavy discounting of all computer models, sales at the high-end have not offset volume sales of less expensive machines as in past years. The 1993 PC market was most heavily affected by severe price erosion, accelerated product cycles, the increasing popularity of portables and workstations, and the success of new distribution channels.

Although abating somewhat, price wars continued to dominate the PC landscape in 1993. Pushed by intense competition among a plethora of PC suppliers, greater use of commodity-based mass marketing channels, and increased focus on the more price-sensitive buyers in homes, schools, and small businesses, vendors continued to slash list prices, cut dealer margins, and introduce low-cost lines aimed at the consumer and home markets. Intense price discounting began in 1991 and accelerated the following year as the industry set records for price reductions. Reductions in street prices, which declined on average by one-third in 1992, were not as steep in 1993. For example, street prices for some 80486-based PCs declined less than 5 percent during the first half of 1993. At some point, profit margins will be cut to the bone, and additional decreases will depend upon reduced component or manufacturing costs. Industry analysts expect price competition to moderate further in 1994.

Shortened, product-life cycles accompanied rapid price reductions. Estimated PC product-life has decreased from 5 years in 1981 to 6 months today, with R&D and market introduction phases shrinking accordingly. Component suppliers have contributed to this phenomenon. In the face of competition from other chip manufacturers, Intel expanded and stepped up product introductions in 1993, while continuing its efforts to move customers to 80486-based PCs with reductions of i486 microprocessor prices. The combination of falling prices and decreasing product cycles put severe pressure on PC suppliers' bottom lines in 1993.

The expansion of the microcomputer industry continued with the introduction of a growing variety of pen-based and hand-held computers at one end and multiprocessor and multiuser systems at the other. Although still in the majority and benefiting from price cuts and the rebirth of the home market, traditional desktop PCs faced stiff competition from the portable and workstation ranks. Because desktop shipments are projected to decline from 80 percent of total PC sales to 65 percent by 1997, vendors are looking for help from the high-growth ends of the product spectrum.

The improved availability of PCs in consumer outlets at attractive prices increased sales to the more volatile, but less penetrated, small business sector, totaling more than 4 million firms with less than 100 employees. According to Link Resources, over 67 percent of these firms had PCs in 1993. Demand for PCs among businesses with less than 10 employees is forecast to grow 20 percent in 1993 to over 1.7 million units.

More than 31 million U.S. households owned PCs in 1993; the installed base was over 38 million. The value of shipments in 1993 exceeded $6 billion, while unit sales grew 5 percent to more than 5 million. Market growth was mostly driven by price cuts of 30 to 40 percent and the introduction of new low-cost PCs targeted at the home buyer. However, more than half of the sales went to satisfy pent up demand for more powerful PCs needed to run new graphical operating environments, such as Windows. Because major brands were sold through mass merchandizing channels, consumers received greater exposure to computers. Buyers also spent an average of $1,750 for their PCs than the previous year, using money saved from price reductions on systems to purchase more performance or additional software and peripherals. With improved system performance, users positioned themselves to accommodate the more power- and storage-hungry software of the future.

INTERNATIONAL COMPETITIVENESS

Foreign markets have become increasingly important to U.S. suppliers as they seek to expand sales. Some producers now sell as much PC equipment overseas as they do domestically. According to IDC estimates, the world market for personal computers totaled $68 billion in 1993, an 8 percent increase in current dollars. Unit shipments grew 14 percent to more than 33 million, with an active installed base of 157 million PCs. The largest national markets were the United States (39 percent of global shipments) and Japan (7 percent), followed by the major Western European countries. By region, the Western Hemisphere represented about 40 percent of the world market; Europe, 33 percent; and Asia, most of the rest. The U.S. share of the world market will continue to decline in the future as computer use expands abroad. While markets in the more developed countries mature, dramatic growth will occur in much of the rest of the world as industrial and government infrastructures are modernized. The potential of these developing markets holds great promise for U.S. companies.

Western Europe. In common with the U.S. market, PC sales in Western Europe have dropped from the steady double-digit growth of the 1980s. Following a 12 percent increase in 1992, IDC estimated that the Western European PC market grew 7 percent in 1993 to 10.5 million units, reflecting slow economic growth in the region. Steep price declines caused market value to remain unchanged at $21 billion. Although market sophistication has lagged behind the United States, Europe is catching up. Representing less than 1 percent of the market in 1993, shipments of PCs with Intel 80xx and 80286 processors have been declining since 1989. As in the United States, PCs with 80486 processors dominated sales with more than 60 percent of the market, while the market share for 80386SX and DX chips dropped precipitously to 21 percent from 53 percent in 1992, according to Dataquest. Sales of PCs with the more powerful RISC and Pentium processors are forecast to reach 2 million units by 1995.

According to Dataquest, the four largest PC markets in Europe last year were Germany (2.4 million units), the United Kingdom (2.3 million), France (1.5 million), and Italy (1 million). Commodore was the leading supplier in Europe, with about 12 percent of unit shipments, followed by IBM, Apple, Compaq, and Olivetti. The future growth of PC sales in Europe is linked to the development of broader distribution networks in each country and to the attractiveness of aftersales service and support packages provided by dealers. The home market also is becoming an important segment.

Japan. Personal computers are not yet as widely used in Japan as in Western Europe or the United States. The PC-installed base at the end of 1993 is estimated to be approximately 14 million units, according to IDC. This is about one-fifth the size of the U.S.-installed base. Factors that have contributed to this limited use include skepticism about the benefits of personal computers among Japanese businessmen, limited office and desk space, and the relatively higher prices for PC hardware and software in Japan compared with the United States.

In 1992, the Japanese PC industry was marked by sluggish export sales, reduced domestic production, and slowing domestic demand. Unit sales to the domestic market were down 6 percent, the first annual decline. But the 1993 market is expected to recover because of escalating hardware and software price wars, the release of the Japanese version of Windows 3.1, growing support for open systems and the DOS-V operating system, and the Japanese government's promotion of PCs in schools. Dataquest has forecast that the 1993 Japanese PC market totaled 2.3 million units and $4.6 billion, up 7 percent and 6 percent, respectively, from 1992. Almost 40 percent of unit shipments were laptop and notebook computers. In 1992, about 25 percent of PCs sold were based on Intel 80486 microprocessors; 80386-based computers accounted for 60 percent; and XT and AT computers fell to 7 percent. Macintosh units made up the rest.

Business users accounted for 60 percent of shipments, where the principal business applications were Japanese-language word processing and spreadsheets. However, Japanese business users have been moving toward networking and more powerful PC platforms with larger storage capacity and more robust operating systems and complex applications. The home and education sectors represent more than 30 percent of sales. Led by demand for high-end PCs and notebook computers, the market is projected to grow at a 9 percent average annual rate through the mid-1990's.

OUTLOOK FOR 1994

The U.S. PC market will experience favorable growth rates in 1994, although less than in 1993. According to Dataquest, the PC market should grow 13 percent, to 16.3 million units, with revenue increasing slightly to $27.6 billion. While unit sales should improve, market competition will continue to put intense pressure on revenue and profit margins. Prices for mainstream 80486 computers should continue to fall during the first half of 1994, especially if Intel further reduces the price of the 486 chip in conjunction with shipments of the new Pentium chip. Prices should begin to stabilize, however, as buyers and vendors evaluate the features and impact of the new PC platforms coming into the market. Marketing requirements will shift as the market matures further. A growing portion of sales will go to the replacement market characterized by more sophisticated buyers, who require more technology-intensive solutions. However, interest from first-time buyers also will increase, stimulated by declining prices and the availability of more useful, easier-to-use software packages.

The next generation of personal computers were introduced in 1993, and will become more widely available in 1994. These systems are characterized by 32-bit multitasking operating systems, 64-bit bus architectures, more powerful RISC-featured microprocessors, multimedia capabilities, more networking and work group computing, instant communications, and mobile computing. IDC predicts that worldwide sales of Pentium-based systems will exceed 700,000 in 1994, while shipments of the Windows NT operating system will approach 1.2 million. During this upcoming technology-intensive phase, PCs will be propelled into application areas once reserved for mainframes and minicomputers.

Sales to national, state, and local governments are a small but growing segment of the market. According to Federal Sources Inc., the Federal Government's spending on computers, communications equipment, and related services will grow 2 percent in the fiscal year that began October 1993. A 4 percent drop at the Department of Defense will be more than offset by a 7 percent increase for the civilian agencies. Future demand will be stimulated by improvements in the procurement process, more emphasis on enhancing Federal employee productivity through technology, and the ongoing modernization of government programs.

Multimedia products will have a greater impact on the PC market in 1994, as the installed base of multimedia-capable and ready PCs expands and the number of multimedia titles proliferates. Multimedia is a broadly defined cornucopia of technologies designed to combine full-motion video, animation, still pictures, voice, music, graphics, and text into a fully integrated and interactive system. These new integrated capabilities bring computers a step closer to realizing their enormous potential. Potential uses include training, education, publishing, entertainment, voice and video mail, teleconferencing, public information, and document-imaging and archival systems. Although estimates vary widely depending upon one's definition, some industry sources foresee a $13 billion market by 1995.

Multimedia is still an evolving set of technologies and products. Many issues concerning technical standards remain, such as those involving video-data compression, graphics and auto file formats, interface and storage specifications, and communications protocols. There is also a question of where the market will take off first, in the home or the office. This is an arena where U.S. computer manufacturers, communication service providers, consumer electronics conglomerates, and entertainment moguls will compete and collaborate to determine the future of the personal computer.

Another growth area is overseas, where PC sales in many countries will grow faster than in the United States. Unit-shipment growth in 1994 is projected to be 16 percent worldwide, including 13 percent each in Western Europe and Japan, according to Dataquest. Factory revenue for PC shipments outside the United States should exceed $45 billion. As a result, U.S. firms will place more emphasis on investing abroad and developing and adapting products for foreign markets.

PORTABLE COMPUTERS

Today's portable computers are divided into three fairly distinct types—laptops, notebooks, and handhelds—that vary broadly by their method of entering, storing, displaying, and processing data. Laptops have been relegated to applications which demand very powerful hardware, such as computer-aided design (CAD) and video presentations. Notebooks serve the more traditional general-purpose user who wants to do a large amount of wordprocessing and manipulate sizable spreadsheets. The handheld systems have less powerful versions of these capabilities combined with more intuitive functions, such as phone lists and messaging.

With the advent of the handheld class of computer, designers are taking advantage of new technologies to bring more functions out of the office and into these personal devices. Most of the functions designed for handheld devices attempt to electronically mimic the functions of some types of office equipment or supplies, such as writing instruments, paper forms, fax machines, or telephones. The next step to computers becoming truly "personal" is to design a handheld system that can bridge the gap between consumer and office electronics, so that the same device will be used in the living room, in the car, or on the beach.

The portable market is experiencing strong overall growth, even as the form factor (shape and size) changes and component technology advances. According to Dataquest, 6.9 million portable computers were shipped worldwide in 1993, with handheld computers comprising less than 10 percent of the total (Figure 10). However, by 1996, handhelds will make up nearly 40 percent of the market.

FIGURE 10 Worldwide Portable Computer
Shipments Will Grow Rapidly

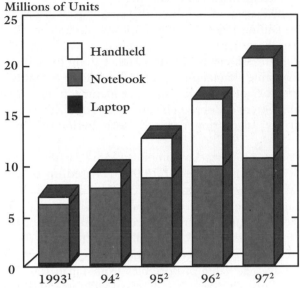

Millions of Units

Legend:
- Handheld
- Notebook
- Laptop

¹Estimate.
²Forecast.
Source: Dataquest, Inc.

In the United States, 50 percent of portable computers are sold through dealer channels, since most notebooks are purchased in large quantities by large corporate users. Product cycles have been reduced to an average of 18 months.

INTERNATIONAL COMPETITIVENESS

Several U.S., European, and Japanese companies are jointly developing products for the handheld area. In most cases, these companies have joined to penetrate more successfully the consumer electronics market with advanced computer-based products. Because breaking into the volume-driven consumer marketplace has proven to be a highly risky venture in the past, companies have formed strategic partnerships to spread the costs and the risk over more than one company. Through these partnerships, vendors also have ensured a supply of strategic components and in some cases gained valuable knowledge of marketing and manufacturing for the consumer market. As in the PC market, the profit margins probably will be established at the thinnest possible point to gain market share. Thus, potential vendors cannot base their market entry on a profit-making scenario, but rather on the potential to sell the follow-on peripherals, services, and software. For many vendors, tie ups are necessary to survive the nonprofitable stage of system development.

Japan's portable computer market is becoming increasingly competitive. The market has been dominated by one proprietary architecture, with a limited amount of useful applications software. The recent introduction of less expensive portables, based on a U.S. standard and its associated massive software library, has greatly invigorated that market. Portables already make up close to half of Japanese PC shipments, compared with around 20 percent of the U.S. PC market. As foreign vendors move into the Japanese market, more portables are being sold directly by the vendor than through traditional dealer distribution channels.

The European market also is experiencing steady growth in spite of its troubled economic picture. During 1993, European portable computer sales grew to 1.9 million units. The European market is very competitive, with many of the leading players holding roughly the same market shares as they do in the United States.

The most remarkable characteristic of the East Asian portable computer industry is the huge number of portable computer manufacturers. Despite an ongoing prediction that third-tier vendors will be driven out of business in price wars, nearly 200 vendors fill the advertising pages of such periodicals as *Asian Computer Sources.*

Domestic imports of portable computers are classified under Harmonized Systems Tariff Schedule number 8471.20.0090. Based on 6 months of data, the United States was expected to import nearly 1.9 million units in 1993, an increase of 58 percent. Imports from Japan will comprise 44 percent of total imports. The rest of Asia will account for another 42 percent. Canada, although increasing by an astronomical 485 percent in 1993, had only 13 percent of the total. In general, portable computer imports are increasing in average value, except for those from Hong Kong. The average value of portables from Japan was the highest—nearly $2,000 per unit—probably due to the high-end systems with color active-matrix displays.

OUTLOOK FOR 1994

The worldwide market for portable computers will be almost 9 million units, with handheld systems growing faster—as much as 100 percent—than notebooks and laptops. Handheld computers will benefit from improved communications and handwriting recognition capability, although they will continue to lack enough software applications to appeal to the general public.

Several different Pentium-based portable systems will be introduced by early 1994, but their market acceptance will be slowed until prices are reduced and other advanced component technology for this high-performance microprocessor (such as the battery) is incorporated. Component shortages will continue to play a role in notebook and laptop products, especially the high end. The supply of active-matrix LCD's, for example, will be tight until several fabrication facilities in Japan are ramped up to full production.

DELL COMPUTER CORPORATION—1994

C A S E

27

BILL J. MIDDLEBROOK,
MICHAEL J. KEEFFE
AND JOHN K. ROSS III
Southwest Texas
State University

Headquartered in Austin, Texas, Dell Computer Corporation (512-338-4400) is a company with skyrocketing sales and new income. Sales and profits for 1993 increased 126 percent and 99 percent, respectively.

Customer satisfaction and customer service are two of the most repeated catch phrases in major corporations. CEO Michael Dell does not want service and satisfaction simply to be repeated by his corporate employees and support staffs; he requires them to practice what he preaches. Dell's commitment to customer satisfaction and service—known at Dell as Direct Relationship Marketing—can be shown through the policies of the corporation. First, there is an unconditional 30-day money-back guarantee for all of Dell's computer systems and a "no questions asked" return policy.

Second, Dell's toll-free technical support organization is available from 7 A.M. to 7 P.M., coast to coast (including Mexico). These technicians solve 95 percent of customer problems in less than six minutes. Additionally, a TechFax system is available twenty-four hours a day, seven days a week. Customers can request technical information through a fax catalogue, and problem-solving instructions are returned by fax. A third-party network of on-site service representatives can be dispatched when problems are not solved over the phone. If necessary, unresolved problems are expedited to the design engineers to ensure complete customer satisfaction. Dell users can also access an on-line technical support group via CompuServe. Finally, Michael Dell openly invites customers to write or call him with comments about the quality of Dell's products and the level of support received from service and support personnel.

This emphasis on quality and service has won accolades from customers and industry analysts. Dell has consistently been recognized as the best in customer support and satisfaction, ahead of all other computer manufacturers. J.D. Power and Associates, known for their automobile rankings, again this year rate Dell number one in customer satisfaction in its third annual end-user survey for the computer industry. Dell's mission statement follows:

> It is the mission of Dell Computer to provide individuals, small businesses, government agencies, educational institutions and large corporations with an affordable alternative within the global PC market.
>
> Dell Computer pledges to provide the highest quality and most technologically advanced personal computers at the lowest possible price and to back those computers with the highest level of customer service.
>
> Dell Computer will continually look for new value added services to provide to its current and future customers.
>
> Dell Computer believes its commitment to service sets itself apart from its competition and helps to give customers in the global PC market a true alternative when making a computer purchase.
>
> Dell Computer strongly believes it must coexist with the environment and will continually work to promote its preservation.
>
> Dell Computer realizes the importance, and its obligation, to its employees and shareholders and will continue to operate in their best interest.

The most publicized story of a company start-up in the computer industry is that of Steven Jobs and Stephen Wozniak designing and marketing Apple computers. These young entrepreneurs took a concept from a garage manufacturing arena and evolved Apple into a multimillion-dollar organization. The story of Michael Dell and the development of the Dell Computer Corporation rivals that of Jobs and Wozniak.

In 1983 Dell, then a freshman pre-med student at the University of Texas, decided to earn additional money by selling disk-drive kits and random access memory (RAM) chips at computer user meetings in Austin, Texas. Within a few months he had sufficient funds to acquire excess personal computers (PCs) at reasonable prices from IBM dealers having difficulties meeting their sales quotas. He modified these machines and began selling them through contacts in the local area and was reported to be grossing approximately $80,000 per month by April 1984. In May 1984, Dell formed the Dell Computer Corporation to sell PC's Limited brand computers and conducted operations out of his dormitory room. After dropping out of school (against his parents' wishes), he began attending computer trade fairs where he sold IBM PC-compatible computers, one of the first custom "clones" on the market.

The results of Dell's endeavors were immediate. During the first year of business, sales were approximately $6 million and grew to $257 million within the next four years. In 1988 the brand name was changed to Dell and sales continued to grow such that by 1990 the organization had sold $546 million in PC compatibles and peripheral equipment and $2.1 billion in fiscal 1993.

In 1987, Dell established its first international subsidiary in the United Kingdom to enter the growing European computer market. European countries had a lower PC saturation rate than the United States, and there were no large PC manufacturers in Europe. From 1988 to 1991, the organization developed wholly owned subsidiaries in Canada, France, Italy, Sweden, Germany, Finland, and the Netherlands and is in the process of launching other subsidiaries in Europe. An Irish manufacturing facility opened in 1991 to provide systems for the European market. In addition, a support center located in Amsterdam provides technical support throughout Europe. By February of 1993, European sales totaled $240 million and constituted 30 percent of total sales. Currently, 40 percent of sales are derived from international subsidiaries after only five years of operations.

In January 1993, Dell made a bold move by entering the Japanese market. Dell computer KK of Japan employs a staff of forty workers to provide a full range of sales, service, and technical assistance. Telephone sales are supplemented with an outside sales force and through two major retailers in Tokyo. As the first computer company to attempt telemarketing in Japan, Dell was met with skepticism by some industry observers. Initial reports indicate that the Japanese are very enthusiastic about the marketing approach and are responding in greater numbers than originally forecasted. Although successful, Dell is expected to have less than 1 percent of the Japanese market in 1993.

Dell Computer Corporation today has approximately 4,200 employees worldwide. Mr. Dell has surrounded himself with people having expertise in computer engineering and marketing; he serves as both chief executive officer (CEO) and chairman of the board of directors. The company currently operates on the principles espoused by Dell during its inception: customer service and a personal relationship with Dell system users.

The short history of the PC industry is one of booms and slumps. The stellar performance of the industry during the early to mid-1980s was followed by a consolidation of existing companies and a slowdown in sales during the 1986–1987 period. Industry sales increased through 1990, and projections show that corporate capital-equipment spending should grow at a 7 to 8 percent annual rate into the early 1990s. Some analysts contend that the growth rate of the PC industry is uncertain as the growth rate of the economy slows. For example, Volpe & Covington, a San Francisco-based PC investment consulting firm, believes that a 15 percent long-term growth in revenues for high-end PCs and a 12 percent compound growth rate for the industry is a reasonable assumption. Other analysts contend that PC sales will grow at only 5 to 7 percent in the 1990s, less than half as fast as sales grew in the late 1980s. In 1992, computer and peripheral sales totaled over $142 billion. This amount grew to $155 billion in 1993 and is projected to exceed $167 billion in 1994.

PC Industry Strategies. Two macroindustry strategies for competing in the PC industry can be combined with two macrosegments of the PC market to assess competitors and competitive approaches. First, PC manufacturers can approach the market as either innovators or imitators. IBM is the accepted innovation leader as both computer manufacturers and customers watch IBM's product development and base production and purchase decisions on current IBM products. Other computer manufacturers approach the market as innovators by developing hardware and software to satisfy specific market segments.

Some firms approach the market building clone PCs. These firms (sometimes called value-added remarketers) use the base MS-DOS technology of innovators and attempt to improve on the system configuration and/or differentiate their product on some basis such as marketing channel used, service and support, product reliability, and/or price. Essentially, value-added remarketers buy components and software from various vendors to configure systems sold under their own brand labels. The success of the imitative approaches is evidenced by the performance of companies such as Compaq, Prime Computer, Inc., CompuAdd, and Dell. Many clone firms believe that to be successful in the PC industry they must be concerned with market pressures to reduce price. They constantly monitor costs and search for ways to reduce those costs.

PC Markets. Macrosegments in the PC industry are usually defined as business, home, government, or education users. Business users want high performance, reliability, and value in a system for their computing needs. State-of-the-art technology, the ability to network and communicate with other systems, customer service and support, and cost are primary purchase determinants for the business user. One of the fastest-growing segments in the business market is the portables market, which is expected to grow at an annualized rate of 20 percent for the next few years.

Home market demand was initially created by innovators, early adopters, and the early majority groups of the adoption or diffusion of innovation cycle. Most home users are price conscious, planning to spend less than $1,200 for a system, and they value ease of operation and service as well as support from the manufacturer. This market should not be as lucrative as it was in the early to mid-1980s, but replacement sales (sales to previous PC owners) and sales to those still intending to buy a home PC should make this market moderately attractive. (For a list of competitors by market share, see Exhibits 27–1, 27–2 and 27–3.)

EXHIBIT 27-1 Worldwide Microsystems Shipped (in millions)

COMPANY	1989	1993*
IBM	2.7	4.4
Apple	1.5	3.2
COMPAQ	0.7	2.5
Sharp	1.4	1.9
NEC	1.1	1.7
Dell	0.1	1.4
Commodore	1.5	1.3
Packard Bell	0.3	0.9
Toshiba	0.4	0.8
AST	0.2	0.8
All others	13.5	22.2

*Projected
Source: infoCorp.

EXHIBIT 27-2 United States Microsystems Units Shipped (in millions)

COMPANY	1989	1993*
IBM	1.5	1.8
Apple	1.1	1.7
COMPAQ	0.4	1.1
Dell	0.1	0.9
Packard Bell	0.2	0.8
Gateway 2000	**	0.6
Hewlett-Packard	0.1	0.4
AST	0.2	0.4
Tandy	0.6	0.4
Commodore	0.4	0.3
All others	5.0	7.2

*Projected
**<100,000
Source: infoCorp.

Government and education users comprise the remaining macrosegments of the PC market. Both of these segments represent large, important segments yet typically yield lower margins than either the business or home markets. Typical purchase decisions are based on a bidding system, with the contract going to the lowest qualified bidder. The education market was considered important for its proposed ability to generate long-term brand loyalty among early users (students). Apple was one of the

EXHIBIT 27-3 Market share, 1992–1993* (percent)

COMPANY	MARKET SHARE 1993 *	MARKET SHARE 1992
IBM	13.9	11.7
Apple	13.5	13.0
COMPAQ	9.5	5.7
AST	6.2	2.7
Dell	5.7	3.8
Top 5	48.8	36.9

*Projected

Source: International Data Corp. *Wall Street Journal,* Thurs., Oct. 21, 1993, page B1.

earliest entrants into this market. It is questionable, however, if the long-term benefits of brand loyalty by early users is actually realized.

This segment, like the business segment, is interested in integrated systems designed to perform to buyers' specific needs. Increased competition for this market has led to increased downward pressures on prices.

Competitors. Major competitors of Dell include most traditional PC manufacturers such as IBM, Compaq, Zenith, and Tandy. These firms rely on selling through a professional sales force or through retail outlets. Competitors of Dell using a direct marketing and/or retailing approach (primarily value-added remarketers) include CompuAdd, which offers a full line of machines; Northgate, which offers machines similar to Dell at savings of up to $2,000 over Dell equipment; and Everex, which offers machines similar to Dell but claim that they are faster than Dell PCs. CompuAdd is located in Austin, Texas; Northgate in Plymouth, Minnesota; and Everex in Freemont, California. None of these firms have the service and satisfaction reputation of Dell.

Changes in the industry will be driven by several factors as the market matures. First, the Gartner Group, a market research firm, estimates that the number of customers replacing their outdated systems are expected to outnumber first-time purchasers by 1995.

Second, an investment report on the PC distribution industry shows that PC saturation rates are relatively low. Only about 33 percent of white-collar workers use PCs on the job, and only 17 percent of all domestic households have a PC. This becomes more important when one considers that the largest growth opportunities are in small to medium-sized accounts (businesses with fewer than 500 employees) that employ more than 70 percent of white-collar workers.

Third, the ratio of price to performance for equivalent functions continues to improve approximately 20 to 25 percent per year, which makes the purchase of state-of-the art machines more attractive to many segments. And fourth, competition should intensify. Value-added remarketers more than doubled during the 1988–1989 period, with the number of firms increasing from 350 to more than 1,000. Coupled with increased demand by business users, improved software and networking capabil-

EXHIBIT 27-4 Dell Computer Corporation, Selected Annual Financial Ratios

	01/31/93	02/02/92	02/03/91
Quick ratio	0.95	1.39	0.90
Current ratio	1.73	2.23	1.67
Sales/cash	21.13	5.75	14.91
Receivables turnover	5.38	5.39	6.09
Receivables days sales	66.86	66.73	59.12
Inventories turnover	6.64	7.03	6.17
Net sales/working capital	5.61	3.15	5.74
Net sales/current assets	2.36	1.74	2.31
Net sales/total assets	2.17	1.59	2.07
Total liab/total assets	0.60	0.51	0.58
Times interest earned	NA	NA	NA
Net income/net sales	0.05	0.06	0.05
Net income/total assets	0.11	0.09	0.10

ities, and increased competition through differentiation and focus-oriented marketing strategies, industry analysts forecast additional changes in both market approaches used by major competitors and further segmentation of the market. The 1990s should be a period of change for the industry, rivaling changes that occurred during the 1980s.

DELL COMPUTER OPERATIONS

Dell's success can be attributed to its commitment to customer service and satisfaction and the marketing of state-of-the-art systems to business users through direct marketing strategies.

Product Line. Dell offers an extensive and competitive product line ranging from inexpensive first-time-user computers to those with the latest technological developments. This strategy has resulted in a continuing evaluation and modification of Dell's product line with new products constantly being offered and other products being discontinued. Currently Dell is working with Microsoft to deliver factory installed Windows NT in high end workstations and networks as the software becomes available. Dell also plans to sell IBM's competing OS/2 operating system preinstalled. The ever changing demands of computer technology and the market have made product forecasting and planning difficult and risky.

Manufacturing. Dell's computers for the domestic market are manufactured in facilities in Austin, Texas. The purchase of a 126,000 square-foot manufacturing facility in 1989 doubled Dell's manufacturing capability. The 135,000-square-foot facility in Limerick, Ireland, is expected to satisfy the growing international demand for Dell Systems.

EXHIBIT 27-5 Dell Computer Corporation Officers

OFFICERS		
NAME	AGE	TITLE
Dell, Michael S.	28	Chairman of the Board, CEO
Kocher, Joel J.	36	President, Worldwide Marketing, Sales and Service
Henry, G. Glenn	50	Senior Vice President
Flaig, L. Scott	48	Senior Vice President
Meredith, Thomas J.	42	Chief Financial Officer, Treasurer
Thomas, Thomas L.	43	Chief Information Officer
Ferrales, Savino R.	42	Vice President
Salwen, Richard E.	47	Vice President, Legal Counsel
Medica, John	34	Vice President, Portable Products Group

The manufacturing strategy utilized at Dell is one of building each computer system to the buyer's specifications. Buyers can add options to customize their system for their own needs. The order is then assembled and shipped with peripherals and upgrades requested by the customer. Manufacturing at Dell actually consists of the assembly and testing of vendor-procured parts, assemblies, and subassemblies. The assembly line is not automated at present, and Dell has not indicated plans to automate. In addition, Dell utilizes a total quality approach where enthusiastic workers compete in product-quality competitions for bonuses and recognition.

Marketing. One factor leading to Dell's success is the organization's marketing style. Dell approaches the market from a service and customer satisfaction standpoint combined with lower prices than comparable brands. Sales leads are generated through several sources, the primary source being advertising in PC and business publications. An outside sales force located in major markets addresses the needs of large corporate customers.

Dell's sales force is channelized according to the market it serves: small/medium business and home users, corporate buyers, and government/education/medical. Each of these sales channels is supported by its own marketing, customer service, and technical support organization. This organizational structure ensures high accountability for the satisfaction of each customer, as well as feedback from daily direct contact with the customer. PC makers dealing through the retail channel do not have this advantage and are not able to respond as quickly to market and service demands as the direct channel. Additional face-to-face exposure occurs at industry shows.

Dell's entire product line is sold by telephone sales representatives who answer more than 8,000 incoming calls on a busy day. In addition to answering customer-initiated calls, the Austin-based sales force responds to sales leads and supports the efforts of its team members in the field.

Sales orders are downloaded to the manufacturing facility several times each day, and all systems are custom-configured according to the customer's specifications. Trucks load at Dell's manufacturing facility throughout the day, and overnight services are utilized for expedited orders. Lead times on systems vary from three to seven days.

Internationally, Dell is similar in marketing approach and culture to its domestic operation. Dell's wholly owned subsidiaries give it access to over 70 percent of the available worldwide market for PCs.

Dell sells to major buyers through a small (twenty-five-person) sales force located in major metropolitan areas throughout the United States and services those accounts with management teams consisting of sales, customer service, and technical support representatives. Dell believes that the small- to medium-sized business represents the greatest growth potential for PC-based systems.

Dell has also arranged to sell its systems through integrators like Electronic Data Systems (EDS) and Anderson Consulting, which will increase its sales potential. This move from traditional channels was prompted by the fact that the mail-order market is only 16 percent of a $35 to $40 billion market, less than one-fifth the size of sales of computer stores. Dell currently has 25 percent of the mail-order market.

RETAIL

Dell has contracted with CompUSA, Inc., a Dallas-based chain of twenty superstores, to sell Dell products. CompUSA is a computer version of Toys " Я " Us, with approximately 21,000 square feet of retail space per store, a service center with a fast service pickup for corporate clients, and over 5,000 items at discount prices. CompUSA is adding new stores in major metropolitan areas and sells Dell systems for the same prices as Dell's direct sales.

Dell has added Staples Office Supply Superstores to its mass merchandising channel. Staples markets to a less sophisticated computer user than does CompUSA. Although Dell systems are sold through this superstore channel, Dell maintains its same level of customer support to these buyers. Users who purchase Dell systems through CompUSA and Staples are entered into Dell's customer data base as if they had ordered directly through Dell.

Dell's mass merchandising move may provide a serendipitous opportunity for the company even though computer retailing is seen by some industry analysts as poised for a shakeout. Dataquest, Inc., believes that traditional retailers will see their share of PC sales shrink through 1994. Analysts state that marketers will have to move toward the ends of the retail spectrum by either concentrating on high-volume, low-price selling or specializing in market niches or other customized services that mass marketers neglect in order to be successful. Smaller operations that emphasize service along with price are already showing the greatest gains. Superstores may be one retail format that not only survives the shakeout but prospers. Dell sells its Precision Line of Computers through Sam's Clubs, a division of Wal★Mart Stores Incorporated, and also through Price Club, another mass merchandising chain.

Research and Development. During the last few years, Dell's revenue growth has allowed the organization to devote considerable resources to building a first-class technological capability. Research and development spending for fiscal 1992 was $31.3 million, up 26 percent from 1991.

Finance. Financial summaries of Dell are presented in Exhibits 27–6 through 27–11. The organization does not pay dividends to investors, relying instead on appreciation of stock price. It has experienced good sales and profit growth. Dell is currently searching for ways to reduce costs without sacrificing customer service and technological performance of its systems.

ISSUES AND CONCERNS

The most pressing concern of investors regarding Dell operations is Michael Dell. Dell has been very successful in building his organization with an entrepreneurial style of management. On a scale of one to ten, Dell rates himself ten as a competitor, innovator, goal setter, entrepreneur, and exporter. He rates himself lowest in the areas of production and finance. Although Mr. Dell was recently cited as Entrepreneur of the Year by *Inc.* magazine, his critics wonder if he is capable of making the transition of moving the corporation from a Stage 1 entrepreneurial mode to a Stage 2 professional management company.

Another concern is Dell's current move to include retail sales in addition to its traditional strength of telemarketing. This move is designed to broaden Dell's appeal to small businesses and the home PC user, but retailers historically have not shown loyalty to any particular brand of machine and may stock several different brands in their stores. Additionally, Dell's emphasis on telemarketing is a double-edged sword.

EXHIBIT 27-6 Dell Computer Corporation, Consolidated Statement of Income (In thousands of dollars, except per share data)

	FISCAL YEAR		
	1993	1992	1991
Net sales	$2,013,924	$889,939	$546,235
Cost of sales	1,564,472	607,768	364,183
Gross profit	449,452	282,171	182,052
Operating expenses:			
Marketing and sales	220,907	142,932	88,662
General and administrative	47,075	39,223	26,354
Research, development and engineering	42,358	33,140	22,444
Total operating expenses	310,340	215,295	137,460
Operating income	139,112	66,876	44,592
Financing and other income (expense)	4,180	6,539	(1,020)
Income before income taxes	143,292	73,415	43,572
Provision for income taxes	41,650	22,504	16,340
Net income	$ 101,642	$ 50,911	$ 27,232
Earnings per share	$ 2.59	$ 1.40	$ .91
Weighted average shares outstanding	39,235	36,274	30,064

Source: Dell Computer Corporation, *Annual Report,* 1993.

Telemarketing does reduce the need for a field sales force and eliminates channel markups, but Dell is considered by some to be little more than a dim, dusty warehouse that sells cheap, undistinguished PCs.

Lastly, the question also arises whether Dell can continue to grow as quickly as it would like and still have the same emphasis on service, performance, and satisfaction. There is intense competition as the industry matures and growth slows. Dell is still one of the infants in an industry populated by giants, and it must be wary of financial and technological colossuses potentially entering its market niche.

EXHIBIT 27-7 Dell Computer Corporation, Consolidated Statement of Financial Position (In thousands of dollars, except per share data)

	JANUARY 31, 1993	FEBRUARY 2, 1992
Assets		
Current assets:		
Cash and cash equivalents	$ 14,948	$ 55,460
Short-term investments	80,367	99,392
Accounts receivable, net	374,013	164,960
Inventories	303,220	126,554
Other current assets	80,239	65,814
Total current assets	852,787	512,180
Property and equipment, net	70,462	44,661
Other assets	3,756	2,722
	$927,005	$559,563
Liabilities and stockholders' equity		
Current liabilities:		
Accounts payable	$295,133	$ 97,389
Accrued liabilities	171,473	114,816
Income taxes	27,233	17,329
Total current liabilities	493,839	229,534
Long-term debt	48,373	41,450
Other liabilities	15,593	14,399
Commitments and contingencies		
Stockholders' equity:		
Preferred stock: $.01 par value; shares authorized: 5,000,000; none outstanding	—	—
Common stock: $.01 par value; shares authorized: 100,000,000; shares issued and outstanding: 36,857,948 and 35,801,620, respectively	369	358
Additional paid-in capital	177,978	165,745
Retained earnings	208,544	106,902
Cumulative translation adjustment	(17,691)	1,175
Total stockholders' equity	369,200	274,180
	$927,005	$559,563

Source: Dell Computer Corporation, *Annual Report*, 1993.

EXHIBIT 27-8 Dell Computer Corporation, Selected Consolidated Financial Data
(In thousands of dollars, except per share and operating data)

	FISCAL YEAR ENDED				
	JAN 31, 1993	FEB 2, 1992	FEB 3, 1991	FEB 2, 1990	JAN 27, 1989
Income statement data:					
Net Sales:					
Domestic	$1,283,899	$566,392	$ 358,877	$300,257	$ 218,204
International	730,025	323,547	187,358	88,301	39,606
Consolidated net sales	$2,013,924	$889,939	$ 546,235	$388,558	$ 257,810
Gross Profit	$ 449,452	$282,171	$ 182,052	$109,586	$ 80,512
Operating income	$ 139,112	$ 66,876	$ 44,592	$ 11,414	$ 21,550
Net income	$ 101,642	$ 50,911	$ 27,232	$ 5,114	$ 14,428
Earnings per share	$ 2.59	$ 1.40	$ .91	$ .18	$ .53
Shares used in per share calculation	39,235	36,274	30,064	28,843	27,019
Balance sheet data:					
Working capital	$ 358,948	$282,646	$ 95,163	$ 57,970	$ 63,126
Total assets	$ 927,005	$559,563	$ 264,222	$171,774	$ 167,032
Long-term obligations	$ 50,621	$ 43,740	$ 4,207	$ 6,041	$ 5,472
Stockholders' equity	$ 369,200	$274,180	$ 112,005	$ 79,761	$ 75,257
Operating data:					
Current ratio	1.7	2.2	1.7	1.7	1.7
Inventories/working capital	.8	.4	.9	1.2	1.6
Debt to equity ratio	.15	.15	.00	.08	.36
Return on average assets	14 %	12 %	12 %	3 %	13 %
Return on average equity	32 %	26 %	28 %	7 %	34 %
Effective tax rate	29.1%	30.7%	37.5%	38.2%	31.8%

Source: Dell Computer Corporation, *Annual Report*, 1993.

EXHIBIT 27-9 Dell Computer Corporation Financial Condition and Results of Operations

	PERCENTAGE OF NET SALES FISCAL YEAR ENDED		
	JANUARY 31, 1993	FEBRUARY 2, 1992	FEBRUARY 3, 1991
Net sales:			
Domestic	63.8%	63.6%	65.7%
International	36.2	36.4	34.3
Consolidated net sales	100.0	100.0	100.0
Cost of sales	77.7	68.3	66.7
Gross profit	22.3	31.7	33.3
Operating expenses:			
Marketing and sales	11.0	16.1	16.2
General and administrative	2.3	4.4	4.8
Research, development and engineering	2.1	3.7	4.1
Total operating expenses	15.4	24.2	25.1
Operating income	6.9	7.5	8.2
Net financing and other income (expense)	.2	.7	.2
Income before income taxes	7.1	8.2	8.0
Provision for income taxes	2.1	2.5	3.0
Net Income	5.0%	5.7%	5.0%

Source: Dell Computer Corporation, *Annual Report*, 1993.

EXHIBIT 27-10 Dell Computer Corporation Consolidated Statement of Cash Flows (In thousands of dollars)

	FISCAL YEAR		
	1993	1992	1991
Cash flow from operating activities:			
Net income	$ 101,642	$ 50,911	$ 27,232
Charges to income not requiring cash outlays:			
Depreciation and amortization	19,597	13,832	8,955
Other	149	5,841	3,660
Changes in:			
Operating working capital	(162,521)	(70,962)	4,036
Non-current assets and liabilities	2,111	871	6,946
	(140,664)	(50,418)	(23,597)
Net cash (used in) provided by operating activities	(39,022)	493	50,829
Cash flow from investing activities:			
Net sales (purchases) of short-term investments	19,025	(99,392)	—
Capital expenditures	(47,251)	(32,630)	(9,485)
Net cash used in investing activities	(28,226)	(132,022)	(9,485)
Cash flow from financing activities:			
Net proceeds from short-term borrowings	8,500	—	—

EXHIBIT 27-10 *Continued*

| | FISCAL YEAR | | |
	1993	1992	1991
Borrowings from long-term debt	7,270	41,450	—
Repayments of borrowings	(711)	(2,577)	(8,791)
Net proceeds from issuance of common stock	—	105,659	—
Issuance of common stock under employee plans	12,244	6,112	2,595
Net cash provided by (used in) financing activities	27,303	150,644	(6,196)
Effect of translation exchage rate changes on cash	(567)	(282)	1,479
Net (decrease) increase in cash	(40,512)	18,833	36,627
Cash at beginning of period	55,460	36,627	—
Cash at end of period	$ 14,948	$ 55,460	$ 36,627

Source: Dell Computer Corporation, *Annual Report*, 1993.

EXHIBIT 27-11 Dell Computer Corporation Consolidated Statement of Stockholders' Equity (In thousands of dollars, except share data)

STOCKHOLDERS' EQUITY					
	COMMON STOCK	PAID-IN CAPITAL	RETAINED EARNINGS	TRANSLATION ADJUSTMENT	TOTAL
Balances at February 2, 1990	$282	$ 51,455	$ 28,759	$ (735)	$ 79,761
Net income	—	—	27,232	—	27,232
Issuance of stock under employee plans	8	2,587	—	—	2,595
Foreign currency translation adjustment	—	—	—	2,417	2,417
Balances at February 3, 1991	290	54,042	55,991	1,682	112,005
Net Income	—	—	50,911	—	50,911
Issuance of 5,762,250 shares of common stock, net	58	105,601	—	—	105,659
Issuance of stock under employee plans	10	6,102	—	—	6,112
Foreign currency translation adjustment	—	—	—	(507)	(507)
Balances at February 2, 1992	358	165,745	106,902	1,175	274,180
Net income	—	—	101,642	—	101,642
Issuance of stock under employee plans	11	12,233	—	—	12,244
Foreign currency translation adjustment	—	—	—	(18,866)	(18,866)
Balances at January 31, 1993	$369	$177,978	$208,544	$(17,691)	$369,200

Source: Dell Computer Corporation, *Annual Report*, 1993.

EXHIBIT 27-12 Dell Computer Corporation Offices

CORPORATE
HEADQUARTERS
Dell Computer Corporation
9505 Arboretum Boulevard
Austin, Texas 78759-7299
Tel: (512) 338-4400, (800) 289-3355
Fax: (512) 338-8700

INTERNATIONAL OFFICES
AUSTRALIA:
Dell Computer Pty Ltd
Unit 13, 25 Frenchs Forest Rd.
Frenchs Forest NSW 2086
Australia
Tel: (61) 2-930-3355
Fax: (61) 2-930-3311

AUSTRIA:
Dell Computer GES.m.b.H
Inkustraße 1-7, Haus H/7
3400 Klosterneuburg
Tel: (43) 2243-34100
Fax:(43)2243-34102

BELGIUM & LUXEMBOURG:
N.V. Dell Computer S.A.
Doornveld 1, Bus 15
1731 Asse-Zellik
Belgium
Tel: (32) 2-466-91-99
Fax: (32) 2-466-47-89

CANADA:
Dell Computer Corporation
121 Granton Drive, Unit 12
Richmond Hill, Ontario
Canada L4B3N4
Tel: (416) 764-4200
Fax: (416) 764-4209

CZECH REPUBLIC:
Dell Computer s.r.o.
Osadni 12a 17000 Prague 7
Czech Republic
Tel: (42) 2-879250
Fax: (42) 2-808237

EUROPEAN MARKETING AND OPERATIONS:
European Marketing & Operations
Dell Computer Corporation
Western Road
Bracknell, Berkshire
U.K. RG12 1RW
Tel: (44) 344-860-456
Fax: (44) 344-714-697

EUROPEAN SUPPORT CENTRE:
European Support Centre
p.a. Dell Computer BV
Zekeringstraat 45B
1014 BP, Amsterdam
The Netherlands
Tel: (31) 20-684-9291
Fax: (31) 20-682-3596

FINLAND:
Dell Computer OY
Vattuniemenranta 2
00210 Helsinki
Finland
Tel: (358) 0-692-3122
Fax: (358) 0-692-2847

FRANCE (MONTPELLIER):
Dell Computer S.A.
BP 9646
34054 Montpellier Cedex 1
France
Tel: (33) 6706-6000
Fax: (33) 6706-6001

FRANCE:
Dell Computer
2, Parc Club Ariane BP-285
78053 St. Quentin en Yvelines Cedex
France
Tel: (33)-1-30 60 69 00
Fax:(33)-1-30 60 69 01

GERMANY:
Dell Computer GmbH
Monzastr. 4
6070 Langen
Germany
Tel: (49) 6103-701-0
Fax:(49) 6103-701-701

EXHIBIT 27-12 *Continued*

IRELAND:
Dell Products (Europe) B.V.
Raheen Industrial Estate
Raheen, Limerick
Republic of Ireland
Tel: (353) 61-304091
Fax: (353) 61 304090

IRELAND(Bray):
Dell Computer Corporation
Boghall Road
Bray
Co. Wicklow
Tel: (353) 1 2860500
Fax: (353) 1 2862020

ITALY:
Dell Computer SPA
Via Enrico Fermi, 20
20090 Assago Milano
Italy
Tel: (39) 2-457941
Fax: (39) 2-45794001

JAPAN:
Dell Computer Corporation
Gotanda Nagase Bldg.
2-8-3, Higashi Gotanda
Shinagawa-Ku, Tokyo 141
Japan
Tel: (81-3) 5420-5901
Fax: (81-3) 5420-7366

MEXICO:
Dell Computer de Mexico, S.A. de C.V.
Blvd. M. de Cervantes Saavedra 61
Colonia Granda
11520 Mexico, D.F.
Tel: (525) 228-7800
Fax: (525) 228-7840

NETHERLANDS:
Dell Computer BV
Zekeringstraat 45 B
1014 BP Amsterdam
The Netherlands
Tel: (31) 20-6812666
Fax: (31) 20-6812751

NORWAY:
Dell Computer AS
Drammensveien 302-304
N-1324 Lysaker
Norway
Tel: (47) 67 12 57 11
Fax. (47) 67 12 55 03

POLAND:
Dell Computer Poland
Stawki Str. 2, XIV Floor
00-193 Warsaw
Poland
Tel: (482) 635-7641
Fax: (482) 635-7162

SOUTHEAST ASIA:
PROCUREMENT OFFICE:
Dell Computer Corporation
Southeast Asia Procurement Office
No. 8, Lane 6 Hang ChouS. Road, Sec. 1
Taipei, Taiwan
Republic of China
Tel: (886) 2-391-2100
Fax: (886) 2-391-3354

SPAIN:
Dell España S.A.
Barajas Park
San Severo s/n
28042 Madrid
Spain
Tel: (34) 1-329-10-80
Fax: (34) 1-329-26-10

SWEDEN:
Dell Computer AB
Kanalvägen 8, Box 709
194 27 Upplands Våsby
Sweden
Tel: (46) 08-590 713 50
Fax: (46) 08-590 737 89

SWITZERLAND:
Dell Computer SA
220 route de Ferney
Ch-1218 Grand-Saconnex-Geneva
Tel: (41) 22-788-40-00
Fax: (41) 22-788-38-66

EXHIBIT 27-12 *Continued*

UNITED KINGDOM:
  Dell Computer Corporation Ltd.
  Milbanke House, Western Road
  Bracknell, Berkshire
  RG12 1RW
  United Kingdom
  Tel: (44) 344 720000
  Fax: (44) 344 860187

Source: Dell Computer Corporation, *Annual Report*, 1993.

C A S E
28

FRED R. DAVID
Francis Marion
University

IBM CORPORATION—1994

The year 1993 was the worst in IBM's history. Net losses were $8.1 billion on revenues of $62.7 billion. Big Blue was a company in Big Trouble. IBM reduced its workforce by 45,000 in 1993 to a total of 256,000. By the end of 1994 and with divestiture of the Federal Systems Company, the IBM workforce should drop to 215,000. Brown Brothers Harriman & Company, an investment brokerage firm, has concluded that "Technological changes in the computer business will preclude IBM from ever returning to its former greatness."

Headquartered in Armonk, New York, IBM's (914-765-1900) CEO Louis Gerstner, Jr., was recently criticized when he made the following comment in a speech:

> The last thing IBM needs right now is a vision. I could spend a lot of time focusing this company on a mission statement, and would love it. But there would be debate instead of action, when the most important thing we have to do is implement better and sooner. I want to stay away from abstractions and deal with the marketplace. Our mission is to be the most successful information technology company in the world. O.K., you want a vision statement? Fine, you got it, now let's go back to work.

IBM does not have a mission statement. Yet CEO Gersner says "Setting strategies is our single highest priority after making IBM profitable. We are hard at work—day and night—developing tough-minded strategies for every one of our businesses." IBM was granted 1,087 U.S. patents in 1993, more than any other company in the world.

OPERATIONS

IBM continues aggressively to restructure its worldwide business operations to reduce costs and regain a competitive posture. As indicated in Exhibit 28–1, more than 90 percent of IBM's revenues are derived from computer hardware, computer software, computer services, and computer maintenance. Revenues from computer services rose 32.1 percent in 1993, but revenues from the other three categories declined as shown. It is interesting that more than 50 percent of IBM's revenues came from non-hardware sources in 1993.

EXHIBIT 28-1 IBM Selected Income and Expense Items

PERCENTAGE OF TOTAL REVENUE				PERCENTAGE CHANGES*	
1991	1992	1993	INCOME AND EXPENSE ITEMS	1993-92	1992-91
			REVENUE:		
57.3%	52.3%	48.8%	Hardware sales	(9.4)%	(9.0)%
16.2	17.2	17.5	Software	(1.1)	5.8
8.6	11.4	15.5	Services	32.1	31.7
11.4	11.8	11.6	Maintenance	(4.4)	3.0
6.5	7.3	6.6	Rentals and financing	(10.9)	11.9
100.0	100.0	100.0	Total revenue	(2.8)	(0.4)
49.5	54.4	61.5	Total cost	10.0	9.3
50.5	45.6	38.5	Gross profit	(18.0)	(9.9)
			EXPENSES:		
33.0	30.3	29.2	Selling, general and administrative	(6.4)	(8.7)
			Research, development,		
10.3	10.1	8.9	and engineering	(14.8)	(1.8)
5.8	18.0	14.3	Restructuring charges	—	—
49.1	58.4	52.4	Total operating expenses	—	—
0.9	0.9	1.8	Other Income, principally interest	94.2	(4.8)
2.2	2.1	2.0	Interest expense	(6.4)	(4.4)
			NET EARNINGS:		
			Before restructuring charges and		
3.5	2.2	0.0	accounting changes	—	—
(4.4)	(7.7)	(12.9)	Net loss	—	—

*Percentage changes displayed as (-) are not meaningful.
Source: IBM *Annual Report*, 1993.

HARDWARE SALES (DOLLARS IN MILLIONS)	1993	1992	1991
Total revenue	$30,591	$33,755	$37,093
Total cost	20,696	19,698	18,571
Gross profit	$ 9,895	$14,057	$18,522
Gross profit margin	32.3%	41.6%	49.9%

Hardware and Software. As indicated above, worldwide gross profit dollars from hardware sales decreased 29.6 percent in 1993, primarily due to a 27.6 percent decrease in processors such as the System 390 processor and the Application/System/400. IBM produces and markets both high-end and midrange processors as well as workstations.

IBM's personal computer systems revenue increased 23.3 percent in 1993 due partly to strong growth in RISC System/6000. IBM shipped about 4.3 million personal computers in 1992 compared to 3.3 million units the prior year. In 1993, other hardware sales revenue increased 68.1 percent, primarily due to higher original equipment manufacturer (OEM) growth.

IBM's 1993 gross profit dollars in software decreased 7.5 percent while revenues declined to $10.9 million (see below).

Services and Maintenance. IBM's services revenue, excluding maintenance, grew 32.1 percent in 1993 while services gross profit dollars increased 10.1 percent. Federal Systems Company, a part of IBM's services operations, was sold in the first quarter of 1994. As indicated in the table on the opposite page, IBM's maintenance revenue decreased 4.4 percent in 1993. A summary of IBM's revenues by classes of similar products or services is given in Exhibit 28–2.

SOFTWARE *(DOLLARS IN MILLIONS)*	1993	1992	1991
Total revenue	$10,953	$11,103	$10,498
Total cost	4,310	3,924	3,865
Gross profit	$ 6,643	$ 7,179	$ 6,633
Gross profit margin	60.7%	64.7%	63.2%

EXHIBIT 28-2 IBM Revenue by Classes of Similar Products or Services (*Dollars in millions*)

	CONSOLIDATED			U.S. ONLY		
	1993	1992[+]	1991[+]	1993	1992[+]	1991[+]
Information technology:						
Processors*	$10,071	$13,916	$14,954	$ 3,179	$ 4,818	$ 4,717
Personal systems*	9,728	7,887	8,505	4,417	3,033	3,210
Other workstations*	2,006	2,671	3,216	689	874	1,040
Storage*	5,122	6,259	7,184	2,101	2,554	2,825
Other peripherals*	2,262	3,026	3,294	971	1,244	1,424
Software	10,953	11,103	10,498	3,898	3,883	3,760
Maintenance	7,295	7,635	7,414	2,726	2,809	2,884
Services	9,711	7,352	5,582	5,100	3,546	2,697
Financing and other	5,568	4,674	4,119	2,622	1,872	1,870
Total	$62,716	$64,523	$64,766	$25,703	$24,633	$24,427

[+]Reclassified to conform with 1993 presentation.

*Hardware only, includes applicable rental revenue, excludes functions not embedded, software, and maintenance.

Source: IBM *Annual Report*, 1993.

SERVICES (DOLLARS IN MILLIONS)	1993	1992	1991
Services	$ 7,648	$ 5,530	$ 4,144
Federal Systems Company	2,063	1,822	1,438
Services revenue excluding maintenance	$ 9,711	$ 7,352	$ 5,582
Cost	8,279	6,051	4,531
Gross profit	$ 1,432	$ 1,301	$ 1,051
Gross profit margin	14.7%	17.7%	18.8%
Maintenance revenue	$ 7,295	$ 7,635	$ 7,414
Cost	3,545	3,430	3,379
Gross profit	$ 3,750	$ 4,205	$ 4,035
Gross profit margin	51.4%	55.1%	54.4%
Total services revenue	$17,006	$14,987	$12,996
Cost	11,824	9,481	7,910
Gross profit	$ 5,182	$ 5,506	$ 5,086
Gross profit margin	30.5%	36.7%	39.1%

Services revenue, excluding maintenance, continued to show overall strong growth, increasing 32.1 percent in 1993 over 1992, following an increase of 31.7 percent in 1992 over 1991.

GLOBAL FACTORS

Exhibit 28–3 reveals that IBM markets its products and services globally. Revenue in the United States was $25.7 billion, up 4.3 percent, while 1993 revenue from non-U.S. operations generated revenue of $37.0 billion, a 7.2 percent decrease from 1992. Note that IBM's Asia Pacific operations increased to over $10 billion in 1993 but the company's Europe/Middle East/Africa revenues declined 12.8 percent to $21.8 billion. In the Europe/Middle East/Africa area, European operations account for about 95 percent of IBM's revenue.

MANAGEMENT AND FINANCE

Members of IBM's top management team are listed in Exhibit 28–4. The company's 1993 financial statements are provided in Exhibits 28–5 through 28–8. Note that the company's long-term debt increased 18.6 percent, partly to cover expenses since net profits were negative $8.1 billion.

PARTNERS

The rush of new technology, the expense of staying on the leading edge, the demands of customers, and worldwide competition have required IBM and other high-tech companies to form a wide range of alliances and partnerships. The costs of developing the 256-million-bit memory chip (in a three-way pact with Siemens and Toshiba) may, for example, reach a billion dollars. With these stakes, sharing costs, risk, and knowledge is essential.

EXHIBIT 28-3 IBM Geographic Areas (*Dollars in millions*)

	1993*	1992*	1991*
United States			
Revenue—Customers	$ 25,703	$ 24,633	$ 24,427
Interarea transfers	7,297	7,524	7,668
Total	$ 33,000	$ 32,157	$ 32,095
Net loss	(5,566)	(5,545)	(2,443)
Assets at December 31	38,333	42,109	43,417
Europe/Middle East/Africa			
Revenue—Customers	$ 21,779	$ 24,971	$ 26,114
Interarea transfers	1,071	1,154	838
Total	$ 22,850	$ 26,125	$ 26,952
Net (loss) earnings	(1,695)	(1,728)	1,256
Assets at December 31	24,566	26,770	30,725
Asia Pacific			
Revenue—Customers	$ 10,020	$ 9,672	$ 9,275
Interarea transfers	1,452	1,875	1,680
Total	$ 11,472	$ 11,547	$ 10,955
Net (loss) earnings	(443)	126	469
Assets at December 31	12,778	12,837	13,241
Americas			
Revenue—Customers	$ 5,214	$ 5,247	$ 4,950
Interarea transfers	3,458	3,452	3,932
Total	$ 8,672	$ 8,699	$ 8,882
Net (loss) earnings	(251)	157	204
Assets at December 31	7,359	6,990	7,121
Eliminations			
Revenue	$(13,278)	$(14,005)	$(14,118)
Net (loss) earnings	(32)	125	(84)
Assets	(1,923)	(2,001)	(2,031)
Consolidated			
Revenue	$ 62,716	$ 64,523	$ 64,766
Net loss	(7,987)	(6,865)	(598)
Assets at December 31	81,113	86,705	92,473

*Net (loss) earnings before effect of changes in accounting for postemployment benefits (1993), income taxes (1992), and nonpension postretirement benefits (1991).

In a decade, IBM has moved from a do-it-yourself, inwardly directed company to an enterprise that reaches out for new ideas and approaches that mesh with its own talents and strengths. The quest to satisfy customers has blurred traditional competi-

EXHIBIT 28-4 IBM's Board of Directors

Harold Brown
Counselor
Center for Strategic and
International
Studies and General Partner
Warburg, Pincus & Company

James E. Burke
Retired Chairman of the Board
Johnson & Johnson

Thomas F. Frist, Jr.*
Chairman, Columbia/
HCA Healthcare Corporation

Fritz Gerber
Chairman and Chief Executive
Officer
Roche Holding Ltd. and
Executive Chairman
Zurich Insurance Company

Louis V. Gerstner, Jr.
Chairman of the Board and
Chief Executive Officer
IBM

Judith Richards Hope*
Senior Partner
Paul, Hastings, Janofsky & Walker

Nannerl O. Keohane
President
Duke University

Charles F. Knight
Chairman of the Board and
Chief Executive Officer
Emerson Electric Co.

Thomas S. Murphy
Chairman and Chief Executive
Officer
Capital Cities/ABC, Inc.

John R. Opel*
Retired Chairman of the Board
IBM

Paul J. Rizzo
Vice Chairman of the Board
IBM

John B. Slaughter
President
Occidental College

Lodewijk C. van Wachem
Chairman of the Supervisory Board
Royal Dutch Petroleum Company

Edgar S. Woolard, Jr.
Chairman and Chief Executive
Officer
E.I. du Pont de Nemours and
Company

*Directors who will be retiring effective
April 25, 1994.

IBM'S MANAGEMENT   MEMBERS OF WORLDWIDE MANAGEMENT COUNCIL

Louis V. Gerstner, Jr.
Chairman of the Board and
Chief Executive Officer

Paul J. Rizzo
Vice Chairman of the Board

James A. Cannavino
IBM Senior Vice President
Strategy and Development

Gerald M. Czarnecki
IBM Senior Vice President
Human Resources and
Administration

Donato A. Evangelista
IBM Senior Vice President and
General Counsel

Ellen M. Hancock
IBM Senior Vice President and
Group Executive

Steven A. Mills
General Manager
IBM Software Solutions Division

Robert J. LaBant
IBM Senior Vice President and
Group Executive

Robert M. Howe
IBM Vice President and General
Manager
IBM Consulting Group and
Business Transformation Services

Dennie M. Welsh
IBM Vice President and
General Manager, Services

Ned C. Lautenbach
IBM Senior Vice President and
Group Executive and Chairman
IBM World Trade Corporation

Hans-Olaf Henkel
IBM Vice President, Chairman of
the Board and Chief Executive
Officer
IBM World Trade Europe/EMEA

Lucio Stanca
President, IBM SEMEA

Nick Temple
President, IBM United
Kingdom

Robeli J. Libero
IBM Vice President, President and
General Manager
IBM Latin America

Robert M. Stephenson
IBM Vice President, President and
Representative Director
IBM Asia Pacific

Kakutaroh Kitashiro
President and Chief Executive
Officer, IBM Japan

G. Richard Thoman
IBM Senior Vice President and
Group Executive

Robert J. Corrigan
IBM Vice President and President
IBM Personal Computer Company

Nobuo Mii
IBM Vice President and President
IBM Power Personal Systems
Division

James T. Vanderslice
IBM Vice President and President
IBM Printing Systems Company

John M. Thompson
IBM Senior Vice President and
Group Executive

Nicholas M. Donofrio
IBM Senior Vice President and
General Manager
IBM Large Scale Computing
Division

William J. Filip
IBM Vice President and General
Manager
IBM RISC System/6000 Division

Leland R. Reiswig, Jr.
President
IBM Personal Software
Products Division

David M. Thomas
IBM Vice President and General
Manager
IBM AS/400 Division

Patrick A. Toole
IBM Senior Vice President and
Group Executive

Michael J. Attardo
IBM Senior Vice President and
General Manager
IBM Microelectronics Division

Lutz F. Hahne
IBM Vice President and General
Manager
IBM Application Solutions
Division

Ed Zschau
IBM Vice President and General
Manager
IBM Storage Systems Division

Jerome B. York
IBM Senior Vice President and Chief
Financial Officer

James J. Forese
IBM Vice President and President
IBM Credit Corporation

Lawrence A. Zimmerman
IBM Vice President and
Controller

Frederick W. Zuckerman
IBM Vice President and Treasurer

David B. Kalis
IBM Vice President
Communications

Abby F. Kohnstamm
IBM Vice President
Corporate Marketing

James C. McGroddy
IBM Vice President
Science and Technology, and
Director of Research

tive boundaries. Today, IBM has more than 20,000 business partnerships worldwide and more than 500 equity alliances with agents, dealers, distributors, software firms, services companies, and manufacturers.

Apple Computer is IBM's partner in Taligent to develop object-oriented software, and in Kaleida to create multimedia standards. Hewlett-Packard and IBM are jointly developing and manufacturing high-speed fiber-optic communications components. Wang and Mitsubishi sell IBM systems under their logos, and Digital Equipment is a partner in offering business recovery services. Alliances not only divide high development and production costs, but also reduce critical time-to-market, pool scarce human skills, provide access to new markets and distribution channels, fill product gaps, and—most of all—help IBM get to the customer first, with the best.

COMPETITORS

IBM is larger than all other U.S. computer manufacturers combined. The top ten computer manufacturers in the United States are listed in Exhibit 28–9 along with their 1993 sales, profits, and R&D expenditures.

CONCLUSION

IBM must reverse trends that otherwise will lead to bankruptcy. In the face of mounting criticism, IBM's chief strategist, Bernard Puckett, resigned in November 1993 and was replaced by James Cannavino. CEO Gerstner is being criticized for

EXHIBIT 28-5 Consolidated Statement of Operations *(Dollars in millions except per share amounts)*

FOR THE YEAR ENDED DECEMBER 31:	1993	1992	1991
Revenue:			
Hardware sales	$30,591	$33,755	$37,093
Software	10,953	11,103	10,498
Services	9,711	7,352	5,582
Maintenance	7,295	7,635	7,414
Rentals and financing	4,166	4,678	4,179
Total Revenue	62,716	64,523	64,766
Cost:			
Hardware sales	20,696	19,698	18,571
Software	4,310	3,924	3,865
Services	8,279	6,051	4,531
Maintenance	3,545	3,430	3,379
Rentals and financing	1,738	1,966	1,727
Total Cost	38,568	35,069	32,073
Gross profit	24,148	29,454	32,693
Operating Expenses:			
Selling, general, and administrative	18,282	19,526	21,375
Research, development, and engineering	5,558	6,522	6,644
Restructuring charges	8,945	11,645	3,735
Total Operating Expenses	32,785	37,693	31,754
Operating (Loss) Income	(8,637)	(8,239)	939
Other income, principally interest	1,113	573	602
Interest expense	1,273	1,360	1,423
(Loss) earnings before income taxes	(8,797)	(9,026)	118
(Benefit) provision for income taxes	(810)	(2,161)	716
Net loss before changes in accounting principles	(7,987)	(6,865)	(598)
Effect of changes in accounting principles	(114)	1,900	(2,263)
Net Loss	(8,101)	(4,965)	(2,861)
Preferred stock dividends	47	—	—
Net loss applicable to common sharcholders	$ (8,148)	$ (4,965)	$ (2,861)
Per Share of Common Stock Amounts:			
Before changes in accounting principles	$ (14.02)	$ (12.03)	$ (1.05)
Effect of changes in accounting principles	(.20)	3.33	(3.96)
Net loss applicable to common shareholders	$ (14.22)	$ (8.70)	$ (5.01)

Average Number of Common Shares Outstanding:
1993—573,239,240; 1992—570,896,489; 1991—572,003,382

EXHIBIT 28-6 Consolidated Statement of Financial Poslition *(Dollars in millions)*

At December 31:	1993	1992
Assets		
Current Assets:		
Cash	$ 873	$ 1,090
Cash equivalents	4,988	3,356
Marketable securities, at cost, which approximates market	1,272	1,203
Notes and accounts receivable—trade, net of allowances	11,676	12,829
Sales-type leases receivable	6,428	7,405
Other accounts receivable	1,308	1,370
Inventories	7,565	8,385
Prepaid expenses and other current assets	5,092	4,054
Total Current Assets	39,202	39,692
Plant, Rental Machines, and Other Property	47,504	52,786
Less: Accumulated depreciation	29,983	31,191
Plant, Rental Machines, and Other Property—Net	17,521	21,595
Investments and Other Assets:		
Software, less accumulated amortization (1993, $10,143; 1992, $8,531)	3,703	4,119
Investments and sundry assets	20,687	21,299
Total Investments and Other Assets	24,390	25,418
Total Assets	$81,113	$86,705
Liabilities and Stockholders' Equity		
Current Liabilities:		
Taxes	$ 1,589	$979
Short-term debt	12,097	16,467
Accounts payable	3,400	3,147
Compensation and benefits	2,053	3,476
Deferred income	3,575	3,316
Other accrued expenses and liabilities	10,436	9,352
Total Current Liabilities	33,150	36,737
Long-term debt	15,245	12,853
Other liabilities	11,177	7,461
Deferred income taxes	1,803	2,030
Total Liabilities	61,375	59,081
Stockholders' Equity:		
Preferred stock, par value $.01 per share—shares authorized: 150,000,000		
Shares Issued: 1993—11,250,000; 1992—None	1,091	—
Common stock, par value $1.25 per share—shares authorized: 750,000,000		
Shares Issued: 1993—581,388,475; 1992—571,791,950	6,980	6,563
Retained earnings	10,009	19,124
Translation adjustments	1,658	1,962
Treasury stock, at cost (shares: 1993—2,679; 1992—356,222)	—	(25)
Total Stockholders' Equity	19,738	27,624
Total Liabilities and Stockholders' Equity	$81,113	$86,705

EXHIBIT 28-7 Consolidated Statement of Cash Flows *(Dollars in millions)*

FOR THE YEAR ENDED DECEMBER 31:	1993	1992	1991
Cash Flow from Operating Activities:			
Net loss	$(8,101)	$ (4,965)	$(2,861)
Adjustments to reconcile net loss to cash provided from operating activities:			
Effect of changes in accounting principles	114	(1,900)	2,263
Effect of restructuring charges	5,230	8,312	2,793
Depreciation	4,710	4,793	4,772
Amortization of software	1,951	1,466	1,564
Loss (gain) on disposition of investment assets	151	54	(94)
Other changes that provided (used) cash:			
Receivables	1,185	1,052	(886)
Inventories	583	704	(36)
Other assets	(10)	(3,396)	5
Accounts payable	359	(311)	384
Other liabilities	2,155	465	(1,179)
Net cash provided from operating activities	8,327	6,274	6,725
Cash Flow from Investing Activities:			
Payments for plant, rental machines, and other property	(3,154)	(4,751)	(6,497)
Proceeds from disposition of plant, rental machines, and other property	793	633	645
Investment in software	(1,507)	(1,752)	(2,014)
Purchases of marketable securities and other investments	(2,721)	(3,284)	(4,848)
Proceeds from marketable securities and other investments	2,387	3,276	5,028
Net cash used in investing activities	(4,202)	(5,878)	(7,686)
Cash Flow from Financing Activities:			
Proceeds from new debt	11,794	10,045	5,776
Payments to settle debt	(8,741)	(10,735)	(4,184)
Short-term borrowings less than 90 days—net	(5,247)	4,199	2,676
Proceeds from preferred stock	1,091	—	—
Common stock transactions—net	122	(90)	67
Payments to purchase and retire common stock	—	—	(196)
Cash dividends paid	(933)	(2,765)	(2,771)
Net cash (used in) provided from financing activities	(1,914)	654	1,368
Effect of exchange rate changes on cash and cash equivalents	(796)	(549)	(315)
Net change in cash and cash equivalents	1,415	501	92
Cash and cash equivalents at January 1	4,446	3,945	3,853
Cash and cash equivalents at December 31	$ 5,861	$ 4,446	$ 3,945
Supplemental Data:			
Cash paid during the year for:			
Income taxes	$ 452	$ 1,297	$ 2,292
Interest	$ 2,410	$ 3,132	$ 2,617

EXHIBIT 28-8 Statement of Stockholders' Equity *(Dollars in millions)*

1991	PREFERRED STOCK	COMMON STOCK	RETAINED EARNINGS	TRANSLATION ADJUSTMENTS	TREASURY STOCK	TOTAL
Stockholders' Equity, January 1, 1991	$—	$6,357	$32,912	$3,309	$(25)	$42,553
Net loss			(2,861)			(2,861)
Cash dividends declared—common stock			(2,771)			(2,771)
Common stock issued under employee plans (1,857,904 shares)		172				172
Purchases (7,306,058 shares) and sales (7,201,997 shares) of treasury stock under employee plans—net			(125)		(6)	(131)
Common stock purchased and retired (2,127,400 shares)		(24)	(172)			(196)
Tax reductions—employee plans		26				26
Translation adjustments				(113)		(113)
Stockholders' Equity, December 31, 1991	—	6,531	26,983	3,196	(31)	36,679
1992						
Net loss			(4,965)			(4,965)
Cash dividends declared—common stock			(2,765)			(2,765)
Common stock issued under employee plans (442,581 shares)		26				26
Purchases (8,097,681 shares) and sales (8,073,124 shares) of treasury stock under employee plans—net			(129)		6	(123)
Tax reductions—semployee plans		6				6
Translation adjustments				(1,234)		(1,234)

EXHIBIT 28-8 *Continued*

1991	PREFERRED STOCK	COMMON STOCK	RETAINED EARNINGS	TRANSLATION ADJUSTMENTS	TREASURY STOCK	TOTAL
Stockholders' Equity, December 31, 1992	—	6,563	19,124	1,962	(25)	27,624
1993						
Net loss			(8,101)			(8,101)
Cash dividends declared—common stock			(905)			(905)
Cash dividends declared—preferred stock			(47)			(47)
Preferred stock issued (11,250,000 shares)	1,091					1,091
Common stock issued under employee plans (3,765,854 shares)		159				159
Common stock issued to U.S. pension plan fund (5,828,970 shares)		258				258
Purchases (6,099,023 shares) and sales (6,452,566 shares) of treasury stock under employee plans—net			(62)		25	(37)
Translation adjustments				(304)		(304)
Stockholders' Equity, December 31, 1993	$1,091	$6,980	$10,009	$1,658	$—	$19,738

EXHIBIT 28-9 Top Ten U.S. Computer Manufacturers 1992 Sales, Profits, and R&D Expenditures (In Millions of Dollars)

COMPANY	SALES	PROFITS	R&D EXPENDITURES
IBM	$62,716	$−7,987	$5,083
Hewlett-Packard	20,317	1,177	1,620
Digital-Equipment	13,636	−92	1,753
Apple Computer	8,445	−34	602
Compaq Computer	7,191	462	173
Sun Microsystems	4,493	188	381
Dell Computer	2,750	−10	372
Quantum	2,002	−510	315
Tandem Computers	2,022	−22	313
Conner Peripherals	2,151	−445	

focusing on cost cutting rather than formulating an overarching vision and strategy for IBM.

The vision thing keeps coming up, too. Jack Cooper, chief information officer of Seagram Company, a big IBM customer, recently remarked, "I give CEO Gerstner another two to six months to work out a strategy. After that, I think its absolutely critical that he have a vision." In a recent Forrester Research Inc., survey of 50 of the 1,000 largest U.S. companies, 42 percent said they plan to cut back on IBM purchases, 26 percent said they are watching IBM closely and may reduce purchases later, and only 2 percent plan to increase their business with IBM.

While IBM and CEO Gerstner are struggling with direction and strategy, the company's competitors are working overtime to muscle IBM out of the market. CEO Platt of Hewlett-Packard says, "We get up every morning and think about killing them." This is a "dog-eat-dog business."

Prepare a strategic plan to guide the IBM Corporation successfully to the year 2000. Include a clear mission statement, a comprehensive internal and external audit, as well as specific recommendations and projected financial statements.

MAGAZINE PUBLISHING INDUSTRY NOTE
ROSE MARIE BRATLAND

The U.S. printing and publishing industry, with approximately 60,000 firms and between 1 million and 2 million employees, remains shadowed by the aftereffects of the 1990–91 recession. With two-thirds of the industry's shipments tied to advertising, a buoyant economy is required to end the gradual erosion of the print media's share of total U.S. advertising expenditures. Rising levels of business and consumer confidence should expand advertising budgets in 1994 and increase the number of advertising pages in the nation's newspapers and magazines.

Printers and publishers serve the nation's communication needs, supplying an array of printed products ranging from almanacs to yearbooks. The industry's cost pressures have led to product specialization in an effort to achieve economies of scale. The 1990–91 recession had a severe impact on industry investment, with estimated 1992–93 capital expenditures 10 to 15 percent below the 1990 peak of $5.8 billion. Capital investment programs focus on increasing plant efficiencies, and have resulted in lowering the ratio of production workers to total employment to 53 percent in 1993 from 65 percent in 1973.

Demand for printed products is determined by a number of factors, including general economic activity, disposable personal income, advertising expenditures, business formations and transactions, and appropriations for schools, libraries, and institutions. The United States is the world's largest market for printed products and a favorable set of demographic factors over the period 1993–98 should reinforce this preeminent position. The U.S. population should reach 270 million in 1998, an increase of more than 12 million over 1993. The number of U.S. households should expand to 101 million in 1998, a gain of almost 5 million from 1993. School enrollments—elementary, secondary, and college—should expand by close to 5 million, to 68 million in 1998, from 63 million in 1993.

Growing competition from the electronic media and a squeeze on leisure time are forcing U.S. printers and publishers to reappraise their traditional markets. Printed products originally issued as books, directories, newsletters, and reference materials increasingly appear in the form of audio books, laser disks, compact disks, software, facsimile, and on-line information. To date, these electronic products supplement rather than supplant demand for printed products, but inroads by these electronic media should become more evident by the close of the decade. Gains by the electronic media are well perceived by leading U.S. printers, several of whom have established facilities to produce electronic materials such as compact disks for their publishing customers.

ENVIRONMENTAL PROFILE

Meeting environmental challenges is affecting the cost structures of both printers and publishers. Printers' concerns with toxins, carcinogens, and volatile organic compounds (VOCs) have led to increased use of alcohol-free fountain solutions, water-based inks, and solvent-less developers and finishers. More use of recycled paper and greater care in the disposal of materials now classified as hazardous result in higher printing production costs. Publishers' environmental issues center on the nation's dwindling space for landfills. Greater use of recycled paper throughout the printed product spectrum, coupled with growing legislative efforts to separate more printed products for recycling purposes from the stream of consumer waste, add to publishers' costs.

Since the United States is the world's largest market for printed products, most U.S. printers and publishers have at best a peripheral interest in international trade. Yet the United States is the second largest exporter of printed products (exceeded only by Germany), with 1993 shipments of slightly more than $4 billion. Major markets for U.S. printed product exports are Canada, the United Kingdom, Japan, and Mexico, with combined purchases accounting for two-thirds of the total. Approximately 60 percent of U.S. printed product exports consist of books and periodicals, but a wide variety of other items, including greeting cards, catalogs, labels, posters, decals, playing cards, calendars, and other trade advertising materials contribute to export markets totaling $1.6 billion in 1993 (Table 1).

Imports of printed products reached $2.2 billion in 1993, with combined shipments from Canada, the United Kingdom, Hong Kong, and Germany representing approximately 54 percent of the total. Shipments of books constituted 46 percent of all U.S. printed product imports in 1993, with some U.S. publishers contracting with Pacific Rim or Mediterranean suppliers who offer attractive pricing.

The next five years should provide significant opportunities for those U.S. printers and publishers seeking an international presence. Successful conclusion of the North American Free Trade Agreement (NAFTA) and the Uruguay Round of the General Agreement on Tariffs and Trade (GATT) will reduce or eliminate trade barriers to

TABLE 1 U.S. Trade Patterns in 1992 Printing and Publishing (SIC 27) (*In millions of dollars, percent*)

EXPORTS			IMPORTS		
	Value	Share		Value	Share
Canada and Mexico	1,940	50.6	Canada and Mexico	473	22.6
European Community	794	20.7	European Community	695	33.2
Japan	295	7.7	Japan	173	8.3
East Asia NICs	203	5.3	East Asia NICs	633	30.2
South America	94	2.4	South America	32	1.5
Other	507	13.2	Other	87	4.1
World Total	3,833	100.0	World Total	2,093	100.0

TOP FIVE COUNTRIES					
	Value	Share		Value	Share
Canada	1,721	44.9	Canada	396	18.9
United Kingdom	408	10.6	United Kingdom	302	14.4
Japan	295	7.7	Hong Kong	251	12.0
Mexico	219	5.7	Japan	173	8.3
Australia	187	4.9	Singapore	120	5.7

Source: U.S. Department of Commerce: Bureau of the Census; International Trade Administration.

exports of U.S. printed products and strengthen protection of international copyrights. By addressing the information requirements of global markets—and assisted by the dominance of English as the world's language of commerce and the professions—the U.S. printing and publishing industry should dominate in providing information services to an increasingly international clientele.

Periodical advertising continued to recover in 1993, but at a slower-than-expected pace. After experiencing an upswing in 1992, the industry expected to see strong growth throughout 1993. Nagging uncertainty about the nation's economic recovery kept advertisers from substantially increasing their advertising budgets for magazines. Circulation was expected to be flat for the year or down slightly. Magazine industry receipts totaled $22.8 billion, up slightly more than 1 percent in constant dollars from 1992 (Table 2).

TABLE 2 Trends and Forecasts: Periodicals (SIC 2721) (*In millions of dollars except as noted*)

| | | | | | PERCENT CHANGE (1991–1994) | | |
ITEM	1991	1992[1]	1993[2]	1994[3]	91–92	92–93	93–94
INDUSTRY DATA							
Value of shipments[4]	20,345	21,667	22,772	24,366	6.5	5.1	7.0
Value of shipments (1987$)	15,735	16,018	16,194	16,517	1.8	1.1	2.0
Total employment (000)	111	108	109	111	-2.7	0.9	1.8
Production workers (000)	20.7	19.5	19.3	19.7	-5.8	-1.0	2.1
Average hourly earnings ($)	13.21	13.64	14.05	14.47	3.3	3.0	3.0
Capital expenditures	223	—	—	—	—	—	—
PRODUCT DATA							
Value of shipments[5]	19,424	20,473	21,517	23,023	5.4	5.1	7.0
Value of shipments (1987$)	15,022	15,292	15,460	15,769	1.8	1.1	2.0
TRADE DATA							
Value of imports	121	136	163	179	12.4	19.9	9.8
Value of exports	705	731	768	829	3.7	5.1	7.9

[1]Estimate, except exports and imports.

[2]Estimate.

[3]Forecast.

[4]Value of all products and services sold by establishments in the periodicals industry.

[5]Value of products classified in the periodicals industry produced by all industries.

Source: U.S. Department of Commerce: Bureau of the Census; International Trade Administration (ITA). Estimates and forecasts by ITA.

Advertising in consumer periodicals during the first half of 1993 recorded its strongest first-half gains in revenue and advertising pages since 1989. However, after a sharp gain in advertising pages during the first quarter, advertising pages were flat for consumer magazines during the second quarter. Advertising gains for the business press were also more impressive early in the year but slowed during the second quarter. Advertisers were cautious in their advertising spending because of lower-than-expected consumer purchasing and their own uneasiness about the health of the economy.

Competition from television, special advertising promotions, and direct mail became more intense as publishers vied for shrinking advertising dollars. Magazines continued to fight their image as a secondary advertising medium by offering advertisers targeted markets for their products through a growing number of special-interest publications and ancillary products.

Industry cost-cutting measures implemented during the recession were expected to boost profit gains during 1993. Over the year, publishers focused on the effectiveness of magazine advertising, the profitability of circulation, and on the growing importance of pleasing their readers. In addition, publishers directed their attention to recycling issues and state and Federal tax proposals affecting magazines.

Advertising Recovery Slows. After experiencing their strongest first quarter in eight years, consumer magazines' advertising growth halted in the second quarter. Publishers Information Bureau reported that for the first quarter, advertising pages rose about 6 percent and advertising receipts climbed about 12 percent from the first quarter 1992 level. During the first seven months of 1993, advertising pages were up nearly 2 percent from the same period in 1992, and advertising revenues increased about 6 percent, reflecting the slowdown in growth during the second quarter and advertising page and revenue declines in July. In many instances, large advertisers reconsidered their advertising commitments to magazines and canceled or cut back their scheduled advertising on short notice as business growth slowed. Publishers resorted to advertising rate discounting and special offers to attract advertisers. For the year, advertising pages grew 1 to 2 percent, and advertising receipts rose 5 to 6 percent. Consumer magazine groups recording the most growth in advertising revenues in 1992 included woman/fashion/service, outdoor and sports, national business titles, and computer magazines. In 1993, advertising recovery for magazines was spotty; some magazines in special-interest segments did well while others in the same group recorded declines.

Most of the top 10 consumer magazine advertising categories recorded revenue gains during the first half of 1993. Categories showing the largest increases were drugs/remedies, direct-response companies, business/consumer services, and toiletries/cosmetics. Computer/office equipment/stationery and cigarettes/tobacco experienced substantial declines.

Business and professional magazines as a group saw no growth in advertising pages in 1992, and very little overall growth in pages was likely in 1993. *International Business Communication's 1994 Business Press Outlook* projected an 8 to 9 percent gain in advertising revenues in 1993, based on the 250 business publications tracked. American Business Press, the major trade association for business publishers, expected advertising revenues to rise about 4 percent in 1993. Advertising recovery for business publications groups was mixed, with some sectors performing very well, and others doing poorly. Groups that did well included computers, electronics, telecommunications, and long-term health care. Those performing poorly included aviation and aerospace, advertising and marketing, and construction-related publications.

From 1982 to 1992, advertising's share of total magazine receipts have declined slightly for both consumer magazines and the business press. In 1982, advertising accounted for 55 percent of total consumer magazine receipts. By 1992 it had fallen to 51 percent. Over the same decade, advertising receipts for business and professional publications dropped from 63 percent of total receipts to 60 percent. A growing number of business and professional magazines have gone from controlled circulation (sent free to industry executives and professionals) to paid circulation as advertising revenues have become more difficult to obtain. As their advertising receipts have become more unpredictable, consumer magazines have looked more to increasing circulation revenues.

Circulation Declines. Economic uncertainty, weak consumer confidence, and modest gains in real disposable personal income took their toll on consumer magazine circulation in 1992 and 1993. Although a record number of new magazines were started in 1992, magazine suspensions increased in a number of magazine groups in 1992 and 1993.

Audit Bureau of Circulation (ABC) data for 1992 reported that for the 570 consumer magazines tracked, total circulation fell for a second consecutive year. Annual combined circulation per issue for single-copy and subscription circulation each declined by about 1 million. Single-copy circulation totaled about 71 million per issue, while subscriptions numbered about 292 million per issue for consumer magazines. This was the first time since 1976 that subscription circulation fell for these ABC-audited magazines, although in 1991 subscription circulation was virtually unchanged from the previous year.

Newsstand magazines accounted for 20 percent of total consumer magazine circulation in 1991, but for 31 percent of total magazine circulation revenues; subscription represented 80 percent of circulation and 69 percent of circulation receipts.

Over the past decade, publishers have charged higher cover prices for newsstand editions of their publications than for subscriptions and have also increased rates on newsstand prices more rapidly. However, higher magazine cover prices in recent years have led to declining newsstand sales as consumers became more cautious in their purchasing. In the past few years, publishers have resisted increasing magazine cover prices but have attempted to make subscription sales more profitable. According to ABC data on the 50 leading magazines' cost to readers, the average single-copy price of a magazine rose from $2.65 in 1990 to $2.67 in 1992, an increase of less than 1 percent. By comparison, the average subscription price rose 2 percent, going from $27.11 in 1990 to $27.77 in 1992. During the 1987–90 period the average yearly single-copy price climbed 20 percent, as the average yearly subscription price increased 11 percent.

Changing Industry Profile. The *Gale Directory of Publications* listed 11,143 U.S. periodicals (consumer, farm, and business) for 1992, 96 fewer than in 1991. The *Consumer & Farm Magazines* publication of Standard Rate and Data Service reported a total of 2,318 consumer and farm publications in 1992, 42 more than in 1991. According to Samir Husni's *Guide to New Consumer Magazines*, a record 679 new magazine titles were launched in 1992, an increase of 126 over 1991. The largest number of startups were erotica and life-style/service magazines, but health, food, and children's publications also recorded strong gains. Many of the new magazines were special issues and one-time publications. *Esquire* launched two special issues in 1992, *Esquire Gentleman* and *Esquire Sportsman*. In early 1993, *Scientific American* published *Scientific American Medicine*, a one-time newsstand publication.

Magazines targeted to the baby boomers or their children, the so-called baby boomlets, were successful launches even during the recent recession. Hot magazine groups in the last five years have been children and teen magazines, which have doubled in number. New titles include *The Simpsons, Disney Adventures*, and *American Girl*. Spinoffs from established magazines have been popular, with such titles as *Discover for Kids, Money for Kids*, and *Field & Stream Jr*. Personal finance titles for the boomers have also done well. New launches, *Smart Money* and *Worth*, were aimed at this group.

A number of magazines targeted age or demographic sectors of the population by publishing a number of special editions. Several parenting magazines, including *Child* and *American Baby*, offered editions tailored to the age of a reader's child. Other recent publications targeted to a niche market include *Emerge*, a newsweekly for Black Americans, *The Senior Golfer*, targeted at aging baby boomers, and *Skiing for Women*.

Several prominent consumer and trade publications ceased to publish in 1993 as cautious advertisers, declining readership, and saturated magazine sectors made the survival of some magazines increasingly difficult. Conde Nast Publications' folding of *HG (House & Garden)*, a 92-year old home magazine, sent shock waves through the magazine industry. Univision publications suspended *Mas*, a general interest, Spanish-language lifestyle magazine with controlled circulation of 630,000. Among business journals, the 120-year old *Home Improvement Center* folded, as did *Magazine Week*, the only weekly trade title serving the magazine industry. Ziff-Davis, a computer publishing giant, closed both *Corporate Computing* and *PC Sources*.

Acquisition activity in 1993 focused on Conde Nast Publications' $170 million purchase of Knapp Communications Corp., publisher of *Bon Appetit* and *Architectural Digest*, giving Conde Nast a dominant position in the home decor and epicurean markets. This followed an announcement late in 1992 that Time Inc. would form a joint venture with American Express Publishing to manage several of AmEx's magazines, including *Travel & Leisure* and *Food & Wine*. Rather than acquiring properties, publishers focused on redesigning their publications, creating spinoff magazines and other products, including fax and videotext editions.

Employment and Production Costs. After a three-year period of downsizing to improve efficiency and cut costs, many magazine publishing companies began hiring in 1993. Publishers sought employees who could perform a number of jobs because of lean hiring budgets. Total employment rose about 1 percent to an estimated 109,000. The number of production workers was about 19,300, slightly less than in 1992.

Overall production and distribution costs rose moderately in 1993. Magazine publishers expected some publication grades of paper to rise as much as 9 percent during 1993, but anticipated no increases in ink prices. No postal rate increases took effect, but Congress passed legislation that would phase in higher postal rates for nonprofit magazines over a five-year period.

ENVIRONMENTAL PROFILE

Recycling has become an important issue. A few publishers have switched to coated recycled paper for their magazines, while others are gradually converting. Still others have no plans to use paper with recycled content. Many publishers are aware that the magazine industry must initiate a voluntary recycling program to keep Congress from enacting mandatory recycling requirements for the industry. Some major publishers are still reluctant to consider using recycled paper because of its higher cost, lower quality, and limited availability. Publishers are beginning to realize that they need to demand more recycled paper before paper producers will begin producing more and better quality recycled paper.

Although the Environmental Protection Agency (EPA) has not proposed any mandatory requirements for printing and writing papers, the agency revised its guidelines for Government procurement of recycled paper in 1993. This was of concern to publishers since any guidelines the EPA sets are likely to become the industry's standards.

According to one industry estimate, U.S. output of recycled printing and writing paper is 6 percent of total production, about the same level as 15 years ago. *Folio Magazine* reports that about 80 percent, or about 6 million tons, of high-grade printing and writing paper is disposed of in landfills annually.

INTERNATIONAL COMPETITIVENESS

Export growth slowed for U.S. magazines in 1993. Exports totaled an estimated $768 million, a gain of about 5 percent from 1992. Between 1989 and 1992, U.S. periodical exports grew at an average annual rate of 18 percent. The principal markets for U.S. magazines in 1992 were Canada (74 percent), the United Kingdom (7 percent), and Mexico (5 percent). While U.S. exports to Canada rose at an average yearly rate of 16 percent between 1989 and 1992, they dropped 1 percent in 1992 from their 1991 level (Table 3). U.S. exports to Mexico, France, the United Kingdom, the Netherlands, and Bermuda recorded strong growth between 1989 and 1992. Most of these markets showed average annual growth rates of more than 25 percent during

TABLE 3 U.S. Trade Patterns in 1992 Periodicals (SIC 2721) (*In millions of dollars, percent*)

	EXPORTS			IMPORTS	
	Value	Share		Value	Share
Canada and Mexico	573	78.3	Canada and Mexico	83	61.1
European Community	95	13.0	European Community	36	26.6
Japan	8	1.1	Japan	8	6.2
East Asia NICs	9	1.3	East Asia NICs	4	3.0
South America	11	1.6	South America	3	1.9
Other	35	4.8	Other	2	1.3
World Total	731	100.0	World Total	136	100.0

	TOP FIVE COUNTRIES				
	Value	Share		Value	Share
Canada	538	73.6	Canada	78	57.6
United Kingdom	52	7.1	United Kingdom	20	14.8
Mexico	35	4.7	Japan	8	6.2
Netherlands	22	3.1	Spain	5	3.7
France	13	1.8	Mexico	5	3.5

Source: U.S. Department of Commerce: Bureau of the Census; International Trade Administration.

this period. Over the past few years, softness in the economies of many industrialized countries curtailed discretionary consumer purchases of items such as magazines. International distributors expect magazine sales to show substantial growth as global economic activity improves.

Some magazine publishers have found that with their revenues declining at home, they must seek readers abroad. More of them are exploring international markets not only in Europe but in Latin America, the Middle East, Africa, and Asia. Recently, Rodale Press, publisher of *Runner's World*, and General Media International, publisher of *Longevity*, launched South African editions of their publications through joint ventures. *Ms.* magazine began distributing in the United Kingdom, Australia, and New Zealand. *National Geographic* and *Time* are exploring the feasibility of launching Japanese-language editions of their magazines. Hearst Corporation has joined with Televisa S.A. of Mexico to have more of its titles translated into Spanish-language editions for the Latin American market. Currently, Spanish-language editions of Hearst's *Cosmopolitan*, *Harper's Bazaar*, *Popular Mechanics*, and *Good Housekeeping* are distributed in Latin America. A Canadian edition of *Sports Illustrated*, launched in 1993, encountered protests from Canadian magazine publishers. Under new Canadian government regulations, U.S. companies will have to obtain government approval for future Canadian editions of their magazines. For nearly 30 years, the Canadian government has imposed a number of restrictions on foreign magazines doing business in Canada.

U.S. publishers have been more cautious in approaching the Eastern European market, although a growing number of European publishers have sought business and investment opportunities in this area. These foreign publishers believe the market offers fast growth potential. The printing and publishing sector in Eastern Europe is in need of technical assistance for its publishing, printing, and distribution operations. Those foreign companies providing assistance are most likely to gain a strong foothold. *Reader's Digest* is planning to launch a Czech edition, and recently *Playboy* started a Polish edition.

Opportunities for U.S. magazine publishers in the world market continue to grow. Many U.S. publications are special-interest titles which are not available in other countries. The United States is the only country worldwide with a sufficiently large, affluent, and educated population to support a large number of special-interest titles. These titles appeal to a small segment of a country's population, and in most countries the population statistics do not support narrowly focused magazines. In addition, since English is widely read and spoken abroad, the language barrier does not greatly impede American magazine sales overseas. Ron Scott, a magazine industry consultant, notes in *Folio Magazine* that for many smaller U.S. special-interest magazines, international newsstand distribution offers an opportunity to sell a sizable number of copies and establish a presence in the international market.

U.S. imports of magazines climbed an estimated 20 percent in 1993, to about $163 million. Major suppliers in 1992 were Canada (58 percent), the United Kingdom (15 percent), and Japan (6 percent).

OUTLOOK FOR 1994

Publishers expect 1994 to be a better year for magazine advertising and circulation as economic activity picks up. Projected growth in Gross Domestic Product (GDP) and corporate profits should encourage companies to increase their advertising budgets. If advertisers and consumers are more confident about the economy in 1994, U.S. magazine industry receipts could rise 2 to 3 percent in constant dollars. Advertising pages will likely increase modestly for consumer and business and professional publications, in the range of 2 to 4 percent, while circulation for both magazine groups will probably be flat or up less than 1 percent.

Even though real disposable personal income is expected to grow at a slightly slower rate than in 1993, increasing consumer confidence could produce more stability in magazine circulation than has existed over the past few years. With so many new titles, the shakeout of weaker titles could continue in 1994, especially in the absence of strong advertising growth.

Major costs, such as for printing, paper, and ink, should increase an average of 2 to 3 percent in 1994, unless demand rises sharply. No postal rate increases are expected before early 1995.

PLAYBOY ENTERPRISES, INC.—1994

More copies of *Playboy* magazine are sold each month than either *Newsweek* or *Cosmopolitan*. The approach to doing business at Playboy Enterprises, Inc. (PEI)(312-751-8000), is characterized by Christie Hefner, chairman and chief executive officer, as "a commitment to think globally and act locally." That statement represents the essence of PEI's business strategy toward the year 2000. Emphasis is being placed on global expansion to take advantage of Playboy's name recognition and the demise of communism worldwide. The Playboy name and logo is the world's second-best known symbol, after Coca-Cola's logo. PEI is headquartered in Chicago, Illinois.

PEI's net income has declined four years in a row, to $365,000 in 1993. The number of U.S. households subscribing monthly to the Playboy Service on television is declining. PEI's newsstand sales declined 13 percent in 1993 and advertising revenues also declined. PEI's magazine circulation revenues declined 2 percent in 1993. U.S. and Canadian newsstand sales of *Playboy* magazine fell 19 percent in 1993. A strategic plan is needed to reverse these recent declines in Playboy's business.

PEI was organized in 1953 to publish *Playboy* magazine. Christie Hefner succeeded her father, Hugh Hefner, as chairman of the board and CEO in 1988. Hugh Hefner still owns 71 percent of PEI's stock. PEI's three divisions are publishing, entertainment, and product marketing.

PUBLISHING

Playboy is the number one selling men's magazine in the world and remains the driving force behind all of the company's businesses. The publishing division reported a 13 percent increase in earnings to $14.4 million on a 7 percent rise in revenues to $162.8 million in 1993. In 1993, PEI launched its 16th international edition of the magazine in Poland, introduced a new line of trading cards, and began developing a CD-ROM product jointly with IBM.

Playboy magazine reported earnings growth of 15 percent in 1993, but magazine revenues fell 1 percent to $101.2 million. The magazine benefitted from lower paper and printing expenses, higher subscription prices, and the rollout of a $4.95 newsstand cover price nationwide. The magazine also announced a 5 percent increase in advertising rates, effective with the January 1994 issue. *Playboy* maintained its 3.4 million circulation rate base for the seventh straight year in fiscal 1993 and experienced a 2 percent increase in advertising pages. *Playboy's* circulation continued to exceed those of major magazines *GQ*, *Esquire*, and *Rolling Stone* combined. The magazine is read by 12 million readers each month and *Playboy's* female audience has grown to over 2.1 million, as given in Exhibit 29–1, the circulation ranking of various consumer magazines done annually by the Audit Bureau of Circulations (ABC).

Subscription sales, which provide 44 percent of *Playboy* magazine revenues, rose 5 percent in fiscal 1993, but the increase did not offset the decline in newsstand sales. Subscription revenues were impacted favorably by a higher average subscription price, and elimination of long-term, discounted subscription rates. Sales from *Playboy's* subscriber file of 2.7 million names also continued to generate high margin income.

PEI publishes the U.S. edition of *Playboy* magazine in 15 advertising editions: eight regional, two state, four metro and one upper-income zip-coded edition. All contain the same editorial material but provide targeting opportunities for advertisers. Net advertising revenues of the U.S. edition of *Playboy* magazine for the years ended June 30, 1993, 1992, and 1991 were $30.4 million, $30.4 million, and $32.7 million, respectively.

PEI has consolidated the printing of *Playboy* magazine and newsstand specials at Quad/Graphics, Inc., located in Wisconsin. Paper is the principal raw material used in the production of *Playboy* magazine and the company uses a variety of types of high-quality coated paper that is purchased from a number of suppliers. Lower negotiated paper prices contribute materially to reduction in manufacturing costs. Paper costs as a percentage of *Playboy* magazine revenues have declined from 22.5 percent in fiscal 1991 to 17.7 percent for the fiscal year ended June 30, 1993.

Consolidation of the convenience store industry and increased competition for display space in traditional retail stores contributed to the decline in newsstand sales in

EXHIBIT 29-1 Circulation Ranking of Various Consumer Magazines

SELECTED U.S. CONSUMER PUBLICATIONS	CIRCULATION (1)	RANKING (2)
Reader's Digest	16.3	1
TV Guide	14.6	2
National Geographic	9.6	3
Time	4.3	9
Sports Illustrated	3.6	10
People	3.5	11
Playboy	3.4	12
Newsweek	3.3	14
Cosmopolitan	2.7	18
Penthouse	1.2	41
Rolling Stone	1.2	45
Business Week	0.9	72
GQ	0.7	98
Esquire	0.7	106

Source: Audit Bureau of Circulations.

fiscal 1993. In an effort to increase sales during the coming year, PEI plans to capitalize on excitement generated by the company's 40th anniversary celebration. PEI is taking an aggressive approach to expand distribution to nontraditional channels such as music, video, and liquor stores, which register high male traffic.

Playboy magazine continues to focus on securing new advertisers from underdeveloped categories, such as fashion, fragrance, automotive, travel, and home electronics, in order to broaden its advertising mix and reduce dependency upon any one advertising category. *Playboy's* advertising sales account for 30 percent of the magazine's revenues. Advertising by category for fiscal 1993 is given in Exhibit 29–2.

The PEI marketing department sponsors a number of annual events with *Playboy* advertisers, such as the Winter Ski Fest and a three-on-three basketball tournament in Daytona Beach. PEI also offers advertisers opportunities to tie in to the Playboy Jazz Festival in Los Angeles through advertising in the Jazz Festival program and corporate sponsorship of certain program elements. Sony was the official consumer electronics sponsor of the 1993 Playboy Jazz Festival.

Playboy magazine's editorial vitality, diversity, and cultural connection are evident in the fiction, articles, investigative reporting, interviews, celebrity profiles, and entertainment and service features that are monthly staples of the publication. Regular columns on politics, books, movies, music, style, men, women, and relationships reflect contemporary social and cultural issues and further the magazine's ongoing dialogue with its readers.

PEI has successfully developed newsstand specials, calendars, international editions, and trading cards, which utilize material from *Playboy's* editorial, art, and photography libraries and capitalize on its loyal customer base.

Playboy-related businesses contributed operating income of $8.4 million in fiscal 1993, but these earnings were down modestly from 1992 due to lower average copy sales for newsstand specials and a smaller 900-number operation (see Exhibits 29–3, 29–4, and 29–5). Royalties from international publishing remained even with last year, although a new trading card deal generated new revenue and operating income.

In fiscal 1993, PEI produced 16 newsstand specials and a *Playmate* calendar. The company also entered into an agreement with Sarah Lazin Books to develop books

EXHIBIT 29-2 *Playboy* Advertising for Fiscal 1993

ADVERTISING CATEGORY	PERCENTAGE OF AD PAGES
Retail/Direct Mail	25
Beer/Wine/Liquor	21
Tobacco	18
Apparel/Footwear/Accessories	10
Toiletries/Cosmetics	8
Automotive	4
Home Electronics	4
Other	10
	100

Source: *Playboy Annual Report,* 1993.

EXHIBIT 29-3 Playboy Publishing Group Revenues and Operating Incomes
(In millions of dollars)

	REVENUES YEARS ENDED JUNE 30,			OPERATING INCOME YEARS ENDED JUNE 30,		
	1993	1992	1991	1993	1992	1991
Playboy Magazine	$101.2	$102.2	$100.3	$7.9	$7.0	$6.1
Playboy-Related Businesses	22.0	21.7	22.3	8.4	9.1	10.3
Subtotal	123.2	123.9	122.6	16.3	16.1	16.4
Catalogs	39.4	28.1	18.1	4.9	2.5	0.7
Administrative Expenses, New Magazine Development and Other	0.2	0.3	—	(6.8)	(5.8)	(4.8)
Total	$162.8	$152.3	$140.7	$14.4	$12.8	$12.3

EXHIBIT 29-4 *Playboy* Magazine's Average Net Paid Circulation Per Issue

	AVERAGE NET PAID CIRCULATION PER ISSUE (*IN MILLIONS*)		APPROXIMATE PERCENT OF CIRCULATION FROM	
FISCAL YEAR	FIRST SIX MONTHS	SECOND SIX MONTHS	SINGLE COPY SALES	SUBSCRIPTIONS
1993	3.4	3.4	21	79
1992	3.5	3.4	22	78
1991	3.5	3.5	23	77

Source: Audit Bureau of Circulations (ABC).

EXHIBIT 29-5 *Playboy* Magazine U.S. Edition Subscription and Worldwide Newsstand Circulation Figures (In thousands, except per copy prices)

	YEARS ENDED JUNE 30,		
	1993	1992	1991
Subscription Revenues	$44,900	$42,600	$40,300
Average Monthly Subscribers	2,816	2,801	2,707
Newstand Revenues	$23,500	$27,100	$25,500
Average Monthly Newsstand Copies	652	781	787
Average Newsstand Cover Price	$ 5.04	$ 4.72	$ 4.39

Source: *Playboy* Form 10K, 1993, p. 5.

around editorial themes from *Playboy* magazine. This deal resulted in the publication of *The Playboy Interviews* in fiscal 1993 and the development of *Playboy Stories*, an anthology of some of the magazine's finest fiction.

Playboy's editorial vision and philosophy are exported globally through international editions published in Argentina, Australia, Brazil, Czech Republic, Germany, Greece, Hong Kong, Hungary, Italy, Japan, Mexico, the Netherlands, Spain, Taiwan, and Turkey. Up to 70 percent of the material in each edition is locally produced, with the remaining text and pictorials originating from the U.S. *Playboy* and other editions. PEI reviews and approves the content of the foreign editions so that they retain the distinctive style, look, and flavor of the U.S. edition, while meeting the needs of their respective markets. The terms of the license agreements for *Playboy* magazine's foreign editions vary, but in general are for a term of at least five years and carry a guaranteed minimum royalty as well as a formula for computing earned royalties in excess of the minimum. Royalty computations are generally based on both circulation and advertising revenues. In fiscal 1993, the three largest-selling editions—Germany, Japan and Brazil—accounted for 48 percent of the total licensing revenues from foreign editions.

Playboy entered into its first overseas publishing joint venture in fiscal 1993, with Autraco Holding Company, to produce a Polish edition. The deal is a departure from the licensing strategy that the company has employed since 1972, when the first foreign edition of *Playboy* was launched, and reflects the company's intent to invest in more global ventures and to become more involved in managing the Playboy brand abroad. PEI plans to launch a South African edition in November 1993 through a license agreement with Times Media Limited, a diversified media company based in Johannesburg.

PEI owns a 20 percent interest in the *duPont Registry*, a monthly magazine and shoppers' guide targeted to collectors of classic, luxury, and exotic cars. In fiscal 1993, this magazine broadened its retail distribution base and reported advertising and circulation increases.

PEI's catalog earnings for fiscal 1993 nearly doubled to $4.9 million, while revenues increased 40 percent to $39.4 million. Catalog operations are the fastest growing segment within the publishing group. The *Playboy* catalog offers Playboy fashions and accessories, home videos, gifts, calendars, art products, back issues of the magazine, and newsstand specials. In fiscal 1993, the catalog expanded its lingerie section to feature the "Romantics by Playboy" line. The growth was largely due to higher sales volume and response rates for *Critics' Choice Video*, which was partially attributable to the acquisitions of assets to two competing catalogs, *Blackhawk Films* and *Postings*, and the merging of their mailing lists with that of *Critics' Choice Video*.

Critics' Choice Video is one of the largest circulation catalogs of prerecorded videocassettes serving the sell-through market, the fastest-growing segment of the video industry. The catalog features more than 2,000 titles, including major theatrical releases and special-interest videos. The company acquired 80 percent of Critics' Choice Video, Inc., in fiscal 1989 and purchased the remaining 20 percent in fiscal 1994 for $3.0 million.

Moving closer to its goal of becoming the catalog leader in home entertainment software, PEI will test a music catalog, *Collectors' Choice Music*, in fiscal 1994. The 100-page catalog will be mailed to 500,000 music customers. It will feature more than 1,300 titles in CD and cassette formats from a wide assortment of music categories—classical, pop, rock, rhythm and blues, jazz, and country. It also will offer an extensive library of hard-to-find recordings.

PEI signed two major agreements in fiscal 1993 to produce new media brand extensions of Playboy products. In conjunction with IBM's Multimedia Publishing Studio, the company will publish *The Playboy Interview 1962–1992*, a CD containing nearly all of the interviews published since the feature's inception in 1962, the subjects' photographs, and a comprehensive index that will allow researchers to quickly access interviews by them. The CD will retail for about $39.95 and will be available through computer retail outlets and via direct mail.

Playboy's entertainment and publishing groups are working together to develop interactive entertainment software through an agreement with Philips Interactive Media of America. Among the releases that PEI will develop and market in fiscal 1994 is *40 Years of Playboy*, a multimedia review of *Playboy's* editorial highlights and an interactive forum through which users can access Playmate photos and create music videos utilizing their favorite pictures.

ENTERTAINMENT

The entertainment division's strategy is to build a library of Playboy programming that can be packaged in multiple formats for worldwide distribution. Today, Playboy programming is available via broadcast, cable and pay television, and direct-to-home technology. It also is offered on video and laserdisc formats and soon will be available on CI-I. To strengthen brand identification of Playboy programming around the world, PEI consolidated all of its television services and programming under the name "Playboy TV" in fiscal 1993 and developed a logo to market the services.

The entertainment division made substantial progress in fiscal 1993. Revenues were up 31 percent to $42.6 million as a result of growth from domestic pay television, international television, and worldwide home video. Earnings declined however to $1.8 million from $3.7 million in fiscal 1992 (see Exhibit 29–6).

Playboy signed important international broadcast license agreements in fiscal 1993 that expanded the audience of Playboy TV to 64 territories and home video to 35 countries. Three new multiyear agreements will result in tiers of Playboy programming being offered on overseas networks for the first time. These deals will enable Playboy to have an ongoing branded presence in international markets and are expected to generate higher and more consistent revenues than selling programs on a show-by-show basis.

The access growth rate of Playboy's domestic pay-per-view service continues to outpace the industry growth rate of homes equipped with addressable cable technology. Access to Playboy TV increased 25 percent, from 7.3 million homes at the start of fiscal 1993 to 9.1 million at the end. Industry analyst Paul Kagan Associates, Inc., estimates that there are now 18 million U.S. addressable homes. Tele-Communications, Inc. (TCI), the largest multiple system operator in the country, entered into its first long-term agreement with PEI in February 1993 to carry the Playboy TV network. As TCI continues to outfit its ten million basic cable homes with pay-per-view technology, the number of Playboy addressable homes should rise commensurately.

PEI's library of 500 hours of programming is available to all of the entertainment division's distribution channels and to launch new media and distribution pipelines. Exclusive programming is a hallmark of Playboy TV and sets the domestic service apart from all other pay offerings. Approximately 60 percent of the network's program lineup is originally produced. The company expects to invest approximately $19 million in new programming in fiscal 1994.

EXHIBIT 29-6 *Playboy* Entertainment Group Revenues and Operating Income (In millions of dollars)

	YEARS ENDED JUNE 30,		
	1993	1992	1991
REVENUES			
Domestic Pay Television:			
Pay-Per-View	$ 8.0	$ 6.0	$ 3.8
Monthly Subscription	8.6	9.8	11.4
Home Satellite Dish and Other	4.7	2.7	2.6
Total Domestic Pay Television	21.3	18.5	17.8
Domestic Home Video	10.1	7.0	2.7
International Television and Home Video	9.8	5.4	3.5
Other	1.4	1.6	1.0
Total Revenues	$42.6	$32.5	$25.0
OPERATING INCOME			
Profit Contribution Before Programming Expense	$15.4	$12.7	$10.4
Programming Expense	(13.6)	(9.0)	(7.5)
Total Operating Income	$ 1.8	$ 3.7	$ 2.9

Source: *Playboy* Form 10K, 1993, p. 9.

Fiscal 1993's programming investment funded approximately 89 hours of new programming, including *Playboy's Love & Sex Test*, *Playboy's Secret Confessions and Fantasies*, and the dramatic, sexy soap opera *Eden*. *Eden*, which was created by the producers of *Falcon Crest*, attracted the interest of USA Network, which licensed and began airing an edited version of the program on its basic cable service in June 1993. *Eden* is the first Playboy TV series to gain national exposure on another network, and the program received good ratings in its late-night time slot. Exhibit 29–7 categorizes the Playboy programs.

Playboy magazine's editorial forum provides both unique programming concepts and cross-promotional opportunities. Some of the magazine's celebrity pictorials and editorial features, such as the "Movies" column and the "Playboy Advisor," have been translated into segments on Playboy TV. Other features provide greater syndication and sponsorship potential. In fiscal 1993, the entertainment group produced the *Reebok Preseason College Football Special* around *Playboy's Pigskin Preview*, and the *1993 Playboy All-American team*. The show aired in September 1993 in 92 television markets nationwide.

Playboy's pay television business reported a 15 percent rise in fiscal 1993 revenues to $21.3 million. However, earnings were down slightly due to increased investments in sales, marketing, and distribution resources, including a new transponder on the Hughes Communications Galaxy V satellite. The new transponder is accessed by more cable operators than was Playboy's previous satellite and provides multichannel possibilities through compression.

EXHIBIT 29-7 Playboy Entertainment Group Company-Produced Series Information

TITLE OF SERIES	FISCAL YEAR FIRST SOLD	LENGTH OF EPISODES (MINUTES)	GENRE
Playboy Late Night			
Series I	1990	60	magazine-format
Series II	1991	30	magazine-format
Series III	1992	30	magazine-format
Inside Out	1991	30	anthology
Eden	1993	30	dramatic series
Playboy's Secret Confessions and Fantasies	1993	30	hosted series
Playboy's Love & Sex Test	1992	30	game show

Source: *Playboy* Form 10K, 1993, p. 9.

Pay-per-view sales growth has slowed due to the uncertainty surrounding the 1992 Cable Act, which affects rates and requires cable systems to obtain permission from broadcasters to retransmit their signals and reserve up to one third of their channels for relaying the signals of local broadcasters. Even though pay television services are not subject to the new regulations, the access growth rate for Playboy TV did not rise as fast as anticipated during the second half of fiscal 1993.

At June 30, 1993, the cable systems where Playboy Television was offered included approximately 16.8 million cable households. Of these households, 12.1 million could purchase Playboy Television on a monthly basis, 2.5 million could purchase only on a pay-per-view basis, and 6.6 million could purchase the programming both ways. CEO Hefner believes that the company's potential pay-per-view audience has grown at a faster rate than the pay-for-view market because Playboy Television has been able to add MSOs by offering a consistent level of "buy rates" (percentage of homes actually purchasing the service) compared to other pay-per-view services, a pricing structure that is profitable to the cable affiliate and a commitment to high quality original programming. Projections by Paul Kagan Associates, Inc., in February 1993 call for 15 percent average annual increases in addressable households through 1995. PEI expects its pay-per-view access to continue to expand at a faster rate than the industry in the near term as additional MSOs make Playboy Television available to their cable affiliates.

The number of monthly subscribers has declined as PEI's marketing focus has shifted to systems that have pay-per-view technology. As of June 30, 1993, Playboy Television had approximately 232,000 monthly subscribing households, down from 281,000 at June 30, 1991. PEI has used its pay-per-view service to gain access to additional MSOs and cable affiliates, some of which were unwilling to carry Playboy Television on a monthly subscription basis, giving the cable affiliates and PEI an opportunity to increase overall revenues. CEO Hefner believes the availability of a monthly subscription option for Playboy Television in addressable systems would benefit the company. (Subscription and pay-per-view figures are compared in Exhibit 29–8.)

In the long run, PEI expects to benefit from the new cable rulings. Cable operators will be encouraged to look for new revenue sources that are not regulated. The recent signing of TCI and Cox Cable Communications to carry the Playboy service is reflective of operators' confidence in the future of Playboy TV and pay-per-view.

EXHIBIT 29-8 Cable Households in Relation to Playboy Television

		CABLE HOUSEHOLDS		PLAYBOY TELEVISION	
	TOTAL CABLE HOUSEHOLDS	ADDRESSABLE CABLE HOUSEHOLDS	HOMES	PAY-PER-VIEW BUYS	MONTHLY SUBSCRIBERS
June 30, 1991	52,550	15,100	4,700	2,118	314
June 30, 1992	54,300	16,750	7,300	3,136	281
June 30, 1993	56,050	18,150	9,100	4,393	232
Compound Annual Growth Rate (1991-1993)	3.3%	9.6%	39.1%	44.0%	(14.0)%

Source: *Playboy* Form 10K, 1993, p. 10.

PEI provides Playboy Television vial encrypted signal, on both a pay-per-view and subscription basis, to home satellite dish viewers. As of June 30, 1993, Playboy Television was available on a pay-per-view basis to approximately 130,000 such viewers, and there were also approximately 67,000 subscription customers. At June 30, 1992, Playboy Television was available to 65,000 home satellite dish viewers on a pay-per-view basis and had approximately 41,000 subscribers. PEI receives an established fee per subscriber, which depends in part on the sales volume of the distributor. In January 1992, PEI began expanding its satellite distribution through agreements with additional distributors to supplement its former exclusive distribution agreement. In December 1992, new encryption technology was introduced by the industry in the home satellite dish market so that former "pirates" are no longer able to receive programming without subscribing to pay television services. CEO Hefner expects this development to continue to have a positive impact on the level of PEI revenues derived from this market.

In fiscal 1994, the entertainment group will explore changes to the pricing, promotion, and advertising mix and plans to test shorter program blocks and 24-hour transmission to boost revenue per home. The Playboy network is predominantly available ten hours a night on a per night and per month basis. The number of monthly subscribers continued to decline in fiscal 1993 primarily from nonaddressable systems. These older systems now represent approximately 10 percent of PEI's total monthly subscriber base. Revenues from monthly subscriptions are expected to increase as more cable systems begin offering Playboy programming on both a pay-per-view and monthly basis.

Playboy's home video business reported a 45 percent increase in revenues in 1993. This business issued 25 new titles, achieved unit volume growth, released the bulk of its titles on laserdisc, and continued its successful video distribution relationship with Uni Distribution Corp. Core releases, such as the *Playmate of the Year* video and *Video Playmate Calendar*, continue to do well. Eleven of the top 100 videos on *Billboard's* 1992 sales charts were Playboy titles. The company extended its product line with the introduction of a *Celebrity Video Centerfold*. The first release featured Jessica Hahn and was a chartbuster, jumping to number two on *Billboard's* top 40 chart list in its third week of release.

The entertainment division plans to produce fewer titles in fiscal 1994 in order to capitalize on its strong backlist of more than 75 titles. New releases will include a *Celebrity Video Centerfold* featuring Diane Parkinson and a video on *Playboy's* 40th anniversary Playmate.

The Playboy-Sharper Image tapes for couples continue to be sold in The Sharper Image's stores and catalogs and through retail distribution. The "For Couples Only" line remains extremely popular with both men and women. The company plans to expand its marketing efforts to women to further increase sales and expand the dual audience for the product.

Playboy moved into the home shopping arena in 1993 by producing and airing its first infomercial, *Secrets of Making Love*, on broadcast and cable television. Starring Morgan Brittany, the infomercial promoted two Playboy videos, an audiotape of music for lovers, and a massage kit. The ongoing successful sales of this program have led to the production of a second infomercial, which promises a new relationship series to be released in fiscal 1994.

The international television and home video operations reported an 80 percent increase in revenues to $9.8 million in fiscal 1993. Playboy's fiscal 1993 agreement with HBO Olé, the first and largest multinational pay television network reaching all of Latin America and the Caribbean, significantly broadened the global reach of Playboy programming. Under terms of the deal, programs such as *Playboy Late Night* and *Eden* will begin airing in a consistent Playboy timeslot.

In fiscal 1993, PEI increased its international television market to 64 countries, from 17, largely as a result of entering into its first multiyear, exclusive agreement to supply blocks of Playboy-branded programming ("programming tier") for exhibition throughout Latin America. While continuing to sell individual series, the company has expanded its existing foreign network relationships by entering into a programming tier agreement with overseas pay television distributors. These agreements enable PEI to have an ongoing branded presence in international markets and are expected to generate higher and more consistent revenues than selling programs on a show-by-show basis. Through separate distribution agreements, PEI also distributes its U.S. home video products to countries in Latin America, Europe, Australia, and Asia. These products are based on the videos produced for the U.S. market, with dubbing or subtitling into the local language where necessary.

At the close of fiscal 1993, the entertainment division formed a strategic alliance with Taurus Programming Services, which plans to launch a pay television service on Spanish cable systems during the latter part of calendar 1993. The agreement calls for the nightly broadcast of a two-hour block of Playboy programming on this new service and grants Playboy advertising time to promote Playboy products, such as home videos and the Spanish edition of *Playboy*.

PEI will pursue other such relationships to further its tier strategy. In fiscal 1994, PEI plans to introduce two new series, *Playboy's Hot Rocks* and *Erotic Fantasies*, to the overseas market. Home video growth from new agreements with distributors in Chile, Columbia, Croatia, Slovenia, and Venezuela will supplement international television sales.

PRODUCT MARKETING

Playboy and the rabbit head design are among the most recognized trademarks in the world. The company leverages the power of its brand recognition, design expertise, art collection, and loyal customer base to develop and market apparel, accessories, and other products to consumers in more than 50 countries.

The Playboy and Playmate product lines consist primarily of men's and women's clothing, accessories, watches, jewelry, fragrances, small leather goods, stationery, and home fashions. These products are marketed in North America, Europe, Asia, Australia, and South America, primarily through mass merchants and other retail outlets, by licensees under exclusive license agreements that authorize the manufacture, sale, and distribution of products in a designated territory. Royalties are based on a fixed or variable percentage of the licensee's total new sales, in some cases against guaranteed minimum. In fiscal 1993, approximately 62 percent of the royalties earned from licensing the company's trademarks was derived from licensees in the Far East, 24 percent from licensees in the United States, and the remainder from Europe, Australia, Canada, and other territories.

The product marketing group reported earnings of $1.0 million on a 7 percent increase in revenues to $9.5 million in fiscal 1993. Revenues grew primarily from expansion in the art products business and significant product marketing growth in Asia. Royalties from international product marketing, which provided nearly half of the division's fiscal 1993 revenues, rose 10 percent. However, earnings declined modestly. Additionally, PEI sustained a loss in its events business, which led to the restructuring of that operation at year-end to significantly reduce future expenses.

Popularity of the Playboy name stems from its association with fun, sexiness, and quality. Aspirational, adventurous, and romantic are a few of the many characteristics that define the Playboy customer. Overseas, the Playboy logo benefits from its strong identification with Western freedoms, American lifestyle, and a desire for "the good life."

The product marketing division worked toward unifying the Playboy brand image around the world in fiscal 1993. The group held its first international product licensing conference, which brought licensees together to meet other executives who manage international Playboy businesses and to exchange ideas about Playboy products. PEI also began developing plans to cross-market products through advertising, public relations, and promotions and through clustering multiple products around themes. An advertising campaign developed around two cluster concepts is expected to be launched in Western Europe in fall 1994.

The major accomplishments of the international product marketing program in fiscal 1993 were continued expansion in China; the development of a relationship with the MBf Group, a multinational Malaysian-based conglomerate, to manufacture and market Playboy condoms; and the restructuring of the licensing program in Japan.

Licensee Chaifa Investment, Ltd. increased the number of Playboy boutiques operating within department stores in China from 34 to 65; opened its first freestanding Playboy shop in Shanghai; and built a factory in Shantou to manufacture Playboy products, provide for direct distribution of merchandise throughout the country, and reduce the cost of Playboy products compared to imports. Chaifa plans to open additional freestanding stores and boutiques during fiscal 1994, bringing the total number of Playboy shops in China to approximately 100.

In Japan, Playboy reorganized its manufacturing and distribution network and established direct relationships with a number of former sublicensees to produce Playboy goods. This increases the company's royalties and allows for greater marketing control.

PEI intends to sign licensees for several new product categories in the European market, including lingerie, swimwear, sunglasses, and bath products. Additionally,

Playboy is moving to a position of active brand management from passive licensing by becoming more directly involved in the development of advertising, merchandising strategies, and store concepts.

Since *Playboy* magazine's founding, the company has provided reliable, factual information on human sexuality and outlined the responsibilities that go along with sexual freedom. With the escalating global health threats posed by AIDS and unprotected sex, the company decided to develop a line of Playboy condoms and use its knowledge and influence on sex-related issues to deliver an important message about safe sex. Playboy condoms were launched late in calendar 1993 under a licensing agreement with the MB*f* Group. A multibillion-dollar financial services and consumer products conglomerate based in Kuala Lumpur, Malaysia. The product line will be introduced initially in Taiwan, with subsequent launches in the Asian region. A portion of the proceeds generated from condom sales will be donated to a newly formed foundation that will distribute grants to locally based organizations supporting sex education and AIDS prevention efforts.

Playboy's decision to upgrade the image of its domestic consumer products to match Playboy magazine standards resulted in the termination and expiration of nearly all product licensing agreements in the United States over the past two years. The loss in royalties from Playboy's former licensees caused a drop in domestic revenues and a related decline in fiscal 1993 operating performance.

The product marketing division has developed several new products, including a line of lingerie marketed under the name "Romantics by Playboy." Playboy also signed designer Becky Bisoulis, known for her elaborate bridal wear and lace fashions, to create a signature collection of Playboy lingerie for the fall 1994 season. PEI is now looking to secure appropriate direct and retail distribution for the product lines.

Special Editions, Ltd. (SEL), which markets original art, limited-edition prints, posters, and art products, reported higher revenues as a result of strong sales from art watches and ties, and a significantly smaller operating loss in fiscal 1993 compared to the prior year. SEL's second watch collection, which featured designs by Keith Haring, Karl Wirsum, and Bas Van Reek, sold exceptionally well, as did the subsidiary's first collection of Keith Haring silk ties.

A collection of art watches utilizing designs by architect Stanley Tigerman and California painter Wayne Thiebaud and a new Keith Haring art tie collection are being developed for sale in fiscal 1994. SEL also plans to release, through an exclusive deal with the Pablo Picasso estate, an art watch featuring the painter's 1924 pen and ink drawing *The Guitar*.

The original art and limited-edition print segment of the business improved in fiscal 1993, due in large part to sales generated by the program SEL developed around emerging artist Charles Dwyer, Jr. SEL also successfully produced and marketed several new limited-edition prints and posters of works by Patrick Nagel and Salvador Dali.

PEI entered the stationery and museum notecard market during 1993. The company produced two series of notecards featuring works by *Playboy* contributing artist LeRoy Neiman—The Equestrian Collection and The Impressionist Collection. Additional works by *Playboy* artists are being considered for new notecard sets planned for introduction in fiscal 1994.

In October 1987, PEI bought the Sarah Coventry brand in order to expand sales by leveraging its brand management expertise. This subsidiary continues to be a solid performer, although fiscal 1993 revenues and earnings growth were inhibited by financial difficulties experienced by its primary jewelry licensee. During 1993, PEI negotiated a more favorable licensing contract with New Dimensions Accessories, Ltd., formerly R. N. Koch, and signed a deal for the distribution of the jewelry line through home parties.

PUBLIC AFFAIRS

PEI established the Playboy Foundation in 1965 to provide financial support for organizations dedicated to protect civil rights and civil liberties, promote First Amendment rights and freedom of expression, and support research and education on human sexuality and reproductive rights. In fiscal 1993, the Foundation awarded nearly $290,000 in grants and in-kind contributions to organizations working in these areas. The magazine provided more than one-half million dollars in free advertising space to nonprofit groups working on AIDS research and services, the First Amendment, and natural environment issues. A basic tenet of *The Playboy Philosophy* is that the First Amendment is the keystone to all other rights. Playboy established the Hugh M. Hefner First Amendment Awards in 1979 to honor individuals who have championed freedom of expression.

Another important component of PEI's philosophy is that the company has a responsibility to give back to its communities—"doing well by doing good." In 1985, the Foundation established the Neighborhood Relations Boards, composed of nonexecutive employees who award grants to small- and medium-sized organizations that serve traditionally disadvantaged people. In fiscal 1993, the Neighborhood Relations Boards awarded grants to 34 groups in Chicago, New York, and Los Angeles.

Playboy actively encourages its employees to get involved in their communities. The Foundation's Matching Gift program matches employee contributions to nonprofit organizations dollar for dollar (up to $350 per employee per year), and the Time Match program provides $2 for each hour that an employee volunteers for a nonprofit group. In fiscal 1993, 21 percent of Playboy's employees participated in the Matching Gift and Time Match programs, resulting in contributions to 121 nonprofit organizations across the country.

FUTURE PLANS

PEI wants to capitalize on trends in Europe and Asia toward democracy and freedom. Which new countries worldwide should be targeted by PEI for entry? Which of PEI's three divisions should receive the greatest emphasis and resources in the early 1990s? Should the company focus more on publishing, licensing, television, telephone, videos, or artwork? How can PEI improve its corporate image among critics who contend that their business is obscene and unethical?

Should PEI make a major acquisition in the near future to begin publishing other magazines, such as *Cosmopolitan*, *Woman's Day*, or *Ladies' Home Journal*, *Gentleman's Quarterly*, or *Esquire*? Which of these magazines could feasibly be acquired? What should be PEI's offering price? There are rumors that PEI itself could be the target of an acquisition soon. How much is the company worth today?

PEI incurred a $4.5 million operating loss in its first quarter of fiscal 1994 and reduced its workforce 10 percent, about 60 jobs. Circulation of *Playboy* magazine slid to 3.4 million in early 1994, down 50 percent from its record 6.8 million copies sold in 1972. The magazine's average reader is a 33-year old male with household income of $33,700; half of its readers are married. Should PEI target other customers? Should PEI enter the gaming business? The company was denied a casino license in New Jersey in 1982 but the gaming industry is a growing business today.[1] What are your recommendations to Christie Hefner to reverse the company's declining profitability and to grow internationally? Ms. Hefner plans to launch the company's 17th foreign edition soon in South Africa. Develop a comprehensive strategic plan for PEI. The company's current mission statement is given as follows:

> PEI is a preeminent international media and entertainment company with a worldwide recognized brand and many windows of opportunity to expand the Playboy franchise and develop other related entertainment franchises globally by leveraging Playboy's strengths of publishing, brand management, and marketing.

NOTES

[1]Carey, Susan. "Playboy Looks Overseas as U.S. Climate Grows Hostile." *Wall Street Journal,* 29 Sept. 1993, p. B4.

EXHIBIT 29-9 Playboy Enterprises, Inc., Consolidated Statements of Operations for the Years Ended June 30 (*In thousands, except per share amounts*)

	1993	1992	1991
Net revenues	$214,875	$193,749	$174,042
Costs and expenses			
Cost of sales	(180,700)	(162,149)	(144,196)
Selling and administrative expenses	(33,149)	(29,116)	(27,556)
Total costs and expenses	(213,849)	(191,265)	(171,752)
Operating income	1,026	2,484	2,290
Nonoperating income (expense)			
Investment income	274	2,086	3,522
Interest expense	(405)	(258)	(298)
Critic's Choice Video minority interest	(860)	(118)	—
Other, net	444	392	376
Total nonoperating income (expense)	(547)	2,102	3,600
Income from continuing operations before income taxes and extraordinary item	479	4,586	5,890
Income tax expense	(114)	(2,764)	(3,479)
Income from continuing operations before extraordinary item	365	1,822	2,411
Discontinued operations			
Loss on disposal	—	—	(120)
Income before extraordinary item	365	1,822	2,291
Extraordinary item—tax benefit resulting from utilization of loss carryforwards	—	1,688	2,219
Net income	$365	$3,510	$4,510
Weighted average number of common shares outstanding	18,871	18,521	18,563
Income (loss) per common share			
Income (loss) before extraordinary item			
From continuing operations	$.02	$.10	$.13
From discontinued operations	—	—	(.01)
Total	.02	.10	.12
Extraordinary item applicable to continuing operations	—	.09	.12
Net income	$.02	$.19	$.24

Source: Playboy Enterprises, Inc., *Annual Report*, 1993.

EXHIBIT 29-10 Playboy Enterprises, Inc., Selected Financial and Operating Data for the Years Ended June 30 (*In thousands*)

	1993	1992	1991
Net Revenues			
Publishing			
Playboy magazine			
Subscription	$ 44,919	$ 42,635	$ 40,314
Newsstand	23,470	27,051	25,518
Advertising	30,406	30,667	32,683
Other	2,386	1,818	1,780
Total *Playboy* magazine	101,181	102,171	100,295
Playboy-related	22,008	21,737	22,283
Catalogs	39,411	28,054	18,135
Other	163	385	—
Total Publishing	162,763	152,347	140,713
Entertainment			
Domestic pay television			
Pay-per-view	8,006	6,031	3,835
Monthly subscription	8,575	9,832	11,400
Home satellite dish and other	4,732	2,591	2,538
Total domestic pay television	21,313	18,454	17,773
Domestic home video	10,133	7,009	2,668
International television and home video	9,822	5,447	3,454
Other	1,329	1,629	1,075
Total Entertainment	42,597	32,539	24,970
Product Marketing	9,515	8,863	8,359
Total Net Revenues	$214,875	$193,749	$174,042
Operating Income			
Publishing			
Playboy magazine	$ 7,947	$ 6,991	$6,122
Playboy-related	8,426	9,097	10,272
Catalogs	4,888	2,472	684
Administrative expenses, new magazine			
development and other	(6,909)	(5,809)	(4,790)
Total Publishing	14,352	12,751	12,288
Entertainment			
Before programming expense	15,364	12,645	10,451
Programming expense	(13,553)	(8,972)	(7,535)
Total Entertainment	1,811	3,673	2,916
Product Marketing	1,015	2,676	3,487
Corporate Administration and Promotion	(16,152)	(16,616)	(16,401)
Total Operating Income	$ 1,026	$ 2,484	$ 2,290

Source: Playboy Enterprises, Inc., *Annual Report*, 1993.

EXHIBIT 29-11 Playboy Enterprises, Inc., Consolidated Balance Sheets as of June 30
(*In thousands, except share data*)

	1993	1992
Assets		
Cash and cash equivalents	$ 1,903	$ 8,773
Short-term investments	50	10,447
Receivables, net of allowances for doubtful accounts of $2,343 and $1,903	22,772	14,824
Inventories	21,666	18,021
Programming costs	31,659	16,197
Deferred subscription acquisition costs	7,608	8,481
Other current assets	7,916	7,509
Total current assets	93,574	84,252
Property and equipment		
Land	292	343
Buildings and improvements	8,032	8,921
Furniture and equipment	19,727	20,206
Leasehold improvements	8,026	6,388
Total property and equipment	36,077	35,858
Accumulated depreciation	(18,490)	(19,530)
Property and equipment, net	17,587	16,328
Programming costs—noncurrent	1,096	7,601
Trademarks	9,449	8,514
Other noncurrent assets	6,061	4,516
Total assets	$127,767	$121,211
Liabilities		
Current financing obligations	$ 322	$ 318
Accounts payable	14,967	14,197
Accrued salaries, wages and employee benefits	4,138	3,677
Net liabilities of and reserves for losses on disposals of discontinued businesses	369	1,128
Income taxes payable	845	358
Accrued retail display allowance	2,417	2,994
Deferred revenues	36,318	39,254
Other liabilities and accrued expenses	5,257	6,416
Total current liabilities	64,633	68,342
Long-term financing obligations	1,347	1,669
Other noncurrent liabilities	6,406	7,944
Total liabilities	72,386	77,955
Commitments and contingencies		
Shareholders' Equity		
Common stock, $.01 par value		
Class A—7,500,000 shares authorized; 5,042,381 issued	50	50
Class B—30,000,000 shares authorized; 16,477,143 and 15,127,143 issued	165	151
Capital in excess of par value	36,344	24,655
Retained earnings	27,401	27,036
Less cost of 341,327 Class A common shares and 1,285,643		
and 1,296,667 Class B common shares in treasury	(8,579)	(8,636)
Total shareholders' equity	55,381	43,256
Total liabilities and shareholders' equity	$127,767	$121,211

Source: Playboy Enterprises, Inc., *Annual Report,* 1993.

EXHIBIT 29-12   Officers of Playboy Enterprises, Inc.

CORPORATE OFFICERS

Hugh M. Hefner
Founder, Chairman Emeritus and Editor-in-Chief

Christie Hefner
Chairman and Chief Executive Officer

David I. Chemerow
Executive Vice President, Finance and Operations,
and Chief Financial Officer

Anthony J. Lynn
Executive Vice President and President,
Entertainment Group

Michael S. Perlis
Executive Vice President and President, Publishing
Group

Richard S. Rosenzweig
Executive Vice President

Howard Shapiro
Executive Vice President, Law and Administration,
and General Counsel

Robert B. Beleson
Senior Vice President and Chief Marketing Officer

Rebecca S. Maskey
Senior Vice President, Finance, and Treasurer

Martha O. Lindeman
Vice President, Corporate Communications and
Public Affairs

Michael R. Nott
Vice President and Corporate Controller

John A. Ullrick
Vice President, Management Information Systems

Robert D. Campbell
Assistant Treasurer

Irma Villarreal
Corporate Counsel and Secretary

GROUP OFFICERS

Publishing Group

Michael S. Perlis
President and Publisher, *Playboy*

Arthur Kretchmer
Senior Vice President, Editorial Director and
Associate Publisher, *Playboy*

Irwin Kornfeld
Senior Vice President, Advertising and Marketing,
and Associate Publisher, *Playboy*

Barbara L. Gutman
Senior Vice President, Circulation and Ancillary
Businesses

Robert F. O'Donnell
Senior Vice President and General Manager,
New York

James P. Radtke
Senior Vice President and General Manager,
Chicago

Haresh Shah
Senior Vice President, International Publishing

Gary Cole
Vice President, Photography, *Playboy*

Marilyn Grabowski
Vice President, West Coast Photography, *Playboy*

Maria D. Mandis
Vice President, Production

Patricia Papangelis
Vice President and Executive Editor, Newsstand
Specials

Tom Staebler
Vice President and Executive Art Director, *Playboy*,
and President, Special Editions, Ltd.

Herbert M. Laney
President, Catalogs

Entertainment Group

Anthony J. Lynn
President

Richard V. Sowa
Executive Vice President, Chief Operating Officer
and President, Distribution

Richard P. Rosetti
President, Production

Richard Bencivengo
Senior Vice President, Programming and
Production, Pay Television

Myron DuBow
Senior Vice President, Business and Legal Affairs

Michael K. Fleming
Senior Vice President and General Manager, Pay
Television

Mary E. Herne
Senior Vice President, International Distribution
and Development

EXHIBIT 29-12 *Continued*

Jeffrey M. Jenest
  Senior Vice President and General Manager, Home Video
Sol Weisel
  Senior Vice President, Production Operations
Stephen M. Astor
  Vice President, Marketing
Marshal Backlar
  Vice President, Production
Suzanne Barron
  Vice President, International Home Video
Michael Hassan
  Vice President, Special Markets, Pay Television
Jeffrey R. Lai
  Vice President, Business and Legal Affairs
Barry A. Leshtz
  Vice President, Sales and Marketing, Home Video
Lawrence L. Logan
  Vice President and Creative Director
Brian W. Quirk

Source: Playboy Enterprises, Inc., *Annual Report*, 1993.

  Vice President, National Sales and Affiliate Relations, Pay Television
Deborah R. Redleaf
  Vice President, Finance

Product Marketing
Robert B. Beleson
  Chief Marketing Officer
Cindy Rakowitz
  Vice President, Public Relations
Lisa L. Weaver
  Vice President, International Licensing

Playboy Foundation
Cleo F. Wilson
  Executive Director
Burton Joseph
  Chairman, Board of Directors

APPLIANCES INDUSTRY NOTE
ARIEH ULLMANN AND JOHN HARRIS
STATE UNIVERSITY OF NEW YORK AT BINGHAMPTON

Product shipments of appliances increased 3 percent in 1993, to a record $17.7 billion. While housing starts increased only about 4 percent during the year, consumer confidence fell from 77 in January, as measured by the Conference Board, to 59 in August (1985=100), a level more typical of a recession year than a recovery year.

The appliance industry is dominated by five major corporations that produce complete lines of basic, major household appliances: Whirlpool, General Electric, White Consolidated Industries, Maytag, and Raytheon, in that order. State-of-the-art major appliances of high quality are offered at low prices because of intense competition among well-capitalized companies, high volume production, heavy capital investment, and a market open to foreign producers. Imports constitute more than 50 percent of the domestic market in several categories of small appliances, because of the high labor content of these appliances.

The major U.S. producers are now moving to become global manufacturers. Most have plants in Western Europe, and some have begun to expand into Central and Eastern Europe and China (Table 1).

Energy Efficiency Standards. The National Appliance Energy Conservation Act of 1987 set national efficiency standards for several categories of major household appliances, including refrigerators and freezers, water heaters, dishwashers, clothes washers and dryers, and kitchen ranges and ovens. The statute directs the Department of Energy (DOE) to tighten the standards in future years, taking into consideration life-cycle costs (initial cost plus operating cost). DOE has since revised energy conservation standards for refrigerators, dishwashers, clothes washers, and clothes dryers. The standards for refrigerators became effective in 1993, and the others are scheduled to take effect in May 1994. The 1994 standards can be met through several changes including more efficient motors, horizontal-axis clothes washers, auxiliary water heaters, lower water temperatures in the rinse cycle, reduced water usage per cycle, and better insulation and automatic heat sensor-controlled shutoffs for clothes dryers.

DOE has proposed new energy efficiency standards for water heaters, room air conditioners, direct heating equipment, televisions, kitchen ranges and ovens, pool heaters, mobile home furnaces, and fluorescent lamp ballasts. The proposed standards are expected to be published early in 1994. After a comment period, the final standards are likely to be published late in 1994 becoming effective before 1998.

ENVIRONMENTAL PROFILE

Energy efficiency and chlorofluorocarbons (CFCs) remain major issues for the appliance industry. For more than 50 years, CFCs have been used as coolants in refrigerators and freezers, as well as in the production of foam insulation. However, because CFCs allegedly damage the earth's protective layer of atmospheric ozone, the United States has pledged to halt CFC production by 1996 under the Montreal Protocol of 1987. In addition, DuPont, a major U.S. producer, has stated that it will end CFC production by the end of 1994. This accelerated phaseout places more pressure on manufacturers to finish testing substitutes, solve problems in material compatibility and toxicity, and meet energy-efficiency requirements. Most manufacturers are

TABLE 1 Trends and Forecasts: Household Appliances (SIC 363) (*In millions of dollars except as noted*)

Item	1991	1992[1]	1993[2]	1994[3]	Percent Change (1991–1994) 91–92	92–93	93–94
INDUSTRY DATA							
Value of shipments[4]	17,692	18,900	19,540	—	6.8	3.4	—
3631 Household cooking equip	2,891	3,064	3,198	—	6.0	4.4	—
3632 Household refrigerators	3,721	3,989	3,972	—	7.2	-0.4	—
3633 Household laundry equip	3,206	3,372	3,352	—	5.2	-0.6	—
3634 Elect housewares & fans	3,112	3,490	3,700	—	12.1	6.0	—
3635 Household vacuums	1,805	1,912	2,048	—	5.9	7.1	—
3639 Home appliances nec	2,958	3,073	3,270	—	3.9	6.4	—
Value of shipments (1987$)	16,826	17,998	18,551	19,210	7.0	3.1	3.6
Household cooking equip	2,914	3,094	3,172	3,270	6.2	2.5	3.1
3632 Household refrigerators	3,688	3,939	3,890	4,060	6.8	-1.2	4.4
3633 Household laundry equip	3,059	3,261	3,394	3,530	6.6	4.1	4.0
3634 Elect housewares & fans	2,892	3,220	3,380	3,460	11.3	5.0	2.4
3635 Household vacuums	1,615	1,720	1,815	1,870	6.5	5.5	3.0
3639 Home appliances nec	2,658	2,764	2,900	3,020	4.0	4.9	4.1
Total employment (000)	104	104	106	107	0.0	1.9	0.9
Production workers (000)	83.8	84.2	85.7	86.5	0.5	1.8	0.9
Average hourly earnings ($)	11.20	11.34	11.29	—	1.2	-0.4	—
Capital expenditures	496	—	—	—	—	—	—
PRODUCT DATA							
Value of shipments[5]	16,089	17,186	17,730	—	6.8	3.2	—
3631 Household cooking equip	2,942	3,118	3,255	—	6.0	4.4	—
3632 Household refrigerators	3,621	3,881	3,865	—	7.2	-0.4	—
3633 Household laundry equip	2,860	3,008	3,114	—	5.2	3.5	—
3634 Elect housewares & fans	2,608	2,926	2,956	—	12.2	1.0	—
3635 Household vacuums	1,834	1,943	2,081	—	5.9	7.1	—
3639 Home appliances nec	2,224	2,310	2,459	—	3.9	6.5	—
Value of shipments (1987$)	15,348	16,417	16,905	17,500	7.0	3.0	3.5
3631 Household cooking equip	2,966	3,150	3,230	3,330	6.2	2.5	3.1
3632 Household refrigerators	3,589	3,832	3,785	3,950	6.8	-1.2	4.4
3633 Household laundry equip	2,729	2,909	3,030	3,150	6.6	4.2	4.0
3634 Elect housewares & fans	2,424	2,700	2,835	2,900	11.4	5.0	2.3
3635 Household vacuums	1,642	1,749	1,845	1,900	6.5	5.5	3.0
3639 Home appliances nec	1,998	2,077	2,180	2,270	4.0	5.0	4.1
TRADE DATA							
Value of imports	3,258	3,830	4,100	4,400	17.6	7.0	7.3
Value of exports	2,139	2,365	2,510	2,700	10.6	6.1	7.6

[1]Estimate, except exports and imports.
[2]Estimate.
[3]Forecast.
[4]Value of all products and services sold by establishments in the household appliances industry.
[5]Value of products classified in the household appliances industry produced by all industries.

Source: U.S. Department of Commerce: Bureau of the Census; International Trade Administration (ITA). Estimates and forecasts by ITA.

expected to use hydrofluorocarbon-134a (HFC-134a) as the refrigerant and hydrochlorofluorocarbon-141b (HCFC-141b) as the foaming agent. The use of HCFC-141b is likely to be only a temporary substitute, since U.S. production is expected to be phased out by Jan. 1, 2003.

Some appliance manufacturers in Europe are already offering CFC-free refrigerators and freezers, most using the mentioned substitutes. Early 1993 models were priced about 7 percent higher than those with CFCs, however.

A U.S. manufacturer may soon use high-insulation vacuum panels in place of foam insulation. The latest versions of these panels reportedly have insulation values up to R-65-80 per inch, far higher than the R-8 achieved with foam produced with CFC-11 or the R-7.5 with HCFC-141b. If the use of these vacuum panels proves to be technologically feasible and cost-competitive, it could result in a substantial increase in a refrigerator's interior space while substantially contributing to energy efficiency. The panels might also be used in other appliances, such as water heaters.

INTERNATIONAL COMPETITIVENESS

Appliance imports and exports increased at nearly the same rate in 1993, imports about 7 percent to $4.1 billion and exports 6 percent to $2.5 billion. The leading suppliers of appliances to the United States were Mexico, China, Japan, South Korea, and Taiwan, in that order (Table 2).

TABLE 2   U.S. Trade Patterns in 1992 Household Appliances (SIC 363)
(*In millions of dollars, percent*)

EXPORTS			IMPORTS		
	Value	Share		Value	Share
Canada and Mexico	1,135	48.0	Canada and Mexico	909	23.7
European Community	323	13.7	European Community	482	12.6
Japan	77	3.3	Japan	464	12.1
East Asia NICs	207	8.7	East Asia NICs	1,725	45.0
South America	177	7.5	South America	40	1.0
Other	445	18.8	Other	210	5.5
World Total	2,365	100.0	World Total	3,830	100.0

TOP FIVE COUNTRIES					
	Value	Share		Value	Share
Canada	732	30.9	Mexico	738	19.3
Mexico	403	17.1	China	726	19.0
Taiwan	89	3.8	Japan	464	12.1
Germany	84	3.6	South Korea	304	7.9
Japan	77	3.3	Taiwan	299	7.8

Source: U.S. Department of Commerce: Bureau of the Census; International Trade Administration.

Mexico is expected to increase its lead regardless of the fate of the North American Free Trade Agreement, because of the growing integration of its appliance industry with that of the United States. Some U.S. appliance manufacturers have established joint ventures with Mexican companies to produce stoves, refrigerators, and laundry equipment in Mexico. These plants are expected to increase production in future years to supply markets in both countries as well as others. Asian countries with lower labor costs will remain the major suppliers of small appliances, for which transportation costs are less of a factor.

The leading markets for U.S. appliances are Canada, Mexico, Japan, Germany, and Saudi Arabia, in that order. Exports to Canada have more than doubled in the past four years as tariffs declined under the U.S.-Canada Free Trade Agreement, under which all Canadian tariffs on U.S. appliances will be eliminated by 1998. Likewise, U.S. appliance exports to Mexico have nearly doubled in the past four years because of major tariff reductions by Mexico and increasing shipments of parts to U.S.-affiliated appliance factories in Mexico.

U.S. export competitiveness depends to a large extent on the value of the dollar with respect to the currencies of its trading partners and competitors. The overall, real trade-weighted value of the dollar has been stable since 1988, after falling 30 percent from its peak in 1985. Even in 1993, the overall, trade-weighted value of the dollar changed only slightly, with strength in European markets offsetting weakness in Japan. During the five years of stability since 1988, U.S. trade in appliances has had time to readjust to the damage caused when an overvalued dollar in the mid-1980s encouraged imports and discouraged exports. The ratio of household appliance imports to exports is currently 1.6. While this is a substantial improvement over the ratio of 2.6 in 1987, it is substantially worse than the ratio of 1.0 which existed in the mid-to-late 1970s. It is unlikely that trade patterns will continue to shift all the way back. Since the mid-1970s, duty-free treatment of imports under the Generalized System of Preferences has resulted in the developing countries becoming major suppliers of many of the small electric household appliances sold domestically.

MANUFACTURING AND DISTRIBUTION

Home appliances are generally classified as laundry (washers and dryers), refrigeration (refrigerators and freezers), cooking (ranges and ovens), and other appliances (dishwashers, disposals, and trash compactors). Many appliance manufacturers also make floor care goods such as floor polishers and vacuum cleaners.

Manufacturing operations consist mainly of preparation of a metal frame to which the appropriate components are attached in automated assembly lines and by manual assembly. Manufacturing costs comprise about 65 to 75 percent of total operating cost with labor representing less than 10 percent of total cost. Optimal-sized assembly plants have an annual capacity of about 500,000 units for most appliances except microwave ovens. Unlike other industries such as textiles, variable costs play an important role in the cost structure; changes in raw material and component costs are also significant. Component production is fairly scale sensitive. Doubling compressor output for refrigerators, for instance, reduces unit costs by 10–15 percent. There are also some scale economies in assembly, but introduction of robotics tends to reduce those while also improving quality, performance, consistency, and flexibility.

Distribution of major appliances occurs through contract sales to home builders or local builder suppliers. Traditionally, these customers were very cost conscious and prefer less expensive appliance brands. Retail sales represent a second distribution channel through which national chain stores and mass merchandisers, like Sears, as well as department, furniture, discount, and appliance stores act as intermediaries. In recent years, independent appliance stores which in the past sold about a third of all white goods are more and more being replaced by national chains such as Sears' Brand Central and mega-appliance dealers such as Circuit City. Consolidation of appliance distributors has led to the current situation in which about 45 percent of the total appliance volume is being sold through 10 powerful mega-retailers, led by Sears with a market share of about 29 percent. A third, less visible channel is the commercial market such as laundromats, hospitals, hotels, and other institutions.

Consolidation. Before World War II, appliance manufacturers produced many varieties of one product. In the mid-1940s, there were over 250 firms manufacturing appliances in the United States, including all the major U.S. automobile firms except for Chrysler. The industry experienced a period of mergers in the 1950s and 1960s while sales grew approximately 50 percent due to increased reliability, advances in technology, and a decline in prices. With the 1970s came high inflation and interest rates, but unit sales still continued to climb.

The last merger wave occurred in 1986 when Electrolux purchased White Consolidated, Whirlpool acquired KitchenAid, and Magic Chef was bought by Maytag. Maytag's acquisition of Jenn-Air and Magic Chef increased its overall revenues by giving brand name appliances to Maytag at various price points. Likewise, Whirlpool's acquisition of KitchenAid and Roper, respectively, broadened Whirlpool's presence at the high-end and low-end of the market. The number of domestic appliance manufacturers today varies by type of product, with seven for home laundry appliances, fifteen for home refrigeration and room air conditioning equipment, and five for dishwashers.

Broad Product Scope. In the 1980s, the market continued to grow primarily thanks to the acceptance by the American people of the microwave oven. Microwave oven unit sales tripled from 1980 to 1989, while washers and dryers increased in sales 34 and 52 percent, respectively. Appliance manufacturers realized that they must offer a complete line of appliances even if they did not manufacture all of them themselves which was one reason for the merger activity and practice of inter-firm sourcing. For example, Whirlpool made trash compactors for Frigidaire (Electrolux/White Consolidated), In-Sink-Erator (Emerson Electric), and Sears. General Electric manufactured microwave ovens for Caloric (Raytheon), Jenn-Air, and Magic Chef (Maytag).

Today, five major competitors control 98 percent of the core appliance market (cooking equipment, dishwashers, dryers, refrigerators, and washers) each of which offers a broad range of product categories and brands targeted to different customer segments. With 33.8 percent domestic market share, Whirlpool is ahead of GE (28.2 percent), a reversal of GE's leadership position two years earlier. Electrolux (15.9 percent), Maytag (14.2 percent), and Raytheon (5.6 percent) follow. Whirlpool holds market share leadership positions in several appliance categories.

Market Saturation. Competition in the United States is fierce. Industry demand depends on the state of the economy, disposable income levels, interest rates, housing starts, and the consumers' ability to defer purchases. Saturation levels remain high and steady; over 70 percent of households have washers and over 65 percent dryers. The market for refrigerators is saturated. Sales of electric ranges have slowed as microwave oven sales have accelerated. With many homes having more than one gas or electric range, the market has become saturated. Yet, even microwave sales, which jumped from 3.5 million units in 1980 to more than 10 million units by 1989, have started leveling out.

Factors of Competition. All rivals work hard at keeping costs down. Over four years, Electrolux spent over $500 million to upgrade old plants and build new ones for its acquisition, White Consolidated Industries. General Electric automated its Louisville, Kentucky, plant which, over ten years, halved the work force and raised output by 30 percent. Had appliance manufacturers been making automobiles, the price of a Cheverolet Caprice would have risen from $7,209 in 1980 to $9,500 in 1990 and not $17,370.

Toward the end of the 1980s, it became even more important to lower costs, monitor margins, and achieve economies of scale. The Big Four were renovating and enlarging existing facilities. Maytag built new facilities in the south to take advantage of lower cost, nonunion labor. Others built twin-plants on the Mexican border to profit from cheap labor. A third trend was towards focus factories where each plant produced one product category only, covering all price points.

Also, all competitors started to push into the high-end segment of the market which was more stable and profitable. Once the domain of Maytag, it became increasingly crowded with the appearance of GE's Monogram line, Whirlpool's acquisition of KitchenAid, and White's Euroflair models. This trend had its roots in the 1980s which brought an increase in new home construction, home expansions, and remodelings. It was estimated that each new home would purchase four to six new appliances. More upscale models were being used as compared to a previous tendency for builders to economize by buying the cheapest national brand appliances.

Quality, too, became an important feature in the competitive game as symbolized by Maytag's lonely repairman. The number of service calls dropped across the board in the wake of rising consumer expectations. Defects rates dropped from 20 per 100 appliances made in 1980 to 10 twelve years later. Relationships with suppliers changed as companies used fewer of them than in years past. Contracts were set up over longer terms to improve quality and keep costs low with just-in-time deliveries.

A recent development is demand by powerful distributors for fast delivery. Distributors seek to curtail inventory costs, their biggest expense.

> We would like to carry even more brands, but we have to find a way to move product more quickly. Sharing information with manufacturers is critical. Logistics is more than distribution; they cover disposal of major appliances, next-day delivery guaranteed in a three-hour period, and emergency repairs. But we have to work with manufacturers to get the costs down,

declared Bernard Brennan, CEO of Montgomery Ward, at a recent meeting of the Association of Home Appliance Manufacturers. As a consequence, General Electric created its Premier Plus Program which guarantees three-day delivery. Also, sales departments are reorganized so one sales representative covers all of a manufacturer's brands of a given product category. Customer information services via 800-telephone lines are now common.

Innovation. Two developments, government regulation and advances in computer software, combined with intense competition have accelerated product innovation. New energy standards to be enforced under the 1987 National Appliance

Energy Conservation Act limit energy consumption of new appliances with the objective to reduce energy usage in appliances by 25 percent every five years. At the same time, the possible ban on ozone-depleting chlorofluorocarbons (CFCs) in refrigerators by 1995 has forced the industry to redesign its refrigerators. Pressures have also been exerted to change washer and dishwasher designs to reduce water consumption.

In 1989, the Super Efficient Refrigerator Program, Inc. (SERP) was organized by the Natural Resources Defense Council, a few utilities, and the Environmental Protection Agency. The SERP organizers created a $30 million price contest financed by 24 utilities to develop a refrigerator prototype free of CFCs and which was at least 25 percent more energy efficient than the 1993 federal standards. Whirlpool won the entire $30 million and has to manufacture and sell over 250,000 refrigerators between January 1994 and July 1997.

Advances in computer technology is the second development accelerating innovation. New programs called fuzzy logic or neural networks, which mimic the human brain's ability to detect patterns, are being introduced in many industries including white goods. In Asia, elevators, washers, and refrigerators using fuzzy logic to recognize usage patterns are already widespread. In late 1992, AEG Hausgeräte AG, a subsidiary of Daimler Benz's AEG unit, introduced a washer using fuzzy logic to automatically control water consumption depending on the size of the load and to sense how much dirt remained in clothes. United Technology is working on a line of air conditioners that automatically adjust room temperature based on the number of people in a room and their preference for comfort, humidity, and air flow.

Outlook. For the future, demand conditions in the United States continue to look unattractive with growth rates forecast around 1 to 2 percent from a level which is 15 percent below 1988 industry shipments. At the prevailing saturation levels, demand is mostly restricted to replacement purchases (79 percent) with the remainder going to new housing and new household formation.

The one positive element in this otherwise bleak outlook is a demographic trend in that the aging baby boomers are demanding more stylish appliances with new features. The late 1980s saw new technologies in cooking surfaces: ceramic-glass units, solid elements, and modular grill configurations. Other new customer-oriented features include the self-cleaning oven, automatic ice cube makers, self-defrosting refrigerators, pilotless gas ranges, and appliances that can be preset. Manufacturers' own brands normally are first accessorized, followed by the national retailers they outfit. Sears and Montgomery Ward usually copy the previous year's most successful products. However, the industry is so competitive that no one manufacturer can keep an innovation to itself for more than a year without a patent. Finally, consumers have become more concerned with the way appliances look. Sleek European styling is fashionable with smooth lines, rounded corners, and a built-in look with electronic controls. Another trend is the white-on-white look which suggests superior cleanability and makes a kitchen look larger.

GLOBALIZATION

The white goods industry is as American as baseball and apple pie. In 1992, 98 percent of the dishwashers, washing machines, dryers, refrigerators, freezers, and ranges sold in America were made in America. Exports represent around 5 percent of shipments. Manufacturing plants of the industry leaders are located in places such as Newton, Iowa (Maytag); Benton Harbor, Michigan (Whirlpool); and Columbus,

Ohio (White Consolidated Industries). Combined, these companies practically own the market for each major appliance with one exception—microwave ovens. These represent the lion's share of imports which make up about 17 percent of total appliance sales.

The acquisition of White Consolidated Industries by AB Electrolux of Sweden in 1986 marked a major change in the industry. Until then, foreign competition was largely restricted to imports of microwave ovens, a segment which was controlled by Far Eastern competitors from Korea (Goldstar, Samsung) and Japan (Sharp, Matsushita). Aware of the fate of other industries, many expected that it was only a matter of time before these companies would expand from their beachhead in microwave ovens and compact appliances into other segments. Indeed, the general manager of the overseas office of Matsushita, the market leader in Japan's white goods industry, stated:

> Foreign makers are right to expect that Matsushita and other Japanese companies will enter the U.S. and European markets soon enough. The traditional makers won't be number 1 and number 2 forever.

Europe's Promise. Of prime attractiveness to U.S. manufacturers is Europe. As a continent, Western Europe represents 27 percent of the global market and, if Eastern Europe and the Middle East and Africa are included, 43 percent; Asia's share is 27 percent; North America follows with 24 percent and Latin America with 6 percent. Western Europe is rapidly moving towards a unified market of some 320 million consumers which is not nearly as saturated as Canada and the United States. Appliance demand is expected to grow at 5 percent annually. Political changes in Eastern Europe have integrated these countries into the world trade system and thus added to Europe's long-term attractiveness.

The European white goods industry has experienced a consolidation similar to that in the United States. In the late 1980s, six companies—Electrolux Zanussi, Philips Bauknecht, Bosch-Siemens, Merloni-Indesit, Thompson, and AEG—controlled 70 percent of the market (excluding microwave ovens and room air conditioners). Until the mid-1980s most companies were either producing and selling in only one national market or exporting to a limited extent to many European markets from one country. Observed Whirlpool CEO Whitwam: "What strikes me most is how similar the U.S. and European industries are." Research by Whirlpool indicates that washers were basically alike in working components around the globe.

However, the European market is very segmented and consumer preferences differ greatly from country to country with regard to almost every type of appliance. For example: The French prefer to cook their foods at high temperatures, splattering grease on oven walls. Thus, oven ranges manufactured for France have self-cleaning ability. However, this feature is not a requirement in Germany where lower cooking temperatures are the norm. In contrast to Americans who prefer to stuff as many clothes into the washer as possible, Europeans overwhelmingly prefer smaller built-in models. Northern Europeans like large refrigerators because they prefer to shop only once a week. In contrast, consumers in the south of Europe prefer small ones, because they visit the open-air markets daily. Northerners like their freezers at the bottom of the refrigerators, southerners on top. Also, the continental European "engineering" mentality dislikes the U.S. and British one-touch button models, but prefers the build-in concept which was developed in the U.S. where it failed to attract buyers. In France, 80 percent of washing machines are top-loaders, while elsewhere in Western Europe, 90 percent are front-loaders. Also, European washers frequently contain heating elements, and the typical European homemaker prefers to wash towels at 95 degrees centigrade. Gas ranges are common throughout Europe, except for Germany where 90 percent are electric.

Given these differences, some observers are skeptical about the possibility of establishing pan-European models which would yield a sustainable competitive advantage through manufacturing, procurement, and marketing efficiencies. They claim that the European market is actually many smaller individual markets made up of the respective countries. Furthermore, many of these national markets feature strong competitors.

AB Electrolux is a force practically in all of Europe with an overall 25 percent market share. Over 20 years, the $14-billion multinational firm from Sweden has undertaken more than 200 acquisitions in 40 countries which span five businesses: household appliances, forestry and garden products, industrial products, metal and mining, and commercial services. Its expertise in managing acquisitions and integrating newly acquired units into the organization is unequalled. For instance, in 1983, Electrolux took over the money losing Italian white goods manufacturer with 30,000 employees, 50 factories, and a dozen foreign sales companies. Within four years, the Swedes turned this company which in 1983 lost Lit. 120 billion into an efficient organization netting Lit. 60 billion. The acquisitions of Zanussi of Italy, Tricity in Britain, and three Spanish companies in anticipation of the changes in Western Europe marked the beginning of a new era in this mature industry. Industrial design centers and research centers are being established in Stockholm, Sweden, Venice, Italy, and Columbus, Ohio, to share product and operation ideas and to accelerate product development among the many brands. Instead of combining production, marketing, and sales on a market-by-market basis, a search for synergies began, first to establish pan-European brands for a unified Europe, and then to explore cross-Atlantic opportunities. The newly formed Electrolux Components Group is charged with taking advantage of the available integration opportunities, primarily by coordinating and developing strategic components worldwide. However, in 1993 Electrolux' pan-European strategy ran into trouble. The recession, combined with Europe's market fragmentation, reduced profits far below the targeted 5 percent margin. In contrast to North America, the varying consumer preferences compelled Electrolux to offer 120 basic designs with 1,500 variants in Europe.

In Germany, Bauknecht (Philips) as well as Siemens-Bosch and AEG-Telefunken are dominant; in Britain General Electric Corporation's Hotpoint leads; and in France, Thomson-Brandt are forces to be reckoned with. Merloni from Italy pursues a different approach by flooding Europe with machines produced in Italy with lower cost labor. In 1987, Merloni gobbled up Indesit, an Italian producer in financial troubles, in order to enlarge its manufacturing base and take advantage of Indesit's marketing position in many European countries. However, in the late 1980s, no brand had more than 5 percent of the overall market, even though the top ten producers generated 80 percent of the volume.

General Electric is another important rival. In 1989, GE entered into an appliance joint venture with Britain's General Electric Corporation (GEC), which has a strong presence in the low price segment of the European market, especially the UK, and thus complements GE's high-end European products.

In the same year, Maytag also entered the European market. It had acquired the Hoover Division through the purchase of Chicago Pacific. Hoover, best known for its vacuum cleaners, in the UK also produced washers, dryers, and dishwashers in a highly integrated process in aging facilities. Hoover is also present in Australia and, through a trading company, services other parts of the world. By acquiring Hoover, Maytag assumed a significant debt load and experienced a negative reaction from the stock market. However, the company's official strategy entails continued globalization via expansion in Europe and the Pacific Rim.

AEG is cooperating with Electrolux in washer and dishwasher production and development; Bosch-Siemens has an alliance with Maytag; the European Economic Interest Group combined several manufacturers with France's Thompson-Brandt as the leader. In spite of this trend toward consolidation, Whirlpool competes among nearly 100 European manufacturers of home appliances.

Asia. Asia, the world's second largest home appliance market, is expected to experience rapid economic growth in the near future primarily thanks to the booming economies of the Pacific Rim countries. Home appliance shipments are expected to grow at least 6 percent per annum through the 1990s—more than in Europe or North America. The market is dominated by some 50 widely diversified Asian manufacturers, primarily from Japan, Korea, and Taiwan, with no clear leader emerging yet. The biggest promise lies in the huge markets of the world's most populous states— China and India.

Latin America. Another market promising attractive growth for appliances is Latin America, once these countries follow Chile's example and emerge from decades of political instability, economic mismanagement, and hyperinflation. The North American Free Trade Agreement (NAFTA) has lowered tariffs and stimulated trade. Appliance shipments to Latin America and Mexico should expand at a faster pace than in North America and Europe.

OUTLOOK FOR 1994

Product shipments of appliances are expected to increase nearly 4 percent in real terms in 1994. Private housing starts are expected to increase 4 percent in 1994, the same rate estimated for 1993. Real improvement is expected in consumer confidence, which in 1993 actually dipped close to the levels last seen during the serious 1981–82 recession. Some argue that these low confidence levels were not a true reflection of the economy, but partly reflected consumer concerns about the federal tax increases, health care reform, and NAFTA, all of which were debated during 1993 and are expected to be settled by early 1994 at the latest.

WHIRLPOOL CORPORATION—1994

Headquartered in Benton Harbor, Michigan, Whirlpool Corporation (616-923-5000) is one of the world's leading manufacturers and marketers of major home appliances. The company's plants are located in twelve countries and its products are distributed in over 120 countries under major brand names. Whirlpool's net earnings for 1993 were $51 million, down 75 percent from 1992. CEO David Whitwam needs a clear strategic plan for the rest of the 1990s decade. Whirlpool's vision statement is:

> Whirlpool, in its chosen lines of business, will grow with new opportunities and be the leader in an ever-changing global market. We will be driven by our commitment to continuous quality improvement and to exceeding all of our customers' expectations. We will gain competitive advantage through this, and by building on our existing strengths and developing new competencies. We will be market-driven, efficient and profitable. Our success will make Whirlpool a company that worldwide customers, employees and other stakeholders can depend on.

HISTORY

Located two hours by car from Chicago, Whirlpool was founded in St. Joseph, Michigan, in 1911. At the time, the company was producing motor-driven wringer-washers under the name Upton Machine, with the hopes of selling them in large quantities to large distributors. In 1916, the first order was sold to Sears, Roebuck and Co. This enduring relationship with its oldest and largest customer continues today with Sears representing 19 percent of Whirlpool's sales. In 1929, Upton merged with Nineteen Hundred Corp., of Binghamton, New York, and plants operated in both locations until Binghamton was closed in 1939. In 1948, the Whirlpool brand automatic washer was introduced. This established the dual distribution system—one product line for Sears, the other for Nineteen Hundred. The Nineteen Hundred Corp. was renamed Whirlpool in 1950 with the addition of automatic dryers to the company's product line.

In 1955, Whirlpool merged with Seeger Refrigerator Co., of St. Paul, Minnesota, and the Estate range and air conditioning divisions of R.C.A. The company, now named Whirlpool-Seeger Corporation, established the RCA Whirlpool brand name which was used until 1967. In 1957, the name was changed back to Whirlpool Corporation. In the same year, the Appliance Credit Corporation was established as a wholly owned finance subsidiary whose name later was changed to Whirlpool Financial Corporation. Also in 1957, Whirlpool, for the first time, entered the foreign market through the purchase of equity interest in Multibras S.A. of Sao Paulo, Brazil, later renamed Brastemp S.A.

In 1967, Whirlpool was the first competitor in the industry to take advantage of AT&T's new 800-line service and created the Cool-Line Telephone Service which provided customers a toll-free number to call for answers to questions and help with service.

Over the years, Whirlpool consistently upgraded its manufacturing capacity by constructing new plants and closing old ones. In 1968, it completed the Elisha Gray II Research and Engineering Center in Benton Harbor thereby establishing a solid R&D basis. In 1986, the KitchenAid division of Hobart Corporation was purchased from Dart & Kraft which marked Whirlpool's entry into the upscale segment of the appliance market. In the same year, Whirlpool sold its central heating and cooling business to Inter-City Gas Corp. of Canada.

Whirlpool diversified in 1985 with the acquisition of Mastercraft Industries Corp., a Denver-based manufacturer of kitchen cabinets. A year later, a second cabinet maker, St. Charles Manufacturing Co., was acquired through the newly formed Whirlpool Kitchens, Inc. In March 1989, Whirlpool Kitchens was sold due to lack of fit. Whirlpool Kitchens had been losing money and had discontinued operations in 1988.

In 1988, Whirlpool's North American operations were reorganized into four brand-oriented business units: Whirlpool Appliance Group, KitchenAid Appliance Group, Kenmore Appliance Group, Inglis Limited. This structure was supposed to allow the company to capitalize on the success of its brands while at the same time reap scale effects through an integrated manufacturing network. KitchenAid served the upscale market based on its reputation for quality blenders and dishwashers, the Whirlpool brand served the mid-price segment, and the Roper brand name, which Whirlpool acquired in 1988 and which was part of the Whirlpool Group, focused on the lower segment and provided Whirlpool with gas range production capability. Thus, within the North American Appliance Group (NAAG) a clear market segmentation existed which ensured complete coverage and minimal overlap. NAAG's scope had been further extended with the acquisition of Emerson Electric's dishwasher and trash compactor business.

In 1992, as a result of a year-long strategic reassessment of the entire company, a new organizational structure was designed for NAAG. Effective January 1, 1993, the new organizational units focus on process management, brand management, customer management, product and service creation, manufacturing, and logistics. The new structure is intended to provide better support for a customer-oriented strategy. The sales and distribution organizations are responsible for brand and customer management for the retail and contract sales business. Marketing focuses on product and service creation and on enhancing brand awareness and loyalty. Logistics is responsible for managing availability and inventory through the warehouses, plants, and vendors. A separate unit, the Kenmore organization, is charged with supporting Sears, Whirlpool's largest single customer.

In June 1993, Whirlpool was named winner in the $30 million Super Efficient Refrigerator Program (SERP), a success which CEO Whitwam attributed to the multidisciplinary team which had been assembled from all over the world: "Each member of the Whirlpool team is an expert in his or her field," Whitwam said. "Their combined efforts and unrelenting focus on bringing a SERP refrigerator to market has resulted in the development of a superior product in a remarkably short time." The first SERP model will be a 22 cubic foot side-by-side refrigerator/freezer to be introduced in 1994. The SERP models eliminate CFCs completely by using a different refrigerant and blowing agent to expand foam insulation between the walls of the refrigerator liner and cabinet. Energy efficiency gains are achieved through better insulation, a high-efficiency compressor, and an improved condenser fan motor in conjunction with a microchip controlled adaptive defrost control which incorporates fuzzy logic. Jeff Fettig, vice president, group marketing and sales for NAAG adds: "I can say that these changes allow us to surpass SERP's very tough requirement that the refrigerators be at least 25 percent more efficient than 1993 federal energy standards." Whirlpool had entered the SERP contest because it was consistent with the company's strategy to exceed customer expectations. Again Fettig: "The SERP program allows us to accelerate the development process and bring these products to the market sooner. Future products will be designed with these consumer expectations [regarding environmental friendliness] in mind, giving people even more reason to ask for a Whirlpool-built product next time they are in the market for a major home appliance."

Since 1988, NAAG had increased its regional market share by nearly a third. The North American business remained Whirlpool's core group: "NAAG has been the source of much of the cash flow required to fund the company's expansion into new markets, and accounts for nearly 60 percent of corporate revenues." Major home appliances constitute a $19 billion basic consumer durable industry in the United States. Exhibit 30–1 traces historical shipment patterns in the main appliance categories. Clearly apparent are the industry's comparatively slow average growth and moderate cyclicality. Refrigerators are the largest product line, followed by washers, dryers, and dishwashers.

Market share data for the years 1988 and 1992 are presented on Exhibit 30–2 and demonstrate the concentrated nature of the industry, Whirlpool's particular predominance in laundry products, and the gradual increases in the company's market shares. The share slippage in refrigeration between 1988 and 1992 partly reflects considerable restructuring in that area, and has probably now reversed.

WHIRLPOOL'S CEO

Among Whirlpool's top management, David R. Whitwam is known as a champion of Whirlpool's globalization. Born in Madison (Wisconsin), Whitwam graduated with honors from the University of Wisconsin with a B.S. in economics. After eight years in the United States Army and the Wisconsin National Guard, he joined Whirlpool as a marketing management trainee in July 1968. One year later, he was named territory sales manager at the South California sales division. From there job descriptions did not change, only the locations. Whitwam spent time in New York and then in Southern California.

A soft-spoken man with midwestern charm, Whitwam was never one to gloat, but his success in California was immense. His forward thinking and innovative spirit sparked Ed Herrelko, vice president of marketing and sales for Caloric, to exalt, "He's a legend out there."

Whitwam moved to corporate headquarters in Benton Harbor in 1977 when he was named merchandising manager for Range Products. From that post came a promotion to director of builder marketing, and then vice president, Whirlpool Sales, in 1983. In 1985, he was elected to the company's board of directors. On December 1, 1987, he assumed his current position as president, CEO and chairman of the board of Whirlpool Corporation. Since then, he has transformed a domestically oriented $4 billion company into a $7 billion global force.

WHIRLPOOL INTERNATIONAL B.V.

Among those most strongly convinced of the promise of the European market was David Whitwam: "The only people who say you can't have a pan-European brand are the people who don't have one themselves." Whitwam elaborates on the company's rationale for globalization:

> The U.S. appliance market has limited growth opportunities, a high concentration of domestic competitors and increasing foreign competition. Further, the U.S. represents only about 25% of the worldwide potential for major appliance sales.

EXHIBIT 30-1 Shipments of Major Home Appliances in the United States (thousand units)

YEAR	DISH-WASHER	DISPOSER	DRYERS	ELECTRIC RANGES	MICROWAVES	REFRIG-ERATORS	ROOM AIR CONDITIONERS	WASHERS	OTHER	TOTAL
1985	3,575	4,105	3,914	3,551	10,883	6,081	3,022	5,279	3,610	44,020
1986	3,918	4,269	4,245	3,741	12,444	6,510	2,816	5,765	3,877	47,585
1987	4,032	4,439	4,637	3,841	12,610	6,972	3,798	5,998	4,325	50,652
1988	3,907	4,233	4,601	3,708	10,988	7,227	4,637	6,190	4,542	50,033
1989	3,668	4,363	4,574	3,529	10,598	7,099	5,091	6,252	4,287	49,461
1990	3,637	4,137	4,320	3,444	8,126	7,101	4,150	6,192	4,516	45,623
1991	3,571	4,002	4,313	3,309	7,012	7,273	2,834	6,197	4,596	43,107
1992	3,820	4,195	4,717	3,574	7,588	7,761	2,910	6,515	5,091	46,171
1993E	4,033	4,366	4,980	3,716	7,697	7,875	3,075	6,728	5,174	47,644
1994E	4,070	4,501	5,098	3,822	7,812	8,076	3,124	6,931	5,230	48,664

Source: Merrill Lynch Forecast.

Most importantly, our vision can no longer be limited to our domestic borders because national borders no longer define market boundaries. The marketplace for products and services is more global than ever before and growing more so every day.

Consumers in major industrialized countries are living increasingly similar lifestyles and have increasingly similar expectations of what consumer products must do for them. As purchasing patterns become more alike, we think that companies that operate on a broad global scale can leverage their strengths better than those which only serve an individual national market. Very likely, appliance manufacturing will always have to be done regionally. Yet the ability to leverage many of the strengths of a company on an international basis is possible only if that company operates globally.

In 1988, Whitwam and Whirlpool made their boldest move so far towards global dominance in the white goods industry. They announced a joint venture with N.V. Philips, the second largest appliance manufacturer in Europe behind Electrolux. The

EXHIBIT 30-2 U.S. Market Shares for Major Appliances

	WHIRLPOOL	GENERAL ELECTRIC	FRIGIDAIRE	MAYTAG	RAYTHEON
Compactors					
92	70%	14%			
88	67	14			
Dishwashers					
92	31	40	20%	8%	
88	19	40	7	7	
Dryers (electric)					
92	52	18	12	15	3%
88	52	16	11	12	3
Dryers (gas)					
92	53	14	10	17	4
88	52	16	11	12	3
Ranges (electric)					
92	30	30	17	17	7
88	13	30	10	10	7
Ranges (gas)					
92		19	25	27	22
88			7	24	15
Refrigerators					
92	25	35	17	13	8
88	28	35	21	10	5
Washers					
92	52	16	11	17	4
88	50	17	10	16	4
Overall 1992	34	28	16	14	6
Overall 1988	31	26	18	15	6

Note: Frigidaire is owned by AB Electrolux.
Source: Appliance Manufacturer Magazine.

deal for a 53 percent interest in Philips' worldwide Major Domestic Appliance Division was consummated in 1989, for $361 million in cash; the new company was called Whirlpool International B.V. (WIBV).

In 1991, Whirlpool exercised its option to purchase from Philips the remaining interest in WIBV. With this move, Whirlpool became the world's largest appliance manufacturer, overtaking archrival AB Electrolux. (Exhibit 30–3 compares Whirlpool market share in the United States and Europe with its competitors.)

Philips' decentralized organization was phased out and WIBV split into two customer-focused business units—one for the Bauknecht brand, and the other for the dual-branded Philips/Whirlpool products and Ignis and Laden products. Brands were thus positioned to fit the niches and conditions in Europe, an approach employed earlier in the United States where each brand was given a particular segment. Bauknecht—Philips' most profitable brand—was aimed at the high end of the market, Philips/Whirlpool at the middle, and Ignis was designed for the lower end. Sales and marketing were kept completely separate for the Bauknecht and Whirlpool appliance groups, yet nonmarketing support from each of the 14 countries was combined. The manufacturing organization was also completely revamped. However, several plants located strategically were maintained—in contrast to Maytag. This turned out to be a significant advantage in a Europe with fragmented consumer tastes. Explained Lisa Mendheim of Maytag, referring to the company's Hoover operations: "We're very limited in adapting washers and dryers made in Wales to European standards." Logistics, distribution, after-sales service, and information were tied together with assembly under one person. Distribution was reconfigured towards a pan-European approach and 10 out of 28 finished goods warehouses were closed.

A global outlook was instilled in the management team. Instead of having primarily Dutch managers, the top seven-member team comprised five nationalities. Managers were rotated between Europe and the United States to foster global thinking. This move paid off recently when the VIP Crisp microwave oven, developed by a

EXHIBIT 30-3 Core Appliance Market Share of Major Competitors in the United States and Europe in 1991 vs. 1989

PERCENT OF MARKET SHARE			PERCENT OF MARKET SHARE		
UNITED STATES	1991	1989	EUROPE	1991	1989
Whirlpool	33.9	32.7	Electrolux	19	20.5
General Electric	28.2	25.5	Bosch-Siemens	13	11.0
Electrolux	15.9	18.4	Whirlpool	10	11.5
Maytag	14.2	14.8	Miele	7	na
Raytheon	5.6	na	Thompson	6	na
Other	2.2	8.6	AEG	5	na
			Merloni		10.0
			Maytag		2.0
			Other	40	40.0

Source: Bray (1993); *Appliance*, September 1992.

new "advanced global technology unit" in Norrköping, Sweden, was introduced and quickly became Europe's best-selling model. The VIP Crisp has a heated base plate which allows Italians to bake crisp pizza crusts and the British to fry eggs. Now the company is starting to import the VIP Crisp to the United States.

WIBV also made a series of moves to establish itself in the emerging markets of central and eastern Europe, which represents about 11 percent of the world appliance market and promises attractive growth opportunities over the long term. Bauknecht was first in setting up a distribution system in East Germany after the opening of the border. WIBV has developed distribution networks in the entire region and established a wholly owned sales subsidiary in Hungary, Whirlpool Hungarian Trading, Ltd. In May 1992, a 43.8 percent minority investment in Whirlpool/Tatramat a.s., a joint venture in Slovakia, was acquired which in October started manufacturing and selling automatic washers and marketing products assembled at other WIBV locations. In 1993, sales subsidiaries were opened in Poland and the Czech Republic adding to WIBV's position in eastern Europe. By the end of 1992, WIBV with headquarters in Eindhoven, Holland, employed 14,000 people and maintained manufacturing facilities in six countries.

WIBV has started redesigning its products in order to increase manufacturing efficiency, improve product quality and customer satisfaction. WIBV, now called Whirlpool Europe B.V. (WEBV), has been restructured. WEBV replaced the Bauknecht and Philips/Whirlpool Appliance Groups with centralized sales and marketing functions which support all of Whirlpool's European brands. National sales subsidiaries have been consolidated into three sales regions in order to take account of the growing European cross-border trade. The marketing function includes separate, brand-oriented components to strengthen brand identity while at the same time ensuring coordination internally. Manufacturing and technology activities are organized around product groups and development centers with Germany focusing on laundry and dishwashing products and Italy focusing on refrigeration and cooking. Key support functions (consumer services, information technology, logistics, planning) are maintained as separate, centrally managed entities. Explained WEBV president Hank Bowman: "The idea is to put systems support in place so we can deliver products more accurately and in a more timely manner." A central account-management function services transnational buying groups. WEBV now has responsibility for the Middle East and Africa which formerly were housed in Whirlpool Overseas Corporation (WOC) and which accounted for $100 million in sales, mainly in the form of kits, in an attempt to boost local content and thus preempt the emergence of the domestic-content rules. WEBV supports WOC by supplying products, components, and technology sold by WOC in its geographic domain. In June 1993, WEBV sold its refrigerator plant in Barcelona (Spain) to an Italian appliance maker in order to make better use of its remaining facilities.

By mid-1993, WEBV had established itself as the third largest appliance manufacturer in Europe behind Electrolux and Bosch-Siemens and anticipated that by achieving increased efficiencies coupled with volume growth it would raise operating margins to the North American level. Exhibit 30–4 illustrates Whirlpool's globalization milestones and Exhibit 30–5 details western European appliance shipments. Excluding microwaves and room air conditioners, aggregate western European volumes are 5 to 10 percent higher than in the United States. Shipments accelerated upward between the mid- and late-80s, and have since flattened. The largest distinct submarket within Europe is Germany (including the Benelux countries and Switzerland), followed by the United Kingdom and France. About one-third of European production takes place in Italy.

EXHIBIT 30-4 1990 Milestones of Whirlpool's Globalization

1990	A program is launched to market appliances in Europe under the dual brands Philips and Whirlpool.
	Formation of a joint-venture company with Matsushita Electric Industrial Co. of Japan to produce vacuum cleaners for the North American market.
	Creation of Whirlpool Overseas Corporation as a wholly owned subsidiary to conduct industrial and marketing activities outside North America and Western Europe.
	Inglis Limited becomes a wholly owned subsidiary.
1991	Whirlpool acquires remaining interest in WIBV from Philips Electronics N.V.
	Creation of two new global business units: Whirlpool Compressor Operations and Whirlpool Microwave Cooking Business.
1992	Creation of Whirlpool Tatramat in the Slovak Republic. Whirlpool Tatramat a.s. will manufacture clothes washers for Slovakia and neighboring countries and import other WIBV major appliances for sale.
	Begins gradual phaseout of dual-branded advertising to sole Whirlpool brand by removing the Philips name in Europe.
	Whirlpool assumes control of SAGAD S.A. of Argentina from Philips.
	Reorganization of Whirlpool Europe. The name is changed from WIBV to WEBV.
	Didier Pineau-Valencienne, chairman and CEO of Groupe Schneider S.A., France, becomes a Whirlpool director, the first non-American on the board.
1993	Reorganization of NAAG. Start of the implementation of a new Asian strategy.
	Sales subsidiaries are opened in Poland and the Czech Republic.
	In May, Whirlpool announces joint venture with Teco Electric & Machinery Co., Ltd., of Taiwan to market and distribute home appliances in Taiwan.

EXHIBIT 30-5 Western European Appliance Shipments (thousand units)

	1988	1989	1990	1991	1992
Refrigerators	11,350	11,845	12,450	12,670	12,750
Freezers	4,205	4,255	4,590	4,680	4,605
Washers	10,140	10,220	10,730	10,800	10,845
Dishwashers	3,335	3,615	3,820	3,925	4,040
Tumble Dryers	2,625	2,400	2,325	2,490	2,475
Cookers	4,840	4,685	4,800	4,615	4,430
Built-in Ovens	3,390	3,405	3,500	3,590	3,765
Total Core	39,885	40,425	42,215	42,770	42,910
Microwave Ovens	7,845	7,615	6,590	7,400	7,300
Total Market	47,730	48,040	48,805	50,170	50,210
Percent Change	11.5%	0.6%	1.6%	2.8%	0.1%

Source: Industry data.

Another initiative which encountered widespread skepticism in the industry was development of a compact washer dubbed the "world washer," which went into production in new manufacturing facilities in Brazil in 1990, and in Mexico and India in 1991. Lightweight, with substantially fewer parts than its U.S. counterpart, it had good test scores and received favorable evaluations based on such features as stainless steel and porcelain baskets. According to Samuel J. Pearson, director international engineering, its performance was equal to or better than anything on the world market while competitive on price with the most popular models in these markets.

Although many of the circumstances surrounding the decision to start world washer production in India, Brazil, and Mexico differed, all three countries saw a clear opportunity. Whirlpool estimated that about 10 to 15 percent of India's 840 million people could afford clothes washers while only about 250,000 lower quality machines were sold annually. Further, a weakened U.S. dollar provided the right "window" that Whirlpool and its partners needed to get the new design into production before competitors could capitalize on the same opportunities. The goal of the world washer effort was to develop a complete product, process, and facility-design package versatile enough to satisfy conditions and market requirements in various countries but with low initial investment requirements. At the same time, the world washer established a beachhead especially against the Far Eastern rivals.

The development was preceded by extensive market research and intensive analysis of almost every washer model marketed in Japan, Korea, Europe, New Zealand, and the United States. Originally, it was planned to replicate the project design in each of the three countries. It eventually proved necessary to develop three slightly different variations. "Each of the affiliates presented different expertise, both in the washer business and in working with various materials," said Lawrence J. Kremer, senior vice president, Global Technology and Operations. "Our Mexican affiliate, Vitromatic, has porcelain and glassmaking capabilities. Porcelain baskets made sense for them. Stainless steel became the preferred material for the others."

Costs also varied widely, further affecting both product and process decisions. "In India, for example, material costs may run as much as 200 to 800 percent higher than elsewhere, while labor and overhead costs are comparatively minimal," added Kremer. Another consideration were the garments to be washed in each country. "Saris—those beautiful, 18-foot lengths of cotton or silk with which Indian women drape themselves—posed a special challenge," recalled Pearson.

The plants also varied subtly from each other, although the goals were identical— minimizing facility investment, avoiding big finish systems and welding stations requiring extensive machinery for material cleanup, and protecting the environment. Brastemp, Whirlpool's Brazilian partner, put its new plant in Rio Claro, 100 kilometers northwest of Sao Paulo. Made of precast concrete, it was designed as a creative convection cooling system to address the high humidity. In India, the new facility was built in Pondicherry, just 12 degrees north of the equator. Although the plant looked similar to that in Brazil—except for the overhead fans—the method of construction was different. Concrete was hand mixed on location, then carried in wicker baskets to forms constructed right next to the building site. The Indian construction crew cast the concrete, allowed it to cure, and, then, using five or six men, raised each three-ton slab into place using chain, block, and tackle. Finally, two plants made up the facility in Monterrey. Internacional de Lavadores housed the flexible assembly lines as well as stamping and a few machine operations. Viplasticos, the adjacent facility, had injection moulding and extrusion processes.

Pearson underscored the fact that the project resulted not only in new plants and a new product, but in team members from very different cultural backgrounds who have gained experience in how to manage a project differently, employing a small team with the authority to do many things. "Our foreign colleagues have become partners in every sense of the word," Pearson said. "When we make the final hand-off to Gopal Srinivasan in India, to Francisco Fiorotto in Brazil, and to Luis Hernandez in Mexico, we will be placing the ventures in the hands of good people, good colleagues, good friends."

WHIRLPOOL OVERSEAS CORPORATION

Whirlpool Overseas Corporation (WOC) is a wholly owned subsidiary that conducts marketing and industrial activities outside North America and Europe. It includes U.S. Export Sales, the Overseas Business Group acquired from Philips in the WIBV transaction, and three wholly owned sales companies in Hong Kong, Thailand, and Australia. Industrial activities encompass technology sale and transfer, kit and component sales, joint venture manufacturing, and project management for affiliates. WOC oversees the activities in Brazil and the joint venture in India.

One of the key responsibilities of WOC is to feed new technologies from Whirlpool's bases in North America and Europe to its other units. A second responsibility is to ensure optimal brand positioning in each country and to analyze specific appliance design for their suitability to various markets. Conditions could vary greatly from country to country requiring design modifications. For instance, the company sold so-called giant ovens in Africa and the Middle East. These ovens were 39" and 42" wide compared to the standard 30" in the United States and were large enough to roast a sheep or goat.

WOC has strengthened its position in South America by taking over control of SAGAD, Philip's white goods operation in Argentina. A joint venture was recently created with Whirlpool's affiliates to distribute Whirlpool's and the affiliates' products to independent distributors. As a result of these moves, Whirlpool and its affiliates are the leading marketers and manufacturers of major home appliances in the region.

WOC's activities are based on the belief that global leadership requires a strong presence in all major markets. Given the company's major presence in North America, Europe, and its 30-year history in South America, Asia represented the last, and what many believed, biggest challenge and opportunity. "In the United States, households are equipped with between seven and nine major appliance products. In Asia, which already accounts for 40 percent of the world market, it's more like four appliances per home," remarked Roger E. Merriam, vice president sales and marketing, WOC. With growing income levels, significant market growth could be expected.

WOC was recently reorganized as a regional structure concentrating on Latin America and Asia. WOC Asia with headquarters in Tokyo was further subdivided into three sub-regions: Asia Pacific (South East Asia, India, Australia), Greater China (Hong Kong, Peoples Republic of China, Taiwan), Japan. This regional structure allows Whirlpool to expand from its infancy position in this region of a market share of 1 percent against the strong local manufacturers. Some of Whirlpool's products are being met with good customer acceptance. For instance, a top-load automatic washer sold in Hong Kong has about one third of the market. Whirlpool moved very quickly in Asia, creating a headquarters in Tokyo and establishing sales subsidiaries and regional offices. Whirlpool realized that a viable position implied more than selling imports from NAAG and WEBV and having kits assembled by licensees. This belief was also reinforced by the fact that consumer preferences in Asia were different from those in the United States and Europe. For instance, Japanese usually wash with cold water. But in order to get their clothes clean, Japanese machines have soak cycles which can range from 30 minutes to several hours. In May 1993, Whirlpool announced a joint venture with Teco Electric & Machinery Co., Ltd., to market and distribute home appliances in Taiwan. Teco is Whirlpool's largest international distributor of Whirlpool products.

To show its commitment to people, Whirlpool has introduced PartnerShare, a stock option plan for its 22,000 U.S. employees, hoping to encourage employee ownership and dedication to building shareholder value. A gain-sharing program at the Benton Harbor components division slashed rework by 31 percent and total scrap cost by 62 percent and its parts-per-million rejection rate by 99 percent over the last 3 years. The program provides each of the plant's 265 employees with an extra $2,700 of pay annually.

The growth objective had resulted in many acquisitions and joint ventures in recent years as well as the aggressive expansion of Whirlpool brands into new territories. The world washer and the SERP win are testimony of the company's growth and innovation orientation.

By 1994, Whirlpool's global direction and assembly of its geographic position were largely complete. However, by its own admission, Whirlpool is not a truly global home-appliance company yet, but has made significant progress towards becoming the leader in the global home-appliance industry.

> But being a real global home-appliance company means more than just trading in countries around the world. It means identifying and respecting genuine national or regional differences in what customers demand from products and services—and simultaneously recognizing and responding to similarities across markets.

CONCLUSION

Prepare a strategic plan for CEO Whitwam who is concerned about Whirlpool's $51 million loss for 1993. Conduct an internal and external strategic analysis and formulate specific strategies that can best assure prosperity for Whirlpool in the latter 1990s. (Exhibits 30–6 through 30–15 provide Whirlpool management and financial information.)

EXHIBIT 30-6 Whirlpool Product Shipments, Revenues, and Operating Earnings

Principal Locations	Principal Products
Affiliates	Automatic dryers
Great Teco Whirlpool Limited	Automatic washers
Taipei,Taiwan	Cooking products
TVS Whirlpool Limited	Dishwashers
Madras, India	Microwave ovens
Manufacturing Facility	Refrigerators
Pondicherry, India	Room air conditioners
Sales Subsidiaries	Major Brand Names
Bangkok, Thailand	Bauknecht
Hong Kong	Ignis
Kuala Lumpur, Malaysia	KitchenAid
Melbourne, Australia	Roper
Singapore	Whirlpool

EXHIBIT 30-7 Revenues by Business Unit

			BETTER/(WORSE)	
	1993	1992	$	%
North American Appliance				
Business	$4,559	$4,162	$ 397	10%
European Appliance Business	2,225	2,463	(238)	(10)
Other	584	472	112	24
Total Appliance Business	$7,368	$7,097	$ 271	4%

Operating Profit by Business Unit

			BETTER/(WORSE)	
	1993	1992	$	%
North American Appliance				
Business	$459	$417	$42	10%
European Appliance Business	123	113	10	9
Other	(78)	(83)	5	6
Total Appliance Business	$504	$447	$57	13%

Other includes Latin America, Whirlpool Asia, European compressor operations, Corporate Center costs and intercompany eliminations.

Source: Whirlpool *Annual Report*, 1993.

EXHIBIT 30-8 Revenue Information (Millions of dollars)

	PERCENT	1993	1992	1991
Major Home Appliances				
Home Laundry Appliances	32.9%	$2,481	$2,489	$2,300
Home Refrigeration and Room Air Conditioning Equipment	34.4	2,588	2,525	2,329
Other Home Appliances	30.5	2,299	2,083	1,921
	97.8	7,368	7,097	6,550
Financial Services	2.2	165	204	207
	100.0%	$7,533	$7,301	$6,757

Source: Whirlpool *Annual Report*, 1993.

EXHIBIT 30-9 Whirlpool 1993 Consolidated Balance Sheets December 31 (Millions of dollars)

| | WHIRLPOOL CORPORATION (CONSOLIDATED) | | SUPPLEMENTAL CONSOLIDATING DATA | | | |
| | | | WHIRLPOOL WITH WFC ON AN EQUITY BASIS | | WHIRLPOOL FINANCIAL CORPORATION (WFC) | |
DECEMBER 31,	1993	1992	1993	1992	1993	1992
Assets						
Current Assets						
Cash and equivalents	$ 88	$ 66	$ 81	$ 52	$ 7	$ 14
Trade receivables, less allowances of $36 in 1993 and $35 in 1992	866	851	866	851	—	—
Financing receivables and leases, less allowances	814	980	—	—	814	980
Inventories	760	650	760	650	—	—
Prepaid expenses and other	102	119	95	98	7	20
Deferred income taxes	78	74	78	74	—	—
Total Current Assets	2,708	2,740	1,880	1,725	828	1,014
Other Assets						
Investment in affiliated companies	320	282	320	282	—	—
Investment in WFC	—	—	239	293	—	—
Financing receivables and leases, less allowances	793	912	—	—	793	912
Intangibles, net	725	795	725	795	—	—
Deferred income taxes	127	—	127	—	—	—
Other	55	64	55	59	—	5
	2,020	2,053	1,466	1,429	793	917
Property, Plant and Equipment						
Land	69	73	69	73	—	—
Buildings	586	588	586	588	—	—
Machinery and equipment	2,181	2,052	2,157	2,031	24	21
Accumulated depreciation	(1,517)	(1,388)	(1,504)	(1,377)	(13)	(11)
	1,319	1,325	1,308	1,315	11	10
Total Assets	$6,047	$6,118	$4,654	$4,469	$1,632	$1,941

EXHIBIT 30-9 *Continued*

| | WHIRLPOOL CORPORATION (CONSOLIDATED) | | SUPPLEMENTAL CONSOLIDATING DATA | | | |
| | | | WHIRLPOOL WITH WFC ON AN EQUITY BASIS | | WHIRLPOOL FINANCIAL CORPORATION (WFC) | |
DECEMBER 31,	1993	1992	1993	1992	1993	1992
Liabilities and Stockholders' Equity						
Current Liabilities						
Notes payable	$992	$1,425	$ 160	$ 322	$ 832	$1,050
Accounts payable	742	688	689	646	53	41
Employee compensation	177	164	172	157	5	7
Accrued expenses	587	495	581	477	6	18
Income taxes	97	87	93	79	4	8
Current maturities of long-term debt	168	28	83	14	85	67
Total Current Liabilities	2,763	2,887	1,778	1,695	985	1,191
Other Liabilities						
Deferred income taxes	167	213	67	109	100	104
Accrued pensions and expenses	219	203	219	203	—	—
Postretirement obligation	318	—	318	—	—	—
Long-term debt	840	1,215	607	862	233	378
	1,544	1,631	1,211	1,174	333	482
Minority Interests	92	—	17	—	75	—
Stockholders' Equity						
Capital stock	79	76	79	76	8	8
Paid-in capital	152	47	152	47	26	26
Retained earnings	1,686	1,721	1,686	1,721	208	236
Unearned restricted stock	(9)	(18)	(9)	(18)	—	(2)
Cumulative translation adjustments	(77)	(49)	(77)	(49)	(3)	—
Treasury stock—at cost	(183)	(177)	(183)	(177)	—	—
	1,648	1,600	1,648	1,600	239	268
Total Liabilities and Stockholders' Equity	$6,047	$6,118	$4,654	$4,469	$1,632	$1,941

Source: Whirlpool *Annual Report*, 1993.

EXHIBIT 30-10 Whirlpool 1993 Consolidated Statements of Earnings (millions of dollars except share data)

YEAR ENDED DECEMBER 31,	WHIRLPOOL CORPORATION (CONSOLIDATED)			SUPPLEMENTAL CONSOLIDATING DATA					
				WHIRLPOOL WITH WFC ON AN EQUITY BASIS			WHIRLPOOL FINANCIAL CORPORATION (WFC)		
	1993	1992	1991	1993	1992	1991	1993	1992	1991
Revenues									
Net sales	$7,368	$7,097	$6,550	$7,368	$7,097	$6,550	$ —	$ —	$ —
Financial services	165	204	207	—	—	—	193	235	233
	7,533	7,301	6,757	7,368	7,097	6,550	193	235	233
Expenses									
Cost of products sold	5,503	5,365	4,967	5,503	5,365	4,967	—	—	—
Selling and administrative	1,433	1,323	1,257	1,305	1,242	1,181	155	113	102
Financial services interest	59	82	91	—	—	—	72	95	101
Intangible amortization	25	27	27	25	27	27	—	—	—
Restructuring costs	31	25	22	31	16	22	—	9	—
	7,051	6,822	6,364	6,864	6,650	6,197	227	217	203
Operating Profit (Loss)	482	479	393	504	447	353	(34)	18	30

EXHIBIT 30-10 *Continued*

| | Whirlpool Corporation (Consolidated) | | | Supplemental Consolidating Data | | | | | |
| | | | | Whirlpool with WFC on an Equity Basis | | | Whirlpool Financial Corporation (WFC) | | |
Year Ended December 31,	1993	1992	1991	1993	1992	1991	1993	1992	1991
Other Income (Expense)									
Interest and sundry	6	38	49	19	21	33	(9)	20	18
Interest expense	(113)	(145)	(138)	(105)	(134)	(130)	—	—	—
Earnings (Loss) Before Income Taxes, Other Items and Accounting Change	375	372	304	418	334	256	(43)	38	48
Income taxes	148	154	130	167	142	113	(19)	12	17
Earnings (Loss) Before Equity Earnings, Minority Interests and Accounting Change	227	218	174	251	192	143	(24)	26	31
Equity in WFC	—	—	—	(28)	26	31	—	—	—
Equity in affiliated companies	16	(13)	1	16	(13)	1	—	—	—
Minority interests	(12)	—	(5)	(10)	—	(5)	(2)	—	—
Net Earnings (Loss) Before Cumulative Effect of Accounting Change	231	205	170	229	205	170	(26)	26	31
Cumulative effect of accounting change for postretirement benefits	(180)	—	—	(178)	—	—	(2)	—	—
Net Earnings (Loss)	$51	$205	$170	$51	$205	$170	$(28)	$26	$31
Per share of common stock:									
Primary earnings before accounting change	$3.19	$2.90	$2.45						
Primary earnings	$0.67	$2.90	$2.45						
Fully diluted earnings before accounting change	$3.11	$2.79	$2.40						
Fully diluted earnings	$0.67	$2.79	$2.40						
Cash dividends	$1.19	$1.10	$1.10						
Average number of common shares outstanding (millions)	72.3	70.6	69.5						

Net earnings (loss) before cumulative effect of accounting change	$231	$205	$170	$229	$205	$170	$(26)	$26	$31
Depreciation	241	275	233	239	271	228	2	3	3
Deferred income taxes	(31)	9	3	(27)	2	(7)	(4)	7	10
Equity in net losses (earnings) of affiliated companies, including dividends received	(14)	16	(1)	(14)	16	(1)	—	—	—
Equity in net loss (earnings) of WFC	—	—	—	28	(26)	(31)	—	—	—
Loss on business disposition	8	—	—	8	—	—	—	—	—
Provision for doubtful accounts	75	55	55	8	15	25	67	40	30
Amortization of goodwill	28	27	27	28	27	27	—	—	—
Minority interests	10	—	5	10	—	5	—	2	—
Other	43	15	(19)	23	(4)	(19)	20	—	—
Changes in assets and liabilities, net of effects of business acquisitions and dispositions:									
Trade receivables	(76)	(83)	58	(75)	(83)	58	—	—	—
Inventories	(145)	(7)	109	(145)	(7)	109	—	—	—
Accounts payable	101	5	162	89	29	139	12	(25)	19
Other-net	158	61	15	165	37	27	—	16	(5)
Cash Provided by Operating Activities	$629	$578	$817	$566	$482	$730	$71	$69	$88

Source: Whirlpool *Annual Report*, 1993.

EXHIBIT 30-12 Whirlpool 1993 Business Segment Information (Millions of dollars)

GEOGRAPHIC SEGMENTS—MAJOR HOME APPLIANCES

	NORTH AMERICA	EUROPE	OTHER AND (ELIMINATIONS)	MAJOR HOME APPLIANCES
Net Sales				
1993	$4,547	$2,410	$ 411	$7,368
1992	$4,266	$2,645	$ 186	$7,097
1991	$4,016	$2,479	$ 55	$6,550
Operating profit				
1993	$ 341	$ 129	$ 34	$ 504
1992	$ 327	$ 101	$ 19	$ 447
1991	$ 274	$ 82	$ (3)	$ 353
Identifiable assets				
1993	$1,742	$1,758	$1,154	$4,654
1992	$1,570	$1,917	$ 982	$4,469
1991	$1,529	$2,284	$ 759	$4,572
Depreciation expense				
1993	$ 137	$ 101	$ 1	$ 239
1992	$ 138	$ 132	$ 1	$ 271
1991	$ 124	$ 104	$ —	$ 228
Net capital expenditures				
1993	$ 188	$ 116	$ 3	$ 307
1992	$ 170	$ 111	$ 3	$ 284
1991	$ 179	$ 104	$ —	$ 283

INDUSTRY SEGMENTS	MAJOR HOME APPLIANCES	FINANCIAL SERVICES	OTHER AND (ELIMINATIONS)	CONSOLIDATED
Revenues				
1993	$7,368	$193	$(28)	$7,533
1992	$7,097	$235	$(31)	$7,301
1991	$6,550	$233	$(26)	$6,757
Operating profit (loss)				
1993	$ 504	$(34)	$ 12	$ 482
1992	$ 447	$ 18	$ 14	$ 479
1991	$ 353	$ 30	$ 10	$ 393

The financial services business segment operates primarily in North America.

EXHIBIT 30-13 Whirlpool 1993 Stockholder Information

	1993	1992	1991	1990
Key Ratios				
Operating profit margin	6.4%	6.6%	5.8%	5.3%
Pre-tax margin[3]	5.0%	5.1%	4.5%	3.3%
Net margin [4]	3.1%	2.8%	2.5%	1.1%
Return on average stockholders' equity	14.2%	13.1%	11.6%	5.1%
Return on average total assets[5]	4.0%	3.3%	2.9%	1.4%
Current assets to current liabilities	1.0	0.9	1.0	1.1
Total debt-appliance business as a percent of invested capital[6]	31.6%	41.7%	46.1%	37.6%
Price earnings ratio	20.8	15.4	15.9	22.6
Fixed charge coverage[7]	3.2	2.6	2.3	1.8
Other Data				
Number of common shares outstanding (in thousands):				
Average	72,272	70,558	69,528	69,443
Year-end	73,068	70,027	69,640	69,465
Number of shareholders (year-end)	11,438	11,724	12,032	12,542
Number of employees (year-end)	39,590	38,520	37,886	36,157
Total return to shareholders (five year annualized)[8]	25.8%	17.0%	6.7%	2.8%

(1)Accounting changes: 1993—Accounting for postretirement benefits other than pensions, 1987—Accounting for income taxes and 1986—Accounting for pensions.

(2)The Company's kitchen cabinet business was discontinued in 1988.

(3)Earnings from continuing operations before income taxes and other items, as a percent of revenue.

(4)Earnings from continuing operations before accounting change, as a percent of revenue.

(5)Earnings from continuing operations before accounting change plus minority interest divided by average total assets.

(6)Cash, debt, minority interests and stockholders' equity.

(7)Ratio of earnings from continuing operations (before income taxes, accounting change and interest expense) to interest expense.

(8)Stock appreciation plus reinvested dividends.

Source: Whirlpool *Annual Report*, 1993.

EXHIBIT 30-14 Whirlpool Senior Management

SENIOR MANAGEMENT

Executive Officers

David R. Whitwam
  Chariman of the Board
  and Chief Executive Officer

William D. Marohn
  President and Chief Operating Officer

Executive Vice Presidents
H.W. (Hank) Bowman
  Whirlpool Europe B.V.

Robert Frey
  President, Whirlpool Asia Appliance Group

Ralph F. Hake
  North American Appliance Group

Ronald L. Kerber
  Chief Technology Officer

Senior Officers
Vice Presidents
Bradley J. Bell
  Treasurer

Bruce K. Berger
  Corporate Affairs

E.R. (Ed) Dunn
  Human Resources
  and Assistant Secretary

Jeff M. Fettig
  Group Sales and Marketing, NAAG

Robert D. Hall
  Global Procurement Operations

Stephen F. Holmes
  Group Manufacturing and
  Technology, NAAG

Halvar Johansson
  Group Manufacturing and
  Technology, WEBV

Source: Whirlpool *Annual Report,* 1993.

James E. LeBlanc
  Chairman of the Board, President
  and Chief Executive Officer,
  Whirlpool Financial Corporation

Charles D. (Chuck) Miller
  Marketing, NAAG

Robert G. Thompson
  Controller

William D. Marohn
  President and Chief Operating Officer

Michael J. Callahan
  Chief Financial Officer

Ralph F. Hake
  North American Appliance Group

James R. Samartini
  Chief Administrative Officer

Bruce K. Berger
  Corporate Affairs

Jeff M. Fettig
  Group Sales and Marketing, NAAG

Edward J.F. Herrelko
  Sales and Distribution, NAAG

Daniel F. Hopp
  General Counsel and Secretary

Kenneth W. Kaminski
  Sears Group, NAAG

Ivan Menezes
  Group Marketing, WEBV

P. Daniel Miller
  President, Whirlpool do Brasil

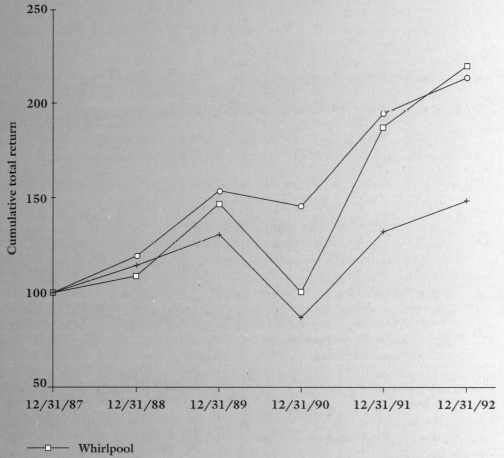

EXHIBIT 30-15 Five-Year Cumulative Return: Whirlpool, S & P Index and S & P Household Furniture and Appliance Group

Whirlpool
S & P 500
S & P Household Furniture Appliance

*Cumulative total return is measured by dividing (i) the sum of (A) the cumulative amount of the dividends for the measurement period, assuming dividend reinvestment, and (B) the difference between share price at the end and the beginning of the measurement period; by (ii) the share price at the beginning of the measurement period.

Source: Whirlpool Corporation, 1992 Proxy Statement.

MATERIAL HANDLING ENGINEERING (SINGAPORE) LTD.—1993

Headquartered in Singapore, Material Handling Engineering (MHE) (phone 65-861-0670, fax 65-861-3271) has subsidiaries throughout the Asian region and a customer base that includes hundreds of companies worldwide. With revenue (called turnover in Singapore) at nearly S$21.5 million (one Singapore dollar is worth approximately U.S. $0.60), MHE is the largest material-handling company in Singapore. Peter Boo, founder and CEO of the company, has a goal of MHE becoming a S$100 million company by the end of this decade. In the short-term, he also has to make sure the 26 percent decrease in 1992 turnover does not repeat itself. Nor does Boo want to incur another year of losing $492,000 as annual net income.

HISTORY

When Peter Boo completed high school, he became a draftsman for a local material-handling (conveyors, automated carts, etc.) company. Boo continued his education by taking technical courses at Singapore Polytechnic and satisfied his compulsory military duty requirement by serving evenings and some weekends. Working in various phases of the company's business gave Boo the experience needed to start his own material-handling company.

With two employees and a small factory having only 32 square meters of usable space, Boo founded MHE in 1975 "to engage in the design, fabrication, and installation of conveyor-based integrated automation systems." Since banks in Singapore were reluctant to lend money to start-ups, Boo used his own funds to purchase and equip his factory.

Boo considered several names for his company, finally settling on Material Handling Engineering because it was descriptive, and the logo he created (see Exhibit 31–1) looked like a conveyor belt. Early customers were companies who knew Boo from his previous company affiliation or those referred by his friends. Those clients generated S$120,000 in turnover for MHE in its first year of operation.

Boo knew the only way his company could grow would be to satisfy its customers who would then refer other customers to MHE. The following mission statement has helped Material Handling Engineering become the leader in its field in Singapore and the Asian region:

> To be a world leader in automated materials handling systems and automation related businesses. To accomplish our mission, we believe in: total and continuous quality service to customers, enhancing the quality of working life for employees, support to suppliers for mutual growth, being good corporate citizens, and providing adequate return on shareholders' investments.

THE COMPANY

Ownership and Organization. MHE has authorized share capital of S$10 million (50 million shares at S$0.20) and has issued 27.5 million shares, most controlled by Peter Boo and his wife Lee Bee Lian. Other investors who own more than 300,000 shares each include the following:

EXHIBIT 31-1 MHE Ltd. Company Logo

Source: Material Handling Engineering, Ltd.

HSBC (Singapore) Nominees Pte. Ltd.	7,052,000 shares
Southeast Asia Venture Investment Co.	1,529,039 "
United Overseas Bank Nominees Ltd.	800,000 "
Venture Investment (Singapore) II Ltd.	396,727 "
Malaysian Ventures Bhad	395,727 "

Eight other non-family investors own more than 100,000 shares.

MHE is listed on SESDAQ (Stock Exchange of Singapore Dealing and Automated Quotation) which is similar to NASDAQ (National Association of Securities Dealers' Automated Quotations System). Shareholders of the company have approved a share option scheme to enable certain senior executives of the company to subscribe for shares in the capital of the company. Under that plan, options to subscribe up to an aggregate of 51,000 ordinary shares of S$1.00 each and 510,000 ordinary shares of S$0.20 each in the capital of the company are offered to executives.

Peter Boo is chairman and chief executive officer of the company, while his wife is the director of purchasing. Serving on the board of directors with them is Derrick Lee Meow Chan, Eric Cheong Yuen Chee, and Robert Iau Kuo Kwong. Since the Boo family controls most of the stock, the board is primarily advisory; however, Boo contends that he does take board members' suggestions seriously. Other departments of MHE are headed by capable executives who also may own part of the company.

Company Structure. MHE is the original company founded by Peter Boo; however, growth needs have been met by acquiring or starting subsidiary companies in Singapore and other parts of the world. MHE and its subsidiaries are referred to as the Group which is composed of ten companies wholly or partially owned by MHE (see Exhibit 31–2). Each subsidiary specializes in different products or services.

Products. MHE manufactures and distributes products to satisfy a wide range of customer needs and has been licensed by several foreign companies to be the exclusive distributor of their products. MHE's products are described below.

Conveyors and Components. Conveyor systems, customized to meet specific customer needs, have always been MHE's bread-and-butter products. The company specializes in turnkey projects designed and manufactured to meet the material handling needs of diverse customers in countries around the world.

Free-flow Chain System. This flexible conveyor system allows operators full freedom in carrying out their tasks at their own pace while the conveyor is running. This is an improvement over the conventional belt system where products move along continuously.

PCB Insertion Conveyors. These provide efficient assembly of components onto printed circuit boards and allow easy adjustments of conveyor widths to suit different boards.

Minibelt Portable Conveyors. This slim-lined range of belt conveyors are designed for light duty automation applications. These portable belt conveyors are among MHE's fastest-selling products.

Factory Automation. MHE has a factory automation unit to deal with products aimed at enhancing the intelligence and productivity of mechanical systems. Robots, palletizers, vision and identification systems, knowledge-based systems produced by MHE and its subsidiaries can be integrated into conveyors presently manufactured by the Group.

Security Systems. Through its subsidiary Premier Security Technology Pte. Ltd., MHE produces security products such as monitoring systems, safes, bank vaults, and prison doors.

Complementary Products. Products that MHE is licensed to manufacture or sell for other companies include the following:

BUSHMAN automatic revolving storage systems

KAWAHARA lift tables

ICAL vibratory equipment

GORING KERR industrial metal detectors

DINGS magnetic devices

FLOVEYOR aeromechanical conveyors

LOGAN baggage-handling systems

MECOM mail distribution systems

EXHIBIT 31-2 Material Handling Engineering Ltd. Group Structure and Current Activities

Source: MHE *Annual Report,* 1992.

RITE HITE dock leveler
KOKI ministar II
CONVERT autowarehouse system
TECHNO PAK high-speed conveyor system

Total System Solutions. Material Handling Engineering's extensive product line and the experience of its people enable it to provide customers with all the services needed for a turnkey project. Mr. Boo explains the steps in a typical project:

Consultancy. "Our years of practical experience in varied turnkey projects has sharpened our skills tremendously in multifarious industries be it bottling, electronics, engineering, mining, or others. MHE's professional team of engineers, through in-depth discussions and extensive consultations, analyzes and identifies the customer's requirements and budget with quality and international standards as main priorities."

Design. "No two customers are alike. With our team of trained designers, together with the computer-aided design systems, we can translate engineering concepts into effective working plans for fabrication. Safety, durability, and competitive operating costs form the basis of the whole system."

Fabrication. "Our new plant houses the fabrication facilities and the manpower necessary to turn our plans into reality. Our highly skilled technical personnel closely follow the blueprints of every design to faithfully reproduce the desired product. Quality assurance is ensured at every stage of the process through careful inspection and testing."

Installation and Commissioning. "Prompt and smooth installation of the total system is ensured through our highly trained and experienced technicians who at no time compromise the quality and reliability of the system. Proper training of the customer's staff is also provided before the final hand-over."

Back-up Service. "A project is not considered complete without an efficient and prompt back-up service to attend to the customer's every need at all times. Our quality service is why many satisfied customers come back to us time and again with repeat orders, sometimes even for their plants outside Singapore."

Turnkey Projects. MHE's ability to do large turnkey projects has enabled it to design, manufacture, and install:

- a coal preparation plant and ship loading conveyor system in Indonesia;
- assembly line systems for computer, television, and other electronics manufacturing plants in Singapore, Malaysia, Indonesia, and India;
- drum-filling handling systems for oil companies in Singapore;
- can- and bottle-handling systems for major beverage bottlers in Singapore and Malaysia;
- an assembly plant for washing machines;
- a mail- and parcel-sorting system;
- airport baggage-handling systems in Singapore and Thailand; and
- a complete loading and unloading facility for a regional refrigerated warehouse.

While the majority of these projects has been in Singapore, MHE does have an expanding client list in other countries (see Exhibit 31–3). For example, in 1991 MHE won contracts for S$10 million worth of work to be done for several companies in Turkey.

EXHIBIT 31-3 MHE's Global Customers

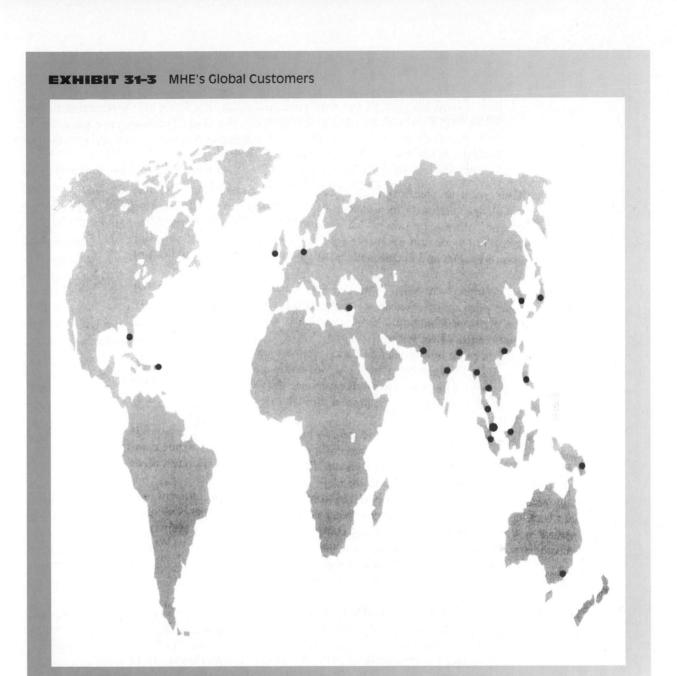

Source: MHE *Annual Report,* 1992.

Facilities. Material Handling Engineering is located at 107 Gul Circle. The building is in one of Singapore's industrial parks and has 6,300 square meters of usable space on 13,400 square meters of land. New factory and equipment worth S$3.8 million is large enough to meet MHE's production needs for the foreseeable future. While MHE owns the building, it only leases the land. The Singapore government owns most of the land in the country and only leases it to residential and commercial builders. MHE has a thirty-year lease on the land.

The new building is large enough to allow most fabricated conveyor systems to be set up and tested before being shipped to customers. There is also ample space to store raw materials and supplies, and there is adequate office space for all MHE's employees. Mr. Boo proudly describes some of the attributes of the new facilities:

■ *Computerization.* "We have invested in computerization of our administration, engineering design, accounting, and inventory systems. With the new computer-aided design (CAD) system, we can now produce two- and three-dimensional layout drawings for presentation to customers. In addition, from the database created, the bill of materials (BOM) can be generated on-line from the drawings. This BOM can be further extended to office automation applications for purchasing, material requirements planning and control, and project management, to ensure delivery promises are kept and material costs controlled. With office automation, administrative work and coordination will be enhanced through the use of local area networks (LAN)."

■ *Autowarehouse.* "We have an automated storage and retrieval system and an automated carousel system which improve operational efficiency. These systems are also used for demonstrations to our customers as we are marketing such systems to meet their storage needs."

■ *Fabrication and assembly.* "We have 1,080 square meters (72m long by 15m wide) of space for fabrication work, as well as a similar amount of space for assembly work. Within the assembly area, we can now preassemble a complete line for customers to inspect before delivery. We are now geared to undertake big turnkey projects in the developed countries as well as the Second and Third World countries."

■ *Spray booth and oven.* "We have our own spray booth and oven, allowing us to do painting that we could not do before. This helps to shorten the through-put time and improve the quality of surface finish."

Markets and Competition. The world automation market is estimated to be about U.S. $38 billion with material transport systems representing about 10 percent of the entire market. Peter Boo wants MHE to capture as much of the market as possible. However, it is difficult to identify a focused target market for MHE since so many different manufacturing and service companies need material handling systems. Companies with assembly lines, packages to be sorted, baggage to be moved, and so forth are potential customers who need to be courted. Mr. Boo believes that "any company with something to move, sort, or handle is a prospective customer."

MHE has no direct competition in Singapore. The few local companies that offer similar products are too small to compete with MHE for large, turnkey projects. The competition is from international companies with the capability to do large projects. MHE competes with other companies when it solicits projects in other countries, and it competes with those same companies for large projects in Singapore.

Many of the major companies in Singapore are large multinationals that often give their material-handling projects to companies from their home countries. For example, Western Electric (Singapore) recently opened a new plant with a state-of-the-art

S$5 million conveyor system that was installed by a U.S. material-handling company. To be as competitive as possible, MHE enters into joint ventures and partnerships with other companies to bid on large projects.

Personnel Relations. MHE's employees are constantly being trained and updated. While most companies pay lip service to the importance of their employees, MHE really means it. There is a severe shortage of workers in Singapore (unemployment is about 2 percent), so there is fierce competition for capable people willing to work. There is no minimum wage in Singapore, but competition for workers keeps average wages high. MHE attracts workers with good working conditions, above average wages, and an aggressive recruiting program. MHE is usually able to fill its manpower needs, but sometimes must hire inexperienced, untrained workers.

Training is something that is very important to MHE. Mr. Boo says, "We have formulated and implemented a three-year training program for employees. To date, more than one-third of our staff has received training. We are setting aside 5 percent of our profits each year for human resource development. Our goal is to have 100 percent of our staff trained." A training room was built in the new facilities where daily training is conducted. Managers, who are trainers, coaches, and counselors, benefit from external programs and in turn teach their subordinates.

MHE has lower than average turnover because the company tries to satisfy employees' needs. The company offers competitive wages and an attractive benefits package. Most workers are members of the Metal Industries Workers' Union which maintains good relations with management. Workers occasionally demand higher wages, but Mr. Boo says, "They can't justify their demands, so we pay them what we think they should get." In addition to above-average pay, workers receive annual bonuses which can amount to as much as three months' pay. In addition, Mr. Boo is working on a profit-sharing plan that will offer more incentive to workers to increase their productivity.

Production. A new building with state-of-the-art manufacturing equipment assures efficient production of MHE material-handling products. Since most projects are unique, MHE manufactures primarily customized products designed by its own technicians. Much of the routine production is done by subcontractors who work at MHE's facilities until a particular project is completed. "We are only interested in value-added production," says Mr. Boo who claims that his previous experience allows him to walk through the facility and identify manufacturing mistakes. He says, "I am a hands-on manager, unlike many people who have management experience but no manufacturing know-how."

Marketing. The company does only minimal formal advertising. There is an advertisement in the yellow pages, and the company has several brochures which are given to prospective customers. Mr. Boo claims that most of MHE's new customers are referred by previous customers, making him a firm believer in the value of word-of-mouth advertising. Mr. Boo and his managers use their networks to secure new projects and to publicize awards the company receives. For example, MHE recently received the National Productivity Award from the National Productivity Council, and Mr. Boo was named Entrepreneur of the Year at an International Entrepreneurship Conference. This kind of free advertising enhances MHE's image and attracts new customers.

Expansion and Diversification. It would be virtually impossible for any company to enjoy meaningful growth if it restricted its operations to Singapore. Mr. Boo knew that when he started his company so, from the beginning, MHE has had a global orientation. At first, MHE bid on turnkey projects in other countries, then as it grew, it began acquiring or building subsidiary companies in other countries (see Exhibit 31–2).

These companies, along with Material Handling Engineering, form the Group, which supplies products and services to each other and to unaffiliated customers. MHE currently generates about 75 percent of the Group's turnover; however, this percentage will decline as subsidiaries grow and others are acquired.

Most of MHE's subsidiaries are in the material-handling business; however, MHE recently incorporated a wholly owned subsidiary, Premier Security Technology (PST), as part of its plan to go into communication electronics. PST agreed to acquire the assets, business, and operations of the security division of Premier Cooperative Society for S$201,716.

The acquisition of PST was soon followed by the establishment of SecureNet (S) Pte. Ltd., a wholly owned subsidiary company providing security services and specialized central alarm monitoring services to PST. PST Security Technology Sdn Bhd was established to tap the vast Malaysian market. Security services were expanded when Australia Safe Company (SEA) Pte. Ltd. was acquired in 1992. ASC deals with safes, bank vaults and prison doors under the established brand name of Australia Safe.

MHE and its subsidiaries now do business in all Asian countries. Approximately 50 percent of 1992 turnover was generated by exports (see Exhibit 31–4) with Japan being the major non-Asian export market. With additional acquisitions and expansion of foreign subsidiaries, Mr. Boo expects more of MHE's turnover to be generated by exports in the future.

FINANCE

From 1975 to 1985, MHE experienced steady but modest growth, achieving turnover of S$3.7 million by the end of 1985. The late 1980s and 1990 saw turnover increase to S$16.8 million (see Exhibit 31–5). The best year in the Group's history was 1991 when turnover increased by more than 70 percent to S$29.2 million. This growth spurt, attributable to acquisition and expansion, was short-lived, however, as turnover for 1992 decreased to S$21.5 million.

Experiencing a nearly S$8 million reduction in turnover from 1991 to 1992 was quite discouraging, but Mr. Boo is confident that the company will prosper as economic conditions improve. He gives the following explanation for the reduction in MHE's turnover:

> The 1992 financial year was a challenging and eventful year for the Group. The effects of recession in most of the industrialized world were felt in Singapore, and slower growth was registered by the economy. The prevailing mood of caution and restraint resulted in a reduced level of capital investment in Singapore and the region. It was under such adverse economic conditions that the Group's turnover decreased by 26 percent to S$21.5 million. This decrease of some S$8 million was due primarily to the absence of sales to Turkey, a reflection of the economic uncertainties in that region. . . .
>
> With completion of a good foundation and the proper definition of future goals and directions for our security business; and the reinforcement of our lead in the material handling industry, I believe we now have prepared the ground for our next stage of growth. Our

EXHIBIT 31-4   MHE's Turnover by Local and Export Markets

Local (50.3%)

Export (49.7%)

Analysis of Export Market

USA (7.7%)

Others (1.2%)

Europe (2.0%)

Japan (16.8%)

Middle East (5.2%)

Asean
(excluding
Singapore)
(67.1%)

Source: Material Handling Engineering Limited, *Annual Report,* 1992.

efforts at growth may, however, be somewhat thwarted by the continuing uncertainties over recovery in the global economic environment.

Financial statements for 1992 (see Exhibits 31–6 through 31–8) show that the S$1.4 million profit (before taxes) in 1991 was replaced with a loss of nearly one-half million dollars in 1992. The company continues to be fiscally prudent. Debt is manageable, and MHE can issue an additional 25 million shares if it has major capital requirements.

FUTURE PLANS

Peter Boo's goal is to control a diversified company with annual turnover of S$100 million by the end of this decade. Material-handling products and security systems have enabled MHE to grow to a S$21.5 million company, but additional acquisitions may be necessary to get the company to its S$100 million goal.

EXHIBIT 31-5 MHE's Five-year Financial Summary

	1992 $'000	1991 $'000	1990 $'000	1989 $'000	1988 $'000
Turnover	21,484	29,171	16,801	16,181	12,897
Net (Loss)/Profit before Tax	(492)	1,428	503	1,790	1,929
Net (Loss)/Profit after Tax & Extraordinary Item Attributable to Shareholders	(599)	1,357	709	1,890	1,383
Shareholders' Fund	13,069	13,979	9,690	9,375	2,473
Total Assets	24,019	24,183	22,226	14,889	8,846
Total Liabilities	10,395	9,510	11,772	5,514	5,073
(Loss)/Earnings per Share (cents) (Note 1)	(2.20)	5.00	2.00	9.00	28.11
Net Tangible Assets per Share ($) (Note 1)	0.48	0.53	0.40	0.44	0.39
Net Dividends	275	385	275	375	82
Gross Rate of Dividend (%) (Note 2)	5.00	7.00	5.00	7.50	10.00

(1). The (loss)/earnings per share and net tangible assets per share are calculated based on the number of shares in issue during the year, or, where there is a movement in the number of shares issued, calculations are based on the weighted average of the number of shares in issue during the year.

	No. of Shares in Issue During the Year	
1988	6,100,000	
1989	20,929,830	(Weighted average)
1990	25,000,000	
1991	27,291,667	(Weighted average)
1992	27,500,000	

(2). The dividend proposed for the year 1992 and dividends paid for the years 1991, 1990 and 1989 are tax exempt. Dividend paid for the year 1988 is non tax exempt.

Source: MHE *Annual Report,* 1992.

One area that has fascinated Mr. Boo for several years is biotechnology. He has not formulated specific plans, but Mr. Boo wants to participate in this rapidly expanding field before it becomes too crowded. His intention is to have MHE assist in food production using relatively new techniques like hydroponics and genetic engineering.

Diversification will not detract from MHE's primary field of material handling. Singapore's manpower shortage leaves the government with two alternatives—import people or encourage automation. The first alternative is not particularly appealing to the government. Officially, the government encourages the immigration of people with professional and technical skills but discourages the immigration of less skilled workers. As for the second alternative, encouraging automation, the government is more proactive. The government of Singapore has established a S$65 million fund to encourage companies to automate their businesses to the fullest extent. Material Handling Engineering Ltd. expects to profit handsomely from that fund.

EXHIBIT 31-6 MHE's Profit and Loss Accounts for the year ended June 30, 1992

	THE GROUP		THE COMPANY	
	1992 $	1991 $	1992 $	1991 $
Turnover	21,484,120	29,171,344	15,728,639	26,460,520
Operating (Loss)/Profit	(455,648)	1,466,542	419,803	1,508,117
Share of Losses of Associated Companies	(36,082)	(39,030)	—	—
(Loss)/Profit Before Taxation	(491,730)	1,427,512	419,803	1,508,117
Taxation	(245,097)	(219,131)	(152,000)	(164,000)
(Loss)/Profit after Taxation	(736,827)	1,208,381	267,803	1,344,117
Minority Interests	137,554	149,100	—	—
(Loss)/Profit Attributable to the Shareholders	(599,273)	1,357,481	267,803	1,344,117
Retained Profits at Beginning of Year	3,067,263	2,298,167	3,548,708	2,589,591
	2,467,990	3,655,648	3,816,511	3,933,708
Exchange Differences Arising on Consolidation	(36,205)	(203,385)	—	—
Profits Available for Appropriation	2,431,785	3,452,263	3,816,511	3,933,708
Dividends	(275,000)	(385,000)	(275,000)	(385,000)
Retained Profits at End of Year	2,156,785	3,067,263	3,541,511	3,548,708
(Loss)/Earnings Per Ordinary Share (Cents)	(2) cts	5 cts		

Source: MHE *Annual Report*, 1992.

EXHIBIT 31-7 MHE's Consolidated Statement of Changes in Financial Position for the year ended June 30, 1992

	1992 $	1991 $
Source of Funds		
From operations:		
(Loss)/profit before taxation	(491,730)	1,427,512
Adjustments for non-cash items:		
Depreciation	1,011,122	746,399
Amortisation of deferred development expenditure	83,704	82,044
Amortisation of goodwill	80,378	6,400
Amortisation of preliminary expenses	28,556	25,404
Development cost written off	1,868	11,328
Fixed assets written off	6,061	—
Other adjustments:		
Exchange differences arising on consolidation	(89,020)	11,049
Profit from sale of fixed assets	(31,830)	(11,709)
Share of losses of associated companies	36,082	39,030
	635,191	2,337,457

EXHIBIT 31-7 *Continued*

	1992 $	1991 $
From other sources:		
Proceeds from sale of fixed assets	**115,153**	87,577
Net proceeds from issue of shares	—	3,520,100
Term loans	**500,000**	—
Staff loan repaid	**47,837**	—
Proceeds from shares issued to minority shareholders	—	78,784
	1,298,181	6,023,918
Application of Funds		
Purchase of intangibles	**410,877**	118,007
Purchase of fixed assets	**1,793,401**	1,811,334
Purchase of investments	**502,593**	—
Repayment of term loans	**321,701**	575,395
Tax paid	**82,646**	67,554
Dividends paid	**385,000**	275,000
Staff loans	—	30,712
	3,496,218	2,878,002
Net (Decrease)/Increase in Working Capital	**(2,198,037)**	3,145,916
Represented by:		
(Decrease)/Increase in inventories	**(588,246)**	1,303,672
(Decrease) in debtors	**(388,934)**	(948,087)
Decrease/(Increase) in creditors	**684,015**	(1,748,288)
	(293,165)	(1,392,703)
Movements in net liquid funds:		
(Decrease)/Increase in fixed deposits	**(876,375)**	233,301
Increase in bank and cash balances	**309,452**	608,989
(Increase)/Decrease in bank overdrafts	**(1,337,949)**	3,696,329
	(2,198,037)	3,145,916

The effects of the acquisition of subsidiaries have been reflected in the separate assets and liabilities of the Group. The effects are analysed as follows:

	$
Net assets acquired:	
Goodwill	319,889
Fixed assets	68,450
Inventories	504,860
Debtors	675,280
Bank and cash balances	753,306
Creditors	(1,423,203)
	898,582
Discharged by cash	898,582

Source: MHE *Annual Report*, 1992.

EXHIBIT 31-8 MHE's Balance Sheets June 30, 1992

	THE GROUP		THE COMPANY	
	1992 $	1991 $	1992 $	1991 $
Non-Current Assets				
Fixed assets	9,627,563	8,882,917	5,415,545	5,338,197
Subsidiary companies	—	—	4,302,948	3,392,848
Associated companies	73,336	109,418	146,437	146,437
Intangibles	545,253	327,818	—	—
Staff loans	11,027	58,864	11,027	58,864
Investments	594,193	219,000	594,193	219,000
Current Assets				
Inventories	3,868,683	4,456,929	2,309,949	3,709,892
Trade debtors	7,198,680	7,274,541	4,138,512	6,645,689
Due by subsidiaries	—	—	2,854,847	569,237
Due by an associated company	9,934	12,186	9,934	2,914
Short term investment	127,400	—	127,400	—
Other debtors, deposits and prepayments	494,532	805,354	213,171	309,104
Fixed deposits with financial institutions	210,149	1,086,524	210,149	450,000
Bank and cash balances	1,258,649	949,197	235,512	885,323
	13,168,027	14,584,731	10,099,474	12,572,159
Less				
Current Liabilities				
Trade creditors	3,465,143	4,391,127	1,645,829	3,943,529
Hire purchase and leasing creditors	389,438	322,153	137,918	138,335
Due to subsidiaries	—	—	—	153,265
Other creditors and accrued liabilities	2,124,039	1,877,623	1,173,340	1,239,144
Term loans	1,047,555	504,806	780,000	280,000
Bank overdrafts	1,561,581	223,632	1,237,065	64,634
Taxation	101,456	51,376	50,451	33,421
Proposed dividend	275,000	385,000	275,000	385,000
	8,964,212	7,755,717	5,299,603	6,237,328
Net Current Assets	4,203,815	6,829,014	4,799,871	6,334,831
Non-Current Assets				
Term loans	867,819	1,232,269	420,000	700,000
Hire purchase and leasing creditors	234,615	306,347	72,491	113,450
Deferred taxation	328,370	216,000	324,000	216,000
	(1,430,804)	(1,754,616)	(816,491)	(1,029,450)
	13,624,383	14,672,415	14,453,530	14,460,727
Share Capital and Reserves				
Share capital	5,500,000	5,500,000	5,500,000	5,500,000
Share premium	5,412,019	5,412,019	5,412,019	5,412,019
Retained profits	2,156,785	3,067,263	3,541,511	3,548,708
Interests of the Share-holders of the Company	13,068,804	13,979,282	14,453,530	14,460,727
Minority Interests	555,579	693,133	—	—
	13,624,383	14,672,415	14,453,530	14,460,727

Source: MHE *Annual Report,* 1992.

FOOD INDUSTRY NOTE
WILLIAM JANIS, CORNELIUS KENNEY, AND ELENA VASQUEZ

The processed food and beverage industry sector (SIC 20) is the nation's largest manufacturing sector. In 1993, the value of food and beverage industry shipments reached an estimated $404 billion, up more than 2 percent over 1992. Exports rose almost 3 percent, while exports of higher value-added processed foods and beverages rose almost 12 percent, a turbulent international economy notwithstanding. Adjusted for inflation, processed food and beverage sector industry shipments rose slightly more than 1 percent in 1993; between 1988 and 1992, real sectoral shipment value rose about 1 percent annually (Table 1).

Industry expectations for 1994 are clouded by concerns about the pace of domestic and international economic recovery, a possible softening in export demand, and increasingly acrimonious food processor-food retailer relationships. Adjusted for inflation, total food and beverage industry shipments are likely to rise about 1 percent in 1994. A rebounding U.S. economy and a pickup in export demand would contribute to accelerated industry growth.

TABLE 1 Trends and Forecasts: Food and Kindred Products (SIC 20) *(In millions of dollars except as noted)* 1991–1994

					PERCENT CHANGE		
ITEM	1991	1992[1]	1993[2]	1994[3]	91–92	92–93	93–94
Industry Data							
Value of shipments[4]	387,601	394,039	404,342	415,406	1.7	2.6	2.7
Value of shipments (1987$)	344,351	347,649	352,013	355,533	1.0	1.3	1.0
Total employment (000)	1,475	1,475	1,461	1,458	0.0	−0.9	−0.2
Production workers (000)	1,070	1,068	1,068	1,066	−0.2	0.0	−0.2
Average hourly earnings ($)	10.10	10.36	10.58	—	2.6	2.1	—
Capital expenditures	9,362	—	—	—	—	—	—
Product Data							
Value of shipments[5]	363,943	369,988	379,661	390,051	1.7	2.6	2.7
Value of shipments (1987$)	323,763	326,835	330,977	334,341	0.9	1.3	1.0
Trade Data							
Value of imports	19,779	20,869	20,785	21,087	5.5	−0.4	1.5
Value of exports	19,918	22,504	23,101	24,307	13.0	2.7	5.2

[1] Estimate, except exports and imports.
[2] Estimate.
[3] Forecast.
[4] Value of all products and services sold by establishments in the food and kindred products industry.
[5] Value of products classified in the food and kindred products industry produced by all industries.

Source: U.S. Department of Commerce: Bureau of the Census; International Trade Administration (ITA). Estimates and forecasts by ITA.

In 1993, aggregate food and beverage industry shipments value increased between 2 and 3 percent (nominal), or slightly more than 1 percent in real terms, as a number of factors dampened growth. Consumers continued to express concern about the overall economy by reducing their spending and, in some cases, by changing buying habits and purchase preferences.

For the first half of 1993, personal consumption expenditures (PCE) for food and beverages consumed at home and away from home rose at an annual rate of more than 2 percent over 1992. Interestingly, expenditures outside the home increased more than in-home food purchases. Many consumers, however, responded to unsettled economic times not only by spending less overall, but also by increasing their purchases of less costly, private-label foods and beverages. In addition, increasing numbers of shoppers have begun trading at "warehouse club" outlets, which stock extra large items at attractive prices.

Most industry analysts consider the U.S. food and beverage processing sector mature and developed. Population growth, economic conditions, and foreign trade patterns affect growth. In 1993, the U.S. population grew by less than 1 percent, consumers were concerned about their economic well-being, and foreign customers struggled with recession.

In addition, an increasing number of food and beverage processors adopted a wholesale pricing strategy centered around lower prices without discounts, merchandise deals, or other purchase incentives. This pricing approach results in smaller gross sales but does not necessarily affect net sales and may even increase them because it reduces promotional costs.

The economic troubles affecting most of the world in 1993 had a dampening effect on U.S. processed food and beverage exports. Total processed food and beverage export value rose only modestly, while exports of lower value-added products, such as meat, poultry, seafood, most dairy products, and grain-based intermediate products declined moderately. Foreign demand for U.S.-produced higher value-added products, such as processed fruits and vegetables, alcoholic beverages, ready-to-eat meals, bakery items, and candy products increased significantly in 1993.

Value-Added. The industry sector is divided here into two groups—higher value-added industries and lower value-added industries—for further analysis. (The Census Bureau derives value added by subtracting the cost of materials, supplies, containers, fuel, electricity, and contract work from the value of industry shipments.) The higher value-added industries manufacture retail-ready, packaged, consumer brand-name products of which at least 40 percent of the industry shipment value is added through sophisticated manufacturing.

Industry analysts attribute the increased foreign demand for higher value-added U.S. products, such as roasted nuts, frozen fruits and vegetables, ice cream, jellies, and canned fruits and vegetables to several factors. A rapidly growing middle class in developing and emerging countries accounted for some of the increased demand. Also, Russia, Ukraine, and other countries of the former Soviet Union had a great appetite for higher value-added foods and beverages, especially alcoholic beverages. Observers believe that some of these shipments moved through brokers and traders in several member states of the European Community.

Mirroring the strength of higher value-added food and beverages abroad, the value of industry shipments of the higher value-added group substantially out-performed lower value-added industries in 1993 (Tables 2 and 3). The value of industry shipments of the higher value-added group increased an estimated 3 percent and

TABLE 2 Trends and Forecasts: Higher Value-Added Foods and Beverages (*In millions of dollars except as noted*) 1991–1994

					PERCENT CHANGE		
ITEM	1991	1992[1]	1993[2]	1994[3]	91–92	92–93	93–94
Industry Data							
Value of shipments[4]	192,654	197,770	203,883	210,218	2.7	3.1	3.1
Value of shipments (1987$)	169,621	174,487	179,024	184,037	2.9	2.6	2.8
Total employment (000)	814	816	813	812	0.2	–0.4	–0.1
Production workers (000)	557	549	549	548	–1.4	0.0	–0.2
Average hourly earnings ($)	11.27	11.60	11.87	—	2.9	2.3	–
Capital expenditures	5,969	—	—	—	—	—	—
Product Data							
Value of shipments[5]	182,570	183,105	188,920	195,154	0.3	3.2	3.3
Value of shipments (1987$)	161,032	165,495	169,798	174,553	2.8	2.6	2.8
Trade Data							
Value of imports	8,719	9,724	9,395	9,535	11.5	–3.4	1.5
Value of exports	5,725	6,660	7,462	8,458	16.3	12.0	13.3

[1]Estimate, except exports and imports.

[2]Estimate.

[3]Forecast.

[4]Value of all products and services sold by establishments in the higher value-added foods and beverages industry.

[5]Value of products classified in the higher value-added foods and beverages industry produced by all industries.

Note: This aggregation includes those industries defined as higher value-added in the text.

Source: U.S. Department of Commerce: Bureau of the Census; International Trade Administration (ITA). Estimates and forecasts by ITA.

accounted for 50 percent of total value; in contrast, the value of the lower value-added group's industry shipments rose about 2 percent.

Adjusted for inflation, the value of shipments of the higher value-added industry group rose more than 2 percent in 1993. The relatively large increase in real shipments value compared with nominal value change (3 percent) reflects processors' price restraints, new efficiencies, and a changing product mix. The lower value-added industry group did not fare as well; adjusted for inflation, group value of shipments contracted fractionally due to declines in the meat and poultry and the fats and oils industries of 1 percent and 3 percent, respectively.

INTERNATIONAL COMPETITIVENESS

Recognizing that domestic markets are expanding slowly, many U.S. food and beverage processors emphasized export sales in 1993. A weaker U.S. dollar and economic concerns abroad have contributed to record export sales in 1993. As U.S. firms become more skillful in cultivating overseas customers and the international economy improves, exports are likely to increase substantially.

TABLE 3   Trends and Forecasts: Lower Value-Added Foods and Feeds (*In millions of dollars except as noted*) 1991–1994

ITEM	1991	1992[1]	1993[2]	1994[3]	PERCENT CHANGE 91–92	92–93	93–94
Industry Data							
Value of shipments[4]	194,947	196,269	200,459	205,188	0.7	2.1	2.4
Value of shipments (1987$)	174,730	173,162	172,989	171,496	–0.9	–0.1	–0.9
Total employment (000)	662	659	648	646	–0.5	–1.7	–0.3
Production workers (000)	513	519	519	518	1.2	0.0	–0.2
Average hourly earnings ($)	8.86	9.07	9.26	—	2.4	2.1	—
Capital expenditures	3,393	—	—	—	—	—	—
Product Data							
Value of shipments[5]	181,373	186,883	190,741	194,897	3.0	2.1	2.2
Value of shipments (1987$)	162,731	161,340	161,179	159,788	–0.9	–0.1	–0.9
Trade Data							
Value of imports	11,060	11,145	11,390	11,552	0.8	2.2	1.4
Value of exports	14,193	15,844	15,639	15,849	11.6	–1.3	1.3

[1]Estimate, except exports and imports.

[2]Estimate.

[3]Forecast.

[4]Value of all products and services sold by establishments in the lower value-added foods and feeds industry.

[5]Value of products classified in the lower value-added foods and feeds industry produced by all industries.

Note: This aggregation includes those industries defined as lower value added in the text.

Source: U.S. Department of Commerce: Bureau of the Census; International Trade Administration (ITA). Estimates and forecasts by ITA.

U.S. exports of processed foods and beverages reached an estimated $22.5 billion in 1993, an increase of about 3 percent over 1992. Despite this marginal gain, U.S. processed food and beverage exports continued to outpace imports, a pattern first established in 1991. U.S. imports of processed foods and beverages edged down an estimated 1 percent in 1993 to $20.8 billion, reversing an increase of more than 5 percent in 1992.

Foreign demand for lower value-added intermediate processed foods and beverages declined slightly in 1993. However, exports of higher value-added products were expected to rise a substantial 12 percent. Because of weakening foreign demand for lower value-added products, which represent the majority of U.S. food and beverage exports, total export value rose almost 3 percent.

Exports of higher value-added processed foods and beverages, including bakery products, breakfast cereal, and chewing gum reached about $7.5 billion in 1993, up nearly 12 percent from 1992. Between 1989 and 1993, exports of these products expanded more than 16 percent annually. Increases in foreign demand boosted the

TABLE 4 U.S. Trade Patterns in 1992 Food and Kindred Products (SIC 20) (*In millions of dollars, percent*)

EXPORTS			IMPORTS		
	VALUE	SHARE		VALUE	SHARE
Canada and Mexico	5,189	23.1	Canada and Mexico	4,694	22.5
European Community	3,659	16.3	European Community	5,187	24.9
Japan	6,077	27.0	Japan	333	1.6
East Asia NICs	2,585	11.5	East Asia NICs	3,146	15.1
South America	682	3.0	South America	2,320	11.1
Other	4,313	19.2	Other	5,190	24.9
World Total	22,504	100.0	World Total	20,869	100.0

TOP FIVE COUNTRIES

	VALUE	SHARE		VALUE	SHARE
Japan	6,077	27.0	Canada	3,667	17.6
Canada	3,244	14.4	Thailand	1,324	6.3
Mexico	1,946	8.6	France	1,083	5.2
South Korea	1,226	5.4	Australia	1,081	5.2
Netherlands	792	3.5	Mexico	1,026	4.9

Source: U.S. Department of Commerce: Bureau of the Census; International Trade Administration.

share of higher value-added food and beverage exports relative to total exports from more than 23 percent in 1989 to more than 32 percent in 1993.

In 1993, exports from five industries among the higher value-added group of industries accounted for 47 percent of the total. Processed nuts led the list with a share of more than 10 percent with exports of $776 million, unchanged from 1992. U.S. manufacturers of processed nuts have strong technical and marketing expertise.

With $729 million in 1993 exports, frozen fruits, fruit juices, and vegetables were second among the top five product categories at nearly 10 percent of the total. Exports of these goods rose almost 5 percent from 1992. U.S. companies operate efficient, large-scale plants to reduce their costs of production. In turn, these enterprises can offer attractive products and prices to foreign purchasers. Major buyers overseas also have developed distribution networks to handle these highly perishable products.

In 1993, U.S. exports of miscellaneous processed foods, including herbal teas, spices, vinegar, and yeast, rose nearly 33 percent to $719 million, or more than 9 percent of total U.S. exports of higher value-added processed foods and beverages. Herbal teas represented about 59 percent of this category.

With a 9-percent share of total U.S. exports of higher value-added processed foods and beverages, 1993 exports of canned fruits, juices, and vegetables reached $675 million, up 3 percent. These shelf-stable products went primarily to Canada ($248 million), Japan ($82 million), Taiwan ($31 million), Hong Kong ($31 million), and Mexico ($28 million).

In 1993, dry, condensed, and evaporated dairy products valued at $605 million accounted for 8 percent of total exports of higher value-added processed food and beverages. Exports increased 22 percent. The leading U.S. customers were Mexico ($159 million), India ($53 million), Canada ($50 million), Japan ($41 million), and Taiwan ($25 million). The United States spent $59 million on export subsidies for powdered milk in 1993, compared with $1.8 billion by the European Community for all of its dairy export subsidies.

Despite recessionary economic conditions in many countries and reduced discretionary income, foreign consumers still purchased more U.S. higher value-added foods and beverages because prices of U.S. foods and beverages compared favorably with prices of similar products.

U.S. food and beverage companies continued to place more emphasis on promoting and exporting their products. Firms devoted more resources to exporting because domestic U.S. demand for processed food and beverages is growing less rapidly than during the 1980s. When the economies of major U.S. customers recover, the industry expects its current promotion and export efforts to lead to increased sales abroad.

Exports of higher value-added foods and beverages to five countries—Canada, Japan, Mexico, Germany, and the United Kingdom—represented an estimated $4.3 billion, or about 57 percent of the 1993 export total. These products often involve sophisticated manufacturing processes. Canada, benefitting from the U.S.-Canada Free Trade Agreement (CFTA), purchased $1.9 billion worth of U.S. higher value-added food and beverages, up 10 percent from 1992. By reducing Canadian tariffs, the CFTA has generated additional U.S. exports to Canada. Japan purchased $1 billion in U.S. higher value-added food and beverages in 1993, down from $1.1 billion in 1992, due in part to a worsening of Japan's recession.

Mexico has emerged as a significant market for U.S. higher value-added foods and beverages. In 1993, U.S. enterprises sent an estimated $634 million worth of higher value-added food and beverages to Mexico, up 36 percent from 1992 (Table 5). This reflects the continuing easing of Mexican trade restrictions during the past several years.

Exports from U.S. processed food and beverage industries selling lower value-added foods and feed, such as meat, butter, cheese, flour, animal feed, fats, and oils, dipped about 1 percent in 1993 to $15.6 billion. Between 1989 and 1993, exports of these items expanded more than 4 percent yearly. The share of lower value-added food and feed relative to total exports dropped from about 76 percent in 1989 to about 68 percent in 1993.

Three factors influenced the performance of U.S. exports of lower value-added processed foods and feed. First, the European Community (EC), a major competitor, spent $4.8 billion in 1993 to subsidize dairy products, eggs, poultry, and refined sugar, an increase of 22 percent over 1992 (Table 6). By contrast, U.S. export subsidies for lower value-added foods came to about $198 million. Most U.S. export subsidies go to raw commodities, such as wheat.

Second, the food and beverage processing industries of some major U.S. customers, such as the EC, Japan, and South Korea, continued to incorporate new technological and marketing techniques, reformulate products, and modernize plants. Distribution and sales channels have become more efficient. Facing sluggish domestic demand in 1993, foreign food and beverage enterprises sought ways to trim costs and prices, thus displacing some U.S. exports of lower value-added processed food and feed.

Finally, exchange rates played a role in slowing U.S. exports of lower value-added processed food and feed in 1993. Many food and beverage companies in countries

TABLE 5 U.S. Trade Patterns in 1992 Higher Value-Added Foods and Beverages (SIC 2023, 2024, 203, 2043, 2045, 2047, 205, 2064, 2066, 2067, 2068, 2082, 2084, 2085, 2086, 2095, 2096) (*In millions of dollars, percent*)

EXPORTS			IMPORTS		
	VALUE	SHARE		VALUE	SHARE
Canada and Mexico	2,173	32.6	Canada and Mexico	2,152	22.1
European Community	1,283	19.3	European Community	4,006	41.2
Japan	1,098	16.5	Japan	161	1.7
East Asia NICs	690	10.4	East Asia NICs	983	10.1
South America	187	2.8	South America	1,046	10.8
Other	1,229	18.5	Other	1,376	14.2
World Total	6,660	100.0	World Total	9,724	100.0

TOP FIVE COUNTRIES

	VALUE	SHARE		VALUE	SHARE
Canada	1,708	25.6	Canada	1,429	14.7
Japan	1,098	16.5	France	995	10.2
Mexico	466	7.0	Mexico	723	7.4
Germany	306	4.6	United Kingdom	622	6.4
United Kingdom	302	4.5	Brazil	592	6.1

Source: U.S. Department of Commerce: Bureau of the Census; International Trade Administration.

with weakening currencies vis-à-vis the U.S. dollar sought to reduce costs by turning to alternative foreign suppliers and reformulated their products.

Japan, Canada, Mexico, South Korea, and the Netherlands, the top five importers of U.S. lower value-added processed foods and feed, accounted for more than 55 percent of total 1993 exports in this category.

In 1993, total imports of processed food and beverages dipped less than 1 percent to $20.8 billion after a rise of more than 5 percent in 1992. The share of higher value-added products was more than 45 percent in 1993, down from more than 46 percent in 1992. Lower value-added goods represented the rest, about 55 percent of all 1993 imports. From 1989 to 1993, imports of higher value-added foods and beverages rose more than 2 percent annually, while those of lower value-added processed food and feed increased about 2 percent yearly.

Imports of higher value-added foods and beverages from five countries—Canada, France, Mexico, the United Kingdom, and the Netherlands—accounted for an estimated $4.5 billion, or 48 percent of the 1993 total. Imports of lower value-added food and feed from five countries—Canada, Thailand, Australia, New Zealand, and Ecuador—represented an estimated $5.3 billion, or 47 percent of the 1993 total.

TABLE 6   U.S. Trade Patterns in 1992 Lower Value-Added Foods and Feeds (SIC 201, 2021, 2022, 2026, 2041, 2044, 2046, 2048, 2061, 2062, 2063, 207, 2083, 2087, 2091, 2092, 2097) (*In millions of dollars, percent*)

EXPORTS			IMPORTS		
	VALUE	SHARE		VALUE	SHARE
Canada and Mexico	3,016	19.0	Canada and Mexico	2,542	22.8
European Community	2,376	15.0	European Community	1,181	10.6
Japan	4,979	31.4	Japan	172	1.5
East Asia NICs	1,895	12.0	East Asia NICs	2,163	19.4
South America	495	3.1	South America	1,274	11.4
Other	3,084	19.5	Other	3,814	34.2
World Total	15,844	100.0	World Total	11,145	100.0

TOP FIVE COUNTRIES					
	VALUE	SHARE		VALUE	SHARE
Japan	4,979	31.4	Canada	2,238	20.1
Canada	1,536	9.7	Australia	1,012	9.1
Mexico	1,480	9.3	Thailand	1,003	9.0
South Korea	1,065	6.7	New Zealand	738	6.6
Netherlands	615	3.9	China	435	3.9

Source: U.S. Department of Commerce: Bureau of the Census; International Trade Administration.

PERSONAL CONSUMPTION EXPENDITURES

U.S. consumer spending for food and beverages appeared to rebound somewhat in 1993, a welcome respite after a lackluster performance in 1991 and 1992. Personal consumption expenditures (PCE) for all food and beverages increased more than 3 percent to $647 billion. Spending for food and drink away-from-home rose 4 percent, while at-home food and beverage purchases gained almost 3 percent.

Adjusted for inflation, PCE for all food and beverages increased 1 to 2 percent in 1993. Away-from-home spending climbed between 2 and 3 percent, as at-home PCE expanded a more modest 1 percent. The estimated 1993 results proved encouraging. Between 1989 and 1992, total food and beverage purchases (in constant dollars) increased only 0.2 percent annually. During the same four-year period, real expenditures for food and beverages consumed at home edged up only 0.1 percent. In contrast, purchases away from home rose almost 1 percent yearly from 1989 to 1992, equalling the real gain in total PCE (Table 7).

Changing consumer demographics, a slowing growth of population, shifting buying habits, and concerns about the economy affected both the amount and types of outlays for food and beverages. The U.S. population is expanding by less than 1 percent annually, and immigrants constitute about one-fourth of this increase. The population is continuing to age as the size of U.S. households shrinks.

Economic concerns not only caused spending restraint but also prompted greater purchases of less costly private-label products and greater patronage of warehouse-club type operations. More women working outside the home and a higher number of single-person households caused a redistribution of the food and beverage dollar away from at-home outlays and toward away-from-home outlays.

Spending for food and drink is declining as a share of all PCE. In 1993, the portion of PCE devoted to food and beverages accounted for an estimated 15 percent of the total, compared with more than 18 percent in 1982. Between 1982 and 1993, the share of away-from-home food and drink purchases decreased minimally from 5.2 percent to 4.9 percent. In contrast, consumer spending for food and beverages at home dropped considerably more, from 13 percent in 1982 to nearly 10 percent in 1993.

More women in the work force, more single-person and single-parent families, and more travel combined to increase the away-from-home market as a share of total consumer spending for food and beverages. During 1982–93, the away-from-home market expanded from 28.2 percent of all food and beverage purchases to 32.6 percent; the at-home market declined by a commensurate amount.

During the 1980s, consumers became more concerned about health, fitness, and substance abuse. These concerns continued to prevail into the 1990s and affected spending for alcoholic beverages. In 1993, the estimated PCE for alcoholic beverages inched up just 0.3 percent and accounted for 11.7 percent of all food and beverage spending, down from 13.3 percent in 1982.

Adjusted for inflation, expenditures for alcoholic beverages declined 0.5 percent annually between 1982 and 1992. Alcoholic beverage spending is likely to continue its decline now that only 50 percent of business meals is tax deductible. Potentially

TABLE 7 Personal Consumption Expenditures for Food, Nonalcoholic and Alcoholic Beverages, 1989–92
(*In millions of dollars*)

ITEM	1989	1990	1991	1992
All food and beverages	565,146	601,351	617,138	630,379
Food and beverages at home	373,675	398,444	407,354	415,281
Food and nonalcoholic beverages	330,129	351,829	359,442	365,625
Alcoholic beverages	43,546	46,615	47,912	49,656
Food and beverages away from home	180,590	191,364	198,503	203,493
Food and nonalcoholic beverages	156,911	165,885	171,889	177,889
Alcoholic beverages	23,679	25,479	26,614	25,603
Other food and nonalcoholic beverages	10,881	11,543	11,281	11,606
Furnished to employees[1]	10,325	10,976	10,769	11,116
Consumed on farms	556	567	512	490

[1]Includes military personnel.

Source: U.S. Department of Commerce, Bureau of Economic Analysis.

higher excise taxes on alcoholic beverages to help pay for health-care reform could further reduce consumption.

Population Changes. Population growth, demographic shifts, and household composition affect food and beverage consumption and spending. Total U.S. population increased slowly throughout the 1980s, and modest growth is continuing in the 1990s. Between 1980 and 1990, total population expanded just 0.95 percent annually and grew 1.1 percent from 1991–92. The Census Bureau estimates that total population is likely to increase about 0.9 percent yearly during the remainder of the 1990s.

An expanding immigrant population (mainly from South America and Asia) will have a notable effect on the industry, which must produce foods and beverages that meet the taste standards of different cultures.

Demographic shifts have also affected demand for food and beverages. The U.S. population is aging. From 1980 to 1990, the median age rose from 30 to 33 years. The fastest-growing age group is the 35-and-over set, with the greatest expansion in the 45–54 age group, which is forecast to increase nearly 45 percent during the remainder of the 1990s.

The 35–44 age group is expected to grow almost 16 percent by 2000, as the 65-and-over group increases by almost 11 percent, reaching an estimated 34.9 million people by 2000. The growing number of older consumers suggests that significant gains in consumer expenditures for foods and beverages will hinge on meeting the needs and preferences of older shoppers.

The changing composition of U.S. households also influences consumer expenditure patterns. In addition to becoming older, the average U.S. household is getting smaller. In 1992, the average household numbered 2.62 persons, a 14-percent decline since 1972.

Between 1985 and 1992, the number of U.S. households reached 95.7 million, increasing more than 10 percent; however, single-person households totaled 24 million, up 16 percent since 1985. In addition, one-parent family households also increased 19 percent since 1985. The trend toward smaller households with increasing numbers of single-person and one-parent households is expected to continue.

The combination of an aging population characterized by decreasing household size and greater numbers of single-person and one-parent households suggests that total spending for food and beverages is likely to increase slowly. More single-person and one-parent households indicate expansion of the away-from-home (food service) market at the expense of the retail grocery industry. Food and beverage processors will be pressed to provide products tailored to older and single-person households to minimize the natural appeal of away-from-home eateries. Because domestic market growth will be limited, manufacturers will likely compete very aggressively for market share and intensify export efforts to fatten sales and profits.

Consumers' Expenditure Survey. In 1991, the typical U.S. household spent $4,568 for food and beverages, including alcohol, at-home and away-from-home, according to the Bureau of Labor Statistics' Consumer Expenditure Survey. The typical household committed 58 percent of total food and beverage spending to food and nonalcoholic beverages for at-home use, 35 percent to away-from-home use, and 7 percent to alcoholic beverages purchased at home and away from home.

The typical U.S. household devoted almost 15 percent of after-tax income to the purchase of food and beverages in 1991. Two-person households spent the least, 13.7

percent, of after-tax income on food and drink, followed by three-person and four-person households, which committed 14.1 percent and 14.8 percent, respectively. The smallest and largest consumer units, one-person and five-or-more persons, spent more after-tax income than average for food and drink, 15.6 percent and 17.9 percent, respectively.

Households of five or more persons chose to spend more after-tax income (11.9 percent) for food and nonalcoholic beverages at-home; four-person households spent 9 percent, while two-person households spent the least for at-home foods, 7.7 percent of after-tax income.

One- and two-person households committed 6.2 percent and 5.9 percent, respectively, after taxes for away-from-home meals and drinks. Three- and four-person households spent the least of after-tax income, 5.1 percent, away from home, while five-or-more-person households spent 5.4 percent.

In addition to allocating more money for restaurant meals, one-person households also spent the most after-tax income on purchases of alcoholic beverages, 1.9 percent, followed by two-person households at 1.1 percent. Three-, four-, and five-person households each spent 0.7 percent on beer, wine, and distilled spirits.

Food and beverage purchase patterns changed somewhat between 1987 and 1991. Consumers elected to dedicate less of their at-home food and beverage budget to meat, poultry, seafood/fish, eggs, fruits and vegetables, and dairy products. Some of the spending shifts, especially in the case of meats, eggs, and some dairy products, reflect shoppers' concerns about health and nutrition.

Shoppers spent more of their 1991 food budget for cereal and bakery products and the so-called "other foods" category, which includes products such as most of the higher value-added prepared foods, nonalcoholic beverages, table spreads, and confectionery products. In 1991, consumers spent 46 percent on "other foods" and cereal and bakery products, compared with less than 42 percent in 1987.

Between 1987 and 1991, the Consumer Price Index (CPI) for red meat rose about 21 percent, compared with increases of 17 percent and 14 percent for poultry and fish/seafood, respectively. Per capita consumption of red meat declined almost 5 percent during this period while poultry per capita consumption increased more than 14 percent.

Prices also influenced shoppers' purchases of fruits and vegetables. During the 1987–92 period, the CPI for fresh fruits and vegetables rose 47 percent and 27 percent, respectively; prices of processed fruits and vegetables also increased, but more modestly, 19 percent and 20 percent, respectively. Per capita consumption of fresh fruit declined almost 8 percent as preserved fruit consumption fell by almost 10 percent.

NEW FOOD AND BEVERAGE LABELING

By May 1994, all U.S. sellers of processed food and beverages must conform to detailed regulations for labeling of nutritional information for their products. The rules, authorized by the Nutrition Labeling and Education Act (NLEA) of 1990, also cover serving sizes, health messages, and descriptive terms such as "light" and "low fat." The new regulations are enforced by the U.S. Food and Drug Administration.

To meet the requirements of the NLEA, most U.S. food and beverage companies have designed new labels to accommodate both NLEA information and commercial messages. Certain processors have completed the changes before the deadline. In turn, these manufacturers have used the new labeling as a selling point to differentiate their products in a crowded marketplace.

The new, more informative labeling regulations may prove especially difficult for many foreign food and beverage processors, particularly companies unaccustomed to such extensive product analysis and disclosure. Some industry analysts view the new requirements as a barrier to trade that could be challenged in the General Agreement on Tariffs and Trade (GATT). Supporters of the rules state that all enterprises, both domestic and foreign, must comply. These observers argue that the NLEA will provide vital consumer information to improve the health of U.S. consumers and that GATT would dismiss any complaint.

In August 1993, the U.S. Department of Agriculture (USDA), which regulates U.S. meat and poultry, issued recommendations on the thawing, handling, cooking, and post-preparation refrigeration of raw meat and poultry. New labels, for both retail consumers, and food service companies, will summarize these suggestions. Simultaneously, USDA will increase the number of meat inspectors, more closely monitor production plants, and accelerate efforts to develop rapid microbiological tests to detect food-borne pathogens. The American Meat Institute estimates that new regulation would cost the entire meat and poultry sector $135 million annually. Several highly publicized deaths from tainted meat contributed to greater public concern about food safety.

FOOD RETAILING

Notwithstanding consumers' overall concerns about the economy, food store and eating/drinking place sales strengthened somewhat in the first six months of 1993. Liquor sales declined, however, by more than 3 percent. Retail sales of all eating and drinking places rose 5 percent during the first six months of 1993, compared with a rise of more than 2 percent in 1992, when restaurant sales rose 3 percent and drinking place sales slumped almost 8 percent. During the first half of 1993, operators of eating and drinking places exercised considerable pricing restraint, which appears to have stimulated sales. For the period, the CPI for away-from-home food sales rose slightly more than 1 percent, compared with an average annual increase of close to 4 percent between 1987 and 1992.

Food store sales also increased by slightly more than 2 percent during the first six months of 1993, compared with a rise of slightly less than 2 percent for all of 1992. The CPI for food-at-home actually declined, about 1 percent for the first half of 1993, compared with an average annual CPI increase of 4 percent. The improved food store sales picture reflects pricing, a growing demand for private-label goods, and the increasing importance of nontraditional food sales outlets.

In 1992, nontraditional grocery sales outlets—hypermarkets, wholesale clubs, so-called deep discounters, and food mass merchandisers—accounted for 7 percent of all commodity volume (ACV) and about 1 percent of competing units, according to Willard Bishop Consulting, Ltd. By 1997, the company estimates, nontraditional outlets will represent more than 11 percent of ACV and 1.5 percent of competitive units.

Owners of food retailing outlets, especially supermarkets, believe that the nontraditional outlets are costing them sales, at least in part because processors and manufacturers sell competitive name-brand items to the warehouse clubs and similar retailers at lower prices. Because the nontraditional food outlets usually buy products in multipacks or larger sizes than traditional outlets, the cost per product unit is less than for goods packaged in conventional sizes. Savings from shopping at nontraditional outlets can be meaningful if shoppers are able to store larger sizes and quantities and are willing to spend extra travel time in exchange for convenience.

Traditional grocery sellers see the threat to their future and hold processors and wholesalers partially responsible. Conventional retailers may seek ways to penalize processors, who remain unhappy with retailers about expensive slotting allowances and penalties for the substandard sales performance of new products. One way retailers are attempting to cope with weak sales and new competition is by upgrading and expanding their private-label products.

In 1992, private-label food and beverages accounted for a reported 19.4 percent of all retail food and beverages sold. The popularity of less costly private-label items usually increases during periods of economic slowdown or uncertainty.

The quality and packaging of private-label food and beverages has been improving for some time. Modern manufacturing technologies, quality control, and improved packaging are ubiquitous throughout the processed food and beverages industry sector. Private-label products are gaining market shares in segments where they earlier had little appeal, including beer, breakfast cereal, and soft drinks. Many consumers perceive little quality difference between nationally branded items and private-label substitutes. The willingness of large numbers of consumers to pay a premium for nationally branded foods and beverages is in question.

Nevertheless, significant forces restrain the further growth of the market for private-label food and beverages. As the share of private-label processed foods and beverages increases, product development and innovation may slow considerably. Advertising, now funded by manufacturers, will likely decrease and the costs of growing the business will fall almost exclusively on retailers. Manufacturers of private-label foods and beverages can finance research and development for new products only by persuading supermarket customers to pay slightly more for the new items, an outcome probably unacceptable to weary and wary consumers.

OUTLOOK FOR 1994

Food and beverage processors and retail food store operators approach 1994 with some concern. While inflation is expected to remain under control, processors and retailers are concerned about the pace of domestic and international economic recovery and the expected growth of nontraditional retail food outlets. Processors of name-brand products will strive to stem the flow of less costly generic goods while retailers will attempt to offset the effects of new, nontraditional competition. Adjusted for inflation, the value of shipments of the food and beverage sector is forecast to rise about 1 percent in 1994 (Table 8).

Processors are also concerned about the passage of NAFTA and the fate of the Uruguay Round of trade talks. Successful conclusion of both trade pacts will mean new export opportunities in future years. However, some processors fear a backlash, which would adversely affect 1994 U.S. export sales in the event of a less-than-successful conclusion of the two sets of trade negotiations. U.S. processors are further concerned about the rate of economic recovery worldwide. For 1994, the value of processed food and beverage exports is forecast to rise about 6 percent to more than $24 billion.

NAFTA would provide at least three significant advantages to the U.S. processed food and beverage industry sector. First, the agreement would begin a series of gradual mutual tariff reductions between the United States and Mexico over a 15-year period. Second, Mexico would abolish all of its import licenses. Lastly, NAFTA would require mutual recognition of distinctive products. For example, Canada and Mexico would both recognize the uniqueness of bourbon and Tennessee whiskey, a condition

TABLE 8 Estimates and Forecasts for the Processed Food and Beverage Sector, 1992–94
(*In millions of dollars*)

| | | | | PERCENT CHANGE |
SIC	DESCRIPTION	1992[1]	1993[1]	1994[2]
201	Processed meat, poultry, and hides	88,856	90,112	91,368
202	Dairy products	51,099	52,274	53,686
203	Preserved fruits and vegetables	47,132	48,907	50,681
204	Grain mill products	48,697	50,591	52,485
205	Bakery products	27,043	27,449	28,025
206	Sugar and confectionery products	22,305	22,982	23,660
207	Fats and oils	18,980	19,260	19,896
208	Beverages	56,037	57,807	59,577
209	Miscellaneous foods	33,890	34,959	36,028
20	Total	394,039	404,341	415,406

[1] Preliminary estimate.

[2] Forecast.

Source: U.S. Department of Commerce, Bureau of Census and International Trade Administration (ITA). Estimates and forecasts by ITA.

predicated upon the elimination of Mexican tariffs on these alcoholic beverages. Only bourbon and Tennessee whiskey distilled in the United States according to U.S. laws and regulations would be sold in Canada or Mexico. In return, the United States would provide similar treatment to Canadian whiskey and Mexican tequila and mezcal.

After many difficulties and delays, the Uruguay Round of multilateral trade negotiations gained new momentum in 1993. Nevertheless, processed food and agricultural issues remain a major hurdle to agreement among the 111 member countries of the General Agreement on Tariffs and Trade (GATT).

The European Community (EC) and, in particular, France, have strong doubts about restricting their food and agricultural export subsidies and reducing barriers to imports from the United States and other countries. Imported processed foods and beverages face a common external tariff throughout the EC. The EC also assesses variable levies on the specific ingredients of imported processed food and beverages to raise prices of these products to levels prevailing in the EC.

A successful conclusion to the Uruguay Round would translate into considerable new export opportunities for U.S. manufacturers of processed foods and beverages. Most of the industry would benefit from a successful GATT agreement by allowing food and beverage manufacturers to invest more easily in GATT-member countries. The proposed investment rules would offer more clarity about the level of business risk for food and beverage companies. For example, a GATT agreement probably would not permit countries to seize assets without compensation, demand export requirements, or set domestic content regulations.

Since 1985, the share of private-label food and beverages sold in the United States has risen consistently, to more than 19 percent of total grocery food and beverage sales in 1992. Perhaps sales of private-label food and beverages will exceed 25 percent of the total in 1994. Many consumers will still search for the best combination of price and value. Industry analysts are debating, on the other hand, whether large numbers of consumers will return to nationally branded goods once the economy improves significantly.

Despite growing sales of private-label food and beverages, important factors may limit further expansion of the market. Many consumers think nationally branded foods and beverages offer greater consistency of quality than private-label substitutes. Major manufacturers of foods and beverages support their products through advertising, marketing, and promotion expenditures to maintain brand loyalty. Private-label goods do not have these advantages.

As the share of private-label processed foods and beverages increases, product development and innovation may slow considerably. Supermarket chains with their own factories do not have incentives to spend money on new product development and innovation for private-label goods because they cannot recover these expenditures over limited production cycles. Manufacturers of private-label foods and beverages could only finance research and development for new products by persuading their supermarket customers to pay a bit more for new products.

C A S E

32

FRED R. DAVID
Francis Marion University

CAMPBELL SOUP COMPANY—1994

Based in Camden, New Jersey, Campbell Soup Company (609-342-4800) saw its earnings fall from $490 million in 1992 to only $8 million in 1993. Campbell's earnings in Europe fell from $44.7 million in 1992 to negative $170.4 million in 1993. Campbell's financial objectives for fiscal 1994 are to achieve earnings per share growth of 12 to 15 percent, maintain return on equity of at least 24 percent, and maintain cash return on assets of at least 24 percent. To reach these objectives, Campbell Soup Company needs a clear strategic plan for the years 1994–2000. A mission statement recently proposed for Campbell follows.

MISSION STATEMENT FOR CAMPBELL SOUP COMPANY

Campbell Soup Company aims to offer nutritional food products to people all over the world. Our worldwide growth strategy focuses on what we do best—soup and biscuits. We are working aggressively to capture tomorrow's opportunities today.

Campbell Soup Company brand power is our pride, our inheritance, our future. With a powerhouse of trademarks that proclaims innovation, quality and consumer trust, Campbell will leverage brand strengths to deliver profitable, sustainable volume.

Campbell will concentrate on using methods and technologies while relying on the skills and experience of our people to build and expand low-cost business systems. This will ensure gains in productivity, quality and service to our manufacturing processes and marketing base.

We will continue to evaluate our business portfolio to ensure that our time, talent and money are applied to areas providing maximum return on investment. The intent is to deliver consistent financial results which keep us in the top quartile versus the best companies in the food industry. We are committed to strengthen our organization, create competitive advantage and achieve our vision, "Campbell Brands Preferred Around the World".

Throughout the 1970s and 1980s, Campbell Soup Company was largely run by the founder's son, John Dorrance, Jr. Dorrance died in early 1989 and disagreement spread throughout the Dorrance family, which owns 58 percent of Campbell's stock. Campbell's chief executive officer at the time, Gordon McGovern, resigned soon after Dorrance's death. Then in 1990, Campbell elected a new CEO, David Johnson, who previously was CEO of Gerber Products Company. After less than two months on the job, Johnson replaced Campbell's U.S. division with a North American division. This decision was based on Johnson's belief that there would soon be a North American free-trade agreement (FTA) to link the United States, Canada, and Mexico. The U.S.-Canada FTA had just been signed by both nations. Johnson continues to serve as Campbell's president and CEO today.

Campbell's philosophy is to "market locally, manufacture regionally, and resource globally—with common technology, knowledge, and supplies." Campbell currently has three major divisions: Campbell North and South America, Campbell Biscuit and Bakery, and Campbell Europe/Asia. In addition, the company has 26 subsidiaries. Each top executive has total responsibility for his or her division, from marketing and developing new products to manufacturing and logistics. These top executives are thus accountable for profits and revenues in their division. The officers as of 1992 are listed in Exhibit 32–1.

Campbell's 70 top executives are required to own at least three times their annual salary in Campbell stock. Members of Campbell's board of directors must purchase/own at least 1,000 shares of Campbell's stock. These two requirements assure that the company's top management team is totally committed to seeing the firm prosper.

Real disposable income for U.S. citizens has dropped in recent years and food as a percentage of total personal consumption expenditures also has decreased. Weak economies worldwide have limited sales of Campbell's premium-priced products such as ready-to-serve soups and Pepperidge Farm cookies. The U.S. population is not growing much, so the fight for food volume growth in the U.S. market is intense. Opportunities to increase revenues are greater abroad than in the United States. In addition to higher population growth and food consumption abroad, some international markets continue to be dominated by small, regional food processors that are sometimes inefficient producers and/or marketers.

Europe is beginning to follow the U.S. trend of seeking convenience in cooking and packaging. This trend allows food companies to offer more "value-added" products such as soups; chicken that already has been cut into pieces, boned, and skinned; marinated meats; ready-to-serve microwavable meals; single-serve portions; and cereals containing fruit and nuts.

Barriers to entry in the food industry are nearly insurmountable since this is a volume-driven business. Economies of scale for production, marketing, and distribution efficiencies are very important. For example, in cereals, the largest players—Kellogg, General Mills, and Philip Morris—are gaining market share at the expense of the three smaller cereal manufacturers—Ralston, Quaker, and Nabisco. There is a consolidation

EXHIBIT 32-1 Campbell Soup Company Officers as of October 1992

David W. Johnson
  President and Chief
  Executive Officer

Herbert M. Baum
  Executive Vice President.
  President, Campbell North
  and South America Division

John M. Coleman
  Senior Vice President—Law and
  Public Affairs and Corporate
  Secretary

James R. Kirk
  Senior Vice President—Research
  & Development and Quality
  Assurance.
  President, Campbell Research
  and Development

Richard A. Shea
  Senior Vice President.
  President, Campbell Biscuit and
  Bakery Division. President,
  Pepperidge Farm, Incorporated

Frank E. Weise, III
  Senior Vice President—Finance
  and Chief Financial Officer

Anthony J. Adams
  Vice President.
  Vice President—Marketing
  Research, Campbell North
  and South America Division

David L. Albright
  Vice President.
  President, Confectionery Group

Stephen R. Armstrong
  Vice President—Human
  Resources

James J. Baldwin
  Vice President—Taxes

Robert F. Bernstock
  Vice President.
  President and CEO,
  Campbell Soup Company Ltd
  (Canada)

Francis A. DuVernois
  Vice President.
  Vice President—Operations,
  Campbell North and South
  America Division

Brenda E. Edgerton
  Vice President—Treasurer

Leo J. Greaney
  Vice President—Controller

Ralph A. Harris
  Vice President—Corporate
  Development

Kathleen MacDonnell
  Vice President.
  Sector Vice President—Prepared
  Foods, Campbell North and
  South America Division

Charles V. McCarthy
  Vice President.
  President, Campbell Sales

Raymond A. Meillier
  Vice President.
  Vice President—Finance,
  Campbell North and South
  America Division

Edward S. Moerk
  Vice President.
  President, Campbell Europe
  Biscuits

Gary S. Moss
  Vice President.
  Vice President—Marketing
  Services, Campbell North and
  South America Division

George P. Nulty
  Vice President.
  Vice President—Purchasing,
  Campbell North and South
  America Division

Carlos Oliva Funes
  Vice President.
  President, Swift-Armour
  Sociedad Anonima
  Argentina

John L. Patten
  Vice President.
  President, Campbell Food
  Service, Campbell North
  and South America Division

Alfred Poe
  Vice President.
  Sector Vice President—
  Condiments & Sauces,
  Campbell North and South
  America Division.
  President, Vlasic Foods, Inc.

J. Neil Stalter
  Vice President—Corporate
  Communications

Robert Subin
  Vice President.
  President, Campbell
  Europe/Asia Division

F. Marty Thrasher
  Vice President.
  Sector Vice President—Soup,
  Campbell North and South
  America Division

Harry Walleasa
  Vice President—Management
  Information Systems

Source: Campbell Soup Company, 1993 *Annual Report*.

of food companies around the world, especially in Europe. As companies develop brand names that sell well around the world, they reap greater marketing efficiencies and profits.

There is a real fight among U.S. food companies for supermarket shelf space and freezer space. Firms that win space have a better chance of capturing the customer's attention and dollars. Price wars are a threat for food companies like Campbell. The areas most sensitive to price wars are frozen dinners and shelf-stable items. Regarding frozen foods, freezer space is particularly limited in supermarkets due to the extra cost of building and maintaining freezers. Thus when ConAgra recently started getting lots of freezer space for its Healthy Choice frozen dinners, price wars broke out. Campbell's Swanson brand frozen dinners compete directly with ConAgra's Healthy Choice.

CEO Johnson is considering a number of acquisitions to increase Campbell's economies of scale and distribution outlets; he is especially interested in European firms. Increases in the value of the dollar versus foreign currencies make it tougher for foreign companies to acquire U.S. firms but make it less expensive for U.S. companies to acquire foreign firms. However, a strengthening U.S. dollar hurts earnings of U.S. food companies with strong international operations.

CAMPBELL BRAND POWER

The year 1993 at Campbell could be described as one of extensive "brainstorming." This is Campbell's term for product development. The company aggressively extended many products using creativity and innovation. New products such as Pepperidge Farm gravy "borrowed" trademarks from other Campbell products. Godiva chocolate, known for luxury and indulgence, "lent" its name to a popular new line of coffees and a liqueur. Prego spaghetti sauce extended its savory benefits to a new pizza sauce line, with first-year results exceeding expectations. These brand-extension successes added more than $30 million to sales.

The volume of Campbell's Home Cookin ready-to-serve soups surged 14 percent in 1993, supported by a new campaign, *It doesn't get any better than Campbell's best*. The line features a redesigned label and two new varieties—New England Clam Chowder and Chicken Vegetable. In the competitive "healthy soup" category, Campbell's Healthy Request 98-percent-fat-free, ready-to-serve varieties captured a leadership position. Campbell's multiuse line added Campbell's Golden Corn and Italian Tomato and relaunched Cream of Asparagus to expand the business. Campbell's Double Noodle dry soup variety debuted in 1993, increasing dry soup volume 11 percent. Campbell introduced Campbell's Cream of Chicken & Broccoli, Chunky Old Fashioned Potato, and Swanson Vegetable Broth in 1993. The company launched a new advertising campaign headlined, *Campbell's Never Underestimate the Power of Soup* in 1993.

Campbell's biscuit and bakery business features many well-known brands. Pepperidge Farm's launch of Goldfish cookies in 1993 offers a novelty Goldfish pack for kids. The company's Distinctive cookie line inspired recent introductions of Double Chocolate and Hazelnut Milano varieties. Frozen garlic bread and rolls were introduced in 1993. Delacre, the pan-European brand, holds number-one market share in cookie assortments, and Arnott's, the Pacific Rim brand, ranks as the world's seventh largest biscuit—or cookie and cracker—brand.

Strong volume performance was posted in 1993 by Swanson frozen dinners, led by Hungry Man entrees and Fun Feast children's meals. In the grocery arena, Franco-

American launched Spaghetti-Os pasta varieties using the kids' cartoon character, Garfield. V8 vegetable juices reached a new audience with the launch of V8 Picante, a mild-flavored salsa drink, in 1993. Meal enhancement introductions included Marie's line of Luscious Low-Fat salad dressings and Vlasic Pickles To Go single-serve pickles.

Campbell increased marketing spending 12 percent in 1993. Helping to build Campbell brands are programs such as *Prego . . . Serving Your Community*, which supports charities with spaghetti dinner fund raisers. "Hearty School Lunch" teamed *Campbell Food Service* with the American Heart Association to offer menus, recipes, and nutrition information to schools nationwide. Celebrating the 20th anniversary of the *Labels for Education* program, Campbell produced an acclaimed television special, *"Portrait of a Teacher,"* hosted by actress Phylicia Rashad in 1993.

GLOBAL MARKETING

Campbell's worldwide growth strategy focuses on what the company does best: soup and biscuits. Campbell is relentlessly pursuing its vision, *Campbell Brands Preferred Around the World*. Currently, 95 percent of Campbell soups are sold in markets with just 5 percent of the world's population. In the United Kingdom, Campbell's condensed varieties are now the fastest-growing soups. Volume climbed a remarkable 18 percent during 1993.

In Mexico, Campbell's new Crema de Chile Poblana condensed soup variety has become a top seller. In Canada, Campbell's "Chunky" soups scored record volume and earnings in 1993. Progress in the Australian market continues with introductions of two new condensed varieties, Mushroom and Bacon and Italian Tomato. Strong growth in Campbell's Hong Kong business has led to expansion of Swanson broths into Taiwan, while markets in Indonesia, Singapore, Malaysia, and Thailand also are growing. Campbell is currently conducting taste tests in Argentina and Poland.

Campbell introduced condensed soups and broths to China in 1993. China's 1.2 billion people each consume almost six servings of soup per week. Campbell is exploring the possibility of manufacturing soup in China to generate additional savings and establish a base for long-term profitability throughout Asia.

Since acquiring a majority ownership in Arnott's Limited in Australia, Campbell's Biscuit and Bakery group derives more than half of its sales and operating earnings from outside North America. Pepperidge Farm, which mainly targets consumers in the Americas, recently expanded into Canada and Mexico. During 1993, fresh bakery items, along with cookies and crackers, were also introduced to Canadians.

In Europe, Campbell's new line of Delacre premium homemade-style cookies, Biscuits Maison de Delacre, is very popular. With simultaneous introductions in France, Belgium, Holland, and Germany, this was the industry's first-ever pan-European launch—in overall coordination of product, advertising, public relations, promotion, and packaging.

Campbell's Golden V8 vegetable juice, rich in beta carotene and made from golden tomatoes, was launched in Japan in 1993. The growing popularity of Mexican salsa in the United States led to the introduction of V8 Picante, a vegetable juice mixture of tomatoes, chilies, jalapeño peppers and lime, to American consumers. In addition, V8 vegetable juice entries to Mexico and China, along with a new uniform formula for V8 in Europe, are contributing to Campbell's revenues. Exhibit 32–2 lists Campbell Soup Company principal subsidiaries, affiliates, and operations around the world.

SUBSIDIARIES AND AFFILIATES

United States
Campbell Finance Corp.
Campbell Investment Company
Campbell Sales Company
Campbell's Fresh, Inc.
Casera Foods, Inc.
Godiva Chocolatier, Inc.
Herider Farms, Inc.
Joseph Campbell Company
Mrs. Paul's Kitchens, Inc.
Pepperidge Farm, Incorporated
Royal American Foods Corporation
Sanwa Foods, Inc.
Vlasic Foods, Inc.

Other Countries
Swift-Armour Sociedad Anonima Argentina *(Argentina)*
Campbell's Australasia Pty. Limited *(Australia)*
N.V. Biscuits Delacre S.A. *(Belgium)*
N.V. Campbell Food & Confectionery Coordination Center Continental Europe, S.A. *(Belgium)*
N.V. Godiva Belgium S.A. *(Belgium)*
Campbell Soup Company Ltd *(Canada)*
Campbell Foods P.L.C. *(England)*
Campbell's U.K. Limited *(England)*
Societe Francaise des Biscuits Delacre S.A. *(France)*
Campbell Soup Asia Limited *(Hong Kong)*
Campbell Japan Incorporated *(Japan)*

Campbell's de Mexico, S.A. de CV *(Mexico)*
Compania Envasadora Loreto, S.A. *(Spain)*

OPERATIONS

Campbell North and South America Division
Atlanta, Georgia *(ramen noodles)*
Barceloneta, Puerto Rico *(canned foods)*
Blandon, Pennsylvania *(mushrooms)*
Bonduel, Wisconsin *(pickles)*
Brampton, Ontario *(distributor refrigerated foods)*
Bridgeport, Michigan *(pickles)*
Chatham, Ontario *(canned foods, ingredients, juices)*
Chestertown, Maryland *(ingredients)*
City of Industry, California *(pickles, ramen noodles)*
Dixon, California *(ingredients)*
Douglas, Georgia *(canned foods, ingredients)*
Dudley, Georgia *(mushrooms)*
Fayetteville, Arkansas *(frozen foods, ingredients)*
Fennville, Michigan *(mushrooms)*
Guasave, Mexico *(ingredients)*
Hillsboro, Texas *(mushrooms)*
Howe, Indiana *(mushrooms)*
Imlay City, Michigan *(pickles)*
Jackson, Ohio *(mushrooms)*
Listowel, Ontario *(frozen foods, distributor ingredients)*
Marshall, Michigan *(canned foods, refrigerated foods)*
Maxton, North Carolina *(canned foods)*
Mexico City, Mexico *(distributor food products)*
Miami, Florida *(frozen foods)*
Millsboro, Delaware *(pickles)*
Milwaukee, Wisconsin *(ingredients)*

Modesto, California *(frozen foods)*
Montevideo, Uruguay *(distributor food products)*
Napoleon, Ohio *(canned foods)*
Omaha, Nebraska *(frozen foods)*
Paris, Texas *(canned foods)*
Pescadero, California *(mushrooms)*
Philadelphia, Pennsylvania *(frozen foods)*
Rosario, Argentina *(meat products, canned foods, frozen foods)*
Sacramento, California *(canned foods)*
St. Marys, Ontario *(ingredients)*
Salisbury, Maryland *(frozen foods)*
Seville, Spain *(olives)*
Sidney, Ohio *(dry foods)*
South Plainfield, New Jersey *(ingredients)*
Stockton, California *(ingredients)*
Tecumseh, Nebraska *(ingredients)*
Thornton, Illinois *(refrigerated salad dressings)*
Toronto, Ontario *(canned foods)*
Villagran, Mexico *(canned foods, frozen vegetables)*
Visalia, California *(olives)*
Wauseon, Ohio *(ingredients)*
West Chicago, Illinois *(mushrooms)*
Worthington, Minnesota *(canned foods, ingredients)*

Campbell Biscuit and Bakery Division
Aiken, South Carolina *(bakery)*
Burbank, California *(bakery)*
Clinton, Connecticut *(mail order)*
Denver, Pennsylvania *(biscuit, bakery)*

EXHIBIT 32-2 *Continued*

Downers Grove, Illinois *(bakery)*
Downingtown, Pennsylvania
 (frozen foods)
Ede, The Netherlands *(biscuit)*
Lambermont, Belgium *(biscuit)*
Lakeland, Florida
 (biscuit, bakery)
Nieppe, France *(biscuit)*
Norwalk, Connecticut *(bakery)*
Pleyben, France *(biscuit)*
Richmond, Utah
 (biscuit, frozen foods)
Salt Lake City, Utah
 (food service products)
Tholen, The Netherlands
 (biscuit)
Willard, Ohio *(biscuit)*

Campbell Europe/Asia Division
EUROPE
Belgium
 Brussels *(confectionery)*
 Lier *(confectionery)*
 Manage *(confectionery)*
 Puurs *(food products)*

England
 Braintree *(frozen foods)*
 King's Lynn *(canned foods)*
 Peterlee *(frozen foods)*
 Salford *(frozen foods)*
 York *(refrigerated foods)*
France
 Thiviers *(canned foods)*
 Bondues *(confectionery)*
Germany
 Cuxhaven *(refrigerated salads)*
 Hamburg *(refrigerated salads)*
 Frankfurt am Main *(canned
  foods)*
 Maisach *(distributor
  food products)*
 Ratingen *(distributor of imported
  foods specialties)*
Ireland
 Middleton *(frozen and
  refrigerated foods)*
Italy
 Stradella *(canned foods)*
 Treviso *(canned foods)*

Scotland
 Glasgow *(frozen foods)*
The Netherlands
 Breda *(confectionery)*
 Raamsdonkveer *(confectionery)*
 Zoetermeer *(trading of imported
  food specialties)*
 Zundert *(frozen foods)*

ASIA
Australia
 Melbourne *(juices)*
 Mernda *(mushrooms)*
 Shepparton *(canned foods)*
Hong Kong
 Hong Kong
  (distributor food products)
Japan
 Tokyo *(distributor food products)*
New Zealand
 Auckland
  (distributor food products)

UNITED STATES
 Reading, Pennsylvania
  (confectionery)

Source: Campbell Soup Company, 1993 *Annual Report.*

INFORMATION SYSTEMS

Campbell concentrates on using methods, technologies and brain power in the most efficient manner possible to eliminate non-value-added steps while improving overall processes. Campbell has upgraded its record-keeping databases to a universal system that tracks every step of the manufacturing process. This marks the transition to a worldwide Campbell Integrated Manufacturing Information System (CIMIS) and looms as the biggest and most promising computer system undertaking in company history. At Campbell's U.S. plants alone, savings from CIMIS are estimated at $22 million annually.

As one of the first companies to adopt Efficient Consumer Response (ECR), Campbell brings value to the grocery shopper while taking costs out of the total supply chain. Driven by every-day-low-procurement pricing, reengineered promotion programs offer incentives without adding cost. In addition, Category Management and Continuous Product Replenishment programs improve overall efficiencies by maximizing return on retail space and reducing inventories, respectively. Total ECR program benefits translate to about a $30-million earnings improvement by 1996.

Campbell's world-class manufacturing and product development technologies rank among the most innovative in the industry. At the new Technology Center in Camden, the best technical and manufacturing concepts are perfected before production begins at plant locations. Along with developing and applying many new technologies—such as fat-sparing and sodium-sparing techniques—the Center is streamlining costs, improving productivity, and providing competitive advantage. During fiscal 1993, savings from new technologies totaled about $25 million.

CAMPBELL NORTH AND SOUTH AMERICA

Operating earnings for Campbell North and South America were $635 million in 1993, compared to $790 million in 1992. Net sales were $4.6 billion in 1993, an increase of 2 percent over 1992. Soup volume was up 2.5 percent despite the one less week, with strong performances by Home Cookin and Healthy Request ready-to-serve soups. In the competitive frozen food business, Swanson kids' meals and Great Start breakfast sandwiches did well. The newly introduced Pepperidge Farm gravies delivered strong volume growth as did Food Service frozen products, Vlasic pickles, and Argentina operations.

The Campbell North and South America Division was formed in January 1992, to take advantage of the emerging "common market" linking Canada, the United States, Mexico, and Argentina. The western hemisphere's eventual emergence as a powerful trading bloc will provide a critical advantage toward competing with trading blocs of the Pacific Rim countries and the European Common Market. Locations in North and South America are identified in the map in Exhibit 32–3.

Major business sectors comprising Campbell North and South America include soup, prepared foods, pork and beans, V8, condiments, and sauces. Soup has made the Campbell name synonymous with quality and convenience has grown. From the days when an ad featuring the famous Campbell Kid proudly boasted "21 kinds of soup . . . 10 cents a can" the familiar red and white labeled condensed soups have since led the way for the more recent introductions of dry, microwavable, and ramen noodle soups. In October 1991, Campbell Soup Company further strengthened its position in the fast growing ramen noodle market when it acquired Sanwa Foods Inc., the third largest marketer of ramen noodle products in the United States.

Americans purchase more than 2.5 billion cans of Campbell's soups annually, and on average have nine cans on their pantry shelf at any time during the year. Campbell Soup brands include Home Cookin, Chunky, and Healthy Request. Integral parts of the soup business are Swanson's canned chicken, beef, and vegetable broths.

Campbell's share of the total prepared soup market is 56 percent, with total wet soup share at 81.8 percent. Campbell's ready-to-serve soups account for almost 10 percent of Campbell's total wet soup share. Other components of the total prepared soup market include dehydrated and ramen noodle soups in several types of packaging including pouches, single-serve cups, and block forms.

Swift-Armour A.S.A., headquartered in Buenos Aires, with production facilities in Rosario, began operation in Argentina in 1907 and has remained a leading producer of beef products. Acquired in 1980 by Campbell Soup Company, the Swift-Armour brand is well known for its beef and other products. Since 1990, Argentina has experienced an economic boom that has benefitted long-suffering Argentines. Consumers now have more disposable income, and as a result Swift-Armour's domestic sales are up strongly. Market share for all Swift-Armour canned meat products has increased from 50 to 62 percent. The present plant at Rosario operates at 100 percent capacity but a new plant is scheduled to open in early 1993 to replace the current facility. Swift-Armour's domestic product lines include canned meats, marmalades, edible fats, ketchup, canned vegetables, and canned fruits under the Swift label, and pastas and edible oils under the La Patrona brand.

In 1992, Swift-Armour began an aggressive marketing campaign to introduce Campbell product lines into Argentina after market tests showed an excellent predisposition for the products among consumers. Argentines prefer cream soups such as Campbell's mushroom, celery, chicken asparagus, and the split pea and bean soup varieties. Campbell's Teddy Bear soup offers appeal for the children's market. V8 juice is an entirely new category to the Argentine market and its introduction offers great growth potential for this popular beverage.

Swift-Armour is the largest beef exporter in Argentina and exports canned meat to some 50 countries. Frozen meat is exported to the United States, Italy, and Japan, and most of the beef which is processed into Campbell's soups in the United States comes from Swift-Armour. In addition, the agribusiness division manages 570,000 acres with over 100,000 head of cattle.

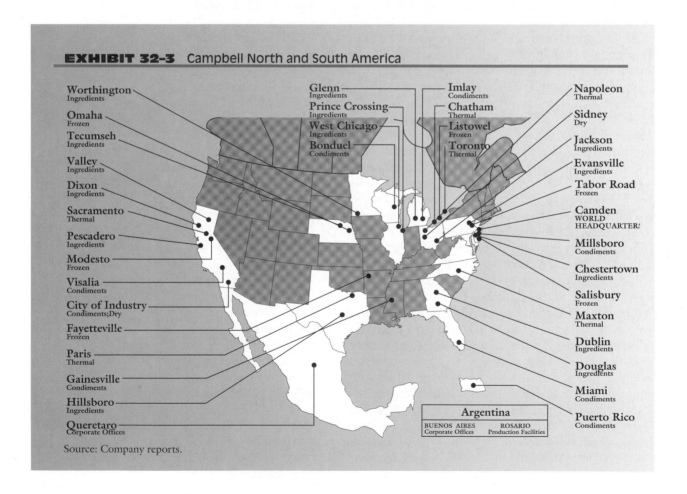

EXHIBIT 32-3 Campbell North and South America

Source: Company reports.

The Biscuit and Bakery Division reported operating earnings of $101 million in 1993. Net sales increased 23 percent to $999 million. These increases stem mainly from attaining 58 percent ownership of Arnotts in fiscal 1993, which contributed $170 million in sales. Previously, Campbell owned 33 percent and accounted for its investment on the equity method. Arnotts has strong earnings growth in the year.

Pepperidge Farm volume increased slightly for the year with sales trends improving significantly in the fourth quarter led by the introduction of Goldfish cookies and frozen garlic bread and rolls. Earnings of Delacre in Europe were down because of a sluggish European economy, the costs of starting up new production lines, and the introduction of the new Biscuits Maison, patterned after Pepperidge Farm's American Collection and Old Fashioned cookies.

In September 1990, Campbell Soup Company consolidated its U.S. and international biscuit and bakery operations into one organization to facilitate the strategic exchange of information between the businesses and, in turn, to grow the company's worldwide brands and products. The new organization comprises Pepperidge Farm, Incorporated; Biscuits Delacre; and Arnotts Biscuits Limited. Campbell Biscuit and Bakery locations are indicated on the map in Exhibit 32–4.

EXHIBIT 32-4 Campbell Biscuit and Gravy

Source: Company reports.

The brands offer a wide variety of fresh baked goods including breads, rolls, croutons, stuffing, cookies, and crackers; snack items including Arnotts' macadamia nuts; and frozen foods including pastries, cakes, pizzas, danish, single-serve desserts, and muffins. The products are offered through traditional marketing outlets as well as, in the case of Pepperidge Farm, through food service, thrift stores, and mail order distribution.

In 1991, Pepperidge Farm completed its $181 million bakery and biscuit plant in Denver, Pennsylvania—the most technologically advanced bakery in the world. The breakthrough technology employed in this new facility provides impetus to drive profitable volume growth through new products.

CAMPBELL EUROPE/ASIA

Campbell Europe/Asia reported an operating loss of $91 million after special charges of $144 million. Before these charges, operating earnings increased 23 percent over 1992 to $53 million, due primarily to significant improvements in the United Kingdom and Germany. Sales increased 2 percent to $1.02 billion in 1993 from $1.0 billion in 1992. Both sales and earnings benefitted from the acquisition of Fray Benthos, the leading premium canned-meat brand in the United Kingdom, and from the company's acquisition of the remaining 50 percent ownership of the Spring Valley juice business in Australia. Campbell Europe locations are shown on the map in Exhibit 32–5.

Campbell's international presence can be found in Great Britain, Europe, and Asia under Betis, Pleyben, Exeter, Unger, Freshbake, Groko, Logro, Beeck, Kattus, Probare, Lacroix, Granny's, Lamy-Lutti, Devos-Lemmens, Imperial, Kwatta, Tubble Gum, Laforest Perigord, Chantenac and many other food and confectionery brands, including world famous Godiva chocolates.

Campbell Frozen Food has four plants located in Glasgow, Salford, Braintree, and Peterlee in Scotland and England servicing the retail and food service markets. The main products are savory pastries and pies, sausages, quiche, sausage rolls, shepherd's pie, ready meals, meat products such as burgers, and snacks and small cake confectionery products. Brand names include Campbell's, Freshbake, and private label for supermarket stock.

Groko (Zundert, Netherlands) was formed in 1957, following the merger of two Dutch food companies. Acquired by Campbell Soup Company in 1979, Groko processes and distributes frozen, prepared vegetable and potato products exclusively to major supermarket chains with distribution contracted through independent frozen food distributors.

Campbell Asia is based in Hong Kong and oversees trading in Hong Kong, Singapore, Malaysia, Taiwan, and Korea. Sales agents and exporters handle sales to the Philippines, Guam, Indonesia, and the Pacific Islands. Campbell brands include Campbell's condensed soups, Chunky Ready-to-Serve, Swanson Broth, Swanson Condensed, Campbell's Beans, V8 and Tomato Juices, Franco-American pasta and gravies, Prego, and Spring Valley juices.

Campbell Australia is headquarted in Melbourne, Australia, with a plant at Shepparton to serve the Pacific Basin island countries including New Zealand, Indonesia, and the Philippines. In addition to Campbell's red and white label soups, the division markets Chunky and Chunky-for-One brand soups, V8 Juice and Spring Valley fruit juices, Campbell's spaghetti sauce, tomato paste, Heat 'n' Serve canned meals, Real Stocks (liquid cooking stock), and Oriental Sauces. Baco luxury flavored milk and Iso-Tonic sports drink are brands featured in the Australasia market. Campbell's commands 26 percent of this market, and another enterprise, Melbourne Mushrooms, command 31 percent of the bulk and prepackaged fresh mushroom market.

Campbell Japan is responsible for the sales of Campbell products throughout Japan. There are three sales offices located in Tokyo, Okinawa, and Osaka. Products sold

EXHIBIT 32-5 Campbell Europe

Glasgow
Campbell's U.K.

Peterlee
Campbell's U.K.

York
Wright's of York

Salford
Campbell's U.K.

Cork
Campbell's U.K.

King's Lynn
Campbell's U.K.

Braintree
Campbell's U.K.

London
Campbell's U.K.
Campbell Europe

Pleyben
Delacre

Thiviers
Continental Foods

Nieppe
Delacre

Tourcoing
Lamy Lutti

Seville
Vlasic Foods

Stradella
Robo

Treviso
Logro

Hamburg
Beeck

Cuxhaven
Beeck

Ratigen
Kattus

Frankfurt
LaCroix

Maisach
Skandinport

Holland

Zoetmeer	Zundert
Boas	*Groko*
Ede	Ramsdonkveer
Delacre	*Verduyjn*
Tholen	
Delacre	

Belgium

Brussels	Puurs
Godiva	*Continental Foods*
Vilvoorde	Lier
Delacre	*Audenaerde*
Lambermont	Manage
Delacre	*Lamy Luti*

Source: Company reports.

include condensed and ready-to-serve soup, premium chocolate, red juices, and biscuits under the Campbell's Godiva Chocolates, V8, Pepperidge Farm, and Delacre brands.

NEW STRATEGIES

Campbell has consolidated its frozen food operations, closed its facilities in Salisbury, Maryland and Philadelphia, Pennsylvania, and shifted certain operations to the Omaha, Nebraska, plant. Campbell plans to divest a number of businesses over several years and to make further acquisitions. Campbell in 1993 acquired the majority interest in Arnotts Limited in Australia. Arnotts was Australia's leading biscuit manufacturer. By virtue of this acquisition, Campbell's Biscuit and Bakery division ranks as the fourth largest biscuit maker in the world. During 1993, Campbell established a biscuit headquarters in Hong Kong, where consumer trials of cookies and crackers have begun. Other test markets include Singapore, Taiwan, and Korea.

Campbell recently acquired Fray Benthos, the United Kingdom's leading brand of premium canned meats. This leverages the company's heat-processing technology used to produce canned soup, as well as its meat-processing expertise. Identify and evaluate some other foreign food companies that Campbell could potentially acquire; make some specific recommendations to CEO Johnson in this regard. Should Johnson alter Campbell's organizational structure? Would a product type structure (e.g., a soup division, a frozen foods division, a cookies division) be more effective than the geographic/product combination type structure? Develop several alternative organizational charts for Johnson and specify the advantages and disadvantages of each design for the company.

Let's say CEO Johnson asks you to go to your college library and gather information necessary to develop a five-year strategic plan for Campbell Soup Company. Include a mission statement for Campbell Soup Company. Include five-year pro forma financial statements to show the impact of your recommendations and an EPS/EBIT analysis to determine whether Campbell should use debt or stock to raise additional capital. (Exhibits 32–6 through 32–11 provide 1993 statements from

EXHIBIT 32-6 Campbell Soup Company Consolidated Statements of Earnings (*Millions of dollars except per share amounts*)

	1993 (52 WEEKS)	1992 (53 WEEKS)	1991 (52 WEEKS)
NET SALES	$6,586.2	$6,263.2	$6,204.1
Cost and expenses			
Cost of products sold	4,027.8	3,963.1	4,095.5
Marketing and selling expenses	1,208.3	1,050.0	956.2
Administrative expenses	306.7	282.3	306.7
Research and development expenses	68.8	59.7	56.3
Interest expense	82.8	101.9	116.2
Interest income	(9.0)	(15.3)	(26.0)
Other expense	28.0	22.2	31.8
Divestiture and restructuring charges	353.0	—	—
Total costs and expenses	6,066.4	5,463.9	5,536.7
Earnings before taxes	519.8	799.3	667.4
Taxes on earnings	262.6	308.8	265.9
Earnings before cumulative effect of accounting changes	257.2	490.5	401.5
Cumulative effect of accounting changes	249.0	—	—
NET EARNINGS	$ 8.2	$ 490.5	$ 401.5
PER SHARE			
Earnings before cumulative effect of accounting changes	$ 1.02	$ 1.95	$ 1.58
Cumulative effect of accounting changes	.99	—	—
NET EARNINGS	$ .03	$ 1.95	$ 1.58
Weighted average shares outstanding	251.9	251.7	254.0

Source: Campbell Soup Company, 1993 *Annual Report*.

Campbell's *Annual Report*.) CEO Johnson must reverse the negative financial trends mentioned at the beginning of this case. Do all you can to help Campbell achieve the specific objectives outlined earlier.

EXHIBIT 32-7 Campbell Soup Company Consolidated Balance Sheets (*Millions of dollars*)

	AUGUST 1, 1993	AUGUST 2, 1992
CURRENT ASSETS		
Cash and cash equivalents	$ 62.6	$ 112.1
Other temporary investments, at cost which approximates market	6.9	5.6
Accounts receivable	646.3	577.1
Inventories	804.2	717.9
Prepaid expenses	166.2	88.9
Total current assets	1,686.2	1,501.6
PLANT ASSETS, NET OF DEPRECIATION	2,264.4	1,965.8
INTANGIBLE ASSETS, NET OF AMORTIZATION	596.0	441.8
OTHER ASSETS	350.9	444.6
Total assets	$4,897.5	$4,353.8
CURRENT LIABILITIES		
Notes payable	$669.4	$ 293.7
Payable to suppliers and others	510.0	497.8
Accrued liabilities	498.9	363.9
Dividend payable	63.5	49.2
Accrued income taxes	108.7	95.1
Total current liabilities	1,850.5	1,299.7
LONG-TERM DEBT	461.9	693.3
NONPENSION POSTRETIREMENT BENEFITS	369.7	—
OTHER LIABILITIES	511.4	333.2
Total liabilities	3,193.5	2,326.2
SHAREOWNERS' EQUITY		
Preferred stock; authorized 40.0 shares; none issued	—	—
Capital stock, $.075 par value; authorized 280.0 shares; issued 271.2 shares	20.3	20.3
Capital surplus	149.1	116.2
Earnings retained in the business	2,002.0	2,224.5
Capital stock in treasury, 19.5 shares in 1993 and 20.1 shares in 1992, at cost	(428.6)	(401.9)
Cumulative translation adjustments	(38.8)	68.5
Total shareowners' equity	1,704.0	2,027.6
Total liabilities and shareowners' equity	$4,897.5	$4,353.8

Source: Campbell Soup Company, 1993 *Annual Report*.

EXHIBIT 32-8 Campbell Soup Company Consolidated Statements of Cash Flows (*Millions of dollars*)

	1993	1992	1991
CASH FLOWS FROM OPERATING ACTIVITIES			
Net earnings	$8.2	$490.5	$401.5
To reconcile net earnings to net cash provided by operating activities:			
Divestitures and restructuring provisions	353.0	—	—
Cumulative effect of accounting changes	249.0	—	—
Depreciation and amortization	242.2	216.2	208.6
Deferred taxes	(48.0)	34.4	35.5
Other, net	41.2	25.1	63.2
Net change in accounts receivable	(73.4)	(16.6)	17.1
Net change in inventories	(90.2)	7.1	48.7
Net change in other current assets and liabilities	(29.6)	(12.4)	30.6
Net cash provided by operating activities	652.4	744.3	805.2
CASH FLOWS FROM INVESTING ACTIVITIES:			
Purchases of plant assets	(366.3)	(336.5)	(361.1)
Sales of plant assets	37.7	25.5	43.2
Businesses acquired	(261.9)	(30.8)	(180.1)
Sales of businesses	9.5	2.6	67.4
Net change in other assets	(19.0)	(55.0)	(57.8)
Net change in other temporary investments	(1.3)	7.2	9.7
Net cash used in investing activities	(601.3)	(387.0)	(478.7)
CASH FLOWS FROM FINANCING ACTIVITIES:			
Long-term borrowings	1.6	5.8	402.8
Repayments of long-term borrowings	(222.7)	(221.6)	(129.9)
Net change in borrowings with less than three month maturities	389.4	80.5	(137.9)
Other short-term borrowings	55.7	77.1	117.3
Repayments of other short-term borrowings	(98.0)	(74.4)	(206.4)
Dividends paid	(216.4)	(166.4)	(137.5)
Treasury stock purchases	(42.3)	(149.6)	(175.6)
Treasury stock issued	35.5	19.2	47.7
Other, net	—	(.1)	(.1)
Net cash used in financing activities	(97.2)	(429.5)	(219.6)
Effect of exchange rate changes on cash	(3.4)	5.4	(8.7)
NET CHANGE IN CASH AND CASH EQUIVALENTS	(49.5)	(66.8)	98.2
Cash and cash equivalents at beginning of year	112.1	178.9	80.7
CASH AND CASH EQUIVALENTS AT END OF YEAR	$62.6	$112.1	$178.9

Source: Campbell Soup Company, 1993 *Annual Report*.

EXHIBIT 32-9 Campbell Soup Company Consolidated Statements of Shareowners' Equity (*Millions of dollars*)

	PREFERRED STOCK	CAPITAL STOCK	CAPITAL SURPLUS	EARNINGS RETAINED IN THE BUSINESS	CAPITAL STOCK IN TREASURY	CUMULATIVE TRANSLATION ADJUSTMENTS	TOTAL SHAREOWNERS' EQUITY
Balance at July 29, 1990	—	$20.3	$61.9	$1,653.3	$(107.2)	$63.5	$1,691.8
Net earnings				401.5			401.5
Cash dividends ($.56 per share)				(142.2)			(142.2)
Treasury stock purchased					(175.6)		(175.6)
Treasury stock issued under Management incentive and Stock option plans			45.4		12.4		57.8
Translation adjustments						(29.9)	(29.9)
Sale of foreign operations						(10.0)	(10.0)
Balance at July 28, 1991	—	20.3	107.3	1,912.6	(270.4)	23.6	1,793.4
Net earnings				490.5			490.5
Cash dividends ($.71 per share)				(178.6)			(178.6)
Treasury stock purchased					(149.6)		(149.6)
Treasury stock issued under Management incentive and Stock option plans			8.9		18.1		27.0
Translation adjustments						44.9	44.9
Balance at August 2, 1992	—	20.3	116.2	2,224.5	(401.9)	68.5	2,027.6
Net earnings				8.2			8.2
Cash dividends ($.915 per share)				(230.7)			(230.7)
Treasury stock purchased					(42.3)		(42.3)
Treasury stock issued under Management incentive and Stock option plans			32.9		15.6		48.5
Translation adjustments						(107.3)	(107.3)
Balance at August 1, 1993	—	$20.3	$149.1	$2,002.0	$(428.6)	$(38.8)	$1,704.0

Source: Campbell Soup Company, 1993 *Annual Report.*

EXHIBIT 32-10 Campbell Soup Company Changes in Number of Shares (*Thousands of shares*)

	ISSUED	OUTSTANDING	IN TREASURY
Balance at July 29, 1990	271,245.4	258,538.0	12,707.4
Treasury stock purchased		(6,790.8)	6,790.8
Treasury stock issued under Management incentive and Stock option plans		2,260.4	(2,260.4)
Balance at July 28, 1991	271,245.4	254,007.6	17,237.8
Treasury stock purchased		(3,986.1)	3,986.1
Treasury stock issued under Management incentive and Stock option plans		1,146.7	(1,146.7)
Balance at August 2, 1992	271,245.4	251,168.2	20,077.2
Treasury stock purchased		**(1,104.5)**	**1,104.5**
Treasury stock issued under Management incentive and Stock option plans		**1,642.5**	**(1,642.5)**
Balance at August 1, 1993	**271,245.4**	**251,706.2**	**19,539.2**

Source: Campbell Soup Company, 1993 *Annual Report*.

EXHIBIT 32-11 Campbell Soup Company Notes to Consolidated Financial Statements (*Millions of dollars*)

	1993	1992	1991
Net sales			
United States	$4,743.6	$4,649.2	$4,495.6
Europe	1,050.2	1,042.6	1,149.1
Other countries	916.7	652.4	656.0
Adjustments and eliminations	(124.3)	(81.0)	(96.6)
Consolidated	$6,586.2	$6,263.2	$6,204.1
Earnings (loss) before taxes			
United States	$ 716.6	$ 809.6	$ 694.8
Europe	(170.4)	44.7	48.8
Other countries	99.4	69.6	55.0
	645.6	923.9	798.6
Unallocated corporate expenses	(52.0)	(38.0)	(41.0)
Interest, net	(73.8)	(86.6)	(90.2)
Consolidated	$ 519.8	$ 799.3	$ 667.4
Identifiable assets			
United States	$2,286.6	$2,802.4	$2,693.4
Europe	668.7	831.0	711.3
Other countries	1,542.2	720.4	744.3
Consolidated	$4,897.5	$4,353.8	$4,149.0

Source: Campbell Soup Company, 1993 *Annual Report*.

BORDEN—1994

Headquartered in Columbus, Ohio, Borden's (614-225-4000) net income for 1993 was a negative $630.7 million, down 73 percent from 1992. A. S. D'Amato, chairman and chief executive officer of Borden, provided his view of Borden in the company's 1992 *Annual Report:*

> My view of Borden operating results—and those since the fourth quarter of 1990 when we last reported improved earnings—can be expressed in two words: totally unacceptable. In my opinion, the reasons for Borden's lack of performance in recent years are fundamental and recurring. They require drastic remedy. The retailers who make up Borden's primary customer base have changed both in composition and operation. Borden's marketing has not. Today's retailers demand a highly-focused, integrated "one-company" approach. Yet, until recently, Borden operated eight sales and seven separate distribution organizations within the Company. In one instance, we had as many as 28 people representing various Borden brands calling on a single nationwide retailer.

Mr. D'Amato resigned in 1993. The new Borden President and Chief Executive Officer is Ervin R. Shames. The new Borden Chairman is Frank J. Tasco. Borden has three major operating divisions: North American Foods, International Foods, and Packaging and Industrial Products. Exhibit 33–1 presents a 1993 summary of the divisions' brands, strengths, and strategies. Exhibit 33–2 lists Borden's principal products by brand.

NORTH AMERICAN FOODS

The North American Foods division of Borden includes North American pasta and sauce, niche grocery products, and U.S. dairy operations. In 1993, these businesses incurred a loss in operating income of $2.3 million, on a sales decline of 12.1 percent to $2.67 billion.

Borden is the leader in a wide range of small-to-medium-sized grocery products that are among the best-known brands in the U.S. food industry—Cracker Jack candied popcorn, Eagle Brand sweetened condensed milk, ReaLemon lemon juice, Wyler's bouillon, and Snow's clam products to name just a few. Together, these products provide Borden with a major presence in North American supermarkets. Borden also is the U.S. foodservice industry's leading supplier of individual-serving products and a major supplier of bulk-size items. Overseas, Borden has a growing European grocery products business, including a joint interest in Spain's number one soup and bouillon producer.

Pasta and Sauce. Borden is the world's largest pasta company. Its flagship Creamette brand is America's best-selling pasta. Borden's Catelli brand leads in Canada; Adria is number one in Brazil; and the Albadoro and Monder brands in Italy are regional favorites. Borden accounts for nearly one-third of North American retail branded dry pasta dollar sales. Borden also is the only major North American pasta company with a full line of pasta sauces, led by Classico—the best-selling U.S. and Canadian premium pasta sauce.

Borden's U.S. and Canadian pasta and sauce sales declined in 1993. However, sales of Classico were up 12 percent in 1993. Classico sales were supported by television advertising and direct mail marketing in key markets. The program will be extended to additional markets in 1994. Classico results also benefitted from the introduction of a seventh flavor, di Sorrento with onion and garlic, and full-year sales of Classico di Parma four cheese sauce and Classico di Salerno with sweet peppers and onions.

EXHIBIT 33-1 Borden at a Glance

NORTH AMERICAN FOODS 1993 SALES: $2,672 MILLION

MAJOR BRANDS AND BUSINESSES	STRENGTHS	STRATEGIES
Pasta and Sauce • Creamette pasta sold across the United States • Catelli pasta and sauce in Canada • Regional U.S. and Canadian pasta brands including Prince, R•F, Anthony's, Gioia and Ronco • Classico premium pasta sauce • Aunt Millie's pasta sauce	• North American pasta leader participating in all market segments—dry branded, private label, foodservice, ingredient • Creamette and Catelli—both number one nationally • Leading regional brands • Only major pasta maker with a full line of sauces • Pasta quality edge • Classico—best-selling premium sauce in United States and Canada • Low-cost production base • Unmatched capacity, distribution	• Recover, expand volume through improved customer service • Improve efficiency, costs through better supply chain management • Strengthen brands with added marketing support, emphasizing quality • Leverage overall advantages in scale, capacity, cost, brand reach • Develop new products
Dairy • Borden, Meadow Gold, Viva and Lite Line milk, ice cream, frozen desserts, cultured products • Borden process cheese and Lite Line diet cheese products	• Strong consumer brand recognition • Dairy leader in many regional markets • Number one in sliced diet cheese domestically • Elsie the Cow—one of the most recognized food trademarks	• Recover lost volume through improved pricing and trade promotion policies • Reduce costs through improved distribution, better plant utilization, lower overhead • Develop new products. Further upgrade ice cream quality
Niche Grocery • Market basket of familiar food brands, including: –Cracker Jack popcorn and peanuts, –Eagle Brand sweetened condensed milk, –ReaLemon juice, –Wyler's bouillon and –Cremora non-dairy creamer	• Number one or strong number two positions in small to medium size grocery categories • Significant presence overall in U.S. supermarkets • Track record of good profits and returns • Opportunities for growth	• Increase advertising and other marketing support behind key products • Reposition products for new appeal, uses • Improve quality and value • Develop new products that offer added value to consumers

EXHIBIT 33-1 *Continued*

INTERNATIONAL FOODS 1993 SALES: $930 MILLION

MAJOR BRANDS AND BUSINESSES	STRENGTHS	STRATEGIES
European Bakery • Nur Hier, Nuschelberg, Stefansback, Lecker Backer, Kamps, and bakeries in Germany; Prima Pek in Hungary • Weber, Jaus and Golden Toast packaged baked goods and breads sold in supermarkets and other retail outlets across Germany	• Unmatched German retail network • Among the leaders in industrial/commercial baked goods • Largest hamburger bun supplier in Germany	• Expand German retail bakery network through internal growth, acquisitions, as well as German hamburger bun business through new plant • Expand further into Central Europe • Lower costs of industrial operation • Develop new products
International Dairy • KLIM milk powder • Dairy and cheese business in Latin America	• World's second-leading milk powder: Borden's most global brand • Well established in growing Pacific Rim and Latin American markets	• Expand recently launched varieties—KLIM Lite Line low fat and KLIM Super Kid and Growing Up specially fortified milk powders • Use joint venture plant in China to support growth in other areas of the Far East as well
European Grocery and Pasta • Joint interest in Spain's Gallina Blanca dry soup and bouillon business • Niche grocery products including ReaLemon juice across Europe and Cocio bottled chocolate drinks in Scandinavia • Monder dry-filled pasta and Albadoro regional pasta in Italy	• Market leadership in Spain in dry soup and bouillon; expanding positions in other nations • Strong positions in most niche markets • Leading European brand of dry-filled pasta	• Build soup and bouillon exports to Africa, Latin America and Asia • Add bouillon business in China via joint venture plant • Expand niche grocery brands to other European countries • Export Italian pasta beyond Europe to Asia and North America

PACKAGING AND INDUSTRIAL PRODUCTS
1993 SALES: $1,904 MILLION

Adhesives and Resins • High performance adhesives and industrial resins for home building, construction, foundry and industrial applications	• World leader in forest products adhesives; presence in most global markets • Major supplier of foundry and industrial resins	• Expand leadership position globally • Selectively expand to meet customer needs • Maintain technical leadership with value-added products

EXHIBIT 33-1 *Continued*

PACKAGING AND INDUSTRIAL PRODUCTS 1993 SALES (CONT.)

MAJOR BRANDS AND BUSINESSES	STRENGTHS	STRATEGIES
Decorative Products		
• The best-known consumer and commercial wallcovering brands including Wall-Tex, Sunworthy, Borden Home, Borges, and Crown	• World leader in wallcovering • Largest share of market in North America and United Kingdom • Strong position across all retail channels of trade	• Grow volume with new products such as coordinated home furnishings and licensed products (e.g. Disney) • Expand distribution with in-store merchandising via mass marketers and home centers • Continue cost reductions
Consumer Adhesives		
• Elmer's adhesives and home improvement products • Krazy Glue instant glues	• Top-selling consumer adhesives and instant glues with strong consumer brand recognition	• Grow sales volume for Elmer's and Krazy Glue adhesives with new products, increased consumer advertising
Plastic Film and Packaging		
• Resinite and Sealwrap vinyl foodwraps; Proponite food packaging; and Loadmaster, Resinex and Resinite palletwrap films	• U.S. leader in vinyl foodwraps • Good position in European and Far Eastern flexible packaging	• Improve profitability with cost reductions and operating efficiencies

Source: Borden *Annual Report,* 1993.

Albadoro S.p.A., one of Borden's two Italian pasta companies, posted higher sales and income in 1992, and increased plant capacity by 20 percent in 1993 to help meet the growing worldwide demand for high quality Italian pasta. Monder Aliment, S.p.A. in Italy, a leading marketer and exporter of dry filled pastas, added several new products in 1993 and achieved a record share of Italian sales.

Gallina Blanca, Borden's joint venture Spanish food company and a world leader in dry soups and bouillon, remained number one in Spain by offering several new varieties, including low sodium and children's soups. Gallina Blanca achieved record sales of Jumbo bouillon in key African markets and began bouillon production in China during 1993 through a joint venture.

Catelli Healthy Harvest pasta and sauces were introduced in 1993 in Canada. The line features whole wheat and other pastas with added fiber and protein, and pasta sauces that are low in fat and sodium.

Borden recently began operations at its St. Louis pasta hyperplant—North America's largest and one of the world's most advanced pasta plants. New pasta lines are being added at hyperplants in Phoenix, Arizona; Lowell, Massachusetts; and Warren, Michigan; and an expansion of a Montreal, Quebec, pasta and sauce hyper-

EXHIBIT 33-2   Principal Borden Products by Brand

NORTH AMERICAN FOODS

PASTA AND SAUCE	NICHE GROCERY	DAIRY

PASTA AND SAUCE

Classico pasta sauce
Creamette
Silver Award
Albadoro

Regional:
 Anthony's (Southern California, Arizona and Nevada)
Aunt Millie's spaghetti sauce (Northeast)
Bravo (western New York)
Dutch Maid (Northeast and North Central)
Gioia (western New York)
Globe A-1 (California)
Goodman's (Northeast and Miami)
Luxury (Gulf Coast)
Merlino's (Pacific Northwest)
Mrs. Grass (Chicago)
New Mill (Midwest)
Prince pasta and sauce (Northeast and North Central)
R•F (Midwest, Southwest and Colorado)
Red Cross (Midwest and Tennessee)
Ronco pasta and sauce (Southeast and Mid-South)
Vimco (Pennsylvania and Ohio)
Winsom (Midwest)

Canada:
Catelli pasta and sauce, Catelli Healthy Harvest pasta and sauce, Creamette, Lancia pasta and sauce, Romi, Splendor, Gattuso pasta and pasta/pizza sauce, Golden Wheat and Bravo sauce

Puerto Rico:
Criada pasta sauce

NICHE GROCERY

Bennett's sauces
Borden egg nog
Borden, Serv, Americana, Chatsworth and Pitch 'R' Pak individual portion control and bulk foodservice products
Campfire marshmallows
Cary's maple syrup
Coco Lopez cream of coconut and fruit drink mixes
Cracker Jack caramel and butter-toffee coated popcorn and peanuts
Cremora and Cremora Lite non-dairy creamer
Eagle Brand sweetened condensed milk
Kava acid neutralized instant coffee
MacDonald's maple syrup
Maple Orchards maple syrup
MBT broth
Meadow Gold sweetened condensed milk
Mrs. Grass soup and dip mixes
None Such mincemeat
ReaLemon lemon juice from concentrate and 100% pure refrigerated lemon juice
ReaLime lime juice from concentrate
Soup Starter, Stew Starter and Minestrone Starter dry soup mixes
Steero bouillon and broth products
Wyler's bouillon and broth products

Regional:
Borden, Gregg's and Re-Mi foodservice mayonnaise, salad dressings and soup bases (Midwest, Southeast and Southwest)

DAIRY

Borden whole, lowfat, reduced lactose, skim and chocolate milks and buttermilk, cottage cheese, sour cream, whipping cream and other creams, egg nog, orange juice and fruit drinks; Hi-Protein lowfat milk; Light sugar-free chocolate lowfat milk and nonfat yogurt; Lite Line protein-fortified skim milk, cottage cheese, sour cream and yogurt; Fat Free sour cream; and Thirstee Smash fruit drinks

Borden ice cream and frozen novelty bars, sandwiches and pops, frozen yogurt and yogurt pops; Eagle Brand ice cream; Fat Free frozen desserts; Lady Borden ice cream; Light ice milk; and Frostick, Mississippi Mud and Juice Stix frozen novelties

Borden process cheese products—regular, light and fat free, Lite Line cheese products and CheezTwo process cheese substitute

Fisher cheese substitute products, Sandwich-Mate slices and Ched-O-Mate, Pizza-Mate, Salad-Mate and Taco-Mate shredded products

Meadow Gold whole, lowfat, skim and chocolate milks and buttermilk, cottage cheese, sour cream, whipping cream and other creams, egg nog, orange juice and fruit drinks; Viva lowfat milks, protein-fortified skim milk, cottage cheese, sour cream and yogurt, sugar-free chocolate lowfat milk, nonfat yogurt and

EXHIBIT 33-2 *Continued*

NORTH AMERICAN FOODS		
PASTA AND SAUCE	**NICHE GROCERY**	**DAIRY**
	Country Store instant mashed potatoes (Midwest and Southwest)	cottage cheese; and Mountain High yogurt
	Dime Brand sweetened condensed milk (Southwest)	**Regional:** KLIM whole milk powder (New York)
	Laura Scudder's natural peanut butter (Mountain, Western and Texas)	**Puerto Rico:** Nevada and Carnaval ice
	Magnolia Brand sweetened condensed milk (New York and Miami)	
	Sippin Pak aseptic fruit drinks (Southeast and Southwest)	
	Star Brand sweetened condensed milk (New York)	
	Canada: Eagle Brand sweetened condensed milk, Cracker Jack caramel and butter-toffee coated popcorn, ReaLemon lemon juice from concentrate, and Milk Mate milk flavorings	
	Puerto Rico: Borden cheeses Coco Lopez cream of coconut and cream fruit drink mixes La Famosa juices and nectars	

Source: Borden *Annual Report*, 1993.

plant was completed. Borden recently closed two small pasta plants at Winnipeg, Manitoba, and Harahan, Louisiana.

To rectify Borden's problems in Pasta and Sauce, a new President and all new sales managers were hired in 1993. A new pasta marketing campaign was launched with television and radio advertising expenditures for Borden pasta brands reaching $8 million annually in 1994, up from $3 million in 1993.

Niche Grocery. Sales and net income of Borden's Niche Grocery operations declined in 1993 although several brands did well, such as Borden's Eagle Brand sweetened condensed milk, Cracker Jack candied popcorn, and Wyler's and Steero

Bouillon. Income was down in ReaLemon juice, Cremora and Cremora Lite non-dairy creamers, Mrs. Grass dry soups, Borden egg nog, Cracker Jack butter toffee, Cremora and Cremora Lite, and Borden's Snow's and Doxsee clam products.

Borden's cheese income was down in 1993 despite the national rollout of the Singleskeeper recyclable/recloseable package for Borden single-wrap cheese slices being completed. Outstanding consumer response to the Singleskeeper package helped Borden maintain its number two position in branded cheese. Borden Fat Free cheese slices in American, Sharp Cheddar and Swiss flavors are popular.

DAIRY

The Borden Dairy incurred a 1993 operating loss of about $25 million, while sales declined to about $1.1 billion. Dairy marketing was reorganized along product lines to provide tighter direction to the fluid milk business and to coordinate the marketing of higher margin ice cream, frozen desserts, and cultured products. A new president of Borden Dairy was hired in September 1993 and a number of new products were introduced, including Cracker Jack ice cream, Borden and Meadow Gold fat-free sour cream, Borden fat-free cheese slices, and Moooore Milk Singles.

The company's Borden, Meadow Gold, Viva, and Lite-Line brands are market leaders in fluid milk, ice cream and other frozen desserts, and cultured products, ranging from regular to lowfat to nonfat. Borden's fluid milk and cultured products businesses are concentrated in the South and West, while ice cream and frozen desserts are distributed across most of the nation. Borden also has dairy operations in Japan and Central America.

Sales of Borden's Lite-Line and Viva protein fortified skim milk have been increasing. A new regional distribution center in Houston, Texas, enables Borden to improve customer service. Sales of the company's Lady Borden premium ice cream have been expanded to the Midwest and Southeast. Increased advertising support and several new flavors have helped to boost Lady Borden ice cream sales. Borden recently launched its Fat Free frozen novelties in three flavors in key Midwest markets. Further expansion is planned for 1994.

Borden and Meadow Gold frozen yogurt and desserts are doing especially well in the Northeast and the Mid-Atlantic region. A major effort to revitalize Borden dairy brands is planned for 1993. The program includes national advertising and public relations campaigns. Packaging for all Borden dairy products has been redesigned to prominently feature an updated Elsie the Cow and a new, bolder Borden trademark. New dairy television commercials featuring an animated Elsie the Cow are appearing.

INTERNATIONAL FOODS

The International Foods division of Borden includes European bakery products, international milk powder, Latin American dairy, and European grocery and pasta products. This division's 1993 sales and net income declined 2.3 percent and 29.9 percent, respectively, to $930 million and $67.3 million. Borden is moving selectively elsewhere overseas—building on existing strengths and longstanding brand franchises, such as KLIM skim milk powder. KLIM International Milk Powder is the world's number-two-selling brand of milk powder. The KLIM brand was instrumental in getting Borden started overseas in the 1920s and is now Borden's most global brand. Sold in over 85 countries, KLIM is among the world's most popular brands of milk powder. Borden is building on KLIM brand strengths through line extensions that take advantage of improved living standards and increased consumer sophistication in many of its markets and by adding to the list of countries where KLIM milk powder is sold.

The first KLIM line extension was KLIM Lite-Line lowfat milk powder launched in 1991. KLIM Lite-Line initially was sold in the Far East, where it quickly became the best-selling brand of lowfat milk powder and is now expanding into the Middle East and Central America.

KLIM Super Kid, a specially fortified whole milk powder for children from the ages of three to seven, followed in 1992 and has done well in its Far Eastern introductory markets. Borden is expanding its presence in China. The company has acquired a joint interest in a Chinese milk powder plant and is doubling its size to produce KLIM brand milk powder.

Borden's KLIM milk powder posted even sales and net income in 1993 compared to 1992. KLIM Lite-Line lowfat milk powder was successful in several Far Eastern markets and in the Middle East and Central America. In its Far Eastern markets, KLIM Lite-Line is the best-selling brand of lowfat milk powder. KLIM Super Kid specially fortified whole milk powder for children three to seven was successful in Taiwan, Hong Kong, Singapore, and Malaysia.

Borden is trying to revitalize Lady Borden ice cream in Japan with more contemporary packaging, new flavors, a new convenience store line, consumer promotions, and increased advertising support. A reformulated Lady Borden Classic premium ice cream has regained much of the distribution in Japan that it had lost after the end of a local licensing agreement in 1991. Borden's Lady Borden Home Made ice cream is being repositioned for maximum appeal to youthful Japanese consumers of superpremium ice cream. A state-of-the art process cheese plant was completed at Nagano, Japan, in June. The plant produces Borden brand sliced cheese in the Singleskeeper package, cheese snacks, shredded natural cheese, and cheese powder for distribution across Japan.

EUROPEAN BAKERY PRODUCTS

Borden is Germany's largest producer and retailer of bakery products, primarily sweet snacks and specialty breads. Borden bought the 17-store Klems bakery in Wuppertal, near Dusseldorf, and the Zo-store Heede chain near Kassel in 1993. In total, Borden operates over 400 retail bakery outlets across Germany.

In Europe, Borden is focusing on promising growth opportunities in sweet snacks. The Company exited from the highly competitive salty snacks category in 1992 with the sale of its U.K. and Spanish units. Sales in Borden's European sweet snacks business have doubled since 1987 and are expected to grow to $600 million annually by 1996. Borden is already a leader in German sweet snacks and is rapidly expanding its presence elsewhere in Central Europe.

The flagship Wilhein Weber GmbH sweet snacks unit is one of Germany's largest commercial bakers, selling packaged products under the Weber, Jaus, and Golden Toast brand names through supermarkets and other retail outlets across the country. Weber manages six German regional bakery chains nationwide and has a joint interest in retail bakeries in Hungary. Borden's European Bakery Products had high sales and net income in 1993.

A sixth retail German bakery chain was acquired in October 1992. Kamps GmbH operates a chain of 23 retail outlets serving the Dusseldorf area. Kamps is being expanded into the nearby cities of Cologne, Duisburg, Essen, and Dortmund. Borden's sales are increasing.

In eastern Germany with the addition of delivery routes for packaged baked goods and growth of the Lecker Backer and Nur Hier retail chains, more outlets are planned for 1994.

Borden's joint venture in Hungary operates five retail stores in Budapest.

PACKAGING AND INDUSTRIAL PRODUCTS/DOMESTIC AND INTERNATIONAL

Borden's packaging and industrial products division has primary responsibility for non-food consumer products, films, resin, adhesives, and includes pasta in Brazil. Sales were up 1.3 percent in 1993 to $1.90 billion, but operating income declined 15.0 percent to $167.7 million. The division's results benefitted from sales and income gains in forest products adhesives and industrial resins, Latin American operations, worldwide wallcoverings, and consumer adhesives. These gains were offset primarily by declines in North American plastic films and packaging. Exhibits 33–3 and 33–4 present products and financials for three years for this division in context with the combined foods divisions.

Consumer Adhesives. Sales and income of Borden's consumer adhesives held steady in 1993 after posting slight gains in 1992. School Glue Gel was added to the Elmer's line of consumer adhesives complementing its popular Glue-All and original School Glue. Results in Krazy Glue instant glues and Accent craft paints declined. Borden's Latin America resin and plastic film sales and income improved. A resin plant in Cubatao, Brazil closed, 1993 as did a Borden pasta plant in Porte Alegre, Brazil. In pasta, Adria remains Brazil's best-selling national brand.

Borden's forest products adhesives, industrial resins, and specialty adhesives were recently consolidated into a single worldwide operation. Borden developed several new forest products adhesives, including low-formaldehyde-emitting resins, and faster-curing and moisture-tolerant phenolic resins. New resin technology also was developed for electronics, advanced composite materials, and high-speed lithography. Borden completed a 50 percent increase in phenolic resin capacity at Louisville, Kentucky, as well as forest products adhesives expansions at Edmonton, Alberta; Springfield, Oregon; and Sheboygan, Wisconsin.

Further expansions are planned at Peterlee in the United Kingdom and at Sarawak in Malaysia. Recent acquisitions in the United Kingdom complemented Borden's position as the leading European supplier of advanced foundry resins and included new technology for an advanced binder system. Borden's forest products adhesives operations in Australia, Malaysia, and the Philippines also posted higher sales and income. Sales and income in Far Eastern films and plastic packaging were up slightly, with expanded film sales throughout the Pacific Rim.

Borden is the world leader in forest products adhesives (used in making plywood, particle board, and other wood products) and pioneered industrial adhesives more than 60 years ago. The company ranks number one in U.S. vinyl food wrap films and is a leader in many of its European and Far Eastern plastic packaging businesses. Borden also has strong positions in foundry and other industrial resins, high-technological coatings, printing inks, and specialty adhesives.

EXHIBIT 33-3

Borden International Foods, and Packaging and Industrial Products

Pasta and Sauce
  Brazil—Adria, Italianissimo, OA, Paty, Raineri, Soltinho and Romanini
  Italy—Albadoro and Monder
  Panama—Imperial Roma and Napoli

European Bakery
  Germany—Weber, Jaus, Kamps, Klems, Klemme, Nur Hier, Nuschelberg, Stefansback, Wriedeler, Lecker Backer, Heede and Golden Toast baked goods and specialty breads
  Hungary—Prima Pek baked goods and specialty breads

Niche Grocery
  Belgium—ReaLemon lemon juice from concentrate, Hemo chocolate drink, Lemaitre chocolate truffles and Vrancaert truffles
  Colombia—Cremora non-dairy creamer
  Denmark—Cocio and Congo bottled chocolate milk, Chocola chocolate drink and Chocolet lowfat chocolate milk
  Spain—Gallina Blanca dry soup mixes, Hoy Menu side dishes and Avecrem bouillon (exported to Middle East and Africa as Jumbo dry soup mixes and bouillon), Salsas ala Carta instant sauce and Sopas Hechas aseptic soups
  Sweden and Norway—Cocio chocolate milk

Dairy
  Worlwide export—KLIM whole, KLIM Line lowfat, KLIM Superkid and KLIM Growing Up milk powders
  Bahamas and Costa Rica—Milk, ice cream and other dairy products, KLIM whole milk powder
  Colombia—KLIM, El Rodeo, Rosemary and Chicolac, whole and active skim milk powders and Borden cheeses
  Panama—KLIM whole milk powder and Borden ice cream, frozen yogurt, cheeses, juices and nectars

Non-Food Consumer
  Decorative Products—Birge, Borden Home Wallcoverings, Borderlines, Borges, Crown, Fashion House, Foremost, Guard, James Seeman Studios, Mitchell Designs, Satinesque, ShandKydd, Storeys, Sun-Tex, Sunwall 54, Sunwall 27, Sunworthy, Trillium and Wall-Tex wallcoverings
  Elmer's household, carpenter's and specialty glues, cements, building adhesives, caulking compounds and sealants, Weather-Tite wood glues and fillers, Fill'N Finish wood filler, GluColors decorative glues, Slide-All lubricant, Squeez N Caulk caulks, Stix-All adhesive and Wonder Bond adhesive
  Krazy Glue instant glues and Aron Alpha industrial adhesives
  Accent, Country Colors and Hobby Craft artist/craft brush-on paints

International:
  Argentina—Cascola, Cascamite and Casco 1002PVA glues, Cascotac contact cement, Rolofreeze, Rolopac, Rolopaper and Rolumino household wraps and Prontoflame fire starter
  Brazil—Adezite sealant putty and specialty vinyl tapes, Cascola, Cascolar, Cascofix, Cascamite, Cascorez, Cascophen and Cola Madeira glues, Cascolor color school glue, Cascor vinyl and acrylic paints, Cascolax floor coatings, Durepoxi epoxy putty, Flexite silicone sealant, Rolopac film and Krazy Glue instant glues
  Canada—Sunworthy wallcoverings, Elmer's household, carpenter's and specialty glues and other products and Krazy Glue instant glues
  Columbia—EGA glues and adhesives, Rally car care products, Al Greco paints and coatings, Chinola shoe and leather care products, Efro, Alpino and Relussiente floor waxes and cleaners, Durepoxi epoxy putty and Chris air freshener
  Ecuador—Elmer's, Blancola, Cascotack, EGA, Parcola and Economicola glues and adhesives, Turbo Rally car care products, Rolopac, Rolopaper, Rolominio and Rolofreeze household wraps. Polo-Shoe leather care products. Poliflex, American Wax and Poligloss household waxes, Clean-All floor cleaners and Durepoxi and Rally epoxy putties

EXHIBIT 33-3 *Continued*

BORDEN INTERNATIONAL FOODS, AND PACKAGING AND INDUSTRIAL PRODUCTS

France—Heller plastic model kits
Germany—Borges wallcoverings
Philippines—Elmer's glues and
adhesives
United Kingdom—Crown and
Storeys wallcoverings,
Humbrol paints and adhesives
and Airfix model kits
Uruguay—Cascola and Cascolax
glues, Cascola contact cement
and Rolopac household wrap

Films and Adhesives
ALpHASET, Betaset and other
foundry resins and refractory
coatings
Astromel, Astrolube, Acat and
other melamine resins and
saturating products
Broadcast banner fabric
Casco, Cascophen, Cascoset and
other forest products
adhesives

Cascamid, Cascolok, Cascote
and other wet strength paper
resins
CILC N KOTE and
Hydrosperse printing inks
LUV and other industrial
coatings and resins
Loadmaster, Resinex and
Resinite palletwrap
films
Ovenex food trays
Proponite and OPPtimum
packaging films
Resinite and Sealwrap foodwrap
films

International:
Film Products—Belgium, France,
Italy, Netherlands, Spain and
United Kingdom; Canada;
Argentina, Brazil, Colombia,
Ecuador and Uruguay;
Australia, Japan, New Zealand
and Taiwan

Forest products adhesives—
France, Spain and United
Kingdom; Canada; Argentina,
Brazil, Colombia, Ecuador
and Uruguay; Australia,
Malaysia and Philippines
Foundry resins—France, Spain
and United Kingdom;
Argentina, Brazil and
Colombia; Australia, Japan,
Malaysia and Philippines
Rigid plastic packaging—France,
Italy, Netherlands and United
Kingdom
Specialty adhesives—France and
United Kingdom; Argentina,
Brazil, Colombia, Ecuador
and Uruguay; Australia,
Malaysia and Philippines

Source: Borden *Annual Report,* 1993.

Worldwide Decorative Products. Borden is the world's largest wallcovering company. Sales held even and net income was slightly higher in 1993. Its Wall-Tex, Sunworthy, Borden Home, Borges, and Crown brands are the best-known wallcoverings in North America and the United Kingdom and hold a strong position in Germany. Borden's business also includes laminated decorative overlays used for interiors and furniture manufacture. Its Elmer's and Krazy Glue brands are favorites among consumers in household adhesives, home improvement products, and instant glue.

Borden wallcoverings improved despite an industrywide slowdown in residential and commercial wallcoverings sales. Particularly strong gains were posted in Borden commercial wallcoverings. A Guard line of environmentally friendly commercial wallcoverings was recently introduced, supported by trade advertising. Borden increased its offerings in the highly profitable coordinated home wallcoverings/bedding ensemble segment of the home fashions market. A new line of licensed Disney character wallcoverings, borders, and wall murals was introduced in 1993, as were Borderlines and Paintable Impressions.

EXHIBIT 33-4 Borden Three-Year Comparison of Division Sales and Operating Income (Dollars in millions)

Year Ended December 31,	1993		1992		1991	
Division Sales						
North American Foods	$2,671.5	48%	$3,039.0	52%	$3,085.9	52%
International Foods	930.4	17	951.9	16	967.0	16
Packaging and Industrial Products	1,904.4	35	1,880.8	32	1,871.2	32
Total	$5,506.3	100%	$5,871.7	100%	$5,924.1	100%
Division Operating Income (Loss)						
North American Foods	$(24.4)	(12)%	$49.8	21%	$337.3	55%
International Foods	51.0	26	41.8	18	90.5	15
Packaging and Industrial Products	167.7	86	142.4	61	186.9	30
Total	194.3	100%	234.0	100%	614.7	100%
Discontinued operations, net of tax	(555.8)		(85.9)		15.0	
Other income and expense not allocable to divisions and income taxes	(269.2)		(512.5)		(334.8)	
Net income (loss)	$(630.7)		$(364.4)		$294.9	

Source: Borden *Annual Report,* 1993.

Plastic Film and Packaging. Results in Borden's North American Plastic Film and Packaging operations were hurt in 1993 by higher raw material costs and strong price competition in all major products. Income in European plastic films and packaging were down due to a sluggish European economy. Dollar sales of Resinite and Sealwrap vinyl foodwrap films were up in 1993 due to higher product pricing and increased demand industrywide. Sales of Loadmaster palletwrap film outperformed industry growth by nearly two to one.

Borden has become the exclusive North American marketer of advanced oriented polypropylene (OPP) films from Moplefan, S.p.A., a leader in European high-technology films. Marketed under the OPPticoat and OPPtiwrap trademarks, the new films are used principally in food packaging and complement Borden's existing line of Proponite OPP films. LUV high technology coatings posted weak sales and income in 1993, benefitting from a growing demand in the United States, Canada, and Europe for Borden's patented fiber-optic coatings.

MANAGEMENT

Borden is a good corporate citizen in protecting the environment and has adopted the Borden Principles of Environmental Responsibility and the Borden Principles of Social Responsibility. Reinforcing these principles are companywide policies and programs regarding fair employment practices, minority purchasing, charitable contributions, environmental protection, and product packaging.

Borden has Equal Employment Opportunity (EEO) programs in place at every U.S. location, with the goal of full representation of qualified minorities and women among the Borden workforce. The result is a diverse domestic workforce in which minorities represent 24 percent of the total, well above the 18-percent national average.

Borden established a pioneering minority purchasing program more than 20 years ago, and it has continued a leadership role by making certain that minority suppliers have opportunities to win business from Borden. In 1993, Borden purchased goods and services totaling $78 million from minority suppliers and made tax payments totaling $51 million through minority-owned banks.

Borden's tradition of caring about people who are less fortunate and in need dates back to Gail Borden. His great concern for people—in particular children who needed a source of pure milk—led him to invent condensed milk and then to found The Borden Company more than 135 years ago. That legacy continues today through the Borden Foundation, which serves as the company's principal conduit for charitable contributions. Among the Foundation's most important efforts is its five-year-old Ten Cities Program with the National Urban League, which allocates special grants to League chapters to enhance the lives of children in their communities. Programs have been conducted so far in 17 Urban League chapters.

Borden devotes considerable resources to meet its environmental responsibilities. It has companywide programs to reduce waste, minimize pollution, and protect the environment. Several Borden plants were recognized in 1993 for outstanding efforts. For example, the state of California recently paid tribute to Borden's forest products adhesives plant at Fremont for cutting its water use in half over a five-year period, even as it expanded production. Other forest products adhesives plants have dramatically reduced waste and have achieved zero discharge of hazardous liquid waste.

Borden's Dallas, Texas, dairy was honored for its perfect wastewater compliance record. Borden's wallcoverings plant in Columbus, Ohio recycles over 4 million pounds of scrap vinyl and corrugated cardboard annually.

Recognizing the growing concern over solid waste, Borden has established a corporatewide product packaging policy. Borden pledges to use packaging that meets environmental concerns while maintaining product quality and safety. Borden has reduced the thickness of packaging materials, used lighter weight materials, and eliminated unnecessary packaging. These include lighter weight containers for Cremora and Cremora Lite nondairy creamers, ReaLemon juice, Eagle Brand sweetened condensed milk, and thinner plastic films for individually wrapped cheese slices and packaged pastas.

Borden uses 100 percent recycled fiberboard for nearly all of its domestic pasta boxes and an increasing amount of recycled content glass, steel, and aluminum in its packaging. New containers are marked with industry symbols to remind and encourage consumers to recycle. Corrugated cartons and shippers used by Borden are made from recycled materials, while shipping boxes from Borden Snacks are reused on average between five and six times. Currently under evaluation is the use of 100-percent recycled polyethylene terephthlate (PET) resin for the Borden Singleskeeper cheese container.

MARKETING

Borden traditionally has gone to market as a group of separate and distinct businesses—without coordinating its efforts to common customers. At a time when many major food retailers are moving rapidly to centralized buying, Borden has had eight separate sales organizations, seven distribution operations, and five distinct information systems in North America alone.

The leading national retail chains want to deal with Borden as one company rather than as a set of separate businesses. This requires Borden to take an integrated approach to sales, marketing, and distribution, and pull together all of its efforts as one company. Borden initiated this new strategy in 1992 when a large retail customer asked to coordinate through one Borden person rather than deal with 28 people as it had in the past. A companywide team was formed to serve this huge national retailer as a single strategic supplier. The result was a substantial increase in overall sales of Borden products, including significant new business. Exhibits 33–5 and 33–6 provide the figures in consolidated statements of income and balance sheets.

Borden will benefit from taking a one-company approach in advertising and promotion, distribution, purchasing, and information management. In advertising and promotion, Borden is consolidating its spending in fewer agencies and firms, and negotiating new arrangements in the way it buys and produces media advertising and sales promotion materials. Until recently, Borden worked with 19 separate advertising agencies and more than 100 sales promotion firms in North America alone. As a bigger client to fewer firms, Borden will receive superior creative work and better marketing support.

In distribution, Borden is moving to integrate its seven separate operations into a single system. The company is consolidating such functions as customer service, accounts receivable, and invoicing. Borden has begun to consolidate warehouse delivery systems for all dry grocery products, including pasta and foodservice, and to establish a one-company management of systems, backhaul, transportation, and warehousing for all Borden operations.

Information management is a crucial element in Borden's one-company approach to sales and marketing. Borden will replace information systems unique to each business with an integrated Borden system. The new system will meet the growing demand for comprehensive sales information on all Borden products and yet provide flexibility to meet the special needs of each business.

Borden is rebuilding the equity in its three biggest, most underutilized assets: the Borden name, the Borden slogan, and Elsie the Cow. Recent research shows that the Borden name has outstanding recognition nationwide. Virtually all consumers sampled nationally recognize the name. The Borden slogan—"If it's Borden–it's got to be good"—continues to represent quality and trust to millions of American consumers. More than seven of every 10 people in a national sample were aware of the slogan. And, despite years of underuse, Borden's 56-year-old Elsie the Cow trademark is still recognized by more than one of every two American adults.

In the past, Borden's approach to its businesses provided little reason to capitalize on the Borden name, slogan, and Elsie. As a result, Borden missed enormous opportunities to reach younger consumers with these still powerful marketing tools. Major new initiatives are underway to put all three back to work behind groups of products. New television advertising will carry the Borden slogan and display a family of Borden products. The Borden name also is being extended beyond dairy, starting with a new Borden snacks line.

Elsie herself has had a makeover, giving her a softer, more contemporary look. She is the focus of an umbrella marketing campaign that began in March 1993 for a full range of Borden dairy products—milk, cheese, ice cream, cultured products, and Eagle Brand sweetened condensed milk. The campaign includes a mix of new advertising, packaging, and public relations, highlighted by Elsie's first national television appearances since the 1970s. The television commercials feature an animated Elsie, husband Elmer, and kids Beauregard ("Beau") and Beulah ("Bea"). They focus on the quality of Borden dairy products and link each product to fresh, wholesome Borden milk.

EXHIBIT 33-5 Borden Business Segments (*In millions*)

YEAR ENDED DECEMBER 31,		1993[a]	1992[b]	1991[c]
Net Sales	Foods	$3,673.8	$4,055.5	$4,119.5
	Non-food consumer and industrial	1,832.5	1,816.2	1,804.6
	Total	$5,506.3	$5,871.7	$5,924.1
Operating Profit	Foods	$ 22.7	$ 92.4	$ 428.8
	Non-food consumer and industrial	171.6	141.6	185.9
	Total segments	194.3	234.0	614 7
	General corporate expense, net	(153.3)	(141.9)	(16.5)
	Interest expense	(125.1)	(116.6)	(167.0)
	Pretax (loss) income from continuing operations	$ (84.1)	$ (24.5)	$ 431.2
Identifiable Assets	Foods	$2,085.6	$3,496.9	$3,689.5
	Non-food consumer and industrial	1,114.3	1,395.4	1,438.1
	Total segments	3,199.9	4,892.3	5,127.6
	Discontinued operations	222.2		
	Corporate assets	449.6	353.7	333.7
	Total	$3,871.7	$5,246.0	$5,461.3
Depreciation and Amortization	Foods	$ 163.7	$ 165.7	$ 157.2
	Non-food consumer and industrial	48.7	49.8	46.2
Capital Expenditures	Foods	$ 102.3	$ 202.9	$ 303.4
	Non-food consumer and industrial	59.1	74.6	66.0
Geographic Information Net sales	United States	$3,620.9	$3,928.7	$3,903.2
	Europe	914.8	979.2	1,083.2
	Other	970.6	963.8	937.7
	Total	$5,506.3	$5,871.7	$5,924.1
Operating profit	United States	$ 82.7	$ 155.1	$ 421.4
	Europe	73.7	54.4	92.1
	Other	37.9	24.5	101.2
	Total	$ 194.3	$ 234.0	$614.7
Identifiable assets	United States	$2,408.0	$3,534.4	$3,602.6
	Europe	695.2	858.0	1,027.4
	Other	546.3	853.6	831.3
	Discontinued Operations	222.2		
	Total	$3,871.7	$5,246.0	$5,461.3

[a]The $38.4 restructuring and other charges to segment operating profit in 1993 is allocated as follows: $38.4 for the foods segment; and $22.1 for U.S. operations, and $16.3 for other foreign operations. The remainder of the restructuring charge not allocable to operating profit: $76.5 is included in general corporate expense.

[b]The $270.7 restructuring charge to segment operating profit in 1992 is allocated as follows: $215.7 for the foods segment and $55.0 for the non-food consumer and industrial segment; and $165.9 for U.S. operations, $38.1 for European operations and $66.7 for other foreign operations. The remainder of the restructuring charge not allocable to operating profit: $27.1 is included in general corporate expense and $79.4 is related to discontinued operations.

[c]The $61.2 restructuring charge to segment operating profit in 1991 is allocated as follows: $48.7 for the foods segment and $12.5 for the non-food consumer and industrial segment; and $34.5 for U.S. operations, $7.4 for European operations and $19.3 for other foreign operations. The remainder of the restructuring charge not allocable to operating profit: $6.0 is included in general corporate expense and $4.4 is related to discontinued operations.

Source: Borden *Annual Report,* 1993.

EXHIBIT 33-6   Borden Consolidated Statements of Income (*In millions except per share data*)

YEAR ENDED DECEMBER 31,	1993	1992	1991
Revenue			
Net sales	$5,506.3	$5,871.7	$5,924.1
Costs and Expenses			
Cost of goods sold	4,078.6	4,301.9	4,268.5
Marketing, general and			
administrative expenses	1,223.7	1,163.6	1,023.9
Restructuring charges	114.9	297.8	67.2
Interest expense	125.1	116.6	167.0
Equity in income of affiliates	(16.0)	(19.4)	(24.0)
Minority interest	40.7	39.7	2.8
Other (income) and expense, net	23.4	(4.0)	(12.5)
Income taxes	(27.2)	14.2	151.3
	5,563.2	5,910.4	5,644.2
Earnings			
(Loss) income from continuing operations	(56.9)	(38.7)	279.9
Discontinued operations:			
(Loss) income from operations	(65.8)	(85.9)	15.0
Loss on disposal	(490.0)		
(Loss) income before extraordinary item and			
cumulative effect of accounting changes	(612.7)	(124.6)	294.9
Extraordinary loss on early retirement			
of debt		(10.8)	
Cumulative effect of change in accounting for:			
Postemploymet benefits	(18.0)		
Postretirement benefits other than pensions		(189.0)	
Income taxes		(40.0)	
Net (loss) income	$ (630.7)	$ (364.4)	$ 294.9
Share Data			
(Loss) income from continuing operations	$ (.40)	$ (.27)	$ 1.90
Discontinued operations:			
(Loss) income from operations	(.47)	(.60)	.10
Loss on disposal	(3.47)		
(Loss) income before extraordinary item and			
cumulative effect of accounting changes	(4.34)	(.87)	2.00
Extraordinary loss on early retirement			
of debt		(.07)	
Cumulative effect of change in accounting for:			
Postemployment benefits	(.13)		
Postretirement benefits other than pensions		(1.32)	
Income taxes		(.28)	
Net (loss) income per common share	$ (4.47)	$ (2.54)	$ 2.00
Cash dividends paid per common share	$ 0.90	$ 1.185	$ 1.12
Average number of common shares			
outstanding during the period	141.0	143.4	147.6

Source: Borden *Annual Report,* 1993.

Borden also will present its dairy products in more contemporary packaging with a unified Borden look. The packaging prominently features Elsie, makes dramatic use of color, and provides a clean, modern, and appetizing look that ties the entire line together. To complement the new advertising and packaging, Borden is gearing up a full-scale national public relations campaign. It will help to re-establish Borden as a flagship brand and to turn a new, younger generation of consumers into loyal Borden customers.

THE BORDEN FUTURE

In Borden's 1993 *Annual Report,* Ervin R. Shames reveals his 1994 plans for Borden as follows:

- We plan to divest 20 percent of Borden's 1993 revenue base, including North American snacks, seafood, jams and jellies, and several other businesses.
- We plan to strengthen dairy and packaging and industrial products and pasta.
- We plan to enlarge our marketing budget, and reduce our costs by $85 million.

EXHIBIT 33-7 Borden Consolidated Balance Sheets (*In millions except share and per share data*)

DECEMBER 31,	1993	1992
ASSETS		
Current Assets		
Cash and equivalents	$ 100.3	$ 186.0
Accounts receivable (less allowance for doubtful accounts of $8.9 and $10.3, respectively)	334.7	889.6
Inventories:		
Finished and in process goods	319.4	400.9
Raw materials and supplies	171.0	240.2
Other current assets	142.6	210.8
Net assets of discontinued operations	222.2	
	1,290.2	1,927.5
Investments and Other Assets		
Investments in and advances to affiliated companies	91.3	96.1
Deferred income taxes	225.4	
Other assets	126.6	255.8
	443.3	351.9
Property and Equipment		
Land	105.5	125.6
Buildings	609.6	815.5
Machinery and equipment	1,949.3	2,389.5
	2,664.4	3,330.6
Less accumulated depreciation	(1,327.7)	(1,542.5)
	1,336.7	1,788.1
Intangibles		
Intangibles resulting from business acquisitions (net of accumulated amortization of $189.8 and $222.9, respectively)	801.5	1,178.5
	$3,871.7	$5,246.0
LIABILITIES AND SHAREHOLDERS' EQUITY		
Current Liabilities		
Debt payable within one year	$410.6	$706.6
Accounts and drafts payable	433.3	589.7
Restructuring reserve	145.9	139.4
Income taxes	56.5	55.1
Other current liabilities	325.2	317.0
	1,371.5	1,807.8
Other		
Long-term debt	1,240.8	1,329.9
Deferred income taxes	47.1	66.8
Non-pension postemployment benefit obligations	353.8	317.7
Other long-term liabilities	103.8	79.3
Minority interest	508.8	518.2
	2,254.3	2,311.9
Shareholders' Equity		
Common stock—$0.625 par value		
Authorized 480,000,000 shares		
Issued 194,983,374 shares	121.9	121.9
Paid-in capital	88.1	83.0
Accumulated translation adjustment	(171.1)	(128.3)
Minimum pension liability	(95.5)	(3.2)
Retained earnings	835.1	1,592.5
	778.5	1,665.9

EXHIBIT 33-7 *Continued*

DECEMBER 31,	1993	1992
Less common stock in treasury (at cost)—53,625,339 shares and 54,342,642 shares, respectively	(532.6)	(539.6)
	245.9	1,126.3
	$3,871.7	$5,246.0

EXHIBIT 33-8 Borden Officers

Frank J. Tasco
  Chairman
Ervin R. Shames
  President and Chief Executive
  Officer

**Corporate Executive Vice
President**
Joseph M. Saggese
  President, Packaging and
  Industrial Products Division
  Domestic and International

Corporate Senior Vice President
Allan L. Miller
  Chief Administrative Officer

Corporate Vice Presidents
Judy Barker
  Social Responsibility
  President, The Borden
  Foundation
W. Bailey Barton
  Health, Safety and Environment
Karen L. Johnson
  Consumer Affairs
Randy D. Kautto
  Human Resources
David A. Kelly
  Treasurer
Philip J. Keuper

Pulic Affairs
George P. Morris
  Chief Strategic Officer
  Vice President, Finance
  North American and
  International Foods
Francis J. Proto
  General Auditor
Eugene N. Skiest
  Science and Technology
Charles N. Timperman
  Corporate Development
George J. Waydo

Operating Executives
North American Foods:
Robert W. Allen
  Senior Group Vice President-
  President, Dairy Products
Peter C. Cline
  Group Vice President,
  North American Snacks
John F. Dix
  Group Vice President,
  Niche Grocery Products
  Vice President, Shared Sales
Craig G. Hammond
  Vice President, Operations

Ronald C. Kesselman
  Group Vice President,
  Foodservice and Seafood
  Products
  Vice President,
  Sales and Marketing Services
Russell S. Mentzer
  Vice President-President,
  North American Pasta Products

International Foods:
Dan O'Riordan
  Senior Group Vice President-
  President,
  International Foods
Ole Norgaard
  Group Vice President,
  Dairy International

**Packaging and Industrial
Products Division
Domestic and International**
Sumner S. Feinstein
  Group Vice President,
  Worldwide Decorative Products
Jerold J. Golner
  Group Vice President,
  North American Plastic
  Operations
Robert G. Jenkins
  Group Vice President,
  Worldwide Resins

EXHIBIT 33-9 Borden Consolidated Statements of Cash Flows (*In millions except per share data*)

	YEAR ENDING DECEMBER 31,	1993	1992	1991
Cash Flows From Operating Activities	Net (loss) income	$(630.7)	$(364.4)	$294.9
	Adjustments to reconcile net income to net cash from operating activities:			
	Depreciation and amortization	224.0	227.6	216.9
	Loss on disposal of discontinued operations	637.4		
	Change in accounting estimates	94.1		
	Restructuring	52.5		
	Non-pension postemployment benefit obligation	36.1	316.5 317.7	(65.0)
	Net changes in assets and liabilities:			
	Trade receivables	47.8	(30.3)	19.9
	Inventories	21.2	1.0	7.6
	Trade payables	(0.5)	(4.4)	(15.1)
	Current and deferred taxes	(242.4)	(175.3)	63.4
	Other assets	(34.2)	(9.6)	(99.0)
	Other, net	(132.9)	14.1	(74.8)
	Discontinued operations	79.9		
		152.3	292.9	348.8
Cash Flows From Investing Activities	Capital expenditures	(177.0)	(286.2)	(376.0)
	Divestiture of businesses	53.4	123.0	94.1
	Purchase of businesses	(9.5)	(20.1)	(29.5)
		(133.1)	(183.3)	(311.4)

EXHIBIT 33-9 *Continued*

YEAR ENDING DECEMBER 31,		1993	1992	1991
Cash Flows From	(Decrease) increase in short-term debt	(536.2)	255.5	(310.4)
Financing Activities	Reduction in long-term debt	(128.7)	(266.1)	(244.2)
	Minority interest			500.0
	Long-term debt financing	274.6	45.2	223.1
	Sale of receivables	400.0		
	Dividends paid	(126.7)	(170.4)	(165.0)
	Issuance of stock under stock options and benefits and awards plans	12.1	3.9	7.2
	Acquisition of treasury stock			(1.6)
		(104.9)	(131.9)	9.1
	(Decrease) increase in cash and equivalents	(85.7)	(22.3)	46.5
	Cash and equivalents at beginning of year	186.0	208.3	161.8
	Cash and equivalents at end of year	$100.3	$186.0	$208.3
Supplemental Disclosures of	Interest paid	$133.3	$130.4	$177.5
Cash Flow Information	Taxes paid	20.5	67.1	102.6

Source: Borden *Annual Report*, 1993.

PILGRIM'S PRIDE—1994

C A S E

34

JAMES L. HARBIN
East Texas State
University—Texarkana

"Sell it or smell it" is the unbending maxim that everyone in the chicken business faces. Because a chicken cannot be stopped from laying or growing, all producers, both literally and figuratively, live or die by the laws of supply and demand.

Headquartered in Pittsburg, Texas, Pilgrim's Pride (903-855-1000) is one of fifty survivors out of approximately 4,000-plus firms in existence a few decades ago. Lonnie "Bo" Pilgrim, one of seven children raised during the Great Depression, has taken his concern from a small-farm supply store forty years ago, to one producing over $888 million in 1993 sales. Currently, Pilgrim's is the fifth largest producer of poultry products and the 22nd largest egg producer in the United States. They produce more that 1.1 billion pounds of dressed poultry and 41 million dozen table eggs, annually, and employ more that 10,000 employees. Net income for 1993 was a record $21 million, up from a $29 million loss in 1992.

This remarkable growth has taken place in a commodity industry about which, every year for the past fifty years, economists have been predicting doom and gloom. Citing industry sales as an indicator, experts have also deduced that the chicken industry has finally matured. The big question facing Pilgrim's today is: can it continue to grow through (1) additional marketing techniques; (2) further cost curtailment; (3) increased integration; and (4) improved genetics and growing techniques; while at the same time facing competitors who are larger and just as savvy.

LONNIE A. "BO" PILGRIM'S BACKGROUND AND PHILOSOPHY

Bo Pilgrim's story is the classic one of deprivation to determination and then to success. Born in Northwest Texas in 1928, he was a middle child of seven. Bo's father died when he was nine; and he left home at twelve to live with his grandmother.

His entrepreneurial spirit has early roots. One of his first goals in life was "to be able to buy a soda when I wanted it. My father would on occasion give me money for a cold drink, but only after I had finished some work he wanted done for it," says Bo. He learned early that he could buy his own soft drinks by buying them from his father's general merchandise store and selling them at a profit to the local factory workers. He later peddled newspapers, raised chickens and hogs, hauled gravel, picked peas and cotton, and sacked groceries—all before he turned eighteen.

Bo is a tireless worker at age sixty-five. Getting up with the chickens would aptly describe Mr. Pilgrim. "Bo" still works 12-hour days, taking time out for a daily exercise regimen of treadmill work and swimming (he had a heart attack about 10 years ago). "People retire too early," says Pilgrim, "they should retire when they don't enjoy working anymore. I won't retire!"

He likens business to "a game, even a war." Commenting on how he spends his time, "I spend one third of my working days dealing with the government, one third with lawyers, and the remaining one third of my time is spent constructively."

"Today we don't appreciate how much we have and how easy it is to get things. I'm definitely hooked on the free enterprise system," comments Bo. "In fact, when I visited with President Reagan a few years ago, I reminded him that the chicken and egg industry had never had any kind of subsidy. I also shared my belief that the government should not be in the business of protecting the inefficient."

Mr. Pilgrim recently expressed his thoughts on entrepreneurship:

It is more than just shooting from the hip. A company has four resources: people, dollars, time, and facilities. Our company's objective is to gain optimum use of these four through planning, building pride, and rewarding your employees.

Educated in a three-room school without electricity, Bo still believes in "old-fashioned Christian values" and the idea that "there is more to life than just making a dollar." He has had three children with his wife of thirty-six years; and for the past thirty-plus years has taught a Sunday school class. When asked about his secret of success, Bo responded:

Take your abilities, season them with experience on the job and combine that with drive and motivation and you will be successful. The way to make a difference in your life is to make that *mind-boggling* decision not to be average.

THE COMPANY

Pilgrim's History. Pilgrim's Pride is engaged in the production, processing, and marketing of fresh chicken and further processed and prepared chicken products. Pilgrim's produces approximately 27 million pounds of chicken per week, establishing it as the fifth largest producer in the United States. Pilgrim's offers a broad range of nearly 250 chicken products across the fresh, frozen-prepared, and individually quick frozen categories. Additionally, they can develop and produce new products to meet specific customer needs.

The company offers a line of processed and prepared chicken products, which includes breast fillets, nuggets, tenders, patties, and deli foods. These products, which undergo one or more further processing steps (including deboning, cutting, forming, battering, breading, and cooking), are packaged in quantities. These are then sold to supermarkets and to food service distributors like Sysco and Kraft General Foods (which resell them to restaurants, hospitals, and the like), fast-food chains, and whole-sale discount clubs.

In large part, because commodity chicken downcycles had almost bankrupted Pilgrim's twice over the years, the company has increasingly emphasized value-added and branded products, including its chill pack and further processed and prepared food lines. In the late 1980's Pilgrim's spent $25 million on a prepared chicken plant. These products generate higher prices per pound, exhibit lower price volatility, and result in higher and more consistent profit margins than non-value-added products such as whole ice-pack chicken.

In order to crack the food service business with processed and prepared chicken, Pilgrim's had to price their products below Tyson Foods, Inc. (their chief competitor), at a loss to Pilgrim's Pride. The company also had to spend approximately $6 to $8 million a year on advertising, promotion, and supermarket slotting allowances to entice this business.

Pilgrim's Pride lost about $50 million over three years trying to enter the prepared chicken market. In fiscal 1988 the company lost a net $8 million on $506 million in sales. Disgruntled investors dumped the stock, which had just had an initial public offering in January of 1987. The value of Bo Pilgrim's stake shrank by 76 percent, to $61 million.

Pilgrim's finally turned the corner with a strategic retreat from the supermarkets and a major advance into the food service market. Retail products now account for a mere 2 percent of Pilgrim's prepared chicken sales. But in food service they have positioned their company as an alternative to Tyson, aimed at those customers leery of being too dependent on one supplier. "A lot of buyers gave us information to help us duplicate the products they were buying from Tyson," Pilgrim says. With customers such as Kraft General Foods, Wendy's, and Kentucky Fried Chicken, the company now has been able to raise its prices to be in line with Tyson.

Pilgrim's Mission. A large group of Pilgrim's employees representing all areas of the company recently met to brainstorm their direction, vision, and mission. The group was fearful that rather than developing a mission, they might end up with a "mission statement." The difference according to Monty Henderson, president/CEO, is "that a Mission Statement becomes very wordy and usually winds up as a long paragraph or two that no one can remember . . . even the authors, and usually winds up in a file somewhere. A Mission by contrast is known by everyone, practiced daily by everyone, and becomes a way of life."

After lots of discussion about their business, their customers, and their competition, they came to a consensus that their vision is "To achieve and maintain leadership in each product and service that we provide." To achieve this vision of product and service leadership, the group felt that their mission must be: "Our Job Is Customer Satisfaction . . . Every Day."

Pilgrim's Marketing. Pilgrim's has a consumer-oriented market strategy. The company's marketing activities and expenditure levels have increased annually as new products and geographic markets have developed. As a result of its marketing activities, the company has achieved significant consumer awareness for the Pilgrim's Pride brand name in southwestern and western metropolitan markets. The company believes that this brand awareness is beneficial to the introduction and acceptance of new products, such as its further processed and prepared food lines.

The company utilizes television, radio, and newspaper advertising, point-of-sale and coupon promotions, and other marketing techniques to develop consumer awareness and brand loyalty for its products. Bo Pilgrim is the featured spokesman in the company's television and radio commercials, and his likeness in a pilgrim's hat appears on all the company's branded products. Advertising slogans have included "Better from the egg to the leg"; "It's a mind-boggling thing"; "The honest chicken from real pilgrim's"; and "Real chickens from real pilgrim's."

The company maintains an active program to identify consumer preferences primarily by testing new product ideas, packaging designs, and methods through taste panels and focus groups located in key geographic markets. This program led to the identification and introduction of new products such as the company's whole boneless chicken, leaner chicken, and the entire further processed and prepared foods line.

Pilgrim's has nineteen regional distribution centers. There are eight in Texas, three in Arkansas, two in Arizona, one in Oklahoma, and five in Mexico.

Pilgrim's Competition. Pilgrim's competes with other integrated chicken companies and to a lesser extent with local and regional poultry companies that are not fully integrated. Pilgrim's has been competing for retail grocery sales of chill-pack products since 1982 and fast-food product sales of whole and precut chickens since 1965. It currently supplies Church's, Kentucky Fried Chicken, Wendy's, Grandy's, and Chili's.

The primary competitive factors in the chicken industry include price, product line, and customer service. Although its products are competitively priced and generally supported with in-store promotions and discount programs, the company believes that product quality, brand awareness, and customer service are the primary methods through which it competes. Pilgrim's produces and markets further processed and prepared chicken products. Currently, Pilgrim's believes that it has only one competitor (Tyson) with a more complete line of value-added products.

The top five chicken producers today, measured by production volume, control more than half the market. They are Tyson Foods, Inc., Springdale, Arkansas; Con-Agra, Inc., Omaha, Nebraska; Gold Kist, Inc., Atlanta, Georgia; Perdue Farms, Inc., Salisbury, Maryland; and Pilgrim's.

The egg industry is more fragmented than the chicken industry with approximately sixty producers accounting for approximately 56 percent of total sales. Pilgrim's competes with many larger and smaller egg producers, primarily on the basis of product quality, reliability, price, and service.

Tyson, the number one poultry processor, solidified its position in 1989 with the purchase of Holly Farms Corporation for $1.3 billion dollars. Since then Tyson has acquired Louis Kemp Seafood and Arctic Alaska Fisheries. "They don't want to just sit on chicken as their core business," says Mark Plummer, an analyst for Stephens, Inc., "if you look at Tyson's strategy they clearly want to be in fish, pork, turkey, and beef; they want to become an international food company." The following is taken from Tyson's 1992 annual report:

> Our marketing strategy for success is simple-segment, concentrate, dominate. We identify a
> promising market segment, concentrate our resources in it and ultimately gain for Tyson
> Foods a dominate share of that segment. Our customers include all of the nation's top 50

food service distributors, 88 of the top 100 restaurant chains, 100 of the top retail super-market chains and every major wholesale club.

Pilgrim's Finances. After enjoying their best year to date in 1986, earning approximately $19 million on $375 million in sales, Pilgrim's arranged for a public offering of seven million shares. This represented nearly 20 percent of existing stock with Lonnie Pilgrim retaining nearly 80 percent. The initial stock offer sold in the $12 range during January of 1987. After the large drop in the Dow during October of 1987, the stock sold in the $3–4 range. It was one of the hardest hit stocks of that period.

In March of 1988 it was announced by the *Wall Street Journal* that Bo Pilgrim was selling his 80 percent stake in Pilgrim's Pride to Tyson Foods for $9 a share, or about $162 million. Most industry analysts weren't surprised that the boss was bailing out. Pilgrim's Pride at that time had one of the most highly leveraged balance sheets of the major poultry producers and wasn't weathering the latest downturn in the chicken industry well. Approximately a week later, the deal fell through and Tyson went on to buy Holly Farms.

Although net sales have increased every year to a high of $887 million in 1993, Pilgrim's finished the previous year with the largest loss in the history of the company.

THE BROILER INDUSTRY

The domestic integrated broiler industry encompasses the breeding, growing, processing, and marketing of chicken products. The production of poultry is one of the largest agricultural industries in the United States. Prior to World War II, the broiler industry was highly fragmented with numerous small, independent breeders, growers, and processors. The industry has experienced consolidation during the last forty-five years resulting in a relatively small number of larger, more integrated companies. Integration of the industry has led to lower profit margins at each independent production stage and enhanced the need for coordination between production stages.

The broiler industry is characterized by intense price competition, resulting in an emphasis on improving genetic, nutritional, and processing technologies in an effort to minimize production costs. These factors, coupled with the feed conversion advantages of chickens, have enabled the industry to enjoy consistently lower production costs per pound than other competing meats. As an example of the adoption of improved methods and technology, certain industry participants have moved toward product packaging at the plant level, including deep-chill processing as an alternative to ice-packing whole chicken and shipping in bulk form. Deep-chill processing rapidly lowers the temperature of chickens to slightly above freezing, thus extending freshness and shelf life.

MARKET OUTLOOK FOR 1994

Industry-wide broiler production appears to be under control moving into 1994. Supply flock data indicate production increases of 5 to 6 percent in early 1994. This modest increase in the level of production should allow for positive net returns to industry players considering per capita consumption is expected to continue to rise. Consumption could get an additional boost from increasing disposable income and the growing popularity of new chicken-based product introductions. For example, early indications are that products such as KFC's Rotisserie Gold are very successful. Typically, new products such as this will generate "copy cat" products, fueling additional demand.

On the expense side of the equation the wild card is grain costs. As a result of this year's flooding in the Midwest, corn and soybean meal have increased more than 30 and 15 percent, respectively. Should U.S. grain exports (particularly to Russia) continue to strengthen, grain supplies could become even tighter. Longer term, higher grain prices can actually be positive for chicken producers as the meat conversion ratio is less than 2 to 1 (2 pounds of feed to produce 1 pound of meat) for broilers versus 8 to 1 for beef. Under such a large divergence poultry clearly has the cost advantage, particularly as feed ingredient costs increase.

In any event, the majority of poultry production consists of value-added product, resulting in earnings and margins that are much more stable than a typical fresh (commodity) broiler producer. As the amount of further processing increases, grain cost as a percentage of the total cost of production is substantially reduced compared to that of fresh product, resulting in greater stability. For example, Tyson's feed ingredient cost as a percentage total is approximately 30 to 35 percent, compared to 60 to 65 percent for most fresh producers.

Broiler exports in 1994 are expected to remain strong. The USDA estimates 1.9 billion pounds of U.S. broiler meat will be exported. Top 1993 markets include Hong Kong, Japan, Mexico, and Poland. Producers are also experiencing increased business from private enterprise in the former Soviet Union. Export markets provide an important outlet for dark meat product, which is less desirable in the United States. In addition, exports reduce domestic broiler meat supplies, helping to support prices.

Industry Profitability. Industry profitability is primarily a function of consumption of chicken and competing meats and the cost of feed grains. Historically, the broiler industry operated on a fairly predictable cycle of about three years, a year of good profits, followed by a year of expanded output and declining profits, followed by a year of losses and production cuts.

The chicken companies have spent much of their energy trying to escape the commodity cycle through marketing. Frank Perdue, with his classic commercials, was the first to demonstrate that a company could charge a premium for a brand-name bird. Today, the biggest producers all play the brand-loyalty game. This leaves the chicken producers in an odd situation; they are commodities concerns trying to behave like consumer-products companies. Prudential-Bache's John McMillin says, "In the 1990's the chicken industry will be better capitalized, more competitive and less profitable."

Industry profitability can be significantly influenced by feed costs, which are influenced by a number of factors unrelated to the broiler industry, including government legislation that provides discretion to the federal government to set price and income supports for grain. Historically, feed costs have averaged approximately 50 percent of total production costs of non-value-added products and have fluctuated substantially with the price of corn, milo, and soybean meal. Assuming that finished product prices and other factors remain constant, very small movements in feed costs may result in large changes in industry profits from non-value-added chicken products. By comparison, feed costs typically average approximately 25 percent of total production costs of further processed and prepared chicken products such as nuggets, fillets, and deli products, and as a result, increased emphasis on sales of such products by chicken producers reduces the sensitivity of earnings to feed cost movements.

Although feed costs may vary dramatically, the cost of producing chicken is not as severely affected by changing feed ingredient prices as are the production costs of beef and pork. Chickens require approximately two pounds of dry feed to produce one pound of live meat, compared to cattle and hogs, which require approximately eight to four pounds, respectively, of feed.

INDUSTRY PROBLEMS

Across the southeastern United States, where 85 percent of the country's chickens are processed, the poultry industry is brooding about a barrage of bad publicity. Chicken processing plants are said to be dirty; rotten meat is reaching the market; salmonella-tainted chickens are poisoning people; and the chicken growers who contract with the processors are being ripped off. Even Ross Perot has publicly lambasted Bill Clinton's record by saying that the Arkansas poultry business is "not an industry of tomorrow."

Leaders of the South's largest agribusiness concede that they have a problem. In September of 1993, a coalition of the Arkansas Poultry Federation, Hudson Foods, Pilgrim's, and Tyson Foods ran full-page ads in several Arkansas newspapers to counter this image problem. Its main caption was "Here in Arkansas, it wasn't a Goose that laid the Golden Egg. It was a Chicken." It further stated such things as: "one out of twelve working Arkansans is employed by the poultry industry; it's a three-billion-dollar-plus industry in Arkansas; salaries and benefits average more than $25,000 each employee; and the poultry industry is the largest taxpayer in Arkansas."

The industry's biggest worry may be microscopic in physical size. Chickens in battery farms (and those in farmyards) often live in their own dung, which encourages the growth of bacteria such as salmonella and campylobacter. These contaminate the meat during processing. About six million Americans are made ill by such bacteria every year, and 1,300 die. Scientists at the Centers for Disease Control say chickens may be the cause in up to half of those cases.

The industry's high-tech, fast-paced production lines—which process some 200,000 birds a day at a single plant—heighten fecal contamination. Bacteria often spread among birds as they speed along conveyors from hot collective baths through wet mechanical feather-pickers to tanks of cold water. Partly to hold down the price of poultry, the industry has not tried to produce cleaner chickens, relying instead on consumers to cook the meat thoroughly.

Injury and illness rates for poultry workers are double the rates of manufacturing generally, according to the Labor Department. And new technology is often used to reduce stress for chickens—to make their meat more tender—rather than for workers. "The industry has one foot in the 21st century when it comes to chickens, but they left one foot back in the 19th century when it comes to people," says Bob Hall, research director of the Institute of Southern Studies, a labor-funded advocacy group in Durham, North Carolina.

Conditions on the production line can be tough. Repetitive motion from such tasks as pulling out chicken guts can cause disabling injuries. Employees frequently spend shifts in either a freezing cooler or 95°F heat. Conditions can be so crowded that blood from a chicken one worker handles can sometimes splash onto a co-worker. The line speed—up to 90 chickens a minute—is double the rate a decade ago.

In the past twenty years the number of major U.S. processors has shrunk from more than 100 to about 30. This consolidation has resulted in a highly centralized and vertically integrated industry in which a half-dozen major players control over 43 percent of American production. As a result, the country has been carved up into regional buying monopolies where each region's dominant processor can dictate terms to the growers.

The processors provide growers with chicks and feed, then slaughter and market the birds. The growers provide chicken houses, the utilities, and labor. Further, the growers receive only short-term contracts from the processors with no formal assurances of long-term business relationships.

A recent report from the Texas Commissioner of Agriculture concluded that while "the grower makes a substantial capital investment and takes most of the risk, he or she is not sharing in the success of the industry." In some cases growers have received as little as $579 in annual income per 20,000-bird-capacity broiler house.

The processors defend their practices. Industry spokesmen point out that growers are guaranteed a price for adult chickens, typically about 3.5 to 4 cents a pound. Thus, the processors contend, growers are sheltered from much of the risk of the volatile chicken market. Bill Roenigk, spokesman for the National Broiler Council, a processor trade group, says studies have shown that broiler farmers' average return on investment is 5 percent, or higher than that in many other agriculture operations.

CHANGING TASTES

Chicken has experienced greater growth in per-capita consumption than most other major meat categories over the last twenty years. From 1965 to 1985, the United States per capita consumption of chicken increased 74 percent while the consumption of beef increased 7 percent. Exhibit 34–3 illustrates per capita consumption of chicken relative to turkey, fish, beef and pork.

The major factors influencing this growth are consumer awareness of the health and nutritional characteristics of chicken, the price advantage of chicken relative to red meat, and the development of more convenient further processed and prepared chicken products. The principal health and nutritional characteristics include lower levels of fat, cholesterol, and calories per pound for chicken relative to red meat. When compared with other meats, chicken has a significant price advantage, which has increased over time.

Recent growth in the consumption of chicken has been enhanced by new product forms and packaging, which increase convenience and product versatility. These products typically undergo one or more further processing steps, including deboning, forming, battering, breading, and cooking. Production of these further processed products is the fastest-growing segment of the broiler industry. The market share of the further processed product group has increased.

In 1987 the United States became a nation of bird eaters. According to the Department of Agriculture, per capita consumption of poultry rose to 78.2 pounds. At the same time, per capita consumption of beef fell to 75.7 pounds. That marked the end of more than three decades of dominance by beef (before that, pork was king).

Notwithstanding an occasional salmonella scare, birds are perceived as more healthful than beef. A 100-gram piece of chicken contains 3.7 grams of saturated fat, compared with 20.7 grams of saturated fat in a piece of T-bone steak weighing the same amount, according to the Agriculture Department.

Chicken is also cheap. Chickens are selling for less than they did in 1923, when Mrs. Wilmer Steele of Ocean View, Delaware, sold what chicken historians say was the nation's first flock of commercial broilers (she got 62 cents a pound).

And perhaps most significantly, chicken companies have lately increased profit margins by producing scores of what the industry calls value-added items: chicken parts that have been boned or skinned or marinated or otherwise processed for the convenience of consumers. Just as anyone can cook a steak, anyone can now cook a shrink-wrapped chicken breast.

The poultry sector isn't solely chicken; it also includes turkey, duck, goose, and quail. But the poultry industry in America is chicken-driven; and, in fact, consumption of chicken alone bypassed beef around 1990 (although beef backers say pounds-per-capita figures aren't strictly fair, because chicken at retail has more bones in it than beef does). Recently chicken nuggets accounted for about 10 percent of total U.S. broiler output. McNuggets showed chicken companies what could happen if they went beyond selling what are called, in the trade, "feathers-off, guts-out birds."

Since McNuggets hit the market nationally in 1982, chicken producers have been swamping supermarkets with value-added products—teriyaki tidbits, breaded wings, whole cooked birds with salt and spices injected into their flesh—and consumers have responded. "Demand has expanded for poultry since 1983 in a way that I've never seen demand for any meat take off since World War II." says Patrick Luby, vice president and corporate economist at Oscar Mayer Foods Corporation in Madison, Wisconsin.

Value-added chicken should, of course, properly be called value-subtracted. It is the whole bird, not its processed parts, that offers consumers the greatest value—and that value is considerable when compared with beef and pork.

Why is chicken, pound for pound, cheaper than the competition? The answer has to do with the fact that a chicken is highly efficient at converting feed to flesh. To produce a pound of flesh, a chicken consumes less than two pounds of feed compared with between six and eight for a cow and three for a pig.

Also, a chicken doesn't live long. The shorter a creature's life cycle, the quicker its generations can be manipulated genetically. Chicken breeders have steadily developed birds that grow bigger on less feed in less time. They may be approaching the limits of practicality on this score; modern chickens have "put on so much weight that they have some real problems mating," says Walter Becker, professor emeritus of genetics and cell biology at Washington State University.

Furthermore, chickens don't graze. Raising cattle requires an investment in land; raising chickens doesn't. Chickens used to need to run around in the sun; otherwise, they would develop a vitamin D deficiency and rickets. But in the 1920s, poultry producers solved the vitamin D problem by adding cod-liver oil to chicken feed. Since then they have been able to raise thousands of chickens in confinement, allowing about 0.7 square foot per bird.

EXHIBIT 34-1 Location of Pilgrim's facilities

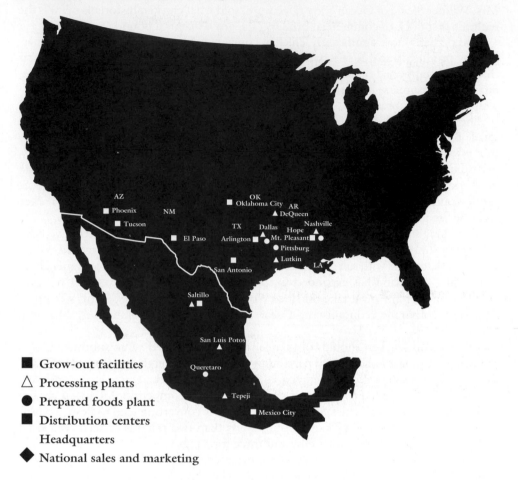

■ Grow-out facilities
△ Processing plants
● Prepared foods plant
■ Distribution centers
  Headquarters
◆ National sales and marketing

EXHIBIT 34-2 Top Chicken Companies, 1993

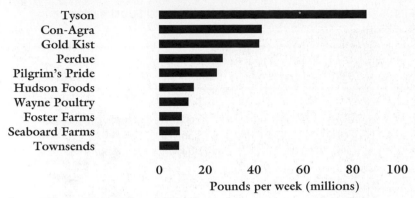

Source: Pilgrim *Annual Report*, 1993.

EXHIBIT 34-3 Per Capita Consumption—*Pounds per Year*

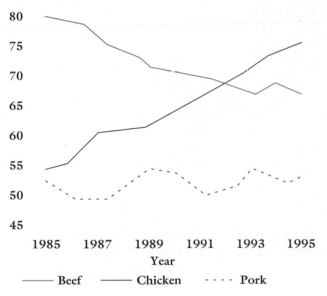

Source: Pilgrim *Annual Report*, 1993.

Exhibit 34-4 Selected Financial Data—Pilgrim's Pride Corporation and Subsidiaries
(*In thousands, except per share data*)

| | YEARS ENDED | | | | |
	1993(a)	1992(b)	1991	1990	1989
Operating Results Summary					
Net sales	$887,843	$817,361c	$786,651	$720,555	$661,077
Gross margin	110,213	34,646	75,567	74,190	83,356
Operating income (loss)	56,102	(13,475)	31,039	33,379	47,014
Income (loss) before income taxes and					
extraordinary charge	32,838	(33,712)	12,235	20,463	31,027
Income tax expense (benefit)	10,543	(4,048)	(59)	4,826	10,745
Income (loss) before extraordinary charge	22,295	(29,664)	12,294	15,637	20,282
Extraordinary charge—early repayment of					
debt, net of tax	(1,286)	—	—	—	—
Net income (loss)	21,009	(29,664)	12,294	15,637	20,282
Income (loss) per common share:					
Income (loss) before					
extraordinary charge	$ .81	$ (1.24)	$ .54	$ .69	$ .90
Extraordinary charge—early repayment					
of debt	(.05)	—	—	—	—
Net income (loss)	.76	(1.24)	.54	.69	.90
Cash dividends per common share	.03	.06	.06	.06	.06
Balance Sheet Summary					
Working capital	$ 72,688	$ 11,227	$ 44,882	$ 54,161	$ 60,313
Total assets	422,846	434,566	428,090	379,694	291,102
Short-term debt	25,643	86,424	44,756	30,351	9,528
Long-term debt, less current portion	159,554	131,534	175,776	154,277	109,412
Total stockholders' equity	132,293	112,112	112,353	101,414	87,132
Key Indicators—As a Percent of Sales					
Gross margin	12.4%	4.2%	9.6%	10.3%	12.6%
Selling general and administrative expenses	6.1%	5.9%	5.7%	5.7%	5.5%
Operating income (loss)	6.3%	(1.6)%	3.9%	4.6%	7.1%
Net interest expense	2.9%	2.8%	2.5%	2.3%	2.7%
Net income (loss)	2.4%	(3.6)%	1.6%	2.2%	3.1%

(a) 1993 had 53 weeks.

(b) During 1992, the Company changed the fiscal year-end of its Mexican subsidiaries from August to September to coincide with that of its domestic operations. 1992 operating results include the operations of the Mexican subsidiaries for the twelve months ended September 26, 1992. Operating results for the Mexican subsidiaries during the month of September, 1991 have been reflected as a direct addition to stockholders' equity.

(c) Excluded from net sales in 1992 is approximately $2.2 million of business interruption insurance proceeds resulting from a fire at the Company's prepared foods plant in Mt. Pleasant, Texas.

Source: Pilgrim's *Annual Report*, 1993.

EXHIBIT 34-5 Consolidated Statements of Income (Loss)—Pilgrim's Pride Corporation and Subsidiaries

	OCTOBER 2, 1993 (53 WEEKS)	YEARS ENDED SEPTEMBER 26, 1992 (52 WEEKS)	SEPTEMBER 28, 1991 (52 WEEKS)
Net sales	$887,843,000	$817,361,000	$786,651,000
Business interruption insurance	–	2,225,000	–
	887,843,000	819,586,000	786,651,000
Costs and expenses:			
Cost of sales	777,630,000	784,940,000	711,084,000
Selling, general and administrative	54,111,000	48,121,000	44,528,000
	831,741,000	833,061,000	755,612,000
Operating Income (loss)	56,102,000	(13,475,000)	31,039,000
Other expenses (income):			
Interest expense, net	25,719,000	22,502,000	19,777,000
Miscellaneous	(2,455,000)	(2,265,000)	(973,000)
Total other expenses, net	23,264,000	20,237,000	18,804,000
Income (loss) before income taxes and extraordinary charge	32,838,000	(33,712,000)	12,235,000
Income tax expense (benefit)	10,543,000	(4,048,000)	(59,000)
Net income (loss) before extraordinary charge	22,295,000	(29,664,000)	12,294,000
Extraordinary charge-early repayment of debt, net of tax	(1,286,000)	–	–
Net Income (loss)	$ 21,009,000	$ (29,664,000)	$ 12,294,000
Net income (loss) per common share before extraordinary charge	$ .81	$ (1.24)	$ .54
Extraordinary charge per common share	(.05)	–	–
Net income (loss) per common share	$ .76	$ (1.24)	$ .54

Source: Pilgrim *Annual Report*, 1993.

EXHIBIT 34-6 Consolidated Balance Sheets—Pilgrim's Pride Corporation and Subsidiaries

	OCTOBER 2, 1993	SEPTEMBER 26, 1992
Assets		
Current Assets		
Cash and cash equivalents	$ 4,526,000	$ 11,550,000
Trade accounts and other receivables, less allowance for doubtful accounts	59,608,000	52,383,000
Inventories	91,794,000	89,428,000
Prepaid expenses	1,260,000	7,179,000
Other current assets	9,843,000	9,979,000
TOTAL CURRENT ASSETS	167,031,000	170,519,000
Other Assets	13,114,000	10,031,000
Property, Plant and Equipment		
Land	14,824,000	15,063,000
Buildings, machinery and equipment	317,657,000	315,392,000
Autos and trucks	25,877,000	24,622,000
Construction-in-progress	7,863,000	2,939,000
	366,221,000	358,016,000
Less accumulated depreciation and amortization	123,520,000	104,000,000
	242,701,000	254,016,000
	$422,846,000	$434,566,000
Liabilities and Stockholders' Equity		
Current Liabilities		
Notes payable to banks	$ 12,000,000	$ 64,979,000
Accounts payable	38,330,000	48,798,000
Accrued expenses	30,370,000	24,070,000
Current portion of long-term debt	13,643,000	21,445,000
TOTAL CURRENT LIABILITIES	94,343,000	159,292,000
Long-Term Debt, less current portion	159,554,000	131,534,000
Deferred Income Taxes	36,656,000	31,628,000
Stockholders' Equity		
Preferred stock, $.01 par value, authorized 5,000,000 shares; none issued	–	–
Common stock, $.01 par value, authorized 45,000,000 shares; 27,589,250 issued and outstanding in 1993 and 1992	276,000	276,000
Additional paid-in capital	79,763,000	79,763,000
Retained earnings	52,254,000	32,073,000
Total Stockholders' Equity	132,293,000	112,112,000
Commitments and Contingencies	–	–
	$422,846,000	$434,566,000

Source: Pilgrim *Annual Report*, 1993.

EXHIBIT 34-7 Consolidated Statements of Stockholders' Equity—Pilgrim's Pride Corporation and Subsidiaries

FOR THE THREE YEARS ENDING OCTOBER 2, 1993	NUMBER OF SHARES	COMMON STOCK	ADDITIONAL PAID-IN CAPITAL	RETAINED EARNINGS	TOTAL
Balance at September 29, 1990	22,589,250	$226,000	$49,890,000	$51,298,000	$101,414,000
Net income for year				12,294,000	12,294,000
Cash dividends declared ($0.06 per share)				(1,355,000)	(1,355,000)
Balance at September 28, 1991	22,589,250	226,000	49,890,000	62,237,000	112,353,000
Net income for the month ended September 28, 1991, excluded below due to the change in fiscal year-end of Mexican subsidiaries				931,000	931,000
Net loss for year				(29,664,000)	(29,664,000)
Common stock issued	5,000,000	50,000	29,873,000	–	29,923,000
Cash dividends declared ($0.06 per share)				(1,431,000)	(1,431,000)
Balance at September 26, 1992	27,589,250	276,000	79,763,000	32,073,000	112,112,000
Net income for year				21,009,000	21,009,000
Cash dividends declared ($0.03 per share)				(828,000)	(828,000)
Balance at October 2, 1993	27,589,250	$ 276,000	$79,763,000	$52,254,000	$132,293,000

Source: Pilgrim *Annual Report*, 1993.

EXHIBIT 34-8 Consolidated Statements of Cash Flows—Pilgrim's Pride
Corporation and Subsidiaries

	YEARS ENDED		
	OCTOBER 2, 1993 (53 WEEKS)	SEPTEMBER 26, 1992 (52 WEEKS)	SEPTEMBER 28, 1991 (52 WEEKS)
Cash flows from operating activities:			
Net income (loss)	$ 21,009,000	$(29,664,000)	$ 12,294,000
Adjustments to reconcile net income (loss) to cash provided by (used in) operating activities:			
Depreciation and amortization	26,034,000	24,090,000	19,860,000
(Gain) loss on property disposals	(2,187,000)	(620,000)	173,000
Provision for doubtful accounts	2,124,000	1,045,000	882,000
Deferred income taxes	5,028,000	(5,382,000)	(2,436,000)
Extraordinary charge	1,904,000	–	–
Net income for the month ended September 28, 1991, excluded above due to the change in fiscal year of Mexican subsidiaries	–	931,000	–
Changes in operating assets and liabilities:			
Accounts and other receivables	(6,555,000)	(9,720,000)	(1,033,000)
Inventories	(2,366,000)	7,807,000	(16,974,000)
Prepaid expenses	4,175,000	(4,416,000)	3,207,000
Accounts payable and accrued expenses	(4,168,000)	14,598,000	3,989,000
Other	(28,000)	(242,000)	(99,000)
Net cash flows provided by (used in) operating activities	44,970,000	(1,573,000)	19,863,000
Investing activities:			
Acquisitions of property, plant and equipment	(15,201,000)	(18,043,000)	(60,518,000)
Proceeds from property disposal	2,977,000	3,766,000	148,000
Other assets	713,000	(536,000)	1,056,000
Net cash used in investing activities	(11,511,000)	(14,813,000)	(59,314,000)

EXHIBIT 34-8 *Continued*

	OCTOBER 2, 1993 (53 WEEKS)	YEARS ENDED SEPTEMBER 26, 1992 (52 WEEKS)	SEPTEMBER 28, 1991 (52 WEEKS)
Financing activities:			
Proceeds from notes payable to banks	28,419,000	163,629,000	210,500,000
Repayments on notes payable to banks	(81,398,000)	(156,150,000)	(197,850,000)
Proceeds from long-term debt	126,468,000	—	31,600,000
Payments on long-term debt	(106,302,000)	(11,502,000)	(8,346,000)
Cost of refinancing debt	(5,510,000)		
Extraordinary charge, cash items	(1,188,000)	—	—
Proceeds from leasing transaction	—	565,000	—
Net proceeds from sale of stock	—	29,923,000	—
Cash dividends paid	(828,000)	(1,355,000)	(1,355,000)
Cash provided by (used in) financing activities	(40,339,000)	25,110,000	34,549,000
Effect of exchange rate changes on cash and cash equivalents	(144,000)	(49,000)	99,000
Increase (decrease) in cash and cash equivalents	(7,024,000)	8,675,000	(4,803,000)
Cash and cash equivalents at beginning of year	11,550,000	2,875,000	7,678,000
Cash and cash equivalents at end of year	$ 4,526,000	$ 11,550,000	$ 2,875,000
Supplemental disclosure information:			
Cash paid during the year for:			
Interest (net of amount capitalized)	$ 23,015,000	$ 22,507,000	$ 20,983,000
Income taxes	$ 3,688,000	$ 1,455,000	$ 2,273,000

Source: Pilgrim *Annual Report*, 1993.

EXHIBIT 34-9 Pilgrim Operations

	OCTOBER 2, 1993 (53 WEEKS)	YEARS ENDED SEPTEMBER 26, 1992 (52 WEEKS)	SEPTEMBER 28, 1991 (52 WEEKS)
Sales to unaffiliated customers:			
United States	$699,089,000	$656,741,000	$645,081,000
Mexico	188,754,000	160,620,000	141,570,000
Consolidated Sales	$887,843,000	$817,361,000	$786,651,000
Operating profit (loss):			
United States	$46,471,000	$ (1,565,000)	$ 19,693,000
Mexico	9,631,000	(11,910,000)	11,346,000
	$ 56,102,000	$ (13,475,000)	$ 31,039,000
Identifiable assets:			
United States	$288,761,000	$297,369,000	$297,473,000
Mexico	134,085,000	137,197,000	130,617,000
	$422,846,000	$434,566,000	$428,090,000

Source: Pilgrim *Annual Report*, 1993.

EXHIBIT 34-10 Pilgrim Corporate Officers

Lonnie A. "Bo" Pilgrim[1]
Chief Executive Officer

Lindy M. "Buddy" Pilgrim[1]
President of U.S. Operations and Sales and Marketing

Monty K. Henderson[1]
President and Chief Operating Officer

Clifford E. Butler[1]
Chief Financial Officer, Secretary and Treasurer

David Van Hoose
President
Mexican Operations

Richard A. Cogdill[1]
Senior Vice President
Corporate Controller

O.B. Goolsby, Jr.
Senior Vice President
Prepared Foods

Robert L. Hendrix
Senior Vice President
Netex Complex

Mike Martin
Senior Vice President
Complex Manager
DeQueen and Nashville, AR Complex

James J. Miner, Ph.D.
Senior Vice President
Farm Production

Robert N. Palm
Senior Vice President
Complex Manager
Lufkin and Nacogdoches, TX Complex

[1] Member of the Executive Committee
Source: Pilgrim *Annual Report*, 1993.

NAME INDEX

Silver, S., 294
Singh, H., 75, 187
Slevin, D. P., 76
Sloan, Alfred, Jr., 6, 23
Slocum, John W., Jr., 352
Smith, Adam, 165, 187
Smart, Dennis L., 25
Smith, Daniel, 148
Smith, John, 109
Snell, Michael, 25
Snow, C. C., 76
Solomon, 306
Sommers, William, 148
Sonnenfeld, Jeffrey, 153
Spencer, William, 236, 272, 294, 357
Spitzer, T. Quinn, 188
Srinivasan, N., 76
Srivastva, Suresh, 8, 24
Stacey, Ralph, 25
Starik, Mark, 4, 120, 256, 265
Stark, Andrew, 25
Starr, Martin, 188
Stearns, Linda Brewster, 267
Stein, J., 366
Steiner, George, 93, 105, 323
Sterling, John, 187
Stewart, Thomas, 148
Stiles, Philip, 267
Stobaugh, Robert, 266
Strati, Antonio, 25
Strickland, A. J. III, 225, 357
Stroh, L. K., 188
Strunk, W., 366
Stuckey, John, 76
Sulter, Malcolm, 212

Taggart, Philip, 294
Tallman, Stephen B., 352
Teets, John W., 86
Telesio, Piero, 266
Tenaglia, 25, 188
Terpstra, Vern, 351
Terry, Robert J., 192
Thakur, Manab, 25

Thomas, Lee M., 149
Thomas, James B., 76
Thomas, H., 76
Thompson, A., 225
Thurston, P. H., 75, 328
Tietz, Fred, 25
Tilles, Seymour, 300, 310, 323
Todor, William D., 266
Toffler, Alvin, 311
Trachtenberg, Jeff, 294
Tregoe, Benjamin, 188
Trenk, Barbara, 266
Trevino, Linda Klebe, 25, 267
Triant, Deborah, 294
Trice, H. M., 160
Truman, Harry, 236
Tucker, Marvin W., 267
Turpin, Dominique, 352

Uttal, Bro, 294

Vandenberg, Robert J., 188
Victor, Bart, 25
Vlachoutsicos, Charalambos, 352
Vogel, David, 25
Vozikis, G., 75

Waalewijn, Philip, 76
Walker, O., 290, 294
Wallace, Marc, 236
Walop, Judith, 148
Waterman, Robert, Jr., 15, 23, 24,
    59, 105, 112, 167, 187, 225,
    265, 266, 314, 320, 323
Watson, Hugh J., 181, 187
Watson, Gregory H., 25
Watson, Charles, 25
Watson, Thomas, Jr., 153, 272
Weidenbaum, Murray, 225
Weihrich, Heinz, 225
Weinstein, Edward, 75
Welch, James A., 76
Welsh, Tricia, 323
West, Richard, 60

West, Philip, 328
Wheelwright, Steven C., 149
White, Merry, 351
White, David, 76
White, E. Z., 366
Whitehall, Arthur, 328, 351
Whiteley, Richard, 86
Wickins, David, 8
Wilersema, Margarethe F., 226
Wilhelm, Warren R., 188
Williams, Jeffrey R., 149
Williams, Gregory, 148
Williams, J. Clifton, 25
Williamson, J. P., 366
Winder, Robert, 148
Winsemius, Pieter, 76
Winter, Fred, 294
Winter, Fred, 278
Wisdom, Barry L., 24
Wolfe, Art, 25
Woodman, Richard W., 25
Wooldridge, Bill, 266
Wright, Richard, 351
Wright, Peter, 69, 75
Wright, Patrick M., 267

Yalowitz, Michael, 148
Yamazaki, Masaleagu, 343
Yanagida, Kovichi, 95
Yavitz, Boris, 245, 265
Yeltsin, Boris, 7
Yeung, Sally, 91, 93, 105
Yip, George S., 351
Young, John, 292

Zahra, Shaker A., 149, 225, 295
Zall, P., 366
Zand, Dale, 323
Zeithaml, Carl P., 225
Zi, Sun, 153
Zimmerer, T. W., 337
Zimmerman, Richard, 29, 325

COMPANY INDEX

3M, 156, 263, 290, 313
A. B. Marabou, 29
Adolph Coors Company, 9, 24
ADVO, 305
Aetna Life & Casualty, 109
Affiliated Pubs., 67
Airbus, 332
Akzo, 67
ALCOA, 305, 313
Allaint Techsystems, 305
Allied Corporation, 17
Allstate, 11, 263
Altantic Richfield, 305
AMAX, 98
American Airlines, 60
American Beauty Brands, 37, 313
American Express, 17, 60, 263
American General, 305
American Home Products, 100
American Italian Pasta Company, 37
Amoco Corp., 91, 92
Anheuser-Busch, 57, 70
Apple Computer, 59, 78, 79, 93, 98,
    99, 100, 109, 340
Archbold Memorial Hospital, 72
Archer-Daniels-Midland, 342
Arco, 70
Armdahl, 305
Arthur D. Little, 196, 338
Asahi Glass, 131
Asea Brown Boveri (ABB), 250, 342
AT&T, 59, 60, 67, 78, 96, 98, 101,
    156, 248, 257, 289, 292,313,
    332, 340
Atlantic Richfield, 251
AttBelo, 67
Audubon, 373
Austin Industries, 262
Australian Consolidated
    Industries, 131
Aviall, 305
Avis, 262

Baldwin Comapny, 122
Banc One, 67, 373
Banco de Bilbao, 348
Banco Vizcaya, 348
Bancorp Hawaii, 98, 101
BankAmerica, 252
Barnett Banks, 90, 279
Bass PLC, 67
Baxter Travenol Laboratories, 18
Bell Atlantic Corporation, 59, 67, 79
BellSouth, 20, 98, 101, 262
Berkshire Hathaway, 313
Bethlehem Steel, 262

BIC, 69
BICC, 131
Biejing Electronic Glass Engineering
    Technology, 131
Black & Decker, 69
Blue Shield of California, 67
BMW, 69
Boeing, 128, 289, 312, 332, 373
Boise Cascade, 233
Borden, 37, 344, 373
Borg Warner, 67
Boston Consulting Group, 225
Bowles Corp, 263
Boy Scouts of America, 302
Bradlees, 305
Braniff Airlines, 302
Bridgestone, 116, 332
Briggs & Stratton, 69
Brown Company, 282
Browning-Ferris, 122
BTR, 116
Burger King, 348
Burlington Resources, 313
Byrne Electric Specialists, 263

Cadbury Schweppes, 67
California Federal Bank, 305
Campbell Soup Corporation, 11,
    215, 263, 343, 373
Cannon, 348
Canon, 61
Carlisle Retailers, 61
Carnation, 348
Carnival Cruise, 79
Carolina Power & Light Co., 106
Caterpillar Tractor, 18, 332, 344
Cayzac & Goudard, 348
Celanese, 18
Chalet Dental Clinic, 263
Chambers Development, 122
Champion International, 128, 263
Charter Medical, 262
Chase Manhattan Bank, 78, 98
    100, 268
Chemical Bank, 18
Chevron, 233, 342
Children's Memorial Hospital, 72
Chris Craft Industries, 67
Chrysler, 57, 109, 332, 339
Church & Dwight, 340
Ciba-Geigy, 131, 340
Cie des Machines Bull, 131
Cie Financiere des Fibres
    Optiques, 131
Cifra, 341
CIGNA, 263

Circus Circus Enterprises, 373
Citibank, 79, 263
Citicorp Venture Captial, 67
Citicorp, 19, 330, 373
Citizen Watch, 116
Classic Car Club of America, 373
Clorox, 263, 340
CML Group, 120
Coastal Emergency Services, 72
Coca-Cola Bottling, 54, 57, 58, 313,
    343, 344
Coldwell Banker, 11
Colgate-Palmolive, 330
Colombia Healthcare
    Corporation, 66
Columbia Hospital, 66
Columbia Gas System Service
    Corporation, 15, 16
Columbia Pictures Entertainment
    Company, 60
Combustion Engineering, 342
Commonwealth Edison, 305
Compagnie des Machines Bull, 218
Compaq Computer, 122, 143, 341
CompUSA, 305
Computervision, 305
Conasupo, 341
Conoco, 256, 317
Consolidated Foods, 316
Continental Products, 61
Control Data, 98
Coors Brewers, 57, 69, 78
Corning Glass, 268
Corning, Inc., 56, 101, 131, 313
CPCC, 37
Cross, 69
Crown Zellerbach, 99
CSX Corporation, 106, 107
Cummins Engine, 233

Dai-Ichi Kangyo Bank, 7
Dai-Ichi Mutual Life, 7
Daimler Benz, 332, 340
Daiwa Securities, 7
Dakota, Minnesota & Eastern
    Railroad, 373
Dallas Morning News, 67
Dana Corp, 167
Dave's Pit Stop Cafe, 373
Days Inn of America, 286
Deere, 313, 332
Del Monte, 343
Dell Computer, 373
Deloitte Haskins & Sells, 348
Delta, 262
Desert Hospital, 72

SUBJECT INDEX

Job specifications, 165
Joint ventures, 56, 60, 65
"Just in time" (JIT) production, 258

Learning by doing, 26
Legal forces, 121–124
Levels of planning, 164
Leveraged buy-outs, 66–67
Leverage ratios, 172, 174
Library, how to use, 133–135
Library publications, 133–135
Linear regression, 137
Linking performance and pay to
    strategies, 251–253
Liquidation, 56, 62, 66
Liquidity ratios, 172, 174
Long-term debt-to-equity ratio. *See*
    Leverage ratios

Machiavellian score, 230
Mach test, 230
Management
    audit, 182
    controlling, 163, 167
    motivating, 163, 165
    organizing, 163, 165
    planning, 163, 165
    staffing, 163, 166
Managing
    by crisis, 197
    by extrapolation, 197
    by hope, 197
    by objectives, 197
    by subjectives, 197
Market development, 56, 58, 64
Market growth (in Grand Strategy
    Matrix), 211–213
Marketing
    audit, 182
    buying supplies, 168
    customer analysis, 168
    distribution, 169
    marketing research, 170
    opportunity analysis, 170
    pricing, 169
    product and service planning, 168
    selling products/services, 168
    social responsibility, 170
Marketing-mix variables, 276
Market penetration, 56, 57, 63
Market segmentation, 276–279
Matching, 199
Matching managers with
    strategy, 268–269
Matching Stage, 197–213
Matching structure with
    , strategy, 246–251
Matrix organizational structure, 251
Measuring organizational
    performance, 309–310
Merchant bankers, 67
Merger, 62, 66–67, 348
Mexico
    natural environment,
    strategies, 339–341
Military strategy, 21–22

Mission statements. *See also* Business
    mission
    broad scope, 93
    components, 97
    customer orientation, 95–96
    declaration of attitude, 93
    declaration of social policy, 96
    definition, 8–9
    Japanese, 95
    process of developing, 91
    resolution of divergent views, 94
    utility, 96
    vision versus mission, 91, 92
    writing and developing, 97–102
Motivating, 163, 165–166
Multidimensional scaling, 279
Multinational corporations
    (MNC), 327–350

Natural environment, 4, 161–162, 213
Natural Environment Perspectives, 19,
    70, 94, 122, 176, 213, 258, 291,
    312, 340
Nominal grouping, 143
Nonprofit organizations
    educational institutions, 71
    government agencies and departments, 72
    medical organizations, 71–72

Objectives
    annual, 11, 241–243
    long-term, 10, 11, 196–197
On-line data bases, 133
Operating profit margin. *See*
    Profitability ratios
Operations management. *See*
    Production/operations
Opportunities, 9
Opportunity analysis, 170
Oral presentation
    answering questions, C9
    content, C8
    controlling your voice, C8
    delivery, C8
    managing body language, C8
    organizing, C8
    speaking from notes, C9
    visual aids, C9
Organizational climate. *See*
    Organizational culture
Organizational culture
    conceptual relationship with
        strategy, 159–162
    creating a strategy supportive
        culture, 256–257
    cultural aspects of strategy choice, 218
    cultural products, 159–160
    of different countries, 162, 207
    dimensions of organizational
        culture, 160, 207
    high-context/low-context, 162
    integrating strategy and culture, 159
Organizational demise, 305
Organizational structure
    divisional, 248–250
    functional, 247

matching structure and strategy, 246–251
    matrix, 251
    strategic business unit (SBU), 250–251
Organizing, 163, 165
Outsourcing, 57

Performance-based long-term
    incentives, 251–253
Personnel management, 166
Personnel policies, 166
Planning, 163–165
Planning process audit, 319
Policies, 12, 243–245
Political access, 220–223
Political forces, 121–124
Political forecast, different countries, 123
Political risk forecast, 123
Politics in strategy formulation, 219–220
Portfolio, 206–209
Price-earnings ratio, 309
Pricing, 169
Prince (Machiavelli), 230
Process decisions, 177
Product development, 56, 58, 64
Product positioning maps, 279–280
Production/operations
    audit, 173–176, 183
Production/operations during
    implementation, 257–259
Profitability ratios, 173–175
Pro forma financial statement
    analysis, 284–286
Proverbs, 306

Qualitative forecasting techniques
    anticipatory surveys or market
        research, 143
    brainstorming, 138, 139, 143
    delphi forecasts, 138, 143
    juries of executive opinion, 143
    sales-force estimate, 143
    scenario forecasts, 143
Quantitative forecasting techniques
    econometric models, 137
    regression, 137
    trend extrapolation, 137
Quantitative Strategic Planning
    (QSPM), 214–218
Question Marks (in the BCG
    Matrix), 207–209

Ratio analysis. *See* Financial ratio analysis
Rational change strategy, 254
Relative market share
    position, 206–209
Research and development
    internal versus external, 177
    issues in strategy
        implementation, 288–292
Research and development audit, 176, 183
Research and development
    spending, 180
    policies concerning, 176, 288–291
    ranking of firms, 289
Resistance to change, 253–255
Resource allocation, 245